The Development of Ethics, Volume II

The Development of Ethics

A Historical and Critical Study

Volume II: From Suarez to Rousseau

TERENCE IRWIN

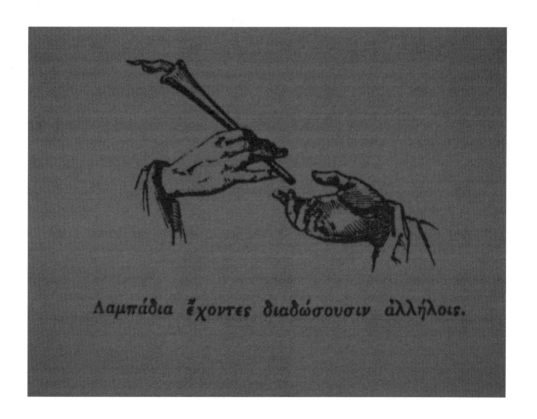

Λαμπάδια ἔχοντες διαδώσουσιν ἀλλήλοις.

OXFORD

UNIVERSITY PRESS

OXFORD

UNIVERSITY PRESS

Great Clarendon Street, Oxford OX2 6DP

Oxford University Press is a department of the University of Oxford.
It furthers the University's objective of excellence in research, scholarship,
and education by publishing worldwide in

Oxford New York

Auckland Cape Town Dar es Salaam Hong Kong Karachi
Kuala Lumpur Madrid Melbourne Mexico City Nairobi
New Delhi Shanghai Taipei Toronto

With offices in

Argentina Austria Brazil Chile Czech Republic France Greece
Guatemala Hungary Italy Japan Poland Portugal Singapore
South Korea Switzerland Thailand Turkey Ukraine Vietnam

Oxford is a registered trade mark of Oxford University Press
in the UK and in certain other countries

Published in the United States
by Oxford University Press Inc., New York

British Library Cataloguing in Publication Data

Data available

Library of Congress Cataloging in Publication Data

Data available

Typeset by Laserwords Private Limited, Chennai, India
Printed in Great Britain
on acid-free paper by
CPI Antony Rowe, Chippenham, Wiltshire

ISBN 978–0–19–954327–4

1 3 5 7 9 10 8 6 4 2

PREFATORY NOTE

This is the second of three volumes. The division into volumes is not meant to be thematically significant, and so the second volume simply begins where the first left off. The numeration of the sections continues from the first volume, and references to §§1–422 refer to the first volume. The preface, dedication, and introduction to the first volume belong equally to the second. In particular, the introduction explains the aims, scope, and limits of the book.

I have benefited from helpful comments and advice by readers for the Press, and from discussion with Stephen Darwall and Nicholas Sturgeon. For help in the Sisyphean task of checking, verifying, and correcting the penultimate draft I am most grateful to Kristen Inglis and Tom Ainsworth.

Faculty of Philosophy

University of Oxford

May, 2008

SUMMARY CONTENTS

CONTENTS

Contents

ABBREVIATIONS

This list includes only the most frequently used abbreviations, and those that might puzzle a reader. I have tried to cite primary texts from sources that will be fairly readily available.

Greek and Latin texts appearing in the OCT, BT, and Loeb series are listed with a reference to the relevant series, but without further details.

I have mentioned only a few of the available translations and editions.

Acronyms are normally used for the titles of books, journals, and collections. Short titles are used for articles and essays.

Page references include 'p.' only in cases where it might avoid ambiguity.

A page number with a letter (e.g., 'Reid, *EAP* 755 H') usually indicates the relevant edition. For less accessible texts available in Raphael, *BM*, or Selby-Bigge, *BM*, a reference to one of these collections is usually given.

ACPQ = *American Catholic Philosophical Quarterly*
AJP = *Australasian Journal of Philosophy*
Aquinas, *in EN* (etc.) = Aquinas' commentaries on Aristotle and on Biblical books.
BCP = *Book of Common Prayer*
BT = Bibliotheca Teubneriana. Greek and Latin texts
Cic. = Cicero
CSEL = *Corpus Scriptorum Ecclesiasticorum Latinorum*
CUP = Cambridge University Press (Cambridge, London, New York)
D or Denz. = Denziger, *Enchiridion Symbolorum*
DM = Suarez, *Disputationes Metaphysicae*
DTC = *Dictionnaire de Théologie Catholique*
EN = Aristotle, *Ethica Nicomachea (Nicomachean Ethics)*
ET = English Translation
Fin. = Cicero, *De Finibus*
G = Kant, *Groundwork*
H = Hutton, edn. of Cudworth; or Hoadly, edn. of Clarke; or Hamilton, edn. of Reid
HJ = *Historical Journal*
HPQ = *History of Philosophy Quarterly*
HS = *Hume Studies*
HUP = Harvard University Press (Cambridge, Mass.)
IPM (or *I*) = Hume, *Inquiry concerning the Principles of Morals*
JHI = *Journal of the History of Ideas*
JHP = *Journal of the History of Philosophy*
JP = *Journal of Philosophy*
KpV = Kant, *Critique of Practical Reason*

Abbreviations

L. = Hobbes, *Leviathan*

Leg. = Suarez, *De Legibus*

Loeb = Loeb Classical Library (Greek and Latin texts with facing English translations, of varying quality). Cambridge MA: Harvard U Press, and London: Heinemann.

M = Sextus Empiricus, *Adversus Mathematicos*

M = *Mind*

Mal. = Aquinas, *De Malo*

ME = Sidgwick, *Methods of Ethics*

NRSV, see Bible. New Revised Standard Version

OCT = Oxford Classical Texts (Scriptorum Classicorum Bibliotheca Oxoniensis). Greek and Latin texts (OUP)

Off. = Cicero, *De Officiis*

OO = *Opera Omnia,* various authors

OT = Ockham, *Opera Theologica*

OUP = Oxford University Press, including Clarendon Press (Oxford, London, New York)

P = Sextus Empiricus, *Pyrrhoneae Hypotyposes*

PAS = *Proceedings of the Aristotelian Society*

Phil. = *Philosophy*

PPA = *Philosophy and Public Affairs*

PQ = *Philosophical Quarterly*

PR = *Philosophical Review*

PS = *Political Studies*

PUP = Princeton University Press (Princeton)

R = Raphael, ed., *British Moralists* (cited by section)

RKP = Routledge; or Routledge and Kegan Paul (London)

SB = Selby-Bigge, ed., *British Moralists* (cited by section)

Sent = *Sententiae* or *Scriptum super Sententiis* (various authors)

SJP = *Southern Journal of Philosophy*

SPAS = *Proceeedings of the Aristotelian Society, Supplementary Volume*

SR = Plutarch, *De Stoicorum Repugnantiis*

ST = Aquinas, *Summa Theologiae*

T = Hume, *Treatise of Human Nature*

TD = Cicero, *Tusculan Disputations*

30

SUAREZ: LAW
AND OBLIGATION

423. The Questions about Natural Law

Discussion of natural law reaches a new level of sophistication in Suarez's elaborate and careful treatment. He takes account of Aquinas, Scotus, Ockham, and their successors, and claims to defend Aquinas' views on the main issues. Since his discussion is usually fuller than Aquinas' discussion, and explores questions that Aquinas does not discuss at length, Suarez deserves careful study.

We may not always agree with his claim to defend Aquinas' position. Indeed, some readers, especially among those sympathetic to Aquinas, have argued that Suarez does not simply disagree with Aquinas on some details, but radically alters Aquinas' views on natural law and the foundations of ethics, and alters them for the worse. This departure from Aquinas is historically significant because—it is suggested—Suarez strongly influences the theory of natural law that has been prominent in post-Reformation Roman Catholic moral theology.

Historians of ethics and political theory have concentrated on Suarez's treatment of law, and especially of natural law. His treatise 'On Laws and God the Legislator' clarifies many issues that his predecessors pass over. Aquinas has relatively little to say on the relation of the principles of natural law to the will of God. Some of his successors, particularly Scotus and Ockham, have more to say. Suarez sets out and discusses in full the major issues that arise in his predecessors; he considers how many separable claims can be made, and what follows from each of them. Since Grotius and Cudworth are probably familiar with Suarez's discussion, it provides a useful basis for comparing modern with mediaeval views.[1]

The prominence of Suarez's discussion of law might lead us to suppose that law is more important in his conception of morality than in Aquinas' conception. If this were so, Suarez would be closer to a modern than to a mediaeval position on one important issue.[2] We should keep in mind, however, the fact that Suarez conceives his treatise on laws as part of a discussion of Aquinas' *Summa*. When he comes to discuss Aquinas' *Treatise on Law*, he

[1] On Grotius' knowledge of Suarez see §463. On Cudworth see §546.
[2] On modern v. mediaeval views on natural law and ethics see §453.

does not need to remind his readers that he is presupposing the previous parts of the *Prima Secundae*; he takes it for granted. His treatise on laws should be understood in the light of his comments on the rest of the Prima Secundae.

A discussion of Suarez's treatment of natural law will lead us to his treatment of moral goodness. For our purposes, his reflexions on this issue are even more important than his views on natural law; for they correct a misleading impression that we might get from exclusive attention to his treatment of natural law.

424. Some Issues and Clarifications

Discussions about the relation of natural law to the divine will involve several distinct questions that are not always kept apart.[3] Since Suarez does most to distinguish the questions and to show how the answers to them are and are not connected, it is helpful to consider the questions as he sees them.

Orthodox Christians agree that all natural facts that essentially refer to contingent particular beings depend on the creative will of God.[4] Since it was up to God whether or not to create human beings, it depends on God's will whether or not there are any good or bad human actions. But does it equally depend on God's will what human actions are good or bad? Was God free to create human beings for whom murder would have been good and generosity bad? Naturalists answer No, because they believe that moral goodness and badness are fixed by the nature of human beings, and that creatures for whom murder was good would not be human beings. Ockham, however, appears to answer Yes, claiming that our rational knowledge of what fits human nature is itself the result of an exercise of God's free will.

But even if facts about what is good and bad for human beings are grasped by the divine intellect and do not result from a choice made by the divine will, a question still arises about moral goodness. Naturalists believe that moral facts are among the natural facts that are fixed for human beings with our nature. Voluntarists argue that, even if natural facts include facts about the human good, moral facts are not natural facts; for moral facts depend on a further exercise of the divine will, beyond its exercise in creation, and the natural facts do not determine this further exercise. Scotus suggests that the moral principles referring to our neighbours (the second table of the Decalogue) are really divine positive laws, and that in this legislation God's will is not determined by any prior requirements of right and wrong. Ockham goes further, and claims that all the requirements recognized by right reason (including the commandment to love God) result from exercises of the divine will undetermined by any divine knowledge of antecedent right and wrong.

Even if we are naturalists about moral facts, we may still be voluntarists about natural law; for we may claim that facts about intrinsic moral goodness (fixed by natural facts) do

---

[3] A survey of different conceptions of the natural law is offered by the commentators on Scotus, *3Sent* d37 = OO vii.2 858.

[4] This clumsy formulation is intended to take some account of Suarez's views on essences (*DM* xxxi).

not imply the existence of natural law, because natural law depends on a further act of divine legislation. If we say this, we raise a further question about the relation of the divine will to intrinsic morality; is it necessary that God legislates in accordance with intrinsic morality, or is God free to legislate differently? Different answers give us different degrees of voluntarism about natural law.

In trying to understand the naturalist and the voluntarist answers to these different questions, we may resort to counterfactual questions. We may ask whether the same things would have been right and wrong if God had not legislated, and we may say that intrinsic natural facts are those that would exist even if God had not exercised legislative will. But this claim needs to be treated carefully. On one way of understanding it, there are no intrinsic natural facts; for, since God is a necessary being, God is necessarily good, and God's goodness requires the exercise of God's legislative will, natural facts cannot exist without God's having legislated. We must, therefore, understand the relevant counterfactual differently. We must hold God's goodness fixed, and assume, contrary to fact, that God's goodness does not require God to legislate; then we ask what intrinsic natural facts there would be on that assumption.

The same point applies to all counterfactuals that consider what intrinsic natural facts would exist if God did not exist. Anyone who believes in God as creator must believe that without God there would be no natural world. Moreover, anyone who believes that God is a necessary being must believe that if God did not exist, there would be no intrinsic natural facts. The counterfactuals that ask what would be the case if God did not exist must be taken to assume the impossible situation in which God does not exist and still the world is in other ways as it actually is.

These questions and distinctions may help us to understand how Suarez sees the main issues, and where he stands on the most important questions in dispute.

425. Suarez's 'Intermediate' Position

Suarez describes his account of natural law as a middle way, which he also takes to be the view of Aquinas, and the common view of theologians (*Leg.* ii 6.5). An extreme naturalist view makes the law of nature purely 'indicative', showing us what is intrinsically good and bad (ii 6.3).[5] An extreme voluntarist view claims that the natural law lies entirely in the commands proceeding from the divine will, and is therefore entirely a prescriptive (praeceptiva), not an indicative, law (ii 6.4).[6] Suarez's view is intermediate because it claims that 'the natural law is not only indicative of good and bad, but also contains its own proper prohibition of evil and prescription of good' (ii 6.5).[7] He agrees with the naturalist view that it is indicative of what is intrinsically good and bad,[8] but he claims that it is also essentially prescriptive.

---

[5] Quoted in §436.　　[6] Quoted in §435.

[7] Suarez takes the gerundive form to mark indicative law, and only the imperative form to mark prescriptive law. See §442.

[8] Since he takes 'indicative of good and bad' to distinguish his position from the voluntarist position he has just mentioned, he must take this phrase to mean 'indicative of what is intrinsically good and bad'.

To see what Suarez means by speaking of an indicative and a prescriptive law, and why he thinks the natural law must have both features, we should consider his description and discussion of the naturalist and the voluntarist views. Then we can ask what his view claims, and whether it is preferable to the two extreme views.

It is easiest to begin with his discussion of naturalism. For once we understood the points on which he agrees and disagrees with naturalism, we can see what he thinks about voluntarism. His critique of naturalism also includes an affirmation of some aspects of naturalism; these show us where he rejects voluntarism.

Suarez claims to hold an intermediate position about the status of natural law, but we also want to know whether he holds an intermediate position about morality. Since he recognizes that the natural law indicates what is intrinsically good and bad, he is a naturalist about some goods and evils. But which goods and evils are these? If they are moral goods and evils, he is a naturalist about morality, though not about natural law. If they are non-moral, he is a voluntarist both about morality and about natural law.

426. Naturalism

For a statement of a naturalist position that treats natural law as purely indicative, Suarez turns to Gregory of Rimini.[9] Suarez relies on Gregory's admission that even if, per impossibile, God did not exist, or did not use reason, or did not judge correctly, lying, for instance, would still be a sin, because it would still be contrary to correct reason. According to Gregory, sin is contrary to divine reason because divine reason is correct, not because it is divine. Gregory infers that whatever is against correct reason is thereby against the eternal law.[10]

Gregory's account is the basis of Biel's instructive discussion of Augustine's definition of sin. This definition might appear to favour a voluntarist, since it mentions divine law (*2Sent* d35 qun a1), but Biel, following Gregory of Rimini, modifies it gradually in a naturalist direction. First, he argues (a1C = 609) that the divine law is essentially connected with divine reason, and that divine reason is essentially correct. Hence he infers that Augustine's

---

[9] 'In this matter the first opinion is that natural law is not properly a prescriptive (praeceptiva) law, because it is not a sign of the will of some superior, but that it is a law indicating what is to be done or avoided, what by its own nature is intrinsically good and necessary or intrinsically evil. And thus many people distinguish two sorts of law: one sort indicating, the other prescribing. And they say that the natural law is a law in the first way, but not in the second. . . . And consequently it seems that these authors will concede that the natural law is not from God as from a legislator, because it does not rest on the will of God, and thus by its force God does not behave as a superior prescribing or forbidding. Indeed, Gregory says (followed by the others), even if God did not exist or did not employ reason or did not judge correctly about things, even so, if there were in a human being the same dictate of correct reason dictating, for instance, that it is bad to lie, this would have the same character of law that it has now, because it would be a law showing the badness that exists intrinsically in the object.' (ii 6.3)

[10] 'Whatever is against correct reason is against the eternal law. If it is asked why I say it is against correct reason without qualification, rather than, more narrowly, against divine reason, I reply: so that it will not be thought that a sin is precisely against divine reason, and not contrary to any correct reason about it. Otherwise it would be supposed that something is a sin not because it is against divine reason in so far as it is correct, but because it is against it in so far as it is divine. For if by an impossibility divine reason or God himself did not exist, or if that reason were in error, still, if anyone acted against correct reason—angelic, human, or any other—he would be in error.' (Gregory, *2Sent*, d34 q1 a2, concl.1 = T&M vi 235. 11–12, quoted by Perena on Suarez, *Leg.* ii 6.3.) Gregory's account of sin is quoted by Biel, *2Sent*. d35 q1 a1 D. See Oberman, *HMT* 105–8.

account means that sin is an offence against correct reason. To the objection that such an account eliminates a reference to divine law, Biel replies that the relevant sort of law need not be imperative in the strict sense that involves a command 'expressed through a word in the imperative mood or something used instead of it to signify similarly' (a1E.1–3). It may be an indicative law, 'by which it is signified only that something is not to be done (non esse agendum), or something <is signified> from which it follows that it is not to be done' (a1D.8–9). An indicative law says or implies that something ought (debere) not to be done (a1D.13), and from that we can infer that the action is in some way prohibited. Hence a reference to a law and a prohibition does not imply a reference to an imperative law. When we speak of a divine or an eternal law commanding and prohibiting, we should not take this to imply an imperative law, but should take 'law' broadly so as to include indicative law (a1E.7–8).

Biel's last step towards naturalism, still following Gregory of Rimini, explains the meaning of 'contrary to correct reason' in his revised definition of sin. He now argues that the reference to correct reason should not be taken to imply that someone's actual correct reason has to oppose the sinful action. Even if, per impossibile, God did not exist, or if God's reason were not correct, or if no one had correct reason, what would be contrary to correct reason would still be wrong (a1E.17–25). We need to make this clear, Biel remarks, so that no one will suppose that a sin is an act contrary to divine reason insofar as it is divine; it is contrary to divine reason only insofar as divine reason is correct (a1E.17–21).[11]

It is difficult to reconcile this naturalist account of sin with a voluntarist account of the basis of the natural law. Biel's account of correct reason implies that the relevant sort of correctness does not depend on the reason of any person, human or divine; correct reason would forbid an action because the action is inappropriate for human nature. If we claim that this is all true because of God's exercise of ordered power, we imply that God is free, by an exercise of absolute power, to change what is appropriate for human nature, or free to command actions that are inappropriate for human nature.[12] Neither result is satisfactory. God could change what is appropriate for human nature only by making human beings have a different nature; but then they would not be the same species. Nor does Biel allow that God could command what is inappropriate for human nature, though perhaps Ockham is willing to allow it.[13]

Neither Gregory nor Biel affirms that what is intrinsically wrong is thereby contrary to the natural law; they speak only of what is contrary to correct reason. But Suarez is justified in assuming that Gregory has intrinsic wrongness in mind. When Gregory speaks of correct

---

[11] 'For if by an impossibility God, who is divine reason, did not exist, or that divine reason were in error, still if anyone acted against correct reason—angelic or human or any other sort, if there were any—they would sin. And if no correct reason at all existed, still if anyone acted against what correct reason, if there were any, would prescribe to be done, they would sin.' (a1E.21–5)

[12] On absolute v. ordered power see §396.

[13] 'This immanent validity, however, is reliable solely for the reason that its justice is derived from the eternal law or divine reason. This eternal law in its turn is dependable because it is not subject to arbitrary decisions of God's will, or reason, but to a final standard of justice that would even endure if there were no divine reason at all; its steadfastness would not be shaken even if the divine reason would deviate from this norm.' (Oberman, *HMT* 107) Oberman tries to reconcile this claim with a voluntarist thesis that the natural law depends on God's ordered power, but it is difficult to see how he reconciles them.

reason, he does not presuppose the existence of anyone who has correct reason—God, angel, or human being. Correctness is not defined by the conclusions of someone's reasoning; on the contrary the correctness of the conclusions of anyone's reasoning is defined by reference to correct reason. Suarez is justified in suggesting that Gregory alludes to the intrinsic rightness and wrongness of actions, in their own nature and apart from anyone's reasoning about them.

These remarks imply only that some actions are wrong intrinsically, and hence contrary to correct reason, whether or not God prohibits them. But Gregory also claims that what is contrary to correct reason is contrary to the eternal law. Whereas he claims that it would still be wrong even if God did not prohibit it, he does not say it would still be wrong even if the eternal law did not prohibit it; hence he seems to infer that what is intrinsically wrong is essentially contrary to the eternal law. If the existence of the eternal law implies the existence of the natural law, whatever is intrinsically wrong is thereby also contrary to the natural law.[14]

Gregory's counterfactual assumption about the non-existence of God makes the implications of the naturalist position clear. Suarez also cites Vasquez's affirmation that the natural law is independent of the will and command of God (*Leg.* ii 5.2).[15] Though Vasquez does not use the supposition of the non-existence of God to explain his point about the natural law, he agrees with Gregory in affirming that the natural law is independent of divine legislation.[16]

Vasquez's main reason for denying that natural law depends on the divine will is his conception of the content of natural law. He insists that it describes things that are good and bad in their own nature, independently of any will. He infers that natural law does not consist in any command; 'for we said that it is primarily rational human nature itself'.[17]

[14] Whether or not Gregory means to say that natural law would still exist even if God did not exist depends on what he means by his claim that whatever is contrary to correct reason is also contrary to the eternal law. He might have either of two claims in mind: (1) Whatever is contrary to what correct reason would say, whether or not anyone's reason says it, is also contrary to what the eternal law would say, whether or not there is any such law. (2) Whatever is contrary to what correct reason would say, whether or not anyone's reason says it, is also contrary to the actual provisions of the actual eternal law. Suarez assumes that Gregory has the second claim in mind; since Gregory does not qualify his claims about eternal law in the way he qualifies his claims about divine reason, Suarez's assumption is fair. I have emphasized the plausibility of Suarez's claims about Gregory because Haakonssen, *NLMP* 20, maintains that 'Suarez's formulation of Gregory's view . . . polemically distorts it in a significant way. Gregory did not say, in the passage referred to by Suarez, that without God the dictates of right reason would still have the same "legal character" . . . He said only that, even without God, there would be sin, or moral evil (peccatum).' This criticism of Suarez does not take sufficient account of Gregory's remarks about the eternal law, which are plausibly taken to say that the dictates of right reason would have the same legal character without God.

[15] Quoted in §427.

[16] 'If, however, one is talking about the natural law, which is said to exist by its own nature, not by decision or by anyone's will, one must speak differently. For since law or right (ius) is a rule that actions must conform to in order to be just (iustae), natural law or natural right will be a natural rule that exists by no will, but by its own nature. And in fact the existence of such a law or right, which is constituted by no will, not even by the will of God, is most of all confirmed by what we said above, in Disputation 97, Chapter 3. That is to say, some things are evils and sins from themselves in such a way that this prohibition depends on no will, even the will of God—this was proved by us more than adequately. Indeed we not only showed this, but we also pointed out that many things are evil from themselves in such a way that their badness is prior in accord with reason to all judgment of the divine intellect. That is to say, they are not bad because they are judged bad by God; rather, they are judged bad because they are such from themselves. From this it results that before any will and command (imperium) of God, indeed before any judgment, some works are good and evil from themselves.' (Vasquez, *Disp.* 150 c.3 §22, p. 7)

[17] nam primarie diximus esse ipsam naturam rationalem hominis, *Disp.* 150 c.4 §29.

In claiming that it is prior to any will, 'we ought not to say on that account that it is any judgment of reason, even of the divine reason; for it is prior to any judgment'.[18] Natural law obliges, simply in virtue of being natural law;[19] obligation requires nothing more than the existence of the rational beings for whom the natural law is natural.[20]

This conception of the source and obligation of natural law supports Vasquez's denial that the natural law is dispensable. If we make it dispensable, we allow, as Scotus and Ockham do, that sometimes the Decalogue requires a specific action, but a particular person is not required to do it. In Scotus' view, dispensations do not dispense from the natural law; for he takes the moral laws concerning our neighbours to be divine positive law. Since, as Aquinas agrees, divine positive law is subject to dispensation, these moral laws are subject to dispensation too. Ockham goes further than Scotus, and takes the whole of the natural law to be subject to dispensation.[21] But according to Vasquez's account of natural law, the whole Decalogue embodies natural law, and therefore is not subject to dispensation.[22] Since natural law is fixed by the facts about rational nature, God cannot make it right to violate natural law simply by dispensation, without any change in the facts about rational nature.

These claims about natural law rest partly on Vasquez's earlier discussion of sin. In connexion with Aquinas' discussion of the account of sin as being contrary to the eternal law (ST 1–2 q71 a6),[23] he asks whether 'all sin is sin by being contrary to law'.[24] He argues that this view overlooks the fact that the badness of sin is prior to any law.[25] God cannot change the nature of things, and the nature of things makes anything good or bad.[26] If goodness or badness were in some way constituted by a law, it would be mutable in a respect in which we know it is immutable.

---

[18] ob id tamen dicendum non est esse iudicium aliquid rationis, etiam divinae; nam quocumque iudicio prior est, Disp. 150 c.4 §30.

[19] 'Now about the natural law, which sometimes does not oblige when one faces the danger of death, our philosophical account must be such that we do not say that the danger of death prevails against the obligation of natural law; for if the obligation and every circumstance of the precept <of natural law> still remained, it would oblige even at the price of death. In this way, the law of nature about not lying, even venially, is to be kept even with the danger of death. By this law the substance of the precept about not lying remains untouched, with all its circumstances, and none of them, even the smallest is removed by the danger of death; for <the substance of the precept> consists wholly in this, that one speaks externally against what one believes internally. Rather, our philosophical account must be such that we say that when the danger of death arises, some circumstance of the natural law is removed, given that the law would otherwise oblige.' (Vasquez, Disp. 161 c.2 §13, p. 111)

[20] This position on obligation is similar to Clarke's. See §617.   [21] See ii 15.3. On Ockham see §395.

[22] 'For the law of the Decalogue, as we said, is natural law. But the natural law is nature itself, which a given thing is said to agree or disagree with, not without qualification but with the required circumstances. And if these circumstances remain, no one, not even God, can so interpret the law that it does not oblige. For—given that rational nature itself cannot be changed—if the facts and circumstances are unchanged, a true and veracious intellect, such as the divine intellect is, cannot interpret the law itself in different ways.' (Disp. 179 §15, p. 268)

[23] Quoted in §235n6.   [24] omne peccatum eo sit peccatum quo est contra legem, Disp. 97 = i 657.

[25] He refers to Part 1, Disp. 104 c.3, on Scotus; and to 1–2 Disp. 179 on dispensations.

[26] 'Moral badness consists in that relation of opposition with rational nature. Moreover, some things are bad from themselves in such a way—that is to say, unfitting to rational nature in the way in which heat is to water—that if they are done with these circumstances, they have this character by their own nature, not by the will of God prohibiting or by his judgment judging. For, just as the essences of things, from themselves and not from the will or intellect of God, do not imply a contradiction, as we were saying above, and one is contrary and unfitting to another, so also hatred of God and perjury are unfitting to a human being from themselves, and not by the intellect or will of God. And therefore not all sins are sins because they are prohibited.' (Disp. 97 c.3, p. 658) On mala quia prohibita cf. §307.

427. Two Versions of Naturalism

According to Suarez, the naturalist position claims that rational nature is itself the natural law.[27] It claims that rational nature is the epistemological basis for the law, since our reason gives us access to the actions that do and do not accord with our rational nature. But it also holds the metaphysical thesis that natural law is rational nature (*Leg.* ii 5.1).

Suarez recognizes two versions of this naturalist thesis: (1) Objective naturalism: As Vasquez claims, natural law is rational nature itself, insofar as different things are appropriate for it, and therefore right, or inappropriate, and therefore wrong. (2) Cognitive naturalism: Natural law is rational nature as grasping what is appropriate for rational nature (ii 5.1).

The two versions appeal to the same underlying facts—the facts about appropriateness to nature that make an action right or wrong. But cognitive naturalism takes the natural law to consist in a further fact, the judgment of correct reason about what is appropriate or inappropriate. The point of cognitive naturalism is not to say that natural law consists in the judgment about rightness rather than in rightness itself; since the judgment must be correct, genuine natural law rests on actual rightness itself. But cognitive naturalism claims that the mere fact of something's being right or wrong does not by itself constitute the existence of a natural law; there would be no natural law if correct reason did not also make a judgment about it.

Suarez agrees with one part of objective naturalism. He believes in intrinsic rightness and wrongness that are constituted by facts about rational nature in its environment, not by facts about anyone's beliefs, judgments, or commands (ii 5.5). Rational nature is the 'foundation' of the objective rightness of actions, but that does not make it law. Similarly, rational nature is the 'measure' or 'rule' of rightness, but not every measure or rule is thereby a law (ii 5.6). Suarez appeals to Aquinas' broad use of 'measure' and 'rule', and asserts that Aquinas would not speak of a law in all these cases (ii 5.6, citing Aquinas, *ST* 2–2 q141 a6 and ad1). Both as a foundation and as a measure, rational nature lacks the essential functions of a law in prescribing, directing, and enlightening.[28] To assert that rational nature lacks these features, but is still natural law, is to use 'law' equivocally, and thereby to undermine the whole discussion (quod evertit totam disputationem, ii 5.5).

Suarez now argues that objective naturalism makes natural law insufficiently dependent on God, since natural law turns out to oblige God. Since lying is no less inappropriate to God's rational nature than to ours, God's nature will also be a measure or rule of the rightness that requires truthfulness. Hence it will be a law for God no less than for human beings. If objective naturalism is right, the same result follows from Aquinas' claim that God owes to himself what is appropriate to his nature (*ST* 1a q21 a1 ad3). Since God's nature provides a measure, and a measure is a law (according to objective naturalism), God will be

---

[27] '...rational nature, in its own right and in so far as it does not involve any contradiction, and is the foundation of all rightness of human acts that are appropriate for such a nature, or, on the contrary, of <all> wrongness of them through inappropriateness for that nature, is itself the natural law' (*Leg.* ii 5.2).

[28] '...rational nature itself, considered precisely, in so far as it is this sort of essence, neither prescribes, nor displays rightness or wrongness, nor directs, nor enlightens, nor has any other effect that is proper to law' (*Leg.* ii 5.5).

obliged by the law of his nature, just as human beings are obliged by the law of their nature; and this, in Suarez's view, seems absurd (*Leg.* ii 5.7).

The independence of natural law from God, as explained by objective naturalism, has the unwelcome result that natural law is not divine law and is not from God (non esse legem divinam, neque esse ex Deo, ii 5.8).[29] The feature of rational nature that makes actions right and wrong does not depend on God for its character (ratio),[30] though it depends on God for its existence; for the fact that lying is inappropriate to rational nature is not from God, does not depend on God's will, and is even logically (in ordine rationis) prior to a judgment of God (ii 5.8). This passage shows that Suarez takes 'from God' (ex Deo) and 'dependent on God' (pendere ex Deo) to be equivalent. He is not claiming that the relevant facts, according to naturalism, are prior to God, but only that they are not posterior to him, as they ought to be (in his view) if they are really a divine law.

Here Suarez agrees that facts about intrinsic rightness and wrongness do not depend on God. He agrees with objective naturalism about rational nature, intrinsic rightness, and their independence of divine commands. That is why he thinks they cannot be natural law.

After these objections to objective naturalism, Suarez turns to cognitive naturalism. According to this view, the existence of natural law consists not merely in the facts about intrinsic rightness and wrongness, but also in the facts about our rational capacity to discriminate intrinsic rightness and wrongness (ii 5.9). Suarez holds that Aquinas, contrary to Vasquez, takes these cognitive facts to be essential to natural law. He believes that Aquinas agrees with him, against Vasquez, in separating a law (lex) from a standard (regula) and a measure (mensura). When Aquinas refers to our capacity to discriminate right and wrong, he describes (according to Suarez) conditions for the existence of the natural law.

This assumption about Aquinas is insecure. Admittedly, he takes a law to be 'some sort of standard and measure of actions' (quaedam regula . . . et mensura actuum) in accordance with which one is led to act or restrained from acting (*ST* 1–2 q90 a1). But he does not say specifically how a law differs from other standards that might guide action. In order to show that reason is a standard and measure of human action, he asserts simply that it is a measure and standard by being a principle of actions; he infers that law belongs to reason. Our rational capacity for distinguishing right and wrong may be necessary for the presence of the natural law in us, but not for the existence of the natural law (q91 a2).

Aquinas, therefore, may accept objective naturalism, and may not be disturbed by the implications that disturb Suarez. But he does not clearly endorse objective naturalism. In claiming that the natural law consists of precepts, he assumes that it requires 'command' (imperium), which is an act of reason presupposing an act of will.[31] Aquinas' claim that command belongs to reason suggests that a fact external to agents does not constitute a precept until it is grasped by some agent, divine or human. Hence the existence of the

---

[29] ET mistakenly puts 'therefore' at the beginning of §8. 'Deinde' marks the second of the 'inconvenientia' mentioned at the beginning of §7.

[30] 'Rational basis' ET. Perena's 'en su esencia' is preferable.

[31] For Aquinas' views on imperium see 1–2 q17 a1; a3 ad1; 2–2 q47 a8; q50; §257. Cajetan on 1–2 q17 a1 defends intellect as the source of imperium, connecting it with the view that prudence itself is prescriptive. He attacks Scotus on this point. Suarez agrees with Scotus in taking command to proceed from the will, in contrast to intellect (*Leg.* i 4.14). See Farrell, *NLSTS* 56; Finnis, *NLNR* 54, 337–43, 347.

natural law seems to require rational agents who grasp it. This aspect of Aquinas' view separates him, as Suarez says, from Vasquez.

Still, Vasquez's view captures Aquinas' belief that natural facts make actions right or wrong, and hence provide the content of precepts of natural law. In Aquinas' view, facts about human nature constitute duties (debita), because they would be prescriptive for us if we grasped them and connected them appropriately with our will.

Suarez, therefore, is right to distinguish the two forms of naturalism found in Aquinas and in Vasquez, and to explore their implications.

428. Suarez's Objection to Naturalism

Suarez criticizes cognitive naturalism, which takes knowledge of right and wrong to be essential for the existence of natural law. According to this view, the natural law proceeds from God as creator, not as legislator; it does not essentially convey God's commands, but indicates what is good or bad in itself.[32]

Both objective and cognitive naturalism would be open to attack if they could not be reconciled with the Scriptural evidence that Suarez accumulates to show that natural law is divine prescriptive law (*Leg.* ii 6.7–8). If a naturalist position could not explain how God can command observance of the natural law, it would have to say that the natural law is purely declarative, and not prescriptive (ii 6.3).

A cognitive naturalist might fairly reply that the indicative character of the natural law does not preclude God's also commanding us to obey it. God's command is a further exercise of divine freewill beyond its exercise in creation. Once we exist as creatures who ought to obey the natural law, we still have a choice about whether to obey it. Moreover, God has a choice about whether to command us to obey it. This does not mean it is possible for God to create us and then to abstain from commanding us to obey the natural law; such an abstention would be contrary to God's goodness. But the fact that God's nature makes it impossible for God, having created us, not to command us to obey the natural law does not imply that God does not freely command us to obey it.

This claim about God's freedom will convince us if we explain divine freedom as Aquinas explains it, but not if we agree with Scotus or Ockham about divine freedom. Since Suarez accepts Aquinas' explanation, he cannot reasonably deny that God commands out of his freewill that we obey the natural law that exists independently of his command.

Suarez has a further objection to the naturalist position; it implies that the natural law is not essentially commanded by God. This claim about essence may be expressed by the counterfactual claim that even if God had not commanded us to obey the natural law, there would still have been natural law. In reply Suarez affirms an essential connexion between the natural law and God's commands. Both versions of naturalism imply that if any divine

---

[32] 'God is, therefore, without doubt the producer and, so to speak, the teacher of the law of nature. But it does not follow from this that he is the legislator, because the law of nature does not indicate God as prescribing but it indicates what is good or bad in itself, just as sight of a certain sort of object indicates that this is white or black, and as an effect of God indicates God as its author, but not as legislator. That, then, is how we will have to think of the natural law.' (*Leg.* ii 6.2)

prohibition were removed, action contrary to the purely indicative principles of goodness and badness would violate the natural law.[33]

Why should we find this result unacceptable? If the naturalist view is right, natural law is not essentially genuine law, as Suarez understands it, because it does not require any command by a superior (ii 6.6). But the best authorities, in his view, understand natural law as genuine law, because they insist that God prohibits offences against the natural law.[34] Suarez misses the mark; a naturalist need not deny that the natural law is in fact commanded by God. The crucial naturalist claim is simply that it is not essential to natural law to be commanded by God.

Suarez now argues that it is not a contingent fact that God commands observance of the natural law. Since God is creator and governor, it is appropriate and necessary for God to command the good and forbid the evil.[35] Given that a rational creature has been created, it is necessary that such a creature is subject to moral government, and therefore to the commands of a superior (i 3.3). Once naturalists concede that the natural law indicates what is naturally right and wrong, and also admit the necessary goodness and rationality of God, they must agree that it is necessary for the natural law to be commanded by God.[36]

These arguments assume a naturalist opponent who believes it is possible that an action violates the natural law and does not violate a divine command. Suarez replies that this conjunction is impossible, because it is necessary that whatever is intrinsically good and bad is commanded and prohibited by God.[37] It cannot simply be a contingent feature of good and bad action that God commands the one and forbids the other; given the nature of good and bad, and the nature of God, something's being good or bad implies that God commands or forbids it. Hence it is not possible for something to be prescribed by the natural law but not commanded by God.[38]

Suarez is open to an objection. Even if the natural law is necessarily commanded by God, it does not follow that it is essentially commanded by God. For not all necessary properties

---

[33] 'Therefore the natural law, as it is in a human being, does not only indicate the thing itself in its own right, but also as prohibited or prescribed by some superior. The consequence is clear, because if the natural law intrinsically consists in the object by itself in its own right, or in showing it, the violation of it will not, in itself and intrinsically, be against the law of a superior. For, if every law of a superior were removed, a human being would <still> violate the natural law by acting against that dictate <of reason simply showing the goodness and badness of the object>.' (ii 6.7)

[34] 'All the things that the natural law dictates to be evil are prohibited by God, by his special prescription and by the will by which he wills us to be required and obliged by the force of his authority to keep these <dictates>. Therefore the natural law is properly a prescriptive law, or introduces (insinuativa) <its> proper precept.' (ii 6.8)

[35] 'God has perfect providence over human beings. Therefore it is proper for him and his supreme governance of nature to forbid evils and to prescribe goods. Therefore, even though natural reason indicates what is good or evil for a rational nature, nonetheless God, as ruler and governor of such a nature, prescribes the doing or avoiding ["vitare" (Perena); OO has "vetare"] of what reason dictates to be done or avoided.' (ii 6.8)

[36] 'Whatever is done against correct reason displeases God, and the contrary pleases him, because, since the will of God is supremely just, what is wrong cannot not displease him, and what is right cannot not please him, because the will of God cannot be irrational . . . Therefore correct reason, which indicates what is good or bad for a human being in its own right, consequently indicates that it is in accord with the divine will that the one should be done and the other avoided.' (ii 6.8)

[37] This is not quite accurate, since it overlooks the distinction between the required (debitum) and the merely desirable, which I will return to later.

[38] 'Finally, the obligation of the natural law is true obligation. Now this obligation is a good in its own way, existing in the nature of things. Therefore, it is necessary that that obligation should proceed from the divine will willing that human beings be required to observe what correct reason prescribes.' (ii 6.10)

11

of a subject are part of the essence of the subject, and hence they do not all belong to it as that subject. The essential properties (according to Aristotelian metaphysics) are those (putting it too simply) that explain the subject's having the other necessary properties it has. Suarez does not seem to have shown why the natural law is essentially commanded by God.

One might try to defend Suarez by arguing that the counterfactual accepted by the naturalist is inconsistent with the recognition of a necessary connexion between the natural law and God's command. The naturalist accepts a counterfactual saying that if God did not command observance of the principles requiring good action, observance of them would still be in accordance with natural law. Since it is necessarily true that God commands observance of the natural law, the truth of the antecedent of the counterfactual implies that these good actions are not in accord with the natural law. Hence the conditional as a whole says that these actions both are and are not in accord with the natural law. Hence the naturalist's supposition leads to a contradiction, so that the whole counterfactual conditional is false.

But we would be wrong to argue in this way against the naturalist thesis, however, since we would misinterpret the counterfactual. If a counterfactual has an impossible antecedent, we need to be careful in saying what features of the actual world we hold fixed in evaluating the counterfactual. In particular, we must not regard as false all the truths about the actual world whose falsity follows necessarily from the truth of the antecedent.[39] We are to suppose that the world is otherwise the same, apart from the fact that God does not command the observance of the natural law. This supposed state of affairs is impossible, given what we know about God, but we ignore this impossibility in considering the counterfactual. We may still affirm that the counterfactual is true, even though it is impossible that God does not command observance of the natural law.

Is this an over-subtle interpretation of the relevant counterfactual, or is it anachronistic for Suarez? It is the interpretation that he applies to the counterfactual claim that if God did not command us to observe the natural law, things would still be good and bad in their own right. He defends the coherence of this counterfactual while agreeing that the antecedent is impossible.[40] The same treatment of the naturalist claim (that even if God did not command us, good and bad action would still violate the natural law) removes Suarez's objection to the coherence and the truth of this claim.

The argument about counterfactuals, therefore, does not refute the naturalist claim that the natural law is not essentially commanded by God, and therefore would still be natural law even if God did not command it. Suarez would have found a strong objection against naturalism if he had shown that naturalism makes it false, or merely contingently true, that God commands the observance of the natural law. Perhaps he believes that this follows for any naturalist who accepts the counterfactual that Gregory uses to formulate the naturalist position. But he would be wrong to believe this. We might reasonably believe that natural law is the natural standard that would have existed even if God had not legislated, but the

---

[39] For Aquinas' treatment of counterfactuals with impossible antecedents see *ST* 1a q25 a3 ad2: 'For nothing rules out a conditional from being true whose antecedent and consequent are impossible, as if it were said, "If a human being is an ass, he has four feet."' (cf. q44 a1 ad2).

[40] See *Leg.* ii 6.14, discussed in §441.

12

world had otherwise been the same. This is consistent with the belief that God necessarily commands the observance of the natural law.

429. True Law

Suarez, therefore, has a cogent argument against the naturalist account of natural law only if he can show that natural law is essentially a genuine law, and therefore essentially commanded by God. To see whether he can show this, we should look more closely at his account of genuine law and of its connexion with commands.

In speaking of 'genuine' or 'true' law, Suarez allows a broader sense. Hooker draws a similar distinction between a law imposed by authority and an 'enlarged' sense of 'law' that refers simply to the principles on which God acts, which are not products of divine legislation, but part of the nature of things.[41] This is the sort of law that Vasquez describes in claiming that law is 'an operation of reason, not of will' (*Comm.* ad90.1, p. 6). He considers the view of those who believe that the connexion of law to obligation requires us to think of natural law as 'the will of God by which he wills us to be obliged' (voluntas Dei qua vult nos obligari, *Disp.* 150 c.3 §21, p. 7). These people think that the existence of law requires an act of legislation, but Vasquez believes they are wrong.

To explain how the natural law is law, Vasquez introduces a further sense of 'law'. It depends neither on the divine will nor on the divine intellect. Hence natural law is law in a broader sense, which Vasquez would prefer to call 'ius' rather than 'lex'. The mark of natural law is its being a rule of just and unjust.[42]

Suarez rejects this treatment of natural law. Though he allows the broader sense of 'law' that includes indicative law, he believes that natural law is law in a more precise sense. In his view, a law is 'a common precept, just and stable, sufficiently promulgated' (*Leg.* i 12.4); in this conclusion he agrees with Aquinas (*ST* 1–2 q96 a1 ad2). The crucial emphasis in this definition, for present purposes, lies on 'precept', which Suarez takes to imply a command expressing the will of a superior.

Suarez reaches this definition by rejecting conceptions of law that he takes to be too broad. The first of these is derived from Aquinas' description of law as a rule or measure that guides action.[43] On this conception, all creatures, not only rational agents, receive and obey law. This would be a mistake, because non-rational creatures 'are not properly capable

---

[41] See §413 on Hooker.

[42] 'From this teaching we infer this noteworthy conclusion, that the name of law (lex) does not fit natural law as well as it fits positive law, whether the word is derived from reading (legere) from a written text, or from election. For the natural law is neither read in a written text, nor is constituted voluntarily by any election, even a divine election; but it exists necessarily by its own nature. Therefore it is more properly called right (ius), because it is the rule of just and unjust.' (Vasquez, *Disp.* 150 c.3 §26, p. 8)

[43] 'Law is a type of rule and measure of acts [Suarez's quotation omits "of acts"] in accordance with which someone is led to action or is restrained from action: for "lex" [law] is so called from binding (ligare), because it obliges (obligat) to action.' (Aquinas, *ST* 1–2 q90 a1) The explanatory clause suggests that Aquinas takes his definition to capture the fact that law binds. But it is difficult to see how the obligatory character of a law, so understood, is captured in Aquinas' description, unless the combination of 'rule' and 'led' (inducere) indicates obligation, or 'a type of rule' (quaedam regula) indicates that he has not fully specified the type of rule that is to be identified with law.

of <receiving> law, just as they are not properly capable of obedience either' (*Leg.* i 1.2).[44] If we speak of non-rational creatures being governed by divine law, when we really refer to 'the efficacy of divine power' and to natural necessity, we are speaking metaphorically (i 1.2). Aquinas takes the eternal law to extend to all creation,[45] but, in Suarez's view, this claim is true only if it is taken metaphorically (i 3.9). Natural law, insofar as it belongs to moral doctrine and to theology, applies only to rational creatures (i 3.10).[46] Aquinas seems to agree, because he distinguishes the way in which rational creatures participate in eternal law from the way in which non-rational creatures do, and concludes that 'natural law is nothing other than participation in eternal law in a rational creature' (*ST* 1–2 q91 a2).

Suarez believes all this because he believes that no command can really be addressed to non-rational creatures; they cannot understand or obey commands as expressions of the reason and will of a superior. This connexion of law with rational will, in both the legislator and the subject, is recognized by Aquinas, according to Suarez, in the derivation of 'lex' from 'ligare', because 'the proper effect of law is to bind (ligare) or oblige (obligare)' (*Leg.* i 1 9).

The reasons that Suarez offers here for taking law to require a command—understood as the expression of the will of a superior—do not seem persuasive, either from Aquinas' point of view or in their own right.[47] We might well agree that rational creatures 'participate' differently in a law, insofar as they are guided by their understanding of it; but this does not mean that it must be addressed to them as a command, or that they must regard it as a command. Similarly, we might agree that a law obliges, but deny that only a command can oblige.

Suarez's arguments make it difficult to identify his basic conviction. Does his whole argument rest on a conception of the nature of law, and does his claim about obligation depend on his view of how law operates? Or does it all rest on his conception of obligation, and does his claim about law depend on his view that law obliges? If we are to accept his claims about natural law we need some independent argument either for his claim about the nature of law or for his claim about the nature of obligation; if this argument is convincing, we must also be convinced that natural law is essentially genuine law, and that it imposes genuine obligation.

430. Obligation and the Natural Law

While the naturalist claims that the natural law would still be natural law even if God did not command it, Suarez denies this claim. He believes that since the natural law essentially imposes a genuine obligation, it essentially proceeds from a divine command.[48] Law requires

---

[44] nam res carentes ratione non sunt proprie capaces legis, sicut nec oboedientiae. (*Leg.* i 1.2)

[45] '. . . since all things subject to Divine providence are ruled (regulantur) and measured by the eternal law, . . . it is evident that all things partake to some degree of the eternal law—namely, in so far as, from its being imprinted on them, they have their tendencies towards their proper acts and ends' (*ST* 1–2 q91 a2).

[46] 'And so natural law properly speaking, which applies to moral doctrine and to theology, is the law that is seated in the human mind for distinguishing right from wrong (honestum a turpi). . .' (*Leg.* i 3.9). For the reference to distinguishing honestum from turpe cf. Aquinas *in EN* §1019.

[47] Aquinas holds a broader conception of command (imperium). See §306.

[48] *Leg.* ii 6.10, quoted in previous section.

commands because law imposes obligation,[49] and obligation requires command; hence if natural law is true law, it requires a divine command. Facts about rational nature fall short of natural law, according to Suarez, because natural law is genuine law. For rational nature in itself does not issue commands, but these are essential to genuine law (ii 5.5).[50]

We might doubt whether rational nature lacks all the features relevant to a law. Natural facts may serve as signs or directives to knowers and agents who understand them appropriately. If Suarez objects that they do not do these things 'considered precisely' insofar as they are these sorts of facts, but only in relation to the appropriate sorts of knowers and agents, we may reply that laws do not enlighten or direct 'considered precisely' in themselves, but only insofar as knowers and agents understand them and care about what they say.

Still, Suarez might fairly maintain that laws mark an intention to display, direct, and enlighten, and that natural facts involve no such intention, and hence do not command. On this point about intention he has found a genuine difference between commands and natural facts. He needs to persuade us that the natural law requires this intention. To be persuaded, we have to accept Suarez's claim that natural law is essentially true law, as he conceives it.

Vasquez's discussion suggests that a naturalist has no reason to concede without argument that natural law is essentially true law. He admits that natural law lacks features that we might readily attribute to law, on the basis of what we know about positive law. But he infers not that he has given the wrong account of natural law, but that natural law is properly called 'natural right' (ius) rather than 'natural law' (lex). Has Suarez an argument to show that Vasquez makes some mistake in this answer to the question about law?

He might have a basis for argument in claims about obligation; for Vasquez assumes that the natural law is obligatory. If, then, Suarez is right about the nature of obligation, and the natural law obliges, it requires a command, and hence is true law. Hence he sometimes argues that since the natural law essentially obliges us, and since obligation requires us to be bound by the command of a superior, we are obliged to follow the natural law insofar as it is commanded by God. The natural law, therefore, is essentially commanded by God.

What does Suarez mean by insisting that genuine obligation requires a command? We might take him to present an account of normative facts and principles. Normative—i.e., reason-giving—principles imply that we ought to act in some way, or we have reason to act in this way. Some have argued that these reason-giving facts must include facts about the will or desires of agents; others have maintained that external natural facts by themselves imply that agents of a certain sort ought to act in a specific way, whether or not a given agent's will is appropriately directed.

According to one interpretation, Suarez's separation of intrinsic natural facts from divine commands separates non-normative natural facts from normative principles of morality.[51]

---

[49] quia de intrinseca ratione eius [sc. legis] est ut aliquam intrinsecam obligationem inducat . . . (i 9.17). See also i 11.2 (the assumption that law obliges is the basis for the claim that it must be promulgated); i 14.1 ('The special effectiveness of law in making human beings good is its obligation, which seems to be especially its intrinsic effect . . .').

[50] Quoted in §427.

[51] This interpretation goes back at least to Culverwell. See §558. It is accepted by (e.g.) Chroust, 'Grotius' 117: 'In order to make any act a truly moral one, we still need the rational insight that this act coincides with the divine will, the author of the natural and moral order.' (Chroust cites Leg. ii 6.7, but I do not see where it supports his claim.) According to this interpretation, Suarez is a 'natural-law moralist' in the sense explained in §455. Culverwell's interpretation suggests

His claims about obligation might be taken to affirm that genuinely normative principles require divine commands. Natural goodness and badness exist independently of God's legislation, and, as he often says, they are the 'foundation' of natural law. But they do not become moral goodness and badness until they are the subject matter of divine commands. The natural is to be distinguished from the normative, because the normative is the area of obligation, and hence of command and legislation.

According to this interpretation, then, Suarez separates the natural from the normative. He believes that without laws and commands, we have no genuine moral obligation, and hence no genuine moral ought or conclusive moral reason. His distinction between the indicative and the prescriptive might be taken to suggest this point; we might suppose that he identifies the indicative with the descriptive and therefore non-normative, and identifies the prescriptive with the normative. If that is what he means, we might suppose that obligation is necessary for genuine norms, so that law and commands are necessary for norms, and hence for the moral ought.[52] If this is Suarez's view, he is a natural-law moralist in a strong sense; he not only believes in natural law, but also believes that morality is essentially and fundamentally natural law.[53] He believes this primarily because he is a prescriptivist about norms.

431. Conceptions of Obligation

To test this prescriptivist interpretation of Suarez, we should see how he understands obligation. If he believes that the moral is to be distinguished from the non-moral by the presence of moral obligation, we might reasonably suppose that his concept of obligation is the concept of a genuinely normative requirement. But we cannot simply take it for granted that this is his concept of obligation. In moral philosophy in English, 'oblige' (or 'obligate') and 'obligation' have been a source of dispute and confusion since the 17th century. We must try to see whether Suarez has a reasonably clear concept, and what it is.

To grasp Suarez's concept of obligation (obligatio), it may be useful to survey some different claims that have been made by writers in English about the concept of obligation. Though they do not exactly capture Suarez's concept, they indicate some of the relevant distinctions.

According to a narrow 'impositive' analysis, an obligation is a special sort of moral requirement, in which the source of the requirement is some voluntary act that imposes the obligation. I have an obligation, therefore, to keep a promise insofar as making a promise is acting so as to bind myself in a particular way. But if I have not done anything to bind myself to refrain from harming innocent people, and no one else has imposed the obligation on me,

---

a division between the merely natural and the moral that is accepted by Locke, Cumberland, and Pufendorf. They all agree that morality depends on natural law, and hence on divine commands, and that the natural foundation of morality consists in natural, but non-moral, goodness and badness. If Suarez anticipates them in marking this division, he is clearly a natural-law moralist, since he takes morality to consist in the obligations that belong to natural law.

[52] This is Finnis's interpretation of Suarez in *NLNR* 47n, 350.

[53] Hence he engages in the 'attempt to understand morality in the legalistic terms of a natural law', Haakonssen, *NLMP* 15. We attribute a natural-law theory in this strong sense to Aquinas, for instance, if we agree that 'for him, the virtues are basically habits of obedience to laws' (Schneewind, *IA* 20). See §315.

I have no obligation to refrain from harming them, even though I nonetheless ought not to harm them.[54]

We accept a 'compulsory' analysis of obligation, in contrast to other sorts of relations between agents and actions, if we concentrate on the necessitating or compulsory aspects of obligations.[55] If I am morally obliged to act in a certain way, it is not simply desirable, or preferable, or a good idea, or attractive, or appealing, to act in that way, but I have no choice about doing it. The sense in which I have no choice is not the physical or the psychological, but the rational sense; nothing else in the circumstances could be a reasonable choice for me. In this way of conceiving it, moral obligations correspond to the compulsory, as opposed to the optional, parts of a syllabus or examination. If we think there are non-moral obligations, they will have the same compulsory character. This contrast between the obligatory and the desirable may be identified with the contrast between the required and the supererogatory areas of morality, if we think morality extends beyond what is required.

In contrast to these analyses, a 'purely deontic' analysis takes an obligation to correspond to every practical use of 'ought'.[56] On this view, since morality and prudence tell us what we ought to do, all true moral and prudential ought-judgments specify obligations.

A 'motivational' analysis might be combined with any of the previous three analyses. It tries to explain the sort of necessity or requirement that belongs to obligations as a motive

---

[54] Hart, 'Obligation' 100, mentions three features of an obligation: '(1) dependence on the actual practice of a social group, (2) possible independence of content, and (3) coercion'. The first feature introduces imposition. Baier, *MPV* 218, agrees with some of this analysis; in his view, 'obligations between people can arise only on account of what has already happened or been done'. Obligations 'arise only when the normal moral relationship between two or more people, that of moral non-involvement, is disturbed, and they end only when the state of moral non-involvement is restored' (216). In 'Moral obligation', Baier rejects Hart's narrowing of 'obligation' and 'duty' (212). But he still maintains that 'obligations arise when and only when a morally binding directive gives rise . . . to a task . . .' (213). A directive is 'the content of speech acts capable of guiding those to whom it applies' (210). He seems to suppose that the existence of directives depends on the existence of the relevant speech acts. Sometimes he even seems to identify obligations with obligation claims: 'All obligation claims are subclasses of general directives with morally binding force, and so are an integral part of a morality, even though some, e.g., promissory or legal obligations, assign tasks which, but for being *thus* assigned, would not be moral tasks' (226). Baier asserts a similar connexion between obligations and speech acts, in *RMO* 315: 'What is peculiar to them [sc. obligations] is that the institutions that generate them have only one role, that the content of the duties generated in this way is determined by the words used by the role player . . . and that the aim of the institution is the generation of such tailor-made duties . . . In promising one obligates oneself, in legislating one obligates others. The most important thing that distinguishes an obligation from other kinds of assumed duty is that it is generated by one's saying something.' In *TJ* 113/97 Rawls accepts a narrow concept of obligation: 'There are several characteristic features of obligations which distinguish them from other moral requirements. For one thing, they arise as a result of our voluntary acts; these acts may be the giving of express or tacit undertakings, such as promises and agreements, but they need not be, as in the case of accepting benefits. Further, the content of obligations is always defined by an institution or practice the rules of which specify what it is that one is required to do. And finally, obligations are normally owed to definite individuals, namely those who are cooperating together to maintain the arrangement in question.' Rawls contrasts duties: 'Now in contrast with obligations, it is characteristic of natural duties that they apply to us without regard to our voluntary acts. Moreover, they have no necessary connexion with institutions or social practices; their content is not, in general, defined by the rules of these arrangements' (114/98). Hence he recognizes natural duties that do not depend on any institutional background. These differentiating features of obligations do not all fit Suarez's concept of obligation. The clearest point of connexion appears in Rawls's reference to an institutional context as the source of the requirement. This is what Suarez has in mind when he takes obligations to presuppose an act of imposition. (He recognizes something like Rawls's division, as a division within obligations, as he understands them, at *Leg.* ii 14.7, 20, 25.) Rawls refers to Hart, 'Legal'; Whiteley, 'Duties'; and Brandt, 'Obligation'. Brandt offers some parallel with Suarez's narrow concept of obligation, by stressing the connexion of paradigmatic uses of 'obligation' with voluntary undertakings and impositions.

[55] See Adams, *FIG* 231–2.

[56] I say 'practical use' to exclude cases such as 'The bread ought to be baked by now', where no obligation is involved.

that inclines the obliged agent to action. If we also accept a purely deontic analysis of obligation, we will take all true moral judgments to imply a motive.

In calling these analyses of the concept of obligation, we distinguish them from claims about the content of obligations. We should especially keep this distinction in mind in considering restrictive analyses of obligation. If one accepts a purely deontic analysis of obligation, and then claims that all obligations are imposed, one makes the restrictive claim that all genuine moral oughts and reasons are imposed. But one is not committed to this restrictive claim if one accepts the impositive analysis of obligation; acceptance of that analysis allows moral oughts and reasons that are not obligations, and are therefore not imposed.

These remarks may help us to be cautious in approaching Suarez's claims. If he offers an impositive analysis of obligation, and claims that obligation, so understood, requires divine commands, he is making a restricted claim about one area of morality; he does not imply that morality in general requires divine commands. But if he accepts a purely deontic analysis of obligation and holds that obligation, so understood, requires divine commands, he holds a broader thesis about the relation of morality to divine commands.[57]

432. Why Obligation Requires Laws and Commands

Suarez clarifies his views on obligation in dissenting from the naturalist claim that obligation follows from the presence of a specific principle in the divine intellect. Naturalists argue that the obligation and prohibition inherent in the natural law consist in the fact that the principles present in God's intellect as creator have been communicated to us as creatures.[58] Suarez argues that the appeal to the divine intellect makes the alleged obligation consist simply in the intrinsic goodness and badness of the actions.[59] A reference to God introduces no more obligation than we find in intrinsic goodness itself; that is to say, intrinsic goodness plus the divine intellect as its source constitutes no obligation whatever. By referring to God's intellect, we assure ourselves that an action really has intrinsic goodness, but we learn nothing more about any obligation. God's intellect recognizes goodness that does not depend on its being recognized, and therefore the goodness itself has to be the source of the obligation.[60]

---

[57] For convenience, I represent 'obligare' by 'oblige' and 'obligatio' by 'obligation', without assuming that these provide the best translation into philosophical English of the Latin terms. What Suarez says about obligations may or may not constitute his account of obligation, in any more idiomatic sense.

[58] 'Some people reply that it suffices for natural law that there is some natural dictate of the divine intellect, by which it judges that these evils are to be avoided and these goods to be done. For about those things that in themselves and intrinsically are such, that prescription is not free but necessary. And from that dictate of divine and eternal law in such a subject matter there necessarily extends a certain participation in it to a rational creature, on the assumption that it has been created. And from this participation and derivation, without any other act of the divine will, there extends to a rational creature, as by a sort of natural consequence, a special obligation, because of which he is required to follow correct reason as indicating the eternal rule that is in God. And thus, whatever may be the case about the free act of the divine will, this obligation and prohibition follow altogether necessarily from divine reason.' (*Leg.* ii 6.22)

[59] 'Further, because that <alleged> obligation does not go beyond the force of an object that is good or bad in itself, from which the action has its being good or bad in itself; the judgment of reason has only the character of applying or showing that sort of object.' (ii 6.22) By 'that obligation' (illa obligatio) Suarez must mean 'that obligation alleged by my opponents', which he does not take (in the light of his previous remarks) to be a genuine obligation.

[60] 'Finally, rational nature showing good and bad obliges neither further nor more strongly from the fact that it is a participation in divine reason than it would oblige considered in its own right and if it were from itself.' (ii 6.22)

Suarez believes that these appeals to intrinsic goodness and badness overlook the distinctive features of obligation. Obliging implies a deliberate attempt by the imposer to move the will of the subject who is obliged.[61] If this attempt succeeds, you have obliged me to act, and thereby you have 'conferred' or 'introduced' a new moral necessity that did not already exist before the act of obliging.[62] Hence 'oblige' does not refer to the fact that it is morally necessary for me to act in a specific way, but to the source of this necessity.[63]

The difference between created and antecedent moral necessity marks the difference between the roles of will and of intellect in law. Intellect recognizes an antecedent requirement that does not depend on intellect. But will is needed for the intention to bind someone else by imposing a moral requirement. Since obligation involves this prospective element, it involves will.[64]

The connexion between law, obligation, and intention to bind is so close, according to Suarez, that law is fundamentally a 'mental law'.[65] The written law simply presents and declares this mental law to the subject, in order to make the legislator's act of will effective. But the act of will that the published law declares is not a mental law unless it is an act of obliging, which is an act of will that creates a moral necessity. Every obligation, properly so called, arises from law.[66] The existence of a moral necessity does not always require a law, but obliging—the imposing of a moral necessity—requires a law.[67]

Given this account of obligation, Suarez denies that God is obliged by the intrinsic goodness of (e.g.) keeping a promise.[68] If God is to be obliged, someone must impose the obligation

[61] 'But this answer cannot be understood, because the dictate of intellect without will cannot by itself have the character of a precept in relation to another, nor can it bring about in the other a special obligation, because obligation is a certain kind of moral moving <of someone> towards acting. Now, moving another to operation is a work of will.' (ii 6.22)

[62] '<We must prove> that some conditions necessary for law are found in an act of will and not properly in an act of intellect. The first condition is initiating motion (movere) and applying a subject to carrying out an action (always including omission under action). For the principle initiating motion and applying something to carrying out an action is will; for intellect rather initiates motion to the extent of specifying <an action>, and therefore is said to direct rather than to initiate motion. The second condition is having the force (vis) of obliging, a force which properly is in will and not in intellect. For intellect is only capable of showing the necessity that is in the object itself, and which the intellect itself could not assign (tribuere) to the object if it were not in it. Will, however, confers necessity that was not in the object, and brings it about that, for instance, in the area of justice, that a thing should have this much or that much value, and in the area of the other virtues brings it about that here and now it is necessary to act, which otherwise would not be necessary in its own right.' (i 5.15)

[63] 'For that will that the superior has of obliging a subject to such an action, or (which amounts to the same thing) of constituting such matter within the necessary limits of virtue, is best called by the name of law . . . Nothing antecedent to this will can have the force of law, since it cannot introduce (inducere) necessity.' (i 5.16)

[64] 'For if one attends to the power of initiating motion that is in law, and thereby one calls law that which is in the ruler which initiates motion, in that way law is an act of will. If, however, one looks at and considers the power in law of directing to what is good and necessary, in that way it belongs to intellect.' (i 5.21)

[65] 'The mental law, so to speak, is an act of a just and correct will in the legislator himself, an act by which the superior wills to oblige to the doing of this or that.' (i 5.24)

[66] i 14.12; 'If obligation is properly and proportionately understood, it always arises from some right (ius) and law (lex), and so in this sense this can be called the adequate effect of law.' We must distinguish the 'foundation' or 'proximate material' of an obligation from the obligation itself. If, for instance, we make a vow, the foundation is a voluntary promise; 'but in so far as it properly obliges us to its fulfillment, it is natural and divine law. . . . And that is also why the jurists say that all obligation that arises from contracts is natural or civil, because it arises from the law of nature or nations or from civil law.' (i 14.13)

[67] On the connexion between obligation and imposition see i 18.1; 'But obligation essentially refers to someone on whom it is imposed.'

[68] ii 2.6; 'And so if a promise is added beyond a general law, God will now be obliged to keep that promise, not by positive law, but by the natural correctness that arises in such an object from the force of a promise.' The sequel

on God. But God has no superior who is entitled to impose the obligation; hence no one can oblige God.[69] Since God acts simply on a judgment of reason, no obligation is involved. The dictates of the divine reason express what is morally right and wrong, and thereby dictate what is to be willed by God (dictant de volendis ab ipso Deo), but they lack the character of law (Leg. ii 3.5) because they reveal, but do not create, moral requirements. The eternal law is law because God imposes it on intellectual creatures (ii 3.8). Hence the eternal law, as law, must introduce an obligation.[70] God introduces an obligation because God has the supreme power to command (ii 4.2), and commands are the only possible source of obligations.

These claims about obligation and acts of binding help us to understand Suarez's account of obligation as a certain kind of 'moral moving'.[71] Some have understood 'moral moving' as 'moral motivation', and taken Suarez to mean that obligation consists in motivation, so that being obliged (i.e., being under an obligation) is being moved (being motivated) to act in the appropriate way. Since (we might suppose) we morally ought to do x if and only if we are obliged to do x, and the appropriate sort of motivation must come from a command, all genuine moral oughts must come from commands.[72]

This interpretation, however, does not fit Suarez. In this context he discusses the active sense of 'obligation', in which someone obliges someone else; as he says, moving someone else to action is a property of the will. His claim does not mean 'Obligation is a certain moral movement[73] towards acting'. The right rendering is 'Obliging is a certain moral moving of someone <else> to act'.[74] Suarez is concerned with the act of obliging, or putting someone under an obligation, not with the state in which someone is under an obligation.[75] The act of obliging, he claims, must involve a will. He does not suggest that you have obliged me only if you have produced a certain motive in me.

shows that Suarez rejects this consequence; though God ought (debet) to do what is naturally correct, God is not obliged to do it.

[69] 'The judgment of reason is necessary in God only from the fact that nothing can be willed except what is foreknown. However, this judgment has not got the function as of obliging or determining the will. Rather the will is in itself correct and right (honesta), and thereby the dictate of reason, the dictate that is understood to be logically (ratione) prior in intellect, cannot have the proper character of law in respect of the divine will. You will say: Granted that it cannot be said to be a compelling (cogens) law, it can be called a law that directs and that shows the appropriateness (convenientiam) or rightness (honestatem) of the object. I answer: This is not enough for a moral law, as is clear from what has been said, and as will be made clearer in what follows on the natural law; but, as agreed, a metaphorical way of speaking is not to be admitted, unless it is commonly used.' (ii 2.8)

[70] Lex autem divina, ut lex, habet potius rationem moventis et imprimentis inclinationem vel obligationem ad opus . . . (ii 3.10).

[71] ii 6.22, quoted in §432.

[72] This is Finnis's interpretation, NLNR 47: 'Aquinas would deplore the confusion (shared by Hume and Suarez!) of obligation with impulse or influence . . .'. In support of this claim about Suarez Finnis cites ii 6.22, translated 'obligation is a certain moral impulse (motio) to action'. This interpretation is accepted and expanded by Moore, 'Good without God' 236–8. Finnis is right to suggest that, if his interpretation is correct, Suarez's account of obligation is similar to Hume's. It is also similar to Hobbes's account; see §485.

[73] Or 'moral impulse' (ET).

[74] For 'moraliter movere' cf. i 5.5, 'that judgment does not bring about a binding or a moral setting-in-motion, but that is necessary in a law'. See also i 4.8, 'obligatio est effectus moralis et voluntarius principis.' This should be rendered 'obliging is a moral and voluntary bringing-about by the prince'. 'Moral effect' (ET) is misleading. See also i 5.7: 'God by making a law does not impel physically to the act prescribed by law, but only lays down an obligation, which is something moral, and it cannot come about in that physical way . . .'. Cf. i 5.17: 'to oblige by a law is a moral bringing about (effectus), dependent on the freedom of the legislator'.

[75] 'Obligatio' is ambiguous between process and product. Cf. Aquinas' discussion of 'perfectum' in his account of God's perfection, ST 1a q4 a1 ad 1.

Suarez assumes this connexion between obligation and the act of binding or obliging whenever he explains the sense in which the eternal law includes obligation.[76] It obliges because it expresses a divine command through which God carries out the relevant sort of moral (as opposed to purely physical) moving. To know that the divine law obliges us we must know that God binds us through the expression of will in commanding obedience to it.[77] Since this act of binding is essential to obligation and to law, the natural law cannot be purely indicative.[78]

433. Obligations v. Duties

This survey of some of Suarez's claims about obligation should help us to decide what question he intends to answer with his account of obligation. Does he use 'obligation' with a broad sense, extending to all moral oughts, and claim that all these obligations require laws and commands? Or is he trying to analyse the concept of obligation as involving will and acts of binding, without claiming that all moral oughts involve these relations?

We have found good reasons for ascribing the second view to him. He never suggests that obligations are the only moral requirements. On the contrary, he takes it for granted that natural facts can provide an indicative law, because they constitute reasons for us to act one way or another. Obligations in his narrow sense are not the only relations that introduce moral requirements; they introduce a different sort of moral requirement from the sorts involved in other moral relations. Obligations introduce a reason for acting that results from imposition, understood to include an expression of the will of the imposer.

Suarez is right to suggest that someone's wanting me to act in a certain way may give me a reason for doing that action beyond the reasons I would have anyhow. If, for instance, I set out to buy you food for a week, I will probably think I should buy you bread and milk among other things and my shopping list will probably not be confined to junk food. If you

---

[76] 'About the eternal law, therefore, ... we say that it has a power of obliging of itself, if it is sufficiently promulgated and applied. The proof is this: because otherwise it would not be a true and proper law, since it belongs to the character of law to oblige. ... Further, because God has the supreme power of commanding (imperare), and therefore of obliging, since the precept of a superior brings in obligation. Now through his eternal law he commands ... Therefore through this same law he obliges.' (ii 4.2)

[77] 'In the divine law, the obligation is immediately from God himself; for, in so far as it is in a human being it does not oblige except in so far as it indicates the divine reason or will.' (ii 4.8)

[78] 'Finally, a judgment indicating the nature of an action is not an action of a superior, but it can be in an equal or an inferior, who has no power of obliging. Therefore it cannot have the character of a law or a prohibition. If it could, then a teacher showing what is bad or good would impose a law; but we cannot say that. A law, therefore, is that command (imperium) that can bring about an obligation. That judgment, however, <that we just mentioned> does not bring about an obligation, but shows the obligation that must be supposed. (Iudicium autem illud non inducit obligationem, sed ostendit illam quae supponi debet.) That judgment, therefore, in order to have the character of law, needs to indicate some command from which such an obligation flows.' (ii 6.6) It is not completely clear what Suarez means in 'That judgment, however ...'. 'That judgment' seems to refer back to the judgment indicating the goodness or badness of an action. In what sense does it 'reveal the obligation (illam) that must be supposed'? Suarez would be destroying his argument if he said that the judgment of goodness or badness in its own right revealed an obligation. Probably, then, he means that it reveals an obligation that must be supposed, if we already believe that God commands what is good and prohibits what is evil. In this case the obligation must be 'supposed', and is not stated explicitly. The next sentence ('Therefore that judgment ...') says what is needed for an explicit statement of an obligation.

have particularly asked for bread and milk, your request is in one way superfluous, since I would have bought it for you anyhow. But it is not altogether superfluous, since it will make me especially careful to make sure I get you bread and milk; it warns me that, even if I had not already included these items on the shopping list, I should include them because you have asked me.

This example does not capture obligation, as Suarez conceives it, which includes necessity. To impose an obligation, the imposer must be in a position to make it true, by the expression of the will for me to act in a certain way, that I have no rational alternative to acting in that way. I oblige myself when I make a promise or some other commitment to another person that expresses my own will to act in a certain way. When another person is in the appropriate position, the expression of her will imposes a necessity on me. This may be true, even if I intend to do the same action anyhow on prudential or moral grounds. The imposition of an obligation makes me aware of reasons that ought to move me even if I were unmoved by the prudential or moral grounds independent of obligation.

Suarez, therefore, does not imply that without an imposed obligation we have no sufficient moral reason for observing the principles of the natural law. God's imposition gives us a further reason, but not the only reason, for observing these principles. This further reason essentially depends on God's expressing the will for us to observe these principles, not on our recognizing that God believes we ought to observe them. Hence natural law requires more than God's intellectual affirmation of the principles of natural law. If Suarez means that we have a distinctive reason to keep the natural law, in addition to other reasons we have, his insistence on the obligatory character of the law, and on the connexion of obligation with God's will, is intelligible.

434. Obligation, Law, and Natural Law

Suarez's introduction of an impositive concept of obligation clarifies some issues about natural law. If we confine 'obligation' to this impositive sense, the element of obligation in the natural law adds moral significance to the moral force that would exist without obligation. God's command, as an expression of God's will communicated to us, introduces a reason for following the principles of natural law that we would not otherwise have.

These observations about obligation justify some of Suarez's objections to some naturalist views. For he is right to suggest that naturalists have not clearly recognized how a divine command affects the moral status of the natural law. His opponents do not make it clear that the natural law includes a divine command, and that this fact alters its moral character. Obligation is morally distinctive because it creates a moral necessity through an act of will, and in particular through an act of the will of a superior. If I recognize an obligation, I recognize that a superior has communicated the will that I do x, and that this expression of the will of the superior leaves me with no rational alternative to doing x. In Suarez's view, this expression of the will of the superior is a command of the superior.

This expression of will differs from a request in its imposition of necessity. If I simply ask you to have dinner with me, I do not claim that my expressing my wish that you have dinner with me should be rationally decisive for you. I might make this simple request even if I am your superior and entitled to give you orders. But in giving a command I imply that the expression of my will is morally decisive for you. If I am not entitled to command you, my issuing a command is inappropriate, since I have no right to expect you to treat the expression of my will as morally decisive for you.[79]

According to Suarez, 'obliging' is the name for the act of introducing a moral necessity by expressing one's will. The only agent who can introduce such a necessity is an agent who is entitled to introduce it, because he has the appropriate authority. Such an agent introduces the necessity by issuing a command. That is why obligation requires a command by a legitimate authority.

He is right, therefore, to claim that divine commands introduce a distinct type of moral necessity. In recognizing imposed necessity, we recognize that God's having communicated his will to us makes what he commands morally necessary, whether or not it was already morally necessary. Suarez believes that if an action is intrinsically wrong, it is morally necessary to avoid it. But this is not the same moral necessity that God attaches to avoiding the action by forbidding us to do it.

But if we agree with Suarez so far, we still face a difficulty in understanding natural law as divine prescriptive law. For we need to be able to understand this conception of natural law without appealing to specific times when God issued instructions, as he did to Moses. The natural law was divine prescriptive law before the Decalogue was revealed to Moses, and revelation is not necessary for us to be obliged. We must, therefore, be able to infer from natural facts not only the existence of natural rightness and wrongness and the existence of God, but also the fact that God commands us to do what is naturally right, and therefore imposes a natural law on us.

It is rather difficult to understand this claim if we stick to a conception of a command as some act of communication that manifests the will of the commander. Perhaps I am a pilot in a dangerous situation, and my commanding officer knows I am in this situation (he is watching my aircraft on the radar), but I am not in direct communication with him. I might well be able to infer that he would order me to act in a particular way, and I might act this way partly because this is what he would order me to do. Still, it is difficult to see how he could give me an order, or how I could act because I had been ordered to, if we were not in communication. This example seems to count against Suarez's claims.

This example may be unfair, however, because it concerns an order to do a particular action about which we do not communicate. An example that helps Suarez more might be derived from claims about what the law requires without explicit commands. According to one view of the US Constitution, the Constitution requires judges to decide legal cases by reference to the correct principles of political morality, in accordance with principles laid down or implied in the Constitution and the Bill of Rights.[80] Judges might, therefore,

---

[79] If we distinguish requests from commands in this way, we can see that the difference between them is not grammatical. If I see something interesting out of the window, and I say 'Come and look at this', I do not suggest that you are required to come and look; I am simply using the imperative to make a vigorous request. If, however, the sergeant tells the private, 'You will do fifty push-ups in the next ten minutes', she is neither predicting nor requesting, but—in most circumstances—giving an order, representing the action as introducing rational necessity.

[80] Dworkin has defended this view in many places, e.g., in 'Hard cases' 86–8.

reasonably claim to be obeying the law, and not simply doing what they think right, when they take account of these moral principles in deciding particular cases on which they have no explicit legislative guidance. Perhaps Suarez can argue that, similarly, we obey God's presumed law, and we act because it is God's presumed law, if we follow the requirements of natural law, on the assumption that God commands their observance.

If this is a reasonable defence of Suarez's claims about natural law and divine commands, he is right to insist that laws and commands introduce a morally distinctive requirement, and demand a morally distinctive response. Acting in response to the command of a legitimate authority is a different action, resting on a different reason, from doing what one regards as right because it is right. The first reason is neither a substitute for the second nor reducible to the second. This is the main point that Suarez clarifies through his doctrine of obligation.

The moral distinctiveness of obligations exposes a flaw in some naturalist accounts of the natural law. If we agree, as naturalists agree, that God commands observance of the natural law, we ought not to regard these commands as simply further evidence of the intrinsic rightness or wrongness of an action. If I know that God believes murder is wrong, I have a further reason to believe that murder is wrong. But the moral basis for avoiding murder is just the same; it consists in the intrinsic wrongness of murder. If we treat divine commands as further evidence of intrinsic wrongness, we miss the fact that they give us a new moral reason, not just further evidence to support the old reason.

Suarez might reasonably point out that the distinctive element of imposed moral requirements is left out of naturalist accounts of natural law in Vasquez and Aquinas. Even if they agree that God commands observance of the natural law, they do not explain how divine commands create a moral necessity rather than simply revealing one. Suarez has good reason, therefore, for claiming that his predecessors have not recognized the significance of the fact that natural law is prescriptive and not simply indicative. His analysis of the narrow concept of obligation makes clear the essential elements of imposed moral necessity.

But if we agree with Suarez on this point, how should we modify a naturalist position? We ought to agree that the natural law includes imposed necessity and obligation because it includes divine commands. We ought further to agree that without divine commands it would include no obligation. But ought we to agree that the natural law essentially includes obligations and commands? In support of his view, Suarez appeals to the general agreement that natural law is genuine law; since genuine law imposes an obligation, natural law must impose one too. But this point does not show that natural law is essentially true law; even if it is necessarily true law, we may argue that it would still be natural law even if God did not command it.

This reply to Suarez suggests a defence of the naturalist position. When Vasquez claims that natural law essentially imposes obligations, he does not use 'obligation' in the narrow impositive sense, but in the purely deontic sense. Since he recognizes narrower and wider senses of 'law', he also uses 'obligation' in a wide sense to match the wide sense of law. Suarez's claims about obligation do not refute Vasquez's claims about obligation, once we distinguish the different concepts of obligation.

A defence of these aspects of Vasquez's position allows us to incorporate Suarez's main conclusions about law and obligation. Whether or not we believe that what would be left without divine commands would properly be called natural law is less important than what we believe about the significance of divine commands. Suarez improves on the naturalist analysis by insisting that insofar as natural law is true law, it involves a new moral relation beyond those involved in intrinsic rightness; it involves the imposed moral necessity that distinguishes prescriptive from purely indicative law.

435. Voluntarism

Suarez, therefore, appears to maintain the naturalist position about intrinsic morality and to criticize the naturalistic analysis of natural law. To see whether this appearance is correct, we may turn to his account of voluntarism. If we are right about his view of naturalism, we ought to find that he disagrees with voluntarism about morality.

He takes the voluntarist to claim not only that the natural law depends on the divine will, but also that the whole natural law consists in divine commands.[81] If that is all there is to natural law, intrinsic rightness is unnecessary. One might ask, then, how the natural law differs from a divine positive law. Suarez answers on behalf of the voluntarist that a divine command constitutes natural law if and only if what it commands is proportionate to the natures of things. If God were to issue commands that are not proportionate to the natures of things, these would not constitute natural law.

How can a voluntarist recognize actions that are proportionate to the nature of things? Is that feature of actions independent of divine commands? If it is, voluntarists deny that being proportionate to nature is sufficient for being intrinsically right. In that case it is possible for God to command actions disproportionate to the natures of things, so that there would be no natural law, and what is right would not accord with the natures of things. Alternatively, the voluntarist might claim that the divine will and command determine what is proportionate to the nature of things.[82]

The voluntarist position that Suarez discusses defends the more extreme view that the divine will determines what actions are proportionate to nature.[83] He takes Anselm to support this position in claiming that all and only what God wills is just.[84] Since at least part of the goodness of a good action consists in its being proportionate to nature, and since all its goodness depends (according to the voluntarist) on God's will and command, proportion to nature must also depend on divine commands.

---

[81] 'The second opinion, the extreme contrary to the first, is that the natural law is placed entirely in a divine command (imperium) or prohibition proceeding from the will of God as author and governor of nature, and consequently this law, as it is in God, is nothing other than the eternal law, as prescribing and forbidding in this sort of area (materia). In us, however (according to this opinion), the natural law is a judgment of reason, to the extent that it signifies to us the will of God about things to be done and avoided as concerns those things that are in accord with natural reason.' (ii 6.4)

[82] See Ockham, §395.

[83] 'They also add that the whole character of good and evil in things to do with the natural law is placed in the will of God, and not in the judgment of reason, even of the reason of God himself, nor in the things themselves that are forbidden or prescribed through such a law. The basis of this opinion seems to be that actions are not good or bad except because they are prescribed or forbidden by God, because God himself does not will to prescribe or forbid this to a creature precisely because it is bad or good, but, on the contrary, this is just or unjust precisely because God willed it to be done or not done.' (ii 6.4)

[84] For Scotus' use of Anselm's remark see §381. As Idziak (123) notices, the list of authorities that Suarez cites in ii 6.4 agrees with Andreas, *1Sent* d48 q1 a2 concl.2 (p. 28).

The same conclusion follows from the view that the natural law is entirely (omnino) placed in the divine command or prohibition. It is assumed that what God commands as part of the natural law is good, and what he prohibits is bad. If, then, God were to command what is antecedently and intrinsically good, the natural law would not be entirely placed in divine commands and prohibitions.[85] Our access to the natural law through our natural reason is a sign of the fact that God's will requires us to do what fits natural reason. The naturalness of the natural law also depends on God's command.[86]

This position is the extreme contrary to the naturalist thesis ascribed to Gregory of Rimini, because the naturalist thesis makes intrinsic rightness necessary and sufficient, and divine commands unnecessary and insufficient, for the existence of natural law. The voluntarist thesis denies intrinsic rightness, and makes divine commands necessary and sufficient, for the existence of natural law.

This voluntarist position discussed by Suarez is more extreme than the one we find in Scotus. For Scotus takes the principles of the natural law, strictly so called, to state what is right independently of any command of God. That is why God cannot dispense from them; the dispensable principles belong to the natural law only in a broader sense. Ockham comes closer to the position described by Suarez; for he takes God's command and prohibition to be the necessary basis of moral right and wrong. Ockham's belief in non-positive morality that can be grasped by natural reason fits the voluntarist position described by Suarez; for this position allows that 'in us the natural law is a judgment of reason'. Suarez notices that

---

[85] The position that Suarez describes matches the one defended by Andreas de Novo Castro. He is most probably to be identified (according to Idziak's edition) with Andrew of Neufchateau (André de Neufchâteau, second half of 13th century). As Suarez's source Perena cites Andreas, *1Sent* d48 q1 a1 concl.4, obj. 3 (Idziak, pp. 16, 21). Andreas discusses the question 'whether every good other than God is contingently good, from the free ordering of the divine will' (p. 3). As an objection he cites Augustine, *Lib. Arb.* i 4 (aliquod est malum non quia prohibetur, sed ideo prohibetur quia est malum). He returns to this at q2 concl.1 obj1 (p.76), where he also cites Aug. *Quaest. in Hept.* iii q68, lb. 19.11. He answers in ad 1 (p. 82) that Augustine simply means that the wrongness of adultery and lying precedes any written prohibition, not that it does not consist in being prohibited by God. His reply to the main question is affirmative. He supports the claim for moral good (concl.1, p. 10): 'because it is good in this way because it conforms to prudence and correct moral reason in accord with natural right (ius), but such reason is correct because the divine intellect and will so prescribes and directs and approves'. Here he follows Ockham's view about the divine will as the basis of correct reason. He considers the objection (obj3, p. 16) that 'it follows that from the standpoint of natural light all actions of a rational creature are indifferent and no act would be good or bad in itself from the nature of the thing'. Andreas replies (ad3, p. 20) that it does not follow 'because God instituted natural right and fixed (certas) laws in accord with which many acts are unqualifiedly good according to rule (regulariter), and some are good in their kind; but if one refers to the unqualified power of God, the conclusion is admitted'.

[86] 'In this way it is taken from Ockham . . . to the extent that he says that no action is bad, except to the extent that it is prohibited by God, and <no action is bad> that could not become good, if it were prescribed (praeceptum) by God, and conversely. . . . Hence he supposes that the whole natural law consists in divine precepts (praecepta) laid down by God, which God himself could remove and change. If someone were to object that such a law is not natural but positive, he would reply that it is called natural because it is proportionate to the natures of things, not because it is not laid down by God from outside. Gerson tends towards this opinion . . . This opinion is defended in a broad form (late) by Petrus Alliacus. . . . The same <is defended> most broadly (latissime) by Andreas de Novo Castro.' (ii 6.4) ET translates both 'late' and 'latissime' by 'at length' without distinction. Perena uses 'largamente' and 'extensismamente'. Perhaps 'most broadly', i.e., 'with fewest restrictions', might be the right rendering. 'Taken (sumitur) from Ockham' and 'to the extent that' (quatenus) may indicate that Suarez is not sure how far Ockham goes in endorsing this position. In 'he would reply', he is not reporting Ockham, but saying what he might say in response to the objection. The passage that Suarez cites and paraphrases in support of his claim about Ockham is *2Sent.* q15 ad3, ad4 = *OT* v 352–3, quoted in §398n67. (This is numbered as q19 in the older edition of Ockham.) The fairness of his judgment is discussed by Kilcullen, 'Natural law' 24. On Cudworth's use of this passage in Suarez see §546.

Ockham takes the requirements of right reason to hold only subject to the present order being maintained by God's ordered power.[87]

Since Suarez rejects this voluntarist position, he accepts some elements of naturalism. But which elements? Since the voluntarism he describes is an extreme position, he might reject it by accepting a naturalist view of proportion to nature, and hence of natural goodness and badness, or he might go further and accept a naturalist account of intrinsic rightness and wrongness. How far, then, does he go towards naturalism?

---

[87] See §395.

31

SUAREZ: NATURALISM

436. The Natural Basis of Natural Law

So far we have not found that Suarez takes every moral ought to require an obligation imposed by the command of a superior. He maintains only that the impositive obligation belonging to the natural law is derived from a divine command. To discover other aspects of his view about the relation between obligation and moral oughts, we need to see what is left of the natural law without the impositive obligation coming from a divine command. His claims about obligation constitute an analysis of a narrow concept of obligation, and do not imply that all moral requirements involve an imposed necessity. In that case, he ought to recognize moral necessity and moral requirements that are independent of obligation (in his sense).

If we abstract from any divine command, what is left cannot meet Suarez's conditions for natural law, since he believes that natural law, as such, includes an obligation derived from a divine command. But we can still consider the actual principles of natural law, if these are understood as the actual principles that constitute natural law when God commands the observance of them. To clarify Suarez's attitude to the voluntarist conception of natural law, we may ask what our moral position would be if we had been created as we are with the nature we have, but God had given us no commands.

According to one voluntarist view, nothing would be morally right or wrong in these circumstances; our natural knowledge of the natural law is simply knowledge of the divine commands. On this view, natural law is natural in the epistemic sense, but not in the metaphysical sense.[1] God was free to make us with the nature we have, but to command something different, and to give us natural knowledge of it; if God had done that, the principles of natural law would have been different, and the morally right and wrong would thereby have been different, even though our nature would have been the same.

A voluntarist view may acknowledge that goods are intrinsic, fixed by the nature of human beings, but deny that the intrinsic character of goods implies a similar fixity in the morally right. Rightness, according to this view, goes beyond natural goodness because it requires a divine command. Good and bad, we might say, can be derived from the

---

[1] This is Ockham's view. See §395. On Aquinas see §308.

requirements of nature, but moral rightness and wrongness must come from a law.[2] If Suarez means this, his claim about the connexion between obligation and law commits him to a controversial, but defensible, position, that morality, rightness, obligation, and law all go together.

We should ask, therefore, what other properties Suarez takes to be connected with natural goodness. It is useful to consider his use of 'right' (honestum), 'wrong' (turpe), 'ought' (debere, debitum),[3] 'required' (teneri ad) and 'sin' (peccatum). If he attaches all these predicates to naturally good and bad actions in their own right, he believes that actions have moral properties apart from divine commands.

437. The Foundation of Obligation

Suarez's description of the natural facts that underlie natural law answers some of our questions. He believes that he follows Aquinas in claiming that divine commands introduce an obligation added to natural rightness and wrongness.[4] Natural law, as divine command, adds 'its own moral obligation'.[5] But it does not add a second obligation to a previous obligation;[6] such a claim would violate Suarez's careful impositive analysis of obligation. Nor does it add morality to a non-moral basis. In Suarez's view, natural law adds moral obligation to the moral rightness and wrongness that exists apart from divine commands. When he calls this rightness and wrongness natural, he does not mean that it is not moral, but that it is based in nature, and not on any human action.[7]

Suarez clarifies this point later, in asking what a divine command adds to the natural properties of actions. A naturalist might claim that obligation is not created by the natural law, but presupposed by it.[8] Suarez rejects this claim, which conflicts with his analysis of obligation; in his view, we are not obliged to do good and avoid evil before any command and prohibition. But he recognizes a moral requirement before any command and prohibition; for natural goodness and badness tell us what we ought (debere) to do. Divine commands, introducing genuine law, oblige us to do something that we already ought to do.[9] Natural

---

[2] This is the view that *DTC* declares to be an element of truth in voluntarism; see §603.
[3] On precept and debitum see Aquinas, *ST* 1–2 q100; *Quodl.* v 19. Cf. §303.
[4] He relies (cf. *Leg.* ii 5.2) on Aquinas, *ST* 1–2 q100 a8, and (cf. ii 6.5) 1–2 q71 a6; q100 a8 ad2.
[5] 'Therefore it is necessary that it add some obligation of avoiding the evil that is evil from itself and by its own nature. Further, there is no contradiction if a thing that is right from itself has added to it an obligation to do it, or if a thing that is wrong from itself has added an obligation to avoid it. . . . Therefore also the natural law, inasmuch as it is genuine divine law, can add its own moral obligation arising from a precept, beyond the natural (if I may put it so) badness or rightness that the matter on which this precept falls has from itself.' (ii 6.12)
[6] Williams's rendering 'some sort of additional obligation' is therefore misleading.
[7] On this sense of 'natural' see ii 9.4, quoted below.
[8] '. . . This law forbids something because it is bad. Therefore before that law there is an obligation of avoiding this sort of bad thing. And the same is true, proportionately, about a command (imperium) and precept to do a good thing because it is good' (ii 9.4).
[9] 'For if this law forbids something because it is bad, it brings about its own special necessity of avoiding it, because this is intrinsic to forbidding. At the same time, however, it proves that this law assumes something, which belongs to the intrinsic duty of nature, because everything in a particular way has a duty to itself to do nothing that conflicts with its own nature. But beyond this duty the law adds a special moral obligation, and we say that this obligation is the effect of this law. The jurists customarily call this a natural obligation, not because it is not moral, but in order to distinguish it from a civil obligation.' (ii 9.4) On natural v. civil obligation, cf. i 14.9.

law, therefore, requires both a divine command and prior intrinsic rightness.[10] The moral judgment and the recognition of moral duty (debitum) are prior to any act of will, by the lawgiver or by the subject.[11]

In all this discussion Suarez distinguishes 'ought' (debere) and 'duty' (debitum) from 'obligation' (obligatio).[12] A class of actions that we ought to do, and that it would be right to do and wrong to avoid, is already fixed by nature; the divine command adds an obligation to do the things we already ought to do. Suarez's use of 'debere' follows Aquinas.[13] We noticed earlier that Aquinas sometimes uses 'oblige' rather narrowly, and seems to have in mind a specific action of laying someone under an obligation. Suarez follows him in this narrow use of 'obligation', and in the broad use of 'duty'.

The obligation imposed by a divine command is binding on our conscience. If we abstract from divine command, the principles of natural law do not give rise to an obligation binding on conscience. But even without divine commands, the inherent rightness or wrongness of certain actions implies that we are required (teneri) in conscience to do or avoid them.[14] Suarez's denial of obligation apart from command and law does not lead him to withhold deontic predicates from naturally good and bad actions.[15]

---

[10] 'Although that obligation which natural law adds, in so far as it is properly prescriptive, is from the divine will, still that will presupposes a judgment about the badness of, for instance, lying, and similar judgments. Still, because from the force of the judgment alone no proper prohibition and no obligation of a precept is introduced, since this cannot be understood without will, for that reason there is added a will to prohibit that action because it is bad.' (ii 6.13) I take 'properly prescriptive' (proprie praeceptiva) to modify 'lex naturalis' (so also Perena). ET renders 'properly preceptive obligation'.

[11] Suarez explains the difference between natural law and other laws: 'Further, this law prescribes what is suitable to rational nature, as rational, and forbids the contrary. But that [sc. what is suitable to rational nature] is precisely the right, as is agreed. Moreover, the natural law differs from other laws on just this point, that the others make something bad because they prohibit it, and make something necessary or right because they prescribe it. But the natural law presupposes in the act or object a rightness that it prescribes or a wrongness that it prohibits; and that is why it is usually said that through this law something is prohibited because it is bad or prescribed because it is good.' (ii 7.1)

[12] ET uses 'obligation' for both 'debitum' and 'obligatio'. Perena uses 'deber' and 'obligacion' to mark the difference in the Latin.

[13] Finnis, *NLNR* 45–6, contrasts Suarez and Aquinas as follows: '. . . Suarez . . . maintained that obligation is essentially the effect of an act of will by a superior, directed to moving the will of an inferior . . . Aquinas, on the other hand, treats obligation as the rational necessity of some means to (or way of realizing) an end or objective (i.e. a good) of a particular sort'. The evidence cited from Suarez deals with his use of 'obligatio'. Hence evidence of a difference between Suarez and Aquinas ought to deal with Aquinas' use of 'obligatio'. However, most of the passages cited by Finnis (46n) do not include 'obligatio' or 'obligare'. Most of them simply deal with the relation of means to the ultimate end. Some of them (*ST* 1–2 q99 a1; 2–2 q44 a1) include 'debitum'. One passage (1–2 q99 a1) says that since a precept of law imposes an obligation (sit obligatorium), it has the character of a debitum; but none of them suggests that Aquinas takes a debitum to imply an obligatio. Later (341n) Finnis contrasts Aquinas with Suarez by saying that 'for Aquinas, obligation is simply a rational necessity of certain sorts of means to certain sorts of ends'. He cites 1–2 q99 a1 and 2–2 q58 a3 ad2. In the latter passage Aquinas says that necessity that is not coaction arises out of the obligatio of a precept or (sive) from the necessity of an end. He implies that an obligatio involves necessity, but does not imply that all teleological necessity, or every debitum, involves an obligatio. Finnis is right to maintain that these passages show something about Aquinas' views on obligation, as we might understand it. But if we want to know Suarez's views on obligation, as we might understand it, we should look at his views on debitum as well as his views on obligatio. If the question about obligation is given the same sense as applied to Suarez and as applied to Aquinas, it is much more difficult to see the difference suggested by Finnis.

[14] 'Hence, if we speak strictly about a natural obligation, it certainly cannot be separated from an obligation in conscience. For if it is <an obligation> to avoid something, it arises from the intrinsic wrongness of an action that is therefore to be avoided in conscience. But if it is to do something, it arises from the intrinsic connexion of such an action with the rightness of virtue, which we are also required in conscience to maintain in our actions. Hence in that case the omission of an action that is a duty is bad in itself.' (ii 9.6)

[15] Ward, *NG* 432–40, summarizes Suarez's position, and presents a generally sound interpretation of it, appropriately emphasizing Suarez's belief in intrinsic morality. He fails, however, to recognize Suarez's distinction between debitum

438. Moral Goodness

These remarks about obligation imply that Suarez rejects voluntarism not only because he recognizes natural goodness apart from the divine will, but also because he recognizes intrinsic morality. If we abstract divine commands from the natural law, what is left is morality (honestas), not just natural goodness. We should examine his conception of moral goodness more closely, to see how strongly he is committed to a naturalist account of honestas, and how far honestas corresponds to morality. In the *De Legibus* he relies on the account of goodness that he expounds more fully in *De Bonitate*[16] and in *Metaphysical Disputation* x.

Suarez places the good as right (bonum honestum) in the threefold division of good into pleasant, useful, and right. Both his account of good in general and his account of the specific good that he identifies with the right commit him to an objectivist and naturalist account; both goodness and rightness belong to the nature of things, and are not constituted by human choice, desire, or judgment. Suarez follows Aquinas' account of the moral good as the honestum; but his specific emphases make clearer the relation of his views on the right and good to issues about voluntarism.[17]

To emphasize this feature of the good, Suarez clarifies Aquinas' claims about the good and the desirable.[18] He follows Cajetan in arguing that goodness cannot be reduced to desirability.[19] This is a reasonable understanding of Aquinas, but the emphasis on the objective character of the good, and its distinctness from anything created or constituted by desire, intellect, will, or command, is characteristic of Suarez. Since many of Aquinas' successors claim that the morally good is the desirable, or what is prescribed by right reason, or what is commanded by God, Suarez tries to be more precise about these connexions between goodness and other properties. He insists that none of these other descriptions gives us the essence of the good or the morally good. He sets out on a meta-ethical inquiry that continues in (among others) Cudworth, Price, and Moore.[20]

Suarez discusses rightness in his exposition of the section of the *Summa* in which Aquinas describes the good to be found in human voluntary actions. Both Aquinas and Suarez take this good to be the moral good.[21] The good as right is to be distinguished from good as

and obligatio; Ward uses the terms without distinction, citing Frassen in his support (449–50). Ward claims that Frassen 'fully admits . . . that the natural law *supposes* an obligation which already exists'. But here Ward uses the words of an objection that Frassen answers. In his answer (*SA* Tract. 4 disp.2 a2 q2 concl.1 = vi 51) Frassen endorses Suarez's view that the natural law presupposes some 'intrinsecum debitum naturae' to which it adds a special obligation. He does not say that the natural law presupposes a prior obligation. In his description of Frassen's view Ward overlooks the difference between obligation and debitum. But he has a stronger basis for his claim about Frassen when he cites a second passage: 'God is not related to the natural law in the way in which a ruler (princeps) is related to positive law. For the ruler confers the entire strength and force (vim et virtutem) of obliging on a law by his will alone. God, however, supposes some obligation on the side of the things, which seems essential to the things themselves, because they are right (honestae) and good from the nature of the thing. For, as we said above, this is the difference between natural and positive law, that the natural law prescribes those things that are right and good in themselves, whereas the civil law only makes right the things that it prescribes, and makes bad the things it prohibits.' (*SA* Tract. 4 disp.2 a3 q1 concl.1 = vi 62. Ward quotes the third sentence of this passage, giving a wrong reference.) Here Frassen forgets or ignores Suarez's distinction between debitum and obligatio. On Ward see also §604.

[16] *De bonitate et malitia obiectiva humanorum actuum = OO* iv 288–305.   [17] Aquinas on the honestum; see §§333–4.
[18] Suarez refers to Aquinas *ST* 1a q5 a1; a3 ad1; a4 ad1; q16 a4 ad1, ad3; *SG* i 4 arg.3.
[19] See *DM* x 1.19 = *OO* xxv 334b = Suarez, *MGE*, ed. Gracia and Davis, 116.   [20] See §547.
[21] 'The moral good, therefore, is the same as the good as right more strictly taken as what is fitting through itself and agrees with a rational nature as such. . . . The natural good is said to be whatever agrees with a given nature, in

perfection that belongs to God in himself. Rightness implies a relation; the bonum honestum is not 'absolute' and 'transcendental', in a sense that would imply the sort of perfection that belongs to a subject in itself. Rightness is a relational good, and so it involves relation to rational nature as such (Bon. ii 2.8 294a).

Like the pleasant and the useful, the right involves some kind of fittingness (convenientia). But it cannot be simply the fittingness that belongs to these other goods. The goods that the Stoics call primary natural advantages (ta prôta kata phusin) and that Aristotle treats as external goods, are not honesta. Suarez supports his claim by referring to Cicero (in De Finibus iii–iv).[22] The right has a special relation to rational nature.[23]

Goodness as rightness belongs to the object of a human will. By belonging to the object it makes an action morally good. This is the kind of goodness that Aquinas had in mind in discussing the morally good.[24] Suarez says 'we call this goodness a right object'; he seems to acknowledge that Aquinas' treatment of moral goodness does not use the term 'right' (honestum), but he assumes, reasonably, that this is what Aquinas intends. He clarifies, but does not alter, Aquinas' doctrine by speaking explicitly of honestas. The relevant kind of goodness belonging to the object of will is the right (honestum), because it is neither the pleasant nor the useful. Since we can recognize that something is either pleasant or useful and still regard it as morally indifferent or morally bad, some further feature is needed to make it morally good.[25]

In distinguishing the moral good from the pleasant and the advantageous, Suarez agrees with Scotus. Scotus, however, infers that the moral good cannot consist in agreement with nature; he opposes the natural affection for advantage to the rational affection for the just. Suarez rejects this opposition, which he traces back to Anselm, between the natural and the right. He argues that fittingness to one's nature does not necessarily imply a reference to one's private advantage; it may realize or express one's nature in its own right apart from any further advantage to the subject. In this respect the Incarnation was fitting for God's nature, though it was not advantageous for God.[26]

---

accordance with what it naturally is or can naturally do. But the moral good is what agrees with a thing, in so far as it acts freely; for custom (mos), from which "moral" is said, consists in free action, as is agreed.' (DM x 2.30 = OO xxv 344b) Suarez cites the commentators on Aquinas, ST 1–2 q18, where Cajetan argues that, according to Aquinas, acts have moral goodness from their objects (Leonine edn. of ST vi 129).

[22] See esp. Cic. F. iii 24, quoted by Maxwell in a relevant context. See §536.

[23] 'Therefore they have them in them some character of goodness, which we properly call rightness, by the character of which such objects are judged through correct reason to be fitting to a human being, and correctly loveable because of themselves.' (Bon. ii 1.5 = 290a)

[24] 'In the objects of human actions that are morally good, some rightness is necessary that fits the object from <the object> itself and not through the action; and that goodness can correctly be called objective goodness. . . . [He cites Aquinas ST 1–2 q19 a1 ad3.] In this <Thomas> says openly that good is presupposed as object before an act of will, and in respect of a morally good action. That good in some way belongs to the genus of morality through direction towards reason. There is therefore in that <good> some goodness that correct reason knows, and this goodness we call a right object.' (Bon. ii 1.3 = 289a) At the end he cites Aquinas, 1–2 q20 a1 ad1; Mal. q2 a3c, ad8.

[25] 'This is proved by reason, because the object of will is good under the character of good; therefore that goodness that moves the will does not flow from the will, but is assumed in the objects. The same, therefore, is true correspondingly in all states or acts of the will, because all tend towards an adequate object of the power in a corresponding way. Therefore it is necessary to say the same about good and correct actions. Therefore they assume in their objects some goodness moving the will towards such actions and formally completing their tendency. Then further, that goodness of such an object does not constitute the useful or the pleasant good; therefore it is right. Therefore in itself it is a certain rightness, sufficient in its kind to give moral goodness to an action, and thereby it is correctly called objective moral goodness.' (ii 1.4 = 289b)

[26] 'For sometimes the fitting is understood as what is expedient for something in such a way that it provides the thing with some perfection and, one might say, usefulness, and this is the way it is used in the objections. In another way,

To identify the kind of fittingness that is moral goodness, we must insist that it is fitting to human nature as a whole as rational nature.[27] Other things that are fitting to human nature are fitting to part of our nature, and in that way are derived from fittingness to our whole nature.[28] Something may be in accord with some aspect of human nature without being unqualifiedly loveable in its own right. In this sense Suarez agrees with Cicero's division between the good of nature and the good as right; it may be morally wrong to love life or health or the other advantages of nature in some circumstances. The moral good that is grasped by correct reason must be appropriate for the nature of human beings as free and rational agents.[29]

Suarez has now affirmed that the intrinsic goodness and badness independent of divine commands is more than the goodness of advantage and pleasure. In appealing to our judgments about moral goodness in order to show that these other two forms of goodness are not moral goodness, Suarez appeals to something that we recognize as distinct from the agent's own advantage. In referring to Cicero's comments on life and health, he relies on moral judgments. Though some later natural-law moralists restrict intrinsic goodness to pleasure and advantage, Suarez does not.[30]

439. The Objectivity of Moral Goodness: An Argument for Naturalism

Suarez believes that the right, as he has described it, is necessarily connected to correct reason, but not relative to correct reason. Relativity to correct reason gives the wrong direction of causation. Correctness in moral judgments is parallel to correctness of judgment in general; it consists in some conformity to some feature of the object judged, rather than

---

however, something is said to be fitting that through itself is suitable in some way and in agreement with the thing's nature and tendency. In this way the Incarnation is said to be fitting for God and for his goodness . . . Hence there are many objects of this kind that either bring nothing expedient beyond the rightness itself of virtue or are not aimed at because of that <expedient result>.' (ii 2.13 = 295b)

[27] Passmore, *RC* 103 cites John of Salisbury, *Metalogicon* i 3 = 829d–830 Webb, satirizing the excessive appeals to *convenientia* among those who try to innovate without much understanding: 'They talked of nothing but "suitability" or "reason", and "argument" sounded in everyone's mouth. To mention an ass or a human being or any work of nature was as bad as a crime, or excessively inept or vulgar and foreign to a philosopher. It was thought impossible to say or do anything appropriately or according to the standard of reason unless a mention of the "appropriate" and "reason" were expressly inserted.'

[28] 'Everything that is loveable (*amabile*) as fitting in itself is derived from (*reduci ad*) the good as right; hence, granted that we concede that that fitting with nature objectively founds the goodness of an action, none the less that is truly called a kind of rightness.' (ii 1.5 = 290a)

[29] 'Therefore in the objects of human actions the advantage of nature alone is not enough for the rightness of the actions. Therefore there is in them some character of goodness, which we call rightness properly, by the character of which goodness such objects are judged through correct reason to be fitting (*decentia*) for a human being, and to be correctly loveable because of themselves.' (ii 1.5 = 290a) 'This right, as such, formally requires fittingness and proportion with rational nature. But we must add that this fittingness must be with rational nature in so far as it is rational and can be governed by correct reason, because this rightness is the supreme goodness that can be present in this sort of fittingness in relation to a human being. Therefore it must be in accordance with the most perfect degree and supreme perfection that is in a human being. Therefore we must look for it in rational nature in so far as it is rational.' (ii 2.11 = 295a)

[30] See §532 on Cumberland; §565 on Pufendorf.

in the creation of such a feature.[31] We ought not, therefore, to define right and wrong by reference to correct reason. Though the right accords with correct reason and judgment, this accord is not what fundamentally makes it right. Reason or judgment is right because it conforms to the nature of a rational agent, but the converse is false.[32]

This argument recalls Suarez's initial discussion of naturalism.[33] He distinguishes 'object-ive' from 'cognitive' naturalism (as we called them) about natural law, and he prefers cognitive naturalism (though he still rejects it). Cognitive naturalism takes the rational grasp of rightness to be necessary for natural law, and Suarez agrees. But when he discusses moral goodness itself, he prefers objective over cognitive naturalism. He agrees with Vasquez's belief in objective rightness independent of anyone's judgment about it; he disagrees only insofar as he refuses to identify it with natural law. Suarez denies that rightness consists in conformity to a law, and affirms that the correctness of a law presupposes rightness distinct from it. Some cases of rightness arise from law, 'to the extent that this very thing, namely subjection to law and conformity to it, is good'. Nonetheless, this special fact about the goodness of obedience still requires conformity to rational nature if it is to constitute a form of goodness (*Bon.* ii 2.7 = OO iv 294a).

Suarez regards this account of rightness as an account of moral goodness, as Aquinas understands it. Aquinas' fullest discussion of moral goodness (*ST* 1–2 qq18–21) does not include Suarez's explanation. Indeed, our suspicions may be aroused by the fact that Suarez explains the right as appropriateness to rational nature. This would be a suitable explanation of the Stoic notion of the right (*kalon*, honestum), since the Stoics believe that living rightly is living in accordance with nature—one's own rational nature and the nature of the universe.

We have found, however, that Suarez is justified in taking Aquinas' remarks about moral goodness to apply to the honestum. Even though Aquinas does not make this clear in his explicit discussion of moral goodness, he makes it clear in his other remarks about the honestum. Nor does Suarez innovate in connecting the right with what is fitting for rational nature; Aquinas recognizes this same connexion between the morally good and rational nature.[34] Both Aquinas and Suarez believe that the right is fitting for rational nature and therefore contributes to the individual rational agent's own ultimate end,

---

[31] 'Objects are not right because they are judged right, but rather, on the contrary, correct reason judges them right just because they are such. For just as in other judgments, their truth is founded in things, if indeed they are such as they are judged to be, so also in this judgment of correct reason that correctness is founded in the object judged. Therefore the rightness of the object cannot consist in conformity to such judgment.' (ii 2.3 = 293a)

[32] '... this good is usually expounded through fittingness to the dictate of correct reason; for that good is right which correct reason dictates as one to be done or loved, etc. Nevertheless, if this statement is understood about correct reason in so far as it states judgment or knowledge of what it is expedient (expedit) to do, in that case rightness does not consist in conformity to the dictate of reason, nor is <correct reason> the first rule or first principle (ratio) of such rightness. For the good is not right because correct reason judges it to be such, but rather the converse: because the good itself truly and in reality is right, consequently it is judged to be such by correct and true reason. Therefore, as far as we are concerned, correct judgment is the rule of the good as right (bonum honestum) because it reveals it to us. However, in its own right, the judgment presupposes a proper fittingness from which the good as right derives its being so; and we say that this is a fittingness to the rational nature in so far as it is such and has such properties or attributes. If, however, the dictate of reason is taken not formally but as it were radically, then it is said correctly and a priori that the good as right is what conforms to reason—that is to say, what conforms to rational nature, which furthermore is naturally <able> to judge that this <good> is to be done or desired for itself' (*DM* x 2.12 = OO xxv 339a). On Gregory's views see §426.

[33] See *Leg.* ii 5, discussed at §426, on two versions of naturalism.   [34] See §334.

her happiness. Suarez accepts both Aquinas' eudaemonism and his naturalism about the morally good.[35]

Admittedly, Suarez would depart from Aquinas if he supposed that we can discover fitness to rational nature by direct intuition, or by reflexion on logical compatibility and incompatibility. If he took this view, he would anticipate Clarke's interpretation of fitness.[36] In his explicit remarks about rightness and fitness, Suarez does not say much about how they are to be discovered. But he interprets them teleologically, by reference to the appropriate ends for a rational agent.[37] Nor does he suggest that fittingness is to be discovered simply by considering actions and rational nature without reference to the circumstances; on the contrary, circumstances are relevant to deciding fittingness, and therefore rightness (*Bon.* ii 3.5 = 298b).

These claims about moral rightness distinguish morality from the content of divine commands. Suarez recognizes moral goodness and rightness as a property of actions themselves in relation to rational nature. If he were to claim that the imposition of some obligation is needed for rightness, morality, or duty, his position would be deeply inconsistent.[38]

440. Metaphysics and Meta-ethics

In speaking of intrinsic natures Suarez refers to his metaphysics. If we look beyond his meta-ethics to his metaphysical treatment of essences and reality, we can confirm and clarify some of our conclusions about moral rightness.

Metaphysical Disputation xxxi discusses the status of essences and their relation to the existence of finite things.[39] The most robustly realist view of essences claims that, whether or not individual human beings and horses exist, their essences have non-temporal being; it is always true that human beings are rational and horses have four legs, and that a chimaera is an impossible combination of man and horse, whether or not the actual world exists or

---

[35] Suarez endorses Aquinas' views about happiness as the ultimate end, against Scotus' objections, in *De Ultimo Fine* iii 6.1–3 = *OO* iv 37b–38a. His views on the ultimate end are discussed by Ward, *NG* 404–18 (who unduly weakens the force of Suarez's claim).

[36] See §619.

[37] 'Some things through themselves and by the character of their essential perfection are in agreement with human nature, either because they are its ultimate end, as God is; or else because a human being achieves them together with that end, such as knowledge or the love of God, because from themselves they correctly dispose a human being in the direction of such an end; or remotely, such as acts of justice (iustitia), etc. For from this it comes about that such things are proportionate to rational nature, in so far as it is capable of happiness and tends towards it, and thereby an action tending towards such objects is also called correct, because through it a human being correctly tends towards the end he ought to tend towards.' (*Bon.* ii 2.14 = *OO* iv 295b)

[38] Suarez's views may influence some of Whichcote's aphorisms on moral objectivism and right reason (cited by Rivers, *RGS* i 64): 'Right is the rule of law; and law is declaratory of right.' (*MRA* §3) 'If we consider what is becoming reasonable nature; then shall we have a rule to guide us as to good and evil.' (§14) 'The rule of right is the reason of things; the judgment of right is the reason of our minds perceiving the reason of things.' (§33) 'There is a reason for what we do, from the things themselves: truth and falsity, good and evil, are first in things, and then in persons. There is a difference in things; and we must comply in all matters with the reason of things and the rule of right, which is the law of God's creation.' (§§455–6). On Whichcote see further §541.

[39] Suarez's views are briefly discussed and compared with other views by Bolton, 'Universals' 180–3, and more fully examined by Wells in Suarez, *EFB* 6–27.

God has created anything. Suarez rejects this most strongly realist view, and argues that 'no Catholic doctor' would maintain that the essences of creatures have some real being distinct from the being of God. Nor did God create them from eternity, since creation takes place in time (*DM* xxxi 2.3 = OO xxvi 230a). The necessary truth that man is a rational animal is to be analysed conditionally: 'if anything is a man, it is a rational animal' (2.8). Things in actuality and in potentiality are to be distinguished formally as being and not-being, not as two kinds of being (3.8). Real actual being depends on a real efficient cause (4.1).

Suarez's discussion seeks to show that essences have no actual being independent of the causal structure of the actual world. Since he takes the efficient cause of the actual world to be God, he believes that the being of essences depends on God as creator. Nothing antecedent to God's freewill makes it true that the appropriate natural kinds for him to place in the world are man, horse, and so on, rather than some other possible kinds.

But after having affirmed the dependence of essences on actual efficient causes and causal laws, Suarez accepts some aspects of the robustly realist case that he has rejected. He allows that essences are real as potential beings, though not as actual beings (2.10). As potential beings, they are independent of the divine will (12.40, 45, 46). Truths about essences include conditionals with impossible antecedents ('if a stone is an animal, it is able to sense') and truths about impossible objects ('a chimaera is both a man and a horse'). All these are true apart from any efficient cause (12.45), and the fact that the conditionals have impossible antecedents does not make them false or incoherent.

In all these cases, Suarez opposes voluntarism about essences. They do not depend on God as creator.[40] The root and origin of necessity in these truths does not depend on divine intellect (12.46). Suarez maintains the position that Descartes takes to undermine divine freedom and omnipotence.[41]

Suarez recognizes different kinds of eternal truths that exist apart from the creative will of God. Some describable kinds are not suitable for being created. Chimaeras are an impossible combination of species, and God could not make it true that they are a possible combination. Man differs from chimaera, apart from the creative will of God, in containing no internal repugnance; its 'non-repugnant' character makes it one of the possibilities among which God chooses (2.2, 10). Just as God could not choose to create round squares, God could not choose to create any other inconsistent combinations.

---

[40] 'Enunciations . . . are known because they are true; otherwise no reason could be given for why God necessarily knows they are true. For if their truth proceeded from God himself, that would happen by means of God's will, and thence it would not proceed by necessity, but voluntarily. Again, with respect to these enunciations, the divine intellect is compared as merely speculative, not as active; but the speculative intellect assumes the truth of its object, and does not produce it. Therefore, enunciations of this sort, which are spoken of in the first, and indeed in the second, way of being spoken of through itself, have permanent truth not only as they are in the divine intellect, but also in their own right, and in abstraction from the divine intellect.' (*DM* xxxi 12.40)

[41] Cf. Descartes's letter to Mersenne, 6 May 1630 = AT i 149.21: 'As for the eternal truths, I say once more that they are true or possible only because God knows them as true or possible. They are not known as true by God in any way which would imply that they are true independently of him. If men really understood the sense of their words they could never say without blasphemy that the truth of anything is prior to the knowledge which God has of it. In God willing and knowing are a single thing in such a way that by the very fact of willing something he knows it and it is only for this reason that such a thing is true. So we must not say that if God did not exist nevertheless these truths would be true; for the existence of God is the first and most eternal of all possible truths and the one from which alone all others proceed.' Cf. letter of 15 April 1630 = AT i 145.10. Cronin, *OB*, ch. 2, compares the views of Suarez and Descartes on essences and eternal truths.

The similarity between the issues arising in this discussion and those in the discussion of goodness is clear in Suarez's use of the same formula, ultimately derived from Plato's *Euthyphro*, of explanatory asymmetry. God knows the eternal truths because they are true, and it is not the case that they are true because God knows them. It is necessarily true that God knows them, and so it is not possible for them to be true without God's knowing them; still, the counterfactual claim is true that even if God were not to know them, they would be true.

Suarez protests that the voluntarist view distorts the status of the relevant truths. For we want it to be part of God's omniscience and wisdom that he knows all necessary truths, and that he is guided by them in his creative activity. But if we make necessary truths subject to his creative will, they lose their necessity. Similarly, we want to attribute some knowledge to his speculative (i.e., theoretical) rather than his operative (i.e., active and productive) intellect; but it is the mark of speculative intellect that it grasps truths independent of it, not that it acts so as to bring them into being. Voluntarism about the eternal truths undermines any reasonable conception of God's wisdom. To express the point in more recent terminology, voluntarism commits us to the wrong 'direction of fit'; it implies that necessary truth requires the conformity of reality to mind, whereas a proper account of necessary truth should make mind conform to reality.[42]

Even this brief survey of Suarez on essences helps to explain how he uses his metaphysics to clarify his claims about goodness. We notice, as we notice in his discussion of natural law, an initial firm statement of an apparently voluntarist claim, safeguarding divine freedom and sovereignty. But after this initial statement, Suarez does not endorse the whole voluntarist position. He insists that the proper recognition of God's sovereignty leaves untouched the belief in essences and truths that are independent of God's will.

The same is true of his views on goodness. The human good is not an eternal essence that God had to bring into the actual world, since God did not have to choose to bring human beings into the actual world. Nor do the various features of the human good exist independently of God's other creative decisions; it is not necessary, for instance, that human beings need water or shelter, since God could have made water and shelter unnecessary for us without creating creatures of a different species. However, God could not both have made human beings and have made all of the human good and human goodness entirely different from what it is. For the human good is fixed by human nature; to make the human good entirely different, God would have had to create an inconsistent state of affairs, by creating creatures who were human beings, but lacked human nature.

This is why Suarez claims that essences of things that do not imply a contradiction have their own being independent of will. While it is up to God to create human beings or not, it is not up to God to make the human essence inconsistent, as the essences of chimaera and of round square are, or to make inconsistent essences consistent. In order to create human beings and make their good something different from what it is, God would have had to make inconsistent things consistent. On this point Suarez is a naturalist.[43]

---

[42] On direction of fit see §256n43.

[43] A doctrine of intrinsic evils 'can be founded in that metaphysical principle that natures as far as their being goes are immutable essences, and consequently also <are immutable> as far as the appropriateness or inappropriateness of natural properties goes' (*Leg.* ii 6.11).

441. Intrinsic Rightness

If we now return to the *De Legibus*, and examine Suarez's remarks about obligation and intrinsic morality in the light of the meta-ethical doctrines we have discussed, we see that he adheres to these doctrines, and recognizes their naturalist implications.

In one place he says that rational nature is the foundation of objective right and wrong in human moral actions.[44] References to a 'foundation' are obscure on the relevant point. The foundation of a house is a necessary condition for a house, but it is not a house; but if we grasp the 'foundations' or 'fundamental elements' of French, we speak French, though we may not grasp it completely. In what sense does Suarez speak of the foundations of right? Does he mean that rational nature is sufficient for it, or only that it is necessary?

He answers this question when he agrees that God's command and prohibition presuppose a necessary rightness and wrongness, not only a necessary goodness and badness, in actions themselves.[45] Hence actions are right and wrong by their own nature, and not because of any divine command.[46] The rules that constitute the principles of right are not natural law, but the foundation of the law.[47] We can know enough about rational nature to discover that some types of actions accord with it and others do not. If this is the foundation of natural law, our knowledge of natural law informs us not only about the divine will, but also about the requirements of rational nature.

Suarez believes that actions are right or wrong insofar as they accord with or violate rational nature, even if we abstract from the fact that such actions are commanded and forbidden by God. To explain the abstraction, he relies on the counterfactual supposition that God does not command or forbid. But this counterfactual, as we have seen, needs to be explained carefully. In making the supposition we must not hold fixed the fact that God forbids all and only what is wrong; if we held this fact fixed, our counterfactual assumption would say that the action violating rational nature but not commanded by God is both wrong and not wrong. Instead, we are to consider the consequences of supposing simply that none of the wrongness of an action comes from God's prohibition, and to ask whether it is still wrong.[48]

Suarez relies on the sort of counterfactual argument that Gregory of Rimini uses to establish the independence of the natural law from the will of God. He rejects Gregory's counterfactual, but he accepts the analogous counterfactual in the case of intrinsic rightness and the will of God.[49] In *De Bonitate* he defends the counterfactual claim in order to show

---

[44] See ii 5.6, discussed in §427.

[45] 'This will of God, prohibition or prescription, is not the whole character of the goodness and badness that is present in the observance or transgression of natural law, but it assumes in the actions themselves some necessary rightness or wrongness, and joins to them a special obligation of divine law.' (*Leg.* ii 6.11)

[46] 'In this opinion, I take to be true the teaching that it assumes in its foundation about the intrinsic rightness or wrongness of actions, by which they fall under the natural law that forbids or prescribes . . .' (ii 5.5).

[47] 'Not everything that is a foundation of the rightness or correctness of an action prescribed by a law, or that is the foundation of the wrongness of an action prohibited by a law, can be called a law. And so, granted that rational nature is the foundation of the objective rightness of good moral actions, it cannot thereby be called a law.' (ii 5.6)

[48] *Leg.* ii 6.14.

[49] 'For let us grant by an impossibility that there is no superior prescribing or prohibiting. This object itself, which is lying, put forward in itself, is wrong, and, on the contrary, speaking the truth is right. And for this reason even in relation to God they are understood to have these characters, and for this reason the latter is repugnant to him and the former is natural. This rightness, therefore, through itself and formally, abstracts from law.' (*Bon.* ii 2.6 = *OO* iv 293b)

that rightness cannot consist in conformity to law. Similarly, in *De Legibus* he takes the truth of the relevant counterfactual to be crucial for settling the issues about the relation between natural law, intrinsic goodness, and divine commands.[50]

He defends the counterfactual against the objection that it involves a contradiction. His opponent suggests that the counterfactual says that lying (a) is a sin, because it is unfitting to rational nature, but (b) is not a sin, because it is not forbidden (ii 6.14). Suarez answers that clause (b) does not follow from the supposition. The supposition simply tries to establish that goodness and badness are prior logically (*secundum ordinem rationis*) to command and prohibition.

One might, however, still object that even though the counterfactual supposition is not self-contradictory in itself, it has contradictory implications: (a) if God does not forbid an action, it is not displeasing to him, and therefore it is not bad; but (b) if it is unfitting to rational nature, it is bad. Therefore (c) it is bad and not bad. Suarez replies that this objection begs the question, since (a) implicitly denies the truth of the counterfactual claim. The counterfactual claim does not imply that being bad and being prohibited by God are really separable (*in re separabilia*) (ii 6.15), and so the actual connexion between wrongness and God's prohibition does not refute the counterfactual.

We might still doubt the truth of the counterfactual once we see that it implies that actions not prohibited by God can be sinful and blameworthy. We might be tempted to reject this implication if we accept Augustine's description of sin as an offence against the eternal law (cf. Aquinas, *ST* 1–2 q71 a6). One reply to this objection asserts that actions not prohibited by God are not sinful or blameworthy, even though they are intrinsically bad (*Leg.* ii 6.16). If Suarez accepted this reply, we might say that intrinsic badness falls short of moral wrongness, since it does not imply sin and blameworthiness. But he rejects this reply, because an intrinsically wrong action would still be a sin (*peccatum*) even if God did not prohibit it; hence neither sin nor blameworthiness (*culpa*) depends on divine prohibition. Both sin and blameworthiness follow from the fact that a voluntary act is contrary to right reason; hence, sin, so understood, is the proper concern of the moral philosopher.[51] The implication that initially appeared unacceptable is not unacceptable after all.

Suarez's conclusion from this discussion sets out the relation between divine command and intrinsic goodness.[52] Moral badness and blameworthiness, from the moral philosopher's point of view, follow simply from contrariety to reason, apart from any divine command.[53]

---

[50] 'For it all turns on this hypothesis: Even if God did not prohibit or prescribe the things that belong to the law of nature, none the less lying is bad, and honouring one's parents is good and a duty (debitum).' (*Leg.* ii 6.14)

[51] Suarez cites Aquinas, *ST* 1–2 q21 a1–2; q71 a6 ad4–5 (partly quoted at §235n6).

[52] 'I reply, therefore, that in a human action there is some goodness or badness from the force of the object considered in abstraction (praecise), as it agrees or disagrees with correct reason. In accordance with that <goodness or badness> [Perena, ET supplies "<correct reason>"] it can be called both a sin and blameworthy in the respects mentioned, apart from its relation to proper law. [Or "law, properly speaking" (Perena, ET).] But beyond this <goodness or badness> a human action has a special character of good and evil in being directed towards God, when a divine law is added, either prohibiting or prescribing, and in accordance with that <character> [Perena; ET supplies "law"] a human action is called a sin or blameworthy action, in a special way, in the sight of God, by its character of transgression of a law that properly belongs to God himself.' (ii 6.17)

[53] 'In that case, therefore, the bad action would be a sin and a fault morally, but not theologically, or as directed towards God.' (ii 6.18)

The divine command adds a special sort of sin and blameworthiness that consist in disobedience to God, but it presupposes the sin and blameworthiness that belong to some actions precisely because of their relation to right reason.[54] Without a divine command or prohibition, actions would lack 'the complete and perfect character of a divine fault and offence, which cannot be denied in actions that are precisely against the law of nature' (ii 6.18). But they would not lack moral properties.[55]

The use of deontic terms for naturally good and bad actions makes it clear that Suarez's division between obligation and intrinsic goodness is not the division between impartial morality and mere self-interest. The use of 'right' and 'wrong', as well as 'good' and 'bad' for actions, apart from any divine command, shows that Suarez refers to the impartial aspect of morality.

These moral properties are 'intrinsic' to actions (ii 16.3). By this Suarez does not mean that they belong to actions irrespective of context or circumstances; the principles of natural law need interpretation so that we can identify the relevant circumstances.[56] Rightness and wrongness are intrinsic because they are determined by rational nature in its circumstances, and not by some external command.

The relation of right and wrong to human nature explains the sense in which natural law is everlasting and immutable.[57] Natural law remains the same because it depends on

[54] ii 6.18 fin. Finnis, *NLNR* 350, suggests that Suarez's distinction between debitum and obligatio is unsatisfactory: 'Since Suarez is under pressure from theological tradition to admit that an action can be identified as contrary to one's obligation, and that the doing of it can be described as guilty, *without reference to God's will*, his effort to be consistent with his own concept of obligation is only verbally successful; again and again in these paragraphs he is brought to the brink of saying that even without reference to any divine precept, acts (or their avoidance) can be obligatory (or guilty/sinful); this is betrayed in his repeated statement that the obligation imposed by the divine will underpinning natural law is "some sort of *additional* obligation" (paras. 12, 13), a "special obligation" (paras. 11, 17, 22).' Finnis's objections are unconvincing. Suarez is not 'brought to the brink of saying' that there can be sin without any obligation imposed by God; he clearly insists on this point. Finnis's claims about an 'added' and a 'special' obligation suggest that he takes Suarez to concede that the divinely imposed obligation is added to an obligation that is already there because of natural goodness and badness. I see no justification for this claim. When Suarez claims that an obligation is 'added', he does not mean that it is added to an obligation, but that it is added to a debitum. When he says it is a special obligation, he does not mean that it is to be contrasted with another sort of obligation, but that obligation is special to command, and not present in a natural duty. Finnis assumes that Suarez takes obligations to be identical to oughts and duties, so that it is awkward for Suarez to admit that actions can be wrong and sinful without violating an obligation. The objections collapse once we recognize that Suarez uses 'obligation' in the narrowly impositive sense; once we see that, his remarks about sins, added obligations, and special obligations are clear and intelligible.

[55] For further discussion of sin as offence against God see *De Peccatis* ii 2.5–8 (= *OO* iv 516b–517a). Though Suarez does not directly address the possibility of sin without infraction of divine law, his remarks are consistent with our present passage. He refers to Aquinas, *ST* 1a q48 a6; 2–2 q10 a3.

[56] 'Human actions, in their rightness and badness, depend greatly on circumstances and occasions of action, and in this there is great variety among them. For some are simpler (so to speak) than others, and need fewer conditions for their goodness or badness to arise. Now the natural law, considered in its own right, does not prescribe an action except in so far as it assumes that it is good, and does not prohibit an action except in so far as it assumes that the act is intrinsically bad. And therefore, in order to understand the true sense of a natural precept, it is necessary to inquire into conditions and circumstances with which that action in its own right is bad or good. And this is called interpretation of a natural precept, as far as concerns its true sense.' (*Leg.* ii 16.6) See §447 on dispensations.

[57] 'I say, therefore, that, properly speaking, the natural law through itself cannot cease or be changed, neither as a whole nor in a particular, given that rational nature remains with the use of reason and freedom. For this latter assumption is always taken as understood and assumed; for, since the natural law is a sort of property of this nature, if this nature were wholly removed, the natural law would also be removed, as far as its existence goes, and it would remain only in accordance with the being of essence or as possible objectively in the mind of God, just as rational nature itself would.' (ii 13.2) Suarez cites Aquinas, *ST* 1–2 q94 a4–5; q100 a8; 2–2 q66 a2 ad1; q104 a4 ad2.

human nature, which remains the same.[58] This reference to human nature explains his claim that intrinsic rightness and wrongness rest on non-contradiction.[59] He does not mean that the principles of natural law are necessarily true in a way that would make their denial self-contradictory in itself; he means their denial conflicts with the relevant facts about human nature. Because of the facts about human nature, the natural law 'presupposes in its material an intrinsic rightness or badness altogether inseparable from this material' (ii 15.4). In metaphysics he argues that essences are in certain respects independent of the divine will. He claims the same independence for moral properties.

442. Theoretical and Practical Reason

We have found that Suarez recognizes two morally significant elements in the principles of natural law; they specify intrinsic rightness and they express divine commands. The 'foundation' of natural law is the set of principles describing the right actions appropriate for rational nature. Obligation is imposed by a divine command.

The division between intrinsic morality and obligation may provoke an objection. We may take it to imply that every ultimate moral principle is divisible into a strictly practical and prescriptive component, requiring a command, and a purely theoretical component, describing rational nature. The identification of moral goodness with some relation of appropriateness or fitness to nature may appear to be alien to Aristotle's and Aquinas' conception of practical knowledge. Suarez seems to make moral goodness a matter of purely theoretical study; once we know what human nature is, we can also discover what is appropriate to it.

This conception of moral goodness seems to reduce moral deliberation to theoretical rather than practical knowledge, and hence seems to conflict with Aquinas' emphasis on the strictly practical character of prudence.[60] Aquinas may appear to avoid Suarez's separation of theoretical and practical components, because he expresses the principles in gerundive form ('good is to be pursued' etc.), and so makes them neither purely theoretical nor purely prescriptive.[61] Suarez, however, seems to leave room for someone to accept the truth of the theoretical principles, while refusing to issue any commands.

This objection, we might suppose, is not obvious to Suarez, because he maintains that God in his goodness cannot both create human beings and command that they act contrary to their nature. But the objection seems damaging if we consider human agents confronted by natural law or by its theoretical basis. It seems that we do not necessarily will what is fitting for rational nature; and we might wonder why the mere knowledge that some action

[58] The natural law is natural 'not because its fulfilment is natural or comes about by necessity, but because that law is a sort of proper characteristic (proprietas) of nature and because God himself has planted it in nature.' (i 3.9)

[59] '... moral actions have their intrinsic natures and immutable essences, which do not depend on any external cause or will any more than do other essences of things which in themselves do not imply a contradiction, as I now assume from metaphysics.' (ii 5.2) Perena ad loc. cites DM x 1.12 = OO xxv 332a, where Suarez explains how goodness adds to being only the convenientia that something has in virtue of its being (ratione entitatis). The metaphysical basis of Suarez's ethical conceptions is explored at length by Gemmeke, MSGFS, esp. Part 2. Cf. §547 on Cudworth.

[60] Suarez's view of prudence is contrasted with Aquinas' view (on tenuous grounds) by Treloar, 'Demise'.

[61] See §425 on ii 6.3. On gerundives and commands in Aquinas see §257.

fits human nature will move us to choose that action. Even if we know that God commands us to do that action, why should that purely theoretical knowledge make a difference to our action?

This objection to Suarez's position is a version of Hume's argument about 'is' and 'ought'. According to Hume, we have given the wrong account of a moral judgment if our account allows someone to believe that a moral judgment is true without having any motive to act on it.[62] If this is a correct constraint on any acceptable account of a moral judgment, Suarez's account is clearly unacceptable. But Aquinas may appear to satisfy Hume's constraint. For he formulates the basic principles as gerundives, and hence (we might infer) not as indicative statements about what is appropriate for human nature; hence they are neither ungrounded commands nor purely theoretical principles. We cannot accept a gerundive (we may suppose) without having some motive to obey it. If this is an adequate defence of Aquinas, he avoids the Humean objection that confronts Suarez.[63]

Sympathy with the Humean objection may encourage an interpreter to accept the account of Suarez's views on obligation that we have rejected. For we may suppose that Suarez believes that purely indicative judgments cannot contain moral oughts, because they do not by themselves motivate the agents who accept them; that he takes prescriptions, and hence commands, to be necessary for motivation, and hence for moral oughts; and that therefore he takes obligations—i.e., moral oughts—to require commands. According to this view, Suarez separates the two components that Hume takes to be necessary for a genuine moral judgment—the descriptive and the prescriptive—and assigns them, respectively, to intrinsic natural facts and to divine commands.

This is not exactly Hume's view, since the existence of a divine command does not guarantee action on it; it still leaves an open question about whether the agent to whom the command is addressed is moved to act on it. But, according to some views, Suarez tries to cover this gap by speaking of obligation as 'moral moving'. If this is to be understood as 'moral motivation', he assumes that obligation requires both a divine command and the motivation to follow it.

---

[62] On Hume see §752. Cf. Finnis, *NLNR* 36–48.

[63] Grisez criticizes Suarez for misunderstanding the character of practical knowledge: 'The theory of law is permanently in danger of falling into the illusion that practical knowledge is merely theoretical knowledge plus force of will. This is exactly the mistake Suarez makes when he explains natural law as the natural goodness or badness of actions plus preceptive divine law' ('First principle' 378). He cites *Leg.* ii 7, and refers with approval to Farrell, *NLSTS* 147–55. The description of Suarez's position in 'when he explains . . .' is not grossly inaccurate, but Grisez makes some contestable assumptions in claiming that this position relies on the mistake that Grisez alleges about practical knowledge. He seems to suggest that, according to Suarez: (1) Knowledge of natural goodness and badness is purely theoretical knowledge. (2) Knowledge of natural law is practical knowledge. (3) The difference between the two kinds of knowledge must lie in the command that belongs to natural law. While (2) is right, (1) is dubious. Suarez nowhere says or suggests that if we are aware of natural goodness and badness and unaware of any divine command, we have neither a reason nor a motive to pursue the good and to avoid the bad. Perhaps Grisez attributes this view to Suarez because Suarez takes natural law, and hence divine command, to be necessary for moral obligation. But, as we have seen, obligation, in Suarez's restricted sense, is not the only source of moral reasons or motivation.

On Suarez as a source of 'Scholastic natural-law theory' see also Grisez, *WLJ* 103–5. According to Grisez and Finnis, Suarez's main mistake is to treat the principles of natural law as theoretical principles that simply state that something is fitting to rational nature. They contrast this with Aquinas' view, according to which the principles have a gerundive form, and so avoid moving from is to ought. This is also relevant to the issue about debitum and obligatio. For we might suppose that the prescriptive aspect of morality enters only with the imperative obligatio and that the merely descriptive debitum is purely theoretical and lacks the appropriate prescriptive character.

We need not examine this interpretation further, since we have seen that it does not fit Suarez's claims about obligation and intrinsic morality. This is not surprising, since we have no reason to suppose that Suarez takes Hume's questions seriously. Still, we might argue that, since Hume's questions are legitimate, Suarez ought to have accepted the view that we have rejected on his behalf about obligations, commands, and oughts. If he takes intrinsic facts to be sufficient for moral oughts, he seems to open himself to Hume's objection, since Hume argues that we cannot move directly from such facts to oughts.

Does Aquinas' gerundive formulation avoid the objections Hume raises to deriving ought from is? The gerundive formulation is ambiguous, and the ambiguity may be resolved in different ways: (1) We may take the gerundive as equivalent to an imperative. In that case, the principles of natural law are really imperatives, and are in danger of being groundless, if they lack what Suarez calls their foundation. (2) We may take the gerundive to say that there are reasons for pursuing certain actions and avoiding others. But if these reasons are connected, for instance, with claims about rational nature, a Humean can ask why we should care about these reasons in particular. (3) We may take them to include both an imperative and a purely descriptive element. But in that case we can ask, in a Humean spirit, how the two elements are related. If the Humean gap is a genuine gap, we cannot accept Aquinas' principles unless we have made the transition from 'is' to 'ought' that Hume challenges.

In deciding how we ought to understand Aquinas' gerundives, and how we ought to connect them with Hume's objections, we need to take account of some complications in his position. At first sight, gerundive formulations may appear to be imperatives; for Aquinas himself says that the propositions expressed with these gerundives are the 'precepts' of the natural law. Precepts belong to the natural law because it is essential to law to command (ST 1–2 q90 a1 sc) and thereby to move us to action. In order to explain how law can have this motive character and still belong to reason, Aquinas relies on his account of command (imperium) as an act of reason presupposing an act of will (q90 a1 ad3; q17 a1).

But Aquinas' account of command precludes an implicit answer to Hume. If he understood all commands as imperatives, he might agree that anyone who accepts a command must be motivated to act on it, by assenting to an imperative. But his actual conception of command is much broader; for commands can be expressed through the indicative mood, with a gerundive ('This is to be done'), and not only through the imperative mood ('Do this') (q17 a1).[64] Hence the fact that he speaks of commands does not imply that he refers to imperatives addressed to oneself or to others.

This broad use of 'command' is relevant to the natural law. For its precepts are in gerundive form, and hence are 'indicative intimations', not 'imperative intimations'. They direct us to act appropriately, and if their directing is to result in action, we must have the appropriate will; but they do not themselves contain any appropriate act of will, and they do not imply that we have engaged or will engage in any such act of will. If all these precepts were imperative intimations that I address to myself, they would constitute attempts to move my will. But we cannot draw this conclusion from the fact that the precepts are indicative intimations. Once we recognize that Aquinas' conception of a command is

---

[64] See §257 on Aquinas.

broader than we might expect, we find that the precepts of the natural law—being indicative intimations—belong on the 'is' side of Hume's division.

If, then, Hume is right to suppose that we cannot move from is to ought without some appropriate desire or motive, Aquinas makes an illegitimate transition. For Aquinas believes it is legitimate to move from 'x is good (in the relevant way)' to 'x is to be done by me' and to 'I ought to do x', without any intervening act of will. The gerundive precept that x is to be done need not arise from, and need not produce, any desire to do x or to achieve the end to which x is a means.

Do Suarez's claims about commands make any essential difference? He agrees with Aquinas in taking gerundive judgments to be indicative (indicantem quid agendum vel cavendum sit, Leg. ii 6.3).[65] But he rejects Aquinas' view that to make a gerundive judgment of this sort is a way of commanding or prescribing. To express a precept, we must use the imperative mood. When he says that many people distinguish an indicative from a prescriptive law (lex indicans v. lex praecipiens, ii 6.3), he takes a law formulated with gerundives to be an indicative law. In his view, such a law is not a law, strictly speaking, because a law, strictly speaking, must contain actual precepts, which must be in the imperative mood. His use of 'command' and 'precept', therefore, is narrower than Aquinas' use, and closer to our usual use.

Once we recognize this disagreement between Aquinas and Suarez about the extent of commands, we see that their apparent agreement about the character of the natural law conceals an important disagreement. They agree that the provisions of the natural law are precepts. But Aquinas believes that the precepts are indicative, since he expresses them in gerundives. According to Suarez, however, a so-called precept in gerundive form is not a genuine precept, since it is indicative. Hence he believes that Aquinas' conception of a precept is too generous. He does not, therefore, take Aquinas' gerundive formulations to express the prescriptive character of natural law.

Suarez, therefore, might appear to accommodate Hume's demands better than Aquinas does. For if I accept any genuine precept of natural law, I accept a command. I must conform my will to the command by moving in the way I am commanded to move. One might, therefore, argue on Suarez's behalf that in accepting the precepts of natural law, I introduce the motive element that, according to Hume, is needed to explain the transition from is to ought.

This defence of Suarez, however, rests on a misunderstanding. For he does not believe that this motive element is needed to justify the acceptance of ought-judgments. He believes, as Aquinas does, that gerundives and ought-judgments are indicative, and do not include any special motivation. Hence he does not believe that any motive element is needed to explain the transition from is to ought. From Hume's point of view, both he and Aquinas make exactly the same illegitimate transition from is to ought without introducing a motive element to explain the transition.

Suarez's claims about obligation and command, therefore, do not result from any concern to exhibit the prescriptive character of moral judgments, or from any other concern that is related to Hume's questions about is and ought. His account of obligation is not meant to be

---

[65] Quoted in §426.

an account of moral requirements, reasons, or oughts in general and is not meant to explain how we can be given reasons or motives to act on moral principles in general. He believes that the moral principles constituting the foundation of natural law are 'merely descriptive', if that is taken to mean that they do not embody an attempt to move one's own will or anyone else's; hence he says they are purely indicative rather than prescriptive. But he does not think they are 'merely descriptive', if that is taken to mean that he thinks they require some further explicit prescriptions, conveyed through divine commands, before we have any reason or motive to act on them. Since these indicative principles include gerundives and oughts, they are already normative (i.e., they already give reasons) without any further prescription.

Suarez makes it clear that he does not think divine commands are needed to give us sufficient reasons or motives to act on the principles of intrinsic morality. The principles that require us to seek good and to avoid evil, to preserve ourselves and to promote the interests of others, and, in general, to act rightly and in accordance with rational nature, are grasped by practical reason apart from divine commands. We need not appeal to divine commands in order to have sufficient reason to choose intrinsically right actions. To suppose that moral reasons and moral motivation belong exclusively to obligations, as Suarez conceives them, is to overlook his narrow concept of obligation, and to underestimate the significance of intrinsic morality without imposed obligation.

Practical, rather than theoretical, reason grasps these principles, because we reach them if we start out from our necessary pursuit of the ultimate good; we discover that these principles achieve the ultimate good for a rational agent. We have reason, therefore, to follow them insofar as we are rational agents; and we recognize we have reason to follow them insofar as we recognize ourselves as rational agents pursuing our ultimate good, and recognize that these principles achieve this good. Aquinas gives reasons for supposing that we are rational agents of this sort, and that we necessarily regard ourselves as such, though we do not see all the implications of attributing this agency to ourselves. Suarez endorses these aspects of Aquinas' position; they are the background for his claims about natural law.

If these are the relevant aspects of Aquinas' doctrine, he has two answers to different parts of a Humean objection: (1) If the question 'Why should I care about these principles?' is a request for a justifying reason, it is answered by the connexion between natural law and practical reason. (2) If it is a request for an exciting reason, it is answered by the features of Aquinas' position that are often taken to constitute psychological egoism.

Neither of these answers to Hume meets Hume's demand for an account of moral principles that guarantees that anyone who believes them has a desire to act on them. But that is a highly disputable demand; failure to satisfy it may not be an error in Aquinas or in Suarez.

443. Natural Rightness and Divine Freewill

We have now explored the two elements that Suarez distinguishes in the natural law: intrinsic morality and divine commands. How are they related? Could they diverge? Even if Suarez agrees with naturalism about the existence of moral reasons based on intrinsic rightness and wrongness, he would still accept a significant part of the voluntarist case, if he were a voluntarist about the relation of intrinsic rightness to God's legislative will. A position we might ascribe to Ockham insists that God is free to command obedience to the principles of non-positive morality or principles conflicting with non-positive morality. By unqualified ('absolute') power God can accept or reject non-positive morality; only ordered power restricts God to the acceptance of non-positive morality.[66] At any given time, God is exercising only ordered power; we do not have to consider both what God might do on the basis of ordered power and what God might do on the basis of unqualified power. Hence we can rely on God to keep on commanding us to follow the non-positive morality that Suarez calls intrinsic morality.

Still, if we rely on God to command intrinsic morality, we rely on God's choice not to change his mind, rather than on his essential goodness. If Ockham is right, it is consistent with God's essential goodness to command us to violate intrinsic morality, though God has told us that he will not command us to do this. If God instructed us to violate intrinsic morality, and gave us innate knowledge of these instructions, there would be no natural law in the metaphysical sense, because God would not command us to act in ways fitting to rational nature; there would only be a natural law in the epistemological sense. The fact that God has created us with the nature we have does not, in Ockham's view, require God to impose any specific laws on us; hence God would have been equally good if God had told us to violate intrinsic morality. That is why God was free to command us to hate God, and hence to give us a command that we could not rationally obey (if we can rationally obey God's commands only out of love of God).[67]

According to Suarez, God was free to create or not to create beings with our nature.[68] The eternal law does not bind God independently of his will; it is a law for creatures arising from God's freewill as legislator. He imposes it on himself, as a craftsman, having decided to make a certain kind of thing, imposes a law on himself (ii 2.4). In this context Suarez speaks of God's ordered power, as Scotus does.[69] Still, God cannot violate his own decrees, because violation would be intrinsically wrong, and therefore is contrary to the intrinsic nature and essence of God (ii 2.7).[70] Suarez relies on this distinction between God's freedom in advance of creation and his lack of freedom after creation, in order to answer the question about whether it is possible for God not to command the observance of intrinsic morality.[71]

Scotus gives a voluntarist answer to this question, by exploiting the distinction between types of power. He claims that general laws come from the divine will, and not from the divine intellect prior to the divine will.[72] Scotus argues that if the divine intellect fixed

---

[66] On absolute v. ordered power see §396. Ockham probably does not suppose that non-positive morality is independent of the divine will (see §395), but if we did suppose that, we could reconcile naturalism about morality (in the form defended by Gregory of Rimini) with voluntarism about the divine will and morality.

[67] See §398.   [68] See §395 on Ockham's objections to Aquinas on God's freedom in creation.

[69] At ii 2.4 he cites Scotus, 1Sent. d44 q1 = OO v.2 1368–9. The passage Perena cites ad loc. is from the commentary in OO, not from Scotus.

[70] Suarez cites Aquinas, ST 1–2 q93 a4 ad1; 1a q21 a1 ad2.

[71] 'Is the hypothesis possible, that God, by the proper act of his will did not attach a proper law forbidding or prescribing the things that belong to the prescription of natural reason?' (ii 6.20)

[72] '...some general laws, prescribing correctly, were prefixed by the divine will and not by the divine intellect as preceding the divine will...; but when the intellect offers the divine will such a law, ... if it pleases God's will, which is free, it is a correct law' (Scotus, 1Sent. d44 q1 §6 = OO v.2 1368 §2 = V vi 365.9–15).

the laws, the divine will would not be free, but would will by necessity.[73] God is free to change these laws by his free will; in such a case his action is not disorderly (inordinatus), but according to a different order that is no less right than the first one.[74] This voluntarist conception of the general laws makes room for dispensations that are no less right than the general laws they violate. Scotus agrees that God cannot dispense from observance of natural law, but argues that our duties to our neighbour do not fall under natural law, and therefore God can dispense us from them. Ockham allows dispensation from each precept of the natural law.[75]

The dispensability of natural law may appear to be a welcome consequence of voluntarism; for familiar Scriptural examples seem to show that God makes exceptions to the precepts of natural law, by dispensing particular people from observance of them. If God is free to make exceptions to the natural law, God seems to be sovereign over natural law, so that natural law does not seem to contain any requirements that are independent of God's legislative will.

Suarez, however, follows Aquinas in discussing the alleged possibility of dispensations from a naturalist point of view. He examines the claim that God can, by absolute power, though not by ordered power, refrain from commanding what is intrinsically right.[76] It is not clear that Scotus holds this view, since he does not agree that the principles of justice with regard to one's neighbour are about what is intrinsically right; these principles depend on God's free will, and for that reason are subject to dispensation. Ockham comes closer to the position that Suarez discusses, since he recognizes non-positive morality. But if even non-positive morality depends on God's having freely ordered his absolute power in a particular way, it does not seem to meet Suarez's conditions for intrinsic rightness. Suarez discusses dispensations on the assumption that he has already shown that natural law includes intrinsic morality, so that dispensations from natural law would have to allow the violation of intrinsic morality.

Instead of directly answering the view he ascribes to Ockham, he turns to Aquinas' view that God cannot change his will on the natural law. In Suarez's view, Aquinas cannot be referring simply to immutability on the assumption of a divine decree, since even divine positive law is immutable in that sense. Aquinas, therefore, must refer to absolute immutability; he should be taken to claim that it is not even within God's absolute power to refrain from commanding the natural law.[77] Against Aquinas, Ockham believes that

[73] In *1Sent* d44 Scotus refers back to his discussion of this issue in d38 = *OO* v.2 1286–7 = V vi 306–7.

[74] 'I say, therefore, that God cannot only act otherwise than is ordered by a particular ordering, but can act otherwise than is ordered by universal order—that is, according to the laws of justice, because things that are beyond that order as well as things that are against that order could be brought about in an orderly way by God, in accordance with unqualified power.' (*1Sent.* d44 = *OO* v.2 1369 §3 = V vi 367.9–14)

[75] See next note.

[76] '... God can in accordance with unqualified power not make such a prohibition' (Suarez, *Leg.* ii 6.20). Perena cites Ockham, *2Sent.* q15 ad3, ad4 = *OT* v 352–3, quoted in §398n67.

[77] 'God cannot not prohibit what is intrinsically bad and misdirected in rational nature, nor can he not prescribe the contrary. This is openly asserted by St Thomas, ... in so far as he says that the decree of divine justice about this law is immutable. This assertion cannot be understood as being only about the immutability that assumes a decree. For in this way any decree at all of God in any positive law whatever is immutable. Therefore St Thomas is speaking of unqualified immutability. Hence his view is this, that God cannot in this case remove the order of his justice, just as he cannot deny himself, or just as he cannot not be faithful in his promises.' (*Leg.* ii 6.21) He cites Aquinas, *ST* 1–2 q71 a6 ad4; q100 a8 ad2.

God's absolute power to impose one or another law is not limited by God's having created creatures with our nature. From Ockham's point of view, the necessity that Suarez maintains of prescribing these specific principles to rational creatures is an inadmissible restriction of divine freedom. The necessity of prescribing these principles would follow from the necessity of choosing the best course of action; but, according to a voluntarist, such necessity is inconsistent with freedom.

Suarez agrees with Aquinas on this point.[78] God was free not to impose the natural law, since God was free not to create us. But if rational creatures exist, God's goodness requires God to prescribe obedience to intrinsic morality. Hence God's absolute power does not extend to imposing another law.[79] The freedom of God is exercised in creation; hence the necessity of imposing observance of the principles of natural law does not cancel divine freedom. Suarez relies on this claim to answer Scotus' objection that the necessity of imposing observance of the second table of the Decalogue would restrict divine freedom.[80]

444. Subordinate Principles of Natural Law

If Suarez holds this naturalist position about intrinsic rightness, he cannot allow dispensations from natural law; for its precepts prescribe intrinsically right actions, which God necessarily (in the respect described) wills that we do. Suarez therefore needs to show that apparent dispensations from requirements of natural law are not real dispensations, and hence do not require us to admit that God can allow violations of natural law.

Apparent dispensations are among apparent exceptions to the natural law. Suarez's careful discussion of the various cases that we might—misleadingly, in his view—include under the head of 'exceptions' explains his view about the ways in which God can or cannot create exceptions. To understand this view, we must understand his general view about the relation of subordinate principles to the higher principles of natural law. This view is worth exploring in its own right, before we see how Suarez uses it to explain apparent dispensations.

Following Aquinas, Suarez recognizes principles of natural law at different levels, and sees that the difference between these levels has to be taken into account when one speaks of the immutability or mutability of different provisions of natural law. As we have seen, he insists especially on the importance of fixing the relevant circumstances in considering what a specific provision says.

He therefore denies that the same action can sometimes be bad in itself and sometimes good in itself. Since an intrinsically bad action conflicts, by its own nature, with the requirements of rational nature, one and the same action with the same nature cannot both

---

[78] On absolute and ordered power see §396.

[79] 'For, speaking without qualification, God could have prescribed or prohibited nothing. However, on the assumption that he willed to have subjects who use reason, he was unable not to be their legislator, at any rate in those things that are necessary for natural rightness of morals.' (ii 6.23)

[80] '. . . it is not inappropriate for the divine will to be necessitated to that prohibition, on the supposition that it decided to establish human nature and to govern it, i.e. (seu), to have appropriate foresight about it' (ii 15.12).

conflict and not conflict with rational nature.[81] To identify the same action, we must fix the relevant circumstances and conditions. The same action, with these fixed, cannot be sometimes good and sometimes bad.[82]

To fix the relevant conditions and circumstances, and hence to find the actions that are intrinsically right and wrong, is the task of prudence, as Aquinas conceives it. Suarez agrees with Aquinas' view that natural law supports some fairly specific rules if the relevant circumstances are built in; hence it supports rules about respect for private property, even though it does not require property. We reach the relevant rules by interpretation (ii 16.6).[83] Suarez's appeal to circumstances and restricting conditions presupposes that the natural law prescribes and prohibits actions with reference to intrinsic goodness and badness, measured by agreement and disagreement with the requirements of rational nature. What rational nature requires depends on circumstances and conditions. Hence, the provisions of natural law take account of the appropriate circumstances and conditions.

A different conclusion would be forced on Suarez if he were to believe that intrinsic rightness and wrongness are intrinsic to action types in themselves, without reference to the agents or the circumstances. This would be a view similar to Clarke's belief in 'eternal relations of fitness'. If such a view were right, then we could infer simply from the fact that A had benefited B that B ought to benefit A in return, without reference to the fact that A and B are rational agents in specific circumstances that affect their rational agency.[84] In appealing to nature, Suarez rejects this explanation of intrinsic rightness, and defends his appeal to circumstances and conditions.

445. Our Knowledge of Natural Law

This discussion of subordinate principles confronts the believer in natural law with a dilemma created by two demands: (1) On the one hand, natural law is supposed to be epistemically accessible and reliable; its principles are readily grasped by everyone and are evidently the basis of any acceptable moral principles. (2) On the other hand, it must yield principles that are applicable to specific questions and practical situations; otherwise it is useless for guiding particular choices and actions.

These two demands seem to conflict. The demand for epistemically accessible and reliable principles encourages us to follow Aquinas in attributing such principles as 'Good is to be done and evil avoided', or 'One must act in accord with reason' to the natural law. But these principles do not include the sort of content that makes them practically applicable. When

---

[81] 'You will say that it can happen that the same action is sometimes bad from itself, but sometimes is not. On the contrary: in that case it will not be able to have both characters with the same circumstances or conditions on the side of the subject matter. For, since goodness or badness arises from the agreement or disagreement of an act with rational nature, it cannot happen that the same act with the same conditions is through itself both in disagreement and in agreement, because opposite relations do not arise from the same foundation.' (ii 15.30)

[82] Suarez explains the sense in which a right action could become wrong: 'And so, if that occasion with all its circumstances remains the same, the precept cannot fail to oblige; for if the occasion and the circumstances change, then the obligation can fail, but not because of a dispensation, but because this is the nature of an affirmative precept, that it always obliges [i.e., invariably on this occasion] but not for always [i.e., for every occasion].' (ii 15.29)

[83] Quoted in §441.   [84] On Clarke see §§618–19.

we try to introduce content without sacrifice of accessibility, we seem to sacrifice reliability. Both Aquinas and Suarez recognize this in the case of the precepts about killing, returning deposits, and keeping secrets; and we might also want to recognize it in the case of the precept against lying. While these precepts seem simple and accessible, they also seem to face counter-examples.

Aquinas answers that some conclusions from the highest principles of natural law hold only usually and have exceptions (*ST* 1–2 q94 a4). He suggests that the precept of returning what you have borrowed holds usually, because we ought to recognize it as valid only subject to certain circumstances that hold usually, but not always. These circumstances do not hold if you are returning a gun to someone who is threatening suicide or murder; in these circumstances you must not return what you have borrowed.

If failure in these circumstances to return what we have borrowed does not violate natural law, the higher principle that supports the usual practice of returning what we have borrowed must support a more complex principle than 'Return what you have borrowed'. If it really supported the unqualified principle, any failure to return what we have borrowed would violate natural law. But any identification of the more complex principle seems to raise a question about accessibility or about applicability. Either (1) the principle is 'Return what you have borrowed unless the lender is suicidal or . . . (listing all the relevant qualifications)'; or (2) the principle is 'Return what you have borrowed in the right circumstances'. In the first case, the relevantly qualified principle does not seem accessible; in the second case, it is not applicable to particular cases, since it still leaves us to list the relevant circumstances.

Suarez considers some of these difficulties in his treatment of the character and content of principles of natural law. In discussing the mutability of natural law, he points out that we need to decide what sorts of principles we are to attribute to natural law. We may formulate the precepts as 'A deposit must be returned', and so on, but these formulations of the precepts are not the precepts themselves.[85] Hence the alleged exceptions to a given precept are really included in the circumstances that are part of the precept (*Leg.* ii 13.7).[86]

---

[85] 'Hence we must further take account of this: The natural law, since in its own right it is not written on tablets or pages, but in minds, it is not always dictated in the mind in those general or indeterminate (indefinitis) words in which we express it orally or in which it is written. For example, the law about returning a deposit, in so far as it is natural, is not judged in the mind so simply and unqualifiedly (absolute), but with limitation and circumspection; for reason dictates that a deposit is to be returned to one who asks for it lawfully (iure) and rationally, or <that it is to be returned> unless some reason of a just defence, a reason applying either to the commonwealth or to oneself, or to an innocent person, prevents it. Commonly, however, this law tends to be expressed only in these words: "A deposit is to be returned". That is because the other things are implicitly understood, and cannot all be made clear in the form of law laid down in a human way.' (ii 13.6)

[86] Suarez's separation of precepts from formulations in rules rests on the sorts of considerations that move Scanlon, WWOEO 199, to deny that principles are to be identified with particular rules that can be applied to settle questions without much further exercise of judgment: 'Principles . . . are general conclusions about the status of various kinds of reasons for action. So understood, principles may rule out some actions by ruling out the reasons on which they would be based, but they also leave wide room for interpretation and judgment.' Scanlon explains his point through an example quite like Suarez's: 'Consider, for example, moral principles concerning the taking of human life. It might seem that this is a simple rule, forbidding a certain class of actions: Thou shalt not kill. But what about self-defence, suicide, and certain acts of killing by police officers and by soldiers in wartime? . . . The parts of this principle that are the clearest are better put in terms of reasons: . . . So even the most familiar moral principles are not rules which can be easily applied without appeals to judgment. Their succinct verbal formulations turn out on closer examination to be mere labels for much more complex ideas.' (WWOEO 199) Scanlon speaks as though the fifth commandment in the Decalogue were an unqualified prohibition of killing. But Christian moralists do not normally understand it in this way, as Aquinas' treatment shows; the usual interpretation makes it a 'principle' rather than a 'rule that can be easily applied without appeals to judgment'.

Here he follows Aquinas' interpretation of the fifth commandment. Aquinas considers an argument to show that the precepts of the Decalogue are dispensable, because the Decalogue forbids killing, but human law allows killing of evildoers and enemies.[87] Aquinas answers that the commandment expresses a principle about wrongful killing, but it does not state a rule that prohibits all killing.[88] If we recognize justifiable killing, we have not found an exception to the commandment; we have found a more accurate statement of it. To find a full statement of the commandment we would need to identify all the circumstances that justify killing. If we cannot confidently claim to have done that, we cannot confidently claim to have formulated the whole content of the principle that forbids wrongful killing.

This conception of principles clarifies Suarez's conception of the precepts of natural law. Since they are precepts of practical reason about what is suitable to human nature, they include circumstances and conditions. Since practical reason does not prescribe unqualified precepts, such precepts do not belong to natural law. Practical reason has to take account of the systematic character of the precepts of natural law. Since natural law, taken as a whole, expresses what is intrinsically right and appropriate for human nature, the different precepts do not express separate moral requirements; they express different aspects of the relevant sort of appropriateness.[89] Reflexion on returning deposits and on other precepts of natural law shows us that we need to limit the circumstances for returning deposits. These limits introduce other precepts and virtues; we have to know whether someone is asking 'lawfully', and whether some 'just defence' requires us to withhold the deposit. We cannot apply the precepts one at a time without reference to the rest of natural law.

The implicit flexibility of the precepts of natural law allows us to understand how they make room for some dispensations. Suarez discusses the papal power to dissolve marriages that have been properly and canonically contracted, but not consummated. He argues that the power to dispense from such a marriage is not a power to dispense from

---

[87] 'Further, among the precepts of the Decalogue is one forbidding murder. But it seems that a dispensation is given by human beings in this precept: for instance, when according to the precept of human law, such people as evil-doers or enemies are permissibly slain. Therefore the precepts of the Decalogue are dispensable.' (ST 1–2 q100 a8 obj.3)

[88] 'The killing of a human being is forbidden in the Decalogue, in so far as it has the character of the wrongful (indebitum): for this is how the precept contains the very character of justice. Human law cannot make it permissible for a human being to be killed wrongfully. But it is not wrong for evil-doers or enemies of the common weal to be killed. Hence this is not contrary to the precept of the Decalogue; and such a killing (occisio) is not a murder (homicidium), which is forbidden by that precept, as Augustine says . . . And similarly, if someone's property is taken from him, if it is right (debitum) that he should lose it, this is not theft or robbery, which are forbidden by the Decalogue.' (1–2 q100 a8 ad3) This way of understanding the commandment has been followed in some modern English versions of the Decalogue. See, e.g., NRSV, REB, at Exodus 20:13. The sense of the Hebrew is not completely clear. See, e.g., Rylaarsdam in IB i ad loc.: 'The verb is not limited to murder in the criminal sense and may be used of unpremeditated killing (Deut. 4:22). It forbids all killing not explicitly authorized. This means that in Israelite society it did not forbid the slaying of animals, capital punishment, or the killing of enemies in war.' Stamm and Andrew, TCRR 99, after criticizing the rendering 'murder', have nothing more precise to suggest than 'illegal killing inimical to the community'.

[89] This systematic character of the natural law, as Suarez conceives it, may be contrasted with an intuitionist view, such as Clarke's or Price's, that recognizes independent, and possibly conflicting, self-evident and equally basic principles, each of which can be grasped by an independent act of intuition. According to an intuitionist view, we can grasp the principles of justice independently grasping the principles of benevolence, and a further intuition is needed in case of conflict between the two sets of principles. See §§620, 823.

natural law; on the contrary, the natural law justifies the dissolution of such marriages by public authority.[90] The ends to which the precepts of natural law are directed warrant the dissolution of some marriages by public authority. This is not a concession that allows the violation of natural law for some other end, but a provision that promotes the ends of natural law.

Suarez's treatment of the precepts of natural law shows that he maintains their reliability even if he makes it more difficult to show that they are accessible or applicable. The teleological and rational character of natural law shows that it includes the reasonable moral judgments that lead us to doubt the simple and unqualified formulations of the precepts. Among these simple and unqualified formulations are those contained in the Decalogue. These Scriptural formulations do not fully express, but simply indicate, the underlying precepts of natural law.

446. Application of the Precepts

If this reasoning shows how the precepts of natural law are accessible to us, does it show that they are applicable to action? They are more difficult to apply than the unqualified precepts, because they require us to recognize what a 'just defence' might be, which is more difficult than recognizing whether we have borrowed something and the time has come at which we agreed to give it back. Suarez implies that the study of apparent exceptions that appear on reflexion to be justified, in the light of all the precepts of natural law, gives us a reasonable basis for recognizing the qualifications implicit in each precept. Consideration of the point of keeping promises, returning deposits, and so on reveals limits that we must recognize in the different precepts.

This view of the precepts of natural law affects Suarez's treatment of specific areas of moral perplexity, including the laws of war. One approach assumes that we have already established the precepts of natural law at a rather high level of abstraction; we know, for instance, that the natural law prohibits killing innocent people, and we examine the circumstances of war to see whether they warrant an exception to this general principle. This is not Suarez's approach. We have a reasonable prospect of grasping the precepts of natural law only when we have examined all the relevant circumstances to see how they affect the content of the precepts.

On the one hand, this may appear a rather flexible approach to the moral questions raised by war. Since we do not examine them in the light of principles whose content we already know, the cases we consider in examining war influence our view of what the relevant principles say. Hence they are part of the process of discovering the principles, not part of the process of applying principles we already know.

---

[90] 'The fact that such a dispensation may be granted by public authority is not contrary to the natural law, but in agreement with it, because nature itself is capable (if I may put it this way) of giving up its own right (ius) because of some greater good that even results in its own advantage. And because the administration of those rights (iurium) that belong to the common good of nature is committed to the power that has charge of the commonwealth, for that reason it is not against natural right (ius) that such an act <of entering into marriage> is dissolved by public authority.' (ii 14.20)

On the other hand, Suarez disallows a familiar means of allowing some moral flexibility in the treatment of war. We might say that in war the normal moral rules are suspended, so that the principles that normally determine the legitimacy of (say) killing or expropriation or deception do not guide our actions in this particular area. According to Suarez, nothing about war makes the ordinary precepts of natural law inapplicable. Hence we have to justify belligerent actions by considerations that we can show to be equally legitimate in other contexts.

If we recognize that the requirements of natural law may be complex, we cannot find them without careful attention to cases in which we see the need for some complication. Hence Suarez's view on natural law leads him directly into the discussion of 'cases of conscience'. His discussion of cases related to lying and deception illustrates his general outlook. He argues that cases of equivocation, ambiguity, and mental reservation should not be classified as lying, since those who speak ambiguously or incompletely (with mental reservation) assert what they really believe, though their audience does not take them to assert this.[91] Hence these misleading ways of speaking are not covered by the prohibition against lying (*Iur.* iii 11.4 = *OO* xiv 700b). But Suarez does not infer that they are permissible simply because they are not lies. Even if one says, strictly speaking, what one believes, the use of equivocation and ambiguity is wrong and contrary to the needs of human society, since it undermines the normal basis of communication. It is justified, however, in cases where one's interrogator has no right to ask the questions, and where one would be open to blame for giving an unequivocal answer.[92] If a dangerous armed intruder asks where his intended victim is, we ought to say 'I don't know', meaning 'I don't know anything I am required to tell you about this'.

Suarez does not apply this casuistical argument to purely imaginary cases. English Roman Catholics put it into practice when they were interrogated by a magistrate who (in their view) was asking questions beyond his legitimate authority.[93] The position Suarez defends was widely criticized, and it is an example of the sort of argument that gave casuistry, and especially Jesuit casuistry, a bad name. But the position is easier to dislike than to refute.[94] His permission for equivocation and reservation is carefully restricted. The restrictions are stated in rules that cannot be applied directly to practice without further moral reasoning. He might be criticized because he leaves room for dispute when he introduces 'necessity' and 'just cause'. But is not clear that such criticism would be justified; perhaps moral rules ought to leave room for further moral reasoning and possible dispute.

Suarez's conception of intrinsic goodness explains his attitude to precepts of natural law. Natural law prescribes what is intrinsically good, and therefore what is suitable for rational nature. The requirements of rational nature help us to see some of the qualifications that

[91] *De iuramenti praeceptis* iii 9.2 = *OO* xiv 695a.

[92] 'Still, one must be careful that people do not take from this excessive permission to speak or swear in this way; for that is without doubt contrary to good morals and contrary to the simplicity of speech, if I may so call it, that is necessary for human society. We must, therefore, add that this way of speaking through ambiguity (*amphibologia*), and especially by speech that is incomplete in the words uttered and in a way (quasi) completed by concepts, is not permitted, unless from some just cause and necessity, and unless otherwise something blameworthy would be done.' (*Iur.* iii 10.10 = *OO* xiv 699b)

[93] See Zagorin, *WL* 182–4.

[94] Kirk, *CP* 205–6, mentions some Protestant casuists who condemn the defence of mental reservation endorsed by Suarez, but do not seem to reject it so absolutely in their own treatment of cases.

are incorporated and understood in the different precepts of the natural law. Since these requirements underlie all the precepts of the natural law, they determine the demands of one precept in the light of the demands of other precepts.

447. Divine Dispensations from the Natural Law?

This discussion of exceptions to general rules shows us how to interpret apparent exceptions so that they are not contrary to principles of natural law, but only contrary to particular formulations of principles. Such an interpretation of apparent exceptions helps Suarez to explain apparent dispensations from natural law.

If it is necessary for God, given the creation of rational creatures, to impose obedience to the principles of natural law because of their intrinsic rightness, God is not free to dispense us from obedience to them.[95] Suarez therefore rejects Scotus' treatment of dispensations. He needs an alternative explanation of the admitted cases in which God either allows or requires someone to violate a common formulation of a precept of natural law; the explanation should show that God does not really dispense from the natural law, because these cases do not really violate natural law. The previous discussion of apparent exceptions to natural law helps Suarez to explain why precepts of the natural law are not subject to God's free will in a way that allows dispensations.

According to Scotus (as Suarez sees, ii 15.8), God cannot dispense us from the natural law, strictly construed; Scotus takes this to extend only to the first table of the Decalogue, from which God cannot dispense us without self-contradiction. God can dispense us, however, from the second table; its precepts are divine positive law that is 'very much in accord' with natural law. Since these precepts are not required by natural law, violation of them is allowed by natural law, and so God is free to dispense us from them.

In reply Suarez argues that the second table of the Decalogue contains the requirements of the natural law in our treatment of other people. We do not vindicate the possibility of dispensations simply by showing that the precepts of the second table, conceived as unqualified prohibitions of action-types described in entirely non-moral terms, have exceptions. The principles of natural law are not unqualified prohibitions of this sort. They declare what is intrinsically right and wrong given certain circumstances, and we need interpretation to find the relevant circumstances. The view that principles of natural law are dispensable, and the view that they are subject to modification by equity (discussed in ii 16) or any human legislation (ii 14), rest on the same error. We fail to understand the immutability of the natural law, if we do not see that it applies to actions in specific circumstances, not to unqualified action types.

Suarez, therefore, rejects an apparently plausible form of argument for dispensations. We might argue that since the natural law forbids killing, but killing is sometimes permissible (ii 15.13), the natural law is dispensable. Suarez replies that the natural law does not forbid

---

[95] Similarly, no human power can abrogate or dispense from the law of nature; '... the natural law, as far as all its precepts go, belongs to the natural properties of human beings. But human beings cannot change the natures of things' (ii 14.8).

all killing; the types of killing it forbids must be decided by interpretation in the light of the fact that all the principles of the natural law aim at promoting good and avoiding evil.

To show that God cannot dispense from observance of the second table of the Decalogue, Suarez argues that apparent dispensations result from a non-legislative action of God. Aquinas argues that the supposition of a dispensation from natural law involves a contradiction, because it requires us to say both that the action is due (debitum), as required by the natural law, and that it is not due, insofar as God's dispensation permits us not to do it.[96] His opponents argue that this argument simply assumes that God cannot dispense; for that is the only basis for the claim that the action we are dispensed from is still a duty. Since the question is about whether God can dispense. Aquinas simply argues in a circle (ii 15.16–17).

To show that Aquinas does not argue in a circle, Suarez distinguishes two sorts of duty (debitum). One is the duty arising from the law as an effect of it. If this were the only duty in question, Aquinas would be arguing in a circle. But that is not all Aquinas means by saying that we still have a duty to do the action from which God allegedly dispenses us. For he appeals to the duty that follows immediately from the intrinsic proportion between the object and the act compared to correct reason or to rational nature. In this case the action in question is intrinsically right or wrong. Hence the relevant duty is inseparable from the actions themselves, because it is antecedent to any law.[97] Since it is not imposed by any law, God cannot dispense anyone from it, since dispensation can only be from an obligation imposed by a law. In Suarez's terms, God's permission not to fulfil an obligation that God has imposed cannot dispense from a duty that exists independently of divine imposition.[98]

This argument alone does not show that God cannot dispense us from the natural law. It shows only that God's dispensation could not prevent the action from being intrinsically wrong. We might argue that if God dispenses, an action is intrinsically wrong, and hence violates one duty, but is permitted by God, and hence by a second duty, which is an obligation. This solution might seem to be suggested by Suarez's distinction between the two types of duty belonging to the natural law.

Such a solution is unwelcome to Scotus and Biel, who deny that God gives permission for intrinsically wrong actions. Biel, in contrast to Scotus, believes that God is free to permit such actions, and simply decides not to permit them.[99] The solution that allows God to permit intrinsically wrong actions might be more congenial to Ockham, who allows a possible

---

[96] In §§16–18 ff both Perena and ET translate 'debitum' by 'obligation', giving the impression that Suarez contradicts his normal view about obligation.

[97] 'This duty, however, is inseparable, not because it is not subject to dispensation (for that would be question-begging), but because it is assumed to exist in things themselves intrinsically before every extrinsic law, and therefore, given that the same things remain, it cannot be removed, because it does not depend on any extrinsic will, nor is it anything distinct, but it is a sort of wholly intrinsic mode, or a sort of relation that cannot be prevented, given that the foundation and term <of the relation> is assumed.' (ii 15.18)

[98] 'But granted that we imagine that the prohibition added by the will of God can be removed, still, it is entirely repugnant for what is in its own right and intrinsically bad to cease to be bad, because the nature of a thing cannot be changed. Hence such an action cannot be done freely without being a bad thing and discordant with rational nature, as we showed there from Aristotle and others.' (ii 15.4)

[99] See §379.

conflict between non-positive morality and divine positive morality. But it is difficult to identify non-positive morality, as Ockham conceives it, with intrinsic morality, as Suarez conceives it. For Ockham seems to believe that even non-positive morality expresses the ordered power of God, and so is subject to change within the unqualified power of God. If Suarez were to attribute to God the power to permit intrinsically wrong actions, he would allow a more direct conflict between the will of God and morality than any voluntarist accounts of dispensations have allowed.

Suarez rejects Scotus' view that violations of the moral law could be in accord with natural law. For the natural law prescribes, forbids, and permits actions insofar as they are intrinsically right, wrong, or neither.[100] It would be self-contradictory for the provisions of natural law to be determined both (i) solely by intrinsic right and wrong, and (ii) by God's dispensations.

This argument does not rule out all dispensations. We might argue that God's dispensation does not say that it is in accordance with the natural law to do something intrinsically wrong. It simply says that in this case we do not violate a duty to God if we violate the natural law. Hence the necessary connexion between natural law and intrinsic right and wrong does not show that God cannot dispense from natural law.

To close this loophole for dispensations, Suarez must claim that God necessarily prescribes and prohibits in accordance with intrinsic wrong and right. Hence, since God prescribes obedience to the natural law, God leaves no room for dispensations from it; there would be room for them only if God prescribed obedience to natural law as a positive divine law. In prescribing obedience to a positive law, God does not prescribe or prohibit on any specific basis, and hence it is up to God to change the prescriptions. But in prescribing obedience to the natural law, God prescribes on the basis of intrinsic right and wrong. Hence God would violate the will expressed in prescribing the natural law if God were free to dispense us from its provisions.

Once he has rejected dispensations, Suarez tries to explain the appearance of dispensations. Dispensations embody a legislator's permission to violate the provisions of a law, but God can alter our moral situation without granting dispensations, For God is not only supreme legislator, but also supreme owner (dominus) and supreme judge. Apparent dispensations really result from God's exercise of the powers of an owner or a judge.[101] The standard examples of Abraham and Isaac, the spoiling of the Egyptians, and Hosea are used to illustrate this explanation of apparent dispensations.

Our examination of Suarez's attitude to dispensations shows how far he accepts voluntarism about the will of God and the natural law. He believes that the obligation imposed by the natural law requires a command expressing God's legislative will, but he intends this point to clarify his strict concepts of law and obligation. Though he disagrees with Aquinas on this point, he accepts the further claims of Aquinas that Scotus and Ockham oppose. He claims that actions are intrinsically right and wrong, and hence are the source of duties, apart from any divine command; God necessarily prescribes and forbids these actions because

---

[100] 'For, as has often been said, the natural law prohibits those things that are bad in their own right, in so far as they are such. And therefore it assumes in the objects or acts themselves an intrinsic duty.' (ii 15.18)

[101] 'Whenever, therefore, God makes permitted an action that by right (ius) of nature appeared to be prohibited, he never does so as a pure legislator, but by using some other power. For that reason he does not dispense.' (ii 15.19)

they are intrinsically right and wrong. Suarez denies, therefore, that morality depends on divine commands.

448. The Natural Law and the Law of Nations

Suarez's exploration of the higher and lower provisions of the natural law leads him into a disagreement with Aquinas over the relation of the 'law' or 'right' (ius) of nations to the natural law. Suarez's views about the extent of law are stricter than Aquinas' views; this is one source of his disagreement with Aquinas about the necessary conditions for the existence of a natural law. Suarez recognizes two distinct sources of the validity of natural law: (1) It is not valid as law unless it expresses the will of the legislator who prescribes it. (2) It is not natural law unless it expresses intrinsic right and wrong. Recognition of different sources of validity also clarifies the status of the law of nations (ius gentium), which belongs to positive law, not to the natural law (*Leg.* ii 19.8). Suarez uses 'law of nations' to refer to two sets of laws: (1) laws common to different nations; and (2) the proper subset of these laws that governs relations between nations. Laws belonging to this second category of the law of nations constitute 'international law', and these include the laws of war.

If the law of nations is positive and not natural, we might infer that all of its provisions owe whatever moral force they have to the fact that they result from some sort of human legislation. If, then, justice in relation to war is a part of the common positive law of nations, different legislation seems to make different kinds of war just and unjust. Suarez, however, qualifies the positive character of the law of nations, by describing it as 'a sort of intermediate' (veluti medium) between natural and civil law (ii 20.10). Though it differs essentially from the natural law, it nonetheless agrees with it on many points (ii 19.1).

Aquinas seems to say, as Suarez acknowledges, that the provisions of the law of nations are conclusions from the higher principles of the law of nature (*ST* 1–2 q95 a4). Indeed, he argues that the provisions of the law of nations are derived from the social nature of human beings. If he is right, the provisions of the law of nations seem to be simply subordinate principles of the natural law, and hence impose duties—with appropriate allowance for circumstances and conditions—in the same way as other subordinate principles do. But if this is what Aquinas means, it is puzzling that he regards the law of nations as positive law; for conclusions from principles of natural law are not merely positive law.

In response to this difficulty in Aquinas, Suarez argues that the law of nations is simply positive law, not part of the natural law (*Leg.* ii 19.3).[102] It is not based on written statues, but on custom (ii 19.6). To explain Aquinas' apparently contrary opinion, Suarez suggests that Aquinas is speaking of 'conclusions' in an extended sense (ii 20.2). Some of the puzzles about Aquinas' position are removed by a distinction he draws when he first distinguishes human positive law from natural law. He says that in this human positive law we can find both conclusions and determinations of natural law. Conclusions have their

---

[102] The law of nations is positive law; 'The negative precepts of the right of nations do not prohibit something because it is bad in its own right—for that [sc. being bad in its own right] is purely natural. Hence, on the side of human reason, the right of nations does not simply reveal badness, but constitutes it. Therefore, it does not prohibit bad things because they are bad, but by prohibiting makes them bad things.' (ii 19.2)

force from something more than human enactment, whereas determinations rest simply on human enactment.[103] They are enacted, by explicit statute or by custom, as part of positive law.

Aquinas' conception of the law of nations is similar to Suarez's conception of the law of nature, insofar as it has two sources of its 'force' (vigor) and of the duties that it requires. Just as Suarez takes natural law to include a divine command, Aquinas takes the law of nations to require more than derivation from the law of nature; it must also be part of positive law. A conclusion from the law of nature that is not recognized by the common custom of the nations cannot belong to the law of nations.

Suarez draws a somewhat similar distinction in his own account of the law of nations.[104] In the case of civil law, something needs to be done to fulfil the requirements of natural law, but it can be done more than one way, and there is no reason to choose this way over that way (as with the rule of the road), or else the reason for choosing this way of fulfilling the law is quite local, referring to the specific circumstances of a particular people. In the case of the law of nations, however, the reason for having this particular rule is clear from the law of nature and rests on considerations that apply to human beings universally. Though the deduction from natural law is not evident, since the rule is not absolutely necessary for right practices, it still fits nature, and the rule is readily agreed on by all (ii 19.9).

Given Suarez's conception of the subordinate precepts of natural law, the law of nations introduces no dispensations from, or exceptions to, natural law. For natural law specifies what is intrinsically right and in accordance with human nature; if any positive law recognized exceptions to natural law, it would permit intrinsically wrong actions, but these actions cannot be morally justified. Still, the provisions of the law of nations cannot be required by intrinsic rightness and appropriateness to human nature; if they were required, they would be part of natural law.[105]

---

[103] 'Both <conclusion and determination> therefore, are found in the human law. But things of the first sort are contained in human law not as simply laid down by law, but they have some force from the natural law also. But things of the second sort have their force from human law alone.' (ST 1–2 q95 a2)

[104] 'For in civil or private right (ius), a determination takes place either (1) that is merely arbitrary, about which it is said that "what pleased the prince has the force of law", not because his will alone suffices as a reason, but because that determination would be rational, if made in different ways, and often there is no reason why it should be made this way rather than that, and thus it is said to be made by will rather than by reason; or (2) certainly when some special reason intervenes, it is considered in relation to the particular and (so to speak) material circumstances, and thus the determination is more in the circumstances than in the substance. But by the right of nations, precepts are more general, because in them the utility of all nature, and conformity to the first and universal principles of nature, is considered. And for that reason they are called conclusions reached from those <first principles>, because from the power of natural discourse appear at once the suitability and moral utility of such precepts, and this <suitability and moral utility> has led human beings to introduce such moral practices (mores), more by the demand of necessity than by will, as the Emperor Justinian has said.' (ii 20.2)

[105] Suarez rejects some inadequate reasons for distinguishing the law of nations from natural law itself. The mere fact that some provisions of natural law presuppose the existence of human society, or private property, does not make them any less provisions of natural law, since, for the reasons we have seen, the subordinate principles of natural law must include a reference to the relevant circumstances: 'Therefore, in order to distinguish the law of nations from natural law, it is necessary that, even when a given sort of material is presupposed, it does not follow through an evident inference, but through a less certain inference, in such a way that human judgment (arbitrium) and moral expediency (commoditas) rather than necessity, intervene. In my opinion, therefore, we must conclude that the law of nations does not prescribe anything as being from itself necessary for rightness (honestas), nor prohibit anything that is bad in its own right and intrinsically—either <bad> without qualification or <bad> on the supposition of a given state and condition of things . . .' (ii 17.9)

The law of nations, like civil law, differs from natural law because it does not prescribe or forbid something as intrinsically right or wrong.[106] But, in contrast to civil law, it is established by 'custom' or 'practice' (usus, ii 19.1; 6), not by formal acts of legislation. This custom is nonetheless legislative; it does not presuppose that this course of action is intrinsically right, but makes it right because of the custom.[107]

Within this law of nations Suarez distinguishes the laws that different nations have in common for dealing with their internal affairs from those that they have in common for dealing with one another; the latter set of laws constitutes 'the law that all peoples and the different nations ought (debent) to maintain between them' (ii 19.8). Some examples illustrate this international aspect of the law of nations: the immunity of ambassadors; free trade between individuals in different states; the law of war; slavery as a punishment for the defeated side in a war; and truces and treaties of peace.

In these cases, natural reason, seeking to discover the implications of natural law, finds some principles to guide international relations, but it cannot give complete answers.[108] A provision of the law of nations rests on three claims about the law of nature: (1) It is intrinsically right to achieve F. (2) It is equally right to achieve F by doing G or by doing H. (3) It is intrinsically right to make an agreement to do G rather than H or to do H rather than G. None of these three claims is subject to human agreement or decision, but human agreement enters in choosing G rather than H.

In this respect civil law shares the positive character of the law of nations. The preservation of life and health requires some rule of the road. It neither favours driving on the left nor favours driving on the right. But it certainly favours driving on the side that is prescribed by positive law. Once the positive law exists, natural law requires a specific type of action—different in different places (driving on the left in Japan, but on the right in the USA)—that it would not require otherwise. Similarly, natural law does not require the

---

[106] 'Hence, on the side of human reason, the law of nations does not simply present badness, but constitutes it; and therefore it does not prohibit bad things because they are bad, but by prohibiting them makes them bad.' (ii 19.2)

[107] Circumstantial dependence does not prevent an action from being intrinsically right or wrong; for, as we have seen, Suarez takes intrinsic rightness and wrongness to belong not to action types described without reference to circumstances, but to action types including all the circumstances that are relevant to appropriateness to rational nature. To fall outside the law of nature a precept must include some further uncertainty. This description, taken by itself, might suggest that a precept falls inside or outside natural law because of its degree of certainty. This seems to be a misleading suggestion. We might not be certain whether the good of human society and of rational nature is advanced by supporting the nuclear family or by encouraging communal upbringing of children (as in Plato's *Republic* or in an Israeli kibbutz). But our uncertainty does not by itself make it false that one sort of arrangement is better than the other. If research and experience prove that one arrangement is better, we have not caused it to be required by natural law; it has been required by natural law all along, and we have just discovered that is required. If we take uncertainty to be sufficient to place a precept within positive law, we violate Suarez's claim that no part of the law of nations prescribes what is intrinsically good; for, despite our uncertainty, some precepts might prescribe what is in fact required by natural law. Once we see that Suarez ought not to be relying on mere uncertainty, we can look for a more satisfactory interpretation of his remarks on the role of human judgment.

[108] 'For this reason they [sc. nations] need some law (ius) to rule them and direct them correctly in this sort of communication and association. And although this comes about to a large degree through natural reason, this is not sufficient and immediate on all questions; and so some special laws could be introduced by the practice of these nations. And this is especially so, because the things belonging to this law are few, very close to natural law, and allow a very easy inference from that law, and one that is so useful and so agreeable to nature itself that, granted that there is no evident inference, as being in itself altogether necessary for rightness of conduct, it is still highly appropriate to nature, and in itself acceptable to everyone.' (ii 19.9)

specific institution of immunity for ambassadors, or slavery as a means of punishment. Other means of communication or punishment could have been devised. The established ways are the right ways to communicate or to punish only because of the general agreement that has established the universal or usual practice.

Suarez believes nevertheless that natural law is relevant to the content of the different practices that belong to the law of nations. The unity of the human race implies a natural requirement.[109] Though each state is a complete community in itself, it is nonetheless a member of the moral and political universe, and therefore subject to moral requirements. Natural law is relevant not only because different states need to co-operate for their own advantage, but also because of a prior moral duty derived from mutual love and mercy.

Suarez believes, therefore, that the law of nations is positive law, but closely connected to the provisions of natural law. The provisions of the law of nations are similar to the provisions of the law of nature, insofar as they result from consideration of what is intrinsically right in the relevant circumstances. But since this consideration shows that we need to make an agreement and establish a custom, our conclusion requires us to establish a course of action that is right because it is commanded, not commanded because it is right. Nonetheless, the provisions of the law of nations must conform to natural law.[110] If we correctly judge that both G and H are ways of achieving an intrinsically right result F, the disjunctive requirement of doing either G or H is right. Suarez's point is that neither doing G rather than H nor doing H rather than G can be defended as intrinsically right, but it is right to do one or the other. It is the choice between these two courses of action that is a matter of practice rather than intrinsic rightness.

The law of nations, however, also permits some actions that are contrary to the natural law; for instance, it permits prostitution and a moderate degree of deception in business dealings, even though these actions are evils prohibited by the natural law (ii 20.3). Not every action prohibited by natural law is also prohibited by the law of nations.

How is this claim to be reconciled with the close connexion that Suarez sees between the law of nature and the law of nations? He argues that though the natural law prohibits prostitution, it does not require positive law prohibiting prostitution, but, on the contrary, justifies us in not legislating against prostitution. Hence it is a conclusion from the law of nature that there ought to be no positive law against prostitution; hence the law of nations contains no such positive law. The absence of this positive law does not make the practice of prostitution right. In this case the reasons for refraining from positive legislation appeal to

---

[109] '. . . the human race, however much divided into different peoples and kingdoms, always has some unity, not only specific, but also, one might say, political and moral; this is indicated by the natural precept of mutual love and mercy, which extends to all people, even to foreigners and to people of every nation. Therefore, granted that any complete state (civitas), either commonwealth or kingdom, is a complete community in itself and consisting of its own members, nonetheless any of them is also a member in a certain way of this universal community, insofar as it relates to the human race. For these communities are never so self-sufficient individually that they have no need of some mutual help, society, and communication, sometimes for their own greater well-being and greater advantage, but also sometimes because of moral necessity and need, as is shown by past practice' (ii 19.9).

[110] '. . . equity and justice must be maintained in the precepts of the law of nations. For this belongs to the character of every law that is a true law, as has been shown above; and the laws that belong to the law of nations are true laws, as has already been explained, and are nearer than civil laws are to natural law; hence it is impossible for them to be contrary to natural equity . . .' (ii 20.3).

the 'fragility and condition of human beings or transactions'.[111] An argument from higher principles of natural law, including the relevant facts about human beings, shows not that these actions are right, but that it is right for positive law to permit them.[112]

This apparent divergence between the law of nations and the law of nature helps to clarify Suarez's position, and to show how he basically agrees with Aquinas. He follows Aquinas in believing that the principles of natural law justify relatively specific conclusions about rules of moral and social behaviour. The positive character of the law of nations does not constitute an objection to this belief about natural law; on the contrary, natural law justifies the existence of the positive law of nations and the ways in which the provisions of the law of nations differ from those of natural law.

449. Natural Law and the Basis of Political Society

Suarez follows Aquinas in believing that a political society (a civitas), no less than smaller social groups, is to be justified by appeal to the law of nature, and, more specifically, to the social nature of human beings.[113] This social nature is the source of our need for positive law (i 3.19–20).[114] Human nature is fulfilled by the different virtues, including justice in relations with other people. The demand for just relations with others is a demand of the law of nature prior to any state or civil law, and the state is needed to fulfil this demand.

Since Suarez derives the state from the law of nature in general, he recognizes no special or overriding claim for self-preservation. He does not suggest, for instance, that the laws of nature incline us towards accepting a state simply because of the dangers and threats to physical security in any condition without a state. They make more specific demands on a state, so that a state does not necessarily fulfil the requirements of the law of nature by ensuring the physical security of its members.

For similar reasons, Suarez does not agree that a state or a government is at liberty to do whatever promotes safety and self-preservation. He takes this view about the liberty of a state to be Machiavelli's view, and he devotes a chapter to refuting it (iii 12). In Suarez's view, Machiavelli wrongly supposes that the preservation of the common weal (res publica) is secured by the preservation of the regime, and that everything promoting this end is to be accepted.[115] This position would be reasonable only if the preservation of a regime could

---

[111] '. . . this very permission may be so necessary, given the frailty and condition of human beings or transactions, that practically all nations agree in maintaining it' (ii 20.3).

[112] Cf. Melanchthon on toleration of error, §412.

[113] At ii 8.4 Suarez follows Aquinas in tracing different aspects of natural law to different aspects of human nature, living, animal, and rational.

[114] 'For <that necessity of law> is founded on this, that a human being is a sociable animal, demanding by his nature a civil life and communication with other human beings. And for that reason it is necessary that he should live correctly, not only in so far as he is a private person, but also in so far as he is a part of a community.' (i 3.19)

[115] '<According to this view>, the subject matter of the laws is that which serves the political order and its maintenance or increase; and directed towards this end these laws are enacted, whether true rightness is found in them, or only pretended and apparent rightness, by concealing even unjust actions, if they are useful to the temporal commonwealth. This is the teaching of politicians of this age; Machiavelli above all has tried to persuade secular leaders of it. It is founded solely on this claim, that the temporal commonwealth cannot be maintained in any other way.' (iii 12.2)

be given absolute priority over every other demand of natural law. But Suarez's conception of natural law assigns no such absolute priority to the preservation of a particular state, or even to the preservation of one's own life, without regard to the other goods and virtues that natural law maintains.

Suarez's answer relies on the prior validity of natural law and the different duties it imposes. Since these duties include more than the preservation of the state, Machiavelli's position cannot be sustained by appeal to the natural law. And since the natural law is prior to civil law, civil law cannot impose a valid obligation that is contrary to natural law (iii 12.4). Hence Suarez endorses the apostles' view that 'we must obey God rather than human beings' (iii 12.5; *Acts* 5:29).

These features of Suarez's views about political society are worth attention not because they are new, but because they are familiar from Aristotle and Aquinas. His contribution is to make clear their implications in the face of the questions, objections, and alternative views presented in Aquinas' successors, including Suarez's own contemporaries. It is useful to keep them in mind so that we can contrast them with the sharply opposed position of Hobbes, and with the more ambiguous positions of Grotius and Pufendorf.[116]

450. The Law of War as Part of the Law of Nations

It is useful to illustrate some of the more specific applications of Suarez's views about natural law and the law of nations by considering his treatment of the law of war, which is part of the law of nations. An account of the rights and wrongs of war is needed to counter the Machiavellian view that war is simply an instrument of national policy, and hence to be judged simply by its effectiveness.[117] This view ignores the fact that war threatens human welfare. A threat to human welfare constitutes a presumption against war, and hence brings it into the area of natural law.

Nonetheless, questions about the legitimacy of war and of particular practices within war cannot be decided simply by appeal to natural law. For natural law does not require resort to war rather than arbitration.[118] On the contrary: the contending parties ought to submit their

---

[116] On Suarez's political theory, and especially the role of consent see Sommerville, 'Suarez to Filmer', esp. 534, who argues that Suarez has a more radical constitutionalist view than is sometimes thought. Since Suarez regards the state as essentially aiming at the public good, he argues that it is legitimate for the community to depose a ruler who acts against the public good. A law professing to authorize a ruler to do what he likes, even against the public good, would not meet the conditions of *Leg.* i 6 for being a genuine law, and so citizens could not be obliged to obey it. See also Skinner, *FMPT* ii 158–66; Hamilton, *PTSS* 62; Tuck, *NRT* 56–7.

[117] 'There was an old error current among the Gentiles, who thought that the laws (iura) of nations rested on arms, and that it was permissible to make war simply to acquire reputation and wealth. This view, even from the point of view of natural reason, is most absurd ... No war can be just unless it relies on a lawful and necessary cause ... This just and sufficient cause is a serious injury that has been inflicted, and that cannot be punished or compensated in any other way. ... A war is permissible so that a commonwealth can guard itself against loss. Otherwise war tends against the good of humankind, because of the deaths, loss of property, etc. If then, that <just and sufficient> cause ceases, the justice of the war will also cease.' (*De Bello* 4.1)

[118] We could have formed a practice of always submitting disputes to arbitration and abiding by the results of the arbitration. But war is 'more in agreement with nature' than arbitration by third parties would have been. Presumably Suarez does not mean that it is more in accord with natural law—for in that case it would be part of natural law, not of the law of nations. Probably, then, he means that it is more in accordance with tendencies in human nature. He clarifies

dispute to 'the arbitration of good men' (*De Bello* 6.5).[119] The duty of recourse to arbitration rests on the natural law, and hence on what is appropriate for rational nature. States do not often resort to arbitration, because they are suspicious of the potential arbitrators (6.6). This may be why Suarez maintains that the practice of resort to war is more in accordance with natural law than resort to arbitration would be. But he acknowledges that resort to arbitration, in cases where the arbitrators are not open to suspicion, is better than resort to war.

For similar reasons, Suarez believes that war is needed for the punishment of injuries.[120] Different states do not agree in acknowledging experts who are sufficiently wise and impartial to find the right solution to their disputes; nor do they recognize any common authority with the right and the power to enforce such a solution. Hence each state is both advocate and judge in its own cause.[121] But though a state cannot normally resort to an independent arbitrator in the confidence that the other party to the dispute will accept the result of arbitration, it is nonetheless required to inquire carefully by consulting 'prudent and learned' advisers (6.6).

Suarez allows defensive war to prevent our being victims of aggression. He also allows aggressive war (1.6), in cases where we are not being attacked by another, in order to punish another state for infliction of an injury, if the other state is not willing to give just satisfaction for the injury (4.5).

In these grounds for war Suarez gives no permission for pre-emptive strikes against an enemy. One might argue that they are covered by the right of self-defence in cases where one can be appropriately certain that an attack is imminent, rather than simply believing that the other side is dangerous. The only other ground that he recognizes besides self-defence is punitive. A pre-emptive punitive attack would constitute an attempt to prevent a prospective wrongdoing.

this point in his discussion of the certainty required about the justice of a cause of war: '. . . the law of war, in so far as it is founded on the power possessed by one commonwealth or a supreme monarchy either for punishment and retribution or for reparation for the injury inflicted on itself by a second <state>, seems properly to belong to the law of nations. For from the force of rational nature alone it was not necessary for this power to lie in the commonwealth that suffered the injury; for human beings could have set up another means of retribution, or committed this power to some third ruler as a sort of arbitrator with power to coerce. Still, because the present way <of exacting retribution> that is now followed is easier, and more in agreement with nature, it has been introduced by custom, and is just in such a way that it cannot be lawfully resisted' (*Leg.* ii 19.8).

[119] 'For they are required to avoid war by morally right (honesta) means, as far as they can. Therefore, if no danger of injustice is to be feared, this [sc. arbitration] is the best means, and hence is to be embraced. This opinion is confirmed. For it is impossible that the author of nature should have left human affairs, which are more often governed by conjectures than by certain reason, in such a state that all disputes between supreme rulers and between commonwealths had to be ended only through war. For that is contrary to prudence and to the common good of humankind, and therefore contrary to justice. Moreover in that case the more powerful side would, according to rule (regulariter), have the greater right (ius), and to that extent the right would have to be measured by arms, which is quite clearly barbarous and absurd.' (*De Bello* 6.5)

[120] '. . . just as within a commonwealth some lawful power to punish crimes is necessary to the preservation of peace, so also in the world as a whole, so that different commonwealths may live in peace, some power is necessary for the punishing of injuries inflicted by one on another. But this power is not present in any superior, because they have none, as we assume. Hence it must be present in the supreme ruler of the injured commonwealth, to whom another ruler is subject because of the crime. Hence a war of this sort was introduced in place of a court assigning just punishment' (4.5).

[121] 'The cause is simply that this act of punitive justice was necessary for humankind, and, naturally and in the human way, no more suitable means could be given, especially because we must anticipate, before the war, the contumacy of the offending party, refusing to give satisfaction—for in that case <the offending party> has only himself to blame if he is subject to the one whom he has offended.' (4.7)

Suarez rejects such attempts. He discusses the justice of killing enemy non-combatants who might be capable of bearing arms and who might renew a war. He argues that this practice is no more justified than pre-emptive punishment would be within a state.[122] Similarly, pre-emptive war would have to be aimed against injustice that is not imminent, but merely prospective. A purely judicial and punitive rationale for aggressive war does not support a war that would violate the ordinary restrictions on punishment.

Is it unreasonably narrow of Suarez to consider only a punitive justification for aggressive war? Should he not also consider a preventive justification? One might argue that in a public health emergency we would be justified in isolating the carriers of a disease, in order to protect other people, even though we might thereby reduce the victims' chances of recovery. Could we not offer the same sort of defence for an aggressive war? Perhaps the enemy is not yet guilty of any specific violation, but we are protecting more innocent people from the danger presented by the enemy.

To see how Suarez might answer this objection and defend his narrow justification for aggressive war, we may consider his views about the threshold for any justifiable war. He sees a presumption against war that needs to be overcome.[123] Since it is certain in advance that a war involves great evils, a justification for a war must offer a sufficient degree of practical confidence that it is necessary for the avoidance of still greater evils. Suarez rejects the demand for complete 'moral certainty' (4.10), but still demands 'the maximum certainty that he [sc. the ruler] can obtain'.

These demands on a legitimate cause of war make it difficult to see how a purely pre-emptive war to avoid a prospective injury could be justified. We have strong reasons for avoiding punishment for merely prospective offences. Given these strong reasons, in addition to the admitted evils involved in war, the credible threat of punitive aggression is preferable to pre-emptive aggression. This is why we do not imprison or punish people simply as a pre-emptive measure.

451. Sedition and Rebellion

Suarez does not believe that war between sovereign states involves the suspension of ordinary moral principles. He therefore argues that the same principles apply to violent conflict within a state. In his view, this is justified within the moral limits that also apply to wars between states. The obligation of obedience and non-resistance to a sovereign is limited; Suarez even defends rebellion and tyrannicide in some circumstances. This aspect of his views did not make Suarez popular in England or France in the early 17th century.[124]

---

[122] '...no one may be punished for a prospective sin, if he does not otherwise deserve death, especially because that presumption <of prospective sin> does not seem sufficient for killing human beings, since especially in a criminal trial there ought to be sufficient proofs, and rather <than being presumed guilty> he who is not proved guilty is presumed to be innocent' (7.16).

[123] '...while a war is not in itself evil, nevertheless, on account of the many disadvantages that it brings with it, it is one of those undertakings that are often executed in an evil way. And that is why it also needs many circumstances to make it right' (1.7).

[124] On the reception of Suarez's DFC in England and France, see De Scorraille, FS ii 189–216. The book was burnt at St Paul's Cross; it was also condemned by the Parlement of Paris and burnt. James I required William Talbort to say

An aggressive war against the ruler of one's own state is justifiable in the appropriate circumstances, if it meets the normal conditions for a just war. Suarez takes it to be obvious that defence against injury by the ruler is justified. He takes it to be easy to justify aggressive action against a tyrant who has no just claim to be the ruler (8.2). It is more difficult to justify aggression against a second kind of tyrant—a ruler who has a just claim to be ruler, but abuses his power and acts unjustly. In this case Suarez holds that individuals have no right to take aggressive action. He relies on the general principle that the common good requires that only a sovereign should have the authority to attack a sovereign (8.2). But in some cases the whole commonwealth (respublica) has the right of revolt against a legitimate ruler acting tyrannically.[125] If the ruler is clearly behaving tyrannically, the commonwealth as a whole has the right to exercise the power that it retained when it made him the ruler. The commonwealth gave him this right and power on the condition of ruling 'politically'.[126]

Natural law requires some sort of government because it requires the promotion of the common good. Since human beings have a common good, and since the uncoordinated actions of individuals do not achieve the common good, some special provision for it is needed.[127] Though individual human beings are not naturally subject to political rule, they are naturally 'subjectible' (subiicibilis) to it (Leg. iii 1.11). The role for human agreement is similar to the role we have already discussed in the law of nations. Natural law does not impose a government independently of human agreement; but it requires us (in normal conditions) to agree to set up a government, and therefore requires us to obey it once we have set it up.

But who are the 'we' who set up a government? In Suarez's view, the legislative power belongs directly to a 'collection' of human beings. It cannot belong to an individual or group unless the 'community' to which it originally belongs has transferred it (iii 2.3). This account might appear to assume the very fact it is supposed to explain. For it seems to assume that some sort of human community is the body that makes the agreement to set up a ruler. But how can we have a community capable of making such an agreement unless we already have a political community with some sort of ruler?

Suarez answers this objection by distinguishing two ways of looking at human beings without government. We can consider them as a mere 'aggregate' (aggregatum quoddam) of individuals with their individual concerns. No legislative power is proper to this collection

what he thought of Suarez's views on the obligations of the subjects of a tyrant deposed by the Pope, before he released him from the Tower. When Talbort did not condemn it, he was given life imprisonment. When John Ogilvie, a Scottish Jesuit, was interrogated, he was also asked to denounce Suarez's views, and refused to do so.

[125] 'The reason is that in this case the whole commonwealth is superior to the king; for since it gave him power, it is regarded as having given it on the condition that he would rule politically, not tyrannically, and if he did not, he could be deposed by the commonwealth.' (8.2)

[126] We might suppose that the ruler is established by a real or implied agreement that requires him to observe the laws and constitution, and that this observance constitutes ruling politically. Suarez, however, does not explain the relation between the ruler and the people in this way.

[127] 'For each individual member has a care for its individual advantage, and these are often opposed to the common good. And sometimes many things are necessary for the common good, which do not belong in the same way to individuals; and though they may at times belong to an individual, he provides for them not because they are common, but because they are proper to him. Therefore in a complete community, a public power is necessary to which it belongs as a matter of duty (ex officio) to aim at and to provide for the common good.' (Leg. iii 1.5)

of human beings; they have only the root of it (quasi radicaliter, iii 2.4). We must consider them in another way, so that even without an actual government, a group of people may form a single political community and 'mystical body'.[128] To form a single body, people need not individually want to set up a government, and they need not make a promise or agreement to set it up. Suarez assumes a less specific shared desire and aim. The human good requires promotion of a common good, and hence requires some agent with the specific task of promoting it. Insofar as human beings recognize a common good, and will an effective means of promoting it, they have a common will that makes a single community.

This common will makes it reasonable for them to agree on constituting some agent with the specific task of promoting the common good. This is the 'special will or common consent' that makes a single political body, and hence makes a body capable of placing its legislative power in some agent with the special task of promoting the common good. Common consent is not necessarily explicit consent to a particular ruler or regime. Suarez does not take such consent to be necessary for a legitimate ruler. He allows tacit or presumed consent, to explain why a ruler who initially rules by tyrannical force may in time acquire legitimate legislative power (iii 4.4). In the case of conquest through a just war, the subject people are required (tenetur) to obey their new ruler. In this case also, according to Suarez, we can see consent, either explicit or owed (debitum, 4.4).

Suarez does not recognize the validity of any complete and unconditional transfer of legislative power to a ruler. Breach of the conditions on which power has been transferred is a justification for the community—in contrast to a private individual—to rebel against a ruler.[129] Even if James VI and I—Suarez's immediate target—could persuade the English people, freely and without coercion, to agree to a complete and unconditional transfer of legislative power, such an agreement would not be binding. If it is not invalid because of ignorance or coercion, it still fails to bind, because it is unjust.

To see why any such agreement would be unjust, and therefore could not cancel the exception that is always understood in any transference of power, we need to return to the sort of common consent that Suarez takes to be the basis of legislative power. The common consent was consent to the promotion of the common good that needs to be promoted by an agent with this specific task. This common consent is justified by appeal to natural law, because it aims at the common good. Any agreement that violated the necessary conditions for a legislative power aiming at the common good would violate the initial common consent. Even if it could obtain actual consent, this would not matter, because such consent would be contrary to the natural law. The aspect of the natural law that is

[128] 'A multitude of human beings should therefore be considered in another way in so far as they are gathered together by a special will or common consent into one political body by one bond of association (societas), and in order to give one another help directed to a single political end. In this way they make one mystical body that can be said, from a moral point of view, to be one in its own right; and this body therefore needs a single head'. (iii 2.4)

[129] 'If, then, a lawful ruler is ruling tyrannically, and if the kingdom has available no other remedy for defending itself, except the expulsion and deposition of the king, the whole commonwealth, acting on the public and common advice of the cities and leaders, will be allowed to depose him. This is true both by virtue of natural law, by which it is permissible to repel force with force, and also because this situation, needed for the preservation of the commonwealth itself, is always understood to be excepted in that first agreement by which the commonwealth transferred its power to the king.' (DFC vi 4.15)

relevant is intrinsic morality, specifying what is suitable for rational and social agents. Suarez's naturalism about morality informs not only his meta-ethics, but also the concrete applications of his moral theory to political questions.

To grasp the role of common consent, we should look more closely at what the political community gives to the ruler. One might expect Suarez to argue that, since the original legislative power belongs to the political community as a whole, and not to any specific government, the government is simply an agent or delegate of the community, and therefore subject to dismissal at the discretion of the people. Suarez, however, denies that all legislative power is delegated by the people. He argues that the community can give away its legislative power to a government, so that the government is not necessarily bound by its own laws, and does not need to seek the continued approval of the community. In such a case the ruler has 'ordinary' power, and not merely 'delegated' power (4.9), and hence the ruler is entitled to delegate power to a subordinate without any special permission from the community.

On this point, Suarez rejects one element of democratic theory; he does not take the moral basis of political society and government to require a conception of legislative power as delegation. But his claims about the transfer of legislative power do not lead him to conclude that the common consent of the community becomes irrelevant once it has established a ruler with ordinary power. A hereditary ruler, for instance, inherits ordinary power together with the conditions on which the ordinary power was originally transferred (4.3). A community cannot transfer legislative power unconditionally; hence it cannot irrevocably abandon any power to restrain or to replace its rulers.

452. The Separation of Morality from Natural Law

Our discussion suggests that Suarez does not differ from Aquinas in any essential point about the nature and basis of morality. His disagreement about the role of divine commands in the natural law does not affect his view about the moral foundation of the natural law, and, in particular, does not lead him to maintain that morality depends on divine commands. In claiming that moral goodness is fixed by rational nature, he follows Aquinas' naturalism. Moreover, in claiming that we are rationally concerned about moral goodness because we aim at our ultimate end, and our ultimate end is realizing our rational nature, he accepts Aquinas' combination of eudaemonism with naturalism. On these basic points, then, he is a traditional moralist, insofar as he stands in the tradition that includes Aquinas. The naturalist and eudaemonist aspects of his conception of goodness and rightness, as opposed to the voluntarist aspects of his conception of natural law, are the essential features of his theory of morality.

We can sum up some of the specific points we have discussed about Suarez by considering the sense in which he is a 'natural-law theorist'. He is clearly a natural-law theorist in the straightforward sense of believing in natural law. One might also say that he is a natural-law theorist to a greater degree than Aquinas and Scotus are, since he has more to say about it, and in particular has a more precise account of what makes it genuine law. It does not follow, however, that natural law is theoretically more important or basic in Suarez, or that his conception of it radically changes the character of his moral theory. The length of his treatment reflects the controversy among Aquinas' successors about the character of natural law and its relation to divine freewill and divine commands. Suarez has to deal with articulated options that do not confront Aquinas.

His examination of the issues about natural law results in some major differences from Aquinas. His view that law and obligation rest on command and on will partly reflects his disagreement with Aquinas about the relation of command to will and to intellect. This disagreement helps to explain Suarez's relatively narrow conception of law, in contrast to Aquinas' view that our share in divine providence also gives us a grasp of divine law.

In moral philosophy, however, Suarez does not take natural law to be theoretically fundamental. His imperative conception of natural law as requiring divine commands is not intended to show that morality requires divine commands. He distinguishes morality, which is independent of divine commands, from natural law, which depends on them. He is not a 'natural-law theorist', if such a theorist gives theoretical priority to natural law in an account of morality. His elaborate discussion of natural law really has the opposite effect. For since he believes that natural law essentially depends on divine commands, and that moral right and wrong do not essentially depend on divine commands, he believes that moral right and wrong do not essentially depend on natural law, but are prior to it. He rejects the view, shared by Aquinas and Scotus, that natural law is essential to morality.

To describe his position in this way is to give a misleading impression of the substantive differences between Suarez's views and the naturalist views of his predecessors. In describing morality he includes the features that Aquinas ascribes to the natural law, and so he retains Aquinas' view of the metaphysical status of morality and of its independence of divine commands. He differs from Aquinas in concluding that morality is also independent of natural law, given his conception of law.

One of the most plausible parts of Suarez's argument about law is his account of the distinctive moral relation that is introduced by law, as he understands it. He recognizes that there is a difference between the sort of reason for actions that is given by facts about rational agents in their circumstances and the sort that is derived more directly from the expression of the will of other rational agents. Law introduces a new moral requirement based on the will of an authority, and not only on the recognition of some moral fact that is prior to any expression of will. We recognize the distinct sort of reason that is derived from law if we recognize that the expression of the will of another person in an appropriately authoritative position gives me a further reason to act, beyond the specific content of that other person's will. Suarez argues that God is a legislator in this sense, and that therefore a further set of moral reasons results from his legislation.

Clarity on this point about the reasons derived from law makes the non-legal character of morality clearer to Suarez. He distinguishes natural law from its basis in intrinsic morality, so that we can both see the distinctive moral reason introduced by law and see the moral reasons that are independent of, but presupposed by, the obligation introduced by law. He therefore emphasizes the natural basis of intrinsic morality no less strongly than he emphasizes the character of imposed obligation. All obligation requires an imposer, whereas morality requires no imposer. On this last point Suarez agrees, as he claims, with Aquinas; but since he distinguishes natural morality from non-natural imposition more explicitly than

Aquinas does, the purely natural character of intrinsic morality appears more sharply in Suarez than in Aquinas.

We would misinterpret Suarez, therefore, if we took him to hold that natural law, as he conceives it, is necessary for morality. Such a misinterpretation would distort his most important claims about the natural status of morality. As we will see, however, some of his early readers misinterpreted his views in just this way.[130]

---

[130] Mahoney, *MMT* 227, describing Suarez's place in the history of moral theology, attributes to him a voluntarist 'view of morality as expressed predominantly in terms of law and the centrality of the will'. See also §461.

32

NATURAL LAW AND 'MODERN' MORAL PHILOSOPHY

453. The Modern Theory of Natural Law

The mid-17th century is often taken to mark the beginning of 'modern' philosophy, because of Descartes's attack on his Scholastic predecessors. Since this is also the period of the 'Scientific Revolution' and of the emergence of the modern nation-state, it would be satisfying (to some historians) to find a similarly sharp break in the history of moral philosophy. This desire to see the origin of a new age in the 17th century is shared by some 17th and 18th-century writers. Hobbes takes himself to turn away from the errors of the 'old moral philosophers' by explaining the virtues as ways of fulfilling natural law. He is not alone in supposing that moral philosophers have taken a new direction by identifying moral philosophy with the study of natural law.

This is why some later writers recognize Hobbes and Grotius as their predecessors. Cumberland mentions Grotius as the first significant writer on natural law.[1] Pufendorf agrees with him; he discusses Grotius in detail and does not bother with writers between antiquity and the 17th century. In his essay 'On the origin and progress of the discipline of natural law', he suggests that no one before Grotius had accurately distinguished natural from positive law.[2] In his view, the Scholastics were too confined by excessive esteem for Aristotle, and so did not add much to the scattered remarks of the ancient philosophers on natural law.[3]

Perhaps Barbeyrac does most to form the view that the modern age in moral theory begins with Grotius' account of natural law. He translated both Grotius and Pufendorf into French, and his valuable notes to the translations were also included in English versions.[4] These notes discuss modern views of natural law, and try to harmonize the views of Grotius

---

[1] See §530.   [2] See Pufendorf, ES, ch.1 §1 = GW v 123.10–12.

[3] ES, ch.1 §4 = GW v 125.34–126.6. The index to ET of JNG contains no references to Suarez or Aquinas, though some to Vasquez. On Pufendorf's tendency to ignore Spanish Scholastic sources see Simons, 'Introduction' 16a. In ES Pufendorf discusses an argument for naturalism by Zentgraf, who cites Suarez in his support; see GW v 209.19–30. He remarks that for Zentgraf the name of Suarez is 'par Apostolis nomen'. Zentgraf was a Lutheran theologian; on his critique of Pufendorf see Palladini, DSSP 217–21. Chroust, 'Grotius', attacks Pufendorf's estimate of the originality of Grotius and his low estimate of mediaeval philosophy.

[4] Barbeyrac's notes appear in Whewell's edn. of Grotius, and in Kennett's translation of Pufendorf. See Tuck, NRT 73n, 160n.

and Pufendorf. Barbeyrac defends the position of Pufendorf against Leibniz's attack.[5] He also defends Pufendorf's conception of natural law through a selective history of moral philosophy that presents Grotius as a pioneer.[6]

In Barbeyrac's view, Bacon inspired Grotius to set moral theory on a new footing based on natural law. By appealing to natural law Grotius 'broke the ice' in moral philosophy. Melanchthon failed to anticipate Grotius, because he was too confined by Scholastic views to make the advance that Grotius made.[7] These Scholastic views are so deeply infected by falsehood that Barbeyrac, like Pufendorf, does not think it worthwhile to try to separate the true elements in them, or even to give an account of their main errors.[8] The honour of emancipating moral philosophy from Scholasticism belongs to Grotius—with certain qualifications to be examined later.[9]

Barbeyrac's view has been taken seriously as a correct estimate of the radical and innovative character of Grotius' and Pufendorf's moral theory in comparison with their predecessors, both the mediaeval Scholastics and the Protestant and Roman moralists of the 16th century. If he is right, these 17th-century theorists of natural law need to be examined, to see where they differ from their predecessors, and whether the differences are improvements.

But while many later critics have agreed with Barbeyrac in treating Grotius as a pioneer, and in taking modern moral philosophy to begin with Grotius, they have not all agreed with him about what makes Grotius a pioneer. In fact, later critics who disagree sharply with Barbeyrac and with one another about what is distinctive of modern moral philosophy have claimed that this distinctive feature begins with Grotius. If they are all right about Grotius, Grotius' position is internally inconsistent. And if they are all right about modern moral philosophy, its distinctive features are inconsistent.

To understand these different claims about Grotius and about modern moral philosophy, we should begin with Barbeyrac, and see how his view compares with other views.

---

[5] On Leibniz see §591.

[6] Barbeyrac's 'Morality' appeared in the 1706 edn. of his translation of Pufendorf's *JNG*. See Tuck, *NRT* 174–7; Hochstrasser, 'Conscience', esp. 294 on Barbeyrac's history of moral philosophy (underestimating the degree of Barbeyrac's commitment to voluntarism). Hochstrasser, *NLTEE* 11–18, discusses other histories of morals that emphasize modern natural law.

[7] 'Tis pretended, that Melanchthon had already given a sketch of something of this kind [sc. a system of the law of nature], in his Ethics; and they tell us too of one Benedict Winckler, who published in 1615 a book intitled Principia Iuris; wherein he entirely departs from the method of the Schoolmen; and maintains against them, amongst other things; that the will of God is the very fountain and foundation of all justice. But 'tis acknowledged that the latter of these two often confounds the law of nature with that which is positive: And that neither the one, nor the other has afforded any more than a small gleam of light; not sufficient to dissipate those thick clouds of darkness, in which the world had been so long inveloped. Besides, Melanchthon was too much prepossessed in favour of the Peripatetic philosophy, ever to make any great progress in the knowledge of the true fundamental principles of the law of nature, and the right method of explaining that science. Grotius therefore ought to be regarded, as the first who broke the ice.' ('Morality', 79) On Melanchthon cf. Stewart, quoted in §462.

[8] 'From thence [sc. the Peripatetic philosophy] sprang the scholastic philosophy, which spread itself all over Europe, and with its barbarous cant became even more prejudicial to religion and morality, than to the speculative sciences. The ethics of the Schoolmen is a piece of patchwork; a confused collection, without any order, or fixed principles; a medley of divers thoughts and sentences out of Aristotle, civil and canon law, Scripture, and the Fathers. Both good and bad lie there jumbled together; but so as there is more of the latter, than the former. The casuists of the succeeding centuries, made it their sole business to out-do their predecessors, in broaching of vain subtilties; nay, what is worse, monstrous and abominable errors, as all the world knows. But let us pass by these unhappy times; that we may at length come to that age, where in the science of morality was, if I may so say, raised again from the dead.' (79)

[9] On the limitations of Grotius see §463.

454. Barbeyrac's View of Grotius

Barbeyrac examines Grotius and Pufendorf in comparison with Hobbes. Though he praises Hobbes, he also attacks him for treating self-interest as the only basis of society. This is the main flaw in De Cive.[10] In the Leviathan, according to Barbeyrac, Hobbes goes even further, making the sovereign the basis of morality and religion.[11] Barbeyrac shares Pufendorf's concern to distinguish natural law theory from Hobbes's position. According to Hobbes, the content of natural law, independent of divine or human legislation, consists of the demands of self-interest. Barbeyrac wants to show that Grotius and Pufendorf offer more than this minimal Hobbesian content.

Barbeyrac's estimate of Grotius may usefully be compared with Gershom Carmichael's opinion. Carmichael agrees that Grotius is important, because he gave a lead in the discussion of natural law.[12] Carmichael excludes Selden and Hobbes from those who followed Grotius' lead. Selden relies on the Noachite precepts, and hence on divine positive law, not on natural law, while Hobbes corrupts the study of natural law.[13] Carmichael agrees with Barbeyrac in treating Grotius and Pufendorf as exponents of the same doctrine. He does not discuss the apparent differences that occupy Barbeyrac; in particular, he does not discuss questions about naturalism and voluntarism.[14]

But Carmichael does not seem to agree with Barbeyrac about why Grotius and Pufendorf are important. He regards the modern treatment of natural law as the true successor, in moral philosophy, of Scholastic ethics. It rightly omits irrelevant elements in Scholastic treatments, including those parts of theology that are known only by revelation (viii). Carmichael seems to suggest, therefore, that the originality of modern treatments of natural law is not primarily any novelty in doctrine, but the clear separation of moral philosophy from other disciplines.

To see whether Barbeyrac or Carmichael is right, we need to compare these modern moralists with the Scholastics. Barbeyrac's claim on behalf of Grotius is initially puzzling, since neither Grotius nor Melanchthon was the first to treat the theory of natural law as a part of

---

[10] '. . . he endeavours to establish, and that too in the geometrical method, the hypothesis of Epicurus, which makes self-preservation and self-interest, to be the original causes of civil society' ('Morality' 88).

[11] 'That the will of the sovereign alone constitutes, not only what we call just and unjust, but even religion also; and that no divine revelation can bind the conscience, till the authority, or rather caprice, of his Leviathan; that is, of the supreme arbitrary power, to which he attributes the government of every civil society; has given it the force of a law.' ('Morality' §29, p. 66)

[12] 'After the ancients moral philosophy was neglected for many centuries, until the work of the incomparable Hugo Grotius, who gave the lead for others to follow.' (Carmichael, PDOH vi) Cf. Moore and Silverthorne, 9–10: '. . . Moral science . . . had been most highly esteemed by the wisest of the ancients, who devoted themselves to its study with great care. It then lay burdened under debris, together with almost all the other noble arts, until . . . it was restored to more than its pristine splendour (at least in that part of moral science which concerns the mutual duties of men . . .) by the incomparable Hugo Grotius. . . . For more than fifty years scholars more or less confined their studies within the limits set by Grotius . . . But then that most distinguished man Samuel Pufendorf, . . . by arranging the material in the work of Grotius in a more convenient order and by adding what seemed to be missing from it to make the discipline of morals complete, he produced a more perfect system of morals.'

[13] [Hobbes] 'iuris naturalis disciplinam non illustrare instituit, sed corrumpere' (PDOH vi). Barbeyrac offers a similar explanation for Selden's failure, despite his merits, to eclipse Grotius; 'he derives not the principles of the law of nature from the pure dictates of reason', but from the Noachite principles, relying uncritically on tradition (80).

[14] The chapter 'On lasting happiness and the divine law' (Suppl. 1 = M&S 21–9) claims that morality expresses divine commands, but it does not say that it essentially expresses divine commands. Though Carmichael knows Suarez (see M&S 41n), he does not discuss the questions that Suarez discusses about voluntarism.

moral philosophy. Natural law is a standard element of Scholastic moral philosophy; Aquinas and his successors discuss natural law in their accounts of law, morality, the Decalogue, and the moral precepts of the Gospel. We have considered the careful reflexions of Suarez on this Scholastic tradition. Since Barbeyrac does not bother to discuss Scholastic views of natural law, he does not say how Grotius' view differs from Scholastic views. But if Grotius is an innovator, we ought to find some major point on which he departs from the Scholastic views.

455. The Fundamental Status of Natural Law

To explore possible defences of Barbeyrac's claim, we might consider different ways of understanding the place of natural law within morality. Moral theories differ according to their views about which aspect of morality is theoretically fundamental and which aspects can be derived from which. Hence one might recognize natural law as an aspect of morality without being a natural-law moralist, if one does not treat morality as primarily and fundamentally natural law. Perhaps, then, Barbeyrac might claim that Grotius is the first to make natural law primary and to reduce other aspects of morality to features of natural law. If Grotius does this, he is the first natural-law moralist.

One might support Barbeyrac by observing that, though the natural law is prominent and important in Aquinas and in his naturalist and voluntarist successors, it is not primary. The *Prima Secundae* begins not with the natural law, but with the ultimate end. Law, including natural law, is introduced only after the discussion of human actions, passions, states, virtues, and sins. It takes us from the sinful condition of human beings to the infusion of virtues that comes from grace. Suarez also places his treatise on law in this sequence; it is 'on God the legislator', in contrast to the treatise on grace 'on God the justifier'.[15]

In one respect, the principles and precepts of natural law are fundamental. In Aquinas' theory, three apparently distinct basic principles are identified: (1) Universal conscience, grasping the ultimate principles from which prudence deliberates. (2) Natural law. (3) Happiness as the ultimate end. They are connected because universal conscience grasps the basic principles of natural law, which enjoin the pursuit of one's ultimate good. Within Aquinas' theory, then, the principles of natural law provide the starting points for prudence; the conclusions of universal prudence are the ends characteristic of the various virtues.

In assigning this basic status to natural law, however, Aquinas does not make it prior to his teleological argument from the final good and human action to the virtues. On the contrary, the argument from the basic principles of natural law just is this teleological argument. The introduction of natural law provides a new description of the argument that has already been given; it does not provide a different sort of argument, let alone an argument for different conclusions. Aquinas' explanation of natural law implies that facts about rational nature are the basis of the precepts of natural law. If we take natural law just to consist in these facts, natural law is not prior to facts about rational nature.

Different questions arise about the place of natural law in Scholastic theories that reject either Aquinas' eudaemonism, or his belief in intrinsic morality (as Suarez calls it), or both.

---

[15] See §302n7; Aquinas, *ST* 1–2 q90 pref.; Suarez, Preface to 'Tractatus de gratia Dei, seu de Deo Salvatore, iustificatore, et liberi arbitrii adiutore per gratiam suam', *OO* vii, p. viii.

Scotus rejects eudaemonism, and takes the affection for justice to be separate from the natural pursuit of happiness. He recognizes intrinsic morality consisting in the precepts of the first table of the Decalogue; these are natural law, strictly speaking, and do not depend on the free will of God. The greater part of morality is strictly only 'highly consonant' with natural law, and is part of divine positive law. Ockham asserts a closer dependence of morality on God's free choice. Both non-positive and positive morality reflect God's choice in different ways. In his theological works Ockham does not identify either of them with the provisions of natural law. Remarks in his political works show that he recognizes natural law; but he does not suggest that belonging to natural law is the crucial test of morality.

Aquinas and his successors, therefore, do not seem to be natural-law moralists. Though they take the precepts of natural law to include fundamental moral principles, they do not take moral facts to be reducible to facts about natural law. On the contrary, Aquinas takes facts about natural law to consist in those facts about rational nature that underlie his account of the virtues.[16] Some of these questions about the status of natural law are obscure because of Aquinas' rather broad conception of law. Since he believes that natural law exists if we are guided by rational principles, it is easy for him to believe in natural law; if there are virtues of the kind Aquinas describes, their principles belong to natural law. From this point of view, it is difficult to see how natural law could be primary in morality.[17]

Different questions arise, however, from Suarez's account of law. Since he takes law to require commands and acts of legislation, he takes natural law to require divine commands imposing obligations (in his narrow sense). Relying on this conception of natural law, he argues that natural law is not primary in morality. Natural law presupposes intrinsic morality, which consists in appropriateness to rational nature. Though the duties that belong to intrinsic morality coincide with the precepts of natural law, their place in natural law is not essential to their being part of intrinsic morality. Suarez, therefore, is not a natural-law moralist.

Barbeyrac would have a plausible case, therefore, for his view that modern moralists are innovators, if he could show that they take morality to consist essentially in principles of natural law, as Suarez understands it. On this view, we have no morality without divine commands and acts of legislation that prescribe actions in accord with nature. Such a view rejects both the strong theological voluntarism that identifies morality with divine positive law and the naturalist view that takes commands and legislation to be inessential to morality. Barbeyrac would vindicate his claim if he could show that Grotius and his successors hold

---

[16] Haakonssen, *NLMP* 15, understands a natural-law moralist as one who engages in the 'attempt to understand morality in the legalistic terms of a natural law'. We attribute a natural-law theory in this strong sense to Aquinas, for instance, if we agree that 'for him, the virtues are basically habits of obedience to laws' (Schneewind, *IA* 20). See §315.

[17] Schneewind, 'Misfortunes' 44–6, argues that emphasis on natural law results from scepticism about virtues and from the reductive project of treating all moral requirements as fundamentally required by rules and laws. The evidence that he offers to show that Christian moralists or moralists who believe in natural law generally endorse this reductive project is not completely convincing. One might agree (as Aristotle agrees) that the requirements of general justice embrace the requirements of all the virtues, and (as Aquinas agrees) that natural law prescribes the actions that accord with all the virtues, without agreeing that the virtues consist fundamentally in tendencies to obey rules. To illustrate his claim Schneewind quotes a passage from William Perkins: 'Universal justice is the practice of all virtue: of that whereby a man observes all the commandments of the Law'. But this passage (recalling Aristotle, Aquinas, and St Paul) does not say what is theoretically fundamental. Schneewind's quotation from Locke, *EHU* ii 28.14, is apposite; but Locke holds a legislative conception of morality (explained in the context), which does not follow from a belief in natural law.

this view about morality as natural law. We will have to see what conception of natural law he relies on in claiming that Grotius and his successors are natural-law moralists.

456. Sidgwick: A Jural Conception of Ethics

It is useful to compare Barbeyrac's interpretation of Grotius and his successors with Sidgwick's description of modern moral philosophy. Sidgwick agrees with Barbeyrac's claim that modern moralists recognize natural law as fundamental. According to Sidgwick, modern moralists take this view because they rely on a 'jural' notion that is largely foreign to the teleological outlook of Greek ethics.[18] According to the teleological outlook, a virtue is fundamentally some kind of good; the theorist's task is to find the connexion between the good that is virtue and other goods (*ME* 106). A jural outlook, on the contrary, conceives moral principles as imperative and inhibitive, rather than teleological.

Sidgwick qualifies his view that jural ethics is characteristic of modern, as opposed to ancient, moral thinking. He argues that Greek philosophers are aware of some idea of moral law, and that Stoic ideas of natural law introduce a transition to a jural conception of ethics. Roman law and Christianity form a jural conception.[19] Mediaeval philosophy, therefore, includes some aspects of a jural conception; Aquinas takes the content of natural law to include the Aristotelian virtues, but, according to Sidgwick, he presents these virtues 'in a new form' (*OHE* 144) that inclines towards a jural conception. Sidgwick, therefore, does not believe in a sharp transition from a teleological to a jural conception of ethics, and does not believe that any sharp transition of this sort separates modern from pre-modern ethics.[20] But he seems to believe that only modern philosophers have clearly stated and articulated this conception.[21] Hence his argument might be taken to support Barbeyrac's view that Grotius begins the modern period in ethics.

[18] 'Ethics may be regarded as an inquiry into the nature of the Good, the intrinsically preferable and desirable, the true end of action, &c; or as an investigation of the Right, the true rules of conduct, Duty, the Moral Law, &c. The former view predominated in the Greek schools, at any rate until the later developments of Stoicism; the latter has been more prominent in English philosophy since Hobbes, in an age of active jural speculation and debate, raised the deepest views of morality in a jural form. Either view can easily be made to comprehend the other; but the second seems to have the widest application.' (*ME* [1] 2–3. *ME* [2] and later editions mention the two views of ethics, but abbreviate the reference to Greek ethics and delete the reference to Hobbes and a jural conception.) '... it is possible to take a view of morality which at any rate leaves in the background the cognition of rule and restraint, the imperative, inhibitive, coercive effect of the moral ideal. We may consider the action to which the moral faculty prompts us intrinsically "good"; so that the doing of it is in itself desirable, an end at which it is reasonable to aim. This ... is the more ancient view of Ethics; it was taken exclusively by all the Greek schools of Moral Philosophy except the Stoics; and even with them "Good" was the more fundamental conception, although in later Stoicism the quasi-jural aspect of good conduct came into prominence.' (*ME* [1] 93) In discussing Sidgwick I sometimes use 'jural' where he uses 'quasi-jural'.

[19] 'Reflexion ... will show that the common notion of what is good for a human being ... includes more than the common notion of what is right for him, or his duty; it includes also his interest or happiness. ... Thus we arrive at another conception of ethics, in which it is thought to be concerned primarily with the general rules of duty or right action—sometimes called the moral code ... On this view, the study connects itself in a new way with theology, so far as the rules of duty are regarded as a code of divine legislation. ... it has a close affinity to abstract jurisprudence ... We might contrast this as a modern view of ethics with the view before given, which was that primarily taken in ancient Greek philosophy generally—the transition from the one to the other being due chiefly to the influence of Christianity, but partly also to that of Roman jurisprudence.' (*OHE* 6–7) See also §224.

[20] *OHE* 144, 160, 163.

[21] Sidgwick is cautious in formulating the jural conception. 'It is ... possible to take a view of virtuous action in which, though the validity of moral intuitions is not disputed, this notion of rule or dictate is at any rate only latent or implicit,

What is a jural conception? Since Sidgwick hesitates to attribute such a conception to the Stoics and to Aquinas, he implies that we do not hold a jural conception simply by believing in natural law. A jural moralist, in his view, treats moral principles as primarily imperative. Since Sidgwick assumes this connexion between law and imperatives, he seems to hold an imperative conception of law; that is why he takes any inclination to believe in moral law to imply acceptance of an imperative conception of morality. Hence he believes that the crucial element of modern ethics is foreshadowed in the earlier views that connect morality with the provisions of natural law.

But what is an 'imperative' conception of a moral principle? Sidgwick's answer is not completely clear, because he seems to combine two conceptions of the imperative: (1) Sometimes he contrasts 'imperative' with 'attractive'. Attractive principles refer explicitly to some desirable goal that the principles secure, whereas imperative principles do not. Hence 'imperative' seems to be equivalent to 'deontological'.[22] (2) Sometimes he assumes that imperative principles depend on acts of legislation.

These two conceptions of the imperative do not seem to pick out all and only the same principles. We may recognize rational principles that are not explicitly teleological, but nonetheless give reasons; if so, we recognize imperatives in Sidgwick's first sense. But it is not clear that we must also regard these principles as products of legislation, and hence as imperatives in his second sense. Scotus, for instance, may believe that our affection for the just commits us to rational principles that are neither teleological nor legislative. It is not clear whether Sidgwick allows the possibility of such principles, or whether he regards them as imperative.

If a jural conception requires only a deontological conception of moral principles, Sidgwick's contrast between the modern and the pre-modern outlook is insecure. Even if we set aside Scotus, Plato and Aristotle and their successors do not hold a purely teleological theory of the virtues. They believe that the virtues count as virtues because of their relation to the agent's good; but they do not assume that the content of the virtues is determined by reference to the agent's good. Aristotle does not suggest that we find out what is just or brave primarily by reflexion on our own good. What we ought (dein) to do, and what it is fine (kalon) to do, are determined by the common good of our community, rather than by our own good, though our reason for caring about justice and bravery depends on their relation to our own good. Aristotle's conception of the fine refers to the tendency of actions to promote a common good. His conception of morality is not directly teleological, and so it satisfies one of Sidgwick's conditions for a jural conception.

Sidgwick's position would have been clearer if he had discussed the character of imperatives more fully. Suarez's fuller discussion of law and imperatives suggests a more precise condition for a jural conception of morality. In Suarez's view, law essentially includes commands because it imposes moral necessity through will, rather than revealing a prior moral necessity. This conception of law makes it clear why a jural conception of morality

---

the moral ideal being presented as attractive rather than imperative. Such a view seems to be taken when the action to which we are morally prompted, or the quality of character manifested in it, is judged to be "good" in itself (and not merely as a means to some ulterior Good). This . . . was the fundamental ethical conception in the Greek schools of Moral Philosophy generally; including even the Stoics, though their system, from the prominence that it gave to the conception of Natural Law, forms a transitional link between ancient and modern ethics.' (ME 105)

[22] On this term see §520.

treats moral principles as products of legislation; for acts of legislation are the acts of will that impose moral necessity. But we have seen that Suarez does not use his imperative conception of law to defend a jural conception of morality; on the contrary, he uses it to distinguish morality from natural law. In his view, morality is the foundation of natural law, and would exist even without natural law, because it does not depend on the imperatives of natural law. Perhaps, then, Sidgwick takes a jural conception of morality to be both deontological and legislative.[23]

457. What is Distinctive of a Jural Conception?

Why does a jural conception of morality, as we have explained it, mark an important change in the understanding of morality? Suarez's division between indicative and prescriptive laws implies that they derive their 'moral necessity', their reason-giving character from different sources. Our reason to follow correct indicative laws depends on their content; they correctly represent the moral reality that exists independently of them. But we have good reason to follow prescriptive laws not because of what they tell us to do, but because of who tells us to do it. We need to look back to their source, whereas we need to look through indicative laws to their content. A competent authority issuing a command through the proper procedure introduces moral necessity.

According to this conception of prescriptive law, a command is legally valid if it is issued by legitimate authority in the appropriate circumstances. It does not necessarily say that I should obey it because of some end I care about. Though I may reasonably ask myself why I should obey the law, this question does not bear on its legal validity. Sidgwick may intend to apply this pattern to morality. A legal view of moral rightness makes moral rightness consist in the appropriate relation to a valid moral principle; questions about whether I have any reason to obey the principle, apart from my being commanded to obey it, do not affect what is morally right. This purely procedural test for the legal validity of a particular law does not apply moral, prudential, or pragmatic standards to the law. If I allege that it is invalid because it is not in my interest, or it is not in the interest of the governed, I fail to grasp the fact that law introduces moral necessity because of its imposer rather than its content; I treat a prescriptive law as though it were purely indicative. Since the necessity imposed by a prescriptive law comes from the will of the imposer, once we know that the imposer has imposed it, we know that it is morally necessary.

This procedural conception of the morally right marks a significant departure from the view that moral principles are essentially indicative laws independent of will. If this is what Sidgwick intends, he isolates an important difference between the jural tradition (as he describes it) and the normal Greek and mediaeval conception. The pre-modern moralists treat moral principles as indicative laws. They usually assume that virtue is some sort of good;[24] in the light of that assumption they try to decide what sorts of states of character and what sorts of

---

[23] Larmore, MM 19–24, defends Sidgwick's division between attractive and imperative approaches (identifying the imperative view with belief in the supremacy of morality over self-interest). He defends Anscombe's view (see §459) on the ground that it recognizes the same division.

[24] 'Usually' is needed because of Scotus' view on the affection for justice.

actions are virtuous. Plato's and Aristotle's question is not primarily about whether the virtues promote happiness, but about whether justice, bravery, and the other recognized virtues are genuine virtues; that question is partly answered by asking whether they promote happiness.

A jural conception immediately raises a question that we will find it useful to pursue in modern moralists. A conception of moral rightness as consisting in legal validity, understood by reference to its source, seems to be incomplete. For if a moral obligation results from a command issued by a legitimate commander with the authority to command, we do not know whether this is a genuine obligation until we know whether the commander is legitimate. To know this, we need to know whether it is morally right for the commander to command. That question cannot be answered by a purely procedural answer directing us to the source of a command. If the first commander commands obedience, that does not decide the question of legitimacy. And if we say that the legitimacy of the first commander is settled by the command of a second commander, we begin an infinite regress.[25]

If this argument is sound, a jural conception seems to answer only some of the questions that we might reasonably want a moral theory to answer. For it is difficult to see how the principles determining the authority of a legislator or commander could be prescriptive laws; if we appeal to their content rather than their source, we treat them as indicative laws. According to naturalism, the test for legal validity is not purely procedural, at least in the case of the natural law. In Aquinas' view, a rule belongs to natural law because it is morally right and prescribes what fits rational nature. Even for positive law, his test of validity is not purely procedural; it must have been enjoined by legitimate authority, but it must also be just. It is even more obvious that for natural law moral rightness is prior to any legislation. The basic principles underlying legal validity, therefore, are indicative laws, moral principles that do not rely on moral necessity imposed by will.

We might defend a jural theory of morality against this objection by arguing that the indicative laws determining the authority of a legislator are not moral principles. If this argument succeeds, we can acknowledge that jural morality rests on a non-jural basis without admitting that the non-jural basis is moral. If we examine jural theories, we also need to consider whether they offer a plausible non-moral basis. The task of finding such a basis is not straightforward. We can see why some legislators might be authorized on the basis of non-moral principles. If, for instance, we are members of a club and we want to settle procedures without endless argument, we might all find it in our interest to authorize a committee to make rules that will be binding on all members of the club. But this sort of authorization does not create a moral obligation to obey the rules. We might think that a properly moral obligation can come only from a legislator who is authorized on moral grounds. If a jural theory does not answer this objection, it seems not to offer an adequate account of morality.

458. Sidgwick and Barbeyrac

If this is a reasonable interpretation of Sidgwick's account of jural ethics, it also offers a reasonable interpretation of Barbeyrac's claim that Grotius is a pioneer in developing the

---

[25] Hart considers the problem of a regress, in *CL*, ch. 6.

theory of ethics as natural law. If Barbeyrac has in mind a jural conception, he is justified in believing that Aquinas and Suarez, for instance, are not part of the tradition that (in his view) begins with Grotius. The mere belief in natural law is not sufficient for Barbeyrac's purposes; for if we treat natural law as a purely indicative law (in Suarez's terms), we do not include the imperative element that is necessary for a jural conception.

Apparently, then, the only conception of natural law that supports a jural theory of morality is a voluntarist conception. If morality essentially consists in the provisions of natural law, and natural law consists essentially in divine commands, morality consists in being commanded by divine authority.[26] If that is Barbeyrac's view, we would expect him to endorse a voluntarist conception of natural law. A voluntarist conception might appear to constitute a distinctive point of view on morality; in contrast to a naturalist conception, it does not identify natural law with an indicative law specifying prior principles about what accords with rational nature, and therefore it does not identify morality with a purely indicative law. This, then, may be the innovation that Barbeyrac attributes to Grotius.

If Barbeyrac has voluntarism in mind, is he ungenerous to mediaeval voluntarists? He might answer that they have not made the voluntarist position clear. Scotus, for instance, believes that some principles of moral rightness are independent of the divine will; these are the parts of the natural law that are not subject either to divine commands or to divine dispensations. Natural law, then, does not primarily constitute moral goodness, since some of natural law recognizes antecedent moral goodness. Ockham seems closer to a purely jural conception, since he seems to regard even non-positive morality as subject to change within God's absolute power.[27] But it is not clear how closely he connects this conception of morality with a theory of natural law. He does not seem to take exactly the view that Barbeyrac ascribes to Grotius.

Whether or not we have accurately captured Barbeyrac's meaning, we have found, with Sidgwick's help, a reasonable interpretation of the claim that morality consists fundamentally in natural law. If Grotius defends the claim, so interpreted, he is a pioneer.

459. The Abandonment of Jural Morality?

Now that we have seen what Barbeyrac and Sidgwick may mean in claiming that modern moral philosophy maintains a jural conception of morality, it is helpful to contrast their view with Anscombe's sharply opposed view of modern moral philosophy. She agrees with Sidgwick in believing that ancient moralists have a non-jural conception. But she argues, contrary to both Sidgwick and Barbeyrac, that mediaeval Christian moralists hold a jural conception. They identified basic moral principles with the precepts of the Decalogue, understood as a body of divine legislation.[28] The Reformers abandon

---

[26] This view seems to be stated by Locke. See *EHU* ii 28.14, quoted in §562.   [27] On Ockham see §395.

[28] 'How did this come about? The answer is in history: between Aristotle and us came Christianity, with its *law* conception of ethics. For Christianity derived its ethical notions from the Torah. (One might be inclined to think that a law conception of ethics could arise only among people who accepted an allegedly divine positive law; that this is not so is shown by the example of the Stoics, who also thought that whatever was involved in conformity to human virtues was required by divine law.) In consequence of the dominance of Christianity for many centuries, the concepts of being bound, permitted, or excused became deeply embedded in our language and thought.' (Anscombe, 'Modern' 30)

this jural conception of morality because of the Lutheran separation between law and Gospel; in contrast to the mediaeval view about the scope of divine law, Luther claims that it applies only to unregenerate humanity.[29] Given this hostility to law (Anscombe claims), Protestants reject a jural conception of morality as a positive guide to life (though it serves to reveal sin). If she is right, we might expect Protestant moralists to look for an alternative way of understanding morality that separates it from divine law. In Anscombe's view, modern moralists have developed a non-jural outlook, but imperfectly, since they have retained beliefs in obligation that presuppose a jural conception.

According to this view, ancient and modern moralists agree, against the mediaeval Christians, in not appealing to divine legislation as the basis of morality. But modern moralists differ from the ancients in their use of a jural conception that they reject. Anscombe argues that the presuppositions, aims, and outlook of Greek ethics, especially Aristotelian ethics, are so radically different from those of modern moral philosophy that they really constitute a different philosophical enterprise. We cannot find room for our concept of the moral in any accurate account of Aristotle.[30] Aristotle uses 'should' and 'ought' with reference to goodness and badness, but not in the special moral sense that these terms have now acquired.[31] Since Aristotle does not use these terms with the special moral sense, he does not have a concept of the moral.

The special moral sense of the modern concepts of obligation, duty, and 'ought' are the remnants of the jural conception of ethics.[32] In its special moral sense, 'ought' is equivalent to 'is obliged', understood in a legal sense.[33] Our use of 'ought' in this special moral sense presupposes a conception of morality that we take to be false. In claiming that we morally ought to do x, we imply that some law obliges us to do x. But if a law obliges us to do x, some legislator must command us to do x. But we (secular modern philosophers) do

[29] '...the belief in divine law...was substantially given up among Protestants at the time of the Reformation.' ('Modern' 31) Anscombe explains this surprising claim in a footnote: 'They did not deny the existence of divine law; but their most characteristic doctrine was that it was given, not to be obeyed, but to show man's incapacity to obey it, even by grace, and this applied not merely to the ramified prescriptions of the Torah, but to the requirements of "natural divine law". Cf. in this connexion the decree of Trent against the teaching that Christ was only to be trusted as mediator, not obeyed as legislator.' She refers to the Council of Trent, Decree on Justification, ch. 11 (De observatione mandatorum; see D 1536–9) and to Canon 21 (D 1571). On the views of the Reformers see §420; they do not justify Anscombe's sweeping claim.

[30] 'If someone professes to be expounding Aristotle and talks in a modern fashion about "moral" such-and-such, he must be very imperceptive if he does not constantly feel like someone whose jaws have somehow got out of alignment: the teeth don't come together in a proper bite.' ('Modern' 26) The term 'moral' itself 'doesn't seem to fit, in its modern sense, into an account of Aristotelian ethics' (26).

[31] '[These terms] have now acquired a special so-called "moral" sense—i.e., a sense in which they imply some absolute verdict (like one of guilty/not guilty on a man) on what is described in the "ought" sentences used in certain types of context...The ordinary (and quite indispensable) terms "should", "needs", "ought", "must"—acquired this special sense by being equated in the relevant contexts with "is obliged" or "is bound" or "is required to", in the sense in which one can be obliged or bound by law, or something can be required by law.' ('Modern' 29–30)

[32] '...the concepts of obligation and duty—moral obligation and moral duty, that is to say—and of what is morally right and wrong, and of the moral sense of "ought", ought to be jettisoned if this is psychologically possible; because they are survivals, or derivatives from survivals, from an earlier conception of ethics which no longer generally survives, and are only harmful without it' ('Modern' 26).

[33] Anscombe claims that a legal conception explains a shift in the sense of the Greek term hamartanein from 'mistake' to 'sin', understood as a violation of law. The same legal conception makes it appropriate to use 'obligation', in a genuinely legal sense, for conformity with the virtues.

not believe that any legislator commands us to do what we morally ought to do.[34] Unlike Aristotle, we have the concepts of morality and the moral, though, unlike the mediaeval moralists, we do not believe in the divine legislator presupposed by our concepts.[35] Since we are—in this respect—post-Christian, we use the term in the moral sense, but our use rests on presuppositions that have been generally abandoned.[36]

This historical sketch makes Anscombe's position more credible. For if the modern use of 'ought' can be shown to rest on assumptions that once were widely shared, but are no longer widely shared, it is easier to understand how we could be relying on presuppositions that we do not recognize and that we even reject. The relevant use of 'ought' has been established in the light of these presuppositions; but, since they are presuppositions rather than explicit premises, we may continue to speak in ways that rely on the presuppositions, even though we do not explicitly appeal to them.[37]

Anscombe is not the only one to claim that legislative concepts have influenced the development and the presuppositions of modern ethics. Schopenhauer argues that Kant's

---

[34] 'So Hume discovered the situation in which the notion "obligation" survived, and the word "ought" was invested with that peculiar force having which it is said to be used in a "moral" sense, but in which the belief in divine law had long since been abandoned: for it was substantially given up among Protestants at the time of the Reformation. The situation, if I am right, was the interesting one of the survival of a concept outside the framework of thought that made it a really intelligible one.' ('Modern' 30–1)

[35] Anscombe, therefore, maintains (1) 'Ought' and related terms ('should', 'must', etc.) have a special moral sense. (2) This special moral sense involves some absolute verdict. (3) The terms have this special moral sense by being equated with 'is obliged' (etc.) in a specific sense. (4) The relevant sense of 'is obliged' is the legal sense. (5) We have the concept of morality only if we use the relevant terms with the special moral sense, so understood.

[36] Does Anscombe mean that whenever we claim we morally ought to do x, our claim is (if measured by our other beliefs) false, so that we actually hold contradictory beliefs about what we morally ought to do? According to this view, my use of the moral 'ought' asserts something that I believe to be false. Perhaps, however, we should not take the use of 'ought' in the moral sense to include a false assertion. It may be more appropriate to connect Anscombe's account with Strawson's claims about presupposition in 'On referring'. Strawson argues that 'The present king of France is bald' does not make the false assertion that there is just one present king of France, and therefore the utterance as a whole is not false. In his view, the utterance lacks a truth-value; it would have a truth-value only if there were just one king of France. In asserting the sentence, I assume that it has a truth-value, because I presuppose that there is just one present king of France. The falsity of my presupposition deprives the assertion of any truth-value. A similar account of the error involved in the moral use of 'ought' might make Anscombe's claims more plausible. It is difficult to argue that an assertion of a moral ought actually asserts that a legislator has issued a command. It may be more plausible to claim that it presupposes such a command, so that it lacks a truth-value if this presupposition is false. Other views of presupposition might suggest different explanations of Anscombe's claim.

[37] To see what Anscombe might have in mind here, we might consider less disputable cases in which we retain attitudes that are intelligible only in the light of presuppositions that we consciously reject. If we have been in the army and under military discipline, we may have learned to dress smartly, with clean belts and boots, to march stiffly, and to conform to parade-ground regulations. If we have had to enforce this military discipline, we have learned to disapprove of failure to conform to these regulations. And we were right (let us assume), for reasons connected with military efficiency, esprit de corps, and so on, to disapprove of such failure. If we return to civilian life, and encounter casually dressed people with scuffed shoes who do not swing their arms, we may continue to disapprove of them. If someone objects that these are civilians and there is nothing wrong with the informality of their dress and manners, we may disagree, insisting that they are dressing or walking improperly. If we deny that the inappropriateness of such dress or manners is restricted to specifically military contexts, we might maintain that it is always more appropriate to have creased trousers, shiny shoes, and a 'military' bearing. In this case, it might be reasonable to conclude that our attitude is unintelligible except in the light of presuppositions that do not hold. To reach something like the situation that Anscombe envisages with the moral 'ought', we would need to suppose that a society retains this respect for 'military' dress and manners even when most people have never been in the army and do not recognize that their respect has this historical basis. The fact that they take these aspects of dress so seriously has no rational basis; but it would have had a rational basis if the military requirements still applied to their situation. As Anscombe suggests, this might all be true even if the people involved were ignorant of it, or explicitly denied it.

views covertly rely on a legal conception of obligation that presupposes a divine legislator.[38] Anscombe agrees with Schopenhauer and Nietzsche[39] in offering a genealogical explanation, showing that what no longer makes rational sense is the residue of practices that relied on assumptions—now rejected—in the light of which they once did make rational sense.

But though Anscombe agrees with many others in connecting legislative concepts with the moral ought, she sharply disagrees with Sidgwick and Barbeyrac. Whereas they take a jural conception of ethics to distinguish modern moral philosophy from ancient and mediaeval outlooks, she takes the abandonment of a jural conception to be characteristic of the Protestant Reformation and of the philosophical views that it has influenced. In her view, the peculiar predicament of modern moral philosophy lies in the combination of a non-jural conception of morality with a concept of obligation that depends on a jural conception.

Further consideration shows that Anscombe and Sidgwick (and Barbeyrac) are not as far apart as they might initially appear. For they agree that a jural conception of ethics results from the influence of Christianity. Anscombe believes that pre-Reformation Christianity holds this jural conception. She agrees with Sidgwick in attributing a non-jural view to the ancient moralists. As we have seen, Sidgwick is not entirely clear about whether he thinks mediaeval moralists hold a jural conception.

One might well suppose that Anscombe's position is more readily intelligible than Sidgwick's. If Christianity is responsible for the acceptance of a jural conception in modern Europe, we might reasonably be surprised if its influence in this direction is delayed for over a millennium and a half. In Anscombe's view, Sidgwick has overlooked the historical evidence showing that a jural conception is prevalent in mediaeval Christian moral philosophy.

460. Who Holds a Jural Conception?

To answer the questions raised by these different views of early modern philosophy, we need to discuss Grotius and his successors. But since some of these views rest on an interpretation of mediaeval moral philosophy, we can usefully ask which views fit better with our account of the Scholastics.

We have good reason to doubt Anscombe's view that a jural conception of morality is characteristic of Scholasticism. The prominence of natural law in Aquinas' account does not imply that he takes acts of legislation to be essential to morality. Given his broad conception of natural law, his belief that morality is essentially natural law does not commit him to a jural conception of morality. He holds a naturalist view that makes natural law essentially an indicative law, but not essentially a prescriptive law.

---

[38] 'In the centuries of Christianity, philosophical ethics has generally taken its form unconsciously from the theological. Now as theological ethics is essentially *dictatorial*, the philosophical has also appeared in the form of precept and moral obligation, in all innocence and without suspecting that for this, first another sanction is necessary.' (Schopenhauer, *BM* §4 = Payne 54)

[39] 'In *this* sphere, of legal obligation, then we find the breeding-ground of the moral conceptual world of "guilt", "conscience", "duty", "sacred duty"—all begin with a thorough and prolonged blood-letting . . . And may we not add that this world has really never quite lost a certain odour of blood and torture? (not even with old Kant; the categorical imperative smells of cruelty . . .)' (Nietzsche, *GM* ii 6 = Ansell-Pearson 45)

In describing Aquinas' view in this way, we rely on distinctions that are clearly drawn not by Aquinas, but by Suarez. Suarez disagrees with Aquinas in making natural law essentially prescriptive. But he maintains Aquinas' naturalist view of morality by denying that morality is essentially natural law. Reflexion on the views of Aquinas, Vasquez, and Suarez (to go no further) makes it clear that a naturalist, non-jural conception of morality is one prominent tendency in Scholasticism.

One might easily form the opposite impression, however, if one takes a different view about where Aquinas and Suarez agree and disagree. If one supposes that Aquinas shares Suarez's essentially prescriptive conception of natural law, his belief that natural law is essential to morality commits him to a jural conception of morality. Similarly, if one overlooks Suarez's claim that natural law is inessential to morality, one will attribute a jural conception of morality to Suarez as well. From this point of view, Scholasticism offers powerful, though not unanimous, support for Anscombe's account of the mediaeval Christian view.

461. Alleged Contrasts between Aquinas and Suarez

To see how one might defend Anscombe's view that mediaeval moralists hold a jural conception, it is useful to turn to a comparative discussion of Aquinas and Suarez. Walter Farrell compares them from a Thomist point of view, and he regards Suarez's departures from Aquinas as errors. The main differences Farrell mentions are these:[40] (1) According to Aquinas, 'a precept or proposition of natural reason is a true secondary cause, producing a real effect, sc. a real obligation'. Suarez, by contrast, claims that human judgment can only manifest obligation coming from the will of God. (2) According to Aquinas, 'eternal law—an act of divine reason—is the cause of all morality'. According to Suarez, 'this act of will of God—the Eternal Law—supposes in human actions a certain necessary honesty and malice'. (3) According to Aquinas, 'on the hypothesis that God never issued this precept which is Eternal Law and the Natural Moral Law, there would be no honesty or malice, for these consist formally in the accord or discord of human acts with a law or precept'. (4) According to Aquinas, 'in the absence of this divine precept these acts have no morality'. (5) According to Aquinas, 'the Natural Moral Law presupposes no goodness or malice; goodness or malice is the result of obedience or disobedience of this law'. (6) 'The idea of a "natural honesty" preceding all law is an evident contradiction in terms, since a morality would then be constituted without any norm or rule and morality consists precisely in the commensuration with a rule of morality. But the falsity of these propositions of Suarez is too evident to need refutation.'

Farrell is right to suppose that Aquinas and Suarez differ over the status of the natural law, and especially over whether it meets the conditions that Suarez lays down for being a true law. It is difficult to find any support in Aquinas for the view that it is law because it is commanded by the legislative will of God. But, given this difference, we ought to look

---

[40] Quotations are from Farrell, *NLSTS* 148–52. I have discussed Farrell both because he states some issues clearly, and because Grisez and Finnis follow him. See §§437, 442.

for Suarez's views on morality by considering his account not of natural law, but of the foundation of natural law. This foundation consists in the principles of intrinsic morality, which are the principles of the natural law, considered apart from its status as expressing God's legislative will. Once we attend to this aspect of Suarez's position, we see that his views on morality are close to Aquinas' views, despite their disagreement on the relation of intrinsic morality to natural law. For they agree in believing that the duty (debitum) to follow the actual principles of the natural law holds because of the nature of the relevant actions themselves, not because of a specific command from God's legislative will.

It is not exactly false, therefore, but it is misleading, to rest content with Farrell's second point of contrast. It is true that, according to Suarez, the eternal law requires an act of legislative will. But if one considers the eternal law as expressing the intellect and will of God the creator, Suarez and Aquinas agree that it is the cause of all morality; there would be no morally good and bad actions if there were no rational agents with our nature. Suarez does not believe that once God had decided to create human beings with our nature, it was still possible for him to prescribe a different natural law; but Aquinas does not believe this either.

The most surprising part of Farrell's case is the view expressed in points (3)–(5). His claim about Aquinas is defensible, provided that we do not assume that conformity to natural law essentially involves conformity to God's legislative will. Aquinas does not maintain that rightness and wrongness essentially involve conformity to divine legislative precepts. On the contrary, divine precepts prescribe actions that are intrinsically right insofar as they conform to rational nature.

Farrell's first point, therefore, gives a one-sided picture of Suarez's views on obligation. It is true that Suarez does not take natural law, apart from its being commanded by God's legislative will, to impose any 'obligation' (obligation); but he believes that the foundation of natural law contains its own duty (debitum). When Farrell cites evidence to show that Aquinas takes the natural law to include an obligation, he cites a passage in which Aquinas uses 'duty' (debitum) and not 'obligation' (obligatio).[41]

Farrell's sixth point also overlooks this distinction between duty and obligation. He rejects Suarez's belief in intrinsic natural rightness or wrongness presupposed by law, on the ground that rightness essentially consists in conformity to a rule or norm. He disagrees with Suarez only if every rule (regula) must also be a law (lex). Given his narrow use of 'law', Suarez need not agree that if intrinsic rightness is separate from law, it must also be separate from every sort of rule.[42]

Some of Farrell's objections may reflect misunderstanding of the sort of concession Suarez intends in considering the nature of intrinsic rightness on the supposition of God's non-existence or inaction. Suarez does not mean this supposition to show that right or wrong acts do or could exist independently of the creative will of God. They are only independent of God's legislation, which expresses a further act of freewill in addition to the act that results in creation. This does not mean that it is possible for God to have created us without

[41] Farrell, 130, cites 1–2 q100, and *Quodl.* v 19, both of which use 'debitum'.

[42] Farrell's account tends to assimilate Aquinas' views about morality to the modern Roman view that formal and complete morality requires obligation and legislation. The points on which he criticizes Suarez mark Suarez's deviations from the modern Roman view, on which see §602.

also legislating that we should observe the law of nature. Creation without legislation is impossible because of God's goodness and providence, not because God's creative will is identical to God's legislative will.

For these reasons, Farrell's comparison of Suarez with Aquinas exaggerates disagreements with Aquinas, in ways that distort both Suarez's and Aquinas' views. If we take account of Suarez's narrow conception of obligation, and the crucial deontic elements that he takes to be distinct from obligation, his belief in intrinsic rightness as the basis for God's legislation agrees with Aquinas' view. To deny that Aquinas agrees with Suarez on this point is to miss an essential element in Aquinas' conception of the basis of natural law. Some of Farrell's 'Thomist' criticism of Suarez relies on a voluntarist treatment of Aquinas, supposing that he takes divine legislation to be necessary for morality.

This treatment of Aquinas makes it intelligible that someone might suppose, as Anscombe supposes, that Aquinas holds a jural conception of morality and that Suarez gives it up. For Aquinas takes morality to be inseparable from natural law, whereas Suarez takes it to be separable. If we attend simply to this difference, without understanding its basis, we may infer that Suarez's belief in intrinsic morality represents a departure from Aquinas. We may even suppose that it marks a secular, non-jural conception of morality that Aquinas would reject.[43]

462. Grotius as a Secular Moralist

If we take this view of the contrast between Aquinas and Suarez, we may be ready to follow Anscombe in supposing that the modern conception of morality consists in the separation of moral right and wrong from the precepts of divine law. This outlook on modern morality suggests a corresponding account of the originality of Grotius. Though Anscombe does not support her thesis about modern moral philosophy with a detailed account of 17th-century theories, one might claim that some features of Grotius' position support her claims about the modern outlook. According to some modern readers, Grotius is similar to Hobbes in trying to defend a minimal conception of natural law, shorn of its Scholastic elaborations and addressed to opponents who reject the Scholastic outlook as a whole.

This picture of early modern moral philosophy underlies Dugald Stewart's account of Grotius. He maintains that Grotius follows the suggestion of Melanchthon, who is the first to maintain a naturalist view. Relying on Cudworth's reference to Ockham and other Scholastics, Stewart takes the Scholastics in general to have maintained a jural view.[44]

---

[43] Villey, FPJM 346–7, holds a rather similar view of how 16th-century Jesuits depart from Aquinas. In his view, they make right ('droit') independent of God, contrary to Aquinas, 'qui situait en Dieu les racines du droit naturel . . . Dans l'excès de leur polemique antiprotestante, nos jesuites déjà prêtent la main à ce futur rationalisme qui va déferler sur le monde moderne et mènera la plus grande partie de "l'école du droit naturel moderne" dans un laïcisme intégral.'

[44] At DPMEP 38 Stewart claims that Melanchthon's view 'like the other steps of the Reformers, . . . was only a return to common sense, and to the genuine spirit of Christianity, from the dogmas imposed on the credulity of mankind by an ambitious priesthood. Many years were yet to elapse before any attempts were to be made to trace, with analytical accuracy, the moral phenomena of human life to their first principles in the constitution and condition of man . . .' In a footnote, referring to Cudworth's remarks on Ockham, Stewart allows that Ockham was among the first to maintain a voluntarist view, but he says nothing about Scholastic views before Ockham. He acknowledges that 'the Catholics have even begun to recriminate on the Reformers as the first broachers of it [sc. Ockham's view]'.

Hence he takes Grotius to have been an innovator in his conception of natural law (171), and to have broken fundamentally with mediaeval views (174, 177). He agrees with Barbeyrac in treating Grotius as a pioneer; but his reason is the exact opposite of Barbeyrac's reason.

Hobbes and Grotius may be taken to present a new, secular account of morality that differs from the mediaeval account in two ways: (1) It develops a theory of obligation that avoids any reliance on divine commands. As Grotius puts it, even if God did not command observance of the natural law, we would still be obliged by its provisions. Similarly, Hobbes argues that the traditional laws of nature are defensible as means to peaceful and commodious living, apart from any question about divine commands. (2) It abandons dubious Scholastic claims about agreement with human nature, insofar as these claims cannot be expressed in claims about self-interest. Both Grotius and Hobbes suppose that sceptics who reject Scholastic claims about what suits rational nature cannot deny that facts about self-interest give reasons for action. Hence they defend the traditional content of natural law (or some of it) by appeal to self-interest and utility.[45]

If Grotius and Hobbes agree on these points, modern natural-law theory is a substitute for a traditional jural conception. The distinguishing feature of modern moral philosophy, on this view, is not the formulation of a jural conception of ethics, but the abandonment of it. Such an interpretation of Hobbes and Grotius fits Anscombe's general view, and casts doubt on the picture of modern moral philosophy that we find in Barbeyrac and Sidgwick. According to the views of both Stewart and Anscombe, on one side, and Barbeyrac and Sidgwick, on the other side, Grotius is an innovator, but the two sides give exactly opposite reasons. His recognition of morality apart from divine commands may be held to support Anscombe's claim that modern moral philosophy abandons a jural conception.

These contradictory views about modern moral philosophy agree in attaching special importance to a jural conception of morality. According to Anscombe, the primary error of modern moral philosophy is its rejection of a jural conception. According to Stewart, this is its primary advance. According to Anscombe, mediaeval moralists hold a jural conception. According to Barbeyrac, the formulation of a jural conception is the primary advance of modern moral philosophy. The different views reflect different judgments both about the historical developments and about the philosophical merits of a jural conception. But they all agree in supposing that the decision about whether to accept or to reject a jural conception is crucially important.

Our previous discussion counts against Anscombe and Stewart. Mediaeval moral philosophers do not characteristically hold a jural conception of morality. Given Aquinas' broad conception of law, he does not differ from Suarez about the status of intrinsic morality, and hence he does not hold a jural conception of morality. Anscombe's claim might fit Scotus and Ockham better, but it conflicts with the positions of Aquinas and Suarez. Equally, then, we have no reason to believe that a non-jural conception of morality is an innovation. Suarez's

---

[45] See Tuck, 'Modern'; Haakonssen (quoted in §464); Schneewind, *IA* 67. Korkman, *BNL* 81–115, argues against their reasons for thinking Grotius original (because of his response to scepticism); he does not discuss whether Grotius is original for some other reason. Shaver, 'Grotius', argues against Tuck that Grotius does not maintain an egoist position in his argument against Carneades.

non-jural account expounds Aquinas' non-jural account. Stewart is mistaken to claim that a non-jural account was an innovation by Melanchthon or Grotius.

To see whether Barbeyrac is right to claim that Grotius is the pioneer of a jural account, we must look more closely at what Grotius says and at what Barbeyrac takes him to say.

33

GROTIUS

---

463. Grotius and his Predecessors

We have seen that Pufendorf, Barbeyrac, and some later writers treat Grotius as the founder of a distinctively modern theory of natural law, even though they do not agree about what is distinctive in his position. They regard his theory not only as an innovation, but also as an advance. To see how far they are right, we should compare Grotius with his Scholastic predecessors, and especially with Suarez, whose work he knew.[1] Though Barbeyrac praises Grotius as a pioneer, he admits that Grotius was not completely emancipated from Aristotle and Scholastic errors.[2] If, then, we compare Grotius' account with Suarez's account, we may be able to decide whether Barbeyrac is justified either in his criticism or in his praise.

Some of Grotius' comments on Aristotle and on the Scholastics tend to confirm Barbeyrac's description of him. He does not dismiss them as curtly as Barbeyrac does, though he does not treat them as his primary authorities. He relies not on Scholastic but on Patristic authority, claiming that the general consent of the clearly orthodox writers, especially the earlier ones, ought to have significant weight in clarifying what is obscure in the Scriptures.[3] He claims to follow these Christian writers in their eclectic attitude to philosophical sources, picking out the elements of truth scattered in different writers. He contrasts this attitude with the Scholastic subjection to Aristotle that made him an intellectual tyrant. But he does not take this misuse of Aristotle to imply any objection to Aristotle himself, who deserves the first

---

[1] On Grotius' knowledge of Suarez see Scott, in Suarez, *STW* 19a–21a; Suarez, *Leg.* ed. Perena, iv, pp. lxviii–lxx. Grotius cites Suarez in *JBP*, at i 4.15.1; ii 4.5.1; ii 14.5; ii 23.13, but not specifically on the natural law. St Leger, *EDHG*, ch. 5, discusses the influence of Suarez on Grotius, suggesting that Suarez's reputation as a supporter of regicide may have discouraged Grotius from citing him too prominently. He quotes (110) a letter of 15 Oct. 1633 = *Briefwisseling* v 194, in which Grotius criticizes polemics against the Jesuits, and especially against Suarez, 'a man of such subtlety in philosophy . . . that, in my judgment, he scarcely has an equal'. Cf. the letter of 1 Aug. 1635 = vi 121, mentioning the Jesuits 'among whom the not undistinguished Francisco Suarez writes . . .'.

[2] 'Grotius saw what was the fundamental principle of the law of nature: But he does no more than just point it out in his Preface, and that in such a manner too, as gives us reason to conclude, that his ideas on that head were not altogether clear; nor enough disengaged from the prejudices of the Schools.' (Barbeyrac, 'Morality' §31, p. 70)

[3] *momentum non exiguum habere debent*, *JBP*, Prol. §51. Grotius' attitude to the Fathers as 'witnesses to the truth' is common, though not unchallenged, among Protestant writers. See Backus, 'Scholarship', and Meijering, 'Theology' (esp. 868–70 on Daillé and Rivet). I cite *JBP* from Whewell's edition, based on the one published in 1631. I sometimes modify Whewell's translation. On the editions of *JBP* see Tuck, *NRT* 73n.

place among philosophers.[4] He follows both Platonists and Christians, among whom he cites especially Lactantius,[5] in dissenting from Aristotle's doctrine of the mean, to which he devotes some less than penetrating criticism (Prol. §§43–5).

Still, his attitude to the Scholastics is not entirely hostile. They lived in unfavourable times and were handicapped by their ignorance of 'good learning' (artes bonae), so that it is not surprising that they made mistakes. Still, he takes much of what they say to be praiseworthy. They are good critics, attacking one another with a degree of moderation not found in contemporary controversy, and agreement among them is unlikely to be mistaken (§52).[6]

These remarks from Grotius' preface do not suggest that he rejects the views of his predecessors as a whole. On the contrary, he claims to accept the views generally accepted by the Scholastics, insofar as these agree with the common consent of the Christian Fathers. He does not suggest that either of these groups of authorities has gone radically wrong in its conception of the law of nature. Barbeyrac suggest that so much falsity is present in the Scholastics that it is not worth trying to extract the truth. Grotius holds the opposite view, that there is enough truth, and little enough falsity, to make the effort of extraction well worthwhile. This conciliatory attitude to the Scholastics might lead us to expect both that Grotius will try to find the position that commands most general assent among them, and that he will be sympathetic to such a position.

464. Naturalism

Grotius affirms the existence of a natural right (ius) that proceeds 'from principles internal to a human being' (Prol. §12). They are internal to us not only because we know them by nature, but also because they are appropriate for rational agents with our nature. To prove that something belongs to natural right, we need to show its 'necessary appropriateness or inappropriateness to rational and social nature' (i 1.12.1).[7]

---

[4] 'Among the philosophers the first place is deservedly assigned to Aristotle . . . Only it were to be wished that his authority had not, some ages ago, been converted into a tyranny; so that truth, in the pursuit of which Aristotle faithfully spent his life, suffers no oppression so great as that which is inflicted in Aristotle's name. I, both here and in other places, follow the liberty of the old Christians, who had not sworn allegiance to any sect of philosophers—not because they agreed with those who say that nothing can be firmly grasped (percipi), which is the most foolish view possible, but because they thought that there was no sect that had seen the whole of the truth, and none that had not seen some part of the truth. They therefore believed that to collect the truth, scattered among different philosophers among sects, into one body: would indeed be nothing other than handing on truly Christian teaching.' (Prol. §42) The last sentence quoted is taken from Lactantius, DI vii 7.

[5] See Lactantius, DI vi 15–17, cited by Whewell ad §43. Grotius quotes him in §45.

[6] . . . ubi in re morum consentiunt, vix est, ut errent, Prol. §52. Leibniz approves of Grotius' favourable remarks about the Scholastics, in Theod. 77.

[7] Grotius' early work JP (see Tuck, PG 170–6; Saastamoinen, MFM 110) appears to take a more voluntarist view of natural law. As his first rule Grotius states: 'What God has shown to be his will, that is law' (ch. 2 = ET 8). But this appearance of voluntarism may be misleading. It is not clear whether Grotius distinguishes the creative from the legislative will of God. Sometimes he seems to refer simply to God's creative will: 'The will of God is revealed . . . above all in the very design of the Creator; for it is from this last source that the law of nature is derived' (8). He might mean that the natural law consists in facts about the nature of creatures: '. . . since God fashioned creation and willed its existence, every individual part thereof has received from him certain natural properties whereby that existence may be preserved and each part may be guided or its own good, in conformity one might say, with the fundamental law inherent in its origin' (9). Grotius does not consider the dispute between voluntarism and naturalism, and does not state the naturalist position that he states in JBP; but it is not clear that JP maintains a voluntarist position.

On this point Grotius agrees with Scholastic naturalists. He signals his agreement when he says that his remarks would still have some standing even if we were to grant that God does not exist or that he is not concerned with human affairs.[8] This concession about God's non-existence is familiar; Suarez quotes it as part of the case presented by Gregory of Rimini and others, to display the distinctness of the natural law from God's commands.[9]

Grotius adds two points to Gregory: (1) He says this proposition cannot be granted without extreme wickedness (summo scelere). It would indeed be wicked to grant God's non-existence, if 'grant' meant 'accept it as true that God does not exist'. Grotius insists that he does not commit this wickedness, because he does not grant the non-existence of God, but simply entertains it counterfactually. (2) In contrast to Gregory and Suarez, one of his suppositions is that God does not care for human affairs; this is the supposition denounced by Plato in *Laws* X and later accepted by Epicurus. Grotius' familiarity (direct or indirect) with Plato or with Epicurean sources may explain why he modifies Gregory's supposition.

These two additions, then, do not make a significant difference to the issue raised by the counterfactual supposition. But what does Grotius mean by affirming the truth of the counterfactual? We may compare him with Suarez, who discusses two relevant counterfactual assertions: (1) Even if God did not exist or did not issue commands, there would be natural law, and obligation. (2) Even if God did not exist or did not issue commands, actions would be intrinsically right and wrong. Suarez rejects the first assertion, but accepts the second. Hence he holds a partly voluntarist conception of natural law, but a naturalist conception of morality.

Grotius does not say which counterfactual he accepts. He would endorse a more strongly naturalist position than Suarez accepts if he claimed that there is a natural law (lex), properly so called, apart from the legislative will of God, and that this law imposes a genuine obligation apart from God's command. This is Vasquez's naturalist position.[10] Grotius does not discuss it.

His initial discussion is confined to the existence of a right (ius), not a law (lex), of nature. In asking whether there is a right (ius) of nature, he takes himself to be asking whether anything is just (iustum) by nature, apart from positive legislation; in affirming that there is something just by nature, he rejects Carneades' sceptical position (Prol. §5). If his claim about the right of nature means only that something is just by nature, not as a result of divine legislation, Suarez agrees.[11]

When Grotius considers 'ius' in the sense in which he takes it to be equivalent to 'lex', he describes it as 'a rule of moral acts obliging to what is correct'.[12] Obligation, in his view,

---

[8] 'And certainly these things that we have just said would have some standing even if we were to grant what cannot be granted without extreme wickedness (locum aliquem haberent, etiamsi daremus, quod sine summo scelere dari nequit), that God does not exist, or that he is not concerned with human affairs.' (Prol. §11) In the first edition (1625) Grotius has 'locum haberent'. He added 'aliquem' in the edition of 1631 (presumably to make it clear that the non-existence of God would not leave everything unchanged). See Molhuysen, 'First edition' 106. Tuck, NRT 76, PG 197–8 ('All we have said now would take place . . .') follows the first edition.

[9] On Gregory see §436.

[10] On Grotius' knowledge of Vasquez see St Leger, *EDHG* 141–2, and Chroust, 'Grotius' 117. They take Grotius to agree with Vasquez rather than Suarez, because they hold a more voluntarist view of Suarez than I would think plausible.

[11] For the distinction between ius and lex in this context see Vasquez (quoted in §429); Suarez, *Leg.* i 2.11 fin.; Grotius i 1.9.1.

[12] '. . . regula actuum moralium obligans ad id quod rectum est.' (i 1.9.1).

implies some necessity that distinguishes it from advice (consilium). But he does not say whether this necessity also belongs to a duty (debitum). Hence he does not say whether every duty is also an obligation. Suarez distinguishes duty from obligation, taking obligation, but not duty, to involve imposed necessity, and therefore command. If Grotius believes that duty implies obligation, and that obligation implies command, he holds an imperative conception of duty. But if he believes that duty implies obligation, and some duties are independent of commands, he holds a non-imperative conception of obligation. It is not quite clear where Grotius stands on these questions.

Grotius describes natural right—understood as law (lex)—as including two elements: the moral wrongness or necessity of some action, because of its inappropriateness or appropriateness to rational nature, and the consequent divine prohibition or command.[13] Hence, insofar as he takes natural right (ius) to be law (lex), he takes it to require a divine command. On this point he seems to agree with Suarez.[14]

465. The Will of God

Though Grotius believes there would be natural right (ius) without law (lex), and hence without the legislative will of God, he does not believe that the existence of God is irrelevant to moral requirements. For we know that God exists and that he offers rewards and punishments (Prol. §11). Grotius now mentions different ways in which the will of God is relevant to questions of right (§13). (1) Right has another origin, besides nature, in the free will of God, whom we must obey. (2) But even natural right, which proceeds from principles internal to a human being, can be ascribed to God, since he willed that such

---

[13] 'Natural right is a dictate of correct reason indicating that some action, from its agreement or disagreement with rational nature itself, has in it moral wrongness or moral necessity, and for that reason such an action is either forbidden or commanded by God the author of nature. Actions about which such a dictate exists are required or impermissible in themselves, and therefore are understood to be necessarily commanded or forbidden by God.' (i 1.10.1) For 'rational nature' Barbeyrac and Whewell substitute 'rational and social nature', appealing to 12.1. Sidgwick, OHE 161n, gives good reasons for rejecting this change.

[14] Schneewind, MP i 88–9, describes the alleged innovation in Grotius' position as follows: '. . . he claimed that there would be binding laws of nature even if God did not exist. . . . If Grotius had claimed only that there are goods and ills independent of the existence of God, his view would not have been particularly original. Such claims had been made in one form or another by various earlier thinkers. They were what Suarez had in mind when he asserted that goods and ills alone do not give rise to obligation and that a sanction imposed by a lawgiver must be added if there are to be obligations. Grotius' innovation was his assertion that there would be obligations, and not simply goods and ills, even if God did not exist.' Schneewind refers to Prol. §11 in support of his claim; but this passage says nothing about obligation. The passage on the law of nature (i 1.10.1) includes a reference to a divine command; hence it does not show that Grotius takes a divine command to be unnecessary for natural law. In any case, even if Grotius maintained the position that Schneewind ascribes to him, it would not be an innovation; it would simply be the position of Vasquez (and probably the implicit position of Aquinas); see §426. Haakonssen, NLMP 29, contrasts Grotius with Gregory of Rimini: 'The scholastic point was that human beings have the ability to understand what is good and bad even without God's command, but have no obligation proper to act accordingly without God's command. Grotius is suggesting that people unaided by religion can use their perfect—and even imperfect—rights to establish the contractual and quasi-contractual obligations upon which social life rests.' The epistemic thesis that Haakonssen mentions captures neither Vasquez's conception of natural law nor Suarez's views about intrinsic rightness and wrongness. His claim about 'obligation proper' is correct only if it refers to obligation in Suarez's narrow sense. Suarez distinguishes obligations from duties and recognizes duties without reference to divine commands. In this narrow sense of 'obligation', however, it is not clear that Grotius recognizes natural law and obligations without divine commands. Both Schneewind's and Haakonssen's attempts to separate Grotius from a familiar Scholastic position rest on inadequate evidence.

principles should exist in us.[15] (3) God made these principles more conspicuous to us, by giving the laws (leges) he has given for the guidance of people who are less capable of reasoning.[16]

The first and third of these claims seem to refer to God's revealing of a legislative will in the Decalogue. Grotius seems to contrast the role of God's will in legislation (in the first and third claims) with its role in natural right itself (in the second claim). He suggests, then, that God's legislative will has no role in the existence of natural right, but simply makes natural right clearer by issuing specific commands. He speaks of laws (leges) only when he mentions the laws that God gives us to make the requirements of natural right clearer.

Grotius' second claim intervenes, rather confusingly, between two claims about God's legislative will. The first claim mentions God's free will as a source of right distinct from natural right. The second claim suggests that even natural right is derived from the will of God, because he willed that such principles should exist in us. 'Principles' here does not refer to our knowledge of the natural law, but to the basic facts about human nature that Grotius has already mentioned. God is introduced here not as the source of our knowledge of natural right, but as the creator of human beings with the nature that is the objective basis for natural right.

Here, therefore, Grotius refers to God as creator, not as legislator; he does not endorse voluntarism about natural law or morality. Like Suarez, he acknowledges God's creative will as the source of human beings with their nature, and hence as the source of naturally right and wrong actions; but this does not imply that natural right and wrong are the result of divine legislation. Though it is up to God whether there are any human beings, and hence whether any human beings act rightly or wrongly, it is not up to God to decide what is good or bad, or right or wrong, for creatures with the nature that is essential to human beings.

It would have been helpful if Grotius had been as careful as Suarez is to separate questions about (i) the natural foundation of natural law (lex); (ii) the essential features of natural law; (iii) the relation of the natural foundation and of the law to God's creative will; (iv) their relation to God's legislative will. His treatment suffers from abbreviation, and he introduces the different points in an unhelpful order. We have no reason, however, to attribute any confusion to him.

He agrees with Suarez and Aquinas in recognizing a natural basis for what they call natural law. This basis is what he calls natural right (ius), and what Suarez calls naturally right (honestum).[17] He seems to agree with Suarez in recognizing duties (debita) that are independent of any divine command.[18] He may be closer to Vasquez's and Aquinas' view, that the existence of natural law (lex) consists in the existence of what is naturally right and wrong, than to Suarez's view, that the existence of natural law requires a divine command. This is the conclusion we will draw if we take Grotius' remarks about the role of God to be exhaustive; for he does not mention, as Suarez does, an act of God's legislative will

[15] See Pufendorf's use of this aspect of divine freedom, discussed in §566.

[16] On divine laws (leges) see Prol. §1. Cf. Aquinas on the function of the Decalogue, §319.

[17] On Grotius' use of 'honestum' see i 2.1.2.

[18] This also seems to be implied by i 2.1.1. Law (lex) introduces new duties (debita), but Grotius does not suggest that there are no duties prior to law.

prescribing observance of natural right, apart from the expression of God's revealed will in the Decalogue. But we have seen that his remarks on the role of God are less than completely clear. It might be wisest to attribute to him no clear view on whether the natural law is prescribed, as such, by God's legislative will.

The extent of a philosopher's commitment to naturalism about natural law is often clarified in his treatment of alleged dispensations. Aquinas, followed by Suarez, claims that genuine dispensations are impossible, since the provisions of the natural law specify what is right and wrong intrinsically, apart from God's legislative will. Grotius follows Aquinas on this issue. In his view, the intrinsic rightness and wrongness of actions does not depend on any divine legislation; God prescribes and forbids actions as being intrinsically right and wrong.

In saying that natural right indicates both intrinsic rightness and the divine precept, Grotius appears to agree with Suarez's claim that the natural law, as such, is prescriptive, and not purely indicative, law. With Aquinas and Suarez, he infers that the natural law is immutable, and cannot be changed by God without self-contradiction.[19] Since God cannot change natural law, apparent dispensations cannot be dispensations. Grotius agrees with Aquinas and Suarez that if God commands us to kill someone or take their goods, God does not make murder (homicidium) or theft lawful in this instance, but changes the circumstances so that the action of killing or taking is no longer murder or theft (i 1.10.6).

Though Grotius is less clear and less systematic than Suarez, he agrees with him on the naturalist claims about morality, on which Suarez also agrees with Aquinas. For he recognizes natural right and wrong, resting on the nature of human beings, apart from any divine legislation.

466. Natural Sociality

If Grotius agrees with Suarez so far on the relation of natural law to human nature, does he also agree with him about the basic features of human nature and about the principles that can be derived from it? Grotius begins by asking: Is there any such thing as right (ius) in the dealings of one people (populus) with another, whether this right is derived from nature or from divine laws (leges) or from custom and tacit agreement (Prol. §1)? Some people have denied that there is any such right beyond a mere name, on the ground that usefulness to a state is the measure of justice, or that a common weal

---

[19] 'Now the Law of Nature is so immutable that it cannot be changed even by God. For although the power of God is measureless (immensa), yet some things can be spoken of to which it does not extend. For things that are spoken of in this way, they are simply spoken of, but they have no sense that would express any reality (res), but are repugnant to themselves. Therefore, just as twice two's not being four cannot be brought about by God, so also it cannot be brought about that what is bad by its intrinsic character is not bad. . . . For as the being (esse) of things when they exist and by which they exist depends on nothing else, the same applies to the properties that necessarily follow on that being. Now such a property is the badness of certain actions, when they are compared with nature using sound reason. Therefore God himself allows judgments about himself in accordance with this norm . . . .'. (i 1.10.5) In the omitted passage Grotius cites, as Suarez (see §447) does, Aristotle on adultery etc. Pufendorf (JNG i 2.6), Barbeyrac, and Whewell object to his use of this passage. On Pufendorf's criticism of the appeal to self-contradiction see §579.

cannot be administered without doing wrong (iniuria).[20] The second of these opinions is the view of Machiavelli, which Suarez discusses as 'the doctrine of politicians of our time' (*Leg.* iii 12.2).

Grotius seeks to answer this objection to the belief in any right that could impose a moral restraint on a particular state. He follows Lactantius and Vasquez in beginning with the objections to justice that are presented by Carneades.[21] According to Carneades' argument, rights (iura) simply embody calculation of utility, and therefore vary in accordance with practices (mores) and different times and occasions, so that there is no natural right (ius). Since everyone naturally pursues utility above all, either there is no justice (iustitia), or justice is foolishness, since consideration for someone else's advantage involves harm to oneself.[22]

Carneades' argument may be initially puzzling, since he says (i) that right reflects a calculation of utility, but (ii) it is foolish to be just. The first claim implies that it is sometimes sensible to follow provisions of right, since they promote utility. The second claim, however, maintains that it is not sensible to be just. The two claims are consistent because they refer to the advantage of different people. In the first claim Carneades asserts that right reflects a society's view of its advantage. In the second he suggests that in following the advantage of society, I harm myself. This combination of claims is familiar from *Republic* ii, which is Carneades' ultimate source; Glaucon, like Carneades, moves from the first claim, that justice embodies the advantage of a society, to the second claim, that it is 'another's good', and harmful to the individual just person.

This second claim can be answered if we have some reason for being just apart from the advantage of a larger society whose advantage may not coincide with our own. We may have such a reason, if principles of justice embody natural right—something that is right because of its agreement with human nature, apart from the advantage of any particular society. Grotius, therefore, tries to prove that there is such a natural right. On this point, his aim is similar to Suarez's aim in answering Machiavelli. He gives Carneades' scepticism about justice a more prominent place in his argument than Suarez gives it. This may be because he thinks it especially urgent to answer scepticism, or because, in fulfilling his aim of using Patristic sources, he relies on Lactantius, who preserves Carneades' critique of justice.

Grotius answers Carneades by denying that a society's view of its advantage is the only basis for right. In his view, there is a natural basis of right. It is founded on human nature, and especially on the human desire for society. This 'social' aspect of human nature is,

[20] 'In practically everyone's mouth is the remark of Euphemus in Thucydides, that for a king or city holding an empire nothing that is useful is unjust. And similar to that one is the remark that in supreme power (fortuna), whatever is stronger is more just (aequius), and the remark that a state cannot be managed without injustice.' (Prol. §3)

[21] Vasquez mentions the Pyrrhonians, ad *ST* 1–2 q94 a1 (p. 35), and quotes Cicero, *Leg.* i 42–7 against them. Lactantius summarizes Carneades' arguments against justice in Cicero, *Rep.* at *DI* v 12, 15. For Lactantius' views on natural law and pagan virtue see §§206, 228.

[22] 'Human beings established rights in accordance with their utility, rights that varied as their customs (mores) varied and even among the same people often changed with time; but there is no natural right. For all human beings and all other animals tended towards their own advantages (utilitates) under the guidance of nature, so that either there is no justice, or if there is any justice it is the height of folly, since one harms oneself in considering the advantage of others.' (Prol. §5)

according to Grotius, what the Stoics have in mind in speaking of 'conciliation' (*oikeiôsis*) of each person to himself and of one person to another.[23]

He describes this aspect of human nature in Stoic rather than purely Aristotelian terms. But, as Barbeyrac sees, the main idea has an Aristotelian source.[24] Grotius seeks to capture Aristotle's conception of a human being as a 'political' (*politikon*) animal, or, as the mediaeval sources render it, a 'social' (*sociale*) animal.[25] He ascribes to human nature both this social aim and the capacity to plan for present and future; in the light of this aim and this capacity we find principles that belong to natural right.

By appealing to the social nature of human beings Grotius seeks a natural basis for our pursuit of the right (*honestum*) as well as the advantageous (*utile*). Following Stoic sources, he claims that our recognition of the right arises from the growth of reason, as we discover a proper object for 'conciliation'. Our conception of the right is our recognition of what accords or conflicts with a rational and social nature.[26]

These claims about sociality and natural right do not necessarily reject Aristotelian eudaemonism. For Aristotle, the Stoics, and Aquinas, the social nature of a human being is part of the human nature that has to be fulfilled in human happiness; hence, the claim that a human being ought to take an appropriate role in a society does not conflict with the claim that each human being pursues his own happiness above all. Scotus rejects Aquinas' view that the pursuit of one's own ultimate good is the proper basis for concern for justice. Grotius does not mention this dispute between Aquinas and Scotus. He says nothing to suggest that he rejects the eudaemonist explanation of the duties belonging to natural right.

Whatever he thinks about eudaemonism, he rejects Carneades' view that utility is the only rational aim that can be founded in human nature.[27] As soon as he has introduced the Stoic notion of sociality (*oikeiôsis*), he rejects Carneades' claim about utility (Prol. §6 fin.). Against Carneades' claim that utility is the mother of the just and fair, he maintains that human nature is the mother of natural right, and would produce a desire for society even if we could satisfy our basic needs for survival without combining with other people (§16). Utility supports natural right, because we cannot supply our basic needs for survival

---

[23] 'And among these things that are proper to a human being is the desire (*appetitus*) for society, in other words for a community, not of just any sort, but a tranquil one that is ordered in accordance with the character of human intellect, with those who are of the same kind. This is what the Stoics called *oikeiôsis*.' (Prol. §6) Grotius cites John Chrysostom and Marcus Aurelius.

[24] On §6 Barbeyrac comments: 'But all these points seem to have flowed from what Aristotle said, "that every human being is akin to and a friend to every other"' (quoted in Greek from *EN* 1155a21–2).

[25] This point is borne out by Grotius' recollection of Aristotle in §7: 'But a human being of mature age knows to treat like cases alike, and has a dominant desire for society, and is the only animal who has language, as a special means to fulfil this desire. Hence it is reasonable to suppose that he also has a capacity for knowing and acting in accordance with general precepts; the things that turn out to be appropriate for him do not belong to all animals, but are suitable for human nature.' This is partly derived from Aristotle, as well as from the Stoic and Patristic sources that Grotius cites.

[26] i 2.1–3. Tuck, 'Modern', argues that Grotius and Pufendorf differ from mediaeval theorists about natural law, because they intend natural law to answer Renaissance scepticism. According to this interpretation, they maintain that some points about self-interest survive the sceptical critique of objective and non-relative values. However, the view that self-interest is the basis of natural law seems as old as Aquinas' eudaemonism; it is not an innovation by Grotius. Saastamoinen, *MFM* 114, fairly criticizes Tuck's view. Haakonssen, *NLMP* 28–30 maintains a view similar to Tuck's.

[27] Grotius' early work, *JP*, ch. 2 (= Williams 14), affirms the social character of human beings, and cites Aristotle.

without the help of others; but it is not the only basis on which we can reasonably assess a particular state.

In all these claims, Grotius never denies that the natural desire for society is subordinate to one's desire for one's own good. He does not defend this eudaemonist thesis against Carneades. Nor does he suggest that it needs defence.[28]

467. Natural Law and Political Principles

Examination of the foundations of Grotius' theory does not suggest any radical innovation in comparison with Suarez. On the contrary, he offers an abbreviated and simplified version of the central naturalist aspects of Aquinas' and Suarez's theory of morality. The elements that Grotius adds from Stoic and Patristic sources supplement the Scholastic position, but they neither conflict with it nor modify its essential claims.

Even though Grotius agrees with Suarez on these basic issues, he does not agree with all his political conclusions. Suarez asserts claims about natural right in opposition to Machiavelli. Though Grotius agrees with him on some points, he does not follow Suarez in allowing a right of resistance.[29] In his long chapter 'On the war of subjects against superiors' (i 4), Grotius further limits even the limited permission that Suarez gives for rebellion.

One of Grotius' arguments against rebellion relies on a conception of rules and principles that Suarez rejects.[30] Grotius speaks as though we should regard principles as rules that give the right answer in most cases, and we should assume that if they do this, it is better to observe them even when they give the wrong answer than to modify the rule.

Grotius' argument is sometimes acceptable; for it may indeed be better to recognize a class of cases where we will not question a rule, even if our violating it would give better results in individual cases. But it does not follow that whenever we have a rule that most often gives the right answer, we should follow it even when it gives the wrong answer. It may be more reasonable to modify the rule so as to take account of the cases where some modification would give a better answer. This is Suarez's point when he argues that the precepts of natural law are not to be identified with the general rules that most often give the right answer. In his view, the precepts of natural law include the circumstances that introduce qualifications into simple generalizations. Grotius overlooks this aspect of Suarez's doctrine here.

Still, he does not adhere rigidly to his general rule. He acknowledges that 'it is a more difficult question, whether the law about non-resistance obliges us in a most serious and most certain danger' (i 4.7.1). He mentions David's rebellion against Saul and the rebellion of the Maccabees against Antiochus. In both cases he argues that only

---

[28] Contrast Darwall, *BMIO* 6.   [29] On Suarez see §451.

[30] 'If the rulers at any time are misled by excessive fear or anger or other passions, so as to deviate from the right road that leads to tranquillity, this is to be held as one of the less frequent cases, which are to be estimated...by the occurrence of better cases. Now laws take it to be sufficient to take account of what most frequently happens. ... For this is preferable to living without a rule (norma) or leaving the rule to the judgment of everyone.' (i 4.4.3)

extreme and most certain danger (summum certissimumque periculum, i 4.7.5) could justify their action; he rejects every other argument that might be given to support the Maccabean rebellion. He then adds a final doubt about the legitimacy of rebellion for Christians (i 4.7.8).

If, therefore, Grotius allows any right of resistance at all, he limits it to self-defence. He does not allow the form of aggressive war that Suarez allows, when the commonwealth deposes the ruler. He rejects the arguments of contemporaries who allow this power of deposition to inferior officials speaking on behalf of the commonwealth (i 4.6.1). In his view, they have only the status of private persons in relation to the supreme ruler whom they claim the right to depose.

These objections to the right of resistance and deposition ignore Suarez's main argument for attributing a right of aggressive war to the commonwealth against the ruler. Suarez argues that natural law does not permit ruling without regard to the common good, and that therefore the condition of ruling in accord with the common good always qualifies the legitimate transfer of power from the people to the ruler. Grotius accepts Suarez's grounds for founding political society in natural law and the common good. But he does not consider these grounds in his discussion of the right of rebellion. This sharp political difference from Suarez's claims about legitimacy and resistance is all the more striking in the light of the agreement between Grotius and Suarez on moral foundations.[31]

Grotius does not improve on Suarez here. For in agreeing that natural right precedes any right created by a state and its laws, and that natural right includes more moral demands than those referring to survival and physical security, he implies that states, governments, and political institutions may be judged by reference to the social nature of human beings, and to the success or failure of different states in fulfilling it. This judgment may not always justify obedience. An argument for obedience has to rely on empirical premises that are sometimes open to dispute.

If this objection to Grotius' political doctrine is justified, the Scholastic and naturalist foundations of his moral theory of natural right tend to undermine his political claims. This conflict in his position is apparent to Pufendorf, who sees that the foundations need to be modified in order to remove the elements of natural right that limit the claims of a particular state on the obedience of a subject. Hobbes attacks the political theorists who rely on Aristotelian principles to support their foolish and dangerous objections to the established regime. If Grotius' position were harmonious, Hobbes's criticisms would be unwarranted, because Aristotelian principles would warrant unrestricted obedience. But when we examine the moral foundation of Grotius' position, we find that Hobbes is right, since Aristotelian principles do not warrant the unrestricted obedience that Grotius advocates. This is not a reason to prefer a Hobbesian over an Aristotelian position.

---

[31] On this particular issue Rousseau's comparison of Grotius and Hobbes contains a grain of truth in a large distortion: 'When I hear Grotius praised to the skies, and Hobbes covered with abuse, I perceive how little sensible men read or understand these authors. The truth is that their principles are exactly alike, they only differ in expression. Their methods are also different: Hobbes relies on sophisms; Grotius relies on poets; all the rest is common to them.' (*Emile* v = Pleiade iv 836 = Foxley, 421–2)

468. Is Grotius a Pioneer?

Examination of Grotius' basic claims about the moral character of natural law does not show that he is the pioneer of a new approach to natural law.[32] His exposition of natural law is brief and simple, in comparison with Suarez's, and it is not embedded in the moral and metaphysical context of Aquinas' Treatise on Law. But these non-Scholastic features of Grotius' exposition do not result in a new view of the relation of natural law to the legislative will of God and to natural rightness and wrongness.[33]

The obscurities in Grotius' views about the connexion of obligation, duty, and right sometimes make it difficult to say where he agrees or disagrees with Aquinas or Vasquez or Suarez. But they do not cast doubt on one central point of agreement; he believes, as they do, that natural rightness precedes any act of God's legislative will, and that natural law essentially corresponds to the requirements of natural rightness. Since he takes morality to consist in observance of what is naturally right, he holds a naturalist conception of morality.

On these basic issues, Grotius agrees with the naturalists, though it is not clear whether he agrees more closely with Vasquez or with Suarez. These points of agreement refute Barbeyrac's claim that Grotius is a pioneer. He does not introduce a jural conception of morality, but rejects a jural conception in favour of Scholastic naturalism. Nor does his belief that there would be morality even if God did not exist make him a secular moralist; since he shares this belief with leading Scholastics, he is no more secular on this point than they are. His reply to Carneades' scepticism about justice does not reduce justice to utility, but sticks to a Stoic and Peripatetic naturalist conception.

On these points in his theory of morality, therefore, Grotius is no pioneer. The most plausible assessment of his position is Gershom Carmichael's judgment that Grotius extracts from Scholastic views on natural law and moral theology the essential points that are relevant to moral and political philosophy. We have noticed that both Aquinas and Suarez recognize questions and forms of argument that belong to moral philosophy in particular; but they do not gather these questions and arguments in a separate treatise. Grotius may make a different impression on a reader because he collects some of the main elements in Scholastic moral philosophy, and clarifies them with references to Greek and Latin writers and to the Christian Fathers. But the doctrine that he expounds is a naturalist doctrine of morality such as we find both in Aquinas and in Suarez.

---

[32] Tierney, INR, ch.13, offers a balanced discussion of what is and is not distinctively modern in Grotius (without detailed discussion of Barbeyrac's interpretation). The 'natural law' view that Schneewind traces to Grotius in 'Kant and natural law' 56–8 is closer to Pufendorf than to Grotius. I am not taking a position on whether Grotius is in some way an innovator in political theory, as argued by Haakonssen in 'History'. Haakonssen acknowledges that Grotius' views about intrinsic morality and natural law are traditional (248–9); contrast his view quoted in §464 above.

[33] Beiser, SR 276, describes an interpretation of natural law theory. 'It assumed that human beings are self-sufficient atoms with a fixed nature prior to the social whole. Rather than depending on the social whole for the formation of their needs and capacities, individuals enter into society with them already formed, and then construct a social order and state according to their self-interest... Although this interpretation is indeed correct for the social contract theory developed by Hugo Grotius, Hobbes, John Selden, and Samuel Pufendorf earlier in the seventeenth century, it would be incorrect to generalize it and to apply it to the great majority of natural law theorists in the post-Restoration era.' Apart from the oddity of contrasting Pufendorf with the post-Restoration era, this description unjustifiably assimilates Grotius to Hobbes and Selden, in opposition to Cumberland and the others.

Barbeyrac, therefore, misunderstands Grotius in presenting him as a pioneer. To see why Barbeyrac is so wrong about Grotius, we need to consider his view of Pufendorf. He could hardly have reached his view about Grotius if he had not already accepted the views of Pufendorf, and set out to reconcile Grotius with Pufendorf in a distinctively modern theory of natural law. His efforts to make Grotius the first modern moralist, and a rebel against Scholastic views of morality, are basically misguided.

HOBBES: MOTIVES AND REASONS

469. Hobbes's Aims

Hobbes is dissatisfied with the error and disagreement among moral philosophers, in contrast to the consensus that natural philosophers have reached. In natural philosophy, inquiry proceeds from indisputable and undisputed first principles, and secures agreement at each step. Moral philosophy, by contrast, presents us with unresolved controversy, because inquirers begin from common beliefs and apparently plausible views.[1] The Aristotelian dialectical approach to moral inquiry begins from 'appearances' and does not confine itself to evident and indisputable starting points.[2] Hobbes believes that it leads to insoluble and fruitless disputes.

He does not believe that this difference between the progress of natural philosophy and the relative backwardness of moral philosophy marks a difference in the subject matter or in the appropriate method. Nor does he draw the sceptical conclusion[3] that knowledge of moral questions cannot be found, or the nihilist conclusion that there is no moral reality to be known. He believes that disputes result simply from failure to apply the method of natural philosophy.[4] We should begin with clear and indisputable axioms about human nature, and avoid the dialectical method that relies on common beliefs.[5]

---

[1] '[Those men who have taken in hand to consider nothing else but the comparison of magnitudes, numbers, times, and motions, and how their proportions are to one another]. . . proceed from the most low and humble principles, evident even to the meanest capacity; going on slowly, and with most scrupulous ratiocination.' (EL 13.3) '[Moral and political philosophers]. . . take up maxims from their education, and from the authority of men, or of custom, and take the habitual discourse of the tongue for ratiocination; and these are called dogmatici.' (EL 13.4) For Hobbes's rejection of appeals to received opinion cf. Civ. 1.2 (on human beings as naturally political); 10.8, 12.12 (on rhetoric). Skinner, RRPH 263, gives parallels from Bacon and others. References to EL follow Gaskin's numeration, which includes Human Nature and De Corpore Politico, with chapters numbered continuously (so that De Corpore Politico i 1 = EL 14).

[2] On Aristotle's method see §67.

[3] Tuck, PG 285–306, discusses the influence of scepticism on Hobbes's philosophical development. Skinner, RRPH 8–9, 299, expresses doubts about the extent of such influence.

[4] '. . . amongst all the writers of this part of philosophy, there is not one that hath used an idoneous principle of tractation.' (commodo usus sit docendi principio, Civ., Ep. Ded.) I quote from the translation of Civ. by 'C.C', published in 1651 and printed by Warrender and Lamprecht. Warrender, ed. of DC (Eng), 4–8, discusses the early evidence on the authorship of the English version, and argues that Hobbes is probably the translator; some of the variations between the Latin and the English versions are difficult to explain as decisions or errors of a translator other than Hobbes. Tuck, ed. of DC, pp. xxxiv–xxxvii, argues that Hobbes is not the translator, but he does not satisfactorily answer Warrender's arguments. Silverthorne's translation is in Tuck and Silverthorne's edition.

[5] Hobbes's method is discussed by Skinner in RRPH 294–375, who is criticized in Gauthier's review.

Hobbes expects his inquiries to settle moral disputes by offering new solutions. He will not show that (for instance) Aristotle is right against Chrysippus on one issue, or that Ockham is right against Aquinas on another. He believes that his answers will fall outside the range of answers that have been subjects of controversy in moral philosophy. The method of natural philosophy will produce consensus in moral thinking too.[6]

Some of Hobbes's complaints about disagreement in moral philosophy are familiar. The persistence of philosophical disputes is a source of one Sceptical argument for suspension of judgment. Sextus does not draw exactly Hobbes's contrast between natural and moral philosophy; he treats all sciences as open to Sceptical doubt. But he has something corresponding to Hobbes's distinction, since he recognizes instances of disagreement about specific cases ('Ought I to eat or to bury or to cremate my parents?') in the area of morality more than in the area of beliefs about the physical world ('Are ripe tomatoes red or blue?'). Hobbes answers the Sceptic by urging that something like the method of natural science will settle disputes about morality.

It would be unreasonable of him to claim that the persistence of disputes in moral philosophy implies lack of progress. Even if his contemporaries do not agree about the explanation of incontinence, the progress of debate shows that it will not do simply to assert either that the Socratic analysis is obviously true or that it is obviously false. Similarly, though the Scholastics disagree about the relation of natural law to the will of God, the debate summed up by Suarez makes it clear what each side needs to say to defend its position. Examination of the nature and sources of the disputes casts doubt on Hobbes's claim that the discipline has made no progress in 2,000 years.

His main objection to his predecessors is not that they disagree with one another, but that their doctrines are dangerous. A reconstruction of moral philosophy is necessary for the proper understanding of the moral basis of political life, since the mistaken moral philosophy of his predecessors has led to political error. Mistaken theories of Greek and Latin writers have encouraged citizens to believe that they have rights against their rulers. Citizens claim the right to judge their rulers by standards derived from moral principles, and so they try to replace their rulers by agitation or revolution.

Such dangerous claims may be traced back to Aristotle's objections to unjust regimes.[7] Though Aristotle does not derive these objections from a general theory of the rights of the citizen, and does not use them to defend disobedience or revolution, his claims about justice

---

[6] 'And truly the geometricians have very admirably performed their part . . . If the moral philosophers had as happily discharged their duty, I know not what could have been added by human industry to the completion of that happiness, which is consistent with human life. For were the nature of human actions as distinctly known (cognita pari certitudine), as the nature of quantity in geometrical figures, the strength of avarice and ambition, which is sustained by the erroneous opinion of the vulgar, as touching the nature of right and wrong, would presently faint and languish. . . . But now on the contrary, that neither the sword nor the pen should be allowed any cessation; that the knowledge of the law of nature should lose its growth, not advancing a whit beyond its ancient stature; that there should still be such siding with the several factions of philosophers, that the very same action should be decried by some, and as much elevated by others; these I say are so many signs, so many manifest arguments, that what hath hitherto been written by moral philosophers, hath not made any progress in the knowledge of the truth. . . . So that this part of philosophy hath suffered the same destiny with the public ways, which lie open to all passengers to traverse up and down . . . ; so that what with the impertinencies of some, and the altercations of others, those ways have never a seed time, and therefore yield never a harvest.' (Civ., Ep. Ded.)

[7] Aristotle discusses instability in different forms of government in Politics v.

suggest possible defences. The Scholastics develop Aristotle's arguments. Suarez uses them to support a qualified defence of rebellion and tyrannicide.[8]

Contemporary experience in England, Scotland, Ireland, and Continental Europe suggests to Hobbes that this critical attitude to rulers undermines states and societies.[9] Grotius shares some of Hobbes's fears about the effects of philosophical arguments for disobedience, and so he tries to blunt the critical edge of some Scholastic theories.[10] Hobbes, however, does not share Grotius' view that the Scholastic doctrines can be largely maintained without endangering civil peace.[11] He believes they are so dangerous that they should be discarded. Once we discover the true basis of morality, we can explode the moral theories that support dangerous political demands.

These moral theories assert that some things are important enough to justify disobedience. No Scholastic argues that civil peace does not matter, but Scholastics who rely on Aristotelian arguments assert that extremely unjust rulers should not be obeyed. If we have to balance the importance of maintaining peace against the importance of maintaining justice, we are not (from Hobbes's point of view) reliable supporters of peace. To prevent this sort of balancing, we need to show that nothing matters enough to justify the disturbance of civil peace. Hobbes argues, therefore, that peace is absolutely prior to all other moral considerations; they all presuppose the maintenance of peace, and therefore cannot justify disturbances of the peace.

This is an over-simple summary of the practical and political aim of Hobbes's moral philosophy. In support of this aim, he goes back to human nature as the foundation of moral philosophy, because he believes that his predecessors go wrong at this basic level. Nor does he confine himself to moral and political philosophy. He does not, for instance, try to defend the priority of peace by a dialectical argument to show that, on reflexion, we really believe peace matters more than anything else. He does not suggest that if we reach 'narrow reflective equilibrium' among our moral and political views, we will accept the supremacy of peace.[12] He believes that if we recognize the true foundation of moral philosophy, we can

---

[8] On Suarez see §451.

[9] 'And now, considering how different this doctrine is, from the practice of the greatest part of the world, especially of those western parts, that have received their moral learning from Rome, and Athens; and how much depth of moral philosophy is required in them that have the administration of the sovereign power; I am at the point of believing this my labour as useless, as is the commonwealth of Plato. . . . But when I consider again, that the science of natural justice, is the only science necessary for sovereigns, and their principal ministers; . . . and that neither Plato, nor any other philosopher hitherto, hath put into order, and sufficiently, or probably proved all the theorems of moral doctrine, that men may learn thereby, both how to govern, and how to obey; I recover some hope, that at one time or other, this writing of mine, may fall into the hands of a sovereign, who will consider it himself . . . without the help of any interested, or envious interpreter; and by the exercise of entire sovereignty, in protecting the public teaching of it, convert this truth of speculation, into the utility of practice.' (L. 31.41) 'And by reading of these Greek and Latin authors, men from their childhood have gotten a habit, under a false show of liberty, of favouring tumults, and of licentious controlling the actions of their sovereigns; and again of controlling those controllers; with the effusion of so much blood, as I think I may truly say there was never anything so dearly bought as these western parts have bought the learning of the Greek and Latin tongues.' (L. 21.9) I cite L. by chapter and section in Curley's edition, which also quotes some of the significant variants in the Latin version (cited as 'LV'). LV is discussed at length by Tricaud, xvii–xxix (and briefly by Laird, H 33, and Curley, lxxiii). He argues (despite the absence of external evidence) that some parts of it antedate the English, which expands the Latin, whereas other parts postdate the English. Cumberland (see §530) cites the Latin version on the assumption that it is later.

[10] On Grotius see §467.

[11] On Hobbes and Grotius see Tuck, PG 305. We lack direct evidence to show that Hobbes read Grotius.

[12] On narrow reflective equilibrium see Rawls, TJ 42–5.

dismiss any confident and reflective moral judgments that threaten the supremacy of peace; all such judgments rest on errors about the foundation.

We have spoken of Hobbes's opposition to an 'Aristotelian' and 'Scholastic' view. But it is not easy to say whom he has in mind; for, in contrast to Scholastic writers, he does not compare his views systematically with the views of his predecessors. His explicit targets include Greek and Latin historians, orators, and philosophers. He often mentions Aristotle, both because of his historical prominence and because contemporary writers have relied on him.[13] It would have been instructive if he had discussed Grotius, who shares Hobbes's concern with peace and war, but defends a largely traditional moral theory. But he does not engage Grotius. Nor does he discuss the moral and political views of Scholastic writers—perhaps because he does not think much of them—and so it is not clear how well he knows them. It is reasonable to assume that he knows the *De Legibus* and the other political writings of Suarez, since Suarez became notorious in both France and England as a supporter of regicide, and the Civil War that led to the execution of Charles I made his views rather topical.[14] But though Hobbes refers to Suarez's works on free will, he does not cite his political writings.[15]

We therefore have to present the dispute between Hobbes and his opponents by considering where his views disagree with theirs, and what one might say on behalf of each side.

470. Passion v. Will

Hobbes believes that his new method demands an understanding of human action; if we grasped it as clearly as we grasp the basic elements of geometry, we could resolve

[13] See Laird, 'Aristotle'. Barker, *PTPA* 523, mentions a newspaper published briefly in 1654, entitled *Observations, Historical, Political and Philosophical upon Aristotle's First Book of Political Government*, which seeks to show 'the happiness of those people that live under such a government, where it is the duty of the governors to rule by law, as the Lord Protector here hath sworn to do'.

[14] On Suarez see §451.

[15] He sometimes mentions Suarez as a typical example of Scholastic unintelligibility. After quoting the long title of a chapter of Suarez's work 'Of the concourse, motion, and help of God' (the first opusculum in Suarez, *OO* xi), he comments: 'When men write whole volumes of such stuff, are they not mad, or intend to make others so?' (*Hom.* 8 = *EW* iii 70). In his view, Scholastic writers, such as Peter Lombard, Scotus, and Suarez, support the authority of the Pope by writing incomprehensible works that only a priestly class can read (*Behemoth*, Part 1 = *EW* vi 185). He does not expect them to have a wider appeal: 'But for the multitude, Suarez and the Schoolmen will never gain them, because they are not understood' (*EW* iv 330). He has more than a passing knowledge of Suarez's work on human freedom and divine foreknowledge. He attacks its account of some Scriptural passages (*EW* v 10) and its absurd conclusions: 'Whereof one conclusion is in Suarez, that God doth so concur with the will of man, that "if man will, then God concurs", which is to subject not the will of man to God, but the will of God to man' (*EW* v 18). He claims to find in this work the source of most of Bramhall's arguments on free will: '. . . whoever chanceth to read Suarez's Opuscula, where he writeth of free-will, and the concourse of God with man's will, shall find the greatest part, if not all, that the Bishop hath urged in this question' (*EW* v 37). Bramhall replies: 'It is indifferent to me whether the greatest part of what I urge in this question, or all that I urge, or perhaps more than I urge, be contained in Suarez his Opuscula. . . . In all my life, that I do remember, I never read one line of Suarez his Opuscula, nor any of his works the sixteen years last past. I wish he [sc. Hobbes] had been versed in his greater works, as well as in his Opuscula, that he might not be so averse from the Schools.' (*CMH* = *Works* iv 259–60) Bramhall implies that he had once read Suarez's major works, and that he still finds them reasonable. See also Hobbes, *EW* v 176; 266 (distinguishing Suarez, Scotus, and other Scholastic writers, whom Hobbes slights, from Protestant theologians, whom he respects). Suarez's works, then, seem to give us a fair idea of the style, method, and substantive positions that Hobbes rejects. Martinich, *TGL* 102, 132–4, 379–80, mentions the relevance of Suarez's views on law and political obligation to Hobbes's concerns, but mentions no references or allusions to Suarez in political contexts.

controversies about morality.[16] His predecessors have obscured the facts by their appeals to unintelligible faculties and abilities. He tries to correct them by reference to facts about desire, pleasure, and motivation that he takes to be indisputable.

Hobbes agrees with the Scholastics that an account of morality should rely on an account of action. We have seen how Aquinas' conception of the final good rests on his account of will, rational agency, and freedom. His distinctive contribution lies in his particular views about the nature of action.

To grasp the role of Hobbes's theory of action in his whole position, we might try to answer these questions: (1) Is his account of action plausible? (2) Is it an independent foundation for his moral theory, or should it persuade us only if we already accept his moral views? (3) Does it support his moral theory? (4) Are his moral claims plausible?

These questions suggest that Hobbes's views may not all stand or fall together, and that we might try different partial defences. If we agree with Hobbes's theory of action, but disagree with his moral theory, we may seek to construct another account of morality on a Hobbesian foundation. If we disagree with his theory of action, but agree with his moral theory, we should defend his moral claims independently of his foundation.

Hobbes rejects a basic point of agreement between Scholastics. Both intellectualists and voluntarists hold that human action essentially proceeds from the will and not only from passions. They believe that will, understood as rational desire (appetitus), differs from passion (sensory desire) because it is guided by rational deliberation, and does not simply follow sense-perception. This is not a Scholastic innovation; it simply develops Plato's and Aristotle's division between rational and non-rational desire.[17]

Hobbes denies this distinction between passion and will, by denying that will is a distinctively rational desire. In his view, will is simply the last 'appetite' (i.e., desire, appetitus) in deliberation.[18] Aquinas believes that will is a rational desire confined to rational agents, because it results from deliberation. But Hobbes believes that non-rational agents also deliberate, so that if will is desire resting on deliberation, it is not confined to rational agents. Scholastics claim that human agents act voluntarily because they act on their will and deliberate desire, whereas non-rational animals lack fully voluntary action because they lack deliberation and will. But if Hobbes is right, the will is not an intrinsically rational desire aiming at the good rather than the pleasant.

His account of deliberation assumes that desire is simply anticipatory pleasure or pain, which is the internal movement explaining action (*EL* 7.1–2). We move towards ends (7.4) that differ in their closeness or distance. We deliberate by being struck in succession by different attractive features of a situation.[19] The strongest appetite that emerges from that process immediately precedes action; this is the will.

---

[16] *Civ.*, Ep. Ded., quoted in §469. [17] On intellectualism and rationalism see §§256, 389.

[18] More fully: 'In deliberation, the last appetite, or aversion, immediately adhering to the action, or to the omission thereof, is that we call the will; the act, not the faculty, of willing. And beasts, that have deliberation, must necessarily also have will. The definition of the will, given commonly by the schools, that it is a rational appetite, is not good. For if it were, then could there be no voluntary act against reason. For a voluntary act is that, which proceedeth from the will, and no other. But if in stead of a rational appetite, we shall say an appetite resulting from a precedent deliberation, then the definition is the same that I have given here.' (*L.* 6.53) Cf. *EL* 12.2; *Hom.* 11.2.

[19] 'When in the mind of man, appetites, and aversions, hopes, and fears, concerning one and the same thing, arise alternately; and divers good and evil consequences of the doing, or omitting the thing propounded, come successively into our thoughts; so that sometimes we have an appetite to it; sometimes an aversion from it...the whole sum

Non-rational agents, therefore, also deliberate. They hesitate at the idea of something repellent and advance at the idea of something attractive; hence they deliberate, and act on their wills. Our goal-directed movements, therefore, do not rely on a rational appearance of an overall good (*EL* 7.5). Hence the Scholastic distinction between will and passion is misguided.[20]

This account of deliberation refers only to non-normative states; it does not mention our estimate of the value of the different options that occur to us in deliberation. It does not distinguish our being more attracted to one of two options from our believing that it deserves to be preferred. If we believe (as we suppose) that one option deserves to be preferred, we believe that the reasons for it are better than the reasons for the other option. This aspect of deliberation and will has no place in Hobbes's account; he does not suggest that our will results from the judgment that one option is better than the other, or from the judgment that we have stronger reasons for pursuing it.

471. Hobbes and Greek Scepticism

Hobbes's non-normative conception of deliberation recalls the Greek Sceptics' account of living without belief.[21] Sceptics take themselves to abandon the dogmatic aim of forming attitudes to the world on the basis of evidence and the weighing of reasons; they do not consider whether p is true before they assent to p. They claim to assent to appearances only to the limited extent that is implied by 'yielding', according to how the appearances strike them. Hobbes believes that we ought to treat deliberation and desire in purely psychological and non-normative terms. Deliberation and will, in his account, result from yielding successively to a sequence of appearances about different options, without any rational assessment of their value.[22]

This comparison between Hobbes and the Greek Sceptics is misleading on one point. The Sceptics agree with their dogmatic opponents that belief (*doxa*) is to be understood as a normative state; we form a belief by an attempted assessment of the evidence, and if we change our view about the evidence, we change our belief. Sceptics agree that dogmatists have beliefs, since their view of the world rests on an attempted rational assessment of the evidence. The dogmatists are wrong, however, to suppose that they rationally assess the evidence. Since Sceptics see the dogmatists' error, they give up forming beliefs. Their yielding to appearances is not belief, because it does not rest on an assessment of evidence, and therefore it is non-normative. The meat in the display case looks bright red, but if we are dogmatists we may not infer that it is red, if we remember that a red light is shining on it. The evidence that would otherwise persuade us to believe that the meat is red is open to question once we remember the red light shining on the meat, and so we will not hastily infer that the meat is fresh. But we yield to appearances when we find that the meat looks

---

of desires, aversions, hopes and fears, continued till the thing be either done, or thought impossible, is that we call deliberation.' (*L.* 6.49)

[20] Hobbes's rejection of the division between will and passion is discussed by James, *PA* 135; Tuck, 'Moral philosophy' 184.

[21] On Scepticism and belief see §139.   [22] On Scepticism and modern moral philosophy see §462.

red and do not question whether it is red, and we yield to them again if we find (when we get it home, in normal light) that it looks dull and dark; in neither case do we take the further step of considering whether it is really how it looks.

The Sceptics' account of the antecedents of action is equally non-normative; they describe a sequence of appearances causing us to yield to one appearance that results in our choice of one option. But the Sceptics, in contrast to Hobbes, do not regard this as deliberation. Aristotelian deliberation involves a rational estimate of grounds for preferring one or another option, and our election is guided by this rational estimate. Sceptics accept this description of deliberation, and therefore give up deliberation, because they make no rational estimates.

Hobbes, however, does not claim to reject deliberation. He does not agree with the Sceptical view that deliberation is a normative activity that dogmatists engage in because of their mistaken normative views. He claims to identify the intelligible elements in deliberation, and hence to describe and to analyse the activity that he and his opponents all engage in. His description is meant to be reductive, since it gives a clear, non-mysterious account of the character of deliberation, by identifying it with a series of simpler and more intelligible mental states. This reduction to something simpler is meant to vindicate the reality of deliberation, not to deny it; Hobbes intends us to agree that his analysis captures what we do when we deliberate, not to conclude that we do not deliberate.

He is right, therefore, to claim that his account of action excludes the Scholastic account, and the Scholastic ethical theory that rests on it. For his analysis of deliberation implies that the Scholastics are wrong to treat will as a distinctively rational appetite.

472. Objections to Hobbes's Account of Will

But ought we to accept Hobbes's account of deliberation? This question divides into three: (1) Is deliberation as described by Hobbes (let us call it 'H-deliberation') really deliberation, so that he gives a vindicating reduction of deliberation? (2) If not, is he right to reject a normative account of deliberation and will? (3) If he is right to reject it, is H-deliberation a good substitute for deliberation?

If we agree that H-deliberation is possible, why should we identify it with deliberation? H-deliberation is not the kind of practical thought that we take to be distinctive of rational agents; for we suppose that they reach a decision in favour of one action or the other in the light of some conception of the overall costs and benefits of their actions. Hobbes does not show that any such conception underlies the advances and hesitations of non-rational agents; hence the advances and hesitations of H-deliberation do not seem to be sufficient for deliberation.

H-deliberation makes a deliberating agent insensitive to any distinction between the strength and the rational weight or 'authority' of desires.[23] This distinction is Butler's formulation of the point underlying Plato's and Aristotle's division between rational and non-rational parts of the soul. It seems to capture a feature of our ordinary deliberation that separates it from H-deliberation. We might, for instance, first H-deliberate, and then ask

---

[23] See §683 on Butler, §831 on Reid.

ourselves whether we should do what our H-deliberation has inclined us to do. If the police are investigating a crime that I believe my friend George has committed, I may be inclined to lie to protect George, but also inclined to tell the truth because I am afraid of being prosecuted, and because I am angry at George and sympathetic to his victim. But after this H-deliberation, I may reconsider what to do, and ask myself which of these inclinations I should follow. This reconsideration seems to be deliberation; it does not seem to be further H-deliberation, since it examines the reasons for and against the different options.

H-deliberation, therefore, does not seem to be deliberation, and so Hobbes does not seem to have found a vindicating reduction of deliberation to H-deliberation. But what does he think about people who claim to engage in deliberation rather than H-deliberation? Are they mistaken about the character of their mental states, so that they falsely believe they are thinking about the merits of an action when they are really only experiencing a sequence of inclinations and aversions? If this is his view, any alleged deliberation beyond H-deliberation is an invention of the Scholastics, with no basis in the real antecedents of action.

Alternatively, Hobbes might take the view of the Greek Sceptics, admitting that some people deliberate and do not simply H-deliberate, but arguing that these people's deliberation lacks the basis that they think it has. Dogmatists suppose that we can discover reasons that do not simply register the strength of our preferences; but if we cannot find any such reasons, it is pointless to deliberate, though we will still H-deliberate.

If Hobbes took this line, suggesting that we will abandon deliberation when we see it is baseless, he would undermine his argument to show that will is simply the last appetite in H-deliberation. If deliberation is not simply H-deliberation, will is not simply the last appetite. If Hobbes held the Sceptical view, he would agree that we are capable of acts of will, but argue that we have no reasonable basis for them.

It is worth comparing Hobbes with the Greek Sceptics in order to see that he is committed to the eliminative view of deliberation; his claims about the will go beyond the apparently more plausible view that deliberation is possible but pointless. He takes himself to hold a vindicating reductive view of deliberation. He seems, however, to be committed to an eliminative view. He offers a mental substitute for deliberation that fails to mark the distinctions, especially those based on power and authority, that we mark in deliberation, as normally understood.

To support his eliminative position, Hobbes needs to show that we lack the mental capacities that would allow us to engage in more than H-deliberation. But he does not try to show this, and it seems difficult to show. Quite ordinary choices seem to presuppose some capacity for deliberation that involves weighing merits. We need quite strong arguments if we are to be convinced that we misconceive what we are doing when we suppose we are weighing merits. In comparison with the Scholastic account of deliberation and action, Hobbes's account is clear and simple; but it does not explain the choices and actions it seeks to explain.

473. Deliberation and Practical Reason

These doubts about Hobbes's account might matter less if we thought it deprives us of nothing that is practically important. If some H-deliberation results in choices that we normally regard as reasonable, we can still distinguish reasonable from unreasonable action by appealing to different patterns of H-deliberation.

Hobbes faces a question analogous to a question that arises for the Greek Sceptics who claim to live without beliefs. We may concede, for the sake of argument, that the Sceptical outlook is consistent, and that it is logically possible for someone to live by yielding to appearances without beliefs about good and bad. But how can someone claiming to adopt such an outlook claim to live an ordinary life? For our ordinary life seems to rely on the beliefs that the Sceptic abandons; we often think we see more reason to believe and to do one thing rather than another. Sometimes I have a vivid impression of an elliptical coin, but I do not believe that the penny is elliptical. I pick it up and put it in a slot machine designed for a round coin. Do I not rely on beliefs that the Sceptic abandons?

Sceptics deny that such cases raise any difficulty. In their view, Sceptics do not yield to all appearances. In the case we have mentioned, they have a more vivid and more forceful appearance of the coin being round, and so they yield to that one, and put the coin in a slot machine, just as they would have if they had believed it to be round. Hence, they claim, the Sceptic can live an ordinary life. But this conclusion is plausible only if Sceptics have an appropriately forceful appearance in all or most of the cases where ordinary people form a given belief. Why should we expect they will have such an appearance? I may have a very strong and forceful appearance that this is real fruit in the bowl, but I may not try to eat it if I suspect that it is made of wax.

The Sceptic might deal with such cases by arguing that if I do not yield to the appearance of its being real fruit, the appearance cannot have been as strong as the appearance of its being made of wax. This answer is unconvincing. If strength of appearances is determined by phenomenal features distinct from whether or not I act on the appearances, my yielding to the strongest appearances may not lead me to follow ordinary life. If, however, an appearance is strongest in virtue of the fact that I act on it, the strength of the appearance may depend on the rational assessment of the evidence; but that basis for determining strength is not available to the Sceptic. Neither conception of strength (or forcefulness, or vividness) suggests that the Sceptic's yielding to the strongest appearance agrees with ordinary life.

Just as Sceptics claim to agree with ordinary life, Hobbes assumes that H-deliberation reaches the conclusions that we reach by ordinary deliberation. He claims that deliberation results from the foresight of good or evil consequences, and better deliberation results from the foresight of more consequences.[24] He assumes that if we foresee more of the consequences, we take account of their goodness and badness in our deliberation and in any decision that is based on deliberation. This is a reasonable assumption about ordinary deliberation, but not about H-deliberation. In ordinary deliberation we consider the goodness and badness of the consequences of an action, and our eventual choice results from our estimate of the overall goodness of an action. But H-deliberation is not guided by a comparison of the net balance of future expected good in different courses of action. H-deliberation is a series of advances and hesitations resulting from the appearance of

[24] 'But for so far as a man seeth, if the good in these consequences be greater than the evil, the whole chain is that which writers call apparent, or seeming good. . . . so that he who hath by experience, or reason, the greatest and surest prospect of consequences, deliberates best himself; and is able when he will, to give the best counsel unto others.' (L. 6.57)

expected pleasures and pains, and we choose the proposed action that arouses our strongest appetite as a result of these advances and hesitations.

Even if we confine goods to pleasures, we have no reason to assume that in the H-deliberating agent the apparently larger sum of future pleasures always arouses the stronger appetite. We may, for instance, be irrationally indifferent to the remoter future, or irrationally obsessed by it at the expense of shorter-term benefits, and these irrational tendencies may determine the course of H-deliberation. Consideration of more consequences may not improve my deliberation. If I am thinking about travelling by air, and I consider all the possible consequences, I may think about the possibility of the aircraft's crashing or exploding, and this thought, however improbable I may take the event to be, may turn me irrationally against travel by air. I would have reached a more reasonable conclusion if I had ignored these prospects.

If the apparently larger sum of future pleasures may not arouse the stronger appetite, H-deliberation may not follow the apparent balance of future pleasures. H-deliberation considers whatever happens to excite desire or aversion. We do not necessarily deliberate best, therefore, if our H-deliberation considers the 'greatest and surest prospect of consequences'; for the sparse equipment of H-deliberation includes no provision for the rational consideration of these prospects; if we are not guided by the expected balance of future good, the consideration of more consequences may produce irrational desires.

H-deliberation, therefore, does not seem to justify Hobbes's claims about the character of deliberation. His remarks about better and worse deliberation rely on a normative conception of deliberation, taking it to consider what is best overall and what we ought to do in the light of what seems best overall. H-deliberation has no room for this normative conception. If deliberation is guided by consideration of what promotes the overall good, the consideration of more consequences results in better deliberation, as Hobbes claims. But, if we are to accept this claim about deliberation, we can hardly confine it to H-deliberation. It is difficult, therefore, for Hobbes to show that H-deliberation reaches the conclusions that we reach from deliberation in ordinary life. The question that arises for the Greek Sceptics also arises for him.

474. Conflicting Views on Incontinence

Hobbes could answer these objections if he could assume that when we consider different consequences of an action, our advances and hesitations result from an estimate of overall goodness and badness. He may assume that the prospect of a larger sum of pleasures always arouses a stronger desire, so that deliberation and will result in an effort to get the apparently greater pleasure. If we assume that pleasantness and goodness are the same, both ordinary deliberation and H-deliberation are guided by belief about the overall good. This assumption makes H-deliberation appear less unlike ordinary deliberation than it really is, since it comes to somewhat similar conclusions.

This reconciliation of H-deliberation with ordinary deliberation is open to doubt if we are not always guided by overall goodness. The examples we have given suggest that the strength of our desires may diverge irrationally from our beliefs about overall good. Hobbes might try to reject our examples by arguing that in cases such as the 'irrational' fear of flying we are really exaggerating the probability of a crash. If we are more afraid of flying than of driving on a dangerous road, we must hold false beliefs about the probabilities. Relative to our estimate of probabilities, then, our fear of flying is rational, and it does not refute Hobbes's empirical assumption about H-deliberation.

But however plausible or implausible this empirical assumption may be, it raises a difficulty for Hobbes. If our last appetite is always directed towards the apparently larger sum of pleasures, we cannot act contrary to our view about what will maximize the net balance of future pleasure. This is the view that Socrates holds in the *Protagoras*; he uses it both to reject the possibility of incontinence and to explain the appearance of incontinence. In his view, we appear to be incontinent in choosing the apparently lesser pleasure over the apparently greater only because we actually exaggerate the pleasure of whatever is temporally closer.[25] Hobbes, however, criticizes the Scholastic view because it excludes incontinence, and so he cannot accept the Socratic dissolution of incontinence.

To show that the Scholastics cannot allow incontinence he claims that they are committed to accepting this argument: (1) Incontinent action is voluntary. (2) All voluntary action is initiated by the will. (4) Hence no voluntary action is contrary to our will. (5) But our will aims at what appears best all things considered. (6) In acting incontinently we do not aim at what appears best all things considered. (7) Therefore incontinent action is impossible. Hobbes believes that the Scholastics are committed to the first six steps. Since he assumes that the conclusion is unacceptable, he assumes that incontinence is possible.

Hobbes is right to suggest that incontinence raises difficulties for Aquinas' view of the will.[26] One might suppose that his account is preferable to the Scholastic account in this respect, since H-deliberation leaves room for incontinence. But the empirical assumption that brings H-deliberation closer to ordinary deliberation requires the denial of incontinence.

Hobbes's views on deliberation and will, therefore, present him with a dilemma. On the one hand, his description of H-deliberation supports his objections to the Scholastic account of will, and also allows the possibility of incontinent action. But his description does not fit his claims about the connexion between deliberation and consideration of overall good. On the other hand, he may support his claims about deliberation and overall good by the empirical assumption that we always pursue the greater apparent good; but this empirical assumption conflicts with the possibility of incontinence.

The dilemma raises a question about Hobbes's general position. He cannot easily abandon his view that deliberation is simply H-deliberation; for that is the central element in his anti-Scholastic account of the will. But since H-deliberation does not support all his claims about better and worse deliberation, we may doubt whether his non-normative description of H-deliberation supports his ethical theory.

475. Will, Passion, and Freewill

Hobbes's views about the will support his position in the controversy about freewill. His views on this controversy are most clearly seen in the dispute with Bramhall. Since Bramhall

---

[25] On Socrates see §27.   [26] On Aquinas see §295.

is sympathetic to Scholastic views about will and passion that Hobbes rejects, we might expect Hobbes to give reasons for rejecting the account of freewill that Aquinas offers. This, however, is not exactly what we find. Aquinas' view cuts across the dispute between Hobbes and Bramhall.

The disagreements between Hobbes and Bramhall recall those between Aquinas and Scotus. Both Hobbes and Bramhall reject Aquinas' intellectualism, the view that the will is determined by the greater good presented by reason. Bramhall, however, follows both Aquinas and Scotus in affirming the rationalist view that separates will from passion; on this point Hobbes is an anti-rationalist, in contrast to the mediaeval voluntarists. Bramhall is also an incompatibilist and indeterminist, since he believes in acts of freewill that cannot be parts of sequences of necessitating causes (i.e., sequences in which the earlier member is in each case sufficient for the later). Against Bramhall Hobbes defends the compatibilist view that we have attributed to Aquinas, and goes further by accepting soft determinism.

The mediaeval dispute draws our attention to possibilities that Hobbes and Bramhall overlook. Bramhall maintains a voluntarist, indeterminist, and rationalist position. He assumes that intellectualism is incompatible with rationalism, because intellectualists reduce the will to a passion, by taking it to be determined by the greater apparent good. In his view, then, the difference between will and passion matters because the will has to be free of all determination. For the same reason he assumes that rationalism requires indeterminism. Hobbes replies by rejecting both rationalism and indeterminism. Neither Hobbes nor Bramhall seems to consider rationalist compatibilism.

Bramhall holds the indeterminist view that a free agent is 'that, which, when all things are present which are needful to produce the effect, can nevertheless not produce it' (Hobbes, *LN* §§32, 35).[27] He is an indeterminist because he is a voluntarist; he appeals to the possibility of choosing the lesser good when one knows the greater good. Hence he offers Medea as an example of incontinence supporting voluntarism (§23). He takes this voluntarism to support rationalism (i.e., the rejection of Hobbes's sentimentalism) about the will. He contrasts spontaneous agents with rational and deliberative agents, and claims that only the latter are free. (Bramhall, *DLN* §6; *DTL* §8; Hobbes, *LN* §8.) He assumes that if the will is free from necessitation by passions, it is free from causal necessitation altogether.

This combination of views allies Bramhall with Scotus and Ockham, not with Aquinas. Since Aquinas believes that the will is not necessitated by passions, he speaks of freedom from necessitation, and so his remarks might suggest that he is an indeterminist. But he does not rely on indeterminism. In his view, we have freewill because the will is moved by rational deliberation rather than by the strength of the passions; this is what makes human beings masters of their own actions. Aquinas does not commit himself to Bramhall's incompatibilist indeterminism.[28] If Hobbes simply wanted to affirm determinism and compatibilism, he would have no reason to reject Aquinas' conception of freewill, since it is consistent with the compatibilist arguments against Bramhall. Similarly, Bramhall might reasonably reject Hobbes's anti-rationalism without rejecting determinism and compatibilism.

---

[27] Scotus and Ockham accept this assumption; see §§369, 388.   [28] On Aquinas see §270.

Hobbes argues for anti-rationalism against Aquinas' conception of freewill. He argues that deliberation is found in animals, and so belongs both to rational and to non-rational agency.[29] Even in human beings deliberation is not necessary for voluntary action, since impulsive and rash actions are also voluntary.[30] Hobbes suggests the reply to this claim about impulsive action; for he acknowledges that we treat it as voluntary because we assume it is subject to deliberation on some occasions, even if not immediately before acting. Aquinas' distinction between directly and indirectly voluntary actions helps to show that unpremeditated action is voluntary if is suitably connected to deliberation, even if deliberation has not immediately preceded.[31]

Hobbes's case against rationalism, then, relies primarily on his first objection, that deliberation is found in non-rational no less than in rational agents. He would be right, if his account of deliberation were right. But if his account is wrong, a Scholastic may fairly distinguish rational deliberation from the succession of impulses that makes H-deliberation. Butler reasserts this distinction as the distinction between authority and power.[32] Bramhall assumes some such distinction; Hobbes undermines it only if he shows that H-deliberation is deliberation.

Since this is Hobbes's only direct argument against the rationalist distinction between will and passion, and since it is a weak argument, a rationalist intellectualist such as Aquinas may reasonably reject Hobbes's case. Hobbes may suppose that he also has a strong indirect argument against rationalism, in his argument against indeterminism. Perhaps he assumes that an argument against indeterminism refutes not only voluntarists, who deny that anything necessitates the will, but also rationalists, who only deny that the passions necessitate the will. But an argument against indeterminism does not affect rationalism.

The weakness of Hobbes's objections to rationalism casts doubt on his account of freedom. He believes that freedom cannot intelligibly be ascribed to the will, and that human freedom cannot intelligibly consist in anything more than determination by the will; moreover, he thinks the will is nothing but the 'last appetite'. He sees no contrast between motivation by the will and motivation by the passions. Hence, since he believes in freedom, the relevant sort of freedom is internal determination by desire. If H-deliberation is not deliberation, his inferences about freedom are insecure.

476. A Hedonist Account of Desire and Emotion[33]

Hobbes links his account of deliberation to his views about pleasure and good; but it is not clear how he understands the link, and so it is not clear which of his various views is prior to

---

[29] '...horses, dogs, and other brute beasts, do demur oftentimes upon the way they are to take, the horse retiring from some strange figure that he sees, and coming on again to avoid the spur. And what else doth a man that deliberateth, but one while proceed toward action, another while retire from it, as the hope of greater good draws him, or the fear of greater evil drives him away' (Hobbes, LN §8).

[30] 'Besides, I see it is reasonable to punish a rash action, which could not be justly done by man to man, unless the same were voluntary. For no action of a man can be said to be without deliberation, though never so sudden, because it is supposed he had time to deliberate all the precedent time of his life, whether he should do that kind of action or not.' (LN §25)

[31] On Aquinas see §255.   [32] On deliberation and will see Hom. 11.2.

[33] On egoism and hedonism see Hampton, HSCT 17–24. She does not consider all the possible versions of egoism and hedonism one might attribute to Hobbes.

which. We have to try to clarify his view of the connexions between his moral psychology and his conception of value.

He treats deliberation as a succession of advances and retreats consisting in desires and aversions. He understands a desire as an advance towards anticipated pleasure. Perhaps he believes that this conception best fits an account of desire that will apply both to human beings and to animals. Or perhaps he relies on the fact that, generally, if I believe x will please me more than y, or I will enjoy x more than y, I will want x more than y. He generalizes the connexion between desire and pleasure into a general account of the nature of desire, so that he maintains psychological hedonist egoism as a theory of motives.

He applies psychological hedonism to his description of the emotions, taking their objects to be connected with the pleasure or pain that may arise in different circumstances. The objects of our passions are means to our satisfaction or security, or in some other way directly related to it. Since our security involves our relation to other people and their security, many of the passions that Hobbes considers involve comparison between myself and others on the points that affect my security. Hence he describes various passions by reference to the feelings arising at different stages in a race or competition (*EL* 9.21).

Other passions seem to have a less direct relation to one's own satisfaction and security. If I pity someone quite unrelated to me who will not affect my security, I do not believe that this person or what is happening to him actually affects my security. In this case Hobbes believes that I think of what I would feel if my security, for instance, were threatened. In thinking of the counterfactual situation, I actually have some of the feeling that I would have if the situation were actual, and so I have the feeling even when my security is not involved.[34]

But even if this appeal to self-confined pleasure is legitimate, it does not vindicate psychological hedonism; it explains the genesis of the passions, not their nature or their objects.[35] It is not clear whether Hobbes sees this, and so it is not clear whether he recognizes non-egoistic passions. At any rate, he acknowledges no exceptions to a psychological hedonist account of desires and motivation. He believes that the non-egoistic passions (if there are any) motivate us only if they seem to affect our prospects of pleasure and pain. Hobbes does not modify a psychological hedonist account of desire and action.

His hedonism includes a distinctive view about pleasure. We might connect pleasure with satisfaction or contentment, and take this to be the ultimate end of desire. This is Epicurus' account of 'static' pleasures.[36] But Hobbes argues that this view does not explain why we go on desiring and acting and would not regard the cessation of desire as a welcome outcome (*L.* 11.1). Hence, we ought not to identify pleasure with Epicurean satisfaction or contentment; we ought to identify it with Epicurean 'kinetic' pleasure. We seek means to 'secure the way of our future desire'. But securing the way of our future desire cannot be our ultimate end; for we do not want to secure the way of our future desire for its own sake.

---

[34] This particular appeal to association is not extensively used by Hobbes. Hume exploits its possibilities for explaining the other-regarding feelings and sentiments.

[35] Those who argue that Hobbes is not, or is not consistently, an egoist appeal to the difference between the source and the objects of the passions. See Gert in Hobbes, *MC* 5–13 (citing *L.* 6.46; *Hom.* 12.10); Hampton, *HSCT* 21–4; Kavka, *HMPT* 44–51; Gert, 'Egoism'; 'Mechanism'; McNeilly, 'Egoism'; Watkins, *HSI* 110–14.

[36] On Epicurus see §151.

Presumably we want the uninterrupted sequence of particular satisfactions, and we secure the way of our future desire in order to ensure that the sequence continues.[37]

477. Pleasure and Good

Hobbes's view of the relation between good, desire, and pleasure expresses self-confined egoist hedonism.[38] The different kinds of good—beautiful, delightful, and profitable—are analysed with reference to one's own pleasure.[39] This list omits the honestum, which most people regard as a good that is not assessed by reference to the agent; Hobbes leaves no room for such a good. These remarks imply that every desire is a desire for one's own pleasure or for an apparent means to one's own pleasure.

This hedonist claim seems to rest on a subjectivist analysis of judgments about goodness. In saying that everyone applies 'good' to whatever pleases himself, Hobbes may simply mean that people apply 'good' to things 'at their pleasure' (as we might say), so that their judgments about goods reflect what they desire and prefer. This alleged fact does not show that the only object of their preferences and desires is pleasure. Perhaps Hobbes moves from the general use of 'pleasure' (as in 'at their pleasure'), referring to desire and choice quite generally, to the specific use, referring to one particular object of desire and choice.

But in any case it is not clear what he means by his claim that we call 'good' whatever pleases us. He might be asserting that 'x is good' means 'x pleases me'. If, then, we grasped the meanings of our words clearly, we would realize that if I say 'What pleases me is good', I express an analytic truth that means the same as 'What pleases me pleases me'. This account of the meaning of 'good' is doubtful, for reasons suggested by Price, Sidgwick, and Moore. When anti-hedonists claim that not all goods are pleasant, they seem to disagree about a question that can be discussed on the basis of some shared assumption about the meaning of 'good'. They seem to need more than a reminder of what 'good' means.[40]

Hobbes may intend the more plausible claim that all the things we call 'good' (in the ordinary sense) really have nothing in common beyond the fact that the person calling them 'good' finds them pleasant. This claim recognizes that 'good' does not mean the same as 'pleasant to me'. When we use 'good' in the ordinary sense for actions, people, institutions, and so on, we suppose that we are ascribing to them some property beyond their being pleasant to us. But Hobbes believes that when we use 'good' with this objective sense, we

[37] On the concerns of Hobbesian prudence see Hampton, *HSCT* 37–42.

[38] 'But whatsoever is the object of any man's appetite or desire, that is it which he for his part calleth good; and the object of his hate and aversion, evil; . . . For these words of good, evil, and contemptible, are ever used with relation to the person that useth them: there being nothing simply and absolutely so; nor any common rule of good and evil to be taken from the nature of the objects themselves . . .' (*L.* 6.7) 'Every man, for his own part calleth that which pleaseth, and is delightful to himself, good; and that evil which displeaseth him: insomuch that while every man differeth from another in constitution, they differ also from one another concerning the common distinction of good and evil. Nor is there any such thing as *agathon haplôs*, that is to say, simply good. For even the goodness which we apprehend in God Almighty, is his goodness to us.' (*EL* 7.3) On 'self-confined' egoism cf. Broad, 'Egoism'.

[39] 'So that of good there be three kinds; good in the promise, that is pulchrum; good in effect, as the end desired, which is called iucundum, delightful, and good as the means, which is called utile, profitable.' (*L.* 6.8)

[40] For similar arguments see §812 on Price.

are misled, since good things have no objective goodness distinct from their pleasing the person who judges them good.

Perhaps, then, Hobbes argues: (1) All that good things have in common is their being desired by the agent who calls them 'good'. (2) All that we desire is our own pleasure. (3) Therefore, when we call things 'good', all that we are actually talking about is what we take to promote our own pleasure. The basic illusion about 'good' is the belief that it refers to something that good things have in common beyond being desired. This connexion between calling x 'good' and finding x pleasant follows from the truth of psychological hedonism (whether or not people believe it is true). It does not rest on an implausible claim about the meaning of 'good' (though Hobbes may accept such a claim).[41]

If Hobbes is right about the connexion between judgments of goodness and apparent pleasure, judgments about goodness vary not only among different people, but also within a single person at different times. He sometimes suggests that if I desire x more strongly than y, x appears pleasanter to me than y, and hence I judge x better than y. But if he believes this, it is difficult to understand how I can desire x more strongly than y while believing y to be pleasanter and better than x; hence it is difficult to see how I can be incontinent. Since Hobbes allows the possibility of incontinence, it is not easy to reconcile all his views about desire, pleasure, and goodness.

478. Practical Reason and Prudence

Hobbes's account of will, passion, and pleasure excludes one traditional role for practical reason. According to Aquinas, will differs from passion by being rational desire, formed by practical reasoning that seeks to discover the constitution of the ultimate good and the means to it. Practical reason, therefore, reaches conclusions that guide rational desire. Hobbes disagrees because he denies that will is essentially rational desire. In his view, practical reason simply discovers means to our future-directed desires for pleasure.[42]

In confining practical reason to this function Hobbes avoids questions about how practical reason and prudence (as Aristotle conceives them) can discover what is really good for us, and therefore can discover the external reasons that we already have, independently of our desires, for choosing one course of action rather than another.[43] In order to reject the Scholastic division between mere passion that is guided by pain and pleasure, and rational will that is guided by deliberation about the good, Hobbes argues that all motives either express a passion or result from deliberation about the means to satisfy a passion. He relies on his hedonistic analysis of desires.[44]

The instrumental role of reason in discovering means to future pleasure and the avoidance of future pain explains how reason can 'prescribe' (praecipere) an action and can declare an

---

[41] Cf. Hampton, *HSCT* 29.

[42] On practical reason see *Hom.* 12.1 (quoted in this section); *Civ.*, Ep. Ded. 3.31 (quoted in this section).

[43] 'And this knowledge is called experience; and the wisdom that proceedeth from it, is that ability to conjecture by the present, of what is past and to come, which men call prudence.' (*EL* 27.13)

[44] More precisely, it depends on the truth of some theory that, like hedonism, helps to explain how practical reason could be purely instrumental. Hobbes offers hedonism to fulfil this role.

action to be good, favouring the principles that Hobbes identifies with the laws of nature. Once we desire peace, reason tells us how to achieve it.[45] The laws of nature are 'precepts of reason' or 'precepts of rational nature' (*Civ.* 3.32) because they are 'certain conclusions understood by reason' (3.33) about the means to self-preservation.

In Hobbes's view, reason does not simply take for granted an antecedent desire for peace. It also declares peace to be good.[46] But it is not clear why reason should declare this without qualification; should it not say that peace is good if and only if you want the further pleasures that peace brings?

The attitude of reason to peace reflects the more general preference of reason for prudence. A preference for some present good over a greater long-term good is irrational, in Hobbes's view; it is rational to focus on the long-term rather than the short-term good. The Stoics are right to say that passions disturb the operations of reason, because they distract us from the aim that reason approves—pursuit of a long-term good.[47] Reason, therefore, directs us towards the pursuit of our long-term good, which Hobbes identifies with self-preservation.

Hobbes is right to suggest that passions lead to irrational action if they cause us to act blindly without considering all the consequences that would turn us against the passions. If anger makes us forget some goal that we prefer over revenge, it makes us frustrate our dominant desire, and hence makes us act against reason. But suppose we are well aware of the costs of acting on anger, and still have a stronger desire to act on it. What is irrational, on Hobbes's account, in acting on anger in such cases?

Hobbes avoids this objection if he restricts his claim about reason to situations in which everyone agrees in desiring peace. Since one counts as good simply whatever seems to promise one pleasure, different people's judgments about good differ, just as their pleasures differ. Hence they disagree, and their disagreement leads to strife and discord.[48] But they all dislike this strife that puts them in a state of war, and in this state of war they all prefer peace, and hence agree that peace is good.[49] Peace is not good apart from their different desires,

[45] 'And thus much for the ill condition, which man by mere nature is actually placed in; though with a possibility to come out of it, consisting partly in the passions, partly in his reason. The passions that incline man to peace, are fear of death; desire of such things as are necessary to commodious living; and a hope by their industry to obtain them. And reason suggesteth convenient articles of peace, upon which men may be drawn to agreement.' (*L.* 13.13–14)

[46] 'They therefore who could not agree concerning a present, do agree concerning a future good, which indeed is a work of reason; for things present are obvious to the sense, things to come to our reason only. Reason declaring (or 'prescribing' (praecipiente) peace to be good, it follows by the same reason, that all the necessary means to peace be good also . . . But because men cannot put off this same irrational appetite, whereby they greedily prefer the present good (to which, by strict consequence, many unforeseen evils do adhere) before the future, it happens, that though all men do agree in the commendation of the foresaid virtues, yet they disagree still concerning their nature . . .' (*Civ.* 3.31–2)

[47] 'They are called perturbations because they frequently obstruct right reasoning. They obstruct right reasoning in this, that they militate against the real good and in favour of the apparent and most immediate good, which turns out frequently to be evil when everything associated with it hath been considered. . . . Therefore, although the real good must be sought in the long term, which is the job of reason, appetite seizeth upon a present good without foreseeing the greater evils that necessarily attach to it. Therefore appetite perturbs and impedes the operations of reason; whence it is rightly called a perturbation.' (*Hom.* 12.1) 'Therefore in this instance the emotions need to be governed by reason. For reason is that which, by measuring and comparing both our powers and those of the objects regulates the amount now of hope and then of fear, so that we may neither be mocked by hopes nor lose by fear without just cause those goods that we have.' (*Hom.* 12.4) See also 12.9.

[48] On this argument see §490.

[49] 'We must know therefore, that good and evil are names given to things to signify the inclination, or aversion of them by whom they were given. But the inclinations of men are diverse, according to their diverse constitutions, customs, opinions; as we may see in those things we apprehend by sense, as by tasting, touching, smelling; but much

but in the state of discord that (according to Hobbes) results from disagreement, everyone's desires coincide, because everyone sees that strife frustrates their attempts to secure the way of their future desire.

In this specific case, therefore, reason says just the same thing to everyone, since it tells everyone truly that peace is a means to satisfying their desires. This does not mean that in all circumstances reason prescribes one single course of action to everyone irrespective of their desires. Hence, when reason declares peace and the means to it to be good, it is not really saying more than Hobbes's theory allows it to say. It simply takes for granted the agreement of desires for peace in this state of general disagreement, and issues its precepts on that assumption.

This is a rather elegant result that Hobbes might well take to confirm the soundness of his method. We might reject his simplifying reduction of good to pleasure, on the ground that we make objective judgments about goodness; and do we not need objective judgments in order to find a rational moral basis for political society? Hobbes answers that we do not need the sort of objectivity that he denies about goodness. On the contrary, once we recognize the consequences of his subjectivist view, we can see an acceptable substitute for objectivity. The subjectivity of value judgments, given the actual differences between human beings, leads to discord; but discord, given the similarities between human beings, leads to the unanimous desire for peace.

Hobbes's account of the role of reason, therefore, fits his general view of motivation. He does not revert to the Scholastic view of practical reason that conflicts with his normal view of the role of reason.[50] If we have an overriding desire for self-preservation, we discover the means to it only by reasoning about future goods. If we do not consider the long-term consequences of our action, we frustrate our desire for self-preservation. In the same way we may expect reason to regulate hope and fear; for baseless fear is based on a false supposition about the future, and reason is needed to find true or plausible beliefs that guide our fears. Someone who acts on a fear resulting from groundless beliefs about the future acts 'against reason' by acting contrary to beliefs about what promotes the satisfaction of the overriding desire for self-preservation, or by failing to consider what promotes the satisfaction of this overriding desire.

And so when Hobbes says that reason declares peace to be good, the declaration by reason is elliptical; it means that in these circumstances of strife where everyone wants to get rid of strife, reason declares that peace is a means to the ending of strife. Since human beings are always either in a state of war or in danger of relapsing into a state of war, they always want to avoid strife, and therefore reason declares peace to be good. The declaration is not categorical, in Kant's sense, by being independent of human inclinations; it is a hypothetical imperative that applies to actual situations.

---

more in those which pertain to the common actions of life, where what this man commends, (that is to say, calls good) the other undervalues, as being evil; Nay, very often the same man at diverse times, praises, and dispraises the same thing. Whilst thus they do, necessary it is there should be discord, and strife: They are therefore so long in the state of war, as by reason of the diversity of the present appetites, they mete good and evil by diverse measures. All men easily acknowledge this state, as long as they are in it, to be evil, and by consequence that Peace is good.' (*Civ.* 3.31)

    50 Gert in Hobbes, *MC* 14–16, discusses Hobbes on practical reason.

Hobbes's view does not imply that it is irrational to act for the sake of revenge rather than self-preservation, if one acts in the light of true beliefs about the consequences of both courses of action. But Hobbes assumes that reason favours the means to self-preservation, because he assumes that when we see that we must choose between an action that promotes our self-preservation and an action that threatens our self-preservation for some shorter-term end, we desire the first course of action more strongly. If, then, we see the consequences for self-preservation, we choose the action that promotes it. Exposure to reason always results in self-preserving action. 'Irrational' action is chosen with less than full awareness of the consequences.

These assumptions about motivation, however, revive the difficulty that arises from Hobbes's views about incontinence. For reason speaks in favour of peace only if our strongest desire is for self-preservation and the means to it. But if we desire something else more strongly than we desire the means to self-preservation, reason should tell us to do what satisfies this other desire. Since Hobbes recognizes that we sometimes have other desires stronger than the desire for self-preservation, he should also agree that reason does not always declare that peace is good. His own views cast doubt on the empirical assumptions that support his claims about practical reason.[51]

Hobbes's treatment of practical reason, therefore, displays two aspects of his reductive outlook. He wants to reduce claims about reason and morality to psychological claims grounded in his account of human nature. This reduction is partly eliminative, showing that there is no sound basis for some traditional beliefs, and partly vindicative, showing that traditional beliefs obscurely grasp some genuine features of human nature. Hobbes's account of the distinction between will and passion is eliminative, arguing that scholastic rationalism is misguided in drawing a distinction. But he intends his reduction of prudence to vindicate it.

The first aspect of his position, however, raises questions about the second. His eliminative treatment of will and passion implies that he can endorse prudence as rational only because he makes an implausible assumption—implausible even within his own account of the passions—about motivation. His position would be more consistent if he were to deny that prudence itself is rational, and to argue that it is rational to follow the prudent course of action only if we have the relevant desire. He ought to agree that when our desires are relevantly different, prudence is not rational, since we will not adopt the prudent course of action when we are informed about the consequences of the choices open to us. Hobbes does not draw this conclusion from his account of practical reason, but Hume draws it.[52]

479. Pleasure, Reason, and the Human Good: Rejection of Eudaemonism

Hobbes's views about motivation and practical reason require the rejection of Scholastic views about the human good. Aquinas follows Plato and Aristotle in taking happiness to be

---

[51] On reason and motivation see Hampton, *HSCT* 34–42. She introduces an appeal to physiological abnormality to explain why passions are against 'reason' (what one would want if one were in a normal physiological condition). This appeal disguises the controversial move as a physiological speculation.

[52] On Hume see §736.

the goal of rational will as opposed to non-rational passion. Reason approves what is good for oneself as a whole, as opposed to the more limited end sought by a particular passion. Greek eudaemonism asserts that whatever I choose for its own sake I regard as either a means to, or a part of, the good for me; but this restriction does not imply that the only thing I can choose for its own sake is a state exclusively of myself. We can consistently accept eudaemonism and value our friend's good for our own sake, if we regard our friend's good as part of the life that is best for us. While all the goods that I choose for their own sake are self-referential, they need not all be self-confined. Whether they are all self-confined is a further question to be answered by an account of what happiness consists in.

Hobbes's rejection of a division between will and passion and between good and pleasure commits him to the rejection of the ultimate good as an object of will. His views require him to go further than most of his hedonist predecessors go in rejecting eudaemonism.

Some hedonists take hedonism to be subordinate to eudaemonism. Epicurus agrees with Aristotle and Aquinas in taking the ultimate good to be a proper starting point for ethical argument; then he argues that pleasure meets reasonable formal criteria for the final good.[53] According to Aristotle, these criteria include completeness and self-sufficiency, measured by reference to the fulfilment of human nature. Epicurus accepts these criteria, and argues that pleasure—with certain qualifications—satisfies them.

Hobbes, however, does not subordinate pleasure to happiness, since he does not recognize any more general or more ultimate end than my own pleasure. He appeals to pleasure, as the Cyrenaics do, as an alternative to the eudaemonist's ultimate good. In his view, everything I choose for its own sake is some pleasure of my own, and so must be some self-confined condition; it must be a state of myself that does not include (though it may causally depend on) a state of someone or something else.[54]

He opposes eudaemonism by rejecting belief in an ultimate end beyond the continual pursuit of pleasure. He argues that if there were a last end we could reach, our desires would come to an end, and that would not be a desirable life.[55] He recognizes a difference between close and distant ends, but he recognizes no ultimate end. In claiming that the felicity of this life does not consist in the repose of a mind satisfied, Hobbes alludes to the familiar fact that human life is subject to changes and vicissitudes, and that it is not reasonable to look for complete satisfaction in these circumstances. Aquinas agrees with Hobbes on this point (SG iii 48);[56] that is part of his reason for concluding that the degree of happiness that we can achieve in this life is incomplete (imperfecta).

Hobbes, however, draws the more extreme conclusion that complete satisfaction is not only unavailable, but undesirable. When we achieve any end we were pursuing, we stop acting. If, then, the ultimate end were attainable, it would require the cessation of activity.

---

[53] Socrates may agree with Epicurus. See §21.

[54] Kavka, HMPT 40–1, discusses this aspect of self-confined egoism. See also Gert, 'Psychology'.

[55] 'To which end we are to consider, that the felicity of this life, consisteth not in the repose of a mind satisfied. For there is no such finis ultimus (utmost aim) nor summum bonum (greatest good,) as is spoken of in the books of the old moral philosophers. Nor can a man any more live, whose desires are at an end, than he, whose senses and imaginations are at a stand.' (L. 11.1) 'But for an utmost end, in which the ancient philosophers have placed felicity, and disputed much concerning the way thereto, there is no such thing in this world, nor way to it, more than to Utopia; for while we live, we have desires, and desire presupposeth a further end.' (EL 7.6)

[56] On Aquinas see §280.

Since a life without activity is not good for a human being, the achievement of an ultimate end is would not be good for a human being.

In this objection to the eudaemonist belief Hobbes does not distinguish process from activity, as Aristotle understands them.[57] Hobbes assumes that action, as opposed to passive enjoyment, is instrumental, aimed at the achieving of some end separate from it. Aristotle rejects this assumption, since he recognizes activities that are parts of happiness and to be chosen for their own sakes. If we achieve the ultimate end, we still have a motive for action; for we want to perform the activities that are characteristic of being happy. Aristotle's conception seems ridiculous from Hobbes's point of view only because Hobbes cannot see the point of Aristotle's distinction between process and activity. He cannot see the point of it because it conflicts with Hobbes's view that action is all purely instrumental.

Even if Aristotle avoids Hobbes's objection on this point, Hobbes has a further objection to a traditional view of the ultimate good. In his view, it requires a definite list of activities constituting the human good; but any such list fails to recognize that human desires and aims are varied and mutable. According to Hobbes, our conception of the good always changes and develops, according to how much we have already got. Since the achievement of one end leads us to look for something beyond it, we cannot determine any fixed final good.

Perhaps eudaemonism does not require the sort of list that Hobbes rejects. The mere recognition of an ultimate good does not commit us to any definite claims about its content. But this defence of eudaemonism concedes Hobbes's main point; it seems pointless to recognize a final good if we cannot form any fairly definite and defensible views about its content. As Aristotle says, we recognize a final good and ask what it is so that we can use our answer to this question in deciding what to do. Hence we expect our inquiry to discover desirable activities specifying the human good.

Still, Hobbes's objection misinterprets the eudaemonist's commitment to a 'fixed' final good. Aristotle need not recognize any determinate set of particular activities that constitute the good. He need only claim that the activities in question fall into some relatively definite types. It might well be true that if we achieve our aim of knowing one language, say, we set ourselves to learn another; but these are two exercises of our language-learning capacity. Similarly, if the continual progress of desire from one object to another stays within the types of capacities whose fulfilment Aristotle takes to constitute the good, such progress does not count against the Aristotelian view.

480. The Instability of Desire

A cogent objection to Aristotle, then, requires us to deny that the fulfilment of any definite types of capacities constitutes the human good. To see why Hobbes might deny this, we may point to the instability of desires for long-term goals. If a ten-year-old child wants to be a pilot, it would be unwise for her to form, or for us to form on her behalf, a plan for her to be a pilot; for by the time she can do anything to put the plan into effect, she may have lost her enthusiasm for being a pilot and decided to be a rock star instead, and may

---

[57] Aristotle on activity; see §95.

then have abandoned this second enthusiasm in order to be a stockbroker. In this case the best advice would perhaps be to secure the way of her future desire, not to tie her to one specific plan of life. Hobbes may believe that all our long-term desires, apart from the desire for pleasure, are unstable in this way, so that it is futile to try to construct a conception of an ultimate end. The only sensible long-term plan, therefore, is to secure the way of our future desire.

This does not refute an Aristotelian view of the final good. Even if people change their minds about long-term ends, they may still have a sufficiently determinate ultimate good.[58] We may be able to see why, in their different circumstances, they change their conceptions of their good; as Aristotle suggests, different circumstances and experiences make the value of one or another good more obvious to them (EN 1095a23–5). We may be able to correct the one-sided conceptions they form as a result of different experiences. Such variation, therefore, does not undermine the claim that an Aristotelian conception of the good fits human capacities.

This defence of Aristotle conflicts with Hobbes's explanation of variation in people's views about the good. He believes that the different things that are good for us are good because we happen to desire them; hence we cannot discover which things are good for us whether or not we happen to desire them. This desire-based conception of the good, however, needs some defence; the bare assertion of it to begs a crucial question against the Aristotelian conception. Hobbes believes we accept a desire-based conception as soon as we accept psychological hedonism and reject any division between the will and the passions. If, however, we are sympathetic to an Aristotelian conception of the good, we have a good reason for rejecting some of the premises of Hobbes's argument for these other positions.

Does Hobbes derive psychological hedonism from the assimilation of will to passion, or does he argue in the reverse direction? Perhaps he takes psychological hedonism to be so obvious in its own right that it is a firm basis both for the assimilation of will to passion and for a desire-based conception of the good.[59] He accepts hedonism because it expresses the basic fact (in his view) that people's judgments about goodness simply reflect what they prefer, and hence (as he supposes) what pleases them. If his argument relies on the subjective character of judgments about goods, it rests on a claim that he does not defend fully against an Aristotelian alternative.

From an Aristotelian point of view, therefore, Hobbes is one of the people who argue too hastily from variation in evaluative judgments to metaphysical subjectivism (EN 1094b14–19). He does not show that observed variations in judgment require the subjectivist explanation. As Aristotle points out, if sick people value health more than habitually healthy people value it, that disagreement is easily explained by their different perspectives. Again, if some people prefer lobster and others prefer cheese, and we cannot show that one is really better than the other, that may be because they are equally good.[60]

Hobbes's convictions about goods reflect a more general feature of his moral psychology. Aristotelian eudaemonism includes a belief in external reasons. If external reasons must be accessible in principle to deliberation, Hobbes's purely psychological account of deliberation

---

[58] It needs to be determinate in the sense previously explained (allowing for different ways of achieving the same good).

[59] Butler on Hobbes on pleasure and happiness; see §688.   [60] See Reid's comment on this example; §829.

rules out external reasons; for recognition of reasons, in his view, consists in the awareness of the comparative strength of our desires. Perhaps this is why Hobbes takes his specific points about the insatiable character of desire to refute the whole Aristotelian conception of the human good.

Aristotle believes that in attributing a nature to a human being, we attribute desires with a particular rational structure, because we recognize not only mere desires, but also rational desires that are guided by comparative evaluations derived from a final good. In Aristotle's view, the examination of human capacities and circumstances results in the discovery of a conception of the good. This conception shows what desires a rational agent has good reasons to acquire. Such reasons are external to an agent's desires.

In Hobbes's view, examination of human nature does not reveal these external reasons. We examine human desires, and discover their relative strength, and the means to their satisfaction. This disagreement with Aristotle rests partly on the analysis of deliberation and reasons that we have examined. Since deliberation simply records a series of inclinations of different strengths, it cannot find a course of action that rests on the best reasons. The reasons that emerge from Hobbes's analysis of human nature are strictly internal and dependent on desires.[61]

481. Aristotelian Teleology

Hobbes's rejection of the traditional conception of the ultimate end, and of the whole Aristotelian conception of human nature that supports Aristotelian eudaemonism, rests partly on his broader reasons for doubting the whole Aristotelian argument. In Aristotle's view, we can discover a creature's good from examining its nature. In both human and non-human cases we can discover the characteristic activity that is essential to this organism, distinguishes it from others, and is the goal of its other processes and actions. This argument is summed up in the appeal to the human function.

Hobbes agrees with many of his contemporaries that Aristotelian teleology is incompatible with the truth of corpuscular explanations, because they believe the Aristotelian claims to require empirically undiscoverable non-bodily causal mechanisms with no corpuscular basis. This belief underlies Locke's criticism of substantial forms, entelechies, and so on,[62] on the assumption that they involve the mechanical explanation as we find in corpuscular explanations (in Aristotelian terms, involving material and efficient causes). Since teleological claims do not describe corpuscular mechanisms, they must (it is assumed) be attempts to describe occult, non-corpuscular mechanisms. The interpretation rests on dubious assumptions, accepted by Hobbes, about the Aristotelian conception of formal and final causation.

These doubts about Aristotelian teleology do not imply the rejection of teleology. Boyle objects not to teleology itself, but to Peripatetic views of nature that (he supposes) introduce additional agents besides God, and conflict with the freedom and transcendence of God;

---

[61] On external reasons see §259 (Aquinas), §684 (Butler).
[62] See, e.g., Locke, *EHU* ii 23.3; 31.6–8 (on substantial forms); iii 10.14.

these views reflect an 'idolatrous' conception of nature.[63] Hobbes agrees with Boyle in rejecting agents distinct from God that have their own inherent goal-directed natures. He treats the study of human action as part of the study of 'motion'. Deliberation and desire should be understood, in his view, as the result of the interplay between motions of varying strengths that determine the motion of the human being as a whole. He regards desire as genuine motion, and attacks those who treat it as merely metaphorical motion (L. 6.2).

He has a further reason for scepticism about Aristotelian teleology in morals and politics. Teleological claims about the proper functions and aims of the political community and of the ruler were used to support demands for reform or for limits on the power of the ruler, or for revolutionary action in support of such claims. Hobbes regards such claims as dangerous errors.[64] Even those who agreed with Hobbes's support for the Royalist side in the Civil War did not welcome him as an ally, since they welcomed neither his rejection of traditional arguments nor his use of arguments that appeared to them to place the state on the wrong basis.[65]

Hobbes, then, follows Aristotle in arguing for a conception of the human good from claims about human nature.[66] He disagrees with Aristotle on the conclusions that can be drawn about the human good from an appeal to human nature. In particular he denies that we can discover anything like an Aristotelian ultimate end.

He therefore approaches the task of describing moral good and evil without Aristotelian assumptions. He does not believe that the human good consists in a life that realizes human capacities under the control of practical reason. The examination of human capacities and their relations does not help us to discover the virtues. Nor does he claim that the good for a human being essentially includes the good of others, because he cannot rely on the argument about self-realization that leads Aristotle to this conclusion. Hence he denies that a human being is naturally social.[67]

Though Hobbes's opposition to Aristotelian eudaemonism reflects a broader opposition to Aristotelian teleology, this broader opposition does not wholly explain the dispute about the human good. If Hobbes had agreed with Aristotle about the good, he could have expressed his agreement within a non-Aristotelian account of the physical world. His attempt to reduce deliberation to a process that can be understood in purely psychological and non-normative terms is not required by post-Aristotelian physical science; it seems to reflect doubts about practical reason that are independent of general doubts about teleology.

Perhaps, therefore, we should explain Hobbes's opposition to Aristotelian ethics by going back to his initial complaint about contemporary moral philosophy, that its appeals to practical reason, natural ends, objective goods, and so on, simply lead to disagreement. To resolve the disagreement, he tries to go below the normative level to purely psychological

---

[63] See Boyle, FE iv 48–51. Leibniz answers accusation of idolatry, in 'On nature itself'. In general I assume that Hobbes accepts his professed theological doctrines and puts them forward as seriously meant. Whether or not (as a matter of biography) he sincerely accepted them, we can account for their content and presentation, and for the hostile reaction of many Christian readers, without assuming that they were either insincere or were meant to be recognized as insincere. Martinich, TGL, offers an elaborate defence of the sincerity of Hobbes's Christianity. Curley's opposing position is briefly set out in Hobbes, L., pp. xii–xiv, xl–xlvi.

[64] See Laird and Barker, cited in §469.   [65] Some of these critics are discussed by Mintz, HL and Bowle, HC.

[66] On the appeal to nature cf. §675 (Hobbes v. Butler); §§727–8 (Hume).

[67] See Civ. 1.12; L. 17.6–12. On Cudworth's criticism see Passmore, RC 72; Hampton, HSCT 10. See also §§531, 564, 610.

descriptions. He agrees with the Greek Sceptics in separating the normative from the purely psychological, but he uses the separation for different purposes. In the Sceptics' view, reflexion on normative disagreements causes us to abandon the normative outlook in favour of simply 'yielding' to appearances. Hobbes believes that a purely psychological description allows him to interpret normative claims in psychological terms, and so to formulate normative claims that we will accept, once we form the enlightened view of human nature.

We might argue that Hobbes's psychological picture is simpler than Aristotle's. He begins from the desire for pleasure; we already recognize this as a desire that sufficiently explains an action. According to Hobbes, we need not recognize any further desires, irreducible to this one, in order to understand our actions in general. The task of arguing from an Aristotelian account of the ultimate good to specific virtues is difficult; many of the obscurities in Aristotle's arguments remain in Aquinas' arguments. Since Hobbes's argument avoids Aristotelian obscurities, it is worth examining, to see whether it offers a plausible account of moral good and evil.

35

HOBBES: FROM HUMAN NATURE TO MORALITY

482. Moral Philosophy, Old and New

Hobbes tries to follow an 'idoneous principle of tractation' in moral philosophy, by beginning with an account of human nature and human motives.[1] On this basis he hopes to improve the lamentable situation in which knowledge of the law of nature has failed to grow 'beyond its ancient stature'.[2] He assumes that sound moral philosophy will discuss natural law, but will reject previous views of natural law. In claiming that knowledge of natural law has not advanced beyond its ancient stature, Hobbes implies that Scholastic discussions of natural law have not advanced moral philosophy. We can perhaps clarify his aims in moral philosophy if we see what he rejects in Scholastic views of natural law.

Aquinas introduces natural law as part of an Aristotelian and eudaemonist theory. The moral virtues are the states of character that constitute the appropriate control by practical reason, aiming at the good of the agent or the good of others or the good of the community; the good of others and of the community enter because they are parts of the good of the agent. Virtuous actions are all connected to natural law (*ST* 1–2 q94 a3). Natural law prescribes the first principles of ethics, grasped by universal conscience (q94 a1 ad2), because 'everything to which a human being tends in accordance with his nature belongs to the law of nature' (q94 a3). The principles of natural law are those that human beings grasp in the rational pursuit of the ultimate end to which they tend by nature. We tend naturally towards our ultimate end, and we are capable of rational understanding of the means to it; in exercising this rational understanding correctly, we grasp the principles of natural law.

Aquinas does not believe, then, that natural law introduces a source of moral principles apart from the rational pursuit of one's own happiness. He does not introduce a deontological element in morality that is separate from his teleological account of the moral virtues. He believes that a correct grasp of the ultimate end for a human being also grasps the principles of natural law. We grasp the natural law insofar as we grasp the first principles of practical

---

[1] *Civ.*, Ep. Ded.; see §469. On Hobbes's aims see Hampton, 'Naturalism'.   [2] *Civ.*, Ep. Ded.

reason.[3] Since the task of practical reason is to discover what constitutes and promotes the human good, our view about the content of natural law will match our view of the nature and scope of practical reason.

Aquinas' successors disagree about the relation between the natural law and the will of God. Scotus and Ockham allow more of what Aquinas counts as natural law to depend on the free will of God; they take the rightness of the various precepts to consist in their being prescribed by God. Suarez's discussion of disputes about divine commands leads him to distinguish two aspects of natural law: its status as law depends on divine commands, but it is natural because it prescribes and forbids actions that are intrinsically right and wrong apart from divine commands.

These different aspects of Scholastic discussion of natural law influence Hobbes. Indeed, the extent of their influence makes it initially surprising that he believes the Scholastics have made so little progress. He agrees with Aquinas' claim that we grasp the principles of natural law by grasping the end to which human nature is naturally inclined. Insofar as he derives an account of the virtues from an account of human nature Hobbes agrees with Aquinas. Hence he identifies moral philosophy with the science of the laws of nature. The true doctrine of the laws of nature specifies the virtues and vices that are the subject matter of moral philosophy.[4]

Hobbes suggests that traditional views do not regard moral philosophy as the doctrine of the laws of nature. As we have seen in discussing Grotius, this suggestion is ambiguous. Scholastic views certainly connect the requirements of the virtues with the provisions of natural law. But it is not so clear whether they regard morality as essentially or fundamentally natural law. Suarez argues that though intrinsic morality is prescribed by natural law, this is not essential to intrinsic morality. According to Suarez, moral philosophy is primarily the science of the honestum, of what is fitting for rational nature; it is the science of natural law only because it is necessarily true that natural law prescribes what is fitting for rational nature.

The sense Hobbes attaches to the claim that moral philosophy is about natural law depends on the sense he attaches to claims about natural law. Suarez distinguishes morality from natural law because he believes that natural law is essentially law, and that law essentially requires the command of a legislator, whereas intrinsic morality is prior to natural law. How does Hobbes understand the natural basis of natural law—the facts that Suarez takes to constitute intrinsic morality? And how does he take natural law to be related to divine commands?

483. Human Nature and Natural Law

Hobbes believes that natural law rests on the requirements of human nature. On this point he agrees with Aquinas and his successors. But he departs from Aquinas in claiming this law

---

[3] On Aquinas see §272.

[4] 'The science of them [sc. the laws of nature] is the true and only moral philosophy. For moral philosophy is nothing but the science of what is good, and evil, in the conversation and society of mankind.' (L. 15.40)

simply prescribes means to self-preservation.[5] Past philosophers did not see this essential connexion with self-preservation.[6] They were roughly right about which traits are virtues, but they were wrong about what makes them virtues, not seeing their essential connexion with 'peaceable, sociable, and comfortable living'.[7]

It would be misleading to suggest that previous philosophers thought the virtues do not contribute to peaceful and sociable living. Aquinas and others suppose that this contribution is essential to the virtues, because peaceful and sociable living fulfils the nature of human beings as rational and sociable creatures. But Aquinas believes that the study of human nature allows us to form a conception of the human good that shows us how the moral virtues perfect human nature and achieve the good; peaceful and sociable living is only part of this good. Hobbes denies that when we study human nature we discover that human beings have a natural ultimate good that supports an account of the virtues. If he is right, we cannot discover from the examination of human nature and the human good that we have good reason to follow the principles of natural law. Suarez and Grotius[8] must therefore be wrong to believe that some actions are intrinsically right (honesta) by being appropriate for rational nature. Since their view presupposes that the human good consists in more than the satisfaction of desires, it is not open to Hobbes.[9]

To reach his account of the virtues, therefore, Hobbes appeals to his account of human nature. He rejects the Aristotelian view—later revived by Butler—that human nature constitutes a system, rather than a collection of desires, and that the task of practical reason

---

[5] A law of nature is '. . . a precept, or general rule, found out by reason, by which a man is forbidden to do that which is destructive of his life or taketh away the means of preserving the same . . .' (L. 14.3).

[6] 'Now the science of virtue and vice, is moral philosophy; and therefore the true doctrine of the laws of nature is the true moral philosophy. But the writers of moral philosophy, though they acknowledge the same virtues and vices: Yet not seeing wherein consisted their goodness; nor that they came to be praised, as the means of peaceable, sociable, and comfortable living; place them in a mediocrity of passions: as if not the cause, but the degree of daring, made fortitude; or not the cause, but the quantity of a gift, made liberality.' (L 15.40) 'But because men cannot put off this same irrational appetite, whereby they greedily prefer the present good (to which, by strict consequence, many unforeseen evils doe adhere) before the future, it happens, that though all men doe agree in the commendation of the foresaid virtues, yet they disagree still concerning their nature, to wit, in what each of them doth consist; for as oft as another's good action displeaseth any man, that action hath the name given of some neighbouring vice; likewise the bad actions, which please them, are ever entitled to some Virtue; whence it comes to pass that the same action is praised by these, and called virtue, and dispraised by those, and termed vice. Neither is there as yet any remedy found by philosophers for this matter; for since they could not observe the goodness of actions to consist in this, that it was in order to peace, and the evil in this, that it related to discord, they built a moral philosophy wholly estranged from the moral Law, and unconstant to itself; for they would have the nature of virtues seated in a certain kind of mediocrity between two extremes, and the vices in the extremes themselves; which is apparently false . . .' (Civ. 3.32). On the doctrine of the mean cf. EL 17.14. For further discussion see Skinner, RRPH 322–6.

[7] 'Yet reason is still the same, and changeth not her end, which is peace and defence; nor of the mind which the means to attain them, to wit, those virtues we have declared above, and which cannot be abrogated by any custom or law whatsoever.' (Civ. 3.29) 'But forasmuch as all men are carried away by the violence of their passion, and by evil customs do those things which are commonly said to be against the law of nature; it is not the consent of passions, or consent in some error gotten by custom, that makes the law of nature. Reason is no less of the nature of man than passion, and is the same in all men, because all men agree in the will to be directed and governed in the way to that which they desire to attain, namely their own good, which is the work of reason: there can therefore be no other law of nature than reason, nor no other precepts of natural law, than those which declare unto us the ways of peace, where the same may be obtained, and of defence where it may not.' (EL 15.1)

[8] On Hobbes and Grotius see Tuck, 'Modern', cited at §466n27. His comparison does not mention this important difference over the honestum.

[9] On the relation of Hobbes's position to the voluntarism of Scotus and Ockham see §391.

is to discover what is appropriate for the needs of the system as a whole.[10] In Hobbes's view, human nature is a collection of desires without a system; practical reason, therefore, must simply look for the means to satisfy one's predominant desire. If our predominant desire is to secure the way of our future desire, we care most about our self-preservation. Practical reason justifies the laws of nature if it shows that they specify means to self-preservation. This is what Hobbes tries to show about the laws of nature.[11]

When Hobbes attributes the laws of nature to reason, he means that reason prescribes means to ends that, in the circumstances Hobbes describes, everyone will want more than they want any other ends. These precepts and prescriptions, in his view, depend on our desires, but they are nonetheless genuine precepts of reason and rational nature.[12] When 'reason prescribes peace to be good',[13] its prescription is the empirical proposition that peace promotes the satisfaction of our desires in the specific circumstances of the state of nature.

We might think that this empirical proposition falls short of a precept of reason, since it does not assert that we ought to seek peace, that we have a reason to seek peace, or that we have a duty or obligation to seek peace. Hobbes, however, believes that he can answer this objection, since he believes that natural laws impose obligations. To see what he means by this, we need to grasp his conception of obligation. Since he defines obligation by reference to rights, we need to discuss his view of rights before trying to understand his view of obligation.

484. Freedom and Rights

Hobbes explains an obligation by contrasting it with a right. Being obliged to do F is incompatible with being free to do either F or not-F, and therefore incompatible with having the right to do F or not-F. Hence, if we are obliged to do F, we lack the right to do F or not-F. These connexions between obligation, freedom, and rights make it reasonable for Hobbes to explain obligation as the absence of freedom. Obligations require some restriction of the right of nature, which is one's freedom to use the means of self-defence.[14] Hobbes does not treat this right as a morally protected or justified freedom; he means simply that an individual is not physically prevented from doing what he thinks will preserve him. If someone has a right to preserve himself, it does not follow that it is wrong to prevent him.

Elsewhere, however, Hobbes seems to treat a right as a morally protected liberty, something that we are morally permitted to do, or a 'blameless liberty'.[15] We might suppose

---

[10] On human nature as a system rather than a collection see §77 (Aristotle); 679–80 (Butler).

[11] Hobbes's restricted conception of natural law, confining it to the preservation of peace, may be compared with Selden's conception, as described by Tuck, *PG* 216–17.

[12] In *L.* 14.3 'praeceptum . . . sive regula generalis' is used for 'precept or general rule'.

[13] *Civ.* 3.31 (quoted in §478). The EV has 'declares'. Silverthorne translates 'teaches'.

[14] 'The right of nature . . . is the liberty each man hath, to use his own power, as he will himself, for the preservation of his own nature; that is to say, of his own life; and consequently, of doing any thing, which in his own judgment, and reason, he shall conceive to be the aptest means thereunto.' (*L.* 14.1) '. . . right consisteth in liberty to do, or to forbear; whereas law determineth and bindeth to one of them: so that law and right differ as much as obligation and liberty, which in one and the same matter are inconsistent' (14.3). Pufendorf, *JNG* i 6.10, criticizes Hobbes's account of right and obligation. See also §624 on Clarke.

[15] 'Neither by the word right is anything else signified, than that liberty which every man hath to make use of his natural faculties according to right reason. Therefore the first foundation of natural right is this, that every man as much

that in claiming that we 'must' be allowed a right to all necessary means to an end that we have a right to pursue, Hobbes introduces a moral claim. If he were talking about purely physical freedom, the claim about means would apparently not follow. If I am not physically prevented from pursuing my self-preservation, it does not follow that I am free to use all the necessary means to it; if I am in the middle of a desert, I may not have access to water.

But perhaps Hobbes will reject this argument. He might reply that if I am physically prevented from using all the necessary means to an end, I am also prevented from pursuing the end, and hence I lack the freedom to pursue it. And so he might still defend a non-moral interpretation of his claims about natural rights.

What does he mean by claiming that we have the natural right to use our faculties 'according to right reason' for our self-preservation?[16] We might take this clause to restrict our right to do whatever we think will promote our preservation; perhaps 'right reason' confines our right to means that accord with right reason. In that case, the use of a rationally unjustifiable means to preserve ourselves (e.g., by practising unnecessary cruelty on our opponents) would exceed our right. Rights, therefore, seem to be confined to legitimate liberties, those that others ought to respect.

But the reference to right reason does not require Hobbes to restrict rights to legitimate liberties. He may simply mean that human beings are free by nature to preserve themselves to the best of their ability, because in the state of nature nothing impedes our taking this course of action. To say this is not to exclude our being free to do other things; hence our right is not confined to prudent action.[17]

Hobbes, however, does not believe—or at least does not always believe—that our natural right extends to everything that is physically possible in the state of nature. Some remarks (outside *Leviathan*) about violations of the law of nature in war suggest ways of exceeding our natural rights. We are physically at liberty to act cruelly or to get drunk, but we violate

as in him lies endeavour to protect his life and members. But because it is vain for a man to have a right to the end, if the right to the necessary means be denied him, it follows, that since every man hath a right to preserve himself, he must also be allowed a right (consequens est . . . ut unusquisque ius etiam habeat, LV) to use all the means, and do all the actions, without which he cannot preserve himself.' (*Civ* 1.7–8) At *EL* 14.6 Hobbes describes a right as a blameless liberty: 'And forasmuch as necessity of nature maketh men to will and desire *bonum sibi*, that which is good for themselves . . . it is not against reason, that a man doth all he can to preserve his own body and limbs both from death and pain. And that which is not against reason, men call *right* or *jus* or *blameless liberty* of using our own natural power and ability. It is therefore a right of nature, that every man may preserve his own life and limbs, with all the power he hath.' *EL* 14.10 seems to imply that statements about rights have some moral content: 'For seeing all things he willeth, must therefore be good to him in his own judgment because he willeth them, and may tend to his preservation some time or other, or he may judge so, and we have made him judge thereof, . . . it followeth that all things may rightly also be done by him. . . . insomuch that *jus* and *utile*, right and profit, is the same thing.' *EL* 14.13 suggests that might makes right: 'A man therefore that hath another man in his power to rule or govern, to do good to, or harm, hath right, by the advantage of this his present power, to take caution at his pleasure, for his security against that other in time to come'. Some of these rights are retained in the commonwealth: 'As it was necessary that a man should not retain his right to every thing, so also was it, that he should retain his right to some things . . . Nor doth the law of nature command any divesting of other rights than of those only which cannot be retained without the loss of peace.' (*EL* 17.2) On Hobbes on the right of nature see Tuck, *NRT* 120–32; §535 (Cumberland).

¹⁶ See Darwall, *BMIO* 62.

¹⁷ *Civ.* 1.9–10 makes each person the judge of what is needed for the preservation of his life. 1.14 allows a right to the stronger that is not restricted by considerations of morality or prudence. On Hobbes's treatment of rights see further Hampton, *HSCT* 51–7; Kavka, *HMPT* 297–303, 319–22.

the law of nature in doing so, and Hobbes infers that we do not act 'with right'.[18] He justifies this inference by arguing that such actions do not promote one's self-preservation, and that one cannot honestly claim that they do.[19] In this case, then, physical freedom does not seem to be sufficient for a right.

485. Obligation as Renunciation of Rights[20]

These different claims about rights complicate our understanding of obligation, because Hobbes understands obligation as the 'laying down' of a right.[21] Sometimes he explains laying down a right as my refraining from exercising a liberty to interfere with your pursuit of a goal that we are both free to pursue. If a 100-euro note is lying in front of it, we are both free to try to pick it up. I lay down my right, and divest myself of my liberty, to hinder your picking it up, if I stand out of your way.[22] If laying down my right is sufficient for obligation, I oblige myself to let you pick up the note by standing out of your way.

But Hobbes usually suggests that this physical renunciation of a right is not the same as obligation. In his view, I lay aside my right by renunciation or by transfer, not by actually standing out of your way, but by saying I will stand out of your way.[23] Once I have done this, I am obliged to stand out of your way and I ought to stand out of your way; if I do not stand out of your way, I act without right.[24] Words and actions

---

[18] 'There is a little ... to be said concerning the laws that men are to observe one towards another in time of war, wherein every man's being and well-being is the rule of his actions. Yet this much the law of nature commandeth in war, that men satiate not the cruelty of their present passions, whereby in their own conscience they foresee no benefit to come. For that betrayeth not a necessity, but a disposition of the mind to war, which is against the law of nature.' (EL 19.2) 'But there are certain natural laws whose exercise ceaseth not even in the time of war itself; for I cannot understand what drunkenness, or cruelty (that is, revenge which respects not the future good) can advance toward peace, or the preservation of any man. Briefly, in the state of nature, what is just and unjust, is not to be esteemed by the actions, but by the counsel and conscience of the actor. That which is done out of necessity, out of endeavour for peace, for the preservation of ourselves, is done with right; otherwise every damage done to a man would be a breach of the natural law, and an injury against God.' (Civ. 3.27n)

[19] Hobbes does not make this point about drunkenness, but he makes it about cruelty (EL 19.2). Hence his prohibition of cruelty is consistent with his claim in Civ. 1.9 that each person is to be allowed to judge what promotes his own self-preservation. If someone believed that cruelty is expedient (by making people less eager to oppose him in future), Hobbes would presumably have to allow him a right to act cruelly.

[20] See Darwall, BMIO 56.   [21] For further discussion see Barry, 'Warrender'; Gauthier, LL 40, Kavka, HMPT 303.

[22] 'To lay down a man's right to any thing, is to divest himself of the liberty, of hindering another of the benefit of his own right to the same. For he that renounceth, or passeth away his right, giveth not to any other man a right which he had not before; because there is nothing to which every man had not right by nature: but only standeth out of his way, that he may enjoy his own original right, without hindrance from him.' (L. 14.6)

[23] 'The way by which a man either simply renounceth, or transferreth his right, is a declaration, or signification, by some voluntary and sufficient sign, or signs, that he doth so renounce, or transfer, or hath so renounced, or transferred the same, to him that accepteth it.' (L. 14.7)

[24] 'And when a man hath in either manner abandoned, or granted away his right; then is he said to be obliged or bound [LV 'debet' is all that corresponds to 'obliged or bound'] not to hinder those, to whom such right is granted, or abandoned, from the benefit of it: and that he ought, and it is his duty, not to make void that voluntary act of his own: and that such hindrance is injustice, and injury, as being *sine jure*; the right being before renounced, or transferred. So that injury, or injustice, in the controversies of the world, is somewhat like to that, which in the disputations of scholars is called absurdity.' (L. 14.7) In Civ. 3.3 wrong is compared to contradiction, on the assumption that it involves violation of a promise.

signifying the transfer of right are 'the bonds by which men are bound, and obliged'. Hence words are 'the verbal bonds of covenant' in contrast to natural bonds (chains; EL 22.3).[25]

What we have said so far might suggest that I have obliged myself once I have told you I will lay down my right. This would be a surprising use of 'oblige'. If I tell you that I will eat a boiled egg for breakfast, but then I change my mind and eat a fried egg instead, have I obliged myself to eat a boiled egg and do I violate my obligation by eating a fried egg? His other remarks do not suggest that it is quite so easy to oblige myself. I oblige myself to you through a valid covenant of mutual trust, involving the future performance by both parties. Such a covenant requires some assurance that the other party will also keep the covenant (L. 15.3). We can acquire this assurance more easily by recognizing that once A has performed A's part of the covenant, it is reasonable for B to perform B's part (L. 15.5).[26] When both A and B have the appropriate assurance, each obliges himself by signifying his intention to lay aside his right.[27]

It is difficult, however, to understand this obligation as a case of laying aside my right, if we stick to Hobbes's initial account of a right as a physical liberty. For if I oblige myself by covenant to repay my debt to you, I do not abridge or 'lay aside' my physical freedom to refrain from paying my debt; on the contrary, if I did not keep that physical freedom, there would be no need for me to make a covenant. The freedom that I abridge or lay aside is my moral freedom. But my moral freedom to keep my money seems to consist simply in the fact that I am not obliged to give you the money. In that case, the account of obligation as laying aside moral freedom is not very illuminating; it simply says that when I oblige myself I make it no longer true that I am not obliged.

Moreover, if Hobbes's claims about liberties and rights must be taken to refer to moral rather than physical liberty, he has not vindicated his claims about the right of nature. For the mere fact that nothing stops me from trying to preserve myself does not show that I am morally free to do whatever I think will preserve me. If Hobbes argues for the right of nature from the mere fact of physical freedom, he is wrong to say that the obligation incurred in making a promise is the laying aside of a right. If his position is consistent, his claim about the right of nature should assert my moral freedom in the state of nature. But then he needs some defence of the claim; the mere fact of physical freedom is not a sufficient defence.[28]

---

[25] Raphael, 'Obligation', calls this 'artificial' obligation, and Barry, 'Warrender', thinks it is the main kind of obligation that Hobbes is talking about (except in passages where he speaks of natural obligation). L. 14.7 (just quoted) is used by both Barry and Raphael. According to Raphael 'A man is artificially obliged to keep his covenants by the mere fact of having made them, but this obligation has little or no force' (348). 'Force' comes from prudential natural obligation. Raphael compares this to the view that it is logically true that we ought to keep our promises, but only utilitarian reasons can be given to justify the practice of making and keeping promises (351). It is not clear, however, that Hobbes takes the making of a promise all by itself to constitute an obligation. This claim has to be restricted to cases where the promise is not 'invalid'. The obligation involved here is also prudential, provided that we think in the indirect prudential way that we must adopt in order to explain why the laws of nature are obligatory in foro externo in a commonwealth. Cf. Kavka, HMPT 338–49, on 'rule-egoism', and §501.

[26] This passage is used by Barry, 'Warrender' 50. See also Darwall, BMIO 72.

[27] On obligation v. ought-judgments see Kavka, HMPT 307, 309.

[28] This point tends to support Clarke's objection. See §§624–5.

486. Obligation as Motivation

In the case we have considered, obligation arises from a voluntary action of binding oneself by covenant. This is to be contrasted with the physical obligation that obliges us to stay where we are if we are bound hand and foot. Sometimes Hobbes suggests that a voluntary act is necessary for all non-physical obligation.[29] But how, we might ask, could this be true of the obligation arising from the laws of nature? And what does the obligation consist in? We have found that it is unhelpful to say simply that it is the renunciation of moral liberty, and then to say that moral liberty is simply the absence of obligation.

Hobbes throws some light on his view of obligation by connecting it with motivation. In non-physical obligation 'liberty is taken away . . . by hope or fear', rather than by physical restraint.[30] When we recognize that something promotes our self-preservation, we have (according to Hobbes's account of motivation) a predominant desire for it, and in that respect our recognition of the effects of the action takes away our liberty not to perform the action and 'binds' us to perform the action. We act freely in choosing the action, in the sense of 'free' that Hobbes applies to actions, because our desires cause our action; but since our desires necessitate our action, they take away (in one respect) our liberty not to act.

This explanation of obligation helps to explain how voluntary agreement may contribute to obligation. We might suppose that the agreement creates the obligation, so that I am obliged to keep my promise in virtue of having made the promise to you and your having accepted it. But this is not Hobbes's view. He believes that we are obliged only when our acts of agreement are made in circumstances that offer us sufficient benefits and assure us of mutual compliance. When these conditions hold, we have a predominant desire to keep the agreement; this predominant desire is the motive that is the obligation. The agreement does not create the obligation; words or other signs are means, but not the source, of obligation.[31] The words contribute to our being obliged only insofar as we have sufficient motives for doing what we say we will do.

In this sense the laws of nature also oblige us. We see that observance of them (in foro interno or externo, as appropriate to the situation)[32] promotes our interest. When we see this, we are moved by hope and anticipation of future good to ourselves; and since

[29] 'For in the act of our submission, consisteth both our obligation and our liberty; which must therefore be inferred by arguments taken from thence; there being no obligation on any man, which ariseth not from some action of his own; for all men equally, are by nature free.' (L. 21.10)

[30] 'Now if God have the Right of Sovereignty from his power, it is manifest, that the obligation of yielding him obedience lies on (incumbere) men by reason of their weakness; for that obligation which rises from contract . . . can have no place here, where the right of ruling (no covenant passing between) rises only from nature. But there are two species of natural obligation, one when liberty is taken away by corporal impediments, according to which we say that heaven and earth, and all creatures, do obey the common laws of their creation; the other, when it is taken away by hope or fear, according to which the weaker, despairing of his own power to resist, cannot but yield to the stronger. From this last kind of obligation, that is to say, from fear, or conscience of our own weakness (in respect of the divine power), it comes to pass, that we are obliged to obey God in his natural kingdom; reason dictating to all, acknowledging the divine power and providence, that there is no kicking against the pricks.' (Civ. 15.7)

[31] 'And the same [sc. words and actions in an agreement] are the bonds, by which men are bound, and obliged: bonds, that have their strength, not from their own nature, (for nothing is more easily broken than a mere word,) but from fear of some evil consequence upon the rupture.' (L. 14.7)

[32] In the state of nature the laws of nature bind only 'in foro interno': 'that is to say, to a desire they should take place: but in foro externo; that is, to the putting them into act, not always' (L. 15.36).

this motive always dominates every other motive, it compels us to act. This obligation removes our freedom to violate the laws of nature once we realize what they say.[33] They oblige us only if we recognize that they are counsels of self-preservation. If we do not know this about the laws of nature, their mere existence does not restrict our freedom.[34] Only ignorance of the content and implications of the laws of nature can explain their violation.

The laws of nature and the virtues connected with them are eternal; they oblige, and are laws, in the court of conscience (*Civ.* 3.29).[35] The fulfilment of the natural law is 'all we are obliged to by rational nature' (*Civ.* 3.30). This is why the sovereign is subject to the laws of nature, though not to the civil law (*L.* 24.7, 29.9). The laws of nature oblige him (*L.* 30.1; *Civ.* 13.16), just as they oblige all mankind (*L.* 30.4, 15).[36]

By making obligation include psychological necessitation, Hobbes fulfils his basic aim of reducing moral to psychological claims.[37] If we assume that we form a predominant desire for every action that appears to promote our self-preservation, we see why reason prescribes the means to self-preservation, and why we are obliged to follow the principles that tell us to follow these means. According to Hobbes's moral psychology, all predominant motives necessitate; hence we are obliged insofar as we have a predominant motive necessitating our action. In this sense the laws of nature oblige us.

How is this type of obligation related to the type that belongs to voluntary undertakings such as covenants? It is different since it does not require any specific act of agreement between two parties. It is not so clear, however, whether it violates the principle that all obligation arises from one's voluntary action. The laws of nature do not oblige any agents who do not seek to preserve themselves and to secure the way of their future desire; for they do not tell us to preserve ourselves, but only what we need to do if we want to preserve ourselves. Perhaps, then, the voluntary action that is presupposed is our self-preserving endeavour; this is not an act of agreement or consent that underlies the obligation (as in covenants), but it is still a voluntary action.

Apparently, then, Hobbes holds a unified conception of non-physical obligation as the removal of liberty through voluntary action that results in a predominant motive. Within this conception, he can explain why the laws of nature prescribe and create obligations, by being empirical propositions about means to self-preservation. If they were not propositions about self-preservation, we could not explain how reason could prescribe them, or how they could oblige everyone who understands what they say.

---

[33] On Hobbes's confusions about freedom, as (i) metaphysical, hence consistent with being psychologically compelled, and (ii) moral, giving permission to act otherwise, see Pufendorf, *JNG* i 6.10; Barry, 'Warrender' 62n.

[34] This is made clear by *Civ.* 3.26, where Hobbes argues that everyone is obliged by the natural law, because everyone can easily see that the provisions of the natural law promote self-preservation. Cf. *Civ.* 2.1n4: '. . . the whole breach of the laws of nature consists in the false reasoning, or rather folly of those men who see not those duties they are necessarily to perform towards others in order to their own conservation'.

[35] Conscience; cf. *Civ.* 12.2.

[36] This is the type of obligation that Oakeshott, 'Introd.' p. lix, calls 'rational obligation' in contrast to 'physical obligation'. Gauthier, *LL* 67, discusses Oakeshott, and concludes: 'Although there is only dubious justification in Hobbes's writings for erecting this concept of rational obligation, we have no major quarrel with Oakeshott, if he wishes to suppose that rational precepts are rationally obliging'. In Gauthier's favoured sense of 'obligation', the laws of nature do not oblige. Cf. Hampton, *HSCT* 242.

[37] On freedom see Barry, 'Warrender' 60, with further references.

487. Natural Law and Divine Commands

This discussion of the laws of nature shows that Hobbes agrees with some of Suarez's claims about intrinsic morality. The laws of nature are precepts of reason in their own right, apart from divine commands, and so we ought to observe them.[38] Hobbes takes a more naturalistic position than Suarez accepts, since he agrees with Vasquez's view that the laws of nature create obligations apart from divine commands; this view follows from Hobbes's motivational account of obligation together with his account of human motivation. Whereas Suarez confines obligations to laws issued by a legislator, and attributes only duties to intrinsic morality, Hobbes finds obligation without legislation. Hobbes's claim that the laws of nature oblige (L. 15.3, 36; Civ. 3.26, 27, 29) precedes his claims (in Civ. 4) about their divine origin and the obligation resulting from it. The obligation to keep the laws of nature does not require them to be laws commanded by God.[39]

But Hobbes also sometimes agrees with Suarez's account of a law, taking it to require the command of a legislator. When he maintains 'true reason is a certain law' and the laws of nature are dictates of reason,[40] he speaks of law in the broader sense allowed by Hooker and Vasquez. But sometimes he claims the laws of nature are laws only because they involve a divine command.[41] Without a divine command, the laws of nature would

---

[38] 'A law of nature, (lex naturalis,) is a precept, or general rule, found out by reason, by which a man is forbidden to do, that, which is destructive of his life, or taketh away the means of preserving the same.' (L. 14.3) 'Therefore true reason is a certain law, which (since it is no less a part of human nature, than any other faculty, or affection of the mind) is also termed natural. Therefore the law of nature, that I may define it, is the dictate of right reason, conversant about those things which are either to be done or omitted for the constant preservation of life and members, as much as in us lies.' (Civ. 2.1)

[39] See Nagel, 'Obligation'; Plamenatz, 'Warrender' (answered by Warrender, 'Reply').

[40] Civ. 2.1, quoted in §486.

[41] The evidence in L. is not clear: 'These dictates of reason (dictamina rationis), men use to call by the name of laws; but improperly: for they are but conclusions, or theorems concerning what conduceth to the conservation and defence, of themselves; whereas law, properly is the word of him, that by right hath command over others. But yet if we consider the same theorems, as delivered in the word of God, that by right commandeth all things; then are they properly called laws.' (L. 15.41) Nothing corresponds to the last sentence, however, in LV. Nor does Hobbes say anything similar in 26.8, where it is the commonwealth that makes the laws of nature genuine laws. A similar question arises about a later remark: 'The office of the sovereign, be it a monarch or an assembly, consisteth in the end for which he was trusted with the sovereign power, namely the procuration of the safety of the people, to which he is obliged by the law of nature, and to render an account thereof to God, the Author of that law, and to none but Him' (L. 30.1). Here again the crucial phrase ('the author of that law') is absent from LV. Indeed, the sense of the Latin is much clearer than that of the English. The Latin reads: Summi imperatoris officia . . . manifeste indicat institutionis finis, nimirum salus populi: quam lege naturae obligatur, quantum potest, procurare: et cuius rationem Deo, et illi soli, tenetur reddere. This might be translated: 'The duties of the supreme commander . . . are indicated by the end of his institution, namely, the safety of the people, which he is obliged by the law of nature to procure as far as he can, and of which he is required to render an account to God and to him alone'. This makes it clear that the safety of the people is not the sovereign's office, but the end for which he was instituted, and that the sovereign is not obliged, but required (teneri) to render an account to God.

On the laws of nature as commanded by God see EL 17.12: 'And forasmuch as law, to speak properly, is a command, and these dictates, as they proceed from nature, are not commands, they are not therefore called laws, in respect of nature, but in respect of the author of that law, God Almighty'. Cf. Civ. 3.33. Civ. conceives divine legislation as positive, given through the Decalogue. This may also be what Hobbes has in mind in L., in speaking of 'theorems, as delivered in the word of God'. But in Civ. 15.8 he agrees with Suarez in taking God to have commanded observance of the natural law through our natural reason: 'Because the word of God ruling by nature only, is supposed to be nothing else but right reason, and the Laws of Kings can be known by their word only, its manifest that the Laws of God ruling by nature alone, are only the natural laws; namely those which we have set down in the second and third chapters, and deduced from the dictates of reason, humility, equity, justice, mercy, and other moral virtues befriending peace . . .'

be advice about self-preservation, but they would not carry the obligation that belongs to a law.[42]

What does Hobbes take to be added by a divine command? Suarez believes that a command is needed to create genuine law, and to create obligation, since obligation requires the imposition of necessity through a command. Hobbes agrees with him on the first point, since he claims that the laws of nature are not properly laws unless they are commands. But he does not seem to agree that commands are necessary for obligation. God's commands take away freedom through hope of rewards and fear of punishments; this hope and fear is the source of the obligation. Once we recognize that there is a God and that he is the creator, and that he rewards and punishes for obedience and disobedience to the natural law, we are obliged to obey the natural law.[43] God's commands are relevant because God supports them with sanctions. The command itself does not create the obligation, but the obligation consists in the motives that are excited by the sanctions.[44]

[42] Taylor, 'Hobbes' 40, notices that Hobbes speaks of laws of nature as dictamina. See, e.g., *L.* 15.41 (quoted in §487); *Civ.* 2.1 ('Therefore the law of nature, that I may define it, is the dictate of right reason, conversant about those things which are either to be done, or omitted for the constant preservation of life, and members, as much as in us lies.'). *L.* 14.3 calls a law of nature a 'precept or general rule' ('praeceptum sive regula'). As we have seen (§478), this does not mean that laws of nature are categorical requirements. As the passage in *Civ.* makes clear, they are dictates only for something that we are all presumed to want. From the fact that they are called dictamina, Taylor infers that they are not simply consilia. But this inference conflicts with *Civ.* 14.1, where Hobbes distinguishes counsel from command: 'Now counsel is a precept in which the reason of my obeying it, is taken from the thing itself which is advised; but command is a precept in which the cause of my obedience depends on the will of the commander'. The laws of nature, abstracting from divine commands, are the first sort of praeceptum, and hence are consilia. This aspect of Hobbes, and the critics who have emphasized it, are discussed by Boonin-Vail, *THSMV* 92–106.

[43] Hobbes ascribes obligatory force to divine power: 'The right of nature whereby God reigneth over men, and punisheth those that break his laws, is to be derived, not from his creating them, as if he required obedience as of gratitude for his benefits, but from his irresistible power . . . To those . . . whose power is irresistible, the dominion of all men adhereth naturally by their excellence of power; and consequently it is from that power that the kingdom over men, and the right of afflicting men at his pleasure, belongeth naturally to God Almighty; not as Creator and gracious, but as omnipotent.' (*L.* 31.5) '. . . the divine laws, or dictates of natural reason . . . the same laws of nature, of which I have spoken already . . . ; namely, equity, justice, mercy, humility, and the rest of the moral virtues.' (31.7). Though Hobbes does not use the phrase 'natural obligation' in this chapter, his view seems to be the same as in *Civ.* 15.7, where the phrase occurs. On natural law and the natural kingdom of God see *Civ.* 15.4–5 (not only Christians and Jews recognize the laws of nature as laws).

[44] Bramhall objects to this remark on our obligation to obey God: '. . . it is an absurd and dishonourable assertion, to make our obedience to God to depend upon our weakness, because we cannot help it, and not upon our gratitude, because we owe our being and preservation to him' (Hobbes, *EW* iv 291). Hobbes replies (295) that Bramhall has misinterpreted him. He agrees that he says in *L.* 'that the right of nature whereby God reigneth over men is to be derived not from his creating them, as if he required obedience, as of gratitude; but from his irresistible power'. But he denies that this is dishonourable to God, since all power is honourable and the greatest power is most honourable. Bramhall's view suggests that God needs gratitude. Hobbes claims that Bramhall misinterprets the passage in *De Cive*: '. . . and [he] says I make our obedience to God depend upon our weakness; as if these words signified the dependence, and not the necessity of our submission, or that *incumbere* and *dependere* were all one' (*EW* iv 295). Hobbes's objection to Bramhall's use of 'depend' is not clear. We might suppose that he appeals to his own use of 'incumbere' to indicate that God's power creates an obligation directly, and not through our fear of him; but this cannot be his point, since he goes on at once in *De Cive* to say that fear is the source of obligation. We might look for some clarification to Hobbes's footnote on his claim about obligation: 'If this shall seem hard to any man, I desire him with a silent thought to consider, if there were two Omnipotents, whether were bound to obey; I believe he will confess that neither is bound: if this be true, then it is also true what I have set down, that men are subject unto God because they are not omnipotent' (*Civ.* 15.7n). (Silverthorne translates 'ideo . . . quia' ('precisely because') as 'primarily because' without any warrant.) The supposition of two omnipotents raises some difficulties. If each has the power to do everything, one might suppose that it has the power to do what it wants to despite what anyone else wants. But this cannot be true of either of them, if the other is also omnipotent. So perhaps we must infer that the will of two omnipotent beings must always agree, and that each is omnipotent insofar as it can do what it wants to despite what any non-omnipotent being wants. This point, however,

Since God's commands create an obligation only through providing us with a motive, the motive, rather than its source in a command, is the obligation.[45] Since obligation is imposition of necessity, and since the relevant type of necessity is psychological necessity, we are obliged wherever we have compelling motives, whether or not they result from commands. This is why the laws of nature oblige us, whether or not they are genuine laws. Whether or not God exists or commands them, they are counsels of self-preservation, but they are laws insofar as they are commanded by God (*L.* 15.41).[46]

Our obligation consists in our overriding desire to obey natural laws as means to self-preservation, both because of their intrinsic character (apart from divine commands) and because we fear punishment, since God, even more than the sovereign (*L.* 26.8, 22), can enforce his will by force. A commander is necessary to turn the laws of nature into genuine laws, and their status as genuine laws provides us with a further source of obligation. It does not, however, provide us with a different kind of obligation; in both cases our obligation consists in the prospective benefits of following the laws of nature and the consequent desire to follow them.

Though divine commands do not create a new type of obligation, they are not superfluous. Since we may not always recognize that the laws of nature promote our self-preservation, we may be tempted to violate them. But if we recall that they are also divine commands, we face a further sanction apart from their natural effects, and therefore we have a further motive to obey them.[47]

We might doubt whether this is a realistic appeal to a second source of prudential motivation. For if we believe God commands observance of the natural law because it is a means to our self-preservation, would not any doubts about whether a type of action promotes self-preservation result in doubts about whether God commands it? In that case, both sources of prudential motivation would disappear at once.

Hobbes might answer this objection by denying that God commands observance of the natural law because it promotes our self-preservation. If we thought that this is God's reason, we would be assuming that God is the source of natural law as the creator who aims at the benefit of the creatures, and that we have a reason to obey God as a benevolent creator. Hobbes denies that this is God's relation to the natural law. In his view, we have a reason to obey God simply because of God's power. God is not bound to command one thing rather

does not seem to bear on Hobbes's argument. Perhaps he introduces the two omnipotent beings to suggest that neither would have any motive to obey the other; since we are not omnipotent, and God is, we have a motive to obey God. But this point does not challenge the accuracy of Bramhall's presentation of Hobbes. Bramhall seems to be justified, therefore, in claiming that Hobbes derives obligation from weakness and fear.

[45] Hobbes's claims about obligation have aroused some dispute. Gauthier thinks Hobbes faces a difficulty if the laws of nature oblige irrespective of divine commands. He assumes that 'if obligatory, they must be genuine laws' (*LL* 67). But Hobbes's remarks about obligation do not support this assumption. See Plamenatz, 'Warrender'.

[46] Bramhall accuses Hobbes of contradicting himself about whether the laws of nature are genuine laws. See *CL*, ch. 3, 577–8. He argues that an appeal to divine commands conveyed through the Scriptures will not make Hobbes's position consistent: 'But this will not salve the contradiction, for the laws of nature shall be no laws to any but those who have read the scripture, contrary to the sense of all the world' (578).

[47] Warrender, 'Reply' 95, acknowledges that, contrary to Taylor's view that Hobbes's position is strictly deontological, we can interpret the obligation created by divine commands as prudential. Hence Warrender's defence of Taylor's interpretation seems to amount to the claim that divine commands are the only source of obligation. This claim, however, conflicts with Hobbes's clear remarks. One need not infer that God is irrelevant as a source of obligation (Nagel and Plamenatz sometimes seem to come close to this).

than another, but simply exercises power in commanding what God wills. In that case, we have no reason to infer that God commands an action only if that action seems to us to promote self-preservation; the character of the natural law shows nothing about necessary features of God's will.

In this respect, then, Hobbes is a voluntarist about the divine will and the content of morality. He implies that it is logically possible for God to command us to violate the counsels of self-preservation that we have overriding reason to pursue (apart from any beliefs about divine commands). On this point, he agrees with Ockham's views about divine power and morality.

Our obligation to follow the laws of nature, both as counsels of prudence and as divine commands, differs in its origins from the obligation arising from contract. I do not acquire a natural obligation by any voluntary act of agreement to the obligation. But the character of the obligation itself is not different. Whether or not I enter into the obligation by an act of agreement, the obligation consists in the overriding prudential motive to do what I am obliged to do. Hobbes has a unified account of non-physical obligation, and the laws of nature fit into it, both as counsels of self-preservation and as divine commands.

While Hobbes agrees with Suarez in taking obligation to impose necessity, he differs from Suarez about the nature of the necessity. Suarez believes the necessity is moral necessity, leaving us with no reasonable alternative to compliance.[48] This is a normative necessity, to be explained by reference to reasons and oughts, not further reduced. Hobbes does not allow any irreducible normative necessity; the necessity imposed by obligation is psychological. In Suarez's view, God's communicating a command to me is sufficient to oblige me to obey it, whether or not I want to obey it. According to Hobbes, however, it is not sufficient; my motivation is also necessary.

This disagreement with Suarez is closely connected with Hobbes's rejection of Suarez's view of the 'foundation' of natural law. Suarez identifies this with moral principles recognized by natural reason, and consisting in the requirements of the honestum. Hobbes does not recognize the honestum as an aspect of morality distinct from the pleasant and the useful; hence he takes the natural foundation of natural law to consist wholly in counsels of self-preservation.[49] This disagreement with Suarez also reflects Hobbes's aim of reducing facts about reasons to facts about motives. Natural law is prescribed by correct reason only insofar as we have an overriding motive to obey it; and we have such a motive only towards counsels of self-preservation.

Hobbes's views on natural law are criticized by Sharrock from a more traditional point of view.[50] Sharrock mentions the classical and patristic sources of the doctrine of natural law that recognizes natural rightness (honestas); he connects them all with St Paul on the Gentiles who are a law to themselves. He also points out that the 'more recent' theologians,

---

[48] Suarez's view would be much more similar to Hobbes's view if Finnis's interpretation of 'moraliter movere' and related phrases were correct. See §442. Bramhall uses 'moral motion' (LN 46, ed. Chappell) in the way Suarez uses it. Hobbes, EW v 293, professes to be unable to make sense of the expression: 'Moral motion is a mere word, without any imagination of the mind correspondent to it.'

[49] Cf. Pufendorf, discussed in §571.

[50] The full title of Sharrock's work explains its point: Hupothesis ethike, de officiis secundum naturae ius, seu de moribus ad rationis normam conformandis doctrina. principia item et rationes Hobbesii Malmsburiensis ad ethicam et politicam spectantes, quatenus huic hypothesi contradicere videantur, in examen veniunt.

both Roman and Protestant, agree with this position.[51] On this basis he argues, against Hobbes, that the laws of nature are properly called laws even without commands (*HE* 46). Here he seems to take Vasquez's position against Suarez. He argues that the laws of nature are laws, because obligation requires law, and the natural dictates of conscience oblige everyone; no command could oblige unless we were already obliged to obey the command. This objection is effective only if Sharrock assumes that all moral requirements and oughts imply obligation, and so fails to draw Suarez's distinction between obligation and ought (debitum). On this assumption he argues against Hobbes's view that self-interest (*philautia*) is the only basis for obligation; in Sharrock's view, we are not required to pursue our self-interest, and hence self-interest cannot yield the sort of necessity that belongs to morality and obligation.[52]

Though Sharrock does not explore the different options that are open to someone who claims that obligation requires commands, and in particular fails to consider Suarez's position, he presents a reasonable alternative to Hobbes's view about the extent of obligation. We will need to consider whether Hobbes can consistently or reasonably maintain a purely psychological conception of obligation in his discussion of the obligatory character of practical reason.

488. Why Moral Principles are Laws of Nature

We can now return to Hobbes's claim that moral philosophy is simply the science of the laws of nature, and ask whether this claim is as distinctive as he suggests it is. He believes that the principles of morality are fundamentally laws of nature, if 'law of nature' is understood as he understands it, as a counsel of self-preservation. Given this understanding, he claims that the principles of morality are counsels of self-preservation.

In Hobbes's view, this account of morality captures the ways in which morality contains precepts that generate obligation. If a genuine virtue includes an obligation to perform some range of virtuous actions, it must conform to the conditions that generate obligations. We cannot specify the virtues simply by considering human nature and the human good. We must also add the fact that we need peace, and have an opportunity to secure it, so that we have good reason to follow the principles that secure it for us.

Hence we have no reason to act on the laws of nature until we can expect the appropriate sorts of effects. Hobbes suggests that if we simply consider the moral virtues by themselves, they tell us nothing more than what we need to do if we are to observe the laws of nature. They do not tell us that we have any reason to observe the laws of nature; and indeed, in Hobbes's view, we have no good reason to observe the laws of nature except insofar as they actually advance our desire for self-preservation.[53] Hence our reason to practise the

---

[51] 'Idem etiam sine ulla refragatione omnes ex omni secta iuniores affirmant theologi' (*HE* 44). He cites, among others, Suarez, *Leg* i 3.9, 9; Aquinas, *ST* 1–2 91 a2, 93 a4; *in Rm* 2.14; Calvin; and Melanchthon.

[52] 'Nemo enim necessario obligatur ad utilitatem suam, quia iuste possit ab ea recedere et iuri suo commodisque quibuscumque ad placitum et pro arbitrio renuntiare.' (52)

[53] When the observance of them does not directly promote our self-preservation, it may still promote our self-preservation indirectly, if the observance of the laws of nature is commanded by God. When Hobbes says that God 'by

moral virtues is extrinsic to them. We cannot find a reason if we simply consider human nature as shaped by the virtues; we must also consider it in the specific circumstances where we find a predominant desire to practise the virtues.

We might suppose that this difference between Hobbes and Aquinas does not make any practical difference; do they not defend the same virtues by different routes? One important practical difference is that they do not necessarily defend the practice of the same virtues in the same conditions. Hobbes sees that the traditional virtues do not always promote self-preservation. He does not conclude that he is wrong to defend them by appeal to self-preservation, or that the laws of nature are not counsels of self-preservation; instead he concludes that we have no reason to practise the traditional virtues when they do not promote self-preservation.

The aim of demonstrating that the laws of nature are counsels of self-preservation may appear misguided. For Hobbes's conception of the content of these laws is mostly quite traditional; he recognizes that they are different ways of treating other people fairly and with respect. The laws of nature prohibit arrogance and prescribe truthfulness, the keeping of promises, living in harmony with one's neighbours, and so on. Many of these principles require individuals to perform actions that are disadvantageous to them and to refrain from actions that would benefit them.

Hobbes deals with this feature of morality by connecting it with self-preservation in two stages: (1) The observance of moral principles tends to preserve a commonwealth, a stable society offering protection from aggression by others. (2) It is always better for me if the commonwealth is preserved than if it is dissolved or weakened. The connexion with self-preservation does not belong to moral principles directly, but to the commonwealth that they preserve. Hence we need not be surprised that moral principles say nothing directly about self-preservation; we see the connexion with self-preservation only when we consider the cumulative effects of all moral principles. We must see how the observance of moral principles preserves the commonwealth if we are to see how it preserves ourselves.

The two stages in Hobbes's argument suggest that in one respect it is misleading to maintain that the moral virtues are essentially concerned with self-preservation. If we are looking for a goal that will allow us to understand the character of the moral virtues, we ought to turn not to self-preservation, but to the preservation of the commonwealth. A virtue prescribes actions and traits of character insofar as they promote this end, and that is the end that unifies the efforts of the virtuous person. To see whether we have cultivated the virtues in a society we need to see whether we have promoted the traits that tend to preserve the commonwealth. For this purpose, reference to individual self-preservation is beside the point.

Self-preservation enters when we raise a different question: why are these traits that preserve the commonwealth prescribed by correct reason? According to Hobbes's psychological reduction of reason, what is prescribed by correct reason is what produces an overriding motive, and hence creates an obligation; only counsels of prudence do that. If we were not interested in knowing the connexion between morality and correct reason, we could ignore

right' commands the observance of the laws of nature, we must take him to mean that God has a right to command this observance; and if we apply Hobbes's account of a right to this claim about God's right, we must take Hobbes to mean that God is free, since nothing prevents him, to command obedience and to enforce compliance with his command.

the reference to self-preservation. But if we were not interested in this question, we would overlook an essential feature of morality; for genuine morality is recommended by correct reason, and so Hobbes has to show that it meets his conditions for correct reason.

489. The Reduction of Morality

In connecting the laws of nature, as he understands them, with morality, Hobbes seeks to reduce morality to counsels of self-preservation. We can ask two questions about Hobbes's account of morality: (1) Does it provide an explanatory reduction? Hobbes seeks to show what all the recognized moral virtues have in common. By doing this he believes he can explain what other theorists dimly recognized, even though they claimed to construct the list of virtues on some other basis. (2) Does it provide a vindicating reduction? if the moral virtues specify the means of peace and security, have we sufficient reason to follow them?

Hobbes's explanatory account of the moral virtues is worth discussing and criticizing in its own right, apart from his psychological and political views. According to his analysis of the moral virtues, moral considerations are characteristically about the public good, narrowly conceived as the preservation of the commonwealth. Hobbes's egoism and his restrictive conception of reasons do not affect this account of morality. He recognizes—at least implicitly—objective moral properties.[54] He may be right about what these properties are even if he is wrong about the mental states of moral agents.

Still, the questions about explanation and about justification are not completely separable, either in Hobbes's view or in fact. Hobbes would find it unwelcome if he had to conclude that the foundations of morality are quite unconnected with his psychological theory. If Hobbesian agents had no reason to care about morality, Hobbes's theory would separate morality from the principles that might rationally guide our actions. If a theorist reaches this conclusion, we have some reason to suppose that he is wrong about either morality or rationality or both.

The traditional account of the virtues assumes that the virtues are conditions that a rational agent has good reason to acquire. If we had no reason to cultivate the conditions that Hobbes calls moral virtues, that would be a reason for rejecting his account of the virtues. Since he wants to avoid this objection, Hobbes does not separate moral from rational considerations; and so he argues that Hobbesian agents have reason to take moral considerations seriously on some occasions.

Hobbes, therefore, seeks an explanatory and vindicating, not an undermining, reduction. When we see what moral principles really are, we ought to see thereby that we have good reason to follow them in the appropriate circumstances. Hobbes's account of human nature shows why Hobbesian agents have reason to follow counsels of self-preservation. If moral principles simply are these counsels, Hobbesian agents have reason to follow moral principles.

---

[54] Cf. Hampton, *HSCT* 42–51, on 'objectivism'. Recognition of some form of objectivism does not make Hobbes's position deontological. We have seen that he does not give a deontological ground for our obligation to obey divine commands. Nor does he assess moral rules deontologically. He assesses them with reference to the public interest, and this assessment depends on a rule-utilitarian explanation.

Most moral agents and moral theorists do not believe Hobbes's claim about the character of morality and moral philosophy. Many people suppose that moral obligations extend beyond the circumstances in which their fulfilment promotes peace. We might suppose, for instance, that in some circumstances it is better to rebel than to conform to a government, despite the danger to peace and self-preservation. In Hobbes's view, such beliefs about morality rest on failure to examine the rational grounds of moral obligation. If morality is rationally justifiable to rational agents, and if Hobbes's analysis of human nature is right, he is right about the character and basis of morality.

Hobbes believes that his account of human nature and its pursuit of peace both unifies and justifies the different moral virtues.[55] Hence his theory of human nature influences his account of morality. We could accept his views about which states are virtuous without accepting his claims about the connexion between the virtues, the preservation of peace, the laws of nature, and self-preservation. But if we did not accept these other Hobbesian claims, we would not, according to Hobbes, have explained why the virtues are important for rational agents. Hobbes believes we can see why his defence of the moral virtues is the only plausible defence, once we have accepted his views about the nature of human action and practical reason.

To see whether Hobbes's reduction of morality succeeds, we can raise two questions: (1) Have Hobbesian agents good reasons to follow Hobbes's rules? (2) How far do Hobbes's rules capture morality? The same questions arise for Plato and Aristotle.[56] But Hobbes rejects the solution that they prefer; for he does not adjust his conception of human nature to take account of apparently plausible views about the value of morality. He takes his theory of human nature to be fixed independently of beliefs about morality. This assumption makes the character of his argument, and the criteria for success, clearer than they are in Plato and Aristotle.

This difference between Hobbes and Plato and Aristotle reflects a difference in moral epistemology that we have seen in Hobbes's statement of his method for reaching consensus in moral philosophy and moral thinking generally. He claims that if we follow a 'geometrical method', we begin with simple and indisputable principles and advance from them by uncontroversial steps. Since morality is an area of dispute, we should begin with non-moral foundations, fixing the nature of human action and deriving an account of morality. His procedure is open to question, however, if the non-moral foundations themselves are not simple and indisputable; if they are open to reasonable dispute, they do not offer a decisive reason for accepting the moral consequences that Hobbes draws from them.

A fair estimate of Hobbes's success in his moral theory will take account of the restricted place that he allows for justification. While it is helpful and appropriate to say that he tries to 'vindicate' and to 'justify' morality, and to show that we have 'reason' to follow it, it is also misleading; Hobbes has no room for these normative claims, except insofar as they can be reduced to claims about motivation. A justification of morality and a demonstration that we have reason to follow morality is simply a true prediction that in the specified circumstances we will have an overriding motive to follow it.

---

[55] This also explains their universality. See *Civ.* 3.32.   [56] See §60 (Plato); §114 (Aristotle).

But can we perhaps ignore this reduction of the normative to the psychological, if we are considering Hobbes's defence of morality as counsels of self-preservation? Might this defence not succeed even if the reduction of the normative to the psychological fails? If it were to succeed, one of Hobbes's attempts at a vindicating reduction would be more plausible than the other.

It is not quite so easy, however, to separate Hobbes's different reductions. For his view that morality consists simply in counsels of self-preservation rests partly on his conception of human nature. He rejects the Aristotelian view that natural law is about what is appropriate for rational nature, because he denies that human nature is the rational system that Aristotle and Aquinas take it to be. He denies that it is a rational system because he does not recognize essentially rational desires, or decisive reasons that are not reducible to overriding motives. He connects morality with self-preservation because he takes the desire for self-preservation to be our overriding motive; hence, his argument for reducing morality to self-preservation depends on his reduction of the normative to the psychological. If we reject the latter reduction, we have good reason to question his defence of morality.

490. The State of Nature

Hobbes's reduction of the moral virtues vindicates them within limits. For his account of human nature implies that the human good and the moral virtues are not connected in all possible circumstances, or even in all circumstances that need to be considered in practical reflexion. Hobbes allows us to consider only the demands of self-preservation, and it seems obvious that, as Thrasymachus, Glaucon, and Adeimantus point out to Socrates, we often promote our self-preservation more effectively by acting against the virtues.

Hobbes deals with this objection in three stages: (1) It is sometimes correct. The state of nature sums up the circumstances in which we have no reason to practise the moral virtues. (2) However, we are worse off in these circumstances than if we are members of a commonwealth. Hence we ought to become members of a commonwealth and to follow the rules for the construction and the preservation of a commonwealth. The relevant rules are counsels for the preservation of peace, which are embodied in the moral virtues. (3) If we are members of a commonwealth, our self-preservation requires us to do whatever preserves peace, and hence requires us to practise the moral virtues.

Glaucon and Adeimantus agree with Hobbes about the first and second stages. They agree that we have no reason to be just outside a commonwealth, and that the existence of a commonwealth requires general observance of justice. They argue, however, that for a reasonably astute individual in an ordinary commonwealth, injustice remains advantageous. Epicurus tries to answer this defence of injustice by arguing that injustice brings fear of punishment and that this fear makes injustice inexpedient for us. His reply is unconvincing. Hobbes's account of the third stage is meant to give a better reply to critics of morality.

Hobbes does not argue that the moral virtues are good for each human being who is rationally concerned with his own good, irrespective of circumstances. He tries to describe the conditions in which the moral virtues are good for us. He does this by contrasting the situation in which the moral virtues do not benefit us with the one in which they do benefit us, and by arguing that we are better off in the second situation than in the first. The first situation is the state of nature; the second is life under a commonwealth.

Hobbes is not the first philosopher to appeal to a state of nature as a starting-point for understanding the basis of moral principles and political obligation. The 16th-century Scholastics and 17th-century natural law theorists also rely on a state of nature.[57] But agreement in appealing to a state of nature does not imply agreement on the sort of theory that emerges; for different theorists describe the state of nature differently.

According to Aquinas' account of human nature and the law of nature, an appeal to the state of nature helps to explain the moral constraints on the formation of a state. For characteristics of human nature explain why it is reasonable to form a state; and the provisions of the law of nature determine the sorts of powers that people can legitimately assign to the state.[58] Hobbes, by contrast, appeals to the state of nature to show why no moral constraints can reasonably be imposed on the state. He rejects Scholastic conclusions because he relies on a different account of human nature and of the place of moral considerations in the state of nature. For his purposes, he needs to show that the state of nature is a state of conflict or potential conflict.

The state of nature, according to Hobbes, is a state of war.[59] This conclusion relies on his account of human passions and of their effect in the circumstances where no power coerces each individual alike. Given what we know about human nature, we can predict that in the absence of equal coercion each person will try to get what he wants by attacking others. People will not generally observe the principles embodied in the moral virtues. Moreover, given Hobbes's account of the human good, people are right to believe they are better off by not observing the virtues.

Why is the state of nature a condition of perpetual conflict? Hobbes's most general argument rests on one aspect of his views about the subjectivity of goodness.[60] Since I use 'good' for what pleases me (oysters), and you use 'good' for what pleases you (cheese), we differ in our judgments about what things are good. Hence our judgments about goodness display 'discord and strife'. Hobbes argues that this discord in judgments explains the discord that marks the state of nature.

This argument is open to objection; for variation in judgments about goods need not lead to the sort of discord that makes peace seem good. If you find x pleasant and I do not, we are not really disagreeing about any property of x; my report of my reaction to x does not conflict with your report of your reaction to x. The mere fact that we have different reactions does not produce the sort of disagreement that results in strife and war. Again, if I judge x good (because it pleases me) and you judge y good (because it pleases you), this discord in our judgments seems to protect us from any practical conflict or competition. Indeed, agreement in judgments about goodness seems far more likely to produce practical conflict. If you and I both agree that it is good for an ordinary person to possess the 100-euro note on the ground in front of us, our agreement is more likely to produce strife and discord.

---

[57] Scholastic views on the state of nature are described by Skinner, *FMPT* ii 154–66.

[58] On the state of nature see §§449–50 (Suarez).

[59] 'Hereby is it manifest, that during the time men live without a common power to keep them all in awe, they are in that condition which is called war; and such a war as is of every man against every man.' (*L.* 13.8)

[60] On goodness see §477.

When Hobbes suggests that the subjectivity of goodness results in discord, he seems to confuse variation of taste, disagreement in judgment, and conflict in action. Perhaps he fails to distinguish (1) the 'discord' that consists in failure to agree in objective judgments about which things are good, from (2) the discord that consists in conflicting plans and actions. The first sort of discord is not the source of the most serious conflicts in the state of nature.

491. Competition and Conflict

Hobbes needs a better argument to show that practical conflict is inevitable in the state of nature. He does not show that his description of the state of nature applies to all of us outside a commonwealth. We all desire to assure the way of our future desire; but this desire does not involve conflict with other people, unless their desires threaten our assurance of being able to satisfy ours. If none of us wants unshareable goods that others want, we have no motive, according to Hobbes's account, for competing with other people, and so we are not forced into conflict and instability.

Hobbes's argument, therefore, turns on the prevalence of competition. Competition enters only because we desire 'unshareable' goods—objects that other people also desire and that we cannot share without some of us getting less than we want—and because there are too few of them for each of us to have all we want. These are what Plato and Aristotle call 'contested (*perimachêta*) goods'. The contest over them causes aggression, or at least the constant danger of aggression.

Why can we not all be satisfied with some quota of unshareable goods? Hobbes might have two explanations in mind: (1) Though our desires for them are limited, the supply is even more limited. If I want a loaf of bread to keep me alive, and you want the same for yourself, but there is only one loaf of bread, we will compete for it. But we will no longer compete if two loaves are available. (2) We have essentially competitive desires, so that each of us desires more than the other has, however much the other has; hence, however much you get, I still want more.[61]

Which of these views does Hobbes maintain? Sometimes he seems to believe that some universal human desires are essentially competitive and that these desires are strong enough to produce competitive behaviour even when it threatens our security. If we desire not only to secure the way of our future desire, but also to secure our future superiority over others, the state of nature implies conflict, however abundant the unshareable resources may be. Clarke rightly suggests that, according to Hobbes, the desire for power over other people is 'one of the first and most natural principles of human life'.[62] Glory seems to rest on a desire for eminence in comparison.[63] In general, the analysis of passions and desires

---

[61] Cf. Rousseau on inflamed amour propre (§884).   [62] Clarke, *DNR* = H ii 635 = R 258. Cf. Hobbes, *L.* 11.2, 17.1.

[63] 'First, that men are continually in competition for honour and dignity; which these creatures are not; and consequently among men there ariseth on that ground, envy and hatred, and finally war . . . Secondly, that amongst these creatures the common good differeth not from the private; and being by nature inclined to their private, they procure thereby the common benefit. But man, whose joy consisteth in comparing himself with other men, can relish nothing but what is eminent.' (*L.* 17.7–8) Cf. *EL* 9.1. On competitive desires see McNeilly, 'Egoism' (who underestimates their importance in *L.*). Cf. §675.

gives a prominent place to competition.[64] It might suggest that the passions are essentially competitive, involving a desire to do better than other people, whether or not I gain any further benefit.

This view conflicts with psychological hedonism; for if we essentially take pleasure in power, we desire power for its own sake, and so pleasure is not the only thing we desire for its own sake.[65] But the conflict may not be obvious to Hobbes; it is not a good reason for doubting that he believes in essentially competitive desires.

A better reason for doubt emerges from his discussion of the desire for power. Though he treats this desire as a general inclination, he treats it as a consequence of the desire for assurance of the way of one's future desire.[66] He suggests that power is valued only for the sake of assurance. We pursue greater and greater power as a means to assurance, but if we have this assurance, we may abandon the pursuit of power.[67] In contrast to naturally social animals, human beings can distinguish private from public good; foresight allows them to recognize future dangers to their well-being, and they seek superiority over others as a means of protection against these future dangers. Similarly, competitiveness and desire for glory result from the search for assurance.[68] Men 'naturally love liberty and dominion over others' (L. 17.1) because they want assurance; the same search for assurance brings them into the state, from 'foresight of their own preservation'. Competition does not rest on a desire for superiority for its own sake, but on a desire for assurance.[69]

But in what sense does Hobbes subordinate competitive desires to the desire for assurance? Does he believe that they originate in it, or that it controls them? Even if the desire for assurance makes us competitive, competitive desires may become independent of it, so that, even if we are assured about the future, we may persist in competition beyond the demands

---

[64] See EL 14.3.   [65] On this argument against hedonism see §95 (Aristotle); §688 (Butler); §804 (Price).

[66] 'Felicity is a continual progress of the desire from one object to another, the attaining of the former being still but the way to the latter. The cause whereof is that the object of man's desire is not to enjoy once only, and for one instant of time, but to assure forever the way of his future desire. And therefore the voluntary actions and inclinations of all men tend not only to the procuring, but also to the assuring of a contented life, and differ only in the way, which ariseth partly from the diversity of passions in diverse men, and partly from the difference of the knowledge or opinion each one has of the causes which produce the effect desired. So that in the first place, I put for a general inclination of all mankind a perpetual and restless desire of power after power, that ceaseth only in death.' (L. 11.1–2) 'So that . . .' in the last sentence suggests the subordination of the desire for power to the desire for assurance.

[67] The passage quoted earlier in this section from L. 11.2 continues: 'And the cause of this is not always that a man hopes for a more intensive delight than he has already attained to, or that he cannot be content with a moderate power, but because he cannot assure the power and means to live well, which he hath present, without the acquisition of more. And from hence it is that kings, whose power is greatest, turn their endeavours to the assuring it at home by laws, or abroad by wars: and when that is done, there succeedeth a new desire; in some, of fame from new conquest; in others, of ease and sensual pleasure; in others, of admiration, or being flattered for excellence in some art or other ability of the mind.' (L. 11.2)

[68] 'Competition of riches, honour, command, or other power inclineth to contention, enmity, and war, because the way of one competitor to the attaining of his desire is to kill, subdue, supplant, or repel the other.' (L. 11.3) 'Moreover, considering that many men's appetites carry them to one and the same end; which end sometimes can neither be enjoyed in common, nor divided, it followeth, that the stronger must enjoy it alone, and that it be decided by battle who is the stronger. And thus the greatest part of men, upon no assurance of odds, do nevertheless, through vanity, or comparison, or appetite, provoke the rest, that otherwise would be contented with equality.' (EL 14.5)

[69] If this explanation is right, Rousseau is unjustified in attacking Hobbes for presupposing desires that are essentially 'social' and 'competitive'. See §883. Similarly, we have reason to doubt Oakeshott's claim that Hobbes treats pride and competition as basic motives: '. . . although men and animals are like in their self-centredness, the characteristic difference between them lies in the competitive nature of human appetite and passion: every man wishes to out-do all other men' (RP 253).

of assurance. But if the desire for assurance controls competition, passions have a stable hierarchy.

The choice between these two views about assurance and competition affects our view about practical reason and the desire for peace. Reason is uniquely concerned with finding the means to peace if and only if the desire for peace is always dominant; if other desires were sometimes dominant, reason would be equally concerned with finding means to satisfying these desires whenever they are dominant. Hobbes's assumptions about practical reason and peace may rely on a more basic assumption about assurance. The desire for assurance is not an inherently rational desire (since Hobbes recognizes no such desires), but (he may assume) it controls the strength of other desires.

If Hobbes does not take competitive desires to be essential to human nature, his state of nature does not include every logically possible condition of human beings outside a commonwealth; it includes only the circumstances in which there do not appear to be enough unshareable goods to go round. Hence Hume believes that justice is appropriate only in specific external circumstances that do not follow from human nature itself.[70] The competition that leads to a state of war results from human nature only in conditions of scarcity.

This may seem a relatively trivial objection to Hobbes, since it concerns what we say about human motives in the rather unlikely counterfactual situation in which there are enough unshareable goods to satisfy everyone's desires (not modified by consideration of other people's desires and needs). It may be important, however, for considering Hobbes's view about the difference between the state of nature and the commonwealth. If our desires are only contingently competitive, it may be more difficult for Hobbes to prove that the state of nature is so insecure that we need to create a commonwealth with unrestricted power to coerce. He may remove this difficulty if he is allowed to assume essentially competitive desires as part of human nature. But that assumption may make it more difficult to explain the stability of a commonwealth of Hobbesian agents. A commonwealth may remove some conflicts, by assuring each of us of protection for our unshareable resources; but it does not prevent conflicts that arise from essentially competitive desires.

492. Why a State of War?

To explain why the state of nature is a state of war, Hobbes might appeal to different sorts of beliefs and desires that suggest three different explanations:[71] (1) In the state of nature no agency compels mutual non-aggression, or compliance with promises, or observance of any of the other laws of nature. Since we lack the necessary assurance that others will behave peaceably to us, it is not in our interest to behave peaceably to them. Hence it is in our interest to violate the laws of nature that we would observe if we were in a commonwealth. (2) In the state of nature we can see that peace is good, and so we want to live at peace. But not everyone sees this all the time. Sometimes it appears that I would be better off

---

[70] See Hume, §770.
[71] Hampton, *HSCT*, chs. 2–3, discusses these different explanations. Pufendorf implicitly notices them in *JNG* ii 2.8–9.

if I cheated my neighbour this time; I do not attend to the remoter consequences of my actions, or I do not think carefully about their impact on my future desires. In these cases our passions distort our conception of our interest. (3) Even though I recognize that peace is good and that it is in my interest to observe the laws of nature, I sometimes care more about satisfying some particular passion—anger, spite, gratitude, for instance—and so I knowingly act against my perceived interest. In this case my passions do not distort my conception of my interest, but they cause me to act against it nonetheless, and so I violate the demands of peace.[72]

These different explanations for violation of the laws of nature in the state of nature are consistent; each may explain violations of natural law on different occasions in the state of nature. They may suggest different and mutually supporting arguments for establishing a commonwealth. But they may also confront Hobbes with difficult choices; for aspects of the state that remove one source of instability and war may encourage others, and therefore may both remove and create instability.

Hobbes believes that in the state of nature peace seems good to us. Within his moral psychology this claim is true to the extent that peace appears to us to fulfil our overriding desire. If the desire for the end to which peace is a means always dominates us, we always think peace good. But if this is true of us in the state of nature, why do we need to be compelled to keep the peace? Why do we not recognize that we all have an overriding desire for peace, so that we keep the peace? Hobbes argues that we lack assurance that others will keep the peace if they are not compelled to keep it, and therefore we need a coercive power over us. But why should I lack assurance, if I know that everyone else desires peace as strongly as I do?

To answer this question, we need to assume that we are prone to mistakes about the sorts of actions that undermine peace. If (contrary to Hobbes's assumptions) we found ourselves at peace, but without any coercive power over us, I would be strongly tempted to believe that I could gain some benefit for myself by aggression against you—cheating, stealing, or assaulting—without disturbing the peace; for I might predict that, even if you found me out, I could defend myself against retaliation from you, and that others might not find it in their interest to take the trouble to help you retaliate against me. Since I know that you think in just the same way about me, I lack the relevant sort of assurance about you. Since you know that I think in just the same way about you, you lack assurance about me. When we lack assurance, it is not in our interest to make and to keep agreements. Hence we lapse into a state of war.

Hobbes believes we are liable to these errors within a commonwealth. We tend to resent the disagreeable aspects of government and authority, because we do not take a wide enough view to see that these are needed to keep the peace.[73] Though we want peace above all, we have unrealistic views about the necessary means to peace. We need a coercive power over us to deter us from putting our unrealistic views into practice by evading our taxes or cheating our neighbours. In the state of nature, we are prone to equally unrealistic views;

---

[72] This seems to be Spinoza's view, given his views on reason and self-preservation. See §515; Curley, *BGM* 124.

[73] 'For all men are by nature provided of notable multiplying glasses (that is their passions and self-love) through which every little payment appeareth a great grievance, but are destitute of those prospective glasses (namely moral and civil science) to see afar off the miseries that hang over them and cannot without such payments be avoided.' (*L* 18.20)

but since we have no coercive power over us, nothing stops us from acting on them, and so we cannot get out of the state of war.

This account of the instability of the state of nature fits best into Hobbes's theory. It explains why we can be in a state of war despite our predominant and universal desire for peace; hence it justifies his claims that we think peace good and that practical reason uniquely prescribes the means to peace. It fits his reduction of reasons to motives and his analysis of goodness by appeal to desire.

But it does not fit all his moral psychology. Some of his views commit him to the second explanation of the state of war. For he does not always maintain that our strongest desire is for the long-term assurance that is secured by peace. He allows that we sometimes have stronger desires for short-term satisfactions; according to his account of judgments about goodness, we must judge these short-term satisfactions good when we desire them more strongly. He cannot consistently claim that we steadily judge peace good, even when we desire something else more strongly. Nor can he claim that reason always prescribes the pursuit of peace; for if some desire other than the desire for self-preservation dominates us, reason prescribes pursuit of the means to that dominant desire.

Still, even if Hobbes's moral psychology does not entirely fit his claims about goodness and about practical reason, it may not damage his argument for the commonwealth. He may reasonably rely on the second claim about the state of nature, appealing to varying judgments about goodness that result from the predominance of different passions at different times. On the occasions when we judge peace to be good, we can see the point of taking steps to protect ourselves against the occasions when we or others will judge some short-term gain to be better than peace. We can even use this variation in judgments about goodness to explain why in the state of nature we lack assurance about other people's intentions. Since they are liable, just as we are, to unstable judgments about good, we cannot be assured that we or they will retain a dominant preference for peace. Hence we have a reason to make it difficult for ourselves and others to undermine peace when we or they desire something else more strongly. We need a commonwealth, to make the benefits of peace so clear that we will not be easily persuaded to violate the laws of nature, and to coerce people who do not constantly see the benefits of peace.

The third explanation of the state of war is more difficult to reconcile with Hobbes's views about goodness, but he seems to be committed to it. For he claims that we can sometimes desire one option more strongly even if we believe that the other option is better. This is why he claims, against Bramhall, that incontinence is possible. This claim about incontinence is inconsistent with Hobbes's view that our judgments about goodness correspond to the strength of our desires.

Hobbes appears, therefore, to be committed to different explanations of the state of war that rest on conflicting elements in his moral psychology. It is not yet clear, however, whether the conflicts in his moral psychology make a difference to his argument from the state of nature to the commonwealth. For all three explanations of the state of war agree about how we can escape it. When we are in our far-sighted moods, we agree that peace is good and that we would like to bring it about. We see that to bring it about, we need to counteract the effect of the near-sighted deliberation that sometimes causes us to overlook the long-term benefits of peace, and the effect of near-sighted desires that cause us to choose some immediate goal at the cost of a longer-term goal. The commonwealth counteracts the effect of the beliefs and desires that divert us from the pursuit of peace.

If we recognize these features of motivation in the state of nature, we may be tempted to infer that Hobbes offers two different sorts of arguments for the state. The first argument asserts that there are moral reasons for establishing the state and that the social contract gives it moral legitimacy. Hence the argument from the goodness of peace and the rationality of pursuing it might be taken to show that the state is morally required. The second argument simply identifies the motives that underlie the foundation of a state, implying that fear of other people is the psychological basis for obedience to law and governments. According to this argument, the social contract establishes only the psychological possibility of the state, saying nothing about whether the state is morally legitimate.[74]

It is plausible to claim that Hobbes offers both sorts of arguments; for he wants to explain both how the state is possible and what makes it morally legitimate. But it is also misleading to distinguish two sorts of argument; for in his view, they are not really distinct. He speaks of the laws of nature as precepts of reason, and says that reason helps us out of the state of nature; but he also believes that this role for reason depends on the appropriate sorts of passions. His account of morality and obligation implies that recognition of reasons demonstrating the goodness of something is simply a dominant motive to pursue it. Hence we recognize that peace is good just insofar as we have a dominant desire for it. With this in mind, we can consider the arguments that he offers to justify a commonwealth, and the motives that he appeals to.

493. Arguments for a Commonwealth

The laws of nature are counsels for securing and preserving peace. Given that we fear death, and seek 'commodious living', we agree that peace is good, and that it is in our interest to join in the formation of a commonwealth.[75] If we cannot secure an agreement that leads to peace, we are allowed to violate the laws of nature.[76] Our overriding desire for peace leads us to accept (in the right circumstances) the agreement to set up a sovereign and the associated covenant that requires all the contractors to give up their freedom to commit aggression on each other by using the 'helps and advantages' of war.

If we make and keep a covenant to live at peace with one another, we gain all the benefits of peace. But our simply making it does not ensure that we will keep it. For some of the different beliefs and desires that explain aggression in the state of nature also explain why some people may not keep a covenant to live at peace. And if the people who lack these misguided beliefs and desires know that other people are likely to break the covenant, they will also be less disposed to rely on it, because of their lack of assurance. If each of us

[74] Passmore, 'Moral', discusses these two tendencies in Hobbes. He finds rational, moral argument ('rationalism') mainly in *Civ.*, and purely psychological argument ('naturalism') in *L.*, but with elements of the rationalist position still present and creating a conflict with the naturalist elements.

[75] *L.* 13.14, quoted later in this section.

[76] '. . . every man, ought to endeavour peace, as far as he has hope of obtaining it; and when he cannot obtain it, . . . he may seek, and use, all helps, and advantages of war' (*L.* 14.4).

oscillates between a peaceful outlook and one of the outlooks that causes violations of a covenant, we will all agree, in our peaceful periods, that we need to be assured that other people will keep their covenants.

The making of an agreement, therefore, cannot by itself generate the sort of community that removes conflict.[77] As a Hobbesian agent, I have a good reason to agree to end the state of war, if other people will comply with the agreement. But I also have a good reason to gain as much as I can from my imperfect compliance with the agreement. For the very best outcome for me would be the one in which other people avoid aggression against me, but I am free to commit aggression on them when it suits me; hence I have a reason for violating the agreement when I can get away with it.

This argument for violating agreements is over-simplified, since we cannot completely separate reasons for making an agreement from reasons for keeping it. I benefit from an agreement insofar as other people keep it; but if my keeping it contributes to their keeping it, and my breaking it contributes to their breaking it, I have reason to keep it. Hence, since I value the survival of the commonwealth, I have a reason to comply to the extent that my compliance encourages other people to comply.

But how much compliance does this principle justify? Questions about the effects of my compliance or violation are not always easy to answer.[78] If very few people make the agreement, and if they will know not only that the agreement has been broken but also who broke it, reflexion on the ways in which my violation would undermine general compliance with the agreement might encourage my reliable compliance. But if the effects of violation are not so easily known, I seem to have a better reason to violate agreements. Moreover, everyone else has these reasons for compliance and for violation, and hence for wariness about other people's likely behaviour. In such conditions, it is difficult to form reliable estimates of consequences, even if we assume that we are all very good at estimating them. Moreover, if we assume, plausibly, that some people may be less good at this than others are, it becomes even more difficult to form a reliable estimate. Hence our collective situation is still unstable, because we have not removed all the sources of instability that are present in the state of nature.

Hobbes infers, therefore, that we must not only agree to live at peace, but also assure compliance with agreements. Hence we must agree on a coercive power to enforce the terms of peace. He defends this claim when he considers 'laying down our arms'.[79] In the

---

[77] 'Nevertheless, in contracts that consist of such mutual trust, as that nothing be by either party performed for the present, when the contract is between such as are not compellable, he that performeth first, considering the disposition of men to take advantage of every thing for their benefit, doth but betray himself thereby to the covetousness, or other passion of him with whom he contracteth. And therefore such covenants are of none effect. For there is no reason why the one should perform first, if the other be likely not to perform afterward. And whether he be likely or not, he that doubteth, shall be judge himself . . . as long as they remain in the estate and liberty of nature.' (EL 15.10)

[78] See Hampton, HSCT, ch. 2, esp. 78. She cites Cudworth, TISU, ch. 5, part 5 = iii 499–502. In ch. 3 Hampton accepts the 'short-sighted' account of instability in state of nature. But perhaps it becomes more rational to cheat and distrust in the state of nature, if the laws of nature rest on indirect egoist arguments (cf. Hampton 93). If I benefit from observing the laws of nature only insofar as I live under a system in which we all forgo direct egoistic deliberation, it seems rational for us to be direct egoists in the state of nature. Hence it is rational for us to distrust one another; hence it is rational to behave in ways that make the state of nature a state of war. That is why we can only wish we were in circumstances in which we could observe the laws of nature in foro externo; in the state of nature we have not made ourselves indirect egoists.

[79] In the state of nature, 'Reason suggesteth convenient articles of peace upon which men may be drawn to agreement' (L. 13.14). 'Therefore before the names of just and unjust can have place, there must be some coercive power to compel

state of nature, we must grasp the arguments justifying the setting up of a coercive power; for they explain how Hobbesian agents could set up a sovereign.

If we set up a sovereign with sufficient coercive power, violation will no longer be so attractive to people who might otherwise be inclined to violation. Coercion alters the options in two related ways: (1) The commonwealth compels me to comply, and punishes me for non-compliance, in cases where it would appear beneficial for me to cheat if I were not going to be punished. Since I now face a threat of punishment, it no longer appears to be in my interest to do what would otherwise appear to be in my interest. (2) I will now be assured that potential violators will be deterred from violation, and so I will be confident about making and keeping agreements. I need no longer refuse to make the agreement out of fear that others will not comply. Moreover, they can reach the same estimate about my behaviour.

According to Hobbes, the second effect of coercion is more important than the first. The main difficulty lies not in giving me a reason to keep my agreements, but in assuring me that others will keep their agreements if I keep mine. I am sufficiently assured only if I know that others will be punished for any violations. The obligation to keep a promise precedes any legal sanction.[80] The coercive power of the commonwealth is relevant, not primarily because it coerces me to do my part, but because it assures me that others will do their part for fear of being punished (L. 14.18–19). With this assurance about others, I have sufficient reason to keep my part of the promise. According to Hobbes, I am obliged to keep it, whether or not I will be punished if I do not keep it.[81]

The obligation to keep a promise, apart from the threat of punishment, arises from the law of nature. When we understand the law of nature, we see that the universal keeping of promises promotes the preservation of society; and since the preservation of society promotes my preservation, I have a reason for agreeing to the universal keeping of promises.[82] According to Hobbes's view of reasons, motives, and obligations, my obligation—apart from any threat of punishment—to keep my promise consists in my having a sufficient motive to keep it, when I bear in mind all the relevant consequences of keeping it and of breaking it. Coercion has to be applied to us, not because we have no reason to keep our agreements otherwise, but in order to give everyone sufficient reason to believe that others will keep agreements.

494. Objections to the Prudential Argument

This is a plausible argument to show that a Hobbesian agent has an overriding motive, and therefore (according to Hobbes's analysis of reasons) a sufficient reason, to join in the

men equally to the performance of their covenants, by the terror of some punishment greater than the benefit they expect by the breach of their covenant . . . and such power there is none before the erection of a commonwealth.' (15.3)

[80] 'In contracts we say, I will do this; In laws, Do this. Contracts oblige us, laws tie us fast, being obliged. (lege obligati tenemur.) A contract obligeth of it self, the law holds the party obliged by virtue of the universal contract of yielding obedience. Therefore in contract it is first determined what is to be done, before we are obliged to do it; but in law we are first obliged to perform, and what is to be done is determined afterwards.' (Civ. 14.2) Cf. Taylor, 'Hobbes' 55.

[81] This point is emphasized by Barry, 'Warrender' 54.

[82] This is what Kavka, HMPT 358, calls 'rule-egoism', discussed by Boonin-Vail, THSMV 82–92.

creation of a commonwealth. But it is open to objections, or at least to qualifications, if we look more carefully at the motives of such an agent.

Hobbes compares two situations: (1) We are in the state of nature and we have made no agreement to set up a commonwealth (including the laying down of our arms). (2) We are living in a commonwealth set up as a result of our agreement. He argues plausibly that if we are in the first situation, we prefer the second. But it does not follow that we can replace the first situation with the second. The commonwealth comes into existence only if we have both made and fulfilled an agreement to lay down our arms and to resign the use of force to the sovereign. Can Hobbesian agents be expected to fulfil such an agreement? Will it appear to them to be in their interest to comply with the provisions setting up a sovereign with a monopoly of the use of force?

Hobbes introduces coercion to counteract people's tendencies to violate agreements, but the only mechanism for introducing coercion seems to be an agreement. The sovereign monopolizes the use of coercive force only after we have all laid down our arms, and so the laying down of our arms cannot be coerced. I must lay down my arms without coercion, in compliance with an agreement, before we have a mechanism to assure compliance with agreements. But if agreements without coercion are unstable, the agreement to establish a coercive mechanism is unstable.

Hobbesian agents create this instability. Each one has a good reason for making an agreement that requires all to lay down their arms, but also a good reason for breaking the agreement. Since we are still in the state of nature, it is to my advantage to induce other people to disarm before I do; once they have done that, I have gained a competitive advantage, and the resulting situation will be better for me than either unilateral disarmament by me or simultaneous disarmament by all would be.[83] The analogous position involving sovereign states who try to agree on disarmament seems to suggest the difficulties of securing an effective agreement, given the benefits of inducing others to disarm first.

This suggestion may appear unrealistic. It implies that we can take Hobbes's picture literally enough to imagine the situation in which we are all disarmed, but the sovereign is not yet in a position to exercise coercive power. But perhaps we cannot really distinguish these two stages. Perhaps we should think of the agreement to lay down our arms, to set up the sovereign, and to authorize him to act for us, as a single indivisible agreement enacted all at once, and not in stages.[84] We cannot, then, assume a situation in which all are disarmed and so unable to protect themselves, while waiting for the sovereign to protect them. And even if we could legitimately think of distinct stages in setting up the sovereign, would it really be to my advantage to be the last one to disarm? If the others have a reasonable prospect of setting up a sovereign with the power to coerce, would it not be hazardous for me to hesitate to join them, since I would be exposed to the danger of retaliation? In this

[83] See Hampton, HSCT 135.

[84] Hobbes describes authorization: 'This is more than consent, or concord; it is a real unity of them all, in one and the same person, made by covenant of every man with every man, in such manner, as if every man should say to every man, I authorize and give up my right of governing myself, to this man, or to this assembly of men, on this condition, that thou give up thy right to him, and authorize all his actions in like manner' (L. 17.13). See Hampton, HSCT, ch. 5; Kavka, HMPT 391. Cf. Cudworth (§551).

respect, the comparison between Hobbesian individuals and sovereign states considering disarmament may be misleading.

But Hobbes may face a related difficulty. His argument assumes individuals thinking about forming an agreement to act collectively. But he does not consider the possibility of groups of people who may see a benefit in remaining armed while others disarm. A group may be strong enough collectively to defend itself against punishment, especially if it can organize its aggression so as to prevent the disarmers from forming effective means of coercion.

One might ask on Hobbes's behalf whether this appeal to groups does not take for granted an answer to his question. How can a group be stable enough if it has not already made the sort of agreement that he describes? If unwillingness to disarm prevents the formation of a commonwealth, will it not prevent the formation of smaller groups as well? As Plato remarks, even the members of an aggressive group must refrain from injustice against one another; but how can they manage that without a Hobbesian covenant?[85]

This defence against the objection does not seem adequate. For even if a Hobbesian commonwealth is needed for complete assurance in making and keeping covenants, assurance may come in degrees. We might see enough mutual advantage in the short term to warrant a short-term agreement. Even if an armed gang can manage only a short-term agreement, it may still disrupt the formation of a commonwealth by attacking the people who disarm.

This objection to Hobbes does not assume that the members of a gang are correct in believing it is in their interest to attack the disarmers who are trying to form a commonwealth. It is enough if they believe it. For Hobbes acknowledges that the sovereign needs to coerce people who form false views of their interest even when they are within the commonwealth. Before we form a commonwealth, people are liable to errors about their interest; that is why we need to bring a commonwealth into being. But if some people's false views encourage them to form armed gangs, it is difficult to see how others can bring the commonwealth into being. The very existence of armed gangs makes it more reasonable for those who would like to form a commonwealth to form their own armed gangs instead.

Hobbes might try to turn this objection to his advantage. The difficulty that we face in starting the process of disarmament will be apparent to a Hobbesian agent. He will see that the formation of gangs may leave him and everyone else stuck in the state of nature, which they all recognize to be worse than the commonwealth. Since he recognizes this, can he not also see that they would all be better off if they all refrained from this line of thought and simply accepted the agreement to set up the commonwealth?

We may grant that any individual Hobbesian agent can see this, and that everyone can see this sometimes. But it does not follow that enough people can share this insight for long enough to make disarmament effective. Hobbes seems to rely on an unrealistic assumption about stable and correct shared beliefs; and so he does not show that the process that sets up a commonwealth is accessible to Hobbesian agents. He could ensure stable and correct shared beliefs if he simply postulated that each individual has only true beliefs about his own interest; but he does not intend to postulate this, since he defends the coercive power of the state by arguing that it is needed to coerce individuals with false beliefs about their interest.

---

[85] Cf. Plato, *Rep.* 352b–c.

This argument tends to show that Hobbes relies on unrealistic claims, as measured by his description of Hobbesian agents, about the people who are supposed to establish the commonwealth. He does not seem to show that Hobbesian agents can establish a commonwealth. Reliance on unrealistic assumptions may in some circumstances be reasonable, as we will see in considering later appeals to a social contract. But it needs to be justified by showing that the unrealistic assumptions give the argument an appropriate rational or moral significance.[86] Hobbes takes its rational and moral significance to be derived from its psychological realism. An attempt to derive rational and moral significance from something other than psychological realistic assumptions requires us to depart from Hobbes's basic aim of reducing moral reasons to overriding motives.

495. Prudence and Motivation in the State of Nature

Our objection to Hobbes has assumed that, as he sometimes assumes, everyone's dominant motive pursues the long-term satisfaction of one's desires; in short, prudent desires dominate. We ought now to withdraw this assumption, and allow, as Hobbes sometimes allows, that people have other motives, concerned with shorter-term satisfaction, that may be stronger than prudent motives. As he acknowledges, it is possible for us, when we deliberate about our interest, to decide in favour of an imprudent action.

If Hobbes agrees that imprudent desires may be stronger than prudent desires, he should not be satisfied with an argument to show—even if he could show—that self-interested and prudent people will form and maintain a commonwealth. Such an argument does not show that the laws of nature always oblige us; for they may not always engage our prevalent motives. The mere knowledge that forming a commonwealth promotes my longer-term interest does not necessarily move me to try to form a commonwealth.

The comparative weakness of prudent desires does not refute Hobbes's claim that we can act on the laws of nature. For if we recognize that in the future we may want to act imprudently, we can do something to prevent ourselves from undoing our prudent choice. If I want to stop drinking whisky, and recognize that I will want to drink more in the future, I may take steps to frustrate my future desire, by pouring the whisky down the sink now, or by making it difficult in the future for me to buy more. These methods of tying my hands in the future explain why it is sensible, from Hobbes's point of view, to join in forming a commonwealth that can coerce me if I try to break its rules. If I foresee that I and others may want to break the rules, I act now to frustrate that future desire.[87]

Moreover, the recognition of imprudent desires may help Hobbes to solve the difficulty that we have raised about starting the process that creates a commonwealth. The instability of our prudent reasoning makes it difficult to see how we could agree to lay down our arms if disarmament must result from an uncoerced agreement. But we can avoid this difficulty about an agreement if we do not assume that submission to coercion must be the product of agreement. Previously we have mentioned the possibility of armed gangs as an objection to Hobbes's argument for the state. But we might try to use them in his favour. If some people form a

---

[86] Cf. Rawls, *TJ* §§24–5.   [87] Cf. Hume on justice, §768.

gang that is stable enough to compel the rest of us to obey, a Hobbesian agent might see that it is in his interest and everyone else's to submit to the gang and make its leader the sovereign.

This attempt to make an armed gang the nucleus of the commonwealth rather than a threat to its formation raises further questions. (1) Why should we trust the gang to avoid aggression against us if we submit? (2) If the gang is made up of Hobbesian agents, how, on Hobbes's view, could it form a stable enough association to be able to compel the rest of us?[88] These questions about assurance do not show that Hobbesian agents cannot form a short-term alliance in a gang; but they become relevant when we consider the gang as a possible basis for a sovereign.

We avoid some difficulties if we exploit Hobbes's admission (sometimes) that our dominant motive is not always prudent. Suppose that A and B form a temporary association in the state of nature. But then A's forceful personality causes B to form a passion of fanatical loyalty to A. A and B then become a strong team, since their partnership is immune to the normal Hobbesian sources of instability; B's fanatical loyalty makes him forgo opportunities to betray A, and A sees that B is too useful to be mistreated; hence the association benefits each of them. Now they see that they will be even better off if they can capture other members, in whom they can form the fanatical attachment to A and B collectively that B had to A. Fanaticism helps to remove the distrust that would be left by a purely prudent desire, and the result of it would be in everyone's interest. A band of fanatics may steadily improve its competitive position against non-fanatics, since non-fanatics lack the rigid and imprudent outlook that would be needed for concerted action against the fanatics. Hence fanaticism might spread.

Rejection of the primacy of prudence, therefore, makes one aspect of Hobbes's account of the basis of morality more plausible. Fanaticism is possible if short-term passions are sometimes stronger than long-term desires. These passions are more attached to their objects than they would be if we were purely prudent. We discover on reflexion that we are all better off because some or all of us are sometimes moved by imprudent passions. Recognizing this, we might try to cultivate some irrational passions so that we benefit in the ways we would not benefit if we were always prudent.[89] Imprudent passions help Hobbes to explain those aspects of the origin of the commonwealth that do not fit his claims about the primacy of prudence. If, therefore, Hobbes recognizes imprudent passions, he can more easily explain the formation of a commonwealth in the state of nature.

496. Reason and the Laws of Nature

But the argument about the state of nature is not merely intended to show how the formation of a commonwealth is psychologically possible; it is also intended to show that

---

[88] On alliances in the state of nature see *EL* 19.4. Hobbes's views on agreements resulting from submission to force (*EL* 22.2) suggest what he might say about gangs or 'protection associations'. Hampton, *HSCT* 169–82, suggests that gangs can be formed without any appeal to fanaticism, because there are enough sufficiently far-sighted people around to form them. But this does not ensure their stability; if their members are Hobbesian agents, they seem to have the normal motives for treachery. The difficulty that Plato takes to arise for thoroughly unjust members of gangs seems to arise for Hobbesian gangs.

[89] Cf. Parfit's argument for being irrational on occasions, *RP* 12–13. Cf. Hampton, *HSCT* 63–8, on non-rational passions.

the laws of nature are 'precepts of reason' (*Civ.* 3.32). In Hobbes's view, this is because the laws of nature concern a future good, which is the concern of reason; in violating the principles that secure this future good, we act on 'irrational appetite' (*Civ.* 3.32).[90]

All these claims about the laws of nature presuppose that it is rational to do what must be done to preserve peace and to secure commodious living, in preference to acting on desires that threaten our prospect of peace. This presupposition would be correct if we always preferred peace and commodious living over any other end. In that case, the laws of nature would oblige us; our dominant desire for the end to which they secure the means would move us to observe them. But Hobbes is not justified in claiming that it is especially rational to desire peace, or to follow the laws of nature rather than principles that further our imprudent desires at times when they dominate us. Nor are we always obliged, even in foro interno, to follow the laws of nature. For, according to Hobbes's conception of obligation as motivation, we are sometimes obliged to follow the laws of nature, but we are also sometimes obliged to follow principles that conflict with them; our obligations follow our dominant motives.

These aspects of Hobbes's position do not conflict with his claim that the laws of nature are precepts of reason. But they imply that violations of the laws of nature are also precepts of reason. For since precepts are rational insofar as they identify means to satisfy our desires, precepts that prescribe means to satisfy imprudent desires are no less rational than the laws of nature. It is rational to establish a commonwealth, when our prudent desires dominate, and rational to frustrate its establishment, when imprudent desires dominate. When we are prudent, we can take steps to frustrate our imprudent desires when they arise; hence, for instance, we pour the whisky down the sink if we believe we will want to drink too much of it. But equally we can take steps when we are imprudent to frustrate our prudent desires; if I am angry enough at you, I may insult you, even though I know I will want your help in the future and that the insult will turn you against me. Both attitudes to our future desires are equally rational, given the purely instrumental account of rationality.

The position that Hobbes is committed to, therefore, is different from the one he puts forward. It is close to Hume's position. Hume goes further than Hobbes goes in tracing the implications of a purely instrumental view of practical reason. Since Hobbes sometimes accepts this purely instrumental view, he is committed to acceptance of the conclusions that Hume draws from it.[91] But he does not draw these conclusions. In particular he does not apply them to his defence of the laws of nature.

Questions about self-preservation expose some of the basic difficulties in Hobbes's argument. His account of the laws of nature and our obligation to seek peace seems to require the primacy of self-preservation. But that primacy both lacks support in Hobbes's account of deliberation and conflicts with some of the mechanisms that are apparently needed to bring a commonwealth into existence. No easy modification allows Hobbes to defend all his main claims.

---

[90] Quoted more fully in §493.   [91] See Hume (§736) and §496 above.

36

HOBBES: MORALITY

497. Hobbes's Attitude to Morality

Hobbes believes that the difference between the state of nature and the commonwealth explains why the true moral philosophy is the science of the laws of nature. If Hobbesian agents form a commonwealth that has the power to compel the observance of rules preserving the peace, they have sufficient reason, according to Hobbes, to observe these rules. The benefits of stability and non-aggression are so large and so evident that we must, if we think clearly about our interest, want them to continue at any cost. Since the laws of nature are also the principles of morality, we have good reason to accept morality.

If we attend to Hobbes's defence of morality, we may be surprised that his early critics attacked him for his allegedly immoral conclusions.[1] Did they simply misunderstand him, or did they perversely refuse to give him credit for his aims, or did they believe that he failed in his aims?

Hobbes's approach to morality is reductive; he attacks those who believe that morality rests on justified claims about human nature that go beyond his psychological account. But such a reduction might be intended either as a vindication or as a rejection of morality. It is a vindication if it shows that the main claims of morality are justified within Hobbesian psychology. It is a rejection of morality if it shows that there is no place for morality within Hobbesian psychology.

Some criticisms of Hobbes are unfair because they do not recognize that he seeks a reductive vindication of morality. They treat him as an enemy of morality because he traces morality to these specific psychological foundations; but Hobbes believes that his exposure of these psychological foundations supports morality, by showing that it does not need the indefensible psychological claims invoked by Scholastic theories.

It is unfair to treat Hobbes as an enemy of morality, if we consider only his intentions. But it may not be unfair, if we also consider the implications of his arguments. For if Hobbesian psychology tends to undermine morality, critics fasten on a genuine feature of Hobbes's position, even if he does not intend it.

---

[1] His critics include Cudworth, Clarke, Cumberland, and Pufendorf. See also Bowle, *HC*; Mintz, *HL*, ch. 6.

498. Hobbes's Defence of Morality

Hobbes's restricted conception of practical reason limits his vindication of morality. Even if he shows that it is instrumental to self-preservation, he does not show that it is uniquely rational; it is rational only on those occasions when the desire for self-preservation is dominant. On other occasions some other principles are rational. But this restriction might not make much difference. If our desire for self-preservation is often dominant, it will be especially useful to find the principles that further this desire rather than others. If morality can be shown to further this desire, that is a significant vindication.

To vindicate morality in this way, we must also restrict its scope. Some of the 'old moral philosophers' claim that morality is good for human beings without qualification, because it suits human nature; it relies on reasons that we can see to be good reasons for rational agents as such. Hobbes believes that this defence of morality is too ambitious, and therefore tends to undermine morality. In some circumstances moral considerations do not give us good reasons, and so the moral virtues are not suitable for human beings as such. In the state of nature we have no reason to accept the principles we intuitively regard as moral principles. It is too dangerous to treat other people well, since we may just increase their ability to harm us when they double-cross us. Since we cannot be assured that they will observe the laws of nature towards us, we are unwise if we observe the laws of nature towards them. Moreover, since our motives and aims are all self-interested, we have no reason to treat other people in accordance with moral principles; for it will not be in our interest to do this in the state of nature.

But though we have no reason to follow moral rules in the state of nature, we can defend them in more restricted circumstances. The commonwealth reduces the costs that deter us from following moral principles in the state of nature; for it coerces violators, and so removes the competitive advantage that others might gain from double-crossing me after I treat them well. In these circumstances morality is not only less dangerous, but also rational; for moral principles are those that informed self-interested agents want to be the rules governing a Hobbesian state. Since a Hobbesian state is in their interest, acceptance of these moral principles is in their interest too.

Only part of this argument presupposes Hobbes's psychology. Even if we are not Hobbesian egoists, we might agree that in the state of nature, as he describes it, the normal moral requirements do not apply, because the cost of fulfilling them is too high. We might agree with Hobbes's view that morality costs us too much, because we lack mutual assurance. If we agree that we ought not to observe the ordinary moral rules if they are ruinous or dangerous to us, we agree that self-preservation imposes some limits on the observance of these rules. But it does not follow that the observance of moral rules must always be in my interest; they may often require some sacrifice of self-interest, as long as it is not ruinous.

Hobbes's psychology supports his further claim that we have reason to observe moral rules only if it promotes our self-preservation. That is why he believes that our agreement to form a commonwealth, to assure mutual compliance, must also be in the interest of each agent. In his view, we are obliged to follow morality if and only if we have a dominant motive to follow it; we have a dominant motive if and only if we recognize that it is in our interest. If we are members of a commonwealth, we find that morality promotes the preservation of the commonwealth that is in our interest.

499. Indirect Arguments for Morality

Within a commonwealth, therefore, Hobbes argues that we have self-interested reasons to observe ordinary moral principles. But he does not argue that the observance of every single moral principle on every occasion benefits me, or even that it preserves the state. The different moral principles and virtues constitute a set of rules for the preservation of the state and for the preservation of 'peaceful, sociable, and comfortable living' within the state. He mentions justice, gratitude, modesty, equity, mercy, and the other recognized virtues. But none of these virtues explicitly limits itself by the requirements of the preservation of the state.

Hobbes's appeal to these virtues implies that we preserve the commonwealth better if we follow rules that do not aim directly at its preservation. He offers an indirect consequentialist defence of morality. It is indirect because it gives us reasons to follow a specific rule on a particular occasion without attention, on that occasion, to the consequences of our action or of the observance of the rule. The benefits of this inattention are familiar in non-moral action. If we are looking for means to enjoyment, we may discover that whole-hearted absorption in an activity is sometimes the best way to enjoy it. We may interfere with this absorption if we turn our attention to the pleasant consequences of the activity, so that we make it a less effective means to our enjoyment. Something similar may be true about moral rules. If we are acting bravely or kindly, for instance, we may do better if we act spontaneously and immediately; attention to the consequences of our actions may prevent them from achieving the consequences we attend to.

To explain such cases we may introduce a 'two-level' argument. We may distinguish the context of immediate deliberation about what to do here and now from the context of reflexion. We do not consider consequences in our immediate deliberation, but we consider them in reflexion about what virtues we ought to cultivate, what habits of action we ought to strengthen or weaken, and what patterns of immediate deliberation we ought to use. Butler suggests that in the context of reflexion—'in a cool hour', as he puts it—we can appropriately ask questions that ought not to intrude into immediate deliberation.[2] This form of two-level indirect justification is the most plausible way of understanding the relation of the Aristotelian virtues to the pursuit of one's own happiness.

Two-level arguments may involve two different sorts of relations between the two levels. In a 'transparent' theory the principles underlying the two levels are consistent, and the second-level principles explain the truth of the first-level principles, even though we ought not to consider them in immediate deliberation. We can reflect on our first-level principles when we are not engaging in first-level activities, and then we can recognize the second-level basis of the first-level principles; we vindicate our first-level principles. In an 'opaque' theory, however, one level relies on principles that we reject when we think at the other level.

---

[2] See §708.

The second-level principles do not explain why the first-level principles are true; they might advise us to behave as if they were true, or to induce ourselves to believe in their truth, or to close our eyes to reasons for disbelieving them. In this case the two levels are 'opaque' to each other.

Our previous example of enjoyment illustrates the difference between transparent and opaque theories. Perhaps I regard enjoyment as a worthwhile end, and I recognize that I will gain most enjoyment by pursuing an activity that I value apart from its enjoyment, and by excluding thoughts of enjoyment when I am engaged in the activity. With this in mind, I might play the violin, valuing it for itself. I hold a two-level conception, but the levels are transparent to each other. When I reflect in a cool hour on the fact that I play the violin for my enjoyment, I do not undermine my pursuit of the activity; nor do I question my belief that it is valuable apart from my enjoyment. If, however, I regard enjoyment as the only end worth pursuing for its own sake, and the rest of the story is the same, the two levels are opaque to each other. For when I reflect in a cool hour, I must recognize that I not only believe (at the first level) that playing the violin—something other than enjoyment—is to be valued as an end, but also believe (at the second level) that nothing except enjoyment is to be valued as an end. My belief at one level conflicts with my belief at the other level.

An opaque two-level theory is easy to understand if different people occupy the two levels. If you are trying to educate me, you may want to teach me not only to act in certain ways, but also to act for certain reasons and to follow certain rules. But if you teach me to do this, you may not tell me why you want me to follow these rules or to recognize these reasons; you may have your own reasons for teaching me to follow the rules that I follow. If I learn your reasons, I may or may not change my mind about whether the reasons I act on are good reasons.

But how can a two-level theory be opaque if the same person holds the theory at both levels? If I recognize both levels, how can I avoid rejecting one or the other when I see the conflict between them? We can answer this question once we see that we may fail to recognize the conflict between our beliefs at different levels, or we may fail to confront it. Even if we confront it, we may not abandon either level of the theory; perhaps the opaque theory is the best we can do. One might even argue that, having recognized the conflict, we ought to try to forget about it. A troop of soldiers sent on a dangerous mission with only a slight chance of success might want to try to disregard the evidence showing that they are very likely to be killed. They might prefer to expose themselves to influences that will make them more prone to believe they will succeed in their mission. If they thought about why they form these beliefs in themselves, they would come to see that the beliefs are false; hence it is better if they do not think about this.

These reflexions on two-level theories may help us to identify some of the questions that arise about Hobbes. His definition of a law of nature connects it with one's own preservation (L. 14.3); but his discussion of the individual laws of nature does not connect them directly with one's own interest. He connects the individual laws of nature with the preservation of peace and the stability of the commonwealth, and therefore connects them indirectly with my self-interest, because I gain from the preservation of peace. Even if the preservation of the commonwealth is in my interest, it does not follow that everything that is required of me to preserve the commonwealth is more in my interest than anything else I might do. Hobbes's argument, then, is indirect.

Similarly, the connexion between specific moral principles and the preservation of peace is indirect. Hobbes does not suggest that each principle aims at the preservation of peace. He needs to explain why it is better to follow the recognized moral virtues, which do not refer to the preservation of peace, than to follow rules aiming explicitly at this end. An indirect defence of morality may be more or less plausible if it is a two-level theory, transparent or opaque. An opaque theory is most flexible in accommodating intuitive objections to a consequentialist defence, since the theory implies that we will hold lower-level beliefs inconsistent with the higher-level principles. But an opaque theory raises the prospect of instability between the two levels, if reflexion at one level tends to undermine the beliefs we hold at the other level.

500. Morality and the Preservation of Peace

Hobbes's argument about morality succeeds only if each of his two indirect arguments succeeds. The indirect argument connecting peace with self-interest proves the point about morality only if the indirect argument connecting morality with the preservation of peace succeeds. We may therefore begin with the argument about morality.

Hobbes can show that moral principles tend to preserve peace, if he offers a plaus-ible account of the content of moral principles and he shows that precisely these prin-ciples preserve peace. He is justified in claiming that the accepted moral rules help to preserve peace, since observance of them reduces the tendency to conflict. But this fact about the moral rules does not explain their character, unless we can show that no other rules would preserve peace as well or better. If we have reason to prefer the accepted moral rules over other rules that preserve peace as well or better, the tendency to preserve peace cannot be our whole reason for accepting the moral rules or their sole justification.

To see whether Hobbes is right, we need to consider apparent exceptions to the requirements of the traditional virtues. Might we protect the state better and preserve peace better if we followed less sweeping rules with more exceptions? These rules might allow, for instance, the breaking of promises on the right occasions, or might allow public officials to break the law when it is expedient. Machiavelli argues that a ruler should sometimes violate the requirements of justice, gratitude, and mercy, to secure the stability of the state.[3] In his view, steady adherence to moral rules makes the state too inflexible to meet emergencies, and so we ought not to commit ourselves to them.

Hobbes agrees with Machiavelli's claim that my obligation to follow the rules of conventional other-regarding morality is strictly limited, and in particular that it depends on my view of how far I can rely on other people to follow the same rules. Following Machiavelli, he believes that self-preservation and the preservation of the state are the basic

---

[3] See §404. Influence of Machiavelli on Hobbes's moral and political theory has not been shown, though it has sometimes been suggested. Saxenhouse, 'Modern' 124–37, suggests that the case for such influence is strengthened by consideration of a discourse on Tacitus (which she takes to be an early essay by Hobbes, published in 1620).

aims that give us good reason to follow or to break a moral rule.[4] Machiavelli particularly wants to show that it is legitimate for a ruler (individual or collective) to advance the interests of the ruler or the state (not always clearly distinguished) even by immoral means. Hobbes tries to convince subjects that they have no good reason to disobey the ruler. He believes that if we understand the moral virtues, we see that we have good reason to observe them, in the appropriate circumstances, and in particular we see why we are not justified in disobeying the ruler. Here, then, he is not concerned directly with Machiavelli's concerns. But he also assumes that subjects of the commonwealth can expect their rulers to observe the laws of nature in relation to them. He does not endorse Machiavellian rules that violate the laws of nature.

But Hobbes does not try to show that there are no occasions of the sort that Machiavelli describes. This is a gap in his argument. If his claims about peace commit him to acceptance of Machiavellian rules, he cannot justify the traditional moral rules, which do not allow Machiavellian restrictions on promise-keeping and so on. If Hobbes has reason to reject the traditional moral rules in favour of Machiavellian rules, or if he gives no reason for preferring the traditional rules over Machiavellian rules as means for keeping the peace, he does not explain the moral virtues. Morality, therefore, may not be a system of Hobbesian laws of nature, designed to secure a Hobbesian state. In that case, Hobbes has no good reason to assume that traditional moral principles preserve the state better than Machiavellian rules would.

Hobbes might argue, however, that people are more likely to accept the ordinary moral rules than to accept the more efficient Machiavellian rules, and that therefore the adoption of ordinary moral rules is more likely to lead to the law-abiding habits that increase stability in the commonwealth. Perhaps it is better, he might argue, if people are trained simply to accept ordinary moral rules than if they are trained to consider the preservation of peace all the time. This is a two-level justification.

Are the two levels transparent or opaque to each other? That depends on why ordinary moral rules (requiring, say, that promises be kept and that punishment be inflicted only when guilt has been settled) are better at preserving peace than more flexible rules (allowing public officials to break promises or to inflict penalties on the innocent) would be. If the reason is that most people think there is some reason, apart from preservation of peace, for observing the stricter rules, the two levels are opaque to each other. For, according to Hobbes, the preservation of peace is the only reason for accepting one moral rule rather than another; if we believe that some rules safeguard rights that belong to human beings apart from any commonwealth, we are mistaken.

Hobbes does not go into this question in detail. It is difficult to believe, however, that he can plausibly maintain all these claims: (1) Preservation of peace is the only good reason for prescribing a particular moral rule. (2) Ordinary moral rules are better than Machiavellian rules would be at preserving peace. (3) The two levels are transparent to each other.

If the third claim is true, our readiness to believe ordinary moral rules, and to suppose we have reason to act on them, is not undermined by our coming to believe that they are justified only to the extent that they preserve peace. But this is quite unlikely. We are

---

[4] On criticisms of Machiavelli by some Scholastics see §449.

relatively stable in our observance of moral rules, apart from what we may regard as the best means to preserve peace, because we think we have some distinct reason for observing them. If this is so, Hobbes's claim to defend ordinary moral rules by appeal to their role in preserving peace depends on our observing them for reasons that, in the light of his theory, are bad reasons. His defence, then, raises some serious objections that he does not try to answer.

These considerations suggest that we might prefer Hobbesian laws of nature over Machiavellian rules on the ground that they preserve the peace more effectively. If Hobbesian laws of nature are generally accepted, and known to be accepted, in a commonwealth, people will trust one another more, and trust their rulers more. There will be less injustice, conflict, and suspicion, and so the commonwealth will be more stable than the sort of republic that Machiavelli imagines. Hence, we might argue, rulers will not need to resort to Machiavellian devices. But this defence of Hobbes is not decisive. For the Machiavellian might still answer that Machiavellian rules allow the rulers to react more flexibly to dangers to the peace.

This dispute between a Hobbesian and a Machiavellian view suggests a possible compromise. Why not allow the rulers to violate Hobbesian laws of nature while teaching their subjects to observe them?[5] In that way we seem to get the benefits of both Machiavellian flexibility and Hobbesian stability. We can reduce the danger of instability arising from distrust if the rulers conceal their violations of the laws of nature as far as possible. Such an arrangement would give us an opaque two-level theory of morality, but the two levels would reflect the outlook of different people. The subjects would accept moral rules without reference to their usefulness for preserving peace, while the rulers would impose them on the subjects, not on themselves, as means to preserving peace. Any moral objections to this arrangement are irrelevant unless they can be expressed in Hobbes's terms, as arguments to show that the arrangement threatens the preservation of peace.

We need not try to settle this dispute between Hobbes and Machiavelli. It is enough to point out that the dispute seems to turn on empirical questions. If Hobbes wants to defend the laws of nature as means to the preservation of peace, he should compare them with more Machiavellian rules and strategies, and explain why he has a better empirical case for the laws of nature. Since he does not do this, he gives us no Hobbesian reason for preferring the laws of nature.

We may overlook this weakness in his case if we evaluate it from the moral point of view. We may be inclined to reject Machiavellian rules, however effective they may be, once we see that they are immoral. Once we see that, further inquiry (we may suppose) is unnecessary. This sort of reply, however, is not open to Hobbes. Since he intends to explain and to justify moral claims by reducing them to rules for the preservation of peace, he cannot reject alternative rules for the preservation of peace on the ground that they are immoral.

Hobbes's claims about morality anticipate some of the difficulties that arise for moralists who try to explain moral principles as maxims for promoting the general good or for maximizing utility. They have to show that the promotion is indirect, and explain why this

---

[5] Some of Machiavelli's remarks suggest that this is his view. See §§403, 410.

is preferable to more direct promotion. Hobbes is in a weak position, since he takes the laws of nature to aim not at the public good, but simply at the preservation of the state. It seems easier to show that the relatively narrow aim of preserving the state may diverge from morality than to show that the broader aim of maximizing the good of all those affected may diverge from it; for the broader aim is more plausibly connected with the outlook of universal benevolence. But the general question arises for later utilitarians no less than it does for Hobbes.

501. Revolutionary Objections

Let us now suppose that Hobbes succeeds in his indirect consequentialist defence of morality as a means to preserve peace. The next indirect argument in his defence of morality seeks to link preservation of peace with one's individual interest.

To show that it is always in my interest to prefer the preservation of peace over any other prospective benefit, Hobbes needs to answer three different sorts of objections: (1) Some members of a commonwealth might decide that they would be better off if the commonwealth were dissolved and replaced either with the state of nature or with a different commonwealth. This is a 'revolutionary' threat. (2) Some might decide they would be better off if the state were deliberately made less efficient in enforcing its rules, so that they could benefit from the loopholes that would be created. This is a 'libertarian' threat. (3) Some might decide they would be better off if the state remained as efficient as it is, but they disobeyed the laws when they could get away with it. This is a 'non-conformist' threat.

Hobbes answers the revolutionary threat by arguing that since peace and stability are better than war and the state of nature, it is always better to put up with the commonwealth we have. This answer aims at two types of revolutionary: (a) One revolutionary plans a civil war, and therefore a return to the state of nature, as a means to improving the commonwealth. (b) Another takes the risk of war, and hence the risk of returning to the state of nature, as part of the strategy of improvement. The 1917 Bolshevik Revolution followed the first strategy. The Parliamentary leaders in England in the early 1640s followed the second strategy, and found that they had to fight a civil war. In 1688 the risk of a civil war did not result in a war in England, but resulted in one in Ireland. Hobbes's argument is primarily concerned with the second type of revolutionary, since a refutation of this strategy will also refute the first type.

He asks us to compare the worst possible result of pursuing either of the options open to us. The two worst results are: (1) We put up with the commonwealth we have, even though it is extremely oppressive. (2) Our revolutionary strategy returns us to the state of nature. Since the worst outcome of acquiescence in an oppressive state is better than the worst outcome of the revolutionary strategy, we ought to prefer acquiescence. This is an instance of the 'maximin' attitude to risk.

This maximin attitude seems to assume an unjustified degree of aversion to risk. The argument proceeds without any attention to the probability of any of the results, and so it prohibits us from considering the probability in deciding which option to prefer.

Hobbes offers the same argument against those who break rules without intending to cause a revolution. But it seems irrational to ignore probability altogether. Even if peace advances self-preservation more than anything else does, and we value self-preservation above everything else, it does not follow that we should never accept the smallest risk to self-preservation in order to gain some other good. Hobbesian agents who took such an attitude to risk would never cross the street.

Hobbes might answer that this objection misses the point of his attitude to risk. He is not necessarily advocating a maximin attitude to risk in deciding whether to cross the street. But the special features of choices involving the dissolution of the state justify an extremely conservative attitude to the risks involved. In some cases we face a choice between Option 1 (with possible outcomes 1a and 1b) and Option 2 (with possible outcomes 2a and 2b) that satisfies these three conditions: (i) The probabilities are unknown, or difficult to fix with any confidence. (ii) The worst outcome, 2b, is catastrophic. (iii) Neither 1a nor 1b is catastrophic. (iv) 2a is the best outcome, but it offers us comparatively trivial gains over 1a and 1b. In these conditions the maximin attitude is reasonable, and we ought to choose Option 1 over Option 2, even though Option 2 offers us the best of the possible outcomes (2a).

In Hobbes's view, the choices that face us in deciding whether to risk a return to the state of nature have this character. The importance of peace and self-preservation, compared to other goods, ensures that the third and fourth conditions are satisfied. The first option is preservation of the peace with the current unsatisfactory regime either a bit improved (1a) or no better (1b). The second option is revolution, either leading to a much better regime (2a) or back to the state of nature (2b). In this case the second option offers us the prospect of improvement (2a), but this advantage over the first option is small in comparison to the disadvantage of reversion to the state of nature (2b). Hence we should prefer the first over the second option.

Hobbes's argument suffers from his failure to show that the first condition is satisfied. In some cases, may we not reach a reasonable estimate of the probabilities of different outcomes that might justify us in proceeding on a more optimistic assumption than the maximin attitude underlying the choice of the first option? Hobbes might fairly point out that revolutionary action sometimes proceeds on a foolishly optimistic judgment about probabilities, or on a negligent failure to consider them. But it would be difficult to show that all revolutionary action faces this objection. Hence a maximin attitude is unjustified.

But even if we concede Hobbes's assumptions about probabilities, his moral psychology makes it difficult to see how Hobbesian agents could reliably satisfy the second and fourth conditions for a maximin attitude to revolution. In his view, the reasonable course of action is fixed by reference to what promotes our dominant desire at a particular time. But our desire for self-preservation may not always dominate us. Hobbes sometimes maintains that other desires sometimes cause us to act imprudently (from the point of view of self-preservation). From the point of view of such desires, the difference between Option 2a and Option 1 might not be as small as it would need to be to justify the choice of Option 1. Since these other desires may sometimes be stronger than the desire for peace, and since Hobbes treats claims about obligation as predictions about motivation, he is not justified in claiming that everyone always has an overriding obligation to preserve peace and to choose the means to it. We have seen that some 'fanatical' desires are needed to set up the commonwealth. If some members of a commonwealth still have fanatical desires, they are not always obliged to seek peace above all. Even if the desire for self-preservation is always overriding, it may not override strongly enough to make the difference between Option 2a and Option 1 small enough.

Might Hobbes concede that our desires do not always result in a maximin outlook, but argue that they ought to, and that they would if they were rational? If he claims that a refusal to adopt a maximin outlook in these circumstances is irrational, he relies on an irreducibly normative conception of rationality. But then he violates his aim of reducing reasons to motives.

Hobbes succeeds in his aim of vindicating morality only if he can show that his assumptions about aversion to risk are psychologically correct; they must be true descriptions of the outlook of agents in the situations he describes. But his argument fails this condition. He may still be right to claim that morality rests on assumptions about aversion to risk. If these assumptions cannot be justified on psychological grounds, they may be understood as aspects of the moral outlook; morality refuses to subject certain kinds of protection to gambling. Hobbes notices that these attitudes are characteristic of morality, but he cannot explain, within his psychological assumptions, why they are reasonable.[6] He fails to include them within a vindicating reduction of morality; for Hobbesian psychology makes morality sometimes irrational.

502. Libertarian Objections

Hobbes's defence of morality presupposes that we want an efficient state. He assumes that I will be ready to observe moral rules that require me and everyone else to forgo some immediate advantages for the sake of peace, if I believe that general observance of such rules increases efficiency. But might I not benefit from a less efficient system? If I could gain some advantages over other people, by greater prudence and more acute calculation of my interests, might I not benefit if the state were inefficient enough to allow me to violate the conditions of agreement on occasions when it suited me? I seem to have no sufficient reason for keeping the rules if I am not forced to keep them; and I seem to have no sufficient reason to prefer a very efficient mechanism of enforcement.

Such libertarian arguments fail if it is better for me to live in a state that enforces compliance on its citizens predictably and efficiently than to live in a less efficient state. One might argue in Hobbes's defence that the libertarian argument ignores the corrosive effects of giving other people the opportunity that I want for myself to break the rules. I may be harmed if other people have this opportunity, even though I would benefit if I alone had the opportunity. Though I might want Gyges' Ring for myself alone, I might not want it if everyone else had it too. Hence I might prefer no one's having it over everyone's having if, if these were my only options.

---

[6] These assumptions are prominent in Rawls, *TJ*, ch. 3. Rawls tries to show why they provide an appropriate basis for a moral theory, without claiming that they are realistic.

This argument does not secure Hobbes's conclusion. We cannot always assume that everyone will be equally astute or active in breaking the rules when it suits him. Hence an opportunity for me to break the rules may not allow a greatly increased scale of rule-breaking. The more astute or unscrupulous or energetic might have reason to welcome an arrangement that they would not welcome if everyone were to exploit it in the way they propose to exploit it.

Hobbes faces a further difficulty from the possibility of fanaticism. We saw earlier how fanaticism might help the formation of a state that would be in the interest of Hobbesian agents. Fanaticism equally makes it easier for the Hobbesian agent to reject the Hobbesian state in favour of a more inefficient one. We could defend an efficient Hobbesian state, if a loophole for even one Hobbesian agent created massive instability; and an inefficient state might leave this dangerous loophole, if all citizens were equally clear-sighted and well-informed Hobbesian agents. But if this is not so, a Hobbesian agent might well prefer a less efficient state. If some citizens are fanatical enough, they will not break the rules even if it is in their interest to do so, and even if they see that it is. If their compliance can be relied on, the Hobbesian agent has good reason to observe the rules less than he would have to if these other people were less fanatical. Evidently, the more disloyal one citizen is, the greater the fanaticism required in the rest of the citizens. It suits him best if other people are so attached to moral rules that they can be relied on to follow them without worrying about their good consequences.

These objections to Hobbes assume that one person takes advantage of the fact that other people are less astute, or lazier, or more fanatical. By taking advantage of these facts, I can do better than I would do if I followed the rules that Hobbes takes to be in each person's interest. From the moral point of view, we clearly take unfair advantage of the differences between people. But the Hobbesian basis of morality does not explain why we should not take this unfair advantage.

503. Non-conformist Objections

The objections of non-conformists to morality raise further questions about the effect of one individual's action on the actions of others. The non-conformist does not want the state to become less efficient, but he wants to take advantage of the opportunities for breaking the rules. If not everyone is equally astute or energetic, not everyone will take advantage of the opportunities for injustice that are open to different people; and so the system need not collapse. Hence Hobbes's 'fool' denies that it is always in his interest to keep the rules of justice. He accepts Hobbes's reasons for agreeing to the commonwealth in the first place, but he points out that these reasons do not justify him in doing what the commonwealth requires of him, if he can gain some greater benefit by unjust action and can avoid punishment for it.[7]

---

[7] 'He does not therein deny that there be covenants; and that they are sometimes broken, sometimes kept; and that such breach of them may be called injustice, and the observance of them justice: but he questioneth, whether injustice, taking away the fear of God (for the same fool hath said in his heart there is no God), may not sometimes stand with that reason, which dictateth to every man his own good; and particularly then, when it conduceth to such a benefit, as shall put a man in a condition, to neglect not only the dispraise, and revilings, but also the power of other men.' (L. 15.4) The fool's argument is discussed by Gauthier, MD 136–7, 144–6.

Hobbes argues that the fool's strategy is not rational, since it is not based on a prudent calculation of the fool's interest. The fool assumes that other people make a mistake about his trustworthiness.[8] But Hobbes answers that the fool makes a mistake here, because he 'could not foresee nor reckon upon' these errors by others. What sort of mistake does the fool make?

Hobbes might intend any of three replies to the fool: (1) His assumptions are so unrealistic that his strategy can never be founded on a reasonable estimate of the facts and probabilities. This reply seems empirically unwarranted. (2) An ordinary estimate of probabilities supports the fool. Still, the dangers of being found out are so severe that we ought to be strongly risk-averse in our calculations about breaking rules. This point, anticipated by Epicurus,[9] is reasonable, but it does not justify Hobbes's claim.[10] Even an appropriate allowance for the costs of discovery, or for the fear of discovery, seems to leave us room to break rules. If Hobbes assumes a maximin attitude, he raises the difficulties that we have already noticed. (3) Perhaps 'cannot' in 'cannot reckon upon' refers to a moral prohibition rather than an impossibility or an error in calculation. Perhaps we are morally required to assume that others are as intelligent as we are, and are likely to find us out. Here an assumption of equality plays an important role.

The second and third of these replies might be taken to rest on some basis other than mere empirical prediction. Hobbes might mean that the fool takes unjustified risks, or that he takes unfair advantage of other people's conformity to rules. But such a reply fails to refute the fool, from Hobbes's self-interested and purely psychological point of view.

In answering the fool, Hobbes assumes that from the self-interested point of view we can see the truth of the assumptions on which justice depends, and that therefore we can see the correctness of the laws of nature from the point of view that showed us why we ought to agree to the setting up of this society. He does not vindicate this claim. He does not justify a stable commitment to morality for the sorts of agents he describes.

504. Indirect Prudence

These replies to the fool assume the legitimacy of his question. They assume that it is reasonable for Hobbesian agents within the commonwealth to appraise a particular action with reference to their individual advantage. In order to answer the fool on this assumption, we must show that the observance of rules is directly beneficial. We have seen, however, that an analogous assumption about the relation between moral rules and the preservation of peace does not support Hobbes. It seemed more plausible to maintain the two-level view that peace is preserved best if we observe moral rules without thinking about this effect. Does this sort of indirect strategy refute the fool?

It may be difficult to see the point of observing the laws of nature, if we consider one action at a time; for then it is easy to see how we may profit by violating them. But we see

---

[8] '...if he live in society, it is by the errors of other men, which he could not foresee, nor reckon upon; and consequently against the reason of his preservation.' (L. 15.5)
[9] See §158.   [10] Darwall, *BMIO* 75, accepts this account of the answer to the fool.

their point if we consider the benefit of having them observed as a whole, in contrast to having them violated as a whole. This point of view shows us why it is better to have some mechanism for compelling obedience to the laws of nature. A coercive mechanism ensures obedience, obedience ensures peace, and we all benefit from peace. If this indirect, global reflexion shows us the benefits of observing the laws of nature, it ought to influence our choice of the motives we want to encourage.

The argument with the fool shows us some motives that we ought not to encourage. We will all be better off if we are all unlike the fool, so that we do not calculate our advantage in particular situations. We will be better off if we confine our calculation of advantage to the initial calculation of the benefits of peace and general observance of the laws of nature. Hobbes suggests that when we enter the state we give up the condition in which 'private appetite is the measure of good and evil'.[11]

Here Hobbes continues his ambiguous and perhaps confused argument about 'discord and conflicts' in our evaluations in the state of nature.[12] He has argued that since what each person calls good is simply what he desires, we are in 'discord' about goods, because our desires differ. This discord results in a state of war. We resolve the discord by agreeing that peace is good, because it fulfils each person's overriding desire. The commonwealth is founded on this common point of view, and requires us to agree in our judgments about goods.

Agreement about goods is not enough, however. For we might agree that it is good for the fool to violate justice. If this is the judgment on which the fool acts, he is not relying on purely private appetite. Similarly, he agrees with other people in thinking peace is good, though he does not agree in observing all the rules designed for preserving peace. We do not require him simply to agree with us in our judgments about what is good; we also require him to agree in being guided by what is good for all of us. Hobbes obscures this point in his claims about private appetite and agreement.

We might, then, treat the claim about abandoning private appetite as an indirect consequentialist claim; in the commonwealth we abandon the policy of considering the costs and benefits of each particular action prescribed by a moral rule. We take a two-level attitude. At the deliberative level, we accord supremacy to the moral rules, and we do not think about whether we gain most for ourselves by observing them. At the reflective level

---

[11] 'And therefore, so long a man is in the condition of mere nature, (which is a condition of war), as private appetite is the measure of good, and evil: and consequently all men agree on this, that peace is good, and therefore also the way, or means of peace, which (as I have showed before) are justice, gratitude, modesty, equity, mercy, and the rest of the laws of nature, are good: that is to say: moral virtues; and their contrary vices, evil.' (*L.* 15.40) '. . . one [seditious doctrine] is that every private man is judge of good and evil actions. This is true in the condition of mere nature, where there are no civil laws; and also under civil government in such cases as are not determined by the law. But otherwise, it is manifest that the measure of good and evil actions is the civil law . . . From this false doctrine, men are disposed to debate with themselves and dispute the commands of the Commonwealth, and afterwards to obey or disobey them as in their private judgments they shall think fit; whereby the Commonwealth is distracted and weakened.' (*L.* 29.6) 'And when men that think themselves wiser than all others clamour and demand right reason for judge, yet seek no more but that things should be determined by no other men's reason but their own, it is as intolerable in the society of men, as it is in play after trump is turned to use for trump on every occasion that suit whereof they have most in their hand. For they do nothing else, that will have every of their passions, as it comes to bear sway in them, to be taken for right reason, and that in their own controversies: bewraying their want of right reason by the claim they lay to it.' (*L.* 5.3) *Civ.* 3.32 (quoted in §478) also suggests that when we recognize that the laws of nature aim at peace, we resolve disagreements about what things are good, because we see that the laws of nature aim at peace, which we all take to be good.
[12] See §478.

we observe that in according supremacy to morality at the deliberative level we preserve peace, and therefore gain more for ourselves than we would gain if we were to think about our own advantage at the deliberative level. We do not follow the fool in assessing the consequences of this or that particular violation of the laws of nature; we bind ourselves to accept the laws of nature as the measure of good and evil.

This is a legitimate two-level indirect consequentialist move. We may be able to see that we are better off if we adhere to the laws of nature without consideration of our own advantage. In that case, just people do better for themselves than fools do. The fact that everyone else has equally good reason to draw the fool's conclusion, and that everyone will be worse off if everyone draws it, can be turned to Hobbes's advantage. Prudential calculation, carried out at the right level and in answer to the right question, shows why we are better off if we do not think as the fool thinks.[13]

This two-level argument, however, does not entirely answer the fool. Even if he agrees to abandon his practice of calculating his advantage in particular cases, he might ask whether it is in his interest to keep this agreement. Even if he agrees that people ought to be trained to obey the laws of nature without question, he might still find that his training leaves him aware of the advantages he might gain by violating the laws of nature. He certainly benefits if other people obey the laws of nature and abandon the calculating of advantages. He also benefits if he appears to be like other people in these ways. Still, he may benefit even more if he is different from other people and is ready to take advantage of opportunities for disobedience.[14] The fool takes unfair advantage of others; but why should this concern him from the point of view of his self-interest?[15]

A further argument for indirect prudence might try to exploit the fool's reasoning. Since we can see that everyone, arguing as a direct egoist, may reach the fool's conclusion, we can see that once we allow ourselves the licence to deliberate as direct egoists, we undermine the system that we try to set up in our collective interest. It is in everyone's interest, therefore, to advocate a system of moral education that trains everyone not to think of their individual interest. While we may advocate this system for indirect egoist reasons, we ought not to allow people to ask about its indirect egoist basis; for once they ask that question, they will see that it is rational for each of them not to follow the requirements of the system.[16]

---

[13] Gauthier, 'Theorist' 21; 'Three' 142–3, suggests this line of argument. He argues that in emerging from the state of nature we must give up the right of nature to think for ourselves about the means to our self-preservation: 'In place of natural reason, one must accept the conventional reason of the law, which directs one to adhere to one's covenants' (143). He quotes from Hobbes's discussion of Bramhall (EW v 193): 'We choose no further than we can weigh. That is good to every man, which is so far good as he can see. All the real good, which we call honest and morally virtuous, is that which is not repugnant to the law, civil or natural; for the law is all the right reason we have, and . . . is the infallible rule of moral goodness. The reason whereof is this, that because neither mine nor the Bishop's reason is right reason fit to be a rule of our moral actions, we have therefore set up over ourselves a sovereign governor, and agreed that his laws shall be unto us, whatsoever they be, in the place of right reason, to dictate to us what is really good. In the same manner as men in playing turn up trump, and as in playing their game their morality consisteth in not renouncing, so in our civil conversation our morality is all contained in not disobeying of the laws.'

[14] Gauthier, 'Three' 144–5, acknowledges that these questions arise for his argument. He discusses them in MA, ch. 6. See also Hampton, HSCT 209–14.

[15] On the fool see Kavka, HMPT 137–56. On rule egoism see 358, 380, discussed by Gauthier, 'Taming'.

[16] This would be the moral equivalent of giving up our right to self-defence once we enter the state, also on indirect egoist grounds. See Hampton, HSCT 201. An indirect argument could answer the difficulty she raises for Hobbes, but only at the greater cost I describe.

If Hobbes went this far, he would endorse an opaque two-level theory. Once we understand the reason—based on collective self-interest—for the moral rules that we must (for reasons of collective self-interest) obey from non-egoistic motives, we must also see that our individual self-interest sometimes justifies the breaking of the rules. Hence our commitment to the rules cannot survive discovery of their basis.

If Hobbes had to reach this conclusion, he could still maintain that knowledge of his theory of human nature and the basis of morality is useful for the cultivation of the moral virtues. But it will be useful only for the cultivation of moral virtues in people who do not know his theory. If we have the task of constructing and teaching a moral code for a given society, and we are convinced by Hobbesian arguments about the importance of peace and the importance of rigid adherence to the laws of nature, we will try to train citizens, in their collective interest, to adhere rigidly to the laws of nature without raising any questions about their own interest. If they start to ask whether rigid adherence promotes their own interest, they will start thinking like the fool.

We will reach this conclusion from Hobbesian premises, if we reject his reasons for believing that the deliberative and the reflective point of view are transparent to each other. These reasons underlie his confidence in answering the fool. But if Hobbes were to abandon his belief in transparency, he would have to abandon the psychological assumptions that make it seem plausible to base morality on self-preservation in the first place; for an indirect argument assumes that we can act for reasons that do not seem to us to promote our own interest. If Hobbes were to admit that, he would be abandoning his reason for believing that the desire for self-preservation is the basis of the laws of nature.

Even if Hobbes were to retreat from his actual position to an opaque two-level theory of morality and self-interest, he would face some difficulty in defending a stable commitment to morality. How could a reflective agent be expected not to ask about the relation between her own interest and the moral rules she has been trained to accept? Once she raises the question, she seems to have good Hobbesian reasons for taking the fool's point of view. This conclusion vindicates some of the objections of Hobbes's opponents who regarded his views as dangerous to morality.

To answer these objections Hobbes might appeal to his further claim that the laws of nature are divine commands. If people are trained to recognize this, they have a motive to follow them even if they do not think about their natural consequences (apart from divine sanctions) for the preservation of peace. If Hobbes took this view, he would reach a position rather similar to the one that Berkeley defends in his sermon 'Passive Obedience'.[17] Perhaps God has chosen to exercise divine power by commanding obedience to rules that in fact promote the preservation of peace; but we need not take this consideration into account, since we have a sufficient motive in the prospect of divine punishment for disobedience. If Hobbes took this view, the appeal to divine commands would bear more weight than it bears in his actual argument.[18] He does not consider this possibility; he relies on a transparent two-level defence of morality.

---

[17] On Berkeley see §699.

[18] This might be regarded as a grain of truth in Warrender's emphasis on divine commands in Hobbes's position. See §487.

505. Psychology and Morality: The Presumption of Equality

In considering objections to Hobbes's defence of morality, we have relied on his psychological assumptions, and on his attempt to reduce norms and obligations to facts about overriding motives. If he maintains this part of his position, he has to rely on some rather strong psychological assumptions that have no obvious basis in his own account of human nature.

It is therefore worth considering a different interpretation of Hobbes's assumptions. We might suggest that, though they are empirically implausible, they deserve consideration as procedural assumptions about morality. Perhaps Hobbes is not describing what is historically or psychologically likely or realistic, but setting out the conditions in which the correctness of a moral rule or system should be assessed. Hobbes seeks to explain the characteristics of moral principles by reference to the state of nature. Demands and assumptions characteristic of moral principles are, in his view, intelligible responses to the specific circumstances of the state of nature. Hence they are intelligible devices for dealing with the threats to peace that arise in the state of nature; since they preserve a commonwealth, they keep us out of the state of nature. So far we have taken arguments from the state of nature to appeal to psychological necessity and plausibility, as determined by Hobbes's psychology. But it is also worth considering them as procedural arguments about the moral point of view.

We can make these different possibilities clearer by examining some of the difficulties that arise for Hobbes's claim that morality presumes equality. The ninth law of nature requires every man to acknowledge every other man as his equal. The tenth law, relying on this acknowledgment, asserts that people have equal rights on entry into the state.[19] People in the state of nature are disposed to demand equal treatment for themselves, and no agreement can be made on any other basis. Hence the rules accepted in the state of nature capture the recognized principles of justice and morality.

---

[19] 'If nature therefore have made men equal, their equality is to be acknowledged; or if nature have made them unequal, yet because men that think themselves equal will not enter into conditions of peace but upon equal terms, such equality must be admitted. And therefore for the ninth law of nature, I put this: that every man acknowledge another for his equal by nature. The breach of this precept is pride. On this law dependeth another: that at the entrance into conditions of peace, no man require to reserve to himself any right which he is not content should be reserved to every one of the rest.' (L. 15.21–2) On equality and justice see also: EL 16.5: '. . . injury, which is the injustice of action, consisteth . . . in the inequality that men, contrary to nature and reason, assume unto themselves above their fellows'. On this point Hobbes believes Aristotle is completely mistaken. See EL 17.1: 'The question, which is the better man, is determinable only in the estate of government and policy, though it be mistaken for a question of nature, not only by ignorant men, . . . but also by him, whose opinions are at this day, and in these parts of greater authority than any other human writings. . . . For though there were such a difference of nature, that master and servant were not by consent of men, but by inherent virtue; yet who hath that eminency of virtue, above others, and who is so stupid as not to govern himself, shall never be agreed upon amongst men; who do every one naturally think himself as able, at the least, to govern another, as another to govern him. And . . . as long as men arrogate to themselves more honour than they give to others, it cannot be imagined how they can possibly live in peace: and consequently we are to suppose, that for peace sake, nature hath ordained this law, That every man acknowledge other for his equal. And the breach of this law, is that we call pride.' Hobbes interprets the commandments of Jesus as requiring that a man 'should esteem his neighbour worthy all rights and privileges that himself enjoyeth; and attribute unto him whatsoever he looketh should be attributed unto himself: which is no more, but that he should be humble, meek, and contented with equality.' (EL 18.6) Failure to acknowledge equality is the source of perpetual war in the state of nature: 'But it is easily judged how disagreeable a thing to the preservation either of mankind, or of each single man, a perpetual war is: But it is perpetual in its own nature, because in regard of the equality of those that strive, it cannot be ended by victory; for in this state the conqueror is subject to so much danger, as it were to be accounted a miracle, if any, even the most strong should close up his life with many years, and old age.' (Civ. 1 13) On the importance of equality see Hampton, HSCT, 24–7.

If moral rules must satisfy a demand for equality, we can see why not all possible rules for maintaining peace are principles of morality. Hobbes's position on this point is not completely clear. He believes that peace is worth any price; if we can secure peace only by accepting someone's offer to make us his servants on any condition he chooses, that is what we have to do. Hence we have no reasonable objection to tyranny. Hobbes does not regard this condition as slavery, since he believes slaves have given no promise to submit to their captors; but it need not differ from the condition of a slave in any other respect.[20]

But despite this attitude to tyranny and oppression, Hobbes does not consider principles that maintain peace by forcing some people into miserable conditions in order to make others better off, even though this arrangement is not necessary for maintaining peace. This is not a purely theoretical possibility that he neglects; many oppressive governments violate many of Hobbes's laws of nature while still maintaining peace. Still, he does not consider the possibility of these principles that maintain peace, but violate the laws of nature. The presumption of equality explains why we might rule out these principles; if they allow oppression of some people simply for other people's benefit, we would not accept them from a starting point of equality.

Hobbes claims that the presumption of equality is realistic because it expresses the actual facts about individuals in the state of nature, and the terms on which they must be supposed to enter the commonwealth. Is he justified in this claim? Perhaps people in the original position would be sensible not to count too heavily on their physical or mental superiority to other particular individuals. But they surely need to consider the possibility that people are unequal in their capacity to grasp the benefits of peace; for the commonwealth is set up to counteract the effects of miscalculation about the effects of grasping at short-term advantage. This question about inequality arises even if we accept Hobbes's assumption that the desire for self-preservation is dominant among people in the state of nature.

But we have also found reasons to question the assumption about self-preservation. The shared desire for self-preservation is not enough to remove distrust and instability in the state of nature. To explain the formation of the commonwealth, it is more plausible to assume some degree of fanaticism in members of gangs who might coerce or persuade others to submit to them. If this is the most plausible mechanism for generating a Hobbesian commonwealth from the state of nature, Hobbes's defence of the presumption of equality is open to doubt. For if a gang can coerce other people for long enough to set up a relatively stable order, individuals have good reason to accept the benefits of peace without equality.

---

[20] 'Dominion acquired by conquest, or victory in war, is that which some writers call despotical. . . . And this dominion is then acquired to the victor when the vanquished, to avoid the present stroke of death, covenanteth, . . . that so long as his life and the liberty of his body is allowed him, the victor shall have the use thereof at his pleasure. And after such covenant made, the vanquished is a servant, and not before: for by the word servant . . . is not meant a captive, which is kept in prison, or bonds, till the owner of him that took him, or bought him of one that did, shall consider what to do with him: for such men, commonly called slaves, have no obligation at all; but may break their bonds, or the prison; and kill, or carry away captive their master, justly: but one that, being taken, hath corporal liberty allowed him; and upon promise not to run away, nor to do violence to his master, is trusted by him. It is not therefore the victory that giveth the right of dominion over the vanquished, but his own covenant.' (L. 20.10–11) 'And because the name of tyranny signifieth nothing more nor less than the name of sovereignty, be it in one or many men, saving that they that use the former word are understood to be angry with them they call tyrants; I think the toleration of a professed hatred of tyranny is a toleration of hatred to commonwealth in general, and another evil seed, not differing much from the former.' (L., Review 9)

This is a case of 'despotical dominion';[21] Hobbes believes that we must accept it if it is the only option open, since any condition that ends the war of all against all is better than the state of nature.

If this is true, a tyrannical regime, violating the laws of nature but preserving the peace, seems to be the most probable alternative to the state of nature. It is difficult to agree with Hobbes's assumption that facts about the state of nature justify his presumption of equality. The ninth and tenth laws of nature, therefore, do not seem necessary for the preservation of peace. Since these two laws of nature are plausible and important moral principles, Hobbes's failure to explain them as means to the preservation of peace tends to undermine his attempted explanation of the traditional virtues. The unrealistic character of the presumption of equality—regarded from the point of view of Hobbes's state of nature—raises a doubt about Hobbes's account of morality.[22]

Hobbes is right to suggest that it is morally appropriate to insist that some equality 'must be admitted' in specifying the terms of social co-operation. A social institution or practice or law that was designed entirely for the benefit of some people without reference to any benefit of the others would be open to objection on moral grounds. Similarly, one might defend a presumption of equality and equal rights as a basic constraint on the preservation of peace; the only peace that deserves to be maintained, one might argue, is the peace that safeguards equal rights. If Hobbes were entitled to that presumption, it would be easier for him to reject some apparently immoral but efficient measures for preserving peace.

We might offer the same defence of assumptions about the equality of individuals within a commonwealth. Hobbes seems to assume equal astuteness and energy in different individuals; without such an assumption his arguments against the libertarian and the non-conformist collapse. The assumption is not empirically plausible, but we might argue that it describes the right point of view for evaluating moral claims. Hobbes rules out calculations that take advantage of other people's lack of astuteness and energy in breaking rules. We might defend him by arguing that it is unfair to take advantage of people in these ways. To avoid taking advantage of them, we ought to assume the same high level of astuteness in everyone.[23]

Hobbes speaks as though the presumption of equality rests simply on people's presumed unwillingness to accept unequal treatment. Such a presumption is difficult to defend on empirical grounds, and that is the only defence he allows. But his emphasis on the presumption highlights a feature of morality that might be defended apart from Hobbes's psychological assumptions.[24] We might take the presumption of equality to mean that a moral principle is acceptable if and only if it can be defended to a group of rational self-interested, non-benevolent agents who regard themselves as equal to each other. This interpretation of Hobbes explains why he sometimes appeals to reciprocity, and advises us to take the other person's point of view.[25] If we do this, we use a social contract as a point

---

[21] See §§494–5.   [22] On Hobbes on equality cf. Green, PE §190.

[23] Kavka, HMPT 188–208, 400, offers a moral interpretation of Hobbes's contract. Gauthier, 'Taming', objects that the state of nature is not a privileged situation for choice (analogous to Rawls's original position).

[24] Hume's account of justice also rests moral demands on empirical psychological claims See §770.

[25] '. . . there is an easy rule to know upon a sudden whether the action I be to do, be against the law of nature or not. And it is but this: that a man imagine himself in the place of the party with whom he hath to do, and reciprocally him in

of view for appraising rules from the impartial, and hence (supposedly) the moral point of view.

506. Psychology and Morality: Risk and Reciprocity

This approach to Hobbesian assumptions as features of the moral point of view may also throw light on his treatment of risk. He relies on a strong aversion to risk in his answer to the revolutionary, but it seems empirically implausible to assume that everyone who contemplates revolutionary action is strongly averse to risk. Nonetheless, this attitude may express the morally right point of view for considering the risk of catastrophe. Since moral rules are supposed to insure us against catastrophe, rather than simply to improve our chances of increasing our welfare, perhaps we should appraise them from a point of view that is strongly averse to the risk of catastrophe. This policy might be justified from a moral point of view, if it is assumed that morality requires us to make our decision without reference to the specific circumstances and risks that we face.

Similarly, the reply to the fool is more plausible if Hobbes's assumptions about risk are not empirical, but procedural assumptions that define the considerations that a moral argument should take into account. If the fool ought to assume that others are his equals in astuteness, he ought not to act on the assumption that he can deceive them. Similarly, if he ought to be extremely averse to the dangers of being found out, he ought not to act on ordinary calculations about the probability of being found out. His attitude, on this view, does not necessarily rest on false empirical assumptions, but it violates the procedures that define the moral point of view.

These procedural attitudes to equality and to probability are summed up in Hobbes's treatment of the Golden Rule.[26] He suggests that if we observe it, we can save ourselves the trouble of working out the long-term benefits of observing each law of nature on each occasion. I ought (rationally) to assume it is probable that other people will treat me in the way I treat them, and so I ought (rationally) to treat them in the way I would want them to treat me; if I do this, I will be following the laws of nature. In observing the Golden Rule, I follow a pattern of equal treatment between others and between others and myself. I rely on an assumption of reciprocity that has not been shown to be probable. The thought that other people might not be as malevolent or exploitative or clever as I am may suggest to me that I do not need to worry about retaliation for bad treatment. But Hobbes insists that I ought to exclude any such thought from my moral calculation, since it would allow me to give an unfair advantage to myself.

We might claim that if morality can be seen to be reasonable in the light of these assumptions about knowledge and motives, Hobbes has justified morality. For he has shown (we might suggest) that morality can be justified to a 'hypothetical' egoist, in the light of specific assumptions about the agent's motives, knowledge, and circumstances.

---

his. Which is no more but a changing, as it were, of the scales. For every man's passion weigheth heavy in his own scale, but not in the scale of his neighbour.' (*EL* 17.9).

[26] See *EL* 17.9, just quoted; *Civ.* 3.26; *L.* 15.35.

If this suggestion can be defended in detail, it is an important result. It captures an important aspect of the moral point of view by reference to a special kind of hypothetical egoist.

But even if we could design a hypothetical egoist to whom it would appear reasonable to choose all or most of morality, we would not have reached Hobbes's intended result. For why is the hypothetical egoist relevant? If the constraints that distinguish him from ordinary people are reasonable only from the moral point of view, how do they explain or justify the moral point of view?

Hobbes does not intend to raise these questions. He intends to describe actual agents and to justify morality to them. If he only describes hypothetical agents whose differences from actual agents are not psychologically plausible, he does not justify morality. If moral principles rely on assumptions that he cannot defend from his account of the state of nature and the commonwealth, his explanation and justification collapse. Still, one might argue that Hobbes's main insight is not the psychological theory that is meant to explain morality, but the moral constraints that capture the moral point of view.[27]

507. Moral Theory in Hobbes's System

The difficulties in Hobbes's account of our reasons for observing morality within the state expose some difficulties in his broader aim of reconciling his account of morality with his psychology. His account of morality as a set of rules for the preservation of peace and the public good departs from older conceptions of morality, by recommending the practice of the moral virtues only within the framework of the commonwealth. Still, the principles that he accepts are a part of morality, as understood by older views.

Moreover, if he is committed to a two-level opaque theory, the first-level reasons for observing these principles may be close to those given by the old moral philosophers. Hobbes's account of morality as consisting of principles for preserving the commonwealth is more plausible at the second level than at the first; it may give reasons for cultivating the virtues and the reasons for acting that the old moral philosophers defend. Similarly, his account of morality as counsels of self-preservation is more plausible at a still higher level, telling us why we have good reason to design principles whose observance preserves the commonwealth.

Hobbes does not clearly distinguish the different roles of his claims about preservation of the commonwealth and about self-preservation. Once we distinguish them, we see that he stays closer to the old moral philosophers than at first he appears to. The possibility of an opaque two-level theory resolves some of the difficulties that face Hobbes's actual theory with its assumption of transparency; but it also raises further difficulties for him.

Human nature itself, as Hobbes understands it, gives us no reason for observing moral rules. Nothing about human nature itself makes morality suitable for it in its own right;

---

[27] In this way one might support the judgment that he is 'the father of British ethics in its greatest period, although most of his progeny were anxious to show why and in what ways they could not live down to so disreputable an ancestor' (Laird, *H* p. v).

hence knowledge of human nature does not show that morality is a non-instrumental element in the human good.[28] A correct account of human nature shows, in Hobbes's view, that no correct conception of the human good supports claims about the first principles of natural law. To this extent, he is a radical sceptic about morality.

He believes, however, that, given the actual circumstances that face human beings, he can avoid general scepticism about morality. His analysis of the content of morality implies that it aims at the public good; hence, if we find a reason, from an egoistic hedonist point of view, to pursue the public good, we find a reason to observe moral rules. He thinks he has found an appropriate reason in the desirability of peace. Peace is attractive to human beings in the state of nature. Once we see that the moral rules are means to attaining and to preserving peace, we see reason to take them seriously.

This argument fails, if it is intended as a realistic prudential argument aimed at a reasonably astute and well-informed agent who is not already committed to morality for its own sake. It fails, whether it is meant to show that such an agent has overriding reason to enter a commonwealth, or to show that such an agent within a commonwealth has overriding reason to observe the moral rules that preserve the commonwealth.

This objection would confront Hobbes even if he had a traditional conception of practical reason, and did not try to reduce reasons to motives. But he also faces a more serious objection. For he cannot easily begin the appropriate sort of instrumental argument for morality. His argument requires an account of practical reasoning that is alien to his explicit account. In defending morality, he assumes that in order to grasp the instrumental role of the laws of nature we must form a conception of our overall, long-term good and keep this steadily in mind. But we cannot form such a conception if we rely on Hobbesian deliberation. The function of Hobbesian deliberation is simply to discover the means to the satisfaction of our currently strongest desire; the results of this sort of deliberation do not match the results of deliberation about our long-term good.

Hobbes cannot reasonably predict, then, that people who conform to Hobbesian psychological laws will accept morality. If he argues that nonetheless such people have good reason to care about morality, he introduces normative considerations that have no basis in the practical reason that he recognizes. We have reason to doubt Hobbes's claim that if his account of human nature and rationality is right, we can justify a firm commitment to morality. It turns out that we cannot even justify a firm commitment to prudence, as ordinarily understood. Hobbes's attempt to explain and justify morality from an empirically respectable (as he supposes) account of human nature neither explains nor justifies prudence or morality.

When Hobbes sets out to explain why the traditional moral virtues are genuine virtues, he assumes that traditional views are right in supposing that we have good reason to acquire and to practise these virtues, so that the 'fool' and similar doubters are mistaken. In his view, reasons and obligations are reducible to motives. Hence he argues that we have good reason to practise the virtues by arguing that moral obligation is a form of prudential motivation. He does not suppose he could give a correct account of the moral virtues without also showing that we have reason to cultivate them.

---

[28] Hobbes and Butler on nature; see §675.

If Hobbes does not find a vindicating reduction of the moral virtues, where has he gone wrong? His critics give different answers. According to sentimentalist critics, he has appealed to the wrong non-normative facts, because he is wrong about the motives that actually influence us. Hutcheson treats normative facts as facts about the reactions of our moral sense.

According to rationalist critics, Hobbes is more deeply mistaken. Cudworth and Clarke attack all attempts to vindicate morality by reducing normative facts (i.e., facts about what we ought to do, and what we have reason to do) to non-normative psychological facts (about what we are in fact moved to do). This rationalist criticism of Hobbes also raises a question about Hutcheson's reductive position.

If we are convinced by Cudworth's and Clarke's arguments against Hobbes, and if we reject the reduction of moral obligation to motivation, we open a gap that he keeps closed. We cannot give Hobbes's reason for believing that if we have a moral obligation to do x, we thereby have a sufficient reason and motive for doing x. But if the appropriate connexion between obligations, reasons, and motives does not appear immediately in our account of moral obligation itself, where are we to find it? Once we raise this question, we can see both why the reductive aspirations of Hobbes's account of obligation remain attractive to many theorists, and why theorists who reject these reductive aspirations raise difficulties for themselves.

How far does Hobbes keep his promise to practise a new method in moral philosophy? He offers something new in seeking a vindicating reduction of moral obligation to non-moral psychological facts about motivation. If he had succeeded in his vindicating reduction, he would have discovered the nature of moral virtues and our reasons for practising them, by reference to an account of human motives that does not itself rely on any normative non-psychological assumptions about morality or about rationality. But his reduction fails. His attempted account of deliberation and practical reason is not even descriptively adequate; what he describes is not deliberation, but only the mental processes that are allowed within his psychological theory. Hobbes's psychological theory is questionable; and if it were correct, it would undermine, rather than vindicate, morality. The difficulties that he encounters in practising his new method suggest objections to the method.

37

SPINOZA

508. Spinoza's Attitude to Ethics

Both the title of the *Ethics* and some of its contents imply that Spinoza intends to contribute to moral philosophy. The last three parts of the *Ethics*, on the affects and on human freedom, are directly about ethical questions. The first two parts, on God and on the origin and nature of the mind, are on topics that many philosophers take to be relevant to moral questions. Moreover, Spinoza suggests that his philosophy supports important practical conclusions. It shows us why we should depart from some ordinary assumptions and outlooks on life. We should not care as much as most people care about the goals, aims, and concerns that we adopt under the influence of emotions. Human bondage consists in 'man's lack of power to moderate [or "govern", moderari] and restrain the affects' (*Ethics* 4Pref. = C 543).[1] Spinoza agrees with one of the main tendencies of Platonic and Aristotelian moral philosophy. Aquinas, for instance, clearly believes that the outlook we form under the influence of our passions misleads us about what is worth pursuing in life.

Spinoza, however, rejects Aquinas' alternative to domination by the passions. Aquinas believes that our main ethical task is to exercise our will in free and responsible action that restrains and controls our emotions; we should form our will in accordance with a true conception of the proper ultimate end of a human being, and if we freely choose to adapt, modify, or restrain our passions in the light of this end, we achieve the virtues. These claims about choice and action appear to Spinoza to be basically misguided.

Spinoza exposes the basic errors of traditional eudaemonist moral philosophy, in the parts of the *Ethics* that might appear to be less relevant to ethics. For he believes that a true account of the nature of the universe and of human beings exposes the errors in a Scholastic view of agency. Scholastic errors rest on false conceptions of freedom and of teleological order. Once we reveal these errors, we can understand human freedom and the human good without reference to indefensible claims about will and agency.

This summary of Spinoza's conclusion also raises a question about his position. In rejecting a Scholastic view of will, freedom, and agency, Spinoza agrees with Hobbes. But Hobbes

---

[1] I will normally omit the title of the *Ethics*, and cite by part and subdivision, with the page in Curley's edition. Thus, 4d1 = C 546, refers to Part Four, Definition 1, on p. 546 of Curley. Quotations are taken from (or based on) Curley.

also tries to replace the Scholastic view with a view of human nature and human agency that supports different ethical conclusions from Spinoza's. We have found reasons for doubt about Hobbes's criticism of the Scholastic view, about his own account of agency, and about the moral theory that he rests on it. We may ask, therefore, whether Spinoza does better than Hobbes on these points.

He argues that, as Hobbes also believes, the Scholastic view implies that human actions are entirely outside the natural order of cause and effect and of natural law. Since Spinoza believes that human actions cannot have this status, he rejects the Scholastic conception of agency. But he does not thereby undermine belief in agency; he might still allow an account that avoided the Scholastic non-naturalist assumptions.

He seems to hold, however, that Hobbes repeats the errors of the Scholastics; for Hobbes retains their assumption that we can affect our behaviour by our will, deliberation, and election. This seems to be a common-sense assumption about will and action, not confined to any particular philosophical theory. If Spinoza rejects this common-sense assumption, he seems to leave little room for agency, and hence little room for ethics. If, then, we are convinced by Spinoza's metaphysics, and we agree that it undermines traditional ethics, perhaps we will find that it undermines his own ethics too. On the other hand, if we interpret the metaphysical conclusions so that they leave room for Spinoza's ethical outlook, perhaps we will find that they lose their force against traditional views.

Spinoza does not believe that he faces this dilemma, because his ethical views seem to him to be defensible without common-sense assumptions about agency. This is perhaps the most challenging aspect of his conception of ethics. Though we might claim that Hobbes undermines agency through his views about deliberation and action, this is not how Hobbes sees it; he takes himself to vindicate agency by explaining it in non-Scholastic terms. Spinoza goes beyond Hobbes in rejecting common-sense views about action. But he still believes, as Hobbes does, that he vindicates ethics. We need to see whether he can reconstruct ethics so that it can do without agency.

This is one reasonable way to approach Spinoza. But we might also consider whether his moral outlook is plausible without reference to the metaphysics views that precede it in his argument. Some of Hobbes's moral views can be evaluated without reference to his claims about action and human nature. It is worth seeing whether the same is true of Spinoza.

509. Mind and the Limits of Agency

To understand how Spinoza argues for his ethical proposals, we have to grasp his distinctive views about agency. We normally assume that we are capable of actions, and that ethics matters because it concerns (among other things) the regulation of actions. Among the sorts of actions that matter to ethics are my walking on your toes, helping you up if you have fallen, signing a cheque to pay you what I owe you, saying something that offends you. Each of these actions includes a bodily movement, and each of them may, in the appropriate circumstances, be right or wrong, virtuous or vicious. The acceptance and improvement of moral judgments seem to matter for action because we seem capable of different bodily movements in the appropriate circumstances. Similarly, when we praise or blame people, we often praise or blame them not only for having good or bad thoughts, but for forming these thoughts into intentions that normally produce bodily movements of the relevant sort.

Spinoza rejects these claims about agency. They rest on the assumption that mental states can cause bodily movements, but this assumption, in his view, is false. He especially attacks Descartes for his belief in the possibility of interaction between mind and body. Descartes believes in interaction through the medium of the pineal gland, and Spinoza rejects this account of how interaction is possible (5Pref = C 596). But he does not merely reject Descartes's account; he also believes that what Descartes tries to explain cannot be explained, because there is nothing to explain.

Interaction between mind and body is impossible, according to Spinoza, because we cannot recognize the appropriate sorts of necessitating relations between mental and bodily events.[2] We find the appropriate sort of necessitation in the relation of different features of a triangle. The angles of a triangle add up to 180 degrees because a triangle has three sides; the fact about its angles follows from the fact about its sides. Similarly, the conclusion of a syllogism is true because its premises are true and the conclusion follows from the premises. According to Spinoza, genuine causation includes this sort of necessity.[3] If we understand the nature of the universe, we see how all of its states of affairs are related by this sort of necessity. If mental and bodily events are not related by this sort of necessity, the genuine states of the universe do not include causal connexions between mind and body.

If mind and body are not causally connected, how are we to explain our stubborn conviction that they are closely related in some way, so that we mistakenly suppose they are causally connected? Spinoza explains our error by claiming that the body is the object of the idea constituting the human mind (2p13d = C 457). What we are aware of, then, in a mental state is some state of the body.

To say that everything we are aware of is some state of the body is to reject a version of mind-body dualism. Spinoza denies that our awareness of an act of will or thought gives us knowledge of a purely mental event with no bodily aspect at all. But even if he is right about this, mind and body may interact; for if mental events are also bodily events, they seem to be capable of causing bodily events. In this respect, we might be tempted to express Spinoza's position as a form of materialism, affirming that all mental events are also physical events with physical causes and effects.[4]

This materialist view, however, does not take account of all of Spinoza's views. He goes further insofar as he also denies interaction between mental and bodily events. For he does not agree that a mental event can cause a physical event, even if the mental event is itself physical. He suggests that the mental event is simply the awareness of a bodily event. When we think our intention of raising our arm has caused us to raise our arm, we are wrong; our intention is simply the awareness of a physical event that has really caused the rising of our arm. The causal connexion holds not between our intention and the rising of our arm, but between the physical event our intention makes us aware of and the rising of our arm.

---

[2] See Bennett, *SSE* 29–32, on causal rationalism, referring to 1a3.   [3] Cf. 4p57s = C 578.
[4] This is Hampshire's view of Spinoza in *S* 55–61; *TTM* 58.

This account of mental events conflicts with ordinary assumptions about agency. If I am watching an assembly line by closed-circuit television, I may have mental states that are aware of every state of the assembly line, but the content of these mental states does not causally explain anything about the assembly line. In this case the direction of causation and explanation goes from the assembly line to my awareness of it. If I were also provided with a panel of buttons to push while I watch the process on the assembly line, and I did not know what was going on, I might be deceived into believing that I control the assembly line by pushing the buttons. If I had the same sort of access to states of my own brain, but they operated quite independently of the mental content of my awareness of them, I might be under the illusion that I control them through my mental content, but in fact the mental content would be causally irrelevant to the states of my brain; this would still be true even if the states of awareness were themselves further brain states.

This conception of my mental states as merely epiphenomenal states of awareness of physical states fits Spinoza's attack on ordinary assumptions about agency. But it does not completely fit his views about mind and body; for our comparison with the television implies causal interaction between physical states (of the assembly line or brain) and states of awareness. On Spinoza's view, connecting causation with necessity, this direction of causation from body to mind is no less unintelligible than the direction that goes from the mind to the body. He does not explain how he can avoid some sort of causation in his claims about objects and ideas. But since this direction of causation is not the most important one for claims about agency, we need not pursue this objection to his position; we can concentrate on the other direction of causation.

We believe we have reliable access to agency, because we are aware of causal influence of our mental states on our actions. We take this to be familiar from experience.[5] Moreover, we take it to be obvious that the intentional and rational content of our mental states explains intelligent action.[6] This common conviction does not rest on metaphysical dualist assumptions. It asserts that mental properties are relevant to explaining those physical events that are also actions. If the object to be explained is a picture or a temple, it needs to be explained—we assume—by certain kinds of aims and intentions.

Spinoza attacks common convictions about mental explanation and causation on different grounds. Some of his attacks seem to be directed at the conviction that choices and decisions are free.[7] We might take him to mean that our false beliefs about freedom reflect ignorance of the causes of our mental states; if that is all he means, he need not deny that the mental states cause bodily movements.

---

[5] 'But they will say that—whether or not they know by what means the mind moves the body—they still have experience that unless the human mind were capable of thinking, the body would be inactive.' (3p2s = C 495)

[6] 'But they will say that it cannot happen that the causes of buildings, of paintings, and of things of this kind, which are made only by human skill, should be able to be deduced from the laws of nature alone, insofar as it is considered to be only corporeal; nor would the human body be able to build a temple, if it were not determined and led by the mind.' (3p2s = C 496)

[7] 'So the infant believes he freely desires (appetere) the milk; the angry child that he wills (velle) vengeance; and the timid, flight. So the drunk believes that it is from a free decision of the mind that he speaks the things he later, when sober, would will (vellet) not to have said. . . . So experience itself, no less clearly than reason, teaches that men believe themselves free because they are conscious of their own actions and ignorant of the causes by which they are determined, that the decisions of the mind are nothing but the desires (appetitus) themselves, which therefore vary as the disposition of the body varies.' (3p2s = C 496–7)

But if this were all Spinoza meant, he would not have argued for his more sweeping claim that 'the body cannot determine the mind to thinking, and the mind cannot determine the body to motion, to rest, or to anything else . . .' (3p2 = C 494). He believes that our illusions about freedom reflect general ignorance about causation. Our belief that we are free depends on our ignorance of causal facts about our mental states. When we discover how ignorant we are, we should also admit that we have no good reason to make dogmatic claims about the effects of our mental states, or about the explanatory role of their intentional content. Hence we ought not to assert dogmatically that the body is incapable of producing the relevant events by itself, since we do not know how much the body is capable of by itself. Since we are ignorant of how the mind moves the body, we ought not to assert that it moves the body.

The argument from ignorance is open to question. We might concede that we are sometimes wrong in claiming that our intentions cause our actions, and that they do not cause actions except through a physical process that we are unaware of or do not know in detail. But this does not give us a good reason to doubt that we sometimes know that we act because we intend to act. I do not know everything about how my pressing the accelerator pedal causes a car to move forward, and it is logically possible that the car is really controlled by a computer that is also linked to my brain; perhaps the computer both moves the car forward and depresses the accelerator when I decide to press it, but my deciding to depress the accelerator is entirely epiphenomenal in relation to the movement of the car. But though it is logically possible that all the states of my brain are related to my intentions and my actions in this indirect way, we should not take this logical possibility seriously. We have no reason to believe it, and we have no reason to abandon our initial conviction that the content of my intention to raise my arm is causally relevant to my raising my arm.

Spinoza's argument, then, appears to rely on a questionable sceptical strategy. He argues that since we are sometimes wrong about mental causation, it is logically possible that we are always wrong, and hence we never know, and are never justified in believing, that any mental events explain any bodily events on any occasion. This is a Cartesian form of sceptical argument; it seems to exaggerate the significance of logical possibility.

Perhaps, however, Spinoza finds this Cartesian sceptical argument plausible in this case, because it fits some of his views about causation and logical necessity. If we admit that it is logically possible (for all we know) that our intention to raise our arm does not cause our arm to rise, we admit that it is not logically necessary (for all we know) that our intention causes our arm to rise. But since Spinoza thinks of causation as logical necessitation, our inability to defend a logically necessary connexion implies inability to defend a genuine causal connexion.

We may reply by challenging Spinoza's conception of causation. If we have good reason to believe that intentions cause actions, but we do not assert a logically neces-sary connexion between intentions and actions, have we not found counter-examples to Spinoza's claim about causation? Spinoza would not allow this form of objection by counter-example. His account of causation is not intended to offer the most plausible understanding of intuitively accepted examples of causes and effects. On the contrary, it is part of a foundationalist argument. The account of causation is supposed to be certain and evident in itself; it is not intended as an analysis of an intuitive concept of causation, but it is a basis from which intuitive concepts can be criticized, and, if necessary, rejected.

If this is so, we have no good reason to agree with Spinoza's conclusions about agency unless we accept some of the most disputable aspects of his metaphysical system and of its underlying epistemology. He does not seem to have any plausible argument that can be defended independently of his whole system.

But if we accept his conclusions what do they commit us to? If we claim that intentions cause actions, we claim that they cause physical movements and processes, and that their content is causally relevant. But to which movements and processes is it relevant? When we speak of intentions causing actions such as raising my arm or writing a cheque, we are not picking out a type of movement that a physicist's or biologist's or physiologist's description is likely to recognize. The actions caused by our intentions are classified into types partly by the intentions that cause them. At a physiological level, we have no reason to assume that all the actions we distinguish as instances of writing a cheque have something in common that distinguishes them from all other movements of our hands and arms. But if our normal classification of actions rests on the illusory assumption (according to Spinoza) that our intentions cause our actions, we must also be mistaken in believing that some of our bodily movements are actions.

Spinoza introduces this question implicitly, in stating the common beliefs about mental causation. His opponent mentions paintings, buildings, and temples as cases where we need mental causation. Spinoza replies that we are too ignorant to be entitled to rule out the possibility of purely physical causation of these events; but this reply does not seem to grasp the main point of the objection. Suppose that we knew enough about marble, mules, ropes, beams, human physiology, and so on, to explain the events that resulted in the existence of the Parthenon and St Paul's Cathedral, without reference to any human intentions or aims. This is difficult to conceive, but even if we could conceive it, would such an explanation explain the existence of a temple and a cathedral? Temples and cathedrals are similar in some respects (as religious buildings), and different in others (since the Parthenon was intended to house a statue of Athena, whereas St Paul's was build for a congregation and for the bishop's chair). In some respects—external appearance—St Paul's is more similar to the Parthenon than to Notre Dame de Paris, but in other respects—as a Christian cathedral church—it is more similar to Notre Dame. It is difficult to see how we could understand or explain the relevant respects of difference and similarity between these different buildings if we did not refer to anyone's aims and intentions.

This point applies more generally to action. We might concede to Spinoza that a complete physiological non-mental explanation could be found for all the physical events that happen when I go for a walk or sign a cheque. But such an explanation does not explain why I go for a walk or sign a cheque. The properties of going for a walk and signing a cheque belong to events because of particular beliefs, desires, and intentions. Spinoza does not say where he stands on this question. He speaks as though we would face no special difficulty in conceiving purely physical explanations of everything that we explain by appeal to mental states. But once we see the difficulties that arise in eliminating mental causation of physical events, we might reasonably find his argument for elimination over-simplified.

Spinoza's views about agency, therefore, go beyond the assertion of materialism. They imply that we are quite mistaken in our beliefs about the causal relevance of our mental states. We believe that the fact that our intention is an intention to raise our arm is causally relevant to the fact that our bodily movement is a raising of our arm. But, according to Spinoza, this belief is false. We know that some bodily changes are happening, but we cannot say, on the basis of our mental states, which bodily changes they are, or what causes them.[8]

510. Errors about Freedom

In regarding ourselves as agents, we assume that the content of our mental states is causally relevant to bodily movements. We also assume that we cause these bodily movements in a particular way. We take ourselves to have a will that is distinct from our intellect and does not necessarily follow it. We therefore attribute to the will some sort of freedom that we do not attribute to the intellect.[9] The freedom of our will is a distinctive feature of the agency that we ascribe to ourselves.

In Spinoza's view, this belief in freedom conflicts with facts about the causal order of the universe. He takes the essential element of freedom to be self-determination (the 'liberty of spontaneity') rather than the capacity for opposites (the 'liberty of indifference'). A free agent would have to be determined entirely by itself without any external determination. God is the only free cause, because God acts only from the necessity of the divine nature, and so is determined by nothing external (1p17c2 = C 425). Since God is identical to the whole universe, nothing external to God can compel God to act. But Spinoza denies that God has the capacity for opposites, and so he rejects the mediaeval views that allow God to have created something different from what has been created.[10] God cannot do anything different from what actually happens; for such a capacity would commit us to saying that God can make it false that from the nature of a triangle it follows that it has two right angles.[11]

We might be puzzled by this argument. Spinoza seems to assert that if we attribute any capacity for opposites to God, we must accept Descartes's extreme voluntarism, ascribing to God the capacity to make logical necessities false. His assertion is intelligible in the light of his conception of causation. If God has the capacity for opposites, it could have been false that God caused tortoises to exist. But if tortoises were caused to exist, it is logically

---

[8] Though Spinoza rejects the common belief that mental states are causally relevant to bodily actions, he does not deny that they are causally relevant to something. He believes that mental states cause mental states. In his view, it is possible to find the right sorts of logical connexions between bodily states and events, and also between mental states and events. Each of these mental states is also the idea of a bodily state.

[9] This is true even if we accept Aquinas' intellectualism. See §286.

[10] On these mediaeval views see Wolfson, PS i 308–19; Gueroult, S i 272–95.

[11] 'Others think that God is a free cause because he can (so they think) bring it about that the things which we have said follow from his nature (i.e., which are in his power) do not happen or are not produced by him. But this is the same as if they were to say that God can bring it about that it would not follow from the nature of a triangle that its three angles are equal to two right angles; or that from a given cause the effect would not follow—which is absurd.' (1p17s = C 425–6)

necessary that tortoises came into being; hence, if God had the power not to cause tortoises, a logically necessary truth could be false.

God, therefore, is self-determined, being identical to the whole universe, but lacks the capacity for opposites. We are not identical to the whole universe, but are finite modes of it; hence we are determined externally, and so we cannot be free.[12] Since we do not know the causes of our acts of will, we believe they are uncaused, and therefore we believe we are self-determined and free. Since we do not know the effects (or lack of them) of our acts of will, and do not know the causes of our bodily movements, we believe that our acts of will cause our bodily movements.[13]

In Spinoza's view, we should not simply deny that we know we are self-determined; we should also recognize that we are not self-determined, and are therefore not free. God exists necessarily, and acts by the necessity of God's nature. Everything else exists necessarily because of the necessity of God's nature.[14] Hence everything follows from facts about the divine nature, which is the nature of the universe as a whole.

We do not know how everything is necessary in such a way that we can exhibit its necessity. Some people are convinced that things are contingent, but this is because they are influenced by imagination (2p44c = C 480). Imagination picks out superficial features of situations in ways that make them appear different from how they really are, and therefore it obscures the features that make them necessary. But the point of view of reason regards things as necessary, setting aside the appearances that arise from imagination.

This does not mean that everything is necessary in the same way. Spinoza leaves room for recognizing a difference that might partly match the ordinary distinction between the necessary and the contingent. Unlike the facts about the divine nature, which are absolutely necessary in their own right, particular events and objects in the universe are not absolutely necessary in their own right, because they depend on the divine nature, and hence on the laws of the universe, and on prior events. Spinoza expresses this feature of contingent (as we might call them) things and events by saying that they are 'necessary through their causes', though not in their own right.[15]

This recognition of things that are not intrinsically necessary suggests a way of reconciling Spinoza with Aquinas on contingency in creation. Aquinas does not believe that if God's existence is necessary and everything else depends on God, there cannot be any freedom in the world. For, in his view, God creates secondary causes that have a causal role appropriate for their type of agency, and this role allows contingency.[16] We might think that something like this view would be open to Spinoza. But he seems to reject it.[17] He argues that the

---

[12] '...men are deceived in that they think themselves free, [i.e., they think that of their own free will they can either do a thing or forbear doing it], an opinion which consists only in this, that they are conscious of their actions and ignorant of the causes by which they are determined. This, then, is their idea of freedom—that they do not know any cause of their actions. For what they say, that human actions depend on the will, is words for which they have no idea. For all are ignorant of what the will is, and how it moves the body ...' (2p35s = C 473. Curley includes the bracketed passage, inserted from the Dutch version). '...men think themselves free, because they are conscious of their volitions and their desire, and do not think, even in their dreams, of the causes by which they are disposed to desiring and to willing, because they are ignorant of <those causes>' (1appx = C 440).

[13] See Curley, BGM 78–82.

[14] 'In nature nothing contingent is given, but all things have been determined from the necessity of the divine nature to a definite way of existing and of producing.' (1p29 = C 433)

[15] See Bennett, SSE, ch. 5.   [16] On Aquinas see §270.   [17] See 1p26–9.

modes of the divine nature depend on God both for their existence and for their action.[18] It follows that particular things cannot determine themselves without God, and cannot make themselves undetermined. From this Spinoza takes his proposition about necessity to follow.

This argument does not directly address Aquinas' position. For Aquinas does not claim that secondary causes make themselves undetermined or self-determining. He claims that God makes them and the rest of the universe in such a way that what happens to them depends on their states—sensory or rational. Since they are not necessitated by the rest of the universe apart from their sensory and rational states, they determine things contingently. Spinoza does not argue clearly against this possibility. If his conclusion that things necessarily produce effects in a certain way follows from his claims about God, it does not rule out Aquinas' view; Aquinas is free to say that God necessarily makes things such that they are necessitated to be secondary causes, and sources of contingent events.

Spinoza can answer this objection to his argument if he appeals to his account of causation. For if causation requires logical necessitation, the suggestion that God could create contingent events—those that could not be shown to be necessary in the light of a complete understanding of their antecedents—must be rejected. If God is the cause of everything, it follows that everything can be known to be necessary in the light of the nature of God.

It is not clear how much room for contingency Spinoza leaves in his account of things that are necessary through their causes. Hobbes's views are hard to follow because he does not always seem to distinguish the claim that one event necessitates another from the claim that the first event makes the second necessary. We can speak of necessitation when the first event is a sufficient condition for the second; hence necessitation follows from the truth of determinism. But necessitation does not imply the necessity of the second event unless the first event is itself necessary, and Hobbes does not make it clear why he thinks human actions that are necessitated are also necessary. Spinoza is perhaps obscure on the same points as Hobbes; but he has a better answer to our question about why necessitation implies necessity. In his view, the initial condition, referring to facts about God or the universe as a whole, is absolutely necessary; and he might believe that whatever is necessitated by the absolutely necessary is itself absolutely necessary.[19] It is reasonable, then, given Spinoza's conception of freedom, for him to believe that facts about causation exclude freedom.

How much of the ordinary conception of freedom does Spinoza undermine with his arguments? If we are incompatibilists, we must deny freedom once we accept his determinism. If we are compatibilists who believe in contingency without indeterminism (as Aquinas does), we must deny freedom if we are convinced by his argument against contingency in secondary causes. But we might be compatibilists who are willing to admit that all our actions are necessary. We might agree that states of our will are caused, but argue that they are caused in the way appropriate for freedom. If our rational capacities make a difference to what happens, and they are not causally idle in the causal chain,

---

[18] '...God is the cause of these modes, not only in so far as they simply exist, but also...in so far as they are considered to be determined to produce something' (1p29d = C 433).

[19] Bennett, *SSE* 111, finds evidence for Spinoza's acceptance of this transitivity of necessity in 1p21–2.

then—according to some views—we act freely. We would indeed face a threat to freedom if the causation of our actions were entirely independent of our will, choice, and rational capacity; but we need some reason to believe this, beyond the reasons for believing that states of our will are caused.

Spinoza also rejects this aspect of compatibilism, because of his rejection of mental causation.[20] Apparently, then, his case against mental causation is the most important part of his argument against ordinary beliefs about freedom. Compatibilists might try to fit beliefs about agency into a deterministic word, even into a world of necessary events. But the compatibilist core (or, as incompatibilists would say, remnant) of freedom is rational agency, which cannot be reconciled with the truth of Spinoza's claims about mental causation.

511. Intellect and Will

If we are mistaken in believing that our will is free and that it causes our actions, what is left of our initial belief that we have wills? Spinoza does not take the initial belief to be entirely false. It is entirely false to believe that the will is causally relevant to bodily movements. But we are right to attribute some mental states to the will; the truth in our initial belief is clear once we reject any distinction between will and intellect.[21] To show that volitions and ideas are the same, Spinoza considers a volition 'by which the mind affirms that the three angles of a triangle are equal to two right angles' (2p49d = C 484). He argues that this affirmation cannot be distinguished from the idea of a triangle; for we cannot have the relevant idea without the affirmation about its angles.

This may not seem an apposite example of a volition. It involves assent to something's being the case; in this particular instance, we assent to something that we must assent to in order to have the idea of a triangle. But even if we concede Spinoza's claim that we cannot distinguish idea from volition in this particular instance, we may not agree that all volitions can be treated in the same way. My volition to write a cheque may be understood as my assenting to its being good to write a cheque here and now. This assent depends on my having the idea of its being good to write a cheque here and now, and on my having the idea of a cheque and the idea of good. But none of these ideas seems to involve my assenting to its being good to write a cheque. Spinoza, therefore, seems to have generalized inappropriately from an untypical example.

His example seems to us to be untypical because it involves assent to something's being the case, and necessarily being the case. When we exercise our will, we assent—as it seems

---

[20] This claim about compatibilism needs to be qualified in the light of Spinoza's remarks on freedom. But those remarks do not vindicate a version of compatibilism that relies on mental causation. See Sleigh et al., 'Determinism' 1227–9; Garrett, 'Ethical' 299–301.

[21] 'The will and the intellect are nothing apart from the singular volitions and ideas themselves. But a singular volition and an idea are one and the same thing. Therefore the will and the intellect are one and the same thing.' (2p49dem = C 485) Bolton, 'Universals' 198–9, discusses Spinoza's view of the divine intellect and will. While he rejects voluntarism, he also rejects the naturalist view that God wills in accord with the good: 'For they seem to place something outside God, which does not depend on God, to which God attends, as a model, in what he does, or at which he aims, as at a certain goal. This is simply to subject God to fate, than which nothing more absurd can be maintained about God, whom we have shown to be the first and only free cause, both of the essence of all things, and of their existence.' (1p33s2 = C 438–9) Those who claim that God acts for the sake of an end imply that God is imperfect (1appx = C 442–3).

to us—to something's coming about that is not necessarily the case and that depends on our assenting or dissenting. In Spinoza's view, we might also think in this way of the triangle; we might ignorantly interpret our assent to the size of the angles of the triangle as a decision of ours. Our illusion is dispelled once we recognize that the truth about the triangle is necessary, not up to us. Until we recognize the necessity, we lack adequate knowledge of the triangle, because our idea of it is not clear and distinct (2p35dem = C 473). But when we have adequate knowledge, we see that we cannot have an adequate idea of a triangle without assenting to the truth about its angles.

According to Spinoza, we should explain our beliefs about the will in the same way. We suppose that it is up to us whether something happens, because we believe it does not happen necessarily, and hence independently of our will. But if we knew more about the event that we assume to be up to us, we would recognize that it is necessary, and indeed that we cannot have an adequate idea of it without recognizing its necessity. The appearance that willing is different from assent to a necessary truth is simply the result of our ignorance of the relevant necessity.

Spinoza does not suppose that it is easy to dispel the illusion that makes us think willing is different from recognizing a truth. Indeed, the difficulty of dispelling the illusion helps to explain some of the ethical value of the *Ethics*. Because we form our ideas on the basis of our imaginations, the way things appear to us does not always reflect adequate ideas. Even if we know the real distance of the sun from the earth, it still appears to me to be only 200 feet away (2p35s = C 473). But if we know the real distance, we do not act on the illusory appearance that proceeds from the imagination; we do not set out to reach the sun, as we might set out to reach something that we believe to be only 200 feet away. Though adequate knowledge does not dispel the illusion, it deprives the illusion of the cognitive results it would have if we did not correct it.

The example of our distance from the sun is meant to illustrate our errors about the will. We think things depend on us because we do not know what they really depend on. When we know the truths about the relevant necessities, we still have the appearance of things depending on us, but, because of our adequate knowledge, we no longer take the appearance seriously.

What knowledge is relevant for dispelling the illusions based on imagination? Spinoza might have two answers: (1) When we recognize that the causes of our action are outside us, we see that the action is not up to us, and we simply assent to it as something that is going to happen. (2) When we recognize that it is necessary, we see that it is not up to us, and we assent to it as a necessary truth.

The first answer assumes that freedom and causal determination by external causes are incompatible. If one rejects this incompatibilist assumption, one need not accept Spinoza's argument to show that our belief in freedom rests on ignorance of causes. This defence of freedom does not cope with Spinoza's second answer; for this answer asserts not just that our action is causally determined, but that its occurrence is a necessary truth. He is right to assume that if something is a necessary truth, we are not free to change it.

Spinoza may well not distinguish these two answers, because of his conception of causal explanation. If he believes that causal explanation of an event demonstrates its necessity, he will not admit the possibility of allowing causal determination without necessity. An adequate explanation of my action will show that it is necessary. The appearance of its not being necessary is simply the result of my not having an adequate explanation.

This case for the identification of intellect and will has the advantages and disadvantages of several of Spinoza's arguments. On the one hand, his most surprising claims about agency and freedom are defensible, indeed unavoidable, within his metaphysical system. On the other hand, the elements of his metaphysical system that support his claims about freedom are quite disputable. Many apparent objections to Spinoza collapse if we accept his views about causation, explanation, and necessity; but these views do not seem so obviously true that we ought to withdraw all our doubts about his views on agency.

512. Emotion and Freedom from Emotion

From these views on agency and freedom, we can understand some of the ethical conclusions that Spinoza draws from his views on the emotions. In his view, it is misguided to deplore the emotions and their destructive effects.[22] We need to understand them and to see how they are a part of nature.[23] Since the emotions have natural causes, we ought to identify these causes. Since they can also be modified by natural causes, we ought also to find the appropriate causes so that we can modify our emotions in accordance with reason.

It is not surprising, in the light of what he has already said, that Spinoza rejects the attitudes of praise and blame that depend on assumptions about freedom, or that he tries to replace these 'active' attitudes with the 'passive' conditions of knowledge and understanding. We may be surprised, however, that after recommending the passive cognitive attitudes, he re-introduces activity and passivity and recommends the active outlook. How can he do this, if he has already undermined the convictions underlying our conception of agency?

Activity regains a place within Spinoza's system once he connects the division between activity and passivity with the division between adequate and inadequate ideas. The passions are essentially passive, and are the results of inadequate ideas.[24] Since inadequate ideas result from the imagination, and adequate ideas from intellect, passions are products of the imaginative point of view.

---

[22] 'And they attribute the cause of human weakness and inconstancy not to the common power of nature, but to some defect (vitium) or other of human nature, which they therefore bewail, or laugh at, or disdain, or (as usually happens) curse. And he who knows how to censure more eloquently and cunningly the weakness of the human mind is held to be godly.' (3Pref = C 491)

[23] '... nothing happens in nature which can be attributed to any defect in it; for nature is always the same, and its virtue and power of acting are everywhere one and the same—that is to say, the laws and rules of nature, according to which all things happen, and change from one form to another, are always and everywhere the same ... The affects, therefore, of hate, anger, envy, etc., considered in themselves, follow from the same necessity and force of nature as the other singular things' (3Pref = C 492).

[24] '... in so far as the mind has inadequate ideas, it necessarily undergoes certain things. ... From this it follows that the mind is liable to more affects to the extent that more of its ideas are inadequate, and conversely, is active in more ways to the extent that more of its ideas are adequate.' (3p1dem, cor = C 494) 'But in so far as the mind has inadequate ideas, it necessarily is passive (patitur). Therefore, the actions of the mind follow from adequate ideas alone, and the mind is passive only because it has inadequate ideas. ... We see, then, that the affects are not related to the mind except in so far as it has something which involves a negation, or in so far as it is considered as a part of nature which cannot be perceived clearly and distinctly through itself, without the others' (3p3dem, sch = C 498). On the passivity of the passions cf. Aquinas, §244.

The inadequate ideas of passion differ from the adequate ideas of intellect insofar as they do not include a grasp of the causes of events. To the imagination, many events appear contingent that will appear necessary if we look at them from the point of view of intellect; for since intellect grasps their causes, it also grasps their necessity.

We may be surprised that Spinoza connects activity with adequate ideas and passivity with inadequate ideas.[25] For we may suppose that the conviction of activity depends on belief in one's active power, and that this belief, according to Spinoza, rests on inadequate ideas. The replacement of inadequate by adequate ideas, according to this view, implies awareness of our own passivity, not of our activity. The position that Spinoza attributes to the passions seems to be a precondition for agency. He seems to acknowledge this point implicitly; for he uses the inadequacy of the ideas of imagination, which are the sources of the passions, in order to explain why we are subject to the illusions of free will (3p2sch = C 494–5) The same inadequate ideas seem to make us liable both to passions and to the conviction of agency.

From Spinoza's point of view, this close connexion between ideas of agency and the ideas that form passions is not so surprising. Passions and illusions of agency are different sides of a single mistaken picture of the mind and its relation to the world. If I take myself to be injured or affronted, I believe that something has happened to me that ought not to have happened; to that extent I think of myself as a victim of the contingencies of the world, and more specifically of the wills of other people. I react with anger; and in my anger I decide that I ought to do something about it. But if I form a more adequate idea of events, I see that they are necessary. In this respect, I abandon the idea that I interact with them as a free agent. I also abandon the idea that I am a victim of the contingencies of the world. Hence I should infer that neither activity nor response to contingency is part of an enlightened view of myself and the world.[26]

Spinoza might reasonably point out to us that we often connect activity and freedom with independence from passions. We say that we ourselves are acting and are not dominated by passions, if we are guided by our rational convictions and are not distracted by passions. Independence from passions is normally taken to be an aspect of self-government. If I am guided by reasons that seem good to me, and I do not vacillate from moment to moment under the influence of different passions, I am the one who decides and acts.

To be guided by adequate ideas is to be guided by reason, because recognition of the causes of things is recognition of their necessity. Recognition of necessity involves a rational transition of thought in which we see that the conclusion necessarily follows from the premisses. We do not come to believe that we ought to try to modify the influence of our passions on our thoughts and actions; any such belief rests on the illusory idea of free agency. Instead of causing beliefs about what we ought to do, the growth of adequate knowledge inevitably results, without any further action, in the decay of our passions. The conviction

---

[25] James, *PA* 145–7, discusses Spinoza's treatment of passivity and the passions.

[26] '...it [sc. knowledge of Spinoza's doctrine] teaches us how we must conduct ourselves concerning matters of fortune, or things which are not in our power, that is to say, concerning things that do not follow from our nature—that we must expect and bear calmly both faces of fortune. For all things follow from God's eternal decree with the same necessity as from the essence of a triangle it follows that its three angles are equal to two right angles' (2p49sch, iv(b) = C 490).

of necessity reduces the incidence of passions, or at least reduces their influence on our thoughts. We no longer believe that events in the world are contingencies that we ought to respond to with free actions that involve bodily movements. If we are guided by inadequate ideas, we are irrationally impressed by misleading appearances. But insofar as we are guided by adequate ideas, we become reasonable.

Since guidance by adequate ideas implies guidance by reason without the influence of misleading appearances, it makes us independent of the variations of our passions, and causes us to act as we ourselves think best. In these respects, guidance by adequate ideas makes us more active, and less subject to our passions. But this is not all that we normally include in being active. Normally we take more rationality to imply more freedom and more agency because we assume that our reason is applied to action; we think of guidance by reason as a source of action. Spinoza leaves out this aspect of our intuitive views about freedom and activity, but he assumes that he is still entitled to speak of freedom and activity. He replaces freedom in action with freedom of mind.[27]

But he does not abandon freedom of action altogether. Though he denies interaction between mind and body, he allows interaction among mental states. If we restrict 'action' to mental interaction, Spinoza allows action guided by reason. If this is the only freedom worth having, it is reasonable of him to claim that he allows us the freedom that is worth having, and that he allows us to be active rather than passive. He believes we can be free of the influence of the passions only if we give up the idea of acting (moving our bodies) for reasons altogether.

This is a high price to pay for freedom from disturbance by passion; it precludes Spinoza from giving ethical advice about external actions, and precludes us from giving such advice to ourselves. Perhaps this conclusion attributes too extreme a view to Spinoza; but if we retreat to a more moderate view that does not preclude advice about action, we raise difficulties for his views about freedom from passions. Freedom from passions comes from recognizing the necessity of things that we had previously taken to be contingent; these include the actions that are matters for moral deliberation and choice (before we agree with Spinoza).

But even if we could accept the implications of Spinoza's position and cease giving ourselves ethical advice, it is not clear how far we would modify our passions. Spinoza seems to assume that a change in our beliefs will weaken our passions, because we will recognize the falsity of the beliefs that are presupposed by the passions. But it is not clear that this will happen. Though recognition of the falsity of a belief results in our no longer holding the belief, we may still retain a false appearance, just as we do when we are afraid of being poisoned by a grass snake even after we learn that it is not poisonous.

We might try to defend Spinoza by arguing that adequate knowledge gives us a reason and a motive to try to moderate our passions, once we recognize that they have so far depended on false beliefs and now depend on false appearances. But a deliberate effort to moderate our passions rests on a false assumption about agency. Moreover, the assumption is not only false, but it conflicts with the main point of Spinoza's claims about adequate knowledge. He rejects the aim of deliberately modifying the passions; that aim depends on

---

[27] Cf. Hampshire, *TTM* 74.

the mistaken belief in freewill. A passion can be removed only by a stronger and opposite passion (4p7dem). Changes in the passions follow, without any further intervention of the will, from adequate knowledge of the necessary connexions in the world.

Spinoza's claims about the passions overlook the attitude of the ancient Sceptics. Sextus agrees with Spinoza, for different reasons, that we have no reason for acting in one way rather than another. He infers that we will give up acting on considerations that seem rational to us. But he does not infer that we will be free of passions. For even if passions include false beliefs or rely on them, recognition of the falsity of the beliefs does not imply the end of the passion. Even if we agree with Spinoza, and decide that we cannot respond as free agents to the contingencies of the world, our passions may not follow this conclusion. It is not clear, therefore, how the mental freedom that Spinoza describes will necessarily result in the modification of the passions.

513. Desires and Tendencies

Spinoza believes that some version of psychological egoism is correct; each person pursues his own good, because every being essentially tends towards its own continuance.[28] We might take him to be referring to a basic desire for one's own preservation; his statement of the basic 'striving' (conatus) may remind us of Aquinas' claim that all things 'desire' (or 'aim at', appetunt) being. But such a claim raises some difficulties for Spinoza.

The difficulty arises from an apparent conflict with his general opposition to all teleological claims.[29] His general view is that there are no final causes in nature. In his view, believers in final causes make the future exercise causal influence on the past, in defiance of the real order of causal influence.[30] They imagine that this is so in nature because they take nature to be a means of satisfying their own desires, and so they ascribe to nature the ends that they pursue for themselves.[31] But we have no reason to accept this anthropomorphic conception of nature.

The conclusion of Spinoza's argument raises some doubt about his premisses. For if all final causes are fictions, what about our belief that we have desires? If he explains our attitude to nature by reference to our desires, does he not explain them by reference to an end we pursue, and hence explain them teleologically, in defiance of the proper direction of causation? He might reply by denying that explanation by desire is teleological. A desire is a mental state earlier than the action, and so the causal influence goes in the proper direction. But this is not a complete reply to the objection. We normally suppose that the desire explains the action because of its goal-directed character; we choose that action as a means to

---

[28] 'So the power of each thing, *or* the striving by which it (either alone or with others) does anything, or strives to do anything—i.e., the power, *or* striving, by which it tries to persevere in its being, is nothing but the given, *or* actual, essence of the thing itself.' (3p7 = C 499)

[29] See Bennett, *SSE* 245.

[30] '...nature has no end set before it, and...all final causes are nothing but human fictions. ... This doctrine concerning the end turns nature completely upside down. For what is really a cause, it considers as an effect, and conversely.... What is by nature prior, it makes posterior' (1appx = C 442).

[31] '...men act always because of an end, namely, because of an advantage they desire. That is why it happens that they always seek to know only the final causes of things that have been done ...' (1appx = C 440).

an end that we pursue. The future-directed goal is causally relevant to this action; whether or not the action achieves the end, I chose it because of a desire with this future-directed character. If Spinoza allows this explanatory role to future-directed desire in human action, he leaves open the possibility of states that are future-directed in the same way in other natural explanation.

To avoid this teleological description of desires, Spinoza might argue that we have given the wrong account of their relation to action. Though we think they explain through their teleological content, we are wrong, just as we are wrong more generally in believing that the intentional content of our mental states explains our action. In desire we are simply aware of a bodily state that explains movements non-intentionally.

But what movements does it explain? We might be tempted to say that our desire for self-preservation is our awareness of states that result in our self-preservation, and that in general we can refer to the actual result of our bodily movement to identify the character of our desire. But this account of desire does not cope with the fact that someone's desire for self-preservation may also explain (as we suppose) actions that do not result in his self-preservation, but seem to him to be likely to result in it. The relevant movements are those that are directed towards self-preservation, and we cannot identify these except by reference to their intentional character and aim. If Spinoza adheres strictly to his ban on teleological explanation, he should apparently allow a desire for F only in cases where F is really achieved. This restricted appeal to desire limits the role of desire in explaining action.

A non-teleological reconstruction of desire also raises doubts about the universality of the desire for self-preservation. Since we all succeed in preserving ourselves for some time, Spinoza can consistently claim that we all act on the desire for self-preservation. But he also seems to treat this as a universal desire on all occasions.[32] Since we do not preserve ourselves on all occasions, it is not clear how the desire can be universal. If Spinoza claims that we all try to preserve ourselves even when we fail, he re-introduces a teleological concept. If he tries to remove the teleological content from trying, and replaces it with a mere tendency, he raises the difficulty about unsuccessful action again.

It is not clear, therefore, how much is left of the 'striving' (conatus) that Spinoza attributes to all human beings, once we remove the teleological content that conflicts with his metaphysics.[33]

514. Desire and Goodness

Some of Spinoza's views about the nature of desire affect his claims about the relation of desire and goodness. We might suppose that the desire for self-preservation rests, as Aquinas claims, on an assumption about goodness; in desiring something we see it in a particular light, in relation to other things that we count as good and worthy of desire, and that is why we try to get it. These intentional concepts do not fit Spinoza's attitude to teleology, and so he does not try to explain desire by reference to goodness. Our basic tendency towards

---

[32] See the passage just quoted. [33] On Spinoza's conception of desire see Broad, *FTET* 23; Curley, *BGM* 107–9.

self-preservation does not rest on any conviction about goodness; we do not desire our own continuance, or anything else, because we take it to be good. On the contrary, desire is prior to belief about goodness.[34] Joy and sadness result from the recognition of something that satisfies this desire, by promoting or hindering our preservation.[35] This connexion between self-preservation and pleasure also explains why we identify good things with causes of pleasure.[36] Since Spinoza rejects teleology, he does not believe that we act from the idea of self-preservation. Pleasure is a feature of my awareness of states that promote my preservation, and this is the sort of state that I call good.[37]

So far, Spinoza agrees with the egoistic aspects of Aristotelian ethical theory, once they are re-interpreted to fit his own views about the character of desire. He agrees with Aristotle that human beings necessarily pursue their own good, and he identifies this with happiness. He assumes that the appropriate end for ethics is happiness, and that the dispute is about where it is to be found and how it is to be achieved. He does not say much about the composition of happiness, or about hedonistic, subjectivist, and objectivist conceptions of it. He claims that 'happiness consists in man's being able to preserve his being' (4p18s(i) = C 556). In speaking of happiness as satisfaction (acquiescentia), he seems to treat it as consisting in a state of mind, however it is achieved.

515. Passions as the Sources of Conflict

How can we acquire the relevant sort of satisfaction? Spinoza believes that we cannot acquire it if our passions dominate us. For passions rest on a naive and misguided view of the world; we think it is worth our while to be angry or resentful at what happens to us, to feel strong attachment to other people or strong dislike of them, and especially to try to change other people and the world for our own advantage. This outlook rests on the assumption that things happen contingently, and hence are up to us to change, and that we know how to change them because we know that our mental states causally affect external reality. Moreover, since our passions result from imagination, they result from superficial views of the world that are liable to vary from person to person. If we look at the same object from different angles, and we do not try to correct our first impressions, it will appear to us that we see different objects. Similarly, different people's passions fasten on different aspects of the same situation and form different aims. Conflicts result from these different aims, since each person's passions differentiate him from other people in accordance with his imagination.

---

[34] '... we neither strive for, nor will, nor desire, nor have an appetite for, anything (nihil ... conari, velle, appetere, neque cupire) because we judge it to be good; on the contrary, we judge something to be good because we strive for it, will it, desire it, and have an appetite for it' (3p9s = C 500).

[35] 'By joy, therefore, I shall understand ... that affect by which the mind passes to a greater perfection. And by sadness that affect by which it passes to a lesser perfection.' (3p11s = C 500–1)

[36] 'We call good or evil what is useful to, or harmful to, preserving our being, i.e., what increases or diminishes, aids or restrains, our power of acting. Therefore ... in so far as we perceive that a thing affects us with joy or sadness, we call it good or evil. And so cognition of good or evil is nothing but an idea of joy or sadness that follows necessarily from the affect of joy or sadness itself.' (4p8 = C 550–1)

[37] On goodness see Garrett, 'Ethical' 272–4.

The condition of people who are dominated by their passions is therefore a Hobbesian state of nature, in which their disagreements in judgment lead to conflicts in action.[38] Spinoza agrees with Hobbes's view that a state of nature is the result of motives that are naturally present in human nature. But he does not agree exactly with Hobbes's account of why the state of nature is a state of war; his disagreement with Hobbes points to his distinctive view of how to emerge from the state of nature.

Hobbes takes both reason and passion to be sources of potential instability and conflict. Our lack of assurance makes it reasonable for us, from the point of view of self-preservation, not to observe the laws of nature in the state of nature. Hobbes reaches this conclusion because he assumes that reason requires us to compete with others for goods that cannot be shared but must be possessed by one individual to the exclusion of others (we cannot both be adequately nourished by eating a meal that is enough for just one person). Since reason requires us to enter the competition that we recognize as dangerous and destructive, it requires us to set up a commonwealth to restrain competition.

Spinoza's account of the state of nature is similar to Hobbes's account. He speaks of the 'right' of nature and 'law' of nature as one's freedom to exercise one's natural capacity; this is rather similar to Hobbes's view of the right of nature, which has no essentially moral character.[39] But his account of how to escape from the state of nature reflects the difference between his view of reason and Hobbes's.[40] Conflicts arise in the state of nature not because of reason (as Hobbes supposes), but only because of passions, which cause people to act on their partial views of things. But these same passions also tell us that we are better off if we listen to reason, since we dislike the effects of acting on our passions. We turn to reason because it considers the true good of human beings and promises to end conflicts.

We need the state, in Spinoza's view, because of our passions. If we listened to reason, we would be ready to keep promises, avoid deceit and violence, and observe the other Hobbesian laws of nature. We need a state with the power of coercion because of the people who are liable to be swayed by their passions into violating the laws of nature.[41] Spinoza is

[38] 'Men can disagree in nature in so far as they are assailed by affects that are passive, and to that extent one and the same man is also variable and inconstant.' (4p33 = C 561) On Spinoza and Hobbes see Curley, BGM 124–6.

[39] 'Since it is the supreme law of nature that each individual thing should strive (conetur) to preserve itself in its state, as much as lies in it, taking no account of another, but only of itself, it follows from this that each individual has the highest right to this, that is . . . to exist and act as it is naturally determined. . . . Hence among human beings, so long as they are considered as living under the command of nature alone, the one who has not yet come to know reason, or who has not yet acquired the state of virtue, lives with the highest right solely by the laws of desire, no less than the one who orders his life by the laws of reason.' (TTP 16 = S 527) 'The natural right of each human being is thus determined, not by sound reason, but by appetite and power.' (TTP 16 = S 527) I cite TTP by chapters and pages of Shirley.

[40] 'Nevertheless, no one can doubt how much more advantageous it is for human beings to live according to the laws and certain dictates of our reason, which . . . aim at nothing except the real advantage of human beings. Moreover, everyone is eager (cupiat) to live as far as possible without anxiety, free from fear, which, however, is quite impossible so long as everyone is permitted (licet) to do what he likes, and nothing more is allowed to the right (ius) of reason than to hatred and anger . . . When we reflect that human beings without mutual help must necessarily live most miserably and without the cultivation of reason . . ., we shall plainly see that men ought (debuisse) to have conspired together to live well and without anxiety . . . But their efforts to do this would have been vain if they willed (vellent) to follow what desire (appetitus) urged on them (for by the laws of desire each person is drawn in a different direction); they ought, therefore, to decree and pledge most firmly that they will direct everything by reason (which no one dares to oppose openly, lest he seem to lack any mind), and to restrain desire insofar as it urges anything harmful to another, and to do nothing to another that one does not will to have done to oneself, and to defend the right of another as one's own.' (TTP 16 = S 528)

[41] 'However, if all men could be easily led by the leading of reason alone, and could recognize the highest advantage and necessity of a commonwealth, everyone would repudiate deceit; for everyone would faithfully adhere altogether

justified in claiming to differ from Hobbes on this point, by taking reason to be always on the side of peace.[42] Hobbes sometimes suggests that reason may be the source of violations of the laws of nature, and so it needs coercion to change the rational attractiveness of the different options. Spinoza's claims about reason and passion are much clearer and less ambiguous. If he is right, we need the commonwealth to reduce the influence of the passions, not to make it rational for rational agents to make and keep covenants. He therefore seems to overlook the questions about assurance that lead Hobbes to argue that reason may be a source of conflict in the state of nature.

Spinoza's disagreement with Hobbes partly reflects his acceptance of the Stoic claim that happiness consists in living in accordance with nature.[43] To show how rational perfection is connected to moral virtue, he argues that if we live according to our own nature as rational beings, we live in ways that benefit others as well as ourselves.[44] Our passions tend to create conflicts, but reason resolves them, by giving us a common point of view that appreciates the benefits we gain from each other. Sometimes he suggests that reason presents to us the means of self-preservation, as Hobbes supposes. But his main reason for claiming that reason removes conflict rests on his distinction between the partial outlook of the passions and the insight of reason into general laws, giving it a common point of view.

Conflict does not arise, therefore, from two individuals' desiring the same thing, but from their having different passions towards it.[45] They may be right in both desiring the same thing; that is not the cause of their conflict. Conflict requires the idea of a gain

to their agreements because of their appetite (cupiditate) for this highest good, namely, the preservation of the commonwealth. ... But it is far from being true that all can always be easily led by the leading of reason alone; for everyone is drawn away by his pleasure, while avarice, ambition, envy, hatred, and the like most often occupy one's mind so much that no room is left for reason. That is why, though human beings promise with certain signs of a sincere mind and undertake to keep their word, still no one can be certain about the good faith of another unless something is added to the promise, since everyone by the right of nature can act deceitfully, and is not required (tenetur) to stick to his agreements, except by the hope of a greater good, or the fear of a greater evil.' (*TTP* 16 = S 529–30)

[42] 'Whatever sort of state (civitas) a human being lives in, he can be free. For certainly a human being is free to the extent that he is led by reason. But reason (though Hobbes thinks otherwise) altogether urges peace; this, however, cannot be attained unless the common laws (iura) of the state are kept. Therefore the more a human being is led by reason—that is to say, the more he is free—the more constantly he will keep the laws of his state, and carry out the commands of the supreme power to which he is subject.' (*TTP* 16n33 = S 580–1)

[43] 'In so far as a thing agrees with our nature, it cannot be evil. Necessarily, then, it is either good or indifferent. In the latter case, namely that it is neither good nor evil, then nothing will follow from its nature that aids the conservation of our nature, i.e. (by hypothesis) that aids the preservation of the nature of the thing itself. But this is absurd. Hence, in so far as it agrees (convenit) with our nature, necessarily it is good.' (4p31d = C 560–1) '... what is most useful to a human being is what most agrees with his nature ... But a human being acts entirely from the laws of his own nature when he lives by the leading of reason ...' (4p35c1 = C 563)

[44] 'But because each one, from the laws of his own nature, desires what he judges to be good, and strives to avert what he judges to be evil, and moreover, because what we judge by the dictate of reason to be good or evil is necessarily good or evil, it follows that in so far as human beings live by the leading of reason, to that extent necessarily they do only those things that are necessarily good for human nature, and hence for each human being, i.e. those things that agree with the nature of each human being. Hence, in so far as they live by the leading of reason, necessarily they always agree.' (4p35d = C 563)

[45] '... it is far from true that they are troublesome to one another in so far as they love the same thing and agree in nature. Instead ... the cause ... is nothing but the fact that they are supposed to disagree in nature. For we suppose that Peter has the idea of a thing loved and already possessed, and Paul, on the contrary, has the idea of a thing loved and lost. That is why the one is affected with joy and the other with sadness, and to that extent they are contrary to one another. In this way we can easily show that the other causes of hate depend only on the fact that men disagree in nature, not on that in which they agree' (4p34s = C 562–3).

that causes another's loss; and that idea comes from their passions. The point of view of reason, however, endorses a common and non-competitive good. Hence 'men will be most useful to one another, when each one seeks his own advantage' (4p35c2 = C 563). The common point of view is common to different people who are guided by reason, since it presents the same conclusions to A and to B; it is free from the distorting influence of the passions that give A and B different points of view on the same situation. But it is also a common point of view because it prescribes whatever is for the common good of A and B.

It is difficult, however, to see why Spinoza supposes that a point of view that is shared by different people will necessarily prescribe a common good. Suppose, for instance, that reason tells us that each person needs to eat 3 kg of food per day to stay alive. Since this is true of everyone, reason tells A that each of A, B, and C, needs to eat 3 kg per day; and it tells B and C the same thing. Hence they can agree on its being good for each person to eat 3 kg. But if there are only 3 kg available to divide, the 'common' conclusion that each person ought to eat 3 kg does not tell anyone what to do; still less does it say what policy it will be good for everyone to adopt. In this respect, reason does not seem to present a common good; the good that it presents does not remove competition between individuals. One might say that the competition is only contingent, resulting from the lack of resources; but contingent competition is enough for Hobbes's argument about the state of nature to get started.

Spinoza is perhaps misled (as Hobbes sometimes is) by indiscriminate references to 'agreement' between individuals. We may concede his claim that reason leads to agreement; if two people equally exercise their reason on arithmetic or geometry and reach true conclusions, they will agree on the conclusions. But it does not follow that this agreement points out the sort of common good that eliminates competition between individuals. It may be true that if different people proceed rationally, free from the influence of their particular emotions, they will reach the same conclusion. But why will they not conclude that, for instance, it is good for you to attack me, and good for me to attack you? Why will they agree on a course of action that is good for all of them?

516. The Good of Rational Beings

Spinoza answers this objection through his conception of the nature of the common good. He considers the possibility that the good of one person is not the good of another, but he dismisses the possibility, on the ground that the very nature of human beings makes their good non-competitive. On this point he departs from Hobbes. According to Hobbes, peace is a non-competitive instrumental good; we all benefit from it in pursuing our various sources of pleasure and satisfaction, but our ends are not essentially non-competitive. Even from the rationally enlightened point of view, the non-competitive good is good only insofar as it is a means to other goods. Spinoza, however, believes that the ultimate good is essentially non-competitive. The good for a human being consists in 'an adequate knowledge of God's eternal and infinite essence' (4p36s = C 564). Since human nature is essentially rational nature, he agrees with Aristotle in taking happiness to require intellectual perfection.[46] Each of us loves this good more to the extent that one sees it loved by others also; hence each of us will strive to make others love the same non-competitive good (4p37alt.dem = C 565).

What is the relation of the adequate and intuitive knowledge of God to blessedness? Perhaps Spinoza allows that internal satisfaction achieved by some other means than intuitive knowledge of God is still blessedness, but recommends intuitive knowledge of God as the best means to it. Alternatively, he may mean that only the satisfaction caused by intuitive knowledge of God is blessedness; in that case, he needs to explain why that specific cause should be regarded as a necessary condition of happiness.

His answer depends on the connexion between adequate knowledge and the intuitive knowledge of God. Since God is to be identified (speaking approximately) with the laws of nature, we come to know God by acquiring adequate knowledge of the laws of nature, and so understanding why what happens is necessary. This is the point of view of reason, which gets us away from the instability of the emotions. Since this point of view removes the disturbances that arise from domination by the passions, it is the only source of the satisfaction that is needed for happiness. Epicurus was right, therefore, to believe that happiness consists in freedom from disturbance (*ataraxia*), and that understanding the character of the gods promotes this undisturbed condition. But Spinoza's account of the understanding that achieves happiness is closer to Aristotle's conception of theoretical wisdom, grasping the necessary truths about the universe.

Once we grasp the connexion between happiness and intellectual perfection, we can reject Hobbes's purely instrumental attitude to the moral virtues. Spinoza believes that virtue deserves to be chosen for its own sake. He disagrees both with Hobbes, who believes it is worthwhile only for its natural consequences, and with theological moralists who believe it is only worthwhile on the assumption of divine rewards. All those who take an instrumental attitude to moral virtue fail to see that, as Spinoza understands it, it is the greatest happiness. God does not need to reward us for service, since the service of God is happiness itself.[47] We have no reason to regard the common point of view as simply a means to peace; it is a source of happiness quite apart from its role in providing counsels of self-preservation.

517. Intellectual Love of God

The enlightened common point of view of reason leads us to the intellectual love of God. This is 'the highest good which we can want from the dictate of reason and is common to all men; we desire that all should enjoy it' (5p20 = C 605). It is the common good that Spinoza believes we will want everyone to share (cf. 4p37alt.dem = C565, discussed above).

In speaking of intellectual love, Spinoza alludes to the sort of love that Aquinas attributes to us when we are moved by the intrinsic goodness of the person loved, rather than by

---

[46] 'In life, therefore, it is especially useful to perfect, as far as we can, our intellect or reason, and in this one thing consists the highest human happiness or blessedness, because blessedness is nothing but the very satisfaction (acquiescentia) of mind that arises stems from intuitive cognition of God.' (4app(iv) = C 588)

[47] 'From this we clearly understand how far those people stray from the true valuation of virtue, who expect to be honoured by God with the greatest rewards for their virtue and best actions, as for the greatest bondage (servitus)—as though virtue itself, and bondage to God, were not happiness itself, and the greatest freedom.' (2p49s4a = C 490)

pleasure or advantage.[48] But his conception of intellectual love is so different that we may reasonably wonder whether he is talking about the same thing. Aquinas takes the object of intellectual love to be a person, whether human beings or God. In loving God we love a person who also loves us; indeed, God's love towards us makes us capable of love towards God. In Spinoza's view, however, God is incapable of love and of any other affect of joy or sadness, because these affects would be incompatible with God's perfection (5p17 = C 604).

These adaptations of intellectual love take no account of Aquinas' view that God is capable of intellectual love without passions, because love belongs to God's will. It is reasonable for Spinoza to ignore Aquinas' view, given that he disagrees sharply with Aquinas about God's intellect and will. He denies any distinction between intellect and will, and in particular he denies it in God. Moreover, he denies that God has an intellect. God's nature does not allow the appropriate relation between an intellect and its objects; for a divine intellect could not be either posterior or simultaneous to its objects, as an ordinary intellect is. An ordinary intellect achieves knowledge insofar as it is passive, by grasping an object that exists independently of it; that is how it achieves the right direction of fit, by knowing rather than creating an object. But a divine intellect could not grasp its objects in this way; it would have to be prior to everything, since God is the cause of everything (1p17s(ii) = C 427). Since God is so different from any ordinary intellect, Spinoza concludes that intellect, will, and desire and so on, belong to natura naturata, not to natura naturans (1p31 = C 434–5); that is to say, they belong to 'what follows from the necessity of God's nature', and not to 'God, in so far as he is considered as a free cause' (1p29s = C 434).

The effect of these claims about God and intellect is to curtail the possibility of intellectual love, as Aquinas understands it. For Spinoza in contrast to Aquinas, it is not love directed towards God as a distinct person with intellect, will, and love. The features of distinct personality do not belong to natura naturans, and hence do not belong to God understood in his own right. This does not make intellectual love of God insignificant in Spinoza's system. Given his doctrine of intellect and will, intellectual love is directed towards adequate knowledge. Knowledge of God is knowledge of the structure and laws of the universe and of their necessity, not of a distinct person. Intellectual love is completely satisfied once we have a complete grasp of the necessary system of the universe.

Spinoza accepts one aspect of the traditional doctrine of intellectual love of God insofar as he takes it to involve union with God.[49] If we can be united with God, and if we love God, then apparently God also loves God. But Spinoza rejects this conclusion, because of his previous restrictions on the ways in which we can attribute intellect, will, and love to God. 'God loving himself' is not to be understood as love directed towards a distinct person beyond finite persons; for there is no such distinct person. The total system of the universe does not love itself. God's love of himself must be reduced to love by individual finite persons (who are all modes of God) for finite persons. That is the only sense in which one's

---

⁴⁸ See Aquinas, §336. Wolfson, PS ii 274–9, gives further sources, but he does not emphasize the moral and personal character of intellectual love, as Aquinas conceives it.

⁴⁹ 'The mind's intellectual love towards God is the very love of God by which God loves himself, not in so far as he is infinite, but in so far as he can be explained by the human mind's essence, considered under a species of eternity; i.e., the mind's intellectual love towards God is part of the infinite love by which God loves himself.' (5p36 = C 612)

intellectual love can be part of God's love of himself; it is part of the total of intellectual love present in all the finite persons.[50]

518. Reason and the Good of Others

Spinoza's account of happiness as intuitive knowledge and intellectual love of God helps us to see the good that is revealed by the common point of view of reason. His conception of the good gives him an answer to our earlier objection that the common point of view might reveal a good that is the object of competition. The intuitive knowledge of God is a non-competitive good; if I acquire it, I do not take any of it away from you, and in recognizing it as good for myself I recognize it as good for you also.

But this non-competitive good does not remove all the objections that Spinoza might face. Even if knowledge of God is the whole of a person's good, the resources we need to achieve it might involve competition; and so we still have no reason for being especially concerned for others in such a competition for resources. Moreover, Spinoza does not argue convincingly for his claim that knowledge of God is the whole of the human good. If we really thought that it is all that matters, we seem to have no reason to secure the more mundane goods for other people or for ourselves. The aspect of Spinoza's outlook that introduces a non-competitive good also curtails one's concern for the goods and evils that are normally taken to matter in inter-personal relations.

In his claims about the purely intellectual good of knowing God, Spinoza offers a genuine alternative to Hobbes. According to Hobbes, the only function for reason in the state of nature is to suggest 'articles of peace', on the assumption that the good of different human beings brings them into conflict and that the conflict has to be managed in people's mutual interest. Spinoza departs from Hobbes in not confining the human good to the sorts of self-confined pleasures that Hobbes considers. But it is not clear that it gets us out of a Hobbesian attitude to our social life.

Spinoza believes that Hobbes would be right if human beings could not reduce domination by passion (4p37sch2 = C 566–7). But he argues that reason can be practical in the ways that Hobbes supposes (4p65–6 = C 583), and he believes that his account of the common good pursued by reason explains how reason can remove Hobbesian conflicts. But it is not clear how this is so, if reason simply turns us towards the knowledge of necessary truths about the universe.

Perhaps he intends his account of reason and adequate knowledge to make a further difference to practical reason. If I am dominated by passions, I use reason to secure advantages for myself, as measured from the limited point of view of my own imagination. But if I

---

[50] This is Martineau's conclusion in *TET* i 364: 'So it comes out, that for God to love himself is for him to love men. But his love to himself . . . is equivalent to man's love to him; therefore his love towards man is equivalent to man's love to him. These wonderful transformations are all wrought by the mere verbal device of duplicate denominations of the same thing; one of the same feature, of love, is slipped, now under one name, now under another; the double names being of persons with the personality emptied out; and the result is a tissue of apparent contradictions which, on examination, prove to be a monotonous tautology. It was long before I could find courage to look behind the venerable mask of these empty propositions; and it was not without pain that I found in the guise of mystical devotion, what I can hardly rank higher than logical thimble-rigging.'

acquire adequate knowledge of myself and others, I no longer look at myself or others from the individual point of view that is influenced by my passions. I now look at all of us—it may be supposed—from a strictly impartial view, seeing everything as the necessary result of the laws of nature. One might suppose that, from this point of view, no room is left for any special concern with myself as opposed to others. Hence I have no reason to favour myself over others.

These claims about one's own good and the good of others are not alien to the Aristotelian outlook. Aristotle believes that the self-love of the virtuous person is also directed to the common good of rational agents, because each person recognizes himself as essentially rational. We have considered some of the objections that arise against Aristotle's use of these claims, and some of the replies that might be offered in his defence. Spinoza adds his own distinctive argument, in claiming that the point of view of reason removes the passions that produce conflict.[51] Enlightened people will not only be free of the competitive aspects of the emotions, but will also seek to co-operate with others.

This argument is open to question. If Spinoza's claims about the emotions are correct, we can see why enlightenment about the emotions will result in a less competitive attitude. But one might also suppose it will result in a less co-operative attitude as well. The emotions produce concern for others, since we believe we can (for instance) do something to relieve the sufferings of others. If we lose this belief in our agency, and we are less disturbed by grief at the sufferings of others, why should we still be concerned about their welfare? If the universal point of view resulting from adequate knowledge removes any bias in favour of myself, should we not also expect it to remove concern for others? If I am indifferent to others, and I also recognize that from the universal point of view I matter no more than others do, why should I not also become indifferent to myself? Co-operation requires not only removal of bias towards myself, but also positive concern for others. Spinoza does not explain why we will develop this positive impartial concern simply by acquiring an impartial point of view.

This difficulty in connecting rational impartiality with positive concern for others is not peculiar to Spinoza. It suggests a reasonable question that can also be raised about Kant's position. But the difficulty arises especially clearly for Spinoza, in his claims about the common point of view of reason. He does not seem to recognize that he needs to say more about why reason leads to co-operation.

Similarly, when he claims that virtue is worth choosing without any external rewards, he criticizes moralists who claim that only the prospect of rewards and punishments makes it worth our while to pursue virtue and avoid vice. But these moralists are not concerned with adequate knowledge of necessary truths; they might well concede that these are worth pursuing apart form their rewards. They are concerned with the moral virtues; since these virtues seem to require some sacrifice of our own interest, a divine reward is needed (on this view) to convince us that they are in our interest overall. If Spinoza rejects this view, he implies that the moral virtues themselves promote happiness. Since he has already said

---

[51] 'This doctrine contributes to social life, in so far as it teaches that each one should hate no one, despise no one, mock no one, be angry at no one, and envy no one; and also in so far as it teaches that each one should be content with his own things, and should be helpful to his neighbour, not from womanish compassion, partiality or superstition, but from the leading of reason, as the time and occasion demand.' (2p49s iv (c) = C 490)

that the satisfaction resulting from intuitive knowledge of God is blessedness, he should identify this state with moral virtue and show how it results in concern for the good of others.

Spinoza's metaphysics both suggests some of the most intriguing elements in his moral philosophy and confronts him with serious difficulties. His distinctive ethical recommendations depend directly on some of the elements of his metaphysics that undermine ordinary convictions about agency. When we reject ordinary views about agency, and replace them with adequate knowledge, we undermine the ordinary sources of anger, resentment, and conflict. But we also seem to undermine some of the convictions that lead to morality.

Similarly, Spinoza's conception of intellectual love makes it difficult to see how an appeal to intellectual love could help him at the points where his ethical doctrines are open to question. For even if we restrict it to other finite persons, and do not extend it to God, it is not directed to their characters or personalities or (as we normally conceive them) their interests. It must be confined to assent to the same necessary truths as they are grasped by other finite minds besides our own. If I assent to your grasping the laws of thermodynamics, and in that sense have intellectual love for you, it does not follow that I will enjoy your company, or care about your being free of pain or deprivation. We have seen why it would be unjust to charge Plato with abandoning the love of particular human beings for the intellectual acceptance of abstractions.[52] This charge seems more appropriate for Spinoza's doctrine of intellectual love.

Spinoza, therefore, does not resolve all the doubts that arise about his moral position. The specific metaphysical claims that are meant to free us from the passions that lead to selfishness and conflict seem to free us from too many other things as well. His attack on agency seeks to expose the illusions underlying our passions. But if it succeeded, it would also deprive us of any basis for moral concern, for ourselves and for other people. Spinoza speaks as though we can appeal to his metaphysics to free us from the passions, without drawing its destructive conclusions for morality. But it is not clear how we can reasonably limit the impact of his metaphysics in this way.

---

[52] On Platonic love see §63.

38

THE 'BRITISH MORALISTS'

519. Rationalists and Sentimentalists

Whewell and Sidgwick both recognize a tradition of British moral philosophers whose outlook is defined, explicitly or implicitly, by questions raised by Hobbes. While philosophers in this tradition are also open to influences from outside Britain, they are especially concerned with Hobbes and his successors. Before we discuss, them, therefore, it may be useful to survey some of the different tendencies in the British moralists, and some of the different ways of dividing them into different schools or movements.

While Whewell and Sidgwick already recognize a distinct British tradition in moral philosophy, modern conceptions of this tradition have no doubt been influenced by Selby-Bigge, who published in 1897 a useful anthology of selections from the British moralists.[1] For the next 70 years, until the publication of Raphael's anthology in 1967, Selby-Bigge's collection introduced non-specialists to the works of the moralists whose works were not available in modern editions. It encouraged the wider knowledge of moralists who had often lain unread since the 18th century.[2] Selby-Bigge divides British moralists between Hobbes and Hume into 'sentimentalists' and 'intellectualists', but he does not explain what he means by these labels, or how they fit different moralists.[3] His first volume contains texts from the leading sentimentalist writers, Shaftesbury, Hutcheson, Butler, Smith, and Bentham. He presumably includes Hobbes, Locke, and Hume in this class.[4] His second volume includes the intellectualist writers Cudworth, Clarke, Balguy, and Price.

This division between sentimentalists and intellectualists recalls the standard division between empiricists and rationalists. Indeed, Selby-Bigge's intellectualists are often called rationalists, and they are all rationalists in the sense often used by the student of the history of

---

[1] Selby-Bigge's collection is intelligently reviewed, with appropriate criticism of his arrangement, by Albee.

[2] Butler had not been neglected either in Oxford or in Cambridge. See Garnett, 'Butler'. But knowledge of other 18th-century writers in English does not seem to have been widespread. See Martineau, *ERA* iii 378; Taylor, 'Butler'.

[3] Raphael, *BM*, abandons Selby-Bigge's division into schools in favour of a historical arrangement. Schneewind, *MP*, returns to a division by schools, more complex than Selby-Bigge's; his collection is not confined to British writers.

[4] For chronological reasons he relegates Locke and Hobbes to an appendix. He excludes Hume because he had already edited his two major works.

metaphysics and epistemology. Similarly, the sentimentalists generally hold some elements of an empiricist position.[5]

Not all the philosophers on each side are exclusively rationalist or exclusively sentimentalist. Hobbes, for instance, mostly agrees with later sentimentalists, but he sometimes (perhaps inconsistently)[6] treats moral principles as requirements of right reason; on this point he maintains a connexion between reason and morality that Cudworth and Clarke (for instance) defend and that Hutcheson (for instance) denies. Similarly, Shaftesbury anticipates Hutcheson on many points, and so might be counted as a sentimentalist. But he maintains that moral rightness and wrongness are not dependent on the reaction of observers, and so he accepts one of the main rationalist objections against sentimentalism.

If we recognize these complications, we can still follow Selby-Bigge's division in studying these moralists. His sentimentalists, from Hobbes to Bentham, develop one relatively systematic approach to morality, and his intellectualists, from Cudworth to Price, develop a significant alternative approach. A comparison of the two approaches is philosophically instructive, since mutual criticism by philosophers on each side exposes some basic questions in moral theory. This mutual criticism provokes Hume's full defence of an elaborated sentimentalist position. His defence in turn provokes Price and Reid to a fuller defence of the rationalism of their predecessors.

These debates also help us to see how both sides treat the 'traditional naturalism' derived from Aquinas. Rationalists criticize sentimentalists on several points on which sentimentalists follow Hobbes against traditional naturalism. But they also accept some aspects of Hobbes's attacks on traditional naturalism. We can therefore use these discussions to identify the features of traditional naturalism that are abandoned on all sides, and we can try to see whether their abandonment is justified.

Under 'British' moralists, Selby-Bigge includes English, Welsh, Scottish, and Irish writers. They do not form a homogeneous tradition. The idea of a single British nation was formed only gradually during the 18th century,[7] and the relevant philosophical traditions are distinct. In the Scottish universities moral philosophy was a subject for formal and systematic undergraduate lectures, whereas in England it had no equally secure place in university education. Clarke's major work was delivered as a series of sermons. Within the English and Welsh Dissenting academies that produced Butler, Price, and Godwin, moral philosophy was taught more systematically. Both Scottish Presbyterians and English and Welsh Dissenters seem to have been exposed to Continental influences that did not affect English Anglican writers to the same degree. The study of Grotius and Pufendorf was entrenched both in Glasgow and in Philip Doddridge's Dissenting academy,[8] but English Anglican writers do not refer to them as often. Hutcheson unites these different intellectual traditions. He was educated in a Dissenting academy, and taught in one himself. He took part in the non-academic literary life of Dublin, for which he wrote his main

---

[5] For doubts about the division between rationalism and empiricism see Loeb, *DH,* esp. ch. 1. He does not discuss Platonism, Cudworth, Clarke, Butler, or Price at length. Consideration of them would reinforce doubts about a sharp division, and about the suggestion that empiricism is in some way characteristic of British philosophers.

[6] Hobbes on practical reason; §478.

[7] The Act of Union of 1707 introduced 'one united kingdom by the name of Great Britain'. The growth of a sense of British identity during the 18th century is studied in Colley, *BFN;* see, e.g., 122–4 on Scotland.

[8] On Carmichael in Glasgow and on Doddridge see §585.

works in moral philosophy. He was a professor in Glasgow, where he produced his textbooks.

Even if we doubt whether all these moralists belong to a single 'British' tradition, Selby-Bigge's label is nonetheless justified insofar as the moralists he collects are engaged in debate primarily with one another. In this respect 18th-century writers differ, broadly speaking, both from their 17th-century predecessors and from their 19th-century successors. Though it is reasonable to begin the succession of British moralists with Hobbes, Cudworth, and Cumberland, these three are primarily concerned with the Classical and Scholastic tradition and with its development in natural-law theory. The beginning of the 18th century conveniently coincides with a more purely British intellectual context. Even if we recognize the importance of Grotius, Pufendorf, and the French Quietists, it is still broadly true that the earlier British moralists after Hobbes react to Hobbes, and that the later react to the earlier. Hutcheson's early work supports Shaftesbury, and criticizes Clarke; it provokes a reply from Balguy and Burnet. His later work is influenced by Butler. Price discusses Clarke, Hutcheson, Butler, and Locke. Hume, Smith, and Reid discuss most of their British predecessors. It is worth our while, therefore, to examine some general approaches to this whole British tradition.

It would be unreasonable to insist on a sharp terminal date. One important division is marked by the return of Continental influence, on Bentham and Godwin through Helvetius, and on 19th-century writers through Kant. But despite these non-British influences, Whewell, Mill, and Sidgwick clearly continue the discussions begun by their British predecessors. Hence an understanding of the more exclusively British discussions of the 18th-century helps us to appreciate the 19th-century discussions as well.

520. Whewell: Dependent v. Independent Morality

Selby-Bigge's division relies on moral epistemology and psychology, and hence on the foundations of the theories from which normative moral consequences are derived. A different division might appeal to the tendencies of different normative theories. Whewell sees such a division in 17th- and 18th-century British moral philosophy, between belief in 'independent' and in 'dependent' morality.[9] Morality is independent if it carries its own authority apart from its consequences; it is good in itself and gives us a sufficient reason for observing it, whether or not it also leads to our own pleasure, or the maximum universal pleasure, or to rewards in the afterlife. The authority of 'dependent' morality, however, depends on whether it leads to these consequences (LHMPE 52, 57). Hence Whewell sometimes speaks of 'independent morality' versus 'the morality of consequences' (84), and sometimes of 'the morality of principles' and 'the morality of consequences' (79).[10]

Whewell's descriptions suggest two ways of distinguishing dependent from independent morality. (1) A metaphysical division. Some people affirm, while others deny, that moral

[9] Though one volume of Whewell's lecture, LHMPE, speaks of England, he includes Scotland, Wales, and (through Hutcheson) Ireland as well.
[10] On independent morality see §604 on Ward.

properties can be reduced to such non-moral properties as our own pleasure, or universal pleasure, or the tendency to result in rewards after death. (2) A normative division. Some people reduce moral rightness to a tendency to promote some specific type of consequences (desired independently of morality?), whereas others deny this reduction.[11]

The parenthesis in the second division marks a question about Whewell's meaning. If it expresses his view, independent morality rejects the reduction of moral rightness to a specific non-moral property. In that case, the second division is a special case of the first division.[12] If, however, the bracketed phrase does not capture Whewell's intention, the second division is neither identical to the first nor a special case of it. We might hold that rightness consists in a tendency to promote morally desirable consequences, but deny that these consequences are themselves desirable independently of morality. If, for instance, we say that rightness consists in a tendency to promote goodness, but we hold that goodness is not reducible to a non-moral property, we believe in 'dependent morality' or 'the morality of consequences' according to Whewell's second division, but not according to his first division.[13]

521. Whewell and Utilitarianism

It is not mere pedantry to point out the difference between Whewell's two divisions. He runs them together because he attributes both conceptions of dependent morality to Paley and Bentham, and rejects them both on his own account. He derives the dependent view

[11] In discussing 'independent morality' Whewell speaks of 'conscience or moral faculty', which Hutcheson called the moral sense. Whewell assumes that Hutcheson and Butler refer to the same thing. (Preface to Mackintosh, *DPEP*, p. xxii.) This question concerns Whewell because he believes a non-utilitarian analysis of moral judgment is needed: 'Right, duty, what we ought to do, are not expressed to the satisfaction of any one by any phraseology borrowed from the consideration of consequences' (p. xxiv). This is why Bentham rejects 'ought' and 'ought not': 'These words—if for this one purpose the use of them may be allowed—*ought* to be banished from the vocabulary of ethics' (*Deont.* ii 1, p. 253). Whewell believes 'deontology' might appropriately be used to describe the outlook of independent morality: 'But the term Deontology expresses moral science (and expresses it well) precisely because it signifies the science of duty, and contains no reference to utility. It is a term well chosen to describe a system of ethics founded on any other than Mr Bentham's principle. Mackintosh, who held that *to deon*—what men ought to do—was the fundamental notion of morality, might very properly have termed the science deontology. The system of which Mr Bentham is the representative—that of those who make morality dependent on the production of happiness, has long been designated in Germany by the term Eudemonism, derived from the Greek word for happiness (eudaimonia). If we were to adopt this term we should have to oppose the deontological to the eudemonist school . . . ' (p. xxviii)

[12] It is only a special case, since there are other logically possible ways of reducing moral to non-moral properties that do not appeal specifically to causal consequences.

[13] Whewell discusses his division further in *LSM*: 'All systems which establish moral rules by their tendency to some external object;—happiness, utility, pleasure, interest, or whatever else; may be called dependent systems, in contradistinction to those which deduce moral rules from the constitution of man, not indeed overlooking the objects of human desires, but not governing themselves by these; such systems may be termed systems of independent morality . . . ' (137). Whewell takes Plato to represent independent morality, because he presents justice as desirable for its own sake as the health of the soul (*Rep.* iv) (138). He recognizes that Aristotle's position appears to be dependent morality, but he argues that the appearance is misleading: 'He analyses happiness, as the first step of his discussion of morality, but this step forthwith throws him back upon the constitution of man, the peculiar ground of the opposite school . . . And thus, in order to determine what modes of action tend to this ultimate and supreme good, he has to consider what the active powers of the soul are . . . ' (139). Hence Aristotle really upholds independent morality: 'For . . . the difference of the two schools of morality is not whether they do or do not speak of happiness; nor whether they do or do not allow happiness to be the supreme object of human action; but whether they do or do not establish their moral rules by their reference to some object considered as distinct from the human faculties themselves; be it called pleasure, or happiness, or utility, or by whatever other name' (141).

from Hobbes and voluntarism, and derives his own position from Cudworth and other rationalists. But a closer look at defenders of independent morality suggests that Whewell over-simplifies. Clarke and Balguy are rationalists who reject Hobbesian, voluntarist, and sentimentalist accounts of moral properties, but both of them show some sympathy to utilitarianism, though they do not accept it. They partly anticipate Sidgwick's combination of independent morality, as a metaphysical position, with utilitarianism as a normative position.

Still, Whewell might be right to combine the metaphysical and the normative conceptions of 'independent morality' as he does. For Adams, Price, and (less explicitly) Butler support his view that arguments for the metaphysical independence of moral properties also support a non-utilitarian normative position.

Is Whewell right? Is it a coincidence that these rationalists believe both his metaphysical and his normative position, and are they mistaken in supposing that the two positions are connected? Or do they show that their arguments for the metaphysical position under-mine utilitarianism? Sidgwick implicitly—but perhaps intentionally—disputes Whewell's position, by trying to separate the metaphysical from the normative issue. But he may underestimate the strength and the character of the arguments that Whewell and the rationalists present against utilitarianism.[14]

Whewell's division, therefore, is partly metaphysical (in contrasting realism with anti-realism and voluntarism) and partly normative (in contrasting anti-utilitarianism with utilitarianism). Selby-Bigge's division is primarily epistemological, distinguishing different accounts of the character and basis of moral judgments. Whewell's division matches the epistemological division at some points. For some supporters of independent morality—Clarke and Price, for instance—are rationalists about moral knowledge and motivation. On the other side, some believe that Lockean empiricism commits them to hedonism as an account of motivation.

Whewell's treatment of the moral sense, however, cuts across Selby-Bigge's division between sentimentalists and intellectualists. In his view, some defenders of independent morality try to avoid the obscurities of the rationalist epistemology of Cudworth and Clarke, while still defending their essential metaphysical claims about the irreducibility of morality.[15] Butler is an 'unsystematic' defender of independent morality, whereas Shaftesbury and Hutcheson defend it more systematically, by appealing to a moral sense.

This description of a moral sense theory fits Shaftesbury, since he is a moral realist. Since Hutcheson claims to defend Shaftesbury, we might follow Whewell and suppose that he also defends Cudworth's and Clarke's metaphysical position on moral properties without their moral epistemology. If Whewell is right, Hutcheson rejects rationalism in order to defend realism and independent morality against Hobbesian voluntarism, not in order to defend Hobbes and Locke against the rationalists.

---

[14] Sidgwick, ME, Bk i, chs. 2–3, 8, express his agreement with rationalists on meta-ethical questions.

[15] 'In general the moral realists were aware that they gave their adversaries an advantage, when they ascribed the discernment of moral relations to the reason, narrowed as the domain of that faculty had in later times been. They now found it more convenient to assert that moral distinctions were perceived by a peculiar and separate faculty. To this faculty some did not venture to give a name, but described it only by its operations and results, while others applied to it a term, The Moral Sense, which introduced a new set of analogies and connexions.' (LHMPE 92)

In support of Whewell, we might cite Reid. Reid is a realist and defends independent morality, but he also sympathizes with those who treat moral knowledge as the product of a moral sense.[16] He argues that reference to a moral sense supports realism and independent morality, because it explains how we can form moral judgments and claim moral knowledge of the properties that Whewell has in mind.

Whewell's division helps us to correct a conclusion we might easily reach from Selby-Bigge's division. We may be tempted to believe that the crucial differences between moral theories lie in their epistemological foundations, and that these foundations determine the rest of a theory. Whewell suggests that metaphysical and normative differences are crucial, and that different epistemological positions may take different routes to the same metaphysical and normative position. His division is consistent with Selby-Bigge's; both divisions identify central issues in dispute, and each division identifies points of agreement and disagreement that the other division may obscure.

522. Whewell on Voluntarism

We may illustrate Whewell's point from an issue closely related to the ones he discusses. Moralists between Hobbes and Butler can be classified as naturalists or voluntarists on questions about morality and the will of God. Hobbes—as generally understood—is a voluntarist. Locke the sentimentalist follows him on this point, and naturalists oppose him. But the division between naturalists and voluntarists does not match the division between rationalists and sentimentalists. Shaftesbury and Hutcheson are naturalists about the relation of the divine will to morality, but they are sentimentalists—Hutcheson more clearly than Shaftesbury—about our knowledge of moral properties. These moralists support Whewell's view that the moral sense theory is a way of supporting independent morality. The belief in independent morality is opposed to voluntarism, and these moralists align themselves with naturalists in opposing voluntarism.

Whewell's judgment disagrees, however, with contemporary rationalist critics of Hutcheson. Burnet, Balguy, and Price argue that Hutcheson's belief in a moral sense requires him to reject realism and the metaphysical independence of morality. Whewell admits that Hutcheson's theory faces difficulties in defending independent morality. But he only discusses Balguy's objections to anti-rationalism, and overlooks Balguy's charge that Hutcheson's account of a moral sense leads to anti-realism.[17] Just as Balguy attacks Hutcheson for rejecting realism, he attacks him for his implicit voluntarism. Naturalists normally oppose voluntarism by arguing for natural rightness and wrongness, understood as objective properties of things, not constituted by anyone's acts of choice, preference, or legislation. This objectivist conception of moral properties seems to conflict with the sentimentalist view that moral properties are constituted by the moral sense of observers.

---

[16] Reid on the moral sense; §842.

[17] At *LHMPE* 94–7 Whewell discusses the criticisms brought by Balguy and the other 'remaining adherents of the old realist school' (94) against Hutcheson's sentimentalism, but he does not discuss Balguy's objections to Hutcheson's anti-realism (except that at 95 he mentions some 'more peculiarly realist arguments' offered by Balguy).

Hutcheson's critics argue that his sentimentalism exposes him to the objections that he raises against voluntarism.

If these objections to Hutcheson are sound, Whewell is wrong to suppose that a moral sense theory, as Hutcheson and his critics understand it, is compatible with the realism and anti-voluntarism that are the marks of a belief in independent morality. If Whewell is right to connect a moral sense theory with independent morality, either Hutcheson's critics are mistaken or else Hutcheson's version of a moral sense theory does not support independent morality.

Reid's version of a moral sense theory fits Whewell's account better; for Reid's conception of a moral sense is meant to show why we can reasonably claim knowledge of objective moral properties that are irreducible to acts of approval. From Whewell's point of view, we might take Reid to continue the non-rationalist defence of realism that Shaftesbury began.

But even if Whewell is right about Hutcheson's version of a moral sense theory, Hume's version raises a further question. For Hume intends his moral sense theory to express anti-realism and the rejection of independent morality.[18] Moreover, he believes that he continues and develops Hutcheson's approach to morality, and especially his account of the moral sense. If Whewell is to cope with all the facts, he should allow that a moral sense theory may speak on either side of his debate about dependent and independent morality. His approach to the debate makes Hume the exception to the predominant tendency of moral sense theories to support independent morality. If, however, we listen to Hutcheson's critics and to Hume, Hutcheson's doctrine speaks against independent morality. Shaftesbury and Reid, on this view, are sharply opposed to Hutcheson and Hume.

523. Objections to Whewell: Utilitarianism

A further difficulty for Whewell arises from his normative thesis about independent morality. Balguy both accepts metaphysically independent morality and is somewhat sympathetic to utilitarianism. Hutcheson is a utilitarian, and tries to show that a moral sense theory is committed to utilitarianism. He agrees with Whewell in connecting a meta-ethical with a normative thesis, but the connexion is the opposite of the one that Whewell asserts. Whewell believes that a moral sense theory is an expression of belief in metaphysically independent morality that includes non-consequentialist morality; Hutcheson, however, believes that a moral sense theory supports utilitarian morality.

This counter-example to Whewell's general thesis about independent morality and non-utilitarianism is less damaging, however, if Whewell is wrong to regard Hutcheson as a defender of metaphysically independent morality. If, as rationalist critics allege, Hutcheson's sentimentalism really conflicts with metaphysically independent morality, his acceptance of utilitarianism does not undermine Whewell's general position.

On this point also, Whewell may have in mind the position of Reid, who believes in a moral sense, metaphysically independent morality, and non-consequentialist morality.

---

[18] Whewell's discussion of Hume is very brief (*LHMPE* 181–2). He notices that Hume agrees with Hutcheson in arguing against Clarke's rationalism, and concludes that Hume and Hutcheson 'thus seemed to trample on the very ruins of the old fortress of immutable morality' (182). But he does not try to fit his discussion of Hume into his view that belief in a moral sense constitutes a defence of 'independent morality'.

Perhaps Whewell is misled by this combination of views in Reid, and wrongly attributes it to previous philosophers who reject voluntarism. In his view, the rejection of voluntarism requires belief in independent morality, which is both metaphysically irreducible and normatively non-consequentialist.

Perhaps Whewell is historically incorrect in his claims about how many people see the connexions he alleges between a moral sense, metaphysically independent morality, and non-utilitarian morality. But he is nonetheless philosophically correct, if these positions are connected in the way he suggests. If he is philosophically correct, the failure of some of his predecessors to hold all these components of his view may result from their failure to see how the components are rationally connected.

524. Appropriate Questions

Selby-Bigge's and Whewell's different schemes for classifying moralists after Hobbes point to different and appropriate lines of division among these moralists.

For a start, we have been able to distinguish different views about (1) epistemology, (2) metaphysics, and (3) normative ethics. Sentimentalists and rationalists disagree primarily on epistemological issues. Realists and anti-realists, and voluntarists and naturalists, disagree primarily on metaphysical issues. Consequentialists and non-consequentialists disagree primarily on normative issues. If we mark these different divisions, we need not be surprised if some people are sentimentalists, but also anti-voluntarists.

These divisions may be used either to represent the intentions of different moralists or to represent the positions they are committed to. Whewell tends to use his division between dependent and independent morality for both tasks. His claim that Hutcheson is a moral realist and a defender of independent morality is most plausible as a statement of what Hutcheson is trying to do. It is more difficult to defend as a statement of what Hutcheson actually achieves, for reasons that Balguy and Burnet point out. Whewell agrees with their criticism of Hutcheson, and in doing so casts doubt on his case for treating Hutcheson as a defender of independent morality.[19]

Similarly, Whewell's suggestion that realism and anti-voluntarism leads to non-utilitarian normative conclusions is questionable as an account of what the moralists themselves think; but it may be more defensible as an account of what their positions imply. Some of these divisions, then, need to be defended by exegetical argument, whereas some need to be defended by philosophical argument about the positions that have been distinguished on some reasonable exegetical basis.

525. The Significance of Voluntarism

Whewell distinguishes supporters of 'independent' morality from theological voluntarists, who make morality, and especially moral obligation, dependent on divine commands.

---

[19] See *LHMPE* 94–9. For Balguy's criticism of Hutcheson's anti-realism see §663.

It is useful to include voluntarism, therefore, in our preliminary survey of British moral philosophy after Hobbes. Though none of the major 18th-century British moralists defends this position, voluntarism is remarkably resilient, despite frequent and convincing attacks on it. Theological voluntarists include John Clarke (1726), Gay (1731), Rutherforth (1744), Brown (1751),[20] and Paley (1785). Their rationalist critics include John Jackson and Catherine Cockburn. Both rationalism, as defended by Cudworth, Clarke, Balguy, Price, and Reid, and sentimentalism, as defended by Hutcheson and Hume, oppose theological voluntarism.

Though British defenders of voluntarism are less careful and sophisticated than Pufendorf and Barbeyrac, they present a clear and forceful argument against naturalism, in both sentimentalist and rationalist versions. Paley's *Moral and Political Philosophy*, first published in 1785, summarizes the voluntarist argument. Since Paley influences both the development of utilitarianism and the criticisms of it, it is useful to see why the voluntarist position appears attractive to readers who compare it with the main rationalist and sentimentalist accounts of morality.

526. Tendencies to Voluntarism

In the view of many voluntarists, the voluntarist position is the orthodox Christian position. We might find this surprising among Anglican writers, given the naturalism of such orthodox and influential writers such as Hooker and Sanderson. But it is less surprising in the light of theological and philosophical influences that seem to raise difficulties for naturalism.

From the theological voluntarist point of view, the view that moral goodness is independent of the will of God seems to challenge the sovereignty of God; and the view that human beings can discover moral goodness either by reason or by a moral sense seems to deny the fallen condition of the human will and its need for grace. This voluntarist outlook is not surprising in moralists who are strongly influenced by Lutheran or Calvinist views. We have seen that it does not express the whole truth about either Luther's or Calvin's position, and in particular that it does not capture their views on natural law.[21] Still, their outlook includes voluntarist elements, and some of their successors emphasize these elements. Cudworth defends his naturalist account of rightness against both Descartes and Dutch Calvinists who maintain the position of Ockham.

The history of Anglican moral theology shows a tendency towards voluntarism.[22] Jeremy Taylor, in contrast to Hooker and Sanderson, tends to minimize the usefulness of appeals to natural law and natural reason. He holds a voluntarist view of the relation of natural law to divine commands, and commends the view that Suarez attributes to Ockham.[23] He implies that the appeal to nature and natural reason is inconclusive, and that we do better to appeal directly to the Scriptures for a guide to action.[24] While he does not deny the existence of a

---

[20] Mill expresses admiration for Brown's defence of utilitarianism, in 'Bentham' = *CW* x 87.

[21] See §§399, 412.

[22] See McAdoo, *SCMT*. Urban, 'Revolution', argues that Hooker began a basic shift from Aquinas' naturalism to Butler's belief in the subordination of nature to conscience. The story of this 'development' rests on some disputable interpretations of Aquinas and of Butler. For more evidence see Mautner in Hutcheson, *HN* 16–26.

[23] On Sanderson see §557.   [24] On Taylor and on Maxwell's criticism see §539.

natural moral law, his readers might reasonably conclude that it does not matter much to theoretical or practical ethics whether we believe in it or not.

Taylor's view is not accepted without question; Bramhall, for instance, accepts a more traditional view of natural law.[25] But it marks a tendency in English moral thought that tends to take the philosophical structure of Aquinas' ethics less seriously.

Moreover, questions about natural law and natural reason became entangled with a more specifically ecclesiastical controversy. Hooker defends episcopacy by appeal to reason; he does not represent it as prescribed by Scripture, but argues that it can be justified by appeal to natural reason in the relevant historical circumstances. This sort of warrant was not good enough for Hooker's opponents, who insisted that a form of church order and government is legitimate only if it can be proved from Scripture. This was the defence they offered of the presbyterian order. The defenders of episcopacy conceded this procedural question to the presbyterians. In contrast to Hooker, Bancroft argues that episcopacy is the divinely prescribed form of government.

In the early 17th century, voluntarism in morality may have gained some support from the political use of voluntarism about divine law. According to a voluntarist view, God maintains certain laws within his 'ordered' or 'directed' power (potentia ordinata), and therefore makes them stable on the assumption that he continues to directs his power in the same way. But it is always within his 'unqualified' or 'absolute' power (potentia absoluta) to change these laws. James VI and I relies on this distinction to explain the relation of the king to the laws of the state. The king is not bound to observe the laws; his observance of the law is the result of his directing his power in a particular way by deciding that these will be the laws and that he will observe them, but it is always within his unqualified power to change them.[26]

These issues about episcopacy and about monarchy (themselves closely connected) may have encouraged Anglican writers to abandon Hooker's position, or at least to refrain from strenuous defence of his naturalism. Once they conceded that a proof of something's being reasonable was not good enough, and that a proof of divine command was required, they might reasonably be expected to make the same sort of concession in ethics.

A tendency towards a voluntarist account of morality is consistent with recognition of natural law grasped by natural reason. The opponents of naturalism who identify morality with the revealed will of God go further than they need to go in order to maintain voluntarism. But the appeal to revelation is a further step that a voluntarist is likely to find plausible. For if some divine law is revealed through natural reason, we will find it rationally

---

[25] At Works iv 81 Bramhall affirms Aquinas' account of the natural law 'participated', which is 'the ordination of right reason, instituted for the common good, to show unto man what he ought to do and what he ought not to do'. At iv 329 his description is derived from Reginaldus, PFP: 'The law of nature is the prescription of right reason, whereby, through that light which nature hath placed in us, we know some things to be done because they are honest, and other things to be shunned because they are dishonest'. He quotes a definition by Reginaldus, PFP i 511: 'The natural law ... is said specially of the dictate or judgment of our reason, the dictate by which through the light impressed on us by eternal law, we know certainly that some things are good, or agreeing with our nature, and judge that they ought to be done ... '. Bramhall does not repeat the remark about agreement with nature, but he adds the naturalist point that the things prescribed by the natural law are prescribed because they are good, and not the other way round. At v 15–16 he insists on the immutability and indispensability of the natural law.

[26] See James, PW, pp. xxv, 180, 184, 186. The theoretical and political significance of these claims is connected with questions about divine right, discussed by Russell, 'Rights'.

acceptable independently of its being commanded by God, and then its moral status does not seem to depend on its being a divine command. A defender of voluntarism is wise to deny that morality is essentially accessible to natural reason.

527. Anti-Scholasticism

A different sort of argument for voluntarism rests on scepticism about the philosophical basis of naturalism. In Aquinas and his successors, a defence of a naturalist account of natural law or (in Suarez) of intrinsic morality rests on claims about nature. In claiming that right action is what fits rational nature, they claim that some actions are appropriate for human nature in itself, independently of divine legislation, and that therefore nature itself has properties independently of divine legislation. These are not simply the properties that natural scientists describe, but also include moral properties, and, more generally, teleological properties implying that natural organisms have natural goals.

Seventeenth-century critics attacked this Aristotelian belief in nature and natural teleology, for more than one reason. Some dismissed Aristotelian metaphysics as hopelessly anti-scientific, primitive, and obscure. Such criticisms are familiar in Descartes and Locke. Others attacked Aristotelian natural teleology on specifically moral and theological grounds. Boyle argues that Aristotelian teleology introduces additional agents besides God, and therefore compromises the freedom and transcendence of God. He attacks such a conception of nature as 'idolatrous'.[27]

Whether such a charge is reasonable or (as Leibniz believes) unreasonable, it might be expected to inhibit a moralist from appealing too readily to assumptions that might appear Aristotelian and Scholastic. For a 13th-century moralist, the Aristotelian conception of nature provides an accepted background that makes claims about natural law more readily acceptable. For a late 17th-century moralist, any sign of Aristotelian influence might be a liability, not an asset.[28] Even the moralists (Cudworth, Clarke, Balguy, Adams, Butler, and Price) who reject voluntarism do not defend the Aristotelian or Thomist conception of natural law and first principles. The Aristotelian conception makes the grasp of natural law a part of the rational grasp of the ultimate end by rational agents. The later rationalists do not generally assert this connexion between ethical principles and natural teleology.[29]

This reluctance, on strategic grounds, to appeal to Aristotelian authority, is expressed in the defence of the 'latitude-men' by 'S.P.'.[30] The 'latitudinarians' try to explain Christianity in ways that are broadly comprehensive of Christian doctrine and natural reason. They are indebted to the Platonism of Cudworth and More. S.P. defends the 'mechanical' and 'atomical' philosophy against the Peripatetic.[31] New philosophy should lead to new divinity.

---

[27] Boyle, FE iv 48–51. In CV Boyle does not mention the charge of idolatry, but he alleges (e.g., 17) that the Scholastic outlook inhibits inquiry, and hence inhibits appreciation of the goodness of God in creation. McGuire's discussion of Boyle in 'Nature' connects an anti-Aristotelian view with voluntarism.

[28] On anti-scholasticism cf. Hobbes, §§469, 482.   [29] Cudworth and Leibniz are exceptions. See §§541, 586.

[30] 'S.P.' is usually identified with Simon Patrick. Beiser, SR 283–4, discusses and quotes him on the disadvantages of appealing to Aristotle.

[31] 'But there is another crime which cannot be denied, that they have introduced a new philosophy; Aristotle and the schoolmen are out of repute with them.' (BANSLM 14)

Instead of trying to suppress new philosophy, as the Presbyterians did, the Church of England ought to embrace the new learning as the Roman Church has done in the works of Descartes and Gassendi (22).

S.P. qualifies the sense in which Aristotle and the schoolmen are 'out of favour'. The new philosophy does not reject Aristotle altogether.[32] But sensible defenders of Christian doctrine should avoid the appearance of being stuck in a Scholastic mould.[33] S.P. suggests that one would put off the 'ingenious gentry' by appealing to Aristotle or St Thomas. But he also implies that, if it were not for this strategic disadvantage, one might quite reasonably rely on these sources. He does not suggest that their content is theologically or philosophically unacceptable. Nonetheless, he agrees with Cudworth and More in reclaiming Platonism for Christianity, and thereby freeing the Church from an exclusive dependence on Aristotle.[34] A broader philosophical perspective will make the basic Christian claims seem more plausible, since they will not appear to depend on a questionable Aristotelian framework.

The Latitudinarian outlook described here is not intended to support voluntarism about morality. On the contrary; the rationalism of Cudworth and Clarke is an attempt to carry out the task that S.P. describes, showing that the essential Christian claims about morality fit the truths that can be independently discovered by natural reason about human beings and their actions. Still, some latitudinarian assumptions make it easier to be a voluntarist. For if one is reluctant to advertise any commitment to principles that might appear Aristotelian, one makes it more difficult than it would otherwise be to reject voluntarism. It is difficult to defend naturalism without making claims about the nature of things in their own right; and one might suspect that these claims really presuppose some aspects of Aristotelian teleology.

A proper resolution of this question would require some discussion of which aspects of Aristotelian teleology are needed for naturalism about morality, and of whether these aspects depend on other Aristotelian doctrines that are open to legitimate suspicion in the light of modern science or Christian theology. Leibniz sees that this discussion is needed, but he does not carry it out fully.[35] Clarke and Price try to reject voluntarism in favour of realism and rationalism, but without any commitment to Aristotelian claims about nature. Butler is doubtful about the prospects of this rationalist outlook, and returns to naturalism. We need to see what his claims about nature presuppose, and whether they presuppose questionable aspects of the Aristotelian position.

[32] 'Whatever is solid in the writings of Aristotle the new philosophers will readily embrace, and they that are most accused for affecting the new, doubt not but they can give as good an account of the old philosophy as their most violent accusers, and are probably as much conversant in Aristotle's writings, though they do not much value those small wares that are usually retailed by the generality of his interpreters.' (BANSLM 22)

[33] 'How shall the clergy be able to maintain their credit with the ingenious gentry, who begin generally to be acquainted with the atomical hypothesis, . . . or how shall they encounter the wits of the age, who assault religion with a new kind of weapon? Will they acquiesce in the authority of Aristotle or St Thomas? or be put off with Contra negantem principia? Let not the Church send out her soldiers armed with dock-leaves and bullrushes, to counter swords and guns . . .' (24)

[34] 'True philosophy can never hurt sound divinity. Christian religion was never bred up in the Peripatetic school, but spent her best and healthfullest years in the more religious Academy . . . but the Schoolmen afterwards ravished her thence, and shut her up in the decayed ruins of Lyceum . . . Let her old loving nurse the Platonic philosophy be admitted again into her family; nor is there any cause to doubt but the mechanic also will be faithful to her, no less against the open violence of atheism than the secret treachery of enthusiasm and superstition, as the excellent works of a late learned author have abundantly demonstrated.' (24)

[35] On Leibniz see §586.

This sketch of different forms of opposition to voluntarism suggests why many people might find voluntarism appealing because of its apparent clarity. Appeals to 'the nature of things' might intelligibly appear to involve vague metaphysics, or exploded natural philosophy, or both.

528. Rationalism v. Orthodoxy

Even if the latitudinarian outlook unwittingly helps voluntarism, the main aim of Latitudin-arians is to oppose voluntarism. Hence any doubt about the implications of Latitudinarian views tends to increase sympathy for voluntarism. The connexion between a Latitudinarian outlook and Cudworth's and Clarke's rationalism gives a reason for conservative Anglicans to resist their account of morality. An attempt to recommend Christian moral principles on rational grounds independent of revelation might appear to be part of a general programme of minimizing the dogmatic elements in Christianity. If one supposes that a major part of Christianity is its moral doctrine, and if one then discovers that its moral doctrine rests on rational, non-dogmatic foundations, one may infer that, as one writer puts it, Christianity is 'not mysterious' after all, because there is nothing more to it than we can discover by natural reason.[36]

For these reasons, the attitude to morality and religion that is defended by Cudworth and Clarke, and followed by Balguy, tends to co-exist, in these people, with an attitude to other aspects of Christianity that arouses orthodox objections.[37] Cudworth supports 'undogmatic' Christianity, and Clarke was accused of Arianism.[38] Balguy was a supporter of Hoadly, who wrote an admiring biography of Clarke. All of them were 'Latitudinarians' and defenders of minimalist Christianity (as their opponents conceived it).[39] None of these leading rationalists seemed a completely reliable Christian in the eyes of the defenders of Trinitarian theology. Butler is the exception to this generalization, since he shows no sign of unorthodoxy.[40]

The suggestion that naturalism about morality encourages scepticism about the dogmas of the Christian faith may seem strange if we think of Aquinas or of Suarez. But it is not entirely surprising. Some French Jansenist objections to the Jesuits express similar suspicions and objections.[41] From the point of view of Aquinas, or of the Council of Trent, it seems entirely unwarranted to claim that if Christianity includes basic moral principles that can be justified by natural human reason, it has no essential dogmatic elements that depend

---

[36] See Toland, CNM. Rationalist treatments of Christianity are intelligently discussed by Tulloch, RTCP ii, chs. 1–2. Stephen, HET i, ch. 3, offers a less subtle account. See also Beiser, SR 123–32.

[37] On Cudworth and Whichcote see Passmore, RC 81.

[38] On the connexion between Arianism and rationalism see Wiles, AH, ch. 4, esp. 110–25 (on Clarke, Butler, and Waterland), 149–51 (on Price). On Cudworth's unpopularity in some orthodox quarters Passmore, RC 101, quotes a comment by Warburton, DL, ed.1, Pref. to IV–VI: 'There wanted not country clergymen to lead the cry, and tell the world—That, under the pretence of defending Revelation, he wrote in the very manner that an artful infidel might be supposed to use in writing against it'.

[39] The growth of Latitudinarian views in Cambridge, and their rather heterogeneous sources (Puritan and rationalist), are described by Gascoigne, CAE 32 (on Pearson and Aquinas); 7, 86 (on John Moore, Clarke's patron); 117 (Clarke); 123 (Waterland); 127 (Rutherforth).

[40] In Anal. ii 1.18 Butler refers approvingly to Waterland on the use of the Trinitarian formula in Baptism.

[41] On Jansenism see §417; Knox, E, chs. 9–10; Abercrombie, OJ; Palmer, CU, ch. 2.

on revelation. But the unwarranted claim seems to influence people both for and against voluntarism.

These points help to explain an initially puzzling fact about support for and opposition to voluntarism. During the period of the Reformation, voluntarist tendencies are most marked in Lutheran and Calvinist sources. Voluntarism seems appropriate for a defence of the sovereignty of God, the weakness of human reason, and the dependence of human beings on divine grace. Cudworth still thinks of Calvinists as some of his main opponents. But in 18th-century England, the Dissenters, successors of the Puritans, often support rationalism against voluntarism in morality. The defenders of voluntarism are the orthodox Anglicans, who might have been expected to sympathize with Hooker and his more Thomist views. Butler and Price and (later on) Godwin were all educated in Dissenting academies.[42] Henry Grove and Philip Doddridge were prominent Dissenting ministers who also argued against voluntarism. On the other side, many writers who show most sympathy to voluntarism are Anglican clergy.

This difference between the 17th and the 18th century arises from theological disputes distinct from ethics. The Dissenters were not necessarily complete rationalists about Christianity; Grove and Doddridge clearly were not. But they were sympathetic to some rationalist elements insofar as they appealed to Scripture and reason against the traditional elements in Christianity that supported distinctively Anglican views. An appeal to Scripture and reason seemed to many Dissenters—notably Price—to undermine the dogmas set out in the historic creeds, and in particular the doctrine of the Trinity. Those who minimize the claims of natural reason are not the more extreme Protestants who believe that the Church of England retains too much of the Scholastic framework of mediaeval Christianity, but the defenders of tradition who resist the attempt to replace traditional dogmatic Christianity with a simplified and un-dogmatic appeal to natural reason and morality.

This reversal of attitudes to natural reason, and especially to natural reason applied to morality, helps to explain the curious alliance of orthodox Christianity with tendencies to voluntarism. Aquinas, Hooker, and Suarez would have been surprised, and with good reason. But those who supposed that the rejection of Aristotelian natural philosophy implied the rejection of the Scholastic position as a whole were unwilling to defend Aquinas' views in moral philosophy. They did not try to separate these views from any commitment to obsolete science or to dogmatic positions rejected by the Reformers.

529. Voluntarism and Egoism

The dispute between voluntarism and naturalism tends to be connected with a dispute between an egoistic account of motivation and a non-egoistic account that recognizes disinterested motivation. We might think it is merely accidental that voluntarists tend to be egoists and naturalists tend to reject egoism. The examples of Scotus and Ockham make it clear that voluntarism and egoism need not be combined. But in the 18th-century debates in Britain the connexion is not merely accidental.

---

[42] On Doddridge and Grove see §§877–8.

The controversy aroused in France by the Quietist movement affected British religious and ethical thought in a surprising way.[43] The Quietists advocated totally self-forgetful love of God; they went so far as to condemn any admixture of thoughts about one's own salvation in one's thoughts about God. Bossuet, with the support of the official Church, rejected this extreme attack on eudaemonism.[44] In Britain the Quietist attitude appeared to be an unwelcome manifestation of 'enthusiasm', displaying a tendency to fanaticism in religious thinking. This reaction was reasonable, but opponents of Quietist enthusiasm did not simply reject the total renunciation of self-interested motivation. They also concluded that the basic error of Quietism lay in its appeal to disinterested motivation altogether. Shaftesbury, Maxwell, and Butler all protest against the view that egoism is the only safe alternative to enthusiasm.

Sympathy towards egoism tends to encourage sympathy towards voluntarism, and tends to gain support from voluntarism. If we are naturalists about morality, we believe that we can grasp intrinsic morality—the reasons that are derived from the nature of human beings and their circumstances. But if we think there are no such reasons forming intrinsic morality, and we believe that moral rightness consists in being commanded by God, we need to explain why we have a reason to act on divine commands. If we say that they provide a reason because they meet some further standard for moral rightness, we seem to revert to naturalism; for conformity to this further standard seems to be what makes them right. We avoid this threat of a regress if we take Hobbes's way out and argue that God makes it in our interest to obey these commands.

An egoist explanation of moral reasons and motives makes voluntarism clear and comprehensible. Naturalism, by contrast, might appear both metaphysically and psychologically obscure and misleading. Naturalism in metaphysics appears to appeal to facts about the nature of things 'in themselves'; these facts seem to need some doubtful Aristotelian explanation. Naturalism about moral reasons and motives appeals to obscure reasons for choosing what is right 'in itself'. Naturalists who are eudaemonists seem to find it difficult to explain how concern for rightness in itself is related to one's own happiness. If they are not eudaemonists, they seem to find it difficult to explain how one can be concerned for what is right in itself. Puzzles of this sort in the naturalist position are solved by the combination of voluntarism with egoism. That is one reason why many English moralists find this combination plausible.

---

[43] See Knox, E, chs. 11–12; Ward, NG, ch. 3; Kirk, VG 451–63. On English discussions of enthusiasm see Beiser, SR, ch. 5. See also §588 (Leibniz); §611 (Shaftesbury); §717 (Butler).

[44] For the extreme rejection of eudaemonism see the Quietist views described in their official condemnation by the Pope in 1699 (Denz. 2351): 'A habitual state of love of God is given, which is pure charity and without any admixture of a motive of one's own interest. . . . No longer is God loved for the sake of (propter) merit, nor for the sake of perfection, nor for the sake of the happiness to be found in loving God.' 2355: 'We will nothing for ourselves, and everything for God. We will nothing in order to be perfect and blessed for the sake of our own interest . . .'. In 1687 similar views, attributed to Michael Molinos, were condemned (see 2207, 2209, 2212).

39

CUMBERLAND AND MAXWELL

530. Cumberland's Aims

Cumberland intends his exposition of the laws of nature to supplement the arguments of his predecessors (Grotius and his brother, Sharrock, and Selden) who have argued 'from the effect to the cause', appealing to the shared sentiments of different people at different times to establish the existence of natural law. Cumberland especially commends Grotius' work, 'which was the first of the kind, worthy both of the author and of immortality' (*LN*, Introd. §1 = P 247).[1] But in contrast to Grotius and the others, he argues from cause to effect, by examining 'the causes, which produce in the mind of man the knowledge of the laws of nature' (Introd. §2 = P 248). He begins from the nature of the universe and the first cause, in order to show that our knowledge of the universe makes it reasonable for us to accept certain principles as laws of nature. We will find that the laws of nature are those principles that promote the greatest common good of rational beings, and that they are supported by divine sanctions.

Cumberland intends his account of the laws of nature to refute Hobbes. His book contains lengthy, often acute, discussion of Hobbes's views, both in *De Cive* and in the English and Latin versions of *Leviathan*.[2] He especially attacks Hobbes's account of human nature, of the state of nature as a state of war, and of natural right. At these points Hobbes reveals his basic errors about the content and aim of the laws of nature, and about our reason for following them. Cumberland argues against Hobbes that the laws of nature are not basically counsels of self-preservation, to be justified by their role in preserving the peace of the commonwealth and keeping us out of the state of nature. According to Cumberland, the laws of nature aim at the common good of rational agents, and this aim by itself makes it reasonable for rational agents to observe them.

---

[1] I quote from either Raphael or Maxwell, and give references to the sections of the Latin text and to pages of Parkin's reprint of Maxwell (cited as P). Maxwell's version is vigorous, and his notes are often acute. But he is sometimes misleading about the Latin, both by addition and by subtraction. (This may be partly because he has tried to free Cumberland 'from as many of his scholastic terms as I could, without hurting the sense, explaining such of the rest as seemed most to require it' (Pref. = P 5–6).) The list of subscribers to Maxwell's translation includes: Revd Dr Geo. Berkeley, Dean of Derry; Revd Mr Butler; Revd Dr Samuel Clark, Rector of St James's; Revd Mr John Hutchinson. Tyrrell's *BDLN* is a paraphrase of *LN*.

[2] At 1.26 = P 336 (see Parkin's note) and 3.2 = P 467, he comments on a difference between the English and Latin *Leviathan*, taking the Latin to be later. Cf. §469.

To give an account of the laws of nature, Cumberland enters the controversy about natural law and intrinsic morality. He does not discuss Grotius or Suarez or their predecessors, and he does not seem to acknowledge most of them. He describes Grotius as the first of his predecessors, as though Grotius himself were not a participant in a debate carried on by Vasquez, Suarez, and their predecessors. His explicit remarks might suggest that he ignores the Scholastics and thinks nothing can be learned from them. However, though he does not acknowledge them, he discusses some of the issues that they discuss, and he probably has their views in mind.

Cumberland's relation to the Scholastic discussion is quite complex. On the one hand, he rejects intrinsic morality; like Culverwell, he argues that morality and obligation come together and both require law. On the other hand, he does not agree with Hobbes and Pufendorf in supposing that the non-moral natural goods are simply those that promote one's own advantage.[3]

Cumberland's translator and editor John Maxwell carries the discussion further (as Barbeyrac does in translating and editing Grotius and Pufendorf). He is closer than Cumberland is to a Scholastic naturalist position. He sometimes cites Scholastics, and even when he does not cite them he defends them against Cumberland.[4] It is often instructive to consider Maxwell's criticisms of Cumberland, since they present views that Cumberland does not explicitly discuss.

531. Natural Law as Divine Legislation

Cumberland agrees that natural law involves goods and evils that rationally concern human beings, apart from any divine law. But he also insists that it essentially involves divine law and divine commands. Though he praises Grotius' treatment of natural law (Introd. §1), he takes a voluntarist position, which Pufendorf cites in his support.[5]

He accepts Suarez's strict understanding of 'law' (without mentioning Suarez), and criticizes those who speak of the laws of nature loosely, without deriving them from the will of a legislator. He agrees with Selden's view that if laws of nature were simply rational precepts, they would lack the authority that belongs to law.[6] Laws are 'practical propositions, with rewards and punishments annexed, promulged by competent authority' (Introd. §6 = P 253). To show that there are laws of nature, therefore, is not simply to show that there are rational moral principles, but to show also that they are the work of a legislator who imposes sanctions.[7]

---

[3] Some of the intellectual background to Cumberland's ethics is explored by Parkin, *SRPRE*.

[4] For instance, it is not clear whether Cumberland knows Suarez, but Maxwell cites him in 'Obligation' §1 = P 796n4. Maxwell does not often cite Scholastic sources. Most of his remarks on natural law refer to Selden, but he quite often mentions Grotius.

[5] See §564.

[6] '[Selden] hath well enough corrected our common moralists, who are wont to consider these dictates of reason as laws, without any sufficient proof that they have all the conditions required to make them so, viz., that they are established and declared to us by God as a legislator, who hath annexed to them sufficient rewards and punishments.' (Tyrrell, *BDLN*, Pref. Cf. *LN*, Introd. §3 = P 250.)

[7] 'A law of nature is a proposition quite clearly presented to, or impressed upon, the mind by the nature of things from the will of the First Cause, pointing out an action, of service to the common good of rational beings, the performance of

Cumberland distinguishes two elements of a law of nature. The 'precept' gives the content of a natural law, indicating the particular way in which it aims at the common good of rational beings. The sanction consists of the reward God assigns to observance of the law, or the punishment God assigns to the violation.

The 'sanction' that Cumberland has in mind is not confined to rewards and punishments that God artificially attaches to good and bad conduct, by (for instance) rewarding good conduct with temporal prosperity in this life (as the Psalmists suppose) or with happiness in the afterlife. The relevant sanction also includes the natural and essential contribution of virtue to our own well-being.[8] The fact that, as the ancient moralists claim, virtue promotes happiness appears to Cumberland to support his claim that God attaches a sanction to good and bad conduct. He does not believe that we must regard natural law as divine law if we are to recognize that sanctions are attached to it. In recognizing it as divine law we recognize that the connexion between virtue and happiness is the result of God's intention to impose this law on us. If we left God aside, we could not justifiably treat the natural law as genuine law, but we would still have good reason to obey it because of its natural sanction.

To this extent Cumberland agrees with Hobbes, but he disagrees with Hobbes about what the natural sanction is. Since Hobbes believes we have a good reason to obey the natural law even if we leave God aside, and he believes that the only good reasons are those that appeal to self-interested motives, he argues that it is in my interest to observe the laws of nature. Hence he treats the laws of nature as indirect counsels of self-preservation, because they preserve the commonwealth.

Contrary to Hobbes, Cumberland takes the laws of nature to be prescriptions about the common good of rational beings. They achieve the good of an individual rational being insofar as her good is a part of the common good. Hence observance of the universal law of nature promotes the good of each individual who is part of the whole.[9] This does not imply that in any given society the good of the whole coincides with the good of each part; for in a defective community, no less than in a diseased or injured body, the good of the whole may involve some harm to a particular part.[10] Civil

---

which is followed, owing to the nature of rational beings, by adequate rewards, while its neglect is followed by adequate punishments. The former part of this definition covers the precept, the latter the sanction; and both are impressed on the mind by the nature of things.' (5.1 = P 495–6 = R 112) Maxwell translates (P 495–6): 'The law of nature is a proposition proposed to the observation of, or impressed upon, the mind, with sufficient clearness by the nature of things, from the will of the first cause, which points out that possible action of a rational agent, which will chiefly promote the common good, and by which only the entire happiness of particular persons can be obtained. ["and . . ." has no basis in the Latin.] The former part of this definition contains the precept, the latter, the sanction; and the mind receives the impression of both, from the nature of things.' The reference to a sanction is introduced in a second printing (see Kirk, *RCNL* 31); but this is not an isolated revision. Cumberland also takes sanctions to be necessary at Introd. §§4, 6, 13.

[8] On Cumberland's lack of emphasis on post-mortem punishments and rewards, see Albee, *HEU* 38–40. Tyrrell (*BDLN*, Ep. Ded.) notices this feature of Cumberland, and adds some material from Parker on these sanctions.

[9] 'The endeavour, to the utmost of our power, of promoting the common good of the whole system of rational agents, conduces, as far as in us lies, to the good of every part, in which our own happiness, as that of a part, is contained.' (Introd. §9 = P 256)

[10] '. . . many things may happen, by means whereof this general care of the whole may not always produce the proposed happiness of individuals, without allay; as breathing and eating, however necessary to the whole body, do not ward off all diseases and accidents' (Introd. §22 = P 272).

government, therefore, seeks to prevent the conflict between individual and common good that arises from the misconduct of other people. The laws of nature secure the common good of rational creatures, and thereby secure the good of each rational creature.[11]

532. Cumberland's Voluntarism: Natural Law and Morality

This description of natural law agrees with Suarez's claim that natural law is genuine law, and hence requires a legislator. Cumberland also follows Suarez in taking obligation to require legislation. He rejects Hobbes's view that 'obligation' is properly applied to the mental state of the person obliged. He applies it to the imposer of the obligation, and therefore takes the divine will and command to oblige.[12] If he is right to claim that the natural law essentially carries obligation, and that obligation involves command, he is right to infer that the natural law requires divine legislation.

Suarez's voluntarism is limited to natural law, and does not extend to morality; he recognizes intrinsic morality independent of legislation and therefore (in Suarez's view) independent of obligation. Culverwell and Locke disagree with him, since they argue that morality requires obligation, and hence divine commands. Culverwell follows Suarez in recognizing natural 'conveniences' and 'disconveniences', and even natural rightness (honestas) apart from divine commands, but he takes these to be insufficient for morality. Locke departs further from Suarez; he allows natural 'convenience', but resolves it into pleasure and advantage without any natural rightness.

Cumberland's view is similar to Locke's, but with some qualifications that bring it closer to a naturalist position. He finds talk of 'agreement' obscure until it is explained by reference to the preservation and perfection of the subject with which an action 'agrees'.[13] But once

[11] Cumberland anticipates and rejects the charge that his account of the laws of nature 'has the effect of ranking the common good, and so the honour of God and the happiness of all other men, below the private happiness of each, and of making the common good serve private good as the supreme end' (5.45 = P 605 = R 117).

[12] 'Therefore the whole force of obligation is this, that the legislator has annexed to the observance of his laws, goods; to the transgression, evils; and those natural goods and evils, by the prospect of which men are moved to perform actions, rather agreeing than disagreeing with the laws.' (5.11 = P 519–20) 'I, therefore, think, that moral obligation may be thus universally and properly defined: Obligation is that act of a legislator, by which he declares, that actions conformable to his law are necessary to those, for whom the law is made. An action is then understood to be necessary to a rational agent, when it is certainly one of the causes necessarily required to that happiness, which he naturally, and consequently necessarily, desires.' (5.27 = P 554) 'I, therefore, resolve moral obligation (which is the immediate effect of nature's laws) into the first and principal cause of these same laws, which is the will and counsel of God who promotes the common good, and, therefore, by annexing rewards and punishments, enacts into laws the practical propositions which tend thereto. Men's care of their own happiness, which causes them to consider, and be moved by, rewards and punishments, is no cause of obligation, since that proceeds, wholly, from the law and the lawgiver; it is only a necessary disposition in the subject, without which the rewards and penalties of the law would be of no force to induce men to the performance of their duty.' (5.22 = P 543–4) On Suarez and Cumberland see Schneewind, *IA* 110n (he does not mention the crucial difference between Cumberland and Suarez about natural law and morality).

[13] 'Good is that which preserves, or enlarges and perfects, the faculties of any one thing or of several. For in their effects is discovered that particular agreement of one thing with another which is requisite to demonstrate anything good to the nature of this thing, rather than of others. In the definition of good I choose to avoid the word [agreement] [convenientia] because of its very uncertain significance. Nevertheless, those things whose actions or motions conduce to the preservation or increase of the powers of other things, consistently with the nature of the individual, may justly be said to agree with them.' (3.1 = P 462)

this explanation is provided, he agrees with those who say that natural law prescribes actions that fit human nature.[14]

In recognizing this natural good antecedent to legislation, Cumberland agrees with Suarez. But he rejects Suarez's further claim that this natural good is sufficient for morality. In his view, the moral good requires legislation.[15] This division between the natural and the moral agrees with Culverwell's interpretation of Suarez. But Cumberland disagrees with Culverwell about which goods are natural. In Culverwell's view, natural goods include natural 'honesty' that can be admired and valued from a point of view outside narrow advantage, but is insufficient for moral goodness. Cumberland restricts the range of natural goods further; he agrees with Suarez in taking honestas to be sufficient for morality, but he denies any natural honestas independent of the will of a legislator. He concedes to Culverwell that the perfection of natural goods gives us an intrinsic reason (antecedent to any divine legislation) to pursue them, but he denies that this is honestas or morality.[16]

This division between the natural and the moral good affects Cumberland's explanation of his account of the natural law. When the natural law is defined as aiming at the common good, 'good' refers to purely natural good, not to the moral good. To understand it as referring to the moral good would be to introduce a vicious circle, since moral good has to be defined by reference to natural law.[17] Only non-moral goods constitute the common good of rational agents. Morally right actions, therefore, should be understood teleologically and instrumentally, as means to non-moral goods.[18]

---

[14] 'There is also another manner of expressing the laws of nature, as thus, this or that possible action is most agreeable [convenit] to human nature. But the sense is doubtful; for (1) Human nature either signifies the particular nature of the agent, and then it is not expressive enough of what ought to be considered before action; . . . Or (2) human nature respects all men . . . But if, in either of these notions the public good is by consequence implied, this form of speaking is consistent with the first, which is therefore to be preferred, because it is free from this ambiguity. Again, it is doubtful to what the expression [is agreeable] relates: For (1) An action may be said to be agreeable to any nature, when it is agreeable to the principles of acting . . . (2) An action may be said to be agreeable to human nature, when its effects preserve or improve the nature of one or more men. This latter sense coincides with the form I first proposed, which is free from ambiguity. And the first sense of the agreeableness of actions may, for the most part, be reduced thereto.' (4.2 = P 484)

[15] 'Good of this kind, of which we form an idea without the consideration of any laws whatsoever, I call natural good . . . It is distinguished, by its greater extensiveness, from that good which is called moral, which is ascribed only to such actions and habits of rational agents as are agreeable to laws, whether natural or civil, and is ultimately resolved into the natural common good, to the perfection and increase of which alone all the laws of nature and all just civil laws do direct us.' (3.1 = P 463)

[16] See 5.42 = P 598, quoted in §535. Clarke quotes this in *DNR* = ii 628n H; see §617.

[17] 'The good placed in the definition, I understand that which by the philosophers is usually called natural good, and which I have already defined, with respect to created beings, as that which preserves, or renders them more perfect or happy. . . . The reader is to observe, that I have called these things naturally good, in that sense, in which these words, as being of a more extensive signification, (and, consequently, more general and first known in the order of nature) are distinguished from things morally good; for these are only voluntary actions conformable to some law, especially, that of nature. Therefore good is not to be taken in this sense, which it is inserted in the definition of the law of nature, because it is absurd, to define any thing, by what supposes the thing defined, already known. There are many things naturally good, that is, such as contribute somewhat to the happiness of man, which are not morally good, as being either not voluntary actions, or not commanded by any law. . . . When, afterwards we act in pursuance of these conclusions, and upon comparison, find our actions conformable to them; beside the previously known appellation of natural goodness, there accrues to these actions this, that they are morally good, from their conformity with the laws of nature already enacted.' (5.9 = P 516–17)

[18] 'Such actions as take the shortest way to this effect [sc. the common good] as to their end, are naturally right [rectae], because of their natural resemblance to a right line which is the shortest that can be drawn between any two given points. Nevertheless, the same actions afterward, when they are compared with the law, whether natural or positive, which is the rule of morality, and they are found conformable to it; are called morally good, as also right, that is, agreeing with the rule; but the rule itself is called right as pointing out the shortest way to the end . . . actions conducive

Cumberland does not consider Suarez's view that natural goods are sufficient for intrinsic morality that is antecedent to law. According to Suarez, natural law is just because it corresponds to intrinsic morality, but Cumberland implicitly rejects that view. Perhaps he agrees with Culverwell's view that the distinctive features of moral obligation require law, or perhaps he agrees with Suarez's view that obligation in general requires law. But he does not confront Suarez's reasons for distinguishing the duties (debita) of intrinsic morality from obligations, which depend on law.

Does this matter? Is the disagreement between Cumberland and Suarez about intrinsic morality purely verbal, or can we find some reason for agreeing with one or the other view? To answer this question we need to explore Cumberland's view on the non-moral good.

533. Individual Happiness and the Common Good

Cumberland's case for a legislative view of morality becomes clearer from his discussion of the ancient moralists and their non-legislative conception of the virtues.

He recognizes that the ancient moralists are eudaemonists, who take the ultimate end to be the agent's happiness. But he does not confuse their eudaemonism with hedonism, and he rejects hedonism. He takes activity and pleasure to be inseparably connected, and both to be necessary for happiness. Happiness is 'a certain aggregate, whose parts we are continually enjoying' (5.13 = P 523).[19]

He agrees with the ancient moralists who take virtue to be necessary for happiness.[20] Among these he agrees with those who take virtue to be a component of happiness, not merely a means to it. But he rejects the Stoic view that virtue is the only good; he endorses Cicero's argument[21] that the Stoic view takes away the point of virtuous action by denying that the effects it aims at are good.[22]

Though Cumberland agrees with these aspects of Greek eudaemonism, he is not a eudaemonist, since he does not agree that one's own happiness is or ought to be one's supreme end.[23] His reason for rejecting eudaemonism is not that he believes in a conflict

to this end, as being the best and most beautiful, are in themselves amiable, and highly to be commended by all rational beings, and therefore, upon account of that high honour to which their beneficent nature entitles them deservedly called honest or honourable in themselves [merito dici per se honestas; M omits "in themselves"].' (Introd. §16 = P 264)

[19] On happiness see Albee, HEU 31–2 (who emphasizes the hedonist side of Cumberland's position); Sharp, 'Cumberland' 377–9 (who argues that Cumberland is a hedonist, and claims rather questionably that Shaftesbury is one too).

[20] 'I might here easily show the wonderful agreement between the Peripatetics, the old and new Academy, and even the Epicureans themselves, though some taught virtue to be the only good; others only the chief good; some that it was itself the very end; others that it was the most proper and absolutely necessary means to the obtaining it.' (5.41 = P 593)

[21] See Cic. F. iv 31–3; §187.

[22] 'Upon this head the Stoics are to be reprehended who affirmed nothing to be good but virtue; nothing evil but vice. For whilst they endeavour to establish the transcendent goodness of virtue and the egregious evil of vice, they incautiously entirely take away the only reason why virtue is good and vice evil. For virtue is therefore good (and in truth it is the greatest good) because it determines human actions to such effects as are principal parts of the public natural good...' (5.5 = P 508)

[23] 'Although I have supposed that everyone necessarily seeks his own greatest happiness, yet I am far from thinking that to be the entire and adequate end of anyone.' (5.28 = P 556) 'Therefore, when moral writers speak of every man's happiness as his ultimate end, I would willingly interpret them in this sense, that it is the chief end among those which respect the agent himself only; and I doubt not, but that every good man has an end, that is, intends an effect, that is greater, namely

between one's own good and the common good; on the contrary, he believes that one promotes one's own good by advancing the common good of which it is a part.[24] But he does not believe that the justifying reason for pursuit of the common good depends entirely on its connexion with one's own good. In his view, it is independently reasonable to pursue the common good, and it would be unreasonable to follow some rule that does not aim at everyone's happiness. Even apart from any reference to the will of God, it is unreasonable to claim to be rationally justified in dominating others while admitting that they have an equally good reason for dominating oneself.[25]

Natural law, therefore, not only prescribes actions that promote one's own happiness, as we can see from the arguments of the Greek moralists; it also prescribes actions that are independently reasonable, because they present a common end that rational agents must observe. Since they can all reasonably agree on this end, it is the end that rational beings, as such, must pursue.[26] The 'sanction' of the natural law does not consist simply in its promotion of my private interest. A further 'reward' is the fact that the moral law promotes the common good.

Cumberland's claim about reason is similar to Spinoza's claim that reason expresses a common point of view on which rational beings agree if they use their reason correctly. This claim is plausible. But Cumberland, like Spinoza, is not clear about the difference between different kinds of agreement. We might agree that the same thing is good for me and for you, but it does not follow that we will agree in preferring that both of us pursue it; for if you cannot have as much as you want without leaving me less than I want, I might prefer you not to pursue it, even if I recognize that you have as good reason to pursue it as I have.

Does this objection affect Cumberland's conception of the common end? He might claim that if the common end is the common good, including each person's individual good, we can and should all agree to pursue it, because it is non-competitive. But we might still doubt whether this is so. Perhaps we can agree on pursuit of a common good, because we all hope to get our own good out of it; but it does not immediately follow that I have as good a reason to pursue the common good for its own sake as I have to pursue my own good.

Cumberland's appeal to a common good that is an independently and non-derivatively reasonable object of pursuit for rational agents is a suggestive innovation in a Scholastic

---

the honour of God and the increase of other men's happiness. I conceive the one chief end or best effect to be composed of our own happiness and that of all other rational beings (which we endeavour as opportunity offers).' (5.47 = P 612)

[24] 'The greatest benevolence of each rational agent towards all forms [constituit] the happiest state of each and of all benevolent persons, so far as it can be produced by them themselves.' (1.4 = P 292 = R 107) 'I use the word "forms" to indicate that the aforesaid benevolence is both the intrinsic cause of present happiness and the efficient cause of future happiness, and is necessarily required in respect of both.' (1.4 = P 293 = R 107) '. . . it is . . . perfectly plain that the happiness of each person, e.g. of Socrates, Plato, and all the other individuals . . . cannot be severally separated from the happiness of all . . . because the whole is no different from the parts taken together.' (1.6 = P 295 = R 108)

[25] 'For example, suppose right reason tells Titius that the happiness possible for him, and the end he should pursue, consist in the enjoyment of complete dominion over the land occupied by Seius and Sempronius, and over their persons, and over the land of all others; then true reason cannot dictate to Seius and Sempronius that their happiness, which they are to seek, lies in the enjoyment of complete dominion over the land and person of Titius and likewise of all others. For the precepts involve an obvious contradiction, so that only one of the two can be supposed true.' (5.16 = P 529 = R 115)

[26] 'For there is only one end in the pursuit of which all can agree; and it is most certain that no decision can be in accordance with right reason unless all can agree on it. Therefore there arises from our common rational nature a necessity that each, by exercising universal benevolence, should always seek the common good, and should seek his own as only a part of that and consequently subordinated to it; and this is the sum of natural law.' (5.46 = P 610 = R 118)

account of practical reason. We might argue that Scholastic views on correct reason are not all essentially eudaemonistic, and that they allow actions to be reasonable in themselves apart from one's own interest. But Scotus is the only one who explicitly distinguishes eudaemonist reasons from impartial practical reason, which he connects with the affection for the just.[27] In Butler, Scotus' division is clearly marked with the division between self-love and conscience. In Cumberland the division is not as explicit as it is in Butler, but he makes it clear that he believes in two irreducibly different aims of practical reason.[28]

534. Non-instrumental Goods v. Moral Goods

Cumberland's view of practical reason assumes that some natural goods are both non-instrumental and non-hedonic. These include the virtues of character recognized by the Greek moralists.[29] He therefore rejects the view of Hobbes and Locke, that the only natural goods are the pleasant (iucundum) and the advantageous (utile). But he disagrees with Suarez's view that the morally right (honestum) is one of the natural goods. In Cumberland's view, the natural goods that are good in their own nature also promote the common good, and may be pursued for the sake of the common good, apart from any law. But these goods cannot be the source of an obligation or a duty (debitum), and so cannot be honesta, without reference to a law. Hence he rejects Suarez's belief in natural duties prior to obligation and law.

For this reason, he believes that the views of the ancient philosophers about virtue fall short of grasping its genuinely moral character.[30] The fact that virtue is choiceworthy in

---

[27] On Scotus see §363.

[28] On Butler see §708. Sidgwick's judgment on Cumberland is rather severe, and underestimates his consistency: 'His account of the sanction, again, is sufficiently comprehensive, including both the internal and the external rewards of virtue and punishments of vice; and he, like later utilitarians, explains moral obligation to lie primarily in the force exercised on the will by these sanctions. He considers, however, that while this egoistic motive is indispensable, and is the normal spring of action in the earlier stages of man's moral obedience, yet rational beings tend to rise from this to the nobler motives of love to God, regard for His honour, and disinterested affection for the common good. At the same time it is difficult to put together in a clear and consistent view his different statements as to the connexion between the good of the individual and universal good, and as to the manner in which the rational apprehension of either or both goods operates in determining volition.' (OHE 174)

[29] 'They are indeed in their own nature good, though there were no law, because they conduce to the good state of the universe: But moral obligation, and the nature of a debt [debiti] thence arising, is unintelligible, without a respect to a law, at least, of nature. Nay further; the very honour, from which actions are, by their own nature, distinguished by the title of honestas, laudable practice, or are called honourable, [a quo actus sua natura boni honestatis titulo insigniantur, seu honesti dicuntur; Maxwell omits "by their own nature"] seems wholly to come from this, that they are praised by the law of the supreme ruler, discovered by the light of nature, and honoured with the greatest rewards, among which is to be reckoned the concurring praise of good men. And justly are they called naturally lawful and honourable [liciti et honesti], because the law, which makes them such, does not depend upon the pleasure of the civil power, but arises necessarily, in the manner already explained, from the very nature of things, and is altogether unchangeable, whilst nature remains unchanged.' (8.1 = P 684–5)

[30] 'Much has been advanced by philosophers, especially the Stoics and Academics, which with strength and perspicuity demonstrates that the virtues necessarily bring happiness along with them, as essentially connected therewith: Which I did not think fit to transcribe, as being what the learned are already acquainted with. It is sufficient, that I readily acknowledge them to be the principal parts of human happiness, so that neither without them can any man (though abounding with all other advantages) be happy: Nor, if he possess them, can he be miserable, however unfortunate. They are therefore worthy of pursuit because of the perfection intrinsic to them, even if there were no law of nature that commanded them. (Dignae itaque sunt, quae propter intrinsceam sibi perfectionem appetantur, etiamsi nulla esset

itself as the most important part of happiness does not imply that it has moral goodness, which depends on divine law. The ancients should have seen that since the virtues are choiceworthy for themselves, they must have had this reward annexed to them by the first cause, who must therefore have commanded observance of them. They have moral goodness only because of this relation to a divine command.

535. Utilitarianism?

Cumberland's references to the common good, greatest happiness, and benevolence have given him a place in the history of utilitarianism, or at least among the forerunners of utilitarianism.[31] It is reasonable to connect his views with utilitarianism on some points. He takes principles of practical reason to be impartial, because reason is essentially impartial between rational beings. He offers a teleological theory of virtues, principles, duties, and rights with reference to the end of achieving the common good. On the basis of this theory, he rejects Hobbes's claims about the right of nature. He argues that the exercise of a Hobbesian right to do what I please in the state of nature would violate the demands of practical reason, and therefore go beyond my rights.[32]

We may also take Cumberland to be a utilitarian because of his emphasis on benevolence, which he attributes both to God and to virtuous human beings. He claims, as utilitarians do, that the benevolent agent is concerned with the greatest good of the beneficiaries.[33] Here we may see evidence of the maximizing outlook that defines the utilitarian view. It is not surprising that Hutcheson cites Cumberland in support of a maximizing view.

But it is difficult to show that Cumberland takes a utilitarian view of maximization and distribution. Hutcheson is a genuine utilitarian on these points because he argues that it is permissible to harm some people in order to increase the happiness of others, and thereby

naturae lex quae illas imperaret.) . . . What I would infer from these reasonings or concessions of philosophers is that we have a proof from nature that virtuous actions have a reward annexed to them by the will of the first cause; and therefore that it is the will of the same cause that men whom he has instructed how to foresee the rewards consequent upon such actions should act so as to obtain that foreshown happiness. In this discovery of the divine will consists the promulgation of the law of nature, and thence directly flows natural and moral obligation. And this is what even those philosophers who taught virtue to be the chief happiness seem not sufficiently to have regarded.' (5.42 = P 598–9)

[31] '. . . the fountain of all nature's law . . . is this: The greatest benevolence of every rational agent towards all forms the happiest state of every and of all the benevolent, as far as is in their power; and is necessarily requisite to the happiest state which they can attain, and therefore the common good is the supreme law' (1.4 = P 292). '. . . it is also most evident that the happiness of single persons, for example of Socrates and Plato and other individuals . . . cannot singly be separated from the happiness of all . . . because the whole does not differ from all the parts taken together' (1.6 = P 295).

[32] See, e.g., 1.30 = P 347: '. . . there can be no right of acting contrary to the law of nature, or the dictates of right reason, because right is defined to be a liberty of acting according thereto. But right reason . . . points out the necessity of coming to a division of things; and, according to Hobbes's own confession, forbids the retaining a right to all things.' Cf. Tyrrell, *BDLN* 40: '. . . there is no right conferred upon any man, of doing whatever his own wild fancy, or unbounded appetite may prompt him to, but only what he shall, according to right reason, truly judge necessary to his own or family's happiness and preservation, in order to the common good of mankind. . . . so that it can never be proved, that any one hath a right of preserving himself, unless it be first made out, how this right of self-preservation conduces to, or at least consists with this common good.'

[33] Maxwell's comment on 1.8 = P 297–8 pertinently questions Cumberland's claim that the virtue aiming at the common good is properly called benevolence.

to increase the total happiness. But it is not clear that Cumberland commits himself to these utilitarian claims.[34]

He takes the end to be not the greatest quantity of good, but the common good of all rational beings. We might take the common good to be the quantity of good that is composed of the quantities present in the lives of different agents; in that case, what promotes the common good may not promote the good of all, or even of most, individual agents. But this is not the only way to understand a common good. We might also understand it to refer to a good that is good for everyone in common, and not good for one person to the exclusion of others. This is how Aquinas understands the common good.[35]

We have good reason to understand Cumberland's claims about the common good in this second way. He claims that it is the whole of which individual goods are parts; that is why individual goods do not conflict in principle with the common good (though they may conflict because of some defect in a particular society). The common good is the end on which rational beings can agree and ought to agree. Since it is assumed that individual rational beings care about their individual goods, they have a reason to agree on the pursuit of a common good that embraces all the individual goods that they take to be reasonable objects of pursuit for different individuals. They have no similar reason, as far as we can gather from Cumberland, to sacrifice some people's individual goods simply to increase a total good that is indifferent to distribution.

Neither Hutcheson nor Sidgwick, each of whom takes Cumberland to be a precursor of quantitative utilitarianism, mentions this difference between Cumberland's common good and a utilitarian total good. Cumberland's conception stays quite close to the Scholastic conception of a common good. It even captures one of the most plausible elements in Hobbes's account of morality. When Hobbes suggests that morality preserves the commonwealth, he thereby suggests that it promotes a common good; for the preservation of the commonwealth is a common good for everyone. It is not good for one person in opposition to another; individuals do not need to compete for it, and if one of us has it, there is no less to go round for all the others. Cumberland takes this idea of a good for everyone, and extends it beyond a single society to all rational beings.

---

[34] Albee claims that Cumberland is 'the first English moralist who can properly be termed a utilitarian' (*HEU* 14), and attributes to him 'the first statement by an English writer of the utilitarian principle' (52). He does not say exactly where Cumberland commits himself to utilitarianism, and does not discuss the differences between Cumberland's conception of the common good and the maximizing outlook of utilitarianism. Sidgwick is cautious about treating Cumberland as a utilitarian: 'At any rate he is noteworthy as having been the first to lay down that "the common good of all" is the supreme end and standard, in subordination to which all other rules and virtues are to be determined. So far he may be fairly called the precursor of the later utilitarianism. His fundamental principle and supreme "Law of Nature", in which all other laws of nature are implicitly included, is thus stated: "The greatest possible benevolence of every rational agent towards all the rest constitutes the happiest state of each and all, so far as depends on their own power, and is necessarily required for their happiness; accordingly common good will be the supreme law." It is, however, important to notice that in his "good" is included not merely happiness, in the ordinary sense, but "perfection"; and he does not even define perfection so as strictly to exclude from it the notion of moral perfection or virtue, and thus save his explanation of morality from an obvious logical circle. A notion so incompletely determined could hardly be used for deducing particular moral rules with any precision; but in fact Cumberland does not attempt this; his supreme principle is not designed to rectify, but merely to support and systematize, common morality.' (*OHE* 174) Part of Sidgwick's objection about perfection is curious (and justly criticized by Albee, *HEU* 33), since Cumberland carefully excludes moral good from the good that is mentioned in the definition of natural law and the moral rules belonging to it. In the last sentence quoted Sidgwick correctly notes Cumberland's failure to draw utilitarian conclusions about distribution from his supreme principle.

[35] On Aquinas see §338. Cf. Suarez, §451.

If this is the right way to understand Cumberland, his view is not only non-utilitarian, but even anti-utilitarian. For if a course of action would maximize the total good, but would harm some people simply to achieve this end, it would not achieve a common good, and Cumberland has no reason to endorse it. Hence questions that might be raised about the quantitative and distributive aspects of a utilitarian view do not arise for his view.

536. Maxwell's Criticism of Cumberland's Account of Morality

Still, Cumberland's view of morality and the common good is open to doubt. Maxwell's comments raise some of the most pertinent questions.[36] Maxwell rejects non-normative accounts of goodness that do not make it clear that goodness deserves to be chosen and is a worthy object of pleasure.[37] For similar reasons he finds an account of goodness as 'convenience' unsatisfactory. He takes 'convenience' to refer only to the non-moral good, as Cumberland understands it, and he finds this inadequate to capture moral goodness.[38] If we combine an account of goodness as convenience with a eudaemonist conception of morality, we do not capture the essential features of moral obligation.[39]

It would be unfair to Cumberland to suggest that a non-normative account of goodness as convenience is his account of moral goodness. But Maxwell does not believe that the extra element that Cumberland adds is enough for moral goodness. According to Cumberland, the promotion of non-moral goodness is the whole of morality, if it is prescribed by divine law. But this account still, in Maxwell's view, reduces morality to an instrumental status.[40] Cumberland claims that moral principles are commanded by God simply as means to the public good; but this account of moral obligation makes it a purely prudential, not a moral, bond.[41]

Cumberland's view, according to Maxwell, overlooks the regulative role of morality in relation to the public good. It is morally permissible to pursue the public good only insofar as it does not violate morality.[42] If promotion of the public good requires injustice, for

---

[36] References are given to the sections and pages of Maxwell's 'obligation', printed at the back of the translation of Cumberland and printed in P as Appendix 2 (cited as 'App.').

[37] '[Good] ought not to be thus defined: "good is that which is pleasant to a perceptive life, jointly with the preservation of the perceiver". For the nature and notion of good does not consist in being pleasant, but in being worthy to be pleased with.' (App. §3 = P 799–800) The quotation is from More, EE, Bk. 1, ch. 4

[38] He argues that if something's nature is itself good, goodness cannot be confined to what is convenient for a thing's nature (App. §3(1) = P 800–1).

[39] 'But in the kingdom of God, a kingdom of virtue and of holiness, they . . . are linked together by an adamantine law of right and one agency, and by this legal necessity they are obliged not to be wicked, but to be holy and virtuous. They practise righteousness and true holiness for other ultimate reasons than personal self-respects, and they shun sin for other ultimate reasons than merely because it is a public nuisance and inconvenience.' (App. §3(3) = P 803)

[40] 'Wickedness is to be shunned not only as a public inconvenience, but for its own intrinsic turpitude, as all the virtuous philosophers, in consort with Christians agree.' (App. §3(4) = P 803)

[41] 'This scheme, of the law of nature, and its definition of good, introduceth an institution of morality, not truly moral, but merely politic and prudential. . . . A mere prudential institution of morality careth neither for virtue nor vice, or living well or living ill, as such and for their own sake, nor any further than as they promote or hinder the public convenience. . . . So this institution affirmeth, that the laws of nature, and all the virtues, are nothing else but means of obtaining the common good. It supposeth, that virtue is not good, but only as a means to the common happiness; and that vice and wickedness is not evil, but as productive of public misery, as will further appear presently.' (App. §3(5) = P 804–5)

[42] 'But the common happiness of rational beings must be sought also from a principle of duty and virtue, and consequently it must be sought only in consistency with virtue, nor otherwise than as virtue requireth. A man may not

instance, it is open to moral objection; hence moral requirements are not exhausted by the requirement to pursue the public good.

This objection touches only some views that connect morality with the common good. It applies to Cumberland's view because he restricts the good promoted by morality to natural good, which does not include moral good. But if an account of natural law holds that the common good promoted by morality includes the moral good, Maxwell's objection does not touch it. This is Suarez's account, since he takes moral goodness to exist independently of any legislation. One might argue that Suarez's non-instrumental account of moral goodness is less clear and intelligible than Cumberland's purely instrumental account; but this does not make Cumberland's instrumental account preferable.

Maxwell acknowledges this point. In opposition to the instrumental view of morality that he attributes to Cumberland, he separates the honestum from other forms of goodness. Here he returns to consider convenience, and draws a distinction that he did not draw earlier. He attributes a non-instrumental notion of convenience, understood as appropriateness for a rational agent, from the Stoics.[43] In applying the Stoic doctrine to his own views about goodness, Maxwell implicitly acknowledges that an action may be 'convenient' to rational agents because it is suitable to their nature, without being purely instrumental 'because of the necessity of their affairs'.[44]

537. Morality and its Sanction

Maxwell believes that Cumberland demotes morality to instrumental prudence by subordinating it to the pursuit of the non-moral good; Cumberland does not see that morality deserves to be chosen for its own sake, and carries an obligation within itself. Hence, according to Maxwell, Cumberland overlooks the obligation that belongs to morality in its own right, apart from any sanction that God attaches to it.[45] According to Cumberland, the fact that virtue is a part of happiness is a sanction attached to virtue by a legislator. Maxwell takes this view to assume the character of virtue itself is distinct from the aspect of virtue that promotes happiness; otherwise that aspect of it could not be the result of 'attachment'. He objects that virtue must be right and obligatory independently of the sanction if the sanction is rightly 'attached' to it.

violate virtue nor touch with wickedness, no, not for the happiness of the universe.' (App. §3(6) = P 806) 'To endeavour the common good of rational beings is so far from comprehending all virtue that, unless our endeavours to promote this common good be duly qualified, it is not virtue, but vice and crime.' (App. §3(8) = P 809)

[43] 'The good life and practice must not be thought merely a public self-convenience which is necessary for men only because of the necessity of their affairs, but it is the doing what is simply and absolutely convenient. "Wisdom is a doing what is convenient—. As a stage player must not have any, but a certain action; and a dancer must not have any, but a certain motion: so a man must live not any, but a certain kind of life, which we call convenient and consentaneous."' (App. §6 = P 841) Maxwell quotes from Cic. F. iii 24.

[44] Perhaps Maxwell is influenced by Clarke's doctrine of fitness. See §618.

[45] 'But a man is bound, both when he cannot do a thing without sin and when he cannot do a thing without punishment, and both these obligations are in every law, and both concur to make the obligation of it. But because the obligation of non licet is antecedent to the obligation of non impune, the precept to the sanction, and the sin is made by the law, the law hath so much obligation as to make the sin, before the penalty is enacted; therefore the law has an obligation antecedently to the sanction of it. For everyone is bound to avoid what is sin.' (App. §3(13) = P 815–16)

This argument does not exactly capture Cumberland's view. According to Cumberland, the goodness of virtue is a sanction, even if it is essential to virtue; even if virtue promotes happiness simply by being good in itself, its promotion of happiness is a sanction. Hence the moral goodness of virtue need not be separate from the attached sanction.

But this reply to Maxwell reveals the basic difficulty in Cumberland's claims about sanctions. If the goodness of virtue is essential to it, because of its relation to the nature of rational agents, how can it have been 'attached' to virtue as a sanction? We cannot attach a key to a chain unless the key and the chain already exist; we do not attach trilaterality to a triangle. To recognize the inherent goodness of virtue is to recognize that this is essential to the nature of the agents whom God has created. One cannot legitimately treat such features as having been attached to the creation.

Might we reply on behalf of Cumberland that his remarks about 'attachment' are misleading, but the substance of his position is reasonable? Perhaps his claim that God 'attached' certain properties to virtue just means that he created human beings in such a way that these states of character would be both good for others and good for the virtuous agent. In that case the sanction might be treated as an essential part of virtue and human nature, not something externally attached as a chain is attached to a key.

But if we say this in support of Cumberland, we raise a more basic question about his appeals to divine legislation. As Suarez points out, claims about natural law and the will of God need to distinguish the creative from the legislative will of God. The fact that there are human beings, creatures for whom justice and benevolence are good, depends on God's will as creator; and if morality depends on human nature, the fact that these actions are morally required depends on God's having created rational animals rather than limiting the creation to plants and non-rational animals. But these facts do not show that morality depends on God's legislative will; for since facts about creation are facts about created nature, they are facts about how things are in their own right, apart from any further legislative act of God.

Some of Cumberland's arguments for his legislative thesis about morality seem to be open to this objection from Suarez. The fact that actions have natural consequences affecting our welfare does not show that God is a legislator, or that moral goodness depends on God's communicating divine law through a command. But Cumberland seems to confuse legislation with creation in his claims about sanctions. The fact that virtue has certain sanctions 'attached' to it, in the broad sense of 'attached' that covers essential properties, shows nothing about God's legislative will. It is simply a fact about the natures of created things.

Exploration of Maxwell's objections, therefore, reveals a serious difficulty in Cumberland's position. Maxwell claims that since morality is good and obligatory in itself, it possesses its goodness and its obligatory character independently of the sanction attached by divine legislation. He may have misunderstood Cumberland's broad use of 'sanction' and 'attach'. But if we allow Cumberland a broad enough use of these terms to answer Maxwell, we also cast doubt on Cumberland's claims about the extent of divine legislation in morality. For a broad use of 'sanction' includes non-legislative 'sanctions' that come from God as creator; the presence of these sanctions does not show that morality depends on divine legislation. The confusion between divine creation and divine legislation may be present in Grotius, but it does not undermine his main argument.[46] In Cumberland, and even more clearly in Pufendorf, the confusion creates spurious support for a legislative conception of morality.[47]

538. Divine Goodness and the Stability of Morality

Though Cumberland does not know Cudworth's *Eternal and Immutable Morality*, he considers the objection to voluntarism that Cudworth implies in his title.[48] According to Cudworth, a legislative account of morality makes morality mutable in the wrong way, since it implies that if God had legislated differently, it would have been right (e.g.) to murder, cheat, and torture, and that therefore morality is mutable in relation to divine legislation. Cumberland answers that the law of nature is mutable only in relation to human nature (as Cudworth agrees), not in relation to any possible change in God's legislation; hence it is eternal and immutable in the way that Cudworth claims it is. It depends on the divine will only insofar as the maintenance of creation depends on the divine will; but—though Cumberland omits this point—that sort of dependence on God's creative will is different from dependence on God's legislative will.[49]

Cumberland's argument to show that morality is as immutable as human nature conflicts with Ockham's view that God is free to change what accords with human nature, and with Scotus' view that God is free to command us not to act in accord with human nature.[50] In his view, God necessarily wills that we act in accord with our nature, and therefore necessarily wills the common good of rational beings (with 'good' understood in a non-moral sense).[51]

Hence the natural law is not the product of the arbitrary will of God. Divine legislation reflects the divine goodness and wisdom that give God a right to rule and to legislate. Since the goodness of the common good recommends it to God as an end, God necessarily legislates that we promote the common good.[52] In doing so God manifests goodness, benevolence, and the other virtues.[53] Cumberland does not suggest that the natural law

---

[46] On Grotius see §465.   [47] On Pufendorf see §566.

[48] Cumberland's connexions with Cambridge may have informed him of Cudworth's views, even if not of his writings.

[49] 'All considerate persons, therefore, I believe, will think, that I have proved the law of nature sufficiently immutable, when I have shown, that it cannot be changed without contradiction, whilst the nature of things, and their actual powers, (which depend upon the divine will,) remain unchanged.' (Cumberland, *LN* 5.23 = P 545)

[50] See §384 on Scotus; §397 on Ockham.   [51] Cf. Pufendorf, §580.

[52] '... the dominion of God is a right or power, given him by his own wisdom and goodness, as by a law, for the government of all those things which ever have been, or shall be, created by him. In the divine wisdom is necessarily contained a dictate to pursue the best end by the necessary means; and in the goodness or perfection of the divine will is by a like necessity included a ready consent to promote the same. And these, by a natural analogy, answer to a ratification of the divine law, whence the divine dominion may take its original' (7.7 = P 673). 'For since he himself is rational, and it cannot be conceived how he can act rationally without proposing an end to himself, nor can there be a greater end than the aforesaid aggregate of all good things; we cannot but think he judges this to be the best end he can propose to himself. Nor is it to be doubted, but that the most perfect being will pursue that end which he has rightly judged to be the best, all circumstances rightly considered. For no reason can be assigned why he should stop short of it; nor can the most perfect will act without reason, much less against it. For although here the obligation of a law properly so called, which proceeds from the will of a superior, has no place, yet that perfection which is essential to him and invariable will invariably determine his will to concur exactly with his omniscient understanding. For it implies a contradiction that the same will should at once be divine, or most perfect, and disagree with the most perfect dictates of the divine understanding.' (5.19 = P 537-8)

[53] 'I choose the rather to observe that, from what I have proved concerning the reason and end of God, may be demonstrated that benevolence, justice, equity, and those other attributes which have any analogy with human virtues,

depends on the contingent fact that God is benevolent. If this were a contingent fact about God, it would also be a contingent fact that God legislates rules that promote the common good of rational agents; for if God were malevolent, rules designed to cause suffering to rational agents would be morally right. To avoid making rightness dependent on the arbitrary will of God, Cumberland insists that God is essentially good, and therefore is not free to legislate evil.

In attributing this character to God, Cumberland raises a familiar difficulty that confronts voluntarists: what do they mean in attributing goodness to God? If we say that God is morally good because God's actions are morally right, we can hardly mean that God obeys a law imposed by a superior, since God has no superior. We also face difficulties if we say that God's actions are right because they conform to God's legislation; for if we say that, we must say that they would still be right if God legislated differently and commanded us to act against the common good of rational beings. Apparently, we have to say that God's actions are morally right because they conform to a divine law prescribing promotion of the common good. But even this account of their rightness is not quite satisfactory. For we also believe that God acts rightly in legislating the natural law; since God does not act in conformity to a second divine law (which would lead us into an infinite regress), this morally right action seems to be right independently of legislation.

Cumberland might avoid these difficulties for his legislative account of morality if he gave up his claim that God is morally good and that God's action in legislating pursuit of the common good is morally right. He believes that practical reason, independently of any legislation, requires pursuit of the common good. Hence he might say that God is essentially rational, and so prescribes pursuit of the common good, because of an essentially rational will, though not because of a morally good will.

539. The Authority of Divine Legislation

Cumberland faces a related difficulty in explaining why we ought to obey God. If we claim that morality consists in acting according to a divine command, we need to explain why we are morally required to obey divine commands. If God issued a second-order command to obey all other divine commands, that would not answer our question, since we could ask the same question about the second-order command. If we believe that God has the right to command because God is essentially wise and good, we imply that we ought to obey a commander who is essentially wise and good. But this requirement seems to be antecedent to any command.

This is the basis of Maxwell's criticisms of Cumberland's account of God's authority. He argues that the authority of a human ruler is based on two conditions: (1) the necessity of rule for achieving the public good, and (2) the legitimacy of the ruler, making it right for us to obey. According to Cumberland, this second condition is established by reference to a divine command requiring obedience to the laws of nature that enjoin actions necessary for the public good.

are actually to be found in God and in his actions, and that it is therefore his will to govern men by precepts guarded with rewards and punishments; . . .' (5.20 = P 538)

But, as Maxwell sees, we cannot rely on the same two conditions to show that God is a legitimate ruler. For God's right to command us to do what is needed to promote the public good cannot be derived from any higher authority than God; hence (according to Cumberland's view of legitimacy) God is not a legitimate ruler. God's title to rule must rest entirely on the first condition; since we care, for non-moral reasons, about the promotion of the public good, and obedience to God's commands allows us to promote the public good, we have a non-moral reason to obey God's commands. Hence God's authority is less firmly established than the authority of human rulers.[54]

We might try to reply on Cumberland's behalf by deriving God's authority from the intrinsic rightness, rather than the non-moral attractiveness of promoting the public good. This would constitute a rationalist defence of God's authority. But it exposes Cumberland to a further objection. For if this intrinsic rightness is intrinsic moral rightness, it seems to presuppose morality antecedent to any law of God, since it cannot depend on divine legislation. Maxwell's objection, therefore, though it at first seems unfair, identifies a weakness in Cumberland's position.

Maxwell believes that we can avoid this fault in Cumberland's position only if we recognize a moral obligation—antecedent to any divine commands—to obey divine commands. Hence, in Maxwell's view, we must abandon Cumberland's voluntarism.[55] This argument for the priority of justice to law is very similar to Cudworth's argument against Hobbes; for, while Cumberland seeks to refute Hobbes, he still accepts some of the basic elements in Hobbes's position. Maxwell argues that Cumberland fails to recognize that divine rewards and punishments presuppose the rightness and wrongness of certain courses of action, and so cannot create it. Price endorses this objection to Cumberland.[56]

These observations on Cumberland support a general attack on voluntarism. Maxwell especially criticizes Jeremy Taylor for his endorsement of Ockham's position on divine commands and moral rightness.[57] Maxwell believes, as Cudworth does, that a voluntarist

---

[54] 'To this assumed dominion and sovereignty, assumed merely from necessity of common good and in order thereto, he cannot obtain our subjection, save only from necessity of the common good, and in order thereto. But if this is the whole of the divine dominion and sovereignty, he is far from having the most supreme dominion possible, which the Deity must have . . .' (App. §3(9) = P 810)

[55] 'In this [sc. Cumberland's] scheme of the law of nature, agreeably to its notion of good, the due order of reasoning and of our obligation is inverted. For, antecedently to the law of endeavouring the common good, there is an obligation upon mankind, and therefore a law, of conscientious subjection and obedience to the authority of the lawgiver. He would not make this law for them, if they were not antecedently under such an obligation, if he could not claim subjection and obedience from them. Their subjection to this the supreme lawgiver is, therefore, the first law of nature.' (App. §3(12) = P 813–14)

[56] See Price, RPQM 114–16, discussed in §818.

[57] 'A mistake, touching the rule and measure of good and evil, of greater importance than any of these, is this; that the arbitrary will of God is constitutively the adequate rule and measure of good and evil, just and unjust, and that nothing is good or evil, but because it is commanded or forbidden.' Maxwell now illustrates this mistake by quoting two passages from Taylor's discussion of natural law: 'With which absurd notion Bp Taylor (DD b2 c1 n4, 52, 58) falleth in, affirming, "that nothing is just or unjust of-it-self, until some law of God or man doth supervene. God cannot do an unjust thing; because whatsoever he willeth or doeth, is therefore just, because he willeth and doeth it, his will being the measure of justice. [Though Maxwell treats "that nothing . . ." as a quotation from Taylor, the actual quotation begins only with "God cannot . . .". See DD ii c1 rule 1, #52 = Works xi 224.] It is but a weak distinction, to affirm, some things to be forbidden by God, because they are unlawful, and some to be unlawful because they are forbidden. For this last part of the distinction taketh in all that is unlawful in the world, and therefore the other is a dead member, and may be dropped off. So Occham affirmeth, against the common sentence of the schools (as his manner is,) nullus est actus malus, nisi quatenus a Deo prohibitus est, et qui non potest fieri bonus, si a Deo praecipiatur et e converso: every thing is good or

234

conception of natural law is an aspect of the position that also takes the eternal truths to depend on God's choice; for 'if truth is of so indeterminate a nature, good must be as arbitrary, as some say' (App. §7 = P 843).[58] The voluntarist position is 'absurd' because it undermines the basis of the law that voluntarists take to be the foundation of moral obligation.[59]

In Maxwell's view, as in Cudworth's, the voluntarist position conflicts with the facts about the honestum.[60] He rejects the voluntarist claim that legislation can make something genuinely honestum. His argument seems to be this: (1) The honestum is good in its own right and because of its own nature. (2) If legislation is the sole source of the honestum, it must make some actions good in their own right. (3) But if something is good in its own right, it is good independently of being commanded or legislated. (3) Legislation cannot make something good independently of being legislated. (4) Hence legislation cannot be the sole source of the honestum.

This argument does not show that Cumberland could not be right about natural law being the product of divine legislation. It shows at most that natural law cannot be the sole source of moral goodness, if moral goodness consists in honestas. If one wants to maintain Cumberland's position, one needs to deny the first step of Maxwell's argument. Cumberland, therefore, agrees that some things are good in their own nature and apart from legislation, and denies that these include honesta. But his position is difficult to maintain. For we are confident that God has imposed the right laws because we assume that the actions required by these laws are already honesta, morally good in their own right. Maxwell's argument suggests, therefore, that Cumberland must reject more of our basic beliefs about morality than he admits.

Since he rejects Cumberland's voluntarism, Maxwell also rejects his explanation of the immutability of the natural law.[61] If natural law depended on divine legislation, it could

bad, according as it is commanded or forbidden by God, and no otherwise." [The previous sentences are from *DD* ii c1 rule 1, #58 = 226] These sayings are attended with a self-contradiction (*DD* ii, c rule 9 n 12), "that it is actually and indispensably necessary, that we love God, and that he cannot command us to hate him."' (App. §7 = P 842–3)

Taylor believes that an appeal to a natural or rational basis for morality introduces too much uncertainty, and that we avoid such uncertainty by relying directly on the revealed will of God. He recognizes that the natural law has a rational basis: 'And when wise men say This is naturally understood: it must mean thus, naturally men find it reasonable, but not naturally to be a law; naturally the consent to it, but not naturally find it out, or naturally we may be instructed, but not naturally bound; but when God changes science into conscience, then he makes that which is reasonable to become a law.' (ii rule 1, §40). Taylor ignores the questions that are raised, e.g., by Sanderson (discussed in §557).

[58] He cites Descartes in this connexion, §7 = P 843.

[59] 'According to this scheme, law is supposed to make justice, whereas, without antecedent justice, it is impossible, that there can be any made law. For no law can be made, but by one, who hath right to be obeyed, and to whom obedience is due; right and due obedience, and consequently just and unjust, is necessarily antecedent to any made law. If nothing is unrighteous but by a made law, mankind must be considered as perfectly at liberty and un-obliged, antecedently to that law; and if we suppose them to be perfectly at liberty and un-obliged, then that law could not oblige them; for no command or prohibition can oblige them to obedience who are persons perfectly at liberty and unobliged.' (Maxwell, App. §7 = P 843)

[60] 'Bonum honestum or virtue is not a mere name, but hath its proper specific nature, which is the beauteous-beneficial [i.e., *kalon kagathon*] practice, as is already proved; which it is as certain that this name [virtue] denotes, as that the word [man] denotes a rational animal. ... Moral good is therefore the beauteous-beneficial practice essentially and in its own nature, and consequently it is necessarily, unchangeably, eternally so. ... hence it appeareth that the good in morality is that which is essentially and in its own nature such, and is not a matter of arbitrary determination.' (App. §8 = P 844–5) Perhaps Clarke is Maxwell's source for the claim about essences. But cf. §547 on Cudworth.

[61] 'The law of nature therefore, besides that it is imposed by a superior authority, appeareth to be a comprehension of what is, in its own nature, matter of law or obligation, antecedently to that authority; whence three honorary

be changed by a change in divine legislation, whether or not divine legislation will in fact change. If we make natural law depend on divine law in this way, we reverse their proper order; for the legitimacy of divine legislation presupposes an independent natural law giving God the right to legislate.[62]

If we recognize rightness independent of divine law, we also allow the possibility of a non-mercenary love of God as a morally perfect being, not simply as supremely powerful. Maxwell takes himself to be avoiding the extravagant appeals of 'enthusiasts' who claim to be moved by the disinterested love of God, and their 'rational' opponents who over-emphasize the pursuit of non-moral rewards. He agrees with Shaftesbury's efforts to defend the disinterested love of God without endorsing any harmful and irrational 'enthusiasm'.[63] In his view, we can maintain this position only if we recognize moral rightness independent of divine legislation.

540. Morality and Practical Reason

One might argue that Maxwell's objections to Cumberland ignore the differences between Cumberland's moderate voluntarist position and the more extreme voluntarism of Ockham or Hobbes. For Hobbes, the question about why we ought to obey God is easily answered. He derives the obligation (and hence motivation) to obey God from God's overwhelming power; he recognizes no distinction, for moral purposes, between power and authority (or legitimacy). Cumberland agrees with Cudworth in rejecting this basis for the moral requirement to obey God.[64]

Maxwell points out that it is difficult to find any genuinely moral basis for the requirement without violating Cumberland's legislative conditions for morality. But Cumberland might appeal to God's essential reasonableness; though we have no moral obligation, strictly speaking, to obey divine commands, we recognize a rational requirement, since we

attributes necessarily belong to it, immutability, eternity, universality, which Cicero hath conjoined. "All nations are at all times within the extent of one law sempiternal and immutable. In opposition to its immutability, which is generally acknowledged by philosophers, lawyers, and divines, some dispute (or rather loosely declaim), that the laws of nature can be dispensed with by divine power. But these will have (what none will allow them) an altering the case and a changing the matter, to be a dispensing with the law."' (App. §11 = P 854) A footnote to 'some dispute . . .' cites Taylor, *DD* ii1 rule 9. Taylor appeals to dispensations in support of voluntarism: 'I am willing publicly to acknowledge that I was always, since I understood it, a very great enemy to all the questions of the Schools which inquire into the power of God . . . But yet here I am willing to speak in the like manner of expression, because the consequent and effect of it goes not to a direct inquiry concerning the divine power; for it intends to remonstrate that because God does actually dispense in his own law, this prime law, or the law of nature, is nothing else but the express and declared will of God in matters proportionable to right reason and the nature of man.' (rule 9 §1) The last phase ('in matters . . .') agrees with naturalists that the natural law in fact prescribes what accords with reason and nature. Maxwell goes on to discuss polygamy and other alleged cases of dispensation.

[62] 'But, antecedently to this obligation from superior authority, it is of an obligatory nature, and must be considered as what is, in its own nature, matter of law, or of obligation; for, that this law is of this nature, will appear, as from other considerations, so from a due explanation of the good, which it requireth, and of the evil, which it forbiddeth.' (App. §1 = P 796)

[63] He quotes a long passage from Shaftesbury; see §611.

[64] As Whewell, *LHMPE* 54, notices, Cumberland does not say much about post-mortem rewards and punishments, though he mentions them. A fuller statement appears in the first of the introductory essays bound with Maxwell's translation; see §671.

believe it is reasonable to obey a wise and reasonable commander who prescribes actions promoting the common good. Cumberland can save his legislative account of morality if he rejects non-legislative moral requirements in favour of requirements of practical reason.

But if we defend Cumberland's legislative account of morality by these appeals to non-moral practical reason, we raise a deeper question about his position. Why should we not simply by-pass morality, as he conceives it, in favour of the requirements of practical reason? These are the requirements that Suarez attributes to intrinsic morality; Cumberland denies that they belong to intrinsic morality because they are independent of divine legislation, but his reasons for insisting that morality requires obligation (in the narrow sense) and legislation are not clear.

He might claim that, as Culverwell suggests, practical reason without legislation lacks the compulsory character that we ascribe to morality. But this claim would be difficult to defend in the light of the role that Cumberland ascribes to practical reason. He surely believes that it is compulsory, in whatever sense morally right action is compulsory, for us to obey God's commands; but if this requirement is not based on legislation, the compulsory character of morality does not depend on legislation. Similarly, the requirement on God to prescribe pursuit of the common good seems no less stringent than the requirement on us to promote the common good.

If, then, we are moved by the requirements of practical reason to promote the common good and to obey divine legislation that promotes it, we seem to recognize the stringency of moral requirements. Should we not identify moral rightness with action on the demands of practical reason? If Cumberland agreed, he would return to the Scholastic belief in intrinsic morality. Though he criticizes the Scholastic position for ignoring the legislative aspect of morality, the role that he assigns to practical reason brings him closer to the Scholastic position than he recognizes. His voluntarism implies that the promotion of the common good of rational agents would not be the supreme principle of morality unless it had been commanded by God. But he seems to agree that, apart from any divine command, it is recognized as the supreme principle of practical reason. He must claim, then, that this supreme principle, even though it is impartially concerned for the good of rational agents, is not a moral principle until God has commanded it. It is difficult to justify this restriction on the scope of morality.

Maxwell concludes that we can maintain the legitimacy and authority of divine legislation only if we accept a naturalist view of natural law.[65] He agrees with the position of Vasquez and (apparently) of Cudworth, who take natural law and its obligation to precede any divine command. Maxwell does not consider the 'intermediate' position of Suarez, who argues that law and obligation rest on commands, but moral right and wrong do not. Maxwell seems to agree with Cumberland and Pufendorf in taking morality to be inseparable from moral obligation, and so he does not consider the possibility that morality might be distinguished from moral obligation. Suarez's position would avoid the faults that Maxwell sees in Cumberland as well as Maxwell's more extreme naturalism answers them. The most

---

[65] 'The law of nature, therefore, is the comprehension of what is in its own nature matter of obligation, and ought to be, abstracted from the preceding authority of command, or the subsequent sanctions of rewards and punishments.' (Maxwell, App. §11(3) = P 859–60)

serious objections that face Cumberland arise from his rejection of intrinsic morality; but his emphasis on practical reason raises the legitimate suspicion that he appeals to intrinsic morality after all.

These aspects of Cumberland's position make it intelligible that different people react differently to its voluntaristic and naturalistic elements. On the one hand, Maxwell treats him as a voluntarist; Cumberland gives him the occasion for a general attack on voluntarism, and he believes that some of his attack applies to Cumberland. On the other hand, Clarke cites Cumberland in support of his own naturalist position; though he quotes quite selectively, his quotations pick out a genuine element in Cumberland's view. Though Cumberland defends some elements of voluntarism against Grotius and the Scholastics, his arguments against Hobbes bring him closer to naturalism than he recognizes.

40

CUDWORTH

541. Cudworth's Place in the History of Moral Philosophy

Cudworth died in 1688, but his main work on moral philosophy, *A Treatise concerning Eternal and Immutable Morality*, was not published until 1731. The first major moral philosopher who is clearly influenced by this book is Price.[1] Cudworth's *Treatise of Freewill* was published only in 1838. These facts about his posthumous works, however, may give a misleading impression of Cudworth's influence on the development of ethical thought. For Locke and Clarke may have been acquainted with Cudworth's main ideas, either through reading his manuscripts or through oral dissemination of 'Cambridge Platonism'.[2]

The fact that Cudworth exercised his direct and indirect influence on ethical rationalists may give a one-sided impression of his contribution.[3] Some historians place him in a Cambridge Platonist tradition of which Culverwell is presented as an earlier member. It is appropriate to connect Cudworth with Culverwell, but it is doubtful whether the connexion lies in their Platonism. It is Culverwell's Scholastic Naturalism, rather than his supposed Platonism, that provides the right context for understanding Cudworth's main arguments.[4] The Scholastic aspects of Cambridge Platonism were recognized by Anthony Tuckney, a rigid Calvinist. Tuckney's letters to Benjamin Whichcote show that Tuckney was disturbed by the deviations he saw in the outlook of Cambridge Platonism; he attributed these deviations to a preference for the study of Scholastic philosophy over the Scriptures.[5]

---

[1] Price; see §802.

[2] On Locke and Cudworth see §555. Scott, 'Introd.' 59–62, presents a series of alleged parallels between Cudworth and Butler. None of them suggests the direct influence of Cudworth on Butler; they can all be explained by reference to Clarke. But they are evidence of similarity between Cudworth and Clarke.

[3] Passmore, *RC* 100–3, argues that Cudworth's position is more sentimentalist than purely rationalist. Hence he connects Cudworth with Shaftesbury as well as with Price, and argues that Price misunderstands him.

[4] On Culverwell see §558.

[5] These informative letters appear in Whichcote, *MRA*, App. In his second letter Tuckney says he has heard that 'you in a great measure for the year laid aside other studies, and betook yourself to philosophy and metaphysics, which, some think, you were then so immersed in, that ever since you have been cast into that mould, both in your private discourse and preaching, both for words and notions; both which, I fear, have rendered your ministry less edifying...' (36). He mentions that in Cambridge Whichote was influenced by Field, Jackson, and Hammond: 'Whilst you were fellow here, you were cast into the company of very learned and ingenious men, who, I fear, at least some of them, studied other authors more than the Scriptures; and Plato and his scholars above others: in whom, I must needs acknowledge, from the little insight I have into them, I find many excellent and divine expressions ... And hence in part hath run a vein of

Cudworth's reflexions on both free will and morality may have been stimulated partly by Hobbes, whom he often quotes. Hobbes intends his views on the will and its freedom to undermine Scholastic intellectualism and rationalism. He intends his account of morality to undermine the Scholastic view, stated by Suarez, that the morally right is what is appropriate to rational nature. Cudworth tries to refute these two aspects of Hobbes's attack on the Scholastic position.

To understand Cudworth in this way is not to imply that he is a thoughtless or uncritical supporter of Scholasticism. Like Simon Patrick, he thinks of Platonism as a way of compensating for the defects of Scholastic Aristotelianism as a defence of orthodox Christianity.[6] But he takes himself to defend Aristotle as well. On the crucial points about the freedom of the will and the natural character of morality, he believes Aristotle is right and Hobbes is wrong. Hobbes's errors reflect not only a mistaken approach to ethics, but also a mistaken approach to basic questions of epistemology and metaphysics. His position is a revival of the 'Democritic doctrine' that Cudworth sees in ancient atomism and empiricism. In Cudworth's view, the ancient doctrine of Democritus and Epicurus, recently revived by Gassendi and Hobbes, rests on an indefensible metaphysics. Hence *Eternal and Immutable Morality* begins and ends with discussion of ethics, but includes a long defence of rationalism in general.[7]

doctrine which divers very able and worthy men . . . are, I fear too much known by.—The power of nature in morals too much advanced—Reason hath too much given to it, in the mysteries of faith—A recta ratio much talked of, which I cannot tell where to find—Mind and understanding is all; heart and will little spoken of—The decrees of God questioned and quarrelled, because, according to our reason we cannot comprehend how they may stand with his goodness, which, according to your phrase, he is under the power of . . . A kind of moral divinity minted, only with a little tincture of Christ added; nay, a Platonic faith unites to God.' (38)

In his second letter Whichcote replies to Tuckney by denying that he has studied the suspect divines and schoolmen as much as Tuckney alleges: 'I should lay open my weakness if I should tell you how little I have read of the books and authors you mention: of ten years past, nothing at all. . . . And for schoolmen, I do not think I have spent four and twenty hours in them divisim these fourteen years. . . . and truly I have more read Calvin, and Perkins, and Beza, than all the authors, books, or names you mention.' (53) Tuckney, however, does not let the point drop. In his third letter he says more precisely whom he includes among Schoolmen: '. . . as to that about the Schoolmen, when I spake of them, I understood not only that narrower compass of them which some make from Albensis to Biel, but so as to take in Vasquez, Suarez, and other later authors of that kind; your perusing of whom so little in so many years, but that you say it and I believe you, I cannot but wonder: and must conclude that either those few hours of your converse with them made a very deep impression in you, moulding you much that way, or as "nascitur non fit poeta", that the natural frame of your head was much in that channel, which must keep us from wondering or finding fault if in your discourse the streams do so much answer the fountain.' (58) (For 'Albensis' Jeffery conjectures 'Alensis' (i.e., Alexander of Hales) or 'Albertus' (i.e., Albertus Magnus).) Whichcote does not answer this point about the later Scholastics, and does not deny the similarity of his views to theirs. Tuckney mentions both the Platonic and the Scholastic character of Whichcote's views; he does not suggest that Whichcote draws on one source rather than the other.

On the influence of Suarez cf. the life of Isaac Barrow, in *Works* i (unpaged). Barrow was appointed a lecturer in geometry at Gresham College, but '. . . when he commented on Archimedes, he did not forbear in discourse to prefer and admire much more Suarez for his book De Legibus . . .'.

6 On Simon Patrick see §527.

7 'But the Aristotelic system is right and sound here, as to those greater things; it asserting incorporeal substance, a Deity distinct from the world, the naturality of morality, and liberty of will. Wherefore though a late writer of politics do so exceedingly disparage Aristotle's Ethics, yet we shall do him this right here to declare, that his Ethics were truly such, and answered their title; but that new model of ethics, which hath been obtruded on the world with so much fastuosity, and is indeed nothing but the old Democritic doctrine revived, is no ethics at all, but a mere cheat, the undermining and subversion of all morality, by substituting something like it in the room of it, that is a mere counterfeit and changeling; the design whereof could not be any other than to debauch the world.' (*TIS* i 1.45 (= 95 Harrison)). To illustrate Hobbes's attacks on Aristotle, Mosheim cites Hobbes, *L.* 46.23 (LV).

542. Reason and Will[8]

Cudworth's sympathetic but critical attitude to Scholasticism appears in his treatment of the psychological foundations of Hobbes's moral theory. He rejects three positions: (1) Hobbes's version of determinism and anti-rationalism; (2) the intellectualist position of Aquinas; (3) the voluntarist and libertarian conception of the will. On the first two points he agrees with Bramhall, but disagrees with him on the third, since Bramhall accepts the voluntarist claims that Cudworth criticizes. His criticisms of these three positions and his attempts to develop a fourth position are worth considering, even though it is not clear exactly what position he eventually maintains, or how it differs from the three positions he rejects.

Cudworth presents two Scholastic views under the head of 'the vulgarly received psychology' (FW, ch. 5 = H 167).[9] Both of them treat the will and understanding as mutually exclusive; hence they treat the will as 'blind', because it includes no element of understanding. The pure intellectualist view claims that the understanding alone determines the will. A more complex view claims that the will 'determines the understanding both to exercise, and specification of objects'.[10]

He rejects the pure intellectualist view as denying freewill. He rejects the more complex view for two reasons: (1) It is viciously circular, because it treats the will as 'blind' in itself; the will determines the understanding only insofar as the understanding presents something to it, so that it is really determined by the understanding.[11] (2) It does not safeguard freewill, because an undetermined but blind will would act capriciously and randomly, which is contrary to genuine freedom.[12]

Both Scholastic views are wrong, in Cudworth's view, because they treat the will and the understanding as though they were two distinct subjects (FW, ch. 7 = H 170–1). To speak of the understanding 'propounding' to the will, or 'alluring' or 'inviting' the will, and of the will as 'following' or 'refusing to comply' is to treat them as two distinct agents. But this treatment would be reasonable only if each of them were a real agent, and hence had both understanding and will. If we treat the will as an agent without understanding, we cannot find a satisfactory account of freedom. For if it is entirely blind, either it thoughtlessly follows understanding (as the pure intellectualist view claims) or it thoughtlessly and capriciously chooses to follow or not to follow understanding. In trying to explain intelligible choices by a real agent, who is a person with both understanding and will, we resort to unintelligible choices by a spurious agent, the blind will.

Are these objections to the Scholastic views justified? In Aquinas' view, the will is blind insofar as it pursues an object that is understood to have an appropriate character; it is the

---

[8] On different views about reason and will see §256 (Aquinas); §389 (Ockham); §470 (Hobbes).

[9] I cite FW and EIM by the pages of Hutton's edition (H).   [10] FW, ch. 5 = H 168 = R 142.

[11] 'They maintaining that the will can will nothing, but as represented to it first by the understanding, (since otherwise it must will it know not what), and again that the understanding cannot act about this or that but as it is moved and determined thereunto by the will, so that there must be both an action of the understanding going before every act of the will, and also an act of the will going before every act of the understanding, which is further contradictious and impossible.' (FW, ch. 6 = H 169 = R 143)

[12] 'But if the blind will does not only at first fortuitously determine the understanding both to exercise and object, but also after all is done remains indifferent to follow the last dictate of it or not, and doth fortuitously determine itself either in compliance with the same or otherwise, then will liberty of will be mere irrationality, and madness itself acting or determining all human actions.' (FW, ch. 6 = H 145 = R 144)

intellect that causes the object to appear in the right light. The ultimate object of the will is the final good, and it is this desire that initiates practical reasoning to find out what is really good, and how different goods can be combined in the final good. This desire for the final good has to be focussed on the conclusion of deliberation if deliberation is to result in action.

These features of Aquinas' view appear to match Cudworth's description of intellectualism. But Aquinas also accepts some of the claims that Cudworth uses to describe voluntarism, since he allows the will to 'determine the understanding both as to its exercise and objects' (FW, ch. 6 = H 169). Aquinas recognizes this distinction between exercise and specification, and allows the will some freedom in each respect; hence he argues that the will is not necessarily moved by the object that intellect presents to it (ST 1–2 q10 a2).[13] But Aquinas does not infer the will is undetermined in choosing what to do as a result of deliberation.

Aquinas' position is consistent if he denies that freedom of exercise and of specification require an act of the will that is independent of or prior to every act of the understanding. When we decide what to deliberate about, or whether to act on the conclusion of our deliberation, or what aspect of an imperfect good or evil to focus on, we decide independently of this particular act of understanding or deliberation, but we may still be determined by previous thought and deliberation. Cudworth is unjustified, therefore, in claiming that the Scholastic position involves a vicious infinite regress.

It would be more plausible to claim that Aquinas allows a circle, by taking the relevant acts of the will and the understanding to depend on each other. Though it is up to the will to decide to consider a question, and to deliberate again about a conclusion reached by the understanding, these acts of will may be determined by intellect. I may decide to consider or not to consider a question because I judge it better to do one thing or the other. But if Aquinas must recognize this circle, the circle is not vicious, since the relevant acts of will and understanding need not be temporally distinguishable.

Cudworth is mistaken, therefore, if he believes that recognition of freedom of specification and of exercise precludes an intellectualist account of the will. We reject intellectualism only if we take the will to be undetermined even by the last act of judgment,[14] so that in the same circumstances the will is capable of going in different directions.[15] Cudworth correctly describes Scotus' position in attributing indeterminism to the voluntarists.

He is rather hasty in assuming that indeterminism implies random and capricious motion that could not be a subject for praise and blame. The voluntarist might reply that when we choose the apparently greater good, we choose it because it appears greater, even though the causal connexion is not deterministic. We might fairly ask the voluntarist, however, why the non-deterministic character of the causal connexion is necessary for the choice to be free and responsible; on this point Cudworth has identified a reasonable objection to voluntarist indeterminism.

---

[13] On Aquinas see §258.

[14] '... this scholastic definition of freewill, viz., that it is, after all things put, besides the volition itself, even the last practical judgment in the soul too, an indifferency of not doing or of doing this or that' (FW, ch. 6 = H 170).

[15] 'This is an upstart thing, which the ancient peripatetics, as Alexander and others, were unacquainted with, their account thereof being this, that *autois periestôsi*, the same things being circumstant, the same impressions being made upon men from without, all that they are passive to, being the same, yet they may, notwithstanding, act differently. The last practical judgment also, as according to these, being that which as men are not merely passive to, so it is really the same thing with the *boulêsis*, the will, or volition.' (FW, ch. 6 = H 170)

But if Cudworth rejects voluntarist indeterminism, where does he stand on determinism? This is rather difficult to say. He rejects determinism, if this is understood as the doctrine that everything is necessitated by previous events; he takes Buridan's ass to show the presence of contingency in some choices (*FW*, ch. = H 164). He does not believe, however, that voluntary and responsible action is to be identified with this sort of contingency (*FW*, ch. 5 = H 166). Sometimes he suggests that we are responsible for an error if further consideration would have caused us to avoid the error by better judgment (*FW*, ch. 10 = H 179). He adds, however, that this further consideration must also be possible for us, and that this possibility requires the absence of determination by 'antecedent necessary causes' (*FW*, ch. 10 = H 179).

This demand might be an affirmation of indeterminism, or it might simply be the demand that causes external to the agent's deliberation and choice must not by themselves adequately explain the action. Cudworth sometimes expresses his view by saying that a person is a 'sufficient cause' (*FW*, ch. 22 = H 203). By this he means neither that we are sufficient irrespective of prior conditions, nor that we cannot fail to produce the effect; he means but that we are capable of producing or not producing it.[16] The possibility of praise and blame requires something more than the necessity of nature.[17] It is difficult to say how strongly or how consistently Cudworth believes that freedom from the necessity of nature requires the absence of determination.

543. The Hegemonicon

Cudworth suggests that the intellectualist Scholastic view that the will is determined by the greater apparent good is a threat to freewill (*FW*, ch. 2 = H 158). But it is difficult to see how far he departs from the intellectualist position. After rejecting the 'blind will' presupposed by both intellectualism and voluntarism, he suggests that we need a different account of the first mover that underlies rational action. In his view, this first mover is the desire for happiness.[18] This is not a desire for some specific object such as pleasure, but a more general desire explaining our particular desires; we want the different particular goods we want on the assumption that they achieve happiness.[19]

---

[16] 'Nothing is produced without an efficient cause, and such an efficient cause as had a sufficiency of power to enable it to produce it. But yet that person, who had sufficient power to produce an effect might notwithstanding will not to produce it. So that there are two kinds of sufficient causes. One is such as acteth necessarily and can neither suspend nor determine its own action. Another is such as acteth contingently or arbitrarily, and hath a power over its own action, either to suspend it or determine it as it pleaseth.' (*FW*, ch. 22 = H 203)

[17] '...it is plain that if we be determined by necessity of nature here, then is there nothing in our own power, nor can we be blameworthy or deserve punishment. ... These things are imputed to the men themselves, as the causes of things, and as not being determined by necessary causes as much as the notions [sic; motions?] of a watch or clock are.' (*FW*, ch. 11 = H 183)

[18] 'Wherefore, we conclude that the *to prôtos kinoun*, that which first moveth in us, and is the spring and principle of all deliberative action, can be no other than a constant, restless, uninterrupted desire, or love of good as such, and happiness. This is an ever bubbling fountain in the centre of the soul, an elator and spring of motion, both a primum and perpetuum mobile in us, the first wheel that sets all the other wheels in motion, and an everlasting and incessant mover.' (*FW*, ch. 8 = H 173 = R 147) Remarks such as this one lead Passmore, *RC* 52–6, to claim that Cudworth is not an unqualified intellectualist.

[19] '...a certain vaticination, presage, scent, and odour of one summum bonum, one supreme highest good transcending all others, without which they will be all ineffectual as to complete happiness, and signify nothing, a certain

This description of the desire for happiness captures the Aristotelian conception of a final good. This conception underlies Aquinas' intellectualist account of the will. Hence it is difficult to see how Cudworth's appeal to a desire for happiness marks a disagreement with intellectualism. Perhaps he rejects it by denying that the desire for happiness is always predominant; in that case he agrees with Scotus' critique of eudaemonism. He seems to endorse the Scotist position in his description of the other powers of the soul. He mentions the concupiscible and irascible parts over which we have no 'despotic' power, but which the 'hegemonicon' may gradually control. Similarly, the hegemonicon may support or reject the demands of conscience.[20] Cudworth does not suggest that the hegemonicon necessarily follows either particular impulses or the desire for happiness or the demands of conscience.

What, then, is the hegemonicon? Cudworth takes it to be the ultimate basis of freedom and of praise and blame.[21] He argues that it cannot be the Scholastic blind will, because it is indifferent and 'fortuitously' determines itself. But he acknowledges that it is guided by the appearance of good.[22] Here he seems to refer to Aquinas' account of the will rather than to Scotus' account. He objects to the explanation of our capacity to choose the lesser good in the case where we choose between two objects that do not appear good in every respect. He suggests that in cases where x appears much better than y, but both x and y have some pros and cons, the will may nevertheless, according to the Scholastics, choose y because of the relatively small apparent good in it. Cudworth objects that this description of the blind will and 'active indifference' makes it no more than 'active irrationality and nonsense', and hence unsuitable to be the hegemonicon (FW, ch. 9 = H 177).

Cudworth raises a reasonable question about Aquinas' explanation of the will's capacity for opposites. But he has not offered the most plausible account of Aquinas' position.[23] Aquinas does not seem to intend the situation described by Cudworth, in which it is perfectly

philosophers' stone that can turn all to gold. Now this love and desire of good, as good in general, and of happiness, traversing the soul continually, and actuating and provoking it continually, is not a mere passion or hormê, but a settled resolved principle, and the very source, and fountain, and centre of life. It is necessary nature in us, which is immutable, and always continues the same, in equal quantity. As Cartesius supposes the same quantity of motion to be perpetually conserved in the universe, but not alike in all the same bodies, but transferred, and passing from one to another; so, more or less, here and there, is there the same stock of love and desire of good, always alive, working in the soul by necessity of nature, and agitating it, though by men's will and choice, it may be diversely dispensed out, and placed upon different objects, more and less' (ch. 8 = H 174 = R 147).

[20] 'Then fancy or imagination, sudden passions and hormae, and commotions called concupiscible and irascible . . . we have no absolute, despotic, easy, undisputed power over them, notwithstanding which the hegemonic of the soul may, by conatives and endeavours, acquire more and more power over them. Above all these is the dictate of honesty, commonly called the dictate of conscience—which often majestically controls them [and] clashes with the former. This is necessary nature too, when here the hegemonic sometimes joins its assistance to the better one, and sometimes takes part with the worser against it.' (FW, ch. 8 = H 174–5) Allen's edition (31) prints a different text in the last two sentences just quoted: 'Above all these is the dictate of honesty, commonly called the dictate of conscience, which often majestically controls them, and clashes with the former; this is necessary nature too, being here the hegemonic, sometimes joining its assistance to the better one, and sometimes taking part with the worse against it.'

[21] 'For here, or nowhere else, is to be found the to eph'hêmin and the to autexousion, sui potestas, self-power, or such a liberty of will as whereby men deserve praise or dispraise, commendation or blame. This hegemonic of the soul is a thing that was much taken notice of by the Greek philosophers after Aristotle, and to this is ascribed by them the original of those moral evils that deserve blame and punishment.' (FW, ch. 9 = H 175) Cudworth supports his claim by discussing a passage in Origen.

[22] 'Nevertheless they themselves acknowledge that there is so much of necessary nature even in this blind and fortuitous will, that it is notwithstanding always determined to good, or some appearance of it, and can never possibly choose evil when represented to it by the understanding as wholly such.' (FW, ch. 9 = H 176)

[23] On Aquinas see §§266–7.

clear to us that x is much better than y, but we choose y nonetheless for the sake of the trivial good (or the extremely small chance of a more significant good) that it offers. He seems to intend the quite different situation in which, even though x might at first appear better than or as good as y, we attend selectively to the advantages of y and the disadvantages of x, so that we come to believe y is better than x.

Does this description avoid Cudworth's charge of attributing to the will some indifference that amounts to 'active irrationality and nonsense'? One might object that Aquinas' appeal to selective attention does not resolve the main difficulty; either this attention to the good features of the inferior option is an exercise of 'active irrationality', or else it is bound by our prior beliefs about the good, and so does not really introduce freedom. But perhaps this objection relies on false alternatives. At any rate, Aquinas' actual position raises a series of further possibilities that are not covered by Cudworth's objection to the Scholastic position.

In opposition to the Scholastic position, as he interprets it, Cudworth argues that the hegemonicon cannot be 'utterly devoid of all light, and perception, or understanding' (FW, ch. 9 = H 177). But he believes it cannot simply be reason, which is never mistaken; it must include the possibility of error, together with the possibility of directing one's attention and of beginning and ending one's deliberation.[24] These capacities in the hegemonicon explain why it is not simply a passive recipient of judgments of understanding.[25] Since we may make more or less effort to deliberate, and may deliberate more or less carefully, we may judge what is in fact worse to be better, and hence may make a culpable mistake; for it was in our power to deliberate more carefully.[26] The hegemonicon is fallible, and when it goes wrong it is responsible for a person's choosing badly.

This description explains why the hegemonicon is the source of freewill. Its good or bad deliberation about good and evil is the basis for praise and blame. But this is not because it possesses the liberty of indifference.[27] On the contrary: if our deliberation about the best thing to do did not determine our choice, but we had some natural and unpredictable tendency to choose the worse outcome for no reason when we were presented with the

---

[24] 'I say, therefore, that *to hêgemonikon* in every man, and indeed that which is properly we ourselves, (we rather having those other things of necessary nature than being them), is the soul as comprehending itself, all its concerns and interests, its abilities and capacities, and holding itself, as it were, in its own hand, as it were redoubled upon itself, having a power of intending or exerting itself more or less, in consideration and deliberation, in resisting the lower appetites that oppose it, both of [i.e., in consideration and deliberation both of . . .] utility, reason, and honesty; in self-recollection and attention, and vigilant circumspection, or standing upon our guard, in purposes and resolutions, in diligence in carrying on steady designs and active endeavours, in order to self-improvement and the self-promoting of its own good, the fixing and conserving itself in the same. . . . Wherefore this hegemonicon always determines the passive capability of man's nature one way or other, either for better or for worse; and has a self-forming and self-framing power by which every man is self-made into what he is, and accordingly deserves either praise or punishment.' (FW, ch. 10 = H 178 = R 150)

[25] '. . . though perception be nature or necessary understanding in us, yet for all that, we are not merely passive to our own practical judgments and to the appearances of good, but contribute something of our own to them, to make them such as they are' (FW, ch. 10 = H 179).

[26] The hegemonic power that Cudworth describes here seems to have the role that Locke attributes to reason, in suspending the operation of particular impulses and deciding which of them it is on the whole better to follow. See §555.

[27] 'But this not because it had by nature an equal indifferency and freedom to a greater or lesser good, which is absurd, or because it had a natural liberty of will either to follow or not follow its own last practical judgment, which is all one as to say a liberty to follow or not follow its own volition. For upon both these suppositions there would have been no such thing as fault or blame.' (FW, ch. 10 = H 179 = R 150) On the liberty of indifference see Passmore, RC 59. He thinks it raises difficulties for Cudworth.

choice between it and the better outcome, we could not reasonably be praised or blamed for anything. The fact that we made the worse choice would just be something about us that we could not be expected to alter; for no deliberation about altering it would be effective.

Instead of trying to find responsibility in indifference, we should place it in the agent's capacity to deliberate. This power to deliberate is inconsistent with the claim that everything is necessary.[28] Our use of this power determines whether we follow the dictates of conscience or the suggestions of other impulses.[29] Since we can choose to use our deliberative capacity well or badly, we can reasonably be blamed for the way we use it.

544. Does Cudworth Improve on the Scholastic View?

If our description of Aquinas' view was right, Cudworth's view differs far less from Aquinas' actual view than from the positions that Cudworth ascribes to the Scholastics. In particular, Aquinas' explanation of the non-necessity of deliberation and election does not seem to rely on the sort of indifference that Cudworth attacks as irrational. When Aquinas argues that it is possible for us to 'consider' the different aspects of good and bad in different options, he seems to mean what Cudworth means in saying that we are not merely 'passive to our own practical judgments', but contribute something to their character (*FW*, ch. 10 = H 179). Aquinas believes that our will influences our consideration of one or another aspect of a situation, but he does not suggest that this influence of the will is altogether independent of our judgment about what it would be best to consider.

So far, then, Cudworth's account of the will rests on justified objections to a doctrine of indifference that implies 'active irrationality and nonsense', but it does not rest on justified objections to Aquinas' position. In fact, he agrees with Aquinas in believing that one can attribute some sort of indeterminacy to deliberation and election without taking the will to be altogether independent of beliefs about better and worse.

Cudworth's major difference from Aquinas seems to be his rejection of the priority of the desire for happiness. In his view, the freedom of the will consists in its being bound neither by the desire for happiness nor by the demands of conscience. The hegemonicon considers the various aims that belong to us by nature—particular impulses, the desire for happiness, and concern for the honestum. Whereas Scotus identifies (at least sometimes) the freedom of the will with the affection for justice, Cudworth makes the hegemonicon superior to conscience as well as to self-love.

---

[28] 'But because he might have made a better judgment than now he did, had he more intensely considered, and more maturely deliberated, which, that he did not, was his own fault. Now to say that a man hath not this power over himself to consider and deliberate more or less, is to contradict common experience and inward sense.... But if a man have this power over himself to consider and deliberate more or less; then is he not always determined thereunto by any antecedent necessary causes. These two things being inconsistent and contradictious, and consequently there was something of contingency in his choice.' (*FW*, ch. 10 = H 179 = R 150)

[29] 'Again in that contest betwixt the dictate of honesty or of conscience and the suggestion of the lower appetites urging and impelling to pleasure or present good or profit, I say in this contest there is no necessary understanding interposing and coming in to umpire between, that does unavoidably and irresistibly determine one way or the other. But the matter wholly depends on the soul's hegemonic or power over itself, its exerting itself with more or less force and vigour in resisting these lower affections ... Whereas it is plain that if we be determined by necessity of nature here, then is there nothing in our own power, nor can we be blameworthy or deserve punishment.' (*FW*, ch. 11 = H 182–3)

How, then, does the hegemonicon estimate the claims of conscience and of self-love, and how does it choose between them? This question seems to face Cudworth no less than it faces Butler; for both of them seem to take conscience to be (in Butler's words) superior to self-love, but they do not take superiority to imply that we necessarily prefer the demands of conscience over those of self-love. Cudworth does not want to conclude that the hegemonicon prefers self-love or conscience for no reason; that would be a return to 'active irrationality and nonsense', which he tries to avoid in denying indifference to the will. But apparently it cannot decide on the basis of self-love or of conscience, if it is capable of deciding between the two.

To resolve this difficulty, Cudworth might try to distinguish two aspects of conscience: (1) It takes an impartial point of view, standing outside the desire for one's own happiness, and considering the value of pursuing one's own interest in comparison with other values. (2) It endorses the specific principles prescribed by morality, embodying the honestum. If we consider the first aspect of conscience we might claim that it captures the point of view of the hegemonicon, because we are capable of looking at practical questions from a broader view than the view of self-love. To this degree we might identify the outlook of the hegemonicon with the outlook of conscience. But since our taking this point of view need not lead us to endorse the requirements of morality, we may still separate the outlook of the hegemonicon from the honestum.

But though this Butlerian solution offers a reasonable account of the deliberative standpoint of the hegemonicon, Cudworth does not present it. Though his account of freewill is suggestive, he does not develop it far enough to make it clear how he intends to answer the questions that can reasonably be raised about it.

545. What is Cudworth's Objection to Determinism?

Our discussion of Cudworth's criticism of the Scholastic view, and our survey of the positive view that he develops to answer these criticisms, should help us to see what he rejects in Hobbes. His conception of the hegemonicon makes it clear why he rejects Hobbes's anti-rationalism as an account of the will and as an account of freedom. For the hegemonicon is the source of freedom precisely insofar as it differs from a Hobbesian will; it is not simply the last appetite in Hobbesian deliberation, but it is the reflective and deliberative source of the comparative judgments that underlie rational action.

It is more difficult to see why Cudworth rejects Hobbes's determinism; for his description of the hegemonicon and of the source of freedom does not seem to conflict with determinism. He argues against Hobbes's claims about necessity with a counter-example. We are capable of choosing between qualitatively identical objects (20 gold coins at the same distance from the agent: *FW*, ch. 4 = H 163–4 = R 140). Since nothing about the situation itself determines the agent to choose one rather than another, Cudworth infers that he is not necessitated and that he chooses 'contingently'.[30] But this fact (if one grants it) does not

---

[30] 'But if being necessitated by no motive or reason antecedently to choose this rather than that, he must determine himself contingently, or fortuitously, or causelessly, it being all one to him which he took.' (*FW*, ch. 4 = H 164 = R 140)

refute determinism. It shows simply that some cause within the agent, and some cause that is not reflected in the agent's reasons, must be assumed.[31] Cudworth infers that human agents are not necessarily determined 'by causes antecedent' (FW, ch. 4 = H 164). If 'causes antecedent' are causes external to agents, his inference is plausible, but it does not refute determinism.

It is difficult to decide where Cudworth disagrees with Hobbes, because neither of them clearly distinguishes two claims: (1) Every event is necessitated by antecedent events, i.e., for every event there is some antecedent event that is causally sufficient for it. (2) Every event is necessary, i.e., it is not possible for it not to happen. Hobbes seems to confuse the two claims in saying that 'every sufficient cause is a necessary cause' (discussed by Cudworth in ch. 22 = H 203). If he just means that every sufficient condition necessitates its effect, this is an analytic truth. If he means that every sufficient condition is a condition that could not possibly not have obtained, and that therefore its effect could not possibly have not obtained, this does not follow from the definition of a sufficient condition.

Cudworth does not point out precisely this flaw in Hobbes's argument. He observes that an agent may be sufficient to bring about an action, by having sufficient power, to bring it about, but may nonetheless choose not to bring it about. This answer does not meet Hobbes's argument; when Hobbes speaks of a 'sufficient cause', he probably means an event that is a sufficient condition, but when Cudworth speaks of a sufficient cause, he does not refer to an event, but to an agent (who does not provide a sufficient condition). Hence he does not grasp exactly where Hobbes goes wrong.

For present purposes, however, it does not matter whether Cudworth is exactly right in his inferences from presumed facts about choices between equally choiceworthy alternatives. For, whatever kind of contingency he sees in these choices, he does not take it to be characteristic of moral responsibility. He argues that the liberty of indifference between equally balanced alternatives is irrelevant to moral responsibility, since no one is reasonably praised or blamed for choosing either one of x or y rather than the other when there is nothing to choose between them.[32] Hence his eventual position on the issues about determinism is this: (1) Examples involving indifference show that determinism must be false for some human choices. (2) But this sort of indifference is irrelevant to moral responsibility. (3) Responsibility requires a type of spontaneity that excludes necessity.

This position is still obscure. Does Cudworth take his third claim to exclude determinism? This is obscure because of his obscurities about necessitation and external determination. If deliberation has the role he attributes to it, external events do not necessitate human actions apart from how we deliberate and choose. But he could say this without rejecting determinism. Since some of his obscurities about necessitation and necessity correspond to Hobbes's obscurities, he fails to distinguish the Hobbesian views that are

---

[31] Cudworth answers this suggestion: 'But if you will say there was some hidden, necessarily determinating in this case, then if the trial should be made a hundred times over and over again, or by a hundred several persons, there is no reason why we must not allow that all of them must needs take the same guinea every time, that is either the first, or second, or third, etc., of them, as they lie in order from the right or left hand.' (FW, ch. 4 = H 164)

[32] 'But this contingent liberty of self-determination, which we have hitherto spoken of ... where there is a perfect equality in objects and a mere fortuitous self-determination, is not that *autoexousion*, that *liberum arbitrium*, which is the foundation of praise or dispraise ...' (FW, ch. 5 = H 166 = R 141)

inconsistent with his position from the determinist view that is (apparently) consistent with it.[33]

Still, Cudworth effectively attacks Hobbes's account of what free choice ought to consist in, from a compatibilist point of view. In Cudworth's view, human action is free and responsible to the extent that it is determined by practical reason and deliberation picking out the action that seems better on the whole. He rejects the Hobbesian view that prudent, rational action is simply the product of the strongest desire. Hence Cudworth infers that, given a correct account of freewill and rational choice, the Hobbesian account of action implies that there is no freewill. Hobbes's anti-rationalism about action and motivation raises a serious difficulty for human freedom, once we combine it with a plausible account of freewill. Hobbes conceals this difficulty only because he combines his anti-rationalist account of action with an account of freewill that is open to Cudworth's objections. On these questions Cudworth shows, both intentionally and unintentionally, that some aspects of the Scholastic position are more plausible than Hobbes's position.

546. The Nature of the Will and the Basis of Ethics

Cudworth sets out to defend neither the intellectualist nor the voluntarist conceptions of freedom embraced by different Scholastics. But his conclusion is closer than he realizes to the intellectualist position of Aquinas. He does not place freedom in an arbitrary choice that is indifferent to the comparative value of different options. He ascribes this freedom of arbitrary choice both to human and to divine wills, but he does not take it to be the sort of freedom that supports praise and blame. He does not take God's choices to result from the freewill that supports praise and blame; for the ways in which human choice goes beyond certain knowledge are alien to divine perfection.[34] God has liberty, but not freewill. Descartes's doctrine of the creation of the eternal truths makes these truths the result of God's arbitrary and contingent choice. Cudworth argues, on the contrary, that God's liberty consists in acting in accordance with the nature of the goodness and wisdom that necessarily belong to God.[35]

This opposition to voluntarism connects Cudworth's doctrine of the will with his conception of the basis of morality. If we accept a voluntarist account of divine freedom, we object, as Scotus and Ockham object, to a naturalist conception of natural law, on the ground that it limits divine freedom. Hence we treat the principles of natural law as the products of divine commands that are not constrained by any prior standards of goodness or rightness.

---

[33] Price's discussion of freewill (see §809) is obscure on the same questions about 'necessity'.

[34] 'So that it cannot belong to God or a perfect being to have a self-intending and self-remitting power, a self-improving and self-impairing power, a self-advancing and self-depressing. . . . Moreover a perfect being cannot have any such power of stretching its judgment beyond certain knowledge . . .' (*FW*, ch. 14 = H 185–6)

[35] 'Whereas according to Scripture God is a nature of infinite love, goodness, or benignity, displaying itself according to infinite and perfect wisdom, and governing rational creatures in righteousness, and this is liberty of the Deity, so that it consisteth not in infinite indifferency blindly and arbitrarily determining all things. There is a nature of goodness, and a nature of wisdom antecedent to the will of God, which is the rule and measure of it.' (*FW*, ch. 14 = H 187)

In Cudworth's view, the voluntarist account of morality reflects an error about the nature of freedom in general, about the sort of freedom that belongs to the divine will, and about the nature of morality. Voluntarists mistakenly believe that a naturalist account of morality would limit divine freedom. Once we find the correct account of freedom, we see that a correct naturalist account of morality does not limit divine freedom.

Against voluntarism, therefore, Cudworth affirms 'eternal and immutable morality'. This is certainly part of the general philosophical outlook that he claims to derive from Plato. But it is also relevant to the qualified defence of Scholastic views against Hobbes; in this respect it is continuous with the aims of his work on freewill.

Cudworth attacks Hobbes from two directions. On the one hand, internal difficulties in Hobbes's position, as judged by Hobbes's standards and by the standards of ordinary moral judgment, show that we must recognize objective moral properties and facts. On the other hand, Platonic metaphysics provides an account of reality that makes the existence of such properties and facts intelligible. Cudworth does not systematically distinguish these two directions of argument. But for our present purposes we may examine his arguments on the assumption that we are not antecedently convinced of his metaphysical framework.

He enters a debate about voluntarism and the basis of morality that is partly defined by Suarez's examination of the merits of different forms of voluntarism and naturalism about natural law. Culverwell's discourse shows that Cudworth's contemporaries in Cambridge were familiar with the Scholastic disputes. Though it is not clear how much Hobbes knew directly about these disputes, he accepts a voluntarist account of the relation between divine commands and morality.

But though Cudworth takes part in this debate, he also extends it to embrace questions that the Scholastics do not explicitly discuss. These questions arise in the discussion of nature and law (or convention; *nomos*) that he finds in Plato. Protagoras maintains that justice is determined by the law of a particular state, and Cudworth finds this position both in the outlook of the 'vulgar' and in Hobbes.[36] Against this 'positive' view of morality he defends the Platonic view that morality is eternal and immutable.

He believes that the Protagorean position opposed by Plato makes the same basic errors as those he finds in theological voluntarism. A positivist view makes morality 'mutable' because it implies that morality changes with the provisions of positive law in different places and times. The theological voluntarist tries to avoid this sort of mutability by treating morality as the unchanging commands of an eternal legislator. Hobbes accepts voluntarism by treating the laws of nature as the commands of God.[37] Descartes accepts voluntarism for the eternal truths, by treating them as the products of the divine will (*EIM* i 3.1–5 = H 22–5).

---

[36] 'As the vulgar generally look no higher for the original of moral good and evil, just and unjust, than the codes and pandects, the tables and laws of their country and religion; so there have not wanted pretended philosophers in all ages who have asserted nothing to be good and evil, just and unjust, naturally and immutably; but that all these things were positive, arbitrary and factitious only.' (*EIM* i 1.1 = H 9 = R 119) As Cudworth describes Hobbes's position, '. . . there are no authentic doctrines concerning just and unjust, good and evil, except the laws which are established in every city: and that it concerns none to inquire whether an action shall be reputed just or unjust, good or evil, except such only whom the community have appointed to be the interpreters of their laws.' (*EIM* i 1.4 = H 13) He quotes from Hobbes, *Civ.*, Pref. 8.

[37] '. . . certain it is, that divers modern theologers do not only seriously, but zealously contend in like manner, that there is nothing absolutely, intrinsically and naturally good and evil, just and unjust, antecedently to any positive

Cudworth answers that theological voluntarism repeats the mistake of Protagoras and Hobbes.

Cudworth attributes voluntarism both to modern theologians and to Scholastics; the Scholastics he cites are Ockham, Pierre d'Ailly, and André de Neufchâteau.[38] He quotes a passage in Latin to summarize Ockham's views. This is not a direct quotation from Ockham; nor does Cudworth say it is. The passage appears in Suarez's presentation of the voluntarist position. Suarez also mentions Cudworth's other two authorities.[39] Cudworth repeats Suarez's paraphrase of Ockham. He omits Suarez's reference to Gerson, who is said simply to 'tend' towards the voluntarist view, but he retains the references to the two authorities who, according to Suarez, maintain it 'broadly' and 'most broadly'. He has probably read Suarez, since he summarizes precisely the remarks that describe the extreme voluntarist view.[40]

Cudworth agrees with Suarez in defending moral properties that are eternal and immutable, in the sense that they are not subject to change either by human legislation or by the unqualified power of God. Suarez offers an account of moral properties, to explain why they are eternal and immutable in this sense. Does this account influence Cudworth, and does Cudworth change it significantly? These questions would be worth asking even if Cudworth had never heard of Suarez, but they are especially worth asking if Cudworth read Suarez and tried to make up his mind about Suarez's position.

He goes beyond Suarez in his conception of the history and philosophical significance of voluntarism. Cudworth connects the mediaeval debate with disputes in ancient philosophy about nature and convention, and so he allows himself to use the arguments for naturalism against voluntarism as arguments for objectivity. The connexion between positivism and voluntarism may have occurred to him because of his reflexions on Plato. He believes that the arguments inspired by Suarez support Plato's rejection of a positive and legislative conception of morality. He refers primarily to the *Theaetetus* and to the *Laws* (*EIM* i 1.1 = H 9), and he discusses the statement and refutation of Protagoras' position in the *Theaetetus* (esp. ii 1–3).[41] It is surprising that he does not consider Plato's discussion of theological voluntarism in the *Euthyphro*. He does not point out that the Scholastic voluntarists revive the position attacked by Socrates in the *Euthyphro*.[42]

---

command or prohibition of God; but that the arbitrary will and pleasure of God (that is, an omnipotent being devoid of all essential and natural justice) by its commands and prohibitions, is the first and only rule and measure thereof. . . . For though the ancient fathers of the Christian Church were very abhorrent from this doctrine . . . it crept up afterward in the scholastic age, Ockham being among the first that maintained "nullum actum malum esse nisi quatenus a Deo prohibitum, et qui non possit fieri bonus, si a Deo praecipiatur; et e converso". . . . And herein Petrus Alliacus and Andreas de Novo Castro, with others, quickly followed him' (*EIM* i 1.5 = H 14).

[38] Hutton, *EIM* 14n, suggests that these references are a sign of a seventeenth-century revival of Scholasticism in England, but she does not mention Suarez. The quotation from Ockham, and references to Pierre d'Ailly and André de Neufchâteau (among others) appear in Suarez, *De leg.* ii 6.4. On Ockham cf. §399.

[39] Quoted in §435n88.

[40] The summary of Ockham appears in Taylor, *DD* ii c1 rule 1 = *Works* xi 226. See §539. Like Suarez, but unlike Cudworth, Taylor refers to Ockham 2.19 ad3–4. It is likely, then, that both Taylor and Cudworth had read Suarez. Culverwell and Cudworth were both in Cambridge in the 1640s and 1650s. Taylor had been an undergraduate there in the early 1630s.

[41] He also refers to the attack on legal positivism in the *Minos* (*EIM* iv 6.3 = H 144).

[42] Passmore, *RC* 41, comments on Cudworth's treatment of positivism and theological voluntarism: 'Against all such theories he asserts a general logical principle, derived, as he points out, from Plato's *Euthyphro*: "It is a thing which we

Though Cudworth's silence is surprising, it is explicable. The Scholastic disputes, as summarized by Suarez, provide him with a well-defined problem that can be discussed without explicit reference to Plato. He may nonetheless recall the fact that Plato discusses both voluntarism and positivism.[43] Plato does not suggest that both positions rest on the same errors, but his treatment of them may have suggested the connexion that Cudworth asserts.

547. The Question about Immutability

In attacking the theological as well as the legal conception of morality, Cudworth clarifies his views on eternity and immutability. If God has commanded these laws from eternity, and always will command them, morality is apparently eternal, and no more subject to change than any laws of nature that God decides not to change. But this sort of eternality and immutability does not satisfy Cudworth.[44] Theological voluntarism ensures only that morality is unchanging, not that it is immutable; if it is to be immutable, it must be immune to changes in some counterfactual circumstances as well as in the actual world. The positivist and the theological moralist must agree that if the legislator changed his mind, right and wrong would change too.

shall very easily demonstrate, that moral good and evil, just and unjust, honest and dishonest, (if they be not mere names, without any significance, or names for nothing else but willed and commanded, but have a reality in respect of the persons obliged to do and avoid them), cannot be arbitrary things, made by will without nature, because it is universally true that things are what they are not by will but by nature." ' This passage from *EIM* i 2.1 contains no explicit reference to the *Euthyphro*; nor does the context. Hence Passmore's claim that Cudworth 'points out' the derivation of his argument from the *Euthyphro* is puzzling. The significance of Cudworth's argument is discussed by Tulloch, *RTCP* ii 284–90 (who underestimates the force of the argument), and Prior, *LBE* (who attaches it too closely to Moore's argument about the naturalistic fallacy). See §815.

[43] Cudworth quotes the *Euthyphro*, in his Sermon before the House of Commons: 'Now I say, the very proper character and essential tincture of God himself is nothing else but goodness. Nay, I may be bold to add, that God is therefore God because he is the highest and most perfect good: and good is not therefore good, because God out of an arbitrary will of his would have it so. Whatsoever God doth in the world, he doth it as it is suitable to the highest goodness; the first idea and fairest copy of which is his own essence. Virtue, and holiness in creatures, as Plato well discourseth in his Euthyphro, are not "therefore good because God loveth them", and will have them be accounted such; but rather, "God loveth them because they are in themselves simply good". Some of our own authors go a little further yet, and tell us; that God doth not fondly love himself, because he is himself, but therefore he loveth himself because he is the highest and most absolute goodness: so that if there could be any thing in the world better than God, God would love that better than himself: but because he is essentially the most perfect good; therefore he cannot but love his own goodness, infinitely above all other things.' (Sermon to House of Commons = Patrides, *CP* 102. I have used inverted commas where Cudworth uses italics, apparently indicating an intended quotation or paraphrase.) Shorey, *PAM* 201, notices the connexion with Plato: 'Another fundamental Platonic trait in Cudworth is his insistence on the sovereignty of ethics and the autonomy of the moral law. Against many mediaeval and Renaissance thinkers he reaffirms in substance the principle of the *Euthyphro* (10a ff) that right is right not because God loves it or wills it but God wills it because it is right and the whole of his *Immutable Morality* and many passages of his *True Intellectual System of the Universe* are in effect reiterations of Plato's faith that morality is of the nature of things, and his assurance that the moral law is as certain as the existence of the island of Crete (*Laws* 662b).'

[44] He quotes and criticizes Descartes's attempt to safeguard immutability: '[Descartes:] 'I do not think that the essences of things, and those mathematical truths which can be known of them, are independent on God; but I think nevertheless that because God so willed, and so ordered, therefore they are immutable and eternal'; [Cudworth replies] which is plainly to make them in their own nature mutable.' (*EIM* i 3.3 = H 24) On Descartes's voluntarism and the eternal truths see Bolton, 'Universals' 197; Descartes, *Replies* vi = AT vii 432–6; Letters to Mersenne, 15 April, 27 May 1630 = AT i 143–54. Cf. Ockham, §396.

Cudworth argues, therefore, that if F-ness and rightness are identical, it follows that if x changes from being F to being not-F, x ceases to be right. Conversely, if it is not the case that if x changes from being F to being not F, then x ceases to be right, it follows that F-ness and rightness are not identical. In the latter case, rightness is immutable in relation to F-ness. To see what Cudworth means by claiming that morality is eternal and immutable, we need to find the range of properties in relation to which it is immutable.

Does this range include all properties, so that moral properties are absolutely immutable? Such a broad range would rule out necessary connexions between any one moral property and any other. If it is necessarily true that good is what ought to be chosen by a rational agent, and that the right is what is required by impartial reason, good and right are mutable in relation to these other properties. If they were not mutable even to this extent, they would be absolutely simple.[45]

Cudworth, however, does not seem to affirm their absolute simplicity. Asserting the mutability of right and wrong, in his view, is parallel to asserting the mutability of the nature of a circle or a cube.[46] He takes his opponents to hold something more than the trivial thesis that we might decide (or God might tell us) to apply the name 'cube' to something spherical. He takes them to believe that the same thing would still be the nature of a cube even though its essence would be being spherical. If he believed that the nature of a cube is immutable in relation to everything, he would infer that it would not change even if the nature of sides and right angles changed; but he does not infer this.[47]

The extent of immutability is relevant to the question of Cudworth's agreement with Suarez. The claims about intrinsic morality, about non-contradiction, and about immutability, reflect Suarez's views as well. But Suarez maintains that intrinsic morality consists in actions that are appropriate to rational nature. He explains appropriateness to rational nature teleologically, as Aquinas does, with reference to one's final good. He must, therefore, recognize some limits on the logical immutability of moral properties; they do not depend, as Ockham sometimes suggests they do, on God's continuing to exercise his unqualified power in the same ordered power, but they depend on human nature remaining the same, and hence on human happiness remaining the same. Moral properties are therefore mutable in relation to human nature and human happiness.

The reference to happiness is not alien to Cudworth; we have seen that the desire for happiness has a central role in explaining rational action, though its relation to the hegemonicon is left obscure. Similarly, the connexion between claims about happiness, rational nature, and moral properties is left obscure. If we notice Cudworth's obscurity, we can identify some central questions that arise in the treatment of immutability by Clarke, Balguy, Butler, and Price.

Once we raise this question about Cudworth, we must also raise a question about Whewell's attempt to divide moralists of this period into supporters and opponents of

---

[45] Cf. Price, §814.

[46] 'For though the names of things may be changed by any one at pleasure . . . yet that . . . the self-same body, which is perfectly cubical, without any physical alteration made in it, should by this metaphysical way of transformation of essences, by mere will and command be made spherical or cylindrical; this doth most plainly imply a contradiction, and the compossibility of contradictions destroys all knowledge and the definite natures or notions of things.' (EIM i 3.4 = H 25)

[47] On the issue about immutability see §§678–9.

'independent' morality. He puts Cudworth firmly on the 'independent' side, and he is clearly justified by Cudworth's opposition to Hobbesian voluntarism. But it is not clear what degree of mutability is allowed by Whewell's notion of independence.[48] Though he takes Cudworth to claim that goodness is an 'absolute and inherent quality' of actions, he does not make it clear what such a claim implies. Must a believer in independent morality claim that moral goodness is absolutely independent of every other property, and hence absolutely simple? Or is it independent and absolute if it depends only on rational nature? Suarez believes that moral goodness is intrinsic to actions, but is not a non-relational property of an action; it implies a relation of the action to rational nature.

Cudworth defends Suarez's belief in intrinsic morality; but Suarez holds that belief as part of a naturalist account of moral properties. Cudworth does not make it clear whether this version of naturalism makes morality eternal and immutable in the sense he intends. In Clarke, Price, and Reid, the belief in intrinsic morality is separated from naturalism, whereas Butler maintains the connexion asserted by Suarez. It is difficult to place Cudworth in this sequence.

Still, this obscurity about naturalism does not affect his main objection to legislative theories of morality; for naturalist and non-naturalist theories of intrinsic morality agree that morality is non-legislative. Legislative theories take moral properties to be mutable in relation to legislative acts, whereas, in Cudworth's view, moral properties are not mutable in this respect. The legislative theory is no more plausible, he suggests, than the claim that we can decide that a triangle will no longer have three sides. Since the nature of a triangle is not mutable in relation to legislative acts, we have no reason to suppose that moral properties are mutable in relation to legislative acts.[49] To suppose that moral properties are mutable, then, is to suppose a manifest contradiction.[50]

548. Legislation and Morality

A supporter of a legislative theory might object that Cudworth's argument begs the question. Admittedly, we might agree that white, equal, and so on have essences that are immutable in relation to legislation, and that someone who claimed to decide that from now on whiteness is going to be the darkest colour would be claiming something contradictory, since he would be claiming that the colour that is essentially lightest is no longer lightest. But those who hold a legislative view of moral properties deny that the essence of moral properties is equally immutable in relation to legislation. The property of being legal or fashionable is clearly not immutable in relation to laws or fashions. The concept is immutable, since 'legal' always means (let us say) 'permitted by the laws currently in force', but the properties

---

[48] Whewell contrasts two schools: '. . . those who held that goodness was an absolute and inherent quality of actions, of whom was Cudworth; and those who did not venture to say so much, but derived morality from the nature of man and the will of God jointly; and so doing, introduced more special and complex views' (*LHMPE* 52). See §520.

[49] 'Now things may as well be made white or black by mere will, without whiteness or blackness, equal and unequal, without equality and inequality, as morally good and evil, just and unjust, honest and dishonest, debita and illicita, without any nature of goodness, justice, honesty.' (*EIM* i 2.1 = H 17 = R 120)

[50] Cf. Suarez's claims about immutability, *Leg.* ii 13.2.

of legal actions that make them legal vary with the laws. Why not suppose that morality is parallel to legality in this way?

Cudworth does not directly consider a property such as legality in comparison with right and wrong. Nor does he give any reason for believing that there cannot be any properties or concepts whose conditions for exemplification essentially mention beliefs, rules, customs, or conventions. But he asks whether moral properties are or are not among the properties that involve conventions. A legislative or conventionalist account might appeal to the fact that in some cases legislation seems to create right and wrong; a law prescribing driving on the right rather than the left makes it wrong to drive on the left and obliges us to drive on the right. Might we not understand all moral rightness and obligation in the same way? Cudworth's argument proves too much, if it implies that—contrary to fact—no legislation affects what is right or wrong.

He answers that, even in cases where legislation makes an action right or wrong, legislation alone does not create right and wrong. If it is wrong for me to drive on the left in the USA, then (1) the legislator has prohibited it, and (2) it is right to obey the legislator.[51] The second condition depends on what is right in itself, apart from any legislation. The rightness of obedience cannot itself be the result of legislation or command; for if the legislator commanded us to obey him, that command itself would have no moral authority unless it were already right to obey the legislator.[52]

Hence, the attempt to create moral obligation simply from commands involves a vicious regress. A command telling us that we are obliged to obey the orders of the commander cannot create the obligation to obey them. For anyone can issue commands of this sort, but they impose an obligation on us only if the commander has the authority to issue them. This authority cannot come from a further command to treat a commander as authoritative; for the commander issuing that command would create an obligation only by having the authority to issue it. Hence not all obligation can be entirely the result of commands.

A comparison with promises clarifies the role of authority prior to commands. A's promise to B creates an obligation for A not simply because A has made the promise, but because it is already true that we are obliged to keep promises.[53] Similarly, B's giving A an order imposes an obligation on A to carry out this particular order only if B is a legitimate commander with

[51] 'For though it will be objected here, that when God or civil powers command a thing to be done, that was not before obligatory or unlawful, the thing willed or commanded doth forthwith become obligatory; that which ought to be done by creatures and subjects respectively; in which the nature of moral good or evil is commonly conceived to consist. And therefore if all good or evil, just or unjust be not the creatures of will (as many assert) yet at least positive things must needs owe all their morality, their good and evil to mere will without nature: Yet notwithstanding, if we well consider it, we shall find that even in positive commands themselves, mere will doth not make the thing commanded just or obligatory, or beget and create any obligation to obedience; but that it is natural justice or equity, which gives to one the right or authority of commanding, and begets in another duty and obligation to obedience.' (*EIM* i 2.3 = H 18 = R 122)

[52] 'And if it should be imagined, that any one should make a positive law to require that others should be obliged, or bound to obey him, every one would think such a law ridiculous and absurd; for if they were obliged before, then the law would be in vain, and to no purpose; and if they were not before obliged, then they could not be obliged by any positive law, because they were not previously bound to obey such a person's command.' (*EIM* i 2.3 = H 18–19 = R 122)

[53] 'As for example, *to keep faith and perform covenants*, is that which natural justice obligeth to absolutely; therefore upon the supposition that any one maketh a promise, which is a voluntary act of his own, to do something which he was not before obliged to by natural justice, upon the intervention of this voluntary act of his own, that indifferent thing

the proper authority that A has already recognized independently of being told to recognize it by B.[54] So far from command creating all obligations of morality, it could not create any unless there were some obligations antecedent to any command.[55]

Some aspects of right and wrong, therefore, are mutable in relation to legislation, because they presuppose the existence of immutable rightness and wrongness determining whether or not it is right to obey a legislator or this particular legislator. If something can become right by being legislated, something else is non-legislatively right and wrong. A purely legislative theory, therefore, is self-defeating.

This argument assumes that any obligation created by a command must depend on some prior obligation to obey a command. Cudworth does not consider the distinction suggested by Suarez, between obligations created by commands and non-obligatory duties prior to commands. We might use Suarez's distinction to undermine Hobbes's attempt to found obligations simply in commands, by claiming that obligations (in Suarez's narrow sense) presuppose intrinsic rightness and wrongness (distinct from obligation). Perhaps, indeed it would have been better if Cudworth had observed Suarez's distinction, instead of using 'obligation' indiscriminately to refer to every sort of moral requirement. Suarez's position allows us to agree with Hobbes's view that the expression of the will of a superior, embodied in a command, introduces a distinctive type of moral requirement. We might agree with Hobbes this far, and still agree with Cudworth's argument to show that some moral requirement precedes any obligation generated by a command.

549. Cudworth and Plato

Cudworth's combination of an attack on Protagorean subjectivism with an attack on theological voluntarism raises a question about Plato; is Plato influenced by anything like Cudworth's argument for the immutability of moral properties?

Concern with mutability is clearly relevant to Plato's treatment of moral properties. According to Heracleitus and Protagoras, good and just are mutable, because the changing character of different circumstances or different conventions wholly determines the goodness or justice of different actions. In Plato's view, this belief in flux is true to some extent, but basically false. It is true, insofar as 'the many justs', the different sensible properties that embody justice in different situations, undergo flux; paying back what you have received is sometimes just, sometimes unjust. But justice itself does not change according to circumstances or conventions. Plato agrees with Cudworth insofar as he argues that the

promised falling now under something absolutely good, and becoming the matter of promise and covenant, standeth for the present in a new relation to the rational nature of the promiser, and becometh for the time a thing which ought to be done by him, or which he is obliged to do.' (EIM i 2.4 = H 19–20 = R 123) On Scotus and promises see §382.

[54] 'And that is not the mere will of the commander, that makes these positive things to oblige or become due, but the nature of things; appears evidently from hence, because it is not the volition of every one that obligeth, but of a person rightly qualified and invested with lawful authority.' (EIM i 2.4 = H 21 = R 124)

[55] Cf. Price's discussion of obligation, RPQM 106. See §818. Smith cites Cudworth's criticism of Hobbes with qualified approval, at TMS vii 3.2.4–5 (318–19). See §786. Some of Cudworth's criticisms of obligations created simply by commands are relevant to Hart's discussion of legal obligation in CL, ch. 5 (though Hart is more sympathetic to a positivist solution, he endorses the criticisms of a Hobbesian theory). Hart and Hobbes are discussed by Hampton, HSCT 107–10.

Protagorean and Heracleitean view makes moral properties mutable, contrary to our belief that they are immutable.

This point about mutability does not apply exactly to the divine legislator. It is easier for Plato than for Cudworth, since he can fairly appeal to disagreements among the gods; if morality were simply a matter of divine legislation by gods who disagree, moral properties would vary among different gods, just as they vary among different human legislators. Plato, however, also anticipates the problem as it arises for monotheists, since Socrates waives the point about disagreement among the gods, and asks whether piety is adequately defined as what all the gods love (Eu. 9d). This makes the problem similar to Cudworth's, since there is no question, for Cudworth or his opponents, of God's actually changing his mind.

Cudworth, however, presses the question about divine legislation further than Plato does. In the Euthyphro Socrates easily gets Euthyphro to agree that the gods love what is pious because it is pious. The mediaeval discussion shows that Euthyphro need not have conceded Socrates' point so readily. Voluntarists maintain that right actions are right because they are commanded. They therefore force Cudworth to make clear a point that Plato takes for granted in the Euthyphro.

Cudworth's argument against the legislative theory helps to explain why both the Euthyphro and the Phaedo discuss questions about explanation. According to Cudworth, what makes it just to drive on the left is the fact that this legislator has commanded it and it is just to do what this legislator commands. We would give the wrong explanation if we said that it is just to drive on the left because it is driving on the left—for that is often unjust. We would also give the wrong explanation if we said that it is just to drive on the left because it is commanded; for not every command ought to be obeyed. These two wrong explanations, as Plato says in the Phaedo, refer to properties that are present no more in just than in unjust actions. To find the right explanation, we have to appeal to the immutable property of justice.

It is sometimes puzzling that Plato argues for non-sensible forms by appealing both to flux and change in sensibles and to features of correct explanations. Cudworth's discussion makes it easier to see the connexion between Plato's different points. In particular, we can see that the appeal to explanation is fundamental. Flux is relevant because we cannot appeal to mutable properties to explain what makes something immutably right. Cudworth's argument against the legislative theory shows why Plato is entitled to insist on an explanatory property that is not in flux; unless we recognize such a property, we cannot explain why it is right to obey a command (for instance) in the cases where it is right.

550. Cudworth and Hobbes

Cudworth refutes any legislative theory that concedes that something makes it right to obey a commander in the cases where it is right.[56] This concession forces a purely legislative theory into a vicious regress. But perhaps Hobbes can avoid the concession. If he claims that right is determined by what the sovereign commands, he need not allow any further

[56] On Hobbes's view of obligation see §487.

question about whether it is right to obey the sovereign. According to Hobbes, it should be neither right nor wrong to obey the sovereign.

Cudworth replies that Hobbes cannot avoid a further question about the rightness of obeying the sovereign. Hobbes agrees that the mere fact of A's commanding B does not by itself create any obligation on B; if I meet a perfect stranger in the street and order him to hand over his money to me, he is not obliged to obey me. Authoritative commands—those that oblige—are different from commands issued by someone without authority. To distinguish the obligatory from the non-obligatory commands, we have to ask whether it is right to obey the commander; and so we raise the question that Hobbes seeks to avoid.

In Hobbes's view, however, Cudworth is wrong about the difference between a non-obligatory and an obligatory command. According to Hobbes, a command imposes an obligation if and only if the commander creates a sufficient motive. He creates the motive if he can attach a credible threat of punishment for violation of the command. Hence Hobbes can distinguish obligatory from non-obligatory commands without conceding that if a command imposes an obligation, obedience to the commander must be right.

Such a reply to Cudworth fits Hobbes's general view that to be obliged is to have a desire strong enough to move us to do the action we are obliged to do. This is why Hobbes believes that the winning side in a war imposes valid obligations on the losing side, insofar as it has the superior power. We have no obligations to obey anyone's commands in the state of nature; for, since no one has the power to compel us, no one can produce in us a strong enough desire to obey the command.

A theological voluntarist might answer Cudworth in the same way. If what is right is what God commands, no further reason explains why it is right to obey God's commands. Admittedly, we need some reason to obey God's commands rather than the commands of just anyone who chooses to issue idle commands. But the Hobbesian answer is available to the theological voluntarist too. According to this view, our reason may be that we love God[57] or we fear him; love or fear gives us an obligation insofar as they provide a motive, but they do not require any further claim about the rightness of obeying the command. This is a voluntarist answer, and perhaps a Calvinist answer. Cudworth regards the Calvinist emphasis on the inscrutable and totally sovereign will of God as the result of a voluntarist conception of the will, and he believes that such a conception undermines any moral reason for obeying God. In his view, the voluntarist cannot give a satisfactory account of the goodness of God.[58]

[57] On the love of God as the basis of obligation see §398 on Ockham.

[58] One sign of the influence of Cudworth's opposition to voluntarism is John Edwards's sermon, EIRGE, delivered at Cambridge in 1699, against theological voluntarist views. Edwards speaks, as Cambridge Platonists speak, of God as having ideas in mind and giving them to us. Most of his argument is not about how right and wrong are distinct from the divine will, but about how they are innate; hence much of his sermon deals with arguments of Locke, Selden, and others against innateness. He argues for universality and innateness from the regret and remorse of wrongdoers, from the tendency to conceal wrongdoing, and to the tendency to offer excuses for it. He uses his claims about innateness to argue against extreme Calvinist views of the total depravity of human beings; he quotes Calvin in his support. (His Calvinism apparently caused conflict with the post-Restoration master of his college; see ODNB sv.) But his acceptance of naturalism against voluntarism becomes clear in his arguments against the power of dispensation from the requirements of morality. He claims that Roman Catholics allow the Pope to dispense from moral obligations, and he attacks this view as immoral: 'Judge whether they do not ascribe more to their great Pontiff than can be attributed to God himself: for certainly it is so far from being in the power of any man to alter the natural and moral law, and to take away the

The claim that our obligation to obey commands rests on a non-moral basis raises a possibility that Cudworth does not properly take into account. Cudworth is less careful than Suarez, since he assumes, with Vasquez, that the moral basis for obeying an obligation must itself be an obligation. Suarez rejects this assumption; he agrees with Hobbes to the extent of holding a legal and imperative conception of obligation, but he recognizes a non-obligatory basis in intrinsic right and wrong. Culverwell suggests a modification of Suarez's position, suggesting that obligation rests on some intrinsic basis, but a non-moral basis.[59] Hobbes and the theological voluntarist exploit this possibility. We avoid an infinite regress of obligations and commands if we recognize an intrinsic (in Suarez's sense), but non-moral, reason for accepting an obligation.

But this voluntarist answer does not defeat Cudworth's main point. Hobbes distinguishes idle commands from those that we have some reason to attend to. But he does not, in Cudworth's view, draw the distinction that we need to draw. Hobbes has simply pointed out that we have a sufficient motive for obeying a command if the commander has enough power. But we normally distinguish this case from the case where we think the commander has the authority to command. It is often reasonable to believe that A has the power, but lacks the authority, to compel B to comply, or that A has the authority and lacks the power.

Since these two features of a commander are separable, authority cannot be the same as power.[60] Since Hobbes's account of obligation cannot distinguish authority from power, it is mistaken. Hence we should identify the proper authority as the one whom it is right to obey; rightness does not consist simply in being commanded by a commander backed by a sanction.

Hobbes might be expected to reject this claim about the nature of authority. For, in his view, a civil authority is created by authorization. We authorize the sovereign by submitting our wills and judgments to his will and judgment.[61] This requirement of authorization might be understood in two ways: (1) Authorization is simply permission and acquiescence; the only difference between authorized and unauthorized domination is the fact that the authorized ruler has been accepted. (2) Authorization is the product of a promise and so creates a moral reason for obedience independent of anyone's power to compel obedience.

Neither understanding of authorization suggests a good answer to Cudworth's objections. (1) If the first is assumed, we can distinguish a case in which we acquiesce in someone's domination from a case in which we believe someone is entitled to our obedience; only the second case implies a real moral obligation to obey him. (2) If the second understanding is assumed, Hobbes traces the obligation to obey back to the obligation to keep a promise, and so he still needs to explain that obligation. If he claims that it is a moral obligation independent of any commonwealth and independent of concern for my self-preservation, he concedes Cudworth's main point. If he claims that the obligation is simply

obligation of it, that it is not within the verge of divine power itself. It is the decision of the famous Grotius . . . God himself cannot change this law of natural goodness, he cannot make that which is intrinsically evil to be no evil. And the reason is, because he would not be God, for his nature would be changed . . .' (21). Among others he attacks (22) the 'great Gallic philosopher' (presumably Descartes).

[59] See §558.
[60] Once Cudworth's objection is developed in this way, it becomes Butler's distinction between power and authority.
[61] On authorization see §494.

the result of concern for my self-preservation, he faces the previous objection that actions motivated by this sort of concern are different from actions that involve respect for genuine authority.

551. Obligation, Reason, and Motive

Even if Cudworth is right so far, the force of his argument is limited. If we distinguish submission to someone's superior power from recognition of someone's authority to command us, Hobbes is wrong to identify obligation with submission to superior power. He can still, however, claim that he captures all that is intelligible in our conception of obligation and authority. For though we might think we have some basis for obeying a command besides recognition of the sanction attached to it, we have no such basis, if Hobbes is right.

This reply to Cudworth's objections requires us to choose between different interpretations of Hobbes's general aim of reducing normative concepts and properties to psychological ones. He claims that a statement about an obligation is simply a statement about what we are motivated to do in the circumstances. Such a reduction might include three different claims: (1) He provides an analysis of the relevant moral concepts, claiming that his psychological concepts are the same concepts. (2) He provides an account of the relevant moral properties, claiming that they are identical to the psychological properties he describes. (3) He argues that there are no moral properties, and proposes that we speak of psychological properties instead.

Cudworth's objections show that it is difficult to maintain the first claim; we distinguish moral obligation from the motives created by fear and self-preservation, in ways that a Hobbesian account of the concepts does not allow. Still, Hobbes might maintain the second claim; he might argue that though our distinctively moral concepts embody some errors, they nonetheless pick out those properties and features of situations that he describes in psychological terms. We suppose that we have moral obligations to obey the law, to seek peace, to keep promises, and (in general) to obey the laws of nature; Hobbes believes that we are correct to believe all this, though wrong to believe that these obligations are different from motives created by fear and self-concern. Since Hobbes believes that the obligations he recognizes are close to the moral obligations we normally recognize, though not coextensive with them, he maintains the second claim. Even if he does not capture the concepts we use to refer to moral properties, he might still identify the properties themselves, avoiding the errors implied by our ordinary concepts.

Do Cudworth's criticisms refute Hobbes's claim to identify moral properties? If moral properties are those whose existence explains something's being morally right and wrong, the nature of moral properties is reflected in the sorts of moral reasons and explanations that can be given by appeal to them. To see whether Hobbes identifies moral properties, then, we need to look for cases in which something seems to be morally right or wrong but Hobbes cannot explain how it is right or wrong. If there are enough of these cases and they seem to be important enough in our basic beliefs about morality, Hobbes has not identified moral properties.

Whether or not this conclusion disturbs Hobbes, it apparently ought to disturb theological voluntarists. For they do not normally seek to reduce the area within which we can recognize moral obligation. Hobbes might not mind if he were convinced that his theory tends to undermine our antecedent conviction that we have moral reasons for obeying a sovereign. But theological moralists ought to mind if they undermine our conviction that we have moral reasons for obeying God; the point of divine command theories is to explain, not to undermine, our moral convictions.

Cudworth's attacks on Hobbes are not conclusive; they often rest on questionable interpretations of Hobbes, and when Hobbes is correctly interpreted, he has an answer to the criticisms. Still, the criticisms point to a central difficulty in Hobbes's position, and a correct interpretation of Hobbes only makes the difficulty clearer. Hobbes tries to reduce normative claims (about what we ought to do and have reason to do) to psychological claims that are grounded in Hobbes's account of action and motivation. Cudworth's criticisms raise reasonable objections to this attempted reduction.

The scope of this argument is broader than the controversy with Hobbes. Cudworth's examination of legislative accounts makes clear a difficulty in any reductive account of moral properties that identifies them with non-moral properties—those that can be applied without raising any further questions requiring moral assessment. Cudworth attacks Hobbes's legislative theory by presenting Hobbes with what we may call an 'open question'. But he does not rely on a purely semantic open question such as we find in Price and Moore.[62] He does not argue that we can doubt without explicit self-contradiction whether what a stronger party commands is right. He claims to find an open moral question; for he argues that we have good moral reasons for regarding some further property as the proper basis for our judgment that a command is right. To see whether this is so, it is not enough to consult our linguistic intuitions about what is trivial, nearly tautologous, or self-contradictory; these tell us only whether we have found an open semantic question. To identify an open moral question, we need to rely on our moral judgment, to see whether we seem to have some reasonable basis for judgment in specific counterfactual circumstances (e.g., where the party giving the commands has no legitimate authority).

Cudworth argues, then, that Hobbesian sufficient conditions for placing us under a moral obligation do not close the question about whether we really are morally obliged. If Hobbes says that rightness consists in being legislated, we can raise a reasonable question about whether a particular legislator legislates rightly. If we try to answer this question by appeal to a further legislator, we face a vicious regress. Hence we must recognize some non-legislative standard of rightness. It is right to obey a commander only if the commander has a moral right to obedience; this further question is not settled by the fact that the commander issued a command.

Recognition of this open question rests on a claim about explanation. Cudworth argues that if what a legislator commands is right, that is not because it has been commanded, but because it has been commanded by a legislator with the appropriate authority; hence commands alone do not explain why an action is right. This diagnosis of the explanatory failure of a positivist account of moral properties applies equally to theological voluntarism.

---

[62] On open questions see §§661, 812.

Moral properties are mutable only in relation to the nature of things, not in relation to anyone's judgments or beliefs or desires. To make them mutable in relation to anything other than the nature of things is to fail to explain what makes actions right and wrong.

To say that moral rightness consists in being willed by God is to make it mutable in relation to the will of God. But we can see that it is not mutable in this respect. For if nothing about the nature of things were different, but the will of God were different from what it is, God would will what is wrong rather than what is right. If God were to will injustice and hatred rather than justice and love, and nothing were different about the nature of human beings and their environment, God would will wrong actions rather than right ones. Since we can recognize that what God willed in these conditions would be wrong, we can see that being right does not consist in being willed by God.

Cudworth's argument does not show that voluntarists are inconsistent if they simply deny his counterfactual supposition and affirm that if God willed something different, that would be right. Ockham sometimes expresses this view.[63] If Cudworth objects that this voluntarist position fails to capture the explanation that we provide by appeal to rightness, voluntarists might reply that rightness does not provide the sort of explanation he supposes; it does not really mention the aspect of the nature of things that makes an act of will right or wrong.

This voluntarist reply to Cudworth rejects some intuitive beliefs about rightness and its explanatory role, in order to maintain a basic principle about divine freedom and sovereignty. It thereby treats metaphysical and theological claims as absolutely fundamental in relation to moral claims, so that it first fixes the metaphysical and theological basis and then accepts or rejects moral claims that do or do not fit this basis. In accepting this hierarchy, it affirms a foundationalist rather than a holist account of morality and metaphysics. Cudworth's view, on the contrary, might be defended as an expression of a holist attitude to morality and metaphysics. In his view, meta-ethics ought to respect those intuitive beliefs about morality and about the explanatory role of moral properties that a voluntarist view has to override.

Cudworth's objection to Hobbes's claims about the legislator is a special case of this general point about immutability and explanation. A voluntarist claims that a legislator or commander can create rightness and wrongness, without any prior moral basis of legitimate authority. Cudworth objects that we can recognize the difference between a command's being backed by overwhelming force and its being morally justified, and that in the first case we do not think it necessarily includes moral obligation. A defender of Hobbes might answer that though we think we see this difference, there really is no difference. To take this view is to reject the intuitive beliefs that make the difference clear to us in the cases that Cudworth describes. From Cudworth's point of view, the Hobbesian position is bound to be mistaken about what makes it right, when it is right, to obey the commands of an authority.

Cudworth's argument, therefore, is powerful, even if it does not convince all possible opponents. It appeals to reasonable assumptions about the explanatory character of moral properties, and to reasonable assumptions about the appropriate method for moral theory in relation to metaphysics. It shows that anyone who wants to revise moral theory in a

---

[63] See §396.

Hobbesian or a theological voluntarist direction must pay a price. The price is steep enough to raise legitimate questions about whether the assumptions underlying the revision are as plausible as they might at first have seemed. For this reason, his argument is a source of important objections to anti-objectivist views. He applies it to Hobbes and to theological voluntarism. His successors apply it to moral sense theories.

41

LOCKE AND NATURAL LAW

552. Disputes about Scholastic Naturalism

This chapter is chronologically anomalous and its title may be misleading. It discusses Sanderson and Culverwell, writing in the 1640s, before the publication of Hobbes's *Leviathan* in 1651, but it also considers Locke's *Essay*, which reached its fifth edition in 1706, just after Locke's death in 1704. It discusses both Locke's essays on natural law, which belong to the 1660s, and his *Essay*, which first appeared in 1690. This period of nearly 60 years also includes some of the works of Hobbes, Spinoza, Pufendorf, Cumberland, and Cudworth. A more exact chronological arrangement, therefore, would place different sections of this chapter in their historical relation to the chapters on other 17th-century writers.

The chronological anomaly is defensible, however, if it allows us to appreciate a debate in English moral philosophy about Scholastic naturalism. Locke's views are intelligible if we connect them not only with Hobbes, but also with Cudworth and with others who reflect on Scholastic claims about reason, will, and morality. The reflexions of Sanderson and Culverwell on natural law form part of the intellectual background to Cudworth as well as to Locke, and so they might reasonably have been considered in the chapter on Cudworth. But since the connexions, both intellectual and probably also historical, between Culverwell and Locke are especially instructive, it is useful to consider Locke's views on the law of nature immediately after considering Culverwell's.

The special difficulties about Cudworth increase the possible chronological anomalies. He probably knew of the general position set out by Culverwell, and even of Culverwell's presentation of it, since Culverwell was his contemporary in Cambridge. It is more difficult to place him in relation to Locke. Cudworth's main work on morality was not published until 1731, but we have reason to believe that Locke was influenced by his reading of some of Cudworth's unpublished work.[1] It may be helpful, then, to compare Locke with Cudworth.

This comparison with Cudworth will be easier if we abandon chronology further. If we follow the order we have used with Hobbes, Cudworth, and earlier philosophers, and begin with moral psychology before discussing normative moral theory, we have to begin with Locke's later work, the *Essay*, and proceed to his earlier and unpublished works on natural

---

[1] See §555.

law. Our composite account of Locke's position, therefore, may not describe anything that Locke believed at any one time. Still, if these cautions are understood, and we do not take this chapter to present an intellectual biography of Locke, we will find some connexions in Locke's thought that are quite relevant to our main questions.

553. Locke, Hobbes, and Cudworth

Locke's views on moral psychology and morality set out from Hobbes's rejection of Scholastic doctrines of the will and the basis of morality. If we are intellectualists about will and reason, as Aquinas is, we have a good reason to accept a naturalist doctrine about natural law and the will of God; for if the divine will follows the divine intellect in accepting moral truths that do not depend on the divine will, we do not reduce God's freedom. If, however, we are voluntarists about will and intellect, we have good reason to be voluntarists about God and the natural law; for the naturalist position will seem to us to deny freedom to God.

Hobbes rejects both intellectualism and voluntarism in favour of his anti-rationalist account of the will. His revised moral psychology inclines him towards some voluntarist claims about the natural law; he does not believe that God recognizes any rational principles that are independently right, or that we can see to be right independently of God's commanding them. We see reason to observe them because of God's irresistible power and the sanctions that God imposes. But God's actual commands are also rules of our self-preservation that we can see reasons to obey apart from the divine will. Hobbes's position, therefore, contains elements of both naturalism and voluntarism.

In opposition to Hobbes, Cudworth maintains a position much closer to intellectualism in moral psychology and to naturalism in moral theory. Though we have seen that he claims to reject Scholastic views of the will, his own position is quite close to Scholastic intellectualism. His moral doctrine is even closer to Scholastic naturalism. He maintains that the obligations of eternal and immutable morality are not the products of divine will.

It is useful, though no doubt too simple, to understand both Locke's moral psychology and his moral theory as an uneasy and unstable compromise between Hobbes and Cudworth. The main outlines of his views seem Hobbesian, but the qualifications that he introduces bring him closer to Cudworth, and therefore to the Scholastic position. The Hobbesian outlines are more influential; they explain Shaftesbury's judgment that Locke struck 'the home blow' for Hobbesian principles.[2] But the qualifications show why one might not be content with the Hobbesian outlines.

554. Reason and Will

Hobbes's predominant view asserts that ends are set by desire apart from reason, and that the function of practical reason is to find instrumental means to the ends pursued by desire.[3]

---

[2] For Shaftesbury's judgment see §608.
[3] I say this is Hobbes's 'predominant' view because he also makes broader claims about reason. See §478.

His sentimentalist successors largely agree with him. Not all of them, however, explicitly endorse all of Hobbes's position. Further questions arise from their treatment of the will.

Some of the questions can be traced through Locke's discussion. He begins by claiming that recognition of the greater good does not move us to action.[4] Here he rejects an extreme intellectualist view that the mere belief that x is better than y moves me to choose x over y. We might prefer the moderate intellectualist view that some desires moving us to action depend essentially on practical reason, and hence on beliefs about the good. According to this view (held by Aquinas), we would not be rational agents if we lacked these desires, constituting a will.[5]

Locke rejects this moderate intellectualist view as well. He does not merely insist that knowledge without desire is insufficient for action. He also holds an anti-rationalist conception of desire as 'an uneasiness of the mind for want of some absent good' (EHU ii 21.31 = R 174). An 'uneasiness' is some desire independent of reasoning about the good. Any exercise of practical reason influencing our desire presupposes some desire, not formed by practical reason, for some end. In each action our end is pleasure, forming our conception of good; our ultimate end is happiness,[6] which is an extreme of pleasure.

The identification of the ultimate end with happiness agrees verbally with Aquinas. But Locke rejects Aquinas' view of the character of happiness and its role in explaining desire. Aquinas regards happiness as ultimate because it is universal; it is not a specific end that excludes the pursuit of other things for their own sake. Hence, our pursuit of happiness for its own sake does not yet give us any specific goal of our desire. On these points Locke disagrees, since he treats happiness as pleasure. If we pursue pleasure as our only ultimate end, we do not pursue types of actions or states of character for their own sake, since these other things cannot be components of pleasure in the way they can be components of happiness (as Aristotle and Aquinas understand happiness).[7]

In identifying happiness with extreme pleasure, rather than simply with pleasure, Locke recognizes that 'pleasure' and 'happiness' are not synonyms. But he suggests that the difference is simply a difference of degree, so that our desire for happiness simply manifests our desire for maximum pleasure. If we desire pleasure as our ultimate end, we cannot desire actions and states of character for their own sake; for these other things cannot be parts of pleasure, though pleasures can be parts of happiness.

Locke does not think it necessary to argue for the identification of happiness with pleasure, but takes it for granted. If we suppose that—contrary to extreme rationalism—motivation

---

[4] 'It seems so established and settled a maxim by the general consent of all mankind, that good, the greatest good, determines the will, that I do not at all wonder, that when I first published my thoughts on this subject, I took it for granted; and I imagine, that by a great many I shall be thought more excusable for having then done so, than that now I have ventured to recede from so received an opinion. But yet upon a stricter inquiry, I am forced to conclude, that good, the greater good, though apprehended and acknowledged to be so, does not determine the will, until our desire, raised proportionately to it, makes us uneasy in the want of it.' (EHU ii 21.35 = R 175)

[5] On intellectualism and rationalism see §§256, 391.

[6] 'If it be further asked, what it is moves desire? I answer happiness and that alone. Happiness and misery are the names of two extremes, the utmost bounds of which we know not . . . But of some degrees of both, we have very lively impressions, made by several instances of delight and joy on the one side; and torment and sorrow on the other; which, for shortness sake, I shall comprehend under the names of pleasure and pain. . . . Happiness then in its full extent is the utmost pleasure we are capable of, and misery the utmost pain.' (EHU ii 21.41–2 = R 176–7)

[7] This question about components of happiness also arises in Mill, U, ch. 4.

and action presuppose desire for an ultimate end, and we suppose—contrary to moderate rationalism—that this ultimate end must be some specific object of desire independent of reason, then pleasure seems the most obvious candidate for ultimate end.[8]

This hedonist conception of the ultimate end is easier to accept if we do not distinguish moderate from extreme rationalism. Equally, it is easier to reject moderate as well as extreme rationalism if we have already identified pleasure as the ultimate object of non-rational desire. It is difficult to say whether hedonism or anti-rationalism comes first in Locke's argument. Each claim supports the other, but both are open to dispute.

555. Freedom[9]

Locke's views on rational desire affect his views about freedom. They both underlie several points of agreement with Hobbes and support some of his objections to Hobbes.[10] He uses Hobbesian arguments to show that we cannot intelligibly attribute freedom or unfreedom to the will, and that we act freely as long as we act on our desires rather than being forced by external pressure (*EHU* ii 21.23 = R 170).[11] He agrees with Hobbes and Hutcheson that action depends ultimately on some non-rational impulse, which Locke calls 'uneasiness'. Apparently, then, he ought to say that action is the result of the strongest desire, so that the greater uneasiness always determines our action.

Locke, however, suggests that this appeal to strength of desire is too simple. We can 'suspend' the execution of our desires; we consider whether it is really good or bad to satisfy them, and we try to decide which ones it is better on the whole to satisfy.[12] This is 'not a fault, but a perfection of our nature' (47). Here we find freedom that is no less genuine than the sort of freedom that implies indeterminism. Determination in itself is no obstacle to freedom.[13]

---

[8] Cf. Hobbes, §478.

[9] On Locke's and Cudworth's views on freedom and autonomy see Darwall, *BMIO*, ch. 6.

[10] On some of these points Locke agrees with Cudworth. This is not surprising if Passmore, *RC* 93, is right to suggest that Locke was acquainted with Cudworth's views.

[11] 'Concerning a man's liberty, there yet therefore is raised this farther question, Whether a man be free to will? which I think is what is meant, when it is disputed whether the will be free. And as to that I imagine, that willing, or volition, being an action, and freedom consisting in a power of acting or not acting, a man in respect of willing or the act of volition, when any action in his power is once proposed to his thoughts, as presently to be done, cannot be free. The reason whereof is very manifest: For it being unavoidable that the action depending on his will should exist or not exist: and its existence or not existence, following perfectly the determination and preference of his will; he cannot avoid willing the existence, or not existence of that action; it is absolutely necessary that he will the one, or the other; i.e. prefer the one to the other; since one of them must necessarily follow; and that which does follow follows by the choice and determination of his mind, that is, by his willing it; for if he did not will it, it would not be. . . . But the act of volition, or preferring one of the two, being that which he cannot avoid, a man in respect of that act of willing is under a necessity, and so cannot be free; unless necessity and freedom can consist together, and a man can be free and bound at once. This then is evident, that in all proposals of present action, a man is not at liberty to will or not to will, because he cannot forbear willing: liberty consisting in a power to act or to forbear acting, and in that only.' (*EHU* ii 21.22–4)

[12] 'For the mind having in most cases, as is evident in experience, a power to *suspend* the execution and satisfaction of any of its desires, and so all, one after another, is at liberty to consider the objects of them, examine them on all sides, and weigh them with others. In this lies the liberty man has; . . . in this seems to consist that, which is (as I think improperly) called *free will*.' (*EHU* ii 21.47 = R 179)

[13] 'This is so far from being a restraint or diminution of freedom, that is the very improvement and benefit of it; it is not an abridgement, it is the end and use of our liberty; and the farther we are removed from such a determination,

The capacity for 'suspension' and rational consideration raises a difficulty for Hobbesian simple compatibilism. It conflicts with Hobbes's view that all action caused by desire is equally free; for someone who acts on passion without the reflexion that Locke describes is less free than someone who acts as a result of rational reflexion. And so a Hobbesian compatibilist account of action deprives us of a type of freedom that is morally significant. Locke implies that, within a compatibilist account of freedom, rationally determined actions are freer than others.[14]

We might think that Locke's views about suspension are easily combined with simple Hobbesian compatibilism. A simple compatibilist can easily admit that rational reflexion tells us whether a proposed action will achieve our end. The result of this reflexion may guide our action by exciting a strong enough desire.

It is difficult, however, for a simple compatibilist, and for Locke, to explain how we examine competing desires and weigh one of their objects against another. Locke argues that when we recognize that there is more to be said for choosing x than for choosing y, we also recognize that it is more reasonable to choose x rather than y, and that in choosing x we choose the better. He therefore recognizes some special connexion between reason and the choice of the better.[15] If we choose the better, we do not simply choose on the basis of instrumental reasoning; for we also rely on instrumental reasoning in choosing the means to satisfy an incontinent desire.

Sentimentalism faces this difficulty even if we accept Locke's identification of good with pleasure. He can say that when reason judges that x is on the whole better than y, it simply judges that x promotes our overall pleasure in life as a whole more effectively than y promotes it. Instrumental reason, however, is equally involved, in showing us what is instrumental to satisfying an incontinent desire. Since Locke insists that our desire for maximum overall pleasure is not our strongest desire on every occasion, he cannot say that we will always act on the judgment about what maximizes overall pleasure.

Why, then, is it more rational to act on this prudent desire (the one for maximum overall pleasure) than to act on the incontinent desire? Contrary to a Hobbesian account, practical reason seems to tell us which end it is more reasonable to pursue; hence it does not seem to be confined to deliberation about instrumental means to some end that appeals to us independently of reason. The same question arises for Hobbes in his attempts to connect practical reason with judgments about the future.[16]

Locke, therefore, raises serious objections to Hobbes's position. He recognizes the existence of rational desires for the better, which do not allow a sentimentalist analysis. These desires cast doubt on the sentimentalist account of freewill and of the virtues; for if the sentimentalist conception of virtue does not make rational desire primary, it seems to undermine freewill.

---

the nearer we are to misery and slavery. . . . Nay were we determined by any thing but the last result of our own minds, judging of the good or evil of any action, we were not free.' (*EHU* ii 21.48 = R 180)

[14] 14 Hence Hume has to deny Locke's comparative claim in order to maintain a Hobbesian view of freedom. See §741.

[15] 'If to break loose from the conduct of reason, and to want the restraint of examination and judgment, which keeps us from choosing or doing the worse, be liberty, true liberty, mad men and fools are the only freemen; but yet, I think, no body would choose to be mad for the sake of such liberty, but he that is mad already.' (*EHU* ii 21.50 = R 181)

[16] See Hobbes, §478.

Though Locke develops the moral psychology of Hobbes in the direction in which later sentimentalists develop it further, he also suggests some reasonable doubts about it. These doubts influence the views of Butler, Price, and Reid. Hence, both sentimentalist and rationalist accounts of action develop suggestions by Locke.

556. Disputes on Natural Law

Hobbes assumes that the non-rational desire presupposed by practical reason is the desire for one's own pleasure. Free and deliberate action consists simply in action aimed at one's own pleasure, If, then, morality has any reasonable claim on an individual, it must also maximize one's own pleasure. Moral properties, therefore, must be the sorts of properties that we will attend to when we become aware of them in relation to our desire for pleasure and the absence of pain. In Hobbes's view, actions that promote our self-preservation meet this condition, since he assumes that we desire a greater long-term pleasure over a lesser one.

Locke accepts Hobbes's hedonist starting-point. His anti-rationalism about motivation and action presumes a non-rational desire for an end, and he agrees with Hobbes in identifying this end with pleasure. Hobbes's next step is to reduce moral principles to counsels of self-preservation. But Locke does not follow Hobbes on this point. For Locke's views on these questions about the foundations of morality we can rely not only on the brief discussion in the *Essay* but also on the earlier treatment in his *Essays on the Law of Nature*. In both structure and content this early work fits into Scholastic debates on natural law. Though it is not clear how much of it Locke still accepts when he puts forward the views in the *Essay*, it is worth discussing in its own right and because it may throw some light on the moral doctrine of the *Essay*.

Locke's account of moral properties arises from the dispute between voluntarists and naturalists about natural law. According to Suarez's 'intermediate' position (as Suarez describes it), some aspects of natural law are independent of the divine legislative will and some depend on it. Natural law is law, and imposes an obligation, insofar as it depends on the divine will, whereas the rightness and wrongness of the acts that it prescribes and prohibits are features of the nature of things in themselves, apart from the divine will. Emphasis on one side or another of Suarez's position results in a more strongly voluntarist or naturalist account.

Grotius accepts the naturalist side of Suarez's position, and Cudworth agrees with him. It is difficult to say whether Grotius goes further than Suarez in maintaining that obligation and law, as well as rightness, belong to the nature of things apart from the divine will. It is clearer that Cudworth goes beyond Suarez on this point, and reverts to Vasquez's view that obligation, as well as duty, belongs to nature and not primarily to will. Cudworth's view is shared by Maxwell and Clarke.

The voluntarist side of Suarez holds that, since the natural law is genuine law, and since law presupposes a command, the natural law, as such, expresses God's legislative will and command. This claim about law does not lead Suarez very far in a voluntarist direction, because he does not take the moral principles prescribed by the natural law to depend on the will of God.

This view that some aspects of the natural moral law, distinct from its status as law, are independent of will and command, whereas its strictly legal aspects depend on will and command, is accepted by several 17th-century moralists. Their degree of commitment to voluntarism depends on their characterization of the aspects, or parts, or preconditions, of morality that are independent of will and command. None of them accepts Ockham's view that what accords with right reason and human nature is itself the result of God's legislative will. Even Hobbes, who goes furthest in a voluntarist direction, believes that what fits human nature is independent of God's legislative will; that is why the laws of nature are counsels of self-preservation. But Hobbes does not believe that God commands obedience to these natural laws because they preserve human society; the commands are not an exercise of God's benevolence or of God's care for creation, but of God's power.

Culverwell, Locke, Cumberland, and Pufendorf reject this part of Hobbes's view; they agree that in some way God necessarily chooses to command observance of the natural law that preserves human society. On this point they agree with Suarez. They differ from Suarez, and from one another, in their views about whether the element of natural law that is independent of command and will is also morality. None of them defends Suarez's combination of naturalism (about right and wrong) and voluntarism (about obligation and law). As we will see, some of the distinctions that he draws make some of the issues between voluntarists and naturalists clearer than the partisans of each side make them. The failure to use Suarez's distinctions may result from the fact that Culverwell and Cudworth do not understand him completely, and the fact that their successors do not seem to be aware of his discussion.

557. Sanderson

Sanderson's lectures on the obligation of conscience do not mention Suarez, but they discuss some of the issues about natural law that Suarez raises. Sanderson is generally sympathetic to the Aristotelian tradition in ethics, and to natural reason as a source of moral truth independent of the Scriptures.[17] He appeals to mediaeval sources and arguments.[18] Like Hooker, he defends this view about natural reason against those who insist on explicit Scriptural authority for any principle or norm binding on Christians. But he is closer than Hooker to voluntarism.[19] His voluntarist tendencies result partly from his emphasis on

[17] Walton, 'Life of Sanderson' = *Sermons* i 50: 'This minister [a friend of Sanderson] asked the bishop what books he studied most, when he laid the foundations of his great and clear learning? To which his answer was, that he declined reading many books; but what he did read were well chosen, and read so often that he became very familiar with them; and told him they were chiefly three, Aristotle's Rhetoric, Aquinas's Secunda Secundae, and Tully, but chiefly his Offices, which he had not read over less than twenty times, and could at this age repeat without book.'

[18] Sanderson shares Selden's attitude to the use of 'Popish' sources: 'Popish books teach and inform what we know; we know much out of them; the fathers, church story, schoolmen; all may pass for popish books and if you take away them: what learning will you leave? . . . Those puritan preachers, if they have anything good: they have it out of popish books, though they will not acknowledge it for fear of displeasing the people. He is a poor divine that cannot sever the good from the bad.' (Selden, *TT* 23) ' . . . without school divinity a divine knows nothing logically, nor will be able to satisfy a rational man out of the pulpit . . . The study of the casuists must follow the study of the schoolmen, because the division of their cases is according to their divinity . . . ' (*TT* 80) As an example of school divinity Selden mentions Scotus.

[19] On Hooker's conception of natural law and his rejection of voluntarism see §414. Gibbs in Hooker, *LEP* (ed. Hill), vi 97–108, 483, exaggerates the differences between Hooker's view and Aquinas' conception of law. It is difficult to see a

obligation. Unlike Suarez, he is not clear on the relation between obligations and oughts, and so it is difficult to say how far he goes towards voluntarism.

In Chapter 4 of *On the Obligation of Conscience* he discusses the rule that guides conscience. He claims first that obligation comes primarily from the command of God, which is the only thing that properly obliges (4.5–6). Correct reason is a secondary rule (4.12). Though it is secondary to the Scriptures in authority, it is also independent of them, so that it guides those who do not know, or do not accept, the Scriptures. In one way it is even prior to the Scriptures; for we need something apart from the Scriptures to identify the moral principles in the Scriptures. Since the Scriptures combine moral precepts with purely ceremonial and judicial precepts, and since they do not tell us which ones are the moral precepts, we need natural reason to say what makes some principles morally required.[20]

The 'innate light' for practical reason comes from the natural law, which moves us to live according to nature as rational beings (4.24). To support this claim from the Scriptures, Sanderson cites the standard passage from *Romans* (4.12, 24). In allowing that the natural law requires us to live in a particular way, Sanderson seems to concede that its principles constitute moral requirements apart from any divine legislation. They depend on the will of God as creator, since beings with our nature would not exist without God's choosing to create us; but they do not seem to depend on divine legislation, since they would still (we might suppose) be moral requirements for us even if God had not also ordered us to obey them.

Sanderson does not say exactly what he thinks on this question. For he maintains that the provisions of natural law are also a law imposed by God, thereby producing obligation. In connecting law with an obligation imposed by a command of the legislator, he agrees with Suarez. It is more difficult, because of the brevity of his discussion, to say whether he also agrees with Suarez's view that God's commands necessarily agree with the intrinsic morality that belongs to actions by their nature independently of divine commands. In speaking of action in accordance with nature, Sanderson may be taken to recognize intrinsic morality independent of obligation (as he conceives it); but he does not emphasize it. His failure to emphasize it may reflect his legislative approach to conscience.

Sanderson's silence on intrinsic morality weakens some of his arguments against those who recognize no moral principles apart from divine commands. He argues that we cannot even use the Scriptures intelligently if we do not rely on moral judgments and principles that are not explicitly announced in the Scriptures (4.16–17). This argument would have been stronger if he had insisted that moral principles are commanded by God because of their intrinsic rightness. If that is true, and if some intrinsic rightness is accessible to natural reason, we ought to be able to recognize at least some elements of morality without having to resort to explicit divine commands. While Sanderson may have this point in mind against his opponents, he does not make it clear.

---

sharp difference between Hooker's 'non-authoritarian' conception of law and Aquinas' conception. Gibbs speaks of 'the traditional idea of a superior imposing his will on inferiors and the coercive sanctioning of the imposition of that will by reward and punishment' (97–8). Aquinas' account of the essential features of law is non-authoritarian in the same sense.

[20] He cites *Leviticus* 9:16, where precepts of different types come in sequence, with no indication of the difference. See §204.

558. Culverwell and Suarez

Culverwell discusses more fully some of the issues that Sanderson implicitly raises; his discussion is especially helpful because it refers explicitly to Suarez. Culverwell is sometimes described as an early Cambridge Platonist, but his sermons published in *On the Light of Nature* do not express a specifically Platonist position.[21] He mentions and discusses Plato among other ancient, Patristic, and Scholastic sources, but does not give him a special place. He defends some aspects of Scholastic naturalism, and especially of Suarez's version of it, against a voluntarist interpretation of Calvinism. He is a Calvinist himself; he opposes both Arminians and Antinomians, and argues that Calvinist views on nature and grace do not rule out, but support, reliance on natural law and natural reason.[22] Though Culverwell's work was presumably known to Cudworth, it did not persuade Cudworth to make similar concessions to voluntarism. It is relevant to Locke's view of the role of divine commands in morality.

Culverwell is not an extreme voluntarist holding the position of Selden or (in some respects) Hobbes. He takes himself to agree with Suarez about the natural goodness and badness, or 'convenience' and 'disconvenience' of things. This aspect of morality is independent of God's legislative will.[23] But, as Suarez and Sanderson argue, a divine command is necessary for genuine moral obligation; the 'height and perfection of a law' depends on a divine command. Culverwell claims that, according to Suarez, natural goodness, without divine commands, imposes a 'natural obligation', but not a moral obligation, to pursue it.[24] Morality and moral obligation depend on a law, and hence a divine command.[25]

---

[21] Culverwell was a Fellow of Emmanuel with Cudworth and Whichcote in the 1640s. Against the view that Culverwell is a Platonist see *LN* xi–xii; Schneewind, *IA* 58n2 (though *ODNB* still describes him as a Platonist). The combination of naturalism and Calvinism is also found in John Edwards; see §550.

[22] Against Arminians see *LN* 14, 187.

[23] 'So that grant only the being of man, and you cannot but grant this also, that there is such a constant conveniency and analogy which some objects have with its essence, as that it cannot but incline to them, and that there is such an irreconcilable disconvenience, such an eternal antipathy, between it and other objects, as that it must cease to be what it is before it can come near them.' (*LN* 55)

[24] 'This Suarez terms a natural obligation, and a just foundation for a law; but now, before all this can rise up to the height and perfection of a law, there must come a command from some superior power, from whence will spring a moral obligation also, and make up the formality of a law.' (*LN* 55)

[25] Some of the reasons that move Culverwell and others to introduce divine commands are expressed by Selden. In his view, only the command of a superior makes actions honesta and officia as well as useful (*JNG* i 4, pp. 46, 50, 52–3). Without commands we lack the relevant sort of moral necessity: 'Pure, unaided reason merely persuades or demonstrates; it does not order, nor bind (obligat) anyone to do their duty (officium), unless it is accompanied by the authority of someone who is superior to the man in question . . .' (*JNG* i 7, pp. 92–3) 'When the Schoolmen talk of recta ratio in morals, either they understand reason as 'tis governed by a command from above, or else they say no more than a woman, when she says a thing is so, because it is so, that is, her reason persuades her it is so. The other acception has sense in it. As take a law of the land, I must not depopulate; my reason tells me so. Why? Because if I do, I incur the detriment.' (*TT* 115–16) Selden infers that morality and religion are inter-dependent: 'They that cry down moral honesty cry down that which is a great part of religion, my duty towards man. . . . On the other side, morality must not be without religion, for if so it may change as I see convenience. Religion must govern it. He that has not religion to govern his morality is not a dram better than my mastiff dog. So long as you stroke him and please him and do not pinch him, . . . he's a very good moral mastiff, but if you hurt him, he will fly in your face and tear out your throat.' (*TT* 83) Similarly, he doubts whether the natural law can be distinguished from the divine: 'I cannot fancy to myself what the law of nature means, but the law of God. How should I know I ought not to steal, I ought not to commit adultery, unless somebody had told me, or why are these things against nature? Surely 'tis because I have been told so. 'Tis not because I think I ought not to do them, nor because you think I ought not, if so our minds might change; whence then comes the

This account misunderstands Suarez on natural and moral obligation.[26] Suarez says that natural law presupposes a natural duty (debitum), to which it adds a natural obligation. By this he means that it is natural as opposed to civil, but not that it is natural as opposed to moral. Contrary to Culverwell, Suarez allows no obligation without law, and no natural obligation without moral obligation; natural obligation is natural because it is the moral obligation imposed by natural law. He distinguishes duty (debitum) from obligation, and makes duty independent of law. Law is not necessary for morality. Though law introduces a moral obligation, it does not introduce moral duties.

The error in Culverwell's summary of Suarez may be expressed in two ways. (1) If he intends to follow Suarez's use of 'obligation', he is wrong to suppose that Suarez recognizes any obligation independent of the will of an imposer who imposes the obligation by a command. (2) If he uses 'obligation' in a broader sense, matching Suarez's use of 'duty', he is wrong to suppose that Suarez recognizes no moral obligation in nature.

Perhaps the second description of Culverwell's error is more accurate. English moralists tend to use 'obligation' more broadly than Suarez uses it, so that 'obligation' applies where 'duty' and 'ought' apply.[27] This broad use of 'obligation' is intelligible, but it may lead us to misunderstand Suarez; for 'obligation' (in the broad English sense) includes both duties (as he describes them) and the proper subset of duties that he calls obligations.

559. Culverwell and the Character of Morality

Culverwell's misunderstanding of Suarez reflects his own views about the necessary conditions for morality. He accepts Suarez's alleged view that non-moral natural obligations are independent of law, but he believes (again supposing that he follows Suarez) that morality requires law, because morality requires moral obligation, and reason cannot bind (oblige) us without reference to the will of God. In acknowledging my action as morally wrong, I acknowledge that it is liable to punishment. If I did not take its wrongness to imply the transgression of a divine command, I would not, according to Culverwell, take it to be liable to the sort of punishment that I ought to accept as justified.[28]

His argument is open to doubt. Culverwell argues that without a divine command I could not regard any of my actions as deserving punishment at all. But why is this? If I understand that action contrary to rational nature is contrary to the good of human society, I can explain why a human society ought to have the power to punish such action; hence I can explain

restraint? From a higher power. Nothing else can bind. I cannot bind myself (for I may untie myself again) nor an equal cannot bind me (we may untie one another). It must be a superior, even God almighty.' (*TT* 69–70) For discussion of Selden see Sommerville, 'Selden'.

[26] See Suarez, *Leg.* ii 9.4, quoted and discussed at §437.   [27] See §818.

[28] 'But what are the goodly spoils that these men expect, if they could break through such a crowd of repugnancies and impossibilities? The whole result and product of it will prove but a mere cipher; for reason, as it is now, does not bind in its own name, but in the name of its supreme Lord and Sovereign, by whom reason "lives and moves and has its being". For if only a creature should bind itself to the observation of this law, it must also inflict upon itself such a punishment as is answerable to the violation of it; but no such being would be willing or able to punish itself in so high a measure, as such a transgression would meritoriously require, so that it must be accountable to some other legislative power, which will vindicate its own commands, and will by this means engage a creature to be more mindful of its own happiness than otherwise it would be.' (*LN* 53)

why action contrary to rational nature deserves punishment. If wrong action also violates a divine command, it is more wrong than it would have been if it did not violate a divine command; but even without a divine command it would not be (as Culverwell suggests) a 'mere cipher'.

Suarez does not offer Culverwell's argument to show that morality requires law; for it rests on assumptions that he rejects. Suarez does not believe that morality requires divine commands. He agrees with Culverwell's view that moral offences would be, in one important respect, less grave, and that we would lack one important reason for avoiding them, if we ignored the legislative and punitive will of God. But this point of agreement does not warrant Culverwell's conclusion.

Culverwell also claims that without a divine command the natural law is a 'mere cipher' because not everyone is moved to obey it on all occasions.[29] This claim proves too much. A divine command and a threat of divine sanctions do not always move everyone to obey the natural law; that is why we need human law with a threat of more immediate sanctions. But Culverwell would destroy his own position if he were to agree that the natural law depends on human commands. To avoid agreeing to this conclusion, he must apparently abandon the argument against naturalism that relies on motivation. Suarez is well advised to avoid this argument, since it raises greater difficulties than it solves.

Culverwell now qualifies his objection to naturalism, by allowing that recognition of intrinsic (but non-moral) rightness influences our action. Even without any divine command, we can recognize intrinsic goodness, and this recognition affects our motives and actions, because of the inherent attractiveness and beauty of the right (honestum).[30] Without commands and obligations, we can still be attracted to some actions and repelled by others, without recognizing any requirement to be attracted and repelled. Perhaps obligation introduces the requirement to choose some actions and avoid others, irrespective of whether or not we are attracted or repelled. Mere awareness of natural rightness and wrongness does not explain the distinctively necessitating element of moral right and wrong. To explain that element, according to Culverwell, we must introduce divine commands.

Culverwell's argument seems to include both metaphysical and psychological (or perhaps epistemological elements). His metaphysical claim asserts that without divine commands intrinsic goodness and rightness lack the element of necessity that is essential to moral rightness. His psychological claim asserts that awareness of intrinsic goodness and rightness lacks the sense of necessity that is essential to a moral judgment, and that this sense of necessity comes from awareness of divine commands.

---

[29] 'For though some of the gallanter heathen can brave it out sometimes in an expression, that the very turpitude of an action is punishment enough, and the very beauty of goodness is an abundant reward and compensation; yet we see that all this, and more than this, did not efficaciously prevail with them for their due conformity and full obedience to nature's law; such a single cord as this will be easily broken.' (*LN* 53–4) Culverwell alludes to *Eccl.* 4:12, which Warburton applies to make a similar point; see §875.

[30] '... there is such a magnetical power in some good, as needs must allure and attract a rational being; there is such a native fairness, such an intrinsical loveliness in some objects, as does not depend on an external command, but by its own worth must needs win upon the soul; and there is such an inseparable deformity and malignity in some evil, as that reason must needs loathe and abominate it. Insomuch, as that if there were no law or command, yet a rational being of its own accord, out of mere love, would espouse itself to such an amiable good, it would clasp and twine itself about such a precious object; and if there were not the least check or prohibition, yet in order to its own welfare, it would abhor and fly from some black evils that spit out so much venom against its nature' (*LN* 54).

We might agree with Culverwell's metaphysical and psychological claims about intrinsic rightness even if we do not agree about the role of divine commands. From the metaphysical point of view, we may say that the distinctive necessity belonging to morality cannot belong to intrinsic rightness; for the necessity of morality is essentially imperative, and so has to depend on will and command, which do not belong to intrinsic rightness. The attempt to build imperativity or 'to-be-done-ness' into states of affairs independent of will involves a mistaken projection of states that can only belong to wills.[31] If we believe in divine commands, we can believe in objective imperativity, because the relevant commands are independent of human wills and choices. If we do not appeal to divine commands, we have to regard the imperative aspect of morality as a feature of human wills, not of the facts they are directed towards.[32]

From the psychological view, we might defend Culverwell by saying that a moral judgment cannot simply consist in a statement about an objective state of affairs. To bind us to action it must motivate us appropriately, through the acceptance of some imperative. It is not enough, therefore, if we simply assert that someone commands us to act; we must accept the command and apply it to ourselves.

If Culverwell had correctly described Suarez's reason for separating natural law from intrinsic rightness, we might have credited Suarez with recognition of the distinctive necessity that belongs to morality. But no such credit is due to Suarez. He does not believe that we can recognize intrinsic rightness without recognizing a requirement (debitum). Suarez takes it to include rational necessity, and hence to support natural duties (debita) in the absence of any obligation (as he understands it). In his view, the rational necessity of natural duties depends on their relation to what is suitable for rational nature. He does not claim that a moral judgment necessarily includes motivation. Hence he does not share Culverwell's metaphysical and psychological assumptions. His claim that natural law requires divine commands, because obligation requires divine commands, is a narrow claim about the distinctive kind of reason given by obligation, in Suarez's narrow sense. He takes obligation, in this narrow sense, to be inessential to morality.

Culverwell's attempt to express the difference between intrinsic rightness and obligation does not capture Suarez's position; it rejects one of his central claims. Though Culverwell believes he expounds Suarez, his exposition incorporates voluntarist assumptions, alien to Suarez, about morality, obligation, compulsion, and command. These voluntarist assumptions conflict with Suarez's basic division between intrinsic morality and natural law. The assumptions are more prominent and explicit in Hobbes, Locke, Cumberland, and Pufendorf; they all abandon Culverwell's unsatisfactory compromise, and prefer a more thoroughly voluntarist position that rejects intrinsic rightness.

560. Parker

Samuel Parker's defence of natural law, in his *Demonstration of the Divine Authority of the Law of Nature*, reveals conflicting tendencies similar to those we have found in Culverwell.[33] He

---

[31] See Mackie, E 40. [32] Suarez on gerundives and imperatives; §442.
[33] Parker's treatment of obligation receives Waterland's approval. See §869.

complains that not much progress has been made in the study of the law of nature, and that Grotius and Pufendorf have not grasped the most important aspects of it.[34] He believes Cumberland has the right conception of the basis of natural law; he seeks to make this conception clear without Cumberland's abstruseness and difficulty. But it is not clear that he adheres to the voluntarist elements of Cumberland's view.[35]

Sometimes Parker argues that we need a demonstration of the existence of God and knowledge of God's designs, if we are to support claims about the obligation of natural law. An appeal to our moral conceptions and our presumed recognition of an inward law is too insecure and unreliable (DA 5); Parker seems to agree with Culverwell's suggestion that without divine commands we have a 'mere cipher'. But he also claims that as long as we 'act sincerely and meditate impartially upon the nature of things', we can find out our duty (DA 9).

He often repeats both of these claims, but he does not reconcile them. He asserts that the existence of God is necessary for obligation.[36] But when he argues against Hobbes's view that there are no moral obligations in the state of nature, he takes facts about the human condition and human nature to require respect for property.

His claims are consistent if he agrees with Culverwell, Cumberland, and Pufendorf in claiming that without a divine command some courses of action are unreasonable, and others are rationally appropriate, but no action is morally right or wrong because none is obligatory.[37] But he also seems to allow obligations and morality independent of divine commands. He speaks of right reason requiring something, and about the extent and limits of its obligation, on the assumption that it imposes some obligation (DA 39). Similarly, an obligation follows from the principle of seeking the public good (DA 40). Nature, not only God, is a source of obligations.[38] Even if obligation includes the necessity of acting in accordance with a law, Parker does not infer that we must assume a divine legislator. He believes that our recognition of x's being necessary for happiness can be source of obligation to x for us (DA 60). Though God adds sanctions, or 'enforcements', to laws, they would apparently still be laws without these enforcements (DA 63).

[34] 'Even Grotius himself has so far mistaken it, as to suppose it obligatory without the supposition of a Deity. Pufendorf has indeed of late harped upon its right definition in general, but has neither described its particular branches nor demonstrated any of the grounds and reasons of its obligation.' (DA viii)

[35] Cumberland is not entirely free of ambiguity. See §532. Tyrrell, BDLN, Ep. Ded., criticizes Parker for insufficient acknowledgment of Cumberland, and for having 'fallen very short of the original from whence he borrowed it, both in the clearness as well as choice of the arguments or demonstrations, and in the particular setting forth of those rewards and punishments derived (by God's appointment) from the nature of men and the frame of things'.

[36] 'For if there were no God, 'tis certain we can be under no obligation; but if there be one, and if he have so clearly discovered his will in all the effects of his providence, he has done all that can be required to establish it into a law, and declare it a matter of our duty.' (DA 23)

[37] '. . . though we should remove the divine providence out of the world; yet not withstanding the right or at least the necessity of propriety [i.e. property] would arise from the natural constitution of things; which will direct every man to confine his desires to his appetites, and when he has his own share of happiness to content himself with its enjoyment, and not to disturb himself or defraud his neighbours without increasing his own felicity . . .' (DA 37).

[38] '. . . nature, and God by nature, informs mankind of these great and fundamental duties of justice and morality; their knowledge is so obvious as to make their obligation unavoidable.' (DA 42) '. . . it is as natural to it [sc. the mind of man] to act suitably to the condition of its nature, as it is to all other creatures to follow the instincts and appetites of theirs; . . . so is man inclined to act rationally by that inward assurance he has that he is endued with reason and understanding; and that alone is sufficient to bring an obligation upon him without any other express and positive command' (DA 42–3).

But despite these apparent concessions to naturalism, Parker reasserts his initial claim that God is the source of all moral obligation. Since God is the author of all the causal relations in the world, we can judge from the good effects of some actions and the bad effects of others what the will of God is; and all our obligation depends on this will.[39] Perhaps he has in mind the role of God as creator, rather than legislator; in that case he may make Pufendorf's mistake of assuming that insofar as God created beings who have moral duties to God, God is the legislator who creates obligations by legislation.[40]

Parker combines these two roles of God in his account of why divine commands introduce obligation. His answer appeals to rewards and punishments both in this life and after death.[41] We can see some reason to follow the laws of nature in their natural consequences in this life; these facts about the world manifest God's creative will. But they are not enough, because (in his view) we have no obligation to be virtuous unless virtue infallibly assures our happiness (86). We would secure the relevant obligation if the Greek moralists were right to believe that virtue is sufficient for happiness or for the most important parts of it (88–9). But Parker disagrees with the Greek moralists. His argument against them assumes a broadly hedonistic conception of happiness, which leads him to misunderstand the Stoic and the Aristotelian and Platonic position. Clarke and Balguy agree with Parker's conception of happiness, and hence with his assertion that Greek moral philosophy cannot assure the appropriate connexion between virtue and happiness.[42] Having rejected these Greek views, he argues that virtue can secure happiness only in an afterlife, and that therefore we are obliged to be virtuous only if we are assured of an afterlife in which virtue results in happiness. According to this view, morality is obligatory not simply because God commands the observance of certain principles, but because God both commands them and attaches sanctions to them.

In taking obligation to rest on divine rewards and punishments, Parker seems to hold a more extreme position than he sometimes holds. He argues against Hobbes that we can see reasons for being virtuous if we reflect on human nature and the human condition, and that these reasons introduce obligations independent of belief in God and an afterlife. In his attempt to show the importance of Christian belief for sound morality, Parker seems to attack some of the grounds for obligation that he has recognized.

Parker's views about the afterlife commit him to a rather extreme version of theological voluntarism. We might argue, as Pufendorf does, that morality requires laws, and therefore

---

[39] 'So that the natural trains and results of things being laid and formed by his providence, when they thrust themselves upon the observation of our senses or our minds, they only inform us . . . upon what rules and principles he has established the government of the world, and by consequence instruct us how to behave ourselves suitably to his will in all our designs and actions. So that it is past all controversy that whatsoever force the law of nature carries along with it is derived upon it purely by virtue of the divine authority. And therefore they cannot pass any proper obligation upon any of his creatures, but only such as are capable of knowing that they proceed from himself, in that all their obligatory power depends purely upon that supposition . . .' (DA 71) The antecedent of 'they' is not clear, but probably 'the laws of nature' should be understood.

[40] On creation and legislation see Suarez, §432; Pufendorf, §566.

[41] 'And now this concernment of the divine providence in our actions being taken into the consideration of our affairs, as it resolves the total obligation of the law of nature into the will of God, so it backs and enforces it with the most powerful and effectual sanctions in the world, viz., the pleasures or torments of conscience, or the judgment of a man's mind upon his own actions in reference to the judgment of God; and this of all things has the most irresistible influence upon every man's happiness or misery.' (DA 72)

[42] On Balguy and Clarke see §673.

requires a lawgiver; but that argument still leaves open questions about why we ought to obey the lawgiver. Parker seems to imply that only one answer is open to us: we have to obey the laws of nature as divine commands, because God has attached rewards and punishments to them. This purely instrumental attitude to morality is open to the objections that Shaftesbury directs against some orthodox Christian moralists. It is also open to objections that Parker suggests; for he argues against Hobbes that we have non-instrumental reasons to care about morality.

Parker's discussion, therefore, usefully presents some conflicting lines of thought. On the one hand, he rejects the voluntarist position that he attributes to Hobbes. He attacks Hobbes on grounds that rely on Grotius' naturalism. On the other hand, he believes that Grotian naturalism leaves too small a role for God in the foundation of moral obligation. He does not reconcile these views. His position supports Shaftesbury's contention that some orthodox defences of moral obligation concede too much to Hobbes.

561. Locke's Voluntarist Account of Natural Law

Locke's *Essays on the Law of Nature* are more careful than Parker's work, but they also display conflicting reactions to the naturalism of Suarez and Grotius.[43] Locke accepts Suarez's claim that natural law expresses facts about what is appropriate (conveniens) to rational nature, and that these facts do not depend on God's legislative will (*ELN* 198).[44] But obligation requires divine commands, because the natural law is a genuine law. To be a genuine law, it must declare the will of a superior, it must prescribe what is to be done and not to be done, and it must oblige (obligare) (*ELN* 110–12). The natural law meets all these conditions.

How much morality, if any, is left if we set aside divine commands? Suarez believes that the foundation of natural law is intrinsic rightness and wrongness, duty, and sin. Culverwell recognizes intrinsic rightness and wrongness, but he gives them a quasi-aesthetic interpretation that is alien to Suarez. Locke seems to see even less place for natural rightness without obligation. If we are not under an obligation, our only reason for action is self-preservation (sui ipsius cura et conservatio). If that is our only reason, virtue is no longer a duty (officium), but a mere advantage (commodum), and the right is reduced to the advantageous (nec homini quid honestum erit nisi quod utile). If we feel like disregarding the law of nature, it will not be blameworthy (crimen), though it may be disadvantageous (*ELN* 180).[45]

---

[43] On the influence of Culverwell and Suarez see *ELN* 36–43.

[44] 'Hence, this law of nature can be described as being the decree of the divine will cognizable by the light of nature, indicating what is and what is not fitting (conveniens) or unfitting to rational nature, and for this very reason commanding or prohibiting.' (*ELN* 111)

[45] 'Since there are some who trace the whole law of nature back to each person's self-preservation and do not seek its foundations in anything higher than that love and instinct by which each single person embraces himself and, as much as he can, seeks to be safe and unharmed, . . . it seems worth our labour to inquire what and how great is the obligation of the law of nature. For if the source and principle of all this law is the care and preservation of oneself, virtue would seem to be not so much a human being's duty (officium) as his advantage (commodum), nor will anything be right (honestum) except what is useful to him; and the observance of this law would be not so much our task (munus) and duty (debitum) to which we are obliged by nature, as a privilege and an advantage, to which we are led by utility, to such an extent that, whenever it pleases us to claim our right (ius) and give way to our own inclinations, we can certainly disregard and transgress this law without blame (crimen), though perhaps not without disadvantage.' (*ELN* 180–1)

Contrary to Carneades, Locke argues that advantage and disadvantage are an inadequate basis for justice. Carneades' view has never convinced anyone with any consciousness of humanity and any concern for social existence.[46] Duties (officia) do not arise simply out of one's own advantage; in fact many virtues are disadvantageous, since they benefit others at our own expense.[47] Since different people's advantages conflict, it is impossible to aim at everyone's advantage at the same time.[48]

Locke's argument seems to neglect a possibility that Suarez allows. For Locke seems to suggest that if obligation (proceeding from the command of a superior) is set aside, all that is left is advantage. Since advantage is an insufficient basis for duties, Locke assumes that we need the command of a superior. But his assumption is unjustified, if we allow natural intrinsic rightness (honestas) as well as natural advantage.[49] Both Suarez and Culverwell allow natural rightness, though they disagree about whether it can support duties. Locke does not discuss their disagreement, because he seems to reject their shared belief in natural intrinsic rightness. Hobbes, Cumberland, and Pufendorf all reject intrinsic rightness. Though Locke does not endorse their position explicitly, he seems to agree with it.

If a divine command is necessary for obligation, what difference does it make? Locke answers that a law is 'vain' or 'pointless' (frustra) if it is not backed by a threat of punishment (ELN 174); this is why the existence of God and the immortality of the soul are necessary for the existence of natural law. We might suppose, then, that natural law obliges us because of God's power, which makes the threat of punishment credible. This is Hobbes's position. Parker agrees with this element in Hobbes, despite his opposition to Hobbes on other points. Locke also seems to agree with Hobbes.

562. Morality and Pleasure

Locke's voluntarism about natural law fits the account of action and motivation that we considered earlier. His examination of natural law supports the moral outlook of the *Essay*, where he describes the morally good and evil as conformity to a law that offers pleasure as a reward for obedience and pain as a penalty for disobedience.[50] He prefers this view to the Hobbist view, and the view of the 'old philosophers', the Aristotelians who believe in intrinsic morality, and take immorality to consist in violations of the dignity of human nature. Against these views Locke asserts that morality is based on divine commands and

---

[46] 'Such an unjust opinion as this, however, has always been opposed by the sounder part among mortals, in whom there was some sense of humanity, some concern for society.' (ELN 204–5)

[47] 'But the obligation of other laws does not depend on this foundation [sc. utility]; for if you run through the duties of the whole of human life, you will find none that has arisen from utility alone and that obliges simply from the fact that it is advantageous, since many virtues, including the greatest, consist only in this, that we benefit others at our own expense.' (ELN 206–7)

[48] 'But if the private utility of each person is to be the foundation of this law, it will necessarily be broken, since it is impossible to attend to the utility of all at the same time.' (ELN 210–11)

[49] Darwall, BMIO 42, reproduces this unjustified assumption in passing from 'utilitas' to 'interest' and 'good'. Advantage is not the only possible element of interest and good; we may also recognize the bonum honestum.

[50] 'Morally good and evil then, is only the conformity or disagreement of our voluntary action to some law, whereby good and evil is drawn on us from the will and power of the law-maker; which good and evil, pleasure or pain, attending our observance, or breach of the law, by the decree of the law-maker, is that we call reward and punishment.' (EHU ii 28.5 = R 183)

sanctions.[51] Conformity to divine law is 'the only true touchstone of moral rectitude' (*EHU* ii 28.8 = R 185); the other laws that Locke recognizes, the civil law and the law of reputation, may be mistaken in their rewards and punishments, but the divine law is always right.[52]

Though Locke accepts Hobbes's basic claims about motivation, he disagrees with Hobbes about how morality appeals to the desire for pleasure. Hobbes believes the laws of nature can be shown to promote self-preservation even without reference to divine commands. He offers his two indirect arguments—from morality to preservation of the commonwealth and from preservation of the commonwealth to self-preservation—to connect morality with self-preservation and hence (according to Hobbes's views on motivation) with one's own pleasure.

It is not clear where Locke disagrees with Hobbes. He believes that divine sanctions are necessary for morality because he does not assume, as Hobbes does, that divine laws prescribe actions that we would see to be advantageous for us in any case. He ought, then, to question at least one of Hobbes's two indirect arguments, but it is not clear which of them he doubts. Since he assumes it is possible to secure one's own advantage by violating moral rules, he may accept the argument that Hobbes ascribes to the fool. He regards morality as a way of securing the public interest, but not of securing everyone's interest.

He even argues that it would be unreasonable to expect God to command us to do anything that we would have sufficient reason to do anyhow; he thinks such a command would be superfluous.[53] This argument about superfluity is weak. Divine commands are not superfluous if they add further reasons. Even if they carried no sanctions, the knowledge that God has ordered us to do something would give some people a further reason to do what they have some reason to do already; the addition of sanctions gives yet another reason.

563. A Return to Naturalism?

So far Locke has rejected any intrinsic morality that by itself gives us moral duties (debita) and moral reasons that do not depend on an extrinsic source of obligations. He takes

---

[51] 'That men should keep their compacts, is certainly a great and undeniable rule in morality. But yet, if a Christian, who has the view of happiness and misery in another life, be asked why a man must keep his word, he will give this as a reason; because God, who has the power of eternal life and death, requires it of us. But if a Hobbist be asked why, he will answer, because the public requires it, and the Leviathan will punish you, if you do not. And if one of the old philosophers had been asked, he would have answered, because it was dishonest, below the dignity of a man, and opposite to virtue, the highest perfection of human nature, to do otherwise. . . . it must be allowed, that several moral rules may receive from mankind a very general approbation, without either knowing or admitting the true ground of morality; which can only be the will and law of a God, who sees men in the dark, has in his hand rewards and punishments, and power enough to call to account the proudest offender.' (*EHU* i 3.5–6)

[52] *EHU* ii 28.14: 'Whether . . . we take that rule from the fashion of the country, or the will of a law-maker, the mind is easily able to observe the relation any action hath to it; and to judge, whether the action agrees, or disagrees, with the rule; and so hath a notion of moral goodness or evil, which is either conformity, or not conformity of any action to that rule: and therefore is often called moral rectitude.' Cf. Schneewind, *IA* 287. Fraser's notes (as usual) try to qualify Locke's commitment to voluntarism here. Fraser cites a letter of Locke's (4 Aug. 1690 = De Beer iv, no. 1309). Locke maintains, as a result of questions by Tyrrell and others (nos. 1301, 1307), that he believes in a natural law, distinct from the will of God revealed in the Scriptures. But he does not qualify his voluntarism about the natural law.

[53] 'It would be in vain for one intelligent being, to set a rule to the actions of another, if he had it not in his power, to reward the compliance with, and punish deviation from his rule, by some good and evil, that is not the natural product and consequence of the action itself. For that being a natural convenience, or inconvenience, would operate of itself without a law. This, if I mistake not, is the true nature of all law, properly so called.' (*EHU* ii 28.6 = R 184)

obligation to come from divine commands supported by sanctions. He assumes that we can reasonably ask why we ought to follow the requirements of morality, and that we have no reasonable answer to this question until we appeal to divine commands. Why, then, ought we to obey divine commands?

We might expect that Locke would agree with Hobbes's answer to this question. Hobbes appeals to God's power. Since God is capable of effective reward and punishment, we have good reason to obey God's commands, whatever they tell us to do. But in the *Essays on the Law of Nature* Locke is not satisfied with this answer. We are required in conscience to obey God (in his view), apart from any rewards and punishments that make obedience advantageous (utile, commodum). Locke agrees with Cudworth's objection to Hobbes, and argues that we are morally required to obey only a command that comes from a legitimate commander, who has 'power and dominion' (*ELN* 184).[54] To explain the nature of this dominion, Locke distinguishes disobedience to a legitimate ruler from disobedience to the orders of a pirate or robber. In the second case, conscience approves our exercise of our right (ius) in consulting our own safety; but in the first, it condemns our violation of the right of another (*ELN* 184). In Locke's view, God is a legitimate commander who is entitled to command.

Why, then, is God entitled to command? Locke seems to see that if we ought to obey God's commands simply because God commands us to, we face the infinite regress that Cudworth urges against Hobbes.[55] The moral basis of God's right to command cannot itself lie in God's command. Locke, therefore, argues that since God is supreme over us and we owe (debere) everything to God, it is proper (par) for us to live by the command of God (*ELN* 186).

This requirement of propriety cannot simply be a fact about God's power. If it is to explain why we ought to obey God's legislative will, it cannot be simply a product of this same legislative will. Hence the requirement to obey God seems to be based in facts about our nature. According to Locke, it is inseparable from the nature of human beings that they are required (teneri) to love and worship God and to fulfil the other things that are appropriate (convenientia) to rational nature (*ELN* 198).

If a principle based on natural appropriateness is the moral basis of our obedience to God's commands, the obligation of the law of nature rests on a principle of natural morality. This cannot be simply a principle of natural utility; for that might require submission to a pirate or robber no less than to a legitimate ruler. If we are required in conscience to obey God, obedience is required by natural rightness (honestas), and therefore by a principle of natural intrinsic morality.

If Locke allows this moral principle requiring obedience to God, he should also recognize other principles of natural morality that we are required (teneri) to observe. Though he does not speak, as Suarez does, of natural duties (debita) in these cases,[56] they must be duties,

---

[54] 'Since nothing else is required to impose an obligation but the dominion and just power of the one who commands and the disclosure of his will, no one can doubt that the law of nature obliges human beings. In the first place, since God is supreme over everything and has such right and command (ius habet et imperium) over us as we cannot have over ourselves, and since we owe our body, soul, and life—whatever we are, whatever we have, and even whatever we can be—to him and to him alone, it is proper (par) that we should live according to the prescription of his will.' (*ELN* 186–7)

[55] See §539 (Maxwell), 548 (Cudworth), 576 (Pufendorf).

[56] He uses 'debitum naturale' at 180, where Von Leyden cites Culverwell and Suarez.

if they are to include some moral basis for obedience to God. Here, then, Locke implicitly agrees with Suarez's distinction between natural morality and the obligation that results from divine command.

Locke, therefore, faces a conflict. When he argues that divine commands provide the only foundation for morality, he agrees with Culverwell and Pufendorf in rejecting natural morality.[57] But he also demands a moral basis for obedience to divine commands, and so apparently has to accept natural morality.[58] Hence his attitude to natural intrinsic rightness is inconsistent, because he refuses to accept the implications of a consistently voluntarist account of the legitimacy of laws and legislators.[59] He raises a difficulty that the critics of Pufendorf expose more clearly.[60]

Intrinsic morality holds this tenuous, but indispensable, place in the *Essays on the Law of Nature*. The same is true in the *Essay*. Even though the *Essay* moves away from the Scholastic framework of the earlier work towards an explicitly Hobbesian position, Locke still maintains that our reason for obeying God depends on something more than our recognition of God's irresistible power.[61] Our recognition of God's right as creator and the recognition of God's goodness and wisdom seem to give us two reasons, apart from God's power, for obeying God.

This remark seems difficult to reconcile with Locke's claim that God would not command us to do actions we could see a reason to do anyhow; for if God commanded no such actions, could we maintain our belief in God's goodness and wisdom? If Locke were right, our belief in God's wisdom and goodness would have to be wholly independent of any views we might form about the tendency of the actions that God actually commands and forbids.

If we believe God has a right over us, and that God exercises that right with wisdom and goodness, we cast doubt on Locke's claim that moral rectitude consists wholly in observance of divine commands. For he implies that it consists at least partly in the recognition of these further facts about God, and therefore in the recognition of further facts about moral rightness beyond divine command. Here as in his earlier work, Locke argues that morality cannot rest solely on servile fear of God, and so he assumes some intrinsic morality. This aspect of Suarez's theory has not disappeared entirely from Locke's *Essay*.

It is difficult, however, to see how Locke can consistently allow intrinsic morality within his moral outlook. Given his hedonist account of motivation and value, some connexion with pleasure and pain is necessary for reasons and motives. If moral properties were entirely divorced from the prospect of pleasure and pain, they would be irrelevant to our action. Since Locke rejects Hobbes's natural connexion of moral rightness with pleasure and pain, he has to assume an artificial connexion through divine commands. This focus on hedonic

---

[57] Von Leyden, *ELN* 39, suggests that Pufendorf may have influenced Locke. Cf. Schneewind, 'Locke' 208–15.

[58] Ibid. 54–8, suggests that Locke offers two accounts of the nature of law and its binding force. He does not consider whether the so-called 'voluntarist' account may not rest on the 'naturalist' account, because of Locke's view about the moral basis for obedience to God.

[59] Ibid. 51, argues that Locke holds an inconsistent combination of voluntarism and intellectualism. Colman, *JLMP* 38–47, objects reasonably to some of Von Leyden's arguments, but does not explain how Locke's claims about God's authority are consistent with a voluntarist position.

[60] On Pufendorf see §580.

[61] 'That God has given a rule whereby men should govern themselves, I think there is no body so brutish as to deny. He has a right to do it, we are his creatures; he has goodness and wisdom to direct our actions to that which is best; and he has power to enforce it by rewards and punishments . . .' (*EHU* ii 28.8 = R 185)

consequences has no place for natural rightness as Suarez conceives it; for natural rightness by itself has none of the relevant connexions to pleasure and pain. Locke recognizes a place for natural rightness in his discussion of God's right and God's wisdom. But if he is right to recognize such a place, the rest of his views about pleasure, value, and morality are open to question.

These views on ethics are not developed at great length in Locke's *Essay*. But they are worth considering, because they bring out clearly the attractions of a Hobbesian position, even for a philosopher who rejects it. Locke presents some clear choices and difficulties that face a philosopher who accepts a Hobbesian account of action and wants to avoid a Hobbesian conception of morality. His views on action and on morality are an unsatisfactory and inconsistent combination of Hobbesian views with some Scholastic naturalist views on natural law and intrinsic morality. Though he goes further than Culverwell goes towards Hobbes, he retains enough of Culverwell's naturalism to cast doubt on the Hobbesian aspects of his position.

42

PUFENDORF

564. Pufendorf on Morality and Law

When Barbeyrac praises Grotius as the pioneer in the theory of natural law, the standard against which he compares Grotius is the doctrine of Pufendorf. His comparisons of Grotius and Pufendorf argue that their two positions agree in substance. We have found some reasons to question his interpretation of Grotius. It will be useful to examine Pufendorf's views, and then to consider Barbeyrac's reasons for claiming that Grotius and Pufendorf agree.

Barbeyrac's view of Grotius and Pufendorf appears to differ from Pufendorf's view of his relation to Grotius. For Pufendorf rejects the naturalist position that he ascribes to Grotius. He rejects intrinsic rightness, and claims that whatever is right is right only because it is imposed by divine command. On this point he agrees with Cumberland (whom he cites). But he departs further than Cumberland departs from Grotius and the Scholastic position, by rejecting Grotius' use of natural sociality as a basis for the evaluation of political society.

In rejecting these two elements of Grotius' position Pufendorf comes closer to Hobbes's view. He disagrees with Hobbes in believing that moral rightness is irreducible to advantage, and therefore is imposed by divine law. But he follows Hobbes in denying that natural properties include any intrinsic moral rightness that is irreducible to advantage. To a limited extent, Hobbes believes in intrinsic moral properties, since he believes that the moral virtues are simply those states that promote self-preservation as means to peaceful and commodious living. But he does not believe that rightness (honestas) consists in anything beyond advantage (commodum); on this point Suarez, Grotius, Cumberland, and Pufendorf all disagree with him.

Pufendorf also agrees with Hobbes in rejecting Grotius' belief in natural sociality as the basis of a commonwealth. To show that the only legitimate moral demand on a commonwealth is the requirement to preserve peace, and that we need a commonwealth in order to preserve peace, he disagrees with Aristotle, the Stoics, the Scholastics, and Grotius. According to these defenders of natural sociality, facts about human nature itself, and not simply about competition, aggression, and self-preservation, make political life appropriate for human beings. Since Pufendorf agrees with Hobbes in rejecting the Scholastic appeal to natural sociality, he has to decide how far he accepts the rest of Hobbes's views about the moral basis of political society.

These claims of Pufendorf might encourage us to conclude that he is really a disciple of Hobbes, and that his disagreements with Hobbes about morality and divine commands are relatively superficial.[1] This is not the conclusion that Pufendorf and Barbeyrac draw from the comparison with Hobbes; they both regard Pufendorf's position as a reasonable alternative to Hobbes's views. We should try to see whether they are right about the significance of Pufendorf's disagreements with Hobbes.

565. Pufendorf's Voluntarism

Pufendorf affirms voluntarism as part of his argument about 'the certainty of the disciplines that deal with morals' (*JNG* i 2).[2] He rejects the view of (allegedly) most of his predecessors, who are misled by Aristotle into believing that moral science is necessarily uncertain. In his view, it is capable of demonstration.[3] Moral entities are imposed by God, but we do not rely on any special revelation of the divine will to know about them.[4] Natural law is natural in the epistemological sense, since we know its requirements innately. But it is not natural in the metaphysical sense; it consists essentially in divine commands, not in facts about our nature. The certainty of moral principles is secured by the fact that they are imposed by a wise and benevolent God in view of the needs resulting from the human condition.[5]

In this statement of his position Pufendorf does not simply affirm that the natural law depends on the legislative will of God. On this issue Suarez and Pufendorf agree against the naturalist view of Vasquez (perhaps followed by Grotius). Suarez believes that the aspect of the natural law that creates 'obligation' (as Suarez understands it) depends on divine commands. Pufendorf's denial of any right and wrong independent of God's legislative will goes further than Suarez goes in the direction of voluntarism; he rejects Suarez's and Grotius' belief in intrinsic rightness and wrongness (honestas and turpitudo) apart from any imposition.[6]

Pufendorf rejects Suarez's view on the role of natural goodness and badness in moral goodness and badness. Suarez derives morality from natural goodness and badness, so that rightness and wrongness are properties of actions promoting or harming the common good of rational agents. Suarez, therefore, takes divine commands to be necessary for natural law, but not for moral rightness. Pufendorf takes them to be necessary for moral rightness as well.

---

[1] See Palladini, *SPDH*.

[2] I cite the 1688 edn. of *JNG*. It includes references to Cumberland, added in the 1684 edn. See Tuck, *NRT* 160n. 'K' indicates Kennett's translation, which I have sometimes altered.

[3] Cf. Locke, *EHU* iii 11.16.   [4] On Pufendorf and autonomy see Darwall, 'Autonomy'; Haakonssen, 'Protestant'.

[5] 'For the introduction of a number <of moral entities> was demanded by the very condition of a human being, which was assigned to him by the greatest and best Creator, in accordance with his goodness and wisdom. And so these, at any rate, cannot at all be called unsure and unstable.' (*JNG* i 2.5)

[6] The naturalist view: '... that some things in themselves, apart from any imposition, are right or wrong, and these constitute the object of natural and everlasting right, whereas those things that are right are wrong because the legislator willed, come under the heading of positive laws' (i 2.6).

Pufendorf presents several different arguments against intrinsic morality: (1) Naturalism denies the appropriate sort of freedom to God. (2) It is wrong about which properties belong to nature apart from will. (3) It is wrong about the nature of moral obligation and its connexion with the command of a superior. If we take these arguments in order, we can identify the main questions that he raises.[7]

566. Nature, Creation, and Divine Freedom

In Pufendorf's view, naturalists believe in some principle independent of, and co-eternal with, God, restricting God's freedom, because they believe in natural rightness and wrongness apart from God's will. Their position is theologically unsound, since God created us by the exercise of free will, and God was free to do otherwise than create us with this nature. Nothing can be good or bad by intrinsic necessity, apart from the pleasure and the imposition of God.[8] When we speak of natural rightness and wrongness, we do not refer to anything independent of the will of God; we simply refer to what is required by the natural condition that the Creator has freely given to us.[9] Human beings with their nature are creatures of God, and so the nature of right actions depends on God's will as creator.[10] A naturalist position makes the existence of human beings with their nature independent of God's will as creator, but Grotius has overlooked this unwelcome result of naturalism.[11]

The view that Pufendorf attributes to naturalism is more extreme than the view of mediaeval naturalists, Suarez and Grotius. All of these naturalists distinguish the creative from the legislative will of God. The voluntarists Scotus and Ockham maintain that, for some aspects of morality, rightness depends essentially on a legislative act of God beyond creation. Suarez is justified in taking voluntarism to assert that the legislative will of God is essential to rightness and wrongness. Against this voluntarist position, Suarez defends naturalism; he claims that once God has created us, no further divine legislative act is needed for some actions to be right and others wrong, because rightness and wrongness are intrinsic to certain actions (in the appropriate circumstances) insofar as they are fitting or unfitting to rational nature. If some creatures have rational natures, some actions are right and others wrong, without any further legislation. The laws that God gives for creation are (as Suarez puts it) 'indicative' rather than 'prescriptive'.[12]

While we may regret that Pufendorf does not follow Suarez by marking the difference between God's creative will and God's legislative will, we might think this does not matter.

---

[7] Schneewind, *IA* 121–2, takes the first of these arguments to express Pufendorf's main concern.

[8] Boyle and Leibniz discuss questions related to this claim. See §586.

[9] 'And truly, as for those who would establish an eternal rule for morality of the actions without respect to the divine injunction or constitution, the result of their endeavours seems to us to be the joining with God Almighty some coeval extrinsical principle, which he was obliged to follow in assigning the forms and essences of things. Besides, it is acknowledged on all hands, that God created man, as well as everything else, according to his own free will. From whence it evidently follows that it must needs have been his power and pleasure to indue this creature with whatever kind of nature his wisdom thought fit. And how then should it come to pass that the actions of mankind should be vested with any affection or quality proceeding from intrinsical and absolute necessity, without regard to the institution and to the good pleasure of the Creator?' (i 2.6 = K 17)

[10] Grotius on creation; §465.   [11] Unde adparet, non satis expendisse hanc rem Grotium, i 2.6.

[12] On Suarez see §425.

Do the Scholastic naturalists concede the essential point to him once they allow that human beings with their nature depend on God's creative will?

The difference between God's creative and legislative will matters for this purpose, because dependence on God's creative will does not distinguish moral rightness and wrongness from other features of the natural world. Pufendorf intends to distinguish moral properties from other properties of natural subjects, events, and processes; but God's creative will and indicative law are present in every part of creation alike. Morality is legislated no more than any other feature of the natural world is legislated; all alike depend on the creative will and indicative law of God, but it does not follow that any of them depend on the prescriptive and legislative law of God.

Dependence on God's creative will does not refute a naturalist belief in 'eternal and immutable' morality. The claim that 'morality' depends on the divine will might mean that it depends on the divine will whether or not any creature behaves morally; this follows from the Christian doctrine of creation. But it does not imply the further claim that what morality is for any creature depends on the divine will. If the principles fixing what is morally right for different creatures do not depend on divine acts of will, the content of morality does not depend on the divine will, even if the existence of these creatures depends on the divine will. And so, even if the existence of human beings for whom justice is good depends on the divine will, it does not follow that the fact that their good requires justice also depends on the divine will. Naturalists are right to argue that Christian doctrines about creation do not affect their claims about the independence of morality.[13]

If, therefore, Pufendorf simply asserts that created things depend on God's creative will and indicative law, he has not refuted the naturalism of Suarez and Grotius.

567. Nature and Imposition

Some of Pufendorf's arguments, however, go beyond the claim that creation implies dependence on the divine will. He allows that some properties belong to nature apart from divine 'imposition', and argues that moral properties are not among them. The properties that he takes not to be imposed are the result of creation; hence imposition implies some further act of the divine will beyond creation. Here he recognizes the distinction between creation and legislation, even though he overlooked it in accusing naturalists of recognizing a principle independent of God and of restricting divine freedom.

To separate natural from imposed properties, Pufendorf distinguishes nature itself from the further properties imposed on nature by the divine will. He argues that nature itself consists simply in bodies in motion, and their effects on one another. No morality can be found simply in movement, and application of physical power; hence rightness and wrongness do not belong to nature in itself, but are imposed.[14] The properties that belong to

---

[13] Contrast Korkman, *BNL* 183–229.

[14] 'So that in reality all the motions and actions of men, upon setting aside all law both divine and human, are perfectly indifferent: And some of them are therefore only said to be honest or dishonest because that condition of nature which God has freely bestowed on man strictly enjoins the performance or the omission of them. Not that any morality inheres of itself, and without all law, in the bare motion; of the mere application of natural power: And therefore we see beasts

nature in itself are those recognized by physical science. Since right and wrong are not among these properties, they do not belong to nature in itself, and therefore they are imposed.

This contrast between moral and purely natural properties relies on a division that has strongly influenced modern meta-ethics.[15] It implies that a post-Aristotelian scientific view of nature rules out the Aristotelian view that normative, and especially moral, properties are parts of nature in itself. The anti-Aristotelian view is summarized in the claim that values 'are not part of the fabric of the world'.[16]

Are the properties recognized by physical science the only ones that belong to nature in itself? Many biological and medical properties fail this condition for belonging to nature in itself; but it does not follow that they are imposed. Drinking sea water is unhealthy for cattle; this fact is not part of physics, but it does not seem to be the result of legislation. Apparently, then, facts about the welfare of human beings may also be natural rather than imposed.

Pufendorf accepts this argument. He agrees that the properties defining natural benefit and harm to human beings precede divine legislation. Natural goodness is distinct from moral goodness (as Cumberland argues[17]), and natural goodness is not imposed.[18] From the creation of human beings it follows that certain things are naturally good and bad for them. Hence 'prudential properties' (concerned with benefit and harm to oneself) belong to nature and are not imposed on it.

These remarks about the natural and non-imposed character of prudential properties cast doubt on the argument to show that moral properties are imposed. For since prudential properties are natural, but are not explicitly recognized in a physicist's description of matter in motion, the absence of moral properties from such a description does not show that moral properties are imposed and not natural.

One might answer that though the physicist's description of the world does not explicitly mention prudential properties, it nonetheless implicitly includes them. The unhealthiness of sea water for cattle is a non-imposed natural property, even though physics does not explicitly mention it as such; for it is wholly constituted by the properties recognized by physics.[19] Nothing more than the sorts of properties recognized by physics, in the appropriate combination, is needed to yield the fact that sea water is unhealthy for cattle, even though such facts are not the concern of physics. Hence no further properties besides those recognized by physics are needed in order to yield prudential properties.

If we accept this argument, however, we cannot be sure that moral properties are imposed. At first it may seem obvious that the worldview of physical science has no room

every day doing such things without fault or sin, in committing which man would have been guilty of the highest wickedness.' (i 2.6 = K18)

[15] On moral entities see Schneewind, *IA*, 120; Korsgaard, *SN* 21–7, esp. 27: 'The legislator is necessary to make *obligation* possible, that is, to make morality normative'.

[16] Mackie, *E* 15.   [17] On Cumberland see §530.

[18] 'But...since God Almighty hath been pleased to create man, a being not possibly to be preserved without the observation of this law, we have no manner of reason or colour to believe that he will either reverse or alter the law of nature, so long as he brings no change on human nature itself; and so long as the actions enjoined by this law do by a natural consequence promote sociality, in which is contained all the temporal happiness of mankind...and therefore supposing human nature and human affairs to be fixed and constant, the law of nature, though it owed its original institution to the free pleasure of God, remains firm and immovable.' (ii 3.5 = K 122, altered)

[19] One might also speak of unhealthiness being 'realized' in properties recognized by physics. The relevant conception of realization is discussed by Shoemaker, 'Realization' (in connexion with mental properties).

for rightness and wrongness. But if it has room for healthiness and unhealthiness, it may also have room for moral properties; for these may be constituted by facts about what is healthy or unhealthy, or in other ways good and bad, for rational agents. The constitutive relation between physical properties and healthiness suggests a way of explaining how rightness and wrongness might be natural and non-imposed properties.

Even if we can conceive how rightness and wrongness might be natural because they are somehow constituted by physical properties, it does not follow that they are natural. Some difference between natural goodness and moral goodness may exclude moral goodness from the natural world. We have shown only that the absence of moral properties from a physicist's description of the world does not make them non-natural or imposed entities.

To defend Pufendorf's claim that moral properties are imposed, we also need to show that (as later defenders of his claim have said) they are 'queer' entities.[20] They are queer, relative to the scientific world-view, if they have characteristics that a scientific world-view gives us no reason to expect. If, for instance, morality required us to believe that some particular things can be wholly in two places at once, but the scientific world-view gave us no grounds for believing that any particular can be in two places at once, morality would require us to believe in queer entities.

This example suggests that queerness might be understood in two ways: (1) One might regard an entity as queer relative to a given science if that science gives us no positive reason to believe in such things. One might agree that moral properties are queer in this weak sense; but many other things are also queer in this sense, and still belong to the natural world. Since physics gives us no reason to recognize the properties recognized by medicine, these properties are queer relative to physics. If moral properties are queer only in this weak sense, they may still be part of nature. (2) Alternatively, one might regard an entity as queer relative to a science only if that science gives us positive reason to disbelieve in such things, or to believe that they are impossible. Queerness in this strong sense would be a more serious objection to an alleged entity; the existence in the natural world of such queer entities would introduce serious tensions into our scientific theories. One theory would tell us that the world is radically different from what another theory tells us it is like, since one theory tends to rule out entities of the sort that another theory accepts.

These remarks about queerness may clarify Pufendorf's arguments about moral entities. To show that they are not natural properties, he needs to show more than that they are queer in the weak sense that his argument about nature and motion has supported. The arguments for queerness in a stronger sense depend on closer attention to the essential characteristics of moral properties.

568. Natural v. Moral Goodness

Pufendorf argues that prudential goodness is natural, but moral goodness is imposed. He no longer tries to exclude morally good and bad actions from nature simply because they are not

---

[20] Mackie, *E* 38, describes the metaphysical part of the 'argument from queerness' in this way: 'If there were objective values, then they would be entities or qualities or relations of a very strange sort, utterly different from anything else in the universe'. Mackie does not intend to rule out the possibility of finding good reasons for recognizing queer entities; see §606.

merely physical movements, since he agrees that prudential properties belong to nature, even though they do not belong to mere physical movements (in the sense previously discussed).

Moral goodness differs from non-moral goodness because morality is imposed on some human actions through law (i 2.6). God's creation of us makes certain actions expedient or inexpedient for us, given our nature, but not thereby right or wrong. We cannot derive morality from our nature as rational animals; for if we consider reason without reference to law and moral norm (legis seu normae moralis), it is simply more efficient in supplying our natural needs. If we try to find what is fitting for rational nature, we simply find that instrumental reasoning is fitting, and this has nothing to do with morality. Hence the Scholastic claim that morality consists in what is fitting for rational nature is mistaken. Until we take account of law, we cannot find morality in human actions any more than the blind can see colour (i 2.6).[21]

Pufendorf here agrees with Suarez and Grotius that actions are beneficial and harmful to human beings apart from legislation. Hence he agrees with Grotius that Stoic claims about conciliation (ii 3.14) are both true and important.[22] But they refer only to natural goodness, and not to moral goodness; the natural benefits and harms of human actions do not place them in the area of morality.[23] Giving a cup of water to an innocent person dying of thirst is beneficial to a human being and has natural goodness, but it is morally indifferent unless someone has legislated it. To show that natural goodness is not sufficient for moral goodness, Pufendorf observes that actions may be naturally good even if they are not voluntary, and even if they are not done by human beings at all; no such actions are morally good.

This observation, however, does not support Pufendorf's legislative thesis. We may well agree that moral goodness and badness in actions requires not only the appropriate property in the action itself, but also the appropriate property in the agent. Since the human good is the good of a rational agent, it is intelligible that the actions that primarily promote this good are voluntary actions for which the agent is appropriately held responsible. Moreover, the fact that we are rational and responsible agents makes it possible for us to be obliged to action by legislation. None of this implies that actions can be morally good only if a legislator has prescribed them.

569. Morality, Obligation, Law, and Command

Pufendorf agrees with naturalists about the content of morality, insofar as he derives its provisions from facts about human nature and what is harmful or beneficial to it (ii 3.13–15).[24]

---

[21] 'For if we considered reason as uninformed with the knowledge and sense of law, or of some moral rule, it might perhaps even in this condition furnish man with the faculty of acting more expeditiously and more accurately than beasts, and might assist the natural powers by an additional shrewdness or subtlety. But that it should be able to discover any morality in human actions, without reflecting on some law, is equally impossible as that a man born blind should make a judgment on the distinction of colours.' (i 2.6 = K 18)

[22] Pufendorf quotes Cic. F. iii 5 and other Stoic texts (and Barbeyrac adds further passages).

[23] 'But this very natural goodness and badness of actions in themselves does not at all place them in the area of morals.' (i 2.6)

[24] As Barbeyrac says (note 1 on ii 3.14), 'The very name of natural right shows us that the principles ought to be deduced from the nature of man, as many of the ancients have acknowledged'. He quotes Cic. Leg. i 5; Marcus Aurelius × 2.

But he denies that these facts alone constitute morality. To explain where a naturalist account of moral properties fails, he asserts: (1) The relevant deontic concepts—right, wrong, duty, and so on—presuppose some reference to a norm and a law. (2) A law requires a command by a superior. On the second point, he follows Suarez. But on the first point he follows Selden against Suarez.[25]

Pufendorf does not defend himself on the first point, but his claim needs defence. To say that right and wrong (honestum, turpe) presuppose some norm (norma) or (as Suarez puts it) some rule (regula) is plausible. But to assert without argument that this rule must be a law is to overlook a distinction that Suarez maintains.

If one believed that Suarez is too rigid in separating laws from rules and norms in general, one might accept Pufendorf's first point. Selden says that the distinction of good and evil, or rightness (honestas) and wrongness (turpitudo), comes from 'right' (ius). One might agree with this claim, but still deny that moral properties require legislation; that is why Vasquez, for instance, asserts that not every ius is a lex.[26] But if we accept Pufendorf's first point, so understood, we will not immediately accept his second point. For if we take 'law', 'norm', 'right' (ius), and 'rule' to be equivalent, we agree with Aquinas' view (sometimes) that none of these requires any command by a superior.

Pufendorf's two claims, therefore, undermine each other. They are consistent, but it is difficult to see a good reason for accepting both of them in the sense that Pufendorf intends. Reflexion on Vasquez and Suarez suggests that the best argument for accepting either of them is an equally good argument for rejecting the other.

If we ignore the broad use of 'law', and so concede Pufendorf's second point, the issue turns on Suarez's naturalist claim about rightness and wrongness, also accepted by Grotius. According to Suarez, actions are right and wrong, and we have a duty to perform and omit them, because of their own nature (in relation to rational beings), apart from any law. Pufendorf disagrees; even if we do not rely on any human law in regarding actions as right and wrong, we nonetheless (in his view) rely on a divine law.

Why should we agree with Pufendorf on this point? Against his view Suarez claims that God imposes the natural law only by commanding actions that are right and wrong in themselves. The counterfactual supposition used by Gregory of Rimini, Suarez, and Grotius to show that we would recognize intrinsic morality apart from beliefs about the existence of God or God's concern for human good and harm raises a reasonable doubt about Pufendorf's legislative thesis.

570. The Errors of Naturalism

Pufendorf defends his legislative view by arguing that naturalism is inconsistent. If we were to recognize intrinsic morality antecedent to any law, we would be committed, in his view,

---

[25] 'For since (1) rightness (honestas)—or moral necessity—and wrongness are characteristics of human actions, arising from agreement or disagreement with a norm or a law, and since (2) law is a command of a superior, it is not clear how rightness or wrongness could be understand before law and in advance of imposition by a superior. As Selden says: "From right (ius) the distinction of good and evil, or wrong and right (honestum) is produced in actions. From this there arises in persons obligation (obligatio) and requirement (debitum) to fulfil a duty (officium)." ' (i 2.6; reference numbers added)

[26] On Vasquez see §429.

to these inconsistent claims: (1) All obligation is imposed by a superior. (2) If A's action is morally good or evil, A is obliged to do or refrain from the action.[27] (3) Actions are morally good or evil apart from legislation. (4) Hence we are obliged, apart from legislation, to do or avoid them. (5) Hence not all obligation is imposed by a superior.

A naturalist, however, need not accept all these claims. If we agree with Suarez, we accept the first, but not the second. If we agree with Vasquez, we accept the second, but not the first. As we have seen, it is not clear which position Grotius takes, and so it is not entirely unfair for Pufendorf to suggest that Grotius is committed to both (1) and (2). He is right to maintain that the acceptance of both steps conflicts with the belief in intrinsic rightness and wrongness. But both Suarez and Vasquez offer Grotius ways to preserve intrinsic rightness. Since naturalists have good reasons for rejecting either (1) or (2), they can avoid the inconsistency that Pufendorf ascribes to them.

Pufendorf replies that naturalists avoid an inconsistency only if they argue in a circle. In his view, Grotius is committed to these claims: (i) Natural law prescribes the good and prohibits the bad. (ii) 'Good' is to be understood here as 'morally good' (honestum). (iii) 'Morally good' is to be defined as 'what is prescribed by natural law', or as involving obligation, which in turn involves a reference to law. (iv) Therefore claim (i) simply says that natural law prescribes and prohibits what it prescribes and prohibits.[28] We ought to avoid this circle by rejecting the naturalist interpretation of the claim that the natural law prescribes the good and prohibits the bad. The naturalist understands 'good' as 'morally good', but, because of (iii), this affirmation of intrinsic morality involves us in a circle. We must therefore take the naturalist (in claim (i)) to say that natural law prescribes the natural good, which is only prudentially and not morally good. Pufendorf follows Cumberland in favouring this interpretation, which denies intrinsic morality.[29]

But is Pufendorf entitled to the claim in (iii), that moral goodness must be defined by reference to a law? Suarez's discussion of intrinsic morality rejects this claim. Pufendorf's objection relies on a legislative conception of moral goodness; but since the naturalists reject this conception, their account of natural law is not circular.

571. Self-Interest v. Morality

So far, then, Pufendorf's arguments for his legislative conception of morality rest on unsupported assumptions about conceptual connexions between morality, obligation, law, and commands. But he also argues in support of these assumptions, to show that morality involves a distinctive sort of reason that requires a command.

---

[27] This seems to be what is meant in 'nam bonum et malum morale involvit respectum ad personam, quae istam actionem edit' (i 2.6, quotation from Osiander).

[28] '. . . if the definition of natural law is to be founded on that necessary honesty or turpitude of some actions, it must be always perplexed and obscure, and must run around in an unconcluding circle, as will appear to any man who considers the definition laid down by Grotius [i 1.10.1]. And Dr Cumberland excellently remarks [5.9] that in defining the law of nature, when we use the word Good, we must mean natural and not moral good; since it would be the highest absurdity to define a thing by such terms as suppose it to be already known; [those very terms being derived as consequences from it, and depending on it as to their own evidence and certainty]' (ii 3.4 = K 122). The bracketed clause is Kennett's addition.

[29] Cf. Cumberland, discussed in §532.

He clarifies his conception of morality by opposing Grotius' view that natural rights (iura naturalia) would have some place even if God did not exist. Without God the dictates of reason could not have the 'force' (or 'significance', vis) of law, since that presupposes a superior. Grotius claims that even without God there would be a natural right (ius). Pufendorf infers that Grotius believes there would be natural law (lex) even if God did not exist.[30]

Pufendorf ascribes to Grotius the extreme naturalist position defended by Vasquez and rejected by Suarez. Pufendorf does not explicitly distinguish this extreme position from the moderate naturalist position of Suarez, that actions would still be right and wrong (honestum, turpe) even if God did not exist. But he implicitly rejects moderate naturalism; for he cites Cicero's remark that mutual trust and justice would perish if we abandoned belief in gods. He recognizes that we might observe the provisions of the natural law 'from a view of advantage' (intuitu utilitatis), just as we take medicines for the sake of health. He allows this basis for action even in the absence of any divine command. But he does not believe that this suffices for mutual trust and justice. Contrary to the naturalists, natural properties include prudential properties, but not moral properties.

Pufendorf takes a step towards naturalism, by maintaining that moral principles require only those actions that are already required by our natural good. In prescribing morality, divine law prescribes actions that we can already see reason to do. This naturalist claim about the content of morality is common to Hobbes, Suarez, and Grotius. But they believe it for different reasons, because they have different views about whether natural goods include moral good (honestum) that is irreducible to the pleasant and the advantageous. Hobbes believes that (1) moral good is reducible to the naturally advantageous, and so he believes that (2) the content of morality is simply what is naturally advantageous. Suarez and Grotius, however, believe that (3) natural properties include irreducible moral properties, and so they believe that (4) the content of morality goes beyond the advantageous.[31]

Pufendorf does not agree entirely either with Hobbes or with Suarez and Grotius. He agrees with Hobbes about (2), but not about (1). He agrees with Suarez and Grotius in rejecting (1), but disagrees with them about (3). Since he agrees with all of them that the content of morality is determined by natural good, and he holds Hobbes's narrow view of the content of natural good, he also holds Hobbes's view that morality consists only of principles prescribing what is advantageous for the sake of peace. He does not allow that the honestum is part of the natural good antecedent to divine commands. But he believes, against Hobbes and with Suarez and Grotius, that moral properties are irreducible to natural

---

[30] '... to give these dictates of reason the force and authority of laws, there is a necessity of supposing that there is a God, and that his wise providence oversees and governs the whole world, and in a particular manner the lives and the affairs of mankind. For we cannot by any means subscribe to the conjecture that Grotius starts ... that the laws (iura) of nature would take place, should we (as we cannot without the most horrid impiety) deny either the being of God or his concern with human business. For, should any wretch be so horribly senseless as to maintain that wicked and absurd hypothesis in the rankest way ... the edicts of reason could not rise so high as to pass into a condition of laws (legum), in as much as all law supposes a superior power.' (ii 3.19 = K 141–2) 'But to make these dictates of reason obtain the power and dignity of laws, it is necessary to call in a much higher principle to our assistance. For though the usefulness and expediency of them be clearly apparent, yet this bare consideration could never bring so strong a tie on men's minds but that they would recede from these rules whenever a man was pleased either to neglect his own advantage or to pursue it by some different means which he judged more proper, and more likely to succeed.' (ii 3.20 = K 143)

[31] Cf. Suarez's comment on the Incarnation, §438.

advantage. Since he disagrees with the naturalist account (in (3)) of how this is so, he must give a different account.

His account relies on assumptions about reasons or about motivation. Though the advantage of following a dictate of natural good is clear, human beings will act against this dictate if they are induced to act against advantage, or if they think they see greater advantage in acting some other way. A dictate of natural good acquires the necessary binding force only from the will of God. Pufendorf agrees, therefore, with Hobbes about the content of morality, but not about its essential motive. He believes that the Hobbesian motive of self-preservation is insufficient for morality. He argues: (a) Calculation of advantage is not the appropriate basis for morally good action. (b) Hence, consideration of natural good is not the appropriate basis for morally good action. (c) The only appropriate basis comes from divine law.

This argument is open to naturalist doubts. Suarez and Grotius believe the first claim; for though they take morally good action to depend on considerations of natural good, they deny that such considerations are confined to considerations of advantage. In their view, reasons of pleasure and advantage are not the only reasons derived from natural good. Hence they deny Pufendorf's second claim.[32]

572. Natural Goodness v. Natural Morality

It is somewhat difficult, therefore, to see where Pufendorf argues against naturalism. He simply asserts that morality requires legislation and command, and that natural properties are prudential, but not moral. It is not clear why he believes that we can give a naturalist account of non-moral goods, but not of morality. If he had denied that natural goods fix the content of morality, and had found morality in divine commands unrestricted by nature, he might have said that nothing can be inferred from human nature about the content of a true morality. But that is not what he says. For, in his view, all that Suarez says about appropriateness to nature is true, and necessary for morality. According to Pufendorf, all the facts about nature that Suarez takes to be moral facts are simply facts about mutual advantage; moral facts require the addition of divine commands.

Pufendorf's argument implies that Scholastic claims about appropriateness to nature fit the pleasant and the useful, but not the honestum (the morally right). When Suarez speaks of the honestum, he speaks of actions that are appropriate for rational nature without necessarily being advantageous. What is advantageous for me is instrumentally beneficial for some end that I already recognize. But in choosing the honestum, I recognize that it is part of my good to act in accordance with standards that refer to a common good distinct from my self-confined good.

---

[32] If one identifies moral good with a certain kind of natural good, one may do this for eudaemonist reasons, as Aristotle, Aquinas, and Suarez do, taking moral goods to be those that make a specific sort of contribution to one's own happiness. But even if one rejects this eudaemonist account of moral goods, one may still resist Pufendorf's claim (2); for one may recognize natural moral goods whose goodness can be explained without reference to the agent's happiness. To agree with Pufendorf about (2), we must believe, as Scotus does, that moral considerations necessarily go beyond any natural good. Scotus believes this because he believes that moral considerations are rational and impartial in ways that no natural good can be.

Aquinas and Suarez find the basis for moral rightness and justice in this common good, determined by the nature of human beings as rational and social animals. This aspect of human nature makes it appropriate to form communities in which individuals regard one another as proper objects of concern for their own sake, and not simply as means to one's own self-confined ends.[33] According to this naturalist view, the recognition of these facts about human beings gives us sufficient reason to pursue the honestum as part of our own good, and hence to accept morality. If these claims about nature and rational agency are correct, neither the advantageous nor the honestum depends on divine commands.

Grotius accepts this naturalist view. He combines the Aristotelian appeal to the social nature of human beings with Stoic claims about conciliation (*oikeiôsis*), and forms his own view of natural human sociality.[34] He agrees that acceptance of human sociality is a sufficient basis for the acceptance of natural rightness. Cumberland agrees with him, except that he takes facts about human sociality to make it rational, not morally right, to pursue the common good.[35]

In claiming that natural good is confined to pleasure and advantage, Pufendorf agrees with Hobbes against Aquinas, Suarez, and Grotius about what can be justified by appeal to nature. But it is difficult to see why Pufendorf agrees with Hobbes. One might reject natural morality because one denies that appeals to nature support claims about human good; but Pufendorf does not deny this. On the contrary, he appeals freely to nature as a source of prudential reasons; if he gave up these appeals, he could not explain why God is good to us in commanding us to obey these particular principles.

Pufendorf's position on natural good, therefore, is consistent, but unstable. Once he concedes the natural character of prudential properties, he has no good reason to deny the natural character of moral properties. If he is right to deny the natural character of moral properties, he apparently ought to reject any appeal to nature to explain prudence. Instead of saying that appeals to nature support reasons of advantage, but not moral reasons, he should say that appeals to nature do not support reasons at all. The only source of reasons supporting practical principles—he ought to say—is desire for some end. If human beings in their natural state want self-preservation, they have reasons of advantage; but the reasons come from their desires, not from their nature, since they do not remain in the absence of the relevant desire. This is Hobbes's position (or one of his positions) about reasons and natural goods.

But it is not Pufendorf's position. He could not accept it without serious damage to his whole outlook. That is why his position is unstable. His anti-naturalist account of morality does not give a good reason for rejecting natural morality while accepting natural prudence. Hence he needs to reject natural prudence as well as natural morality. To reject natural prudence is to take Hobbes's predominant view about reasons; the full implications of this view commit us to a Humean account of practical reason.

Though Pufendorf does not give convincing reasons for being a naturalist about prudence and a voluntarist about morality, we may find his position appealing. For some people doubt whether appeals to human nature could justify moral principles, even though they allow appeals to nature to justify concern for the longer-term as well as the shorter-term future,

---

[33] On Aquinas see §339. On Suarez see §449.   [34] On Grotius see §466.   [35] On Cumberland see §532.

concern for one's bodily health, mental development, and so on. In the latter cases, it does not seem implausible to claim that facts about our nature give us reason to aim at certain ends, whether or not we actually care about them. It is not so obvious that this is true of the ends characteristic of morality.

Naturalist defences of morality argue that the extension of natural reasons to morality is correct, even if it is not obvious. Grotius sums up these defences of morality in appealing to Aristotelian and Stoic claims about the natural sociality of human beings. If these claims are reasonable, we ought not to take Pufendorf's step towards Hobbes's and Hume's conclusions.

573. Divine Law as a Source for Morality

But suppose that we agree with Pufendorf's views about the sorts of reasons that can be grounded on natural good, and we agree that these are insufficient for moral reasons. Does his account of moral principles as divine law backed by sanctions cope with the relevant features of morality? To see whether he satisfies the demand that he thinks naturalists cannot satisfy, we should consider the distinctive sort of reason introduced by divine commands, and then ask whether that is a moral reason.

According to Suarez, divine commands give us a reason derived from the fact that a superior has expressed his will about what we are to do. This is God's function as a legislator, as distinct from a teacher making clear to us what we ought (in any case) to do. We should therefore follow the natural law not only because—as Suarez believes—it prescribes intrinsically right actions, but also because God wills and commands that we are to follow it. Divine commands give us a moral reason because it is already right to obey divine commands. Since this moral reason requires antecedent intrinsic morality, not all morality depends on divine commands.

Let us concede to Pufendorf that if we simply consider natural goodness, apart from any reference to divine commands, we will act only on self-interested concerns. Why should the introduction of divine commands change that? If our attitude to natural goods is self-interested, why should we expect that our attitude to God's commands will be less self-interested? An appeal to God does not seem to offer an escape from purely self-interested motives.

Perhaps Pufendorf simply means that people will have strong enough motives to follow moral principles only if they treat them as divine commands. If he means this, two answers are possible: (1) People ignore the commands of God from the motives that also lead them to ignore the dictates of natural good and evil. (2) Even if divine commands are needed to provide stable motives that deter us from violating natural law, this is irrelevant to the dispute with naturalists. For they might agree with Pufendorf's claim about motivation, while still believing that moral goodness is intrinsic to actions conforming to human nature.

574. The Form of Moral Requirements

One might argue that these claims about motivation are beside the point, and that commands are relevant not because they appeal to certain motives, but because they have a certain form. Facts about natural goods, we may argue, have the wrong form for moral facts; they simply specify what we need to achieve certain ends. Legal requirements have a different form; they do not say 'Drive on the right if you want to avoid a fine', but tell us without qualification to drive on the right. In this respect we might say that legal requirements have a categorical rather than a hypothetical form.[36]

This is the respect in which moral principles may seem more similar to legal requirements than to facts about natural goods. For we do not expect moral principles to say 'Do not steal if you want to keep out of prison' or 'Do not steal if you want to act appropriately to rational nature'; they simply tell us not to steal (etc.) without qualification. Since they are similar to laws, we may infer that they are laws. But since they are not merely human laws, they are divine laws.

If this is what Pufendorf means, he holds a natural law theory of morality, in the sense we have discussed.[37] He gives priority to law, since he makes morality consist essentially in laws validly enacted by a legitimate authority.[38] A rule of morality is valid insofar as God has commanded it. Moral obligations differ from counsels of prudence because they contain an element of necessity that we cannot release ourselves from, just as we cannot release ourselves from obligations that are validly imposed on us by the law. This conception of morality explains why naturalism is mistaken; the requirements fixed by suitability to rational nature lack the appropriate sort of necessity.

This objection would be cogent, if requirements of nature had the form of hypothetical imperatives, so that they explicitly referred to our preferences and desires; in that case we could release ourselves from them by simply changing our preferences. But Pufendorf does not show that this is the form of a natural requirement (naturale debitum), as Suarez understands it. If intrinsic morality consists of requirements of rational nature, naturalists need not concede that it lacks the non-hypothetical necessity that Pufendorf ascribes to moral principles.

575. The Authority of Divine Legislation

Perhaps, then, Pufendorf is no better off than a naturalist in accounting for the form of moral principles. But a naturalist may also argue that Pufendorf is worse off. For the comparison of moral principles with laws should not only account for the necessity and unqualified character of moral principles; it should also ensure the legitimacy of the authority imposing the necessity. In the legal case, legitimacy cannot be established by reference to the laws that are commanded; hence, in the moral case, the legitimacy of the moral authority cannot be established by reference to the moral laws that it commands.

How, then, can it be established? The parallel with law is not entirely helpful. Conditions for legitimacy of a legal authority are partly moral; no vicious circle is involved if we are trying to explain legal, not moral, authority. If, however, we find that the conditions for

---

[36] This distinction is not the same as Kant's division between categorical imperatives and hypothetical imperatives. Kantian hypothetical imperatives need not be either imperative or hypothetical in form, and hence the imperatives just mentioned might still be hypothetical, according to Kant's division.

[37] On morality as natural law see §455.   [38] On this 'jural' conception see §457.

the legitimacy of a moral authority are partly moral, we are in worse difficulties. These principles authorizing the authority cannot themselves be legal commands; if they were, they would take us into a vicious regress. If they are moral principles, not all moral principles are commands of a lawful authority.

This argument—derived from Cudworth and Maxwell—suggests that Pufendorf has to recognize intrinsic morality. If God is to be an authoritative legislator, a principle of intrinsic morality must require obedience to this legislator. If not all moral principles are commands of a divine legislator, we may argue for further principles of intrinsic morality.[39]

576. Pufendorf v. Hobbes on Legitimate Rulers

This argument for naturalism has assumed that a morally legitimate authority rests on a moral basis. But we might reject that assumption, as Hobbes does. In his view, God is a legitimate legal authority because God has power to compel us to obey, on pain of punishment. Fear of God's superior power causes us to accept God's rule over us; the legality of God's commands is established not by any further moral principle, but simply by the fact that God makes them known to us in the standard way. Hobbes does not hold a pure natural law theory, since he also claims that the natural laws whose observance is commanded by God are counsels of prudence, and that this fact makes them moral rules. But his test for God's being a legitimate ruler and legislator is simply divine power.

Cudworth objects that Hobbes's test for legitimate authority is too weak, because it does not distinguish the orders of a tyrant from the laws of a legitimate authority.[40] Pufendorf agrees with Cudworth's objection, and attacks Hobbes for resting obligation simply on power and fear (*JNG* i 6.9–17).[41] An obligation presupposes a just basis for our accepting the limitation of our liberty by the superior who imposes the obligation.[42] We are obliged to look on God not simply with servile fear, but also with veneration (*EJU*, Def. 12, §1); we recognize not only his power, but also his goodness. We should love him as the author and giver of every good (*DOH* 1 4.6).

If Pufendorf demands a just basis for accepting God's rule over us, he seems to force himself into an infinite regress or into a contradiction. He faces an infinite regress if it is just to accept God's rule only because God commands us to accept it; this command will itself need a just basis, which will require a further divine command, and so on. He contradicts himself if this just basis for accepting God's rule is a principle of morality prior to any divine command; for any such principle shows that not all morality rests on divine commands.

577. A Non-moral Basis for Morality?

Pufendorf might avoid this dilemma (or we might avoid it in a revised version of his position) by arguing that 'just reasons' (iustae causae) for accepting God's rule are not moral reasons,

---

[39] For a similar argument see Cockburn in §876.   [40] See Cudworth, §548.

[41] Pufendorf discusses Hobbes, *Civ.* 15.5.

[42] 'Obligations are laid on human minds properly by a superior, that is, by such an one who not only hath sufficient strength to denounce some evil against us upon non-compliance, but hath likewise just reasons (iustae causae) to require the retrenching of the freedom of our will by his own pleasure (arbitrio).' (i 6.9 = K 63)

but appropriate reasons in a more general sense. If he takes this view, he avoids Hobbes's account of legitimacy, but he does not endorse moral conditions for legitimacy. A purely procedural account of law rests on a moral foundation for legitimacy (we may concede), but a purely procedural account of morality rests on a non-moral foundation for legitimacy.

Cumberland seeks this sort of foundation in his claims about practical reason. As rational agents, we are concerned for the common good of rational beings, and when we recognize that God legislates for this common good, we see good reason to observe God's commands. But this is not a moral reason, since, in Cumberland's view, legislation is necessary for morality. Pufendorf lacks Cumberland's doctrine of impartial practical reason; he suggests that apart from divine commands practical reason simply pursues one's own advantage. Can he offer some other non-moral basis for the legitimacy of divine legislation?

He may suggest that we find this non-moral basis if we reflect on the nature of God, as discovered by natural reason. We respond with love and reverence, not because our response fulfils an obligation God lays on us, but simply because God evokes these attitudes. Kindness and benevolence in another may evoke such reactions without any mediating belief that I am obliged to respond in this way to the other person.[43]

But is this an appropriate reason for accepting God as a legitimate ruler? We might accept someone else's instructions because we are grateful to them or we love them; these responses are not based on moral judgments (we may grant to Pufendorf). But such responses do not imply that the person to whom we are grateful (say) is a legitimate moral legislator. Hence they do not seem to support Pufendorf's conception of God as a moral legislator. If we are to treat someone as a moral legislator, it is difficult to avoid reliance on moral judgments.

Sometimes Pufendorf seems to appeal to a more overtly moral basis for accepting God as legislator. He demands that we love God for his goodness, so that we obey him out of admiration for his goodness, not simply out of gratitude for his beneficence to us.[44] This demand seems to introduce a moral judgment about God. For we do not simply admire God's imposition of these laws on us, or God's own observance of them. The mere fact of being a legislator or of observing one's own laws does not justify admiration for someone's goodness. Nor can we simply be moved by a desire to show our appreciation of the benefits God has conferred on us. The fact that you have benefited me does not justify me in doing whatever you want me to do from a desire to repay you or to show my appreciation. If you save me from being murdered, that does not justify me in murdering someone else just because you ask me to.

If gratitude to God is to be a suitable foundation for moral obligations and duties, we must act out of a warranted belief that God can be trusted to ask us to do right rather than wrong actions, and that therefore obedience to God is an appropriate way to show our gratitude. But this belief cannot simply be the belief that God is an almighty legislator who has created us; it presupposes that God prescribes actions that can (at least sometimes) be

---

[43] Schneewind, 'Pufendorf' 145–6, discusses this attempted solution.

[44] The inadequacy of an appeal to gratitude, even within Pufendorf's system, is remarked by Palladini, *SPDH* 56–62, who also notices that the mere fact of God's having created us should not, according to Pufendorf, establish God's right to rule. Saastamoinen, *MFM* 105–10, replies that Pufendorf does not appeal to any independent idea of justice to find a 'just cause' for God to rule, but derives our idea of justice from our idea of God. According to ii 1.3, we do not apply 'justice' to God with its ordinary sense.

seen, on distinct grounds, to be morally right. In that case we appeal to intrinsic rightness and wrongness, which Pufendorf claims to have repudiated.[45]

These questions about legitimacy reveal a basic difficulty in Pufendorf's attempt to treat morality as a type of law, satisfying a purely procedural condition for moral validity. If moral considerations affect the legitimacy of a moral legislator, morality does not consist only of the laws imposed by a legitimate moral legislator. If we defend Pufendorf by appealing to non-moral conditions for legitimacy, the defence seems inadequate; we seem to need moral conditions that cannot be derived from commands.

Pufendorf, then, seems to be open to the objections that Cudworth raises against Hobbes. Kant summarizes these objections in claiming that positive law presupposes natural law.[46] We might not agree with Kant's claim that the ground of the authority of a legislator of positive law must be moral, and therefore must be part of natural law. But his claim is plausible if we consider a legislative theory of the natural moral law itself; the non-moral grounds that Pufendorf offers do not vindicate the authority of a moral legislator. Hence at least one natural law cannot itself be valid simply because it has been legislated by a divine legislator. This is why Kant, while conceding that we may call God a legislator, denies that God is the author of the moral law.

578. Divine Commands as a Substitute for Morality

Pufendorf need not accept this objection to his legislative conception of moral rightness. He could reply in the way in which Hobbes could reply to Cudworth. Hobbes might concede that we think our moral judgments rest on something more than fear of punishments imposed by human or divine sanctions; but he might still argue that they actually rest on nothing more. If we cannot find a morally acceptable basis (by his opponents' standards), we should abandon our initial assumptions about morality. Similarly, Pufendorf might claim that our obedience to God does not rest on moral reasons, but simply on the causal and psychological effects of our awareness of God's power and beneficence, and our dependence on him. He might claim to be retaining all that can reasonably be maintained of our initial assumptions about morality.

It is more difficult, however, for Pufendorf than for Hobbes to try this revisionary approach to morality. For he does not accept Hobbesian psychology. Nor does he question the initial assumptions about morality that he takes himself to share with his opponents. For he assumes that morality involves some sort of norm, rule, and obligation, and hence imposition by a superior. Without these connexions his argument collapses; he assumes that if we reject them, we are not talking about morality, but about some other sort of belief and practice.

He therefore relies heavily on conceptual claims about the nature of morality, as opposed to (for instance) prudence; his arguments are futile if the conception of morality that he relies on is eccentric. But he seems to violate basic beliefs about morality if he claims

---

[45] Hutcheson argues in this way for the insufficiency of gratitude, SMP ii 3, 266, quoted at §645.
[46] See Kant, MdS 224.

that the authority of a moral legislator rests on a non-moral basis—fear or gratitude or a combination of them. He seems not to have explained morality, but to have recommended that we replace it with something else.

Perhaps Pufendorf ought to accept this consequence. He would have a consistent position if he claimed that nothing has the properties that we attribute to morality. He might concede that it is part of the concept of morality that it rests on natural rightness and wrongness, which provide a basis for determining the legitimacy of a legislator. If there is no natural rightness and wrongness, there is no morality. It is sensible (he might argue) to replace moral principles with divine commands resting on non-moral conditions for legitimacy. We argued that Hobbes would hold a more consistent and less easily refuted view if he claimed to be replacing morality rather than describing or explaining it. The same is true of Pufendorf; in this respect as in others, he is closer to Hobbes than he would prefer to be.

We have no reason, however, to replace morality with Pufendorf's position, unless we believe he has exposed some error in a naturalist conception of morality. His attacks on naturalism do not show that a naturalist who agrees with Suarez and Grotius faces serious difficulties. His attempt to formulate an alternative to naturalism seems to face more serious difficulties, especially if it implicitly relies on naturalist claims that do not fit into his theory.

579. Grotius on Nature and Contradiction

Grotius agrees with Cudworth and with Suarez in believing that a voluntarist conception of divine commands and morality leads to further unwelcome results besides those we have already noticed in Pufendorf. In their view, the voluntarist position implies that God can make contradictions true. According to voluntarists, cruelty is wrong because God forbids it; hence, if God were to command it, cruelty would be right, and in that case a contradiction would be true. But this result is impossible; just as God cannot make twice two something other than four, God cannot make something that is intrinsically wrong not wrong (Grotius, *JBP* i 1.10.5).[47]

Pufendorf rejects this argument. He replies that the impossibility of making twice two something other than four is that twice two and four are identical and differ only in description. No such impossibility can be found in actions that conflict with the natural law. The naturalist may be accused of an error in evaluating the counterfactual, (1) 'If God were to command deliberate killing of innocent people,[48] then this deliberate killing (which is wrong) would be right'. The naturalist reads (1) as (2) 'If God were to command deliberate homicide, it would be both right and wrong'. But (2) does not follow from (1), because the crucial clause 'which is wrong' is the aspect of deliberate homicide that is supposed to be changed in the counterfactual supposition; we cannot legitimately hold it fixed in evaluating

---

[47] Grotius; §465.
[48] It would be shorter simply to use 'murder'. But since it might be argued that murder is essentially wrongful homicide, the use of this term might appear to result in a sound but trivial argument.

the counterfactual. We would be entitled to hold it fixed only if we could not identify deliberate homicide without its being wrong. The supposition that deliberate homicide is not deliberate is unintelligible; but the supposition that it is not wrong is not unintelligible in the same way.

The argument about contradiction might appear to be more effective if we substituted 'vice' for 'deliberate homicide'. For (we might argue) the supposition that vice is not wrong is unintelligible, and therefore the supposition that God could make vice right is self-contradictory. Though this is true, it does not really help naturalism. For voluntarists need not say that God could make vice right; they need only say that he could command actions—e.g., deliberate homicide, taking pleasure in the infliction of pain—that are actually wrong, and then these actions would be right.

Pufendorf's objections are effective against a superficially tempting defence of naturalism by appeal to contradiction. We may confuse the trivial result that God cannot make things both right and wrong with the non-trivial result that God cannot make things right that are actually wrong. One might reasonably attribute to Clarke some arguments that misconstrue trivial results as non-trivial, and one might fairly criticize Cudworth for failing to distinguish the two sorts of result.[49]

It is less clear, however, that Pufendorf answers Suarez's argument, which both Grotius and Cudworth seem to have in mind. Suarez argues as follows: (1) Deliberate homicide is morally bad because it conflicts with rational nature. (2) God cannot change the facts about what conflicts with rational nature. (3) Therefore God cannot change this fact making deliberate homicide bad. (4) Hence, if God makes deliberate homicide not bad, God makes it simultaneously bad and not bad.

Suarez tries to establish the relevant sort of contradiction not by appealing to the alleged internal inconsistency of 'deliberate homicide is not bad', but by appealing to the conflict between this claim and the needs of rational nature. The voluntarist supposes that God can change deliberate homicide from being wrong to being right without changing rational nature; the naturalist claims that this supposition is self-contradictory, given the connexion between wrongness and rational nature.

This argument may be accused of begging the question in favour of naturalism. For the first step asserts that conflict with rational nature is what makes deliberate homicide bad. A voluntarist does not accept this step, but affirms instead that God's prohibition is what makes deliberate homicide bad. Hence Pufendorf maintains that nothing is right or wrong before it is made so by a law.[50] In the face of this voluntarist claim, the argument about contradiction is neither the mistake that Pufendorf alleges nor an independent argument against voluntarism.

Voluntarists might take different views about where the naturalist argument about contradiction goes wrong. Ockham sometimes seems to suggest that it is within God's unqualified power to make deliberate homicide accord with correct reason. In that case God's creation of human beings with this nature still leaves God free to prescribe actions that conflict human nature, or else it leaves God free to make deliberate homicide accord

---

[49] Cudworth; §547. Clarke; §619.
[50] 'We have already shown in our former book [i 2.6] that no actions are in themselves required or illicit (debita aut illicita) before they are made so [sc. required or illicit] by some law.' (ii 3.4 = K 121 altered)

with human nature.[51] Whichever view Ockham takes, God is free to make it no longer true that deliberate homicide is wrong without making a contradiction true.

580. Divine Freedom and Natural Goodness

These voluntarist answers, however, do not seem to be open to Pufendorf. For he rejects the Ockhamist view, and prefers the account of divine freedom that Cajetan and Suarez maintain in defence of naturalism. He argues that, while God was free to create or not to create human beings, he could not both have created them and imposed a different natural law on them; the Ockhamist supposition 'clearly involves a contradiction'.[52]

Here Pufendorf relies on Grotius' conception of a contradiction as conflict with rational nature. If Ockham says it is possible for deliberate homicide to be contrary to rational nature and yet not morally bad, Ockham affirms (according to Pufendorf) the possibility of a contradiction.[53] If God had created a species with duties (officia) contrary to the actual principles of natural law, he would not have created a social animal, but a different species. In creating the human species, God thereby created an animal for whom not all actions ought to be indifferent, and thereby (eo ipso) constituted a law for this species. The contradiction in Ockham's view lies in the combination of these two claims: (1) The species for whom deliberate homicide would be required would be the human species. (2) The human species is essentially the species of social beings for whom deliberate homicide is bad.

Pufendorf believes, therefore, that Grotius is committed to a more voluntarist position than he acknowledges, because of his claims about divine freedom. But he also believes that his own voluntarist thesis avoids any commitment to a conception of morality as simply the product of arbitrary divine choice. Not only is Grotius, according to Pufendorf, less of a naturalist than he supposes; Pufendorf, according to himself, is also less of a voluntarist than some earlier voluntarists have been.

It is puzzling, however, that Pufendorf uses this argument against Ockham; for the claim that a species for which deliberate homicide is not wrong could not be the human species seems to undermine Pufendorf's legislative account of morality. If the creation of human beings is the creation of animals for whom not every action ought (deberet) to be indifferent, the existence of human beings itself implies some natural duties (debita, officia); and so duties do not all depend on divine legislation.[54]

---

[51] See Ockham, §395.   [52] 'non obscure contradictionem involvere', ii 3.4.

[53] 'For although God was not obliged by any necessity to create man . . . yet when he had once decreed to create him a rational and a social animal, it was impossible but that the present natural law should agree to him; not by an absolute, but by an hypothetical necessity. For should man have been engaged to the contrary performances, not a social animal, but some other species of barbarous and horrid creature had been produced. Notwithstanding all which, it remains for a certain truth, that antecedently to the imposition of any law, all actions are indifferent. For by decreeing to create man, that is, to create an animal whose actions ought (deberent) not all to be indifferent, God immediately constituted a law for him [sc. man].' (ii 3.4 = K 121 altered)

[54] The close connexion that Pufendorf recognizes between human nature and the provisions of the natural law is still clearer in his treatment of dispensations. 'Therefore we cannot properly call it a dispensation of the law of nature, when a man by express command from heaven, executes God's right upon other men, merely as his instrument. . . . None, I believe, can be so simple as to imagine that when the object is changed, or the circumstances varied, the law itself suffers alteration.' (ii 3.5 = K 123) Following Aquinas, Suarez, Grotius, and Cumberland, he denies that God can dispense from the natural law, for just the reasons given by the naturalists.

581. What Sort of Voluntarist is Pufendorf?

We might reply on behalf of Pufendorf that the argument against Ockham does not rule out every sort of voluntarism.[55] Perhaps nothing is morally wrong without a divine command, but still the human species could not exist unless deliberate homicide was morally wrong. These claims are consistent if it is not possible for God to create human beings and not to prohibit deliberate homicide. The resulting position is still voluntarist, since it maintains, against Suarez and Grotius, that deliberate homicide would not be wrong unless God had prohibited it.

The claim about God's necessary will separates this view from the more extreme voluntarism of Ockham and Hobbes. In Hobbes's view, nothing about the divine will and morality makes it necessary for God to command the observance of the principles that preserve human society and individual human beings; that is why God's commanding it is an exercise of divine power rather than divine benevolence. Contrary to Hobbes, Pufendorf takes God's choice of principles to be necessary.[56]

But how are we to understand the necessity of God's choosing to prohibit deliberate homicide among human beings? Pufendorf cannot answer that God sees that deliberate homicide is intrinsically wrong and therefore prohibits it. Cumberland answers that God is essentially rational, and therefore necessarily aims at the common good of rational beings; but Pufendorf does not endorse Cumberland's views about reason and the common good. In his view, God is aware of the non-moral badness (i.e., disadvantage) of deliberate homicide, and necessarily prohibits it for that reason. Instead of saying, as Cumberland says, that God is essentially rational and therefore benevolent, Pufendorf seems to say that God is necessarily benevolent, but for no further reason.

This conception of divine benevolence raises further questions for Pufendorf. It commits him to identifying morality with benevolence. Maxwell argues effectively against Cumberland, as Butler argues against utilitarianism, that benevolence is not the whole of morality. If he is right, a benevolent God cannot be guaranteed to legislate all and only what is morally right.

But if we leave aside this question about the relation between benevolence and morality, Pufendorf still needs to explain the relation of benevolence to God's freedom and God's essence. If God is contingently benevolent, so that benevolence is an aspect of God's ordered power, subject to changes resulting from the exercise of God's unqualified power, God is free not to be benevolent. In that case, if God had not been benevolent, but had commanded human beings to act contrary to their rational nature, would such action have been right? If Pufendorf believes that right and wrong depend on divine legislation, he must answer Yes. But then it cannot be essential to morality that it requires what accords with rational nature, and Pufendorf is back to an Ockhamist view that he rejects.

Apparently, then, Pufendorf needs to say that God is not free not to command actions that accord with rational nature. How, then, can Pufendorf maintain that God is still genuinely free? Aquinas and Suarez have an answer to this question, relying on their view that certain

[55] Korkman, *BNL* 183–229, distinguishes Pufendorf from an extreme voluntarist by saying that he is not a voluntarist at all, but holds a divine command theory.

[56] On this version of voluntarism see §604.

things are intrinsically right, given the nature of human beings. The fact that God is not free not to do what is intrinsically right does not reduce God's genuine freedom; for it is not a diminution of freedom to recognize truths about what one ought to do and what it is best to do, any more than it is a diminution of freedom to recognize truths about the world. God's knowledge of the truth and willing of the good are aspects of his perfection. Pufendorf, however, does not agree that God is guided in legislating by truths about what it is right to do, since there are no such truths apart from God's legislation. Must he not admit, therefore, that God's freedom is limited? The refusal to recognize natural rightness and wrongness raises difficulties for his attempt to safeguard divine freedom. He claims that naturalists cannot reconcile their doctrine of intrinsic morality with divine freedom;[57] but it seems more difficult to reconcile divine freedom with the version of voluntarism that would support Pufendorf's objections to Ockham.

He might answer these questions about freedom by asserting that God is essentially benevolent, and that action in accordance with one's essence is not a limitation on one's freedom. But then he needs to explain why God is essentially benevolent. This is explicable from a naturalist point of view; benevolence is an aspect of God's perfection because it is required by intrinsic rightness. But it is more difficult to see how God's essential benevolence is to be explained from a voluntarist point of view, without reference to intrinsic rightness. Pufendorf does not explain why God would not be God without benevolence, since benevolence does not seem to be among God's perfections.[58]

It is not clear, then, that Pufendorf has found a plausible version of voluntarism that avoids the aspects of naturalism and Ockhamism that he rejects. Though his position might be made consistent, it is difficult to defend on the basis of any plausible conception of a divine legislator. Once he rejects the naturalist view that God legislates on the basis of intrinsic morality, it is difficult to find a credible account of why God necessarily prescribes just those principles that naturalists ascribe to intrinsic morality.

582. Divine Freedom, Creation, and Legislation

Pufendorf, however, does not believe that it is difficult to reconcile his views about morality and nature with his legislative account of morality. Sometimes he removes any difficulty by relying on the broader notion of 'legislation' that we have seen in his discussion of creation. He claims that in the very act of creation God at the same time constituted a law for human beings (ii 3.4, quoted above), and therefore morality can be understood as the result of divine legislation.

This claim about creation, however, does not help Pufendorf's legislative thesis about morality. The only sort of law that follows from the act of creation is the sort that Suarez calls indicative law, including every sort of norm or rule. Suarez denies that law in this broad sense is genuine law; for if it were genuine law, it would be trivially true, given Suarez's view of rightness, that rightness presupposes law. When Pufendorf claims that rightness

---

[57] See §566.   [58] A similar question arises about Hutcheson's treatment of God's benevolence. See §662.

presupposes law, he does not mean the claim in the trivial sense; hence facts about creation do not by themselves vindicate him.

Pufendorf's tendency to speak of law in both narrower and broader senses helps to explain why he sometimes rejects Grotius' position, but sometimes suggests that Grotius really agrees with him. Though he sometimes rejects Grotius' argument to show that voluntarism gives God the power to make contradictions true, he sometimes seems to endorse this argument. He recognizes that Grotius takes the relevant contradictions to result from the relation of some actions to 'nature using sound reason' (*JBP* i 1.10.5) and 'rational and social nature' (i 1.12.1).[59] The reference to sound reason, in Pufendorf's view, refers to the law of sociality that the Creator enjoined on human beings. Grotius must admit that human beings receive their rational and social nature not from immutable necessity, but from God's pleasure; hence they must have received the morality of actions that fit or do not fit human beings, as rational and social, from God also.

This is a puzzling argument; for it implies that the legislative account of morality is irrelevant to Pufendorf's essential claims. All that he shows by appealing to God's pleasure is that the existence of human beings with rational and social natures depends on God's creative will. But none of the naturalists whom he attacks denies this claim about dependence; since on this point they are orthodox Christians, they agree that God's creative will determines what sorts of agents exist.

Pufendorf's argument is intelligible if we recall his disputable assumption that naturalists must admit some principle external to God that limits God's freedom.[60] Perhaps he assumes that their claims about what God cannot do commit them to some restriction of God's freedom as creator. This assumption needs some defence. In any case, recognition of the point that Pufendorf insists on about God's freedom as creator falls far short of acceptance of his claims about morality and legislation.

We have found, therefore, that Pufendorf defines his relation to naturalists about morality in two ways. (1) Sometimes he agrees with them in recognizing natural goods, but disagrees with them in excluding moral goods from natural goods; that is why he thinks morality requires additional legislation. (2) He agrees with them in recognizing natural morality, but he thinks that this proves his legislative thesis if we agree that God created human beings. These two claims are inconsistent, since the first denies natural morality, and the second accepts it.

Pufendorf does not believe he is inconsistent, because he uses 'law' and 'legislation' equivocally. The first claim contrasts moral properties, which depend on legislation, with natural properties, which do not. But the second claim takes law to embrace all the properties that are required by the indicative laws of creation. The difference between these two claims about nature and legislation marks the difference between the voluntarist and the naturalist view of morality. According to the naturalist, nothing needs to be added to created nature for moral properties to exist; according to the voluntarist, divine legislation has to be added. Pufendorf's different conceptions of law and legislation sometimes lead him into

---

[59] In understanding Grotius this way Pufendorf undermines his objection to the argument about contradiction, which (as we have explained) does not apply to the explanation of 'contradiction' that he attributes to Grotius here.

[60] See §566.

disagreement with naturalism; but sometimes he represents the naturalist view as though it were his own (because of his broad use of 'law' for indicative law).

583. Sociality and Society

Questions about Pufendorf's attitude to naturalism affect his claims about nature in his social philosophy. He accepts some of the appeals to human nature that the naturalists use as the basis for their account of societies and states; but he rejects the naturalist claims that would separate his position from Hobbes's claims about the moral basis of the commonwealth.

He maintains that naturalist principles, abstracted from the will of God, provide counsels of advantage with no moral force. But once we know that God commands us to preserve and to develop rational human nature, these naturalist principles can be used to support moral principles. He therefore takes over Grotius' Stoic principle of 'sociality', and takes this to provide a moral basis for the formation of communities with their own moral principles.

In taking sociality to be a central aspect of human nature, apart from any society, Pufendorf departs consciously from one of Hobbes's basic assumptions. In Hobbes's view, if we do not presuppose a government that secures peace for us, the rule of self-preservation has absolute priority, and no other aspect of human nature has any practical standing except insofar as it promotes self-preservation. Self-preservation is the ultimate and dominant end; in this respect, it corresponds to happiness, as Aristotle and Aquinas conceive it. Since Hobbes rejects the Aristotelian view that the ultimate end includes more than self-preservation, the other laws of nature oblige only in foro interno in the state of nature.

Pufendorf agrees with Cumberland in rejecting this view about human nature in the state of nature.[61] Human beings are not only naturally concerned for their own safety, but also naturally social; hence other principles besides self-preservation have moral standing in the state of nature. As Clarke sees, this does not imply that we are required to neglect self-preservation in the state of nature; but it implies that we are required to act on social principles even if they do not promote self-preservation, as long as they do not undermine it.[62] Pufendorf takes the neglect of natural sociality to be one of Hobbes's major errors about the state of nature.

He therefore rejects, as Grotius does, the argument of Carneades seeking to prove that utility is the origin of justice (*JNG* ii 3.11–12). He agrees with Grotius in appealing to the social aspect of human nature.[63] This is the aspect that Hobbes forgets in his account of the

---

[61] On Cumberland see §535. Pufendorf cites him in the discussion of sociality at ii 3.15.

[62] Clarke on Hobbes; §629.

[63] 'This then will appear a fundamental law of nature, every man ought, as far as in him lies, to promote and preserve a peaceful sociableness with others, agreeable to the main end and disposition of human race [sic] in general. For by sociableness we do not here mean a bare readiness or propension to join in particular societies, which may possibly be formed on ill designs, and in an ill manner; as the confederacies of thieves and robbers; as if it were sufficient only to join ourselves with others, let our intentions be what they will. But by this term of sociableness we would imply such a disposition of one man towards all others, as shall suppose him united to them in benevolence, by peace, by charity, and so, as it were, by a silent and a secret obligation.' (ii 3.15 = K 137)

state of nature.[64] Pufendorf acknowledges[65] and endorses Cumberland's detailed critique of Hobbes's view that it is rational for people in the state of nature to behave to one another in ways that keep them in a state of war.

584. The Limits of Sociality

If we rely on natural sociality, we do not confine evaluation of a state to its success in keeping the peace. If we take communities, including political communities, to be appropriate means for fulfilling human nature, including its rational and social aspect, we can rely on other criteria for assessing the moral acceptability of a state apart from its success in defending us from aggression.

This is the basis of Suarez's argument against Machiavelli's case for putting the state beyond moral criticism. He also appeals to natural sociality in arguing that the subject's obligation to obey the ruler has limits, even if the ruler does not actually threaten the subject's life. This is the basis for Suarez's qualified defence of rebellion and tyrannicide, applied especially to England under James I.[66]

Grotius' attitude to this appeal to nature is cautious. He uses it, as Suarez does, to argue against the view that there is no place for considerations of right and justice in the state of nature, and especially in relations between states (*JBP*, Prol. 25). To this extent, he agrees with Suarez against Machiavelli. But he rejects Suarez's use of the argument from nature to support rebellion.[67] He recognizes the right to refuse to obey orders to act unjustly, but denies any right to depose a ruler who rules badly. He limits the right of rebellion (i 4.8), though he allows it in extreme circumstances (i 4.7.4).

Grotius' position, therefore, exemplifies Hobbes's charge that naturalist Aristotelian conceptions of the role of the state are dangerous (from his point of view), since they leave room for criticism, and, in some circumstances, for rebellion on the basis of this criticism. Hobbes's complaint applies to Suarez, and, to a significant though lesser degree, to Grotius.

Pufendorf takes a further step away from the aspects of naturalism that disturb Hobbes. He believes that human beings are naturally social, and therefore he recognizes a natural basis for communities, but he halts any appeal to social human nature when he reaches civil society. Though human beings are naturally social, they are not naturally political.[68] Hence we cannot justify or understand or criticize political society by considering how well

---

[64] 'For since the natural state of man includes the use of reason, we must by no means separate from it those obligations which reason tells us we lie under. And because every man may discover it to be most for his own interest and advantage so to manage his behaviour as to procure rather the benevolence than the enmity of others; he may easily presume from the likeness of nature, that other men have the same sentiments about the point as himself. Therefore it is very foul play, in describing this imaginary state, to suppose that all men, or however, the greatest part of them do act with disregard and defiance to reason, which is by nature constituted supreme directress of human proceedings; and such a state cannot, without the highest absurdity, be called natural, which owes its production to the neglect or the abuse of the natural principle in man.' (ii 2.9 = K 114)

[65] In a footnote to this paragraph. See Cumberland, §535.   [66] See Suarez, §451.   [67] See *JBP* i 3.9.1; i 4.1.3.

[68] '... allowing him a natural desire of society, since this may be gratified by the primary societies already described, this infers not his desire of civil society, any more than his general love of employment bespeaks his affection for that of a scholar in particular.' (*JNG* vii 1.3 = K 625)

or badly it fulfils the natural sociality of human beings. The social aspect of human nature can only justify smaller communities, such as families, voluntary associations, and so on. It cannot be used to justify civil society.

This distinction between the merely social and the civil is supported by an examination of Aristotle's remarks on human beings as political animals. Pufendorf correctly points out that some of these remarks do not refer specifically to the state, and therefore do not support Aristotle's claims about the specifically political nature of human beings.[69] But his criticism of Aristotle is incomplete. In the *Ethics* (in the passage quoted by Pufendorf) Aristotle claims that the complete good requires fellow-citizens (*politai*) as well as family and friends. Pufendorf does not comment on this claim; he speaks as though Aristotle had mentioned only family and friends. Aristotle recognizes the difference between the city and other sorts of community, and argues that the functions peculiar to a city are necessary to fulfil human nature. These arguments in *Politics* i and iii are not answered by Pufendorf.

In restricting the appeal to sociality, Pufendorf accepts part of Hobbes's conception of the moral basis of the state. His view about the state is more Hobbesian than we might have predicted from his views about sociality and from his criticism of Hobbes's neglect of sociality in the state of nature. He takes the function of the state to be limited by the demands of security, which is needed to remedy the evils that result from the blind impulses of individuals in the state of nature.[70] The provision of security against these evils is the only function of the state; no further basis for evaluation or criticism of a state is recognized. By abandoning the critical aspects of naturalism, Pufendorf avoids Hobbes's criticisms of appeals to nature.

On this point, as in his treatment of divine commands and natural law, Pufendorf abandons some, though not all, naturalist claims. He takes the demands of human nature to be relevant to natural law, but insufficient for morality. He takes human sociality to be important for understanding elementary human societies, but not for understanding the moral basis of the state.[71] Pufendorf's partial rejection of naturalism brings him closer to Hobbes. His reasons for abandoning some aspects of naturalism are not convincing, in the light of his moral and theological premises.

It is not surprising that Pufendorf both appeals to natural human sociality and strictly limits his appeal. For we have noticed that Grotius' belief in natural sociality is the basis for

---

[69] 'But now his affection for civil government can never be inferred from the bare desire of company; since this . . . may be equally gratified by primary societies, such as may well be supposed without admitting a commonwealth. So again, the Philosopher proves man to be a political creature from the reason of speech, which else had been assigned to him to no purpose; whereas the use of speech is not confined to a commonwealth; men having lived and conversed together long before the institution of government. In like manner is to be understood that passage in his first book of Ethics to Nicomachus: "That good may deserve the name of perfect, which appears to be sufficient; and that we call sufficient, which answers not only to the wants of a single man in a solitary life, but those of our parents, our wife, our children, our friends and fellow subjects, . . . because man is by nature a political creature." And yet, there is room for the several relations of parents, children, wife, and friends, without supposing a commonwealth.' (vii 1.3 = K 626)

[70] On Hobbes see §492.

[71] Saastamoinen, *MFM* 82–94, argues that Pufendorf's case for civil society is not egoistic, based on individual benefit, but theocentric; we have to do what is needed to fulfil God's intention to have human beings live a distinctively human life in society. This view brings Pufendorf closer to Grotius (except for the necessity of appealing to God's intention).

his belief in natural morality. If Pufendorf completely endorsed Grotius' belief, it would be difficult to reject natural morality. If, however, he completely rejected Grotius' belief, he would lose his main ground for disagreement with Hobbes. The limited endorsement of natural sociality makes Pufendorf's position unstable at the crucial points. This instability is yet another sign of the difficulty that Pufendorf faces in maintaining his voluntarism against the main objections urged by naturalists.

585. Influence of Pufendorf

Pufendorf's position deserves careful study not only for its contribution to the long debate about naturalism and voluntarism, but also because of its influence on later moral philosophy. It was influential in Scotland, partly because Gerschom Carmichael published an annotated edition. Since Carmichael was a professor in Glasgow, his edition helped to make *De Officio Hominis* a textbook in Glasgow, where Hutcheson became familiar with it.[72] Carmichael's notes suggest general agreement with Pufendorf, especially on the main questions about the relation between morality and divine commands.[73]

Pufendorf's work was also widely used in England. Some of the specific evidence of its use comes from the accounts of Dissenting academies (where Butler, Price, and Godwin received their education).[74] Samuel Palmer recalls that the books studied in the academy he attended included Suarez in metaphysics, and in ethics Hereboord (the main textbook), More, Marcus Aurelius, Epictetus (with Simplicius), Solomon, and 'the moral works of the great Pufendorf'.[75] Philip Doddridge mentions Grotius and Pufendorf as a principal source of the ethics that he learned in his academy.[76] He includes Pufendorf in a list of books recommended to John Wesley as suitable reading for young preachers. Though he recommends Hutcheson only with reservations, he does not qualify his commendation of Pufendorf.[77]

Among his English and Scottish readers Pufendorf does not seem to have received any explicit criticism of the voluntarist foundations of his theory. Some of them are sympathetic to voluntarism. But even among those who oppose voluntarism, no one attacks Pufendorf

---

[72] On Hutcheson see §676.

[73] In Suppl. i. Carmichael represents the natural law as God's instructions to us for our happiness. He takes divine commands to be necessary for genuine morality: 'But in order for any human action or its omission to be a moral act and thereby imputable to a human being as good or evil, in accordance with what has been said above, a law must be added, prescribing or forbidding that action' (§13). This law has to come from the divine will.

[74] See Lincoln, *SPSIED*, esp. 83.   [75] Bogue and Bennett, *HD* ii 80–1.

[76] 'Our ethics are interwoven with pneumatology and make a very considerable part of it. They are mostly collected from Pufendorf and Grotius, and contain no very surprising discoveries, but seem to be built on a very rational foundation, and comprise a great deal in a few words.' (Doddridge, *Corr.* i 43) 'Our ethics were a part of pneumatology. The principal authors whom Mr Jennings referred to were Grotius and Pufendorf. But, upon the whole, I know of no book which resembles it [sc. our ethics?] so much, both in matter and method, as Wollaston's Religion of Nature Delineated.' (*Corr.* ii 469)

[77] 'For ethics, Whitly and Carmichael's edition of Pufendorf's De Officio Hominis, to which Hutcheson's ethics may be added, which is an elegant piece, though some of his principles are not in my judgment good, as he goes on the foundation of the necessitarian scheme.' (*Corr.* iii 484–5)

as an influential defender of voluntarism. German critics are more explicit on this point, and Pufendorf defends himself against them in his controversial works.[78] Some of the right questions are raised by Leibniz, who defends the aspects of Scholastic ethics that Pufendorf rejects. We may therefore turn to the ethical position that is the basis for Leibniz's critique of Pufendorf.

[78] See §587.

43

LEIBNIZ: NATURALISM
AND EUDAEMONISM

586. Scholasticism

Leibniz defends some aspects of the naturalist position against voluntarism. His defence is worth comparing with the arguments of Suarez, Grotius, and Pufendorf. His naturalism in theology and in the foundations of ethics is part of an overall outlook that revives an Aristotelian and Scholastic point of view, by combining naturalism with eudaemonism and with a teleological conception of morality.[1]

Modern philosophers were too hasty, according to Leibniz, in rejecting the Scholastic outlook. 'The incomparable Grotius' was right to say that there is gold in the rubbish of the monks' barbarous Latin (*Theod.*, Prelim. Disc. = G vi 53 = H 77). Modern critics have unjustly attacked Aristotelian teleology, and Aristotelian attempts to understand human nature with reference to the natural and immanent ends of human beings. Boyle and Pufendorf accuse naturalist views of setting up a principle that is independent of God.[2] Belief in a free and sovereign God appears to rule out, as a restriction on God's freedom, any inherent goals in natural substances.

Leibniz argues that this modern criticism of Aristotelian views misunderstands divine freedom and natural goals. In 'On nature itself', he turns the theological argument back on his opponents; they diminish God's creative power if they deny that God has created substances that are capable of initiating their own goal-directed movements. If we agree that God creates substances that are sufficiently complex to have natures and ends, we have some reason to agree that their nature also fixes what is good and right for them.[3]

---

[1] Leibniz's scanty references to Aristotle are discussed by Mercer, 'Ethical knowledge'. Though she emphasizes the Platonic aspects of his epistemology, she recognizes his Aristotelian conception of nature (146–7). This conception helps to explain some of the main tendencies of his moral outlook.

[2] On Boyle see §481. Pufendorf on divine freedom; §566.

[3] 'If the law set up by God does in fact leave some vestige of him expressed in things, if things have been so formed by the command that they are made capable of fulfilling the will of him who commanded them, then it must be granted that there is a certain efficacy residing in things, a form or force such as we usually designate by the name of nature, from which the series of phenomena follows according to the prescription of the first command.' ('On nature itself' §6 = G iv 507 = L 501) Leibniz's conception of nature is compared briefly with the outlook of the Cambridge Platonists by Cassirer, *PRE* 150–4.

Leibniz suggests that his opponents' view tends towards the occasionalism of Malebranche.[4]

This dispute in natural philosophy helps to explain why Pufendorf opposes naturalism on behalf of divine sovereignty; he applies Boyle's general objections to a teleological view of nature to the particular claims of naturalists about right and wrong. Leibniz answers this theological attack on a teleological conception of nature.

Though Leibniz's thoughts on questions in moral philosophy are brief and scattered, his outlook is quite systematic. Moreover, it is familiar to Kant—at any rate, in its Wolffian form—as a representative of the traditional naturalist point of view.[5] But he may not present the traditional eudaemonist view in its most plausible form. He connects naturalism and eudaemonism with some doctrines that are absent from Aquinas and Suarez, and that might reasonably arouse Kant's suspicion.

587. The Reformation

Leibniz's sympathy towards mediaeval Scholasticism is relevant not only to philosophy but also to his theological outlook. In his comments on the Lutheran Reformation, he acknowledges Luther's antagonism to Aristotle, including Aristotle's ethics. But he points out that this is not the only Lutheran attitude to Aristotle. He cites the favourable reference to Aristotle's ethics in the most conciliatory of early Lutheran documents, the *Apology*, of which Melanchthon was a principal author. As we might expect, Leibniz commends Melanchthon's general attitude to Aristotelian philosophy.[6]

In his view, the moderate outlook of Melanchthon is a suitable model for an enlightened Christian philosophical position. Pufendorf attacks those Lutheran theologians who defend naturalism by appeal to Suarez, whom (he alleges) they regard as equal to the Apostles.[7] He suggests that naturalism belongs to the mediaeval Scholastic outlook that has been discarded in theology and philosophy. Since Leibniz believes that the Scholastic outlook does not deserve to be wholly discarded, he agrees with those who take a Lutheran and a naturalist outlook to be compatible.

This sympathy towards mediaeval Scholasticism also influences other aspects of Leibniz's attitude to contemporary divisions among Christians. In discussion with Bossuet, he suggests

---

[4] Leibniz believes his opponents have to say: '...things do not act but...God acts in the presence of things and according to the fitness of things, so that things are occasions, not causes, and merely receive but never effect or produce' ('Nature' §10 = G iv 509 = L 502).

[5] See Schneewind, *IA*, ch. 22. Wolff's role as intermediary between Leibniz and Kant is discussed by Beck, *EGP* 256–75. Schmucker, *UEK*, ch. 1, esp. 42–7, describes the importance of Wolff in forming the early stages of Kant's moral philosophy.

[6] 'But at last he [sc. Luther] curbed his vehemence and in the *Apology for the Augsburg Confession* allowed a favourable mention of Aristotle and his *Ethics*. Melanchthon, a man of sound and moderate ideas, made little systems from the several parts of philosophy, adapted to the truths of revelation and useful in civic life, which deserve to be read even now.' (T, Prelim. Disc. §12 = G vi 57 = H 81)

[7] In *ES* Pufendorf discusses an argument for naturalism by Zentgraf, who cites Suarez in his support; see *GW* v 209.19–30. He remarks that for Zentgraf the name of Suarez is 'par Apostolis nomen'. Zentgraf was a Lutheran theologian; on his critique of Pufendorf see Palladini, *DSSP* 217–21.

that differences between Protestants and Roman Catholics are not irreconcilable.[8] Leibniz's conviction about the possibility of reconciling the Protestant and Roman positions on fundamentals presupposes that neither side is properly charged with the errors that the other side urges against it, so that the mutual anathemas are not deserved. On this point he is about three centuries ahead of his time.

588. Egoism and Eudaemonism

Leibniz revives the eudaemonism of Aristotelian ethics. He accepts it as a psychological doctrine; hence he claims that we always pursue our own good, and that allegedly incontinent action is really the result of ignorance of our good. Sometimes he appears to be a psychological egoist, and even a hedonist. He understands happiness (felicity) as 'a lasting state of pleasure'.[9] He understands love in the same way, but he allows it to include 'disinterested' love, which nonetheless is inseparable from one's own pleasure.[10]

This conception of disinterested love allows Leibniz to endorse the pursuit of virtue for its own sake. He approves of most of Shaftesbury's attitude to morality and the moral motive. In his view, non-mercenary love is possible insofar as the happiness of those in whose happiness we take pleasure becomes a part of our own happiness. If we find pleasure 'in' the good of another, the happiness of others turns into our own happiness.[11]

This position shares some of the obscurities of Shaftesbury's position. It is not clear whether Leibniz's claims about happiness rest on hedonist assumptions or not. Indeed, he seems to raise some difficulties for a strictly hedonist account of happiness. If happiness consists entirely in pleasure, we can find pleasure 'in' some object only insofar as the object is a source of pleasure, but not something valued for its own sake. In this sense, an Epicurean hedonist can find pleasure 'in' the pleasure of another.[12] But this construal of 'pleasure in'

---

[8] '. . . these differences would be still less considerable than some of those which are tolerated within the Roman Church, such as for example, the point concerning the necessity of the love of God, and the point of probabilism. . . . If, however, the matter were treated as it should be, I believe that the Protestants would one day be able to explain their views concerning dogma more favourably than seems at first . . .' (Letter to Bossuet, 18 Apr. 1692 = Foucher de Careil i 344–5 = R 189). Leibniz's proposals for reunion are discussed by Jordan, *RC*. See esp. ch. 6 on the correspondence with Bossuet.

[9] R 83 = 'Felicity', in Grua, *TI* ii 579. Cf. *NE* i 2.4; i 2.9 (perhaps less hedonist).

[10] 'To love is nothing else than finding one's pleasure (I say pleasure, and not utility or interest) in the good (bien), perfection, happiness of another; and thus, though love can be disinterested, it can nonetheless never be detached from our own good, into which pleasure essentially enters.' (R 19 = to Bossuet, 6–16 Oct. 1698 = Foucher de Careil ii 199)

[11] 'I find it well said, . . . that true virtue must be disinterested, that is to say, as I interpret it, that one ought to be brought to find pleasure in the exercise of virtue, and disgust in that of vice, and that this should be the aim of education.' ('Judgment on Shaftesbury', R 196 = Dutens v 34 (Letter 11)) 'Our [own] good is no doubt the basis of our motives, but quite often we find not only our utility but even our pleasure in the good of another; and in this last case there is precisely what ought to be called disinterested love . . .' (R 197) 'Love (amare sive diligere) . . . is rejoicing in the happiness of another, or, what amounts to the same thing, converting (adsciscere) the happiness of another into one's own. With this is resolved a difficult question, of great moment in theology as well: in what way non-mercenary love is given, which is separated from hope and fear, and of all regard for utility. In truth, those whose utility delights us, they are the ones whose happiness turns into (ingreditur) our own happiness; for since things that please us are desired for their own sake.' ('Codex Iuris Gentium' = Dutens iv 295 = L 421–2 = R 171)

[12] On Epicurus see §159.

does not explain how the happiness of others could 'turn into' our own happiness. However important your pleasure may be in causing my pleasure, this causal role does not make it either the whole or a part of my pleasure.

Alternatively, if I take pleasure in something as the essential object of this pleasure, the object is not simply causally related to the pleasure, but internally connected to the value of the pleasure itself. If this is what Leibniz means, he cannot consistently identify good exclusively with pleasure; for I identify my good with pleasure in this specific object, on the assumption that this object is intrinsically appropriate, and hence valuable in its own right.

The obscurity in Leibniz's views about pleasure and happiness infects his attempt to clarify them with an example. We may find it pleasant to look at a beautiful painting, apart from any further gain; when this disinterested pleasure takes a person as its object, it becomes (in his view) pure love.[13] In distinguishing our attitude to things not capable of happiness from our attitude to persons Leibniz recalls Aristotle; our attitude to non-agents does not include a concern for their interests, since they have none, but is simply a concern for their preservation for us (EN 1155b27–31). But if we grant this difference, we may still be puzzled by Leibniz's remark about the painting. Paintings and jokes may be sources of pleasure by themselves, apart from any further instrumental benefit, but Leibniz does not seem to treat our attitude to the painting as parallel to our attitude to the joke. In contrast to a joke, he seems to suggest that we attribute some non-instrumental goodness to the painting, apart from the fact that we find pleasure in it; we find pleasure in it because of this non-instrumental value. But if this is what he means, he does not always hold a hedonist view of happiness.

Perhaps, then, Leibniz really means that happiness consists in pleasure taken in appropriate activities and states. If this is what he means, it is more intelligible to regard the object of the pleasure as part of one's happiness. Hence it is more intelligible to regard the good of another person as a part of one's own good.

Though Leibniz recognizes the possibility of love for another person for the other's own sake, and hence of non-mercenary love, he does not identify this with purely disinterested love. He avoids the Quietist conception of pure love, as Fénelon describes it. According to Quietism, love of God ought eventually to renounce all considerations of self-interest, so that genuine love of God excludes any concern for one's own interest, or perfection, or salvation. Bossuet argues against Fénelon that disinterested love, understood in this way, is neither possible nor desirable. Leibniz takes Bossuet's side in this controversy.[14] He rejects any disinterested love that is separated from one's concern for one's own good. But his composite view of happiness allows love of another to be essential to one's own

---

[13] 'And just as the contemplation of beautiful things is itself pleasant, and a painting of Raphael affects a person who has understanding, even if it brings him no gain, so that some image of his love remains in his eyes and in his pleasures; so also, when the beautiful thing is capable of happiness, the affection passes over into true love.' ('Cod. Iur. Gent.' = Dutens iv 295 = L 422 = R 171)

[14] '. . . This is the controversy about whether love which is disinterested, and seeks the well-being of the beloved, nevertheless depends upon the impulsion toward one's own well-being. . . . I should answer that whatever is pleasant is sought for itself, as opposed, that is, to what is useful to the good ends of producing the well-being of another. . . . the impulse to action arises from a striving towards perfection, the sense of which is pleasure, and there is no action or will on any other basis. . . . Nor can anyone renounce (except merely verbally) being impelled by his own good, without renouncing his own nature' (Pref. Mantissa Cod. Iur. Gent. = L 424). On Quietism see §§529, 611, 717.

good, and not simply instrumental to it; in this sense, Leibniz believes in disinterested love of God.

He complicates his views about motivation and reason still further by describing pleasure as the 'sense' of perfection. Here he suggests that perfection is the end and pleasure is just the sign of our having achieved it. If this is what he means, he avoids a purely hedonist conception of the ultimate end, and thereby allows a more intelligible notion of disinterested concern. His modifications of hedonism help to explain why Leibniz is sympathetic to traditional eudaemonism, which treats disinterested concern for another as part of one's own good. He shares this sympathy with Shaftesbury, and so endorses some of Shaftesbury's defence of unselfish moral attitudes.

But he stops short of endorsing Shaftesbury's claim that virtue promotes happiness in the present life.[15] He objects to philosophers' arguments about virtue and happiness on the ground that they are not effective enough among most people.[16] Leibniz speaks as though he were pointing out some flaw in the argument about virtue and happiness in this life. But he seems to point out only that people find the argument difficult to believe. He does not explain why an appeal to God and to divine rewards and punishments would be the only cogent argument for the claim that virtue always promotes happiness. He seems to suggest that this appeal is more likely to weigh with most people.

Leibniz might intend to object that Shaftesbury's claim is too restricted to be very useful. If we identify happiness with pleasure, virtue promotes our happiness only if we find enough pleasure in being virtuous; but if we happen to be unmoved by that sort of thing, virtue does not (according to this argument) promote our happiness. In that case Shaftesbury's argument applies only to people who already take pleasure in virtue; but they do not need to be convinced by an argument to show that virtue promotes happiness. For the people who need an argument, Shaftesbury's argument is useless.

This objection to Shaftesbury rests on a subjectivist and hedonist conception of happiness. But it is not clear that Leibniz accepts this conception of happiness. He implicitly agrees (for the reasons we have mentioned) that our happiness consists in what is really good; if some or most people find it difficult to recognize what is really good for them, that does not affect the fact that it is good for them. He also agrees that one can find one's own good in the good of others; this is not because everyone finds more pleasure in the good of others, but

[15] 'But that we ought to hold this life itself, and all that makes it desirable, second to the great advantage of others, so that it behooves us to bear the greatest pains for the sake of others—this is beautifully prescribed by philosophers rather than firmly demonstrated (magis pulchre praecipitur a philosophis quam solide demonstratur).' (G iii 388 = R 173 = L 423)

[16] 'For the dignity and glory, and our mind's sense taking pleasure in virtue (animi sui virtute gaudentem sensus), to which they appeal under the names of honestas, are certainly goods of thought or the mind, and indeed great ones. But they are not such as to prevail over all men, or over all the bitterness of evils, since not all men are equally moved by the imagination, especially those who have not grown used to the weighing of virtue or the cherishing of goods of the mind, . . . In order really to establish by a universal demonstration that everything honourable is beneficial, . . . we must assume the immortality of the soul and the ruler of the universe, God.' (G iii 388 = R 173 = L 423) 'One can say that this serenity of spirit, which finds the greatest pleasure in virtue and the greatest evil in vice, that is, in the perfection and imperfection of the will, would be the greatest good of which man is capable here below, even if he had nothing to expect beyond this life. For what can be preferred to this internal harmony, this constant pleasure in the purest and greatest, of which one is always master and which one need never abandon? Yet it must also be said that it is difficult to attain this disposition of spirit and that the number of those who have achieved it is small, most men remaining insensible to this motive, great and beautiful though it is.' (R 58 = L 569–70)

because those who recognize worthwhile pleasures in the appropriate objects take these pleasures in their own genuine good, which includes the good of others. If disinterested love (as Leibniz understands it) promotes one's own good, the disinterested pursuit of virtue should promote one's own good. This is nonetheless true even if virtue does not yield greater pleasure than any other way of life, according to some neutral measure of quantity of pleasure. Shaftesbury's case seems to rely on arguments and assumptions that Leibniz endorses; and so Leibniz does not explain why Shaftesbury is wrong.

If Leibniz concedes this point to Shaftesbury, he need not withdraw his claim that divine rewards and punishments are important. Even if they are not necessary to make virtue promote one's happiness, they may provide significant further reasons for believing this claim, and especially for believing that virtue does not require a long-term sacrifice of happiness. Shaftesbury agrees on these points. But it does not follow that divine rewards and punishments are needed to demonstrate that virtue promotes happiness.

This comparison of Leibniz's claims about disinterested love with his objections to Shaftesbury suggests that he has not explored the implications of his various views on pleasure and happiness. His opposition to Shaftesbury seems to reflect a hedonist and subjectivist conception that does not account for all of Leibniz's claims and arguments about happiness. His arguments seem to bring him closer to the Aristotelian position on this question than his objections to Shaftesbury might would suggest.

589. The Right and the Just

Leibniz's conception of one's good as involving one's own perfection allows concern for the good of others for their own sake. He believes that one's own good also requires such concern for the good of others. This is the basis of goodness and beneficence.[17] These connexions between goodness, perfection, and justice imply that if we have a true conception of our own good, we also seek the good of others for its own sake. This is why enlightened concern for the perfection of the intelligent substance that is myself leads to concern for the perfection of intelligent substances generally.

Why does Leibniz believe that concern for one's own perfection results in concern for the perfection of others? Perhaps he assumes that one's conception of one's own perfection is non-egocentric from the beginning. My concern for myself, on this view, is concern for my perfection simply as the perfection of an intellectual substance; hence any other intellectual substance will appear to me to have the same claim on my concern. Alternatively, he may assume that my conception of my own perfection may be egocentric, but a proper understanding of this perfection requires me to engage in the activities that extend my concern to others. This is the strategy of Aristotle and Aquinas, who take friendship and intellectual love to mediate between self-concern and concern for others. They argue that an egocentric concern for my own perfection as a rational being leads to the co-operative

---

[17] 'Justice is nothing but what conforms to wisdom and goodness combined. The end of goodness is the greatest good. But to recognize this we need wisdom, which is merely the knowledge of the good, as goodness is merely the inclination to do good to all and to prevent evil. . . . we may ask what is the true good. I reply that it is merely whatever serves the perfection of intelligent substances.' (R 50 = L 564)

activities that require non-instrumental concern for others. It is not clear whether Leibniz accepts this argument.

His account of the basis of concern for others in concern for their perfection affects his account of justice. While he accepts traditional 'nominal definitions' of justice, he argues that we find its real essence only by understanding it teleologically.[18] A nominal definition might be negative, defining just actions as those that are not open to reasonable complaint by others. But this definition does not show us what would be a sound basis for reasonable complaint, or why a good person sees a reason for acting justly. To answer these further questions, we need to recognize the basis of justice in love for others and in concern for their perfection.

Leibniz, therefore, describes justice as 'the charity of the wise'.[19] It is the expression of love for others, aiming at the proper end of such love, which is the perfection of intellectual substances. This is the right way to conceive justice, because it is the right way to understand the rational basis of concern for others. Since this basis rests on a true conception of self-interest, Carneades is wrong to believe in a conflict between justice and self-interest.

The connexion of justice with charity means that we cannot separate justice from beneficence. Justice does not consist simply in refraining from harm, and it does not leave other virtues to confer positive benefits on others. On the contrary, if the Golden Rule gives the content of justice, justice includes beneficence, since we would reasonably want others to be beneficent to us, and not simply to avoid harming us.[20] Leibniz argues that we are not simply required to refrain from harm, but also to prevent harm to another if we can easily prevent it.[21] Moreover, we are required not only to prevent harm, but even to benefit another, if we can easily do it (R 55 = L 567–8). If we refuse to provide this benefit, the other person can reasonably complain. We can see that other people would reasonably complain of us, if we notice that we would think it reasonable to complain of them if we were the

[18] 'Everyone would agree, perhaps, on this nominal definition—that justice is a constant will to act in such a way that no person has reason to complain of us. But this is not enough unless the method is given for determining these reasons. Now I observe that some people restrict the reasons for human complaints very narrowly and that others extend them. There are those who believe that it is enough if no harm is done to them and if no one has deprived them of their possessions, holding that no one is obligated to seek the good of others or prevent evil for them, even if it should cost us nothing and give us no pain.' (R 53–4 = L 566)

[19] '...justice is the charity of the wise man, that is, a goodness towards others which ought to conform to wisdom. And wisdom, in my opinion, is nothing but the knowledge of happiness.... we have a right to learn the reasons which... <anyone> has for being what he calls just, in order to see whether these same reasons will not bring him also to be good and to do good.' (R 54 = L 567) 'By moral...I mean something equivalent to natural for a good man, for...we should believe we are incapable of doing things which are contrary to good morals. A good man is one who loves all men, so far as reason permits. Therefore, if I am not mistaken, we may most fittingly define justice, which is the virtue governing that affection which the Greeks call philanthropy, as the charity of the wise man, that is, as charity which follows the dictates of wisdom. So the assertion attributed to Carneades, that justice is the highest folly because it bids us consider the interests of others while neglecting our own, is based on ignorance of its definition. Charity is universal benevolence, and benevolence is the habit of loving or of cherishing. But to love or to cherish is to find pleasure in the happiness of another, or what amounts to the same thing, to accept the happiness of another as one's own' (R 171 = L 421).

[20] At MdS 386 Kant describes the pursuit of one's own perfection and the happiness of others as duties of virtue, as opposed to right. His division between duties of virtue and of right seems to affirm a division that Leibniz rejects.

[21] 'Would one not hold him for a bad man and even for an enemy if he did not want to save us in this situation? I have read in a travelogue of the East Indies that a man being chased by an elephant was saved, because another man in a neighbouring house beat on a drum, which stopped the beast; supposing that the former had cried to the other to beat [the drum], and that he had not wanted to out of pure inhumanity: would he not have had the right to complain?' (R 54–5) Loemker omits this example.

victims in a similar situation. We would think it unreasonable if others were to refuse to benefit us when the cost to them would be trivial and the benefit to us would be large, simply because they did not feel like it or because they wanted us to suffer.[22]

In this reasoning about when a complaint would be reasonable, Leibniz relies on the Golden Rule as a guide to the requirements of justice. He answers the objection that the rule requires the judge not to sentence the criminal, since the judge would not want to be sentenced if she were in the criminal's position.[23] Leibniz argues that we should not apply the Golden Rule simply by putting ourselves in one other person's position, but by considering the results of being all the people affected by the action. A proper application of the Golden Rule requires the judge to sentence the criminal, and requires unequal distribution of profits in a partnership.[24]

Leibniz makes a good case for refusing to confine justice to abstention from harming. But he does not explain his reasoning from the Golden Rule in any detail. It seems to be open to Butler's objection that utilitarianism allows unfair treatment of one person simply for the benefit of others.[25] Leibniz's example of punishment might suggest this result. If I put myself in the position of A, B, and C and recognize that the proposed action would harm A, but benefit B and C, does it follow that I would want it done if I were in B's and C's position, but would not want it done if I were in A's, so that the action turns out to be just? If this is how Leibniz argues, he must assume that in applying the Golden Rule, I take a purely self-interested point of view. Such reasoning seems to justify cutting up one person for spare-part surgery on five others, or killing one innocent person to encourage others not to break a law.

If Leibniz intends this interpretation of the Golden Rule, he assumes that it requires some quantitative calculation of overall benefits and harms. In that case, his perfectionism and his teleological conception of charity and justice lead him into utilitarianism. He does not try to defend this conclusion against the objection that it may violate the requirements of justice to the individual.

One might, however, apply the Golden Rule differently. If I am proposing to imprison or execute an innocent person as a scapegoat, Leibniz might ask me to recognize that this innocent person has something to complain about, because I can see that I would have something to complain about if I were the innocent victim. I would resent being made a scapegoat. If, however, I were guilty of a crime, I would not resent being punished for it; I would prefer not to suffer the harm of punishment, but I would not claim to have any basis for resentment.

---

[22] 'We may say, then, that justice, at least among men, is the constant will to act as far as possible in such a way that no one can complain of us, if we would not complain of others in a similar situation. From this it is evident that when it is impossible to act so that the whole world is satisfied, we should try to satisfy people as much as possible. What is just thus conforms to the charity of the wise man.' (R 56–7 = L 568)

[23] Cf. Kant's discussion of the Golden Rule, G 430.

[24] 'The judge must put himself not only in the place of the criminal but also in that of the others whose interest lies in the crime being punished, and he must determine the greater good in which the lesser evil is included. The same is true of the objection that distributive justice demands an inequality among men . . . Put yourself in the place of all and assume that they are well informed and enlightened. You will gather this conclusion from their votes: they will regard it as fitting to their own interest that distinctions be made between one another. For example, if profits were not divided proportionally in a commercial society, some would not enter it at all, and others would quickly leave it, which is contrary to the interest of the whole society.' (R 56 = L 568)

[25] Butler; §702.

The appeals to the Golden Rule and to possible complaints suggest two different questions that Leibniz might be asking: (1) If you are a purely self-interested agent in each of the relevant positions, do you think the proposed action benefits or harms you? (2) If you apply your sense of legitimate bases for complaint to each person's position, what do you say? In some cases the two questions might support the same conclusion, as they do in Leibniz's case of deserved punishment. But sometimes they seem to support different conclusions, as they do in cases of scapegoats.

The interpretation of the Golden Rule suggested by the second question gives more plausible answers, since it does not lead to the violations of justice that seem to be allowed by the first question. But the second question does not provide an independent test of justice; for legitimate bases of complaint and resentment presuppose some views about justice, rather than explaining them by some independent principle. The function of the second question is to separate these views about justice from any possible distorting effects of our own interest and our own point of view. The first question, by contrast, offers an independent test of justice. But the test that it offers seems to lead to unjust results.

Leibniz's appeals to the Golden Rule and to the possibility of legitimate complaint anticipate later applications of these tests both by utilitarians and by their opponents.[26] His discussion is too simple, since he does not suggest that his tests for justice need interpretation, or that any questions can be raised about their implications.

The questions that arise about Leibniz's test for justice also raise doubts about whether justice can be identified with the charity of the wise, as he understands it. If charity is to be understood as generalized concern with human interests, it does not seem to be the same as justice. For charity, so understood, seems to lead to a utilitarian conclusion, through the first interpretation of the Golden Rule. Justice, however, seems to stop short of this utilitarian conclusion. Leibniz is right to say that justice is not confined to refraining from harm, and so cannot be distinguished from charity on that basis, but he is wrong to infer (if he means to infer this) that justice is simply generalized benevolence.

This objection does not show that justice is not the charity of the wise; for it may be unfair to Leibniz to identify charity with generalized benevolence, understood as a strictly utilitarian outlook. One might reply that love of other people includes concern for their rights and obligations as individual persons, and so it should make us responsive to complaints founded on convictions about fairness. In describing God's outlook as impartial love for persons, we do not imply that God is indifferent to justice, or that God is ready to impose extreme harm on some simply to benefit others. Similarly, if justice is the charity of the wise, and charity is not concern for maximum total welfare, justice is not utilitarian concern either. But if considerations of fairness and justice regulate charity, an understanding of charity is not entirely prior to an understanding of justice. Hence the account of justice as the charity of the wise may be circular.

Leibniz's remarks on justice and charity are suggestive, but inconclusive, since they do not examine these questions that they inevitably raise. He neither endorses a purely utilitarian conception of charity nor distinctly repudiates it. He leaves this issue about divine and human benevolence for others to discuss.

---

[26] Cf. Hare, MT, chs. 5–6.

590. Naturalism v. Voluntarism

Leibniz often rejects a voluntarist account of the basis of moral principles, for theological, metaphysical, and moral reasons. Though he writes in ignorance of Cudworth's *Eternal and Immutable Morality*, his statement of the issue and of the reasons for naturalism is close to Cudworth's.[27] He formulates the issue in the *Euthyphro*, and, for Cudworth's reasons, takes Socrates' side.[28] Leibniz claims that Lutheran ('our') theologians all reject voluntarism, and most Roman and Reformed (Calvinist) theologians reject it, on both Scriptural and philosophical grounds.[29] If Leibniz is right, his report indicates that Lutheran theologians reject the voluntaristic elements in some of Luther's remarks.[30] He rejects Pufendorf's claim to be defending an orthodox Lutheran position.

In Leibniz's view, the voluntarist position 'would destroy the justice of God'.[31] A correct conception of God must rest on a belief in the divine perfections. These perfections must be recognized as perfect for some other reason than the fact that they belong to God (T, Pref. = H 53, 59). We must not defend God's dealings with human beings by arguing that he is above justice, or that his superior power automatically makes his actions just (T = H 95). Like Cudworth, Leibniz connects voluntarism with the views of some of Socrates' opponents in the Platonic dialogues. Where Cudworth mentions Protagoras, Leibniz mentions Thrasymachus, revived by Hobbes (R 47 = L 562).

Voluntarism, according to Leibniz, makes justice 'arbitrary', whereas the opposed view makes it part of the nature of things, and no more dependent on will than arithmetic is (R 49 = L 563). In the light of views such as Cumberland's and Pufendorf's, more needs to be said to show that these two views exhaust the possibilities. A moderate voluntarist argues that God has reasons for preferring one law over another, and that these reasons rest on facts about human beings, but still they are not moral principles until they are affirmed by God's will. Leibniz's discussion suffers from his failure to consider this argument to show that not all voluntarist views make justice arbitrary.

Nonetheless, it is difficult to escape some version of his objection. Even if we grant that, as Pufendorf supposes, God's commands agree with (roughly speaking) natural good, we still need an explanation of why this is so. Does God command freely or necessarily? If God is free, by his unqualified power, to command something else, and (by hypothesis) is not guided by what is objectively right, it does not seem unfair to regard God's choice as arbitrary. Alternatively, if God commands necessarily, what is the source of the necessity? If

---

[27] Leibniz knew Cudworth's *TIS*, which suggests a naturalist view about the goodness of God at, e.g., ch. 5 §5 = iii 461.

[28] 'It is generally agreed that whatever God wills is good and just. But there remains the question whether it is good and just because God wills it or whether God wills it because it is good and just; in other words whether justice and goodness are arbitrary or whether they belong to the necessary and eternal truths about the nature of things, as do numbers and proportions. The former opinion has been held by certain philosophers and by theologians, both Roman and Reformed. But the Reformed theologians of today usually reject this teaching, as do also all our own theologians and most of those of the Roman church as well.' (R 45–6 = L 561)

[29] 'All our theologians, therefore, and most of those of the Roman church, as well as the ancient Church Fathers, and the wisest and most esteemed philosophers, have favoured the second view, which holds that goodness and justice have grounds independent of will and force.' (R 46 = L 562)

[30] See §412.

[31] 'Common conception of justice' = R 46 = L 561.

(by hypothesis) it is not the objective rightness of the action, but a psychological necessity in God, the choice of this action over others still seems arbitrary.[32]

591. The Errors of Pufendorf's Voluntarism

Leibniz does not think highly of Pufendorf in general, and the judgments in his letter 'Opinion on the Principle of Pufendorf' are directed to his short work *De officio hominis*. Since he does not carefully examine Pufendorf's fuller statement of his case in *J De iure naturae et gentium*, he sometimes distorts Pufendorf's position or overlooks some complications in it. Some of his questionable claims are attacked by Barbeyrac in his defence of Pufendorf. Barbeyrac's comments give us an opportunity to consider the merits of each side in this dispute about natural law.[33]

Leibniz attacks Pufendorf's view that obligation requires a superior, so that there are no moral requirements without the command of a superior. After remarking that this would commit Pufendorf to Hobbesian views about the state of nature and about the possibility of international law, Leibniz considers the obvious reply. Pufendorf claims to avoid a Hobbesian conception of the state of nature by arguing that moral requirements are not, as Hobbes supposes, obligations imposed by a state, but obligations imposed by God. The state of nature is a state in which we have no superior, but, since God always commands obedience to the moral law, we are never in a state of nature. We may pass over questions about whether Pufendorf and Leibniz give a fair account of Hobbes's position. Even if Pufendorf improves on Hobbes on this point, Leibniz still believes that Pufendorf's voluntarism is open to objection.

His first objection mentions Grotius' 'etiamsi' clause, but does not explain the point clearly.[34] As he describes Grotius' view, even without reference to God care for one's own well-being would create a natural obligation. But he does not explain what he takes Grotius to mean by 'well-being'. We might take him to suppose, as Barbeyrac does, that Grotius recognizes only prudential, not moral, reasons, in abstraction from God. If this is what Leibniz means, he plays directly into the hands of Pufendorf and Barbeyrac. Alternatively, we might intend 'well-being' in the broader sense intended by Grotius, so that it does not embrace simply the pleasant and the advantageous, but also includes the morally good. In that case, his appeal to Grotius implies opposition to voluntarism. But he does not defend it fully enough to give any argument against the voluntarist position.

He states a second objection more carefully, arguing that voluntarists cannot give an acceptable account of the goodness of God. If divine justice is simply the product of the

---

[32] See Ward's discussion of voluntarism, NG 71–110, discussed in §604.

[33] Schneewind, 'Barbeyrac', Saastamoinen, *MFM*, and Korkman, *BNL*, discuss Barbeyrac's criticism of Leibniz. Korkman is the most sympathetic to Barbeyrac. Buckle, *NLTP* 60–4, defends Pufendorf against Leibniz's criticism: 'It could perhaps be said that, for Pufendorf, the will of a superior, without just reasons, is only coercion; while just reasons, without the will of a superior, are only reasons for law, but not law itself' (61). This feature of Pufendorf's position, however, does not answer Leibniz's questions about why it is honestum to obey God's commands.

[34] 'Indeed, not to mention that which Grotius justly observed, namely that there would be a natural obligation even on the hypothesis—which is impossible—that God does not exist, or if one but left the divine existence out of consideration; since care for one's own preservation and well-being certainly lays on men many requirements about taking care of others . . .' (R 71)

divine will, God is not essentially just.[35] If we recognize that God is essentially just, and we do not simply mean to define 'just' as whatever God wills, we must recognize eternal truths about justice that are not products of the divine will. If Pufendorf denies these independent eternal truths in the case of justice, he ought also to maintain that God creates all the eternal truths, as Descartes did; he has no good reason to single out truths about goodness and justice (R 71–2).

Pufendorf might regard this as an unfair criticism. It ignores his arguments for distinguishing moral properties from others, and hence for avoiding voluntarism in relation to all the eternal truths. In his view, the properties that belong to matter in motion belong to nature itself. We need not treat physical properties as the result of divine imposition; the imposed properties are the ones that do not belong to nature itself.

This argument about the difference between natural and moral entities is inconsistent (as we have seen) with Pufendorf's claim that his voluntarism about morality follows from the recognition of God's freedom in creation. Hence it creates as many difficulties for Pufendorf's overall position as it resolves. But if we ignore these broader difficulties, does the treatment of moral entities offer a plausible reply to Leibniz on eternal truths?

To answer this question, we need to evaluate Pufendorf's reasons for refusing to include moral properties among the properties of 'nature itself'. If he were to refuse to treat any teleological properties—about goals, welfare, good, or health—as properties of nature itself, he would disagree with Leibniz over the general questions about nature that Leibniz discusses in 'On Nature Itself'. But in fact Pufendorf does not disagree with Leibniz on these broader issues in natural philosophy. For he allows prudential properties as part of nature; he could not retract this view without destroying his account of the content of natural law.

If, therefore, Pufendorf is to reply convincingly to Leibniz, he needs a good reason for drawing the sharp distinction he draws between prudential and moral properties, and for treating moral properties alone as the products of divine legislation. We have found reason to doubt Pufendorf's arguments for his sharp distinction.

592. Pufendorf's Legislative Account of Morality

According to Leibniz, Pufendorf's claims about the necessary connexion between morality and legislation betray a misunderstanding of the status of morality. Virtuous people do not need to regard their action as required by any act of legislation.[36] Reference to law may be necessary to move those who are reluctant to act virtuously, but it is not appropriate for the

---

[35] 'Neither the norm of conduct itself nor the essence of the just depends on <God's> free decision, but rather on eternal truths, objects of the divine intellect, which constitute, so to speak, the essence of divinity itself; and it is right that our author is reproached by theologians when he maintains the contrary; because, I believe, he had not seen the wicked consequences which arise from it. Justice, indeed, would not be an essential attribute of God, if he himself established justice and law by his free will.' (R 71)

[36] 'Thus he who acts well, not out of hope or fear, but by an inclination of his soul, is so far from not behaving justly that, on the contrary, he acts more justly than all others, imitating in a certain way, as a man, divine justice. Whoever, indeed, does good out of love for God or of his neighbour, takes pleasure precisely in the action itself (such being the nature of love) and does not need any other incitement, or the command of a superior; for that man the saying that the law is not made for the just is valid. To such a degree is it repugnant to reason to say that only the law or constraint makes a man just . . .' (R 72)

virtuous. Leibniz alludes to a Scriptural passage commonly used in Lutheran argument to contrast the outlook of the Christian with the outlook of those moved by fear of the law.[37]

Leibniz seems to be unfair to Pufendorf here, by running together different claims: (1) If something is morally right, it must be required by an act of legislation. (2) If we are morally virtuous, we must regard morally right actions as required by an act of legislation. (3) If we are morally virtuous, we must perform morally right actions out of fear of the legislator. The criticisms of Pufendorf attack the third claim, but Leibniz does not show that Pufendorf is committed to it; it does not follow from either of the first two claims.

But Leibniz's objection suggests a fair question. If Pufendorf does not accept the third claim, why is an act of legislation needed? We might grant, and we might concede that Leibniz has overlooked, some element of compulsoriness in morality. When Leibniz says that a virtuous person does the right actions out of love for God or his neighbour, he does not seem to give an adequate account of the virtuous person. I might do many things out of love of actions or people without regarding them as required by morality. In taking them to be part of morality, I recognize that they do not depend on my preference; I am required to form my preference by these demands. In that respect—we might say on Pufendorf's behalf—I ought to look on them as a matter of law rather than choice or liking.

But to agree with Pufendorf on this point is not to agree that we must look on right actions as products of legislation. To recognize an action as required and non-optional, I need not believe that anyone has legislated it. To agree with Pufendorf we would have to overlook Suarez's distinction between the due (debitum) and the obligatory (in his narrow sense). We could correct Leibniz's neglect of the compulsory element in morality, and the recognition of compulsoriness in the moral consciousness, without accepting Pufendorf's claim that the compulsoriness of morality must arise from legislation.

Leibniz alludes to this issue; he argues that Pufendorf's views on necessity overlook the fact that moral situations themselves can present us with practical necessities without reference to any law.[38] But despite this plausible objection to a purely legal conception of moral necessity, Leibniz concedes Pufendorf's restriction of duty to what is prescribed by law (R 73). It is not clear what this concession means, however. Does Leibniz also agree with Pufendorf's claim that law requires an act of legislation by a superior? If he agrees on this point, he seems to give up a basic point to Pufendorf.

Though Leibniz's position is stated too briefly to be clear or convincing, it suggests a fair criticism. If Pufendorf claims that the specific necessity characteristic of legislation is essential to morality, and that other sorts of necessity or compulsoriness are insufficient,

---

[37] 'But we know that the law is good, if a man use it lawfully, as knowing this, that law is not made for a righteous man, but for the lawless and unruly, for the ungodly and sinners.' (1Tim. 1:8–9) In commenting on this passage Aquinas explains the sense in which just people are not under the law: 'It would seem that not all are subject to the law. For those alone are subject to a law for whom a law is made. But the Apostle says (1Tim. 1:9): "The law is not made for a just person." Therefore the just are not subject to the law. . . . This argument is true of subjection by way of coercion: for, in this way, "the law is not made for the just person": because "they are a law to themselves," while they "show the work of the law written in their hearts," as the Apostle says (Rm. 2:14–15). Consequently the law does not have a coercive force on them as it does on the unjust.' (ST 1–2 q96 a5 obj1 ad1)

[38] 'Nor is Chapter 2, part 4 [of Pufendorf's DOH] correct in saying that he who recognizes no superior cannot be constrained by necessity: as if the very nature of things and care for one's happiness and safety did not have their own requirements; and many things which are ordained by reason itself in order that, following the guidance of our best nature, we will not attract evil to ourselves, or come to lose the good.' (R 73)

324

what feature of legislation is relevant? A distinctive feature of legislated necessity is the fact that it is imposed on us by someone, so that it represents someone's demands on me. Why should this be distinctive of morality?

We can try different answers to this question: (1) Other people's demands impose a distinctive sort of requirement, and the virtuous person must recognize this. (2) Legislation represents the demands of a superior, who deserves respect and obedience. (3) Legislation comes from a legislator who imposes sanctions.

None of these answers vindicates Pufendorf. The first two seem to be self-defeating. For if he means that the demands of other people or of a superior create a special sort of requirement, he seems to rely on further assumptions: (a) We can distinguish legitimate from illegitimate demands. (b) We can distinguish the sort of superiority that creates moral authority. (c) We already acknowledge a moral requirement to listen to the legitimate demands of others or of a superior. All of these assumptions defeat Pufendorf's purpose because they appeal to some moral requirement antecedent to any legislation. Hence Pufendorf cannot consistently rely on any of these three assumptions.

Since this objection shows that Pufendorf cannot give either of the first two answers to Leibniz's objection, he is left with the third, making morality consist in the arbitrary will of a legislator supported by sanctions that provide the reason for obedience. But we might reasonably doubt whether the threat of a sanction is either necessary or sufficient for morality or for moral virtue. It is difficult to refute Leibniz's suggestion that Pufendorf relies on a perverse conception of morality and of moral virtue.

593. Barbeyrac's Defence of Pufendorf on the Content of Morality

Barbeyrac believes that Leibniz's attack on Pufendorf is misguided because it ignores Pufendorf's account of the content of morality. According to Leibniz, Pufendorf's rejection of naturalism commits him to the view that God exercises arbitrary power. For if God does not necessarily will what is right independently of the divine legislative will, God's choice to enjoin these laws on us rather than others must (according to Leibniz) be an arbitrary choice, in the sense that it does not rest on any knowledge that it is better to enjoin these laws than to enjoin any others.[39]

Barbeyrac correctly objects that Leibniz has failed to acknowledge two points on which Pufendorf repudiates Ockhamist claims about God's unqualified power: (1) The content of the natural law is fixed by natural good and harm. (2) God can neither act nor want to act unjustly (Pufendorf, DHC 459). From these two claims it follows that God's imposition of these laws is not an exercise of 'arbitrary will' (volonté arbitraire, 458), but an expression of God's necessary goodness and justice. Barbeyrac needs both of these claims. If the first were true without the second, God would be free to impose some different law with a different

---

[39] Barbeyrac's answer to Leibniz appears in Pufendorf, DHC 429–95. See Schneewind, 'Barbeyrac'; IA 250–9; Buckle, 'Voluntarism' 110–14. Barbeyrac refers to Leibniz as an anonymous writer in the body of his essay, but names him on the title page.

content, and the provisions of that law would be morally right. But Barbeyrac interprets the second claim in such a way that God necessarily chooses justice, with its specific content fixed by natural good.

Here Pufendorf and Barbeyrac come close to acceptance of the naturalist view that the content and existence of the natural law do not result from God's legislative will. If we claim that God cannot choose to act unjustly, either this claim says simply that God's choosing something makes it just, or it implies that something is just independently of his choosing it. In the first case, the necessity of God's choosing just action still allows the divine will to be arbitrary; hence Barbeyrac must admit that something is just independently of God's choosing it. But such an admission conflicts with the claim that nothing is right independently of God's legislation.

But perhaps Pufendorf and Barbeyrac do not mean this. Perhaps they mean that the content of the natural law is fixed independently of God's legislative will, but its character as morality depends on God's legislation. This legislation, however, is necessary; it is not an exercise of God's free will. The attempt to replace arbitrary will with necessary will raises further objections. For Barbeyrac cannot say that God's choice of laws aimed at natural goods is necessary because God necessarily chooses the right; for if he said that, he would admit that right is independent of God's choice, and so he would concede the whole point to Leibniz. But if it is a mere psychological necessity, not based in rational necessity, it does not seem less arbitrary in the relevant sense.

Barbeyrac's defence of Pufendorf on this point is therefore open to question. He is right to accuse Leibniz of not taking account of everything that Pufendorf says and of over-simplifying his position in ways that make it easier to refute with well-worn anti-voluntarist arguments. As Barbeyrac sees, Pufendorf modifies the voluntarist position in ways that escape criticisms that apply to Ockhamist voluntarism. But these modifications do not result in a defensible alternative to Leibniz's naturalism. Either they collapse into naturalism or they are open to a modified version of the naturalist objections to Ockham.

594. God's Right to Rule

Barbeyrac sees a further unfairness in Leibniz's claim that Pufendorf is inconsistent in his claims about the relation of God to morality. On the one hand, Pufendorf claims that morality requires divine legislation. On the other hand, he claims that we should not treat God simply as a Hobbesian sovereign whose right consists simply in superior power to coerce us; we should also recognize that God has 'just cause' for his justified claim to power over us (R 73). Leibniz objects that Pufendorf's claims are inconsistent; if we have just cause to obey God, some moral obligation is antecedent to divine legislation, and it does not all depend on divine legislation. This objection relies on one of Cudworth's objections to Hobbes; if we need to distinguish legitimate from illegitimate rulers in order to identify authoritative legislators, not all standards of legitimacy are products of legislation.[40]

---

[40] See Cudworth, §548.

Pufendorf has a way out of this objection only if the 'just cause' for God's rule is non-moral. This may be what he has in mind; if we deny that God's superiority rests simply on superior force, a moral basis is not the only alternative. We may also recognize someone as superior out of gratitude, love, admiration, or reverence, none of which necessarily rests on recognition of moral rightness. Leibniz's objection, then, is too simple.

But it may nonetheless be basically correct. For the non-moral attitudes that we have mentioned do not seem to provide a sufficient basis to show that God is an appropriate moral authority, or that his will could produce moral rightness. To be moved to obey someone out of gratitude, admiration, and so on is not to have any basis for believing that their commands will be morally right; and action exclusively from such motives is not the action of a morally virtuous person.

It is difficult to see, therefore, how any non-moral explanation of 'just cause' could provide a morally appropriate basis for obedience to God. Any moral explanation faces Leibniz's objection that it makes Pufendorf's position inconsistent. A fuller examination of Pufendorf's position shows that Leibniz is careless in his interpretation, but nonetheless sees the essential weakness in Pufendorf.

He adds a pertinent question about what Pufendorf takes force to contribute to moral obligation. He suggests that Pufendorf has not worked out the relation between force and the reasons that hold independently of force.[41] Sometimes Pufendorf seems to say that obligation requires a superior because a superior introduces force; but he also insists that we are required to obey God independently of the Hobbesian reasons based on God's power and on force. Hence Pufendorf seems to allow that the moral reasons supporting God's right to rule are independent of divine sanctions. Though the sanctions provide a further motive to obey, they do not in themselves provide an additional moral reason to obey, and so they do not explain the moral character of our obedience to the laws that are backed by sanctions. Hence Pufendorf has failed to explain the character of the moral reasons that he presupposes in arguing that we are required to obey God. He looks in the wrong direction for an account of the distinctive features of morality.

595. Barbeyrac's Objections to Eudaemonism

Barbeyrac not only defends Pufendorf against Leibniz's attack, but also attacks the point of view from which Leibniz criticizes Pufendorf. Part of his defence of voluntarism relies on his arguments to show that naturalists cannot capture the distinctive features of morality. He believes that naturalists who take nature without divine legislation to be sufficient for morality hold an impoverished conception of morality. Since divine legislation introduces the morally right (honestum), a naturalist must reduce everything to pleasure and advantage. To show that Leibniz does this, Barbeyrac attacks his eudaemonism.

[41] The steps of Leibniz's criticism are difficult to follow in detail, but his conclusion raises a fair question: 'Supposing, for example, that a sick Christian fell into the power of a Turkish doctor, by whom he was compelled to practise salutary precepts that he already knew for some time, but which are now strengthened by necessity (necessitate armatis). If he were given an opportunity to escape, would he be obliged to temperance more than he had been before his imprisonment? One or the other, then: either reasons oblige prior to force, or they do not oblige any longer when force ceases.' ('Pufendorf' = Dutens iv 282 = R 75)

Barbeyrac over-simplifies the questions about eudaemonism. Both Aquinas and Suarez deny his assumption that eudaemonism subordinates everything to one's own advantage and pleasure; for they regard the right (honestum) as distinct from the advantageous (commodum), but regard both as promoting the agent's ultimate good. In overlooking this feature of the eudaemonist position, Barbeyrac weakens his defence of Pufendorf against the objections of Leibniz. Though Leibniz, as we have seen, tends to represent his eudaemonism as though it were hedonism, he does not consistently do this; and if he did, he would misrepresent the possibilities open to a eudaemonist.

To show that eudaemonists reduce the good to the pleasant and the useful, Barbeyrac alleges that Leibniz overlooks the distinction that 'the wise pagans' have drawn between the right (l'honnête) and the useful (l'utile) (445). In his view, Leibniz's account of motivation reduces all value to the useful. Whether or not this is true of Leibniz, it is clearly false of the traditional eudaemonist position that Leibniz seeks to defend. Like many others, Barbeyrac fails to acknowledge that traditional eudaemonists claim to distinguish the right and the advantageous without abandoning eudaemonism.[42] Some argument is needed to show that they are wrong.

Let us, however, concede to Barbeyrac that concern for morality cannot be explained by reference to concern for one's own ultimate good. Why should we not reject eudaemonism, but believe in intrinsic rightness, recognizing that some reasons derived from natural good and evil are distinct from reasons of advantage? An appeal to natural good and evil does not necessarily confine itself to what is good and evil for me, and so it does not necessarily confine itself to self-interested reasons (narrowly understood). Pufendorf gives us no reason to believe that only a divine command could introduce a different sort of reason.

This objection gains force from Barbeyrac's objection to Leibniz's eudaemonism. According to Barbeyrac, the wise pagans, in contrast to Leibniz, recognized the honestum as distinct from the advantageous. How did they do this? Barbeyrac and Pufendorf believe that the distinctive feature of moral goodness is its dependence on a divine command. If, then, the wise pagans recognized moral goodness, must they not have recognized the dependence of morality on laws and divine commands?[43] But this was not part of their conception of morality. If Pufendorf is right, then Barbeyrac is wrong to allow that the wise pagans recognized the honestum.

His claim is nonetheless plausible; perhaps he simply means that when the ancients speak of the honestum, they recognized reason independent of considerations of one's own interest. But if this is what it takes to recognize the honestum, divine commands do not seem to be necessary for morality. Barbeyrac's praise of the wise pagans conflicts with his acceptance of Pufendorf's necessary conditions for morality; he would be well advised to abandon Pufendorf's view.

Barbeyrac's account of the honestum exposes a central issue in views of morality. Suarez follows a traditional naturalist view in supposing that, since the honestum is independent of the divine legislative will, moral goodness is independent of it too. Culverwell tries to

---

[42] Reid is also obscure on this question; see §§854–5.
[43] Barbeyrac does not deal with this aspect of ancient moral philosophy in chs. 27–8 of his 'Morality', which discuss the Stoics and Cicero. He criticizes the Stoics for taking virtue to be sufficient for happiness without reference to rewards in the afterlife. Given his views about the importance of moral goodness, it is not clear that this criticism is altogether fair.

avoid this inference; he suggests that to recognize the honestum is to recognize something appealing and attractive in its own right, but not to recognize the rational necessity that belongs to morality. Cumberland agrees with Culverwell in recognizing intrinsic perfection worthy of pursuit, but he denies that this is sufficient for the honestum.[44] Pufendorf agrees with Suarez in identifying the honestum with the morally good, but he disagrees with him in taking moral goodness to require law. While Barbeyrac agrees with Pufendorf on this point, he undermines his position by allowing that the wise pagans could recognize the morally good without recognizing divine commands. He could retreat from this position to Culverwell's position, but, if he did that, he would weaken his argument against Leibniz.

596. Barbeyrac's Argument from Obligation

To support his claim that naturalists cannot consistently recognize the distinctive character of the honestum, Barbeyrac argues that they cannot capture moral obligation. In the naturalists' view, obligation must rest on one's own reason. But this view cannot account for the fact that obligation must be imposed on us. For our reason is simply ourselves, and we cannot impose an obligation or duty (dette) on ourselves (473).[45] Hence, the maxims of reason, however much they may conform to the nature of things, carry no obligation until our reason has discerned God as its source; only the will of God can produce a genuine obligation (473–4).[46]

This argument about the source of obligation rests on the questionable assumption that an obligation must be imposed through some act of imposition; that is why Barbeyrac assumes that if naturalists reject God as the imposer, they must claim that they impose the obligation on themselves. But self-imposition, he suggests, is an idle performance; for obligation must be imposed on us irrespective of our own wishes, whereas something we impose on ourselves depends precisely on our own wish to impose it or to release ourselves from it. Whereas we cannot release ourselves from a genuine moral obligation, we can always release ourselves from something we impose on ourselves. Hence imposition on oneself cannot create genuine obligation.

We might dispute the assumption that we can always release ourselves from what we impose on ourselves. If we make a promise, we cannot release ourselves from it, but do we not impose it on ourselves by voluntarily making the promise? Barbeyrac might fairly reject this example. Though I freely undertake to do x, by promising to do x, I do not impose on myself the obligation to do x; for I am obliged to do x only if I am obliged to keep my

---

[44] Cumberland; §532. Culverwell; §558.

[45] Barbeyrac cites Seneca's remark, at Ben. v 8, that one cannot be one's own debtor, which, however, Seneca does not use to draw Barbeyrac's conclusions. The same argument about self-imposed obligations is used by Warburton; see §875.

[46] According to Schneewind, Barbeyrac's voluntarism rests on his belief in the incommensurability of moral and prudential justification and motivation: 'Like Pufendorf, Barbeyrac offers no positive account of the inherent strength of duty, or of how awareness of "the beauty of virtue" (Devoirs, p. 447) can motivate us. But he is quite insistent that the motivation cannot come solely from reason's awareness of the nature of things. Reason is, in the end, only ourselves reasoning; and "no one can impose on himself an indispensable necessity of acting in such and such a manner". What I impose I can remove. Necessity holds only if I cannot at my own pleasure escape from it. If I can release myself there is "no true obligation" (Devoirs, pp. 472–4). Only the command of another imposes necessity.' (Schneewind, 'Barbeyrac' 188)

promises, and that is not an obligation I impose on myself. Hence Barbeyrac is right to reject any appeal to self-imposed obligation.

But this argument damages naturalism only if naturalism implies that imposed obligation is the only possible source of moral requirements. Suarez rejects Barbeyrac's assumption. He distinguishes indicative from prescriptive law, and argues that only prescriptive law introduces moral necessity by imposed obligation. Morality and moral necessity require only indicative law; they involve duties (debita) that are not imposed. Barbeyrac assumes that if obligations are imposed, duties (dettes) are also imposed; but he is not entitled to rely on this assumption in arguing against Suarez. If he argues against naturalists who agree with Cudworth in identifying duty and obligation, he is not entitled to assume that obligations are imposed.

If we state Suarez's doctrine, but use Cudworth's broad conception of obligation, we claim that some moral necessity involves obligations that are not imposed. A voluntarist may now ask where obligations come from if they are not imposed. According to a naturalist, our own reason discerns and conforms to the nature of things, but it does not impose any obligation arising from the nature of things. Our reason must recognize the obligation; but, according to the naturalist, the nature of things itself makes it true that we are obliged to act a specific way. No one imposes the obligation on us.

To answer this defence of naturalism, Barbeyrac might argue that the alleged obligation existing in the nature of things does not constitute a genuine obligation until we impose it on ourselves; for until we do that, it has no influence on our actions, and obligation implies some sort of motivation. But this internalist assumption about obligation and motivation undermines Barbeyrac's claims no less than it undermines naturalist claims. If he accepts internalism, must he not say that our recognition of the will of God, rather than the will of God itself, imposes the obligation on us? If he refuses to say this, and distinguishes—quite reasonably—the existence of the obligation itself from our recognition of it, he should allow the same distinction to the naturalist.

597. Leibniz v. Traditional Eudaemonism

Our discussion of Leibniz and Barbeyrac shows that Leibniz's eudaemonist and naturalist position is defensible against voluntarist objections. Leibniz does not present a full statement and defence of his ethical outlook, but he says enough about it to suggest that it deserves to be taken seriously.

Leibniz's remarks on ethics justify his claim to defend the insights of Scholastic philosophy. But he does not simply repeat traditional eudaemonism. We have seen that some of his arguments go beyond the views of Aristotle and Aquinas. His main innovations are these:

(1) We have sometimes found it difficult to distinguish his eudaemonism from hedonism. Though a consistent hedonist position undermines his claims about self-love and the love of others, he is not careful to avoid hedonism.

(2) His eudaemonism is combined rather awkwardly with an appeal to perfection as an end, and it is not clear how the two principles fit together. Aquinas introduces perfection as an aspect of one's ultimate good, and so combines eudaemonism and naturalism with

perfectionism. It is not so clear that Leibniz does this. The fact that his conception of the good sometimes tends towards hedonism makes it even more difficult to see how perfection and happiness are connected. A conception of happiness closer to Aristotle's makes the connexion easier to grasp. Sometimes, however, Leibniz's principle of perfection seems rather similar to one of Clarke's principles of fitness—as though it were intended as a principle that we can just see to be correct, without reference to our nature as rational agents.

(3) He assumes that the appropriate extension of eudaemonism is some maximizing concern; at least he neither examines nor rejects this assumption. Hence his claims about justice and charity may easily suggest a utilitarian conception of the morally right.

It is useful to pick out these features of Leibniz's position, for two reasons: (a) They are not features of Aristotle's or Aquinas' position. (b) Kant criticizes them severely (in the form in which he knows them from Wolff and his successors).[47] It is not surprising if Kant believes that his arguments against these aspects of Leibniz's position also refute the traditional eudaemonist position, or if readers of Kant believe this. But if we are right about the differences between Leibniz's position and the traditional eudaemonist position, we ought not to suppose, without further argument, that Kant's objections to the Leibnizian position apply to the traditional eudaemonist position.

Equally, we ought not to assume that Leibniz's particular interpretation of the eudaemonist position is mistaken, simply because it seems to lead to conclusions that face powerful Kantian objections. Perhaps traditional eudaemonism really justifies these conclusions, or perhaps it is so vague that it cannot justify any specific conclusion on the questions that Leibniz discusses. But it is worth noticing that these controversial features of Leibniz's position in moral psychology, the metaphysics of perfection, and normative ethics, have no basis in traditional eudaemonism.

---

[47] See Schneewind, *IA*, ch. 22. On the development of Kant's critical ethics in relation to his predecessors see Schmucker, *UEK*, ch. 5.

44

PUFENDORF AND
NATURAL LAW

598. Barbeyrac's Attempt to Assimilate Grotius to Pufendorf

Though Leibniz's attacks on Pufendorf from a naturalist point of view do not convince Barbeyrac to abandon Pufendorf's position, naturalist arguments influence Barbeyrac's interpretation of Pufendorf. He believes that once we understand Pufendorf, we will see that he already captures the plausible elements of the naturalist position, so that naturalist criticisms are beside the point. For this reason Barbeyrac believes that Grotius is the pioneer who makes some progress towards the position that Pufendorf articulates fully. Now that we have examined both Grotius and Pufendorf, we can return to Barbeyrac's argument to show that they basically agree, and that they together achieve an important advance in moral theory.

This synthesis of Grotius and Pufendorf is historically influential and philosophically significant. As we will see, it persists in later moral theories that reject extreme voluntarism, as Pufendorf does, but retain a voluntarist account of obligations and moral requirements. Since we have considered some reasons for believing that Pufendorf's position blends naturalist and voluntarist elements in an incoherent combination, it is worth examining Barbeyrac's synthesis. Even if it requires some modification of Pufendorf, it might remove the grounds for taking Pufendorf to be incoherent. If it succeeds on this point, Barbeyrac has gone some way towards defending his claim to combine Grotius and Pufendorf. Even if he deserves more credit for the synthesis than he gives himself, and Pufendorf deserves less than Barbeyrac gives him, it would be important if such a coherent synthesis could be found.

The different aspects of Pufendorf's position on nature and morality help to explain Barbeyrac's confidence that Pufendorf and Grotius really agree on the main questions about natural law. His belief in their agreement underlies his estimate of Grotius as the pioneer of an enlightened theory of natural law. If he had recognized that Grotius maintains the naturalist view that Pufendorf rejects, he could not have treated Grotius as a defender of Pufendorf's position. He would have had to admit that on this basic point Grotius had not cleared himself from the 'vulgar prejudices' (as Barbeyrac describes them) of the Scholastics. Pufendorf believes that Grotius accepts these vulgar prejudices, and so he develops his position by contrast with Grotius. Barbeyrac, however, believes that Pufendorf and Grotius agree more closely than we might gather from Pufendorf's comments.

To reconcile Grotius with Pufendorf, Barbeyrac re-interprets passages that appear to commit Grotius to a form of naturalism rejected by Pufendorf. He argues that they can reasonably be interpreted in a sense that favours Pufendorf's voluntarism. An example of his treatment of Grotius is his interpretation of Grotius' 'etiamsi' clause. Grotius claims that there would still be right and wrong even if there were no God. Since Pufendorf criticizes Grotius for defending this claim, it seems difficult for Barbeyrac to argue that Pufendorf and Grotius really agree.

Barbeyrac, however, takes the appearance of disagreement to be misleading. He suggests that Grotius' really wants to say that even if there were no God and no divine legislation, things would still be naturally good and bad.[1] Grotius (as Barbeyrac interprets him) exaggerates this correct claim by asserting that without divine legislation there would be moral facts (iustum, ius, honestum, turpe), but this is an exaggeration of his main point that there would still be prudential facts.

If Barbeyrac were right to say that Grotius really means only that there would be prudential facts without divine legislation, and does not really believe there would also be moral facts, he would indeed have reconciled Grotius' view with Pufendorf's voluntarism. But he gives us no reason to believe that Grotius does not mean what he says.

599. Barbeyrac's Attempt to Assimilate Pufendorf to Grotius

We may be surprised that Barbeyrac relies on this apparently forced and arbitrary interpretation of Grotius to reconcile him with Pufendorf. But we will be less surprised if we notice that he also interprets Pufendorf so as to fit Grotius' views. He endorses Grotius' view that the right is what conforms to rational and social nature. As Barbeyrac sees, this account of the right frees Grotius from Pufendorf's charge of circularity.[2] Barbeyrac supposes that it also distinguishes Grotius' position from the Scholastic view, which involves the circle that Pufendorf mentions. It is difficult to see the difference that Barbeyrac alleges; Grotius simply refers briefly to what Aquinas and (especially) Suarez discuss at length.

---

[1] 'Mr de Couverin, the translator of Grotius, explains these words, but something obscurely, and seems also to mistake him, telling us, that he maintains, that man's natural light, without any star of God, would carry a man in a most efficacious manner to seek good and avoid evil, by all means possible, in obedience to that law only which reason prescribes, and with the execution of which conscience is charged. I suspect that Grotius never designed to express himself with so much philosophical exactness, and that there is [a?] little rhetoric in that passage, if the sense being rightly understood has that meaning, that the maxims of the law of nature are founded upon the condition of mankind, and necessarily contributing to the advantage of every one, will not cease to take place, and be practised outwardly in some measure, although no Deity be acknowledged; but then they can't be looked upon as duties, nor can be put into practice, but upon the assumption of some interest or vain-glory.' (Barbeyrac on Tufendorf, JNG ii 3.19)

[2] 'Our author [sc. Pufendorf] proves this in his Apology, §19, thus, If we demand of them who define the natural law so, What things are the matter of this law? They'll answer, Such as are honest or dishonest in their nature. If we again ask them, What are those? They can answer nothing else, than that they are the matter of the natural law. This makes well for the schoolmen. But can't we speak something here in the behalf of Grotius? I own, that the notions of this great man are not sufficiently cleared and freed from vulgar prejudices: But I am very much mistaken, if he has not found out the truth, and can't explain his notion so, that when the thing is searched to the bottom, the difference between him and our author will prove a verbal dispute only. The right of nature, says Grotius, ... [Barbeyrac quotes JBP i 1.10.1; see §464] ... So that it is no circle, for if you ask Grotius whence comes that necessary honesty or baseness of the actions commanded or forbidden by the law of nature, he'll answer you, From the necessary agreement or disagreement with a reasonable and social nature.' (Barbeyrac on Pufendorf, JNG ii 3.4 (122 K))

Here Barbeyrac admits, or at least concedes, the truth of Grotius' account of moral goodness. He implicitly abandons Pufendorf's and Cumberland's objection that moral goodness presupposes a reference to law. 'Agreement with rational and social nature' needs some further explanation. One might suspect that it cannot be fully explained without reference to what is right for rational and social beings, or what they ought to do, or need to do. But that sort of circularity among moral concepts is not necessarily vicious; and in any case it is different from a reference to law.

Though Barbeyrac offers the correct explanation of Grotius' meaning, in opposition to Pufendorf's explanation, he nonetheless asserts that Grotius really agrees with Pufendorf. He believes that both Grotius and Pufendorf escape the circle that (allegedly) follows from the Scholastic view, and so he assumes that Grotius is not open to Pufendorf's criticisms. He infers that the difference between Grotius and Pufendorf is only verbal, because Grotius accepts Pufendorf's main point. Since Grotius refers to natural sociality, which depends on the will of God, he admits that moral goodness depends on the will of God, which is the voluntarist position.[3]

It is difficult to see how this attempt to reconcile Grotius with Pufendorf could be consistent with Barbeyrac's explanation of Grotius' 'etiamsi' clause. He tries to interpret that clause so as to avoid admitting natural morality, because he agrees that Pufendorf does not believe in natural morality. But now he agrees that Grotius believes in natural morality, and he claims that Pufendorf also believes in natural morality. After assimilating Grotius to Pufendorf, he now assimilates Pufendorf to Grotius; his two claims seem to involve ascribing inconsistent positions to Pufendorf.

For his assimilation of Pufendorf to Grotius Barbeyrac might fairly claim support from Pufendorf. For Pufendorf also tries to assimilate Grotius' position to voluntarism by appeal to these claims about creation. Barbeyrac follows him in identifying (sometimes) God's creative will with God's legislative will.[4] This identification explains why Pufendorf asserts that any reference to God as creator is an admission of the truth of his voluntarist thesis. His assertion gives a misleading picture both of Scholastic views and of Pufendorf's view. Every orthodox Christian thinker, including Aquinas, Vasquez, Suarez, and Grotius, agrees that human beings with rational and social natures exist because of God's will, and not because of some necessity that is independent of God. But to say that the morality of actions proceeds from God in this way is not to concede Pufendorf's legislative thesis. Indeed, Pufendorf admits this point when he agrees that prudential facts depend on God's creative will, but do not imply moral facts.

The importance of sociality is suggested by Barbeyrac's inconsistent arguments for reconciling Grotius with Pufendorf. According to his first argument, facts about human nature, including sociality, require the observance of moral principles; this fits voluntarism because human nature is the result of creation, and hence of the divine will. According to the second argument, Grotius really means that concern for advantage, but not concern for the right, is

---

[3] 'He [sc. Grotius] seems to acknowledge also, with our author, that this necessity is not absolute and independent upon the will of God. . . . This right, I say, although it flows from the internal principles of man (i.e. from the conditions of the human nature) may nevertheless, and that with reason, be attributed to God, because he has implanted such principles in us. I will now leave it to any man, whether the commentators upon Grotius have not mistaken his sense, and if when he speaks of honest or dishonest actions, he does not mean them in the same sense that our author allows them . . .' (Barbeyrac on Pufendorf, *JNG* ii 3.4 = K 122)

[4] Cockburn discusses this issue. See §876.

justified without reference to divine commands. These arguments accurately represent two inconsistent tendencies in Pufendorf. On the one hand, he retains naturalist claims about sociality, since these claims help to vindicate God's goodness to us in issuing the commands that he actually issues; he is good to us because he commands us to do what fits our nature. On the other hand, he sees that if he concedes the naturalist claims about natural sociality, he has no reason to deny that pursuit of the right, as well as the expedient, is justified without reference to the will of God.

Pufendorf needs to decide in favour of Barbeyrac's second argument. The first really abandons voluntarism; only Pufendorf's confusion about God's creative and legislative will conceals this fact from him. The second argument rests on the controversial claim that facts about human nature justify action for the sake of the expedient, but do not justify action for the sake of the right.

The identification of creation with legislation underlies Barbeyrac's argument to show that Pufendorf recognizes natural rightness and wrongness. He agrees with the naturalist view that human nature itself makes some actions naturally right and others naturally wrong. This position seems to conflict with the voluntarist thesis about legislation and morality. But Barbeyrac, following some of Pufendorf's remarks, denies any conflict; indeed, he argues that we concede the voluntarist thesis once we concede that nature depends on God as creator. In speaking of God's role as creator he speaks of 'the laws which God hath imposed on us as creator', as though these were the laws that Pufendorf takes to be necessary for the truth of voluntarism.[5] But this explanation of natural law does not help Pufendorf. For if he refers only to the laws that follow from the fact that God has created us with this nature, he needs no further legislative action by God.

600. Barbeyrac's Modern Theory of Natural Law

Barbeyrac's assimilation of Grotius and Pufendorf is instructive, therefore, because it develops an argument in Pufendorf far enough to expose a basic difficulty in Pufendorf's position. Though Pufendorf attacks the naturalism of Grotius, he also tries to assimilate it to his own position; these two views of Grotius depend on Pufendorf's two views about legislation. When Barbeyrac assumes that creation implies legislation, he reconciles (as he supposes) Grotius with Pufendorf by abandoning voluntarism.

This dubious element in Barbeyrac's interpretation of Grotius and Pufendorf is the basis of his history of natural-law theory. He places Grotius at the head of the natural-law tradition

---

[5] 'To remove all equivocations, and leave no place for cavil, we ought to observe, that we must own things honest or dishonest of themselves, or in their own nature. 1. By way of opposition to human appointment, as the agreements or opinions of men. 2. In respect of the subject, with relation to which they are thought so. As for example, there are some acts which agree to God no way, i.e., which he can't do without derogating from his perfection, and so contradicting himself. There are actions also, which of themselves agree, or disagree with the human nature, in our present state. But if we understand that an action is honest, or dishonest in its own nature, without any relation to the appointment of God, or the laws which God hath imposed upon us, by our creation, in that sense the proposition is false.' (Barbeyrac on Pufendorf, *JNG* i 2.6 = K 17n) Barbeyrac cites ii 3.4–5, and *ES* 5.7 = *GW* v 168–9, where Pufendorf rejects intrinsic honestas insofar as it implies that 'Deus, eiusque voluntas a prima origine moralitatis excluduntur'. But his defence of his position does not distinguish the creative and the legislative aspects of God.

because he separates him from the Scholastics; this separation assumes falsely that Grotius differs from Scholastic naturalism in his explanation of intrinsic morality. In separating Grotius from the Scholastics, Barbeyrac assimilates him to Pufendorf, by his questionable interpretation of both Grotius and Pufendorf.

Barbeyrac's history has encouraged the view that modern moral philosophy marks a sharp break from Scholasticism, and that a modern theory of natural law, beginning with Grotius, is distinctive of the modern outlook. This view about modern natural-law theory has no plausible basis. On the main points Grotius accepts Scholastic naturalism. Barbeyrac does not show that he is a pioneer of the modern natural-law tradition.

He might more plausibly have argued that Grotius and Pufendorf continue the debate between naturalism and voluntarism whose main lines are clearly drawn by Suarez. Grotius belongs on the naturalist side of the debate. Hobbes, Locke, Cumberland, and Pufendorf, in different respects and to different degrees, defend voluntarism. Barbeyrac supports Pufendorf's attempts to defend a voluntarist position that accommodates plausible naturalist views about the natural basis of morality; but his arguments rest on misunderstanding and confusion.

An examination of Pufendorf's doctrine of natural law helps to explain why Barbeyrac regards natural law theory as a revolution in moral philosophy. Pufendorf comes much closer than Ockham or Scotus comes to a purely procedural conception of morality as law. Both Scotus and Ockham recognize some natural aspects of morality, and so they do not need a non-moral basis for the legitimacy of a moral legislator. Pufendorf goes further, since he recognizes only non-moral goods in nature, and takes moral right and wrong to be products of legislation. He thereby gives natural law priority in morality, because it is not subordinate to the ultimate human good, or to natural rightness and wrongness. Hence, Pufendorf's theory lives up to Barbeyrac's advertisement of natural-law theory as a significant innovation in moral theory. The difficulties that arise in Pufendorf's position suggest that the innovation is not an advance.

601. Burlamaqui on Pufendorf

Some of the weaknesses in Pufendorf's position, as explained by Barbeyrac, are identified in Burlamaqui's comments. Burlamaqui agrees with Pufendorf's view that law requires a prescription by a superior (*PNL* 78), and that this feature of laws distinguishes them from counsels; while counsels are drawn from the nature of things, laws also require commands (79). Hence the 'laws' recognized by naturalists are simply counsels. But though Burlamaqui follows Pufendorf here, his attempts to expound and to modify Pufendorf's position reinforce doubts about whether Pufendorf and Barbeyrac hold a consistent position.

According to Pufendorf,[6] laws express only the end of the legislator, whereas Burlamaqui claims that law has a double end, relative both to the sovereign and to the good of the subjects.[7]

---

[6] *JNG* i 6.1.
[7] '. . . it would be doing injustice to the sovereign to imagine that he thinks only of himself, without any regard to the good of those who are his dependents. Pufendorf seems here, as well as in some other places, to give a little too much into Hobbes's principles' (Burlamaqui, *PNL* 100).

He follows Pufendorf in believing that a connexion to law constitutes the moral goodness, as opposed to the merely natural goodness, of actions (114). But he describes moral properties in the way Suarez describes intrinsic morality; we discover them by rational reflexion on what our nature requires.[8] Hence we learn about morality through a moral sense, as Hutcheson supposes (145), but also through reason (150). The foundation of natural law is human nature (157). One important aspect of nature is sociability.[9] Unlike Pufendorf, Burlamaqui takes natural sociability to be a foundation of the state as well as of smaller societies.

Burlamaqui emphasizes the non-arbitrary character of God's commanding observance of the natural law. The natural and necessary differences in actions explain why God commands some rather than others (184).[10] On this basis we can answer the standard question about whether an action is just because God commands it, or the other way round. Since justice is obedience to the command of a superior, justice depends on God's command; but since God commands only what is reasonable in itself, God's commands require some prior reasonableness in nature.[11]

But what is the character of this prior reasonableness? If Burlamaqui accepts the voluntarist elements in Pufendorf, he ought to say that the reasonableness antecedent to divine commands is merely prudential and not moral. Pufendorf and Cumberland believe that we must say this to avoid a vicious circle in defining moral properties. Burlamaqui, however, does not follow them. He agrees with Barbeyrac in denying that Grotius is committed to any vicious circle, and on this basis he defends Grotius' 'etsi daremus' clause (217). He argues that Grotius' account of natural morality is non-circular, because it appeals to rational and social nature, and not to any legislation.[12] Moral qualities (honesty and turpitude) do not essentially depend on legislation.

Burlamaqui's remarks confirm our suggestion that Barbeyrac's defence of Pufendorf exposes the basic conflict in Pufendorf's views; the conflict is even clearer in Burlamaqui's concessions to Grotius. Sometimes he seems to take Pufendorf's view that the natural basis for divine commands is not natural morality, but only natural prudential goodness; that is why moral goodness requires divine commands. But if Burlamaqui consistently stuck to this

---

[8] He explains this in his description of natural law: '. . . a law that God imposes on all men, and which they are able to discover and know by the sole light of reason, and by attentively considering their state and nature' (126).

[9] 'Ethic writers have given it the name of sociability, by which they understand that disposition which inclines us to benevolence towards our fellow creatures, to do them all the good that lies in our power, to reconcile our own happiness to that of others, and to render our particular advantage subordinate always to the common and general good.' (169)

[10] 'To conceive it [sc. natural law] therefore as depending on an arbitrary will would be attempting to subvert it, or at least it would be reducing the thing to a kind of Pyrrhonism; by reason we could have no natural means of being sure that God commands or forbids one thing rather than another.' (185)

[11] 'A thing is just because God commands it; this is implied by the definition we gave of justice. But God commands such or such things, because these things are reasonable in themselves, conformable to the order and ends he proposed to himself in creating mankind, and agreeable to the nature and state of man.' (223) 'Tis so much the more necessary to admit these two sorts of obligation and morality, as that which renders the obligation of law the most perfect, is its uniting the two species; being internal and external both at the same time. For were there no attention given to the very nature of the laws, and were the things they command or prohibit not to merit the approbation or censure of reason; the authority of the legislator would have no other foundation but that of power; and laws being then no more than the effect of an arbitrary will, they would produce rather a constraint properly so called than any real obligation.' (215)

[12] 'Here I can see no circle: For putting the question, whence comes the natural honesty or turpitude of commanded or forbidden actions? Grotius does not answer in the manner they make him; on the contrary, he says that this honesty or turpitude proceeds from the necessary agreeableness or disagreeableness of our actions with a rational and social nature.' (187)

view, he would not agree with Grotius on natural moral goodness without divine legislation. When he demands divine commands in addition to natural goodness and badness, it is not clear whether he relies on Pufendorf's argument (that morality needs laws and commands) or on Suarez's argument (that natural law, but not morality, needs them).

It is easy for Burlamaqui to fall into this ambiguity, because Pufendorf and Barbeyrac also fall into it. Sometimes they speak as though they appealed only to God's creative will; in that case they would recognize natural and intrinsic morality. Sometimes they take God's legislative will to be essential to morality; in that case they reject intrinsic morality. Burlamaqui does not see the conflict between his support of Pufendorf and his defence of Grotius, because he accepts two inconsistent elements of Pufendorf's view of natural law and natural morality. The conflict between these two elements becomes still clearer in the efforts of Barbeyrac and Burlamaqui to expound Pufendorf's views.

602. A Defence of Voluntarism: Fundamental v. Formal Morality

These conclusions about Pufendorf deserve to be borne in mind if we consider the later influence of his views on Roman Catholic moral theology. We may find such an influence surprising in the light of his objections to Scholastic views. We have seen that he is right to contrast his position with some Scholastic views, and especially with the views of Aquinas, Vasquez, and Suarez. But his views are much closer to those of Scotus, Ockham, and Biel, and so we might expect this side of Roman Catholic thought to be more sympathetic to Pufendorf's voluntarism.

Suarez's treatment of natural law and intrinsic morality exercises an uneven influence on later Roman Catholic moral theology. The clearest sign of his influence is the acceptance of his claim that natural law is genuine law requiring a divine legislator. Aquinas does not endorse this claim; his understanding of the sense in which the natural law is law allows the existence of a law without a legislator.

Aquinas' understanding of the legal character of the natural law persists in some later Roman moral theologians. According to Alphonsus Liguori, the natural law states what is to be done and avoided.[13] He states natural precepts in gerundive form. He does not suggest that if it is a precept of a law, it must present itself as the command of a legislator. Alphonsus rejects some voluntarist accounts of the content of natural law; he implies that, in contrast to positive law, it is not laid down by the free will of God or man.

This conception of natural law is not accepted in all later Roman sources. Its opponents do not endorse extreme voluntarism, which might reasonably be taken to encourage

---

[13] 'A natural precept, or precept of natural right (ius), is a dictate or a judgment of our reason, by which, through the light impressed on us by the author of nature, we settle what is to be done and what is to be avoid. For example: good is to be done, evil is to be avoided. From this general precept particular precepts are derived—e.g., God is to be worshipped, no one is to be injured, and in fact all the precepts of the Decalogue (except for the circumstances of the Sabbath) and many others. A positive precept or precept of positive right, is one that has been laid down by the free will of God or of human beings and depends on it—e.g., the precept about baptism, the Lenten fast, etc.' (Alphonsus Liguori, *TM* i, Tract. 2, ch. 1 §102 = p. 69)

Jansenist errors about morality and God. But for those who tend to sympathize with Scotus, Pufendorf's version of voluntarism might seem attractive, since it combines some elements of naturalism with a firmly voluntarist conception of morality. In 1860 W. G. Ward remarks that many Roman Catholics believe that some form of voluntarism is the most appropriate position for a Roman Catholic to hold.

His remark is confirmed by the *Syllabus Errorum* of Pope Pius IX (1864), which supports voluntarism without explicit endorsement of it. The Pope condemns a threefold error about morality, which (a) denies that moral laws need a divine sanction, (b) denies that human laws ought to conform to the natural law, and (c) denies that they derive their obligatory force from God.[14] The Pope presents these three claims as part of a single error, but they appear to be separable. One might believe the first claim while rejecting the second, if one accepts an account of natural law that does not necessarily imply a divine legislator. Rejection of the second claim does not require acceptance of a divine legislator.

Leo XIII's account of the natural law officially corrects the error condemned by his predecessor. He emphasizes the natural character of the natural law in saying that human reason itself commands and forbids. But he also seems to present human reason as expressing itself in an imperative form that presupposes a divine source of the commands.[15] Fifty years later, Pius XII reaffirms these claims about morality and the natural law.[16]

A more recent official Roman discussion does not explicitly mention natural law, but it relies on St Paul's remark about being a law to oneself. It speaks of conscience as a means of access to a law written in the human heart by God, but it does not discuss the way in which the law presents itself, or has to present itself in order to count as morality or as natural law.[17] It does not emphasize the imperative character of the law as requiring a divine legislator; nor does it follow Alphonsus in asserting that moral right and wrong are independent of the free will of God. The difference between morality and divine positive law is not explained.

The statements of the three popes on natural law affirm some version of voluntarism, but it is not clear what version they have in mind. One might argue that, strictly speaking, they only affirm voluntarism about moral laws, and do not reject the possibility of intrinsic morality. If this is what they mean, their position would be consistent with Suarez's division between morality and natural law. It is doubtful, however, whether the popes mean to

---

[14] (a) Morum leges divina haud egent sanctione, (b) minimeque opus est, ut humanae leges ad naturae ius conformentur aut (c) obligandi vim a Deo accipiant. (Denz. §2956; reference letters added)

[15] 'Such a law is, first among all, the natural law, which is written and engraved in the minds of individual human beings, because it is human reason itself, commanding to do right actions and forbidding to sin. But this prescription of human reason cannot have the force of law unless because it is the voice and interpreter of a higher reason to which our mind and our freedom must be subjected. For since the force of law is this, to command duties (officia) and to ascribe rights (iura), it depends entirely on authority, that is, on a genuine power (potestas) to fix duties and to set out rights, and also of attaching a sanction to its commands by rewards and punishments. Now all these things clearly cannot be found in a human being, if as his own supreme legislator he were to give himself the norm for his actions. It follows, therefore, that the natural law is the eternal law itself, implanted in those who use reason, and inclining them towards the required (debitum) action and end; and this is the eternal reason itself of God the creator and ruler of the whole world.' (Denz. 3247, Leo XIII, *Libertas Praestantissimum*)

[16] 'This natural law rests on God as its foundation, the almighty creator and father of all things, and also the supreme and most perfect legislator and the wisest and most just judge of human actions. Once the eternal Deity is rashly rejected, then the principle of all rightness (honestas) collapses and falls, and the voice of nature is silent or gradually weakens . . .' (DS 3781, Pius XII, *Summi Pontificatus*, quoted by Mahoney, *MMT* 82)

[17] See *Gaudium et Spes* §16, in Alberigo et al., *COD*. Quoted in §206.

allow the possibility of morality that is independent of divine commands. Pius XII affirms that if the existence of God is denied, the principle of all rightness (honestas) also collapses. Similarly, the other two popes would have failed to discuss an important and pertinent question about morality and God if they believed that their remarks allowed the possibility of intrinsic morality. They may reasonably be taken to affirm the voluntarist position that Ward takes to be widespread among Roman Catholics.

The version of voluntarism that is endorsed by the popes and opposed by Ward may be explained more clearly by reference to the division between fundamental and formal morality. Ward finds this in some of the Scholastic writers (from the 17th and 18th centuries) whom he cites as supporters of voluntarism. These writers distinguish two sets of facts and properties relevant to morality: (1) Fundamental morality: we grasp this when we grasp what is good and bad for human beings because of their nature. These facts about human nature are independent of divine legislative will. God could not have created human beings for whom murder was good. (2) Formal and complete morality: this includes obligation, which requires divine legislation. Since divine legislation is needed for formal and complete morality, merely fundamental morality does not give us morality.

In recognizing intrinsic goodness and badness apart from legislation, the Roman writers show that they do not separate facts from values, or 'is' from 'ought'. For they allow that facts about human beings, their nature, and circumstances, suffice for (we might say) prudential facts, and for true judgments about what promotes human welfare and about what we ought to do, from the prudential point of view. These prudential facts are the subject matter of ancient ethics. But since these facts are not sufficient for true moral judgments, natural goodness lacks an essential ingredient of morality. It gives us only fundamental morality, because it does not include the legislative element that is needed for formal morality.

603. What is Fundamental Morality?

To understand what 'fundamental morality' means, we need to distinguish two sorts of 'fundamentals' or 'foundations': (i) We might claim that knowledge of an earlier period of history is the necessary, or the best, foundation for learning about a later period, because it is a prerequisite for understanding the later period; but it does not by itself give us knowledge of the later period. (ii) We might claim that if we get a first class degree in philosophy, we have grasped the fundamentals of philosophy. In that case we have actually learned philosophy, not just a prerequisite to philosophy, even though we have not learned the whole of philosophy.

Roman Catholic writers take 'fundamental morality' to be fundamental only in the first sense. It falls short of formal morality because it lacks the form, the essential characteristic, of morality. It is the foundation on which morality is built, and hence a prerequisite for morality, but not morality itself. Without divine legislation things would be intrinsically good and bad, and hence there would be prudential facts and prudential reasons; but nothing would be morally good or bad, or morally right or wrong, without divine commands.[18]

---

[18] 'Or, nous pouvons être assurés qu'un tel ordre moral existe dans l'exemplarisme divin, répondant à la nature même des choses, et avant toute intervention de la volonté de Dieu. Rien qu'en considérant la nature raisonnable ordonnée vers

'Fundamental sins', therefore, are intrinsically bad, because they are inappropriate to rational nature. Hence they have 'to-be-prohibitedness' (prohibenditas), and demand prohibition. But they are not wrong (inhonesta) or sins without a divine prohibition.[19]

This division helps to clarify the relation between these later Roman writers and the positions of Suarez and Pufendorf. Where Suarez speaks of intrinsic morality, Gonet speaks of fundamental morality, which is only the basis of morality and not yet genuine morality.[20] Fundamental morality is independent of the divine will, but obligation depends on the divine will; here Gonet recalls Suarez. But Gonet's formulation includes an element of voluntarism that goes beyond both Aquinas and Suarez. In claiming that without divine law lying would not be morally bad 'formally and completely', he implies that 'fundamental morality' is really just the foundation on which morality is built rather than the fundamentals that belong to morality (the first rather than the second conception of 'fundamental' that we distinguished above). Without divine legislation things would be intrinsically good and bad, but not morally good or bad, and hence not right or wrong. Though Gonet derives some of his position from Suarez, his eventual position coincides with Pufendorf's.

The influence of this moderate voluntarist position, and some of the difficulties that arise in making it clear, can be noticed in the brief presentation in textbooks. Rickaby accepts Suarez's naturalism insofar as he recognizes natural good and evil; God could not have created human beings for whom murder was good.[21] But he argues that obligation

le vrai et vers le bon, ou encore la marche normale de la société humaine, on saisit facilement la nécessité et l'existence d'un ordre moral, droits et devoirs réciproques, parce que ce sont là des relations essentielles de la nature raisonnable, laquelle, sans ces relations, serait un tissu des contradictions. C'est là ce que les théologiens thomistes appellent la moralité considérée *initiative et fundamentaliter*. Mais ces relations essentielles, dont notre esprit saisit la nécessité et existence, manqueraient de fondement et de caractère obligatoire, s'il n'existait pas un être qui soit le prototype, l'idéal de l'ordre auquel tout homme doit se conformer, s'il veut demeurer dans la moralité: prototype idéal, à la fois cause exemplaire—et d'abord cause exemplaire—et cause efficiente, transformant, en le rendant obligatoire, le bien *rationnel* en bien formellement *morale*. En bref, la morale naturelle ne se réduit pas à des commandements divins. Au lieu de rapporter, comme Descartes le fait, les essences en général a la volonté divine "Leibniz a vu la vérité en faisant de *l'entendement* divin le lieu des essences, et du *vouloir* divin la source des existences ... Si donc on nous pose cette question: le fondement du devoir est-il en Dieu, oui ou non? nous répondons: il est en Dieu comme en son dernier support, mais son support immédiat est l'ordre des relations, l'ordre des fins." Mgr Hubst *Carême 1891, 4e conférence*. Cet ordre des relations et des fins trouve lui-même son fondement en Dieu, mais à ne connaître que le support immédiat de la moralité qu'il constitue, on n'est pas encore lié par la conscience de l'obligation, mais on peut en soupçonner l'existence. ... [Omitted passage quoted in n22 below.] Cette position sauvegarde à la fois le caractère rationnel de la morale naturelle et en même temps son fondement divin, tout en éliminant les excès du voluntarisme. Sauvegarder le caractère rationnel de la morale naturelle tout en montrant le fondement divin, ce n'est pas, quoiqu'on ait dit, ouvrir les voies à la constitution d'une morale laïque, c'est-à-dire d'une morale sans Dieu.' (*DTC* xv.2, col. 3317)

[19] 'Do those things that are intrinsically bad formally have the character of sin or <in other words> of moral badness and wrongness (inhonestum) because of opposition to a prohibiting law, or instead because of unfittingness to rational nature? On this point they more commonly teach that these things are only fundamentally sins because of unfittingness to rational nature, and that they have only to-be-prohibitedness (prohibenditas), or <in other words> a demand that they be prohibited. But they have the formal character of sin because of violation of a prohibiting law, so that for that reason they would lack formal badness if they were not prohibited, whether it were possible for them not to be positively prohibited by God, or impossible—which latter view I take to be truer, with Suarez ... against Ockham and others.' (Domenico Viva, *In propos. 48 et 49 Innocent. XI.* no. 1, quoted by Ward, *ONG* 459) Viva was an Italian Jesuit (1648–1726).

[20] 'Toute cette doctrine est résumée par Gonet en cette proposition: Si enim lex aeterna, subindeque omnes aliae leges tollerentur, mendacium non esset malum morale nec peccatum formaliter et complete (voilà le "moral"), sed fundamentaliter et initiative, quia esset contrarium naturae rationali (voilà le "rationnel") et ex sua natura aptam, ut prohiberetur a legibus, si ponerentur. *De Vitiis et Peccatis*, n.66; cf. Salamanticenses, ibid. disp. vii, dub 1, n.11.' (*DTC* xv.2, col. 3317)

[21] 'As it is not in the power of God to bring it about, that the angles of a triangle taken together shall amount to anything else than two right angles, so it is not within the compass of Divine omnipotence to create a man for whom it

341

requires an imperative, and that Kant is mistaken in trying to find the imperative within the individual agent. A genuine command requires a commander distinct from the subject of the command, and so it requires divine commands.[22] Hence we have to distinguish an 'initial and fundamental obligation' from 'an obligation formal and complete', which requires a divine command. These remarks mark Rickaby's agreement with Pufendorf against Suarez. He does not acknowledge any moral oughts without laws and commands.[23] Hence he does not agree with Suarez's belief in intrinsic morality. 'Fundamental obligation' includes no oughts and therefore allows no genuine morality.[24]

The question about whether genuine morality requires obligation and command introduces more than a verbal dispute about the extent of morality. Our answer to the question determines whether anyone who is doubtful about the existence of an external legislator should be equally doubtful about the existence of moral oughts and duties. Suarez answers that morality is independent of an external legislator. Pufendorf disagrees with him. The Roman Catholic writers who contrast 'fundamental' with 'formal and complete' morality go further towards Pufendorf than, from Suarez's point of view, they ought to go.

Anscombe's diagnosis of modern moral philosophy, therefore, emerges naturally from this modern Roman view. She takes morality to require a concept of 'ought' and obligation that implies legislation. Those who believe in divine legislation are justified in using moral concepts. Those who do not believe in divine legislation will find that they use moral concepts they cannot justify, since they reject the beliefs that these concepts presuppose; hence they would be better off if they stuck to 'fundamental' and incomplete morality.[25]

---

shall be a good and proper thing, and befitting his nature, to blaspheme, to perjure himself, to abandon himself recklessly to lust, or anger, or any other passion. God need not have created man at all, but He could not have created him with other than human exigencies. . . . The denial of this doctrine in the Nominalist and Cartesian Schools . . . Still less are moral distinctions between good and evil to be set down to the law of the State, or the fashion of society. Human convention can no more constitute moral good than it can physical good, or mathematical or logical truth.' (Rickaby, MP 113–14)

[22] 'Kant . . . contends . . . that the Categorical Imperative, uttered by a man's own reason, has the force of a law, made by that same reason; so that the legislative authority is within the breast of the doer, who owes it obedience. This he calls the autonomy of reason. It is also called Independent Morality, . . . The doctrine is erroneous, inasmuch as it undertakes to settle the matter of right and wrong without reference to external authority; and inasmuch as it makes the reason within a man, not the promulgator of the law to him, but his own legislator. For a law is a precept, a command: now no one issues precepts, or gives commands, to himself. To command is an act of jurisdiction; and Jurisdiction . . . requires a distinction of persons, one ruler, and another subject. . . . If this [sc. Kant's view] were true, there would be no sin anywhere except what is called philosophical sin, that is, a breach of the dignity of man's rational nature . . . A man may transgress and sin, in more than the philosophical sense of the word: he may be properly a law-breaker, by offending against this supreme Reason, higher and other than his own. . . . apart from God we shall prove certain acts wrong, and other acts obligatory as duties, philosophically speaking, with an initial and fundamental wrongness and obligation. In the present section we have proved once for all, that what is wrong philosophically, or is philosophically a duty, is the same also theologically. Thus the initial and fundamental obligation is transformed into an obligation formal and complete.' (MP 116–17)

[23] The full notion of what a man *ought*, is what he *must do under pain of sin*. Sin is more than folly, more than a breach of reason. . . . he is not his own master; he is under law . . .' (MP 116)

[24] The position of DTC and Rickaby is similar to that of Cathrein, PM, ch. 5. His account of obligation agrees with Suarez against Vasquez and Kant. But he seems to agree with Leo XIII and DTC in rejecting the possibility of 'lay' morality. Here he seems to go beyond Suarez. It is not clear whether his position is consistent, since he also seems to attribute intrinsic honestas to actions without reference to the divine will. Perhaps he means that without obligation derived from divine command such honestas lacks normativity, and fails to provide the right sort of reason for action. This is similar to Culverwell's position.

[25] On Anscombe see §459.

We have argued that mediaeval Scholasticism does not support this modern Roman Catholic view; we can align Aquinas and Suarez with the modern Roman view only by misinterpretation. But even if this is true, the modern Roman view may still be correct about the nature of morality. To show that it is correct, we need to see what, if anything, is wrong with the naturalist account of morality that we have ascribed to the Scholastics.

We now find that the modern Roman position converges with Barbeyrac's position in a surprising way. Though the two positions disagree about the source of the jural conception of morality, they agree in accepting the jural conception. The view that Barbeyrac attributes to modern theorists of natural law is just the view that the modern Roman view ascribes to the Scholastic tradition. But we have found that Barbeyrac is right to deny that the jural conception is the Scholastic conception.

The modern Roman position, then, accepts Pufendorf's central distinction (on which he agrees with Cumberland) between natural goodness and morality, takes obligation to be necessary for morality, and takes divine legislation to be necessary for obligation. Pufendorf takes himself to defend a Lutheran position against earlier and contemporary Scholastic writers, but his position commends itself to later Roman Catholic writers.[26]

604. Defence of Naturalism

In our discussion of Pufendorf, we found that his voluntarism faces serious objections when it seeks to explain how God is an authoritative legislator whose commands deserve to be obeyed. How far do later Roman writers answer these objections? The naturalist side of the argument is supported by Ward, who argues that Roman Catholics are permitted to believe in 'independent morality' if they think a cogent philosophical case can be made for it, and that in fact a cogent case can be made. In speaking of 'independent morality', Ward agrees with Whewell, who treats theological voluntarism as a version of dependent morality.[27] Since Ward notices that many Roman Catholics believe that voluntarism is the only tenable position for them to hold, he believes it is worthwhile to collect evidence from the 17th-century Scholastics and from later Roman sources to show that no valid ecclesiastical authority prohibits Roman Catholics from believing naturalism if they take it to be rationally superior.[28] Since his book appeared in 1860, a few years before Pius IX's *Syllabus* (1864), Ward does not try to reconcile his defence of naturalism with the Pope's endorsement of voluntarism about natural law.

---

[26] ' . . . it is remarkable that some of his expositions remind us of the works of modern Catholic authors. He himself, however, was always emphatic in his profession of pure Lutheranism and never appealed to the views of Catholic authors.' (Simons, in Pufendorf, *JNG*, tr. Oldfather, 17a)

[27] On Whewell see §522.

[28] At *NG* 429–90 Ward presents a long series of Roman Catholic authorities defending what he calls 'independent morality' (using Whewell's expression): 'Certain Catholics . . . are under the impression, that there is some overwhelming amount of theological authority for the thesis, that all moral obligation proceeds from God's command. The first and principal part of this section then will be devoted to establishing the contradictory of this. I will show that so considerable a number of the greatest Catholic writers oppose themselves to any such thesis that at all events any Catholic who may regard it as opposed to reason has the fullest liberty of denying it' (429). I know most of his authorities only from the long quotations he gives (he does not always give precise references to their works).

Ward's defence of naturalism deserves the praise it receives from Mill.[29] In defence of naturalism he adduces cogent arguments from Suarez as well as Vasquez.[30] He underestimates the extent of mediaeval support for voluntarism; Ockham is the only mediaeval writer whom he acknowledges as a voluntarist, and he does not discuss Scotus. But he emphasizes the mediaeval and Catholic sources of naturalism in order to refute the absurd suggestion of Dugald Stewart that naturalism is a Protestant innovation.[31] Stewart's view (in which he agrees with Barbeyrac) that mediaeval philosophers are not worth discussing does not seem to rest on knowledge of their actual views. As his Roman Catholic critics point out, he does not even seem to remember Pufendorf's attack on the Scholastics for having maintained naturalism.[32] It is reasonable of Ward to attack Stewart's completely mistaken account of mediaeval views.

Against all voluntarist views, he argues that the Church recognizes 'moral' or 'philosophical' sin which consists simply in acting against rational nature.[33] It thereby recognizes that action against rational nature is wrong in its own right, apart from any divine command. Independent morality consists in right action, which is in accord with rational nature, and wrong action, which is contrary to it. Ward argues that the recognition of independent morality conflicts with the view that 'moral obligation implies the command of a superior' (450).

This presentation of the dispute about independent morality seems to overlook a distinction drawn by Suarez. According to Suarez, morality is not sufficient for natural law, because natural law includes obligation, and therefore depends on command and legislation. Hence his doctrine of independent morality is consistent with the view that moral obligation implies the command of a superior, if 'obligation' is used in Suarez's narrow sense. From

[29] Mill expresses his respect for Ward's argument, in *ESWHP*, ch. 10 = *CW* ix 164–5n: '. . . a book the readers of which are likely to be limited by its being addressed specially to Catholics, but showing a capacity in the writer which might otherwise have made him one of the most effective champions of the Intuitive school. Though I do not believe morality to be intuitive in Dr Ward's sense, I think his book of great practical worth, by the strenuous manner in which it maintains morality to have another foundation than the arbitrary decree of God, and shows, by great weight of evidence, that this is the orthodox doctrine of the Roman Catholic Church.' Mill's reference to the 'arbitrary decree' of God misunderstands Ward's target. Ward sees clearly that most of his opponents reject the Ockhamist view (as he understands it) that morality results from God's free choice.

[30] Ward, *NG* 71–111.   [31] On Stewart see §462.

[32] Ward quotes from Perrone's comment on Stewart (430): 'This teaching [sc. voluntarism] was the master-stroke of Pufendorf, which he in turn derived from his parent Luther. Following him, all these Protestant jurists vigorously ridicule and attack the scholastic teachers because they maintain intrinsic distinction between moral goodness and badness founded in the very essences and nature of things, and because they defend an eternal law in God, independent of the free will of God. And so we cannot sufficiently wonder how a Scottish philosopher of great reputation among recent philosophers, Dugald Stewart, in the preface that he wrote for the first supplementary volume to the Encyclopaedia Britannica, could ascribe this glory to Melanchthon, on the ground that he was the first of all to teach that the distinction between moral goodness and badness is derived not from revelation, but from the intrinsic nature of things. . . . Was this very doctrine not previously common to practically all the scholastics? And was not the contrary opinion, which does away with moral distinctions altogether, preached by Luther and his followers? See how Protestant prejudices could so far mislead Stewart, a philosopher, and in other ways a commendable one!' In stressing the Protestant sources of voluntarism, Perrone seems to commit the opposite error to Stewart's and to underestimate the strength of mediaeval voluntarism; 'practically all (omnibus fere) the scholastics' is rather an over-statement.

[33] He cites (450) the definition by Alexander VIII: 'A philosophical or moral sin is an action unfitting to rational nature and to correct reason. A theological and mortal sin, however, is a free transgression of a divine law.' (DS §2291). Though this definition introduces the condemnation of a proposition, Ward argues that the definition itself is not part of what is condemned, but an accepted view on the basis of which the condemnation was issued.

Suarez's point of view, then, Ward has confused the issues in dispute, by maintaining that independent morality precludes the view that obligation rests on command.[34]

It would have been useful if Ward had noticed and used Suarez's distinction between duty and obligation. For if he had drawn the distinction clearly, he could have asked his voluntarist opponents what they meant in claiming that moral obligation depends on divine commands. The voluntarist claim may appear appealing because it contains a true claim (as Suarez supposes) about obligation; but this true claim does not justify a voluntarist account of morality and moral duties in general.

In defence of Ward, one might reasonably argue that his opponents do not seem to confine themselves to the narrow claim about obligation that Suarez accepts. The papal documents we have discussed seem to maintain a broader claim about the basis of morality. Similarly, the division between fundamental and formal morality does not concede the possibility of moral duty and moral rightness apart from legislation. Against these opponents Ward might fairly claim to be denying what they assert when he claims that moral obligation does not require divine commands. Though he misses an opportunity to clarify the opponents' position, and thereby to identify its mistake, he does not misrepresent it. Both he and his opponents seem to assume a broad sense of 'obligation' covering all moral oughts and duties.

Part of Ward's argument consists in the exposition of naturalism, to show that it is a viable alternative to voluntarism. Another part maintains that naturalism is preferable, because it offers reasonable answers to questions that voluntarism cannot answer so reasonably. For this purpose, he sets aside the extreme voluntarist view that morality consists in conformity to the free commands of God. He attributes this view to Ockham, and rejects it, agreeing with the Scholastic writers who believe it is repugnant to a reasonable conception of God and morality.[35] But he also contests the moderate voluntarist view that morality consists in conformity to the necessary commands of God. This view cannot fairly be accused of identifying morality with the arbitrary will of God, but Ward believes that it is still open to serious objection.

Moderate voluntarism concedes that God is not free to command injustice and cruelty. But how, Ward asks, can it explain why God is not free? We can understand why lack of freedom to violate necessary truths is not an improper restriction on divine freedom; for we take it to be essential to the divine intellect to grasp these necessary truths unalterably, and we would not take it to be a divine intellect otherwise. But this explanation is not available to voluntarists, since they deny that the wrongness of cruelty and lying is a necessary truth grasped by the divine intellect apart from the divine legislative will. Since, according to voluntarism, the wrongness of wrong actions is not intrinsic, but depends on their being violations of God's commands, we still do not understand why these commands are necessary exercises of God's legislative will.

Ward sets out this objection to the moderate voluntarist view by considering Viva's account of 'fundamental sins'.[36] According to Viva, they are (i) intrinsically bad, because they are inappropriate to rational nature, and hence (ii) worthy of being prohibited or

---

[34] On Ward on Suarez see §437.

[35] This is the version of voluntarism that Mill has in mind in his repudiation of Mansel's account of divine goodness, at *ESWHP*, ch. 7 = *CW* ix 103.

[36] See §603.

demanding prohibition, but (iii) not really wrong (inhonesta) or sins without a divine prohibition, but also (iv) necessarily prohibited by God. In the fourth point, Viva rejects the Ockhamist position that it is possible for God not to prohibit those actions that are in fact morally wrong; he does not concede that God might have made murder, theft, and cruelty right. But Ward suggests that Viva's voluntarism deprives him of a justification for his claim that intrinsically bad actions have 'deservingness of prohibition' (prohibenditas). Why do they deserve prohibition if they are not intrinsically wrong? If one claims that naturally bad actions deserve prohibition precisely because they are intrinsically bad, do we not concede that it is intrinsically wrong to permit them? Viva answers this question by rejecting naturalism, but still maintaining that permission for intrinsically bad actions would be incompatible with God's holiness. Ward pertinently asks why this permission would be incompatible with God's holiness, unless the actions that would be permitted were intrinsically wrong in advance of being prohibited.

Ward's objections to Viva's moderate voluntarism are not original; they revive Cudworth's objections to Hobbes and Leibniz's objections to Pufendorf. All these criticisms maintain that voluntarists need some non-legislative morality if they are to say what they need to say about divine legislation. Cudworth argues that we need to explain how God is an authoritative legislator, and that we cannot explain this unless we suppose it is right to obey God. But how can it be right to obey God unless what God commands is right, independently of what God commands? Moderate voluntarists do not argue that God's authority requires or allows him to start with a blank cheque. On the contrary, they argue that God's necessary holiness requires approval of intrinsically good actions.

605. The Persistence of Voluntarism

These difficulties that face moderate voluntarism suggest that the division between fundamental and formal morality does not refute naturalist criticisms of voluntarism. On the contrary, it simply revives Cumberland's and Pufendorf's views about divine legislation and morality. Pufendorf accepts moderate voluntarism in order to avoid the extreme voluntarism of Hobbes; but it does not give him a satisfactory position. Ward's discussion shows how the modern Roman position reproduces the weaknesses in Pufendorf's position.

We might, then, be surprised that moderate voluntarism has been so tenacious, and has even been accepted in modern Roman Catholic statements on moral questions, despite the fact that it departs from the traditional Catholic position of Aquinas and Suarez by accepting some of Pufendorf's most questionable claims. How are we to explain this rather puzzling development? Some answers are worth considering.

First, Aquinas' position is not completely clear. One might take him to support the modern Roman position if one supposed that he takes natural law to depend essentially on the divine legislative will. We saw that this was Farrrell's interpretation of Aquinas, and that it tends to obscure the reasons for ascribing a naturalist position to Aquinas.

Second, it is easy to misinterpret Suarez's position, and therefore easy to overlook his agreement with Aquinas on the essential points about naturalism. Since he claims that obligation and natural law require divine legislation, we may take him to affirm voluntarism about morality, if we overlook his distinction between duties and obligations. Alternatively, if we notice his naturalism about morality without natural law, we may (following Farrell) suppose that naturalism about morality is a deviation from Aquinas' position. In fact he deviates from Aquinas about necessary conditions for natural law, not about necessary conditions for morality. But since even Ward misunderstands Suarez on these questions, it is not surprising that Suarez's naturalism about morality receives less attention than it deserves. Moderate voluntarists may well suppose that they are following Suarez in separating fundamental from formal morality; they do not notice that he recognizes formal and complete morality without divine legislation.

Third, the 19th- and 20th-century popes are especially concerned to defend the place of Christian theism in morality and to refute the error (as they understand it) of moral thinking that omits any reference to God. This concern might be satisfied in different ways, but one might argue that voluntarism does most to satisfy it; if morality itself refers essentially to divine legislation, we cannot abandon reference to a divine legislator without abandoning morality itself. One might dispute whether this extreme claim about God and the basis of morality is the best way to fulfil the aims of these popes; Aquinas avoids the extreme claim, but he certainly does not take theism to be irrelevant to morality.

Fourth, even those who do not share the aims of the popes may believe that they are right to connect morality with legislative will. Pufendorf's claims that moral duties involve obligations and commands, and that one's own will cannot provide the relevant obligation, may seem plausible, even if we do not agree with the ways in which Pufendorf exploits this claim. Similarly, we might claim that the modern Roman position is right to connect morality with obligation and with legislation, even if we do not draw all the Roman conclusions about divine legislation.

If these four points help to explain the persistence, and even the advance, of voluntarism within Roman Catholic Scholastic moral philosophy and theology, we may helpfully return to them when we consider the persisting voluntarist trend in 18th-century English moral philosophy.

But, whatever we say to explain the persistence of voluntarism, we seem to need some explanation apart from its philosophical merits. Once the alternative presented by Suarez is clearly understood, naturalism about morality seems to have clear philosophical advantages over voluntarism. These advantages are clear to Leibniz, but his criticism of voluntarism is too brief and careless, as Barbeyrac shows, to expose all the difficulties that arise for a defender of voluntarism. Ward's defence of naturalism convincingly argues both from Catholic philosophical tradition and on broader philosophical grounds. His defence casts serious doubt on the decision of the three popes to go as far as they go in acceptance of voluntarism.

606. Mackie's Defence of Pufendorf

The modern Roman Catholic version of voluntarism relies on the claim that moral oughts require obligations and commands. We might accept this claim even if we are not theists, on the ground that this is the only way to explain the necessity that seems to belong to moral principles. To see why some elements of this position might seem plausible, we may turn to modern defenders of Pufendorf's claim. Two 20th-century philosophers have tried to answer this question, by arguing that a divine-command theory of morality deserves to be taken seriously, and that it does better than other views in capturing the special force of moral requirements. Their arguments are especially instructive because they draw opposite conclusions from them. Mackie believes that since there would be real moral facts only if there were divine commands of the right sort, and since there are no appropriate divine commands, moral judgments are not true. Adams believes that since moral facts require divine commands, and moral judgments are true, we have a good reason to believe in divine commands. Does Mackie or Adams give a good reason for agreeing with Pufendorf about the role of divine commands in morality?

Mackie agrees with Pufendorf's claim that moral properties are not part of the natural world that we understand through the physical sciences; Mackie expresses this point by claiming that moral entities are 'queer'.[37] He does not mean to rule out the logical possibility of objective values. He suggests that there would be objective values within a specific theological framework (which he rejects). Theological moralists might argue that God created human beings with a specific good; this would be an objective fact, but not an objective value. Objective values, however, enter with 'objective prescriptivity', which results from divine commands.[38]

This suggestion that divine commands introduce objective prescriptivity and objective values might be held to capture Pufendorf's view that morality depends on divine commands; without divine commands there are only descriptive truths embodying no objective prescriptions. Suarez insists that without divine commands there are only 'indicative' facts, and that divine commands are needed for genuine prescriptions, but he believes that the right sorts of indicative facts are sufficient for moral facts. Pufendorf and Mackie agree against Suarez that genuine moral principles must be prescriptive.

Pufendorf and Mackie, therefore, may both accept this argument: (1) Moral rightness exists if and only if there are objectively prescriptive truths.[39] (2) If there are no divine commands, there are no objectively prescriptive truths. (3) Hence, if there are no divine commands, there is no moral rightness, and moral nihilism is true. (4) If, however, there are divine commands (with the right content), there are objectively prescriptive moral truths, and hence there is moral rightness.[40]

---

[37] See §567.

[38] 'It might be that there is one kind of life which is, in a purely descriptive sense, most appropriate for human beings as they are—that is, that it alone will fully develop rather than stunt their natural capacities and that in it, and only in it, can they find their fullest and deepest satisfaction. It might then follow that certain rules of conduct and certain dispositions were appropriate (still purely descriptively) in that they were needed to maintain this way of life. All these would then be facts as hard as any in arithmetic or chemistry, and so logically independent of any command or prescriptive will of God, though they might be products of the creative will of God, which, in making men as they are, will have made them such that this life, these rules, and these dispositions are appropriate for them. But, further, God might require men to live in this appropriate way, and might enjoin obedience to the related rules. This would add an objectively prescriptive element to what otherwise were hard, descriptive truths, but in a quite non-mysterious way: these would be literally commands issued by an identifiable authority.' (E 230–1)

[39] These truths must have the right content; neither Pufendorf nor Mackie endorses the extreme voluntarist thesis that any logically possible commands by God would thereby constitute moral rightness.

[40] Mackie may not agree entirely with Pufendorf about the role of divine commands. He may, for instance, believe that it is a purely empirical fact that there are no objective values apart from divine commands, whereas Pufendorf might believe (if he were to confront the question) that this can be known a priori.

To accept this argument, we must agree that morality requires objective prescriptivity. and that divine commands secure precisely this objective prescriptivity. But Mackie's different remarks about objective prescriptivity make it difficult to agree on both points at once: (1) He suggests that objective values both give us knowledge of what to do and cause us, through our recognition of them, to try to do it; our recognition by itself ensures correct action.[41] (2) His second clarification of objective prescriptivity turns to Kant's notion of a categorical imperative. A categorical imperative rests on a reason that is independent of any desire of the agent that would be satisfied by acting on the imperative.[42] Mackie takes his denial of objectively prescriptive entities or truths to be the denial of categorical imperatives.[43] If he takes objectively prescriptive entities to require the internal connexion between knowledge and motivation that he attributes to Plato's Forms, he must also take categorical imperatives to involve reasons that we cannot recognize without being motivated to act on the imperatives. (3) In his discussion of categorical imperatives, Mackie sees that an imperative, understood as a simple command in the imperative mood, need not be an objectively prescriptive categorical imperative. If the command presupposes that the agents addressed have some specific desire or inclination, it is really a hypothetical imperative.[44] (4) His next clarification of objective prescriptivity rests on partial acceptance of a non-naturalist analysis of some moral terms in some of their uses. The non-natural element indicates the action-guiding aspect of the alleged objective value, and hence introduces objective prescriptivity.[45]

But do divine commands introduce objective prescriptivity? Mackie's most stringent test for objective prescriptivity requires an internal connexion between knowledge of objective values and motivation to follow their prescriptions; it must be logically impossible to know them and not to act on them. Divine commands fail this test; for it is logically possible to know that something has been commanded by God without wanting to do anything about it.

Even if the demand for a categorical imperative does not require such a tight internal connexion, divine commands do not automatically count. As Mackie agrees, commands might presuppose different sorts of motives or desires in the person commanded. The mere

[41] 'Conversely, the main tradition of European moral philosophy from Plato onwards has combined the view that moral values are objective with the recognition that moral judgments are partly prescriptive or directive or action-guiding. Values themselves have been seen as at once prescriptive and objective. In Plato's theory the Forms, and in particular the Form of the Good, are eternal, extra-mental entities . . . But it is held also that just knowing them or "seeing" them will not merely tell men what to do but will ensure that they do it, overcoming any contrary inclinations.' (23) Mackie makes it clear that the causal role of 'seeing' does not require the co-operation of desires; it is supposed to be causally sufficient by itself.

[42] 'A categorical imperative, then, would express a reason for acting which was unconditional in the sense of not being contingent upon any present desire of the agent to whose satisfaction the recommended action would contribute as a means—or more directly . . . ' (29)

[43] 'So far as ethics is concerned, my thesis that there are no objective values is specifically the denial that any such categorically imperative element is objectively valid. The objective values which I am denying would be action-directing absolutely, not contingently . . . upon the agent's desires and inclinations.' (29)

[44] 'Indeed, a simple command in the imperative mood, say a parade-ground order, which might seem most literally to qualify for the title of a categorical imperative, will hardly ever be one in the sense we need here. The implied reason for complying with such an order will almost always be some desire of the person addressed, perhaps simply the desire to keep out of trouble.' (28–9)

[45] ' . . . the description "non-natural" leaves room for the peculiar evaluative, prescriptive, intrinsically action-guiding aspects of this supposed quality' (32).

fact that divine commands are commands, and therefore are imperatives of some kind, does not make them categorical imperatives.

What, then, makes them categorical imperatives? Two answers seem possible: (1) God can be relied on to command us to observe principles that are (whether or not God commands them) categorical imperatives. (2) Since it is a categorical imperative that we ought to obey God's commands, God's commanding us to act in various ways presents us with categorical imperatives, and hence introduces objective prescriptivity.

Neither of these answers supports Mackie. The first answer admits categorical imperatives apart from God's commands. The second answer presupposes at least one categorical imperative apart from God's commands—the requirement of obedience to God. In either case, God's commands cannot be the only source of objective prescriptivity, but presuppose that some principle other than a divine command is objectively prescriptive.

For this reason, Mackie's development of Pufendorf's position does not help Pufendorf. Mackie suggests a reason for believing that divine commands introduce the normativity of morality, because they ground the specifically moral 'ought'. But this is not an adequate reason. If we believe that divine commands are necessary for morality because they introduce moral normativity, we face two objections: (1) If normativity is understood as objective prescriptivity, we have quite good reason to doubt whether morality really needs to be normative after all. It is not clear that morality requires the internal connexion that Mackie describes between knowledge and motivation. (2) If morality requires objective prescriptivity, divine commands do not give us morality, because they do not give us objective prescriptivity.

We might infer, therefore, that Pufendorf is better off without the defence that Mackie offers through his appeal to objective prescriptivity. But this inference is open to question. If Pufendorf does not mean to claim that divine commands introduce categorical imperatives, he does not show that divine commands themselves are the source of morality. Apparently, we need some categorical reason, independent of divine commands, for following divine commands. This basis belongs to intrinsic morality, as Suarez understands it. Alternatively, Pufendorf might deny that we have a categorical reason for obeying divine commands, and so might agree that our basis is prudence, fear, or gratitude; but in that case he fails to show that he does any better than other people in capturing the distinctive features of morality. He does not refute Suarez's claim that the basic principles of morality belong to intrinsic morality, and are inherently indicative, rather than prescriptive.

607. Adams's Defence of Pufendorf

A different defence of Pufendorf is offered by Robert Adams, who agrees with him in claiming that genuine obligations are the result of divine commands. This claim, as we have seen, might be taken to be simply Suarez's claim; and indeed Adams cites Suarez (cautiously) in his support.[46] But his position is a defence of Pufendorf rather than of Suarez, because Adams's concept of obligation is broader than Suarez's on the crucial point.

---

[46] Adams, FIG 251n5.

According to Adams, obligation coincides with moral rightness and wrongness.[47] His concept of obligation is the broad concept that connects the obligatory with the required and the compulsory, rather than the narrow impositive concept that we found in Suarez. Since obligation, understood broadly, extends to the various moral properties that Suarez takes to be antecedent to divine commands, Adams must agree with Pufendorf's view that intrinsic goodness and badness are antecedent to divine commands, but moral rightness and wrongness depend on divine commands.

This description of Adams's relation to Suarez disagrees with Adams's view of Suarez. Adams quotes Suarez's remark that divine commands presuppose intrinsic honestas and turpitudo in the actions. He takes this remark to refer only to intrinsic goodness, not to moral rightness and wrongness; hence he translates 'honestas' and 'turpitudo' as 'honourableness' and 'shamefulness', rather than by 'rightness' and 'wrongness'.[48] On this point he differs from Pufendorf, who denies any intrinsic honestas and turpitudo antecedent to divine commands. Adams seems to agree with Culverwell's interpretation of Suarez, which treats honestas and turpitudo as intrinsically attractive and repulsive features antecedent to divine commands. According to Adams, these features constitute natural goodness and badness, but they do not constitute moral requirements.

Adams argues as follows that obligations need divine commands: (1) Obligations involve social requirements that are the basis of justified praise and blame, guilt, and shame. (2) These social requirements depend on the demands that other persons actually make, not simply on those that they are entitled to make.[49] (3) Such requirements would be too variable and alterable unless they expressed divine commands.[50] (4) Therefore moral requirements express divine commands.

For present purposes, we may concede Adams's first premiss, and accept a tight connexion between moral requirements, social requirements, and inter-personal attitudes. To accept all this is to agree that moral requirements depend on facts about human society and especially about human nature in society—the sorts of facts that Grotius describes as 'sociality'. One might reasonably claim that these facts are the basis of the moral requirements that Suarez calls 'duties' (debita). Adams's second premiss, however, is open to doubt. It does not seem obvious that what I owe to people, or what I am required to do for them, always and essentially depends on what they actually demand of me or on what someone else actually

[47] '['Right'] can have . . . a strong sense in which a right action (or perhaps more often *the* right action) is one that it is *wrong* not to do. For that reason it is commonly clearer to speak of an action as permissible, in the former case, or *obligatory*, in the latter case . . . I will generally speak of the part of ethics that we take up at this point as the realm of "moral obligation" (or simply of "obligation") . . .' (Adams, FIG 231–2)

[48] FIG 251n5, quoting Suarez, *Leg.* ii 6.11 (quoted at §441n45). I am pursuing Adams's line of thought for its intrinsic interest, without meaning to suggest that he necessarily subscribes to it all. He also says that Suarez 'is less thoroughly a divine command theorist of the nature of obligation than Cumberland, Pufendorf, and Locke'. In my view, this claim is false, if 'obligation' is understood in Suarez's impositive sense, but true if it is understood in Adams's broad sense.

[49] 'If we are thinking about the nature of obligations, and about the reasons we have to comply with possible demands, it matters that the demand is actually made. It is a question here of what good demands other persons do in fact make of me, not just of what good demands they could make. The demand need not take the form of an explicit command or legislation; it may be an expectation more subtly communicated; but the demand must actually be made.' (FIG 245–6)

[50] FIG 247–8. I have over-simplified here. Adams says he is not ruling out other ways of avoiding the problem of variability, but the way he chooses is a natural move for a theist. He regards this as a 'more powerful theistic adaptation of the social requirement theory' (248). I take him to mean that it is more powerful than a non-theistic explanation of the relevant social requirements.

demands on their behalf. It seems to depend on what they need, or on what they are entitled to, apart from anyone's actual demands.[51]

Adams seems to sympathize with this objection, since he also refuses to allow obligations to depend on actual demands of actual human agents. That is why he affirms his third premiss. But if we see some force in the objection, why should we not reconsider the second premiss, rather than draw Adams's conclusion?

Adams's view is not as extreme as Pufendorf's, since he does not take the scope of obligation to be the scope of morality. He is willing to allow that it would be morally good and admirable to give a cup of water to an innocent person dying of thirst, but he does not believe it could be morally required unless someone actually demanded it of me. This is difficult to see. If I deliberately poured the water on the ground, other people would justifiably censure me whether or not they believed that someone was demanding that I give the water; and I would appropriately feel guilty about what I had done whether or not I believed that someone was making this demand. The salient facts here seem to be that the dying innocent person needed the cup of water and that I could easily give it to him.[52]

Adams, therefore, does not give us a good reason to agree with Pufendorf against Suarez on the basis of moral requirements. When Suarez recognizes intrinsic honestas and turpitudo, he thereby recognizes intrinsic moral rightness and wrongness. Similarly, Pufendorf believes that if there is no intrinsic morality, there is no intrinsic honestas and turpitudo. According to Suarez, intrinsic honestas and turpitudo are also the basis for duties (debita), sins (peccata), and blameworthiness (culpa). Suarez disagrees with Adams's view about the source of moral requirements; Adams's arguments ought not to persuade us that Suarez is mistaken.

This basic disagreement between Suarez and Pufendorf—even in the improved version of Pufendorf offered by Adams—does not imply that divine commands do not matter in an account of the moral requirements that actually apply to us. Suarez evidently attaches moral importance to the requirements that result from divine legislation. But divine commands, in his view, do not have the specific moral importance that they would have if they were the source of moral requirements. The recent defences of Pufendorf's voluntarism should not change our previous conclusion that Ward gives some good reasons for preferring naturalism.

[51] One might agree that what people actually demand is indeed morally relevant, not for the reason Adams gives, but because there are moral reasons—though not always decisive ones—to respect people's actual demands.
[52] Leibniz offers some examples (for a different purpose) that illustrate this point well. See 'CCJ' = R 54–5. See §589.

45

SHAFTESBURY

608. Platonist, or Sentimentalist, or Both?

Shaftesbury is the first to use the terms 'moral sense' and 'moral realist'. Since later believers in a moral sense, Hume and Hutcheson, reject moral realism, we may be surprised that Shaftesbury uses both terms to describe his own position. His philosophical allegiances also seem to lead him in different directions. On many points he agrees with Locke, but he also draws extensively on Platonic and Stoic sources. We may wonder whether he combines these different influences into a consistent position.

These different strands in Shaftesbury have led to different views about where he stands, and about which of his moral doctrines are the most significant or fundamental. Some later critics treat him as the first sentimentalist. Hutcheson is the first of these critics; he designs his *Inquiry* as a defence of Shaftesbury's principles.[1] The principles he defends are disinterested affection and a moral sense—two prominent themes in Shaftesbury's defence of the moral outlook.

Following Hutcheson's lead, Martineau regards Shaftesbury and Hutcheson as the representatives of 'aesthetic ethics'.[2] This position includes the metaphysical claim that the object of moral judgment is not external reality, but some state of oneself. That is why the judgment of conscience does not involve the mind's 'submission to the truth of external things'. Aesthetic ethics also includes the epistemological claim that moral judgment belongs to emotion not to reason, so that the right is known because it is felt.

Selby-Bigge takes a similar view of Shaftesbury, since his collection prints works by Shaftesbury, Hutcheson, and Butler as 'three principal texts of the sentimental school' (Pref., p. vi).[3] Sidgwick's appreciative account of Shaftesbury does not mention Platonism or realism. In Sidgwick's view, Shaftesbury's *Characteristics* marks 'a turning-point in the history of English ethical thought', because he is 'the first moralist who distinctly takes psychological experience as the basis of ethics' (Sidgwick, *OHE* 190).

---

[1] See Hutcheson's title page, quoted in §632.

[2] 'Whether the term which they emphasize is the moral sense or disinterested affection, they seek their key to the judgments of conscience in some form of inward emotion, and not in the mind's submission to the truth of external things; so that the right is not . . . felt because it is known, but known because it is somehow felt.' (Martineau, *TET* ii 485–6)

[3] On Selby-Bigge's view of Butler see §712.

We form a different picture of Shaftesbury, however, if we attend to the influence of Cambridge Platonism and of Stoicism.[4] Whewell emphasizes this influence in treating Shaftesbury as an early supporter of 'independent morality' and in treating Shaftesbury's realism to be part of the defence of this position.[5] Since Hutcheson supports Shaftesbury, Whewell takes Hutcheson to be another defender of realism and independent morality.

These different elements in Shaftesbury suggest a complex picture of his relation to Locke. He was a pupil of Locke, and remained an admirer. But the tendency of Locke's moral philosophy is sharply opposed to Platonist views; for Locke agrees with Hobbes's psychological egoistic hedonism and theological voluntarism. Though Shaftesbury agrees with Locke in general about the reasonable character of Christianity, and about the folly of opposing natural reason to revelation, Locke's moral position outlook seems to agree with the 'orthodox' Christian outlook that Shaftesbury deplores.

Shaftesbury seems to maintain a Platonist metaphysics of morality together with a Lockean epistemology and moral psychology. On the one hand, he defends the reality of moral properties, apart from the will or preferences of agents, and the reality of moral virtue, apart from self-confined desires. These two claims constitute his 'moral realism'. On the other hand, he seems to follow Locke's views about the basis of knowledge and motivation; knowledge is based on the senses, and motivation on non-rational desire rather than reason. How can we be confident that the sensory basis of cognition, as Locke understands it, will support the belief in the independent reality of moral properties?

Shaftesbury's position, therefore, includes different elements that might seem attractive to different people. In distinguishing these different elements, we will see why both Hutcheson and Butler might reasonably claim to defend central elements in Shaftesbury's position.

All of his critics and interpreters agree that he criticizes Hobbesian egoism. We may usefully begin with the criticisms that mark points of agreement with later sentimentalists; then we can ask whether he also criticizes Hobbes from a Platonist direction, and whether these criticisms fit a sentimentalist outlook.

609. The Sense of Right and Wrong

According to Shaftesbury, we are immediately aware of moral goodness and rightness; we do not come to believe actions are right, or that people are good, as a result of considering whether they promote someone's pleasure. We approve of them from an unselfish point of view that considers the public interest.[6] Those who are appropriately sensitive to moral goodness have more than a tendency towards benevolent actions; they also have the capacity to reflect on this tendency and to 'take notice of what is worthy or honest; and make that notice or conception of worth and honesty to be an object of his affection' (ICV i 2.3 = K 173).

---

[4] Platonist and Stoic influence is emphasized by Passmore, RC 96–100; Walford, Introd. to ICV, p. xv; Rivers, RGS ii 94.

[5] On independent morality see §520.

[6] '. . . we call any creature worthy or virtuous, when it can have the notion of a public interest, and can attain the speculation or science of what is morally good or ill, admirable or blameable, right or wrong' (ICV i 2.3 = K 173). References to Shaftesbury cite the relevant treatise followed by the page in Klein's edition of Char., cited as 'K'.

Shaftesbury seems to intend this description to fit both the virtuous moral agent and the sound moral judge of moral agents (including oneself).

This recognition of moral properties may be compared to sense-perception. Conscience expresses itself in judgments about the rightness of this or that action, as well as in the grasp of general principles. Both aspects of conscience are often immediate, not involving any explicit reasoning and derivation. Hence they may be described as a sense of right and wrong.[7] Shaftesbury uses such expressions to refer to these immediate reactions to particular situations.[8]

A different basis for belief in a moral sense is the assimilation of moral to aesthetic awareness. We have found this assimilation in Culverwell, who describes natural rightness (honestas) and wrongness (turpitudo) as proper objects of admiration and disgust; he regards them as appealing and repellent, apart from any narrow self-interest. Aesthetic responses offer a useful parallel to moral reactions in being both immediate and disinterested. If we find something beautiful, appealing, repulsive, or disgusting, we do not seem to be recording a conclusion we have reached on the basis of any reasoning; nor do we seem to be reporting on our own interest. The disinterestedness of our appreciation of beauty suggests how we might appreciate moral goodness and badness in a similarly disinterested way. According to Shaftesbury, we recognize beauty and charm in moral as well as natural objects apart from any views about our own interest (*Misc.* 5, ch. 3 = K 466). Ancient moralists who speak of the *kalon* might be taken to rely on this parallel between aesthetic and moral reactions; Shaftesbury treats their remarks as evidence of the parallel.[9]

The comparison between a moral sense and the sense of beauty helps to explain why virtuous people refuse even to consider certain kinds of questions. Shaftesbury compares the question 'Why be honest in the dark?' with the question 'Why keep yourself clean if no one can smell?' In the second case, he answers that he would not care to associate with someone who needed to ask himself this question and did not take it for granted that he should keep himself clean. The appropriate reaction to not keeping clean is not reflective, but aesthetic—an immediate sense of disgust. Similarly, virtuous people are not those who can always explain why we should be honest in the dark and therefore always act honestly; they would not dream of asking the question. To be a virtuous person is to be repelled by the very

---

[7] 'There is in reality no rational creature whatsoever, who knows not that when he voluntarily offends or does harm to anyone, he cannot fail to create an apprehension and fear of like harm, and consequently a resentment and animosity in every creature who observes him. So that the offender must needs be conscious of being liable to such treatment from every-one, as if he had in some degree offended all. Thus offence and injury are always known as punishable by every-one; and equal behaviour, which is therefore called merit, as rewardable and well-deserving from every-one. Of this even the wickedest creature living must have a *sense*. So that if there be any further meaning in this *sense* of right and wrong; if in reality there be any *sense* of this kind which an absolute wicked creature has not; it must consist in a real antipathy or aversion to *injustice* or *wrong*, and in a real affection or love towards *equity* and *right*, for its own sake, and on the account of its own natural beauty and worth.' (*ICV* i 3.1 = K 178)

[8] '... there must in every rational creature be yet further conscience, namely, from sense of deformity in what is thus ill-deserving and unnatural and from a consequent shame or regret of incurring what is odious and moves aversion.' (*ICV* ii 2.1 = K 209) 'A man who in a passion happens to kill his companion relents immediately on the sight of what he has done ... If, on the other side, we suppose him not to relent or suffer any real concern or shame; then either he has no sense of the deformity of the crime and injustice, no natural affection, and consequently no happiness or peace within: or if he has any sense of moral worth or goodness, it must be of a perplexed and contradictory kind' (*ICV* ii 2.1 = K 209–10). On Shaftesbury's use of 'moral sense' see Rivers, *RGS* ii 124; he uses the expression rarely in the text, but sometimes inserts it in the marginal summaries.

[9] Cf. Maxwell's reference to the *kalon kagathon* as the 'beauteous-beneficial', §539.

thought of taking this question seriously as though it needed an answer in particular cases (*Sens. Comm.* 3.4 = K 58). 'The sense of right and wrong', therefore, captures Stoic claims about the fine.[10] Shaftesbury agrees with the Stoics' appeal to the immediate recognition and admiration of actions and characters that benefit others or promote a common good, independently of any benefit to the agent.[11]

Shaftesbury claims, then, that we are aware of moral rightness and wrongness by some sort of quasi-aesthetic sense that includes some pleasure sufficient for motivation. Our 'inward eye' distinguishes fair and foul in actions and characters no less than in other beautiful and ugly objects. Disputes about what is fair and foul presuppose that we have some conception of the relevant qualities; otherwise we could not identify the area of dispute.[12] Our ordinary moral sentiments of gratitude, resentment, pride, and shame presuppose some conception of the relevant moral qualities that are the proper objects of the sentiments. To explain the connexion between sentiment and principle, Shaftesbury alludes to the Stoic doctrine of 'preconceptions' or 'anticipations' (*prolêpseis*); he claims that we have 'a natural presumption or anticipation on which resentment or anger is founded' (*Mor.* 3.2 = *Char.* ii 419 = K 329).[13] This natural 'presumption' embodies an implicit principle that guides our sentiment, and attention to the sentiment reveals the underlying principle.[14]

The aesthetic character of the moral sentiment does not compromise the objectivity of moral properties or the rationality of moral principles. Shaftesbury accepts the Stoic doctrine of the *honestum* as what deserves praise in its own right, apart from whether it is actually praised.[15] He advocates the cultivation of moral taste and a sense of moral appropriateness that will be as keen as the cultivated person's sense of the appropriate and suitable in clothes, or paintings, or music, because he believes that this sense of appropriateness will make us aware of moral facts, and especially of the admirable characteristics of actions and characters that are concerned for others. The sense of moral appropriateness is not a substitute for grasp of the right principles, but it is an essential support for it; if our sentiments diverge sharply from the actions enjoined by our principles, they will counteract the effect of our principles.[16]

---

[10] This connexion with the Stoic doctrine is clear from the section on the beautiful (sub-heading: '*To kalon*') in Shaftesbury's PR 244–52.

[11] Cf. Cic. *Off.* i 14–15.

[12] 'No sooner are actions viewed, no sooner the human affections and passions discerned . . . than straight an inward eye distinguishes and sees the fair and shapely, the amiable and admirable, apart from the deformed, the foul, the odious or the despicable. How is it possible therefore not to own that as these distinctions have their foundation in nature, the discernment itself is natural and from nature alone? . . . Even by this [sc. disagreement] it appears there is fitness and decency in actions since the fit and decent is in this controversy ever presupposed.' (*Mor.* 3.2 = K 326–7)

[13] On Stoic preconceptions see §165.

[14] In PR 214–20 Shaftesbury discusses *prolêpseis*, which he translates as 'natural concepts'. The chapter begins with references to Epictetus on preconceptions.

[15] 'Is there no natural tenor, tone, or order of the passions or affections? No beauty or deformity in this moral kind? Or allowing that there really is, must it not, of consequence, in the same manner imply health or sickliness, prosperity or disaster? Will it not be found in this respect, above all, that what is beautiful is harmonious and proportionable, what is harmonious and proportionable is true, and what is at once both beautiful and true is, of consequence, agreeable and good?' (*Misc.* 3.2 = K 415) A footnote quotes Cicero's account of the fine ('per se ipsum possit iure laudari') at *Fin.* ii 45. The aesthetic aspect of the *kalon* and honestum is explored at length in PR 244–52 (referring to Epictetus on the aesthetic and the moral aspect of the *kalon*, at 246).

[16] 'Thus, we see, after all, that it is not merely what we call *principle* but a *taste* which governs men. They may think for certain, "This is right or that wrong"; they may believe, "This is a crime or that a sin", "This punishable by man

610. Moral Motivation, Virtue, and Happiness

In arguing for a moral sense Shaftesbury intends a claim about motivation as well as judgment. We are not only capable of judging from an impartial point of view, but also capable of acting on this point of view. Awareness of cruelty or injustice moves us to action because it is cruelty or injustice, whether or not it affects our own interest. This capacity for action on disinterested motives conflicts with Hobbes's psychological hedonism.

In the light of this affirmation of non-egoistic motivation, some readers have been surprised by Shaftesbury's discussion of our 'obligation' to virtue. This term often causes confusion in the British moralists; but in this context Shaftesbury explains himself by identifying our obligation with our 'reason to embrace it' (*ICV* ii 1.1 = K 192).[17] He answers this question by explaining why virtue promotes the agent's happiness. He does not directly say that this is the only reason we could have for embracing virtue; but since he suggests no other reason, he seems to assume that a sufficient reason for being virtuous must at least include a warranted belief that virtue promotes one's happiness.

We might be surprised that Shaftesbury mentions only this reason for being virtuous, after what he has said about the disinterested character of the moral sense.[18] Martineau voices this disappointment strongly; he suggests that after affirming the possibility of disinterested motivation, Shaftesbury reverts to a self-interested hedonist outlook.[19] Martineau cites the remarks about the moral sense in order to show that Shaftesbury recognizes a basis of moral goodness that is independent of any appeal to self-interest. A virtuous person is one who regards the moral properties of actions as the sources of sufficient reasons in their own right. Why, then, should some reason based in self-interest be needed?

Shaftesbury's acceptance both of a disinterested conception of a moral sense and of a self-interested defence of morality should not surprise us as much as it surprises Martineau. We need only recall the structure of eudaemonist ethical theories. If we understand the pursuit of happiness as the pursuit of rational structure and harmony in our different activities, it is reasonable to examine the contribution of virtue to happiness.

Still, Martineau would be right to say that asking this question conflicts with the disinterested appreciation of virtue, if Shaftesbury were suggesting that virtue maximizes pleasure. Is this what Shaftesbury means? We can certainly find passages where Shaftesbury seems to accept Locke's moral psychology, including his hedonist conception of happiness.

---

or that by God''; yet, if the savour of things lies cross to honesty, if the fancy be florid and the appetite high towards the subaltern beauties and lower order of worldly symmetries and proportions, the conduct will infallibly turn this latter way.' (*Misc.* 3.2 = K 413)

[17] On the use of 'obligation' see §818. For Shaftesbury's use cf. *Mor.* ii 1 = K 255 ('an enlarged affection and sense of obligation to society'); *Sens. Comm.* iii 1 = K 51 ('It is ridiculous to say there is any obligation on man to act socially or honestly in a formed government and not in that which is commonly called the state of nature').

[18] Cf. John Brown's comments, §867.

[19] 'The idea of obligation, in the form of an ultimate authority, intuitively known, after being affirmed and justified, is again lost: the question being raised, "What underlies this bottom of all?" "where are the credentials of this power which legitimates itself?" If it is disappointing to find this question asked, it is still more so to hear the answer, viz. that what binds us to the right is the balance of personal happiness it brings us;—an answer at which the independent base of virtue suddenly caves in, and the goodly pile that seemed immovable is shifted on to the sands of hedonism.' (Martineau, *TET* ii 508)

Sometimes he seems to be an anti-rationalist about motivation and action.[20] He argues that the choice of one end over another, in cases where instrumental reasoning cannot decide the issue, must be the outcome of the different impacts of desires of different strengths. It is not clear, however, whether he believes that every desire must be the outcome of some prior non-rational desire focussed by instrumental reasoning. Hutcheson commits himself to this aspect of anti-rationalism, but Shaftesbury does not go so far.

His attitude to hedonism is also imprecise. He distinguishes the virtuous person from the straightforwardly calculating hedonist who considers, as Hobbes's 'fool' does, whether this or that virtuous action will promote his own interest. To reject the attitude of the fool, however, is not to reject one's own pleasure as a ground for pursuing the virtues in general. And Shaftesbury seems to rely on a hedonist assumption. In his view, happiness 'is generally computed' from pleasures or satisfactions (*ICV* ii 2.1 = K 201).

He agrees with Cumberland that virtuous people's outlook does not subordinate the common good to their own pleasure. In his view, the affection for the public interest is a source of pleasures.[21] These pleasures arise partly from sympathetic participation in the pleasures of others (*ICV* ii 2.1 = 202 K), and partly from reflexion on and approval of our own benevolent attitudes. This reflective conscience is distinct from fear of punishment, even of divine punishment; someone who observes the requirements of morality simply from the fear of divine punishment lacks a necessary condition for conscience (*ICV* ii 2.1 = K 207).[22]

This is a hedonist defence of virtue only if Shaftesbury means that the social and sympathetic pleasures enjoyed by a virtuous person are greater than those enjoyed by others, as estimated from a neutral point of view. The virtuous person, on this view, gets more pleasure than the vicious person, just as we get more pleasure from savouring each bite of a well-cooked dish than we get from bolting it down without tasting it properly.

Shaftesbury, however, does not seem to intend his claims about pleasure to be understood in this way.[23] He suggests that it is trifling to say that pleasure is our good, because 'will' and 'pleasure' are synonymous. To say that we do what we please, or that we aim at our pleasure, simply means that we choose what we think eligible. In asking where we should seek our pleasure, we are asking what is really eligible; we should be asking how to distinguish good from bad pleasure (*Mor.* 2.1 = K 250–1). If we identify happiness with pleasure, we are saying that our good consists in doing what we like; but since our preferences and likings change, identification of our good with the satisfaction of our preferences makes our good variable and unstable (*Sol.* 3.2 = 138–9 K).

Sometimes, therefore, Shaftesbury argues that our happiness consists not simply in achieving our preferences and likings, but in achieving our good. A true conception of

[20] 'It has been shown before, that no animal can be said properly to *act*, otherwise than through affections or passions, such as are proper to an animal . . . Whatever, therefore is done or acted by any animal as such, is done only through some affection or passion, as of fear, love, or hatred moving him. And as it is impossible that a weaker affection should overcome a stronger, so it is impossible but that where the affections or passions are strongest in the main, and form in general the most considerable party, either by their force or number; thither the animal must incline: and according to this balance he must be governed, and led to action.' (*ICV* ii 1.3 = K 195–6)

[21] '. . . the natural affections, duly established in a rational creature, being the only means which can procure him a constant series or succession of the mental enjoyments, they are the only means which can procure him a certain and solid happiness' (*ICV* ii 2.1 = K 201).

[22] Butler on conscience and divine punishment; §717. He agrees with Hutcheson (§636).

[23] Cf. Hutcheson's attack on hedonism, which may be partly directed at Shaftesbury. See §633.

our interest shows that expression of concern for others is a vital part of our interest. Opponents of this claim about virtue and happiness rely on a narrow conception of interest and happiness that obscures the real questions.[24]

We can clarify the issue about happiness once we recognize that a person's good is not to be defined simply by reference to the satisfaction of desires. As Shaftesbury puts it, the good does not depend entirely on 'fancy', because 'there is that in which the nature of man is satisfied, and which alone must be his good' (*Mor.* iii 3 = *Char.* ii 436 = K 335). In the light of our conception of human nature, we can see which passions are suitable to us, and find an appropriate 'balance of . . . passions', constituting 'beauty and decorum' in one's internal states (*Mor.* ii 4 = *Char.* ii 294 = K 277). Contrary to Hobbes, we find that society and the aims and affections that support it are natural to human beings. The pleasures that belong to social sentiment are part of a human being's happiness not because they are greater than any other pleasures, but because of their role in the human good.[25]

Since the good appropriate to human nature consists in the right internal order of self-regarding and other-regarding sentiments and passions, happiness comes from within and not from outside a person (*Mor.* iii 2 = K 335). Non-moral goods benefit us only if they are used properly. The moral good, by contrast, is good in its own right; it is most agreeable in itself, and preferable to all these external goods (*Mor.* iii 2 = K 332). The awareness of good order in one's own nature is the source of a higher enjoyment than we receive from other sources (*Mor.* iii = K 331).

These aspects of Shaftesbury's account of the human good suggest that his references to pleasure fall short of hedonism. A hedonist defence claims that virtue is the best policy for an agent who takes his pleasure as his ultimate end, because virtue, apart from any further result, is the source of the greatest pleasure.[26] Since we have sympathetic feelings, and since we find pleasure both in the satisfaction of our sympathetic feelings and in the awareness of their satisfaction, the virtues that express and satisfy these sympathetic feelings are the best means to maximum pleasure. This argument fits some of Shaftesbury's remarks on virtue and happiness, but it does not fit the passages where he subordinates the pursuit of pleasure to the pursuit of one's genuine good.

Sidgwick notices some of the variations in Shaftesbury's claims about happiness, and claims justifiably that he seems to incline in different passages towards both a hedonistic and a non-hedonistic conception of a person's good. But Sidgwick does not justify his conclusion

---

[24] 'Now if these gentlemen who delight so much in the play of words, but are cautious how they grapple closely with definitions, would tell us only what self-interest was, and determine happiness and good, there would be an end to this enigmatical wit. For in this we should all agree, that happiness was to be pursued, and in fact was always sought after; but whether found in following nature, and giving way to common affection; or in suppressing it, and turning every passion towards private advantage, a narrow self-end, or the preservation of mere life; this would be the matter in debate between us. The question would not be "Who loved himself, or who not", but "Who loved and served himself the rightest, and after the truest manner".' (*Sens. Comm.* 3.3 = K 56) Similarly, after explaining why one separates concern for the interests of others from one's own interest, Shaftesbury replies that 'to be well affected towards the public interest and one's own is not only consistent but inseparable' (*ICV* ii 1.1 = K 193).

[25] '. . . we may with justice surely place it as a principle, 'that if anything be natural in any creature or any kind, it is that which is preservative of the kind itself, and conducing to its welfare . . . If any appetite or sense be natural, the sense of fellowship is the same' (*Sens. Comm.* 3.2 = K 51).

[26] This is the view that Brown attributes to Shaftesbury. See §867.

that Shaftesbury's predominant view of happiness is hedonistic.[27] This conclusion ignores the places where Shaftesbury criticizes a hedonist account of a person's good; such criticism implies that Shaftesbury sometimes rejects hedonism, not just that he sometimes speaks in non-hedonist terms.

If Shaftesbury were a hedonist, his position would be unstable. His claim about the virtuous person's pleasure might be understood as a purely causal and psychological claim, that being virtuous produces a larger quantity of the same sort of feeling of pleasure that everyone seeks. If that is what he means, his claim about the virtuous person involves the empirical claim that the virtuous person gets more pleasure on the whole than Hobbes's fool could get.

This empirical claim is open to doubt. The fool need not leave his sympathetic feelings completely undeveloped, and so he need not entirely forgo the pleasures of the virtuous person. But he can control these feelings enough to take advantage of the prospect of cheating when it seems to offer especially large rewards. This strategy seems at least as good as Shaftesbury's strategy, if the question is to be decided by a neutral measure of quantity of pleasure.

Alternatively, Shaftesbury might mean that virtuous people gain more pleasure from being virtuous because they value it most; the good of others, as such, is the object, not merely the cause, of a virtuous person's pleasure.[28] In that case, we can value something for some other feature besides its pleasure. Shaftesbury implicitly departs further from hedonism than he explicitly acknowledges.[29]

But if Shaftesbury simply measures an agent's pleasure by reference to the agent's own values, he does not show that the virtuous person is better off than others who gain what they value most. If virtuous people are really better off than other people, their judgment about the value of virtue must be correct, and our account of a person's good must make the truth of this judgment relevant to well-being. In that case, we accept a non-hedonist account of what is actually valuable, not simply a non-hedonist account of what an agent can value. Shaftesbury seems to recognize this point when he discusses the human good. In claiming that the human good includes the satisfaction of the social affections, he does not claim that by satisfying these affections we gain more pleasure, or that people always or often care most about satisfaction of these affections. He claims that these are the affections that deserve to be satisfied.

On this issue, therefore, Shaftesbury is closer to Platonism than to Locke. Though many remarks suggest that he takes Hobbes's and Locke's view on virtue and happiness, the main tendency of his position agrees with the Greek moralists whom he cites with approval. His account of our 'obligation' to virtue is expressed as a claim about enjoyment, but it is really an argument for the position of the Greek moralists, that virtue is a part of the human

---

[27] 'In the greater part of his argument Shaftesbury interprets the "good" of the individual hedonistically, as equivalent to pleasure, satisfaction, delight, enjoyment. But it is to be observed that the conception of "Good" with which he begins is not definitely hedonistic; "interest or good" is at first taken to mean the "right state of a creature" that "is by nature forwarded and by himself affectionately sought" . . . Still, when the application of this term is narrowed to human beings, he slides—almost unconsciously—into a purely hedonistic interpretation of it.' (Sidgwick, *OHE* 185n)

[28] On object and cause see Plato §53; Aristotle §95; Butler §688.

[29] Green, *CW* i 323–5, discusses Shaftesbury's views on pleasure and self-interest unsympathetically, but not altogether unfairly.

good, correctly conceived. A Lockean interpretation of Shaftesbury is easy and attractive; it leads Hutcheson to his defence of Shaftesbury. But closer inspection shows that it does not capture Shaftesbury's position.

Admittedly, some of Shaftesbury's remarks are imprecise, so that it is not easy to see what he thinks about why morality is reasonable. In appealing to happiness he agrees with Cudworth, who also gives some sort of primacy to the desire for happiness. He also agrees with the Stoics, who believe that we achieve our happiness by fulfilling our nature. Since Shaftesbury follows traditional eudaemonism and naturalism on these questions, it is not surprising that Leibniz generally approves of his position.[30]

But what does he take to be the connexion between our reason for pursuing morality and our inclination to be moral? Does he believe that we have reasons, independent of inclination, to strengthen inclinations that favour morality? Or does he believe that if our inclinations favouring morality weakened, we would have less reason to pursue morality? The choice between these two views determines how far Shaftesbury goes in accepting rationalism about reasons and naturalism about the human good. We might reasonably expect him to favour the naturalist answer that takes reasons to be distinct from strength of desire; for he normally claims that human happiness depends on human nature, not that it depends on human desires. But he does not seem to reach a clear view about the nature of our reasons to favour morality. This is the basis of Butler's objection to Shaftesbury. Since Butler sympathizes with Shaftesbury's naturalism, he notices the place where Shaftesbury fails (in Butler's view) to recognize the implications of a naturalist defence of morality.[31]

611. Platonism, Realism, and Voluntarism

We may now turn to some aspects of Shaftesbury's position that display his Platonist outlook even more clearly. His first publication was his preface to the *Select Sermons* of Whichcote. As Shaftesbury presents him, Whichcote opposes the tendencies in Christian theology that dismiss natural reason, and especially the natural reason that recognizes moral goodness independently of the Christian revelation. Whichcote agrees with Cudworth in opposing the 'modern theologers' who treat moral goodness as simply the product of the divine will, without any further basis in the nature of reality.[32] Shaftesbury follows the Platonists in regarding the theological voluntarist position as both philosophically unsound and theologically dangerous.

He also agrees with Cudworth's view that theological voluntarism repeats the errors of Hobbes's combination of egoism and positivism. He supports Cudworth's criticism of Hobbes by attacking Hobbes's psychological egoism. His attack on Hobbes also opposes the tendency of theologians to represent morality simply as a means to rewards in the afterlife. The theologians suppose they have answered Hobbes if they replace a human will with a divine will as the source of moral right and wrong, and if they replace this-worldly rewards of virtue with other-worldly rewards. Voluntarism and egoism encourage the same basically mistaken attitude to morality.

---

[30] On Leibniz see §588.   [31] On Butler see §677.   [32] See Cudworth, quoted in §546.

To explain the errors of voluntarism, Shaftesbury examines the legislative view of moral properties, according to which actions are morally good or bad only insofar as they are determined to be so by legislation.[33] This view has infiltrated orthodox divinity as well (*Sens. Comm.* 3.1 — K 57). It is attractive to those who regard the moral outlook as a potential rival to a theological view that regards God as absolutely sovereign (*Mor.* ii 2 = K 262). If the demands of some independent morality limit what it is possible for God to do, God does not appear to be absolutely sovereign. And if these demands can be known by natural reason, divine revelation is not the only source for knowledge of God.

Shaftesbury describes both Hobbesians and theological voluntarists as 'nominal' moralists, as opposed to moral 'realists'.[34] This use of the mediaeval contrast between realism and nominalism recalls Cudworth's assimilation of Hobbes to Ockham.[35] In calling his opponents 'nominal' moralists Shaftesbury does not mean that they deny the reality of moral distinctions; since they believe in the reality of human or divine legislation, they also believe in the reality of the distinctions marked by this legislation. But they are nominalists because they do not believe that moral properties belong to things by their own nature. To be a realist, as opposed to a nominalist or conceptualist, about universals is to believe that things fall into natural kinds because of what they are in themselves, and not because anyone's names or concepts classify them as they do. Similarly, a moral realist believes that moral properties belong to good and bad actions, agents, and so on, in their own right, not because of their relation to any legislative will.

According to Shaftesbury, the legislative view is bad philosophy and bad theology. His opponents mistakenly suppose that if they take a servile and flattering attitude to God apart from any belief in divine moral attributes, they honour God. Shaftesbury answers that they do not honour God appropriately unless they recognize God's inherent goodness, as measured by standards of goodness distinct from any divine command (*Sens. Comm.* 2.3 = K 46).[36] If they make moral goodness depend on divine legislation, the

---

[33] 'That all actions are naturally indifferent; that they have no note or character of good or ill in themselves; but are distinguished by mere fashion, law, or arbitrary decree.' (*Sol.* 3.3 = K 157) 'He [sc. Hobbes] did his utmost to show us that "both in religion and morals we were imposed on by our governors", that "there was nothing which by nature inclined us either way, nothing which naturally drew us to the love of what was without or beyond ourselves" . . . ' (*Sens. Comm.* 2.1 = K 42)

[34] 'For 'tis notorious that the chief opposers of atheism write upon contrary principles to one another, so as in a manner to confute themselves. Some of them hold zealously for virtue, and are realists in the point. Others, one may say, are only nominal moralists, by making virtue nothing in itself, a creature of will only or a mere name of fashion.' (*Mor.* ii 2 = K 262) 'For being, in respect of virtue, what you lately called a realist, he endeavours to show that it is really something in itself and in the nature of things; not arbitrary or factitious (if I may so speak), not constituted from without or dependent on custom, fancy, or will; not even on the supreme will itself which can no-way govern it; but being necessarily good, is governed by it, and ever uniform with it. And, notwithstanding he has thus made virtue his chief subject and in some measure independent on religion, yet I fancy he may possibly appear at last as high a divine as he is a moralist.' (*Mor.* ii 3 = K 266–7)

[35] On Shaftesbury and mediaeval voluntarism cf. Whewell, *LHMPE* 88. Passmore, *RC* 98, suggests that Shaftesbury's use of 'factitious', with the parenthesis recognizing that it may be found unfamiliar, indicates the influence of Cudworth. This is one of Cudworth's favourite words. As Passmore notes, *OED* cites as the first to use the word in the sense of 'arbitrary' (but this 'sense' does not seem sharply distinct from the first sense, for which an instance is quoted from Sir Thomas Browne in 1645).

[36] On Shaftesbury's realism see Norton, *DH* 33–43, and Winkler, 'Realism' 192. Winkler points out that Shaftesbury connects realism especially with the affirmation of the reality of disinterested affections, and that therefore Hutcheson might claim to accept this aspect of realism in rejecting Hobbes's view of motivation. However, Shaftesbury seems to intend a realist position that goes beyond Hutcheson's claims about the relation of the moral sense to moral properties.

voluntarists are no better than those who make morality the result of legislation or convention.[37]

To show that we need these distinct standards, Shaftesbury argues that if we attribute moral goodness to God, and we do not believe that God can make contradictions true, we must reject voluntarism.[38] In his view, the voluntarist must believe both that (1) justice prohibits punishment of one person for the crimes of another, and that (2) if God were to punish one person for the crimes of another, that would be just. Hence the voluntarist must say that (3) if God were to punish one person for the crimes of another, God would make the same action both just and unjust. Hence in saying that God acts justly in punishing one person for the crimes of another, we say that God acts justly and unjustly, and hence we 'say nothing' or 'speak without a meaning'.[39]

A voluntarist might reply that Shaftesbury misunderstands the relation between the categorical claim in (1) and the counterfactual in (2). In (1) we refer to what is just, according to God's ordered power. In (2) we refer to what would be just if God had not exercised absolute power in the way God has in fact exercised it, but had made it just to punish one person for the crimes of another. This is how Scotus exploits Anselm's claim that what God wills is necessarily just.[40] If this is a legitimate reply, Shaftesbury does not demonstrate that voluntarists are committed to the truth of contradictions.

But if voluntarists try this answer to Shaftesbury, they need to explain what they mean in claiming that God is just or that God's decisions are just. If we entirely separate justice from the traits and actions that involve fairness, reciprocity, respect for desert, and so on, we are not claiming what we might initially have appeared to be claiming in saying that God is just; it is not clear that we ascribe any definite moral property to God at all.

Voluntarists would be better off, therefore, if they denied that God is essentially just. By an exercise of absolute power God chooses to be just, but not because it is better to be just than to be unjust; if God had chosen differently, it would have been better to be unjust than to be just. This is a consistent position that avoids Shaftesbury's objection about contradiction. Has he any other argument against this position?

His argument against theological voluntarism is part of his general discussion of the relation between morality and religion. He relies on his argument for a moral sense. Since

---

[37] '...fashion, law, custom or religion...may be ill and vicious itself, but can never alter the eternal measures and immutable independent nature of worth and virtue' (*ICV* i 2.3 = K 175). Cf. Hutcheson, §636.

[38] '...whoever thinks there is a God and pretends formally to believe that he is just and good, must suppose that there is independently such a thing as justice and injustice, truth and falsehood, right and wrong; according to which he pronounces that God is just, righteous, and true. If the mere will, decree, or law of God be absolutely to constitute right and wrong, then are these latter words of no significancy at all. For thus if each part of a contradiction were affirmed for truth by the supreme power, they would consequently become true. Thus if one person were decreed to suffer for another's fault, the sentence would be just and equitable. And thus, in the same manner, if arbitrarily, and without reason, some beings were destined to endure perpetual ill, and others as constantly to enjoy Good; this also would pass under the same denomination. But to say of any thing that it is just or unjust, on such a foundation as this, is to say nothing, or to speak without a meaning' (*ICV* i 3.2 = K 181). On Hutcheson's use of this argument about contradiction see Balguy, §660.

[39] This is one of the passages cited by Prior, *LBE* 18 (see §815), as examples of anticipations of Moore's argument about the naturalistic fallacy. But it makes a different point from the one that Prior suggests. Shaftesbury's claim that voluntarists would speak 'without a meaning', or that the words would be 'of no significancy' rests wholly on his claim that they are committed to the truth of a contradiction, not on the claim that 'God wills what is right' would be meaningless if 'right' meant 'what God wills'.

[40] On Scotus see §381.

we have a natural sense of right and wrong apart from any religious beliefs, we cannot accept the voluntarist's counterfactual claims without violating our intuitive judgments about morality. According to the voluntarist, it is possible for these intuitive judgments to be grossly mistaken; for rightness consists in conformity to the will of God, and the qualities we intuitively recognize as right are right not in themselves, but only because they conform to the will of God. In that case, we commit ourselves to lie, cheat, and deceive if those actions conform to the will of God. We do not conceive the goodness of God as consisting in conformity to distinct standards of goodness; we conceive it simply as consisting in God's following his own will.

This argument does not show that the voluntarist position is inconsistent, but it shows that religious morality, as voluntarists conceive it, departs sharply from intuitive moral convictions. We have to say that injustice and cruelty are wrong not because of what they are in themselves, but because they are contrary to the divine will; facts about unjust actions, their agents, and their victims do not settle whether these actions are right or wrong. Shaftesbury is justified, therefore, in suggesting that acceptance of voluntarism tends to undermine intuitive convictions about injustice and cruelty.[41] Theological voluntarism does not claim that malignity and so on are morally good qualities, but it requires us to be prepared to recognize them as good qualities even if nothing about the agents and victims of the relevant acts and dispositions were to change.

If goodness is distinct from what is approved by the legislative will of God, the appropriate attitude to God is love of his goodness, not hope of reward and fear of punishment (*Mor.* 2.3 = *Char.* ii 271 = K 268). We ought to learn about the nature of virtue and merit before we learn about the goodness of God and the rewards for virtue (*Mor.* 2.3 = K 271). If we rely on our moral sense, we become capable of a disinterested love of God.

Shaftesbury acknowledges that aspirations towards disinterested love of God have aroused the suspicion that they involve irrational fanaticism.[42] The French Quietists give disinterested love a bad name, because they reject the self-interested attitude, arguing that we ought to love God entirely without reference to thoughts of our own salvation.[43] The demand for

---

[41] 'But if . . . he comes to be more and more reconciled to the malignity, arbitrariness, partiality, or revengefulness of his believed Deity, his reconciliation with these qualities themselves will soon grow in proportion; and the most cruel, unjust, and barbarous acts will, by the power of this example, be often considered by him not only as just and lawful, but as divine, and worthy of imitation.' (*ICV* i 3.2 = K 181)

[42] 'Though the disinterested love of God be the most excellent principle, yet, by the indiscreet zeal of some devout well-meaning people, it has been stretched too far, perhaps even to extravagance and enthusiasm, as formerly among the mystics of the ancient Church, whom those of latter days have followed. On the other hand, there have been those who, in opposition to this devout mystic way, and as professed enemies to what they call enthusiasm, had so far exploded everything of this ecstatic kind as in a manner to have given up devotion; and in reality have left so little of zeal, affection, or warmth, in what they call their rational religion, as to make them much suspected of their sincerity in any. For, though it be natural enough for a mere political writer to ground his great argument for religion on the necessity of such a belief as that of a future reward and punishment; yet it is a very ill token of sincerity in religion, and in the Christian religion more especially, to educe it to such a philosophy as will allow no room to that other principle of love; but treats all of that kind as enthusiasm, for so much as aiming at what is called disinterestedness, or teaching the love of God or virtue for God or virtue's sake.' (*Mor.* 2.3 = K 268) Maxwell quotes and endorses this passage; see §539. On enthusiasm see §529.

[43] On Quietism see §717. On its influence in 18th-century England see Duffy, 'Wesley'. Quietism influenced some important English Protestants in the 18th century, e.g., William Law and John Wesley. Duffy comments on the late 17th century: 'At the end of the century the "Quietist" writers, Fénelon and Madame Guyon, became something of a Protestant cult in England as elsewhere, having a profound and on the whole destructive influence on the emergent school of half-baked Protestant mystics' (2). Duffy mentions an approving reference to Fénelon by Wesley (16). This

completely self-forgetful motivation appears fanatical, both in religion and in morality. But we ought to avoid the excessive reaction of the defenders of 'rational religion' who assert that disinterested moral approval is neither possible nor desirable.[44] If we do not recognize God as a proper object of moral admiration, our attitude to God is the servile fear that undermines morality.

612. Realism and the Irreducibility of Morality to Self-Interest

Our discussion of Shaftesbury's attack on voluntarism has revealed two aspects of the position that he calls 'realism'. He opposes it not only to the legislative thesis that moral properties depend on will and legislation, but also to the reductive thesis that reduces the moral motive to the desire for one's own pleasure. Hence he regards Hobbes as a merely nominal moralist both because of his voluntarism and because of his egoism. Similarly, he accuses theological voluntarists not only of denying that moral facts are independent of God's legislative will, but also of denying the possibility of disinterested morality.

Shaftesbury believes that Locke has encouraged both aspects of nominalism. While most people reject Hobbes's moral views, they do not see that Locke endorses Hobbes's basic principles, and so makes it easier for other people to accept them. Locke argues illegitimately from his rejection of innate ideas to the conclusion that there are no natural moral properties that we naturally recognize.[45] Shaftesbury rejects Hobbes's and Locke's assumption that an adequate defence of morality must connect morally good action with some further source of pleasure beyond itself—either (as in Hobbes) some further advantage to the agent in this life or (as in Locke) some further advantage in the afterlife.

We might suppose that Shaftesbury is simply confused in treating his opposition to voluntarism and his opposition to egoism as parts of one 'realist' doctrine. His two claims seem quite separable. Apparently we might be metaphysical realists about moral properties, taking them to be independent of legislation, while still supposing that we pursue morality

sympathy with Quietism fits Wesley's doubts about rationalist ethics. See Rivers, *RGS* i 224, on Wesley's objections to Clarke and Butler: 'It were to be wished that they were better acquainted with this faith who employ much of their time and pains in laying another foundation, in grounding religion on "the eternal fitness of things", on "the intrinsic excellence of virtue" and the beauty of actions flowing from it—on the reasons, as they term them of good and evil, and the relations of beings to each other' (Sermon 17). According to Wesley, if this morality corresponds with the Scriptures, it simply creates unnecessary perplexity, and if it does not correspond with them, it is dangerous and misleading. A different strand in Wesley's outlook appears in his attack on Hutcheson; he is especially appalled by Hutcheson's emphasis on the importance of disinterested motives, especially in his objections (shared with Shaftesbury) to the grounding of morality in the hope of reward from God. See Rivers, *RGS* i 230.

[44] Berkeley implicitly accuses Shaftesbury of endorsing the enthusiasm of the French Quietists (see §717), because of his emphasis on disinterested moral motivation. Berkeley compares the Quietists to the Stoics who 'have made virtue its own sole reward, in the most rigid and absolute sense' (Alc. 3.14 = *Works* 136). Cf. §180n27.

[45] 'It was Mr Locke that struck the home blow, for Mr Hobbes's character and base slavish principles of government, took off the poison of his philosophy. 'Twas Mr Locke that struck at all fundamentals, threw all order and virtue out of the world, and made the very ideas of these (which are the same as those of God) unnatural and without foundation in our minds. . . . Thus virtue, according to Mr Locke, has no other measure, law, or rule than fashion and custom: morality, justice, equity, depend only on law and will: and God indeed is a perfect free agent in his sense; that is, free to any thing, that is however ill: for if he wills it, it will be made good; virtue may be vice, and vice virtue in its turn, if he pleases. And thus neither right nor wrong, virtue nor vice are any thing in themselves; nor is there any trace or idea of them naturally imprinted on human minds.' (*Letters to a student* 77–8 = *PR* 403–4. Partly quoted by Whewell, *LHMPE* 88)

for the sake of our own interest. Might we not say that moralists such as Suarez who are both realists and eudaemonists accept one part of Shaftesbury's 'realism' without the other?

We might explain Shaftesbury's combination of the metaphysical with the motivational thesis by regarding them as two sides of his attack on opponents who are both voluntarists and egoists. If we think moral goodness is what God approves of, we have no reason to care about moral goodness beyond our reason to care about what God approves of. Christian writers opposed to enthusiasm suggest that our reason to care about what God approves of is egoistic; the only rational ground for doing what God approves of is the prospect of reward and punishment.

But even if Shaftesbury's conception of realism is excusable as a reply to opponents who are both voluntarists and egoists, is it nonetheless confused in treating two separable views as aspects of a single realist position? Perhaps something further can be said in his defence. If we are realists about moral properties, holding them to be independent of will and legislation, we must also hold them to be irreducible in certain ways. If some people think moral goodness is purely instrumental goodness promoting the agent's pleasure, they may claim to be moral realists insofar as they think moral goodness is a real property of things. Still, they do not recognize the distinct reality of moral properties in contrast to pleasure-promoting properties. We therefore have a good reason for denying that Hobbes's belief in real pleasure-promoting properties makes him a moral realist, even though he claims that they are moral properties.

Suarez, by contrast, is a moral realist even though he is a eudaemonist, because he recognizes the moral good (the honestum) as a distinct sort of good besides the pleasant and the advantageous (dulce and utile). His belief in 'intrinsic' moral goodness recognizes moral goodness as a further property besides pleasure and advantage. He therefore passes both of Shaftesbury's tests for being a moral realist. Though Shaftesbury does not explain why a single realist position requires the rejection of both voluntarism and Hobbesian egoism, he has a good reason for his view. He is entitled to criticize those whom he calls the 'modern Epicureans' because they reduce social sentiments to selfish ones (Sens. Comm. iii 3 = K 55). Those who degrade 'honesty' (i.e., moral goodness)[46] by making it only a name are the selfish moralists (Sens. Comm. iii 4 = K 58). These moralists treat the difference between the honest person and the knave as simply a matter of instrumental calculation (Sol. i 2 = K 78).

This connexion between the metaphysical and the motivational sides of Shaftesbury's realism tends to support his claim that his theological voluntarist opponents are egoists. If all moral distinctions rest on the legislative will of God, it is difficult to see how obedience to God's legislative will could have any moral basis. This does not imply that a disinterested love of God is impossible; for moral attitudes are not the only disinterested attitudes. Shaftesbury goes too fast, therefore, in suggesting that his opponents who derive morality from the legislative will of God cannot allow a disinterested love of God. Nonetheless, his position is defensible. For if they deny any moral basis for obedience to a legislative will, they remove the main reason one might offer for taking disinterested love for God to be appropriate.[47]

---

[46] Shaftesbury uses 'honesty' with the broad sense of 'honestas'.　　[47] Cf. Pufendorf, §577.

If, then, disinterested love (apart from the influence of sanctions) for God is the morally appropriate basis for obedience to divine commands, not everything that is morally appropriate is the product of legislation. If disinterested love is appropriate only because of legislation, we can still ask why we should obey that legislation. The demand for non-mercenary love of God is much more reasonable on the realist assumption than on the voluntarist assumption.

Shaftesbury, therefore, deplores the tendency to combine a purely legislative theory of morality with a purely external account of obligation (taking it to depend on rewards and punishments). In seeking some natural basis for morality, he rejects some versions of orthodox Christianity. Some of his remarks suggest that he rejects orthodox Christianity altogether, and not merely some versions of it; and his opponents take his unorthodox views to be a ground for rejecting his view of morality.[48] But his views about morality and its sanctions do not seem to be unorthodox in themselves. He insists that belief in post-mortem rewards should be a secondary motive to virtue, but he agrees that it is an appropriate motive in its proper place. He argues that belief in a conflict between virtue and happiness in this life cannot be reconciled with sound theism, because it would imply doubts about the goodness and providence of God. For similar reasons he agrees with the belief in post-mortem rewards for virtue.[49]

Though Shaftesbury does not allow the prospect of rewards and punishments, in this life or the next life, to be the sole or primary motive for virtue, he allows it an important role. In his view, virtue contributes to happiness, and thereby lays the foundation of distributive justice in the world; but it is only a foundation, and we are right to look for the completion of the building in the afterlife.[50] The disinterested recognition and love of virtue provides an argument for an afterlife and for a God who matches virtue to happiness. Contrary to the modern theologians who appeal exclusively to the legislative will of God, the realist view does not threaten the truth of Christian doctrine. Shaftesbury sketches a defence that is

---

[48] Berkeley, *Alc.* 3.14 = *Works* 136, attacks Stoics, Quietists, and Shaftesbury all together as dangers to Christian morality: 'The Stoics, therefore, though their style was high, and often above truth and nature, yet it cannot be said that they so resolved every motive to a virtuous life into the sole beauty of virtue, as to endeavour to destroy the belief of the immortality of the soul and a distributive providence. After all, allowing the disinterested Stoics (therein not unlike our modern Quietists) to have made virtue its own sole reward, in the most rigid and absolute sense, yet what is this to those who are no Stoics? If we adopt the whole principles of that sect, admitting their notions of good and evil, their celebrated apathy, and, in one word, setting up for complete Stoics, we may possibly maintain this doctrine with a better grace; at least it will be of a piece and consistent with the whole. But he who shall borrow this splendid patch from the Stoics, and hope to make a figure by inserting it into a piece of modern composition, seasoned with the wit and notions of these times, will indeed make a figure, but perhaps it may not be in the eyes of a wise man the figure he intended.' See also Balguy's objections to Shaftesbury, §668.

[49] '... whoever has a firm belief of a God, whom he does not merely *call* good, but of whom in reality he *believes* nothing beside real good, nothing beside what is truly suitable to the exactest character of benignity and goodness; such a person believing rewards or retributions in another life, must believe them annexed to real goodness and merit, real villainy and baseness, and not to any accidental quality or circumstances . . . These are the only terms on which the belief of a world to come can happily influence the believer. And on these terms, and by virtue of this belief, man perhaps may maintain his virtue and integrity even under the hardest thoughts of human nature, when either by ill circumstance or untoward doctrine he is brought to that unfortunate opinion of virtue's being naturally an enemy to happiness in life. This, however, is an opinion which cannot be supposed consistent with sound theism' (*ICV* i 3.3 = K 189–90).

[50] 'For, if virtue be to itself no small reward and vice in a great measure its own punishment, we have a solid ground to go upon. The plain foundation of a distributive justice and the order in this world may lead us to conceive a further building.' (*Mor.* 2.3 = K 270)

developed more fully, and with more specific reference to orthodox Christianity, by Clarke and Balguy.[51]

613. The Moral Sense as Support for Realism

In the light of Shaftesbury's realism, we may reconsider his belief in a moral sense. It is relatively easy to see why he uses the moral sense to support the motivational aspect of realism; our direct reaction to moral goodness and badness moves us to act on these features of actions and people, without calculating their effects on our interest. But how does it support the metaphysical aspect of realism?

According to Shaftesbury, our intuitive conviction that moral properties are real and irreducible has an epistemological basis in the way we are aware of moral properties. When we claim that right and wrong are intrinsic qualities of things, independent of any legislation, we can legitimately appeal to the sense of right and wrong that is directed to actions and characters themselves, irrespective of any legislation that may prescribe them.[52] The regularity and constancy of our immediate awareness of right and wrong give us reason to believe that they belong to the nature of things and are not products of legislative will, human or divine.

These claims about a moral sense allow objective moral properties. If we are immediately aware of them, they may still be aspects of fitness to rational nature, as Suarez supposes. Shaftesbury's suggestion that we have a natural sense of the honestum might indicate that he agrees with Suarez's conception of the nature of moral properties.

Belief in a moral sense conflicts with realism, however, if we hold a Lockean conception of a sense and its objects. According to Locke, or one common interpretation of Locke, senses whose objects are secondary qualities do not tell us about objective features of the world, but only about our own ideas. If Shaftesbury accepts a Lockean conception, his belief in a moral sense commits him to claims about moral knowledge that conflict with metaphysical realism about moral properties. But belief in a moral sense does not by itself require Lockean epistemological claims. As Reid points out later, belief in a moral sense does not push us towards realism or anti-realism until we decide how we are to conceive the relevant sort of sense.[53]

Hutcheson makes up his mind on this question, by accepting a Lockean conception of a sense, and therefore rejecting realism about moral properties.[54] But Shaftesbury does not commit himself to this Lockean doctrine, and so he does not take his claims about a moral sense to conflict with realism.

---

[51] See Balguy, §668.

[52] 'However false or corrupt it [sc. the mind] be within itself, it finds the difference, as to beauty and comeliness, between one heart and another, one turn of affection, one behaviour, one sentiment and another; and accordingly, in all disinterested cases, must approve in some measure of what is natural and honest, and disapprove what is dishonest and corrupt.' (ICV i 2.3 = K 173) Shaftesbury attributes this natural tendency to disinterested approval to the moral sense: 'As to atheism, it does not seem that it can directly have any effect at all towards the setting up a false species of right or wrong. For, notwithstanding a man may through custom, or by licentiousness of practice, favoured by atheism, come in time to lose much of his natural moral sense, yet it does not seem that atheism should of itself be the cause of any estimation or valuing of anything as fair, noble, and deserving, which was the contrary.' (ICV i 3.2 = K 179–80)

[53] On Reid see §842.   [54] See Hutcheson, §642.

614. The Moral Sense and Mutability

Even apart from Locke's views about senses and their objects, belief in a moral sense raises difficulties for realism if we take moral properties to be essentially what the moral sense approves of. This view implies that approval by the moral sense constitutes rightness, so that if there were no moral sense, nothing would be right or wrong, and if our moral sense were to change, moral rightness and wrongness would change with it.

Shaftesbury's failure to maintain these metaphysical claims about the moral sense is not simply a sign of his theoretical imprecision. His limited use of a moral sense makes his Platonist metaphysics of morality consistent with his epistemology. Since he does not take moral properties to be essentially those that are grasped by the moral sense, he does not claim that if our moral sense changed, right and wrong would change. He treats the moral sense as our means of access to properties that exist independently of it. He introduces the natural sense of right and wrong to argue that even false religious beliefs cannot take away our sense of right and wrong actions existing in their own right apart from legislation, inducements, or threats (ICV i 3.1 = K 179).

If Shaftesbury took approval by the moral sense to constitute moral properties, he would undermine his realism and his arguments against voluntarism. He would be subject to the argument that he aims at the theological voluntarists. In his view, we recognize God's will as morally perfect because we regard moral properties as distinct from what God approves. Similarly, we recognize that someone's moral sense is right because we believe in moral properties that are distinct from what the moral sense approves. Balguy uses this argument effectively against Hutcheson's belief in a constitutive relation between the moral sense and moral properties.[55] But it does not affect Shaftesbury, since he treats the moral sense as a sign of objective moral properties, not as their metaphysical basis. His defenders are right to argue that he does not make moral rightness (the honestum) depend on its being approved. Though Berkeley criticizes him on this point, the criticism rests on misinterpretation.[56]

He seems, therefore, to leave open the logical possibility of a clash between what we approve of and what is really right. Realism implies that our moral sense—even an idealized sense (in which the idealization does not include a reference to real moral qualities)—does not constitute moral rightness; hence it is logically and metaphysically possible for it to be wrong. But if we have no access to any other means of knowing moral properties, we cannot

---

[55] Hutcheson; §643.

[56] Wishart, *Vindication*, severely criticizes Berkeley on this point, urging ironically that Berkeley could not have written *Alciphron* because of its gross errors. Among these errors are Berkeley's misinterpretation of Shaftesbury on the honestum: 'But what man who had but tasted of these fountains [sc. the ancients] could have been capable of attempting to palm upon us such an account of their sentiments concerning the *to kalon*, the pulchrum and honestum, the moral beauty, as he has given us from a single detached word or two of Plato and Aristotle? From which he would bear us in hand, that there was no moral beauty independent of the actual esteem and applause (of the opinion) of our neighbours, or of profit or pleasure; nay, that the very notion of the honestum, according to them was what was actually commended, or was pleasant and profitable, merely because Aristotle says what is beautiful is *epaineton*, laudable; and Plato says, what is beautiful is pleasant or profitable, This is such an account of the sentiments of the ancients concerning the honestum, the moral beauty, as many a clever schoolboy who has never learned a syllable of Greek is capable of confuting out of his Tully, Off. i. Honestum: quod etiam si nobilitatum non sit, tamen honestum sit, quodque vere dicimus, etiamsi a nullo laudetur, laudabile esse natura. Et De Finib. Lib. 2. Honestum id intelligimus, quod tale est ut, detracta omni utilitate, sine ullis praemiss fructibusque, per se ipsum possit iure laudari.' (26–7) Stewart, 'Critic' 7, ascribes this anonymous work to Wishart on the basis of a shorthand copy in Wishart's papers.

correct our moral sense (except within limits that assume the reliability of the moral sense). If, then, it were mistaken, we could not know this. How, then, do we know that it is not mistaken now? Realism plus a moral sense theory seems to encourage scepticism.

This argument needs more careful consideration. One ought not to dismiss a theory simply because it leaves some room for scepticism; every realist theory does that. But Shaftesbury is in a stronger position if he believes that the moral sense is not our only means of access to moral properties in the world. If he believes we can correct our moral sense by reason, he can answer critics who ask why we ought to trust our current moral sense, but ought not to trust our moral sense if it began to approve of injustice and cruelty. Shaftesbury's metaphysical and epistemological claims about moral reality and the moral sense raise these questions that he does not pursue.

The limited scope of Shaftesbury's claims about the moral sense helps to explain the debate among his successors. Hutcheson takes a step that Shaftesbury does not take, by defining moral goodness as essentially what is approved by the moral sense. He takes the moral sense to be disinterested, and therefore he supposes that he defends Shaftesbury. This interpretation of the moral sense and its relation to moral goodness is also Berkeley's interpretation of Shaftesbury, and it is the basis for Berkeley's criticism.[57] But Hutcheson overlooks the fact that he defends only the motivational part of Shaftesbury's realist doctrine, and that he undermines the metaphysical part. Balguy points out this consequence of Hutcheson's modification of Shaftesbury; he shows that Hutcheson's position exposes him to Shaftesbury's argument against theological voluntarism.[58]

615. Shaftesbury as a Source of Sentimentalism and Realism

Our discussion of Shaftesbury shows why it is unwise to be firmly attached to a division between rationalism and sentimentalism, or to Whewell's division between independent and dependent morality. A short way to describe his position is to say that he maintains realism and sentimentalism; but this short description is misleading, since he does not formulate his position clearly enough to help us to decide exactly where he stands on some of the main issues.

Some of his explicit defenders emphasize the metaphysical and Platonic side of his position. Among these is Richard Fiddes, who connects Shaftesbury with Malebranche's theological naturalism, treating their views as an answer to voluntarism and to doubts about the reality of moral properties. In the Preface to his General Treatise of Morality, Fiddes defends some of Shaftesbury's position against attacks by Mandeville. He especially discusses Mandeville's arguments against Shaftesbury's defence of the objectivity of moral distinctions. He rejects Mandeville's arguments based on variation in customs between different societies, arguing that such variations are irrelevant to questions about objectivity. In defining the part of

---

[57] See Berkeley, Alc. 3.5 = Works 120: '[Moral beauty] . . . is rather to be felt than understood—a certain je ne sais quoi. An object, not of the discursive faculty, but of a peculiar sense, which is properly called the moral sense, being adapted to the perception of moral beauty, as the eye to colours, or the ear to sounds.' The following discussion of Shaftesbury's conception of the kalon assumes that it is simply beauty. See Rivers, RGS ii 157. See also §632.

[58] Balguy on Hutcheson; §653.

morality that is invariant, Fiddes defends naturalism against theological voluntarism: basic principles of morality are those of primary obligation, and these are commanded because they are good, not good because they are commanded.[59]

In contrast to Fiddes, Hutcheson develops the psychological side of Shaftesbury's argument. He believes he defends Shaftesbury's realism by insisting on the irreducibility of moral properties and sentiments to Hobbesian self-interest. He relies on Shaftesbury's defence of the moral sense against Hobbesian egoism, and formulates his account of the metaphysics and epistemology of morality on the basis of a Lockean account of the moral sense. This account requires the rejection of the metaphysical independence of moral properties from beliefs, sentiments, and legislation, and so abandons one aspect of Shaftesbury's realism.

If we accept Shaftesbury's metaphysical realism about moral properties, we should not accept all of Hutcheson's views about the moral sense; for we should not take the reactions of a moral sense to be constitutive of moral properties. Since Shaftesbury is not clear about the metaphysical relation between moral rightness and approval by the moral sense, he does not make it clear what role he intends for the moral sense. But he does not commit himself to the claims that would conflict with his realism.

Shaftesbury's position as a whole is primarily realist and naturalist; his remarks about the moral sense do not introduce the aspects of sentimentalism that conflict with realism. Though Hutcheson develops one aspect of Shaftesbury, he does not capture the central elements of Shaftesbury's position. Butler and Price come closer than Hutcheson to an expression of Shaftesbury's main doctrines.

---

[59] '. . . those [sc. subjects of morality] under the first distinction [sc. primary obligation] arise from the immutable reason and order of things, and do not depend even upon the will of the supreme legislator, but are founded in those eternal and essential perfections of his nature whereby his will itself is regulated; and which, in the natural order of our ideas, are therefore antecedent to his will; such things as are not merely good by virtue of his command, or of any circumstances wherein man may accidentally be placed; but such as are commanded because they are absolutely good and under all circumstances, in their own nature' (Fiddes, *General Treatise*, p. lviii). Hence, for instance, pride (as involving false judgment) and hatred of God are always wrong. Fiddes's general position is more metaphysical and less naturalist and psychological than Shaftesbury's. He has less to contribute to understanding the basis for moral realism on non-theological grounds. Following Malebranche, he rests the basis of moral right in recognition of the perfection of God and of God's purposes for the universe. On this support he finds action appropriate to human beings to lie in a combination of their perfection and their happiness.

46

CLARKE

616. Cudworth and Clarke

Clarke sets out his moral theory in one of his major works on natural theology.[1] He addresses those who reject the Christian revelation because it cannot be vindicated by reason. In his view, the basic principles of morality are evident to reason, apart from any appeal to revelation, and these moral principles make it reasonable to believe in the Christian revelation. His success depends on revealing the rational grounds of 'the unalterable obligations of natural religion', which we discover through our moral judgments. To reveal these grounds he defends some elements of a naturalist position against the view of those who claim 'that there is no such real difference [sc. between good and evil] originally, necessarily, and absolutely in the nature of things' (DNR = H ii 609 = R 227).

This description of Clarke's argument suggests correctly that he supports Cudworth's doctrine of eternal and immutable morality. He defends Cudworth's position against the Hobbesian reduction of morality to counsels of narrow prudence and to positive law, and against the voluntarist explanation of morality as an expression of God's legislative will.

Is this similarity to Cudworth evidence of influence? Cudworth's *Eternal and Immutable Morality* was not published until 1731, 26 years after Clarke's Boyle Lectures. None of the major moralists before Price seems to have read Cudworth's book; Price acknowledges it generously.[2] Cudworth's arguments are not adequately reflected in More's *Enchiridion Ethicum*. Despite Cudworth's annoyance at More's allegedly borrowing from Cudworth's

---

[1] Clarke's Boyle Lectures of 1704–5 are printed in Hoadly's edition with a single title: *A Discourse concerning the Being and Attributes of God, the Obligations of Natural Religion and the Truth and Certainty of the Christian Revelation, in answer to Mr Hobbes, Spinoza, the Author of the Oracles of Reason, and other Deniers of Natural and Revealed Religion, being Sixteen Sermons . . . .* The title of the first eight sermons (from 1704) is *A Demonstration of the Being and Attributes of God, more particularly in Answer to Mr Hobbes, Spinoza, and their Followers, Wherein the Notion of Liberty is Stated, and the Possibility and Certainty of it Proved, in Opposition to Necessity and Fate, being the Substance of Eight Sermons . . . .* This work is cited as DBAG. The following eight sermons (or rather their 'substance', from the sermons of 1705) are cited as DNR. This work has its own title page, with the title *A Discourse concerning the Unchangeable Obligations . . . Revelation* (omitting 'in answer to . . .'). This is also the title at the beginning of the discourse. The running head for this discourse is: 'The evidences of natural and revealed religion'. One of the Scriptural mottoes on the title page of DNR is *Is.* 5:20: 'Woe unto them that call evil good, and good evil; that put darkness for light, and light for darkness; that put bitter for sweet, and sweet for bitter' (H 579). This motto fits Clarke's criticism of Hobbes.

[2] See Price, §802.

unpublished work on ethics, More does not give a clear picture of the best parts of Cudworth's meta-ethical argument.[3]

Still, Cudworth's ethical views may have influenced philosophers of quite different doctrinal tendencies who may not have read the whole book. His views on will and freedom may have affected Locke's revisions of the *Essay*.[4] Shaftesbury was acquainted with the views of Cambridge Platonists, and they probably influence his rejection of voluntarism about ethics and divine commands, and his insistence on disinterested appreciation of the morally right and admirable (honestum) for its own sake.[5] Similarly, Clarke was educated in Cambridge, and acquainted with Platonist views. His ethical theory shows the influence of Cudworth's ideas, whether or not they come from Cudworth himself.[6]

It becomes more difficult, but also less important, to estimate the extent of Cudworth's influence once we notice that he is not the only possible source of the views defended in *Eternal and Immutable Morality*. We noticed that he draws on Scholastic sources that were also available to his contemporaries and may have influenced them directly or indirectly. Study of Shaftesbury shows us that many of the realist aspects of Cudworth's position might be reached by reflexion on Stoicism. This is not at all surprising, since Stoicism is one source of the Scholastic position upheld by Suarez, who in turn influences Cudworth. We might, then, argue that the points of agreement between Cudworth and Clarke result either from the influence of Cudworth or from the independent influence of Scholastic or Stoic arguments. From the philosophical point of view, the important point is to see the connexions between Clarke's position and the naturalist doctrines we have mentioned.

Clarke, however, does not defend all the aspects of Scholastic naturalism that Cudworth accepts. He goes beyond Cudworth in a rationalist direction. In his view, moral properties can be grasped by reason without any reference to human nature or human ends. In claiming that they are grasped by reason, he reaffirms the traditional naturalist view. But in claiming that a true description of the relevant facts need not refer to nature, he affirms rationalism without naturalism. His position lacks the teleological elements of Cudworth's view and of Cudworth's Scholastic and Stoic sources. Does Clarke's non-naturalist rationalism present the best part of Cudworth freed from unhelpful accretions? Or does it leave out an important part of Cudworth's view and thereby reach a less plausible view?

617. Natural Law and Obligation

Clarke affirms that laws of nature are obligatory without reference to any divine command. He refers to Socrates' argument against Euthyphro, and uses it against a voluntarist account

---

[3] On Cudworth and More see Passmore, *RC* 16–17.   [4] See Passmore, *RC* 91–6.

[5] Shaftesbury and Platonism; §§608, 611.

[6] Passmore, *RC* 100–1, denies any strong influence of Cudworth on Clarke and, argues that the influence of Whichcote and Cumberland is more significant. He points out that Clarke might reasonably be anxious about being identified with the position of Cudworth, whose orthodoxy was suspect, as Clarke's was (see §869). Moreover, Clarke was sympathetic to modern tendencies in science, and might be expected to find Cudworth's metaphysical outlook old-fashioned. Though Passmore is right to emphasize Clarke's respect for Cumberland (whom Clarke often quotes), he does not comment on the two striking respects in which Clarke departs from Cumberland, in rejecting both (1) a legislative conception of obligation, and (2) the identification of benevolence with morality. Sharp, 'Cumberland', also emphasizes Clarke's debt to Cumberland without recognizing these important disagreements. See below §617.

of natural law.[7] To show that the natural law is prior to any will or command, he cites a catena of Stoic passages, especially from Cicero.[8] Following Cicero, he insists that natural law describes what is praiseworthy whether or not it is actually praised. Since actual praise does not determine the content of natural law, actual will cannot determine it either; hence it is not up to a human or a divine legislator to change what is right or wrong.[9]

These claims constitute a position that Shaftesbury calls 'realist'.[10] They separate Clarke from the voluntarist aspects of Cumberland's position. Clarke does not openly disagree with Cumberland, however. Instead, he quotes Cumberland selectively, choosing a passage in which Cumberland denies that the natural law is arbitrary or mutable. Following Cumberland, Clarke asserts that God's goodness constrains the scope of divine willing.[11] But he neither mentions nor discusses the voluntarism in Cumberland's views on obligation.[12]

Clarke maintains his selective approval of Cumberland in his discussion of moral goodness. He claims that everyone who has any just sense of the difference between good and evil must acknowledge 'that virtue and goodness are truly amiable, and to be chosen for their own sakes and intrinsic worth' (H ii 628 = R 248). He quotes a similar remark from Cumberland.[13] But Clarke draws Shaftesbury's conclusion, that this intrinsic goodness constitutes morality. He does not even mention Cumberland's view that without an imperative law mere amiability constitutes neither moral goodness nor obligation. He implicitly rejects Cumberland's view that obligation lies in the act of the person imposing the obligation.[14] He agrees with Cudworth, and with Maxwell's criticism of Cumberland, in taking obligation to lie in facts

[7] 'As this law of nature is infinitely superior to all authority of men, and independent on it, so its obligation, primarily and originally, is antecedent also even to this consideration, of its being the positive will or command of God himself... As in matters of sense, the reason why a thing is visible is not because it is seen, but it is therefore seen because it is visible, so in matters of natural reason and morality, that which is holy and good ... is not therefore holy and good because it is commanded to be done, but is therefore commanded of God because it is holy and good.' (H ii 626 = SB 507) In a footnote Clarke cites the relevant passage from the *Euthyphro*, and criticizes Ficinus' translation.

[8] These quotations are omitted by R and SB. R omits all the quotations in Clarke's footnotes. SB's selective treatment of quotations gives the wholly misleading impression that Clarke quotes hardly anyone besides Hobbes and Cumberland.

[9] 'This is that law of nature, which being founded in the eternal reason of things, is as absolutely unalterable, as natural good and evil, as mathematical or arithmetical truths, as light and darkness, as sweet and bitter: the observance of which, though no man should commend it, would yet be truly commendable in itself.' (H ii 626) At 'mathematical...' Clarke quotes Cic. *Leg.* i 45: 'For just as true and false, consequence and contrariety are judged by their own character (sua sponte) and not by the character of anything else, so also constant and steady reason in life, which is virtue, and likewise inconstancy, which is vice, <are judged> by their own nature'. At 'observance...' he quotes Cic. *Off.* i 14 'which [sc. the honestum] we truly say is praiseworthy by nature, even if it is praised by no one'. SB and R both omit the passage in which Clarke refers to Cicero.

[10] See Shaftesbury, §611.

[11] 'To this law, the infinite perfections of his [sc. God's] divine nature make it necessary for him ... to have constant regard. And (as a learned prelate of our own has excellently shown,) not barely his infinite power, but the rules of this eternal law, are the true foundation and the measure of his dominion over his creatures. ...' (H ii 627 = R 247). Clarke quotes from Cumberland, *LN* 7.6–7 = P 671–4. Cumberland's influence on Clarke is discussed by Sharp, 'Cumberland' 384–7 (who does not remark on the most important differences).

[12] Price endorses Clarke's naturalist view of obligation, *RPQM* 118. See §818.

[13] At H ii 628n Clarke quotes from Cumberland, *LN* 5.42 = P 265, quoted in §535. This occurs in Cumberland's discussion of the agreement among ancient moralists who claim that virtue is choiceworthy in itself as the most important part of happiness. Clarke does not mention Cumberland's view that this feature of virtue is insufficient for its having moral goodness, which depends on being part of a law commanded by God. Cumberland alludes to this part of his view in the context, arguing that the ancients should have seen that since the virtues have this feature, they must have had this reward annexed to them by the first cause, who must therefore have commanded observance of them. But he does not repeat his normal view that they have moral goodness only because of this relation to a divine command.

[14] See Cumberland, §532.

about right and wrong apart from any act of obliging or any motive created in the person obliged.[15]

This is the extreme naturalist view of obligation, as Suarez understands it. Vasquez accepts this view in claiming that the natural law, understood simply as objective rightness and wrongness, implies obligation.[16] Clarke follows Vasquez, in opposition to the voluntarist view of Culverwell, Locke, Cumberland, and Pufendorf, that both morality and obligation require imperative law. He does not explain why he prefers the extreme naturalist view to the moderate naturalist view of Suarez (and perhaps Grotius). Suarez argues that obligation depends on imperative law, but moral facts, properties, and duties (debita) depend only on natural facts.

Clarke agrees with Cudworth in treating 'obligation' as interchangeable with 'duty'. In affirming a naturalist, as opposed to a voluntarist, position about morality and the divine will, he speaks indifferently of duty and obligation.[17] Apart from all divine or human legislation, there is a difference between good and evil, and some things are more fit and appropriate than others. These naturally fit and good things include an obligation. To show that things have an obligatory power, nothing more needs to be shown, in Clarke's view, than that they are good and reasonable and fit to be done in themselves.[18]

One might argue, on Suarez's behalf, that Cudworth and Clarke over-simplify the relevant questions, and obscure some arguments for voluntarism. Voluntarists are right, according to Suarez, to argue that a prescriptive law introduces a new moral relation of imposed obligation; they are wrong to assume that moral rightness and moral duty depend on imposed obligation. In his view, we cannot see why voluntarists are wrong about moral rightness until we see why they are right about obligation. If we do not draw the relevant distinctions, we do not see the difference between prescriptive law, which imposes moral requirements, and indicative law, which reveals them.

But if Clarke's position is over-simplified, that does not seem to affect his main point. Despite his favourable references to Cumberland, he does not agree with Cumberland's view that imposed obligation is necessary for morality. In affirming that obligation follows from facts about nature rather than will, he neither accepts nor rejects the substance of Suarez's view of obligation, but he accepts the substance of the naturalist view of morality.

618. Eternal Fitnesses

Clarke agrees with Cudworth in believing that the law of nature and the moral properties it involves are eternal and immutable. He takes these properties to be eternal and necessary

---

[15] This is one issue on which Clarke is closer to Cudworth than to Cumberland.

[16] On Vasquez see §427.

[17] '...these eternal and necessary differences of things make it fit and reasonable for creatures so to act; they cause it to be their duty, or lay an obligation upon them, so to do; even separate from the consideration of these rules being the positive will or command of God; and also antecedent to any respect or regard, expectation or apprehension, of any particular private and personal advantage or disadvantage, reward or punishment, either present or future; annexed either by natural consequence, or by positive appointment, to the practising and rejecting of these rules' (H ii 608 = R 225).

[18] 'Some things are in their own nature good and reasonable and fit to be done; such as keeping faith, and performing equitable compacts, and the like; and these receive not their obligatory power, from any law or authority; but are only declared, confirmed and enforced by penalties, upon such as would not perhaps be governed by right reason only.' (H ii 611 = R 228)

fitnesses in things that result from their eternal and necessary relations.[19] These eternal fitnesses are the grounds of obligations on us apart from any positive will or command of God.

Clarke believes that the recognition of eternal relations between things commits us to the recognition of eternal fitnesses in their relations as well. Just as 'the properties which flow from the essences of different mathematical figures, have different congruities or incongruities between themselves' (H ii 608 = R 226), certain acts are fitting to the essences and relations of the different things involved. When we grasp the essence of squares and circles, for instance, we can understand that the squaring of a circle is incongruous for the square and the circle, even though this has not always seemed obvious.

Clarke offers a list of moral principles that embody fitnesses. Since God is infinitely superior to us, it is fit for us to honour, worship, obey, and imitate God. It is fit for God to govern the universe 'according to constant and regular ends' and to do what is best for the whole creation, rather than to design the misery of the whole. Similarly, in relations among human beings, benevolence is more fit than universal destructiveness;[20] it is more fit to treat one another justly than to consider only one's own advantage; and more fit to preserve the life of an innocent person than to kill him or to let him die without any reason or provocation (H ii 609 = R 226).

These claims about fitness are familiar. Suarez takes the morally right (honestum) to be what is fitting (conveniens) for rational nature, and we might take Clarke to have the same sort of fitness in mind. His mathematical example of truths that 'flow from the essence' of a given figure suggests that judgments about fitness rest on an account of the nature of the agent who does the fit or unfit action. His examples of actions fit for God suggest the same basis for judgments of fitness. God's infinite superiority to us implies (Clarke may suggest) that benevolent motives must guide God, and that motives that might interfere with benevolence can have no place.

Clarke combines this claim about the source of eternal fitnesses with a claim about our knowledge of these fitnesses; he believes that they are perfectly evident to an unprejudiced subject. In speaking of what is clear 'in the nature of the thing itself', Clarke seems to mean that simple inspection of the relevant proposition convinces us of its truth. Someone who denies that there is light while he is looking at the sun fails to recognize something that is as obvious as anything could be.[21] If someone entertains doubt on this point, it is pointless to argue with him, or to try to convince him on any question that depends on the evidence of

[19] 'The same necessary and eternal different relations, that different things bear to one another; and the same consequent fitness or unfitness of the application of different things or different relations one to another; with regard to which, the will of God always and necessarily does determine itself, to choose or act only what is agreeable to justice, equity, goodness and truth, in order to the welfare of the whole universe; ought likewise constantly to determine the wills of all subordinate rational beings, to govern all their actions by the same rules, for the good of the public, in their respective stations.' (H ii 608 = R 225)

[20] 'In like manner; in men's dealing and conversing one with another; it is undeniably more fit, absolutely and in the nature of the thing itself, that all men should endeavour to promote the universal good and welfare of all; than that all men should be continually contriving the ruin and destruction of all.' (H ii 609 = R 226)

[21] 'These things are so notoriously plain and self-evident, that nothing but the extremest stupidity of mind, corruption of manners, or perverseness of spirit, can possibly make any man entertain the least doubt concerning them. For a man endued with reason, to deny the truth of these things; is the very same thing, as if a man that has the use of his sight, should at the same time that he beholds the sun, deny that there is any such thing as light in the world; or as if a man that understands geometry or arithmetic, should deny the most obvious and known proportions of lines or numbers,

the senses, just as there is no point in arguing about geometry with someone who rejects its basic assumptions.[22]

It is not clear why judgments about what is fit in itself should have this degree of evidence. Perhaps Clarke is combining two conceptions of fitness 'in itself'. (1) In saying that things are fit in themselves or in their own nature, he is opposing the view that their rightness depends on divine or human legislation or on their promotion of some further end—maximum utility, for instance. (2) But he also seems to mean that their rightness belongs to them entirely without reference to anything else; it resides simply in the character of an action, taken by itself.

This second conception of fitness may be interpreted so as to support Clarke's epistemological claim. For if we grasp 'the character of an action, taken by itself' simply by grasping the concept of the action, anything that 'flows from the essence' follows necessarily from the concept. Hence, anyone who clearly grasps the concept of the relevant action thereby grasps what flows from its nature.

619. Clarke v. Naturalism

These two conceptions of fitness 'in itself' are not equivalent. We can see the difference between them if we compare earlier versions of naturalism with Clarke's position. From the point of view of Aquinas and Suarez, some actions are fitting for rational nature in their own right, apart from any legislative will. Hence we attribute 'intrinsic rightness' to them, but we do not imply that they are self-evidently fit for rational nature. To show that self-preservation is fit for rational nature is, according to Aquinas, quite easy. It is also a basic fact that human beings are social animals, but the implications of this fact are not immediately obvious. Some argument about the human good is needed before we can see how justice and friendship are fitting for rational nature.

The teleological argument favoured by Aquinas and Suarez does not fit Clarke's view that we ought to be able to see the rightness of benevolence simply by considering what it is. In their view, we must consider how benevolence fits into other aspects of human nature. We cannot simply consider benevolence by itself, but we must also consider its relation to human nature.

Clarke's idea of intrinsic morality may be defended by appeal to Cudworth's demand for eternal and immutable morality. If the rightness of sparing the life of an innocent person is immutable, it belongs to the action simply insofar as it is sparing the life of an innocent person. If it depended on some further facts about the agent or the beneficiary of the action, it could change from being right to wrong if these further facts changed; hence its rightness would not be immutable. If it is to be immutably right, the mere fact that it is sparing the life of an innocent person must be the sole and sufficient basis of its rightness. Though Cudworth does not connect immutability with the intrinsic character of an action in exactly Clarke's terms, Clarke might intelligibly claim to capture Cudworth's implicit position.

---

and perversely contend that the whole is not equal to all its parts, or that a square is not double to a triangle of equal base and height.' (H ii 609 = R 227)

[22] Ross, FE 52–4, is sympathetic to Clarke and Price on fitness.

Clarke, therefore, agrees with Suarez and Cudworth insofar as he relies on claims about intrinsic morality, fitness to nature, and immutability, and explains these claims in opposition to a legislative conception of morality. He departs from them, however, in supposing that intrinsic and immutable morality is intrinsic to actions themselves, without reference to their relation to agents of a certain kind.

This understanding of intrinsic morality is connected—whether as cause or as effect—with an epistemological tendency that is prominent in Clarke, but not in Cudworth and Suarez. He wants to show that the principles of intrinsic morality are not only right in themselves, but also known in themselves, and known beyond any possibility of reasonable doubt. This does not follow from the claim that the rightness of actions is intrinsic to the actions themselves. When Aquinas speaks of truths that are known 'in themselves' or of cases in which the predicate is present in the subject, he does not mean that the relevant truths are obvious on inspection, or that they are evident facts about the meaning of terms.[23] Clarke seems to add an epistemological claim that is intended to expose the error of doubters such as Hobbes.

These aspects of Clarke's views on intrinsic morality suggest how he accepts parts of Suarez's and Cudworth's position, but nonetheless alters it significantly. Teleology is present in Suarez's naturalism no less than in Aquinas' naturalism; hence, Suarez's claims about morality as fitness to rational nature include a teleological element that is absent from Clarke's claims about eternal fitnesses. Clarke offers no account of rational nature that might make it reasonable to claim that one or another action is fitting to rational nature.

Clarke, therefore, abandons Suarez's naturalism.[24] Cudworth stands between Suarez and Clarke on these issues. He does not speak of fitness as they do, and so he does not make it clear whether he takes the immutability of morality to require the strong immutability demanded by Clarke or the more qualified immutability allowed by Suarez.

These three moralists explain claims about morality by appeal to some notion of contradiction, but they understand 'contradiction' in different ways that match their conceptions of fitness. Suarez explains the sense in which God would be making a contradiction true if he were to change moral rightness and wrongness. Given the facts about rational nature and the fact that, necessarily, right and wrong are what accords with and conflicts with rational nature, a change in right and wrong, without a corresponding change in human nature, would make it true that the same action both is and is not in accord with rational nature. To make the killing of innocent persons cease to be wrong is not contradictory in itself, but it leads to a contradiction, given the facts about rational nature, about killing, and about rightness.[25] Cudworth also speaks of contradiction, but he does not explain so clearly where the contradiction lies. Clarke resolves the obscurity in Cudworth, but he does not return to Suarez; he asserts a direct contradiction between the idea of killing an innocent person and the idea of moral rightness, similar to the contradiction between having angles adding up to 200 degrees and being a triangle. This version of an appeal to contradiction, as opposed to the naturalist version, is effectively criticized by Pufendorf.[26]

---

[23] See Aquinas, §309.   [24] Contrast Finnis, *NLNR* 42–8.
[25] Suarez on contradiction; §441.   [26] See Pufendorf, §579.

Fitness and contradiction, therefore, according to Suarez, are three-term relations, involving an action, an essence, and human nature. Being innocent and being deliberately killed are incompatible, because they do not fit the requirements of human nature, and in particular do not fit the social aspects of human nature, which require us to refrain from harming others (except in circumstances specified by the requirements of human nature). According to Clarke, the relevant relations have only two terms; they involve the action and the essence that it contradicts. Since a triangle essentially has angles adding up to 180 degrees, a triangle with angles adding up to 200 degrees contradicts this essence. Since an innocent person is one who has a right not to be killed, the rightness of deliberate killing of the innocent contradicts the essence of innocence.

In contrast to Suarez and Cudworth, therefore, Clarke separates rationalism and object-ivism from naturalism. He agrees with naturalism insofar as he rejects voluntarism and a legislative conception of moral rightness, and therefore accepts intrinsic morality. Moreover, he believes that intrinsic morality can be grasped by rational reflexion on the objective facts about agents and actions. But he seems to have a more restrictive conception of the facts and the reflexion that are relevant. He replaces deliberation about the goal-directed nature of rational agents with inspection of the inherent character of acts apart from their context and their ends.[27]

620. The Metaphysics and Epistemology of Eternal Fitnesses

It is difficult to separate metaphysics from epistemology in Clarke's conception of eternal fitnesses, and it is difficult to say which is prior to which. He seems to connect two controversial doctrines: (1) He explains the sort of contradiction and fitness relevant to naturalist ethical claims by appeal to logical and conceptual relations. (2) He explains our grasp of logical and conceptual relations by appeal to self-evidence and obviousness.[28] The first move is disputable, but not surprising, since the appeal to contradiction can be clearly and intelligibly explained by reference to mathematical entities. The second move is initially appealing, since it seems to show that an opponent who denies claims about fitness is simply failing to see something that should be obvious to any mind free of confusion.

But this apparent advantage of Clarke's conception of fitness has severe costs. Three disadvantages are especially evident: (1) Clarke makes it difficult to explain how there could ever be reasonable dispute or uncertainty about what is morally right. His explanation of fitness through immediacy makes it look as though moral disputes must always result from

---

[27] Passmore, *RC* 102, compares Clarke with Cudworth: 'Neither Cumberland nor Clarke after him felt Cudworth's difficulty in working out a theory of immutable morality within a theological framework; for their ethics is legislative through-and-through. Thus, in Clarke, what is eternal and immutable is a system of duties, not the goodness of a certain way of life.' Passmore's second sentence is correct, but his first sentence is mistaken about Clarke. For Clarke repudiates (without drawing attention to the fact) the view of Cumberland (and Pufendorf; see §565) that obligation and moral rightness depend on divine legislation. On this point he follows Cudworth and (once allowance is made for different concepts of obligation) Suarez. The disappearance of the teleological element, and hence of the appeal to goodness that Passmore mentions, cannot be explained by Clarke's acceptance of a legislative conception of obligation. Instead, we need to appeal to his epistemology.

[28] On the tendency to identify conceptual truths with introspectively obvious truths see Bennett, *LBH* 247–9.

gross confusion or irrationality. The naturalist explanation of fitness by appeal to nature at least shows why it might sometimes be difficult to answer moral questions. (2) As Clarke understands the obvious, it seems rather uninformative. If we ask what is wrong with deliberately killing innocent people, Clarke seems to answer that the meaning of 'innocent person' includes a reference to the wrongness of deliberately killing them. Hence the answer to our question will be that it is wrong to kill an innocent person because an innocent is one whom it is wrong to kill. If we want to know why it is wrong to kill a person who has done us no wrong, Clarke's appeal to the definition of innocence does not answer our question. (3) The appeal to obviousness suggests that the appeals to fitness and to nature are idle; the recognition of obviousness seems to provide all the explanation that Clarke takes to be available.

Some moral disputes might be settled by the means Clarke offers. If, for instance, we wonder whether murder is wrong, we might simply be forgetting that the concept of murder is the concept of an unjustifiable homicide. Moreover, significant and complex moral disputes might turn on conceptual issues—if answers to conceptual questions may be difficult to find. Clarke's particular understanding of conceptual issues, however, seems to ensure that the only truths he can offer about fitness will be trivial and uninformative.

When Clarke replaces fitness to rational nature with bare fitness, it is difficult to see that a claim about fitness explains or justifies the claim that an action is morally right. Reference to fitness does not seem to introduce any further feature that might support the judgment about rightness. Clarke's conception of fitness may lead us in the wrong direction, if we try to explain it through self-evidence. For the most plausible explanation of the self-evidence that he attributes to judgments of fitness treats them as purely conceptual judgments. We may well find that this is too restrictive a conception of moral judgment.

Disagreements among later rationalists about appeals to fitness highlight this difficulty in Clarke's position. While Balguy defends fitness as a morally relevant and significant feature that makes actions right, Adams appeals directly to the immediate judgment that actions are right and wrong, without trying to explain this through fitness and unfitness.[29]

621. The Content of Moral Judgments

Clarke believes that we can grasp eternal fitnesses partly because he is sure that we agree on basic moral principles and that we recognize them as describing appropriate and fit conduct. He believes that the strongest argument against his position is 'the difficulty there may sometimes be, to define exactly the bounds of right and wrong', and the different views that have been held on these questions in different historical periods and in different societies. He offers an analogy with colours. Though two colours may blend into each other so gradually that we cannot say definitely where one begins and the other ends, we can nonetheless agree that there is a clear difference between red and blue, or white and black. Similarly, the recognition of difficult or indeterminate cases in morality should not persuade us that we cannot recognize a clear distinction between right and wrong.[30]

---

[29] Adams; §665.

[30] 'But as, in painting, two very different colours, by diluting each other very slowly and gradually, may from the highest intenseness in either extreme, terminate in the midst insensibly, and so run one into the other, that it shall not be

The basic principles require us to honour and to obey God, to deal with everyone equitably, as we desire that they will deal with us, and to preserve ourselves to perform these other duties. Anyone who rejects these principles is no less irrational than someone who rejects basic arithmetical principles about addition.[31] We are not necessitated to observe moral principles, because we have free will and because we are liable to passions that distract us from a clear grasp of these principles. But the effect of these passions is to make us 'endeavour . . . to make things be what they are not, and cannot be' (H ii 613 = R 232). When we clearly consider basic moral principles and understand them, we cannot help but assent to them in conscience; this is what St Paul means in speaking of our being a law to ourselves.[32]

In some of these cases we can perhaps see why Clarke thinks the denial of a basic principle involves a contradiction. Perhaps he thinks it is part of the concept of God that God deserves honour and obedience from creatures like us. Similarly, he might argue that if we both accept a duty and reject the necessary means to carrying out we do not really believe that it is a duty. But it is more difficult to find such an account of the principle of equity. If I want to harm others for my advantage and want them to benefit me for my advantage, my will does not contradict itself.

To reach a contradiction in cases such as this one, we have to begin from a different starting point, drawing on Cumberland's claims about the impartiality of practical reason.[33] If I claim that it is reasonable for me, as a rational agent, to treat other rational agents, as rational agents, without regard for their interests, but unreasonable for others, as rational agents, to treat me, as a rational agent, without regard for my interests, then I contradict myself. I begin from claims about how it is reasonable for one rational agent to treat another, but then I contradict these claims in different cases, even though I have already agreed that the principles apply to all rational agents.

---

possible even for a skilful eye to determine exactly where the one ends, and the other begins, and yet the colours may really differ as much as can be, not in degree only but entirely in kind, as red and blue, or white and black: so, though it may perhaps be very difficult in some nice and perplext cases (which yet are very far from occurring frequently), to define exactly the bounds of right and wrong, just and unjust, and there may be some latitude in the judgment of different men, and the laws of divers nations, yet right and wrong are nevertheless in themselves totally and essentially different, even altogether as much, as white and black, light and darkness.' (H ii 611 = R 229)

[31] 'He that wilfully refuses to honour and obey God, from whom he received his being, and to whom he continually owes his preservation, is really guilty of an equal absurdity and inconsistency in practice, as he that in speculation denies the effect to owe any thing to its cause, or the whole to be bigger than its parts. He that refuses to deal with all men equitably, and with every man as he desires they should deal with him, is guilty of the very same unreasonableness and contradiction in one case, as he that in another case should affirm one number or quantity to be equal to another, and yet that other at the same time not to be equal to the first. Lastly, he that acknowledges himself obliged to the practice of certain duties both towards God and towards men, and yet takes no care either to preserve his own being, or at least not to preserve himself in such a state and temper of mind and body, as may best inable him to perform those duties, is altogether as inexcusable and ridiculous, as he that in another matter should affirm one thing at the same time that he denies another, without which the former could not possibly be true; or undertake one thing, at the same time that he obstinately omits another, without which the former is by no means practicable.' (H ii 613 = R 232)

[32] 'For no man willingly and deliberately transgresses this rule, in any great and considerable instance, but he acts contrary to the judgement and reason of his own mind, and secretly reproaches himself for so doing. And no man observes and obeys it steadily, especially in cases of difficulty and temptation, when it interferes with any present interest, pleasure or passion, but his own mind commends and applauds him for his resolution, in executing what his conscience could not forbear giving its assent to, as just and right. And this is what St. Paul means . . .' Clarke now quotes *Rm.* 2:14–15. (H ii 615 = R 234).

[33] Cumberland; see §533.

Perhaps, then, we could formulate a principle of equity that would be contradicted by the sort of outlook that Clarke has in mind. But this is a relatively uninteresting result. My rejection of a principle of equity involves me in self-contradiction only if I already accept a principle of equity. But why must anyone who rejects a principle of equity also accept it? Clarke would have an answer to this question if he could show that in recognizing someone as another person, and hence a possible victim of unfair treatment for my own advantage, I must also recognize the other as having a right to equitable treatment. But how can he show this?

He sometimes suggests that we inevitably judge from an impartial and equitable point of view. This point of view appears most clearly in our judgments of other people. Sometimes we set aside our special interest in an action, and we examine it impartially, taking the moral point of view. Even if we pretend that the impartial point of view has no authority for our actions, we acknowledge its authority when our own interests are not involved. Why, asks Clarke, should we suppose that it loses authority when it appears to conflict with our own interest? No reason can be given, from the impartial point of view, to show that the impact on my interest should matter so much.[34]

In reply to Clarke's question one might ask why one should suppose that my interest does not make all the difference. To understand this question, we need to understand the force of 'why one should suppose'. Does this 'why' ask for a reason from the impartial point of view, or a reason from my self-interested point of view? Or can we identify some third point of view? This question underlies the argument that leads Sidgwick to affirm an ultimate dualism of practical reason.[35] Clarke does not pursue the questions that arise about his principle of equity.

Even if we agree with Clarke's view that we necessarily accept some principle of equity, we might doubt whether it has any significant moral content. He does not explain how more specific moral principles might emerge from this impartial point of view. Some of his remarks, however, suggest that he intends to derive them from impartiality. He claims that the principle of equity requires us 'so to deal with every man, as in like circumstances we would reasonably expect he should deal with us' (H ii 619 = R 241). He does not say simply that we should treat others as we would prefer them to treat us; for our preferences may themselves be self-centred and warped. He requires us to take an impartial view of our own desires as well.

622. Benevolence

Clarke does not rely on equity alone to derive positive moral content. He also recognizes 'universal love or benevolence', which requires us to aim at the greatest good we are capable

---

[34] 'But the truth of this, that the mind of man naturally and necessarily assents to the eternal law of righteousness, may still better and more clearly and more universally appear, from the judgment that men pass upon each other's actions, than from what we can discern concerning their consciousness of their own. For men may dissemble and conceal from the world, the judgment of their own conscience; nay, by a strange partiality, they may even impose upon and deceive *themselves*; (for who is there, that does not sometimes allow himself, any, and even justify himself in that, wherein he condemns another?) But men's judgments concerning the actions of *others*, especially where they have no relation to themselves, or repugnance to their interest, are commonly impartial; and from this we may judge, what sense men naturally have of the unalterable difference of right and wrong.' (H ii 616 = R 237)

[35] See Sidgwick, *ME*, concluding chapter.

of achieving for everyone.[36] His first argument seeks to derive this principle from the fitness of aiming at the greater rather than the lesser good. But he does not explain why this good consists in achieving the welfare of persons (rather than some good to which their welfare is not essential). His second argument is derived, as he remarks, from Cicero's account of the Stoic doctrine of conciliation.[37] This begins from the natural human desire and need for society, and appeals to the reasonableness of extending society until it includes everyone.[38]

Clarke does not point out the possibility of deriving a principle of benevolence from the obligation to prudence combined with the obligation to equity.[39] If we rationally wish to promote our own interest, and we recognize that what is rational for us to want for ourselves is equally rational for others to want for themselves, an appeal to equity justifies the extension of benevolence to everyone. Clarke's explicit argument appeals to the principle of equity to justify universal benevolence, but he does not appeal to the rationality of prudence. This may be because he treats the principle of prudence as derivative from other duties, not as a rational principle in its own right. Here Butler improves on him.[40]

Some aspects of Clarke's position are quite similar to Cumberland's. They both recognize a benevolent God who aims at the welfare of the whole universe. Indeed Clarke maintains that the fact that morality promotes the universal welfare is both obvious in itself and a clear proof that morality is in accord with the will of God (H ii 621). He cites Cumberland in his support.[41] Moreover, they both reject Hobbes's attempt to reduce the natural basis of the laws of nature to mere counsels of narrow prudence.[42]

Still, Clarke disagrees with Cumberland—more sharply than he makes clear—on some central issues. We have already seen that he rejects Cumberland's voluntarism about morality and about obligation, and affirms that eternal fitnesses create obligations apart from any divine or human will. He also rejects utilitarianism more clearly than Cumberland rejects it. The eternal fitnesses that Clarke recognizes cannot all be captured by the principle of utility. In explaining why he rejects utilitarianism as a general account of morality, Clarke makes his conception of eternal fitnesses clearer.

---

[36] 'For if (as has been before proved) there be a natural and necessary difference between good and evil, and that which is good is fit and reasonable, and that which is evil is unreasonable to be done, and that which is the greatest good, is always the most fit and reasonable to be chosen: then, as the goodness of God extends itself universally over all his works through the whole creation, by doing always what is absolutely best in the whole, so every rational creature ought in its sphere and station, according to its respective powers and faculties, to do all the good it can to all its fellow-creatures.' (H ii 621)

[37] Conciliation; §166. Clarke refers to Cic. *Fin.* v 65.

[38] 'Wherefore since men are plainly so constituted by nature, that they stand in need of each other's assistance to make themselves easy in the world, and are fitted to live in communities, and society is absolutely necessary for them, and mutual love and benevolence is the only possible means to establish this society in any tolerable and durable manner, and in this respect all men stand upon the same level, and have the same natural wants and desires, and are in the same need of each other's help, and are equally capable of enjoying the benefit and advantage of society: 'tis evident every man is bound by the law of his nature, and as he is also prompted by the inclination of his uncorrupted affections, to look upon himself as a part and member of that one universal body or community, which is made up of all mankind, to think himself born to promote the public good and welfare of all his fellow-creatures, and consequently obliged, as the necessary and only effectual means to that end, to embrace them all with universal love and benevolence . . .' (H ii 622)

[39] See Sidgwick's comments on Clarke, *ME* [1] 360.   [40] Butler on prudence; §686.

[41] He quotes Cumberland, *LN* 1.15 = P 312: '. . . the truth of moral philosophy is founded in the necessary connexion between the greatest happiness human powers can reach, and those acts of universal benevolence, or of love towards God and man, which is branched out into all the moral virtues'.

[42] See Schneewind, *IA* 312, 317, 320, citing Sharp, 'Cumberland', 386–7.

He gives a central place to benevolence, which he conceives in a way that allows a utilitarian interpretation. In his view, love requires that 'we endeavour, by an universal benevolence, to promote the welfare and happiness of all men'. God shows the same benevolence towards us. In this description of benevolence Clarke recalls Cumberland's view that practical reason aims at a common good; like Cumberland, Clarke does not say whether this should be understood in utilitarian quantitative terms.

Utilitarianism, however, does not capture Clarke's view of rightness and fitness as a whole. He recognizes principles connected with justice, and takes them to limit the application of the utilitarian principle. It would be difficult for him to avoid this position, given his moral epistemology. For his rationalism rests on intuitive convictions that certain kinds of actions and relations are fit and reasonable in themselves. We have to reject such convictions if we treat the principle of utility as the supreme moral principle. Hence the believer in eternal fitnesses had better not be a utilitarian.

Clarke believes, for instance, that it is fit and reasonable in itself to keep a promise, show gratitude to a benefactor, avoid pain to an innocent person, and so on. But if the principle of utility is supreme, we may have to violate these principles of fitness; breaking promises, violating ties to particular people, overriding the rights of the innocent, may all be needed to maximize utility. Even if utility will not in fact require us to override these principles, a utilitarian has to deny that the relevant actions are fit and reasonable, and so morally obligatory, in themselves; they are reasonable only if they fit into an indirect utilitarian argument.

Since Clarke rejects a utilitarian explanation of the rightness of actions that he regards as fit in themselves, he argues that the general or common good is not the only basis for obligation. Another basis rests on the demands of equity, which requires that 'we so deal with every man, as in like circumstances we would reasonably expect he should deal with us' (H ii 619 = R 241). Since he is not a sentimentalist, Clarke sees no need to explain how the reciprocity connected with equity has any basis in our sentiments.

Equity and benevolence seem to be distinct. The characteristic of equity is reasonableness plus impartiality between myself and each other person, whereas the characteristic of benevolence is concern for the welfare of every other person. If, for instance, I would reasonably not want someone else to do what a benevolent person would do in my interest, then the rule of equity imposes some limit on the practice of benevolence.

Clarke does not say whether universal benevolence aims at maximizing the quantity of good irrespective of its distribution. If this is the aim of benevolence, it may clash with equity. It is not clear why I would 'reasonably expect' someone else to treat me unequally simply because unequal treatment would increase the total happiness. Nor does Clarke suggest that reasonableness should be assessed purely by utilitarian criteria. Apparently, then, equitable treatment might conflict with maximizing utility.

Clarke agrees that on the whole the good of the universal creation coincides with what is right, and that God wills virtue to be rewarded by happiness. But he rejects an appeal to utility as the criterion of rightness. He mentions three features of utility: (1) It is sometimes very difficult to tell what maximizes utility. (2) Public utility varies from society to society. (3) Public utility must be judged by the governors of each particular society. In contrast, the moral law has none of these features.[43] Clarke adds specific objections to the breaking of promises on utilitarian grounds, pointing out that these breaches of faith may have bad consequences (H ii 630–1). Without directly criticizing Cumberland, he implicitly anticipates Maxwell's explicit criticisms of Cumberland's neglect of non-teleological moral principles.

A sophisticated utilitarian might try to answer Clarke's objection about consequences. Hutcheson's indirect utilitarian defence of more specific principles and traits suggests that we need not face the uncertainties of calculating utility on every occasion on which we have to decide what it is right to do.[44] But one may doubt whether the indirect utilitarian defence succeeds, if it is applied to the specific rules and traits that Clarke takes to be clearly right.

Clarke's second and third objections raise the most important issues. He does not merely mean that it is unwise to rely on something as difficult to discover and as variable as public utility. He means that we know moral principles lack features that they would have if they were really maxims for the promotion of utility. Moral requirements are clear and uniform in some cases where the demands of utility are obscure and variable. If a utilitarian view were correct, we would need to answer some complicated questions about utility before we could know that a certain type of action is morally right; but we do not need to answer all these questions. Even if the answers would eventually favour our moral principle, the fact that we do not need them shows that the principle is not based on predictions about utility.[45]

Indirect utilitarianism does not entirely overcome this objection. Even if it avoids the difficulty of facing obscure and difficult questions about particular actions, it faces similar questions about rules and character traits. If our reason for accepting certain specific rules or virtues is clear independently of our beliefs about their contribution to utility, Clarke's objection stands.

The objection raises a serious question about one defence of a utilitarian account of morality. Sometimes utilitarians suggest that if they can give plausible arguments to show that recognized moral rules tend to maximize utility, they have vindicated a utilitarian position. In suggesting this, utilitarians imply that extensional equivalence between utilitarianism and recognized principles provides a sufficient defence of utilitarianism. If Clarke is right, however, extensional equivalence is not enough. If our reason for accepting the moral principles is independent of utility, mere extensional equivalence would not show that our moral principles are utilitarian, or that the principle of utility is the supreme moral principle.

Clarke need not claim that all moral requirements are always clear, or that utility is never relevant to questions of moral rightness. He has a strong case if he can show that moral

---

[43] 'Others have contended, that all difference of good and evil, and all obligations of morality, ought to be founded originally upon considerations of public utility. And true indeed it is, in the whole; that the good of the universal creation, does always coincide with the necessary truth and reason of things. But otherwise, (and separate from this consideration, that god will certainly cause truth and right to terminate in happiness;) what is for the good of the whole creation, in very many cases, none but an infinite understanding can possibly judge. Public utility, is one thing to one nation, and the contrary to another, and the governors of every nation, will and must be judges of the public good, and by public good, they will generally mean the private good of that particular nation. But truth and right (whether public or private) founded in the eternal and necessary reason of things, is what every man can judge of, when laid before him. It is necessarily one and the same, to every man's understanding; just as light is the same to every man's eyes.' (H ii 630 = R 251)

[44] See Hutcheson, *SMP* 66, 85, discussed in §647.

[45] Cockburn emphasizes these anti-utilitarian aspects of Clarke's theory in her attack on Rutherforth. See §876.

principles are sometimes clear independently of considerations of utility. If he is right about this, the utilitarian criterion is not the correct criterion of morality.

This argument is another version of Cudworth's objection to Hobbes. Cudworth rejects the view that (1) the true principles of justice are those commanded by the sovereign, and (2) are true because they are commanded by the sovereign. Clarke argues against the view that (3) the true principles of morality maximize utility, and (4) are true because they maximize utility. Both Cudworth's pair and Clarke's pair of claims recall the pair of claims about piety and what the gods love that are discussed by Socrates and Euthyphro. Just as Cudworth argues that the truth of the first claim does not imply the truth of the second, Clarke argues that the truth of the third does not imply the truth of the fourth. Indeed, he argues that the third may be true, but the fourth is false.

Clarke does not refute utilitarianism, but he identifies a question that a utilitarian has to answer. A true moral theory should offer not only a criterion that identifies morally right actions, but also an account of the property that makes them right. Clarke argues that utilitarianism fails in the second task because we can see that the right-making property of right actions is a property that would still make them right even if they did not maximize utility.

A utilitarian might argue that we are simply wrong in supposing that true moral principles would still be true if they did not maximize utility. Clarke points out, however, that it may be difficult for a utilitarian to support this claim. A utilitarian theory has to appeal to some of our moral beliefs and convictions against others; indeed, it seems plausible because it relies on our strong convictions about the goodness of benevolence. But if it violates our strong convictions about the sort of property that makes right actions right, we may reasonably ask whether our convictions about benevolence ought to override our convictions about right-making properties.

Though Clarke offers this strong argument against utilitarianism, he does not consider an obvious utilitarian reply. He concedes that morality prescribes universal benevolence; but if universal benevolence must aim at maximum utility, how can the requirements of morality be clear independently of questions about utility?

Clarke might try different replies to the utilitarian: (1) He might concede the utilitarian point for benevolence, but deny it for equity, and claim that equity sometimes overrides benevolence. (2) He might deny that benevolence aims at maximum utility.

The first reply is hazardous.[46] For if utilitarian considerations take such a firm hold on one aspect of morality, they may cast doubt on Clarke's claim that some crucial moral principles are clear independently of benevolence. We might doubt whether equity really overrides benevolence; and Clarke does not face this question. It might be better to challenge the utilitarian analysis of benevolence,[47] and to argue that benevolence does not imply the additive attitude to welfare that the utilitarian assumes.

Clarke's case would be stronger if he had relied on this defence. If he accepts the utilitarian analysis of benevolence, he concedes one apparently important area of our moral attitudes to utilitarianism. But he ought not to concede this as being obvious without argument, since

[46] Cf. Butler's treatment of benevolence, §698.

[47] Hutcheson (*IMGE* 3 §4 = L231 = R 331) traces his use of 'benevolence' to Cumberland. But we have found reason to doubt whether Cumberland is a utilitarian; see §535.

the utilitarian interpretation of benevolence is open to question. If utilitarians reject our actual attitude of benevolence in favour of a more utilitarian attitude, they owe us some further argument.

623. Moral Principles and Motivation

Our comparison of Clarke with Suarez and Cudworth has shown that Clarke relies on claims about immediacy in the metaphysics and epistemology of intrinsic morality. In his view, eternal fitness is a property of actions in themselves, apart from their relations to ends or to human nature, and it can be known immediately, by inspection of the actions themselves apart from these further relations. He lays a similar emphasis on immediacy in his account of how moral properties are relevant to motivation and action. According to Aquinas and Suarez, the relevance is mediated; rational agents pursue their ultimate end and what they take to promote it, and intrinsic morality promotes this end through its connexion with human nature and human good. This indirect connexion is less clear, but apparently still present, in Cudworth. He may accept the eudaemonist framework of Scholastic ethics; even if he does not, he suggests that the hegemonicon regards moral rightness as a consideration to be considered along with other considerations bearing on action. He does not suggest that the bare awareness of moral rightness is sufficient to explain acting on it.

Clarke, however, takes bare awareness to motivate us. He believes that the simple grasp of a moral principle motivates a well-ordered will to choose the right action. A sound understanding necessarily grasps the true moral principles, and a sound will necessarily acts on them.[48] We need no special explanation, involving some non-cognitive element, of why someone's will follows principles of morality; that is just a fact about a well-ordered will. We need an explanation only when the will goes wrong.

In saying this Clarke rejects psychological hedonism; he denies that an action becomes intelligible only by being traced back to a desire for pleasure. The hedonist argues that the non-hedonist stops with a brute fact; and the non-hedonist replies that this allegedly brute fact is no less intelligible than the desire for pleasure. Clarke defends his rationalism about motivation in the same way. In his view, no further desire should be introduced to explain why a well-ordered will adheres to the true moral principles. The sentimentalist offers a further explanation, in claiming that some specific desire or sentiment is characteristic of the well-ordered will. Clarke suggests that the further explanation sought by an anti-rationalist is no better than the further explanation for moral motivation sought by a hedonist. If we stop with a non-hedonist desire, why not stop with motivation without desire?

This argument from parity raises a large question about the assumptions that underlie the whole dispute between rationalists and sentimentalists. The two sides seem to differ partly about when and why it is appropriate to end explanations by appeal to brute facts. But how is this dispute to be resolved? If we stop with brute facts, how do we tell that one is intrinsically

---

[48] 'And by this understanding or knowledge of the natural and necessary relations, fitnesses, and proportions of things, the *wills* likewise of all intelligent beings are constantly directed, and must needs be determined to act accordingly; excepting those only, who will things to be what they are not and cannot be; that is, whose wills are corrupted by particular interest or affection, or swayed by some unreasonable and prevailing passion.' (H ii 612 = R 230)

more intelligible than another? Even if we are not psychological hedonists, we may think it is arbitrary to stop with Clarke's brute facts about motivation. The stopping point should not be arbitrary; we want some better reason for regarding a certain motive as characteristic and appropriate for morality than the mere claim that it is no more unintelligible than others that have been picked.

In this sharp contrast between pure rationalism and hedonist anti-rationalism about motivation, eudaemonism deserves consideration, though Clarke does not consider it. The point of eudaemonism is not to trace all desires to some single type of desire that is taken to be intelligible in itself; on this point it differs from hedonism. Its point is to make one motive intelligible by its connexion with other motives in the pursuit of a final good. A similar conclusion about justification is worth considering. A hedonist account of the basis of morality claims to show not only how morality is psychologically possible, but also that it is rationally justifiable, since it promotes a genuine good. A non-hedonist account of moral motivation seems to leave a reasonable question unanswered, if it does not show how it is reasonable to act on the motives of the virtuous person. Clarke seems to leave unanswered an important question that both hedonists and non-hedonist eudaemonists try to answer.

624. Against Hobbes: Morality and the Right of Nature

So far we have discussed Clarke's account of the basic principles of morality in the light of his metaphysical and epistemological claims. We have left out of account his defence of his belief in eternal fitnesses against the voluntarist position that he attributes to Hobbes. Though it may be misleading to separate Clarke's positive views from his critical discussion of opponents, it may also be useful. For if we decide that Clarke's criticisms of Hobbes are plausible, we should not at once infer that they support his own conception of moral principles.

Clarke agrees with Cudworth in using Suarezian arguments against voluntarism to attack Hobbes. Some of the questions that he intends to answer with his own account of moral properties are clearer from his criticism of Hobbes. Cudworth argues that Hobbes's legislative view of morality forces him into a vicious regress; but, as we saw, Hobbes might avoid a vicious regress of legislation based on morality based on legislation if he claims that legislative morality has a non-moral basis. Clarke attacks this answer by arguing that we have moral obligations in situations where, according to Hobbes, we have none. If Cudworth is right, Hobbes must acknowledge at least one moral obligation in the state of nature, and hence prior to any legislation—the obligation to obey a legitimate legislator. If Clarke is right, Hobbes must recognize many obligations prior to legislation. Clarke tries to show that (1) Hobbes admits moral obligations in the state of nature, and (2) Hobbes gives no good reasons for denying such moral obligations.

In support of his first claim, he considers Hobbes's remarks about the right of nature. According to Hobbes, it is not wrong, but morally permissible, for me to kill you if that is necessary for my preservation. In killing you I exercise the right of nature.[49] But how,

---

[49] For Hobbes's account of the right of nature as a liberty see L. 14.1, quoted in §484.

asks Clarke, can Hobbes speak of a 'right of nature', and hence recognize a morally justified liberty, without assuming that some moral principles apply to the state of nature? For if I have a moral right to do x, I am morally protected in doing x, and you would be wrong to prevent me from doing x.[50] How, then, can Hobbes claim that people have rights in the state of nature, while denying that there is anything that it is morally right or wrong to do?

If Hobbes were clearly using 'right' so as to mean 'moral right', so that it implies some moral protection for some liberty, Clarke would be justified. But Clarke has imported moral content that Hobbes does not intend. For Hobbes identifies the right with a liberty, which is simply the absence of external impediments. His explicit use of 'having a right', therefore, does not imply that the liberty in question is morally justifiable. In his explicit sense of 'right', we have a right to preserve ourselves in the state of nature, if we are not overcome by superior individuals or groups. We have the right because we are free, and we are free simply insofar as we are not prevented. But this sort of right does not imply that other people are morally obliged to leave me alone, and Hobbes does not recognize any such obligation.

If Hobbes sticks to this non-normative conception of the right of nature, he must allow this right to extend beyond self-preservation. If our right to kill for self-preservation simply means that nothing prevents killing for self-preservation in the state of nature, it is equally true that there we have a natural right to kill and torture just for fun. Clarke points out that Hobbes is committed to this broad conception of the right of nature.[51] But in fact Hobbes does not allow as broad a right of nature as he would have to allow if he stuck to a non-normative sense of 'right'.[52] In picking out the right of self-preservation and remaining silent about the other natural rights that follow from his non-normative sense of 'right', he seems to restrict the scope of rights in ways that his theory does not justify.[53] If he restricts our rights because he believes we have a morally justified or blameless liberty to pursue the means to our self-preservation, but no such liberty to behave with wanton cruelty, he recognizes moral constraints in the state of nature.[54]

Hobbes might reply, however, that in speaking of rights, he is referring to what is allowed by right reason, but right reason is purely prudential, referring to the agent's own interest. If the only rational considerations applying in the state of nature are prudential considerations, Clarke has not shown that moral considerations apply in the state of nature. Clarke is right, therefore, to criticize Hobbes's appeal to the right of nature, but his criticisms do not force Hobbes to recognize morality in the state of nature.

---

[50] 'For instance; if every man has a right to preserve his own life, then it is manifest I can have no right to take any man's life away from him, unless he has first forfeited his own right, by attempting to deprive me of mine. For otherwise, it might be right for me to do that, which at the same time, because it could not be done but in breach of another man's right, it could not be right for me to do: which is the greatest absurdity in the world.' (H ii 631 = R 253)

[51] '. . . if there be naturally and absolutely in things themselves, no difference between good and evil, just and unjust; then in the state of nature, before any compact be made, it is equally as good, just and reasonable, for one man to destroy the life of another, not only when it is necessary for his own preservation, but also arbitrarily and without any provocation at all, or any appearance of advantage to himself; as to preserve or save another man's life, when he may do it without any hazard of his own. The consequence of which, is; that not only the first and most obvious way for every particular man to secure himself effectually, would be (as Mr Hobbes teaches) to endeavour to prevent and cut off all others; but also that men might destroy one another upon every foolish and peevish or arbitrary humour, even when they did not think any such thing necessary for their own preservation' (H ii 609–10 = R 227).

[52] On Hobbes's use of 'right' and on the right of nature see §484.   [53] On drunkenness and cruelty see §484.

[54] Pufendorf, *JNG* i 6.10, also criticizes Hobbes effectively on the right of nature.

625. Morality and Self-Preservation

But Clarke offers an objection that replies to this appeal to prudence. He argues that Hobbes cannot plausibly claim that the only rational constraint on behaviour in the state of nature is prudential. In Clarke's view, we recognize moral obligations in the state of nature. We give them some weight, even if they do not guide our conduct in the same way as they would in a more stable situation.[55]

Hobbes argues: (1) Some ordinary moral rules do not bind us when they impede self-preservation. (2) Therefore, they are not binding in the state of nature, in which they impede self-preservation. (3) Therefore, the only rational principles binding us in the state of nature are principles of self-preservation. Clarke points out that Hobbes's first claim does not justify the second or the third; it shows only that ordinary moral rules do not bind us in the state of nature on occasions when they impede self-preservation. But even in the state of nature, observance of ordinary moral rules does not always impede self-preservation; when it does not, we are obliged, for anything that Hobbes has shown, to observe them.

Hobbes may acknowledge the considerations mentioned by Clarke, since he does not treat the right of nature as a right to do immoral actions that are not justified by appeal to self-preservation. Why should he refuse to allow that we have a natural right to amuse ourselves in every way, however immoral, that neither advances nor threatens our self-preservation? He seems to agree, at least implicitly, with Clarke's view that the obligation to observe moral rules is still in force whenever it does not impede self-preservation.

Hobbes points out that we take some ordinary moral rules to be in abeyance in the state of nature because observance of them might threaten self-preservation. Clarke answers that the peculiar dangers of the state of nature modify our ordinary moral obligations, but do not cancel moral obligations that do not impede self-preservation. If moral considerations matter even in the state of nature, and even when they are not means to self-preservation, they are not simply rules derived from self-preservation.[56] If Hobbes were right, some actions would be morally indifferent that, in our ordinary view, are not indifferent.

626. Moral Obligations in the State of Nature

Clarke argues further that Hobbes must recognize moral obligations in the state of nature, if he is to justify the formation of a state. If we all killed and tortured whenever we felt like it, the result would be the destruction of humanity. The sort of obligation that Hobbes must assume to get us out of the state of nature is the very sort whose existence he denies.[57]

---

[55] 'Nay, I believe, there is no man, even in Mr Hobbes's state of nature, and of Mr Hobbes's own principles; but that if he was equally assured of securing his main end, his self-preservation, by either way; would choose to preserve himself rather *without* destroying all his fellow-creatures, than *with* it; even supposing all impunity, and all other future conveniencies of life, equal in either case . . .' (H ii 616 = R 236)

[56] In some places Hobbes seems to come close to agreement with Clarke. See *EL* 16.8 on 'accommodation' to others (this seems not to allow a purely psychological sense of 'obligation'); 17.10 on obligation in foro interno; *Civ.* 3.27 (and n.).

[57] 'Which being undeniably a great and unsufferable evil; Mr Hobbes himself confesses it reasonable, that, to prevent this evil, man should enter into certain compacts to preserve one another. Now if the destruction of mankind

Hobbes, therefore, picks and chooses arbitrarily among the laws of nature, claiming that some of them do not oblige in foro externo outside the commonwealth, whereas the law enjoining us to seek peace obliges us in the state of nature, since it is the basis for the social compact. Hobbes has no good reason to single out this one law of nature.[58] Clarke takes Hobbes to assume that observance of the other laws of nature is obligatory if their observance does not impede self-preservation, and that therefore self-preservation cannot justify the aggression of the person who has not yet suffered aggression. And so he argues that Hobbes must recognize moral obligations that he professes to reject.

Clarke's argument is effective if Hobbes is arguing from the moral wrongness of the state of war to the moral obligation to form a commonwealth. The moral judgment about the badness of the state of war implies, as Clarke points out, a judgment about the badness of unprovoked aggression in the state of nature. To show that we have a moral obligation to seek peace, we need to recognize moral obligations that are not reducible to counsels of self-preservation.

Similarly, according to Clarke, Hobbes's attempt to rest the foundation of the commonwealth on a covenant requires recognition of moral obligations that Hobbes professes to deny. Clarke assumes that Hobbes wants the covenant to impose some moral obligation, and he argues that it cannot do this unless we already recognize some obligation, apart from the covenant itself, to keep covenants.[59] Just as Cudworth argues that a command cannot itself create the obligation to obey commands, Clarke argues that a promise cannot create the obligation to keep a promise.

This argument presupposes that Hobbes argues for the commonwealth on moral grounds. We might take him to argue that morality demands peace so that the other demands of morality can be properly fulfilled. To say this is to express a moral demand that Kant identifies with the postulate of public right.[60] Such a demand implies that some moral obligations apart from counsels of self-preservation already hold in the state of nature.

by each other's hands, be such an evil, that, to prevent it, it was fit and reasonable that men should enter into compacts to preserve each other; then, before any such compacts, it was manifestly a thing unfit and unreasonable in itself, that mankind should all destroy one another. And if so, then for the same reason it was also unfit and unreasonable, antecedent to all compacts, that any one man should destroy another arbitrarily and without any provocation, or at any time when it was not absolutely and immediately necessary for the preservation of himself.' (H ii 610 = R 227)

[58] 'Now if men are obliged by the original reason and nature of things to seek terms of peace, and to get out of the pretended natural state of war, as soon as they can; how come they not to be obliged originally by the same reason and nature of things, to live from the beginning in universal benevolence, and avoid entering into the state of war at all? He must needs confess they would be obliged to do so, did not self-preservation necessitate them every man to war upon others: but this cannot be true of the first aggressor; whom yet Mr Hobbes, in the place now cited, vindicates from being guilty of any injustice: and therefore herein he unavoidably contradicts himself.' (H ii 632–3 = R 255)

[59] '. . . if the rules of right and wrong, just and unjust, have none of them any obligatory force in the state of nature, antecedent to positive compact; then, for the same reason, neither will they be of any force after the compact, so as to afford men any certain and real security; (excepting only what may arise from the compulsion of laws, and fear of punishment, which therefore, it may well be supposed, is all that Mr Hobbes really means at the bottom.) For if there be no obligation of just and right antecedent to the compact; then whence arises the obligation of the compact itself, on which he supposes all other obligations to be founded?' (H ii 634 = R 257).

[60] 'If you are so situated as to be unavoidably side by side with others, you ought to abandon the state of nature and enter, with all others, a juridical state of affairs.' (Kant, *MdS* 307)

627. The Role of Self-Preservation in Morality

Clarke shows that Hobbesian counsels of self-preservation cannot cover all the moral properties we recognize; for we recognize moral obligations that cannot be reduced to counsels of self-preservation. Hobbes himself seems to recognize them, if he believes we have moral reasons for getting out of the state of nature and into a commonwealth.

Clarke defeats one argument that might seem to support Hobbes. We might well be attracted to Hobbes's general position because we agree with him in supposing that the existence of a stable commonwealth makes an important difference to our moral obligations. Hobbes argues as follows: (1) One salient feature of the state is its monopoly of the use of force. (2) Moral obligations differ inside and outside the state. (3) The state's monopoly of the use of force explains the different moral obligations it generates, since it raises the price of aggression and increases the rewards for non-aggression. (4) Therefore the state is needed to give me a reason to follow morality.

Clarke answers Hobbes by accepting the first three claims and rejecting the fourth. He offers a different defence of the state's monopoly of the use of force. Compulsion removes temptations to violate moral obligations, but it does not necessarily create the obligations that would otherwise be easy to violate.[61]

The existence of a state may also imply new obligations. Perhaps, for instance, I ought to be ready to commit myself more unreservedly when I know that other people will be compelled to keep their part of the bargain.[62] But recognizing these facts about compulsion does not make compulsion necessary for obligation.[63] Hobbes's insistence on compulsion shows us one reason why a state is necessary to fulfil some moral demands, but it does not tell us as much as he supposes about the nature or basis of these demands. Apparently, then, people in the state of nature still have reason to act on moral principles, even though circumstances may dictate that they will not act in the ways they would act in a state. To show that we have no moral obligations in the state of nature, Hobbes needs some further argument besides the arguments that Clarke refutes.

628. Prudential Obligation

Hobbes might answer this criticism by a route that Clarke suggests for him. Clarke recognizes that the 'obligatory force' that Hobbes ascribes to covenants may be simply 'what may arise from the compulsion of laws and fear of punishment'.[64] Fear of punishment suggests a prudential reason for keeping a covenant, and Hobbes may claim that the only sort of reason he recognizes is a prudential reason. In the state of nature, he may claim, our only obligations are non-moral. If the laws of nature are simply counsels of self-preservation,

---

[61] 'It is true, men by entering into compacts and making laws, agree to compel one another to do what perhaps the mere sense of duty, however really obligatory in the highest degree, would not, without such compacts, have force enough of itself to hold them to in practice; and so compacts must be acknowledged to be in fact a great addition and strengthening of men's security.' (H ii 632 = R 254)

[62] Hobbes on assurance; §485.   [63] Mackie, HMT 14, 40, defends Hobbes.

[64] See H ii 634 = R 257, quoted in §626.

self-preservation gives us the only principles that guide our behaviour in the state of nature and justify our attempts to get out of the state of nature.

This claim that the only obligations in the state of nature are prudential cannot be justified by appeal to ordinary moral convictions; as Clarke has shown, we recognize obligations independent of self-preservation, even if we are not required to fulfil them when they conflict with self-preservation. How can Hobbes show that we are mistaken in allowing such obligations? Even if we set aside specifically other-regarding moral considerations, might we not recognize other reasons to act in ways that would improve our lives? Some of these other reasons, distinct from reasons of self-preservation, might apparently give us reasons for actions independent of self-preservation in the state of nature, and for attempts to escape from the state of nature.

Hobbes is right to reject all these sources of obligation, if he shows that all obligation requires motivation, and that the only possible form of motivation rests on beliefs about self-preservation and the means to it. In that case, the obligation to join in making a compact must be an actual motive in each person in the state of nature; it must mean that each person has a strong enough desire in the state of nature to join in making the compact and to stick to it. If obligation results from practical reasoning, it emerges from instrumental reasoning about the means of satisfying one's currently strongest desire.

These assumptions about motivation belong to Hobbes's account of human nature, which he defends before he raises any questions about obligations in the state of nature. His account of human nature allows him to reject the claims about obligation in the state of nature that Clarke urges against him. Hobbes claims that if the nature of human action is clearly understood, moral disputes will be settled. In this case moral disputes arise because of the erroneous belief that we have moral obligations in the state of nature; the error in this belief is exposed by Hobbes's views on obligation and motivation.

629. Prudential Obligation and Hobbesian Motivation

But if Hobbes appeals to his account of human nature in order to answer Clarke, he exposes himself to further objections. For the claims about human nature that answer Clarke are difficult to defend.

Hobbes claims that self-preservation is the basis of all obligation in the state of nature. This is because he treats obligation as motivation, and takes the desire for self-preservation to be our strongest motive. Agents in the state of nature, however, do not seem to follow the demands of prudence, as Hobbes understands them. He describes deliberation as the result of anticipating various future pleasures and pains; the outcome of this process is motivation by the prospect of pleasure and pain that is psychologically most compelling. Hobbes does not justify his claim that the prospect of maximum long-term pleasure will always be most compelling; in fact such a claim conflicts with his belief in the possibility of incontinence.

Hobbesian psychology has to make room for Hobbes's apparent admission that people are sometimes moved by competitive motives even contrary to the demands of prudence and self-preservation. This admission gives us a further reason for doubting whether deliberation will reach the results that it has to reach if Hobbes is to treat claims about obligation as predictions about the results of deliberation.

If Hobbes's account of deliberation applies to the state of nature, how can he predict that agents will be moved to make and to keep the compact that sets up the common-wealth? To show that they will have the appropriate motives, Hobbes needs to argue that my desire to make and observe the compact is stronger than my desire to gain something for myself by deceiving people into laying down their arms, and stronger than my desire to protect myself against the possibility that they will think they can gain something for themselves by deceiving me. Even if I would be better off if I and everyone else could make and observe the compact, it is unlikely that everyone could be expected to see this or to keep it in mind constantly enough to allow the institution of a commonwealth.

Clarke is right, then, to suggest that if Hobbes were willing to reduce any normative force in the obligation of keeping promises to purely psychological inducements,[65] he could avoid reliance on a moral obligation whose existence he denies.[66] But this Hobbesian reply would be unsatisfactory. Hobbes rejects moral obligations in the state of nature, because he reduces normative statements to statements about actual feelings and desires. But this reduction of normative statements undermines some of his normative claims.

Defenders of Hobbes might reject Hobbes's reductive claim about normative statements in general, and might allow that prudential obligations are normative because they contain reasons that are not reducible to desires. Then they might tell Clarke that the principles that he interprets as moral principles are really prudential principles. Such a defence of Hobbes would not claim that statements about prudential obligation are really statements about motivation; but it would support Hobbes's claim that in the state of nature, and therefore in the construction of the commonwealth, the only obligations are prudential. Would this be a good defence of Hobbes's central claim?

Such a defence has to explain why normative prudential principles are acceptable in the state of nature while normative moral principles are not. If we confine ourselves to the claim that self-preservation takes priority in the state of nature, Clarke has already answered us; for he has pointed out that morality makes room for self-preservation without losing its normative force. But if we go further, and claim that moral principles give good reasons only if they are derived from prudential principles, we must defend that claim. Hobbes defends it by arguing that prudential principles describe our actual overriding desires in the state of nature, whereas moral principles do not. But here he relies on his reduction of the normative to the psychological.

If, therefore, we abandon that reduction, how can we reject Clarke's reasons for claiming that, even in the state of nature, we have moral obligations that are irreducible to the requirements of self-preservation? It is not easy for a Hobbesian to escape Clarke's criticisms, if they are suitably developed, and if the costs of the Hobbesian replies are made clear.

---

[65] Inducements need not involve punishment. See §493.
[66] Hume tries to avoid this objection to Hobbes; see §769.

630. The Significance of Clarke's Criticism of Hobbes

Clarke's discussion of Hobbes argues effectively against a voluntarist account of moral obligations, against Hobbes's reduction of moral to prudential obligation, and against his further reduction of obligation to motivation. But does it argue so effectively for Clarke's own view that morality consists in eternal relations of fitness that can be grasped intuitively from an understanding of the relevant concepts?

We can see some reasons for doubting Clarke's view if we ask ourselves why his criticisms of Hobbes are plausible. For example, we may agree with him that in the state of nature we have moral obligations independent of self-preservation. Even if we cannot reasonably be expected to ignore the demands of self-preservation, we can reasonably be expected to treat other people with some consideration for their interests in circumstances where we neither gain nor lose anything by it. The moral obligation or permission to preserve ourselves does not include a moral permission to violate moral principles that do not affect our self-preservation. If we find Clarke's arguments plausible on these points, we can readily explain why they are plausible, by pointing out that even in the state of nature people benefit from considerate treatment by others. Our needs and interests are similar in some ways both inside and outside a commonwealth that has the power to coerce.

This explanation suggests that facts about human nature and human needs are relevant to the presence of moral obligations. Since nature and needs are constant, in these respects, in the state of nature and in a commonwealth, moral obligations are constant too. The differences that Clarke recognizes between moral obligations within and outside a commonwealth also suggest the same view of the basis of these obligations. When he suggests that behaviour leading to the destruction of mankind is a clear evil (H ii 610), he suggests that good and evil are relevant to the benefit and harm of human beings.

If we are convinced by this explanation of the moral obligations that Clarke recognizes in the state of nature, we may doubt his account of the character of moral principles. He suggests that it is fit in itself to keep promises and to show gratitude to benefactors. He might make this uninterestingly true by making the relevant obligation part of the definition of 'promise' and 'benefactor'; but if he defends himself in this way, he invites us to ask why we should recognize such things as promises and benefactors (as he defines them). His discussion of Hobbes suggests that obligations belong to promises and to benefactors because of their relation to human nature and needs. In that case, the keeping of promises is not really fit 'in itself'; it is appropriate to human nature and needs.

Clarke does not reject this naturalist account of the basis of moral obligations. In his discussion of benevolence and universal love, he first offers an explanation that relies on the inherent fitness of seeking the greater good, but then, as we saw, he appeals to Stoic views on nature and conciliation.[67] These are naturalist views, and Clarke speaks here of the natural constitution and needs of human beings. He does not see that this account of moral obligations conflicts with his claims about the inherent fitness of certain actions. Butler

---

[67] See H ii 622, quoted in §622.

contrasts a naturalist position with the a priori rationalism of Clarke. Butler's naturalism is all the more plausible in the light of Clarke's tendency to rely on it.[68]

631. Rationalism v. Naturalism in Clarke

Clarke's tendency to naturalism suggests a possible answer to objections that would otherwise confront his account of moral properties. It is not very satisfactory to be told that certain actions are evidently fit, if we are not told how to defend this claim about fitness. Clarke answers that the only objectors will be those whose minds are grossly perverted or deluded. But if the only sign of their alleged perversion or delusion is their rejection of the allegedly self-evident judgments of fitness, it does not seem altogether plausible to dismiss their objections.

Moreover, the application of Clarke's moral epistemology to these disputes exposes a more basic difficulty in his appeals to fitness. His attempt to explain such appeals by his mathematical examples suggests that those who dispute his claims about rightness overlook basic conceptual truths. But if this is what he means, he seems to imply that we cannot intelligibly formulate moral disputes about, say, the truth of utilitarianism. If utilitarianism is true, it must be a conceptual truth. Those who claim, for instance, that what is right does not always promote utility must be claiming that what always promotes utility does not always promote utility. Conversely, if utilitarianism is false, those who claim that rightness is what promotes utility must be claiming that some property that necessarily diverges from what promotes utility is what promotes utility. We might suppose, however, whichever side of the dispute about utilitarianism we favour, that our opponents are mistaken without contradicting themselves, and that we need to offer more than trivial conceptual truths if we are to answer them.

One might argue that this is an unfair objection to Clarke, because it assumes that conceptual truths are trivial, and so could not be the subject of a complex moral dispute. The assumption is indeed false, but it does not result in unfairness to Clarke, since he accepts it. The same assumption underlies his assumption that people who make moral errors are parallel to those who deny that a triangle has two right angles. If he gives up the assumption about the obviousness of conceptual truths, he also needs to revise his views about how we can be aware of fitness, and, more generally, his claims about the place of self-evidence in moral knowledge.

Not all of Clarke's argumentative strategies are limited by his explanation of fitness. He tries a more plausible strategy when he compares those who reject basic judgments of fitness with those who reject basic sensory judgments. The error that people make if they deny that there is light while they are looking at the sun is a crippling error, since anyone who denies this will be unable to count anything as evidence for asserting anything. Similarly, someone 'who would in good earnest lay it down as a first principle, that a crooked line is as straight as a right one' (H ii 609 = R 227) could not draw any distinction between crooked

---

[68] Butler and Clarke; §678.

and straight. If, then, some people rely on arguments from the senses, but are willing to reject basic sensory judgments, we can convict them of inconsistency.

Clarke could convict his opponents of a parallel inconsistency if he could show that while they reject the moral truths he puts forward, their own arguments depend on the acceptance of truths that are no more certain than the ones he defends against them. This is one line of argument that Clarke uses against Hobbes. He argues that Hobbes has to rely on some moral judgments that apply in the state of nature, and that he cannot consistently both do this and deny the basic truths that Clarke puts forward.

Similarly, if utilitarianism can be shown to conflict with this impartial point of view on claims of right, Clarke's opposition to utilitarianism does not rest simply on the dogmatic claim that some true judgments of fitness conflict with utilitarianism. These judgments rest on the point of view on ourselves that underlies our relations with others as objects of praise, blame, resentment, indignation, and so on. This is a sketch of an argument developed by Butler and Kant. But as soon as we try to support judgments of fitness in this way, we remove their self-evidence and their immediacy; fitness has to be assessed by reference to the sorts of relations and contextual facts that Clarke normally excludes. Some of his most interesting claims about knowledge of specific moral principles raise difficulties for his more general epistemology and metaphysics of morality.

Because Clarke fails to examine his appeals to self-evidence any further, he fails to present a clear alternative to sentimentalism. By appealing simply to claims of self-evidence, he leaves himself open to the objection (urged by Hutcheson against Burnet's defence of Clarke) that what strikes a rationalist as self-evident is simply what appeals to the moral sense, and that rationalists misrepresent their affective reactions as the conclusions of some purely rational argument. Clarke has no good defence against this objection unless he goes beyond a mere appeal to self-evidence. He needs to show why the appearance of self-evidence is a reasonable one, and why there are some rational grounds for believing that the appearance is correct in one or another case. But if we show these things, we find that an appeal to self-evidence is unhelpful. Clarke's position, then, is unstable; but it offers some room for a more thorough criticism of sentimentalism resulting in a more systematic and more convincing alternative. His remarks on Hobbes suggest that this alternative requires a more favourable attitude to naturalism than Clarke normally displays.

Comparisons between Clarke and the naturalism of Cudworth and Suarez reveal ways in which Clarke—consciously or not—carries out his aim of saving what he regards as essential in the anti-voluntarist conception of morality that opposes Hobbes, without incorporating what he might regard as Scholastic accretions that obscure its main point. This attitude to ethics offers a useful parallel to his attitude to the dogmas of Christianity. In Clarke's view, the essential features of Christianity are more convincing when they are set out without some of the traditional doctrines; hence many regarded him as unsound or equivocal on the doctrine of the Trinity, for instance. In transforming the anti-voluntarist belief in intrinsic morality into a rationalist rather than a naturalist position, he might well suppose he is doing a similar service to moral understanding.

One might agree with Clarke in supposing that the replacement of naturalism by a more unqualified rationalism is a desirable simplification of the Scholastic and Suarezian position; it seems to serve Clarke's announced purpose of making the basis of morality clear beyond doubt or cavil. Aquinas and Suarez make judgments about rightness depend on some quite complex and disputable judgments about human nature and the human good. These, however, are the sorts of judgments that Hobbes disputes. One might infer, therefore, that our moral judgments are secure and certain even when these judgments about natures and ends are open to doubt; hence, from Clarke's point of view, it is better to exhibit the clarity and certainty of judgments about intrinsic morality, freed of the disputes that might arise about natures and ends. Apparently, we should not have to agree with Aquinas or Suarez or Cudworth about natures and ends in order to be assured of the truth of judgments about intrinsic morality.

This is a reasonable defence of Clarke, especially given his aim of refuting Hobbes. But it succeeds only if Clarke has found a satisfactory account of the epistemological and metaphysical basis of judgments of intrinsic morality. If his non-naturalist claims about fitness raise more difficulties than we raise with teleological judgments about fitness to rational nature, he has not improved on Suarez. Indeed, he does not seem to have avoided naturalism at all. We have seen that some of the most plausible aspects of his critique of Hobbes and of his explanation of benevolence rely on naturalist claims that do not fit Clarke's metaphysics and epistemology of morality.

These questions will concern us further in discussing Balguy, Price, and Reid, who develop and defend Clarke's rationalism in more detail, and examine some of the objections about moral knowledge, motivation, and justification that seem to arise for Clarke. They will also concern us in discussing the sentimentalists who take the difficulties in the rationalist programme to show that moral principles are not grasped by reason at all, and in discussing Butler and Kant. For Butler believes Clarke goes too far in rejecting naturalism; the restoration of some aspects of traditional naturalism is Butler's answer to sentimentalism. Kant's objections to rationalism are similar to Butler's in some important ways that are not completely obvious. Once we see these similarities, we can more easily see the ways in which Kant's answers to the objections do and do not differ from Butler's return to traditional naturalism.

47

HUTCHESON: FOR AND AGAINST MORAL REALISM

632. Hutcheson's Aims

Hutcheson believes, as Cumberland and Shaftesbury do,[1] that Hobbes's position undermines morality.[2] He agrees with Shaftesbury and Clarke in rejecting Cumberland's and Locke's view that morality consists in laws imposed by divine commands.[3] In his view, we can understand moral obligation without reference to any law, by understanding our approval of benevolence. This approval is disinterested; Hutcheson rejects attempts to defend morality within the limits of a hedonist psychology. But he also rejects Clarke's account of moral judgment and motivation as aspects of rational understanding grasping the fitness of things and properties. He reaches his own position by reflexion on his objections to Clarke.[4] Hence he rejects the extreme rationalism of Clarke by insisting on a role for both reason and desire in moral motivation and justification.

In the *Inquiry*, therefore, Hutcheson supports Shaftesbury rather than Clarke. He undertakes to defend the principles of Shaftesbury against Mandeville, and to present the ideas of moral good and evil according to the views of ancient moralists.[5] He argues that

---

[1] On Shaftesbury see *IMS* 160, 174 (= SB 447); *IMGE* 4.4, L 141 = SB 139. I cite *IMGE* by the original sections and by pages of Leidhold's edition (L), which indicates the changes in Hutcheson's later editions. These changes were sometimes considerable. SB follows the second edition, R the third. I cite *IMS* by pages of Peach's edition, and *SMP* by original sections and pages. Rivers, *RGS* ii 154–64, describes the influence of Shaftesbury on Hutcheson. Berkeley's description of the moral sense in *Alc.* fits Hutcheson at least as well as it fits Shaftesbury (cf. §614). Berman, *AF* 4, suggests that Berkeley had Hutcheson in mind, and points out that in the 4th edn. of *IB* (= L 208–9) Hutcheson replies to Berkeley.

[2] On the popular exploitation of Hobbesian views in support of immoral conclusions see Mintz, *HL*, ch. 6.

[3] 'If any one ask, can we have any sense of obligation, abstracting from the laws of a superior? We must answer according to the various senses of the word obligation. If by obligation we understand a determination, without regard to our own interest, to approve actions, and to perform them; which determination shall also make us displeased with our selves, and uneasy upon having acted contrary to it; in this meaning of the word obligation, there is naturally an obligation upon all men to benevolence; . . . So that no mortal can secure to himself a perpetual serenity, satisfaction, and self-approbation, but by a serious inquiry into the tendency of his actions, and a perpetual study of universal good, according to the justest notions of it.' (*IMGE* 7.1 = L 176 = R 346)

[4] See Leechman in *SMP*, Pref. p. iv.

[5] The full title of the first edition (1725) is: 'An Inquiry into the Original of our Ideas of Beauty and Virtue; in Two Treatises, in which the Principles of the late Earl of Shaftesbury are Explained and Defended against the Author of *The Fable of the Bees*: and the Ideas of Moral Good and Evil are established, according to the Sentiments of the Ancient

Shaftesbury's views about morality do not justify the objections that Shaftesbury and his followers raise against Christianity. Hutcheson believes Shaftesbury is right to defend the possibility of disinterested moral judgment and moral action, and he supports Shaftesbury's position by appeal to the ancients.[6] In speaking of 'the ancients' Hutcheson, like Shaftesbury, especially has in mind the Stoics, in whom he maintained a life-long interest.[7]

Hutcheson defends Shaftesbury by rejecting all attempts to reduce moral judgments to calculations of self-interest. Against reductive views that treat moral judgment as the result of instrumental reasoning, he argues that some moral judgments are immediate judgments of a moral sense. This argument defends Shaftesbury's 'moral realism' (though Hutcheson does not use Shaftesbury's phrase). Shaftesbury follows traditional naturalists in claiming that the morally right (the honestum) is really distinct from the pleasant (dulce) and the advantageous (commodum, utile). Hutcheson is also a realist on this point.

The *Inquiry* also describes the content of our moral judgments. Hutcheson takes the basis of moral judgment to be utilitarian. His utilitarianism helps his anti-reductionism. For it is especially clear that utilitarian principles cannot be reduced to self-interested principles. If we are ultimately, and not just instrumentally, committed to utilitarian principles, our commitment is fundamentally disinterested. This utilitarian side of Hutcheson's position goes beyond Shaftesbury and Cumberland, but Hutcheson might reasonably claim that it offers a further defence of their position.

This picture of Hutcheson, derived from the *Inquiry*, matches part of Whewell's assessment of him. Whewell treats him as a defender of 'independent' morality. This view of Hutcheson is reasonable, insofar as these aspects of his position seem similar to Butler's views. Sometimes, indeed, Hutcheson emphasizes his agreement with Butler. In his late *System of Moral Philosophy*, he accepts or adapts several of Butler's claims about conscience and moral judgment.[8] Several of his arguments against the reductive aspects of Hobbes's moral psychology are similar to Butler's. Whewell therefore, places Hutcheson among the 'moral realists' who support Cudworth and Clarke, taking morality to be independent of legislation, will, and private advantage.[9]

Moralists, with an Attempt to introduce a Mathematical Calculation in Subjects of Morality' (L 199). This is followed by a quotation from Cic., *Off.* i 4 (including the remark that the honestum is praiseworthy even if it is not praised). On Shaftesbury and Mandeville see Kaye, in Mandeville, *FB* i, pp. lxxii–lxxv.

[6] 'It is indeed to be wished that he had abstained from mixing with such noble performances some prejudices he had received against Christianity; a religion which gives us the truest idea of virtue, and recommends the love of God and of mankind as the sum of all religion. How would it have moved the indignation of that ingenious nobleman, to have found a dissolute set of men, who relish nothing in life but the lowest and most sordid pleasures, searching into his writings for those insinuations against Christianity, that they might be the less restrained from their debaucheries, when at the same time their low minds are incapable of relishing those noble sentiments of virtue and honour, which he has placed in so lovely a light! Whatever faults the ingenious may find with this performance, the author hopes nobody will find anything in it contrary to religion or good manners . . . The chief ground of his assurance that his opinions in the main are just is this, that as he took the first hints of them from some of the greatest writers of antiquity, so the more he has conversed with them, he finds his illustrations the more conformable to their sentiments.' (*IMGE*, Pref. = L12)

[7] Scott, *FH* 246–54, emphasizes (indeed exaggerates) Hutcheson's closeness to Stoicism. On Hutcheson's teaching of Stoic texts see Ross, *LAS* 54.

[8] The subscribers to *SMP* include: Balguy of St John's College, Cambridge; two John Maxwells (one MA, one DD); Thomas Reid, Esq.; Adam Smith. A large proportion of the subscribers seem to be Irish and Scottish. On Hutcheson and Butler see §714.

[9] On Whewell see *LHMPE* 94–9 and §§520–1. Norton has revived Whewell's view, without mentioning Whewell. See §643.

Whewell's view of Hutcheson is open to question, however, insofar as Hutcheson is a utilitarian, and so makes morality 'dependent' on universal pleasure. Whewell takes opposition to utilitarianism to be one mark of independent morality, but he does not discuss Hutcheson's elaborate statement of utilitarianism. He is right to connect Hutcheson's defence of immediate and disinterested moral judgment with independent morality, though he argues that the introduction of a moral sense tends to compromise a defence of independent morality. Before we ask whether Whewell is right, it will be useful to discuss the position of the *Inquiry*.

633. Psychological Hedonism

Hutcheson follows Shaftesbury in rejecting Hobbes's psychological hedonism. He denies that the desire for one's own pleasure is the only ultimate non-rational desire, and so he rejects Hobbes's view that both exciting and justifying reasons are ultimately derived from the desire for one's own pleasure. But he believes Shaftesbury does not go far enough. He argues that Shaftesbury's attempt to allow unselfish virtue within hedonist assumptions is not a defensible view of the relation between morality, desire, and pleasure.[10] To derive our unselfish motives from our desire for pleasure, we have to reflect on the remote and indirect consequences of our actions and motives. Such a reflexion, aided by the arguments of Cumberland and Pufendorf, might vindicate the cultivation of benevolence, but Hutcheson believes it is a wildly implausible explanation of our actual benevolent outlook. We do not need to be convinced by the conclusion of any complex prudential reasoning in order to feel and to approve benevolent motives.[11]

The next line of defence for psychological hedonism claims that moral goodness appeals to us not because its remoter consequences appear pleasant, but because it appears pleasant in its own right, apart from its consequences. Hutcheson answers that this hedonist argument is self-defeating, because our pleasure in virtuous action needs to be explained by an antecedent concern for virtuous action.[12] Pain in the absence of a desired object and pleasure in our success in getting it are the by-products of our desire for the object itself; they are not the objects of the desire.[13] Though moral sentiments often cause pain and uneasiness, this

---

[10] On Shaftesbury's view see §610.

[11] 'Some moralists, who will rather twist self-love into a thousand shapes, than allow any other principle of approbation than interest, may tell us, that whatever profits one part without detriment to another, profits the whole, and then some small share will redound to each individual; that those actions which tend to the good of the whole, if universally performed, would most effectually secure to each individual his own happiness; and that consequently, we may approve such actions, from the opinion of their tending ultimately to our own advantage. . . . But must a man have the reflexion of Cumberland, or Pufendorf, to admire generosity, faith, humanity, gratitude? Or reason so nicely to apprehend the evil in cruelty, treachery, ingratitude? Do not the former excite our admiration, and love, and study of imitation, wherever we see them, almost at first view, without any such reflexion; and the latter, our hatred, contempt, and abhorrence?' (*IMGE* 1.4 = L 93–4 = SB79)

[12] Against the claim 'That virtue perhaps is pursued because of the concomitant pleasure', he objects: 'To which we may answer, first, by observing that this plainly supposes a sense of virtue antecedent to ideas of advantage, upon which this advantage is founded; and that from the very frame of our nature we are determined to perceive pleasure in the practice of virtue, and to approve it when practised by our selves, or others.' (*IMGE* 2.8 = L 110 = SB 103)

[13] 'It would be absurd to say that this joy in the success was the motive to the desire. We should have no joy in the success, nor could we have had any desire, unless the prospect of some other good had been the motive. This holds in all

feature of them does not support hedonism; for we would not be uneasy unless we objected, on some non-hedonist ground, to the situation that makes us uneasy. That is why we respond to our uneasiness by trying to get rid of the situation we object to, not by trying to remove our uneasiness at it. We do not, for instance, try to remove our uneasiness at someone's distress by trying to care less about it; instead, we try to remove their distress.[14] Our moral sentiments include pleasure and pain in certain situations, but they do not aim primarily at pleasure and the absence of pain.[15]

Hutcheson objects fairly to an aspect of Hobbes's and Locke's position that may appear to persist at some places in Shaftesbury.[16] He defends Shaftesbury's predominant position and eliminates any concessions to hedonist egoism. He accuses Hobbes and Locke, as opponents of Scholasticism, of introducing worse confusions than the Scholastics ever introduced, by their attempts to reduce unselfish motives to desires for one's own pleasure.[17]

In opposing indirect hedonism and egoism, Hutcheson also attacks Shaftesbury's other opponents, the theological moralists who try to explain moral motivation by appeal to the desire for rewards and punishments. He argues that such motives cannot explain our admiration for morally good action. If we believed that virtuous people act entirely from the desire for further rewards after death, we would admire them no more than we admire people who do the right actions only for the sake of more immediate rewards.[18] Following Shaftesbury, he allows mixed motives, if the moral motive is sufficient for morally right action and the desire for reward is simply a further incentive.[19] He opposes both the French Quietists and Mandeville, who argue from the prevalence of mixed

our desires, benevolent or selfish, that there is some motive, some end intended, distinct from the joy of success, or the removal of the pain of desire; otherways all desires would be the most fantastic things imaginable, equally ardent toward any trifle as towards the greatest good; since the joy of success and the removal of the uneasiness of desire would be alike in both sorts of desires.' (*SMP* i 3.2, 42 = SB 471) Similar remarks on egoism appear at *SMP* i 2.4, 23; i 3.4, 45; i 3.6, 50. Hutcheson's argument against hedonism is developed more fully and more carefully by Butler, whose influence is clear here and elsewhere in *SMP*; see §715.

[14] 'If our sole intention, in compassion or pity, was the removal of our pain, we should run away, shut our eyes, divert our thoughts from the miserable object, to avoid the pain of compassion, which we seldom do: nay, we crowd about such objects, and voluntarily expose ourselves to pain . . .' (*IMGE* 2.8 = L 111 = SB 104) See §810.

[15] Hutcheson attacks the Cyrenaics and Epicureans, *SMP* i 7.16, 148.   [16] See Shaftesbury, §610.

[17] 'Whatever confusion the schoolmen introduced into philosophy, some of their keenest adversaries seem to threaten it with a worse kind of confusion, by attempting to take away some of the most immediate simple perceptions, and to explain all approbation, condemnation, pleasure and pain, by some intricate relations to the perceptions of the external senses. In like manner they have treated our desires and affections, making the most generous, kind and disinterested of them to proceed from self-love, by some subtle trains of reasoning, to which honest hearts are often wholly strangers.' (*NCPA*, Pref. = Garrett 4) Just as the rationalists try to abandon the division between intellect and will, egoists try to explain away the division between self-regarding and other-regarding affections.

[18] 'But that the approbation is founded upon the apprehension of a disinterested desire partly exciting the agent is plain from this, that not only obedience to an evil deity in doing mischief, or even in performing tri-fling ceremonies, only from hope of reward or prospect of avoiding punishment, but even obedience to a good deity only from the same motives, without any love or gratitude towards him, and with a perfect indifference to the happiness or misery of mankind, abstracting from this private interest, would meet with no approbation.' (*IMGE* 2.4 = L 222)

[19] 'Secular rewards annexed to virtue, and actually influencing the agent further than his benevolence would, diminish the moral good as far as they were necessary to move the agent to the action, or to make him do more good than otherwise he would have done; for by increasing the interest . . . to be subtracted, they diminish the benevolence. But additional interests which were not necessary to have moved the agent, such as the rewards of a good being for actions which he would have undertaken without a reward, do not diminish the virtue.' (*IMGE* 7.9 = L 188–9 = SB 181) On Shaftesbury and Balguy on mixed motives see §§612, 669.

motives to the rarity of genuine virtue.[20] Still, simple desire for rewards cannot constitute a morally admirable motive by itself; our admiration presupposes some disinterested motive.[21]

634. Prudential Hedonism

Hutcheson believes that psychological hedonism is false, because it gives a false account of other-regarding action. But, in contrast to Shaftesbury, he also rejects the traditional eudaemonist view that one's happiness may include actions and states of character. He accepts prudential hedonism—the identification of one's own good and one's own happiness with pleasure.[22] For a prudential hedonist, self-interested reasoning is about ways of maximizing pleasure; any aims that do not aim at maximizing my pleasure do not aim at my happiness or my good.

Prudential hedonism, however, does not seem plausible without psychological hedonism.[23] It seems arbitrary to identify one's own good with pleasure, and to ignore the objects apart from pleasure that we recognize as possible objects of pursuit. Hutcheson does not explain why he accepts prudential hedonism. He argues that our moral sentiments and moral sense are not expressions of desires for our own pleasure, and he infers that they are not self-interested desires. He assumes that psychological egoism collapses with psychological hedonism. Similarly, he assumes that the supremacy of the desire for one's own happiness would imply the supremacy of a selfish desire.

This assumption makes it difficult for him to understand the eudaemonism of the ancient moralists. He interprets it in two different ways: (1) He suggest that eudaemonists recognize unselfish desires not arising from self-love, but 'subject' these desires to the selfish desire for one's own pleasure.[24] (2) He suggests that the ancients treat the desire for one's own happiness as the starting-point of action, from which we may develop desires that are not focussed on happiness. In his support he appeals to their views on friendship and on patriotism.[25]

He acknowledges that eudaemonist views, whichever way we interpret them, do not deny unselfish desire and action. But he still assumes that their conception of the ultimate end is selfish. He overlooks the possibility that some of the ends of unselfish affections are parts of perfection and happiness, not simply means to it; for he assumes that if the 'kind'

---

[20] On Mandeville see Kaye in *FB*, pp. lii–lvii; cxxiv–cxxviii. Kaye's account of Mandeville's opponents does not distinguish (i) those who deny that a virtuous person can have any non-moral motive for a virtuous action from (ii) those who deny that a non-moral motive by itself is insufficient for virtue. Since Kaye speaks as though both classes held the first view, he gives the impression that most moralists held a more rigorous view than they really held. Some moralists, however, seem to accept Mandeville's conception; see §669.

[21] Here Waterland disagrees with Mandeville. See §872.   [22] On Shaftesbury see §610.

[23] Sidgwick, *ME* i 4, rejects psychological hedonism, but in Book ii and in iii 14 he defends prudential hedonism.

[24] 'Or shall we deny any original calm determination toward a public interest; allowing only a variety of particular ultimate kind affections; not indeed arising from self-love, or directly aiming at private good as their natural termination, and yet in all our deliberate counsels about the general tenor of our conduct, subjected, in common with all the particular appetites and passions of the selfish kind, to the original impulse in each one toward his own perfection and happiness? This last seems to be the scheme of some excellent authors both ancient and modern.' (*SMP* i 3.6, 51)

[25] *IMGE* 3.15 = L 237.

affections are subordinate to happiness, they are subordinate to an essentially selfish end. He maintains that moral sentiments are independent of our desire for our own happiness; but, given the possibility of non-hedonistic eudaemonism, his argument against psychological hedonism does not rule out every egoist account of the basis of morality.[26]

635. Arguments for a Moral Sense: Against Egoism

If moral reasons are not derived from self-interest, they must provide sufficient reasons by themselves, without reference to any more ultimate reasons. Our recognition, for instance, that this action promotes the public good must provide—in conjunction with the relevant desire—a reason for doing it, without appeal to any further self-interested consideration. But a simple desire for the good of others for their own sake does not make someone morally good. Even if such a desire is entirely non-self-regarding, we could have it without approving of our action. It is characteristic of a morally good person, however, to approve of this desire, whether in himself or in someone else; that is the essentially reflexive element of morality. To make a moral judgment on an action is not simply to add another desire to our initial desire to do the action; it is to express the view that this desire is right and appropriate for an agent in these circumstances.

A rationalist might accept these arguments. If promotion of the public good is a sufficient justification and admits no further justification, perhaps reason recognizes this justification.[27] Similarly, the reflexive character of moral judgment may result from rational recognition of the appropriate desire.[28]

Hutcheson, however, believes that his arguments against psychological egoism also refute rationalism. Our moral judgments do not rest on reasoning about consequences because they do not rest on reasoning at all; they are too immediate to be the product of reasoning. If we had to depend on reason, our moral judgments would be wavering and unreliable. God's goodness provides us with a moral sense, so that we are not left to work out the right actions by our limited rational capacities.[29] If we are as acute as Cumberland and Pufendorf, reflexion on our own advantage will lead us to the actions that the moral sense approves; but the moral sense, directly approving benevolent actions, reaches the same conclusion more immediately and reliably.[30]

---

[26] Cf. Kemp Smith, PDH 35–8.

[27] Reid rightly points to this gap in the argument from the limits of justifying reasons to the existence of a moral sense. See Reid, EAP v 7 = H 675b = R 939, criticizing Hume, who at this point relies on Hutcheson's argument.

[28] Butler and Reid agree with Hutcheson on the reflexive character of moral judgment. But they do not infer that moral judgments are not a product of reason. See §§715, 842.

[29] 'The weakness of our reason, and the avocations arising from the infirmities and necessities of our nature are so great, that very few men could ever have formed those long deductions of reason, which show some actions to be in the whole advantageous to the agent, and their contraries pernicious. The author of nature has much better furnished us for a virtuous conduct than some moralists seem to imagine, by almost as quick and powerful instructions as we have for the preservation of our bodies.' (IMGE, Pref. = L 9)

[30] 'For, even upon the supposition of a contrary sense, every rational being must still have been solicitous in some degree about his own external happiness: reflexion on the circumstances of mankind in this world would have suggested, that universal benevolence and a social temper, or a certain course of external actions, would most effectually promote the external good of every one, according to the reasonings of Cumberland and Puffendorf; while at the same time this perverted sense of morality would have made us uneasy in such a course, and inclined us to the quite contrary, viz.

This argument for the moral sense as opposed to reason, directly addresses only those opponents who identify reason with strictly self-interested calculation.[31] Hutcheson assumes that moral properties can be matters for rational judgments only if they are found to promote one's self-interest.[32] But his observations on the immediacy of moral judgments could also be used against opponents who treat them as the product of non-egoistic reasoning. Hutcheson legitimately insists that any adequate account of moral judgments has to explain their immediacy.

But this requirement does not rule out all rationalist views known to Hutcheson. The appeal to immediacy does not seem to count against Clarke's views. For Clarke does not believe that moral judgments are rational because they are the conclusions of complex calculations of self-interest, or because they depend on any other complicated process of reasoning. As he points out, many mathematical and logical judgments appear to be immediate, but do not seem to belong to a sense.

Since the *Inquiry* considers only egoism as a viable alternative, Hutcheson tends to speak as though we must believe in a moral sense if we are to allow disinterested action. This is how he presents the issue in his early essay on Mandeville. According to Mandeville, all apparently virtuous action is really self-interested, resulting from the desire for one's own pleasure or for some means to it.[33] Hutcheson answers by defending 'kind affections' and a moral sense, without distinction.[34] We might suppose, therefore, that belief in a moral sense commits us only to recognition of disinterested action. But Hutcheson intends more than this; he also means to assimilate moral judgments to the senses rather than reason.

He connects the immediacy of moral judgments with their passivity. We seem to receive them from external reality just as we receive ideas of sensory qualities.[35] We might, then, take

barbarity, cruelty, and fraud; and universal war, according to Mr. Hobbes, would really have been our natural state; so that in every action we must have been distracted by two contrary principles, and perpetually miserable, and dissatisfied when we followed the directions of either.' (*IMGE* 7.12 = L 196 = SB 186)

[31] 'This moral sense of beauty in actions and affections may appear strange at first view. Some of our moralists themselves are offended at it in my Lord Shaftesbury; so much are they accustomed to deduce every approbation or aversion from rational views of private interest . . .' (*IMGE*, Pref. = L9)

[32] Cf. Grove's argument for a basic sentiment of benevolence, §878.

[33] See Mandeville's attack on allegedly disinterested action: 'There is no merit in saving an innocent babe ready to drop into the fire; the action is neither good nor bad, and what benefit soever the infant received, we only obliged our selves; for to have seen it fall, and not strove to hinder it, would have caused a pain, which self-preservation compelled us to prevent: nor has a rich prodigal, that happens to be of a commiserating temper, and loves to gratify his passions, greater virtue to boast of, when he relieves an object of compassion with what to himself is a trifle.' (*FB* i 56(Kaye) = R 270)

[34] 'Suppose the scheme of almost all moralists except Epicureans to be true; "that we have in our nature kind affections to different degrees, that we have a moral sense, determining us to approve them whenever they are observed, and all actions which flow from them; that we are naturally bound together by the desire of esteem from each other, and by compassion; and that withal we have self-love or desire of private good." What would be the consequence of this constitution, or the appearances in human nature? All men would call those actions virtuous which they imagine do tend to the public good: where men differ in opinions of the natural tendencies of actions, they must differ in approbation or condemnation; they will find pleasure in contemplating or reflecting on their own kind affections and actions; they will delight in the society of the kind, good-natured, and beneficent; they will be uneasy upon seeing or even hearing of the misery of others, and be delighted with the happiness of any persons beloved; men will have regard to private good as well as public; and when other circumstances are equal, will prefer what tends to private advantage. Now these are the direct and necessary consequences of this supposition; and yet this penetrating swaggerer, who surpasses all writers of ethics, makes those very appearances proofs against the hypothesis.' (*TL*, Letter 6, 119–21)

[35] 'We must . . . have other perceptions of moral actions, than those of advantage; and that power of receiving these perceptions may be called a moral sense, since the definition agrees to it, viz., a determination of the mind,

belief in a moral sense to support moral realism. Hutcheson argues, following Shaftesbury, that we have a sense of right and wrong that cannot be extinguished by a theoretical commitment to egoism.[36] Even if we try to be Hobbesians, we have to admit that we immediately recognize and approve of moral goodness in people and actions.

Not every sort of sensory awareness, however, includes detection of external reality. Hutcheson argues that beauty is an idea 'raised in us' by objects (IB 1.9 = L 23), to which nothing similar in the objects corresponds. If we recognize beauty in an object we are aware of objective properties of it, such as order, symmetry, and proportion; but though these properties give us the idea of beauty, they are not the beauty in the object.[37]

A subjectivist analysis would cast doubt on part of Shaftesbury's defence of his 'moral realist' view that moral properties are aspects of reality and not simply creations of our minds through choices, desires, or legislation. The Inquiry does not show what Hutcheson thinks about this part of Shaftesbury's position. He does not discuss the conflict between Shaftesbury's aims, which he shares, and the result he has reached.[38] One might argue that

to receive any idea from the presence of an object which occurs to us, independent on our will.' (IMGE 1.1 = L 90 = R 307; cf. Passions §1 = R 356) 'These determinations to be pleased with certain complex forms, the author chooses to call senses; distinguishing them from the powers which commonly go by that name, by calling our power of perceiving the beauty of regularity, order, harmony, an internal sense; and that determination to approve affections, actions, or characters of rational agents, which we call virtuous, by the name of a moral sense.' (IMGE, Pref. = L 8–9) 'The quality approved by our moral sense is conceived to reside in the person approved, and to be a perfection and dignity in him: approbation of another's virtue is not conceived as making the approver happy or virtuous or worthy, though 'tis attended with some small pleasure.' (IMGE 1.8 = L 218 = R 314)

[36] Turnbull defends Shaftesbury by similar arguments, defending belief in a moral sense against 'nominal moralists' (as Shaftesbury calls them): 'On the one hand, if there be no such sense in our make, virtue is really but an empty name; that is, the fitness or approveableness of affections, actions, and characters in themselves is an idle dream that hath no foundation, but advantage or interest is all that we have to consider or compute in our determinations. But, on the other side, if there be really a sense of beauty, fitness, or agreeableness in affections, actions, and characters in themselves, independently of all other considerations, then it plainly follows that we are made not merely to consider our private good, or what quantity of external safety, ease, profit, or gratification an action may bring along with it; but to rise higher in our contemplation, and chiefly to inquirewhat is fit and becoming, agreeable, laudable, and beautiful in itself.' (PMP 134). In support of his belief in a moral sense Turnbull (138–9) cites Cicero on natural law (quoted in §197). Cf. §715.

[37] '. . . by absolute or original beauty, is not understood any quality supposed to be in the object, that should of itself be beautiful, without relation to any mind which perceives it: For beauty, like other names of sensible ideas, properly denotes the perception of some mind; so cold, heat, sweet, bitter, denote the sensations in our minds, to which perhaps there is no resemblance in the objects that excite these ideas in us, however we generally imagine that there is something in the object just like our perception' (Beauty 1.17 = L 27). This discussion of beauty appears in the first treatise in An Inquiry into the Original of our Ideas of Beauty and Virtue. The second treatise is An Inquiry concerning the Original of our Ideas of Virtue or Moral Good. It has nothing similar to the remarks about beauty in the treatise on beauty. Hence it is not clear whether Hutcheson accepts a subjectivist analysis of moral goodness parallel to his analysis of beauty.

[38] Doddridge sees this difference between Hutcheson and Shaftesbury, and takes Shaftesbury to be closer to the rationalist position of Balguy (which Doddridge favours): 'It may be observed by the way, that though Lord Shaftesbury uses many expressions which Dr Hutcheson has adopted, yet it seems that he in the main falls in with the [rationalist] account given above; since he considers virtue as founded on "the eternal measure and immutable relation of things", or in other words as consisting "in a certain just disposition of a rational creature towards the moral objects of right and wrong."' (Course i 190 [1794 edn.].) Doddridge refers to Shaftesbury, ICV i 2.3 = K 175, quoted in §611. These differences between Shaftesbury and Hutcheson are obscured in the brief treatment by Fowler, SH 183–200, who emphasizes the similarities without considering the significant differences. His emphasis partly results from his attention to the features of Shaftesbury that are close to Hutcheson: 'The analogy drawn between beauty and virtue, the functions assigned to the moral sense, the position that the benevolent feelings form an original and irreducible part of our nature, and the unhesitating adoption of the principle that the test of virtuous action is its tendency to promote the general welfare, or good of the whole, are at once obvious and fundamental points of agreement between the two authors' (183). Similarly, Fowler's chapter on Shaftesbury (102) does not discuss the metaphysical aspects of Shaftesbury's moral realism (though

if his account of the moral sense reaches a subjectivist conclusion, one ought to consider whether (i) something is wrong with his account of a sense, or (ii) he has applied this account wrongly to the moral sense, or (iii) he is wrong to claim that we are aware of moral properties by a moral sense. If we reject the first and second possibilities, and we believe that a realist position is plausible, we may find the third possibility attractive. The *Inquiry* does not pursue these questions any further. Though Hutcheson seems to commit himself to a subjectivist account of the moral sense, he does not develop such an account.

636. Voluntarism and Divine Commands

Hutcheson follows Shaftesbury in rejecting the views of Hobbes and Mandeville that treat morality as the outcome of decisions or conventions or practices.[39] According to Hobbes, morality accords with human nature only in the specific circumstances of the commonwealth. Hutcheson argues that even when circumstances do not make morality beneficial for us (conceiving our benefit in a self-confined sense), morality is still in accord with human nature.

Hutcheson answers Hobbes by appealing to our actual desires and motives, and specifically to sympathy and benevolence, to show that, apart from our selfish advantage, we still have a motive that is strong enough to move us to act morally. He accepts Hobbes's view about what makes something natural; for he argues that we often have a predominant desire to do what is morally right, even apart from any further benefit we gain from it.

Since morality has this natural basis, theological voluntarists are wrong to identify moral rightness with conformity to the divine will or divine legislation.[40] God's arbitrary will and inclination does not make it right to do what promotes the good of humanity. Voluntarism gives a false account of moral knowledge and motivation. In order to know what is morally right, we ought not to ask simply what God requires; nor ought we to act simply out of a desire to conform to divine commands. We should rely on our moral sense, and on unselfish motivation.

Since voluntarism is mistaken, we should also recognize a natural law antecedent to any positive legislation by God or by human legislators. The first principles of natural law are eternal and immutable, and natural law imposes obligations even in the state of nature.[41] Nor are they the result of the arbitrary choice of God and the exercise of divine power. God does not create goodness by arbitrary will; God is necessarily good, and therefore benevolent.

Fowler alludes to them at 89: 'actions being denominated good or just, not by the arbitrary will of God, but in virtue of some quality exiting in themselves').

[39] Mandeville is most plausibly taken to understand morality as the result of evolving conventions and practices, rather than deliberate decisions and artifices. See Kaye in *FB* i, pp. lxiv–lxvi.

[40] 'The primary notion under which we approve is not merely a conformity to the divine will or laws. We seriously inquire about the moral goodness, justice, rectitude, of the divine nature itself, and likewise of his will or laws; these characters make up our common praises of them. They surely mean more than that his will or laws are conformable to themselves. This we might ascribe to an artful impure demon. Conformity to his nature is not conformity to immensity, eternity, omnipotence. 'Tis conformity to his goodness, holiness, justice. These moral perfections then must be previously known, or else the definition by conformity to them is useless.' (*SMP* i 4.3, 56)

[41] *SMP* ii 3.11, 273; ii 4.1, 281.

Hence God approves of some actions rather than others because they benefit humanity.[42] God's goodness ultimately explains our having our moral sense; for since it is good for humanity that we are benevolent and approve benevolence, God, being benevolent, gives us a moral sense that approves of benevolent action.[43] Hutcheson combines Shaftesbury's opposition to voluntarism with his own views about the moral sense and benevolence.

637. Reason, Desire, and Action

Though Shaftesbury anticipates Hutcheson in speaking of a moral sense, his remarks on the sense of right and wrong do not deny that moral judgment is rational; they simply seem to assert that we have some immediate and disinterested grasp of moral goodness. But Hutcheson goes further than Shaftesbury on this point; for he intends his doctrine of a moral sense to refute a rationalist account of moral judgment. We might suppose that he simply means his anti-rationalism to rule out an indirect egoist account of moral judgment. Perhaps he means only that moral judgment is not based on reasoning about good consequences for oneself. If that is all he means, he does not exclude the possibility that moral judgment is based on, or incorporates, some different exercise of reason. But he never recognizes this possibility. The reason for his failure to recognize it becomes clear in the *Illustrations*, where he expands his account of the moral sense in relation to some of Hobbes's and Locke's views on action and motivation.[44]

Hobbes's account of morality rests on his moral psychology, and in particular on his conception of practical reason. He denies that practical reason is the source of any distinctive ends; its only function is to find means to ends that are independently fixed by non-rational desires.[45] Locke and Hutcheson develop this Hobbesian view. We have found it useful, in discussing both the mediaeval disputes and the dispute between Hobbes and Bramhall, to distinguish intellectualism (the view that action depends primarily on intellect rather than will) from rationalism (the view that action depends on passion rather than rational will). Aquinas is a moderate intellectualist, but also a rationalist, whereas Scotus is both a voluntarist and a rationalist. Hobbes's discussion does not distinguish the two positions, and on this point Locke and Hutcheson follow him.

[42] '... "Could not the Deity have given us a different or contrary determination of mind, *viz.* to approve actions upon another foundation than benevolence?" It is certain, there is nothing in this surpassing the natural power of the Deity. But as ... we resolved the constitution of our present sense of beauty into the divine goodness, so with much more obvious reason may we ascribe the present constitution of our moral sense to his goodness. For if the Deity be really benevolent, or delights in the happiness of others, he could not rationally act otherwise, or give us a moral sense upon another foundation, without counteracting his own benevolent intentions.' (*IMGE* 7.12 = L 195–6 = SB 186) Cf. *IMP* 20: God in his goodness has given us a moral sense approving of general good or what is beneficial to the system. '... and the nature of virtue is thus as immutable as the divine wisdom and goodness. Cast the consideration of these perfections of God out of this question, and indeed nothing would remain certain or immutable.'

[43] Hutcheson emphasizes benevolence among God's attributes, and infers that we have to attribute something like the moral sense to God: '... if we can in any way reason concerning the original nature from what we feel in our own, or from any of our notions of excellency or perfection, we must conceive in a Deity some perceptive power analogous to our moral sense, by which he may have self-approbation in certain affections and actions ...' (*SMP* i 9.5, 174–5)

[44] *IMS* was published in 1728, after the second edition of *IMGE* (1726).

[45] This may not be Hobbes's consistent position; he sometimes seems to suggest that prudence is especially characteristic of practical reason. But the anti-rationalist position is his predominant view. See §478.

Hutcheson begins his argument by defending a more moderate position than Hobbesian anti-rationalism. At first he only rejects the extreme intellectualism that makes reasonable action proceed from reason entirely without desire.[46] So far he agrees with Locke. Locke, however, assumes that extreme intellectualism is the 'received opinion', perhaps because he does not distinguish intellectualism from rationalism (which one might indeed take to be a received Scholastic opinion).[47] Hutcheson disagrees with him on this historical point. He claims to support the Scholastic opposition to extreme intellectualism. Authors of 'confused harangues' about motivation by reason alone have shown their historical ignorance.[48]

He claims that desire as well as reason is necessary for action, and that desire is needed for us to aim at an end. In claiming that the ends of action cannot be derived from reason without desire, he believes he follows Aristotle.[49] According to Aristotle, thought by itself moves nothing; the thought that initiates motion must be 'thought for the sake of some end' (*EN* 1139a35–6), which requires desire. Similarly, Aquinas asserts that our cognitive capacity does not move us without desire as intermediary.[50] According to Hutcheson, those who claim that virtue belongs wholly to reason ignore the Scholastic division. The extreme intellectualist claim about virtue is inconsistent with eudaemonism, which assumes an original desire, not derived from reason, for happiness as ultimate end.[51]

In speaking of 'confused harangues' Hutcheson may refer to Clarke and others who believe that the mere awareness of eternal fitnesses moves us to the appropriate action. Clarke's theory of action, no less than his epistemology and his meta-ethics, departs from the Scholastic position, in order to achieve immediacy and certainty. If Hutcheson reasserts the Scholastic view, he does not hold Hobbesian anti-rationalism. The Scholastics distinguish rational will from non-rational passion, but Hobbes rejects that distinction.

---

[46] 'We have indeed many confused harangues on this subject telling us, "We have two principles of action, reason and affection or passion, the former in common with angels, the latter with brutes. No action is wise, or good, or reasonable, to which we are not excited by reason, as distinct from all affections . . ." ' (*IMS* 122) Different varieties of rationalism are helpfully discussed by Wallace, 'Reason'.

[47] Locke; §554.

[48] 'Writers on these subjects should remember the common divisions of the faculties of the soul. That there is (1) reason presenting the natures and relations of things antecedently to any act of will or desire, (2) the will, or *appetitus rationalis*, or the disposition of soul to pursue what is presented as good and to shun evil. Were there no other power in the soul than that of mere contemplation, there would be no affection, volition, desire, action. . . . Both these powers are by the ancients included under the *logos* or *logikon meros*. Below these they place two other powers dependent on the body, the *sensus* and the *appetitus sensitivus*, in which they place the particular passions. The former answers to the understanding and the latter to the will. But the will is forgot of late, and some ascribe to the intellect not only contemplation or knowledge but choice, desire, prosecuting, loving.' (*IMS* 122. Cf. R 357n.) In the penultimate sentence 'the former' might refer to reason and 'the latter' to appetitus rationalis, or (more probably) 'the former' might refer to sense and 'the latter' to sensitive appetite (so that 'answers to' means 'corresponds to' rather than 'belongs to').

[49] 'But are there not also exciting reasons, even previous to any end, moving us to propose one end rather than another? To this Aristotle long ago answered "that there are ultimate ends desired without a view to any thing else, and subordinate ends or objects desired with a view to something else." . . . But as to the ultimate ends, to suppose exciting reasons for them would infer that there is no ultimate end but that we desire one thing for another in an infinite series.' (*IMS* 123; cf. 227)

[50] See *ST* 1a q20 a1 ad1, and §256.

[51] 'They tell us that "virtue should wholly spring from reason"', as if reason or knowledge of any true proposition could ever move us to action where there is no end proposed, and no affection or desire towards that end. These gentlemen should either remember the common doctrine of the schools, or else confute it better; that the *prohairesis* which is necessary in virtuous action is *orexis bouleutikê*; and that virtue needs not only the *logon alêthê*, but the *orexin orthên*. . . .' (*IMGE* 3.15 = L 236) The second sentence is from Hutcheson's footnote, which continues with other Aristotelian references.

638. The Rejection of Rationalism

Hutcheson, however, rejects both moderate intellectualism, and rationalism. He follows Locke in holding that action depends on our having desires for ends that are independent of practical reason. He argues that to avoid an infinite regress of ends in explaining actions, we must recognize basic, non-rational instincts that rest on no further reasons.[52] This argument goes beyond Scholastic moderate intellectualism; for a moderate intellectualist might agree that all action requires desire, but still maintain that reasoning about the good produces the appropriate sort of desire. Though Hutcheson explicitly attacks only extreme intellectualism, his conclusions conflict with both moderate intellectualism and rationalism.

Hutcheson's conception of the relevant options casts doubt on some of his claims about Aristotle and the Scholastics. He relies on Aristotle's claim that deliberation is confined to means to ends, and ends are the objects of wish.[53] He infers that, in this Aristotelian scheme, the most ultimate ends must be taken for granted in any deliberation. And so he concludes that the desire for the highest end, happiness, is not the product of practical reason. All this is a reasonable interpretation of Aristotle. But Hutcheson goes wrong in his claim that the desire for happiness is a non-rational impulse or instinct or, as Locke puts it, 'uneasiness' that is prior to practical reason. In his view, it is a particular instinct, not essential to rational agency.

This is not the Aristotelian view of the desire for happiness. According to Aquinas, the ascription of such a desire is equivalent to the ascription of rational desire to an agent. It is not a particular desire or instinct on a level with a liking for oranges rather than apples. It is the structural feature of other desires that makes them all desires of a rational agent. To have a desire for one's own happiness is to be disposed to pursue each of one's desires to the right degree, so that it does not impede the appropriate satisfaction of other desires. Practical reason, therefore, does not merely find some means to satisfy a non-rational desire that is prior to practical reason. It discovers the nature of happiness by finding the appropriate degree of satisfaction for different desires. In holding this view, Aristotle and Aquinas take a moderate intellectualist view of the relation of reason, will, and desire.

Hutcheson, however, treats happiness as though it were a contingent fact that this is the end of all our desires. He treats extreme intellectualism and his own anti-rationalism as the only options to consider. Both Hutcheson and Locke fail to distinguish extreme from moderate intellectualism, and intellectualism from rationalism, because they look at the traditional view in the light of assumptions that they share with Hobbes.[54]

---

[52] 'Thus ask a being who desires private happiness or has self-love, "What reason excites him to desire wealth?". He will give this reason, "that wealth tends to procure pleasure and ease". Ask his reason for desiring pleasure or happiness. One cannot imagine what propositions he could assign as his exciting reason. This proposition is indeed, true, "There is an instinct or desire fixed in his nature determining him to pursue his happiness". But it is not this reflexion on his own nature, or this proposition, which excites or determines him, but the instinct itself.' (*IMS* 123) 'In the first place the understanding, or the power of reflecting, comparing, judging, makes us capable of discerning the tendencies of the several senses, appetites, actions, gratifications, either to our own happiness, or to that of others, and the comparative values of every object, every gratification. This power judges about the means or the subordinate ends: but about the ultimate ends there is no reasoning. We prosecute them by some immediate disposition or determination of soul, which in the order of action is always prior to all reasoning; as no opinion or judgment can move to action, where there is no prior desire of some end.' (*SMP* i 3.1, 38)

[53] Hutcheson appeals to Aristotle's claims about decision and deliberation, *IMS* 129.   [54] Cf. Hume, §735.

Since Hutcheson assumes that the ultimate end is the object of a non-rational instinct prior to all practical reason, he rejects the traditional conception of happiness as the ultimate object of rational desire. If the desire for happiness is not a distinctively rational desire, happiness cannot be, as Aristotelian eudaemonists suppose, a composite of objects of rational desire. Hutcheson agrees with Locke and Hobbes in substituting a hedonist conception of happiness for the traditional conception.

He approves of the definition of happiness that he attributes to the Old Academy and the Peripatetics: 'constant activity according to the highest virtue in a prosperous course of life' (*IMP* 56). The ancients, in his view, call this the supreme good. Hutcheson agrees with their account for hedonist reasons; he treats it as an account of the source of pleasure and contentment. But he does not agree with Locke and Hobbes in replacing the Aristotelian conception of an ultimate good with a psychological hedonist view that derives all motivation from the desire for one's own pleasure. In his view, motivation must be traced back either to self-love, aiming at our private happiness, or to a special sense or instinct that leads us, as agents and as critics, to take a special interest in benevolence.

The nature of this instinct is not clear. If it moves us because we tend to take pleasure in other people's benevolence, has Hutcheson avoided a hedonist conception of the ultimate end? To understand this aspect of his position, we need to examine his views of motivation more closely, to see how his claims about benevolence and the moral sense fit into his theory.

639. Exciting Reasons and Justifying Reasons

According to Hobbes, deliberation proceeds by anticipation of different degrees of pleasure arousing desires of different strengths, until we reach the last appetite, which moves us to the action. Hutcheson does not treat deliberation as mere anticipation. He marks different roles for reasons and deliberation by distinguishing exciting reasons from justifying reasons: (1) p is an exciting reason for S to do x if and only if p is a truth showing a quality in x exciting S to do x. (2) p is a justifying reason for S to do x if and only if p is a truth showing a quality in x engaging our approbation.[55]

This division might suggest that exciting reasons are those that move me to action, and hence explain my action, and justifying reasons are those that justify it.[56] We can speak of reasons in two contexts: (a) Sometimes we ask 'What is [or was] your reason for doing that?'. We seek an explanation of your action that identifies what motivated or excited you to act. The correct answer is the one that describes what actually moved you. (b) But if we ask 'Why should I do that?' or 'What reason is there to do that?' we do not seek a report on

---

[55] 'When we ask the reason of an action, we sometimes mean, "What truth shows a quality in the action, exciting the agent to do it?" Thus, why does a luxurious man pursue wealth? The reason is given by this truth, "Wealth is useful to pursue pleasures". Sometimes for a reason of action we show the truth expressing a quality engaging our approbation. Thus the reason of hazarding life in a just war is that "It tends to preserve our honest countrymen or evidences public spirit." The reason for temperance and against luxury is given thus, "Luxury evidences a selfish base temper." The former sort of reasons we will call exciting and the latter justifying. Now we shall find that all exciting reasons presuppose instincts and affections and the justifying presuppose a moral sense.' (*IMS* 121; cf. 227)

[56] Hence his distinction seems quite close to Raz's distinction between 'guiding' (= justifying) and 'explanatory' (= exciting) reasons (Raz, ed., *PR* 2–4). See also Smith, *MP* ch. 4.

anyone's actual motive; we seek a justification that could be offered, to provide (let us say) a normative reason.[57]

This distinction appears in the contrast between predicting and deciding. Others may predict what I will do by knowing about the motives that influence me in these circumstances; they rely on knowledge of the reasons that move me. But normally when I ask 'What am I going to do?' I mean 'What am I to do?', a deliberative rather than a predictive question; I look for normative reasons rather than explanatory reasons. I might raise a similar deliberative question by asking 'What do I want?' or 'Do I want that?'. Despite their grammatical form, these questions normally ask for reasons to want one thing rather than another, and so ask for normative reasons. We may have a good normative reason to act, but remain unmoved by it. Equally, a particular reason may have moved us act, but we may see that it gave us no good reason for acting, and so does not justify our action.

Though these are distinct types of reasons, it is not an accident that they are both called 'reasons'. A motivating and explanatory reason appears to justify us to some degree, and a normative reason is capable in some circumstances of motivating us. Still, a motivating reason may not justify us adequately, and an adequate justification may not move us to act.

The division between the two types of reasons becomes even clearer if we recognize external reasons—states of affairs that constitute good reasons for A to do F, even though A's doing F neither satisfies A's desires nor would satisfy them in appropriate counterfactual circumstances.[58] A's needs and A's welfare, for instance, provide good external reasons for A to do F even though they do not satisfy A's actual or counterfactual desires. We can recognize a division between explanatory and normative reasons without also agreeing that some normative reasons are external reasons; but if we recognize external reasons, we must take some normative reasons to be even less closely connected to desires than internal normative reasons are.

According to Hobbes, recognition of sufficient reasons for my action is simply awareness of sufficient motives for doing it, and deliberation is simply the awareness of successive desires resulting in the strongest desire.[59] But if we recognize normative reasons, these are the basis for deliberation and action. If, for instance, we recognize that the contribution of an action to the public good is a good reason for doing the action, the normative reason may become our motivating or explanatory reason. To recognize this consideration as a good normative reason is to recognize that it ought to be our motivating reason; but it was a good normative reason whether or not we recognized it or acted on it. A desire is rational, then, insofar as it responds to the weight of normative reasons that we recognize in the course of deliberation. If we have rational desires, we respond to apparently better reasons, and do not simply register the comparative strength of desires.

---

[57] Hutcheson also discusses justifying and exciting reasons at *SMP* i 4.3, 57.

[58] The appropriate counterfactual circumstances are those that can be specified without circularity, so as not to include 'if A were to recognize the appropriate external reasons'. On external reasons see §268.

[59] If he recognized normative reasons, he would introduce Butler's distinction (anticipated by Cudworth; see §548) between authority and power. In Butler's view, the principle with greater authority is the one that tells us the reasons that make it reasonable to do x rather than y. See §683.

Hutcheson, however, does not accept this account of rational desire, because he does not recognize normative reasons. As he understands justifying reasons, they exist only if I actually approve of something; hence, if I have justifying reasons for benefiting others without regard to myself, I have a moral sense.[60] A search for justifying reasons, as Hutcheson conceives them, is not a search for normative reasons. In looking for normative reasons for an action, we examine the pros and cons of the action itself. But in looking for Hutcheson's justifying reasons, we examine our sentiments to see whether the proposed action arouses a feeling of approval. Since justifying reasons require actual feelings of approval, they move us to action by themselves, so that we sometimes act without exciting reasons.[61]

Sometimes we might reflect on ourselves and our actions in this way. If A asks 'Do I really like B?', A may be asking a question that is to be answered by introspection and recollection; perhaps A will discover on reflexion that A finds B entertaining and charming, but does not really like B. But deliberative questions are not normally like this; they do not normally ask for an accurate report on one's feelings of approval, but for an assessment of the proposed action, on the assumption that one's feelings of approval ought to respond appropriately to the assessment. Hutcheson leaves out this aspect of deliberation and normative reasons.

He does not disagree radically, therefore, with Hobbes's view of motivation and practical reason. For he supposes that the recognition of a reason—exciting or justifying—is simply the recognition that something arouses a particular sort of non-rational desire or sentiment that was present apart from the recognition of this sort of reason. Deliberation, therefore, proceeds by the awareness of desires or sentiments aroused by different considerations that are presented to us. This conception of deliberation prevents us from recognizing distinctively rational desires. Hutcheson's account of reasons matches his anti-rationalism about desire and reason. In his view, the recognition of reasons is simply the recognition of considerations arousing desires. He accepts the most controversial feature in Hobbes's account of deliberation.

640. Freewill

The claim that ends are not the objects of distinctively rational desires explains Hutcheson's view on freewill, and especially his opposition to rationalist views. The rationalist Balguy argues that if we are moved wholly by non-rational desires for ends, we do not act freely and responsibly; he assumes that merit requires freedom, and freedom requires the capacity for

---

[60] 'When we ask the reason of an action, we sometimes mean the truth which excites the agent to it by showing that it is apt to gratify some inclination of his mind . . . At other times by the reason of actions we mean the truth which shows a quality in the action of any person engaging the approbation either of the agent or the spectator or which shows it to be morally good.' (IMS 226–7) ' . . . what reason makes us approve the happiness of a system? Here we must recur to a sense or kind affections' (IMS 129).

[61] 'If this being have also public affections, what are the exciting reasons for observing faith or hazarding his life in war? He will assign this truth as a reason, such conduct tends to the good of mankind. Go a step further, why does he pursue the good of mankind? If his affections be really disinterested, without any selfish view, he has no exciting reason; the public good is an ultimate end in this series of desires.' (IMS 228) No further reason can be given to move us to be concerned about the good of mankind; that is an ultimate concern moving us to action.

rational motivation.[62] Hutcheson answers that non-rational desire is the basis of all action,[63] so that if freedom really required motivation by reason rather than non-rational desire, no action could ever be free. Even if action on 'mere election' without any reason to choose one or another option were possible, it would be morally insignificant, and not a candidate for merit.[64]

Hutcheson believes that his opponents must assume that acting freely is acting without a reason, because he takes 'acting without a reason' to cover three different cases: (1) Choosing x over y without seeing something to choose between x and y. (2) Choosing x over y without desiring x as better than y. (3) Choosing x over y without having a stronger non-rational desire for x. These different cases are relevant to different disputes with different opponents.[65] A voluntarist such as Scotus or Ockham who does not reduce the will to a passion argues that all three types of choice are possible, but an intellectualist such as Aquinas denies the possibility of the first sort of choice. With qualifications, Aquinas also denies the possibility of the second sort of choice; the qualifications depend on the role he assigns to election in incontinent action.[66] But he affirms, as Balguy affirms against Hutcheson, the possibility of the third sort of choice. From either a voluntarist or an intellectualist point of view, free action requires the determination of action by something other than the superior strength of a non-rational desire.

All these views assume that we can avoid acting on our strongest non-rational desire. But, according to Hutcheson, if we could avoid this, we could thereby choose x over y for no reason and on the basis of no recognized difference between them—the first of the three alleged possibilities mentioned above. Since Hutcheson rejects the first possibility, he thinks he is entitled to reject the second and third also. His sentimentalist view traces actions back to impulses and passions rather than to rational choice, but it does not (in his view) threaten freedom. He rejects only the alleged freedom that requires action without a sufficient motive.

This conception of freedom relies on Hutcheson's analysis of action and motivation, which will not persuade anyone who disputes his views on freedom. If we allow distinctively rational motivation, we will deny that we must always act on our strongest non-rational motive. We may allow that we act on our 'strongest' desire, if we take 'strength' to include

---

[62] 'Some will not allow any merit in actions flowing from kind instincts. "Merit", say they, "attends actions to which we are excited by reason alone, or to which we freely determine ourselves. The operation of instincts or affections is necessary, and not voluntary; nor is there more merit in them than in the shining of the sun, the fruitfulness of a tree, or the overflowing of a stream, which are all publicly useful." ' (IMS 165) On Balguy see §657.

[63] 'Now we endeavoured already to show, "that no reason can excite to action previously to some end, and that no end can be proposed without some instinct or affection." What then can be meant by being excited by reason as distinct from all motion of instincts or affections?' (IMS 165–6)

[64] 'Then determining ourselves freely, does it mean acting without any motive or exciting reason? If it did not mean this, it cannot be opposed to acting from instinct or affections, since all motives or reasons presuppose them. If it means this, "that merit is found only in actions done without motive or affection, by mere election, without prepollent desire of one action or end rather than its opposite, or without desire of that pleasure which some suppose follows upon any election by a natural connexion" then let any man consider whether he ever acts in this manner by mere election, without any previous desire. And again, let him consult his own breast whether any such kind of action gains his approbation?' (IMS 166–7) The first sentence above seems to suggest that all action has an exciting reason. This conflicts with Hutcheson's view that when we act on a justifying reason we act without an exciting reason. His claims are consistent if we take 'motive or exciting reason' to be alternatives, not equivalents, and take motives to be justifying reasons.

[65] On different Scholastic positions see §§390–1.   [66] Aquinas on incontinence; §295.

the strength of reasons as well as the non-rational force of desires.[67] But if we understand 'strength' so broadly, it allows action on the desire supported by stronger reasons against a more forceful non-rational desire, contrary to Hutcheson's view.

According to Aquinas and others, the capacity to act on apparently stronger reasons is essential for freedom. If human action rested on a non-rational passion aiming at the ultimate end, it would not be free, but in fact it is free because the desire for the final good is not a non-rational passion. Hutcheson ignores this account of freedom. It depends on a rationalist account of rational will and desire, but he does not recognize rationalism as an option distinct from extreme intellectualism and from his own anti-rationalism. Since he does not refute a rationalist account of freedom, he does not show that questions about freedom are irrelevant to morality.

641. Anti-rationalism and the Moral Sense

Anti-rationalism about reason and desire supports Hutcheson's moral epistemology. In the *Inquiry* it is difficult to see why he ascribes moral judgment to a moral sense, and why he prefers this view to a non-egoist rationalist account. In the *Illustrations*, however, he recognizes Clarke's rationalism as a third option besides his position and the egoism that he has rejected in the *Inquiry*.[68] He rejects this third option, because he believes that anti-rationalism about motivation also requires anti-rationalism about moral judgment. Rational beliefs alone cannot produce either exciting or justifying reasons. Non-rational affections must be presupposed; they explain why our belief that something promotes the public good makes a difference to our action. Since Clarke is an extreme rationalist and intellectualist, he assumes that the rational recognition of fitnesses ensures the right motivation. But since Hutcheson rejects the extreme intellectualist assumptions, he also rejects rationalism about moral judgment.

He does not consider the possibility that moral judgments belong to reason, but are insufficient for motivation. He assumes that a moral judgment must motivate; every time we make a moral judgment that we ought to do a particular action, we must be moved (to some extent) to do that action. He therefore assumes an internal logical connexion between accepting the truth of a moral judgment and being motivated to act on it.

Why should we admit this internal logical connexion? Could we not make a moral judgment about an action, and so cite a normative reason for it, without having any feeling of approbation? Hutcheson answers that moral judgments include awareness of obligation, and since awareness of obligation to do x is awareness of a motive for doing x, moral judgment requires awareness of motivation.[69] He assumes that obligation implies some type

---

[67] Reid speaks of 'animal strength' and 'rational strength'; see §832.

[68] 'There have been many ways of speaking introduced, which seem to signify something different from both the former opinions. Such as these, that "morality of actions consists in conformity to reason, or difformity from it:" that "virtue is acting according to the absolute fitness and unfitness of things", or agreeably to the natures or relations of things, and many others in different authors. To examine these is the design of the following sections; and to explain more fully how the moral sense alleged to be in mankind, must be presupposed even in these schemes.' (*IMS* 119 = R 359).

[69] 'When we say one is obliged to an action, we either mean, (1) that the action is necessary to obtain happiness to the agent, or to avoid misery, or, (2) that every spectator, or he himself upon reflexion, must approve his action, and disapprove his omitting it, if he considers fully all its circumstances. The former meaning of the word obligation presupposes selfish affections, and the sense of private happiness; the latter meaning includes the moral sense.' (*IMS* 130)

of necessity or compulsion, and that the only relevant type of necessity is some necessity in the motives of the person obliged or in the moral judge.

This assumption about necessity and motivation is doubtful. Hutcheson does not consider, as Suarez and Cumberland do, the imposer as the source of obligation. Nor does he consider the rationalist view that the source of the relevant kind of necessity lies in what we are obliged to do, in the obligatory state of affairs itself. [70] But the rationalist view is plausible, since we have good reason to regard the necessity of obligation as a feature of normative reasons rather than motives. Rational deliberators consider the reasons favouring different options, and they act on the reasons that seem best. The reasons that present obligations are those that present the relevant sort of necessity; rational deliberation recognizes this necessity. The appropriate motivation, then, is a response to the recognition of the necessity contained in obligation, but the obligation does not consist in the motivation. According to this picture, we distinguish three elements: (1) the reasons that constitute the obligation, (2) the recognition of the obligation, and (3) the motive resulting from the recognition. Hutcheson, however, seems to collapse the three elements into one.

To explain Hutcheson's treatment of obligation and motivation, we may recall the influence of Hobbes's conception of deliberation. According to Hobbes, deliberation does not include the recognition of reasons and necessities apart from one's desires, but it is a sequence of anticipatory desires elicited by the prospects of pleasure resulting from the different options. Hutcheson's analysis of justifying and exciting reasons also takes deliberation to be a sequence of anticipatory desires. Hence he takes the recognition of reasons to include desire.

Hobbes's understanding of deliberation is part of his reduction of normative facts to psychological facts. Hutcheson disagrees with the specific reduction that Hobbes attempts, since he rejects the reduction of benevolence and moral approval to selfish desire. But he still takes each normative fact to be about a mental state of the subject. Since moral judgments state a reason for acting and an obligation to act, Hutcheson assumes that they describe our motivation.

His internalism about moral judgment and motivation, therefore, rests on his analysis of reasons. From the plausible assumption that connects obligation with reasons he infers an internal connexion between obligation and motives. The connexion between moral judgment and obligation seems to him to require an internal connexion between moral judgment and motives. His Hobbesian account of deliberation makes it difficult to avoid the aspects of a Hobbesian account of obligation that connect obligation with awareness of motivation.

642. A Subjectivist Account of the Moral Sense

Hutcheson defends anti-rationalism and internalism in the *Illustrations*, not in the *Inquiry*. They help him to explain and to support an anti-realist conception of the moral sense.

[70] This is Cudworth's and Clarke's view of obligation. Suarez agrees with it, except that he takes the intrinsic necessity to belong to duty (debitum) rather than to obligation (as he conceives it). His view also provides an account of moral requirements that dispenses with Hutcheson's assumptions about motivation.

In saying that a sense involves reception of an idea he does not mean that every idea we receive corresponds to some genuine feature of the object itself. 'Perceptions' that are 'proper ideas of sensation' do not present any external reality; for, though they are signs of some external reality, the reality need not resemble them.[71] Since objects themselves are not (for instance) coloured, our ideas of secondary qualities do not present actual qualities of the objects; secondary qualities are ideas caused by objects, not qualities in objects themselves.

Similarly, the moral sense is aware of the moral goodness of an action, which is not a feature of the action itself. Hutcheson distinguishes three aspects of a benevolent action: (1) the agent's action; (2) the beneficiary's reaction to the agent's action; (3) the spectator's reaction to the agent's action and to the beneficiary's reaction. The third aspect—the spectator's reaction to the agent and to the beneficiary—involves a feeling of approbation, and this reaction makes it appropriate to speak of a moral sense.[72] The feeling of approval corresponds to the idea of colour in the case of sight.

A moral judgment, therefore, is similar to a sensory judgment because it refers both to the external world and to the state of the person making the judgment. The colours we attribute to external objects are 'only perceptions in our minds, and not images of any like external quality' (IMS 163).[73] In seeing that bodies are red, we see external bodies; but all we are aware of is their effect on us. Since Hutcheson takes this view of the nature of secondary qualities, he takes his comparison of moral judgment to a sense to imply that moral judgments do not reveal objective moral properties of external objects.

Since we may not share Hutcheson's view of the senses, belief in a moral sense does not require this subjectivist conclusion about moral properties. We might defend a more objectivist account of senses and secondary qualities, and hence a more objectivist conclusion about moral properties. We might claim, for instance, that the colour we are aware of is the property of objects that causes such-and-such sensations in us (in most people, or in normal perceivers). This property is relationally defined, since the definition includes a mention of certain sensations; but it does not depend on the existence of such sensations. If, for instance, we ceased to exist, the property that causes such sensations in us would still exist; hence things would still be red even if there were no perceivers to perceive them. Similarly, the

---

[71] 'These sensations, as the learned agree, are not pictures or representations of like external qualities in the objects, nor of the impression or change made in the bodily organs. They are either signals, as it were of new events happening to the body, of which experience and observation will show us the cause; or marks, settled by the Author of Nature, to show us what things are salutary, innocent, or hurtful; or intimations of things not otherways discernible which may affect our state; though these marks or signals bear no more resemblance to the external reality, than the report of a gun, or the flash of the powder, bears to the distress of a ship.' (SMP i 1.3, 5)

[72] 'These three things are to be distinguished, 1. The idea of the external motion, known first by sense, and its tendency to the happiness or misery of some sensitive nature, often inferred by argument or reason, which on these subjects, suggests as invariable eternal or necessary truths as any whatsoever. 2. Apprehension or opinion of the affections in the agent, inferred by our reason: so far the idea of an action represents something external to the observer, really existing whether he had perceived it or not, and having a real tendency to certain ends. 3. The perception of approbation or disapprobation arising in the observer, according as the affections of the agent are apprehended kind in their just degree, or deficient, or malicious. This approbation cannot be supposed an image of any thing external, more than the pleasures of harmony, of taste, of smell. But let none imagine, that calling the ideas of virtue and vice perceptions of a sense, upon apprehending the actions and affections of another does diminish their reality, more than the like assertions concerning all pleasure and pain, happiness or misery.' (IMS 163–4 = R 371)

[73] This view is 'Lockean' according to Hutcheson's interpretation of Locke, whether or not it is actually Locke's. Winkler, 'Realism' 180, discusses Locke's view of secondary qualities, and Hutcheson's understanding of it, and shows how this understanding supports an anti-realist account of Hutcheson.

moral sense is (on this view) aware of the properties of actions and people that cause the reaction of disinterested approval; though these properties are relationally defined, their existence does not depend on our reacting as we do.

Hutcheson agrees that a moral judgment involves some belief about an objective property of some external object—the benevolence of the agent. Ought he not, then, to say that this benevolence itself is the moral goodness that we recognize through the moral sense? It is not implausible (even if it is over-simplified) to claim that morally good agents are good insofar as they are benevolent, and that the goodness we ascribe to them is benevolence. It seems far more implausible to claim that the goodness we ascribe to agents is an idea in our minds; this does not seem to be what we praise them for when we praise their benevolence as the whole or a part of their moral goodness.

Hutcheson rejects the objectivist answer for a good reason, given the rest of his position. For if benevolence were moral goodness, we could judge that an action is morally good, by judging that it is benevolent, and still be indifferent to it. In that case, the moral goodness would not include any obligation, as Hutcheson understands obligation. Since moral goodness includes obligation, and obligation is psychological necessity, moral goodness includes some psychological necessity. The moral judge who ascribes goodness to the agent recognizes an obligation, and hence a motive. Since obligation and motive belong to the judge, the moral goodness that we ascribe to the action must really be a feature of the judge rather than of the action itself.

We can see this difference between benevolence and moral goodness from another point of view, if we appeal to the division between justifying and exciting reasons. Benevolence is one of the affections or instincts that may be exciting reasons, but it does not by itself constitute a justifying reason. Moral goodness is a justifying reason, and so it must be the idea in the judge's mind, not the benevolence in the agent.

Hutcheson, therefore, is a subjectivist because he is an internalist about moral judgment and motivation. He is an internalist because he takes moral goodness to include obligation, takes obligations to include reasons, and reduces reasons to motives. Hence his anti-rationalism about reason and desire supports his subjectivism about moral properties. He does not thoughtlessly import a Lockean conception of sensory qualities into a position that might support realism about moral properties. He needs a subjectivist account of moral properties to maintain his anti-rationalism and its consequences. His interpretation of necessity, obligation, and reasons underlies his discussion of justifying reasons. Justifying reasons must be features of actual desires; hence, if morality provides justifying reasons, moral properties must belong to our desires and feelings, not to the external reality that we react to.

The anti-rationalist theory of motivation underlies different aspects of Hutcheson's position that might seem initially separable. In his criticism of Clarke, he rejects (1) Clarke's rationalism about motivation, (2) his rationalism about moral judgment, and (3) his realism about moral properties. We might think that if we agreed with Hutcheson on the first point, we could still agree with Clarke on the other two points, and that if we agreed with Hutcheson about ascribing moral judgment to a moral sense, we could still be realists about moral properties. In the *Inquiry* it is not clear why Hutcheson prefers his belief in a moral sense to Clarke's rationalism. The *Illustrations*, however, clarifies Hutcheson's version of anti-rationalism about reasons. If we believe—as Clarke believes—that recognition of moral properties includes recognition of obligation, we must also, given Hutcheson's view of obligation and reasons, attribute moral judgments to a moral sense, and accept a subjectivist account of moral properties.

Hutcheson's anti-realist interpretation of the moral sense, therefore, emerges from the assumptions about deliberation, reasons, and motivation that he shares with Hobbes, in opposition to Cudworth and Clarke. On this issue, Hume sees the implications of Hutcheson's position.[74]

643. The Rejection of Realism

We can now distinguish the aspect of Hutcheson's position that supports 'moral realism' or 'independent morality' from the aspect that rejects these positions.

He agrees with Shaftesbury in regarding morality as something distinct and independent, because it is not reducible to self-love. Morality is real because we have distinct and irreducible sentiments that favour morality, and we do not construct them out of self-love. On this point, Hutcheson concludes that Shaftesbury is right and Hobbes is wrong.

But acceptance of this degree of realism about morality does not induce Hutcheson to accept the independent reality of moral properties; he takes their existence to require the appropriate reaction in a spectator or judge. He believes this because he believes Hobbes's reduction of obligation to motivation and he believes that something's having a moral property imposes an obligation. He therefore denies that moral goodness and badness are independent of human sentiments and reactions, just as Hobbes denies that they are independent of commands.[75]

When Shaftesbury defends a 'realist' position against 'nominal moralists', he rejects both Hobbesian egoism and Hobbesian voluntarism; but it is not always clear that he distinguishes these two Hobbesian claims. It is not surprising, therefore, that Hutcheson might take himself to be defending Shaftesbury's whole position even though he actually defends only one part of it and rejects one part of it.

The differences between the *Inquiry* and the *Illustrations* do not show that Hutcheson consciously changed his mind. In the earlier work, the discussion of beauty affirms the subjectivist view that the later work affirms about the moral sense. Hutcheson may have held the same view all along. Still, the earlier work is consistent with Whewell's view that

---

[74] See Hume, §785.

[75] Norton, *DH* 62–6, does not distinguish these two questions about realism. He often speaks of Hutcheson's being a realist about 'virtue', by which he means that Hutcheson rejects the reduction of moral virtue to self-interest. But he also speaks as though this position implied that Hutcheson is not a 'subjectivist'. Norton argues: 'To suppose, as Kemp Smith does, that Hutcheson was a moral subjectivist is to include him among that group of moral sceptics that he sought to refute, and contravenes fundamental aspects of his work' (69). In speaking of moral scepticism Norton refers to the egoism of Hobbes and Mandeville, He mistakenly supposes that opposition to their view implies opposition to subjectivism. But, contrary to Norton, to recognize the reality of distinctively moral sentiments and feelings is not to recognize moral properties independent of these moral sentiments and feelings; and in this sense Hutcheson is not a moral realist. See Winkler, 'Realism'. Norton's description of Hutcheson would actually be a more accurate description of Shaftesbury (whom Norton describes, more accurately, in similar terms at 33–43). Norton's interpretation of Hutcheson is refuted by Radcliffe, 'Subjectivism'.

Hutcheson defends Shaftesbury's moral realism. Having examined the *Illustrations*, we can see that Whewell is also right to claim that Hutcheson tends to undermine his defence of realism. In the later work Hutcheson does not defend a realist position, but analyses moral judgments as judgments about the actual mental states of agents. His position on reasons, motivation, and the moral sense aligns him with Hobbes on the main issues that separate Hobbes from the rationalists. He does not try to reduce morality to facts about what promotes one's own pleasure; but his rejection of Hobbes on this point requires only a comparatively small modification in the basic Hobbesian position. Hence his later work departs from Shaftesbury in ways that also depart decisively from moral realism.

Hutcheson's explication of the moral sense requires anti-realism, since he claims that the goodness we are aware of is a feature of our reactions, not of external reality. He could have avoided this anti-realism, by identifying the moral goodness with a power of the object rather than a reaction of the spectator. What difference would it make if we modified his conception of the moral sense in this way? Would it be a small modification that would affirm realism without rationalism?

If we have correctly explained the connexions between Hutcheson's different views, anti-realism about moral properties does not rest primarily on his conception of a sense. It rests on his views about obligation and motivation, which in turn rest on his views about necessity and reasons. If the moral rightness of an action includes the obligation to do it, this rightness is a feature of the agent rather than of external reality. And so any attempt to revise his position would have to reject much more than his conception of a sense; it would also have to reject his views about reasons and obligation. These views show how deeply Hobbesian assumptions influence Hutcheson, even in his arguments against Hobbes.

HUTCHESON: FOR AND AGAINST UTILITARIANISM

644. Benevolence and Utilitarianism

After arguing that we approve moral goodness in its own right, and not as a means to our own advantage, Hutcheson asks what sorts of actions and characters we approve of from the moral point of view. The answer will tell us what moral goodness consists in. In the *Inquiry* he begins from the claims of Cumberland and Shaftesbury about the general good and the common good. He argues that moral principles are impartial: they are not concerned differentially with the good of some people rather than others, but with the good of all those affected. He takes a teleological view of morality, as both Cumberland and Shaftesbury do. Following Cumberland, but not Shaftesbury, he holds an instrumental version of a teleological view; moral rules and principles are to be observed not for their own sake, but for their causal consequences. He goes beyond both Shaftesbury and Cumberland in holding a maximizing conception of the end to be achieved: the end is the maximum total quantity of good, however it is distributed. By these steps Hutcheson transforms Shaftesbury's and Cumberland's views into a utilitarian outlook.

Hutcheson is not entirely original in accepting a version of utilitarianism. Hobbes's view is broadly utilitarian, insofar as he reduces morality to the 'laws of nature', a set of principles for promoting the security of the commonwealth. This analysis of moral principles captures a central element in morality, insofar as it implies that moral principles essentially aim at some end broader than the good of the agent. Their essential aim explains the merely apparent conflict between morality and self-interest in the commonwealth, and the real conflict between them in the state of nature. In the right circumstances, we will have a self-interested concern to observe rules promoting the public good; otherwise Hobbes could not justify our observance of them.

Cumberland's position is not precisely utilitarian. He argues that moral principles are those that promote the common good of rational agents, and therefore are endorsed by benevolent agents. He and others who reject Hobbesian hedonistic egoism, for Shaftesbury's or for Hutcheson's reasons, also reject Hobbes's third reason for accepting a utilitarian account, and so they need to support moral principles by appeal to some other reason or motive.

Cumberland appeals to benevolence, which includes disinterested concern for the good of others, not restricted to any particular group of other people.

This conception of the basis of morality may appear especially Christian. The view that the whole moral law can be summed up in the requirement to love God and one's neighbour may appear to imply that all moral attitudes can be resolved into forms of benevolence. Cumberland begins his treatise by quoting the second 'great commandment' and St Paul's claim that love is the fulfilling of the law.[1] To love one's neighbour as oneself seems to imply an impartial concern with the interests of different people without discrimination; and this impartial concern seems especially characteristic of benevolence. Hence Cumberland makes benevolence the universal virtue, controlling the others. Hutcheson agrees with him (*IMGE* 3.6 = L 231 = R 331).

Moreover, benevolence seems to fit Hutcheson's belief in the moral sense. For benevolence results from sympathetic pleasure and pain provoked by the pleasures and pains of others, without reference to any further advantage to the agent. Hence it seems to appeal to the moral sense. Hutcheson understands different moral rules as particular expressions of benevolence.

But though benevolence appears to be the right sentiment to support utilitarianism, this appearance may be misleading. For the extent and direction of the benevolence that people actually feel does not seem to extend to utilitarian morality. Even though benevolence is not inherently restricted in the way that, say, parental love or friendship or loyalty to a group is, we may still feel it for some people and not for others; it need not be impartially directed towards the benefit of everyone affected by our actions.

Hutcheson recognizes this difficulty, since he distinguishes different attitudes that might be identified with benevolence. Some of these are discriminatory, directed to some particular people to the exclusion of others, rather than to other people generally. But, in his view, we approve most strongly of the benevolence that seeks to maximize utility.[2] This is 'the calm desire of good, and aversion to evil, either selfish or public, as they appear to our reason or reflexion', in contrast to 'the particular passions towards objects immediately presented to some sense'. The benevolence that we most approve of is not an impulse of (say) generosity or kindness, but a calm desire that does not manifest itself in immediately-felt impulses.[3]

---

[1] See *LN*, title page. Cumberland quotes *Rm.* 13:10 and *Mt.* 22:37–40.

[2] '... to understand this more distinctly, it is highly necessary to observe that under this name are included very different dispositions of the soul. Sometimes it denotes a calm, extensive affection, or good-will toward all beings capable of happiness or misery: sometimes, 2. a calm deliberate affection of the soul toward the happiness of certain smaller systems or individuals; such as patriotism, or love of a country, friendship, parental affection, as it is in persons of wisdom and self-government; or, 3. the several kind particular passions of love, pity, sympathy, congratulation' (*IMGE* 3.6 = L 231 = R 331).

[3] 'Thus nothing can be more distinct than the general calm desire of private good of any kind, which alone would incline us to pursue whatever objects were apprehended as the means of good, and the particular selfish passions, such as ambition, covetousness, hunger, lust, revenge, anger, as they arise on particular occasions. In like manner our public desires may be distinguished into the general calm desire of the happiness of others, or aversion from their misery upon reflexion; and the particular affections or passions of love, congratulation, compassion, natural affection. These particular affections are found in many tempers, where, through want of reflexion, the general calm desire are not found; nay, the former may be opposite to the latter, where they are found in the same temper. Sometimes the calm motion of the will conquers the passion, and sometimes it is conquered by it. Thus lust or revenge may conquer the calm affection towards private good, and sometimes are conquered by it. Compassion will prevent the necessary correction of a child, or the use of a severe cure, while the calm parental affection is exciting towards it. Sometimes the latter prevails over the former.

Moreover, it is not just any calm desire of good that is contrasted with particular passions, but the calm desire for the good of humanity in general.[4]

Our moral sense, then, approves especially of this universal form of calm benevolence. The benevolence of the Good Samaritan was not restricted to people he already knew or had some previous connexion with; we approve of his attitude because it extends to everyone equally. Attention to such cases suggests that our moral sense approves of the impartiality that is characteristic of utilitarian morality.[5] We should not, then, try to rest utilitarianism on a rationalist basis, as Cumberland seems to do. On the contrary, it fits the anti-rationalist belief in a moral sense.[6]

If we grant that our moral sense approves of the impartial aspects of utilitarianism, should we also grant that it approves utilitarian maximizing? Utilitarian morality aims at maximum total good, summed over all the people concerned, irrespective of its distribution. To show that our moral sense approves of this outlook, we may point out that if A gave a large gift to charity that A could easily afford, we would approve of A's action more than we would approve of B's action, if B were in similar circumstances to A, but gave a small gift to charity, and wasted the rest of the money that could have been given to charity. Such cases show that we approve of greater rather than lesser beneficence. Hence, Hutcheson argues, they show that the moral sense approves of the maximizing aspect of utilitarianism.

We might think Hutcheson faces a difficulty in the fact that our moral sense also approves of narrower attachments and of beneficence directed to one's family, or friends, or associates, without reference to broader utilitarian considerations. He answers this apparent difficulty by arguing that utilitarian reasons can be given for our approval of both narrower and wider attachments to the good of others. Agents are more virtuous if they prefer to benefit 'unrelated' people rather than (say) to return benefits to people who have benefited them.[7] But causing harm to 'related' people is worse than causing it to unrelated ones, because someone who cannot even treat friends decently is less likely to develop the expanded benevolence that is characteristic of morality.[8] When we discriminate morally between people who produce the same amount of good or evil by a particular action, we are guided

All this is beautifully presented in the 9th book of Plato's *Republic*. We obtain command over the particular passions, principally by strengthening the general desires through frequent reflexion, and making them habitual, so as to obtain strength superior to the particular passion.' (*Passions* 2.2 = Garrett 31–2, 209 = R 357)

[4] 'Again, the calm public desires may be considered as "they either regard the good of particular persons or societies presented to our senses; or that of some more abstracted or general community, such as a species or system". This latter we may call universal calm benevolence.' (*Passions* 2.2 = Garrett 32 = R 357)

[5] 'Our moral sense, though it approves all particular kind affection or passion, as well as calm particular benevolence abstractedly considered; yet it also approves the restraint or limitation of all particular affections or passions, by the calm universal benevolence. To make this desire prevalent there above all particular affections, is the only sure way to obtain constant self-approbation.' (*Passions* 2.2 = Garrett 33 = R 357)

[6] Hume disagrees with Hutcheson on this point. See §768.

[7] 'In equal moments of good produced by two agents, when one acts from general benevolence, and the other from a nearer tie; there is greater virtue in the agent who produces equal good from the weaker attachment, and less virtue, where there is the stronger attachment, which yet produces no more.' (*IMGE* 7.9 = L 190 = SB 181)

[8] 'But the omission of the good offices of the stronger ties, or actions contrary to them, have greater vice in them, than the like omissions or actions contrary to the weaker ties; since our selfishness or malice must appear the greater, by the strength of the contrary attachment which it surmounts. Thus, in co-operating with gratitude, natural affection, or friendship, we evidence less virtue in any given moment of good produced, than in equally important actions of general benevolence. But ingratitude to a benefactor, negligence of the interests of a friend, or relation; or returns of evil offices, are vastly more odious, than equal negligence, or evil offices towards strangers.' (*IMGE* 7.9 = L 190 = SB 181)

by utilitarian criteria even if we do not notice them; the attitudes we praise more are those likely to produce more good on the whole. Hence the degrees of our approval match the tendency of different traits of character to promote the public good.[9]

How is the public good determined? Hutcheson believes that universal calm benevolence takes a maximizing point of view, and is therefore indifferent to the particular recipients of good and evil. If one action benefits two people I know and another benefits, to the same degree, three people I do not know, universal benevolence prefers the second action. It is also indifferent to the distribution of happiness, and considers only the quantity of happiness resulting from an action.[10] This quantitative conception of public good would have no hold on our moral sentiments unless we were disposed to favour the benevolent attitude that takes this purely quantitative attitude towards the production of good and evil.[11]

Since, therefore, we approve of extended benevolence, we approve of the utilitarian position.[12] Even if we do not initially recognize that we accept utilitarianism, reflexion shows that our moral attitudes presuppose utilitarianism. Since the moral sense approves calm benevolence, we accept the maximizing utilitarian principle. This principle allows us to co-ordinate the demands of ordinary rules and virtues, since we can resolve conflicts between these demands if we have the necessary information about the balance of pleasures and pains.[13]

While Hutcheson insists on the supremacy of the affection towards the universal happiness, he recognizes some mitigation, though not justification, of departures from it. We allow mitigation in cases where some generally admirable trait causes deviation from utility in a particular case.[14] Our attitude is understandable, since we usually do not think about how

---

[9] '. . . calm good-will towards a small system is lovely and preferable to more passionate attachments; and yet a more extensive calm benevolence is still more beautiful and virtuous; and the highest perfection of virtue is an universal calm good-will towards all sentient natures. Hence it is, that we condemn particular attachments, when inconsistent with the interest of great societies, because they argue some defect in that more noble principle which is the perfection of virtue' (*IMGE* 3.8 = L 233).

[10] 'In comparing the moral qualities of actions, in order to regulate our election among various actions proposed, or to find which of them has the greatest moral excellency, we are led by our moral sense of virtue to judge thus; that in equal degrees of happiness expected to proceed from the action, the virtue is in proportion to the number of persons to whom the happiness shall extend . . . and in equal numbers, the virtue is as the quantity of happiness or natural good . . . So that the action is best, which produces the greatest happiness for the greatest number.' (*IMGE* 3.8 = L 125 = R 333) 'Here also the moral importance of characters, or dignity of persons may compensate numbers; as may also the degrees of happiness or misery: for to procure an inconsiderable good to many, but an immense evil to few, may be evil; and an immense good to few, may preponderate a small evil to many.' (*IMGE* 3.9 = L 125 = R 343)

[11] In the 2nd edn. of *IMGE* 3.11 = L 128 = SB 126, Hutcheson sets out six axioms 'to compute the morality of any axioms', expressing them in algebraic formulae. In the 3rd edn., L 234–5 = R 335, he reduces the axioms from six to four and deletes the algebraic formulae. He says that in the fourth edition he removed some mathematical expressions 'which, upon second thoughts appeared useless, and were disagreeable to some readers' (Pref. to 4th edn. = L 201).

[12] 'This increase of the moral beauty of actions, or dispositions, according to the number of persons to whom the good effects of them extend, may show us the reason why actions which flow from the nearer attachments of nature, such as that between the sexes, and the love of our offspring, are not so amiable, nor do they appear as virtuous as actions of equal moment of good towards persons less attached to us. The reason is plainly this. These strong instincts are by nature limited to small numbers of mankind, such as our wives or children; whereas a disposition, which would produce a like moment of good to others, upon no special attachment, if it was accompanied with natural power to accomplish its intention, would be incredibly more fruitful of great and good effects to the whole.' (*IMGE* 3.10 = L 127 = SB 124)

[13] 'In such cases, we should not suppose contrary obligations, or duties; the more important office is our present duty, and the omission of the less important inconsistent office at present, is no moral evil.' (*IMGE* 7.9 = L 191 = SB 181)

[14] 'And yet when some of these narrower kind affections exceed their proportion, and overcome the more extensive, the moral deformity is alleviated in proportion to the moral beauty of that narrower affection by which the more extensive is overpowered.' (*SMP* ii 2.3, 243)

to promote the general happiness, but we take it for granted that particular benevolent actions promote it.[15] Some of our narrower affections, both loves and hates, are natural and acceptable on this utilitarian presumption.

Hutcheson concedes, then, that most people's sentiments are non-utilitarian in some aspects. But he does not treat these non-utilitarian aspects as objections to his utilitarian analysis of the moral sense. He treats the utilitarian principle as the single supreme principle of morality that is endorsed by the moral sense.

645. Utilitarianism and Natural Law

The moral primacy of benevolence supports Hutcheson's account of the traditional doctrine of the laws of nature, and helps him to answer the questions in dispute between voluntarists and naturalists. He agrees with Shaftesbury's defence of naturalism, and affirms that the proper foundation of right is God's infinite goodness and wisdom. The moral requirement to obey God rests on the recognition of God's goodness, and not simply on gratitude for the benefits God has given us.[16] Gratitude alone does not justify obedience to God; the fact that a gangster has done me a good turn does not justify me in doing whatever he asks me to, and, similarly, gratitude warrants obedience only if we have reasonable independent assurance of God's goodness.

This comment on gratitude answers Pufendorf's attempted defence of voluntarism. Pufendorf rejects Hobbes's apparent view that our only reason for obeying God's commands is fear of punishment; the alternative he offers is gratitude for God's benefits. Hutcheson replies, quite reasonably, that, unless we know more about the divine will, gratitude is no better than Hobbesian fear as a basis for genuine morality. Justified obedience to God rests on recognition of God's goodness, and hence on the approval by our moral sense of God's moral sense. Since our moral sense is utilitarian, God is a utilitarian, guided by the requirements of universal maximizing benevolence.[17]

This utilitarian principle supports the Scholastic naturalist view that natural law specifies what is suitable for human nature. Since what is suitable for human nature is whatever maximizes utility, the laws of nature are rules for the maximization of utility.[18] Cumberland's view that the laws of nature promote the common good of rational

---

[15] '...we have this just presumption, that by serving innocently any valuable part of a system, we do good to the whole' (244).

[16] 'But benefits alone, are not a proper foundation of right, as they will not prove that the power assumed tends to the universal good or is consistent with it, however they suggest an amiable motive to obedience.' (SMP ii 3.7, 266). Cf. Pufendorf, §577.

[17] Hutcheson's belief in benevolence as God's only basic moral attribute seems to have been formed early in his life. Around 1719, after his return to Ulster from Glasgow, some members of his congregation objected, on Scriptural grounds, to a sermon of his that tried to reduce God's moral attributes to benevolence. See Scott, FH 20–1. In 1737 (Adam Smith's first year as an undergraduate in Glasgow) Hutcheson was prosecuted for heresy by the Presbytery of Glasgow 'for teaching to his students, in contravention of his subscription to the Westminster Confession, the following two false and dangerous doctrines: 1st, that the standard of moral goodness was the promotion of the happiness of others; and 2nd, that we could have a knowledge of good and evil without and prior to a knowledge of God' (Rae, LAS 12–13; cf. Scott, FH 83–4). On Smith on God's benevolence and justice see Balguy, §662; Butler, §701.

[18] '...the proper means of promoting the happiness of mankind by our actions, which is the same thing with inquiring into the more special laws of nature' (SMP ii 1.1, 227). '...let us recollect how it is that we discover the special laws of

agents is correct, if we take the common good to be maximum utility. The maximizing aspects of utility have no clear basis in Cumberland, but Hutcheson takes them for granted.

The utilitarian explanation of the laws of nature implies that, despite their apparently non-utilitarian and exceptionless character, they have exceptions. Even if exceptions are not explicitly stated, we must be ready to recognize them on utilitarian grounds.[19] Similarly, utility is the basis of rights, since utilitarian principles determine and limit the scope of specific rights.[20]

The utilitarian explanation of the laws of nature, and the rejection of voluntarism, support Hutcheson's answer to those critics who claim that we have moral reasons for accepting some specific moral rules without exceptions. He rejects the argument of 'some divines', and in particular Berkeley, for strict observance of moral rules because of our ignorance of utility.[21] Hutcheson argues that if we refrain from utilitarian reasoning to find exceptions to the common laws of nature, we must also forgo the reasoning that allows us to find these 'ordinary rules or laws of nature' in the first place.[22]

One might take Hutcheson to offer a direct utilitarian reply to Berkeley's argument. Berkeley argues for an indirect utilitarian attitude to the rule of obedience to the established government; Hutcheson seems to answer that this indirect argument rests on an unreasonably pessimistic assumption about our ignorance of consequences. But Hutcheson accepts some indirect utilitarian arguments; they support his claims about rights, and they offer useful utilitarian answers to apparent counter-examples.

646. Objections to Hutcheson's Utilitarian Arguments[23]

Does Hutcheson show that we implicitly approve the utilitarian principle, or that we have good reason to revise our moral judgments in a utilitarian direction? He relies on two claims

nature. We have no universal precepts enunciated by God, in words, binding us in all cases where God does not by words declare some exceptions. The laws of nature are inferences we make, by reflecting upon our inward constitution, and by reasoning upon human affairs, concerning that conduct which our hearts naturally must approve, as tending either to the general good, or to that of individuals consistently with it' (SMP ii 17.2, 119).

[19] Cf. Suarez's treatment of alleged 'exceptions' to natural law, §§444–5. His treatment is non-utilitarian, but might be adapted to utilitarian arguments.

[20] 'A man hath a right to do, possess, or demand any thing, "when his acting, possessing, or obtaining from another in these circumstances tends to the good of society, or to the interest of the individual consistently with the rights of others and the general good of society, and obstructing him would have the contrary tendency".' (SMP ii 3.1, 253) 'For the ultimate notion of right is that which tends to the universal good; and when one's acting in a certain manner has this tendency, he has a right thus to act.' (SMP ii 3.7, 266) In the first passage, one clause ('or to the interest...') allows some non-utilitarian considerations. But neither passage allows any net sacrifice of utility for a non-utilitarian reason.

[21] 'They argue as if certain propositions had been ingraved by God on some pillars, telling us what we are to do in all possible cases... and ordering us to commit the event to God, without reasoning about it, while we keep to the letter of the law. Nay, some tell us that "we know not all the remote effects of actions: such as appear to us of good tendency may in the whole have pernicious effects; and those may have good effects in the whole which appear to us of the most hurtful tendency...."' (SMP ii 17.6, 128) See Berkeley, PO. Hutcheson might also refer to Butler. On Berkeley and Butler see §§699–701.

[22] 'For 'tis only by our reasonings, about the tendencies of actions, and these sometimes pretty remote, that we arrive at these conclusions which we call the ordinary laws of nature.' (SMP ii 17.6, 129)

[23] Blair, 'Hutcheson's moral philosophy', is a generally appreciative discussion that raises some useful critical points. Blair contrasts Hutcheson with Clarke in terms that recall Butler's contrast between two methods of moral philosophy

that need to be distinguished: (1) Universal calm benevolence is free of any exclusive or discriminatory attitude that is irrelevant from the moral point of view to the distribution of good. (2) It is free of any non-maximizing discriminatory attitude to the distribution of good.

Hutcheson moves quickly from the first claim, that benevolence is in some way impartial, to his conclusion in the second claim, that it seeks to maximize the good without any further demands on its distribution. His examples support the first claim; for many people, including non-utilitarians, would agree that some differences between possible beneficiaries are morally irrelevant. We may agree, for instance, that a doctor ought to be impartial between different patients with the same needs, and ought not to prefer the richest, or most intelligent, or those most like herself. But we may not agree that she ought to take a maximizing point of view in deciding how to treat different patients with the same needs (for instance, by cutting up the less socially useful people for spare-part surgery on the more useful people). Since it is not clear that impartial benevolence supports the maximizing utilitarian outlook, Hutcheson's argument is incomplete.

Approval of utilitarian benevolence, therefore, does not result in approval of the traits and outlooks that we actually approve of. If we try to cultivate the optimific traits and outlooks (those that have the best prospect of maximizing utility), perhaps we should cultivate some traits that make us less concerned with our obligations to 'related' people, so that we grasp the maximizing considerations. In that case, our beliefs about what maximizes utility may diverge from our beliefs about particular attachments.

Hutcheson should allow this possibility, since he does not show that the particular traits we approve of are those that maximize utility. If our tendencies to approve diverge from utilitarian benevolence, he believes our approval needs to be modified. But it is not clear that our moral sense approves utilitarian modifications.

647. Indirect Utilitarianism

Hutcheson does not discuss this apparent gap between the moral sense and utilitarianism. Sometimes he does not acknowledge that any consideration except the public good affects

(12–13; cf. §678). According to Blair, Shaftesbury gives a eudaemonist answer to the question 'Why be moral?', but Hutcheson rejects it (15–16), because he rejects the primacy of the desire for happiness. Blair's main criticism concerns the demanding character of utilitarianism (18–20). He denies that what we most approve of from the benevolent utilitarian point of view counts as our duty: 'To devote ourselves to death for our country; to sacrifice our own happiness to that of the public; are acts of high disinterested benevolence, which receive the greatest approbation from the moral sense, but are by no means accompanied with that sense of strict duty that attends justice, truth, fidelity, observance of compact, and those other humbler virtues that are primary and essential to society. To them we feel ourselves indispensably obliged; but are not conscious of such an obligation with respect to universal disinterested benevolence; which is indeed considered as the heroism, or sublimity of virtue, which every man's mind approves and admires; but which is not bound upon us by the authoritative sanction of duty, in so strong a manner, as the other virtues just now mentioned. . . . In general, we may observe, concerning the strain of this part of our author's philosophy, that it represents virtue rather in the light of a beautiful and noble object, recommended by the inward approbation of our minds, than as a law dictated by conscience; and may be thought to be calculated rather for making virtuous men better, than for teaching the bulk of mankind the first principles of duty.' It is not clear whether Blair thinks duty is based on non-utilitarian principles or is a subset of what utilitarian benevolence demands.

our judgment about the morality of actions.[24] He takes 'our late debates about passive obedience' to have considered only what course of action would best promote the public good. He does not confront the objection, urged by Maxwell and by Butler, that it is possible to pursue the public good by morally impermissible means, and so he does not allow that some moral questions are distinct from questions about how to promote the public good.

He implicitly answers this objection, however, by arguing that one can explain apparently non-utilitarian judgments on indirect utilitarian grounds. The fact that our moral sense approves of non-utilitarian attitudes is consistent with a utilitarian account of our moral sense, if we promote utility by acting on non-utilitarian attitudes. Our non-utilitarian motives strengthen our attachment to the courses of action that promote utility.[25] The cardinal virtue of justice, as recognized by the ancients, often appears to conflict with utility. But we can see, on closer examination, that its utilitarian basis explains its primacy among the virtues.[26] A similar utilitarian account explains why the other traditional cardinal virtues are virtues.

This account of apparently non-utilitarian principles is not immediately convincing. According to Price, it does not entirely convince Hutcheson, because he does not stick consistently to his utilitarian analysis. Price draws attention to Hutcheson's acknowledgment of our immediate approval of justice and veracity, in addition to our approval of them for their consequences.[27]

Hutcheson might try a utilitarian explanation of his remarks on immediate approval in order to answer Price's objection. Perhaps our approval of justice does not depend on a calculation of its consequences here and now; still, the formation of this attitude of immediate approval towards a just action is justified only by our approval of the consequences of the general observance of justice.

---

[24] 'Again, that we may see how love, or benevolence, is the foundation of all apprehended excellence in social virtues, let us only observe, that amidst the diversity of sentiments on this head among various sects, this is still allowed to be the way of deciding the controversy about any disputed practice, viz. to enquire whether this conduct, or the contrary, will most effectually promote the public good. The morality is immediately adjusted, when the natural tendency, or influence of the action upon the universal natural good of mankind is agreed upon. That which produces more good than evil in the whole, is acknowledged good; and what does not, is counted evil. In this case, we no other way regard the good of the actor, or that of those who are thus enquiring, than as they make a part of the great system.' (IMGE 3.3 = L 118 = SB 112)

[25] This utilitarian explanation of ostensibly non-utilitarian moral virtues and rules is sketched in IMGE, but developed more fully in the later SMP.

[26] 'The course of life therefore, pointed out to us immediately by our moral sense, and confirmed by all the just consideration of our true interest, must be the very same which the generous calm determination would recommend, a constant study to promote the most universal happiness in our power, by doing all good offices as we have opportunity which interfere with no more extensive interest of the system; preferring always the more extensive and important offices to those of less extent and importance . . .' (SMP i 11.2, 222)

[27] '[He] has acknowledged that we immediately approve of private justice as well as of veracity, without referring them to a system or to public interest. But I know not well how to reconcile with this his general method of treating the subject of justice and rights, and particularly his saying, in the same chapter, that the ultimate notion of a right is that which tends to the universal good.' (Price, RPQM 161n) Price also (137–8n) cites Hutcheson's SIMP on veracity as suggesting an exception to utilitarianism: 'Veracity and faith in our engagements, besides their own immediate beauty thus approved, recommend themselves to the approbation and choice of every wise and honest man by their manifest necessity for the common interest and safety.' (SIMP 167) The English version softens the contrast between non-utilitarian and utilitarian approval that appears more sharply in the Latin: 'Veritas autem et fides non solum sua propria nobis se commendant pulchritudine, mendacia vero et fraudes sua nos turpitudine offendunt; verum et manifesta communis utilitatis ratio ad veritatem et fidem, tamquam communi saluti necessarias, bene sanos invitabit . . .' (MPIC 135)

648. Indirect Utilitarianism and Indirect Egoism

An indirect utilitarian defence raises a question about Hutcheson's overall position. For it suggests that we might also try an indirect egoist explanation and defence of our moral judgments. Hobbes seems to accept both indirect utilitarianism and indirect egoism, without exploring either position. In both cases the indirect analysis avoids implausible claims about the explicit content of particular moral judgments, while maintaining the regulative role of the general egoist or utilitarian outlook.[28]

Hutcheson's view is worth comparing with Hobbes's view, because, on the one hand, Hutcheson defends indirect utilitarianism more explicitly, but, on the other hand, he rejects indirect egoism, claiming that we approve things unselfishly without reference to consequences for our own advantage. An indirect egoist might answer that we do not think about our own advantage when we approve things morally, but nonetheless our unselfish approval is justified and supported by consideration of our own advantage. Though Mandeville is wrong (on this view) to deny that we have unselfish motives, he would be right to affirm that our ultimate motives are selfish. If Hutcheson accepts indirect utilitarianism, should he not also accept this indirect egoist argument? If he should, his acceptance of indirect utilitarianism subverts his whole argument about the moral sense.

In answer to indirect egoism, he might deny that our moral approval is concerned with our own advantage, even if considerations of advantage might support it. Even if things changed so that our moral approval did not work to our advantage, we would retain it. This counterfactual judgment reflects the fact that our moral approval is not guided by considerations of advantage. The mere fact that our moral attitudes are advantageous to us does not show that advantage explains or sustains them.

This is a reasonable reply to indirect egoism, but it raises two difficulties for Hutcheson: (1) The counterfactual argument assumes that our moral approval essentially relies on certain reasons. If it were a simple favourable feeling that does not consider one's own advantage, it would not be inherently selfish, but it would not be inherently unselfish either. Whether or not our moral approval is unselfish depends on the considerations that it takes as reasons for approval. Hence it must be essentially open to specific sorts of reasons and not to others. It must have a rational structure that does not easily fit Hutcheson's conception of the moral sense. (2) If we reject an indirect egoist account of the moral sense, can we not offer analogous arguments against indirect utilitarianism? Hutcheson might deny the analogy, since he argues that we respond to utilitarian considerations in our moral reasoning. But he does not show that we rely on the maximizing aspects of utilitarianism. Even if an indirect utilitarian defence of our moral attitudes might be given, it may not explain our attitudes.

Price notices this parallel between egoism and utilitarianism.[29] His argument against egoism is quite similar to Hutcheson's, but he believes that the same sort of argument undermines Hutcheson's utilitarianism. Though his argument does not do justice to indirect utilitarianism, it raises serious questions about Hutcheson's whole system.

---

[28] On Hobbes see §504.   [29] See Price, *RPQM* 136, discussed at §822.

One of these questions arises from a dilemma about the moral sense. On the one hand, if Hutcheson emphasizes the comparison with a sense, and hence takes the moral sense to be simple approval, without essential reference to specific reasons, he makes it easier to defend both the indirect utilitarianism he accepts and the indirect egoism he rejects. On the other hand, if he emphasizes the dependence of moral judgment and approval on specific reasons, he makes it easier to refute both the indirect egoism he rejects and the indirect utilitarianism he accepts.

How should he clarify or amend his position? If moral approval essentially depends on certain kinds of reasons for approval, it differs from an ordinary sense in this respect, and the comparison with a sense is correspondingly less useful. A more plausible conception of moral approval seems to make it easier for Hutcheson to maintain his opposition to egoism, but more difficult for him to maintain indirect utilitarianism.

This conclusion is surprising. For Hutcheson's comparison of moral approval with sensory awareness is intended to support his argument against egoism. He believes that if he shows our reaction to moral good and evil is immediate, and hence independent of complex calculations about advantage, he refutes an egoist analysis. But his discussion of indirect utilitarianism suggests that immediacy does not help his argument against egoism as much as he supposes. To resist an indirect egoist analysis of the moral sense, he needs to give the moral sense more rational structure.

649. How does the Moral Sense Support Utilitarianism?

How much does it matter whether Hutcheson can show that the moral sense accepts utilitarian morality? We have assumed that if ordinary moral judgments diverge from utilitarianism, that is a serious objection to his argument for utilitarianism. But some utilitarians do not believe it is a serious objection. One defence of utilitarianism against objections derived from ordinary moral convictions maintains that the principle of utility is a rational principle. Balguy and Butler distinguish rational benevolence from non-rational passions that might lead us to favour other courses of action. In their view, we need to correct our passions so that we align them with the utilitarian principle.[30] We can resolve conflicts between our initial convictions and the utilitarian principle if we train our passions to follow reason.

Hutcheson's anti-rationalism precludes this defence of utilitarianism. He believes that the misconceived contrast between reason and desire, as rationalists describe them, points to the real division between calm and passionate motions. This division captures, in his view, the division that Plato and Aristotle have in mind in distinguishing parts of the soul by appeal to psychic conflict.[31] Hutcheson does not recognize the good-dependence of desires

---

[30] This is not the whole of what Balguy and Butler think about utility. See §§664, 700.

[31] 'The difference between the calm motions of the will and the passionate, whether of the selfish or benevolent kinds, must be obvious to any who consider how often we find them acting in direct opposition. Thus anger or lust will draw us one way; and a calm regard, either to our highest interest, the greatest sum of private good, or to some particular interest, will draw the opposite way . . .' (SMP i 1.7, 12) In a footnote Hutcheson refers to Plato and Aristotle. See Hume, §735.

of the rational part, as Plato and Aristotle understand them, since his account of motivation precludes good-dependent desires. Calm and reflective desires, his substitute for rational desires, are the source of impartial benevolence.[32]

The utilitarian outlook, therefore, is the moral outlook because utilitarianism expresses benevolence, and the moral sense approves of benevolence. We can correct any non-utilitarian judgments by reminding ourselves that we ought to be trying to take the most benevolent view possible, and that this commits us to consideration of utility.

How should we understand the claim that benevolence is what the moral sense approves of? We might take it in two ways: (1) From our beliefs about morality we might conclude that the basic moral principle is benevolence. Then we might notice that we have the sort of sensory awareness and approval of benevolence that suggests we have a moral sense; if this were not what it approved, it would not be a strictly moral sense. (2) We might define a moral sense as the sensory awareness and approval we feel towards the actions and characters of human agents, considered from a disinterested point of view. Having shown that we have such a sense, we then ask what it approves of and we find that it approves of benevolence.

These two accounts of the relation between benevolence and the moral sense imply different views about the resolution of possible conflicts. According to the first view, our argument about the character of morality shows that the moral point of view is benevolent before we consider whether we have a moral sense or not. Approval of benevolence is a necessary condition for being a moral sense, and we know a priori that the moral sense approves of benevolence. If, then, we are inclined to make moral claims that conflict with those of utilitarian benevolence, we can legitimately reject them on the ground that they do not accurately reflect our moral sense, which approves of benevolence. But if we accept the second view of benevolence and the moral sense, we cannot deal with conflicts in this way. Our belief that the moral sense approves of benevolence is simply empirical, and liable to be falsified by further evidence of what the moral sense (defined independently of approval of benevolence) approves of.

In the *Illustrations* Hutcheson takes this second view, assuming a purely empirical connexion between benevolence and the moral sense. Moral properties are taken to imply obligation, and hence to imply motivation. The properties approved of by the moral sense are simply those that in fact give us justifying reasons; and these have to be states of the agent, according to Hutcheson's subjectivism. According to this view, benevolence is not moral goodness; it is the property that is shown by empirical evidence to arouse our feeling of approval, on which moral goodness depends.

This subjectivist analysis of moral properties requires a utilitarian moralist to claim that all true utilitarian judgments are true predictions about what the moral sense will approve of. We cannot claim to have some other access to what is really right, in the light of which the apparent reactions of the moral sense could be corrected, or shown not to be genuine reactions of the moral sense. The utilitarian believes that the moral sense, as Hutcheson describes it, endorses utilitarianism.[33] For since moral reasons and motives rest primarily on our sympathetic feelings towards the pleasures and pains of others, a survey of more people

---

[32] See Hume on calmness, §738.
[33] According to Stephen, *HET* ii 60, 'Hutcheson uses two standards—the public good, and the approval of the moral sense—and uses them indifferently, because he is convinced of their absolute identity. In his discussion of particular

suffering the same degree of pain or pleasure, or of the same number of people suffering a higher degree of pain or pleasure, results in more intense pain and pleasure. And if our moral sense approves of the benevolence that consists in these sympathetic feelings, it will approve of the desire to achieve the maximum total good. Hence the moral sense will approve of utilitarian benevolence.

But these claims do not secure Hutcheson's conclusion. If two situations differ only in these quantitative respects, we will prefer the one that achieves greater pleasure. But these are not the only features of situations that might affect our sympathetic feelings and our tendency to approve of them. May we not be moved by narrower attachments, or by some specific injuries to specific people, even if they conflict with utilitarian benevolence? Even if utilitarian benevolence is one object of the moral sense's approval, it may not be the only object; for, as Hutcheson agrees, benevolence does not always overcome other passions.[34] In that case, our moral sense may not always agree with benevolence. If other-regarding motives distinct from utilitarian benevolence sometimes influence us, our moral sense might sometimes approve of their influence. If normal observers sometimes approve utilitarian benevolence, but often approve some action or attitude that does not maximize utility, then moral rightness sometimes maximizes utility, but sometimes does not.

Hutcheson might argue that a particular person's moral sense is mistaken if it disagrees with utilitarianism, and that it ought to be adjusted to the utilitarian outlook. The comparison of the moral sense to ordinary senses allows some correction. Particular sensory reactions can be corrected by appeal to the reactions of normal perceivers in normal conditions.[35] Similarly, the reaction of one person's moral sense on one occasion can be corrected by reference to the reactions of the normal spectator on this sort of occasion.

But Hutcheson's theory leaves only limited room for correction. The moral sense is aware of objective properties—the tendency of an action to promote the public good, and the disposition of the agent to promote it. But these properties are not the moral goodness of the action, because the moral goodness is not an objective property of the action, but a feature of the observer's reaction to it. We cannot, then, correct one person's moral sense by reference to objective moral properties that it aims to detect, since there are no such properties for it to detect; we must correct it by reference to the normal observer. For similar reasons, the 'normal' observer cannot be the one who actually detects the relevant objective moral properties; normality must be understood without reference to any beliefs about the objective properties to be detected.

Correction by reference to normal observers may not favour utilitarianism. Their reactions to conflicts between utilitarianism and less universal attitudes (as Hutcheson considers them) are likely to vary, both between different people and in the same person between different occasions. Hence the appeal to the normal observer yields no clear decision. We might

problems, the moral sense passes out of sight altogether, and he becomes a pure utilitarian.' Stephen does not discuss the questions that might arise in trying to defend the 'absolute identity' of the two standards.

[34] 'It is well known, that general benevolence alone, is not a motive strong enough to industry, to bear labour and toil, and many other difficulties which we are averse to from self-love. For the strengthening therefore our motives to industry, we have the strongest attractions of blood, of friendship, of gratitude, and the additional motives of honour, and even of external interest.' (*IMGE* 7.8 = L 186 = SB 180)

[35] For references and discussion see §659 on Balguy.

claim that only the observers who approve of utilitarianism are the normal and healthy ones; but in that case we would presuppose the truth of utilitarianism. If we appeal to the truth of a particular theory to correct our moral sense, we undermine a basic assumption of Hutcheson's theory, since we measure the moral sense by an external moral standard.

If Hutcheson refuses to correct our moral sense by an external moral standard, his defence of utilitarianism commits him to the empirical claim that normal spectators approve of the utilitarian solution of any conflict between utilitarian benevolence and less universal or non-maximizing moral attitudes. But this empirical claim is doubtful.

650. A Conflict between Hutcheson's Normative Ethics and his Meta-ethics

These questions about utilitarianism raise a general difficulty for Hutcheson's sentimentalism, and more generally for his treatment of normative judgments. He treats statements about obligations and rightness as predictions about how normal observers react. He cannot consistently say that normal observers ought to be corrected, or that they ought to take moral distinctions more seriously than they do; for these ought-judgments are also predictions about the reactions of normal observers.

Even if we agree with the reactions of normal observers, Hutcheson's theory prevents us from giving the natural interpretation of our agreement. We are inclined to suppose that if we believe our moral sense is usually right, or that we ought to follow it, we accord authority to the moral sense because it conforms to some standard external to it. But Hutcheson's account of moral judgments as statements about the reactions of the moral sense[36] prevents us from evaluating the moral sense in this way.[37]

Utilitarianism, therefore, both seems attractive from a sentimentalist point of view and raises objections to it. If we believe that morally good and bad action results from benevolence, aiming at the pleasure of others, we may suppose that the best action results from the most extensive benevolence aiming at maximum pleasure. If we did not suppose that some sentiment has to be the basis of morally right action, this argument for utilitarianism would not seem plausible; but if we are convinced by Hutcheson's anti-rationalism about motivation, benevolence seems to be the most plausible sentiment to treat as the basis of morally good action. Once we see that better actions seem to result from more extended benevolence, the utilitarian conclusion seems plausible.

This conclusion about the moral agent, however, commits Hutcheson to the further claim that the enlightened moral judge with the correct moral sense is the one who approves of benevolence, and approves of it more the more widely it is extended. If moral judges lack this utilitarian reaction, Hutcheson faces a difficult choice. To safeguard the utilitarian approach in normative ethics, he needs to abandon sentimentalist meta-ethics. If he retains

---

[36] Here as before, I have understood Hutcheson to be a cognitivist, treating moral judgments as statements. Frankena, 'Moral sense', argues that he is a non-cognitivist.

[37] For rationalist criticisms of Hutcheson on this point see §§656, 812.

his meta-ethics, he casts doubt on a utilitarian account of moral goodness. Some normal judges will approve of utility (we may grant), but others will not. Hutcheson's utilitarian analysis of virtues, rights, and laws of nature may well be a true report of what he approves of. But he cannot claim that this necessarily gives a reason for others to approve of the same things; whether they have a reason or not depends on how they react.

Sidgwick believes that for these reasons Hutcheson cannot adequately defend the objective truth of utilitarianism. In Sidgwick's view, a proper rational defence of utilitarianism, or any other objective moral principle, depends on acceptance of a rationalist account of moral judgments, in contrast to Hutcheson's sentimentalism. He suggests that on this point Hume drew the logical conclusion from Hutcheson's position, and so made people aware of the dangerous consequences of sentimentalism.[38]

Sidgwick wrongly suggests that only Hume's endorsement of Hutcheson's sentimentalism made the implications of Hutcheson's position clear. As we will see, Balguy and Burnet (not to mention Butler) already criticize Hutcheson's sentimentalism for its subjectivist tendencies; they do not need Hume to point out the implications of Hutcheson's position. But Sidgwick is right about the philosophical issue that Hutcheson raises. If we try to defend utilitarianism without sentimentalism, we raise doubts about the sentimentalist assumptions that make utilitarianism seem attractive in the first place.

651. The Significance of Hutcheson's Position

Hutcheson is the first modern moralist to try to work out a systematic theory covering the whole area of moral philosophy, including moral psychology, meta-ethics (the metaphysics of moral properties and the epistemology of moral judgment), and normative ethics. While Hobbes, Cudworth, Shaftesbury, and Clarke have something to say on all these topics, Hutcheson expounds and defends an explicit theory whose different parts are meant to support one another. In his view, his anti-rationalism supports his belief in a moral sense, which in turn supports his utilitarianism.

We have considered Whewell's assessment of the cumulative significance of Hutcheson's position, as a defence of Shaftesbury's moral realism. We have found that while this assessment fits Hutcheson's early work, it does not fit the *Illustrations*, which goes beyond Shaftesbury in a subjectivist direction. This subjectivism in turn raises difficulties for Hutcheson's utilitarian arguments.

This side of Hutcheson makes it easier to see why, as Sidgwick remarks, Hume claims to follow Hutcheson against the rationalists, especially in his views about the role of the

---

[38] '... the attempt to exhibit morality as a body of scientific truth fell into discredit, and the disposition to dwell on the emotional side of the moral consciousness became prevalent. But thus the objectivity of duty, with which its authority is bound up, fell out of view, without its being perceived how serious the loss was: for example, we find Hutcheson, in intention most orthodox of moral professors, innocently asking, "why the moral sense should not vary in different human beings, as the palate does". When, however, the new doctrine was endorsed by the dreaded name of Hume, its dangerous nature, and the need of bringing again into pre-eminence the properly intellectual element of the moral faculty, was clearly seen: and this work was undertaken as a part of the general philosophic protest of the Scotch school against the empiricism that had culminated in Hume' (*ME* [1] 91). Sidgwick modifies and shortens the passage in later editions; see [7] 104.

sentiments, feelings, and passions in moral judgment, motivation, and justification, and in the constitution of moral facts.[39] Hutcheson appears closer to Hobbes, Locke, and Cumberland than to Cudworth and Clarke. He tries to remove the most offensive aspects of Hobbes's views about morality. But Hume's development of Hutcheson's sentimentalist claims brings Hutcheson closer to Hobbes than he wants to be.

The position that Hume thinks he sees in Hutcheson may not be Hutcheson's position. Hutcheson might not agree with Hume about the implications of his position, or might not welcome these implications if he were convinced that they followed from his position. Still, Hume's judgment on Hutcheson is not idiosyncratic; he agrees with Hutcheson's rationalist critics. Burnet, Balguy, and Price argue that Hutcheson is committed to one of the worst features of voluntarism, because his view implies that moral judgments are arbitrary and baseless. In contrast to Whewell, they argue that Hutcheson's appeal to the moral sense does not support moral realism and independent morality, but undermines it.

We might reasonably interpret Hume as conceding these implications that the rationalists draw from Hutcheson's position, but then arguing that these implications do not refute the position. Both Hutcheson and his rationalist critics take these objections to be fatal, if they are warranted; hence Hutcheson defends himself against them. Hume argues that they are not fatal; they simply point out the facts about morality that we have to live with.

Hutcheson's position seems, at first sight, impressively systematic; but closer attention suggests that it is incoherent. His main difficulties arise from several sources: (1) He appeals to the immediacy of the moral sense to refute indirect egoism; but he seems to defend utilitarianism by indirect arguments that seem to offer equal support for indirect egoism. Hence his case against egoism and his case for utilitarianism seem to undermine each other. (2) His anti-rationalism supports his appeal to a moral sense, but his subjectivist conception of the moral sense undermines his utilitarianism.

These difficulties do not show that a moral sense theory is mistaken, or that utilitarianism is mistaken, or that one cannot hold both theories at once. But they suggest that we should question Hutcheson's case for holding both at once. His successors hold different views about where he has gone wrong, and about which elements of his position should be retained or rejected.[40]

652. Fielding, Shaftesbury, and Hutcheson

Hutcheson develops, but also modifies, Shaftesbury's opposition to voluntarism, by presenting a sentimentalist account of disinterested concern. He is not the only reader who believes that Shaftesbury maintains a sentimentalist position. Fielding's novels convey, as contemporary readers saw, a similar interpretation of Shaftesbury, and a defence of the position that Fielding ascribes to him. Though we have no reason to believe that Fielding knew Hutcheson's work, he is worth mentioning to show how one might develop Shaftesbury's position, and why critics objected to the views that they traced to Shaftesbury.[41]

[39] See esp. *Letter from a Gentleman*, discussed in §751.   [40] On Hutcheson and Butler see §714.
[41] Harrison, *HFTJ*, ch. 6, compares Fielding with the moral philosophy of his time: he perhaps underestimates the connexion between Fielding and the sentimentalist interpretation of Shaftesbury.

This attitude to Shaftesbury is evident in *Tom Jones*.[42] Moral reflexions in the novel begin from two opposed and unacceptable theoretical positions defended in the frequent disputes between Squire Allworthy's two companions, Square and Thwackum. Square accepts Clarke's belief in eternal and immutable fitnesses that have been evident to rational people at all times; he often appeals to the ancient Stoics in his support. Fielding supports the critics of Clarke who argue that his eternal fitnesses are too vague to offer any definite practical advice. Square manages to appeal to them to justify all sorts of dubious and self-serving conduct, so that, whatever he feels like doing, he has an eternal fitness to support or to excuse him. Thwackum, by contrast, is a theological voluntarist, a parody of the position that Berkeley defends in *Alciphron* against Shaftesbury's belief in a moral sense.[43] He regards Square's outlook as merely pagan. In his view, morality requires the relentless and rigid enforcement of the duties allegedly derived from the Decalogue, and especially the duties of obedience. Thwackum is a sadist, who is only too pleased to appeal to morality for the infliction of pain; hence he particularly emphasizes Scriptural justifications for a belief in hereditary guilt that will license punishment of Jones.

The most conspicuous product of the joint efforts of Square and Thwackum is their pupil Blifil. He learns enough from them to find excuses and pretexts for his own selfish and treacherous hypocrisy. He becomes incapable of genuine love and friendship, as Sophia Western sees when her aunt tries to arrange a marriage between them. Blifil's pious and canting hypocrisy agrees in its conclusions with the open cynicism of Mrs Western.

We might take Fielding to present generous feelings as the appropriate moral outlook that avoids the faults in rationalism and theological voluntarism. But this view is too simple. For he presents some people moved by generous feelings who are still misguided overall. Squire Western is generous to some degree. He loves his daughter Sophia, and he forms warm and friendly feelings towards Jones. But when Sophia tries to oppose his plans for her, he lashes out at her; he never stops to think about whether her interests coincide with his plans. Similarly, his friendly feelings to Jones count for nothing as soon as he finds out that Jones is interested in Sophia and so presents another obstacle to his plans. He does not understand other people, and so has no conception of how their happiness might not fit with their use to him.

Many people share Squire Western's thoughtless and unstable generous feelings. Fielding often displays the thoughtless and fickle judgments and sympathies of 'public opinion'; though the public is often an impartial observer, to the extent that its interests are not directly involved, it is by no means a judicious spectator. People flit from one judgment to the opposite on the slightest impetus. They condemn someone ignorantly, but as soon as he gets what they thought he deserved, they feel exaggerated compassion for him. Malice, envy, and credulity encourage damaging gossip that harms innocent victims. Though Fielding does not suggest that people are incapable of disinterested and sympathetic judgments, he suggests that their sympathies are thoughtless and easily distorted.

---

[42] Published in 1749. The only relevant comment on Shaftesbury's moral philosophy is in ch. 2, where Square mentions Cicero's *Tusculan Disputations* and 'the great Lord Shaftesbury' as authorities for the view that pain is not evil because it is not morally unfit. Dudden, *HF* 679, remarks that Fielding 'appropriated much of the substance of his [sc. Shaftesbury's] philosophy, which he reproduced with some modifications in unphilosophical terms'.

[43] On Berkeley see §614.

In contrast to these people, Allworthy and Jones both display goodness. Since they are different, Fielding avoids suggesting that only one sort of outlook or behaviour can embody goodness. But it is not completely clear where their goodness lies. In both cases it coexists with obvious imperfections. Allworthy tolerates the endless arguments between Square and Thwackum, and does not entirely dismiss either point of view. He is guided by generous feelings that both of them lack, though his judgments, especially in relation to Jones, are erratic—especially if he listens too much to his advisers.

If Allworthy's faults result from his listening too carefully to bad advice, Jones's faults result from impulsiveness that he would have corrected if he had thought about it. Fielding suggests that his failings are relatively minor, and receive unjustified condemnation; though they are open to blame, the blame ought to be balanced by recognition of his overriding merits and his scrupulous conscience. Both Allworthy and Jones show disinterested sympathy with others, and both are loyal and reliable even when the costs to them are severe; on this point they are different from the people with generous but fickle impulses. Though they both make mistakes with serious consequences, the mistakes do not make their character less reliably good and admirable.[44]

How do they manage this, and why are they admirable for doing it? Our admiration implies that the virtuous person is not simply the one whose natural generous impulses are not corrupted by false theories; that description does not separate the virtuous person from Squire Western. Goodness requires some regulation of selfish impulses by steady and discerning generous sentiments. But it is difficult to see how these sentiments can be steady and discerning in the appropriate way if they are not formed on appropriate principles that have some basis beyond their appeal to our sentiments. We might say that Fielding prefers a morality of sentiments and virtues over a morality of principles. But these divisions do not seem completely accurate; he seems to accept some morality of principles, without saying what the principles are or where they come from.[45]

It is reasonable to attribute Fielding's views to the influence of Shaftesbury. The views that we can reasonably derive from his novels, and especially from *Tom Jones*, correspond to the views he expresses in his explicitly ethical essays.[46] Fielding captures one side of Shaftesbury, the side captured by Hutcheson. He represents the importance of disinterested love of virtue, in contrast to the instrumental calculation of how virtuous action promotes one's selfish interest. But Shaftesbury takes this love to be appropriately directed towards 'eternal fitnesses' grasped by reason. We might say roughly that Hutcheson and Fielding grasp one side of this position and Clarke grasps the other. Perhaps this is unfair to Fielding, since he avoids any naive commendation of generous feelings as a guide to moral character; but he does not say much about the principles that might support the appropriately educated

---

[44] Coleridge points out Fielding's emphasis on character as opposed to mere correct behaviour: 'If I want a servant or mechanic, I wish to know what he does;—but of a friend I must know what he is. And in no writer is this momentous distinction so finely brought forward as by Fielding. We do not care what Blifil does;—the deed, as separate from the agent, may be good or ill; but Blifil is a villain;—and we feel him so from the very moment he, the boy Blifil, restores Sophia's captive bird to its native and rightful liberty.' (*Marg.* ii 693) Dudden, *HF* 683–4, cites and discusses Coleridge's remark.

[45] On this comparison between Thwackum, Square, Blifil, and Western see Harrison, *HFTJ* 28–34, who points out that Fielding does not accept an anti-intellectual view that would regard Western as expressing a sound moral outlook.

[46] See Dudden, *HF* 272–5.

generous feelings. He does not consider Hutcheson's utilitarian answer to this question, and such an answer would be difficult to fit into Fielding's praise of uncalculating sympathy.

The sentimentalist side of Fielding is the side that impresses some 18th century critics. In the view of Johnson's biographer Hawkins, Fielding represents the harmful tendencies of contemporary novels.[47] These books begin with Richardson's *Pamela*, but Fielding provokes Hawkins's sharpest criticism.[48] He attacks Sterne for the same sentimentalist tendencies.[49] In saying that Fielding gives us Shaftesbury 'vulgarized', Hawkins may recognize that he does not give a complete picture of Shaftesbury's position; but he does not say what has been left out.

Hawkins's criticism is unspecific. In suggesting that the sentimentalists leave out a 'sense of duty', 'obligation', and 'virtue upon principle', he leaves room for both rationalist and voluntarist answers. Until the relevant notions are explained more clearly, it is not clear whether rationalists or voluntarists can provide what is missing in the sentimentalist outlook.[50]

---

[47] 'They were mostly books of mere entertainment that were the subjects of this kind of commerce, and were and still are distinguished by the corrupt appellation of novels and romances. Though fictitious, and the work of mere invention, they pretended to probability, to be founded in nature, and to delineate social manners.' (Hawkins, *LJ* 213)

[48] 'He was the author of a romance entitled "The history of Joseph Andrews" and of another, "The foundling, or the history of Tom Jones", a book seemingly intended to sap the foundation of that morality which it is the duty of parents and all public instructors to inculcate in the minds of young people, by teaching that virtue upon principle is imposture, that generous qualities alone constitute true worth, and that a young man may love and be loved, and at the same time associate with the loosest women. His morality, in respect that it resolves virtue into good affections, in contradiction to moral obligation and a sense of duty, is that of lord Shaftesbury vulgarized, and is a subject of most excellent use in palliating the vices most injurious to society. He was the inventor of that cant-phrase, goodness of heart, which is every day used as a substitute for probity, and means little more than the virtue of a horse or a dog; in short, he has done more towards corrupting the rising generation than any writer we know of.' (214)

[49] 'Of the writers of this class or sect it may be observed, that being in general men of loose principles, bad economists, living without foresight, it is their endeavour to commute for their failings by professions of greater love to mankind, more tender affections and finer feelings than they will allow men of more regular lives, whom they deem formalists, to possess. Their generous notions supersede all obligation; they are a law to themselves, and having good hearts and abounding in the milk of human kindness, are above consideration that bind men to that rule of conduct which is found in a sense of duty. Of this new school of morality, Fielding, Rousseau, and Sterne are the principal teachers, and great is the mischief they have done by their documents.' (218)

[50] On Hawkins see Kaye in Mandeville, *FB* i, pp. xxii–xxiii.

49

BALGUY: A DEFENCE OF RATIONALISM

653. Hutcheson and Rationalism

Hutcheson's *Inquiry* provoked intelligent criticisms from rationalists who agreed with Clarke. An exchange of letters between Hutcheson and Gilbert Burnet in 1725 encouraged Hutcheson to write the *Illustrations* (published in 1728).[1] Balguy published his criticism of the *Inquiry* in his *Foundation of Moral Goodness*, in 1728. His further thoughts appear in Part II of the *Foundations* (1729).

Balguy not only criticizes Hutcheson, but also tries to defend Clarke's rationalism against criticisms. Hutcheson argues for his sentimentalism partly by presenting it as the only plausible alternative to Clarke's rationalism, and by claiming that the rationalist can give only false or uninformative answers to the main questions that concern the moralist. Balguy answers that Clarke's appeal to motivation by reason is preferable to Hutcheson's theory of desire and action, and that Clarke's analysis of moral judgment as rational recognition of eternal fitnesses is both true and informative.

The later stages in the defence of rationalism and sentimentalism need to be considered in the discussion of Price and Reid on the one side, and Hume on the other. Some of the disputes between Hutcheson and Balguy allow us to see why the later versions of rationalism and sentimentalism develop as they do.

Balguy's criticism is especially useful because it raises a basic question about the consistency of Hutcheson's position. Hutcheson's early work sets out to defend Shaftesbury's realism against Hobbesian egoism and theological voluntarism. As we have seen, he introduces the moral sense to express his rejection of any egoist and instrumentalist accounts of moral judgment. But he also defends a sentimentalist account of the moral sense in opposition to Clarke's rationalism. Balguy argues that the realist and the

---

[1] See Hutcheson, *IMS*, Pref. The sequence of editions of works by Hutcheson and his critics is this: 1725: *IMGE*, ed.1. 1726: *IMGE*, ed.2; Butler, *Sermons*, ed.1. 1728: Letters between Hutcheson and Burnet; *IMS*, ed.1; Balguy, *FMG*, Part I, ed.1. 1729: *IMGE*, ed.3; Balguy, *FMG*, Part II; Butler, ed.2. 1730: *IMS*, ed.2. 1731: Balguy, *FMG*, Part I, ed. 2. 1733: Balguy, *FMG*, Part I, ed.3. 1734: Balguy, *TMT*. 1736: Butler, ed.3. 1738: *IMGE*, ed.4. 1742: *IMS*, ed.3. Beiser, *SR* 314–19, discusses the dispute between Hutcheson and Balguy and Burnet.

sentimentalist sides of Hutcheson's position conflict, and that we can see the basic conflict by examining Hutcheson's relation to voluntarism. Since Hutcheson sets out to refute voluntarism, he has reason to reconsider his position if Balguy shows that it is open to the basic objections that—as Hutcheson and Balguy agree—make voluntarism morally unacceptable.

654. Free Will and Reason

Hutcheson follows Hobbes in accepting a simple compatibilist account of freedom, claiming that we act freely if we are determined by our own desires. Simple compatibilism fits anti-rationalism about motivation. If we claim that we are free only if we are moved by distinctively rational desires, we commit ourselves, in Hutcheson's view, to denying the reality of freedom, because there are no distinctively rational desires.

Balguy criticizes this sentimentalist view. He agrees with Hutcheson's objections to libertarian accounts of freedom that identify free action with action on no sufficient motive. But he notices that Hutcheson takes these objections to imply the impossibility of action that is not the result of non-rational instinct.[2] Balguy believes that if Hutcheson were right on this point, we could not justify ordinary judgments about merit, which presume rational motivation, as opposed to non-rational motivation by instinct.[3] Internal determination of actions does not ensure the sort of freedom that is relevant to moral merit and demerit; hence the sentimentalist account of motivation fails to identify this freedom. Since some sort of rational motivation is necessary for freedom, motivation by sentiment, as the sentimentalists understand it, is insufficient for freedom.

Can the idea of motivation by reason be made more intelligible than Hutcheson supposes? Balguy suggests that recognition of the intrinsic merits of a course of action may move us to action, without any further appeal to a non-rational instinct.[4] If we are rational agents, we can be moved by the merits of a course of action; that claim is no less intelligible and explanatory than the anti-rationalist appeal to a prior non-rational instinct.[5]

---

[2] See the different formulations distinguished in §637.

[3] 'Now I readily grant that there is no merit in acting without any motive or reason. On the other hand, it may be affirmed that neither is there any merit in actions to which the agent is driven by natural instinct. . . . But determining ourselves freely to act and to do what appears conformable to reason, is making the best use of both faculties that we possibly can.' (FMG i = TMT 93 = SB 574)

[4] 'He wants to be informed what are the motives, inducements, or exciting reasons for the choice of virtue, and what the justifying reasons of our approbation of it. He seems to think these questions are not to be answered upon the scheme I am defending: let us then try whether this difficulty be not surmountable without the help of those instincts which he has introduced for that purpose.—What is the reason exciting a man to the choice of a virtuous action? I answer, his very approbation of it is itself a sufficient reason, wherever it is not over-ruled by another more powerful. What can be more just, what more natural, than choosing of a thing that we approve, and even choosing it for that very reason?—But why then do we approve? Or what justifies our approbation of it? I answer in one word, necessity. The same necessity which compels men to assent to what is true, forces them to approve what is right and fit. And I cannot but wonder, that our author should demand a reason for the one more than for the other. In both cases the mind necessarily acquiesces, without regarding or considering the effects or tendencies of either.' (FMG i = TMT 81 = SB 559)

[5] 'Our author's question amounts plainly to this: what does a reasonable creature propose in acting reasonably? Or what is it that induces his will to take counsel of his understanding? As if this were not the very essence of a rational action! The question therefore might as well have been put thus: what is it that induces a man to be a rational agent, when he has it in his power to be otherwise?' (FMG i = TMT 83 = SB 562)

Balguy suggests that motivation by recognition of merits is distinctive of morality; but he could have argued that it is possible in non-moral cases too. His main point is a fair objection to Hutcheson. On behalf of Hutcheson one might say that simply citing a belief is not enough to explain an action, and that we explain an action better if we cite both a belief and a suitably connected non-rational desire. Balguy suggests that it is no less explanatory to cite a belief in the intrinsic merits of a course of action. To be a rational agent is to be capable of acting on the recognition of intrinsic merits.

The claim that we are rational agents with this capacity is no less informative than the claim that we are creatures with the sorts of instincts that Hutcheson recognizes. This is a reasonable answer to Hutcheson, even if it is not decisive. It effectively answers the claim that only an anti-rationalist can explain action. The anti-rationalist explanation may still be preferable to the rationalist's appeal to intrinsic merits of a course of action; but Hutcheson's arguments do not show why it is preferable. Hume is right to believe that Hutcheson's position needs some further defence than Hutcheson provides.

If Balguy is right to object to Hutcheson's anti-rationalism about motivation, he is also right to object to his analysis of free will. For one might reasonably argue that the capacity to act on the apparent merits of different courses of action, and not simply to be moved by one's strongest non-rational desire, is essential to the freedom that is relevant to praise and blame. Hutcheson's attempt to dissolve questions about freedom by taking all determination by desire to imply freedom is open to objection.

If Balguy's criticisms are justified, they might be taken to show that Hutcheson needs to go further than he actually goes in his defence of anti-rationalism. He claims to respect and to support the common view that moral motivation is an expression of freedom, and is therefore open to praise and blame. But perhaps he ought to claim that common sense is confused in its claims about freedom. Common sense assumes that morality in some way expresses freedom because it involves motivation by reason; but this assumption rests—according to the sentimentalist—on a mistaken view about practical reason.[6] Still, even if a sentimentalist might take this more sceptical attitude to freedom, Balguy still shows that Hutcheson's actual attitude is unsatisfactory; the arguments that Hutcheson offers neither support common views on freedom nor prove that rationalist views are less explanatory than Hutcheson's anti-rationalism.

655. The Moral Sense and Motivation: Hutcheson and Burnet

Hutcheson's account of reason and action, together with the assumption that recognition of moral rightness and wrongness guides our action, supports his belief in a moral sense. He argues that if we are obliged, we must have some feeling that motivates us to do what we are obliged to do. This non-rational feeling is the moral sense, and an action's rightness consists in its being approved by this moral sense.

---

[6] Hume perhaps tends towards this view when he suggests that questions about the connexion between morality and praiseworthiness and blameworthiness are the product of 'verbal disputes'. But he does not make it clear how far he has to go in rejecting common-sense views. See §726.

We might disagree with this claim for different reasons: (1) We might accept Hutcheson's strong internalist assumption—that the recognition of moral rightness implies a motive for acting rightly—but maintain rationalism about motivation, claiming that no non-rational desire is needed to make our recognition of rightness practically effective.[7] (2) We might reject internalism and deny that recognition of rightness by itself moves us to action.

Hutcheson's rationalist opponents seem to be tempted by both answers. Sometimes Clarke affirms the first claim, but qualifies it by restricting it to someone who is not perverted. He sometimes concedes, therefore, that in a sufficiently perverse person recognition of rightness is not internally connected with motivation, but some further state is needed if he is to be moved to act rightly. Clarke may not concede, however, that a further state is needed in the person of sound mind. He may suggest that we need no further explanation of why a person of sound mind acts as he does on recognizing moral rightness; we need the further explanation only for the perverse mind.[8]

Burnet sometimes maintains an externalist version of rationalism, accepting the second rationalist answer rather than the first. In his view, we can conceive someone making the right moral judgments while lacking the affections that would cause a favourable feeling towards these judgments.[9] Burnet does not deny the existence or the general correctness of a moral sense, but he denies that it is necessary for making true moral judgments. He argues that we can recognize that an end and an action are reasonable from the moral point of view without thereby having any favourable feeling towards them.

Hutcheson replies that Burnet's appeal to the reasonableness of one or another end is empty.[10] An end is not reasonable in its own right, but only in relation to some further end for which we have an antecedent desire. Similarly, we cannot judge an end reasonable except relatively to a further desired end. Hence judgments about reasonableness must depend on a further desire; hence we need a moral sense.

To show that an end cannot be reasonable in its own right, Hutcheson argues that it is always appropriate to ask 'What makes it reasonable?'. To say that nothing makes it reasonable, or that it makes itself reasonable, is uninformative. To say what makes it reasonable, we always have to say that it appeals to us on the basis of some further end we care about. In the case of morality, the relevant further end is the public good, which appeals to our moral sense. The mere claim that something is reasonable in itself is an appeal to an alleged brute fact.

---

[7] See Price, §819.   [8] See Clarke, §623.

[9] '. . . the reasonableness of the ends of moral agents does not depend on their conformity to the natural affections of the agent nor to a moral sense representing such ends as amiable to him, but singly on their conformity to reason. Reason would always represent the end in the same manner to the rational agent, whatever his affections or inward sense of amiableness were. And supposing a being framed so as to have only selfish affections and yet to be endued with a faculty of reasoning, such a being, if he employs that faculty, must see it to be highly unreasonable that his private interest or pleasure should take place to the destruction of the interest or pleasure or all other beings like himself, though for want of kind affections he would be void of any collateral disposition to act in that manner which to his understanding must necessarily appear reasonable. Nay, such a being would perceive his natural affections to be very unreasonable affections' (Burnet in Hutcheson, IMS 218).

[10] 'Now what are the justifying truths about ultimate ends? What is the truth by conformity to which we approve the desire of public good as an end or call it a reasonable end?' (IMS 229)

Burnet and Balguy reply that some reasons must be taken as ultimate, since we cannot show their reasonableness by appeal to further reasons. Similarly (according to Clarke and Burnet) no further reason can be given for accepting a mathematical axiom, but we do not infer that mathematical judgment requires a further contribution from the affections. On the contrary, mathematical judgments consist in recognizing axioms as ultimate reasons and in reasoning in accordance with them. It is equally appropriate to recognize ultimately reasonable moral principles and to judge in accordance with them. If they are ultimately reasonable, no more ultimate reasons can be given to show that they are reasonable; but it does not follow that we must appeal to some further non-rational desire. Balguy agrees that if I recognize a moral principle as ultimately reasonable, I will normally want to act in accordance with it; but he claims that the desire results from the recognition, and does not explain it.[11]

If a defender of Hutcheson objects that Balguy is appealing to a mere brute fact, not further explained, Balguy might answer that Hutcheson also appeals to a brute fact—a non-rational desire and a tendency to act on that desire. Can we not ask why we should act on that desire? The question 'Why should I?' suggests that we are looking for some further reason that Hutcheson fails to provide.

In this dispute about brute facts the anti-rationalist complains that the rationalist cannot say why we act on what we see to be ultimately reasonable. The rationalist complains that the anti-rationalist cannot say why we should act on basic non-rational desires for ends. The anti-rationalist, therefore, complains about the rationalist's failure to provide a motivating reason, whereas the rationalist complains about the anti-rationalist's failure to provide a normative reason. At first sight, both complaints seem reasonable. Balguy's discussion shows that Hutcheson's assumptions about explanation and reasons do not define all the legitimate questions that can be raised.

656. Balguy on Reasons and Motives

In these criticisms of Hutcheson Balguy and Burnet make claims about reasons and reasonableness that presuppose that we can recognize a normative reason (answering the 'Why should I?' question) without having some antecedent desire to do what we see the normative reason to do. Hutcheson rejects this presupposition about reasons, and offers his own conception of reasons. In reply to Burnet he argues that reasons must be either exciting or justifying reasons, both of which rely on affections (*IMS* 226–7). Balguy argues against Hutcheson on this point, denying the connexion that Hutcheson alleges between justifying reasons and motivation.

---

[11] 'We find our minds necessarily determined in favour of virtue. But I presume such a determination is not antecedent, but consequent to our perceptions of this amiable object. Even the desire of natural good seems to be in reality no instinct, though commonly called and reputed such. Our affections indeed for particular objects are manifestly instinctive, as it was requisite they should; but I see no need of supposing a previous determination of the mind, either to natural good in general, or to moral. As soon as either comes to be perceived, it necessarily determines the mind towards itself. But this determination being consequent to perception, is, if I mistake not, improperly called instinct. It is indeed affection, but that affection, I suppose, is produced in the mind, not antecedently planted in it.' (*FMG* i = *TMT* 92–3 = SB 573)

To show that a justifying reason does not require a further sentiment, Balguy argues that we can recognize merit in an action without thereby approving of it. The recognition of merit is the ground for approval, but is not reducible to approval.[12] According to Balguy, Hutcheson's definition of merit reduces the normative aspect of praiseworthiness—the fact that it provides a reason for praise—to the non-normative fact that it is actually praised. If Hutcheson were right, we could not distinguish qualities that deserve praise from those that receive praise but do not deserve it.

Hutcheson complains that Balguy's definition of merit by reference to worthiness of praise is useless, because it simply provides a synonymous term. We want something more informative than the nearly tautological claim than merit is worthiness,[13] but Balguy's definition fails to provide the 'explication' that we expect from a definition. Hutcheson rejects accounts that identify moral goodness with 'conformity of affections and actions to truth, reason, true propositions, reason of things'. To distinguish moral goodness from true belief in general, we need to add something about conformity to how things ought to be, and this addition simply reintroduces goodness instead of explaining it.[14] Rationalists, therefore, ought to accept his appeal to a moral sense, once they recognize that their accounts of moral goodness do not give an appropriate explication. If we explain 'good', 'ought', 'worthy', 'fit', and 'obligatory' through one another, we have got no further towards an explication. An explication ought to introduce simpler concepts that can be grasped without grasping the normative concepts that we are trying to explicate.

Sentimentalists are right to object that if we can say nothing more about praiseworthiness than that it merits praise, we have not got very far. But the rationalists need not immediately agree that we should seek reductive explications that include only simpler concepts, and only non-normative concepts. For if we can explain one normative concept through accounts that introduce several others, we may say something informative about the connexions between different concepts, without eliminating normative terms. Rationalists might reasonably have pointed out that the sentimentalists overlook this third option beside mere synonymies and reductions.

---

[12] '... to his query concerning the meaning of the words *merit* or *praiseworthiness*; I answer, that they denote the quality in actions which not only gains the approbation of the observer, but which also deserves or is worthy of it. Approbation does not constitute merit, but is produced by it; is not the cause of it, but the effect. An agent might be meritorious, though it were in the power of all other beings to with-hold their approbation, he might deserve their praise, though we suppose him at the same time under an universal censure' (*FMG* i = *TMT* 59 = R 442).

[13] 'Let those who are not satisfied with either of these explications of merit endeavour to give a definition of it reducing it to its simple ideas and not, as a late author has done, quarrelling with these descriptions, tell us only that it is deserving or being worthy of approbation, which is defining by giving a synonymous term.' (*IMS* 165 = R 373) On this issue about definitions see also Price, §812; Reid, §845.

[14] 'These characters belong to every true judgment. Virtue and vice equally conform to moral truth, in so far as we discern truth about them. But when we add further restrictions, our account becomes empty. 'Tis said that these moral truths intended are only such as show what actions are good, what we are obliged to do, what ought to be done. These words mean no more than the word moral goodness; and then the definition is no better than this, "the moral goodness of an action is its conformity to such true propositions as show the action to be good"; or, "good actions are such about which 'tis true that they are good". In general, all descriptions of moral goodness by conformity to reason if we examine them well, must lead us to some immediate original sense or determination of our nature. All reasons exciting to an action will lead us to some original affection or instinct of will; and all justifying reasons, or such as show an action to be good, will at last lead us to some original sense or power of perception.' (*SMP* i 4, 56–7)

But even if Balguy's account is merely synonymous, it is still informative. For if it is correct, it shows that being praised is not the same as being worthy of praise, and hence it refutes an explication that reduces being worthy of praise to being praised. Moreover, since the recognition of a justifying reason includes the recognition of something deserving approval, it is different from a feeling of approval.[15] If we identify it with a feeling of approval, we obscure the basis on which we approve. We approve an action because we see a good justifying reason for it, not because we have a feeling of approval.[16]

If we distinguish justifying reasons from feelings of approval, we can ask whether the recognition of a justifying reason for doing x is sufficient for being motivated to do x. Hutcheson's answer to this question is Yes, since he identifies the reason with the feeling of approval. Balguy is free to answer No, since his account of justifying reasons allows a possible gap between recognizing the reasons and being moved to act on them. But he answers Yes; in his view, action follows approval, and approval follows recognition of justifying reasons.[17]

This claim must be qualified to recognize a possibility that Balguy mentions: the will may exercise its capacity to rebel against the conclusion that reasonably necessarily assents to. Like Clarke, he allows this possibility, but he has some difficulty in explaining it. Though he agrees that the will sometimes rebels against rational assent, he still assumes that rational assent is normally sufficient for action, without any further approval by the will.

He overlooks, therefore, the possible position that would combine his account of justifying reasons with Hutcheson's account of exciting reasons. Perhaps he would reject such a position because it implies that rational assent always needs some non-rational impulse to produce action. Even if some opposed non-rational impulse might interfere with the normal operation of rational assent, it does not follow that its normal operation depends on a favourable non-rational impulse; it follows only that no interfering impulse is present. Balguy might reasonably observe that we often seem to act on the basis of our belief that we have a good reason to do what we try to do. If Hutcheson replies that we must nonetheless have some further non-rational impulse favouring the rational course of action, why should we agree? Either he argues illegitimately from the absence of interfering impulses to the presence of favouring impulses, or he takes his general anti-rationalist account for granted in order to dismiss apparent counter-examples. Though Balguy's discussion is rather brief,

---

[15] 'Internal obligation is a state of the mind into which it is brought by the perception of a plain reason for acting, or forbearing to act, arising from the nature, circumstances, or relations of persons or things. . . . The reasons of things are to men, in respect of practice, what evidence is in speculation. Assent in the one case, and approbation in the other, are equally and irresistibly gained; only there is this difference, that the will has power to rebel, and the understanding has not.' (FMG i = TMT 68–9 = R 450)

[16] For criticism of Balguy on obligation see Price, RPQM 114. See §818.

[17] 'What is the reason exciting a man to the choice of a virtuous action? I answer, his very approbation of it is itself a sufficient reason, wherever it is not overruled by another more powerful. What can be more just, what more natural, than choosing of a thing that we approve, and even choosing it for that reason? But why then do we approve? or what justifies our approbation of it? I answer in one word, necessity. The same necessity which compels men to assent to what is true forces them to approve what is right and fit. . . . Virtue being intrinsically worthy and excellent, fails not to produce a real affection for itself, in all minds that attentively consider it; it not only makes itself approved, but admired; not only admired, but loved, by those that contemplate it in a proper manner: and the better any one is acquainted with it by contemplation and practice, the more amiable it becomes, and the higher his affection rises. Is it then to be wondered, that rational beings should choose what they love, or, in other words, embrace an object of their affections?' (FMG i = TMT 81–2 = R 453)

it suggests reasonable doubts about the view of action and motivation defended by Hobbes, Locke, and Hutcheson.

657. Moral Judgment v. Moral Sense

To strengthen his case against sentimentalism, Balguy tries to explain how Hutcheson came to suppose that approval depends on some sentiment. He distinguishes the recognition of the beauty (pulchrum) in actions from the recognition of their rightness or fitness (honestum). Though he concedes (without actually agreeing) that the recognition of beauty varies according to different people's sense of beauty, he denies that the recognition of rightness varies in the same way.[18] In his later reflexions Balguy withdraws this concession on beauty. In his view, the qualities that Hutcheson takes to arouse beauty as an idea are really those that constitute beauty in the objects.[19] But he recognizes that Hutcheson's view is a tempting conception of beauty, and he argues that moral goodness is not to be understood by analogy with beauty (as Hutcheson understands it).[20]

Balguy argues against the conjunction of Hutcheson's two claims: (1) To be morally good is to be approved of by the moral sense. (2) The moral sense approves of benevolence. Hence he believes that he refutes Hutcheson if he can show that moral goodness consists in something other than benevolence. One might argue that this objection does not refute Hutcheson's first claim. But it is difficult to see what he could easily substitute for benevolence. Though the moral sense is not benevolence itself, but an attitude towards benevolence, it is similar to benevolence in being a disinterested pleasure at people's welfare. This pleasure is the basis for our approval of disinterested concern in others. Hence it is fair of Balguy to attack the conjunction of Hutcheson's two claims by attacking the second claim.

He argues that sometimes we recognize moral goodness in others without ascribing benevolence to them and without exercising our own moral sense. George and Louis produce the same amount of good, but George does it out of benevolent feelings and Louis does it from a sense of honour and duty. These two rulers rule two communities equally well, but George rules over his extended family, whereas Louis rules over complete strangers. In this case, according to Balguy, George acts from his benevolent affection, whereas Louis acts as he does because it is right, without any particular benevolent feeling (since he does not even know most of the people whom he rules).[21] In such cases, we not

---

[18] *FMG* i §5 = *TMT* 60–1 = R 443–4.

[19] He rejects the view that beauty and order are 'not real and absolute in themselves, but merely relative to our faculties, and ... resulting entirely from the constitution and accommodation of a certain internal sense', so that they 'consist wholly in an arbitrary agreement between the objects and the sense' (*DR* 16 = *TMT* 225). Balguy's views on beauty are discussed by Kivy, *SS*, ch. 7.

[20] A sentimentalist analysis of beauty may appear plausible, if we suppose it is impossible to judge something beautiful without finding it attractive or agreeable. But even if we suppose this about beauty, we should reject (in Balguy's view) an analogous conception of moral goodness. Recognizing that an action is right is not the same as finding it attractive; hence the moral sense has no constitutive role in moral rightness.

[21] 'In the former case, a great share of the merit would be placed in the account of natural affection, commonly so called. In the latter, excepting the weaker attachment of common humanity, we discover nothing but pure virtue, and a sense of honour and duty. ... And if instead of small governments, large and populous kingdoms could have

only attribute moral goodness to an agent who has no inclination in favour of it, but we actually attribute greater virtue to the agent who acts on the basis of recognizing rightness, apart from any inclination.[22]

These claims about the agents whose actions and characters are judged imply conclusions about the judges. If Kurt is the judge considering the actions and characters of George and Louis, does Kurt judge on the basis of approval by the moral sense? Balguy answers No, because Kurt recognizes that Louis acts out of some motive other than benevolence. Kurt recognizes this without any sensory reaction to benevolent affections. Hence Kurt's judgment that Louis acted rightly and has a good character does not consist in Kurt's favourable feeling towards Louis's benevolent affections. Hence Hutcheson's claims about the moral sense are wrong.

Balguy's objection does not depend on all his claims about George and Louis. It is enough for his purposes if we agree that our judgments about the comparative goodness of two agents are to some degree independent of our beliefs about the extent of benevolent affection in each. In such a case, the judgment about the goodness of the agents cannot be simply our feeling of approval of their degree of benevolent affection.

Hutcheson might disallow such counter-examples on the ground that they violate his internalist constraint on moral judgment. In his view, an attribution of goodness that is not a reaction of approval towards benevolence would not imply the relevant motivation in the judge; hence it could not be moral judgment. Rationalists may choose either of two replies: (1) They might simply deny the internalist constraint, and claim that moral judgment ascribes a property to an agent that may or may not arouse a favourable feeling in the judge. (2) Clarke and Balguy argue that in the normal person, in the absence of interfering factors, recognition of what is rationally required or appropriate produces the appropriate motive. If this is true of the moral judge, we can explain why Hutcheson's internalist constraint might appear true, even though it is false. For the real connexion between moral judgment and motivation, in the normal person, is not conceptual (part of what it means to be a moral judgment), but it is still necessary; normal rational agents and judges could not be indifferent to moral considerations that present demands of reason.

Hutcheson's internalist constraint, then, does not seem so clearly true that it disqualifies Balguy's examples of moral goodness and moral judgment without benevolent affections and a moral sense. Balguy argues plausibly that our ordinary moral convictions recognize possibilities that Hutcheson overlooks. Hutcheson might answer that our ordinary moral convictions are mistaken about the nature of moral goodness and of moral judgment. Our belief in the purely rational goodness of Louis and the purely rational judgment of Kurt rests on assumptions about reason that Hutcheson believes he has undermined. But he relies on questionable views about practical reason. He points out the obscurity of rationalist claims about reason and about the properties grasped by moral judgment; but he does not show that anti-rationalism is the right answer.

---

been supposed thus circumstanced, the different merit of the legislators would still have appeared in the same light.' (*FMG* i = *TMT* 57 = SB 534)

[22] 'To do good solely from a love of moral rectitude, without any natural impulse or incitement, seems to me the most perfect goodness that we are capable of framing any idea of; and as such, ought, I think, to be constantly ascribed to the supreme being.' (*DR* 10 = *TMT* 219)

658. Morality as an End

Balguy opposes Hutcheson's account of reasons and motives partly because he believes that it gives us a false view of possible reasons for concern with moral goodness. He agrees with Hutcheson's rejection of a purely instrumental account of morality as a means to fulfilling self-confined aims; hence he agrees that morality is to be chosen and pursued for its own sake. But he disagrees about how this is possible. Hutcheson infers that since we would have no reason to choose morality unless it satisfied some antecedent affection, we have a sense that approves benevolence for its own sake; that is the justifying reason for morality. Balguy believes that this explanation reflects a mistake about how we can choose moral goodness for its own sake. For Hutcheson still makes it subordinate to some prior affection that moves us without reference to moral goodness, so that it is not moral goodness itself that we really care about.

Balguy argues that the reasonableness of morality is the source of our affection for it, and is not derived from some prior affection.[23] Hutcheson reverses the right order of reasons and explanation insofar as he requires some affection that is prior to morality and gives us our reason to pursue it.[24] For a morally virtuous person, the requirements of morality are the source of distinctive reasons, and not derived from prior reasons.[25]

To represent the distinct place of morality in establishing reasons, Balguy suggests that Hutcheson makes moral reasons insufficiently stable. If they depended on our moral sense, we would lose them if our moral sense were to change. But this conclusion is mistaken, for in fact the reasons would remain and we would become worse by failing to recognize them.[26]

---

[23] 'And in respect of the divine laws, what is it that convinces us that they are just, and holy, and good? Is it their conformity to a certain disposition which we suppose in the deity? On the contrary, is it not a perception of the intrinsic reasonableness of them, and their tendency to the public good? If we impartially consult our ideas, I am persuaded we shall find that moral goodness no more depends originally on affections and dispositions, than it does on laws; and that there is something in actions, absolutely good, antecedent to both.' (FMG i = TMT 49 = SB 529)

[24] 'What I contend for at present, is, that without regarding or thinking of the pleasure it may yield, we esteem virtue or moral rectitude upon its own account; that our affection for it, is not an instinctive determination, but raised and produced in the mind by the intrinsic worth and goodness of the object. Most other objects are therefore good, because they are adapted to our faculties, or our faculties to them. But truth and virtue are good in themselves, and necessarily appear so to all beings capable of perceiving them: their excellence is not borrowed or adventitious, but inherent and essential: they reflect not a foreign light, but shine like the sun, with their own proper rays and native lustre.' (FMG i = TMT 79 = SB 556)

[25] 'I affirm and maintain, that though moral good greatly promotes natural good, it is moreover in itself an absolute good. What proof can we give of the absolute goodness of pleasure, but that we approve of it, upon its own account, and pursue it for its own sake? The same proof we have of the absolute goodness of virtue, which, considered by itself, and abstract from every other thing, necessarily extorts our approbation, and appears worthy of our choice. Our approving and admiring it antecedently to those satisfactions which flow from it, is an undeniable proof of its absolute and inherent worth. —And as virtue is absolute good, as well as pleasure, so that it is of a different and superior kind, evidently appears from this single consideration; that whereas natural objects are only therefore good, because they gratify; moral objects therefore gratify, because they are good. Natural good is mere gratification. In moral good there is gratification likewise, and that of the best and noblest kind; but it is the consequence of original and essential goodness. The correspondence or congruity between natural objects and their faculties, is arbitrary and mutable; between moral objects and their faculties, necessary and immutable.' (FMG i = TMT 89–90 = SB 570)

[26] 'He grants, (speaking of virtue) that the lovely form never fails to raise desire, as soon as it appears. But this desire, according to his notion, is only an instinctive affection, suited and accommodated to its object. And even this object, virtue itself, which he calls a lovely form, appears, I think, in his representation, far less lovely than it really is. For he has represented this loveliness, not as absolute and necessarily inherent, but as factitious and communicated. According to him, suppose but the moral sense inverted, and then vice, as we now call it, becomes the lovely form. But surely

On this point Balguy believes the Stoics are right.[27] Though they are wrong to suppose that moral virtue is the only good, they have seen that morality is a source of non-derivative reasons.

These claims about virtue help to explain what Balguy means in saying that virtue is good 'in itself' and that sentimentalism does not show that it is good in itself.[28] To say that it is good in itself is not only to say that it is good non-instrumentally; everything that, apart from its consequences, satisfies an antecedent desire meets this condition. Virtue is good in itself because it is good without reference to anything external to it; hence its goodness is not relative to any affections that it satisfies.[29]

It is not completely clear, however, what Balguy's condition allows and what it excludes. He is right to object to Hutcheson's view that the value of virtue is derived from approval by the moral sense; that view overlooks the fact that we expect morality to form our ends, and not simply to promote or to achieve ends that we already pursue. But does he also mean, for instance, that virtue cannot be worth choosing for any features that we can describe in non-moral terms? Does he, for instance, deny that the value of virtue might consist in its fulfilling the human function or being in accord with human nature? That seems to depend on whether these properties belong to virtue itself, or are simply coincidental to it. Since Balguy does not answer these questions, his demand that we value virtue for itself does not isolate the theories that respect his demand from those that do not. Nonetheless, his demand casts reasonable doubt on a sentimentalist theory.

659. How is the Moral Sense Corrigible?

In claiming that Hutcheson fails to show how moral virtue can be valued for itself, Balguy attacks not only Hutcheson's anti-rationalist moral psychology, but also his epistemology and metaphysics of morality. Hutcheson's account of the moral sense maintains an internal connexion between moral judgment and motivation. It also includes an epistemological claim, that moral judgment is not a kind of rational belief and judgment, and a metaphysical

---

this is a misrepresentation of virtue, the excellence of which is not precarious nor derived, but essential, absolute, and independent.' (*FMG* i = *TMT* 80 = SB 557)

[27] 'Thus it is with right reason, or moral good. It shows indeed how to proceed in our inferior pursuits, and gives weight to our least actions; but at the same time it raises our minds to higher contemplations, and presents itself to our view, as an object of supreme worth, and unrivalled perfection. So great and splendid did this good appear to some of the ancient philosophers, that it dazzled their eyes, and overpowered their senses. All inferior objects vanished before it, and they could find no good in anything else. But as it is not true, that virtue is the only good: so much less is it true that there is no intrinsic goodness in it; or that it is not worthy to be pursued for its own sake.' (*FMG* ii 11 = *TMT* 128)

[28] 'For in virtue there is an inherent worth, an objective perfection. It is essentially good in it self, and has no dependence on any agents, or any faculties. As such, it is upon its own account, and for its own sake, worthy to be chosen and pursued by moral agents, who cannot but acknowledge and admire its intrinsic excellence.' (*FMG* ii 11 = *TMT* 129–30 = SB 724)

[29] 'But let us suppose virtue and interest neither in conjunction nor opposition; or let us suppose a man in possession of all his desires. Would it, upon this supposition, be wrong and foolish in him, to perform several actions, merely because he saw them to be just, fit, reasonable, virtuous? If it would, the consequence must be, that the same action may be right and wrong, reasonable and unreasonable at the same time. I mean, not in different respects, but upon the whole, which is a manifest contradiction.' (*FMG* ii 10 = *TMT* 127)

claim, that moral properties are not features of the actions and people to whom we seem to ascribe them, but are ideas in our minds. Hutcheson derives this denial of externality from his conception of a sense and its objects. But even if he did not deny the externality of moral properties, his conception of the moral sense would commit him to a further metaphysical claim about stability and objectivity. In claiming that moral goodness is essentially what is approved by the moral sense, he implies that any change in our moral sense would also be a change in what is morally right.

Burnet and Balguy appeal to claims about corrigibility that Cudworth uses against Hobbes.[30] Cudworth argues that obligation cannot be reduced to commands, because it is open to us to ask whether the commander has the appropriate authority and a command cannot establish its authority simply by commanding. Burnet uses this argument against Hutcheson's conception of the moral sense. In his view, we are justified in relying on the reactions of the moral sense only insofar as we have some reason to believe that it captures moral rightness. Hence we have to face a real question about moral rightness that is not answered by simply recording the reaction of the moral sense. Since we face such a question, moral rightness is antecedent to the moral sense, not constituted by the reactions of the moral sense.[31] The moral sense is corrigible in principle by reflexion on whether it accurately represents the properties it purports to represent.[32]

Hutcheson answers that he can readily allow the moral sense to be corrigible in the same way as other senses are corrigible. The fact that sight is corrigible does not show that colours are not essentially the objects of a sense. Similarly, the moral sense is corrigible, but moral properties are essentially the objects of a sense. We can correct a particular sense on a particular occasion by taking a closer look, or by reference to how things generally look to that sense. We can even correct one person's senses by reference to how things generally look to normal perceivers. The moral sense is corrigible in the same way. When we learn more about the effects of an apparently benevolent action, for instance, our initial feeling of approval may change to a feeling of disapproval. And if we find we are eccentric in our

---

[30] On Cudworth see §548. On Balguy and Burnet see Winkler, 'Realism' 190, on the 'inverted moral spectrum'. The questions that they raise are relevant to dispositional theories of value, such as those discussed by Smith, Lewis, Johnston, 'Dispositional'. Wright, 'Values' 8–9, briefly discusses the objection that 'if some practice stops having a certain sort of moral effect on us—not because of any change in its manner, circumstances, or other effects, but because *we* change—a dispositional account of moral qualities has no option . . . but to construe that as a change in the moral status of the practice, even if our preferred description of the case would invoke the ideas of improved or deteriorated moral discrimination.' Wright thinks this objection can be answered by an appropriate description of the kind of subject whose dispositions are being considered. He mentions (9n) that one might say that moral rightness is a property that provokes our actual reactions (as opposed to those that it would provoke if we were to change). This suggestion is explored by Lewis, 'Dispositional' 127.

[31] 'The perception of pleasure, therefore, which is the description this author has given of the moral sense, seems to me not to be a certain enough rule to follow. There must be, I should think, something antecedent to justify it and to render it a real good. It must be a reasonable pleasure before it be a right one or fit to be encouraged or listened to.' (*IMS* 204)

[32] 'Thus, as deriving virtue merely from natural affection, implies it to be of an arbitrary and changeable nature; our judging and approving of it by a moral sense implies the same: forasmuch as this sense, as well as that affection, might possibly have been quite contrary to what it is at present; or may be altered at any time hereafter. Accordingly our author grants, there is nothing in this surpassing the natural power of the deity. But I humbly apprehend he is mistaken; and that it is no more in the power of the deity to make rational beings approve of ingratitude, perfidiousness, &c. than it is in his power to make them conclude, that a part of any thing is equal to the whole.' (Balguy, *FMG* i = *TMT* 62 = SB 538)

approvals, we can correct them by reference to the moral sense of other people. Though we can correct our moral perceptions, moral properties are essentially the objects of a moral sense.[33]

Hutcheson is right to say that sometimes we correct a sense by reference to the perceptions of healthy or normal perceivers, even though we take the object of the sense to depend essentially on their reactions. Hence we might say that some jokes are not really funny, because they strike some people, but not most people, as funny. We do not imagine that we are pointing out some feature of a joke that is independent of the reactions of hearers. If we originally found the joke funny, we may not find it less funny when we recognize that it is not really funny, because it affects other people differently from how it affects us. This sort of corrigibility raises no difficulty for Hutcheson.

But this is not the only way we can correct the senses. Even if we took colours to be in some way relative to the usual perceiver, we would not need to endorse Hutcheson's account. We might say that red is essentially the property that causes such-and-such reactions. Our definition would be relative to certain reactions, but the continued existence of the colours themselves would not depend on the continued existence of the perceivers with these reactions.[34] A key that is made to open a lock of a specific shape may still exist even if there is no lock with that shape. Hence we need not infer that the continued existence of colours depends on the reactions of perceivers.

Nor is it clear that we take the objects of sense to be relative to the usual perceiver. When we correct one person's perception of colour by reference to the perceptions of 'normal' and 'healthy' perceivers, we take the 'healthy' perceiver to be not the usual perceiver, but the perceiver who is best at detecting actual redness (whatever we take this to be). If most people were a little colour-blind to differences between red and green, we would not infer that the colours of red and green traffic lights are the same. We rely on the judgments of the people we take to be better at detecting red and green. Hence we believe that colours exist apart from particular perceivers, or the most usual type of perceiver. We rely on this belief when we correct some perceivers, and when we take some to be better than others.

But whatever we think about ways of correcting the ordinary senses, the moral sense seems to be open to corrections that conflict with Hutcheson's conception. A correction of

---

[33] 'We do not denominate objects from our perceptions during the disorder, but according to our ordinary perceptions, or those of others in good health. Yet nobody imagines that therefore colours, sounds, tastes, are not sensible ideas.' (*IMS* 163 = R 371) 'Our reason often corrects the report of our senses about the natural tendency of the external action and corrects rash conclusions about the affections of the agent.' (*IMS* 164 = R 371) 'But must we not own, that we judge of all our senses by our reason, and often correct their reports of the magnitude, figure, colour, taste of objects, and pronounce them right or wrong, as they agree or disagree with reason? This is true. But does it then follow, that extension, figure, colour, taste, are not sensible ideas, but only denote reasonableness, or agreement with reason? Or that these qualities are perceivable antecedently to any sense, by our power of finding out truth? Just so a compassionate temper may rashly imagine the correction of a child, or the execution of a criminal, to be cruel and inhuman: but by reasoning may discover the superior good arising from them in the whole; and then the same moral sense may determine the observer to approve them. But we must not hence conclude, that it is any reasoning antecedent to a moral sense, which determines us to approve the study of public good, any more than we can in the former case conclude, that we perceive extension, figure, colour, taste, antecedently to a sense. All these sensations are often corrected by reasoning, as well as our approbations of actions as good or evil: and yet no body ever placed the original idea of extension, figure, colour, or taste, in conformity to reason.' (*IMS* 134–5 = R 365)

[34] See Hutcheson, §642.

someone's judgment compares it with the judgment of good moral judges, not simply with usual moral judges. Moreover, we assume that good judges are good because they detect the relevant properties. Hence the moral properties exist independently of the reactions of good judges; if they did not, good judges would not detect them. Moral properties, therefore, are not essentially what the moral sense approves of.

We might also suggest, on behalf of the rationalists, that moral properties are different from the objects of the senses in a further way that Hutcheson does not notice. Even if we deny that sensory properties depend on being perceived, or on the existence of a particular type of perceiver, we might argue that they are essentially sensory. If they were not in some way capable of being perceived by the senses, they would not be (we might say) the properties they are. If a property lacked even this connexion to sight, we might conclude that it is not colour. This, however, does not seem to be true of moral properties. For moral goodness seems to be defined by reference to agents and actions, not by reference to the sensory reactions of spectators and judges. If it is essential to colour, sound, and so on that they can be immediately grasped by a special sense, moral properties seem to be disanalogous in this respect, and do not seem to be essentially sensory properties.

Burnet and Balguy argue that we are justified in accepting the reactions of our moral sense to the extent that we believe, for reasons not derived wholly from the moral sense, that it detects moral properties that are not essentially dependent on it. Since we can assess the correctness of our affective reactions by principles that are not derived wholly from these reactions, moral judgment does not seem to be simply the concern of the moral sense. Hutcheson allows that moral judgments are corrigible, and argues that his theory allows for the relevant sort of correction. If he is wrong, a defence of sentimentalism needs to show that the rationalists are wrong about the extent to which we can correct the moral sense.

660. Balguy, Hutcheson, and Euthyphro

If Hutcheson were right to take moral properties to depend essentially on the moral sense, moral rightness would change if our moral sense were to approve different things. The moral sense theory, therefore, does not make morality 'eternal and immutable' in Cudworth's sense. Cudworth attacks Hobbes for making morality mutable in relation to decisions of legislators. Balguy develops Cudworth's argument by applying it to the moral sense. He argues that Hutcheson makes morality inappropriately mutable just as Hobbes does.[35]

This may seem an unfair attack on Hutcheson. For he follows Shaftesbury and (without knowing it) Cudworth in defending the natural character of morality against those voluntarists who make it depend on law, artifice, or convention. In Hutcheson's view, 'our first ideas of moral good depend not on laws'. For when we ask whether laws are just, we are not asking simply whether they are laws; and when we ask whether what God wills is just we

---

[35] Balguy had no direct access to Cudworth's work before the first publication of FMG i in 1728. But he could have derived his argument from reflexion on Clarke.

are not simply asking whether God wills it. We cannot reasonably ask whether God wills what God wills, but we can reasonably ask whether what God wills is just.[36]

Hutcheson observes that voluntarist writers try to reassure us by asserting that since God is good, what God wills is also good, so that we need not worry about whether what God wills might be bad. He remarks that this assertion, as defenders of voluntarism intend it, depends on the non-voluntarist belief that being good consists in something more than in being willed by God; for the voluntarist reassures us only if we take 'God's will is good' to say more than that God's will is God's will. The same objection holds if a voluntarist tries to reassure us by asserting that since God is good, God wills what God ought to will. These claims are reassuring only if we understand 'ought' in ways that are inconsistent with the theological moralist's explanation.[37] Hence the reassurance that voluntarists offer is reassuring only if it is understood so as to conflict with voluntarism.

Balguy acknowledges that Hutcheson presents these arguments against voluntarism.[38] But he believes that, even if Hutcheson tries to avoid voluntarism, sentimentalism repeats the central errors of voluntarism, and is therefore open to Cudworth's objections against Hobbes.[39] For it seems that a reasonable question can be asked about whether what the moral sense approves is good. In asking this question, we are not asking whether the moral sense approves what it approves. The latter question is easily answered, but the question we want to ask is not so easily answered.

The same objection can be expressed through Cudworth's argument about mutability. According to the sentimentalist, what is morally right is right insofar as it appeals to our actual sympathetic and benevolent feelings. What is right would change, therefore, if these feelings changed. If we make morality mutable in this way, we distort the character of moral principles and our reason for observing them.[40] In this objection, Balguy adapts Socrates'

---

[36] 'But to call the laws of the supreme Deity *good* or *holy* or *just*, if all goodness, holiness, and justice be constituted by laws, or the will of a superior any way revealed, must be an insignificant tautology, amounting to no more than this, 'that God wills what he wills. Or that his will is conformable to his will'. It must then first be supposed that there is something in actions which is apprehended absolutely good . . .' (Hutcheson, *IMGE* 7.5 = L 181 (and n17) = R 351) For discussion see Price, §811.

[37] 'The writers . . . who deduce all ideas of good and evil from the private advantage of the actor, or from relation to a law and its sanctions, either known from reason, or revelation, are perpetually recurring to this moral sense which they deny; not only in calling the laws of the Deity just and good, and alleging justice and right in the Deity to govern us; but by using a set of words which import something different from what they will allow to be their only meaning. Obligation, with them, is only such a constitution, either of nature, or some governing power, as makes it advantageous for the agent to act in a certain manner. Let this definition be substituted, wherever we meet with the words, ought, should, must, in a moral sense, and many of their sentences would seem very strange; as that the deity must act rationally, must not, or ought not to punish the innocent, must make the state of the virtuous better than that of the wicked, must observe promises; substituting the definition of the words, must, ought, should, would make these sentences either ridiculous, or very disputable.' (*IMGE* 7.4 = L 180 = R 350)

[38] 'I am as unwilling, as our author can be, that virtue should be looked upon as wholly artificial. Let it by all means be represented as natural to us; let it take its rise, and flow unalterably from the nature of men and things, and then it will appear not only natural but necessary.' (Balguy, *FMG* i = *TMT* 46 = SB 527)

[39] 'Our author . . . has made the following observation, that our first ideas of moral good depend not on laws, may plainly appear from our constant inquiries into the justice of laws themselves; and that not only of human laws, but also of the divine. What else can be the meaning of that universal opinion, that the laws of God are just, and holy, and good? Very right. But I wonder much this sentiment should not have led the author to the true original idea of moral goodness. For after we have made such inquiries, do we find reason to conclude, that any laws are good, merely from their being conformable to the affections of the legislator?' (*FMG* i = *TMT* 48–9 = SB 529)

[40] '. . . it seems an insuperable difficulty in our author's scheme, that virtue appears in it to be of an arbitrary and positive nature; as entirely depending upon instincts, that might originally have been otherwise, or even contrary to

challenge to Euthyphro and Cudworth's challenge to voluntarism, in order to show that Hutcheson has not escaped the basic objection.[41]

This adaptation of the argument against voluntarism assumes that facts about our approval are not relevant to an action's changing from being right to being wrong. If God's changing his mind makes no difference to the facts that determine rightness and wrongness, why should a change in our mind make a difference? The basic objection to voluntarism assumes that the facts relevant to rightness and wrongness are facts about human beings, their nature, and their environment, not facts about anyone's attitude to these things. If this objection defeats voluntarism, it should, as Balguy sees, defeat sentimentalism as well.

661. Hutcheson and Open Questions

To see whether Balguy is right to use Cudworth's arguments about mutability and open questions against Hutcheson, we need to distinguish two ways of understanding the claim that an alleged definition leaves an open question: (1) A semantic open question. When Shaftesbury and Hutcheson suggest that substitution of 'willed by God' for 'good' in 'Good is what is willed by God' reduces a non-tautologous sentence to a tautology, they might be observing that 'good' and 'willed by God' do not mean the same. (2) A moral open question. When Cudworth claims that Hobbes's account of right as what the legislator wills leaves a question open, he means that it leaves open a reasonable moral question, and so does not give a satisfactory account of what rightness consists in, which would be a satisfactory explanation of what makes things right.[42]

We might defend Hutcheson by relying on the difference between these two types of open question. Perhaps Balguy's objection proves only that the moral sense theory creates a semantic open question about 'right' and 'approved by the moral sense', so that we cannot claim that 'right' means 'approved by the moral sense'. But the moral sense theory is not intended—Hutcheson might reply—as an account of the meaning of moral terms, and so the presence of semantic open questions raises no difficulty for it.

But if Hutcheson relies on this defence, he raises a doubt about his objection to theological voluntarism. He seems to say that he has identified a semantic open question (when he says that substitutions would make the sentences either ridiculous or very disputable). But why should theological voluntarists not reply that they do not intend to analyse the meaning of moral terms, but to give an account of what moral rightness consists in? Semantic open questions do not necessarily undermine such an account.[43]

Hutcheson does not attack theological voluntarism simply because he thinks it gives the wrong analysis of the meaning of 'good' and 'right'. He does not intend to concede that it may be a correct account, for all he has said, of what moral goodness and rightness consist in. If he has given a reason to reject voluntarism as an account of moral goodness, he should

---

what they are now, and may at any time be altered or inverted if the Creator pleases. If our affections constitute the honestum of a morality, and do not presuppose it, it is natural to ask, what it was that determined the Deity to plant in us those affections rather than any other?' (*FMG* i = *TMT* 46–7 = R 438).

[41] See Clarke, §617.   [42] On this distinction see §815.

[43] See Adams's defence of theological voluntarism in 'Wrongness'.

take the open questions he has raised to be moral, and not merely semantic. His position is consistent if he maintains that his attack on voluntarism identifies moral open questions, whereas Balguy's attack on him identifies only semantic open questions.

But are Hutcheson's open questions about voluntarism so different from Balguy's open questions about sentimentalism? If Hutcheson rejects theological voluntarism, he agrees that counterfactuals such as 'If God commanded us to kill innocent people for fun, it would be right to kill them for fun' raise legitimate doubts about the voluntarist position. They raise such doubts if we consider a case where nothing about the innocence of the people or the value of their life is different, and only God's attitude to these things is different. If we doubt whether what is right and wrong would change, we assume that rightness and wrongness depend on facts about the victims, their killers, and their environment, not on someone's attitude to these facts. But once we understand our doubts, we seem equally justified in asking similar questions about such counterfactuals as 'If the moral sense approved of killing innocent people for fun, it would be right to kill them for fun'. In this case also, all the morally relevant facts are the same, and someone's attitude to them is the only different feature of the case.

Balguy has a reasonable ad hominem objection, therefore, to Hutcheson, given Hutcheson's use of open questions. It is more than an ad hominem objection, however, if the assumptions underlying Balguy's appeals to open questions are reasonable.

662. Divine Goodness: Bayes and Grove

Hutcheson argues that theological voluntarism cannot give a plausible account of God's moral attributes.[44] Against the voluntarist view, he affirms that God is essentially benevolent. Since we know this about God, we also know that it is not an accident that we have the moral sense that we have. Our approval of benevolence results from God's benevolent choice to give us a moral sense that approves of actions promoting our greatest good.

Hutcheson's claims about God provoke a controversy between Balguy, Bayes, and Grove about whether God acts out of rectitude (Balguy), benevolence (Bayes), or wisdom (Grove) (114).[45] Bayes defends Hutcheson's position, on the ground that it offers the only clear account of the divine nature. He complains that appeals to divine rectitude are too vague unless they are explicated by further attributes of God (DB 8). We cannot appeal to divine justice to show that divine benevolence is limited by other moral criteria; for justice needs a utilitarian analysis (10). Similarly, it is unhelpful to appeal to fitness, as Clarke and Balguy do; for fitness has to be fitness for some end. If (as Bayes supposes) utilitarian benevolence provides the only suitable end, Balguy does not offer a genuine alternative to a utilitarian account (14). If we attribute non-utilitarian aims to God we make God's aims unknowable (18), and we introduce untenable distinctions. Bayes argues that we cannot reasonably

---

[44] The voluntarist seems to be forced to say that God's goodness consists in the fact that God wills whatever he wills, since all goodness consists simply in being willed by God. Even if God cares about the sorts of things we regard as morally good, that is simply a fact about God's will; God does not will them because they are good, since their goodness is nothing more than God's willing them. Hutcheson rejects the conclusion that whatever God willed, it would be good.

[45] See Balguy, DR; Bayes, DB; Grove, WFSAD.

distinguish just punishment from punishment aiming at good consequences (49), and that we cannot distinguish good order in the universe from general happiness. Similarly, Balguy's suggestion that God aims at objective beauty in the universe is misguided, since there is no objective beauty. Balguy confuses beauty itself with the cause of beauty, as if one were to say that heat is the 'intestine motion of particles of bodies', when one really means that this motion is the cause of heat (43).

In reply to Bayes's defence of Hutcheson both Grove and Balguy deny that God's moral nature consists entirely or primarily in utilitarian benevolence. Grove's argument for divine wisdom is directed against voluntarism and anti-rationalism as well as utilitarianism. He claims that if we attribute moral perfections to God, we must also ascribe rightness and wrongness to actions independently of God's choosing them.[46] He also rejects Hutcheson's claim that, since the choice of ends depend on affection rather than reason, God's wisdom consists simply in the knowledge of means, not in the choice of ends. Hence Grove rejects Hutcheson's views on exciting and justifying reasons (18).[47] He agrees with Balguy in believing that Hutcheson's conception of benevolence as a psychological necessity for God is no better than the Cartesian ascription of arbitrary choice to God.[48] A voluntarist cannot explain the difference between God's right and God's power, and hence cannot resist Hobbes's argument for deriving God's right from God's power.[49] Those who accept extreme Calvinist views find themselves in this Hobbesian position.

Those who believe that God's choice of moral principles results from necessary divine benevolence cannot, in Grove's view, explain how either God or human agents choose their actions freely, or how vicious people are responsible for their vice. Vicious people, like God, follow their inclinations; how can they help it if their inclinations are different from God's? They cannot be expected to act so as to change their inclinations, since such action would have to proceed from their present inclination (WFSAD 96).

One difference between naturalists and voluntarists may be expressed in the question whether obedience to God is prior to imitation of God. Grove argues against Warburton that imitation is prior.[50] The priority of imitation implies that we recognize the wisdom of God in preferring actions that are right in themselves, so that we accept the divine law.

---

[46] 'That there are different moral kinds of action, some fit, others unfit to be done, some becoming, others unbecoming the supreme being, and this independently of his choosing or willing them, is as evident, as that there are moral perfections and excellencies belonging to the divine nature.' (Grove, WFSAD 1)

[47] 'As certainly . . . as all the ways of God are wise and righteous and good, they are the result of wisdom and not of unguided inclinations. The same wisdom that discovers the reasonableness of one end, one scheme, one method to another, is inducement enough to a being in whom there is the most perfect rectitude of nature, to prefer that end, that scheme, that method in all his works.' (WFSAD 19)

[48] He quotes at length from Descartes, Reply to Sixth Objections §6, who argues that omnipotence of God implies complete indifference between alternative options. Grove's argument is quite similar to Cudworth's, though it might equally be derived from Clarke (WFSAD 23–5).

[49] 'And if there be no difference between physical and moral power, or between mere power and right . . . we have then no absolute security that God will not thus act [sc. damn his innocent creatures]; and how much better, I pray, is the sovereignty ascribed by some to the most excellent of all beings than this monstrous, this boundless right of Hobbes? For my part, I cannot see wherein they differ; since each, like a vast abyss, swallows up without distinction everything that is thrown into it. In all likelihood, Hobbes had never thought of that absurd notion, or would have been ashamed to broach it, if the then reigning systems in divinity had not given authority to that and several other parts of his wild scheme of religion, morality, and politics.' (WFSAD 26)

[50] 'Imitation is prior to obedience. My reason for asserting this is, that to obey God presupposes our having made a right use of our intellectual powers and faculties, the result of which is a conviction that God hath given us a law which

Doddridge favours the views of Balguy and Grove over the utilitarianism assumed by Bayes's argument for God's necessary benevolence.[51] His conclusion is similar to Butler's view that benevolence is not the only relevant moral attribute of God. Doddridge believes God is perfectly good or benevolent, insofar as God 'promotes the happiness of others so far as it is fit to be promoted' (*Course* 111). The qualification rejects the attribution of a maximizing utilitarian attitude to God.

It would be consistent to agree with Doddridge and Grove about the divine nature against voluntarists and sentimentalists, and still to accept utilitarianism; for one might argue that a perfectly reasonable agent will accept utilitarianism. Cumberland holds that God rationally chooses to promote the common good because this is the reasonable end; and one might defend a parallel claim about utility. Hutcheson's rationalist opponents, however, deny that practical reason supports utilitarianism; Balguy, Butler, Doddridge, and Price all maintain that practical reason imposes some limits on the pursuit of maximum utility. In defending utilitarianism on rationalist grounds Sidgwick accepts a position that his 18th-century predecessors consider and reject.[52]

663. How Sentimentalism Agrees with Voluntarism

Hutcheson's theory implies that God is good insofar as our moral sense approves of his character and actions. This account of God's goodness implies that if our moral sense were to change and no longer approve benevolence, God would no longer be good. This result seems even more surprising than the voluntarist claim that if God were to will that we act cruelly rather than kindly, kindness would no longer be good. Instead of making our goodness depend on God, the sentimentalist seems to make God's goodness depend on ours.

Hutcheson might answer that though this change in us is logically possible, God's goodness prevents it. For God, out of goodness towards us, has given us a moral sense that approves of benevolence, and God will not change his mind. This defence leads Balguy to ask why God maintains his goodness. He raises this question in discussing Hutcheson's account of how God's goodness explains the uniformity of the moral sense. According to Hutcheson God is benevolent, and necessarily communicates to us the moral sense that is best for human beings.

Balguy objects that this account of God's goodness makes God's goodness a mere fact of God's nature that is independent of God's wisdom, and hence implies that God is not free.[53]

---

we are bound to obey, and a resolution to obey it. Now in this right use of our faculties, we evidently imitate the supreme of all beings who constantly exerts his most perfect knowledge and power after the most perfect manner.' (*WFSAD* 101)

[51] 'It seems that a virtuous mind may be as easy, in considering God as a being of universal rectitude, as if we were to consider him as a being of unbounded benevolence: nay it seems, that in some respects the former will have the advantage; as it is impossible for us confidently to say, what will be for the greatest happiness of the whole; but on the other hand, we may naturally conclude that rectitude will on the whole incline God to treat the virtuous man in a more favourable manner than the wicked.' (Doddridge, *Course* 117) Cf. §877.

[52] See Sidgwick, *ME*, p. xx ('a utilitarian on an intuitional basis').

[53] 'But will not that disposition, and that principle in the Deity, which are supposed to correspond to our natural affections, and moral sense, certainly incline him universally to communicate and continue that same sense to all rational

We might think this is a dangerous objection for Balguy to raise; for he does not believe it is possible, given the nature of God, for God to approve of what is evil. Does he not also deny that God is free? If so, his charge against Hutcheson rebounds on him. Balguy, however, might fairly answer that God's recognizing a truth that is not subject to his will is not a limitation on his freedom. Given the nature of God, God chooses freely to act according to true principles of right. But if God is necessitated by a fact about his nature independent of his judgments of truth and right, he is not free.

From the rationalist point of view, Hutcheson's position implies that the ends God achieves in the world do not reflect God's wisdom, since, according to the sentimentalist, wisdom and reason do not apply to the choice of ends. But if we reflect on the wisdom and goodness of God, we must—according to the rationalists—include the ends that God achieves in creation.[54] If, as Hutcheson implies, these ends are not the result of God's wisdom in choosing, God is no wiser in choosing to benefit the creation than he would be in choosing to torture his innocent creatures.[55]

It would not help Hutcheson to answer that God is free not to communicate his moral sense to us. For then Balguy might reasonably ask why God chooses to communicate it. Hutcheson cannot say that God sees that this is the right thing to do, since what is right (according to Hutcheson) is simply what is approved by the moral sense. It must, then, be an arbitrary choice by God.

These arguments seek to show that Hutcheson cannot answer the charge of arbitrariness and positivity by appealing to God; he cannot say that the moral sense is reliable because God has given it to us out of his goodness. If God's goodness is simply God's having the qualities that God's moral sense approves, the resort to God simply pushes the arbitrariness back a step. If, however, this is not the right account of God's goodness, goodness is not simply what elicits the approval of the moral sense.

On the ground that he has chosen, Balguy's objections are powerful. Hutcheson would be well advised to deny him this ground. Balguy assumes that moral properties cannot be arbitrary or mutable in certain ways, because we can give a further reason, in the nature of the properties themselves, for judging the moral sense to be right or wrong. Hutcheson

agents? I answer, that this being the ground or foundation of the supposed demonstration here spoken of, must itself be antecedently proved: . . . Now there is no way to secure this fundamental point, but by showing that such a disposition in the Deity is strictly necessary. And this, I presume, is not possible to be shown. To suppose the benevolence of the Deity strictly necessary is to resolve all his proceedings and dispensations into absolute fatality.' (*FMG* ii 21 = *TMT* 163)

[54] Balguy, *DR* 10.

[55] 'Ends are either ultimate or subordinate. Ultimate ends determine themselves, as being necessarily approved. The ultimate end of the deity in all his acts of creation and providence, I humbly suppose to be moral good. Every thing is to be referred to this, and resolved into it. Why did he at first produce the universe? Why does he still preserve and cherish it? Why replenish it continually with variety of good? Because he sees it to be absolutely right and fit so to do. Or in other words, because the purest and most perfect reason directs him to it. Though therefore reason, or intelligence, considered as an attribute, do not make this end; yet it discovers it to be, what it really is in it self, an absolute, essential, and necessary good; and by consequence, the true ultimate end not only of the supreme being, but of every moral agent.' (*FMG* ii 25 = *TMT* 172 = *SB* 732) Grove agrees with Balguy: 'That there are different moral kinds of action, some fit, others unfit to be done, some becoming, others unbecoming the supreme being, and this independently of his choosing or willing them, is evident, as that there are moral perfections and excellencies belonging to the divine nature.' (*WFSAD* 1) 'As certainly . . . as all the ways of God are wise and righteous and good, they are the result of wisdom and not of unguided inclinations. The same wisdom that discovers the reasonableness of one end, one scheme, one method to another, is inducement enough to a being in whom there is the most perfect rectitude of nature, to prefer that end, that scheme, that method in all his works.' (19)

might reply that Balguy's assumption is unjustified. Since the only intelligible account of moral properties makes them dependent on the reactions of the moral sense, our view that they are non-arbitrary and immutable in certain ways turns out to be unjustified.[56] Balguy's assumptions, we might say, are question-begging, since a defender of a moral sense theory has no reason to concede them.[57]

If this reply is open to Hutcheson, Balguy's argument about mutability and about open questions is not a conclusive refutation of sentimentalism. Still, the reply raises a further doubt. For if a moral sense theory implies radical conclusions about mutability, are the reasons for accepting such a theory so cogent that they justify us in overturning the convictions that conflict with the theory? Hutcheson can hardly answer this question by dismissing the objections based on claims about mutability. For he relies on the same objections in arguing against voluntarism. Hence he cannot reasonably dismiss Balguy's objections as question-begging, since they rely on open questions that Hutcheson takes seriously.

664. Rationalism and Utilitarianism

Balguy is sympathetic to Hutcheson's utilitarianism, though he does not entirely endorse it; but he argues that sentimentalism does not offer a satisfactory defence of utilitarianism. Within Hutcheson's position the passion of benevolence connects sentimentalist meta-ethical theory with utilitarian normative theory. It is a non-rational passion that provides both exciting and (indirectly) justifying reasons; if we act on it and approve of it, we conform to the utilitarian standard. Balguy rejects this view of benevolence, arguing that the moral principle of benevolence is not a passion, but a rational principle.[58]

This rational principle is 'calm, universal benevolence'. In calling it calm and universal Balguy follows Hutcheson, who recognizes that the benevolence required by utilitarianism is not the confined sentiment that we are familiar with. But Balguy argues that utilitarian benevolence, a completely impartial commitment to maximizing the general good, is not simply the result of our particular passions of benevolence. Not only do sentimentalism and utilitarianism fail to support each other; they actually conflict.

Balguy does not object to Hutcheson's account of the content of utilitarianism. In particular, he does not distinguish Cumberland's conception of the common good of rational beings from Hutcheson's maximizing conception that allows us harm one person in order to raise the total good. He speaks of a universal good that 'includes' the private good

---

[56] This is the conclusion Hume draws. See his letter in Greig, *LDH*, no.16, quoted in §759.

[57] We might cope with some objections about mutability by introducing a rigid designator. We might say that what is right is what is approved of now or at some other fixed time or place, and say that what is right remains the same even if people's moral sense differs over time. (See Lewis, §659 above.) But it is difficult to see what would justify picking on one time rather than another. The introduction of a rigid designator seems to imply that we (or any others introduced by the rigid designator) are incorrigible about what is morally right.

[58] 'It cannot, I think be denied, but that calm, universal benevolence, in praise and preference of which our author often speaks, is more owing to reason and reflexion than natural instinct, wherever it appears. And supposing us naturally void of public affection, I doubt not but reason and reflexion would raise such a benevolence as this, in considerate minds.' (*FMG* i = *TMT* 78 = SB 555)

of every individual.[59] He might intend to express Cumberland's conception of a common good, which would require us to aim at the good of every individual, and would prohibit the sacrifice of one individual to another. But it is not clear that Balguy means this. He may mean simply that we calculate the total good by summing the goods and evils of all individuals involved. This way of understanding the universal good is Hutcheson's way; it does not prohibit, but even requires, the sacrifice of some people's good as a means to a higher total. Balguy does not say why this is a reasonable end for morality.

In recognizing a rational principle of benevolence Balguy agrees with Clarke, who regards benevolence as one aspect of what is fit and right. He describes the pursuit of universal good as the 'primary dictate' of right reason. We might assume that the primary dictate is the supreme principle, from which other principles are derived or to which they are subordinate. This, however, is not Clarke's view. Clarke claims that our moral convictions are immediate; they rely on features of a specific situation itself, rather than on calculations, direct or indirect, about consequences. Similarly, Balguy believes that relations of fitness are not confined to the utilitarian principle, and that they impose non-utilitarian requirements. A solitary agent's reasonable treatment of his own needs and desires would display moral virtue, even if no one else stood to benefit.[60]

Balguy takes a non-utilitarian position on divine goodness and rectitude. Against Hutcheson and Bayes, he affirms that God is moved by other considerations besides benevolence. These include the intrinsic beauty of the universe, and considerations of justice and retribution that cannot be reduced to utility. God seeks a proportion between virtue and happiness that is distinct from a desire to maximize utility. Balguy does not consider how far these principles are compatible with utility, or how one ought to resolve conflicts between them. He assumes that justice guides God to act in ways that do not maximize universal happiness; that is why Bayes criticizes him for implying that God cannot be relied on to pursue the primary aim of maximizing our happiness.[61]

665. What is Fitness?

To show that we have a reasonable case for accepting moral principles that conflict with utility, rationalists ought to say what makes it fit, and therefore right, to keep a promise or

---

[59] 'The primary dictate of right reason is that every moral agent intend the good of the whole, or aim at universal good. In this universal good the private good of every individual is included.' (FMG i = TMT 100 = SB 581)

[60] 'But I presume there is other merit besides this, in the discharge of what we may call self-duties. Were any man supposed alone, without any fellow-creatures in the universe; would there be no merit, no moral goodness, in the highest improvement of his faculties, and the exactest government of his appetites and inclinations? Though he conformed all his actions to the rules of right reason; checking every desire, and denying himself every gratification inconsistent therewith; would there be nothing laudable, nothing meritorious in such a conduct as this? On the contrary, would it not be very acceptable to the deity, and procure the man his approbation and favour? Why then, and upon what account would it be thus acceptable? I suppose it will be answered, as the man was hereby better fitted for the discharge of those duties which were owing to his maker. But surely it must be granted, that his maker would be incapable of receiving the least benefit from such a conduct. What advantage therefore, or natural good the man proposed, must terminate in himself, and be directed accordingly. But prior to this view must be supposed his regard to moral good. Those acts of praise, adoration and thanksgiving, which were offered by him to the creator, must primarily and immediately flow from a regard to the intrinsic reason and rectitude of the thing, which is moral good . . .' (FMG i = TMT 98–9 = SB 579)

[61] Bayes, DB 18.

to show gratitude to a benefactor. Clarke sometimes seems to rely on a purely conceptual connexion; he suggests that the concept of a benefactor makes gratitude a fit response, because a benefactor is one who benefits in a way that makes gratitude appropriate.[62] This explanation makes our judgments about fitness dependent on prior judgments about rightness or appropriateness, and so it does not help us to identify obligations independent of utility; the utilitarian simply needs to say that if gratitude is not appropriate on utilitarian grounds, the person who has conferred a benefit is not a real benefactor.

Balguy endorses Clarke's appeal to fitnesses, and takes these fitnesses to be relative to the nature and circumstances of things.[63] He sometimes tries to do better than Clarke's purely conceptual explanation of fitness. He suggests that the Golden Rule suggests a principle of fitness that makes it fit to relieve a person in distress. Relief of distress fits the person in distress because he is similar to me in the relevant respects, and I would think it reasonable for someone to help me in distress.[64] What is fit for a human being depends on the nature of human beings in contrast to non-rational animals.[65]

Bayes follows Hutcheson in criticizing the rationalist appeals to fitness as empty. In his view fitness can only be fitness to some end. We cannot, therefore, speak of God as doing what is fit for the nature of human beings without asking what end it is supposed to be fit for. We get plausible answers, according to Bayes, only if we suppose that God does what is fit for the happiness of human beings, which is Hutcheson's position.[66] Grove rejects this criticism

---

[62] On Clarke see §§618–19.

[63] '. . . Morality of actions consists in conformity to reason, and deformity from it. That virtue is acting according to the absolute fitness of things, or agreeably to the natures and relations of things. That there are eternal and immutable differences of things, absolutely and antecedently; that there are also eternal and unalterable relations in the natures of the things themselves; from which arise agreements and disagreements, congruities and incongruities, fitness and unfitness of the application of circumstances to the qualifications of persons, &c' (*FMG* i = *TMT* 66 = SB 542).

[64] 'Or, supposing us void of natural compassion, as well as benevolence; might we not possibly be induced to attempt the relief of a person in distress, merely from the reason of the thing, and the rectitude of the action? Might we not, by considering the nature of the case, and the circumstances of the sufferer, perceive some fitness, some reasonableness in an act of succour? Might not some such maxim as that of doing as we would be done unto, offer itself to our minds, and prevail with us to stretch out a helping hand upon such an occasion?' (*FMG* i = *TMT* 50 = SB 530)

[65] 'There is likewise a wide difference between the nature of rational creatures, and that of brutes; and between the nature of brutes, and that of inanimate things. They require therefore respectively a suitable treatment. To treat men in the same way we treat brutes, and to treat brutes in the same way we do stocks and stones, is manifestly as disagreeable and dissonant to the natures of things, as it would be to attempt the forming of an angle with two parallel lines. I would not call such a conduct acting a lie, because that is confounding objective and subjective truth, and introducing needless perplexities. I would not call it a contradiction to some true proposition, because that neither comes up to the case, nor is a way of speaking strictly proper; but I would call it a counter-action to the truth, or real natures of things.' (*FMG* i = *TMT* 72–3 = SB 550) In *FMG* ii 8 Balguy argues that infliction of pain is 'directly repugnant to the nature of the object' (*TMT* 122), without any reference to an internal sensation of the agent. 'It is as contrary to nature, and to the truth of things, as to give a thirsty man poison instead of drink. It is contrary to the nature of the object, because he naturally desires indolence and pleasure, and shuns pain. It is contrary to the nature and circumstances of the agent, because he being rational, must act unnaturally whenever he acts unreasonably.' (123) 'To give pain without cause to an innocent person, is an action highly irregular and disorderly, because there is a visible and odious disagreement between action, agent, and object. And upon the same account it is counteracting the truth of things.' (124) In these passages Balguy denies that fitness is always relative to some further end outside the fit or unfit action. But he also introduces some teleological element into fitness, in speaking of the nature of the victim. His explanation of fitness comes closer to Butler's naturalism. See §678.

[66] 'When therefore we say that God is in all his actions governed by the reasons and fitness of things, we must, I think, mean, if we would understand ourselves, that (1) he is moved to every action by a regard to some good and valuable end . . . This seems to be the only notion we have of a wise and reasonable action . . . Thus, for instance, if you suppose with me that (2) the view by which the divine being is directed in all his actions is a regard to the greatest good or happiness of the universe, then the moral rectitude of God may be thus described, viz., that it is a disposition in him to

of fitness, arguing that the deliberate infliction of undeserved pain is unfit for an innocent person, apart from any further end that the agent inflicting the pain might have in mind.[67]

While Balguy and Grove defend, and try to explain, Clarke's appeal to fitness, William Adams tries to defend rationalism without reference to fitness.[68] In his view, an appeal to the truth and fitness of things is either an unhelpful repetition of the claim that some things are objectively right, or a misleading way of trying to explain it. Fitness and conformity to truth can be found in all sorts of knowledge, prudence, and skill, but none of these is concerned with what is morally right.[69] Clarke's conception is therefore too wide to capture the distinctive feature of moral rightness. Virtue has to be understood as 'conformity to what reason dictates as right, not what it teaches for true' (NOV 34). The idea of right is 'a simple uncompounded idea, and consequently cannot be explained but by example' (NOV 62).

In Adams's view, we can distinguish truth from falsity, at the most basic level, only by perception; and this is the only way we can distinguish right and wrong. Facts about rightness can be explained only by further facts about rightness that must themselves be immediately grasped. While moral perception is different from any sort of sense, it has a basic status analogous to that of some sensory judgments.

Adams's objection to fitness would be questionable if it were directed against Aquinas and Suarez. For they try to say something about rational nature, to support their claim that rightness and wrongness can be understood as fitness and unfitness to rational nature; whether or not they succeed, they try to fill the gap that Adams mentions. It is more difficult, however, to defend Clarke against Adams's objection. The claim that we recognize rightness by recognizing bare fitness (as opposed to fitness to rational nature) does not seem to add much to the claim that we simply recognize rightness. Adams, anticipating Price, suggests that the core of the rationalist position is better expressed in claims about rightness than in claims about fitness. But his objections to Clarke might reasonably suggest a different conclusion; perhaps Clarke has an unhelpful account of rightness because his conception of fitness excludes teleological aspects of human nature. This is Butler's conclusion.

666. Adams on Utilitarianism

Adams's confidence in basic judgments of rightness without reference to fitness encourages him to state a clearer position on utilitarianism than Balguy states. Though Balguy accepts non-utilitarian judgments about fitness, he does not emphasize possible conflicts with utilitarianism. Adams, however, agrees with Maxwell's criticism of Cumberland in explicitly rejecting the public good as is the basis of moral virtue or of its obligation.[70] Utilitarianism

promote the general happiness of the universe.' (Bayes, DB 14, reference numbers added.) Bayes passes from a broadly teleological interpretation of fitness in (1) to a more definitely utilitarian interpretation in (2).

[67] Grove, WFSAD 27.

[68] '. . . when virtue is said to consist in a conformity to truth, in acting agreeably to the truth of the case, to the reason, truth, or fitness of things, there is, if not inaccuracy, yet something of obscurity in the expression' (Adams, NOV 32–3). He proceeds to argue that the relevant kind of fitness has to be understood as moral rightness, which therefore cannot be understood by reference to fitness.

[69] Adams does not consider the explanation of fitness offered by Suarez, and defended by Butler. See §716.

[70] On Maxwell see §536.

breaches St Paul's prohibition on doing evil that good may come (*NOV* 29–30), because it allows the possibility of actions that we know to be wrong for the sake of maximizing the good.

This objection is stated rather briefly, so that it is not clear what Adams is assuming about utilitarianism. If he means that every utilitarian position will prescribe wrong actions for the sake of utility, he does not take proper account of Hutcheson's strategy in his *System of Moral Philosophy*. Hutcheson argues that when we look at utility more closely, we can see that some of the rules, for instance those prescribing rights, promote utility in the longer run, even though they violate it in the shorter run. If, however, Adams means that utilitarianism allows the possibility of acting wrongly for the sake of utility, and that a true account of morality cannot allow this possibility, Hutcheson does not refute him.

Sometimes Adams concedes that the practice of virtue generally promotes greater happiness. But he argues that this fact about virtue does not vindicate utilitarianism. If utilitarianism were true, the truth of a given moral principle would be as certain or uncertain as the truth of the claim that its observance promotes utility. But since the truth of a principle is sometimes certain while the truth about its contribution to utility is open to question, the truth of the principle cannot be grounded in contribution to utility.[71] This is a legitimate argument to show that utilitarianism gives the wrong account of why true moral principles are true.

Adams's sharp criticism of utilitarianism is more explicit than the attitude of Clarke and Balguy. The rationalists claim that we have immediate knowledge of what is fit and reasonable. They cannot apply the utilitarian analysis to our moral judgments without undermining the claim to immediate rational insight. This is all the clearer if we agree with Balguy against Adams in believing that the notion of fitness can be usefully explained. Any plausible explanation of this notion seems to give us some reason to suppose that fitness for maximizing happiness is not the only relevant form of fitness.

667. A Plausible Defence of Rationalism?

Now that we have examined some of the disputes between Hutcheson, on the one side, and Clarke and Balguy, on the other side, we may pause to ask what these disputes suggest about the prospects for the sentimentalist and the rationalist positions.

The rationalist arguments in Clarke and Balguy seek to expose the philosophical, moral, and theological inadequacy of both voluntarism and sentimentalism. In particular, Balguy argues that Hutcheson's attempt to counter theological voluntarism by appeal to sentimentalism is unsuccessful. These rationalist criticisms are often telling; they expose serious difficulties in sentimentalist attempts to reduce moral judgments and moral properties to something more easily understood within sentimentalist assumptions.

The sentimentalist position seeks to connect three views: (1) Anti-rationalism about reason and action. (2) Utilitarianism as a normative theory. (3) Reduction of obligation to

---

[71] 'But this connexion is not necessary, nor in many particular cases certain; and the foundation of virtue cannot be anything that is precarious and contingent.' (*NOV* 30)

feeling and sentiment. Though it is possible to believe one of these views without the others, a theorist who believes one finds the others more immediately plausible. Conversely, rationalists tend to attack all these aspects of the sentimentalist view. They argue that a sentimentalist account of moral properties, moral motivation, and moral rightness does not fit what we seem to know about morality.

Balguy's criticism of Hutcheson convinces not only Butler and Price, but also Hume. For Hume implicitly agrees that Hutcheson cannot combine his sentimentalist objections to Clarke with his realist defence of Shaftesbury, because his sentimentalism conflicts with realism. Butler and Price argue that in the face of this we should give up sentimentalism, but Hume decides to give up realism instead. His decision changes the terms of the debate. Balguy takes it for granted, quite fairly, that Hutcheson accepts his arguments against voluntarism and the realist assumptions they rely on. Price and Reid cannot take these points for granted against Hume.

Is it reasonable to take these points for granted? The rationalists deny that what is morally right and wrong is determined either by the commands of a ruler legislating for the public interest or by the affective reactions of a spectator. In their view, we can know that some actions are right and wrong apart from these conditions, and our knowledge gives us a basis for judging both commands and affective reactions as sometimes right and sometimes wrong. So far the rationalists might claim that they are not relying on any abstruse theory, but simply appealing to familiar features of moral judgment that their opponents cannot explain. But they raise difficulties for themselves once they try to explain how we know these moral truths. The obscurity of their explanations may provoke doubts about whether there is really anything to be explained.

Clarke modifies traditional naturalism about fitness to rational nature. He intends his appeals to fitness to secure the immediacy and certainty of our grasp of moral principles, and hence to assure us of the existence of the appropriate moral facts. In response to questions about Clarke's notion of fitness, Balguy tries to give it more content, and in doing so seems to introduce some appeal to facts about human nature; these facts cast doubt upon the immediacy and certainty of moral judgments that claim to recognize fitnesses. Adams takes a different direction, by abandoning any effort to explain the content of basic moral judgments by appeal to fitness. These developments of Clarke's position suggest that his moral epistemology is open to serious objections.

This obscurity in moral knowledge, as the rationalists conceive it, may suggest that they have no good reason for attributing genuine moral knowledge to us at all. This is Hume's conclusion. The necessity of defending rationalist claims against Hume explains why moral epistemology and meta-ethics are so prominent in Price and Reid. When we understand their defences of rationalism, we can see why Kant looks for a different sort of defence.

50

BALGUY AND CLARKE: MORALITY AND NATURAL THEOLOGY

668. Balguy on Morality and God

Rationalism is important for Balguy because it allows him to explain how God is good, and why we can expect the moral demands of God to be morally right. Since basic moral principles are accessible to reason, and since a rational agent who grasps these principles will also be moved to act on them, God, being a rational agent, knows basic moral principles and acts on them. Being wise and just, God also wants us to act on them; hence God enjoins action on the principles that commend themselves to natural reason.

If this argument succeeds, however, it seems to present Balguy with a difficulty. In his defence of intrinsic morality that is accessible to natural reason, he has to explain why he does not make Christianity superfluous to morality. In explaining himself, he defends Clarke both against Christians who impugn his Christianity and against Deists who criticize him for failure to embrace Deism. His 'Second Letter to a Deist'[1] replies to Matthew Tindal's *Christianity as Old as the Creation*.[2] Tindal argues that if Clarke puts Christian morality on a secure rational basis, he makes Christianity morally unnecessary. Why turn to Christianity for moral insight or teaching, if we can already get it from the eternal fitnesses grasped by reason?

This line of thought leads some people to claim that Grotius 'secularizes' morality.[3] But Tindal's objection applies more broadly to moralists who would not normally be regarded as 'secular', such as Aquinas and Suarez. They do not believe that their claims about the rational basis of intrinsic morality make Christian belief morally unnecessary. It is useful to compare their defence of their position with the role that Balguy sees for Christianity.

He argues that, though Clarke takes the basic principles of morality to be contained in the natural law and to be knowable by reference to natural reason, revelation is still needed both to make moral principles more widely known, and to provide a further incentive to obey them. For these reasons natural reason does not make revelation superfluous.

---

[1] *TMT* 271–343.

[2] In his epigraphs Tindal quotes from St Paul on the Gentiles who are a law to themselves, and from Clarke's lectures.

[3] On Grotius see §§462, 464.

For similar reasons, Balguy rejects Shaftesbury's objection—as Balguy conceives it—to orthodox Christianity. According to Balguy's account of Shaftesbury, the appeal to divine sanctions threatens morality, because it encourages us to act on self-interest rather than benevolence.[4] This account does not seem to do justice to Shaftesbury's position.[5] According to Shaftesbury, some Christian opponents of 'enthusiasm' and the self-forgetful love of God react too strongly, by appealing exclusively to rational calculation of rewards and punishments. This attitude to disinterested motives seems to Shaftesbury to destroy morality, including Christian morality. But he does not deny that an appeal to rewards and punishments, in a secondary place, is permissible and appropriate.

Balguy may not be quite fair, then, in picking Shaftesbury as a target for his criticism of Deism. But he is justified in examining the Deist view that rational morality is all that Christianity has to offer.[6] To refute the Deist, Balguy considers someone who is benevolent, but at first does not believe in God or an afterlife. He argues that if such an agent becomes convinced of the truths he previously rejected, we have no reason to suppose that his benevolent impulses will thereby be weakened.[7] The Deist gives no reason for believing that the motives produced by divine sanctions necessarily undermine the motive of benevolence.

669. Morality, Motivation, and Self-Interest

This answer deals effectively with the Deist, but it raises a broader difficulty for Balguy's conception of morality and motives. On the one hand, his answer to the Deist presupposes

---

[4] At *TMT* 9 Balguy quotes from Shaftesbury, *ICV* i 3.3 = K 184: 'Nor can this fear or hope . . . consist in reality with virtue or goodness if it either stands as essential to any moral performance or as a considerable motive to any act, of which some better affection ought alone to have been a sufficient cause. . . . [I]n this religious sort of discipline . . . the principle of self-love, which is naturally so prevailing in us, being in no way moderated or restrained but rather improved and made stronger every day by the exercise of the passions in a subject of more extended self-interest, there may be reason to apprehend, lest the temper of this kind should extend itself in general through all the parts of life. For, if the habit be such, as to occasion in every particular, a stricter attention to self-good and interest, it must insensibly diminish the affections towards public good, and introduce a certain narrowness of spirit.' (Balguy's quotation does not exactly match Klein's text.) Balguy comments: 'Whether by this the author did not mean to show or insinuate the inconvenience and damage that virtue sustains from the future and invisible motives of religion, let the reader judge. My business is to show, if I can, that these apprehensions are groundless; and that in some cases a strict attention to self-good is of great service to the public.' Balguy does not quote the following discussion where Shaftesbury considers the benefits that we may gain from hope of future rewards and belief in providence. This hope and belief inhibits the growth of passions that might interfere with the operation of the 'sense of right and wrong'. Shaftesbury allows an appeal to future reward that promises the appropriate kind of pleasures: '. . . if by the hope of reward be understood the love and desire of virtuous enjoyment, or of the very practice and exercise of virtue in another life; the expectation or hope of this kind is so far from being derogatory to virtue, that it is an evidence of our loving it the more sincerely and for its own sake. Nor can this principle be justly called selfish; for if the love of virtue be not mere self-interest, the love and desire of life for virtue's sake cannot be esteemed so.' (*ICV* i 3.3 = K 187) His position, then, seems more qualified than Balguy allows.

[5] On Shaftesbury see §612.

[6] In his 'First Letter to a Deist' Balguy defends the appeal to divine sanctions: '. . . though interest can never enter into the nature and constitution of virtue, yet why may it not be allowed to accompany and stand beside her. Notwithstanding all that has been granted, I can see no reason why virtue and the rewards of virtue must needs be separated and set at variance.' (*TMT* 7)

[7] '. . . however the new motives may operate, they cannot hinder the efficacy of the old one. Whatever good they may produce over and above (as indeed much may be expected from their conjunction with the former principle), yet still the benevolence being supposed the same in degree must, I think, remain the same in force and influence' (*TMT* 8).

that virtuous motives and self-interested motives may coincide in a virtuous person.[8] On the other hand, he seems to deny that we could remain virtuous if we begin to do virtuous actions on self-interested motives, in addition to the properly virtuous motives that we already have.[9] For he argues that the presence of a self-interested motive subtracts from the worth of the action to the extent that it influences the agent. In saying this Balguy seems to undermine his answer to Deism.

Perhaps this objection is too hasty. Balguy does not believe that human beings in their present condition are capable of the complete disinterestedness that would constitute perfect virtue and that belongs only to God. Perhaps, then, he could reply to Shaftesbury that divine sanctions simply replace some previous self-interested motive that concurred with benevolence. But it is difficult to make this claim seem plausible. The belief in divine sanctions seems to make the motive of self-interest stronger than it was before, so that, if we follow Balguy's rule, we must apparently subtract its increased force from the estimate of the virtue of the agent.

Balguy's acceptance of the principle of subtraction seems to play into the hands of Mandeville, whose claims about the impossibility of genuine virtue rely on this principle. Mandeville's cynical attitude to moral virtue seems irrelevant to a reasonable conception of a moral virtue, but it seems relevant to Balguy's claims.[10] Why, then, should Balguy expose his position to this sort of objection?

He defends his principle of subtraction by offering two examples. (1) A mother rescues her drowning child 'in the transports of her fear, grief, and tenderness'. (2) A brave soldier is challenged to a duel without having given any offence, but 'conscientiously and resolutely refuses to fight' despite 'many vile reproaches, insults, and outrages' (FMG ii 35 = TMT 193). In Balguy's view, the virtue and moral merit of the two actions 'will bear no comparison'; the second action is clearly superior to the first on these points.

But these examples do not support the principle of subtraction. The mother in the first example acts solely from the motives that he mentions, whereas the soldier in the second example does not act simply from shame, or fear of punishment, in refusing to fight a duel. If, therefore, the mother lacked these specific emotions, no rational convictions would move her to save her child. If that is the intended description of the case, our comparative judgment rests on the mother's lack of these rational convictions, not on the soldier's lack of non-rational incentives. Hence our judgment does not support the principle of subtraction.

To justify the principle of subtraction, we would need to suppose that both the soldier and the mother have an equal tendency to act 'conscientiously and resolutely', and that they differ only insofar as the mother's instinct agrees with her conscientious motive and the

---

[8] 'The perfection of moral goodness consists in being influenced solely by a regard to rectitude and right reason, and the intrinsic fitness and amiableness of such actions as are conformable thereto.' (TMT 33)

[9] He seems to accept this consequence of his position, when he discusses the concurrence of reason and instinct: '. . . however actions may be mixed or compounded, as flowing from the united principles of reason and instinct, I cannot but suppose that the worth of such actions is in proportion to the share of influence which reason has in the production of them. The force of the natural impulse, whatever it amounted to, must, I think, be subtracted in the estimate' (FMG ii 35 = TMT 192). On addition and subtraction in the understanding of motives see also Aquinas, §287; Smith, TMS vi 2.3.13, 303, who wrongly attributes the principle to Hutcheson (see Raphael and Macfie's note), but correctly (§16) rejects it; Ross, RG 170–3.

[10] On Mandeville see §633.

467

soldier's instinct disagrees with it. But if we describe the example in this way, is Balguy's judgment right? The soldier's action may be a clearer proof of his moral character, but his action seems to have no more merit than the mother's.

Tipping Silvester and William Adams have good reasons to object to the principle of subtraction. They notice the difficulty it raises for Balguy's defence of appeals to divine sanctions. Silvester argues that agreement between reason and non-moral instincts and motives does not subtract from the merit of an action. If we act on rational benevolence, the presence of other motives—both self-interest and non-rational benevolent instincts—is often appropriate, and they often support the moral motive.[11]

Adams sometimes seems to come close to acceptance of Balguy's principle of subtraction.[12] He seems to rely on subtraction when he suggests that God is not virtuous, because God has no difficulties to overcome. Since God's moral purpose coincides completely with God's other purposes, the principle of subtraction requires us to deny virtue to God. But this conclusion does not satisfy Adams. For he also claims that virtue does not consist in the conquering of difficulties, but in having the power to conquer them; since God has this power, God has virtues.

This claim about God undermines the principle of subtraction. Since a second, concurrent motive does not necessarily diminish our power to act on the first motive alone, it does not necessarily diminish our virtue, and therefore the principle of subtraction must be false. This conclusion is much more plausible than Balguy's. It would allow him to answer Shaftesbury better than he actually does.

670. Obligation and Revelation

Balguy defends Clarke's view that principles of right hold independently of the will of human beings and of the divine will. We discover them apart from revelation, and our confidence in them increases our confidence in revelation.[13] To deny the rational foundation of morality is to deny the integrity of the 'volume of nature'; but revelation cannot stand in the absence of natural principles.[14]

---

[11] 'Such benevolence is indeed a kind of prejudice on the side of goodness; but there must always be something of reason in its acts, which would be like those of a judge, who being prepossessed in his opinion of the right of a case, should determine for a party without weighing minute particulars. His action would go upon the general principle of doing right, though it would not be in all points strictly regular.' (Silvester, MCB 7)

[12] '... [W]hatever good we do [sc. from instincts] and not from reason, so far is lost of the merit and virtue of the action. In prospect as the motives to duty are stronger, a stricter conformity to right will be necessary to give a proof of equal virtue in the agent' (Adams, NOV 15–16). In speaking of 'motives' here Adams has in mind non-moral motives.

[13] 'The two volumes of nature and grace are so divinely perfect; contain so much true beauty, and solid worth; that in order to be thoroughly admired, they can want nothing more than to be well understood. And moreover they correspond so strictly, and tally so exactly in numberless respects, and are so peculiarly fitted to illustrate, unfold, and enforce each other; that nothing can redound more to the credit and esteem of either, than a nearer contemplation of both.' (TMT, Pref., p. xxix)

[14] 'To aim at the subversion of revealed religion, in order to promote the credit and authority of either natural religion, or morality; seems to me like pulling down a noble and beautiful structure, merely to lay open the strength of its foundations. On the other hand, to promote the establishment or advancement of revelation, by weakening the obligations of reason and morality, appears to me just such an undertaking as it would be to undermine a fabric, with a view to support and strengthen it.' ('Law of Truth' = TMT 370–1)

Balguy argues that if we reject natural reason as a source of moral obligation, we cannot explain how religion could oblige our consciences.[15] From divine sanctions we can derive motives causing us to obey God's will, but these cannot show us that it is morally right to obey God's will. Balguy comments that if Hobbes thought God's power by itself implied right, 'he must, I think, have laboured under the greatest confusion of ideas that ever befell any understanding' (391).

For similar reasons Adams argues that divine sanctions do not by themselves have 'the nature of obligation', so that acting from them does not by itself constitute virtue (NOV 25–6). Adams assumes that virtuous agents must recognize some other reason for doing what they do apart from the fact that they are commanded to do it or inclined to do it; they must also recognize that they have some reason to follow this commander's command, because the commander has some right to obedience, or that they have some reason to follow this instinct, because it deserves their attention.

671. Maxwell on Reason and Revelation

A further defence of a position similar to Balguy's and Clarke's on rational morality and revelation appears in Maxwell's two introductory essays in his translation of Cumberland, 'from both which the usefulness of revelation may appear'. In the first essay, 'Concerning the city or kingdom of God in the rational world and the defects in heathen deism', Maxwell tries to take a middle position between those who regard post-mortem rewards and punishments as all-important and those who dismiss them from consideration.[16] He agrees with Cumberland's emphasis on the good resulting from virtue in this life, but he argues (and Cumberland does not deny) that future rewards are also relevant.

His second essay, 'Concerning the imperfectness of the heathen morality', examines some aspects of Greek moral philosophy, to show that the ancients are right about some things, but still full of errors that make revelation necessary.[17] His survey of Greek ethics seeks to show how far natural reason could take people already damaged by sin and without the help of grace. Maxwell deals with the question that concerns Clarke and Balguy, and

---

[15] 'But if the obligations of reason are disowned, and looked upon as mere philosophical fancies, and abstract shadows, I see not, for my part, how any religion can be valid.' (TMT 400)

[16] 'I would not be misunderstood here, as if I thought "That human affairs were so disorderly as not clearly to show plain marks of a governing providence". To say "that the present moral appearances are all regular and good" is false. But "that there is no moral order visible in the constitution of nature" is equally false. The truth seems this, "moral order is prevalent in nature; virtue is constituted, at present, the supreme happiness, and the virtuous generally have the happiest share of life." The few disorders, which are exceptions to this general proposition, are probably left to us as evidences or arguments for a future state.' ('Kingdom of God' §3 = P 29) Maxwell proceeds to quote with approval from Shaftesbury, Mor. ii 3 = K 270.

[17] At the end of the essay, Maxwell states his general aim: '. . . there seems [sic] to me to be two opposite extremes into which men have run. Some cry up reason, and the light of nature, at such a rate, as to think them alone sufficient guides, in consequence of which they think all revelation useless and unnecessary; . . . Others, with a mistaken view of magnifying revelation and faith, undervalue and vilify reason and the light of nature most immoderately, as if they were no proper guides at all, nor fit to be trusted in divine matters and the truths of God. But if that were the case, how should we ever come to the knowledge of God at all? So it is plain St Paul thought, by the passages just now quoted from him.' ('Heathen' = P 231–2) The last sentence refers to Rm. 1:20.

asks whether acceptance of natural law makes revelation useless.[18] He argues that a proper appreciation of the moral truths included in natural law only makes the need for revelation clearer.

The Stoics receive the fullest discussion.[19] Maxwell notices especially the cosmic aspect of Stoic ethics, and praises the Stoics for it.[20] But he attacks their dismissal of the fear of death,[21] and their doctrine of indifferents. He suggests a modification of their position, allowing preferred indifferents to be goods. The modified Stoic position makes it reasonable to see imperfections in our happiness in this life and to hope for complete happiness in an afterlife.[22] Maxwell also rejects the Stoics' pursuit of freedom from passion (*apatheia*), and accuses them of arrogance.[23] He dismisses Epicurus briefly,[24] and does not discuss Aristotle's ethics in any detail.

This examination of Greek ethics introduces Maxwell's discussion of pagan virtues. He agrees that the actions of the heathen are sinful.[25] But he maintains that their virtues are nonetheless genuine virtues, within these limits.[26] In particular, he attributes to the ancients an appreciation of moral value for its own sake.[27] The pervasively sinful character of heathen actions does not prevent this grasp of morality.

Maxwell seeks to show, as Clarke and Balguy do, that a defence of Christianity does not require complete dismissal of pagan morality and moral philosophy. In particular, it does not require us to take the dangerous course of ridiculing all reasons or motives for morality that are accessible to those who do not know the specific rewards and punishments offered by Christianity. Maxwell argues that this course is dangerous, because it erodes the necessary moral basis for appreciation of Christian claims about God.

[18] 'After all these considerations, let any impartial man judge, whether a revelation was useful or necessary for the reformation of mankind. No, says the modern deist; for the light and law of nature, natural religion, and morality are sufficient, as they have been laid down by Plato, Aristotle, Cicero, Epictetus, M Antoninus, and others among the ancients; by Grotius, Pufendorf, Crellius, Sharrock, Wilkins, Cumberland, Clark, Wollaston, and others among the moderns.' ('Heathen' = P 228)

[19] See 'Heathen' §§1–11 = P 68–91.   [20] 'Heathen' §2 = P 70.

[21] 'Heathen' §4 = P 73: 'they ridicule the fear of death, explode the laudable custom of burying the dead, and of mourning for them; all of which is absurdly unpopular and irreligious. Nor could the world be governed if all men entertained a persuasion that death, and consequently the execution of criminals, is no penal evil, no evil at all, as the Stoics suppose.'

[22] 'But, in order to rectify their philosophy of good and evil, it ought to be considered that good things are of two kinds. For some things are good, as constituent parts of our true perfection and happiness of life, and these we call the end. Other things are good, as conducive thereto, and these are called the means. In the first notion, the good things commonly so reputed (life, health, honour, plenty, etc.) cannot be evils, considered in the nature of an end; and the evils commonly so reputed (death, sickness, infamy, penury, etc.) cannot be good. In the second notion of means, the evils, commonly so reputed, may be good, and the good things, commonly so reputed, may be evils; and usually are, not helps, but hindrances to our true perfection and happiness in a future state.' (§5 = P 75–6)

[23] §§7–10 = P 78–87. According to Maxwell, 'Instead of sober morality, they deal much in superlative extravagancies ...' (§9 = P 82).

[24] He cites Bishop Parker in order to 'dispatch' the Epicureans in a few words, §12 = P 91.   [25] See p. cxxxvi.

[26] See P 193–4. He quotes Augustine, *CD* v 19 (see §233); Article 13 of the *English Articles*; and *Rm.* 2:15.

[27] 'A third principle of laudable practices is a respect for worth and virtue; honesty and duty, justice, and equity, reason and ingenuity, civility, decency, and order, and a like respect for ourselves, our own perfection and felicity, without any regard to God or holiness. For, as there is a human-social virtue, which is on this side the holy-social, so there is a regard for worth and virtue, honesty, reason, and justice, which is on this side true holiness and godliness. The pagans practised the virtues which they teach, "*fugiendae turpitudinis causa*" (Cic. *Tusc* ii), to shun that which is base and shameful, "*tou kalou heneka*", (Aristotle, *Ethic. Nicom.* passim) because it was just and good, virtuous or honest. Their maxim was "*honestum per se expetendum*", that which is virtuous is self-desirable, and some of them have said "a feast is nothing else but the doing of one's duty" (Orig. *c. Cels* viii, p. 392).' (P 197)

672. Christian Virtues

These arguments make it reasonable for Balguy to argue that his rejection of voluntarism does not threaten Christian orthodoxy, and that in fact his voluntarist opponents are open to much more serious theological objections. To this extent he reaffirms Aquinas' position. We may be surprised, however, by the omission in Balguy of a further aspect of Aquinas' moral theology.

Once Aquinas has described the acquired moral virtues, he describes the various contributions of grace—infused moral virtues, gifts, theological virtues, and so on, and he discusses their contribution to the moral life. The *Secunda Secundae* describes the requirements of the moral virtues, from the point of view of grace. When we acquire grace, for instance, we acquire the virtue of charity, which differs from ordinary friendship insofar as it causes us to love God, and to love our neighbour for God's sake. Aquinas, then, might reasonably accept Balguy's picture of nature and grace as foundation and superstructure.[28] But he believes that the superstructure includes virtues, and specifications of virtues, that go beyond the virtues studied by moral philosophy.

This aspect of Aquinas' ethics is difficult to discern in Clarke and Balguy. In his 'Second Letter to a Deist', Balguy considers the two claims 'that the law of nature is perfect and unchangeable' and 'that all men are naturally capable of discerning it' (*TMT* 276). He argues that from these two claims we cannot legitimately derive the Deist conclusion 'that the Gospel is needless, and all revelation superfluous' (277). His answer would have been easy to defend if he had agreed with Aquinas' view that a Christian life includes infused as well as acquired virtues and that the infused virtues exceed natural reason. Balguy, however, does not answer in this way.

Most of Balguy's defence of Clarke consists in pointing out that human beings have a defective grasp of the truths contained in natural law, because of their proclivity to various vices. The Deist asks: 'Can the law of nature be clear, and the light of nature dim?' (300). Balguy replies quite convincingly that even if the law of nature is clear in itself, it may still be obscure to people who are negligent or inattentive or distracted. This distinction between the clarity of the law and the weakness of our grasp of it makes revelation intelligible, as Balguy claims. We can understand—if we already understand why God allowed our understanding to weaken—why God would reveal to us principles that we could grasp without revelation, but are unlikely to grasp firmly and clearly. God not only reveals these principles to us, but also makes us aware of the divine command that we observe them, and of the sanctions that support the command.[29] Revelation reinforces what we already know, or encourages us to act on it, or makes up for our defective grasp of what it is open to us to grasp by reason.

Balguy does not seem to suggest that revelation adds any virtues to those that we already know, or that it imposes obligations on us that we could not justify by natural reason. God appears primarily as a legislator reinforcing demands with sanctions. God does not appear as an object of love who might be the focus of the virtue of charity. If this account of Balguy's position is fair, he leaves out an important element in the Christian approach to morality.

---

[28] On this metaphor cf. §§356, 417.   [29] Cf. Aquinas on the Decalogue, ST 1–2 q99 a2 ad 2, discussed in §319.

Silvester supplies Balguy's omission through his discussion of 'moral' and 'Christian' benevolence. He distinguishes the Christian virtue from the moral virtue partly by its different obligations; the Gospel both requires a more universal love than ordinary moral virtue requires and requires a special sort of love of one Christian for another (*MCB* 10). These distinctive obligations refer to God as the primary object of love; the image of God is present in every human being, but other Christians have a closer similarity to God than non-Christians have. To support his claims about the love of God and the love of other people, Silvester appeals to Aquinas and to Calvin.[30] In contrast to Silvester, Balguy seems to allow no distinctively Christian virtues.

Perhaps this objection to Balguy is unfair.[31] For he argues that neither Cicero nor any other ancient author grasped the 'sublime' part of morality, whereas 'there is either a real sublime in Christian morality, or something still greater' (293). If the Christian revelation includes a sublime aspect of morality, it seems to go beyond the reinforcement of truths that are known already.

But what is the extra element in Christian morality? Balguy might mean either of two things: (1) The ancient philosophers could have grasped Christian morality by the natural reason they had, had they been more attentive or less blinded by vice. (2) They could not have grasped Christian morality, since it cannot be grasped without the Christian revelation. The second view is Aquinas' view; it does not suggest that the failure of non-Christian moralists is simply a failure to do their work properly. Balguy, however, seems to endorse the first view, but not the second. While he claims that Christian morality is sublime, he does not suggest that its specifically Christian character is derived from Christian theology.

This particular obscurity in Balguy's position might be explained by the apologetic context. He is arguing with a Deist, not preaching to Christians, and so he might prefer not to appeal to any distinctively Christian virtues. This explanation is not completely satisfactory, however. If Balguy had believed in distinctively Christian virtues, he would have had a much clearer and more decisive answer to the charge of superfluity. He does not entirely dispel the impression that he presents Christianity as ordinary rational morality supplied with rewards and punishments.

673. Reason and Revelation in Moral Understanding

How successful is Balguy's defence of Clarke's attitude to revelation? From Aquinas' point of view, much of what Clarke claims is quite acceptable. He has convincing reasons for

---

[30] *MCB* 15 cites Aquinas *ST* 2–2 q25 a1, and Calvin, *Inst.* iii 7.6 ('. . . we remember not to consider the badness of human beings, but to look upon the image of God in them, which cancels out and effaces their offences, and with its beauty and worth attracts us to love and embrace them.').

[31] He argues that for the heathen the light of nature was insufficient '. . . for bringing mankind to that standard of duty which belongs to their nature, and that state of perfection whereof they are capable'. ('Second Letter' = *TMT* 291). The philosophers did not reach this standard: '. . . not one of them was master of an adequate, perfect rule of life; not one of them has given us grounds to conclude, that he had a clear perception of that entire system of relations, or moral truths, which constitute human duty.' (*TMT* 292) If Cicero had rewritten the *De Officiis* in the light of the Gospel, 'how would such a work appear, in comparison with his *Offices*? As much superior, I doubt not, in every unprejudiced eye, as his *Offices* are to school-boys' themes, or the prattle of children.' (*TMT* 292)

insisting that the law of nature is not the creation of any will, even the divine will, and that its obligations are eternal and immutable. We can legitimately examine Christianity to see whether it meets the demands of the rational morality that we have reason to accept apart from the Christian revelation. To show that the principles he accepts appear reasonable apart from Christianity, Clarke appeals to the testimony of the Greek philosophical tradition, and especially to Stoicism. He does not make revelation superfluous, since he does not claim that unaided reason could have discovered all the truths revealed by revelation. But natural reason is expected to endorse in retrospect the truths discovered by revelation; the revealed truths are supposed to be 'agreeable' to reason.[32]

We might understand 'agreeable' in two ways: (1) Clarke takes a moderate view of the role of natural reason, if 'agreeable to' simply means the same as 'consistent with'. If natural reason restricts the scope of revelation in this way, it refutes the view of Tertullian that Christianity can oblige us to believe doctrines that seem clearly absurd or repugnant from the point of view of natural reason. (2) He takes an extreme view of the role of natural reason if 'agreeable to' means that natural reason must, from its own resources, find a sufficient basis for agreeing with revelation. According to this extreme view, revelation has a purely heuristic or suggestive role in discovery; it is similar to the teacher of arithmetic who gives learners a hint that allows them to find an answer that is defensible independently of any hint they may have been given.

These two accounts of the role of natural reason and revelation do not exhaust the possibilities. Aquinas, for instance, does not confine himself to the moderate claim, but he stops short of the extreme claim. Clarke, however, does not clearly reject the extreme view that natural reason must eventually be able to satisfy itself of the correctness of Christian claims.

The extreme view affects our conception of Christian virtues. Clarke claims that pagan moral precepts are 'improved, augmented, and exalted to the highest degree of perfection' (267) in Christian moral teaching. But who is to judge the improvement, augmentation, and so on? Clarke seems to suggest that the moral precepts of the Gospel must be shown to be reasonable from the natural point of view.[33] He seems to claim that all Christian moral precepts recommend themselves to 'unprejudiced' reason once we consider them more carefully. Hence the Christian creeds and sacraments, as well as Christian moral teaching narrowly conceived, can be defended as ways of promoting moral reform.[34]

If Clarke goes this far, he seems to imply that Christianity may be superfluous for some people. Even if the Christian revelation was historically necessary, why could a rational

---

[32] 'The necessary marks and proofs of a religion coming from God, are these. First, that the duties it enjoins be all such as are agreeable to our natural notions of God; and perfective of the nature, and conducive to the happiness and well-being of men; and that the doctrines it teaches be all such, as, though not indeed discoverable by the bare light of nature; yet, when discovered by revelation, may be consistent with, and agreeable to, sound and unprejudiced reason.' (DNR, Prop. ix = H ii 673)

[33] 'These precepts, I say, are such as no unprejudiced philosopher would have been unwilling to confess were the utmost improvement of morality, and to the highest degree perfective of human nature.' (DNR, Prop. x = H 675)

[34] '... those positive and external observances (the two sacraments) which are instituted in the Christian religion as means and assistances to keep men stedfast in the practice of those great and moral duties which are the weightier matter of the law' (Prop. x = H 675). This is followed by description of baptism as a rite of admission and the Eucharist as a rite of commemoration. 'All the credenda, or doctrines . . . have every one of them a natural tendency, and a direct and powerful influence, to reform men's minds and correct their manners.' (Prop. xiii = H 680)

student of Christianity and moral philosophy (such as Clarke himself) not find a basis in 'unprejudiced reason' for all essential Christian moral precepts, and hold on to them because of their rational grounds, without their Christian grounds? Perhaps most people cannot grasp these rational grounds, or cannot stick to their principles in times of difficulty and temptation, without the support of religious dogma. But why suppose that everyone needs this extra support? Moreover, even if everyone needs religious support, it may not give us the support we need if we once recognize that it has only the supportive role that Clarke allows it.

Some of Clarke's views about the Stoics are relevant here (H 645–6). In his view, a belief in the afterlife is morally necessary once we recognize that God's approval of virtue and disapproval of vice is not completely manifested in this life, where virtue does not always result in happiness. If we deny the afterlife, then, we are committed to downright atheism. Clarke believes that this argument fails if the Stoics are right to identify virtue with happiness; for, if they are right, we suffer no loss of happiness in this life that needs to be made up in an afterlife. He agrees with the Stoics that 'virtue is truly worthy to be chosen, even merely for its own sake, without any respect to any recompense or reward' (H 646), but he rejects the rest of the Stoic position:[35]

His objection to the Stoic position relies on the identification of happiness with feelings of pleasure; Clarke assumes without argument that when the Stoics speak of happiness, they must be referring to a feeling of satisfaction. He points out reasonably that such a feeling of satisfaction may co-exist with severe pain, if the rest of one's life is going badly, and that it is difficult to explain why one is not losing some happiness in that case. This objection, however, rests on a misunderstanding of the Stoic position; Clarke does not recognize that the Stoics regard virtue as identical to happiness, not as a means to a feeling of satisfaction that is identical to happiness.[36] Since Clarke does not show that the Stoics are wrong on this point, he does not show that they are logically required to admit an afterlife.

If Clarke believes that it is difficult to stick to virtue without the assurance of an afterlife, we might think he takes a rather circuitous route to stiffen the resolve of virtuous people. Rather than require them to believe the whole Christian religion, even in Clarke's minimal version, might it not be better to educate them to focus more firmly on the value of virtue in its own right? His claims about what is and is not psychologically realistic seem disputable.

This objection to Clarke does not answer all his arguments for connecting morality with belief in an afterlife. He argues more plausibly that future rewards are an appropriate addition to the moral motive, though they neither replace it nor dilute it.[37] Even if we could

---

[35] 'But it does not from hence follow, that he who dies for the sake of virtue is really any more happy than he that dies for any fond opinion or any unreasonable humour or obstinacy whatsoever; if he has no other happiness than the bare satisfaction arising from the imagination of his resoluteness in persisting to preserve his virtue, and in adhering immoveably to what he judges to be right; and there be no future state wherein he may reap any benefit of that his resolute perseverance.' (Prop. iv = H 646)

[36] Some excuse for Clarke's interpretation is provided by the Stoic doctrine of *eurhoia*. See §182.

[37] 'For though virtue is unquestionably worthy to be chosen for its own sake, even without any expectation of reward, yet it does not follow that it is therefore entirely self-sufficient, and able to support a man under all kinds of sufferings, and even death itself, for its sake, without any prospect of future recompense.' (H 629 = R 249) 'Men never will generally, and indeed 'tis not very reasonably to be expected they should, part with all the comforts of life, and even life itself, without expectation of any future recompense. So that, if we suppose no future state of rewards, it will follow that god has endued men with such faculties, as put them under a necessity of approving and choosing virtue in the judgment of

be sufficiently motivated to follow morality without reference to future rewards, the future rewards support morality by removing objections to it.

Still, Clarke does not give a completely convincing reason for his belief that an enlightened moralist still needs Christian doctrine. He might give the impression that Christianity is necessary only for people in whom the rational motive to morality is weak. This impression may be unfair to Clarke, but closer attention to his argument does not entirely dispel the impression.

Clarke's argument, then, is open to objections from the point of view of an orthodox Christian who believes that Christianity prescribes virtues that are not completely accessible to natural reason. Balguy's defence of Clarke's position does not remove these objections. Balguy explains the relation of nature and grace through the metaphor of foundations and superstructure, but his use of the metaphor is misleading in this case; for he does not seem to recognize a superstructure of Christian virtue built on intrinsic rational morality.

Balguy speaks of Bishop Hoadly's outlook in the same way, arguing that the bishop has been concerned with the fundamentals, and not the 'circumstantials', of both natural and revealed religion (*TMT*, Dedic.) Hoadly was accused of reducing Christianity to a minimal position that, in order to seem rationally acceptable, abandoned some distinctive and vital elements of the Christian position. Balguy's account of the two volumes of nature and grace seems to be open to the same accusation. From the point of view of morality at any rate, the second volume encourages moral improvement by commands and sanctions, but it does not seem to contribute any distinctive insight into morality and its requirements.

It is reasonable, then, for orthodox Christian opponents of Clarke to be dissatisfied with his explanation of the connexion between rational morality and Christian morality. As we will see, Waterland and Butler express some of the objections that might be raised.[38] Should this dissatisfaction spread to Clarke's and Balguy's defence of rational morality as a foundation for Christian morality? The eventual results of such dissatisfaction are visible in (for instance) Kierkegaard's sharp division between the outlook of rational morality and the Christian outlook; in his view, the Christian revelation imposes demands that do not simply go beyond rational morality, but are basically opposed to it. If Clarke and Balguy bring Christian virtues too close to ordinary moral virtues, they raise a question about whether one can defend Aquinas' claim that a Christian superstructure rests on the rational foundation.

---

their own minds, and yet has not given them wherewith to support themselves in the suitable and constant practice of it.' (H 630 = R 250)

[38] On Waterland and Butler see §869.

51

BUTLER: NATURE

674. Butler's Aims

Butler's sermons are intended 'to explain what is meant by the nature of man, when it is said that virtue consists in following, and vice in deviating from it; and by explaining to show that the assertion is true' (P13). He says that this claim about nature is the view of the ancient moralists; they believe that vice is 'more contrary' to human nature than torture and death are.[1]

In the comparative 'more contrary' Butler suggests that torture and death are to some degree contrary to nature.[2] He therefore attributes to the ancients a doctrine of degrees of naturalness, and hence a graded conception of nature, according to which torture and death are indeed contrary to nature, but less contrary than vice is. These remarks about the ancients recall the Stoics, and especially passages in Cicero that assume a graded conception of nature.[3]

---

[1] 'That the ancient moralists had some inward feeling or other, which they chose to express in this manner, that man is born to virtue, that it consists following nature, and that vice is more contrary to this nature than tortures or death, their works in our hands are instances.' (P 13) I cite Butler from Bernard's edition (containing the *Sermons* in vol. i and the *Analogy* in vol. ii). The sermons are cited by roman numeral (or 'P' for the Preface) and paragraph. 'D' refers to the 'Dissertation of the nature of virtue' appended to the *Analogy*.

[2] Cf. iii 2, quoted in §703.

[3] 'For a human being, therefore, to take something from another, and to increase his advantage by the disadvantage of another human being, is more contrary to nature than is death or poverty or pain or the other things that can happen to our body or to external things.' (Cic. *Off*. iii 21) 'Further, if someone wrongs another to gain some advantage for himself, either he supposes that he is not acting against nature, or he estimates that death, poverty, pain, or even the loss of children, kin, or friends, is more to be avoided than an act of injustice against anyone. If he supposes he is not acting against nature by wronging human beings, how is one to argue with him, given that he altogether takes away humanity (hominem) from a human being? But if he estimates that, while such a course is indeed to be avoided, the other things—death, poverty, pain—are much worse, he is mistaken in estimating that any defect (vitium) belonging to the body or to fortune is more serious than vices (vitia) of the soul.' (Cic. *Off*. iii 26)

In his note on P 13 Bernard cites Diogenes Laertius vii 87 and Cic. *Off*. iii 21, and adds: 'Yet it must be observed that by the precept "Follow nature" Butler meant something widely different from the Stoic interpretation of that precept. The Stoics meant by it a wise obedience to the laws of the universe; Butler means obedience to the system of *human* nature, which amounts, in practice, to a following of conscience as its most important and distinctive constituent. The *formula Stoicorum*, in its original import, was far more nearly akin to the ethical principles of Clarke and the rational school of moralists than to those of Butler.' (Bernard's phrase 'formula Stoicorum' is misleading about the syntax of *Off*. iii 20, where 'Stoicorum' depends on 'rationi disciplinaeque' rather than on 'formula'.) Bernard is right to mention the similarity of Stoic views to Clarke, but wrong to suggest that the Stoics and Clarke are not interested in human nature; see §630.

Though naturalism about virtue is characteristic of ancient moralists, it is not the unanimous view of modern moralists. Some simply reject it, while others regard it as trivial and useless, even if it is true (P 13).[4] Butler argues that critics reject or dismiss the Stoic formula because they misunderstand it. If the critics had understood it correctly, their criticisms would be justified. To show why they are wrong, we have to interpret claims about human nature correctly.

Though the *Sermons* are brief, they state or presuppose positions on many issues in moral psychology, meta-ethics, normative ethics, and moral theology.[5] The appeal to nature constitutes a distinctive position in all these areas. A correct account of human nature, in Butler's view, not only vindicates the truth and importance of Stoic naturalism, but also supports it against the three main rival positions that Butler considers: extreme rationalism, sentimentalism, and Hobbesian egoism. It may be helpful, therefore, to sketch some of the relevant controversies and Butler's resolutions of them.

675. Hobbes on Nature and Morality

A proof that morality is natural would refute Hobbes's position. Hobbes's moral and political theory rests on an account of human nature, but he takes this account to refute the view that morality is natural. He rejects the Aristotelian claim that a human being is naturally a political animal.[6] He argues that human beings, in contrast to some other species of animals, need explicit agreements backed up by force in order to maintain a society. Society does not come naturally to human beings, both because they compete for scarce goods and because they struggle for superiority.[7] According to some of Hobbes's remarks, a person's good essentially consists in the awareness of superiority to other people, but does not essentially consist in, for instance, co-operative relations with other people.

Hobbes believes that purely psychological and environmental facts about human nature help to explain why human beings in the state of nature need morality and law; that is why he begins *Leviathan* with an account of human nature and desires. Given human nature, we have a sufficient reason and motive for accepting morality. But morality is not natural; we need it only because it removes some obstacle to achieving our goal, not because it is actually a part of the goal we aim at. We need morality because other people interfere with our own satisfaction, and morality helps to prevent this interference. If we could as effectively achieve the ends achieved by morality in some other way, we would have no reason to prefer morality. Morality is desirable for each individual not because of her own nature, but because of the unwelcome results of other people's behaviour.

---

[4] Quoted in §678.

[5] Pattison's appreciation of Butler's *Analogy* applies equally to the *Sermons*: 'The objections it meets are not new and unseasoned objections, but such as had worn well, and had borne the rub of controversy, because they were genuine. And it will be equally hard to find in the *Analogy* any topic in reply, which had not been suggested in . . . the preceding half century . . . Its substance are the thoughts of a whole age, not barely compiled, but each reconsidered and digested.' ('Thought' 75) See also Rivers, *RGS* i 183.

[6] Hobbes on Aristotle; see §481. On Hutcheson and naturalism see §§714, 716. Hume discusses Hutcheson in his letter of 17 Sept. 1739 = Greig No. 13 = R 631, quoted in §728. On final causes and design cf. Kames, *EPMNR*, Part 1, Essay 2, ch. 1 = Moran 24–6 = SB 910–12.

[7] See *L.* 17.7–8, quoted in §491.

Hobbes's claim clarifies a view that Butler opposes, and hence clarifies the view that he wants to defend. Butler wants to show that being moral has a closer connexion with our nature than Hobbes thinks it has. Given the sort of being that I am, I have good reason, in Butler's view, to prefer morality even if other people are not likely to interfere with me. That is why a better account of human nature should support a better account of why morality is worth having for each human being.

An appeal to facts about human nature appears to undermine morality, since it seems to justify a version of self-confined egoism that casts doubt on the rational basis of morality. Hobbes defends morality by his reduction of morality to prudence and by the assumptions that support his answer to the fool. Others find these defences of morality unconvincing. Just as Descartes raises sceptical doubts that seem more compelling than his answers, so Hobbes raises sceptical doubts about morality that seem more compelling than his attempted vindication of morality against these doubts.

Naturalism, then, has a dialectical role. Butler recognizes that appeals to human nature are used against morality, and so he seeks to refute his opponents by using a form of argument that they also accept. He agrees that the appeal to nature is legitimate, but believes that it justifies conclusions that refute critics of morality.

676. Sentimentalism and Naturalism

Butler is not the first to defend morality against Hobbes by appeal to nature. He follows Shaftesbury and Hutcheson in trying to show that human nature itself, rather than the specific circumstances of our environment, supports morality. Hutcheson's inaugural lecture 'On the natural sociality of human beings' shows how close Hutcheson and Butler are on this question.[8] Hutcheson's thesis marks his agreement with Grotius against Pufendorf and Hobbes.[9] He includes favourable references to the Stoics, reflecting his normal sympathetic attitude to them.[10]

Hutcheson opposes the position of Pufendorf, who restricts the natural to the pleasant and the expedient (§22), and so he defends the naturalist claim of Suarez and Grotius that moral rightness (honestas) is also natural. He takes the dispute between Pufendorf and the naturalists to turn on whether human beings have natural benevolent desires (§24). If they have, then, in his view, morality is in accordance with human nature, and the anti-naturalist position is refuted. Hutcheson, therefore, takes his doctrine of a moral sense to vindicate naturalism.[11] Morality is natural because it is the product of a natural sentiment; it is not

---

[8] See Hutcheson, HN. The lecture was delivered and published in 1730, four years after the first edition of Butler's Sermons.

[9] The lecture takes up an aspect of Pufendorf's position that Gerschom Carmichael had drawn to Hutcheson's attention. See §454.

[10] Prevailing attitudes to Stoicism in the Scottish Enlightenment are discussed by Stewart, 'Legacy'.

[11] 'Our moral sense shows this [sc. universal calm benevolence] to be the highest perfection of our nature; what we may see to be the end or design of such a structure, and consequently what is required of us by the author of our nature; and therefore if anyone like these descriptions better, he may call virtue, with many of the ancients, "vita secundum naturam", or acting according to what we may see from the constitution of our nature, we were intended for by our Creator.' (Hutcheson, NCPA, Pref. = Garrett 8)

simply devised as a means to secure some end that would appeal to us even if we had no moral attitudes. Since this is how he understands the natural character of morality, Hutcheson often contrasts his view with the claim that morality arises from reason; by 'reason' he means instrumental reason.

Many of Butler's claims about nature might be taken to support a sentimentalist account of morality. In his first sermon he endorses Hutcheson's claim that human nature includes not only self-interested but also moral attitudes. He mentions benevolence (i 6), particular passions (i 7), and reflexion (i 8). The principle of reflexion is the principle by which we approve or disapprove of our passions, propensions, and actions; and Butler identifies this principle with conscience.[12]

He claims, then, that the sentimentalist is right about the extent of human motives, against Hobbes's egoism.[13] He disagrees about the character of our moral attitudes, rejecting Hutcheson's view that they consist in a non-rational moral sense. But on other points we might suppose that he agrees with Hutcheson. It is not surprising that Hutcheson endorses some of Butler's arguments, and in his later work takes the moral sense to incorporate some of the features of conscience, as Butler conceives it.[14]

677. The Error of Sentimentalism

But despite these points of agreement with Hutcheson, Butler believes that the sentimentalists offer an inadequate conception of human nature. If human nature were simply a collection of the motives and dispositions recognized by sentimentalists, Hutcheson would be right.[15] But Butler rejects this account of human nature. At first he confines himself to 'the partial inadequate notion of human nature treated of in the first discourse' (P 21); hence he does not treat either self-love or benevolence as superior to the particular passions. Nor does he at first introduce reflexion or conscience as a superior principle, nor explain what its superiority and authority consist in.[16]

---

[12] 'This principle in man, by which he approves or disapproves his heart, temper, and actions is conscience; for this is the strict sense of the word, though sometimes it is used so as to take in more.' (i 8)

[13] 'Mankind has various instincts and principles of action, as brute creatures have; some leading most directly and immediately to the good of the community, and some most directly to private good. . . . The generality of mankind also obey their instincts and principles, all of them; those propensions we call good, as well as the bad, according to the same rules; namely, the constitution of their body, and the external circumstances which they are in. Therefore it is not a true representation of mankind to affirm, that they are wholly governed by self-love, the love of power and sensual appetites: since, as on the one hand they are often actuated by these, without any regard to right or wrong; so on the other it is manifest fact, that the same persons, the generality, are frequently influenced by friendship, compassion, gratitude; and even a general abhorrence of what is base, and liking of what is fair and just, takes its turn amongst the other motives of action.' (P 18–21)

[14] See also §714.

[15] '. . . Brutes in acting according to the rules before mentioned, their bodily constitution and circumstances, act suitably to their whole nature. . . . Mankind also in acting thus would act suitably to their whole nature, if no more were to be said of man's nature than what has been now said; if that, as it is a true, were also a complete, adequate account of our nature' (P 22–3).

[16] 'This faculty is now mentioned merely as another part in the inward frame of man, pointing out to us in some degree what we are intended for, and as what will naturally and of course have some influence. The particular place assigned to it by nature, what authority it has, and how great influence it ought to have, shall be hereafter considered.' (i 8)

To expose the weakness in the sentimentalist position, Butler refers to an argument of Shaftesbury's, which rests on an inadequate conception of nature.[17] According to a sentimentalist view, someone who lacks a strong enough preference to choose virtue over vice thereby also lacks any sufficient reason to choose virtue. Hutcheson holds this view no less than Shaftesbury. The sentimentalists do not mean simply that such a person will not be aware of any reason to be virtuous. They mean that he also has no such reason.

In Butler's view, the sentimentalists are wrong to hold this view, because their account of human nature is incomplete. For practical as well as theoretical reasons, we need to insist on the 'reflex approbation or disapprobation' of conscience.[18] From the sentimentalist point of view, conscience is just one of the motives that make up our nature. We have reason to follow it just to the extent that it is stronger than other motives; but if other motives are stronger, Shaftesbury and Hutcheson believe we have reason to follow those motives. They do not take account of the special character of conscience.

If sentimentalists make reasons depend on the comparative strength of different motives, they need not endorse our acting on cruel or lazy or spiteful motives if they are strongest. If we prefer action on the moral motive, we will want to encourage people to strengthen their tendency to act on their approval of humanity rather than on cruelty. Butler objects that if sentimentalists are right, we cannot justifiably say what we might reasonably want to say about the outlook of humanity. For we cannot say we have any reason to prefer humanity, apart from our preference for it. Nor can we claim that it is especially natural to act on our humane sentiments; whether it is natural or not depends on whether these sentiments are stronger. Butler wants an account of nature that allows us to ascribe the appropriate authority to conscience, and so to defend the claims that sentimentalists cannot defend.

[17] 'The practical reason of insisting so much upon this natural authority of the principle of reflexion or conscience is, that it seems in great measure overlooked by many, who are by no means the worse sort of men. It is thought sufficient to abstain from gross wickedness, and to be humane and kind to such as happen to come in their way. . . . The not taking into consideration this authority, which is implied in the idea of reflex approbation or disapprobation, seems a material deficiency or omission in Lord Shaftesbury's Inquiry concerning Virtue. He has shown beyond all contradiction, that virtue is naturally the interest or happiness, and vice the misery, of such a creature as man, placed in the circumstances which we are in this world. But suppose there are particular exceptions; a case which this author was unwilling to put, and yet surely it is to be put: or suppose a case which he has put and determined, that of a sceptic not convinced of this happy tendency of virtue, or being of a contrary opinion. His determination is, that it would be *without remedy*.' (P 25–6) Shaftesbury uses this phrase in his discussion of the moral effects of atheism: 'Now as to atheism, though it be plainly deficient and without remedy in the case of ill judgment on the happiness of virtue, yet it is not, indeed, of necessity the cause of any such ill-judgment.' (*ICV* i 3.3 = K 189, cited by Bernard)

[18] 'But it may be said, "What is all this, though true, to the purpose of virtue and religion?. These require, not only that we do good to others when we are led this way, by benevolence or reflexion happening to be stronger than other principles, passions, or appetites, but likewise that the whole character be formed upon thought and reflexion; that every action be directed by some determinate rule, some other rule than the strength and prevalency of any principle or passion. . . . it does not appear that there ever was a man who would not have approved an action of humanity rather than of cruelty; interest and passion being quite out of the case. But interest and passion do come in, and are often too strong for and prevail over reflexion and conscience. . . . does not man . . . act agreeably to his nature, or obey the law of his creation, by following that principle, be it passion or conscience, which for the present happens to be strongest in him?"' (ii 3)

678. Naturalism and Rationalism

Butler's claim that sentimentalism cannot explain why we have a reason to follow con-science against other motives is not new. The same objection underlies Balguy's criticism of Hutcheson. We might expect, then, that Butler would support rationalism against sentimentalist naturalism.

His favourable comments on Clarke's rationalism reflect his early interest in Clarke's philosophy and natural theology. But his early interest also led him to some sharp criticisms of Clarke's natural theology. He also refrains from endorsing Clarke's approach to moral philosophy.[19]

He compares Clarke's rationalism with his own naturalism.[20] He grants that the rationalist argument 'seems the most direct formal proof, and in some respects the least liable to cavil and dispute'. The 'seems' and 'in some respects' mark possible reservations. If it were intuitively certain that, for instance, benefaction requires gratitude, that would indeed be a direct formal proof, and it would put the moral principle beyond cavil and dispute. But Clarke's alleged proof of such principles does not seem convincing enough to exclude cavil and dispute. Butler's naturalism implies that moral truths cannot be proved without reference to facts about human nature.

This disagreement with the rationalists may appear to expose Butler to a rationalist objection to Hutcheson's naturalism. According to Balguy, our having a natural tendency to approve morality does not explain what morality consists in or why we ought to follow it. If people are predominantly right-handed, it does not follow that we ought to be right-handed; if they changed to being predominantly left-handed, being left-handed would not thereby become better than being right-handed. If nature is nothing more than a natural tendency of this type, a proof that morality is natural does not clarify the character of morality.

To avoid this objection to the sentimentalist appeal to nature, extreme rationalists avoid any appeal to nature. Sentimentalists make morality appear mutable in a respect that falsifies its character. To preserve immutability, the rationalists sever morality from human nature altogether, and claim that it consists solely in eternal relations of fitness.[21]

Butler recognizes that rationalists object to naturalism. He mentions Wollaston's criticism of appeals to nature that are simply appeals to the strength of particular desires.[22] According

---

[19] The letters between Butler and Clarke on the existence of God are in Bernard, i 311–39. Letters on moral questions are at 331–9.

[20] 'One begins from inquiring into the abstract relations of things; the other from a matter of fact, namely, what the particular nature of man is, its several parts, their economy or constitution; from whence it proceeds to determine what course of life it is, which is correspondent to this whole nature. In the former method the conclusion is expressed thus—that vice is contrary to the nature and reason of things; in the latter, that it is a violation or breaking in upon our own nature. Thus they both lead to the same thing; our obligations to the practice of virtue; and thus they exceedingly strengthen and enforce each other. The first seems the most direct formal proof, and in some respects the least liable to cavil and dispute; the latter is in a peculiar manner adapted to satisfy a fair mind; and is more easily applicable to the several particular relations and circumstances in life. The following discourses proceed chiefly in this latter method. The three first wholly.' (P 12–13) Cf. Hume, §731 on rationalism and naturalism.

[21] See Cudworth, §547.

[22] '... there were not wanting persons, who manifestly mistook the whole thing, and so had great reason to express themselves dissatisfied with it. A late author of great and deserved reputation says that to place virtue in following nature, is at best a loose way of talk. And he has reason to say this, if what I think he intends to express, though with

to this criticism, an appeal to nature is either empty, if it says no more than we would say by mentioning the desire, or misleading, if it suggests that acting on good reasons is simply acting on our predominant desires.

679. Butler's Version of Naturalism

In reply to this rationalist criticism of appeals to nature, Butler argues that both sentimentalists and rationalists have the wrong conception of nature. He seeks to defend the view 'that virtue consists in following, and vice in deviating from it' (P 13). Since this is the view of the ancient moralists, he seeks to clarify their conception of nature. He does not believe that the traditional appeal to nature is genuinely obscure, but he believes that people who are accustomed to speaking of nature as modern moralists speak of it need to grasp the difference between their conception and the traditional conception.[23]

The traditional conception of nature marks the difference between the 'partial inadequate notion of human nature' that Butler assumes in the first Sermon and the more adequate notion that he introduces in the second Sermon (ii 4). If the partial inadequate notion were all that there is to nature, it would be ridiculous for the ancient moralists to claim that deviation from nature is vice; hence we should suppose they have something different in mind.[24]

To see what they have in mind, Butler distinguishes three senses of 'nature' and 'natural'. Two of them are familiar from the debates between Hobbes, the sentimentalists, and the rationalists. We might take 'natural' to mean (i) in accordance with some natural impulse or other, or (ii) in accordance with one's strongest natural impulse (ii 5–6). These two senses capture Hobbes's appeals to nature. Hobbes looks for an account of human nature that identifies the basic moving forces that explain all the varied and complex movements and

---

great decency, be true, that scarce any other sense can be put upon those words, but acting as any of the several parts without distinction, of a man's nature happened most to incline him' (P 13). For Wollaston's objection see R 291. See also Adams's doubts (§665) about whether Clarke's appeal to fitness adequately grasps the sorts of facts that are described by moral truths.

[23] 'Now a person who found no mystery in this way of speaking of the ancients; who, without being very explicit with himself, kept to his natural feeling, went along with them, and found within himself a full conviction, that what they laid down was just and true; such an one would probably wonder to see a point, in which he never perceived any difficulty, so laboured as this is, in the second and third Sermons . . . But it need not be thought strange, that this manner of expression, though familiar with them, and, if not usually carried so far, yet not uncommon amongst ourselves, should want explaining; since there are several perceptions daily felt and spoken of, which yet it may not be very easy at first view to explicate, to distinguish from all others, and ascertain exactly what the idea or perception is. . . . Thus, though there seems no ground to doubt, but that the generality of mankind have the inward perception expressed so commonly in that manner by the ancient moralists . . . yet it appeared of use to unfold that inward conviction, and lay it open in a more explicit manner than I had seen done.' (P 13)

[24] 'Now all this licentious talk entirely goes upon a supposition that men follow their nature in the same sense, in violating the known rules of justice and honesty for the sake of a present gratification, as they do in following those rules when they have no temptation to the contrary. And if this were true, that could not be so which St Paul asserts, that men are by nature a law to themselves. If by following nature were meant only acting as we please, it would indeed be ridiculous to speak of nature as any guide in morals; nay, the very mention of deviating from nature would be absurd; and the mention of following it, when spoken by way of distinction, would absolutely have no meaning. For did ever any one act otherwise than as he pleased? And yet the ancients speak of deviating from nature as vice, and of following nature so much as a distinction, that according to them the perfection of virtue consists therein. So that language itself should teach people another sense to the words *following nature* than barely acting as we please.' (ii 4)

tendencies of a human being. Morality, in his view, depends on facts about human nature, but it is not natural. Hutcheson's naturalism also relies on these two senses of 'natural'. In his view, virtue is natural because it is based on one of our natural sentiments, benevolence, and therefore excites the approval of the moral sense. Wollaston assumes the same sense of 'natural' in criticizing sentimentalist appeals to the natural.

Butler, however, does not believe that naturalism commits us to the errors of sentimentalism. He therefore seeks to isolate the sense of 'nature' and 'natural' that is relevant to the claim that virtue consists in following nature. A third sense of 'nature' and 'natural' introduces a connexion between nature and system.[25] When we study some system, we try to understand it as a whole, and to grasp the point of each part in it. Butler gives the example of a watch, insisting that we do not understand it unless we grasp 'its conduciveness to this one or more ends', which are the ends of the system as a whole.[26]

This point of view on the watch allows us to understand some claims about its nature. We can say both (a) that the nature of a watch is to tell the time, and (b) that it is natural for watches to run fast or slow, break down, etc. The second of these statements fits the first two senses of nature just described. But the first fits neither of them exactly. It is a claim about the system as a whole; its different bits and pieces constitute some organized whole in which they have a particular part to play; and the watch goes against its nature when it is (as we say) 'out of order'.

This first claim about the watch explains Butler's claim about human nature, by clarifying his third sense of 'nature' and 'natural'. The properties that belong to x's nature belong to x as a whole system, and not simply to its parts, and doing F is natural for x if F is required by x as a whole rather than simply a part or aspect of x. This explanation clarifies the claim that virtue is in accord with our nature and vice is contrary to it.[27] Even if vice is natural in one of the first two senses, it is not natural in the third sense.[28]

The third sense of 'natural' relies on a teleological conception of a system and its needs. This conception may be clear enough when we consider an artifact with a known design; for the designer of the watch sets the end for which the system is made. To apply this pattern directly to human beings, we have to assume that they are also artifacts designed for some purpose. Butler certainly believes that human beings are designed by God (ii 1). But his

---

[25] On nature and system cf. Aristotle, §77; Hobbes, §483.

[26] 'Whoever thinks it worth while to consider this matter thoroughly, should begin with stating to himself exactly the idea of a system, economy, or constitution of any particular nature, or particular any thing: and he will, I suppose, find, that it is an one or a whole, made up of several parts; but yet, that the several parts even considered as a whole do not complete the idea, unless in the notion of a whole you include the relations and respects which those parts have to each other.... Let us instance in a watch—Suppose the several parts of it taken to pieces, and placed apart from each other: let a man have ever so exact a notion of these several parts, unless he considers the respects and relations which they have to each other, he will not have any thing like the idea of a watch. Suppose these several parts brought together and anyhow united: neither will he yet, be the union ever so close, have an idea which will bear any resemblance to that of a watch. But let him view those several parts put together, or consider them as to be put together in the manner of a watch; let him form a notion of the relations which those several parts have to each other—all conducive in their respective ways to this purpose, showing the hour of the day; and then he has the idea of a watch.' (P 14)

[27] 'Thus nothing can possibly be more contrary to nature than vice, meaning by "nature" not only the several parts of our inward frame, but also the constitution of it.' (P 15)

[28] 'Man may act according to that principle or inclination which for the present happens to be strongest, and yet act in a way disproportionate to, and violate, his real proper nature.' (ii 10)

ethical argument does not rely directly on this theological premiss; and so he tries to explain his claims about nature and system without appeal to design.[29]

If we treat something as a system rather than simply a collection, we imply that its different traits achieve results that are not only consistent, but also harmonious and mutually co-operative. Consistency requires that different traits do not regularly conflict and do not undermine one another. Harmony requires them to co-exist in such a way that their results support one another. Co-operation requires more active steps to achieve harmony, so that one trait not only supports or facilitates another, but strengthens and helps it.

In claiming that human beings have a nature, Butler claims that we constitute systems of this sort. We discover our nature by looking at a human being to see how the different elements constitute a single system. We grasp the system in human nature not by looking at the several passions and motives in themselves, but from considering their relations.[30]

680. Is Human Nature a System?

What, then, do we discover by looking at the relations between different passions and affections? Do we think of ourselves as simply a collection of impulses, so that none of our impulses belongs to our selves any more than another does? Or can we draw any distinction parallel to the one that Butler draws in the case of the watch?

Some intuitive views seem to support Butler. If a doctor says 'You need an operation', and explains that we need it in order to remove a cancerous growth, we do not disagree on the ground that it would be better for the cancerous growth, taken by itself, to keep growing instead of being killed. Or if I say 'I need to exercise more', the part of me that enjoys being lazy does not need the exercise, but I may still need it. In both cases, we confirm Butler's suggestion that we recognize some difference between the requirements of the system as a whole and the requirements of particular parts of it. We think of ourselves as selves that have some definite aims and interests distinct from a mere collection of the motives, desires, and impulses that constitute us.

But even if we tend to speak in Butler's way, are we speaking loosely? To show that we are not, Butler tries to say what is involved in acting naturally, in his third sense. To see that human nature is a system, we need to understand the role of superior principles in our action; this is the feature of human nature that sentimentalists have left out.[31]

---

[29] Millar, 'Following nature' and 'God and human nature', discusses Butler's teleology. Millar relies on claims about the causal origin of the different traits that Butler calls natural. His discussion shows how such claims may lead Butler into difficulties.

[30] 'It is from considering the relations which the several appetites and passions in the inward frame have to each other, and, above all, the supremacy of reflexion or conscience, that we get the idea of the system or constitution of human nature. And from the idea itself it will as fully appear that this our nature, that is, constitution, is adapted to virtue, as from the idea of a watch it appears that its nature, that is, constitution or system, is adapted to measure time.' (P 14)

[31] 'But that [sc. the sentimentalist account] is not a complete account of man's nature. Somewhat further must be brought in to give us an adequate notion of it; namely, that one of those principles of action, conscience or reflexion, compared with the rest as they all stand together in the nature of man, plainly bears upon it marks of authority over all the rest, and claims the absolute direction of them all, to allow or forbid their gratification: a disapprobation of

Butler claims that 'reflexion' or 'conscience' is a superior principle in human nature. If we simply treat it as one motive among others, we ignore its superiority. Even if we were to claim, falsely, that it is always or usually our dominant motive, we would not have recognized its superiority. We have to acknowledge a superior principle as having authority, and not simply strength.

If we conceive a self as a system governed by superior principles, we can understand the naturalism of the ancients.[32] Consideration of the needs and connexions of the different parts of the system of human nature explains why pain is contrary to nature. But to understand how the unnaturalness of pain differs from the unnaturalness of injustice, we must grasp the difference between superior principles and other principles.

Butler introduces two claims about superior principles: (1) Human nature includes superior principles, those that rely on authority rather than strength. (2) Human nature is a system insofar as it is governed by superior principles. The second of these claims seems to go beyond the first. Since superiority does not imply greater strength, our motives might include superior principles that do not govern us, and we might be inclined to say that they ought not to govern us because they make our lives chaotic; the mere fact that they claim authority does not show that we ought to listen to their claim. But though these are two distinct claims about superior principles, Butler takes them to be closely connected; he believes that once we understand what superior principles are, we also see that we act in accordance with our needs as whole systems only insofar as we act in accordance with superior principles.

Butler's diagnosis of the error of the sentimentalists shows that his conclusion is not to be treated as an analytic truth; the meaning of 'natural' or 'in accordance with our nature' is not to be given by 'in accordance with a superior principle'. Rather, when we understand the meaning of 'in accordance with nature' and of 'superior principle', we recognize the synthetic truth that acting on superior principles is in accordance with nature. To act in accordance with nature is to act in accord with the requirements of ourselves as whole systems.

---

reflexion being in itself a principle manifestly superior to a mere propension. And the conclusion is, that to allow no more to this superior principle or part of our nature, than to other parts; to let it govern and guide only occasionally in common with the rest, as its turn happens to come, from the temper and circumstances one happens to be in; this is not to act conformably to the constitution of man: neither can any human creature be said to act conformably to his constitution of nature, unless he allows to that superior principle the absolute authority which is due to it.' (P 24)

[32] 'Thus nothing can possibly be more contrary to nature than vice; meaning by nature not only the *several parts* of our internal frame, but also the *constitution* of it. Poverty and disgrace, tortures and death, are not so contrary to it. Misery and injustice are indeed equally contrary to some different parts of our nature taken singly: but injustice is moreover contrary to the whole constitution of the nature. If it be asked, whether this constitution be really what those philosophers meant, ... I have no doubt, but that this is the true account of the ground of that conviction which they referred to, when they said, vice was contrary to nature. And though it should be thought that they meant no more than that vice was contrary to the higher and better part of our nature; even this implies such a constitution as I have endeavoured to explain. ... They had a perception that injustice was contrary to their nature, and that pain was so also. They observed these two perceptions totally different, not in degree, but in kind: and the reflecting upon each of them, as they thus stood in their nature, wrought a full intuitive conviction, that more was due and of right belonged to one of these inward perceptions, than to the other; that it demanded in all cases to govern such a creature as man.' (P 15–16)

681. The Law of Our Nature

Butler connects this naturalism with belief in natural law. He follows Stoic precedents, by recalling the passage in *De Officiis* that suggests the graded conception of nature.[33] Both Cicero and Butler assume that the law of nature is not simply about rational agents, but also available to rational agents.

Though Butler does not mention natural law, he introduces it, as Clarke does, by appeal to St Paul's claim that human beings are by nature a law to themselves (*Rm.* 2:15).[34] Aquinas cites this passage as a Scriptural warrant for including a doctrine of natural law in Christian moral theology. Luther and Calvin, among many others, agree with Aquinas.[35] Butler agrees with them in taking St Paul to claim both that rational agents are a law to themselves and that conscience is the means of recognizing the content of the law.[36] We are by nature a law to ourselves because of two connexions between law and nature: (1) It is part of our nature to be guided by law, since guidance by law is one of our natural principles. (2) In being guided by law, we act in accordance with our nature.

Butler sees these connexions between law and nature because he identifies guidance by law with acting on superior principles. A proper understanding of our nature shows that it is natural to us to act on superior principles. If we act on superior principles, we are guided by conscience, and the actions required by conscience are those that accord with our nature.

Is Butler entitled to both of these connexions between nature and law? Even if it is natural to follow superior principles, we might not immediately agree that these principles grasp what is natural for us to do. In claiming that guidance by superior principles implies guidance by conscience, and that we act naturally when we act on conscience, Butler relies on assumptions that need defence.

In Butler's view, a grasp of his claim that we are a law to ourselves reveals the error in sentimentalist naturalism.[37] Contrary to Shaftesbury, he takes the authority of conscience or reflexion to give us a sufficient reason for preferring morality, irrespective of any beliefs

---

[33] 'And this follows even more from the reason of nature, which is divine and human law. If anyone is willing to obey it (and all will obey it who want to live in accord with nature), he will never act so as to seek what belongs to another and to take for himself what he has taken from another.' (Cic. *Off.* iii 23)

[34] Cf. Clark, *DNR* = H ii 615.   [35] See §412.

[36] 'The apostle asserts that the Gentiles *do by NATURE the things contained in the law*. . . . He intends to express more than that by which they *did not*, that by which they *did* the works of the law; namely, *by nature*. . . . [T]here is a superior principle of reflexion or conscience in every man, which distinguishes between the internal principles of his heart, as well as his external actions; which passes judgment upon himself and them; pronounces determinately some actions to be in themselves just, right, good; others to be in themselves evil, wrong unjust . . . It is by this faculty, natural to man, that he is a moral agent, that he is a law to himself. . . . This prerogative, this *natural supremacy*, of the faculty which surveys, approves or disapproves the several affections of our mind and actions of our lives, being that by which men are a law to themselves, their conformity or disobedience to which law of our nature renders their actions, in the highest and most proper sense, natural or unnatural.' (ii 8–9)

[37] 'The practical reason of insisting so much upon this natural authority of the principle of reflexion or conscience is, that it seems in great measure overlooked by many, who are by no means the worse sort of men. . . . The observation, that man is thus by his very nature a law to himself, pursued to its just consequences, is of the utmost importance; because from it will follow, that though men should, through stupidity or speculative scepticism, be ignorant of, or disbelieve, any authority in the universe to punish the violation of this law; yet, if there should be such authority, they would be as really liable to punishment, as though they had been beforehand convinced, that such punishment would follow.' (P 25, 29) These two passages are separated by Butler's argument against Shaftesbury, on which see §714.

about rewards or punishments. The law that we find in ourselves also tells us what is naturally suitable for us, and so we have an obligation to obey it because it is 'the law of our nature' (iii 5).

682. The Difference between Naturalism and Rationalism

Butler's presentation of his position suggests that it is different from both Hutcheson's and Clarke's positions. If his argument succeeds, he vindicates part of the traditional view that he alludes to in his remark on the ancient moralists; both Aristotelians and Stoics regard human nature as a source of moral reasons that do not depend on desires.

Balguy's criticisms of Hutcheson make it clear why rationalists do not appeal to human nature to explain the essential features of moral goodness. The sentimentalist view implies that morality is mutable in relation to facts about human nature. To preserve morality from this sort of mutability, the rationalists sever morality from human nature, and claim that it consists solely in eternal relations of fitness (as Clarke, followed by Balguy, expresses it).

In arguing that a reference to nature is essential to a correct account of virtue and vice, Butler rejects the rationalist attempt to explain virtue without reference to nature. He claims that the naturalist approach 'is in a peculiar manner adapted to satisfy a fair mind; and is more easily applicable to the several particular relations and circumstances in life'. It rests on premises that an unprejudiced reader must accept, since we all have to recognize that there is such a thing as human nature.[38] Once we recognize its structure, we can see that morality conforms to this structure. Even if we are sceptical about Clarke's abstract and eternal relations of fitness and unfitness, we cannot deny the truths about human nature that we assume in our daily life and in our understanding and guidance of ourselves. Butler claims that these truths are sufficient to support a convincing account of the nature and justifiability of morality.

This form of naturalist argument helps us to decide whether rationalism and naturalism are compatible. Butler argues for two claims: (1) Living virtuously accords with human nature. (2) To live virtuously is to live in accord with human nature. He is right to say that a rationalist might agree with the first claim, and that therefore rationalism and naturalism are complementary. But his second claim conflicts with rationalism, because it implies that morality is mutable in ways in which Clarke seems to deny. Even though morality is not mutable in relation to our feelings of sympathy (as Hutcheson supposes), it is mutable (according to Butler) in relation to human nature. For if morality consists in living in accord with nature, it follows that if human nature were to change, morality would change too. Hence morality cannot consist entirely in eternal relations of fitness that are independent of facts about human nature.[39] If rationalists disagree with Butler on this point, his naturalism

---

[38] It may be worth comparing this form of argument with the strategy of Butler's later *Analogy*. In that work he claims to proceed from familiar facts about the 'constitution and course of nature' ('Advertisement', p. xvii Bernard) to conclusions about the divine government of the world. In the *Sermons* he proceeds from familiar facts about human nature to conclusions about the moral government of the individual.

[39] On mutability cf. Suarez, *Leg.* ii 13.2, quoted in §441. On Hume's neglect of the difference between Clarke and Butler see §§744, 747.

is not consistent with the view that morality consists in eternal and immutable relations of fitness. This conclusion seems to conflict with his initial suggestion that his argument and Clarke's are complementary. Though Clarke does not go as far as Wollaston goes in dismissing claims about human nature, Wollaston captures some of the spirit and motivation of Clarke's account of eternal and immutable morality. Clarke differs from Cudworth and Suarez in avoiding any essential appeal to judgments about human nature and the human good. He wants moral judgments to be certain and evident apart from the uncertain support (as Wollaston suggests) of judgments about nature. If Wollaston has correctly expressed the reservations about appeals to nature that inform Clarke's position, Butler reverts to a position that is close to Suarez's naturalism, and apparently incompatible with Clarke's claims about fitness.

Butler's suggestion that naturalism and rationalism are compatible is more intelligible, however, if we contrast both positions with the sentimentalist naturalism that Balguy attacks. If a rationalist agrees that facts about human nature are eternal and immutable in the relevant sense of being independent of changes in human inclinations and choices (other than those that are essential to human nature), Butler's naturalism is compatible with rationalism.

The distance between Butler and Clarke is even smaller if, as we suggested, Clarke relies on naturalist claims.[40] In arguing against Hobbes and in accepting the Stoic doctrine of conciliation, Clarke introduces claims about human nature and the human constitution. He does not see that these claims are inconsistent with the extreme rationalist position that Wollaston develops from him. If Butler sees the naturalist elements in Clarke, and notices that Clarke does not explain his use of them, he is right to explore an alternative to voluntarism and sentimentalism that includes a systematic account of nature.[41]

Butler maintains, against Wollaston, that an appeal to nature makes morality eternal and immutable in the appropriate way, by being independent of human inclinations. If he shows this, he answers Balguy's objections to Hutcheson, and Wollaston's suggestion that any naturalist theory faces the same objections. To see whether Butler has a distinctive position, as opposed to a collection of dubiously consistent positions, we should try to understand his naturalism.

Butler's case rests on his account of a superior principle and of the instructions that are issued by specific superior principles. He admits that his claim is 'somewhat abstruse' (P 17), and his attempt to clarify it (P 18–24) is rather compressed. It will be helpful to set it out in more detail.

---

[40] See Clarke, §630.
[41] Doddridge agrees with Butler in accepting both an appeal to fitness and an appeal to nature. See §877.

52

BUTLER: SUPERIOR PRINCIPLES

683. What is Superiority?

Butler explains his conception of superiority by appeal to the difference between mere power or strength and authority. Authority belongs to the lawful government, even if it happens that a tyrant or brigand has greater power. The lawful authority has the right to command and we have reason to obey it, even if in fact we do not or cannot always obey it.[1]

Butler appeals to the contrast between power and authority in order to emphasize the normative character of superior principles; this is their claim to motivate us by something other than their psychological strength. If there were no superior principles, we would have to suppose 'that there was no distinction to be made between one inward principle and another but only that of strength' (ii 16).

We often draw some distinction between authority and strength. For we often recognize that we have or had reason to do x rather than y, whether or not we had a stronger desire to do x than to do y. The greater strength of desire is one ground for claiming that we had such a reason, but not the only one. Often we recognize a better reason for doing x even when we recognize a stronger desire to do y.

We can draw Butler's distinction if we consider an agent deliberating, and asking 'Why should I do this?'. In these cases we are asking for a reason to do x rather than y. Even though I may ask myself 'What do I want?', or 'Which do I prefer?', this may not simply be a question about what my current preferences actually are. If I ask 'What do I believe?' or 'Do I believe that?', I am not usually asking for further information about my current beliefs; I am usually trying to make up my mind, by considering what it is reasonable to believe. Since belief aims at truth, I answer the question about belief by asking what is true.[2] Similarly, questions about what I want often seek some reason for wanting one thing rather than another, because these desires aim at the good, at what it is reasonable to want.

Butler suggests that in some cases we have a reason for doing x rather than y simply because we want to do x more than we want to do y. Here the relevant principle is just

---

[1] 'All this is no more than the distinction, which every body is acquainted with, between *mere power* and *authority*: only instead of being intended to express the difference between what is possible, and what is lawful in civil government; here it has been shown applicable to the several principles in the mind of man.' (ii 14) Cf. Cudworth on Hobbes, §548.

[2] See C. Taylor, 'Agency' 36 (on 'articulation'); Moran, *AE* 38–42.

strength. Sometimes, however, our reason for doing x rather than y is our belief that y is better than x, not simply that we feel like doing y rather than x. We decide on the basis of strength when we choose, e.g., between red wine and white wine, or we decide to go to one film rather than another; in that case we ask 'Which do I prefer?'. In other cases, however, we deliberate by considering the merits of different courses of action, not by registering our preferences. If I am angry at someone for having, say, got a job I wanted, my strongest desire at first may be to express my resentment in some way, but it may strike me that I have no good reason to take it out on my rival. In this case I do not simply register the comparative strength of my desires; I modify their strength by what Butler calls 'reflexion' on the merits of different courses of action.

Reid points out that Butler's distinction is too simple.[3] In cases where we appear to decide simply by consulting our stronger inclination, we may still be guided by the merits of the different options. Often we consider their merits and decide that both are acceptable, so that it is all right to go by our stronger inclination. Normally it is all right to choose Granny Smith apples over Golden Delicious simply because we prefer the taste; but if we discovered that Granny Smiths were dangerous to health, we would no longer think it all right to be guided by our taste. Reid's point is also relevant to cases where we falsely believe we ought not to follow our stronger inclination. Perhaps, for instance, we have been told we should always drink white wine rather than red wine with fish, and so we follow this rule even though we much prefer red wine to white. If we learn that it is quite all right to drink red wine with fish, we learn that it is all right to follow our preference. Reid's correction of Butler actually strengthens Butler's case, since it shows that judgments of merit are relevant even in some cases where we do not explicitly refer to them.

684. Superior Principles as Sources of External Reasons

Butler's argument for the distinction between power and authority rejects Hobbes's attempt to reduce practical reason and deliberation to a contest of countervailing psychological forces.[4] Hobbes's analysis dissolves the apparent distinction between the strength of desires and the weight of reasons. Butler replies, quite reasonably, that a plausible account of desire and deliberation cannot do without this distinction. If Hobbes were right, we could not decide after reflexion on our action that we have done what we most wanted to do, but failed to do what we had the best reason to do. Since we sometimes reach this conclusion on our actions, Hobbes's analysis is inadequate.

But how far beyond Hobbes does Butler's distinction take us? We might argue that we acknowledge the difference between power and authority even if we allow only internal reasons. Perhaps some desires are based on the weight of reasons rather than mere strength of desires; but might the weight of reasons not be derived from desires? Perhaps we have reason to satisfy one occurrent desire over another if and only if the satisfaction of the first desire promotes the satisfaction of more of our desires in the long run. In choosing between our occurrent desires we are moved by the weight of reasons, but the reasons themselves

---

[3] See Reid, *EAP* ii 2 = H 534b, discussed at §829.   [4] See Hobbes, §470.

are derived from the comparative strength of our different desires, not from any external standard.

This argument does not eliminate external reasons. The proposed principle for judging between occurrent desires seems to be open to reasonable doubt. For if I consider the overall satisfaction of my desires in the long run, I may conclude that I have no good reason to satisfy some of them in accordance with their strength. I may, for instance, see that I have reason to acquire a desire for x and to eliminate a desire for y, because I take x to be better than y. If I foresee that it will take me some time to carry out this change in my desires, I may foresee that for a long time my desire for y will be stronger than I think it ought to be and my desire for x will be weaker. If I were to be guided by the comparative strength of my desires during this time, I would pay more attention than I should to the desire I am trying to eliminate, and less attention than I should to the desire I am trying to acquire or strengthen. The purely 'internal' principle of satisfying my stronger long-term desires is itself open to rational criticism. Hence we cannot identify the rational criticism of desires with criticism in the light of long-term desires.

This argument does not show that we have external reasons, but only that we deliberate on the assumption that we have external reasons. In criticizing our actual and predicted desires, we assume that we can rely on reasons for preferring one to another; and we take these reasons to be distinct from any facts about actual or predicted preferences. If there are no external reasons, or none that we can reasonably believe we have found, our deliberation cannot work in the way we suppose it works. To vindicate our conception of deliberation, we need to show that we have reasons of the sort that we think we rely on.

Butler's argument about power and authority, therefore, answers Hobbes by showing that we take ourselves to be open to external reasons. It shows that a plausible account of deliberation, correcting Hobbes's attempt to reduce deliberation to an interplay of psychological forces, requires us to recognize reasons that are not reducible to facts about the satisfaction of actual or predicted desires. In defending this conclusion, Butler highlights an important feature of deliberation and practical reason. His point is not new; he makes explicit a point that is presupposed by the Aristotelian and Scholastic conception. Reid makes clear the significance of Butler's argument.

Butler's conception of a superior principle separates him not only from Hobbes, but also from the sentimentalists. In distinguishing authority from strength, he grasps a point that Hutcheson blurs in his discussion of justifying and exciting reasons. Awareness of a justifying reason, in Hutcheson's view, is simply the awareness, arising from reflexion, of a feeling of approval of the action or person that we have reflected on.[5] Hutcheson suggests that 'actions done without motive or affection, by mere election, without prepollent desire of one action or end rather than its opposite' (IMS 166) are either impossible or morally insignificant. He reduces awareness of a better reason for choosing x rather than y to awareness of a stronger desire for x.

Balguy notices this weakness in the sentimentalist view, insisting that merit or praiseworthiness is not what is approved, but what deserves approval.[6] Butler generalizes and

---

[5] Hutcheson's view is therefore rather similar to Frankfurt's view about second-order desires, in 'Freedom'. Butler's criticism is similar to the objections by those critics of Frankfurt (e.g., Watson, 'Agency') who insist on evaluation as opposed to mere higher-order desires. Cf. §639 on Hutcheson.

[6] On Balguy see §656.

strengthens Balguy's objections. He sees that the awareness of merit may not coincide with any inclination to do what we regard as having greater merit. If we are guided by authority, we are looking for the best reasons to act, not simply trying to find which actions excite our sentiment of prospective approval. In claiming that human nature includes government by superior principles, Butler reasserts the Aristotelian claim that a human being is a rational agent who deliberates and chooses on the basis of external reasons.

685. Why Do We Need Superior Principles?

To explain why we must recognize superior principles, Butler offers a sort of transcendental argument, seeking to show that they are necessary for the recognition of something that we cannot rationally refuse to recognize.[7] We could not have reason to give up the belief that some things deserve approval more than others; for it would be absurd to believe that any two actions that a human being can do (and are therefore in accordance with nature in either of the first two senses) equally deserve approval. He claims that we face this absurd result if we do not recognize a claim to superiority and authority distinct from the strength of a desire.

If we recognize no superior principles, we lose any basis for drawing distinctions between the worst and the best actions. If I freely do x, I act on my strongest desire for x; if strength is the only basis for approval, I must approve any action that anyone does; but clearly I do not. If we do not distinguish authority from strength, we cannot explain why we should think it is better to do x rather than y, or that there is reason to do x rather than y, in cases where x and y are equally natural in the first two senses. Butler's transcendental argument draws our attention to the absurdity of abandoning normative judgments altogether.[8]

Butler suggests that we cannot really live without recognizing superior principles. If we simply try to live by following the desire that we register as strongest, we will find we cannot do that. We might suppose we can, but only because our views about what is better influence the relative strength of our desires. If this were not so, and we simply acted on whatever desire happened to be stronger at any particular time, we would have no tolerable life at all.

If we do not believe that superior principles guide action, we have no reason to suppose that they guide belief; we must abandon the formation of beliefs on the basis of better reasons. In that case, we have to explain, as the Greek Sceptics try to explain, how we can live simply on the basis of appearances. The Stoics argue that the Sceptical position leads to 'inaction' (*apraxia*).[9] The sources do not always make it clear what the Stoics think the Sceptic is incapable of. But the most plausible Stoic argument points out that though the Sceptic is capable of goal-directed movement, as a non-rational animal is, Scepticism

---

[7] A transcendental argument says roughly: (1) We cannot have sufficient reason to give up p. (2) We cannot accept p without accepting q. (3) Therefore we must accept q. The exact sense of the modal terms in these claims needs quite a bit of explanation.

[8] 'If there be no difference between inward principles but only that of strength, we can make no distinction between these two actions, considered as the actions of such a creature; but in our coolest hours must approve or disapprove them equally; than which nothing can be reduced to a greater absurdity.' (ii 17)

[9] Plutarch, *Col.* 1122a–f. See §139.

removes the possibility of acting on reasons. That is why Scepticism makes a human life impossible, so that Sceptics are mistaken in claiming to follow everyday life. The Stoics are urging the absurdity, as Butler puts it, of equal approval and disapproval of any two actions.

One passage in Sextus considers this Stoic use of Butler's argument about absurdity. The dogmatists argue that if a tyrant threatens the Sceptic with a choice between doing something evil and being killed, then either the Sceptic will refuse to do the evil action or he will do as he is told to avoid torture. In either case he will show that he thinks one course of action better than another, and will assent on the basis of that conviction (Sextus, M xi 164).[10] Sextus answers that the Sceptic does not make up his mind by considering the goodness or badness of what he does; he simply follows the appearance that strikes him more strongly.

The Stoics need not deny that this sort of response is logically possible. They might reasonably urge that it is nonetheless 'absurd', as Butler puts it, because it deprives the Sceptic of the resources that everyone uses to decide such cases. The Sceptic will have to go in one direction or the other without the benefit of the evaluative comparison that we normally rely on. If it is part of a human life to be capable of acting on evaluative comparisons that may alter the strength of our desires, the Sceptic deprives us of a human life. This dispute between Stoics and Sceptics supports Butler's claim that we cannot abandon the distinction between power and authority in our choices.

686. Self-Love as a Superior Principle

So far we have expounded the concept of a superior principle, and the necessity of acknowledging superior principles, without saying which principles are superior, or why it is natural to act in accordance with any superior principles or with the specific ones that Butler recognizes. So far we have assumed only that a superior principle is one that claims authority, because it claims to rely on the weight of reasons; we have seen why Butler believes it would be 'absurd' to claim to live without such principles. But the account we have relied on so far counts more principles as superior than those that Butler regards as superior. He relies on a narrower account of superior principles than the account we have relied on. Someone who decides on the basis of rational reflexion that it is always better to deny satisfaction to all of his immediate impulses, as far as possible, has a superior principle resting on some rational evaluation rather than merely on strength of desires; but he will not act naturally if he always acts in accordance with this superior principle. Perhaps Butler believes that this alleged superior principle is not really superior, because it cannot really be defended by appeal to thorough rational evaluation; it must turn out to rest on some irrational prejudice at some stage. But it will be easier to understand the course of his argument if we allow that this foolishly ascetic principle is a superior principle, and then ask how many correct superior principles there are.

Butler does not assume that every principle that claims authority is a correct superior principle. Correct superior principles are those that appeal to genuinely authoritative

---

[10] Discussed in §140.

considerations, and are supported by the real weight of reasons. Once we recognize what a correct superior principle must be like, our next task is to find the correct superior principles.

Butler applies his claims about nature, system, and superior principles to reasonable self-love.[11] He argues that self-love is a superior principle distinct from particular passions, and that it is natural to act in accord with self-love. These claims are relatively uncontroversial, but it is not superfluous for Butler to defend them. For though most people may agree with them, they may not agree with them for the right reasons. Once we see why self-love is a superior principle, and why it is natural to act on self-love, we will also see what is wrong with some views about the conflict between self-love and morality.

To show that self-love is a superior principle, Butler distinguishes it from the particular passions that pursue specific external objects. A passion pursues its objects 'without distinction of the means by which they are to be obtained' (ii 13). This may lead to a conflict between two appetites in cases where the objects of one 'cannot be obtained without manifest injury to others' (ii 13). Reflexion decides in favour of one course of action rather than the other, by considering which is better.

This reflexion expresses rational self-love, insofar as it expresses our conception of ourselves as more than a collection of episodes of desire. The fact that satisfaction of one desire conflicts with satisfaction of another would not interest us if we did not care about the joint product of satisfying the two desires. We are temporally extended selves, and these selves partly consist in our plans for ourselves; hence we are concerned about the different aspects of ourselves in the present, and about their development in the future. Self-love differs from particular passions in being concerned with the self as a continuant that includes a number of affections. To express this self I have to recognize reasons to make decisions that conflict with one or another present passion, and I have to recognize the possibility of conflict between the weight of reasons and the strength of particular impulses.[12]

Butler assumes that if we were guided exclusively by strength, we would satisfy particular passions without pursuing our own interests. None of the particular passions provides us with a view of what our whole self needs. Since we regard ourselves as whole selves, not just as collections of passions and desires, we must evaluate one passion against another, to see whether the satisfaction of one will damage our whole selves. Since we cannot secure our interests as extended selves if we simply rely on the comparative strength of desires that we register at a particular time, we must consider not only what we happen to care about most now, but also what our future interest requires. If we recognize ourselves as something more than collections of passions, and hence as having concerns that go beyond the satisfaction of this particular desire now, we must acknowledge superior principles that rely on authority rather than mere strength.

[11] I will take 'reasonable' to be understood in what follows. An explanation and defence of the term 'self-love' in Butler's sense is offered by Whewell: '. . . it seems to be not inapt to describe that state of mind in which we regard ourselves as external and detached objects of solicitude, and provide for our own well-being as we would do for that of a friend whose passions we can resist, and whose future and permanent good we try to secure, without losing our calmness of feeling and clearness of view' ('Preface' in Mackintosh, *DPEP*, p. xvi).

[12] If we are psychological egoists, we will regard this possibility as purely logical; but we still must recognize Butler's distinction.

To see what Butler assumes about the connexion between self-interest and superiority, we may ask what would follow if they were not connected.[13] Two of his assumptions can be identified if we consider some logically possible alternatives that Butler ignores: (1) Suppose that we had some particular passion that was magically correlated with our good as whole selves, so that whatever this passion favoured would coincide with what a rational and well-informed bystander would say was best for us. In that case we would not need any superior principle to make our particular choices. Butler assumes that our situation is non-magical in this respect. (2) Suppose that our superior principles were totally incompetent, so that we never gave ourselves the practical advice that a rational bystander would give us, and we never took the view of our previous conduct that a rational bystander would take. If we noticed that things were going badly in this way, we might be well advised to give up acting on superior principles. Butler assumes that we do not suffer such gross incompetence.

Though Butler does not discuss either of these imaginary situations, they actually support his claims about superior principles. For how could we discover the magical success of some particular passion, or the gross incompetence of our superior principles, without some exercise of the sort of reasoning that belongs to superior principles? If we are even to discover the limitations of our superior principles, we must recognize their authority.

687. Self-Love and Nature

Butler believes that when the reflexion of rational self-love conflicts with our particular passions, it is obvious that reflexion should be obeyed, and that this is obvious 'from the economy and constitution of human nature', irrespective of the comparative strength of the relevant desires. Self-love is a superior principle, requiring us to consider ourselves as whole selves rather than mere sequences of impulses. When we act in accord with reasons applying to us as whole selves, we act in accord with our nature. These reasons are external, since they depend on facts about our nature, not on facts about our desire to act in accord with our nature. On this point Butler commits himself to the conception of reasons that is rejected by Hobbes and the sentimentalists.

This argument relies on Butler's third sense of 'nature', since it claims that we act naturally in acting on the reasons that apply to us as whole selves. It is reasonable to identify our nature with the nature and essential characteristics of our selves, taking our selves to be extended, including a number of desires, and embodying some concern for a rational ordering of particular desires. According to this conception of human nature, being a rational agent of the sort who attends to rational self-love is part of the nature of a human being. If we denied this, we would be neglecting the systematic element in human nature.[14] If we were

---

[13] Butler considers some relevant possibilities at *Anal.* i 3.18. He considers some circumstances in which we would not benefit from having reason. His conclusion is: '. . . reason has, in the nature of it, a tendency to prevail over brute force; notwithstanding the possibility it may not prevail, and the necessity, which there is, of many concurring circumstances to render it prevalent'.

[14] 'Thus the body is a system or *constitution*; so is a tree; so is every machine. Consider all the several parts of a tree without the natural respects they have to each other, and you have not at all the idea of a tree; but add these respects,

to neglect the role of superior principles, we would be thinking of a human being as a mere collection of episodes of desire and satisfaction; whatever we described in such terms would not be human agency or human nature.

This conception of nature and the natural explains why it is natural to act on self-love. A rash and self-destructive action is unnatural not because we act against self-love, considered as an impulse, but because we act against self-love as a rational principle concerned for the self as a whole. Self-love is not simply a passion on the level of other passions and desires that might strike us. Its outlook results from reflexion on the merits of satisfying one or another particular passion, and so it expresses a superior principle. Since self-love takes account of our interests as agents with a future to take care of, it is needed to safeguard the interests of our nature as a whole. And so our nature as a whole requires us to follow rational self-love.[15]

Butler's argument is clearer if we distinguish two points that we learn from consideration of rational self-love: (1) The attitude of rational self-love shows us that we regard a rational agent as having a nature in Butler's third sense, because a rational agent is composed of a system of desires and aims extending across time, and is not merely a collection. (2) This same attitude shows us that it is natural to act on this superior principle.

Though we derive both these points from considering the fact that self-love takes a holistic point of view on the agent, they are distinct points. If we could recognize that we care about ourselves as whole systems, but we could not think of what to do to promote our interests as whole systems, we would learn that we have a nature without learning what sort of principle we must follow in order to act naturally. If we could recognize that self-love aims at our interest as whole systems, but we supposed that it is deluded in assuming that we are whole systems, then we would also have failed to find a natural course of action.[16] We must agree that we learn both things about self-love, in order to accept Butler's argument to show that it is natural to act on self-love.

Self-love does not create our nature, as though it were true only from the point of view of self-love that we have a nature. Nor is it purely external to our nature, in the way that someone else's practical reason might be. If I think about how to achieve your interest, I think of you as a system independently of my reflexion on your interest. But I do not think of myself in the same way. Part of the system that I discover in myself through the exercise of practical reason in my own interest is the fact that my nature includes concern for myself and my interest. Among the various elements of my nature that rational self-love considers is itself.

This account of self-love captures a Stoic view about the relation of nature to practical reason. When the Stoics speak of living 'in accord with nature', and claim that reason allows

and this gives you the idea. The body may be impaired by sickness, a tree may decay, a machine may be out of order, and yet the system and constitution of them not totally dissolved. There is plainly somewhat which answers to all this in the moral constitution of man.' (iii 2n)

[15] 'Is it that he went against the principle of reasonable and cool self-love, considered merely as a part of his nature? No: for if he had acted the contrary way, he would equally have gone against a principle of his nature, namely, passion or appetite. But to deny a present appetite, from foresight that the gratification of it would end in immediate ruin or extreme misery, is by no means an unnatural action; whereas to contradict or go against cool self-love for the same of such gratification, is so in the instance before us.' (ii 11)

[16] In that case self-love would be like a politician offering to consider the 'national interest' of several groups of people who happen to be geographically contiguous, but have nothing else in common. Cf. Aristotle, *Pol.* iii 9.

us to do this, they mean that reason is an 'artificer of impulse';[17] its task is to arrange and to regulate impulses that are natural (in Butler's first two senses) so that they achieve a system, and so reveal that we have a nature (in Butler's third sense). But they also believe that practical reason is itself part of the nature we try to conform to; human nature is essentially rational nature, and therefore rational guidance is to be valued for its own sake.

Butler does not assert that reasonable self-love explicitly considers our nature. My judgments about what is in my longer-term interest are not (or need not be) de dicto judgments about what is natural. But they are de re judgments about what is natural, because the outlook of self-love takes account of those features of me that in fact constitute my nature. Self-love favours an action as natural once I have considered how it affects the interests of the self as a whole, as present and future, and as consisting of more than a collection of unordered desires. If I deliberate correctly, the action I choose was natural before I ever deliberated; it already accorded with correct self-love. Correct self-love does not create naturalness, but results from my discovery of it; I discover it, by discovering its impact on the self as a whole.[18]

One might dispute Butler's claim to have proved that one ought to follow self-love over particular passions. Even if one granted that it is unnatural to violate self-love, why does that make it wrong? These questions will seem reasonable from a sentimentalist point of view; for, according to Hutcheson and Hume, I have no overriding reason to do x unless my strongest desire is to do x or for something to which doing x is a means. Butler answers this doubt about his argument by appealing to the distinction between authority and power. Once we recognize that we rely on this distinction, we see that the question about what we ought to do is to be answered by finding what we have an authoritative reason to do, not by comparing the strength of our desires. The authoritative reason comes from self-love.[19]

If Butler has given good reasons to believe that acting on reasonable self-love is natural, what difference should that make to a moral agent? A belief in the naturalness of an action does not seem to be necessary for prudential motivation. Reasonable self-love acts on the reasonable belief that this action is good for me, but (for all Butler has said) does not seem to act on the belief that the action is natural.

Still, recognition of the natural character (in the third sense) of prudent action is practically relevant. I recognize that it is reasonable to care about my longer-term interest even when it conflicts with my desire for some more immediate satisfaction. But what is reasonable about it? A mere preference for deferred satisfaction or a groundless preference for satisfaction twenty years from now over satisfaction two years from now does not by itself seem reasonable. When we reflect more carefully, we discover that the reasonable action is the one that fulfils the desires and needs of myself as a whole; it is because I extend into the future, not because there is something inherently better about delayed satisfaction, that it is sometimes reasonable to delay satisfaction. Though it might not have been obvious to me from the start that I care about my nature and about the naturalness of my action, reflexion

---

[17] See Diogenes Laertius vii 86–7, quoted at §176.
[18] See Sturgeon, 'Nature' 330–1. In his view, self-love differs from conscience in not thinking about the naturalness of actions. But the sense in which this is true or false for self-love also suggests the sense in which it is true or false for conscience. See §707.
[19] See further Hume, §738; Reid, §831.

on familiar cases of prudence makes it clear to me that I have good reason to care about naturalness—indeed that naturalness is the source of prudential rationality. This discovery helps us to understand the character of prudence; Butler also claims that it helps us to understand the character of morality, and helps us to see why we have reason to follow conscience when it prescribes the morally right course of action.

688. Psychological Hedonism

If Butler is right so far, he has raised one important objection against Hobbes. His distinction between strength and authority of desire conflicts with Hobbes's reductive account of practical reason as a process of registering the comparative strength of different desires. Moreover, since he understands self-love as a superior principle, and claims that acting in accordance with self-love is natural, he rejects Hobbes's defence of psychological hedonism; for he does not treat self-love as simply a particular passion aiming at one's own pleasure. Still, we might suppose that all this makes no difference to Hobbes's moral argument. Indeed, we might say that if self-love is the only superior principle, Hobbes's psychological hedonism is vindicated, even if not for Hobbes's reasons. Butler replies that, even if self-love is the only superior principle, Hobbes's psychological hedonism is false.

Hobbes makes four claims: (1) Every action of mine is motivated by the prospect of my pleasure. (2) Self-love seeks my maximum pleasure. (3) Every action is motivated by self-love.[20] (4) Hence every action is motivated by concern for my maximum pleasure. These claims are to some extent independent. We could accept the third, as a eudaemonist does, without necessarily being hedonists and accepting the fourth. And we could agree that some desire for pleasure always moves us, without agreeing that the desire to maximize our pleasure always overrides any other desire.

Butler, however, does not seem to see that these claims are independent. He seems to argue against Hobbes as though the refutation of hedonism implied the refutation of the whole Hobbesian position. This is perhaps a fair ad hominem reply to Hobbes, who does not see that different parts of his position need independent defences. Still, Butler's failure to see the different questions involved in a discussion of Hobbesian egoism exposes a weakness, as we will see later, in his own views about self-love.

Butler seems to think that Hobbes's hedonist thesis is not only empirically false, but logically impossible. In Butler's view, each 'particular passion'—hunger, thirst, revenge, gratitude, and so on—aims at its proper object (being fed, having thirst relieved, etc.), not at the pleasure that results from achieving the object. We take pleasure in achieving the object in question, but we would not get this pleasure unless we desired the object apart from any prospect of pleasure.[21] If, then, I take pleasure, in x, there must be some feature F of x such that (1) I take pleasure in x qua F, and (2) my desiring x qua F precedes and explains

---

[20] Does Hobbes hold the position Butler attacks? See §476. Even if Hobbes holds a less extreme position than Butler ascribes to him, Butler's objections cast doubt on the more moderate theses that some interpreters find in Hobbes.

[21] 'That all particular appetites and passions are towards external things themselves, distinct from the pleasure arising from them, is manifested from hence; that there could not be this pleasure, were it not for the prior suitableness between the object and the passion.' (xi 6)

my taking pleasure in x. Hence I am pleased, for instance, when I have eaten and am full because (1) I want to be full for its own sake, and I have achieved that desire, and (2) I am pleased that (1) is the case.

This analysis of pleasure supports an argument against psychological hedonism:

(1) We take pleasure in F because we want to satisfy our desire for F.

(2) We want to satisfy our desire for F because we care about getting F for its own sake.

(3) Hence, if we take pleasure in F, we care about F for its own sake.

(4) Hence if we take pleasure we care about something other than pleasure for its own sake.

This conclusion conflicts with the claim that the only thing we care about for its own sake is pleasure.

Butler's analysis, however, does not seem to fit all desire and pleasure. If I am given a taste of vodka without knowing what it is, and I enjoy it, it does not follow that I wanted to taste vodka for its own sake. On the contrary, if I find out that it is vodka, I may be disgusted by the thought of tasting vodka, and not want to taste it at all for its own sake; but I still may want to taste it because I enjoy the taste.

Butler suggests that action requires some source other than the conscious desire for pleasure. If I simply contemplated the objects in the world and had no incentive to act one way rather than another, I would not know which would give me pleasure, and I would never get started. But this point does not secure Butler's conclusion. I may have some instinctive tendency to do some things rather than others, before I consider any prospect of pleasure from them; or other people may force me to act. As a result of these other stimuli, I notice that I enjoy some things rather than others, and hence I may go after those things again. Butler's question, 'How can you ever get started?', can be answered without abandoning any of the psychological hedonist's case or accepting Butler's alternative. He has not shown, then, that psychological hedonism is logically impossible.

This fault, however, does not cripple Butler's argument against psychological hedonism. Even though he does not show that it is logically impossible, he undermines our reason for taking it seriously, if he shows that we take it seriously because of an error about pleasure and desire. His argument against psychological hedonism assumes that all pleasure involves taking pleasure in x qua F, and hence desiring F for its own sake, apart from any pleasure in x. This is a stronger assumption than he needs. If some, though not all, pleasures presuppose our valuing something other than pleasure, psychological hedonism is false.

To identify the sort of pleasure that supports Butler, we may distinguish three cases: (1) I simply find a taste pleasant, no matter what I know about (say) the wine that has the taste; in this case I am pleasantly surprised if I learn that the wine came from New York rather than from a chateau in Burgundy. (2) My pleasure is 'belief-dependent', but not 'value-dependent'. I especially enjoy wine from Chateau Supreme, and if I discover that the wine I have just enjoyed comes from New York rather than Chateau Supreme, I am disappointed, and enjoy it less; the surprise is unpleasant rather than pleasant. But I nonetheless acknowledge that my taste for Chateau Supreme is just a taste; I do not imagine it is non-instrumentally good to have this taste, irrespective of whether I enjoy it. (3) My pleasure is 'value-dependent'. I may be especially pleased that you did something for me because I thought it was a spontaneous expression of friendship. In that case I will be much less pleased when I find that your action had some ulterior selfish motive. I show that I value expressions of friendship apart from the pleasure I take in them.[22]

The mere existence of belief-dependent pleasures does not refute psychological hedonism. Hedonists may claim that belief-dependent pleasures rest on beliefs that ultimately rest on further beliefs about what will give me belief-independent pleasure. But it is more difficult to answer Butler if we allow value-dependent pleasures; for in this case our explanation of the pleasure presupposes belief in the non-instrumental goodness of something other than pleasure and hence refutes the claim that we regard only pleasure as non-instrumentally good. A hedonist needs to show that apparent beliefs in non-instrumental goodness are really only beliefs in instrumental goodness, so that (in the case just mentioned) we take pleasure in friendship only because we believe it is instrumentally good as a source of pleasure that is not value-dependent. But why should we believe hedonists about this, if we are not hedonists already?

Butler's attack on psychological hedonism fails to refute it outright, but it raises a formidable objection. He shows that some apparent evidence for hedonism is really evidence against hedonism, since some pleasures are value-dependent. Hedonists can explain away this evidence only by offering an implausible analysis of value-dependent pleasures. By showing what a hedonist is committed to, Butler suggests good grounds for rejection of hedonism.

689. Different Conceptions of Self-Love: Hedonism v. Holism

Butler believes that his refutation of psychological hedonism also refutes psychological egoism—the view that all my actions are motivated by self-love. This is because he relies on a narrow conception of self-love. In his view, self-love, my concern for my own interest, aims at my own happiness, understood as my own pleasure. This is how he distinguishes one's 'general desire of his own happiness' from one's particular affections.[23]

But his further claims about self-love seem to conflict with the claim that it aims at pleasure. He notices that self-love presupposes a capacity for reflexion and self-awareness. I have to be aware of myself as an agent with a number of desires and with some capacity to regulate my pursuit of their objects. If I reflect suitably on my interest, I form a conception

---

[22] Cf. Hutcheson, §633, on pleasure and desire. On belief-dependence see Price, §804. On Aristotle's discussion of similar questions about pleasure see §§88, 95. On Epicurus' hedonism see §156. The dispute between Butler and Hobbes recalls the dispute between Aristotle and Epicurus.

[23] 'The former proceeds from or is self-love, and seems inseparable from all sensible creatures who can reflect upon themselves and their own interest or happiness, so as to have that interest an object to their minds . . . The object the former pursues is somewhat internal—our own happiness, enjoyment, satisfaction . . . The principle we call "self-love" never seeks anything external for the sake of the thing, but only as a means of happiness or good; particular affections rest in the external things themselves. One [sc. self-love] belongs to man as a reasonable creature reflecting on his own interest or happiness. The other [sc. particular passions], though quite distinct from reason, are as much a part of human nature. That all particular appetites and passions are towards external things themselves, distinct from the pleasure arising from them, is manifested from hence; that there could not be this pleasure, were it not for that prior suitableness between the object and the passion . . . ' (xi 5–6; cf. xi 7, 9)

of appropriate action for myself that is based on self-love, not simply on the instinctive or impulsive or unreflective pursuit of the objects of particular desires.

Butler also believes that my interest, or good, or welfare, is not some end that I can achieve without achieving the objects of my particular desires and affections. That is why the idea of someone who is well-off and happy, but has completely failed to achieve any of his particular aims and desires, is self-contradictory.[24] If self-love wholly 'engrosses' us, in such a way that we totally neglect the pursuit of the objects of our particular desires, self-love defeats its own ends.

It does not follow, however, that self-love aims at my own pleasure, as opposed to external objects. In speaking of the 'enjoyment of those objects . . . ' Butler might simply be using 'enjoyment' in the sense of 'achieving or satisfying a desire'. But even if he takes it to imply pleasure, he shows only that the enjoyment of achieving my goal is part of my ultimate end, not that my end is nothing more than enjoyment. If self-love seeks my good and my interest, it values both the achievement of my desires and the value-dependent pleasure that I take in that achievement. Hence Butler should not say that self-love values pleasure alone. On the contrary, since (as he agrees) the pleasure it values is value-dependent, it cannot value pleasure alone.

Butler, therefore, does not justify his claim that self-love values nothing external for the sake of the thing itself, but values an external thing only as a means to pleasure. If value-dependent pleasure in (say) having friends rests on our valuing friendship for its own sake, self-love values the objects of desire for their own sakes. In claiming that self-love aims only at pleasure for its own sake, Butler underestimates his case against psychological hedonism. A fuller statement of his case would perhaps have made clear to him what he ought to say about self-love.

Butler's conception of a superior principle suggests a further objection to the conception of self-love that appears in his remarks on psychological hedonism and egoism. If self-love concentrates on pleasure, it resembles particular passions. To be superior to them, it has to consider the proper proportion between the satisfaction of one desire and of another. It cannot do this if it considers only pleasure; for, as he agrees, pleasure is not the only thing I have reason to value.

690. Self-Love, Pleasure, and Happiness

Sidgwick sees that Butler's hedonist conception of self-love is puzzling enough to need explanation. To explain it, we should, in his view, notice that earlier English moralists normally accept two assumptions: (1) Happiness is to be identified with pleasure. (2) The agent's own good—the object of self-love—is to be identified with the agent's happiness. Either of these claims, taken by itself, might be taken as a trivial analytic truth; but they cannot both be trivial, since the conclusion that (3) one's own good is to be identified with one's own pleasure does not seem to be trivial. Perhaps the fact that the first and second

---

[24] 'Happiness or satisfaction consists only in the enjoyment of those objects which are by nature suited to our several particular appetites, passions, and affections.' (xi 9)

claims both seem trivially true, taken individually, makes people believe that the third claim is also trivially true. But, as Sidgwick remarks, the third claim surely needs some argument.

Sidgwick cites Butler's account of self-love to support his claim that the English moralists accept a hedonist conception of happiness.[25] Butler's argument about the difference between pleasure and the objects of particular passions suggests that he tacitly accepts the identification that Sidgwick attributes to him. But, surprisingly, he does not argue for it. A hedonist conception of happiness is not surprising in Hobbes, who rejects the Greek and mediaeval conception of the highest good. But it is more surprising that so many of Hobbes's successors neither examine nor challenge this part of his view. Cumberland and Cudworth take happiness and the ultimate good to be distinct from pleasure, but they do not make this point a major theme of their elaborate criticisms of Hobbes.[26] Hutcheson rejects Hobbes's psychological hedonism, but does not reject his subjectivism about happiness and the human good. Given the role of Aristotle's conception of the good in his account of the virtues and of our reasons for being virtuous, we should expect the acceptance of the Hobbesian rather than the Aristotelian position to make some significant difference to some aspects of moral theory.

The acceptance of Hobbes's hedonist conception of happiness is especially surprising in Butler, since the argument to show that self-love is a superior principle is considerably weakened if its object is confined to one's pleasure rather than to one's overall good. It might seem plausible to identify one's overall good with one's pleasure, if we accepted a hedonist account of motivation; but Butler rejects any such account. Price follows Butler in claiming both that self-love is a rational principle and that the object of one's self-love is simply happiness, conceived as pleasure.[27]

Butler's position differs sharply from the Greek sources that underlie his naturalism. He draws freely on the Stoic conception of human nature as a system guided by rational principles, one of which is directed to the agent's own good. The Stoics do not accept a hedonist account of one's own good; nor do any other Greek moralists except (as Sidgwick remarks) the Cyrenaics and Epicureans. Against this background Butler's hedonist conception of self-love is surprising. He agrees with Hobbes, Shaftesbury (perhaps not always),[28] and Hutcheson, and so damages his own position. He would have benefited from considering Cudworth's and Cumberland's views on happiness, which are closer to Scholastic, and hence to Greek, eudaemonism than to the hedonist view. Since Butler overlooks these views, his conception of happiness is over-simplified in ways that affect his arguments about self-love and other superior principles.[29]

---

[25] 'We have, in fact, to distinguish self-love, the "general desire that every man hath of his own happiness" or pleasure, from the particular affections, passions and appetites directed towards objects other than pleasure, in the satisfaction of which pleasure consists.' (Sidgwick, *OHE* 192) In adding 'or pleasure' as a gloss on 'happiness', Sidgwick introduces a claim that Butler does not explicitly endorse.

[26] See §§533, 543.   [27] See Price, §805. Contrast Reid, §836.

[28] On complications in Shaftesbury's position see §610. Green, *Introd.* ii §24, 335–6, criticizes Butler's view of happiness: 'Neither Butler nor Hutcheson can claim to have carried the ethical controversy much beyond the point at which Shaftesbury left it. Each took for granted that the object of the "self-affection" was necessarily one's own happiness, and neither made any distinction between living for happiness and living for pleasure.'

[29] Sidgwick comments that Hutcheson falls into the hedonist account despite remarks that seem to conflict with it: 'It is worth noting that Hutcheson's express definition of the object of self-love includes "perfection" as well as "happiness"; but in the working out of his system he considers private good exclusively as happiness or pleasure.' (*OHE* 202n)

691. Psychological Egoism

Rejection of Butler's hedonist analysis of self-love casts doubt on his objections to psychological egoism. He might be rejecting either or both of two claims: (1) The sole and sufficient motive for all my actions is self-love. (2) Self-love is a necessary motive for all my actions. He does not properly distinguish these two claims; and though he has arguments against them both, he does not seem to see that they need different answers.

Butler's point about being 'engrossed' by self-love casts doubt on the first egoist thesis. If we thought that self-love could replace every other desire, Butler would be right to say that domination by self-love, so conceived, is self-defeating. Moreover, if we thought that nothing except the object of self-love is to be valued for its own sake, we would still defeat our aims; for self-love values the achievement of objects that we value for their own sake apart from self-love.

But these objections to engrossing self-love do not refute the second egoist thesis. For, according to this thesis, self-love alone need not be the motive of every action. We may value revenge, say, or friendship for its own sake, and our desire for it may be a motive for some of our actions. The egoist adds that we would not pursue this object of this desire on this occasion if we did not also believe that it would promote our overall good. Since we regard our good as the right combination of the ends of particular affections, we do not cease to value this object for its own sake if we also believe that its pursuit promotes our good.

Butler's refutation of hedonism does not touch this egoist thesis. He needs to argue that concern for our own interest does not regulate all our desires. Two different arguments are worth trying: (1) We may reject self-interest for something inferior. We have irrational desires, which we pursue despite knowing that it is bad for us. We pursue a grievance against someone, for instance, even though we know that the grievance is unjustified and that we will only harm ourselves. (2) We may reject self-interest for something superior. We act on moral motives, if we believe that this is rational action (and hence not included in the first exception to psychological egoism) that is independent of self-love.

Scotus argues for both sorts of exception to the psychological egoist assumption, and Butler agrees with him.[30] He recognizes the first exception by distinguishing self-love as a rational principle from the various 'instincts and principles of action' that human beings share with non-rational creatures (P 18). He also recognizes the second exception. For he thinks that after conscience makes its decisions, self-love may reflect on these decisions when we 'sit down in a cool hour' (xi 20), to see whether or not they benefit us. Even if self-love always endorses the actions chosen by conscience, this endorsement of self-love is distinct from the deliberation underlying the judgment of conscience.

Butler may have good reasons for rejecting psychological egoism as well as psychological hedonism; we need to examine his reasons in considering his claims about conscience and self-love. But he does not make it clear that different arguments are needed to refute egoism from those that refute hedonism; for he does not steadily maintain his view of self-love as a principle of rational prudence. To the extent that he regards self-love as a desire for pleasure, he tends to confuse the issue about egoism with the issue about hedonism.

---

[30] On Scotus see §§360–1, 363.

692. Self-Love and the Passion of Benevolence

Butler's account of the superiority of self-love, and of the difference between self-love and the particular passions, supports one of his aims in the *Sermons*, even before he introduces the special features of morality and conscience. One might argue that morality necessarily conflicts with human nature, on these grounds: (1) Morality requires benevolence—the love of one's neighbour—and benevolence requires concern for others. (2) We act in accord with nature by following self-love. (3) Self-love conflicts with concern for others. (4) Therefore acting in accord with nature conflicts with morality. This is Hobbes's view of the state of nature; to remove the conflict between morality and one's nature, one must be in the circumstances in which benefiting others instrumentally benefits oneself.

Hutcheson answers this argument by conceding the first and third premises and rejecting the second. He argues that, since we have particular passions distinct from self-love, and since these include 'kind affections' concerned with the good of others, it is natural to act on these as well as on self-love. Butler objects to this defence of kind affections because it concedes too much to the critic of morality. Hutcheson agrees that morality conflicts with self-love. In order to show that, nonetheless, it is natural to act on morality, he has to identify natural action with action on one's strongest desire. This conception of the natural relies on the second sense of 'natural', which Butler takes to be inadequate for the defence of the naturalist thesis about virtue. Since Hutcheson's defence rests on strength of desire rather than on authority, it should be rejected.

Contrary to Hutcheson, Butler believes that a proper grasp of the nature of self-love casts doubt on assumptions that suggest a conflict between self-love and morality. Self-love is a superior principle; it reflects on the particular passions and supervises them. Morality requires benevolence, and benevolence requires concern for others even against my private interest—that is to say, against the passions that are entirely self-centred. But it does not follow that morality conflicts with self-love. For self-love frustrates itself if it does not allow the satisfaction of the particular passions that have objects distinct from the object of self-love. It must also regulate the pursuit of the particular passions, since otherwise they may be bad for me. Self-love does not necessarily conflict with our desire for, say, food, or physical security, or other people's esteem. Admittedly, each of these desires may on some occasions be taken to excess, if it interferes disastrously with our other aims. But we have no reason to reject such desires altogether.

Butler's argument against the selfish interpretation of self-love assumes that self-love is a superior principle, trying to harmonize and order the particular passions that have their distinct objects. Self-love would not be doing its work if it ignored our particular passions. To adapt one of Butler's political metaphors, the ignoring of some particular passions would be like trying to reconcile the interests of different people by expelling or not counting some people. Though self-love is distinct from particular passions and regulates them, it does not necessarily conflict with them.

This point about the particular passions applies to benevolence. Insofar as benevolence is a particular passion, it generates no special or necessary conflict with self-love. If we desire the good of others, our good consists partly in the satisfaction of that desire, no less than in the satisfaction of our other desires; there is no special conflict between benevolence and self-love. Admittedly, self-love may (for all we have seen so far) sometimes conflict with benevolence; but the same is true of every other desire that concerns self-love.[31] No good argument for suspicion of benevolence can rest on features of it that are equally features of any particular passion. An opponent of benevolence might point out that because benevolence is concerned with the interest of another, and not with my own interest, it sometimes conflicts with self-love. But this aspect of benevolence does not by itself show that a self-interested person has any special reason to be suspicious of benevolence; for any particular passion may sometimes conflict with self-love, but a self-interested person who rejected all particular passions would also frustrate self-love.[32]

In this defence of benevolence, Butler assumes that the object of self-love is the agent's pleasure, rather than the achievement of the objects of the particular passions. To show the connexion between self-love and benevolence, he appeals to the pleasures resulting from being benevolent (xi 14–15). He argues that, since benevolence is one source of pleasure, self-love has no special reason for rejecting benevolence.

This hedonist conception of self-love weakens Butler's case. If self-love simply seeks pleasure, from whatever source it may come, it apparently does not care whether we get the pleasure from one or another source. Hence self-love might apparently be satisfied by a sufficiently intense pleasure achieved from the pursuit of some of our particular affections rather than others. The opponent of benevolence might argue that, for some people at any rate, more intense pleasures may be gained from non-benevolent passions, and that these may leave no room and no need for the satisfaction of our benevolent desires.

In some places Butler seems to take this objection to be relevant; for he defends himself by arguing that benevolence offers the degree and type of pleasure that might suit someone seeking to maximize pleasure (xi 15). But this is not the best reply that he can offer. A better reply would rely on two other aspects of self-love: (1) The pleasure that we gain from achieving the aim of self-love is value-dependent pleasure. Hence self-love values the objects of our desire for their own sakes, not merely as a means to pleasure. (2) Self-love is a superior principle, aiming at the achievement of our desires in their proper proportion. If benevolent desires are among those that, in their proper proportion, suit our nature, reasonable and enlightened self-love endorses them.

Butler's conception of self-love is difficult to understand. For though he believes it aims at our good, he also suggests that self-love may so 'engross' us that we fail to achieve our good.[33] But if self-love is concerned with my good and my interest, which are fixed by our nature, enlightened self-love will secure my good; for it will secure, as far as it can, the satisfaction of our particular passions in the proportion that is required by our good. If we

---

[31] 'But that benevolence is distinct from, that is, not the same thing with self-love, is no reason for its being looked upon with any peculiar suspicion; because every principle whatever, by means of which self-love is gratified, is distinct from it; and all things which are distinct from each other are equally so.' (xi 11) 'This being the whole idea of self-love, it can no otherwise exclude good-will or love of others, than merely by not including it, no otherwise, than it excludes love of arts or reputation, or of anything else. Neither on the other hand does benevolence, any more than love of arts or of reputation, exclude self-love.' (xi 11)

[32] See, e.g., xi 11, 19.

[33] 'Self-love then does not constitute *this* or *that* to be our interest or good; but, our interest or good being constituted by nature and supposed, self-love only puts us upon obtaining and securing it. Therefore, if it be possible that self-love may prevail and exert itself in a degree or manner which is not subservient to this end, then it will not follow that our interest will be promoted in proportion to the degree in which that principle engrosses us and prevails over others.' (xi 9)

spent so much time thinking about our own interest that we neglected the pursuit of those goods in which our good consists, we would not be guided by enlightened self-love, but by erroneous self-love. We cannot be so engrossed by enlightened self-love that we neglect the pursuit of the goods that enlightened self-love tells us to pursue for the sake of our good.

If, therefore, we reject a hedonist conception of self-love on Butler's behalf, we can argue more effectively than he argues for his claims about self-love and benevolence. The right policy for self-love requires a fair consideration of the objects of all the particular passions. We have no special reason to leave benevolence out of this consideration, if we appeal simply to features that benevolence shares with all the other particular passions.

BUTLER: NATURALISM AND MORALITY

693. Benevolence as a Passion and as a Rational Principle

So far we have seen how Butler applies his naturalist doctrine to moral psychology, to answer the sentimentalist analysis of reasons and motives, and so to undermine some misguided views about the conflict between self-love and benevolence. He might be right about all this, however, and still be wrong in his main claim that virtue is living in accord with nature. To defend his main claim, he needs to show that his conception of nature also provides a plausible account of morality. Even if we agree that the superior principle of self-love prescribes natural actions, we still need to be convinced that some superior principle both prescribes moral virtue, and thereby prescribes natural actions.

We might expect Butler's account of benevolence to answer this question; for he introduces it in Sermon xi to answer those who believe that morality and self-love conflict. He answers some objections to the authority of morality. Many people assume that morality requires benevolence and that benevolence is bound to conflict with self-love. Butler believes that this assumption rests on the errors that he corrects in his account of self-love and the particular passions. Once we see these errors, we see that self-love and benevolence need not conflict, and so we can reject the claims about morality that imply the conflict.

This argument vindicates morality, however, only if (1) morality requires only what the passion of benevolence moves us to do, and (2) the outlook of self-love determines what is natural, because self-love is not only a superior principle, but the supreme principle. Butler accepts neither assumption.

For some of Hobbes's opponents, and especially for Hutcheson, benevolence is the foundation of morality and the moral virtues. According to this view, an argument to show the reality of benevolence is necessary for the defence of the virtues, as Hutcheson conceives them, against Hobbes. But if, as Hutcheson assumes, benevolence and our approval of it are sufficient for moral rightness and obligation, rightness and obligation vary in accordance with the relative strength of the benevolent passion in different people. Hutcheson tries to guard himself against this result by tying moral requirements to the normal agent and judge, but he still leaves morality exposed, as Balguy argues, to changes in the outlook of normal agents and judges.[1]

Butler agrees with Balguy's criticism of Hutcheson's account of benevolence. In contrast to Hutcheson, he speaks of benevolence in two distinct ways. On the one hand, benevolence as a passion is one of the particular affections, involving a desire for the good of another for the other's sake. On the other hand, it is a principle that to some extent is analogous to self-love.[2] It is not simply a collection of benevolent impulses, but something more like a rational principle, directed towards the good of society. A rational principle is the only plausible basis of the claim that benevolence is the sum of virtue.[3]

By distinguishing the passion from the principle, Butler accepts Balguy's position in contrast to Hutcheson's. Though Hutcheson takes benevolence to endorse an impartial, utilitarian attitude,[4] it is difficult to see how he can also claim that his benevolence is a passion, even a passion in a normal person exposed to the appropriate information. For benevolence seems to differ in different people; some are more impartial than others, and it would be rash to claim that the normal agent will invariably take the utilitarian point of view. Butler seems to agree with Balguy in taking benevolence to involve a rational principle that is not to be identified with the reaction of the normal agent.[5]

Still, though Butler distinguishes the passion from the principle of benevolence, he does not take the principle to be independent of the passion. On the contrary, he takes the reality of the passion to vindicate the principle. In his introduction of benevolence he suggests that any extent of the passion 'points out what we were designed for, as really as though it were in a higher degree and more extensive' (i 6). We might doubt this claim. Why does the fact that people naturally tend to care about the interests of their parents, or children, or particular friends, or about particular people's sufferings, prove that a rational concern for the good of others in general is natural (in Butler's third sense) to human beings? Butler's claim seems even less plausible if the rational principle of benevolence may sometimes conflict with the passion of benevolence. If I think about the good of others in general, I may have to restrain

---

[1] See Balguy, §659.

[2] '. . . there is a natural principle of benevolence in man, which is in some degree to society what self-love is to the individual. And . . . if there be any affection in human nature the object and end of which is the good of another—this is itself benevolence or the love of another. Be it ever so short, be it in ever so low a degree, or ever so unhappily confined, it proves the assertion, and points out what we were designed for, as really as though it were in a higher degree and more extensive' (i 6).

[3] 'Thus, when benevolence is said to be the sum of virtue, it is not spoken of as a blind propension, but a principle in reasonable creatures, and so to be directed by their reason, for reason and reflexion comes into our notion of a moral agent. And that will lead us to consider distant consequences, as well as the immediate tendency of an action. . . . Reason, considered merely as subservient to benevolence, as assisting to produce the greatest good, will teach us to have particular regard to these relations and circumstances, because it is plainly for the good of the world that they should be regarded. . . . All these things must come into consideration, were it only in order to determine which way of acting is likely to produce the greatest good. Thus, upon supposition that it were in the strictest sense true, without limitation, that benevolence includes in it all virtues, yet reason must come in as its guide and director, in order to attain its own end, the end of benevolence, the greatest public good.' (xii 27)

[4] See Hutcheson, §644.

[5] Is benevolence a third superior principle, besides self-love and conscience? This is denied by McPherson, 'Development'; Jackson, 'Refutation'; Frey, 'Self-love'. They argue that benevolence is treated as a particular passion. This conception of benevolence does not give appropriate weight to the passages in which Butler treats benevolence as the foundation of utilitarian morality. The view that it is a superior principle is defended by Raphael, 'Conscience' 237–8; Grave, 'Foundations' 75 (who appeals to the conclusion of Sermon i); Penelhum, Butler 31–5. See also McNaughton, 'Benevolence'.

my desire to benefit this particular person at the expense of another for whom I have no passion of benevolence (for instance, my child at the expense of a stranger's child).

To show that benevolence as a principle completes benevolence as a passion, Butler needs to show that the passion is directed not only to people with whom we have some prior relation, such as parents, children, and friends, but also to the good of particular individuals whose sufferings we become aware of. The Good Samaritan helped a particular individual with whom he had no previous connexion. If benevolence extends this far, then Butler might argue it is also reasonably extended to people we have not met; for if we happen to see or meet A and do not happen to see or meet B, but we know that A and B are in equal need, we have reason to extend our benevolence equally to each of them.

The extension of benevolence might be compared to the rational extension of a particular passion. I might initially be fond of eating the wrong food, but once I realize that tofu is both tasty and nutritious, I may come to enjoy eating it, and form an appetite for it that I did not have before. This modification of a particular passion seems to require the intervention of rational self-love, connecting my particular passion with the concerns of the whole self, and modifying them in the light of these concerns. This appeal to nature and to the needs of the whole self explains the modification of a passion by a rational principle. Some parallel intervention by a rational principle seems to be needed to explain how the passion of benevolence grows into the principle of benevolence.

What rational principle could intervene? It cannot be the principle of benevolence whose origin we are trying to understand. To claim that the relevant principle is self-love is to insist on a closer connexion between self-love and benevolence than Butler characteristically recognizes. The only relevant superior principle seems to be conscience, which we have not yet examined.

694. Self-Love and the Principle of Benevolence

These questions about the development of benevolence from a passion to a principle raise a question about Butler's defence of benevolence in Sermon xi. That sermon seems to argue within the limits of Sermon i, which deliberately refrained from relying on the authority of conscience or reflexion, and simply treated it as one aspect of human nature among others. These limits confine Butler's argument, at that stage, to the resources used by sentimentalist defences of morality. Similarly, his defence in Sermon xi does not go far beyond what a sentimentalist might offer. Though he recognizes that benevolence is more than a particular passion, his defence treats it as a particular passion.[6] The defence is legitimate, if the objection against benevolence is simply the fact that it requires us to pursue the good of others. Butler shows that this feature of benevolence does not show that benevolence conflicts with self-love.

---

[6] 'The short of the matter is no more than this. Happiness consists in the gratification of certain affections, appetites, passions, with objects which are by nature adapted to them. ... Love of our neighbour is one of those affections. This, considered as a virtuous principle, is gratified by a consciousness of endeavouring to promote the good of others, but considered as a natural affection, its gratification consists in the actual accomplishment of this endeavour. ... Thus it appears, that benevolence and the pursuit of public good hath at least as great respect to self-love and the pursuit of private good as any other particular passions, and their respective pursuits.' (xi 16)

But we could agree with Butler on this point and still wonder whether the degree of self-sacrifice required by the principle of benevolence might not conflict with self-love. We might agree that self-love frustrates itself if it frustrates our benevolent inclinations, given their actual strength. But the role of conscience does not depend on the actual strength of any motive.[7] The argument of Sermon xi does not seem to consider this aspect of a superior principle. Admittedly, the mere fact that conscience prescribes benevolent action does not show that it necessarily conflicts with self-love; but it is still possible, for all Butler has shown in this sermon, that the degree of benevolence prescribed by conscience conflicts with self-love.

We must, then, inquire further into Butler's view of conscience and morality before we can see why he thinks moral virtue is natural. To grasp his view of moral virtue, we must see how it is related to benevolence; this will help us to understand what principles conscience accepts.

695. Conscience as the Generic Principle of Reflexion

To grasp Butler's views on conscience and morality, we need to survey his different uses of 'conscience' at different points in the *Sermons*. In the Preface and the earlier sermons, he tends to mention 'reflexion' or 'conscience' or both together in a generic sense, referring to the superior principle. An irrational passion is said to conflict with 'reflexion and conscience' (P 14, ii 3). Conscience is 'the principle in man by which he approves or disapproves his heart, temper, and actions' (i 8; cf. P 9 on approbation). This reflexive attitude, assessing different passions by considering weight of reasons rather than strength of desire, matches Butler's characterization of a superior principle in general. Similarly, he speaks of the 'superior principle of reflexion or conscience', which has natural authority as distinct from strength (ii 8). He begins Sermon iii by claiming to have established the supremacy of 'the one superior principle of reflexion or conscience'

In these passages Butler identifies guidance by conscience with guidance by a superior principle. He attaches a very broad sense to 'conscience', so that to act on one's conscience is simply to act on a superior principle. 'Reflexion' (P 24, 25) or 'reflex approbation' (P 26) is his generic term for a superior principle. Sometimes he identifies it with conscience without suggesting that there is any other superior principle.

But when he states his position in more detail, he recognizes self-love as a superior principle distinct from conscience.[8] When he identifies conscience with the supreme principle, he recognizes distinct and independent superior principles. If he did not recognize them, his claim that conscience is supreme would be trivial; for there would be no other superior principle that could rival it.

To explain how acting on 'reflexion or conscience' is natural, Butler does not consider moral judgments directly. Instead he considers a rash action that someone undertakes against

---

[7] 'And the conclusion is, that to allow no more to this superior principle or part of our nature, than to other parts; to let it govern and guide only occasionally in common with the rest, as its turn happens to come, from the temper and circumstances one happens to be in; this is not to act conformably to the constitution of man: . . . one may determine what course of action the economy of man's nature requires without so much as knowing in what degrees of *strength* the several principles prevail, or which of them have actually the greatest influence.' (P 24)

[8] Readers disagree about whether Butler also recognizes benevolence as a superior principle. See §693.

the principle of reasonable self-love. He takes it to be clear that in acting against self-love one violates one's nature, and so he infers that reasonable self-love is a superior principle.[9] He attributes to self-love the sort of authority he has previously attributed to 'reflexion or conscience'.

Butler claims that we can recognize the superiority of self-love 'without particular consideration of conscience' (ii 11). In this claim he uses 'conscience' in a narrower sense than he had in mind in speaking of 'reflexion or conscience'. The argument about self-love was intended to prove the supremacy of the 'faculty which surveys, approves, or disapproves' (ii 9), which is 'reflexion or conscience'. But we cannot prove the superiority of self-love without particular consideration of the faculty that surveys and approves; for self-love is shown to be precisely an expression of that faculty. Reasonable self-love is not distinct from conscience, if conscience is understood as reflex approbation in general; on that understanding of conscience, reasonable self-love is simply a manifestation of conscience. Hence the conscience that is not considered must be conscience in a more specific sense. When Butler explicitly sets aside 'particular consideration of conscience', he signals the fact that he intends to treat conscience as one among a number of superior principles.[10]

Immediately after this passage that distinguishes self-love from conscience Butler returns to speaking of 'reflexion or conscience' (ii 12) in a generic sense that does not distinguish conscience from reasonable self-love. He believes he has made it clear that reflexion or conscience is 'manifestly superior and chief, without regard to strength' (13); but he argues only that it is superior to 'the various appetites, passions, and affections' that do not necessarily follow authority. He does not mention the superior principle of reasonable

---

[9] '. . . it is manifest that self-love is in human nature a superior principle to passion. This may be contradicted without violating that nature; but the former cannot. So that, if we will act conformably to the economy of man's nature, reasonable self-love must govern. Thus, without particular consideration of conscience, we may have a clear conception of the *superior nature* of one principle to another; and see that there really is this natural superiority, quite distinct from degrees of strength and prevalency' (ii 11).

[10] Darwall, *BMIO* 255–61, discusses these passages on self-love and conscience. He explains them by suggesting that 'Butler may not actually believe that one principle *can* be superior to another independently of their relation to conscience' (255). This claim is trivially true if 'conscience' is used in the generic sense I have described, so that it includes every principle relying on authority rather than strength. Darwall, however, also seems to intend the non-trivial thesis that results if we substitute the specific sense of 'conscience', so that conscience is one superior principle among others. Darwall suggests that any superior principle distinct from conscience (in the specific sense) is superior because of authorization or endorsement by conscience. In support of his view Darwall cites ii 8. Here Butler mentions the passion of benevolence as part of human nature, and goes on to discuss other passions: 'Yet since other passions, and regards to private interest, which lead us . . . astray, are themselves in a degree equally natural, and often most prevalent; and since we have no method of seeing the particular degree in which one or the other is placed in us by nature; it is plain the former [sc. benevolence and similar natural dispositions], considered merely as natural, good and right as they are, can no more be a law to us than the latter. But there is a superior principle of reflexion or conscience . . .'. This passage cannot be evidence that reasonable self-love is not a superior principle; for the principles that Butler contrasts with conscience do not include reasonable self-love, but only include 'regards to private interest', which are not said to be reasonable; Butler denies that any of these principles are superior at all. This is Darwall's reason for affirming the non-trivial claim that every superior principle is superior by being authorized by specific conscience. This claim faces an objection in ii 11, where Butler speaks of reasonable self-love as superior 'without particular consideration of conscience'. Darwall (273) emphasizes 'particular' here, and appeals to the argument of ii 10, which he calls a reductio. He explains ii 11: 'There is, I think, a perfectly good explanation of why he would have said just this if he believed what he says in the reductio, namely, that the natural superiority of any principle at all is equivalent to the authority of conscience'. This explanation, however, does not support Darwall's claim, which is about specific conscience; for his account of ii 10 is correct only if it refers to generic conscience. Taylor, 'Features', perhaps (286) anticipates Darwall's view about conscience as the only source of the authority of other principles. He says that conscience is the only source of imperatives, i.e., of 'oughts', as opposed to judgments of probability.

self-love. Butler assumes that the only principle that is guided by rational authority is reflexion or conscience (14).[11] To deny the 'natural supremacy of conscience' (16) is to recognize no difference between inward principles, 'but only that of strength' (16, 17).

The assumption that Butler relies on here (that only conscience expresses rational authority) is false, if he takes conscience to be distinct from reasonable self-love; for he has just pointed out that self-love is a superior principle. If this is true of self-love, Butler is wrong to claim that if conscience—understood as distinct from self-love—were not naturally supreme, there would be no difference between inward principles but only that of strength; for if we had reasonable self-love, we would have a superior principle that relies on authority.

Butler avoids this obvious objection to his argument, if he does not treat conscience as distinct from self-love. If conscience is the generic 'reflexion or conscience', the principle of reflex approbation in general, it is not distinct from reasonable self-love; self-love is simply one particular manifestation of this general principle. Given this generic notion of conscience as reflex approbation, Butler is right to claim that if we had no conscience we would have no reflex approbation, and therefore no superior principles.

This shift from a generic conception of conscience (as the principle of reflexion underlying any superior principle) to a specific conception (of a superior principle distinct from reasonable self-love), and back to a generic conception, does not destroy Butler's argument, unless he takes his argument for the supremacy of generic conscience to prove the supremacy of specific conscience (the principle that takes the moral point of view, in contrast to the view of reasonable self-love). He has not yet argued for the superiority of specific conscience.

696. Conscience as a Specific Superior Principle

In Sermon iii Butler clarifies the distinct place of specific conscience as a superior principle. He begins with generic conscience, by claiming to have established 'the natural supremacy of reflexion or conscience' (iii 1), and takes this to imply that 'mankind hath the rule of right within himself' (iii 5). This rule of right is the generic principle that relies on authority (iii 2). Butler now asks about our obligation to attend and to follow this rule of right. His first answer is that it is the law of our nature; as he has shown in the argument about self-love, superior principles both express our nature (as rational agents) and take account of our nature (by exercising foresight for the needs of a human being as a system).[12] But he now considers an objector who asks why we should follow the law of our nature if it requires us to act against our interest.[13] He therefore considers the possibility of a superior principle that conflicts with self-love.

---

[11] Butler says that 'that principle by which we survey, and either approve or disapprove our own heart, temper, and actions, is ... to be considered ... as being superior, as from its very nature manifestly claiming superiority over all others'. This is a general description of a superior principle. But he immediately infers that this principle is identical to conscience: '... insomuch that you cannot form a notion of this faculty, conscience, without taking in judgment, direction, superintendency' (ii 14).

[12] 'But allowing that mankind hath the rule of right within himself, ...' (iii 5, quoted in §706).

[13] 'However, let us hear what is to be said against obeying this law of our nature. And the sum is no more than this: "Why should we be concerned about anything out of and beyond ourselves? If we do find within ourselves regards to others, and restraints of we know not how many different kinds, yet these being embarrassments, and hindering us from

Butler argues that the objection rests on a false estimate of the conflict between self-interest and 'duty' (iii 8) or 'virtue', because 'self-love . . . does in general perfectly coincide with virtue' (8). When we consider not particular sacrifices imposed by duty, but the course of our life as a whole, even confining ourselves to the present life, we have no good reason to affirm a conflict between duty and interest.

We might understand Butler to claim that the supreme principle is self-love, and that we decide whether an action is natural for us by deciding whether it is in our interest. But this is not his position. At the summary at the end of this sermon, he maintains that natural action must accord with a superior principle. He acknowledges both reasonable self-love and conscience as superior principles (iii 9).[14] He does not argue that the superiority of any superior principle implies the supremacy of conscience; for both reasonable self-love and conscience are superior principles, and conflict with either of them makes an action unnatural. Since they are both superior, and both sources of natural action, any action recommended by conscience and rejected by reasonable self-love would be, to that extent, unnatural. Butler allows the logical possibility of a conflict between self-love and conscience, and deals with it by arguing that it is not a practical possibility that needs to concern us.

697. Does Conscience Support Morality?

This development in Butler's account of conscience in Sermons ii–iii is not surprising; for he tries both to explain the concept of a superior principle and to defend his view of which principles are superior. For the first purpose it is reasonable to speak of 'reflexion' without discrimination, but for the second purpose it is necessary to distinguish different superior principles. Though the generic description of conscience in terms that seem to apply equally to self-love makes Butler's exposition obscure, it does not necessarily betray confusion. For though he recognizes that distinct superior principles belong to generic reflexion or conscience, he does not believe that specific conscience is simply one superior principle among others. On the contrary, specific conscience fully realizes the superiority that is present to some degree in all superior principles. Once we recognize the obligation to follow reflexion and generic conscience, we must also recognize the obligation to follow the principle that most fully realizes the superiority of generic conscience, and hence we must recognize the obligation to follow specific conscience.

This claim about more and less complete realizations of superiority needs some clarification. The degree of superiority of a principle may be assessed by the extent to which it relies on reasons rather than strength of desires, and by the number of relevant considerations it takes into account. Measured by these standards, conscience is the supreme principle of reflexion because it satisfies the generic conception of a superior principle to a higher degree than any other does.

going the nearest way to our own good, why should we not endeavour to suppress and get over them?" Thus people go on with words, which when applied to human nature, and the condition in which it is placed in this world, have really no meaning.' (iii 6–7)

14 Quoted and discussed in §703.

If this is Butler's view of the relation between generic and specific conscience, it should clarify some of Butler's questions and tasks. We need to find an initial description of conscience that allows us to understand the questions Butler is asking and what he needs to prove in order to answer them. We may ask whether these are analytic truths: (1) Conscience is separate from self-love. (2) Conscience approves of morality. (3) Conscience is supreme.

The first claim is false for generic conscience, but analytically true for specific conscience. If the only superior principle were self-love, apparently reflexion (i.e., generic conscience) and self-love would be identical. In that case, self-love would be supreme and we would have disproved the supremacy of specific conscience.

Butler takes the third claim to be synthetic, and to need argument. It is less easy to decide about the second claim; is argument needed to show that conscience and morality agree? If he were convinced that morality is utilitarian, but that conscience is the source of the judgments about fairness that conflict with utilitarianism, he would have to recognize a disagreement between conscience and morality. But he does not seem to contemplate this possibility. He relies on conscientious judgments as a means of access to our moral judgments, and assumes that our moral theory must conform to these judgments.

We can clarify Butler's position if we consider Sidgwick's reasons for believing that Butler's claims about conscience, reason, and nature, are tautological. According to Sidgwick, Butler takes conscience to be essentially reasonable. Since he claims it is natural to live according to conscience, he claims that what is natural is living according to reason. But he believes that living according to reason is living according to nature; hence he simply says that it is natural to live according to nature and reasonable to live according to reason.[15]

This argument is too hasty. Butler claims that specific conscience necessarily prescribes the principles of morality, not simply those of reasonable self-love. Hence his claim that it is natural and reasonable to live according to specific conscience implies that living in accord with one's rational nature as a whole requires living in accord with moral reason. Butler conceives specific conscience as essentially reasonable, but he does not assume it is to be identified with the whole of practical reason; it is moral reason.

Butler's main questions, therefore, are these: (1) Does generic conscience (i.e., the general principle of reflexion) include specific conscience (i.e., the principle that approves of morality)? (2) Is it natural (i.e., in accord with the requirements of the whole nature of an individual) to act in accord with specific conscience? (3) Is specific conscience also supreme (and hence superior to self-love)?

If Butler's claims about morality and nature are correct, a correct account of morality should show how morality is in accord with nature, understood as involving the requirements

---

[15] Sidgwick argues: 'Butler assumes with his opponents that it is reasonable to live according to Nature, and argues that Conscience or the faculty that imposes moral rules is naturally supreme in man. It is therefore reasonable to obey Conscience. But are the rules that Conscience lays down merely known to us as the dictates of arbitrary authority, and not as in themselves reasonable? . . . [Butler] expressly adopts the doctrine of Clarke, that (a) the true rules of morality are essentially reasonable. But if (b) Conscience is, after all, Reason applied to Practice, then Butler's argument seems to bend itself into the old circle: (c) "it is reasonable to live according to Nature, and it is natural to live according to Reason."' (ME 378; reference letters added). Sidgwick's move from (a) to (b) is open to question. The argument requires (b) to be a statement of identity; that is how (c) becomes an uninformative circle. But (a) does not justify taking (b) as a statement of identity.

of the whole system of human desires and capacities. We have already seen how Butler argues that prudence is natural. To see how he thinks morality is natural, we must see, first of all, how he understands the content of morality. His answer to this question may support his claim that morality is natural.

698. Benevolence and Morality

Sermons xi–xii show that Butler takes conscience to be closely connected with benevolence, because he takes morality to be closely connected with benevolence. We might, then, rashly identify conscience with rational benevolence. If that is Butler's view, he agrees with Cumberland against Hutcheson, and either rejects or ignores the objections raised by Balguy and Maxwell against the identification of the moral outlook with benevolence.[16]

Butler examines benevolence and morality when he preaches on St Paul's claim that 'if there be any other commandment, it is briefly comprehended in this saying, namely, Thou shalt love thy neighbour as thyself' (*Rm*. 13:9). Butler takes this to mean that 'to love our neighbour as ourselves includes in it all virtues' (xii 25). He identifies love of one's neighbour with the principle rather than the passion of benevolence.[17] This rational principle is devoted to the public good and to the production of the greatest good.[18]

Is Butler right to identify love of one's neighbour with concern for the public good? At the end of Sermon xii he takes non-utilitarian aspects of morality to constitute 'cautions and restrictions' (xii 31) on St Paul's claim that love of one's neighbour includes the whole of morality. He reaches this conclusion because he believes that love of one's neighbour is benevolence, and that benevolence is concern with the public good. That is why Paul implicitly advocates promotion of the public good.

Butler seems to concede too much to the utilitarian, because of a questionable claim about the passion and the principle of benevolence. The passion is transformed and made rational by extending its scope from particular people (family, friends, acquaintances) to concern for other people in general, until it reaches the outlook of the Good Samaritan. But Butler takes the Good Samaritan's concern to be concern for the public good, whereas the two types of concern seem different. The Good Samaritan is concerned equally with anyone in distress, not simply with people for whom he feels an antecedent passion of benevolence. But the fact that his concern is impartial and general does not imply that he weighs one person's benefits and harms against another in order to achieve the maximum public good.

---

[16] Sidgwick, *ME* 86n, suggests that Butler's views changed on this matter: 'In the first of his Sermons on Human Nature . . . he does not notice, any more than Shaftesbury and Hutcheson, any possible want of harmony between conscience and benevolence. A note to Sermon xii, however, seems to indicate a stage of transition from the view of the first Sermon and the view of the Dissertation'. (In *ME* [1] 70n he does not mention Sermon xii.) Sidgwick's claim is unpersuasive insofar as it relies on Sermon i, which explicitly takes no account of superiority among the principles that constitute human nature.

[17] 'Thus, when benevolence is said to be the sum of virtue, it is not spoken of as a blind propension, but as a principle in reasonable creatures, and so to be directed by their reason; for reason and reflexion comes into our notion of a moral agent.' (xii 27)

[18] See xii 27: 'which way of acting is likely to produce the greatest good'.

We might even go further in an anti-utilitarian direction, and say that love of individual people should make us unwilling to sacrifice one for the sake of many. The story of the Good Samaritan would be quite different if he were to consider whether his effort would be better spent on saving the life of the unknown victim (who, for all he knew, might have been unlikely to do much for the public good) or on some benefit to other people who were more likely to advance the public good. Hutcheson's utilitarianism seems to require the Samaritan to choose the second option;[19] but we might object that such a choice misses part of the point of the demand for love of the individual people who are our neighbours. It is at least as easy to take St Paul's principle in an anti-utilitarian as in a utilitarian direction.

Butler takes the love of one's neighbour to be part of the 'school of discipline' for our particular affections and attachments. In the prayer that concludes this sermon, he implies that the development of particular affections into universal love prepares us for the eventual perfect love of God as the source of all goodness.[20] As we acquire benevolence, we come to love goodness in the form of benevolence, and so we come to love the perfect goodness of God.[21] But this universal aspect of benevolence seems to be distinct from its concern for the public good as opposed to (say) just treatment of individuals.

Butler's assumption that St Paul advocates promotion of the public good shows how far he is influenced by utilitarianism. For he might well have argued that St Paul refers to concern for particular people and their interests and rights, and that such concern is an aspect of our moral sense that underlies our concern for justice and excludes purely utilitarian policies. He could have used a legitimate Scriptural argument to support his own efforts to display the non-utilitarian elements in morality. The utilitarian assumes that benevolent concern for individuals supports a utilitarian maximizing policy. Butler does not challenge that assumption. He shows how deeply the utilitarian assumption is entrenched, even in a moralist who might be expected to question it.

699. Indirect Benevolence and Morality: Berkeley's Argument

Butler qualifies and restricts St Paul's claim by mentioning the various ways in which rational benevolence resists or restrains the operations of the passion of benevolence, and even the operations of a direct concern with the public good. He mentions the importance of friendships that involve discrimination between people, uncertainty of judgments about the public good, the importance of laws and so on (xii 27). In these ways benevolence has to proceed indirectly, if it is not to frustrate its own end. The need for indirectness recalls Butler's arguments about self-love and the particular passions.

---

[19] This claim needs to be qualified to allow for rule utilitarianism in Hutcheson. See §647.

[20] 'O Almighty God, inspire us with this divine principle; kill in us all the seeds of envy and ill-will; and help us, by cultivating within ourselves the love of our neighbour, to improve in the love of Thee. Thou hast placed us in various kindreds, friendships, and relations, as the school of discipline for our affections: help us, by the due exercise of them, to improve to perfection; till all partial affection be lost in that entire universal one, and thou, O God, shalt be all in all.' (xii 33)

[21] 'Thus, to be righteous, implies in it the love of righteousness; to be benevolent, the love of benevolence; to be good, the love of goodness; whether this righteousness, benevolence, or goodness be viewed as in our own mind or another's, and the love of God as a being perfectly good is the love of perfect goodness contemplated in a being or person.' (xii 33)

An argument for this indirect benevolence is presented and defended more fully by Berkeley in his sermon, 'Passive Obedience'.[22] The point of this sermon is to oppose a doctrine of limited obedience to authority. This doctrine is often defended by appeal to a utilitarian argument about the consequences for the public good. Berkeley replies that utilitarian reasoning favours not limited obedience and selective disobedience, but invariable passive obedience. This doctrine does not require us to obey immoral instructions (such as those that the Thirty gave to Socrates); disobedience to these instructions is permissible, as long as we are willing to accept the penalties.[23]

Berkeley begins from the belief in laws of nature, and asks how we are to find out what they prescribe. He does not consider the Scholastic appeal to fitness to rational nature or Clarke's views about fitness.[24] He assumes without argument that happiness, understood as pleasure, is the basis for finding good and evil (5). We seek our own happiness; we find it in agreement with the divine will, because it is our eternal interest to agree with God's eternal will (6). Since God is impartially benevolent, it is in our interest to follow the utilitarian principle that God accepts (6).[25]

The laws of nature, then, aim at maximizing utility, because that is what God aims at.[26] Berkeley agrees with Cumberland's consequentialist account of the laws of nature,[27] but not with Cumberland's view that it is inherently rational to aim at the common good. Berkeley's position is more favourable to voluntarism (though without a definite commitment). He does not suggest that we would have any reason to be utilitarians if God's being a utilitarian did not make it in our interest to share God's aims.

If we share God's aim of maximizing utility, we would be ill-advised to be direct utilitarians, acting on our calculation of the consequences of particular actions. Such calculations are often difficult and fallible, and since different people disagree about their results, direct utilitarianism leads to discord. To avoid this bad effect, we need to be indirect utilitarians, relying on general rules. Hence natural law does not consist only of the single principle of maximizing the good; it also includes the general rules that we are obliged to observe without exception in order to maximize the good (8–12). Since utility requires us to obey them without exception, the fact that in some circumstances observance of them has bad results does not remove our obligation to obey them.[28]

Why, then, should we suppose that passive obedience rather than limited obedience is the rule that we ought to follow? Berkeley's answer shows why Hobbes would be

[22] Since Berkeley delivered this sermon in 1712, Butler might have known it. It is helpfully discussed by Broad, 'Morals'.

[23] 'The fulfilling of those laws, either by a punctual performance of what is enjoined in them, or, if that be inconsistent with reason or conscience, by a patient submission to whatever penalties the supreme power hath annexed to the neglect or transgression of them, is termed loyalty . . .' (3) I cite the sections in *Works*.

[24] Clarke's Boyle Lectures were published in 1706, and so Berkeley could have known them.

[25] '. . . . antecedent to the end proposed by God, no distinction can be conceived between men; that end therefore itself, or general design of Providence, is not determined or limited by any respect of persons. It is not therefore the private good of this or that man, nation, or age, but the general well-being of all men, of all nations, of all ages of the world, which God designs should be procured by the concurring actions of each individual' (7).

[26] 'These propositions are called "laws of nature" because they are universal, and do not derive their obligation from any civil sanction, but immediately from the Author of nature himself.' (12)

[27] See §535 for reasons for doubting whether Cumberland is a utilitarian.

[28] 'And, notwithstanding that these rules are too often, either by the unhappy concurrence of events, or more especially by the wickedness of perverse men who will not conform to them, made accidental cause of misery to those good men who do, yet this doth not vacate their obligation . . .' (13)

well advised to rely on an indirect utilitarian defence of his laws of nature. Berkeley does not suggest (as Hobbes sometimes seems to) that every act of disobedience is likely to lead to the evils of anarchy and should therefore be avoided. But he argues that permission for limited obedience will lead to these evils, and so should be rejected. Loyalty (consisting in passive obedience) is a virtue because of the 'miseries inseparable from a state of anarchy' (15–16). Since it would be so difficult to determine case by case whether disobedience would be expedient, we ought to have an invariable rule to be observed without calculation in particular cases (19). On this ground Berkeley rejects any argument to show that our agreement to obey the law is conditional on (say) the good behaviour of the rulers, and so he affirms that even if the rulers behave badly, the duty of obedience remains (23).

This argument for strict observance of general rules supports, in Berkeley's view, different attitudes to positive and negative rules. Only the negative precepts of natural law carry absolute obligation, because it is always possible to obey the negative commands without exception (26, 32), and no negative precept may be violated for the sake of observing a positive precept (35).

Once he has argued that acceptance of utilitarianism does not justify calculation of consequences in particular cases, Berkeley answers those who argue from the public good to a doctrine of limited obedience. They wrongly apply the utilitarian criterion to particular actions; but they ought to restrict its application to rules, and they ought to observe the rules without the exceptions that would be warranted by calculation in particular cases.[29]

Berkeley's general point is stronger than his application of it to the question about obedience. He does not show that the general aim of maximizing utility requires an absolute rule of passive obedience rather than a rule of selective obedience. He relies heavily on arguments about anarchy, uncertainty, and co-ordination; but it is not clear that he weighs their bad effects accurately against the bad effects of non-resistance to bad regimes. But whether or not we agree with him on this question, we may agree that he has found a possible defence of utilitarianism against some intuitive objections. We may be too hasty in assuming that our acceptance of general rules that make no mention of utility counts against the truth of utilitarianism. If we are indirect utilitarians, we may even find it easier to justify these non-utilitarian general rules, by showing that their observance, without regard to utility, is the best way to maximize utility.

We might, then, take Berkeley's indirect utilitarianism to lie behind Butler's remarks about restrictions on benevolence. Berkeley explains why the utility of accepting the utilitarian principle alone will be lower than the utility of accepting subordinate principles that we refuse to break even for reasons of utility. If this is what Butler has in mind, his restrictions on benevolence might be taken to clarify, rather than refute, the claim that benevolence is the whole of morality.

---

[29] 'In framing the general laws of nature, it is granted we must be entirely guided by the public good of mankind, but not in the ordinary moral action of our lives. Such a rule, if universally observed, hath, from the nature of things, a necessary fitness to promote the general well-being of mankind: therefore it is a law of nature. This is good reasoning. But if we should say, such an action doth in this instance produce much good and no harm to mankind; therefore it is lawful: this were wrong. The rule is framed with respect to the good of mankind; but our practice must be always shaped immediately by the rule. Those who think the public good of a nation to be the sole measure of the obedience due to the civil power seem not to have considered this distinction.' (31)

700. Objections to Indirect Utilitarianism

Indirect utilitarianism, however, does not seem to account for all the restrictions on benevolence that Butler accepts. Sometimes he accepts a sharper distinction between benevolence and virtue (xii 31n; D 8). Clarke argues that, though morality and utility, suitably understood, coincide, they are distinct, and morality is not mutable in accordance with utility.[30] Butler follows him on this question. For he mentions some duties (for instance, fidelity, honour, strict justice, xii 31n) that specify moral virtues, but 'are abstracted from the consideration of their tendency'.

What sort of abstraction has Butler in mind? If he meant simply that we do not think directly about the public good when we decide to follow these moral principles, his abstraction is consistent with utilitarianism. For Berkeley's reasons, we might argue that utilitarianism requires abstraction from considerations of utility in decisions about particular cases. But this does not seem to be the sort of abstraction that Butler intends; for he has already recognized that the utilitarian position leaves room for some indirectness, and he takes these cases (fidelity and so on) to introduce a new question. He seems to mean that in these cases the relevant rules have no indirect utilitarian justification, and we do not accept the rules because we believe they have some non-apparent indirect utilitarian justification. Hence the characteristic motives of virtue are different from benevolence; even if we believe that indirect utilitarianism supports a given virtue, that belief does not explain our belief that it is a virtue.

Butler may seem to weaken his case against utilitarianism when he mentions the possibility that the good of the creation is the 'only end of the Author of it' (xii 31n), and that the author of nature proposes no end to himself but the production of happiness (D 8). We might infer, as Hutcheson does, that since God has given us our moral sense, the rules that it endorses promote the general good that God intends. If we believe that God is a utilitarian, we might argue that moral rules have an indirect utilitarian justification that is not apparent to us, but is apparent to God, and that this is our reason for accepting the rules.[31] We will accept this argument against Butler if we accept Berkeley's case for indirect utilitarianism.

Butler, however, does not affirm that God's only end is the general good and his moral character 'merely that of benevolence'—he concedes this only for the sake of argument.[32] He agrees that if the premiss about God's benevolence is true, God has given us moral rules that have a utilitarian defence. But this defence is nothing to us as moral agents. Our reason for disapproving of injustice does not depend on its effects on general happiness; the production of happiness is a coincidence that may matter to God but does not give us our primary moral reason.[33] Berkeley's indirect utilitarianism does not answer this claim about

---

[30] See Clarke, *DNR* = H ii 630, discussed in §622.

[31] Hutcheson, *SMP* i 256, criticizes Butler's *Anal.* on punishment. See also §645 (his reply to the argument from ignorance of utility to acceptance of non-utilitarian rules).

[32] Broad, *FTET* 81, and McPherson, 'Development (2)' 10–11, go too far in suggesting that Butler thinks God is or may be a utilitarian. Butler does not assert that this is possible; he simply concedes for the sake of argument that it is possible. His concession allows him to claim that he has good reason to deny that it is possible. Broad's view that Butler takes God to be a utilitarian is rejected by Grave, 'Foundations' 85–6, who argues that it conflicts with the attribution of justice to God.

[33] 'And therefore, were the Author of nature to propose nothing to himself as an end but the production of happiness, were his moral character merely that of benevolence; yet ours is not so. Upon that supposition, indeed, the only reason of his giving us the above-mentioned approbation of benevolence to some persons rather than others, . . . must be, that he

moral reasons; for he simply assumes egoism and voluntarism as the basis of morality, and so does not consider the possibility that some moral principles have a non-utilitarian basis, even if a utilitarian can also defend them.

Butler's argument reveals an ambiguity in questions about what makes right actions right. If his hypothesis about God were true, utility would make right actions right by being the causal origin of the presence of right actions in the world and of our true judgments about which actions are right. How, then, can Butler deny that, on this supposition about God, utility would make right actions right?

To see why he might have a good reason, we may consider a parallel explanation of physics. Suppose that God recognizes that it will maximize utility if we understand the causal processes and laws of the physical world, and we act on that knowledge. Even so, it does not follow that the properties we grasp when we understand physics are the properties that maximize utility. Or suppose that the Nobel Foundation infallibly rewards the scientists who find the true theories with Nobel Prizes; it still does not follow that winning the Nobel Prize makes someone's theory true, even if it is an absolutely reliable symptom of truth. Butler believes that an appeal to God's utilitarian outlook to support a utilitarian moral theory would make a similar mistake. We ought not to argue directly from facts about the causal origin of our moral judgments to conclusions about the character of right-making properties.

To explain why utility, in Butler's view, is not the right-making property, we might argue that facts about utility are not always the only relevant facts, or the decisive facts, that bear on whether an action is right. If we tried to be physicists or historians (on the supposition of a utilitarian God) by asking what belief will maximize utility, we would not understand which facts matter for a physical or historical understanding. Similarly, acquaintance with our moral judgments shows us that we do not believe that utility is all that matters, or that it is always decisive.

An indirect utilitarian might answer Butler on two points: (1) Though admittedly we do not always take utility to be all that matters, we are mistaken. (2) The analogy with physics does not work; for Butler agrees that in morality utility sometimes matters, and even that it is sometimes decisive, whereas utility never matters in physics (we may suppose).

The first answer does not refute Butler. Utilitarians cannot afford to reject our judgments of relevance, but must take them to be correct sometimes. If they could not rely on such judgments, they would undermine their grounds for thinking that utility matters. Berkeley assumes that indirect utilitarianism allows us to explain the appearance of our accepting non-utilitarian rules. But if utilitarians admit that we have non-utilitarian as well as utilitarian judgments about moral relevance, they need to show that our non-utilitarian judgments are somehow less reliable than our utilitarian judgments. Butler argues that we have no reason to prefer our utilitarian judgments. Sidgwick argues that common sense is 'unconsciously utilitarian', but Butler disagrees; even if we know about the balance of utility, we do not take that to decide all the questions that arise.

---

foresaw this constitution of our nature would produce more happiness, than forming us with a temper of mere general benevolence. But still, since this is our constitution, falsehood, violence, injustice, must be vice in us, and benevolence to some, preferably to others, virtue; abstracted from all consideration of the overbalance of evil or good, which they may appear likely to produce.' (D 8) Butler should agree that if we believe the rules have an indirect utilitarian justification, that will give us a further reason to approve of them; his point is that such a reason is not necessary for us to have a sufficient reason. He has more to say on human ignorance in Sermon xv 14.

The second answer fails for similar reasons. If we attach some weight to the judgments that favour utilitarianism, we need some reason for discounting the judgments that favour non-utilitarian considerations. A utilitarian would be unwise to discount them simply because they are non-utilitarian; for such discounting would affect utilitarian judgments as well, unless we take the truth of utilitarianism to be settled without reference to common sense. If utilitarians argue from common-sense judgments, they are open to Butler's objections. If they do not argue from common sense, they need to show that their preferred method is preferable to argument from common sense.

701. Divine Goodness and Divine Benevolence

Butler's arguments about divine goodness and moral rightness take a position in the debate that Cumberland and Hutcheson begin. Both of them identify God's goodness with benevolence. Maxwell disputes Cumberland's view. Balguy and Grove agree with Maxwell; they reject the arguments of Hutcheson and Bayes to show that God's moral character is simply benevolent.[34] Butler agrees with Balguy and Grove. Against Hutcheson he argues that the moral sense includes non-utilitarian elements. Hence we have one good reason to believe that God's moral goodness includes non-utilitarian elements of goodness. This reason might be outweighed if we had strong theological grounds for believing that God is benevolent and has no moral characteristics distinct from benevolence. But theological and Scriptural arguments suggest that God is just and merciful towards individuals, not simply benevolent towards the whole human race.[35]

Butler relies on these arguments to show that God's moral government of the world is concerned with virtue and vice for their own sake, and not merely with maximum happiness. In the chapter of the *Analogy* to which the *Dissertation on Virtue* is appended, he insists that we recognize God as just, not merely concerned with happiness.[36] He does not categorically rule out the possibility of discovering, if we knew enough about what would maximize happiness in the universe, that God's character is 'simple absolute benevolence'. But he does not agree that arguments from reason or revelation support this conception of God. On the contrary, he takes these arguments to suggest that God has moral qualities distinct from benevolence. He even claims that we have no clear conception of what benevolence would imply, let alone of its being morally acceptable, if it were not constrained by veracity and justice.[37]

---

[34] On Balguy and Grove see §662.   [35] On Hutcheson see §645.

[36] '. . . perhaps divine goodness, with which, if I mistake not, we make very free in our speculations, may not be a bare single disposition to produce happiness; but a disposition to make the good, the faithful, the honest man happy. Perhaps an infinitely perfect mind may be pleased with seeing his creatures behave suitably to the nature which he has given them . . .' (*Anal.* i 2.3). 'Some men seem to think the only character of the Author of nature to be that of simple absolute benevolence. . . . There may possibly be in the creation beings, to whom the Author of nature manifests himself under the most amiable of all characters, this of infinite absolute benevolence; for it is the most amiable, supposing it not, as perhaps it is not, incompatible with justice; but he manifests himself to us under the character of a righteous governor.' (*Anal.* i 3.3) Price, *RPQM* 83n, quotes the first of these passages.

[37] 'And it [sc. virtue] has this tendency, by rendering public good an object and end, to every member of the society; . . . by uniting a society within itself, and so increasing its strength; and, which is particularly to be mentioned, uniting it by means of veracity and justice. For as these last are principal bonds of union, so benevolence or public spirit, undirected, unrestrained by them, is, nobody knows what.' (*Anal.* i 3.19) This follows the passage on superior principles, discussed in §686.

702. Fairness, Responsibility, and Non-utilitarian Morality

While the *Sermons* show that Butler rejects utilitarianism, only the *Dissertation* makes his reasons clear. These reasons convince Price, who appeals to Butler's arguments against the reduction of morality to benevolence.[38] The *Dissertation* is especially useful because Butler appeals not only to common beliefs about morality, but also to general features of morality that help to clarify his view of conscience and of the connexion between conscience and morality. These are the basis of his anti-utilitarian arguments.

He begins with the difference between authority and strength. Hutcheson's account of moral approval and disapproval overlooks the authoritative character of these sentiments; they do not simply express our favourable feelings or unfavourable feelings, but also claim to be based on the merits of the people and the situation. Butler cites Epictetus as the source of his remarks on the 'approving and disapproving faculty'; he understands this expression as capturing his doctrine of superior principles, as explained in Sermons ii–iii.[39]

In opposition to Hutcheson, Butler distinguishes a rational judgment from favourable feeling. We might feel distressed or upset that someone caused us harm, but we would not make an unfavourable moral judgment unless we thought he had violated some principles that we think he could reasonably be expected to accept. If we decide to drive the wrong way on a one-way street just to save a few minutes, we may be distressed at colliding with a truck coming round a corner, but we can hardly blame the truck driver for anything. We blame people only by appeal to principles that we think we can reasonably expect them to accept.[40]

This observation that moral judgment expresses a superior principle, not simply a feeling of approval, does not refute utilitarianism. But it raises a pertinent question for the utilitarian: how do the rational standards on which the superior principle of conscience relies favour utilitarianism? Cumberland assumes that the rational point of view attends only to the good consequences of actions. Butler looks more closely at the standards defining the outlook of conscience, and finds that they do not support consequentialism, and hence do not support utilitarianism. He therefore agrees with Maxwell's criticism of Cumberland.[41]

In making a moral judgment we assume the agent's responsibility for the action. Butler brings this out clearly in distinguishing punishment from beneficial preventive action.[42] Someone merits blame on the assumption that he is responsible for the relevant action or

---

[38] See Price, *RPQM* 131, quoting from D 8.

[39] 'That which renders beings capable of moral government, is their having a moral nature, and moral faculties of perception and of action. Brute creatures are impressed and actuated by various instincts and propensions: so also are we. But additional to this, we have a capacity of reflecting upon actions and characters, and making them an object to our thought; and on doing this, we naturally and unavoidably approve some actions, under the peculiar view of their being virtuous and of good desert; and disapprove others, as vicious and of ill desert. That we have this moral approving and disapproving faculty, is certain from our experiencing it in ourselves, and recognizing it in each other. It appears . . . from our natural sense of gratitude, which implies a distinction between merely being the instrument of good, and intending it: from the like distinction, every one makes, between injury and mere harm, which Hobbes says, is peculiar to mankind; and between injury and just punishment, a distinction plainly natural, prior to the consideration of human laws.' (D1) A footnote refers to Epictetus.

[40] An appeal to reasonable expectations of acceptance and rejection is explained in Scanlon, *WWO*, ch. 5.

[41] As we saw in §535, Cumberland is not a utilitarian, but some of the questions that arise about his view arise about utilitarianism as well.

[42] 'For if, unhappily, it were resolved that a man who, by some innocent action, was infected with the plague should be left to perish lest, by other people's coming near him, the infection should spread, no one would say he deserved this treatment. Innocence and ill desert are inconsistent ideas.' (D 3)

state. Since our moral judgments appeal to desert, merit, and appropriateness, rather than to the strength of our reactions, they presuppose responsibility. Since these judgments about blameworthiness are different from utilitarian judgments about what maximizes the good, the utilitarian judgments do not capture our moral judgments.

Butler also believes that some moral principles are obligatory apart from considerations of utility. Certain acts are owed to individuals, and agents are praiseworthy or blameworthy for actions or omissions apart from the effects on utility.[43]

Butler does not draw attention to any common feature of these different exceptions to the utilitarian principle. Hence, he might be taken to hold the pluralist intuitionist view defended by Price and Reid.[44] This view recognizes a number of ultimate principles none of which is supreme, and none of which provides any systematic reasoned basis for deciding conflicts among principles.

But Butler may not intend a pluralist position. Though he does not insist on any common feature of the exceptions to utility, he suggests one. For each case involves reciprocity and equality. If we were asked to explain the principles we rely on in the judgments that Butler mentions, we might say that these are fair principles for evaluating both ourselves and others. We would rightly resent being treated badly simply because we had harmed other people, if the harm was either justified or unavoidable. We do not merely apply these judgments to other people; we also expect to have them applied to ourselves, and we apply them to ourselves in considering whether we deserve blame.

Restraint on self-sacrifice is one aspect of fairness that is fundamental in morality, but not fundamental in utilitarianism. Another aspect of fairness, however, goes beyond restraint of self-sacrifice. Butler's remarks on punishment imply that some moral attitudes are retrospective, rather than purely prospective; they consider what individuals have done in comparison with what they could reasonably have been expected to do. Principles that restrained self-sacrifice, but lacked the appropriate retrospective elements, would not be morally acceptable, because fairness to individuals requires retrospective treatment.

These claims about the content of morality matter for two of Butler's further claims: (1) Morality is to be identified with living in accord with nature. (2) Conscience approves of morality. If morality were identical to the requirements of utilitarian benevolence, he would have to prove these two further claims by connecting nature and conscience with utilitarianism. But since he does not accept utilitarianism, he has to connect nature and conscience with moral principles including the non-utilitarian elements we have mentioned. Does he make his task easier or harder by rejecting utilitarianism?

703. Self-Love, Benevolence, and Conscience

To understand some of Butler's claims about nature, morality, and superiority, we should return to his rather complex views on self-love and benevolence. Self-love is superior to

---

[43] 'The fact then appears to be, that we are constituted so as to condemn falsehood, unprovoked violence, injustice, and to approve of benevolence to some preferably to others, abstracted from all consideration, which conduct is likeliest to produce an overbalance of happiness or misery.' (D 8) This passage is quoted with approval by Ross, *FE* 77–9, who describes Butler as 'the most sagacious, if not the most consistent or systematic, of the British Moralists'.

[44] On Price and Reid see §§822, 851.

the passion of benevolence; for benevolence towards particular persons 'may be a degree of weakness, and so be blameable' (P 39). When the passion of benevolence conflicts with self-love, self-love has authority and ought to prevail.

It is not so easy to say what Butler believes about self-love and the rational principle of benevolence. The sort of conflict that arises between self-love and the passion of benevolence also seems to arise between self-love and the principle of benevolence. Rational devotion to the public good may involve neglect of one's own good; Butler sees possible conflict between benevolence and other moral virtues (D 8), and the reasons that persuade him of these conflicts can be used to show that there are conflicts with self-love. Moreover, he recognizes a moral duty to take care of one's own interest (D 6); might not this duty on some occasions override the demands of benevolence?

Butler does not seem to claim that self-love is superior to benevolence in all circumstances. Apparently, then, self-love should sometimes restrain benevolence, but benevolence should sometimes restrain self-love. How are we to decide which should prevail?

Sometimes Butler seems to imply that self-love should always prevail, because it is superior to benevolence.[45] As we have seen earlier, he recognizes self-love and conscience as the two superior principles, and he does not mention benevolence as a third. Moreover, he claims that an action is unsuitable to our nature if it violates either of the two superior principles.[46] If, then, self-love rejected an action, and benevolence were the only principle supporting it, we would be acting unnaturally if we performed it.

Butler implies, therefore, that self-love is superior to the principle of benevolence. If these were the only two rational principles in our nature, it would be appropriate to regulate the demands of benevolence by appeal to self-love. As Butler argues, this does not mean that we would not be benevolent, but only that we would avoid the blameworthy degree of benevolence that requires unreasonable self-sacrifice. Self-love, then, is superior to the principle of benevolence, in its own right.

It does not follow, however, that we ought never to sacrifice our interest to do what benevolence requires. For on some occasions conscience may favour the benevolent action over the prudent action, and on such occasions we ought to follow conscience. If we follow it against self-love, we act unnaturally to some degree, insofar as we violate the superior principle of self-love. But we nonetheless act naturally on the whole, because conscience considers what is and is not suitable to my nature as a whole, whereas self-love considers only a part of my nature.

---

[45] Frey, 'Self-love', defends this view.

[46] 'Reasonable self-love and conscience are the chief or superior principles in the nature of man, because an action may be suitable to this nature, though all other principles be violated; but becomes unsuitable, if either of these are.' (iii 9) It is not clear what possibility Butler envisages in the 'because' clause. He might have either of these two in mind: (1) An action is natural if and only if either self-love or conscience endorses it. (2) An action is natural if and only if both endorse it. In the 'but becomes...' clause he accepts a further claim: (3) If either self-love or conscience opposes an action, the action is unnatural. If he believes both (1) and (3), an action that is endorsed by one superior principle and opposed by the other is both natural and unnatural. Butler excludes this possibility if he accepts two other claims: (4) Conscience approves only virtuous action. (5) Actions are virtuous if and only if they are natural, and vicious if and only if they are unnatural. Butler clearly accepts (4). But does he accept (5)? He has a reasonable alternative: (6) Actions are virtuous to the extent that they are natural and vicious to the extent that they are unnatural. According to (6), naturalness and unnaturalness allow degrees, so that an action that is contrary to nature (to some degree) may still be, all things considered, natural; for it may violate one superior rational principle but be endorsed by another. The context favours (6), by allowing degrees of naturalness.

In appealing to this graded conception of nature, Butler sums up his argument in Sermon iii. He begins the sermon with the suggestion that things may be to some extent contrary to nature, but in accordance with nature all things considered.[47] Butler's conception of nature allows some things to be contrary to important aspects of our nature, but less contrary to our nature as a whole than their opposites would be. Similarly, he speaks of the nature of man 'as respecting' himself only and as respecting society (i 4). These two aspects of nature mark two ways in which something could be natural or unnatural.[48]

If, then, we are sometimes justified in following benevolence against self-love, this is not because benevolence prescribes it, but because conscience requires us to follow benevolence. Hence we are really following conscience, not benevolence. We choose the most natural action by following conscience, which approves the actions that suit our nature as a whole.

704. Non-utilitarian Morality as a Source of Natural Action

To see why Butler thinks the actions approved by conscience are natural, we must attend to the content of morality. If utilitarianism were correct, then, in Butler's view, we ought to identify morality with benevolence and concern for the public good. We would thereby identify morality with a self-sacrificing outlook that treats an individual person as a means to maximizing the total good. Since conscience takes the moral point of view, it would coincide with the rational principle of benevolence, if utilitarianism were correct. Even though the concept of conscience would be different from the concept of rational benevolence, their advice would necessarily coincide.

If Butler accepted this view of morality, his claims about conscience and nature would imply that my nature as a whole requires this maximizing attitude. But he neither affirms nor defends this conclusion. He takes benevolence to be a natural passion, and supposes that it is natural to satisfy it to some degree; but these claims do not support utilitarian benevolence. Since he eventually rejects utilitarianism, he takes the outlook of conscience to be non-utilitarian; hence he takes natural action to be guided by non-utilitarian principles. Do the specific non-utilitarian principles that Butler endorses make it more plausible to claim that the actions prescribed by conscience are natural?

To see why these actions are natural, it is relevant to notice that the non-utilitarian elements in Butler's theory endorse self-love at some important points. Butler believes that it is blameworthy to be too little concerned for one's own good and too ready to sacrifice it for the good of others.[49] Often we need not insist on the moral badness of

---

[47] 'Thus, when it is said by ancient writers that tortures and death are not so contrary to human nature as injustice—by this, to be sure, is not meant that the aversion to the former in mankind is less strong and prevalent than their aversion to the latter, but that the former is only contrary to our nature considered in a partial view, and which takes in only the lowest part of it, that which we have in common with the brutes; whereas the latter is contrary to our nature considered in a higher sense, as a system and constitution contrary to the whole economy of man.' (iii 2)

[48] See also i 14–15, referring to different parts of our nature.

[49] 'It deserves to be considered, whether men are more at liberty, in point of morals, to make themselves miserable without reason, than to make other people so; or dissolutely to neglect their own greater good, for the sake of a present lesser gratification, than they are to neglect the good of others, whom nature has committed to their care. It should seem, that a due concern about our own interest or happiness, and a reasonable endeavour to secure and promote

imprudence, because we often have ample non-moral reasons for being prudent. Still, morality, and not only self-interest, rejects imprudence. It not only endorses proper self-concern, but also rejects those principles that would appeal only to someone who lacked proper self-concern.

The acceptance of proper self-concern makes a difference to our moral judgments. The sacrifice of one person simply to promote the greater good of others is a course of action that reasonably self-concerned people would refuse on their own behalf. Aristotle remarks that the brave person is not the one who is always ready to sacrifice his life, but the one who is ready to sacrifice it for an appropriate cause. In the same spirit, Butler's exceptions to unrestricted maximizing benevolence protect legitimate self-concern against demands for self-sacrifice.[50]

This feature of morality shows why, in one respect, it does not conflict with nature, since it protects those natural requirements that self-love prescribes. But some further reason is needed to explain why the aspects of morality that go beyond self-love are also natural.

One feature of self-love may help to show why agents who recognize self-love as a superior principle in them also have reason to recognize a further principle as superior to self-love. Self-love is essentially fair between the different passions and interests that it has to consider. If we extend Butler's political comparison, we might say that legitimate government by self-love seeks to give the fair and appropriate place to each special interest going with each particular passion, without allowing itself to be dominated by whichever passion can shout most loudly in support of its demands. If one passion is restrained, the restraint is justified by the legitimate interests of the other passions. Rational self-love is impartial between them; it is not biased by the strength of one particular passion.

Similarly, Butler might reasonably claim, conscience deals fairly with the claims of the different individuals whose interests are involved in a situation that concerns it. It is not biased by partiality to oneself, or by a self-sacrificing attitude that considers only the desires of other people. As Clarke suggests, it is characteristic of conscience to take an impartial view of all the people whose interests are involved. To ignore the point of view of conscience would be parallel to ignoring some of our particular passions and interests simply because others are stronger. Just as all the interests relevant to the decision made by self-love are real interests of the self, so all the people relevant to the decisions made by conscience are real persons with claims equal to my own.

Hence, according to Butler, if we acknowledge the reality of other people, the only appropriate point of view to take towards them is the point of view of conscience. A particular passion, according to Butler, has no reason to complain of enlightened self-love. Similarly, the particular agent has no reason to complain about the treatment he is given in relation to other people, if the proper principles of morality are observed.

---

it, . . . is virtue, and the contrary behaviour faulty and blameable; since, in the calmest way of reflexion, we approve of the first, and condemn the other conduct, both in ourselves and others. This approbation and disapprobation are altogether different from mere desire of our own, or of their happiness, and from sorrow upon missing it. . . . prudence is a species of virtue, and folly of vice: meaning by *folly*, somewhat quite different from mere incapacity; a thoughtless want of that regard and attention to our own happiness, which we had capacity for.' (D 6)

[50] This protection for legitimate self-concern may be compared with Rawls's demand for 'mutual disinterest' and his discussion of benevolence, *TJ* 127–9.

705. Why is Conscience Supreme?

Butler's case for the natural character of conscience depends on our being convinced that conscience, rather than self-love, is supreme. We may wonder why the supreme principle should be the one that treats other people as equals. Why should we not regard other people as competitors for scarce resources, with each of us trying to promote his own interest irrespective of the interests of the others? According to this view, self-love is the supreme principle prescribing natural action. Butler's view implies that we can see why we should accept the supremacy of conscience, once we consider the reasons for taking the point of view of self-love. Unless we accept the outlook of self-love, we abandon the distinction between authority and strength; we abandon any view of ourselves as rational, temporally extended, agents. The result of abandoning conscience would be analogous; we would cease to treat other people as people who deserve things, and cease to claim that we deserve anything from them.

Butler needs to show, then, that we essentially regard ourselves in certain ways that turn out, on reflexion, to involve recognizably moral relations to others. If, for instance, we essentially regard ourselves as appropriately treated in certain ways, or as deserving certain kinds of treatment, and not simply as wanting it in our own interest, our nature essentially includes more than self-love recognizes. Butler insists that the recognition of character and responsibility, and the correlative recognition of desert, are essential to the moral point of view (D 2–3). They are essential elements of human nature. If we evaluated ourselves and other people only from the point of view of self-love, we would ignore an essential feature of ourselves. Our failure would be no less grave than the failure to think of ourselves as temporally extended and as more than a mere collection of passions.[51]

This line of thought might reasonably be extended in a direction that would support Butler's claim. To forgo evaluation by any principles applying to ourselves and others, and to forgo beliefs and sentiments connected with resentment, gratitude, praise, blame, desert, and so on, would be to curtail radically the normal expressions of our nature. To consider myself as a whole, as a system constituted by the relation of my desires to superior principles, I must consider myself as taking these attitudes to myself in relation to others. This is why I act in accordance with my nature in taking the principle embodying these attitudes as the supreme principle; that principle is conscience. If I treat myself as a whole self, I cannot confine my non-instrumental concern to myself.

The character of Butler's argument is still easier to grasp if we see the connexion between his account of superior principles and Plato's account of justice in the soul. Butler's use of the political notions of authority and power relies on one part of Plato's political analogy.[52] Butler applies the analogy to self-love, arguing that it reaches a fair arrangement of the various particular passions, because it is guided by rational evaluation that attaches the appropriate value to each of them. If we accepted the guidance of self-love but rejected the guidance of conscience, we would allow superior principles only a partial influence over us, and so would express our nature as rational agents only in one aspect of our lives.

---

[51] The Sermon on resentment (viii) is also relevant in this connexion.
[52] Whewell and Gladstone on iii 1 note the parallel with Plato.

This argument assumes that self-love treats different passions fairly, and integrates their satisfaction in some way that recognizes their legitimate claims. This is a quasi-political conception of self-love. By thinking of self-love in this way, we can argue that it considers incompletely the sorts of claims that conscience considers completely. We might wonder, however, why self-love should not be as 'complete' as conscience in its consideration of other people's claims, but still fail to draw the conclusion that conscience draws. Why should self-love not treat other people's interests in the way it treats the particular passions, modifying and integrating them so as to satisfy my own interests? This self-centred conclusion is not the outlook of the supreme principle that Butler recognizes. But why should this self-centred principle not be supreme?

To close off this possibility, Butler must insist on the essential difference between particular passions and other people. Though we can speak of particular passions as having legitimate claims to satisfaction, they do not themselves put these claims forward as deserving satisfaction; all the claims of desert come from self-love on behalf of this particular rational agent. Other people, however, are rational agents, and make claims that involve considerations that they put forward on their merits; they have the same relation to their particular passions that I have to mine.

This fact about other people implies that if I am to consider the merits of a particular course of action that involves them, I have to recognize them as sources of possible legitimate claims about the merits of this course of action. If I considered my own particular passions in this way, I would mistakenly treat them as though they were people. But if I did not recognize others as sources of possible legitimate claims, I would mistakenly treat them as though they were mere collections of passions or interests.

If this distinction between particular passions and other people is warranted, Butler need not agree that the supreme principle is the self-centred principle that treats other people as means to my own interest. In his view, I do not completely guide my own actions by a principle that carries authority until I treat other people fairly, by a principle whose merits they are also rationally required to accept. Though my self-centred principle considers other people, it does not consider them as agents with legitimate claims; it does not rely, therefore, on considerations of authority rather than strength when it prefers my own interest to their interest.

This attempt to develop Butler's case for the supremacy of conscience requires a good deal of speculation that goes beyond anything he says. Some of the speculation has a much firmer basis in Kant. But it is not simply a Kantian import into Butler. It relies on his conception of a superior principle as resting on authority rather than power, and on his rejection of utilitarianism on grounds connected with praise, blame, responsibility, and justice. Conscience acknowledges other people as sources of legitimate claims. This involves a certain sort of equality, since I regard myself as having legitimate claims against them, insofar as I conceive myself as being rightly subject to praise and blame from them.

706. The Obligation to Follow Conscience

Since Butler has these reasons for claiming that conscience prescribes natural action by prescribing non-utilitarian morality, he is entitled to appeal to the natural character of conscience in order to explain why we should obey it. He considers someone who asks about our obligation to obey conscience.[53] This questioner agrees with (e.g.) John Clarke that the only proper sense to be attached to 'obligation' is some psychological necessity derived from a sanction imposed by a law.[54] A related question might be raised by Hutcheson, who agrees with Butler in recognizing obligation independent of law, but still identifies obligation with a type of motivation.

Butler answers by claiming that we are a law to ourselves apart from any imposed law or sanction. In opposition to both John Clarke and Hutcheson, and in agreement with Samuel Clarke, he takes obligation to require authority, as distinct from psychological strength. Hence, when he claims that conscience carries its own authority with it, and therefore carries its obligation with it, he identifies obligation with the presence of reasons as distinct from motives. He does not mean that conscience infallibly creates a desire to conform to it, but that it is a superior principle that prescribes natural action.

We might infer from this passage that Butler takes obligation to imply awareness of a moral requirement, and that he takes approval by conscience to constitute the obligatory character of an action. This inference would be mistaken. The obligation comes from the fact that in acting in a specific way we follow 'the law of our nature'. Because our following the principles endorsed by conscience accords with our nature, approval by conscience is the mark of an obligation—of a sufficient reason to act as conscience requires.

Butler's argument for the claim he says he has 'proved' is the fact that human beings, in contrast to non-rational animals, are rational agents governed by superior principles. At this stage, then, he appeals to the generic character of conscience as the principle of 'reflexion'. To show that following conscience is natural, he emphasizes the holistic aspect of nature.[55] He relies on the argument at the end of Sermon ii for the supremacy of generic conscience, the general principle of reflexion. It applies to specific conscience only if specific conscience 'adjusts, manages, and presides over' other impulses and principles so as to fulfil the nature of the whole.

This function of conscience must be distinguished from the related, but more limited, function of self-love. For self-love also takes a holistic point of view, adjusting different impulses for the sake of my own interest. But this outlook does not take account of all the

---

[53] 'But allowing that mankind hath the rule of right within himself, yet it may be asked, "What obligations are we under to attend to and follow it?" I answer: it has been proved that man by his nature is a law to himself, without the particular distinct consideration of the positive sanctions of that law; the rewards and punishments which we feel, and those which from the light of reason we have ground to believe, are annexed to it. The question then carries its own answer along with it. Your obligation to obey this law, is its being the law of your nature. That your conscience approves of and attests to such a course of action, is itself alone an obligation. Conscience does not only offer itself to show us the way we should walk in, but it likewise carries its own authority with it, that it is our natural guide; the guide assigned us by the Author of our nature: it therefore belongs to our condition of being, it is our duty to walk in that path, and follow this guide, without looking about to see whether we may not possibly forsake them with impunity.' (iii 5)

[54] On John Clarke see §865.

[55] 'Every bias, instinct, propension within, is a natural part of our nature, but not the whole: add to these the superior faculty, whose office it is to adjust, manage, and preside over them, and take in this its natural superiority, and you complete the idea of human nature.' (iii 2) '[Nature] . . . is the inward frame of man considered as a system or constitution; whose several parts are united, not by a physical principle of individuation, but by the respects they have to each other; the chief of which is the subjection which the appetites, passions, and particular affections have to the one supreme principle of reflexion or conscience. The system or constitution is formed by and consists in these respects and this subjection.' (iii 2n)

considerations that we can see to be relevant from the holistic point of view. It reasons as though the effect on my private good were the overriding consideration, but in fact this is not the overriding consideration. Self-love concentrates on a proper subset of the considerations that matter. We would be wrong, then, if we thought that self-love estimates all the relevant considerations at their proper value.

Butler adds a further comment on the obligation to follow conscience, in his discussion of Shaftesbury.[56] According to Shaftesbury, a strong inclination to virtuous action combined with severe doubt about whether virtue is one's own interest would leave one 'without remedy', because one would have strong inclination both to choose virtue and to choose vice. In Butler's view, this conclusion rests on the sentimentalist error that is exposed by a correct understanding of the superiority of conscience.

If conscience approves a course of action that appears to be against my interest, it follows that the choice of this action is approved from the point of view of my nature as a whole. Since my nature as a whole includes the part of my nature that is the concern of self-interest (i.e., the aspects of my nature that concern my private good), the legitimate claims of self-interest have already been considered, and I have discovered that I have overriding reason to choose the action despite the apparent cost to my own interest. It would therefore be unreasonable to reject this course of action for the sake of my own interest.[57]

Butler's argument highlights the most important aspect of his claims about conscience. He does not claim that Shaftesbury is wrong about how strong a motive results from the recognition of moral obligation. He argues that Shaftesbury is wrong to suggest that a discussion of obligation should consider only the comparative strength of different motives. If we grant that conscience is a supreme principle, with the moral content that Butler attributes to it, we cannot also be in doubt about whether it creates an overriding reason to follow it. This overriding reason follows from Butler's account of supremacy.

Butler moves more quickly than he should in claiming that conscience, as he conceives it, prescribes natural action. It claims supremacy, because moral principles profess to tell us the legitimate extent of self-interested action. But whether this claim is correct depends on whether the moral principles accepted by conscience are those that fulfil human nature. We have considered how Butler might compensate for his over-hasty argument by explaining how morality fulfils human nature.

707. Why Does it Matter Whether Conscience is Natural?

Butler's argument is meant to show that the actions prescribed by conscience are natural, from the point of view of my nature as a whole, and that therefore conscience is the supreme

---

[56] See P 25–6, quoted in §677.

[57] 'But the obligation on the side of interest really does not remain. For the natural authority of the principle of reflexion is an obligation the most near and intimate, the most certain and known: whereas the contrary obligation can at the utmost appear no more than probable . . . the greatest degree of scepticism which he thought possible will still leave men under the strictest moral obligations, whatever their opinion be concerning the happiness of virtue. . . . Take in then that authority and obligation, which is a constituent part of this reflex approbation, and it will undeniably follow, though a man should doubt of every thing else, yet, that he would still remain under the nearest and most certain obligation to the practice of virtue; and obligation implied in the very idea of virtue, in the very idea of reflex approbation.' (P 26–7)

principle. This is an argument about what the moral theorist can discover by reflexion on nature and on the principles of morality. It is not an argument about what the moral agent considers.

In this respect, conscience is similar to self-love. For rational self-love considers (roughly speaking) the multiplicity of my present desires and the effect of my present desires on my future good. In doing so it chooses the natural action, because of the sort of thing I am; but an agent moved by correct self-love need not be thinking about nature. Similarly, conscience considers me in relation to other people from the appropriately impartial view; it need not think about nature in taking this view, but the actions it prescribes are natural because of the sort of thing I am. Hence it pursues natural action de re, but not de dicto.

Butler does not suggest, therefore, that virtuous people ask whether an action is natural before they decide whether to do it. They ask whether it promotes the public good, whether it is just or fair, whether it shows a blameworthy degree of imprudence, and so on. These are the properties of actions that Butler mentions in the Dissertation. Philosophical examination shows that action on these considerations fulfils human nature, and that therefore acting on conscience is natural.[58]

Does this mean, however, that Butler's argument about the natural character of conscience has no practical significance? It vindicates the views of the ancient moralists who identify virtue with acting in accord with nature, and so it refutes those modern moralists who deny any special connexion between morality and nature. A full study of human nature helps us to understand why morality has the content that it has. But does this discovery about the content of morality give us any further reason for choosing the moral point of view?

To answer this question, it is useful to return to the connexion between promoting one's own interest and fulfilling one's nature. Though we may not initially suppose that we care about fulfilling our nature, we discover that fulfilling our nature is a reasonable goal, because that is what we value (when we think about it) in promoting our own interest through reasonable self-love. Reflexion on self-love shows us that the fulfilment of our nature is worth pursuing in its own right, not simply as a means to fulfilling self-love. Hence the discovery that acting on conscience fulfils our nature gives us a reason to prefer the actions prescribed by conscience.

708. The Harmony of Self-Love and Conscience

This explanation of the supremacy of conscience and of the analogy between conscience and self-love helps us to appraise some objections to Butler's overall position. After labouring to understand and to defend his argument for the supremacy of conscience, we may be surprised to find that he also argues for the harmony of conscience and self-love. Sidgwick infers that Butler has no good argument for regarding conscience as superior to self-love, and that his argument for the general harmony between self-love and conscience reveals some

---

[58] Sturgeon, 'Nature', develops some of the awkward consequences for Butler of supposing that (i) conscience decides on an action by considering whether it is natural, and (ii) it decides whether an action is natural by considering whether it is already favoured by some other superior principle than conscience. Even if Butler accepted (i), he need not accept (ii); but we have insufficient grounds for attributing either (i) or (ii) to him.

doubt or confusion on the issues. This is why Sidgwick argues that Butler's real insight is the discovery of a 'duality' in practical reason.[59] He believes that Butler recognizes two ultimate principles and has no good argument for attributing priority to one over the other. This verdict on Butler influences Sidgwick's views on the nature and limits of practical reason.

Sidgwick's verdict overlooks Butler's reasons for believing that conscience, rather than self-love, is supreme. Butler recognizes one 'regulative and governing faculty'. We have seen that he speaks of reflexion or conscience in both the generic and the specific sense. Generic reflexion includes both self-love and conscience, but these are not just two unconnected applications of practical reason. Within this generic principle of reflexion or conscience, specific conscience is supreme. It is not confined to self-love, but neither is it entirely separate from self-love; it takes to a reasonable conclusion the sort of reflective reasoning that self-love applies only to a restricted range of the questions that can be answered by practical reason. That is why (as Butler implies in answering Shaftesbury) the legitimate claims of self-love are already included in the considerations that matter to conscience. Since conscience is superior to self-love, Butler does not treat self-love as a supreme principle incorporating the demands of morality.[60]

We may be surprised, then, that he does not abandon, but actually affirms, the claim that morality and self-love must agree.[61] Sidgwick takes him to affirm that self-love is a rational principle not subordinate to conscience. This, in his view, is why Butler believes that a course of action approved by conscience must still be examined from a different rational point of view, to see whether it meets all the relevant standards of rationality.[62] Is this

[59] 'Butler's express statement of the duality of the regulative principles in human nature constitutes an important step in ethical speculation; since it brings into clear view the most fundamental difference between the ethical thought of modern England and that of the old Greco-Roman world,—a difference all the more striking because Butler's general formula of "living according to nature" is taken from Stoicism, and his view of human nature as an ordered polity of impulses is distinctly Platonic. But in Platonism and Stoicism, and in Greek moral philosophy generally, but one regulative and governing faculty is recognized under the name of Reason—however the regulation of Reason may be understood; in the modern ethical view, when it has worked itself clear, there are found to be two,—Universal Reason and Egoistic Reason, or Conscience and Self-love.' (OHE 197–8) Sidgwick on Scotus and Butler; see §368.

[60] On Aquinas and the superiority of self-love see §365.

[61] '...there can no access be had to the understanding but by convincing men that the course of life we would persuade them to is not contrary to their interest. It may be allowed, without any prejudice to the cause of virtue and religion, that our ideas of happiness and misery are of all our ideas the nearest and most important to us; that they will, nay, if you please, that they ought to prevail over those of order, and beauty, and harmony, proportion, if there ever should be, as it is impossible there ever should be, any inconsistence between them: though these last too, as expressing the fitness of actions, are as real as truth itself. Let it be allowed, though virtue or moral rectitude does indeed consist in affection to and pursuit of what is right and good, as such; yet, that when we sit down in a cool hour, we can neither justify to ourselves this or any other pursuit, till we are convinced that it will be for our happiness, or at least not contrary to it' (xi 20).

[62] Sidgwick, OHE 196. After quoting the 'cool hour' passage Sidgwick continues: 'That the ultimate appeal must be to the individual's interest was similarly assumed in Shaftesbury's argument...'. His account of Butler is defended by Frankena, 'History' 183; 'Concepts' 184. Similarly, Green, IHTHN 327–8, takes Butler to affirm the supremacy of self-love in this passage and in iii 9. Wilson and Fowler, PM 63n, claim that Butler introduces a conflict into his position: 'This passage, which places self-love on even a higher level than conscience, appears to me to be plainly inconsistent with Butler's predominant conception of benevolence and self-love as co-ordinate principles of our nature, both alike being regarded as under the supreme governance of conscience or reflexion'. McPherson, 'Development (1)', takes Butler to maintain the supremacy of self-love in the Sermons (in contrast to the Analogy); he argues that Butler takes self-love and conscience to be identical, and maintains that ' "productive of happiness" may be regarded as the ground of rightness' (327). He thus concludes that Butler is an 'egoistic eudaemonist' (330). This view would bring his position somewhat closer to that of the Greek moralists. McPherson's attribution of eudaemonism to Butler is rejected by Raphael, 'Conscience' 236; Grave, 'Foundations' 83–4.

the right way to understand the reflexion 'in a cool hour' that takes the point of view of self-love?

Butler does not suggest that self-interest is an appropriate motive for virtuous action, since virtue consists in 'affection to . . . what is right and good, as such'. Nonetheless, he allows a defence of virtue that appeals to self-interest. To understand the role of this defence, we should notice that the appeal to self-love is a concession ('let it be allowed . . .') made for the sake of argument. It does not state Butler's view of the proper role of self-love.[63] It simply points out that many people will ask what they have to gain from being virtuous, and that the defender of virtue has no reason to be afraid of this question.[64]

Belief in a conflict between self-love and conscience results, in Butler's view, from mistaken assumptions about the character of self-love. In arguing against these assumptions, he does not concede that self-love is superior to conscience, or that the authority of conscience must be defended by appeal to self-love. On the contrary, he claims that the proof of the naturalness of conscience is itself sufficient proof that we have reason to follow it (iii 5).[65] He relies on this proof in pointing out Shaftesbury's error. We recognize the error once we see how confused it would be to suppose that we could recognize the supremacy of conscience and still think that self-love gives us a conflicting obligation. In this context, Butler's argument for the general, though not universal, coincidence of conscience and self-love is meant to undermine one objection that people commonly urge against conscience. He does not agree that he needs a proof of the coincidence if he is to give us a sufficient reason to follow conscience.

709. The Legitimate Claims of Self-Love

Sidgwick's interpretation, however, may appear more plausible once we notice that Butler, in his own voice and not by way of concession, claims that an appeal to self-interest is the only way of gaining 'access to the understanding'. He does not criticize the tendency of most people to look at their lives from the point of view of self-love. On the contrary, he assumes that we ought to approach even the most enlightened understanding through self-love. He advocates this approach even though he insists on the reality of moral facts, constituted by relations of fitness.

We might argue that Butler is referring to the possibility of access to the understandings of other people who are not convinced of the authority of conscience. Once we are convinced of this authority, why should we still appeal to self-love to justify us in the pursuit of what is right and good as such? This attempt to restrict Butler's appeal to self-love would be an unjustifiably extreme reaction to Sidgwick's view. Butler's view on the nature and relation of conscience and self-love makes it reasonable to appeal to self-love in support of conscience.[66]

---

[63] The concessive reading is supported by the long sentence 'It may be allowed . . .', where Butler makes it clear that he is 'allowing' several things. See Sturgeon, 'Nature' 338; Broad, FTET 80.

[64] Rivers, RGS i 85–6, describes a similar approach to the benefits of religion among latitudinarian writers. See also McAdoo, SA 173–5, who correctly emphasizes the connexions between Anglican writers and traditional eudaemonism.

[65] Broad, FTET 80–1, does not do justice to Butler on this point.

[66] White, 'Conscience and self-love', argues that Butler's appeal to self-love arises from a concern with motivation, and the belief that conscience and recognition of moral rightness provide too weak a motive. Taylor, 'Features', treats

For a successful defence of the harmony of self-love and conscience supports the claim that it is natural to follow conscience. We will be more readily disposed to allow that the attitudes connected with morality are central aspects of our nature, if we are not also disposed to believe that they conflict with self-interest.

Butler's conception of human nature treats it as a system, rather than a mere collection of traits. It is a system because its different features, impulses, and principles include mutual harmony, and co-operation. Rational self-love is natural because it introduces co-operation into a series of impulses and propensities that would otherwise be liable to conflict and mutual frustration. If conscience is natural, it should introduce co-operation between self-love, its subordinate impulses, and the further considerations that are relevant when we consider our relations to other people. A sharp conflict between self-love and conscience would imply that two superior principles tend to impede, or even to undermine, each other. Human nature might form a system under the guidance of self-love, and a system under the guidance of conscience, but if the two systems tended to clash, we would have reason to doubt whether they constituted a single system.

Butler takes our aims, motives, and principles to constitute a system under conscience. But his case for this claim is weaker if they also constitute a system under reasonable self-love, and this system conflicts with conscience. His belief in the natural character of conscience is more plausible if self-love and conscience agree. If we thought that some action violating morality would be in our interest, we might be inclined to suspect that our moral concerns are dispensable, non-essential aspects of ourselves. Butler's argument for the harmony of self-love and conscience neither blurs the distinctness of the two principles nor compromises the supremacy of conscience.

710. Different Conceptions of Self-Love

This stage in Butler's argument revives a question that we raised in discussing his views about self-love and benevolence. We noticed that he relied on a narrow hedonistic conception of self-love, and that this was the basis for his claim that self-love does not care about the objects of first-order desires for their own sakes. This is the conception of self-love that he has in mind in the discussion of the harmony of self-love and conscience. He assumes that when self-love considers whether we should act on conscience, it simply considers the possible yield of pleasure, contentment, and so on. This is why he thinks that someone who chooses morally virtuous action for self-interested reasons is following the Epicurean policy, and does not take the 'religious or even moral institution of life' (P 41). This person does not choose virtuous actions for their own sakes, and so cannot act from the virtuous motive.

This claim assumes that self-love does not care about actions for their own sake, but only for their resulting pain or pleasure. But this view of self-love casts doubt on Butler's claim about the harmony of self-love and conscience. For different people find different

the passage on the cool hour as ad hominem (296: 'dialectical concession to the audience'). He appeals to the passage on Shaftesbury in the Preface, which asserts obligation from conscience independent of self-love. These views of the passage on the cool hour both underestimate the significance of Butler's naturalism.

things pleasant and painful. Why expect that adherence to conscience will maximize each person's pleasure?

Price and Sidgwick agree with this criticism of Butler, and infer that he ought not to have maintained the harmony of self-love and conscience.[67] But the doctrine of harmony is neither an optional extra in Butler's position nor a mere persuasive device for commending morality to those who do not accept it for better reasons. We have seen that it is also part of Butler's defence of the natural character of conscience and morality.[68] If Butler abandoned the doctrine of harmony, he would seriously weaken his naturalism as well. Price and Sidgwick see this, and so they abandon Butler's naturalism when they abandon his doctrine of harmony.

But we might strengthen Butler's overall position if we questioned his narrowly hedonistic conception of self-love. In accepting this conception he departs sharply from the naturalism of the ancient moralists. According to Aristotelian eudaemonism, happiness is the composite human good, and self-love is directed towards this good. This Aristotelian conception justifies the claim that self-love is a superior principle. Self-love takes the point of view of myself as a whole only if its aims include whatever is worth pursuing for its own sake. A holist conception of nature requires a holist conception of self-love. This conception of self-love underlies Aquinas' claims about the desire for happiness. Butler's naturalism about self-love, therefore, seems to require Aristotelian eudaemonism, rather than Butler's hedonist conception of self-love.

Butler, however, also departs from Aristotelian naturalism by separating conscience from self-love; his hedonistic conception of self-love makes it easier to justify this separation. If he accepted an Aristotelian conception of self-love, could he still avoid Aristotelian eudaemonism about conscience?

The narrow conception of self-love that Butler needs in order to make conscience external to self-love recalls Scotus' separation of the affection for justice from the affection for advantage.[69] However, he differs sharply from Scotus; for Scotus connects only the affection for advantage with nature; he attaches the affection for justice to reason and freedom as opposed to nature. In Scotus' view, the rejection of eudaemonism requires the rejection of naturalism. Butler retains naturalism, and, though he rejects eudaemonism, he retains the doctrine of harmony. The difficulties that he faces in retaining the doctrine of harmony tend to support Scotus' view that naturalism and eudaemonism need each other.

In contrast to Scotus, Aquinas rejects the narrow conception of self-love. In his view, any attempt to oppose self-love to the other-regarding virtues rests on a mistake about the character and objects of self-love. Enlightened self-love, in his view, does not value one's own self-confined good above the good of others. One the contrary, once our self-love is enlightened, we will love God more than ourselves.

Aquinas' broad conception of self-love vindicates Butler's claims in Sermon xi about self-love and benevolence. But how does it affect Butler's reasons for taking conscience to be superior to self-love? Does Butler still see some important feature of conscience that cannot be subordinated even to extended self-love as Aquinas conceives it?

Aquinas ought to agree with Butler's claim that conscience is distinct from self-love. The considerations that weigh with conscience are those that make an action morally right.

---

[67] Cf. Price, §805; Sidgwick, *ME* 501–2.   [68] Cf. Reid, §856.   [69] On Scotus see §§364, 368.

Aquinas and Suarez recognize these considerations in their discussion of the honestum. Considerations of my own happiness do not necessarily appear in the deliberation that is required for identifying the morally right action; and, since a virtuous person takes the rightness of an action as a sufficient reason for doing it, virtuous people do not need to consider their own happiness in deciding what to do, when moral questions are involved.

It does not follow, however, that conscience weighs reasons that are entirely outside the scope of self-love. Butler sometimes suggests that self-love considers only my own private good—that is, the good for me in abstraction from any concern for the good of others. Conscience, by contrast, considers the legitimate claims of other people, and treats my private good as only one of the considerations that matter in identifying the morally right action. This view of the relation between conscience and self-love presupposes a narrow view of self-love.

Against Butler one might argue, on Aquinas' behalf, that enlightened self-love accepts the claim of conscience to regulate the relations between oneself and others, and even accepts its claim to override the conclusions that self-love would have reached without reference to conscience. Self-love has good reasons to accept the claims of conscience, on the strength of this argument: (1) Self-love takes a holistic view of my interest, referring to my nature as a whole; that is why action on self-love is natural. (2) My nature as a whole requires me to accept the place that conscience accords to the legitimate demands of other people, since my nature requires me to regard myself as a responsible agent making legitimate demands on them. (3) Therefore, enlightened self-love also accepts this prescription of conscience.

This defence of Aquinas' position is stronger if we accept Butler's case for the second claim. He makes it clearer than Aristotelian naturalists do why the point of view of conscience deserves to be practically overriding from the naturalist point of view. Though the argument we have offered is a defence of Aquinas' views about self-love and morality, the premises are Butler's. The holistic conception of self-love does not fit what Butler says about the relation of self-love to conscience, but it fits his views about the natural character of self-love. Hence, Butler ought to accept the defence of Aristotelian eudaemonism.

Acceptance of Aristotelian eudaemonism requires some revision in Butler's doctrine of the supremacy of conscience, but does not require him to abandon this doctrine entirely. From the Aristotelian eudaemonist point of view, conscience is supreme insofar as it is the overriding guide to action, but self-love is supreme, insofar as it is the principle that decides on the overriding guide to action. Perhaps one might say that conscience is supreme from the practical point of view, but self-love is supreme from a higher-order deliberative point of view.

This account of the relation of self-love and conscience suggests a defence of Butler's claims about their harmony. It does not rest on a narrow conception of self-love. Hence it does not make morality simply a device (from the point of view of self-love) for securing one's own independently determined interests.

711. Questions about Butler and Aristotelian Eudaemonism

This defence of Aristotelian eudaemonism tends to show that Butler's main claims about self-love and conscience are more plausible, and constitute a stronger case for naturalism, without his narrow conception of self-love, and without the specific argument for the supremacy of conscience that depends on the narrow conception of self-love.

The defence may be over-simplified, however. Perhaps it overlooks part of Butler's case for the separation of conscience from self-love and for the supremacy of conscience. Perhaps an assessment from the point of view of self-love gives a different sort of weight to moral considerations from the weight we would give them from the point of view of conscience; for perhaps part of our nature requires a degree of commitment to morality that we might rationally follow even if it conflicts with the other goals that appeal to fully-informed self-love. In that case there would still be some point in claiming that conscience has grounds, based on appeal to our nature as whole selves, for overriding the arguments of self-love.

Butler does not clearly decide between two accounts of why self-love and conscience agree. One picture treats conscience as, in a sense, subordinate to self-love, from the point of view of self-love. According to this picture, self-love is concerned with the agent's private interest above all; but it sees that this interest is best secured by allowing the place to conscience that conscience demands for itself on moral grounds. We can reach this conclusion when we see that the attitude characteristic of conscience is a central part of my nature as a rational agent, and therefore a central element in a true conception of myself and my interest.

A second picture treats conscience as superior to self-love, even from the point of view of self-love. According to this picture, self-love does not place one's private interest above everything, but simply demands fair and appropriate treatment for it, both in relation to one's particular passions and in relation to the demands of other people. Self-love acknowledges the authority of conscience if it recognizes that conscience treats it fairly. We might take this conception of self-love to underlie the demand to be shown that morality 'will be for our happiness, or at least not contrary to it'. Perhaps the second possibility is satisfied if conscience rejects unjust treatment of my claims in relation to the claims of others.

An analogy to illustrate these two conceptions of self-love might be drawn from two sorts of relations between different authorities. In co-operation between independent states, each side must be assured that co-operative action promotes its own private interest. In relations between subordinate and superordinate authorities, a less stringent demand is normal. A provincial government in a federal system, for instance, does not accept each federal law only if it is in the interest of the province, but it expects not to be treated unfairly, and to have its legitimate interests satisfied, by federal legislation as a whole. If self-love is this sort of subordinate authority, it can look out for private interests without asserting the deliberative supremacy of its own point of view.

It is difficult to say which of these pictures of self-love is closest to Butler's intentions. It is therefore difficult to say what the point of view of self-love really considers and what moves it. The obscurities in his view of self-love result in obscurities about the attitude of self-love to the demands of conscience.

Butler does not offer much argument to show that the point of view of conscience on ourselves—as agents who deserve a certain kind of treatment and regard ourselves as entitled to demand it—is rationally inescapable in the way that the point of view of self-love is. Argument of this sort is needed to show that conscience is natural and supreme. Even though Butler's treatment is sketchy, it is worth mentioning the connexions that he sees between moral judgment, conceptions of desert and responsibility, and conceptions of oneself. The connexions are quite suggestive and important in themselves, and they are even more important because Kant develops some of them.[70]

These arguments draw our attention to features of conscience and moral attitudes that Aristotelian eudaemonists do not explore as fully as Butler explores them. Do they constitute an objection, or a supplement, to Aristotelian eudaemonism? If moral attitudes are central in rational agents' enlightened conception of themselves, it seems plausible to claim that they are central in any reasonable conception of one's own happiness; for happiness—as Aquinas understands it—involves concern for oneself and for one's perfection. The more convincing detail we provide in support of Butler's position, the better a case we make for incorporating it within Aristotelian eudaemonism. This conclusion is worth emphasizing about Butler, since it is worth bearing in mind when we consider Kant. Kant departs further than Butler departs from Aristotelian eudaemonism, since he rejects the naturalist account of virtue and the harmony of self-love and conscience. But we need to ask whether the reasons that should persuade Butler to accept Aristotelian naturalism apply in some form to Kant as well.

---

[70] Kant's discussion of morality and the highest good (*KpV*, Bk. ii, ch. 2) is relevant to Butler's questions about the supremacy of conscience.

54

BUTLER: IMPLICATIONS OF NATURALISM

712. Different Views of Butler

Now that we have examined Butler's claims about nature and morality, we can consider their implications for the moral controversies that form the background for the *Sermons*. Butler intends his naturalism as a normative and as a meta-ethical doctrine. We saw earlier that he does not align himself with sentimentalists or rationalists, but claims to defend a naturalist position that is not exposed to the criticisms that, in his view, undermine a sentimentalist version of naturalism. How far does he describe and defend this version of naturalism?

Different critics have taken surprisingly different views of Butler's eventual position and of its relations to other views. In discussing Hutcheson and Balguy we examined some of the contrasts that Selby-Bigge and Whewell draw in their different divisions between schools of moral philosophers. Butler offers us a further opportunity to see how different philosophers take different issues to be connected.

Selby-Bigge places him in the 'sentimental school', perhaps because of his appeal to nature and his view that the operations of conscience involve both the understanding and the heart.[1] The references to nature seem to distinguish him from the rationalists Clarke and Balguy and to align him with Shaftesbury and Hutcheson, whom Selby-Bigge classifies as sentimentalists. The view of conscience that Selby-Bigge imputes to Butler also aligns him with sentimentalists. He suggests that, for Butler, the authority of conscience consists in its reflective character; and that the reflective favour of conscience constitutes rightness.

This interpretation has some contemporary support. Selby-Bigge refers appropriately to Kames's criticism of Butler's view about authority, He also claims, less plausibly, that Price criticizes Butler in the same way.[2] If this is the right view of Butler, his position is a variation on Hutcheson's. Hutcheson seems to understand Butler in this way, and hence uses some of Butler's ideas in developing his own position.[3]

Selby-Bigge recognizes that this classification does not cope with everything Butler says. He suggests that the way Butler states his position 'looks almost like a sop to the

---

[1] See §719.   [2] See §720.   [3] See §715.

intellectualists' (*BM* i, p. xlvi).[4] But this does not lead him to question Butler's place among the sentimentalists; it simply leads him to treat Butler as an ambiguous and reticent sentimentalist.[5]

Whewell, however, treats Butler not as a sentimentalist, but as an 'unsystematic' moralist who recognizes a 'moral faculty' without describing it in as much detail as Hutcheson does (*LHMPE* 108). Butler, in his view, avoids technical expressions for our moral capacities. Among the non-technical phrases that Whewell takes to be equivalent, he mentions 'man's being a law to himself', 'a difference in kind among man's principles of action, as well as a difference in strength', 'an internal constitution in which conscience has a natural and rightful supremacy' (*LHMPE* 108–9). Still, he takes Butler to be a defender of 'independent' morality. As evidence he cites some of the same phrases about superiority and authority.[6] He concludes, therefore, that Butler really belongs with Cudworth and Clarke, and expresses their position unsystematically.[7]

These differences of opinion about Butler may simply show that Butler is reticent and ambiguous, but they may also point out some difficulties in the options that interpreters consider. If a sentimentalist is one who attributes some important epistemic role to sentiments as well as to rational judgment, we might have a good case for placing Butler with the sentimentalists. But if sentimentalism involves the claim that moral rightness is constituted by the approval of some sentiment, emotion, or moral sense, Butler is not a sentimentalist. Whewell is right to treat him as a defender of independent morality, and to emphasize his criticisms of Shaftesbury on authority.

A more extreme version of Whewell's view emphasizes the points on which Butler agrees with Clarke, especially in his rejection of voluntarism and acceptance of intrinsic fitness. The *Sermons* (on this view) presuppose Clarke's position, without stating it at length. On this view, Butler does not take the view that Selby-Bigge and Kames attribute to him, of taking moral rightness to be constituted by the reflective approval of conscience, but believes that

---

[4] On Selby-Bigge's and Darwall's view see §720.

[5] A note on the Dissertation in Angus's edition (320–1, partly quoted by Gladstone) offers a summary of Butler's relation to other moralists: 'Butler's reasoning in this chapter has very much the character of Dr Reid's "philosophy", giving the instinctive principles of our nature a greater prominence than has often been given them by metaphysicians . . . He admits, with Clarke, that the distinction between right and wrong is eternal, and that the distinction is founded on the fitness of things, but with characteristic wisdom he seeks the evidence of this distinction and one foundation for it in human nature. . . . His account of the origin of the idea of merit, and of its connexion with a reflex sense, is probably taken from Shaftesbury . . . By giving prudence a place among the virtues, he opposes Hutcheson, allows whatever of truth is to be found in Hobbes's system, and explains it. . . . Benevolence he reckons a most important virtue, and yet denies, against Leibniz, that all virtue is resolvable into it. In his doctrine of a moral sense he agrees substantially with Hutcheson, his contemporary. . . . he gives an idea of the "fitness of moral acts"; an idea more practical at all events than that of Clarke. . . . [He] answers by anticipation the theory of Bentham, that virtue is a regard for the happiness of others, as the dissertation throughout answers the theory of Paley.' The most serious error in Angus's account is the assimilation of Butler to Hutcheson. He is vague about the relation between Butler's naturalism and Clarke's rationalism. He is right to emphasize the connexion between Butler and Shaftesbury, and Butler's opposition to utilitarianism (which he discusses further at 331).

[6] On Whewell cf. §520.

[7] 'These notions so steadily adhered to—of a difference of kind; a peculiar constitution of man in which each faculty and motive principle has its place; a nature which determines what ought to be as well as what is; relations which are seen and apprehended as manifest by contemplation of the conceptions which they involve—are the proper characters of the school of independent morality, and show how justly Butler, notwithstanding some vagueness, and perhaps some vacillation of expression, is taken as one of the principal philosophers who have upheld that side of the great antithesis of opinion on the foundations of morals.' (Whewell, *LHMPE* 111)

conscience perceives eternal fitnesses and applies this perception to our other motives and principles.[8] According to this view, Butler holds the position that Whewell ascribes to him, but he does not hold it 'unsystematically'; he simply does not parade the views of Clarke, which he nonetheless accepts.

These different views of Butler may be the result of his own inexplicitness and brevity, or they may reflect genuine ambiguities in his position. It may not be Butler's fault, however, if critics find him difficult to classify. They may be asking the wrong questions, or looking for the wrong things in Butler. He cannot be accused of inexplicitness in saying what he is trying to do. He rejects both Wollaston's attempt to discard an appeal to nature and Shaftesbury's attempt to explain moral authority within a sentimentalist framework. If we look beyond Cudworth to Suarez and to Aquinas, we see the connexion between Butler's own intellectual environment and the ancient moralists whose position he seeks to defend. We can now try to see what this form of naturalism implies about the meta-ethical questions that divide sentimentalists from rationalists.

To decide about the implications of Butler's naturalism, it will be useful to return briefly to Butler's arguments against Hobbesian and sentimentalist views about nature and morality, to see what meta-ethical position he arrives at by defending his version of naturalism against these opponents.

713. Butler and Hobbes on Nature

Butler's most explicit attack on Hobbes rejects Hobbes's psychological hedonism, in order to question the basis of Hobbes's belief that we have no reason to be moral unless it is in our interest. But even if Butler proved that, contrary to Hobbes, it is psychologically possible for us to care about morality apart from our self-interest, we might still agree with Hobbes in thinking we have no reason to care about morality apart from our self-interest. A positive defence of morality against Hobbes needs to show that we have some reason that Hobbes overlooks for being concerned about morality even when the state does not make it advantageous for us.

Butler uses his conception of nature against Hobbes's view that morality is not natural for human beings and becomes rational only in a commonwealth. In Butler's view, the facts about nature that appear in Hobbes's argument are relevant only to the first and second senses of 'nature'. Once we grasp the third sense, we see that it is natural to follow the appropriate superior principles. Self-love is an appropriate superior principle, and so we have reason to follow self-love. Since the considerations about nature that support the naturalness of self-love also support the naturalness of conscience, Butler concludes that we have the same reason to follow conscience as we have to follow self-love.

This argument is dialectically effective against Hobbes. For Hobbes agrees that we have reason to follow self-love; but, in Butler's view, he does not give a good account of what that reason is, since he mistakenly relies on a purely psychological conception of strength of desires. He therefore has to endorse the implausible reduction of claims about reasons to

---

[8] See Penelhum, *B* 10–11. He argues that Butler accepts Clark's position, and simply refrains from appealing to it.

predictions about the strength of desires. In fact our reason for following self-love is the fact that self-love is a superior principle that prescribes natural action. Once we see the correct explanation of our reason for following self-love, we see that we cannot consistently agree with Hobbes in thinking we have reason to follow self-love unless we also admit that our nature gives us just the same sort of reason to follow conscience.

714. Butler and Sentimentalism

In rejecting the reduction of all motives to the selfish pursuit of one's own interest, Butler agrees with Hutcheson. It is not surprising that Hutcheson often draws on Butler in his later work.[9] Butler also agrees with Hutcheson in not endorsing the extreme rationalism of Clarke and Balguy.[10] But his argument about nature implies that Hutcheson repeats some of Hobbes's mistakes. Hutcheson agrees with Butler in identifying natural actions and states teleologically and holistically, by reference to the requirements of a human being as a whole.[11] But his argument to show that benevolence is natural does not stick to this conception of nature; he argues only that benevolence arises by nature, and is not derived from the pursuit of the expedient. This claim relies only on Butler's first and second senses of 'natural', and does not take account of the third sense.

Butler's account of human nature assigns an important place to practical reason, both in prudence and in morality, that sharply distinguishes his view from the sentimentalist position. He differs from sentimentalists insofar as he argues from facts about human nature, as opposed to facts about human feelings and sentiments. In his view, facts about nature are relevant because they provide reasons independent of the actual desires of particular human beings. He therefore rejects Hobbes's view of practical reason, and Hutcheson's view of justifying reasons.

The difference between Butler's position and the sentimentalist position on these issues is summed up in his criticism of Shaftesbury for failing to grasp the essential features of the authority of conscience (P 26). Shaftesbury does not hold a purely sentimentalist view on this question; for on several points he anticipates Butler's appeal to nature. Nonetheless, Butler identifies a central difference between Shaftesbury (at least in some of his remarks) and a traditional naturalist view. Shaftesbury tends to argue as though our reason for preferring virtue over vice is the more strongly favourable feeling we acquire towards it when we recognize what it is. This assumption underlies his description of the case 'without remedy'. We may doubt whether Shaftesbury would accept the implications of his position, as Butler describes them, but Butler is justified in objecting that Shaftesbury fails to distinguish the authority from the psychological strength of conscience. Criticisms of Butler's objection to Shaftesbury simply make clear the point that Butler objects to.[12]

---

[9] On Hutcheson see §633. Butler's influence is present in *SMP* at, e.g., i 61, 74, 101, 256.

[10] On the different contrasts drawn by Butler and Hume see §§727–8.

[11] Hutcheson, *HN* §§7–9. On Hutcheson and naturalism see §636.

[12] Part of Wishart's defence of Shaftesbury (see §614) consists of an attack on Butler both for unacknowledged borrowings from Shaftesbury and for the misinterpretation that underlies the objection to Shaftesbury on authority. 'A memorable instance of this kind [sc. of injustice to Shaftesbury] we have in the Reverend Mr Butler, who, after he

Butler argues that when we understand virtue better, we do not simply find that we feel like following it; we see that it deserves to be followed. Contrary to Shaftesbury's view, the authority of conscience consists not in the fact that people tend to feel favourable to it, but in the fact that conscience provides reasons that deserve to be followed in preference to other reasons.[13] To defend this disagreement with Shaftesbury, Butler needs an account of justifying reasons (as Hutcheson calls them) that makes them independent of sentiment.

715. Hutcheson v. Butler on Conscience

Some of the differences between Hutcheson's and Butler's versions of naturalism appear more clearly from Hutcheson's attempt to fit Butler's doctrine into sentimentalism. He notices that, according to Butler, conscience is supreme insofar as it is a 'principle of reflexion' that reflects on the other principles that we act on, and either approves or disapproves of them. In his *Introduction to Moral Philosophy* Hutcheson identifies this principle with the moral sense. He claims that conscience, or the moral sense, is the most divine of the senses, that it is disinterested, and that is directed to the general good.[14] He connects the moral sense with reflexion and approval. If it is capable, as it seems to be, of reflecting on, and reacting to, other practical principles, it is supreme in relation to them.

If we recall the origin and grounds for Hutcheson's doctrine of the moral sense, it is easier to see why he might suppose he could readily incorporate Butler's views, and why other people might tend to assimilate his position to Butler's. In his earlier work Hutcheson takes himself to be defending Shaftesbury's 'moral realism', which he interprets as the doctrine that we are capable of disinterested approval of moral goodness apart from any belief about our own interest. If we use 'moral sense' simply to name our capacity to recognize and to approve this moral goodness, those who disagree with Mandeville and Hobbes believe

had plumed himself up in the borrowed feathers of Lord Shaftesbury and published a volume of curious and elaborate discourses, under the title of Sermons, wherein it may be evident to anyone who reads both, that he has borrowed almost all his light and discoveries from him, without ever making the least acknowledgment to him, has in a second edition published a preface, in which he has misinterpreted him in the grossest manner, and so as it is hard for any man to help thinking the misrepresentations to be wilful and designed.' (*Vindic.* 82–3) In answer to Butler, Wishart simply cites passages on the psychological strength of conscience; 'How clearly and elegantly does Lord Shaftesbury show that the checks and reproofs of one's own conscience are naturally stronger than his sense of the greatest shame and odium from others?' (86) Wishart tries to strengthen his defence by appealing to Shaftesbury's remarks on the moral sense: 'Does he not, in the Inquiry concerning Virtue, show how natural and essential to our frame a moral sense is? Which, as it has a respect to our own actions, is the same thing with conscience, or the foundation of it.' (87) By assimilating conscience to the moral sense (as Shaftesbury understands it) Wishart introduces a further element of obscurity in Shaftesbury's position, and fails to answer Butler's main point. Rivers, *RGS* ii 167, comments on Wishart's attack on Butler. Price, *RPQM* 190n (quoted in §802) agrees with Butler's objection to Shaftesbury.

[13] On Shaftesbury see §610. Adams, *NOV* 17–18, states this distinction of Butler's briefly: 'I am not here speaking of the force and efficacy of this principle, but of its authority and pre-eminence . . . and we are, even when we desert her service, obliged, in spite of ourselves, to acknowledge her authority as a law written in our hearts . . . '

[14] 'That this divine sense or conscience naturally approving these more extensive affections should be the governing power in man, appears both immediately from its own nature, as we immediately feel that it naturally assumes a right of judging, approving, or condemning all the various motions of the soul; as also from this that every good man applauds himself, approves entirely his own temper, and is then best pleased with himself when he refrains not only the lower sensual appetites, but even the more sublime ones of a selfish kind, or the more narrow and contracted affections of love toward kindred or friends, or even his country, when they interfere with the more extensive interests of mankind and the common prosperity of all.' (Hutcheson, *IMP* 23)

in a moral sense. From this point of view George Turnbull, an admirer of Shaftesbury, treats both Hutcheson and Butler as defenders of Shaftesbury, and therefore as exponents of the moral sense. In his view, the differences between rationalists and sentimentalists are simply disagreements about what to call the moral sense, and not about its existence. His position is reasonable if he uses 'moral sense' simply to indicate what opponents of Hobbes all recognize.[15]

This appeal to Butler is instructive because it tries to capture Butler's notion of superiority and supremacy by reference to higher-order attitudes.[16] Martineau argues, indeed, that Hutcheson's later views of the moral sense adopt Butler's position.[17] Hume also takes Hutcheson's claims about the superiority of the moral sense to agree with Butler; he argues that this concession to Butler does not fit Hutcheson's general view.[18]

But Martineau and Hume over-estimate the degree to which Hutcheson agrees with Butler. Though he goes some way towards acceptance of Butler's view of conscience, he stops short on one crucial point. In Butler's view, superior principles essentially appeal to authority rather than mere strength. If conscience is supreme, it is also most authoritative. If it has authority to decide the questions it decides, it appeals to considerations that take legitimate precedence over the considerations that lower principles appeal to. One might infer that a supreme principle, so understood, must be a rational principle. But Hutcheson rejects that inference. He does not treat the moral sense as rational.

Similarly, Hutcheson disallows rational correction of the moral sense. His opponents assume that it is corrigible by reason, and so they infer that the supreme principle, superior to a moral sense, is a rational principle. Hutcheson concedes corrigibility, but denies that

[15] Turnbull defends belief in a moral sense to 'such philosophers as do not deny the thing, but seem to quarrel with the name . . .' (PMP 124). ' . . . it is no great matter for the name, if the thing itself in question be acknowledged. And it certainly is by all, who acknowledge the difference between good and evil; however they may choose to express that difference by calling it truth, reasonableness, fitness, or by whatever other appellations. For if there is truth, fitness, or reasonableness in actions with regard to us, it is perceivable by us; and if we perceive it, we are capable of perceiving it; that is, we have the faculty requisite to perceiving it, or which enables us to perceive it' (125). He allows that this capacity may be described in rationalist terms as reason perceiving fitnesses; 'But moral sense, moral taste, moral discernment, or moral conscience, well express it; and seem to be the properest phrases in our language to answer to those used to signify the same determination in our nature by ancient philosophers.' (128) He refers, as Reid (a pupil of Turnbull's) does later, to ancient sources that mention a 'sensus decori et honesti'. See §§635, 842. Turnbull is discussed by Rivers, RGS ii 179–80.

[16] Some of the difficulties faced by Hutcheson's strategy are parallel to those faced by Frankfurt's account of freedom, in 'Freedom'.

[17] 'In the "System" he calls the "moral sense", in the very heading of the chapter devoted to it, "the *faculty* of perceiving moral excellence, and its supreme objects". [SMP i 4, 53 (Concerning the Moral Sense)] I need not point out that the subjective "sense", or passive susceptibility to a certain "pleasure" relative to men has here become an objective "faculty" or active apprehension of "an *independent quality* immediately perceived in certain affections and actions consequent upon them" (as he shortly afterwards expresses it). [SMP i 4, 58] From a form of sensibility we are handed over to a cognitive power; and instead of a special "pleasure" to be received, we have a mental energy to be put forth. Still more marked is this feature, when he says that the "faculty" carries in its very nature the prerogative of commanding and controlling the other powers, appreciating as it does a quality superior to any with which the others have to do. [SMP i 4.6, 61] Here surely we hear a voice in tune with the deep authoritative tones of Butler, rather than with the soft and winning tenor of Shaftesbury.' (Martineau, TET ii 536–7) Martineau's second reference appears to be inexact. Hutcheson speaks of the moral sense as 'a natural and immediate determination to approve certain affections and actions consequent upon them; or a natural sense of immediate excellence in them, not referred to any other quality perceivable by our other senses or by reasoning' (SMP i 4.4, 58). He does not use 'independent quality', though 'not referred to . . .' might be taken to imply it.

[18] For Hume's criticism of Hutcheson's IMP on conscience see §779.

reason corrects. He argues by analogy, pointing out that theoretical reason is wrong if it judges hastily or on insufficient evidence, but we still use reason to correct reason, by reconsideration. Similarly, the moral sense corrects and regulates itself.[19] According to Hutcheson, Butler's phenomenological tests for identifying conscience as the supreme principle pick out the moral sense; they do not require a rational principle.

Hutcheson assumes that Butler must establish the supremacy of conscience by phenomenological tests. To interpret Butler this way is to over-emphasize his appeal to reflexion and to under-emphasize his appeal to authority. An authoritative principle demonstrates its right to override lower principles, by appealing to the superior weight of the reasons it appeals to, not to the psychological strength of the desires it appeals to. This understanding of authority makes it difficult to see how a feeling of approval could be authoritative.

It is not surprising that Hutcheson overlooks this aspect of Butler's view of supremacy; for it rests on the division between power and authority, which has no place in Hutcheson's conception of reasons. His conception of justifying reasons differs from Butler's conception of authoritative principles on precisely the point that distinguishes their views about supremacy. The difference between Butler's position and Hutcheson's is summed up in Butler's criticism of Shaftesbury for failing to grasp the essential features of the authority of conscience (P 26).

Both Hume and Price notice that Hutcheson's position on authority is unsatisfactory. In Hume's view, the concession to Butler is a mistake. In Price's view, Hutcheson is right to agree with Butler, but wrong to suppose that the moral sense meets Butler's conditions for an authoritative principle.[20] Both critics argue, from their opposite points of view, that Hutcheson can restore consistency to his position only by moving either to a more rationalist or to a more anti-rationalist view.

716. Normative Naturalism v. Rationalism

Though Butler accepts rationalist criticisms of sentimentalist naturalism, he does not agree with extreme rationalist claims about the immutability of right and wrong. For if he is right about morality and nature, right and wrong would change if what is required by a human being as a whole system were to change. In his view, what is right is right because it is required by a human being as a whole system. On these points, Butler is right to claim that he affirms a traditional conception of nature and morality. It is the conception affirmed by Suarez.

These naturalist claims as they stand are not very clear, because 'required' is not clear. But Butler explains what the relevant sorts of requirement are, by introducing his general idea of a superior principle and his specific claims about the correct superior principles that

---

[19] 'This moral sense from its very nature appears to be designed for regulating and controlling all our powers. This dignity and commanding nature we are immediately conscious of, as we are confident of the power itself. Nor can such matters of immediate feeling be otherways proved but by appeals to our hearts. . . . It does not estimate the good it recommends as merely differing in degree . . . But as we immediately perceive the difference in kind, and that the dignity of enjoyment from fine poetry, painting, or from knowledge is superior to the pleasures of the palate, were they never so delicate; so we immediately discern moral good to be superior in kind and dignity to all others which are perceived by the other perceptive powers.' (*SMP* i 4.6, 61)

[20] See Price, *RPQM* 215n, discussed in §816.

he recognizes. Since the requirements he defends rely on authority rather than on strength of desire, they are distinct from Hutcheson's claims about nature.

We might mark this difference between Butler's and Hutcheson's naturalism by saying that Hutcheson is a purely psychological naturalist, but Butler is a normative naturalist. Normative naturalism does not seem to be subject to the open question argument derived from Cudworth.[21] This argument challenges Hobbes's legal conception of moral rightness by pointing out that we can raise a reasonable moral question about whether a legislator has the right to legislate, and that the answer to this question requires judgments about rightness that is not the product of legislation. Similarly, as Balguy argues against Hutcheson, we can reasonably ask whether the moral sense judges correctly, and we appeal to some rightness independent of the judgment of the moral sense. But, in Butler's view, no further reasonable question of this sort arises about the rightness of what is appropriate to nature. The normative element expressed by 'appropriate' leaves no room for the sort of question that Balguy raises about Hutcheson.

If this is the difference between Butler's and Hutcheson's naturalism, does Butler improve on Hutcheson? Is his normative naturalism empty, or question-begging, or does it commit him to uselessly circular accounts of moral properties? The desire to avoid emptiness and circularity is one of Hutcheson's reasons for favouring purely psychological naturalism. When Balguy offers accounts of normative properties that do not reduce them to purely psychological properties, Hutcheson complains that non-reductive accounts are uninformative; they are 'mere synonymies' that do not 'explicate' moral properties.[22]

The dispute between Hutcheson and Balguy is relevant to Butler's normative naturalism. If we accept Hutcheson's objections to Balguy, we may argue that Butler's normative naturalism leads him back to Clarke and Balguy; for perhaps he offers us only the empty and uninformative accounts of moral properties that we find in Clarke and Balguy. Perhaps Butler's version of naturalism is simply a circuitous route to accounts that share the non-explanatory features of rationalist accounts of moral properties.

This conclusion, however, overlooks an important difference between Butler and the rationalists. Even if Butler's naturalism fails to provide a non-normative 'explication' of moral properties, it makes morality more mutable than it appears to be in the rationalists' view. In their view, gratitude is the appropriate and fitting response to a benefaction, and we can see this simply from consideration of the definitions of these actions and attitudes themselves.[23] To deny that benefaction requires gratitude is parallel to denying that being a triangle requires having internal angles adding up to two right angles.

The epistemological and metaphysical implications of these rationalist claims are different from the implications of Butler's claims. According to Butler, rightness and wrongness rest on the requirements of human nature as a system. To know what these requirements are, we cannot simply attend, say, to the relation of benefactor and beneficiary. We need to attend to the further facts that we discover in considering a human being as a system. These

---

[21] On Cudworth see §551.   [22] See Hutcheson, *IMS* 165 = R 373, quoted in §656.

[23] See Balguy, *FMG* i = *TMT*66 = SB 542–5, quoted in §665. It is sometimes difficult to be sure how far Balguy differs from Butler, since he speaks of the 'nature' of the agent or recipient in a morally good or bad action. But he seems to mean (for instance) the agent's nature as a benefactor or the recipient's as a beneficiary—i.e., the bare fact that one is a benefactor and one a beneficiary—rather than their nature as human beings.

further facts are not purely non-normative psychological facts; they are those that Butler appeals to in arguing for the naturalness of self-love and conscience. They show that we have some conception of human nature as a system that justifies self-love and conscience. Normative naturalism, therefore, is not simply Clarke's rationalism in disguise.

But if we vindicate Butler on this point, we might doubt whether Clarke's rationalism and Butler's normative naturalism provide complementary lines of argument. Agreement with Butler seems to require disagreement with Clarke, since Butler implies that morality is mutable in relation to some facts that, according to Clarke, are not sources of mutability.

This contrast between Butler and Clarke, however, may be too sharp to fit everything Clarke says. For Clarke does not say exactly what the eternal fitnesses have to fit. Sometimes he speaks of fitting the nature of the agent and the action; Balguy also explains the relevant type of fitness in this way. It is excusable for Butler to attack Wollaston without attacking Clarke; for Wollaston commits himself much more firmly than Clarke and Balguy commit themselves to a narrow construal of fitness that does not involve reference to human nature.

This assessment of Butler's relation to Clarke suggests a conclusion about Butler's relation to Cudworth. If Butler's account of morality does not introduce the open questions that Balguy takes to be introduced by Hutcheson's account, Butler shows that we can accept Cudworth's argument without accepting Clarke's and Balguy's extreme rationalism. This conclusion is useful, since we might reasonably find Cudworth's argument more plausible than the extreme rationalist conclusions that Clarke and Balguy claim to draw from it.

Butler, therefore, is neither a sentimentalist nor a rationalist nor an unsystematic moralist. His acceptance of traditional normative naturalism places him in an intermediate position between Hutcheson and Clarke; or perhaps one ought to say that it puts him outside the dispute between them, since he denies their common assumption that a naturalist account must be sentimentalist. As Suarez's position shows, a philosopher might intelligibly believe both that moral properties are eternal and immutable in relation to will, command, sentiment, and legislation, while believing that they depend on facts about rational nature. This is a distinctive position, not a mere amalgam of fragments gathered from rationalism and sentimentalism.

717. Voluntarism

Butler further defines his relation to Clarke, on the one side, and Hutcheson, on the other, by his attitude to voluntarism about God and morality. Issues about voluntarism mark one central area of dispute between Hutcheson and his rationalist critics, because of an alleged inconsistency in his position. Hutcheson rejects the sort of voluntarism that identifies morality with the content of divine commands, but he also claims: (1) What is right is right because it appeals to our moral sense. (2) We have a reason to do what is right because it appeals to our moral sense.

According to Burnet and Balguy, these claims commit Euthyphro's error; for they imply that what is right would be different if our moral sense were to change and everything else about us and the world were to remain the same. Burnet and Balguy argue that Hutcheson's sentimentalism inherits the faults of theological voluntarism, making morality subject to inappropriate variations. Though Hutcheson seeks to avoid voluntarism, he commits himself, according to these rationalist critics, to the most serious voluntarist error.

Butler embraces a naturalist position, holding that moral rightness and wrongness are independent of divine legislation. In the *Analogy* he affirms naturalism without discussing it at length, since he is reluctant to engage in speculation about the divine will and intellect.[24] He takes naturalism to be the general view of both ancient and modern moralists.[25] In reply to the objections that appeal to divine dispensations from the moral law, he defends the naturalist view that the command to plunder the Egyptians (for instance) does not constitute divine permission to do wrong. The fact that God has commanded in this case an action that would have been wrong had it not been commanded makes the action no longer wrong. Hence the recognition of these possibilities does not undermine belief in immutable morality.[26]

[24] '...I am far from intending to deny, that the will of God is determined by what is fit, by the right and reason of the case; though one chooses to decline matters of such abstract speculation, and to speak with caution when one does speak of them. But if it be intelligible to say that it is fit and reasonable for every one to consider his own happiness, then fitness of action, or the right and reason of the case, is an intelligible manner of speaking. And it seems as inconceivable, to suppose God to approve one course of action, or one end, preferably to another, which yet his acting at all from design implies that he does, without supposing somewhat prior in that end, to be the ground of the preference; as to suppose him to discern an abstract proposition to be true, without supposing somewhat prior in it, to be the ground of the discernment. It doth not therefore appear, that moral right is any more relative to perception, than abstract truth is: or that it is any more improper, to speak of the fitness and rightness of actions and ends, as founded in the nature of things, than to speak of abstract truth, as thus founded' (*Anal.* i 6.12n).

[25] 'I...have omitted what I think true, and of the utmost importance, because by others thought unintelligible, or not true. Thus I have argued upon the principles of the fatalists, which I do not believe: And I have omitted a thing of the utmost importance which I do believe, the moral fitness and unfitness of actions, prior to all will whatever; which I apprehend as certainly to determine the divine conduct, as speculative truth and falsehood necessarily determine the divine judgment. Indeed the principle of liberty, and that of moral fitness, so force themselves upon the mind, that moralists, the ancients as well as moderns, have formed their language upon it.' (*Anal.* ii 8.11) See also ii 5.6: '...it is by no means intuitively certain, how far these consequences could possibly, in the nature of the thing, be prevented, consistently with the eternal rule of right, or with what is, in fact, the moral constitution of nature.' Bernard (ii 117n) refers to Cudworth and Clarke, See Clarke, *DBAG*, Prop. xii = H 571: 'Further: that there is a fitness or suitableness of certain circumstances to certain persons, and an unsuitableness of others, founded in the nature of things and in the qualifications of persons, antecedent to will and to all arbitrary or positive appointment whatsoever, must unavoidably be acknowledged by everyone who will not affirm that 'tis equally fit and suitable, in the nature and reason of things, that an innocent being should be extremely and eternally miserable, as that it should be free from such misery. There is therefore such a thing as fitness and unfitness, eternally, necessarily, and unchangeably in the nature and reason of things.' Cf. *DNR*, Prop. 1 §3 = H 612: 'And now, that the same reason of things, with regard to which the will of God always and necessarily determines itself to act in constant conformity to the eternal rules of justice, equity, goodness and truth; ought also constantly to determine the will of subordinate rational beings, to govern all their actions by the same rules, is very evident.' H 613: 'Originally and in reality, 'tis as natural and (morally speaking) necessary, that the will should be determined in every action by the reason of the thing, and the right of the case; as 'tis natural and (absolutely speaking) necessary that the understanding should submit to a demonstrated truth.' Cf. Shaftesbury, *Inquiry* i 3.2, quoted in §611.

[26] 'Indeed there are some particular precepts in Scripture, given to particular persons, requiring actions, which would be immoral and vicious, were it not for such precepts. But it is easy to see, that all these are of such a kind, as that the precept changes the whole nature of the case and of the action; and both constitutes and shows that not to be unjust or immoral, which, prior to the precept, must have appeared and really have been so: which may well be, since none of these precepts are contrary to immutable morality. If it were commanded, to cultivate the principles, and act from the spirit of treachery, ingratitude, cruelty; the command would not alter the nature of the case or of the action, in any of these instances. But it is quite otherwise in precepts, which require only the doing an external action: for instance, taking away the property, or life of any. For men have no right to either life or property, but what arises solely from the grant of God: when this grant is revoked, they cease to have any right at all in either: and when this revocation is made known, as surely it is possible it may be, it must cease to be unjust to deprive them of either. And though a course of external acts, which without command would be immoral, must make an immoral habit; yet a few detached commands have no such

The *Sermons* do not discuss the question of voluntarism directly. But Butler affirms his view in the sermon on the love of God. He alludes to the 'enthusiastic' view that the love of God should be entirely disinterested and self-forgetful, so that any thought of the benefits one gains from the love of God is entirely out of place, and incompatible with the proper love of God. This attitude of the French Quietists provokes a sharp reaction from other Christian moralists, who believe that the self-forgetful attitude advocated by Quietists is psychologically impossible and morally dangerous.[27]

An extreme reaction to Quietism is an attack on any disinterested love of God as mere fanaticism or (as Butler's contemporaries describe it) 'enthusiasm'. The opponents of enthusiasm about the love of God sometimes suggest that the safest and most rational attitude to God and morality is to regard God simply as the imposer of morality, and as the source of rewards and punishments for the observation and violation of it.[28]

Butler agrees with Shaftesbury and Maxwell in rejecting this extreme opposition to enthusiasm about the love of God.[29] He believes that, just as benevolence and self-love can and should co-exist, so also the disinterested love of God can and should co-exist with self-love directed to God. The rejection of disinterested love of God is an extreme reaction that reduces religion to purely self-interested calculation.[30] The disinterested love of God is legitimate and appropriate, both from a religious and a moral point of view; it is no less appropriate than love of a good moral character and of a human being who embodies it. Any sound moral outlook includes this reasonable and disinterested love.[31]

Butler's rejection of voluntarism separates him both from enthusiasm and from its opponents. For each side in the dispute has some tendency towards voluntarism about morality. On the one side, exclusive emphasis on the self-forgetful love of God, irrespective of anything else we value, may incline us to ignore any moral basis for the love of God. On the other side, emphasis on the legitimacy of self-interest may incline us to treat

---

natural tendency.' (*Anal.* ii 3.13) Bernard ad loc. criticizes Butler's position rather unfairly. Gladstone ad loc. suggests that 'violence offered by order of law may help to illustrate Butler's meaning'. He defends Butler more fully at *SSWBB* 37–40. On morality and divine commands cf. §869 (Waterland and Butler).

[27] On Quietism see §§611, 864.   [28] See Waterland, §872.

[29] Cf. Maxwell's appeal to Shaftesbury, §§539, 611.

[30] 'Everybody knows, . . . that there is such a thing as having so great horror of one extreme as to run insensibly and of course into the contrary; and that a doctrine's having been a shelter for enthusiasm, or made to serve the purposes of superstition, is no proof of the falsity of it: . . . It may be sufficient to have mentioned this in general, without taking notice of the particular extravagances which have been vented under the pretence or endeavour of explaining the love of God; or how manifestly we are got into the contrary extreme, under the notion of a reasonable religion; so very reasonable as to have nothing to do with the heart and affections, if these words signify anything but the faculty by which we discern speculative truth.' (xiii 1)

[31] 'By the love of God I would understand all those regards, all those affections of mind which are due immediately to Him from such a creature as man, and which rest in Him as their end. . . . And they may all be understood to be implied in these words of our Saviour, without putting any force upon them: for He is speaking of the love of God and our neighbour as containing the whole of piety and virtue. It is plain that the nature of man is so constituted as to feel certain affections upon the sight or contemplation of certain objects. Now the very notion of affection implies resting in its object as an end. And the particular affection to good characters, reverence and moral love of them, is natural to all those who have any degree of real goodness in themselves. This will be illustrated by the description of a perfect character in a creature; and by considering the manner in which a good man in his presence would be affected towards such a character. He would of course feel the affections of love, reverence, desire of his approbation, delight in the hope or consciousness of it. And surely all this is applicable, and may be brought up to that Being, who is infinitely more than an adequate object of all those affections; whom we are commanded to love with all our heart, with all our soul, and with all our mind. . . . there is nothing in it enthusiastical or unreasonable.' (xiii 2–3)

morality simply as the product of divine commands with sanctions attached. Butler rejects both these views. We avoid enthusiasm if we ground love for God in awareness of God's moral perfection, as understood by reference to standards of moral perfection that we do not accept simply because of the love of God. We have to reject voluntarism if we are to understand the righteousness of God and to find a morally acceptable basis for love of God.[32]

Once we grasp the right basis for the love of God, we can also see that it no more excludes self-love than concern for moral goodness excludes self-love. Disinterested love of God is possible and desirable, just as disinterested love of other things is possible and desirable, if self-love itself is not to be frustrated.[33] But the disinterested love of God is not fanatical or irrational, if it rests on the disinterested love of moral goodness in its own right.

Butler's brief references to voluntarism show that he takes his position to be controversial, and he believes that if he engaged in this controversy, he would stray from his main purpose in the *Analogy*. He might well have the same reason for avoiding the controversy in the *Sermons*, since a discussion of it would raise questions not only about meta-ethics, but also about God's intellect, will, freedom, and goodness. A discussion of voluntarism would distract him from the practical and pastoral aims of the *Sermons*.

But he does not take the issues about voluntarism to be irrelevant or practically unimportant. He takes the falsity of voluntarism to be extremely important, since naturalism underlies his whole explanation of the love of God. In claiming that God 'cannot' approve anything except what is right 'in itself' Butler raises the metaphysical questions about divine freedom, creation, and intrinsic morality that Suarez discusses at length.[34] He endorses the naturalist position of Suarez that is familiar to him from Clarke. To understand the *Sermons*, it is useful to keep in mind Butler's clear position on this issue.

718. Naturalism, Constructivism, and Realism

Butler's rejection of voluntarism agrees with Hutcheson's explicit position. According to Balguy, however, Hutcheson's sentimentalist account of moral properties leaves him with a voluntarist position. Is Butler open to the same criticism? The difference between

---

[32] '... suppose that they had a real view of that "righteousness, which is an everlasting righteousness"; of the conformity of the Divine will to the law of truth, in which the moral attributes of God consist; of that goodness in the sovereign Mind, which gave birth to the universe ...' (xiv 14).

[33] 'Some degree of goodness must be previously supposed; this always implies the love of itself, an affection to goodness: the highest, the adequate object of this affection, is perfect goodness; which therefore we are to love with all our heart, with all our soul, and with all our strength. "Must we then, forgetting our own interest, as it were go out of ourselves, and love God for his own sake?" No more forget your own interest, no more go out of yourselves, than when you prefer one place, one prospect, the conversation of one man to that of another. Does not every affection necessarily imply that the object of it be itself loved? If it be not it is not the object of the affection. You may, and ought if you can, but it is a great mistake to think you can love or fear or hate anything, from consideration that such love or fear or hatred may be a means of obtaining good or avoiding evil.' (xiii 13)

[34] 'God cannot approve of any thing but what is in itself right, fit, just. We should worship and endeavour to obey him with this consciousness and recollection. To endeavour to please a man merely, is a different thing from endeavouring to please him as a wise and good man, i.e. endeavouring to please him in the particular way of behaving towards him, as we think the relations we stand in to him and the intercourse we have with him require.' (MS note of Butler's, printed in Bernard ii 305)

Hutcheson's psychological naturalism and Butler's normative naturalism raises a question about their metaphysical claims about the nature of moral properties.

Hutcheson's version of naturalism rejects objectivism, since it asserts that moral properties turn out not to be features of external reality, if 'external' implies independence of the judgments and reactions of moral judges. They are relational properties, and one term of the relation is the actual reaction of a judge's moral sense. Butler opposes this claim about the moral sense. His opposition becomes clearer when he explains his view of conscience.

This difference from Hutcheson, however, still leaves Butler two options: (1) Hutcheson is right to reject objectivism, but wrong in his description of the subjective term of the relation involved in moral properties. Instead of saying that the reactions of the moral sense constitute the rightness of actions (states of character, etc.), Hutcheson ought to have said that the reactions of conscience make actions right. (2) Contrary to Hutcheson's position, rightness is agreement with human nature. Human nature consists essentially in the rational and reflective aspects of human beings, but facts about human nature are not constituted by the reactions or judgments of moral judges. On the contrary, good moral judges are the ones who detect these facts that exist apart from their reactions.

It may be difficult to decide which of these positions Butler affirms against Hutcheson. In either position facts about human beings as rational and reflective agents are relevant. But they are relevant in different ways. According to the first view, the relevant facts are those about human beings as moral judges, because their judgments constitute moral properties and moral truths. According to the second view, however, the relevant facts are not constituted by moral judgments; truths about us as moral judges are simply a subset of the truths about us as rational agents, and these truths as a whole constitute the moral facts.

The first of these positions is a form of constructivism. If Butler accepts it, he follows Hutcheson in rejecting Clarke's realism. If, however, he accepts the second position, he agrees with Clarke in taking moral facts and properties to be independent of our moral judgments. Normative naturalism, on this view, differs from rationalism in its view about which external facts are moral facts, and therefore about the properties in relation to which moral properties are mutable. But it agrees with rationalism in regarding them as external facts.

Butler's views about superior principles, morality, and conscience help us to decide where he stands on this metaphysical issue. A decision on this issue is important not only for understanding Butler, but for understanding Kant; for similar issues arise in trying to fix Kant's position in relation to rational intuitionism and sentimentalism.

Butler's introduction of his position supports the realist against the constructivist interpretation. For he introduces it as a version of the naturalism that he ascribes to the ancient moralists. He is right to ascribe naturalism to the ancients; he might equally have ascribed it to Aquinas and to Suarez.[35]

Naturalism, as Suarez presents it, is a realist rather than a constructivist position. He makes this clear by his treatment of the claims that (1) the good is the desirable, and (2) the right is what accords with correct reason. He believes that both of these claims are correct, if suitably understood, but they give incorrect accounts of what makes things good or right

---

[35] It is not such an accurate picture of Scotus' or Ockham's position. See §§384, 395.

in the constitutive ('formal') sense. He argues (following Cajetan) that rational desire desires the good because it is good, and that this is the direction of explanation that makes clear the relation between good and desirability; he clearly rejects the reduction of goodness to desirability (understood non-normatively). Similarly, he argues that the correctness of correct reason consists in its grasping facts about rational nature that are independent of the reasoning that grasps them (though they are not independent of the rationality that is displayed in this reasoning). He thereby rejects the reduction of rightness to what is grasped by correct reason (non-normatively understood, without mention of its grasping the right).[36]

If Butler and Suarez agree in accepting the claim that virtue is living in accordance with nature, do they interpret the claim in the same way? The fact that Suarez takes it to be a realist claim, and spells out the realist aspects of it, suggests the right questions about Butler. If Butler appears to accept the asymmetries that Suarez accepts (desirable because good; grasped by correct reason because fitting for rational agents), we have some reason to attribute a realist version of naturalism to him.

He seems to accept Suarez's asymmetries. For he agrees with Suarez in rejecting a voluntarist account of the relation between rightness and the divine will. He contrasts voluntarism with belief in 'the fitness and rightness of actions and ends, as founded in the nature of things'.[37] This way of stating the alternative to voluntarism may remind us of Clarke; but it also fits the naturalist position that (we have argued) Butler maintains in opposition to Clarke (whether or not he clearly recognizes this opposition). Constructivism does not fit a belief in rightness as founded in the nature of things rather than the will of an agent; it is difficult to see how an opponent of voluntarism could reasonably be a constructivist.[38] Admittedly, Butler may not agree, or he may not see that his acceptance of naturalism rather than voluntarism is difficult to reconcile with constructivism. Still, his naturalism gives us a reason for ascribing to him a view of rightness similar to the one that Suarez accepts.

719. Conscience, Reasons, and Motives

Butler's conception of conscience requires him to express a view on the dispute between rationalists and sentimentalists about the connexion between moral judgment and motivation. His view is rather carefully balanced between the opposing views, and it is sometimes difficult to see where he stands. If we can grasp his position, we will also be able to see its bearing on the issue about realism. For one of Hutcheson's reasons for rejecting realism is his internalism about moral properties, moral judgment, and motivation. We need to see whether Butler asserts or assumes any internalist doctrine.

Conscience is a prescriptive principle, parallel to self-love. Neither principle is simply the recognition of the relevant truths about practice. Just as self-love includes a desire for one's happiness, conscience includes the desire to express one's nature as a whole. Moreover, conscience accepts the requirements of morality, since it sees that they can be justified with

---

[36] On Suarez see §§438–9.   [37] *Anal.* i 6.12n, quoted in §717.
[38] See the sympathetic treatment of voluntarism in Korsgaard, *SN* 21–7, partly quoted in §567.

reference to my nature as a whole. This implies: (1) If x is morally right, anyone has a reason to do x. (2) If S recognizes that x is morally right, and S is a conscientious person, S recognizes that S has a reason to do x. (3) If S recognizes that x is morally right, and S is conscientious, S has a desire to do x.

But this does not imply that an action cannot be right, or cannot be seen to be right, by an agent who lacks a motive for doing the action. Rightness, therefore, is not an inherently motivating property. Those who have a corrupt conscience might recognize that an action is right without seeing that they have a reason to do it, and without any desire to do it. Hence the analogues of (2) and (3) are false in the case of such people.

Since I can have a reason I do not recognize, (1) is true even of people who have a corrupt conscience. Such people, like everyone else, have a reason (noticed or not) to act in accordance with their nature; since morality is in fact (though they do not recognize it) natural, they have a reason to act morally. Such a view rests on Butler's claims about the connexion between morality and human nature. But it does not imply any special epistemological view about the character of moral properties. Butler does not accept Hutcheson's internalist assumption that a moral property, or the recognition of it, is inherently motivating.[39]

Butler clarifies his views on internalism, in his account of the moral faculties (at the beginning of the Dissertation). Though people agree that we have 'a moral nature and moral faculties of perception and action', they differ about the nature of these faculties and their relation to knowledge and sentiment.[40] He emphasizes that we expect someone's moral outlook to include both understanding and emotion, and to extend to practice as well as theory. In using the terms 'sentiment' and 'perception', he may have deliberately chosen terms that could be used both for cognitive and for affective states.[41] Elsewhere he describes 'moral understanding' as 'as well including a practical sense of virtue, as a speculative perception of it'.[42]

Butler may intend his formula to echo a remark of Aristotle's.[43] In discussing election (*prohairesis*) Aristotle says that it is properly described as 'desiring reason or intellectual

[39] Contrast Mackie, *HMT* 39, 48, 55.

[40] 'It is manifest great part of common language, and of common behaviour over the world, is formed upon supposition of such a moral faculty, whether called conscience, moral reason, moral sense, or divine reason; whether considered as a sentiment of the understanding or as a perception of the heart, or, which seems the truth, as including both.' (D 1)

[41] We ought not to suppose that Butler takes 'sentiment' to be especially proper to emotion, so that his formula is deliberately paradoxical. A simple survey of the excerpts in SB suggests a rather general use of 'sentiment'. It is commonly used by Hutcheson in ways that certainly include affective states. But Shaftesbury, Balguy, and Price, for instance, regularly use it for cognitive states. Price provides an especially striking example of Butler's very phrase: 'No one can avoid owning that he has the idea of unsuitableness; (that is, a sentiment of wrong) in the application of eternal misery to innocence. Let him, if he can, find out a reason for denying it to be a sentiment of his understanding, and a perception of truth.' (*RPQM* 129) Butler may have meant by the phrase just what Price means by it. Cf. §819. Whewell, ad loc. in *BTSHN*, absurdly suggests emendation of the text to reverse 'sentiment' and 'perception'. Beattie and Reid criticize Hume for his non-cognitive use of 'sentiment'; see §842, and Rivers, *RGS* ii 301–2. On Butler's doctrine see Raphael, 'Conscience' 230–1; Taylor, 'Features' 299.

[42] *Anal.* i 5.14. Bernard cites this passage in his note on the passage quoted from Diss.

[43] An allusion to Aristotle is suggested by Bernard: 'Butler's words are carefully chosen, and are intended to indicate the complexity of conscience, which is partly intellectual, partly emotional. If it be called a sentiment, it must not be forgotten that it is a sentiment of the *understanding*; if it be called a perception, it is still a perception of the *heart*. Aristotle's definition of the faculty of moral choice is closely parallel . . .' Bernard goes on to cite *EN* 1139b4–5. (He may misunderstand Butler's use of 'sentiment'; see above.)

desire' (*EN* 1139b4–5). The echo is not exact; for Aristotle is speaking of the origins of moral action, not of the faculty of moral judgment. Still, the two questions, about the origin of action and the origins of moral judgment, are not easily separated. For in Hutcheson and Hume the combination of an anti-rationalist view of motivation and justification with an internalist view of the connexion between moral judgment and motivation leads to an anti-rationalist view of moral judgment.[44] They believe that desire, as opposed to reason, is the source of motivation; they assume that the making of a moral judgment necessarily motivates the agent to act on it; and so they infer that the making of a moral judgment involves some desire or emotion.[45]

Butler is non-committal about rationalism and internalism. He speaks of moral reason and moral sense together, not making it clear which aspect he takes to be primary; and he speaks of moral understanding as including a practical sense of virtue. It is easy to see why anti-rationalists and internalists might think Butler is leaning in their direction.

Butler's remarks, however, suggest to Price that Butler holds a rationalist position, and that he takes the affective aspects of our moral outlook to result from our moral judgment, the cognitive aspects. The fact that we are capable of being moved by our moral judgments does not imply that the moral judgments themselves include the relevant feelings. Though Butler's phrase about conscience combines the cognitive and the affective aspects more closely than Price's adaptation of his phrase does, it does not imply the inseparability of moral judgment from affective reactions. In the conscientious person they are closely connected; just as our belief that something is wrong immediately provokes a feeling of rejection, so also the feeling of unease or distaste helps us to discover that something is wrong. But that is all consistent with recognizing the possibility of true moral judgments that do not include affective reactions. Butler does not affirm or suggest a necessary connexion between moral judgment and motivation; and so he does not accept a crucial premiss in Hutcheson's and Hume's arguments against rationalism.[46]

720. Constructivism and Realism

Conscience approves of morality, and specifically of the content of the moral virtues. Butler seeks to prove that virtue is acting in accordance with our nature, relying on two claims: (1) Conscience approves of virtue. (2) Doing what conscience approves of is in accordance with our nature.

Which of these claims is a matter of definition, and which is a substantive claim, needing more argument than simple clarification of the relevant concepts? It is especially difficult to

---

[44] I intend to use 'internalism' with the sense defined by Frankena (following Falk), in 'Obligation' 49–50. It indicates a conceptual connexion between seeing that one has an obligation (or, even more strongly, having an obligation) and having a motive for doing what one sees one has the obligation to do.

[45] This is Hume's argument in *T* iii 1.1, 5–10. Hutcheson's position is more complicated (*IMS* i, 121–2). But his claim that justifying reasons must actually excite our approbation (and not simply give us reasons for approbation) commits him to some form of internalism about moral judgment and motivation. He asks, e.g., '. . . what reason makes us approve the happiness of a system? Here we must recur to a sense or kind affections' (129). This reference to affection is not directly connected to action (as it is in Hume), but it is at least connected to motivation. Cf. §639.

[46] See Hutcheson, §641; Hume, §745.

decide whether claim (1) is intended as a definition of virtue. It might be taken two ways: (a) What makes something virtue is the fact that it is approved by conscience (understood in some way that does not involve reference to virtue). (b) Conscience approves of something that (on independent grounds) constitutes virtue. If (b) is meant, is it a necessary or a contingent truth about conscience? Would it be conscience if it did not approve of morality?

We have already found reasons to answer No to the last question.[47] Butler seems to believe that conscience is the superior principle that necessarily takes the point of view of morality. Someone who had no moral beliefs would have no conscience. Someone who has mistaken moral beliefs has a mistaken, or perhaps corrupt, conscience. But this aspect of conscience does not settle the more important question about whether morality is reducible to what conscience approves of.

The reductive claim expresses Hutcheson's view that moral goodness is what our moral sense approves of. This is the constitutive claim that our approval is what makes it moral goodness. When we recognize the moral goodness or badness of an action, we recognize the benevolence or malevolence of the agent and the pleasure or pain of the recipient, but these would not be morally good or bad if we did not approve or disapprove of them. Only our approval or disapproval makes them good or bad.

Does Butler hold the anti-realist view that moral rightness is simply what our conscience approves? If he does, his dispute with Hutcheson rests simply on the difference between his conception of conscience and Hutcheson's conception of a moral sense. Alternatively, does he take conscience to recognize things that are right and wrong independently of this recognition, so that the recognition does not make things right or wrong?

In the *Dissertation* Butler suggests that we have some idea of what actions reveal virtue and vice, independently of knowing whether they are or are not approved by conscience. Moreover, this view fits his initial statement of sympathy with the views of Clarke, and his unambiguous repudiation of voluntarism as an account of morality and the divine will.[48] Constructivism is the equivalent of voluntarism at the human level; once the proper outlook of conscience is defined without reference to the fact that conscience grasps what is morally right, the morally right is defined as what is grasped by conscience. This view conflicts with 'the fitness and rightness of actions and ends, as founded in the nature of things',[49] and with Butler's objections to the purely psychological naturalism of Shaftesbury and Hutcheson.

A constructivist interpretation of Butler's claims about conscience is consistent with some of his remarks about conscience. It is not surprising, then, that Hutcheson takes over Butler's claims about the supremacy of conscience, and uses them to describe the moral sense. His *System of Moral Philosophy* shows how a psychological naturalist might try to incorporate some of Butler's views within a constructivist position; for (according to Hutcheson) the moral sense has the reflective supremacy that Butler takes to be the hallmark of conscience.[50]

---

[47] See §697.   [48] See §717.

[49] *Anal.* i 6.12n, quoted in §717. Butler also approves claims about fitness at S xi 20.

[50] A constructivist interpretation of Butler is defended by Darwall, *BMIO*, ch. 9. See esp. 279. In discussing a passage in which he takes Butler to reject Clarke's intuitionism, Darwall comments: 'This . . . suggests he thinks that *normative* ideas refer to no order that is independent of the exercise of autonomous practical reason (conscience) itself.' If 'the exercise of' were omitted, the resulting claim would be similar to the position I have attributed to Butler. 'The exercise of' suggests that Darwall intends a constructivist interpretation. A similarly procedural interpretation of Butler is favoured by Schneewind, 'Use'; but contrast *IA* 353.

A variation of Hutcheson's constructivism might substitute a rational procedure for the reactions of the moral sense. This is approximately the form of constructivism favoured by Kant, according to some views of his position.[51] Butler, however, does not hold this view. If he held it, his meta-ethical position would be inconsistent, since he rejects the assumptions that constructivism shares with voluntarism and with psychological naturalism. It is more reasonable to conclude that he takes conscience to grasp moral truths whose truth does not consist in their being grasped by conscience.

Some relevant questions about the interpretation of Butler's position arise from Kames's criticism. Kames takes the moral sense to be unanalysable and immediate, not susceptible to reductive analysis. He criticizes Butler on the assumption that Butler offers a reductive analysis. In his view, Butler defines morality as what conscience approves of.[52] He criticizes Butler on the ground that this reductive and anti-realist account does not capture the distinctive character of the moral sense.[53] Kames argues that to find an adequate account of the moral sense we must add to Butler's claims about the authority of conscience a specific claim about the source of authority—that we perceive the action to be our duty. Since we must mention the perception of our duty in an account of authority, we cannot find a reductive account of duty by appeal to the authority of conscience.

Kames's criticism underlies Selby-Bigge's treatment of Butler as a sentimentalist.[54] He takes Butler to claim that rightness consists simply in being approved by the reflective faculty of conscience. He agrees with Kames's criticism of Butler on this point (xlii, xlvi).

Whewell raises legitimate questions about the view defended by Kames and Selby-Bigge. He rejects a constructivist account of Butler, in denying that Butler makes conscience 'the ultimate criterion of right and wrong' (Three Sermons, p. xiii). In Whewell's view, conscience is a faculty in the same sense as reason is one: 'a power by exercising which we come to discern truths, not a repository of truth already collected in a visible shape' (p. xiv).

We can confirm Whewell's interpretation of Butler by considering what sorts of things conscience approves. Butler describes them in two ways: (1) They are just, fair, and benevolent actions, which tend to promote the common good of society, and to maintain the appropriate relations of desert, responsibility, and equality, between individual agents.

---

[51] See Rawls, LHMP 236.

[52] 'Dr. Butler, a manly and acute writer, hath gone farther than any other, to assign a just foundation for moral duty. He considers conscience or reflexion "as one principle of action, which, compared with the rest as they stand together in the nature of man, plainly bears upon it marks of authority over all the rest, and claims the absolute direction of them all, to allow or forbid their gratification." And his proof of this proposition is, "that a disapprobation of reflexion is in itself a principle manifestly superior to a mere propension."' (Kames, EPM, ch. 3, 33 (Moran) = SB 931) Thomas Johnson also attributes a sentimentalist position to Butler; see §866.

[53] '...the authority of conscience does not consist merely in an act of reflexion. It arises from a direct perception, which we have upon presenting the object, without the intervention of any sort of reflexion. And the authority lies in this circumstance, that we perceive the action to be our duty, and what we are indispensably bound to perform. It is in this manner that the moral sense, with regard to some actions, plainly bears upon it the marks of authority over all our appetites and passions. It is the voice of God within us which commands our strictest obedience, just as much as when his will is declared by express revelation' (Kames, EPM, ch. 3, 34 (Moran) = SB 931).

[54] 'It is in Butler that the sentimental school really reaches its climax. He is indeed careful not to commit himself to any decision between the claims of reason and sense . . . but it is impossible not to treat his theory as intimately related to the speculation of Hutcheson, who indeed in his last work . . . evidently has taken a good deal from Butler. Man as an organic whole consists not only of parts, but of parts interrelated under a reflective faculty, which is endued not only with power or attractiveness but with authority. . . . To act according to human nature is to fall in with the system imposed by this authority . . . ' (SB i, p. xliv)

(2) These sorts of actions are those that fulfil human nature; we can see this by considering the 'social nature of man',[55] insofar as it includes both benevolence and the outlook connected with responsibility and fairness.

Neither of these two features of morally right actions is imposed or constituted by the approval of conscience. Conscience is supreme only because it identifies and prescribes actions with these properties. As we would expect from Butler's rejection of voluntarism, he agrees with those who defend intrinsic morality.

[55] The title of Sermon i.

55

HUME: NATURE

721. The Experimental Method

Hume's *Treatise* is 'an attempt to introduce the experimental method of reasoning into moral subjects' (title page). Hume recognizes that moral philosophy cannot always make the deliberate experiments that advance other inquiries.[1] We cannot always create the situation in which we can observe the effect that we are interested in.[2] In this area we must find a substitute for deliberate experiments by acquiring 'experiments' in Hume's wider sense—a broader acquaintance, based on observation and reading, with human behaviour and reactions in different situations. Moral philosophy, therefore, should rest on the study of human nature, which Hume calls the 'science of man' (*T*, Introd. 4).

Is this claim about the nature of moral philosophy important or controversial? If it means only that moral philosophy should rest on facts about human beings, we might think it is commonplace. Even rationalists such as Clarke agree that information about these facts is necessary for applying moral principles, even if the principles are independent of facts about human nature. Other philosophers see a closer connexion between morality and human nature. Aristotle, Aquinas, Hobbes, and Butler (for instance) claim that moral principles depend essentially on facts about human nature; they seem to agree with Hume.

But Hume does not merely claim that facts about human nature are relevant to moral theory. He also claims that the science of man can decide all the important questions in moral philosophy.[3] If he means that a purely experimental science can settle all the questions of moral philosophy, he disagrees with many others who take human nature to be fundamental

---

[1] 'Moral philosophy has, indeed, the positive disadvantage, which is not found in natural, that in collecting its experiments, it cannot make them purposely, with premeditation, and after such a manner as to satisfy itself concerning every particular difficulty which may arise.' (*T*, Introd. 10) I cite the *Treatise* (*T*), by book, part, section, and paragraph, from Norton and Norton's edn. I cite the *Inquiries* (*IHU* and *IPM*, the latter sometimes cited simply as *I*) by section and paragraph from Beauchamp's edns. The relations between *T* and *I* are discussed by Selby-Bigge, Introd. to edn. of *I*, fairly criticized by Laird, *HPHN* 237–41.

[2] 'But should I endeavour to clear up after the same manner any doubt in moral philosophy, by placing myself in the same case with that which I consider, 'tis evident this reflexion and premeditation would so disturb the operation of any natural principles, as must render it impossible to form any just conclusion from the phenomenon. We must therefore glean up our experiments in this science from a cautious observation of human life, and take them as they appear in the common course of the world, by men's behaviour in company, in affairs, and in their pleasures.' (*T*, Introd. 10)

[3] 'From this station we may extend our conquest over all those sciences, which more intimately concern human life, and may afterwards proceed at leisure to discover more fully those, which are the objects of pure curiosity. There is no

in moral philosophy. For the science of man, as Hume conceives it, seems to be simply a 'descriptive' (in a sense that needs explanation) account of human behaviour and its causes. Some naturalists do not believe that this is the whole basis of moral philosophy. They take moral philosophy to derive an account of reasons for acting one way rather than another from a theory of human nature. But they do not regard the underlying theory of human nature as purely descriptive—purely 'experimental' in Hume's sense. We might summarize their view by saying that they take their theory of human nature to be inherently normative, because it contains claims about goods and reasons.

A brief statement of Hume's disagreement with other theorists of human nature might say that he rejects the normative aspects of an account of human nature. Since he takes the science of man to settle all the main questions in moral philosophy, he rejects the claims of moral philosophy to be an essentially normative discipline. This division between a 'normative' and an 'experimental' discipline needs to be clarified further, but it suggests the point of Hume's ambitions for a purely experimental science of human nature.

His predecessors in moral philosophy are mistaken, then, to suppose that moral philosophy includes more than this experimental study. They do not take a purely 'experimental' view of moral philosophy, because they regard information about human psychology and behaviour as material for an irreducibly normative discipline. In their view, moral philosophy does not simply describe universal or frequent tendencies, but examines them in the light of principles about how they ought to be.

The normative pretensions of previous moral philosophy appear to Hume to be misguided. But why does he think so? In claiming that the science of man allows us to 'conquer' the sciences that more intimately concern human life, he might mean that the experimental study of human nature provides a basis for better-founded normative claims about how human beings ought to be. Alternatively, he might mean that experimental study conquers moral philosophy by expelling the normative element that is distinct from experimental study. We need to see which of these two views expresses Hume's claim about the significance of experimental moral science.

722. The Experimental Method as a Source of Scepticism and a Reaction to Scepticism

In claiming to follow the experimental method, Hume connects his discussion of morals, in the third book of the *Treatise*, with the discussion of the understanding and of the passions in the first two books, though he also takes it to be somewhat independent.[4] Since all three books claim to follow the same method, some questions that arise about the use of this method in Book i may also be raised about Book iii.

The experimental science of human nature casts doubt on various claims to knowledge, and hence arouses sceptical doubt. Various philosophical and common-sense claims to

---

question of importance whose decision is not comprised in the science of man; and there is none, which can be decided with any certainty, before we become acquainted with that science.' (*T*, Introd. 6)

[4] Book iii 'requires not that the reader should enter into all the abstruse reasonings' of the first two books (*T*, advertisement to Bk. iii).

knowledge imply empirical claims about our impressions and ideas, and about our capacities to form certain kinds of beliefs. The experimental method shows us that these claims are false or groundless. This is the method of the main epistemological inquiries of Book i; it tells us by 'experiment' whether we have any capacity to acquire the sort of knowledge that we must have if some of the theories of other philosophers are true. In Hume's view, an appeal to our available means of forming beliefs reveals no rational basis for various claims to knowledge. On these claims to knowledge Hume reaches a sceptical conclusion.

Sometimes he speaks as though his arguments for scepticism affect philosophical theories rather than common sense. His account of causation undermines claims to knowledge of hidden powers, necessary connexions in the world, and a law of universal causation. A sceptical conclusion about these claims may not appear to undermine our ordinary claim to know that if we light this match and put it on our bare hands, we will burn ourselves.

Sometimes, however, Hume attacks the basis of common-sense beliefs. His discussion of induction seems to affect the rational basis of all our beliefs about 'matters of fact'. His argument about personal identity seems to attack not only metaphysical theories of personal identity, but also the belief that I am the same person through the normal changes in my mental states. Similarly, the sceptical discussion of the senses casts doubt on both the vulgar belief and the more circumspect (as Hume supposes) philosophical belief in external objects. Hume takes his scepticism to be pervasive, since it shows that our beliefs about causes and effects and our beliefs about external objects undermine each other (i 4.7, 4). But we cannot give up either of these sets of beliefs.

If Hume's premises seem to lead by valid arguments to absurd conclusions, ought we to doubt the truth of his premisses? Hume does not think so. In his view, sceptical philosophy and common sense are in permanent tension. Sceptical arguments encourage him to reject all beliefs.[5] Common life does not refute the sceptical arguments, but it weakens their influence. Since we have to act, we cannot (he claims) maintain complete suspension of belief.

Still, sceptical philosophy changes our attitude to our common-sense beliefs. If we are sceptics, we recognize that we hold our ordinary beliefs because they are entrenched and we cannot easily get rid of them, not because we think the evidence warrants them.[6] This is not our normal attitude—before we become sceptics—to our everyday beliefs. If we agree with Hume that sceptical arguments undermine the justification of everyday beliefs, we cannot turn our back on sceptical conclusions when we engage in the activities of everyday life.

A sceptical point of view does not undermine every impulse to philosophical inquiry, but it changes the character of the inquiry. If we are sceptics, we ask psychological rather than normative questions. Instead of asking what is morally good or bad, we ask what causes us to judge one thing good and another bad.[7] We no longer pursue philosophy in

---

[5] 'I am ready to reject all belief and reasoning, and can look upon no opinion even as more probable or likely than another.' (i 4.7.8)

[6] 'In all the incidents of life we ought still to preserve our scepticism. If we believe, that fire warms, or water refreshes, 'tis only because it costs us too much pains to think otherwise. Nay, if we are philosophers, it ought only to be upon sceptical principles, and from an inclination, which we feel to the employing ourselves after that manner.' (i 4.7.11)

[7] 'I cannot forbear having a curiosity to be acquainted with the principles of moral good and evil, the nature and foundation of government, and the cause of those several passions and inclinations, which actuate and govern

the hope of discovering basic truths about reality, but it may still satisfy our curiosity on these psychological questions. Since these are questions for the science of human nature, that science does not finish its work when we have reached the sceptical conclusion; unlike Sextus' sceptical method, it does not eliminate itself with everything else that it eliminates.[8]

The experimental method allows us to construct this science of man that makes no claims about ultimate reality, and does not go beyond the ordinary claims of common life. Even if we are sceptics about the objective truth of claims about the world, our scepticism does not spread to claims about our propensities and tendencies. For the relevant claims belong to the science of human nature, which survives Hume's sceptical doubts.[9]

Is Hume entitled to assume that the 'pre-sceptical' science of human nature that we use to argue for sceptical conclusions is the same science as the 'post-sceptical' science that investigates the questions that survive sceptical conclusions? In his view, the pre-sceptical and the post-sceptical science are the same, because each is an empirical investigation of human abilities. Past philosophers have told us that we can know the world as it really is; in order to know it, we need certain cognitive capacities. The pre-sceptical science of human nature assures us that we lack these capacities, so that it is futile to seek knowledge of the world as it really is. But since the science of human nature tells us about our capacities, we can continue asking about our capacities even when we realize we cannot learn about the world as it really is. The psychological investigation of human capacities—both pre-sceptical and post-sceptical—is not a normative inquiry, and it does not try to answer normative questions about whether we are justified in believing in causes, or necessary connexion, or an external world.

This description shows that the science of man is insufficient for Hume's sceptical conclusions. In Book i his case for scepticism depends on his claims about the cognitive capacities we need in order to acquire knowledge of the world as it is. He claims, for instance, that if we are justified in believing that causal connexions in the world are more than constant conjunctions, we need an impression of necessary connexion in the world. Psychological inquiry shows us (in his view) that we have no such impression. But some argument going beyond psychological inquiry is needed to show that we need such an impression if we are to believe justifiably in causation. Such argument seems to belong to metaphysics and epistemology. Hence the discipline that Hume practises in order to reach sceptical conclusions does not seem to be the purely psychological science of human nature that answers his post-sceptical questions.

The purely psychological science of human nature, therefore, cannot assure us that the only questions worth asking are those that this science of human nature can answer. To convince ourselves to restrict our questions to the science of human nature, we need arguments in metaphysics and epistemology. Questions that can be raised

---

me. I am uneasy to think I approve of one object, and disapprove of another; call one thing beautiful, and another deformed; decide concerning truth and falsehood, reason and folly, without knowing upon what principles I proceed.' (i 4.7.12)

[8] See Sextus, P i 206; §138.
[9] 'Human nature is the only science of man; and yet has been hitherto the most neglected.' (i 4.7.14)

about these arguments are not answered by inquiries in the science of man, as Hume conceives it.

Moreover, we might well suppose that epistemological and metaphysical arguments spread sceptical doubt to experimental science. For experimental science deals with causal relations, relies on induction, and examines relations between external objects and human minds. Why should we not doubt its possibility if we accept Hume's sceptical doubts about causation and so on? We might answer that experimental science does not concern itself with the causal connexions that are open to sceptical doubt. Even if this answer preserved experimental science from doubts about causation, it would be difficult to defend an analogous answer about induction and the external world. But in any case Hume does not offer this answer even about causation; for he agrees that the search for objective causal connexions is inseparable from empirical inquiry.[10] He cannot, then, claim that his sceptical doubts do not apply to experimental science.

To reconcile experimental science with scepticism, he claims that we can concede the cogency of the sceptical argument without doing anything about it. Even if we admit that, strictly speaking, the science of human nature is based on illusions and errors, we do not worry about this sceptical conclusion when we are engaged in our experimental science. But if this is Hume's view, the post-sceptical experimental science is not exactly the same as the pre-sceptical science that we relied on to support sceptical doubts. For in our pre-sceptical phase we do not admit that, strictly speaking, our experimental science is based on illusions, whereas we admit just this about our post-sceptical experimental science. The pre-sceptical science claims to reach justified conclusions about the real world, whereas the post-sceptical science makes no such claims.

Perhaps Hume might reject these claims about pre-sceptical and post-sceptical experimental science. He might say that the experimental science is just the same whether or not we are sceptics; our pre-sceptical and post-sceptical phases affect our epistemological attitude to experimental science, not the outlook of experimental science itself. But it is difficult to defend this division between the science and our epistemological attitude to it. Our experience, as we understand it, of boiling kettles and bare hands placed on them convinces us of claims, based on experience, about the causal relations between boiling kettles and burnt hands. We cannot separate conviction on the basis of experience, taken to be of objects and causal relations, from common-sense beliefs or experimental science. A post-sceptical science needs to replace these beliefs with an outlook that persists after sceptical scrutiny; this outlook does not include conviction on the basis of evidence taken to support the conviction. The scope of Hume's scepticism prevents him from separating experimental science from sceptical attitudes.

---

[10] 'Nothing is more curiously enquired after by the mind of man, than the causes of every phenomenon; nor are we content with knowing the immediate causes, but push on our enquiries, till we arrive at the original and ultimate principle. We would not willingly stop before we are acquainted with that energy in the cause, by which it operates on its effect; that tie, which connects them together; and that efficacious quality, on which the tie depends. This is our aim in all our studies and reflexions: And how must we be disappointed, when we learn, that this connexion, tie, or energy lies merely in ourselves, and is nothing but that determination of the mind, which is acquired by custom, and causes us to make a transition from an object to its usual attendant, and from the impression of one to the lively idea of the other?' (T i 4.7.5)

723. The Experimental Method and Scepticism in Moral Philosophy

These questions about the science of human nature may affect the discussion of the passions and of morality in the second and third books of the *Treatise*. In these books Hume does not defend scepticism about morality; he does not suggest that if we compare the claims of morality with our capacities, as we learn about them through experimental science, we will raise sceptical doubts about morality. But it seems puzzling that he does not suggest this; for moral philosophy seems to offer opportunities for scepticism analogous to those we find in metaphysics and epistemology.

The opportunities are most obvious in Hume's negative arguments about reason and passion and about moral objectivity. Rationalism and objectivism, the two positions that he rejects, imply that moral judgments express knowledge of an objective reality. Clarke claims a priori knowledge of 'eternal fitnesses' that exist independently of our beliefs and preferences. Any other objectivist position that attributes moral properties to external reality itself is also open to sceptical doubts. Hume believes that, once we consider our reasoning capacities and the character of our moral judgments, we can see that we lack the sort of access to objective moral properties that we would need if we were entitled to make objectivist claims. Experimental science of human nature shows us that we lack the capacity to find eternal fitnesses, just as we lack the capacity to find objective causal relations.

The refutation of these objectivist philosophical theories of morality does not, in Hume's view, imply any doubt about morality itself. On the contrary, we may find it reassuring and clarifying to recognize that our moral judgments do not collapse in the face of a refutation of philosophical theories that profess to find some deeper foundation for them. Since the theories are controversial, it is a good thing that our moral judgments do not rely on their truth.

But are common-sense moral convictions independent of philosophical theories, or invulnerable to sceptical criticism? We cannot be sure in advance that they do not rely on assumptions that are refuted through the experimental method. In Book i Hume argued that common-sense views, not only philosophical views, about external reality are subject to sceptical doubt. The same might be true about some moral convictions.

Hume even seems to entertain the possibility of this sceptical doubt about morality. He believes that common sense holds that objects are really coloured. Philosophy shows that this belief is false. Moral philosophy shows that moral properties are similar, in this respect, to secondary qualities. If common-sense beliefs and forms of expression suggest that we initially believe in the objective reality of secondary qualities, do they not suggest that we also initially take moral properties to be objective? If they suggest this, Hume's argument seems to undermine both philosophical theories and common sense.

If common-sense views about morality commit us to claims about objectivity that Hume refutes, we have no reason to believe that anything is right or wrong. What difference might this make? Hume believes that the sceptical argument about secondary qualities makes no practical difference.[11] But his account of the impact of scepticism does not fit this judgment.

---

[11] 'Vice and virtue, therefore, may be compared to sounds, colours, heat and cold, which, according to modern philosophy, are not qualities in objects, but perceptions in the mind.' (*T* iii 1.1.26, quoted more fully in §758)

Once we are sceptics, we stop thinking of our beliefs as warranted; we just notice that 'it costs us too much pains to think otherwise', because our beliefs are entrenched and stubborn. But this is not our pre-sceptical attitude to our beliefs about the physical world. Nor is it our attitude to our moral beliefs before we confront Hume's arguments on moral properties. We do not at first believe murder is wrong and consideration for others is right simply because it costs us too much pains to think otherwise; or at least we do not believe that this is why we hold these beliefs.

If sceptical argument either persuades us that this has always been the basis of our moral beliefs, or causes us to hold them only on this basis, it seems to deprive us of a reason that we thought we had for taking our moral beliefs seriously. If we hold them only because it costs us too much pains to think otherwise, why should we prefer them over strong desires that conflict with them? Should we not expect changes in beliefs about the status of our moral beliefs to affect our moral beliefs, and hence our moral practice?

This is part of the rationalist case against Hutcheson. Balguy argues that sentimentalism implies unacceptable mutability in moral goodness. Though this is a philosopher's objection, it includes a claim about morality; for Balguy claims that our convictions about morality imply the falsity of sentimentalism. One might argue the other way, that if sentimentalism is true, these ordinary convictions about morality are false.

Hume does not believe that scepticism undermines ordinary moral convictions; for he believes, contrary to Balguy, that ordinary convictions do not include the beliefs that are undermined by his sceptical arguments against other philosophers. Changes in beliefs about the status of moral beliefs do not, in Hume's view, affect moral beliefs or their practical significance. But if he is wrong on this point, his sceptical arguments may damage morality more than he recognizes. Such damage would be unwelcome to Hume, since he takes himself to be explaining and supporting moral convictions by revealing their true principles.

We might express Hume's position in terms drawn from 20th-century philosophy, by saying that he treats moral philosophy as a strictly second-order inquiry, with no implications for first-order morality.[12] Epistemology and philosophy of science, we might say, are second-order inquiries; they do not seek to vindicate or refute particular scientific theories in the way a scientist would, but they investigate the epistemological and metaphysical status of these theories. If, for instance, scientific knowledge presupposes the existence of unobservable entities, but we are convinced on philosophical grounds that there can be no such things, we are not advising scientists to stop doing what they are doing; we are simply rejecting false accounts of what they are doing. Even if the scientists themselves, in their avocation as philosophers of science, believe these false accounts, that does not matter to them as practising scientists.

But though we can form a rough idea of the difference between first-order and second-order inquiries from such examples, it is difficult to make the division precise in ways that would support the original claim that second-order conclusions do not affect first-order practice. We can ride bicycles or paint pictures without knowing any theories about bicycles or about perspective or about aesthetics, and these theories might be purely second-order. But the division is not always so clear. Geologists seem to believe that the earth has existed

---

[12] See Ayer, 'Language'; Mackie, E 16–19. On related questions about scepticism and 'insulation' see §141.

for millions of years; they seem to believe in the equal reality of their present observations and of past ages of the earth that cannot be observed. If they came to disbelieve in the objective reality of unobservables, they would have to reject their belief in the past ages of the earth. The belief that they are describing a real past may be regarded as a second-order claim, since it is a claim about the nature of their activities rather than simply a description of them. But it seems to be part of the scientific investigator's view, not simply a belief of the theorist who studies the investigator. And if investigators really ceased to hold this belief, it is not clear why their practice might not be affected.

It is at least as difficult to distinguish first-order morality from second-order moral philosophy in a way that would prevent second-order conclusions from affecting first-order convictions. If we are discussing the behaviour of people in another culture, or in the past, I might say: 'What they did was not wrong, because no one in their culture (none of their contemporaries) thought it was wrong.' You might answer: 'Whether or not anyone thought it was wrong, it was wrong; what's right or wrong doesn't depend on anyone's opinion.' We seem to have engaged in a moral discussion about the rightness or wrongness of someone's action. But the discussion includes expressions of different views about the objectivity of rightness; and a change of mind on this question might lead to a different moral judgment about actions.

It is not surprising that morality includes convictions about the status of our moral convictions. For we assert moral claims on the assumption that they matter, and we can reasonably be expected to say why they matter. If we decide there is nothing to be said for any of them, and they all simply reflect how we have been brought up or the social circles we have moved in, we may change our mind about how much to insist on our moral views, or about what we ought to do to improve them, or about whether they can really be improved. Whether or not Balguy is right to say that morality presupposes a certain kind of immutability, he has good reasons for saying that some claims about objectivity belong to morality, not merely to philosophers' views about morality.

Hume's claim that he applies the science of man to moral subjects is therefore more puzzling than it initially appears. In Book i of the *Treatise*, the questions that are open to the science of man, and the attitudes that are open to us when we consider its conclusions, depend on the conclusions of sceptical arguments. In the later books of the *Treatise* Hume does not mention the impact of scepticism on his pursuit of the science of man. But he offers sceptical arguments on ethics, and it is worth our while to ask whether these arguments affect moral beliefs and practices. Though Hume seems to believe (if we go by his remark on secondary qualities) that metaphysical claims do not affect morality, it is not clear that he can reasonably separate second-order from first-order claims as sharply as he wants to.

724. Errors of the Ancient Moralists

Some of Hume's views about the scope and use of the science of man are clearer if we consider some of his remarks on his predecessors. His explicit references to other philosophers do not cover all the influences on him, but they are a useful starting point.

In a letter that describes his early philosophical development, Hume criticizes the ancient moralists for inattention to human nature. He claims that their views on virtue and happiness rest on groundless assumptions and prejudices, rather than on acquaintance with the relevant experimental details. He proposes, therefore, to pursue the study of human nature with the aim of deriving the whole of moral philosophy from it.[13]

What specific cases might support Hume's claim that the ancients do not attend to human nature? Perhaps he means that, for instance, the Stoics would not have identified virtue with happiness if they had known more about human psychology.[14] Because of their claims about virtue and happiness, they demand a humanly impossible degree of detachment from external goods. Even if some detachment is possible, perhaps it does more harm than good, by weakening morally desirable impulses as well.[15]

But even if this is a defensible criticism of the Stoics, it does not support Hume's general verdict on the ancients. For some ancient critics attack the Stoics for their inattention to human nature.[16] Hence these critics agree with Hume on the relevance of human nature. Moreover, the Stoics themselves have quite a lot to say about human nature, the passions, and human action. They do not agree with Hume on these topics, but they attend to facts about human nature. Chrysippus, Seneca, and Epictetus study our natural reactions to recognized goods and evils, in order to argue that we need different reactions that bring us closer to living a life that accords with nature. Both the Stoics and their critics attend to human nature, though they have different accounts of what nature requires.

Hume might answer that simply talking of what one conceives as 'human nature' is not the attention to human nature that he recommends. Some Greek claims about human nature are not purely predictive, non-normative claims about human constitution or behaviour, but include a normative component. Butler recognizes this feature of ancient conceptions of nature in his own third sense of 'nature', which refers to the requirements of a system as a whole. As Butler says, this third sense tells us what the Stoics have in mind in claiming that virtue consists in living in accord with nature.

Hume's division between the 'experimental' and the 'hypothetical' outlook applies to the normative conceptions of nature that we find in ancient moral philosophy in mind; his attack on the ancients applies no less to Butler.[17] If this is at least part of what Hume means in claiming that ancient moral philosophy is 'hypothetical', he is right about the difference between himself and the ancients.

---

[13] 'I found that the moral philosophy transmitted to us by antiquity laboured much under the same inconvenience that has been found in their natural philosophy, of being entirely hypothetical, and depending more upon invention than experience. Every one consulted his fancy in erecting schemes of virtue and of happiness, without regarding human nature, upon which every moral conclusion must depend. This therefore I resolved to make my principal study, and the source from which I would derive every truth in criticism as well as morality.' (To George Cheyne, March 1734 = Greig ed., i #3. Quoted by Kemp Smith, PDH 16)

[14] This criticism of the Stoics is suggested in Hume's essay, 'The Sceptic'.

[15] See 'Sceptic' §37: 'Another defect of those refined reflexions, which philosophy suggests to us, is, that commonly they cannot diminish or extinguish our vicious passions, without diminishing or extinguishing such as are virtuous, and rendering the mind totally indifferent and unactive.'

[16] This is one point of the criticism of the Stoics in Cic. F. iv 26–9.

[17] Perhaps the Sceptics are an exception. Though Hume is influenced by them, he does not discuss them among the ancient moralists.

725. Achievements of the Ancient Moralists

Hume agrees with Hobbes in rejecting the theories of the ancient moralists and their development by mediaeval Christian moralists. But, in contrast to Hobbes, he does not discuss the Aristotelian and Thomist position in any detail. Hobbes treats ancient and Christian mediaeval views as a single position to be rejected; his view is rather similar to Luther's view that the mediaeval Church has corrupted Christian morality by trying to reconcile it with Greek moral philosophy. Hume's attitude is more similar to Machiavelli's view that the 'monkish' mediaeval moralists have corrupted the sound morality of pagan antiquity.[18]

In this contrast between healthy paganism and the errors introduced by mediaeval Christianity, Hume anticipates Hegel and Nietzsche. But he differs from them about where to find the healthy paganism. Hume finds it in Hellenistic ethics, and specifically in Cicero's account of it. He shows very little acquaintance with the ethical views of Plato and Aristotle.[19] Hegel goes further back, and finds the true Hellenic spirit in Plato and Aristotle. Nietzsche goes back still further, because he believes that Socrates and Plato are already infected with the errors of the Jewish spirit; he turns to pre-Platonic Greek thought for the true Hellenic spirit. The fact that those who want to contrast the pagan with the Christian spirit cannot agree about where to draw the line between them suggests that it is difficult to draw a satisfactory contrast.

Some of the ancients are right, in Hume's view, about the nature and extent of the virtues.[20] He is a 'great admirer' of Cicero; he relies on Cicero's catalogue of virtues, even though he believes that the Stoic moral theory from which Cicero derives his catalogue is hopelessly hypothetical. Perhaps he believes that Cicero's catalogue does not really depend on Stoic moral theory. But if Cicero has a correct catalogue of the virtues, and if such a catalogue depends on accurate experimental science of human nature, how can ancient moralists fail to regard human nature?

Hume tries to reconcile his claims about the unsound and hypothetical character of ancient moral philosophy with his approval and use of the ancient moralists. In his view, the ancients anticipate his view that the virtues are not rational conditions. Their official endorsement of rationalism conflicts with their actual appeal to taste and sentiment. Their abstract theory reflects the mistaken view that moral principles are purely rational, but the descriptions of the virtues reflect an unacknowledged appeal to taste and sentiment.[21] This appeal to sentiment is the aspect of ancient philosophy that Hutcheson revives in his anti-rationalism.[22]

In treating the ancients as anti-rationalists Hume may be influenced by Hutcheson's appeal to Aristotle's claims about reason and desire. But Hutcheson does not say, as Hume says,

---

[18] See §403.

[19] He refers to Aristotle's *Ethics* at *I* 8.9; App. 4.12 ('We need only peruse the titles of chapters in Aristotle's *Ethics* to be convinced . . .'). He mentions Plato in App. 4.20.

[20] See the Letter of 17 Sept. 1739, quoted in §726. On Hume's use of Cicero see Laird, *HPHN* 242–3 (whose list of parallels, however, is not very convincing).

[21] 'The ancient philosophers, though they often affirm, that virtue is nothing but conformity to reason, yet, in general, seem to consider morals as deriving their existence from taste and sentiment.' (*I* 1.4)

[22] See *LG* 30, quoted in §751.

that the ancients hold an official rationalist position that conflicts with anti-rationalism about will and passion.[23] Hutcheson may also be influenced by the fact that actual discussions of virtues refer to tastes, sentiments, and emotions.

Hume's reasons for taking the ancients to be implicit anti-rationalists are as unconvincing as Hutcheson's reasons for taking them to be explicit anti-rationalists. One might identify virtue with control by reason while still recognizing the importance of training one's sentiments and emotions. If Hume had known the ethical works of Aristotle and Aquinas, he would have found that they give an important place to the emotions, and that Aquinas discusses the emotions in some detail. Such attention to the emotions does not conflict with the view that the moral virtues require subordination of the emotions to will and practical reason.

Hume's claims about what the ancients say and mean are brief, but significant; they sketch some of the main features of his own position. He suggests that if we practise the science of man, we will take an experimental approach to human nature, we will be anti-rationalists about action and virtue, and we will abandon the normative pretensions of moral philosophy, both in our claims about human nature and in our claims about the virtues.

726. The Ancients v. the 'Divines' on Voluntary and Non-voluntary Virtues

Hume draws one of his sharpest contrasts between the ancients and the 'monkish' writers in discussing the claim that the moral virtues are voluntary states. He believes that this claim reflects ignorance of the experimental method. It introduces an unprofitable dispute that can be resolved by attention to facts about human nature. In Hume's view, the ancients are right to avoid this dispute, because they do not separate moral from non-moral virtues. A dispute about which virtues are strictly moral is purely verbal. No significant issue rests on a sharp division between genuine moral virtues and other qualities that we may find attractive or admirable to some degree.

In taking this position Hume disagrees not only with earlier Christian moralists, but apparently also with Hutcheson. In Hutcheson's view, the distinctively moral virtues must be founded on benevolence, and he criticizes Hume for allowing natural abilities and other non-voluntary states unrelated to benevolence to count as virtues. Hume takes this to be an artificial and misleading restriction of 'virtue'.[24]

---

[23] Cf. Hutcheson, §637.

[24] 'Whether natural abilities be virtues is a dispute of words. I think I follow the common use of language. *Virtus* signified chiefly courage among the Romans. I was just now reading this character of Alexander the 6th in Guicciardin ... Were benevolence the only virtue, no characters could be mixed, but would depend entirely on their degrees of benevolence. Upon the whole, I desire to take my catalogue of virtues from Cicero's *Offices*, not from the *Whole Duty of Man*. I had, indeed, the former book in my eye in all my reasonings.' (17 Sept. 1739 = Greig, *LDH* i #13 = R 632) Since Hume is replying to Hutcheson's comments on the *Treatise*, Hutcheson presumably said something in these comments about Hume's conception of the virtues. Hume repeats this criticism in his comments on Hutcheson's *MPIC*: 'I always thought you limited too much your ideas of virtue; and I find I have this opinion in common with several that have a very high esteem for your philosophy.' (10 Jan. 1743, Greig i #19). Cf. §779.

Hume gives two reasons for rejecting the division between moral virtues and other good qualities: (1) Self-regarding as well as other-regarding traits, and excellences of intellect as well as of affection, are often counted as virtues. (2) The distinction between voluntary and involuntary does not separate real moral virtues from other qualities.[25] He cites the ancient moralists in support of his first claim.[26] He also takes them to be indifferent to the voluntary character of virtues.[27] He holds that Christian moralists deny both of his claims, and refers to *The Whole Duty of Man*.[28]

Hume's claim that the ancients are indifferent to the voluntary character of virtues is puzzling. He mentions the fact that they regard some bad self-regarding traits as 'ridiculous and deformed, contemptible and odious', and claims that they believe such traits are 'independent of the will'. And he suggests that they value mental traits that are not in everyone's power. But even if he is right about this, it does not show that the distinction between voluntary and involuntary 'was little regarded' in the moral reasonings of the ancients. Both Aristotle and the Stoics take it to be important to show that it is up to us to be virtuous, and they believe that they can show this for the virtues that they endorse as praiseworthy states of a rational agent.[29] Aquinas agrees with them on this point. In his claims about virtue, passion, and will, he tries more systematically than the ancients try to show how the virtues are voluntary. He defends in detail the claims that Aristotle presents in outline.[30]

Hume's view of the ancient moralists is sharply but not unfairly criticized by Beattie. Though some of his objections and citations are of doubtful value, Beattie points out that Aristotle insists on the voluntary character of virtue.[31] The virtue that Aristotle has in mind is the sort of virtue for which prudence is both necessary and sufficient.[32] Even if these points were not clear in Aristotle, they would be clear in the Stoics.[33] It is puzzling that Hume ignores all this evidence about the views of the ancient moralists.

[25] On Aristotle's views on responsibility and virtue see §§90–1, 99–101.

[26] '. . . the ancient moralists, the best models, made no material distinction among the different species of mental endowments and defects, but treated all alike under the appellation of virtues and vices, and made them indiscriminately the object of their moral reasonings' (*I* App. 4.11). Hume adds a long passage from the *De Oratore* in which Cicero clearly recognizes both self-regarding and other-regarding virtues (*De Or.* ii 343–4). 'I suppose, if Cicero were now alive, it would be found difficult to fetter his moral sentiments by narrow systems; or persuade him, that no qualities were to be admitted as virtues, or acknowledged to be a part of personal merit, but what were recommended by *The Whole Duty of Man*.' (*I* App. 4.11n) This also seems to be the point of the references to the Romans on courage and Guicciardini's description of Alexander VI (in the letter to Hutcheson just quoted). These examples do not bear on the point about voluntariness.

[27] 'In general, we may observe, that the distinction of voluntary or involuntary was little regarded by the ancients in their moral reasonings; where they frequently treated the question as very doubtful, whether virtue could be taught or not? [A footnote refers to Plato's *Meno*, inter alia.] They justly considered, that cowardice, meanness, levity, anxiety, impatience, folly, and many other qualities of the mind, might appear ridiculous and deformed, contemptible and odious, though independent of the will. Nor could it be supposed, at all times, in every man's power to attain every kind of mental, more than of exterior beauty.' (*I* App. 4.20)

[28] On this work (probably by Richard Allestree) see Rivers, *RGS* i 18–23, ii 299n. Cf. §751.

[29] On Aristotle see §§99–101. On the Stoics see §169.   [30] On Aquinas see §262.

[31] Commenting on Hume's appeal to the titles of the chapters in the *Ethics*, Beattie remarks: 'True; but if our learned metaphysician had extended his researches a little beyond the titles of those chapters, he would have found that, in Aristotle's judgment, "moral virtue is a voluntary disposition or habit; and that moral approbation and disapprobation are excited by those actions and affections only which are in our own power, that is, of which the first motion arises in ourselves, and proceeds from no extrinsic cause." ' (*ENIT* 335–6).

[32] Beattie, *ENIT* 335.

[33] To show that Cicero insists on the voluntary character of virtues, Beattie cites *Fin* v 36, where Cicero mentions 'the great and genuine virtues, which we denominate voluntary', including the cardinal virtues (*ENIT* 338).

Hume might reply that discussions of the *hekousion* and *akousion* in the ancient moralists are not really about 'the voluntary', if we understand belief in the voluntary to commit us to belief in the will and its freedom. Perhaps he understands the voluntary to include an indeterminist conception of the freedom of the will. In that case he might agree with the later critics who have argued that questions about the will and freewill are inventions of Christian moralists who need to identify the traits and actions that determine a person's status in the afterlife.[34] This would be a questionable historical claim, however. Aquinas does not take his claims about the voluntary to rest on an indeterminist conception of freewill; he does not suggest that he departs from Aristotle's views on the praiseworthiness and voluntariness of the virtues. But if Aquinas does not count as a theological moralist by Hume's criterion, that is a reason for doubting Hume's criterion. Hume does not make it clear what question about freedom interests Christian moralists but does not interest ancient moralists.

Hume is right to assert that Christian moralists affirm the voluntary character of virtues, and so deny his second claim. But it is surprising that he takes them to deny his first claim.[35] Christian moralists do not normally deny that intellectual and self-regarding traits are among the virtues; Aquinas recognizes self-regarding moral virtues, and recognizes intellectual virtues, some of which are connected with moral virtues.[36]

Contrary to Hume, therefore, both the ancients and the Christian moralists endorse his first claim and reject his second claim. This attitude to Hume's two claims is consistent, if some intellectual and some self-regarding traits are voluntary. Hume, however, seems to assume that since the ancients accept his first claim, they must accept his second claim, and that since the Christians reject his second claim, they must also reject his first claim.

Why does Hume not consider the possibility of accepting his first claim without the second? One reason may be that Hutcheson disagrees with him on both claims, and so he tends not to distinguish them. But another reason may be his account of the double error of Christian moralists. In his view, we would agree with him about the range of the virtues if we practised the experimental method. But Christian philosophers have not practised it, because theological presuppositions have turned their attention to questions about praise and blame.[37] Christian influence has made the issue about voluntariness seem important, and has warped the scope and character of moral philosophy so as to make this issue unduly prominent.

The experimental method refutes Christian philosophers on this point (according to Hume). The sentiments of praise and blame that we experience extend to self-regarding traits and to non-voluntary states, but the 'divines' simply ignore this observable fact about our sentiments, and they do not bother to fit their theoretical claims to the facts about human nature. Since Hume believes that both the errors he rejects about the scope of the

---

[34] For this defence of Hume see Williams, 'Voluntary acts'. On doctrines of the will see §§217–18 (on Augustine).

[35] Rivers, *RGS* ii 299–300, notices this feature of Hume's account.   [36] On Aquinas see, e.g., §§291, 313.

[37] 'In later times, philosophy of all kinds, especially ethics, have been more closely united with theology than ever they were observed to be among the heathens; and as this latter science admits of no terms of composition, but bends every branch of knowledge to its own purpose, without much regard to the phenomena of nature, or to the unbiased sentiments of the mind, hence reasoning, and even language, have been warped from their natural course, and distinctions have been endeavoured to be established where the difference of the objects was, in a manner, imperceptible. . . . Every one may employ terms in what sense he pleases; but this, in the mean time, must be allowed, that sentiments are every day experienced of blame and praise, which have objects beyond the dominion of the will or choice, and of which it behoves us, if not as moralists, as speculative philosophers at least, to give some satisfactory theory and explication.' (*I* App. 4.21)

virtues result from failure to follow the facts of experience, he assumes that anyone who disagrees with him on one point will disagree on the other point too.

But if Hume is wrong about the ancients, he undermines his historical explanation of the emphasis on voluntary traits. For if moralists who are not influenced by Christian theology emphasize them, such emphasis cannot be simply a result of Christian influence. He gives us no reason to believe that theological attitudes to morality are responsible for the introduction of concerns about the voluntary character of virtue.

We must postpone a full discussion of Hume's reasons for thinking the divines neglect facts about human nature.[38] But we can make a start by exploring his conception of the experimental method, and in particular his application of it to the understanding of passions and sentiments.

727. Predecessors in the Science of Human Nature

Among Hume's modern predecessors, Hobbes deserves special attention. Though Hume does not discuss Hobbes, he alludes to him prominently. The very title of the *Treatise* recalls Hobbes's work *Human Nature*. The allusion is appropriate, since Hobbes anticipates Hume's ambition of reducing moral philosophy to an experimental and non-normative science of human nature. In Hobbes's view, the moral philosophy of the ancients is misguided, because it does not rest on a true conception of human nature; hence it does not understand the virtues and does not see 'wherein consisted their goodness'.[39] Hobbes tries to set moral philosophy on a firmer footing by starting from an account of human nature that is free of mistaken views in moral philosophy.

Not only does Hobbes anticipate Hume's programme of deriving moral philosophy from the science of man, but he also anticipates many of Hume's specific conclusions. Hume's views on the passions, on free will, on practical reason and deliberation, and on justice, are similar, though not identical, to Hobbes's views. Hume develops both Hobbes's main approach to moral philosophy and many of Hobbes's specific arguments.[40]

Hume, however, does not mention Hobbes in these contexts. Nor does he cite him as a predecessor in applying the experimental science of man to moral philosophy; nor does he list him among those who have made significant advances in moral philosophy.[41] Perhaps Hume's silence about Hobbes reflects Hobbes's continuing unpopularity. To point out that Hobbes had anticipated his approach or his specific conclusions would not be a way to conciliate most readers.

In contrast to Hobbes, Hume cites and praises Butler and Hutcheson as his predecessors. In his published works he does not state any disagreement with either of them, but

---

[38] See §776. [39] L.15.40. See §483.

[40] According to Johnson, Hume was 'a Tory by chance, as being a Scotchman; but not upon a principle of duty; for he has no principle. If he is any thing, he is a Hobbist.' (Boswell, *JTH* = Hill-Powell iv 194 and note; v 272.) Johnson's remark is discussed by Russell, 'Tory'. On Hume's Hobbism see also Russell, 'Hume and Hobbes'; 'Scepticism'; 'Atheism'. (The title page refers to Hobbes's *Elements of Law* and to Spinoza's *TTP*, which alludes to the passage from Tacitus cited by Hume.) Johnson was not the only one who recognized connexions with Hobbes; see the review of the *Treatise* quoted by Mossner, *LDH* 139, and §785.

[41] *IHU* 1.14n (first edition; not in Beauchamp, but in Hendel ed., 23n).

in his letters he recognizes serious disagreements with each of them. His brief remarks on Butler mark some of his main objections to Butler's position. His comments on Hutcheson are fuller, and quite instructive; they show that Hume opposes Hutcheson on some central issues that he does not discuss with specific reference to Hutcheson in the published works. In some cases he refers to non-extant letters of Hutcheson; his references reflect a dispute between two versions of a sentimentalist position. In Hume's view, Hutcheson follows Butler in failing to take a sufficiently experimental approach to human nature.[42]

728. Hume v. Hutcheson and Butler on Nature

Butler begins his *Sermons* with three sermons on human nature, which are presupposed in his arguments about self-love and conscience. Butler argues that morality is natural for human beings as rational agents; he defines an appropriate sense of 'natural', referring to the human system and constitution as a whole, and argues that self-love and conscience both fulfil nature by being rational faculties. He claims that morality is natural, and that it is rational.

In Hobbes's view, we show that morality is rational if and only if we vindicate it by an argument from the specific circumstances described in the transition from the state of nature to the commonwealth. This justification falls short of Butler's aim; for Butler wants to show that morality is justified and appropriate for human nature in any circumstances, not just when it accords with Hobbesian self-interest.

At first sight, Hutcheson and Hume agree with Butler in believing that morality is natural, but reject his belief that morality is rational. They deny that moral judgments and sentiments are simply devices to secure the self-interest of Hobbesian agents; they take morality to have a broader foundation in the operations of human nature and human mental life in general. Hume, agreeing with Hutcheson, accepts Butler's objections to psychological hedonist egoism,[43] and treats Butler's argument as an example of the ways in which philosophical investigation of human nature can lead to a more accurate understanding of the basis of morality.

Hume's sympathy with some of Butler's views helps to explain why he tried to bring his work to Butler's attention. He sought an introduction to Butler, and told a friend that he was 'castrating' his draft of the *Treatise* in order to show it to Butler.[44] He also sent Butler a copy of the published *Treatise*.[45] Butler was reported to have been favourably impressed by Hume's *Essays*,[46] but we do not know whether or how he responded to the 'castrated' *Treatise*, or to the published work, or how the one differed from the other.

---

[42] On Hutcheson and Hume see §781.   [43] *IHU* 1.14n.

[44] Letter in Klibansky and Mossner, *NLDH* #1. Mossner, *LDH* 112, and Penelhum, *TH* 244, assert that the parts of the *T* that Hume removed were about miracles. But the letter gives no evidence of this. Penelhum and Mossner appeal to the previous paragraph of the letter, which deals with a draft essay on miracles. They infer that (a) this essay was intended to be part of the *Treatise*, and (b) it is the part that Hume excised from the 'castrated' version that he showed to Butler. But Hume says nothing to support either inference.

[45] Letter in Greig, *LDH* i #8.

[46] Klibansky and Mossner, *NLDH* #5 ('I am also told that Dr Butler has everywhere recommended them.').

Hume follows Hutcheson in absorbing some of Butler's views within a sentimentalist position. But he rejects other aspects of Butler's position. In particular, he denies that virtue is natural to human beings.[47] He opposes the natural to the miraculous, to the unusual, and to the artificial, and argues that in none of these senses of 'natural' is virtue natural and vice unnatural.[48] Since these senses of 'natural' include all those that are relevant to naturalism about virtue, Butler's system is unphilosophical.

None of Hume's senses of 'natural', however, fits Butler. For Butler's crucial third sense of 'natural' fits none of Hume's senses. This is the sense that is relevant to Butler's claim that what is natural for a natural organism is what is required by its whole constitution and system, as opposed to each particular part.[49] Butler does not mean simply that virtue is non-miraculous, usual, or non-artificial; hence the fact that these features do not distinguish virtue from vice does not affect Butler's thesis.

Elsewhere Hume notices a sense of 'natural' that is more relevant to Butler. He suggests that Hutcheson appeals to nature in a sense that involves some teleological assumptions. This is a reasonable interpretation of Butler's claims too. But Hume adds, without further argument, the more questionable claim that the relevant teleological claims can be defended only by an appeal to design.[50] For reasons that he gives in his *Dialogues*, he believes that no sufficient empirical case can be made for the claim that natural organisms are designed for some end.[51]

To show that Hutcheson's implicit claim about ends involves him in theology, Hume alludes to the first question in the *Shorter Catechism* ('What is the chief end of man?') and to the answer ('. . . to glorify God and enjoy him for ever').[52] Hutcheson tries to avoid any appeal to such dogmatic claims by basing morality on nature; but Hume's questions suggest that this attempt fails, because the teleological aspects of nature raise questions that cannot be settled by natural reason.

A teleological sense of 'natural' fits Butler's claim that some things are natural for an organism because they are appropriate for the organism as a whole. But it is a further step to claim that they are appropriate because they promote the activities for which the organism was designed. Perhaps, then, Hume's main objection to Butler claims that Butler's normative conception of the natural relies on an 'unphilosophical' assumption about design. This assumption is the topic of Hume's *Dialogues* and Butler's *Analogy*. Hume objects to

[47] 'Mean while it may not be amiss to observe, from these definitions of natural and unnatural, that nothing can be more unphilosophical than those systems, which assert, that virtue is the same with what is natural, and vice with what is unnatural.' (*T* iii 1.2.10)

[48] ''Tis impossible, therefore, that the character of natural and unnatural can ever, in any sense, mark the boundaries of vice and virtue.' (*T* iii 1.2.10)

[49] See §679.

[50] 'I cannot agree to your sense of *natural*. It is founded on final causes; which is a consideration, that appears to me pretty uncertain and unphilosophical. For pray, what is the end of man? Is he created for happiness or for virtue? For this life or for the next? For himself or for his Maker? Your definition of *natural* depends on solving these questions, which are endless, and quite wide of my purpose.' (17 Sept. 1739, Greig i #13 = R 631) Hutcheson normally uses 'nature' in a non-normative sense that is quite similar to Hume's. But the conception that Hume questions influences Hutcheson's argument to show that the moral sense is not arbitrary, but actually implanted by God for the good of the human race. See §663.

[51] See Hume, *DNR*, esp. Parts 5–6.

[52] See Schaff, *CC* iii 676. Hutcheson subscribed the Westminster Confession (to which the Shorter and Larger Catechisms were annexed) on taking up his chair in Glasgow; see Scott, *FH* 56.

Hutcheson, as he often does, on a point on which Hutcheson is closer to Butler than Hume thinks Hutcheson ought to be.[53]

Hume is right to believe that both Butler and Hutcheson regard human beings as products of design. It does not follow, however, that a belief in design is needed to support the normative claim that an organism's nature and constitution require one course of action rather than another. Irrespective of beliefs about design, facts about a system and constitution as a whole seem to support claims about what is natural for an organism. We rely on such claims when we say that someone needs to have a tooth extracted or needs an operation.[54] To see how far Hume departs from Butler's naturalistic form of argument, we should consider his views on these claims about needs.

729. Legitimate Appeals to Nature

The *Inquiry* is more conciliatory than the *Treatise* about naturalism. Hume allows that justice is natural, since it tends to arise from the operation of natural human tendencies.[55] If we seek to contrast the natural with the artificial, we must conclude that justice is artificial rather than natural. Still, disputes about naturalness are merely verbal, since justice is also natural in a clear and acceptable sense.

These conciliatory remarks about nature do not mark a difference of substance from the *Treatise*. For, though they allow us to claim that virtues are natural, they do not show that they are distinctively natural; vices might equally be natural in the sense that Hume allows.

Hume goes further towards Butler's position, however, in some of his claims about the moral sense. In the *Treatise* his attack on naturalism about virtue immediately follows his argument to show that the sentiments of morality are natural. According to his account of the senses of 'natural', he need only show that these sentiments are frequently found in human beings. But he says more than this. Though he does not affirm that virtue consists in acting in accordance with nature, he accepts part of the relevant conception of nature. In his view, human beings who have their moral sentiments extirpated and destroyed fall into disease or madness.[56]

Here Hume implicitly acknowledges one clear sense, apart from those he explicitly recognizes, in which an action or condition may be natural or against nature. To say that the removal of some trait is liable to cause disease or madness is not simply to say that the trait is frequent; for many frequent traits might be removed without these effects. In speaking of disease or madness, Hume recognizes that some things are required by, or appropriate for, a human being as a whole system. Disease and madness are not simply infrequent conditions; they oppose the needs of the whole system. What the whole system

---

[53] The connexion between Hutcheson and Butler is especially clear in Hutcheson, *HN*. See §676.

[54] See Butler, §680.

[55] 'The word natural is commonly taken in so many senses and is of so loose a signification, that it seems vain to dispute whether justice be natural or not.' 'In so sagacious an animal, what necessarily arises from the exertion of his intellectual faculties may justly be termed natural.' (*I*, App 3.9)

[56] 'These sentiments are so rooted in our constitution and temper, that without entirely confounding the human mind by disease or madness, 'tis impossible to extirpate and destroy them.' (*T* iii 1.2.8)

needs is what Butler calls 'natural' in his third sense. Hume, therefore, allows that some things are natural, in Butler's third sense. He even regards the moral sentiments as natural, in this sense.

Hume might reject this argument because it assumes that disease and madness must be understood by reference to the needs of a whole system. If he could replace this holistic and evaluative (because of 'needs') claim with an 'experimental' and purely statistical claim, he would show that truths about health and sanity do not concede the substance of Butler's claims about appropriateness to nature. He might claim for instance that madness and disease are conditions that interfere with aims that most people share, irrespective of their upbringing and environment, and that this is what makes them natural. If he defends this claim, he accepts a version of naturalism, though it is not Butler's version.

730. Nature and Rational Authority

But even if Hume agrees with Butler's claim that some actions are naturally appropriate for a human being, he disagrees about which actions these are. In Butler's view, two claims about naturalness are closely connected: (1) What is natural for a human being is what is appropriate for the whole system that constitutes a human being. (2) For a human being as a rational agent, it is appropriate to act in accordance with superior principles appealing to authority rather than strength. Hume accepts neither of these claims.

Butler's first claim assumes that a human being is a system, as opposed to a collection or aggregate of traits, capacities, and desires. We must recognize this system before we can identify principles that aim at the good of the system as a whole. But some of Hume's other claims commit him to the denial of this belief in a system. According to Hume, a human self is simply a collection of mental states and episodes, no subset of which constitutes the essential or fundamental self. We cannot consider or protect the fundamental persistent characteristics of the numerically identical self, since there is no such self and there are no such characteristics.

Perhaps we ought not to introduce Hume's sceptical arguments about personal identity. He does not suggest that his arguments in moral philosophy presuppose his scepticism about personal identity. On the contrary, he allows that the idea of the self accompanies many passions.[57] But he does not make any of the claims about a person as a system that support Butler's claims about natural action. He may recognize that Butler's view involves claims about the self that are too robust for Hume's position.[58]

Since Hume rejects Butler's claims about the self, he also rejects Butler's precise distinction between rational self-love and the particular passions. Though he accepts a part of Butler's argument in favour of benevolence (*IPM* 9.20),[59] he omits Butler's claim that self-love is

---

[57] At *T* ii 1.2.2 he speaks of 'self, or that succession of related ideas and impressions, of which we have an intimate memory and consciousness'. Here 'intimate' is needed to distinguish our idea of the self from our idea of a chair.

[58] This issue about the self becomes important in Hume's discussion of prudence and justice; see *T* iii 2.7.5, discussed in §770.

[59] This passage has no parallel in *T*.

concerned with the whole self as opposed to particular objects of desire. The deliberations of self-love seem to assume something like Butler's conception of its aim and object.[60] But Hume's outlook leaves no room for such a conception. He needs to explain self-love with reference to the agent's predominant desires, not with reference to the whole self.[61]

Butler claims not only that self-love is concerned with the whole self, but also that its concern is rational, since it is a superior principle. In calling it rational and superior, Butler means that it not only registers the strength of our desire for x over y, but also considers the reasons that make a good case for preferring x over y. This rational character of self-love explains why it is better at finding natural actions than the particular passions are; if we were to follow our strongest particular passion, we would not find what is appropriate for the temporally extended self as a whole. The appropriately holistic view requires a superior principle. Since conscience has the same rational character, it also finds natural actions. Both self-love and conscience are rational and authoritative principles that find what is appropriate for one's nature as a whole.

Hutcheson and Hume reject Butler's claims about the rationality of self-love and conscience, because they reject his claims about authority of reasons and strength of desires. In their view, the recognition of a reason for doing x is simply the awareness of a desire to do x or of a sentiment in favour of doing x. If self-love and conscience are not distinctively rational, neither prudence nor morality is distinctively rational.

This is why Hutcheson claims that one needs to attribute a moral sense to us to explain why we approve of some actions and characters rather than others. In his view, we would have been no less rational if we had lacked this attitude to morality. Whereas Butler connects rationality with being moved by a superior principle, Hutcheson denies the connexion, since his views about reasons leave no room for Butler's claims about superiority. Nonetheless, Hutcheson follows Hobbes and treats prudence as especially rational.[62] Moreover, though he rejects Butler's view that authority depends on superior reason, he affirms the authority of conscience.

Hume explicitly disagrees with Hutcheson on the authority of conscience;[63] he implicitly disagrees with him on the rationality of prudence. According to Hume, reason does not guide us to act in accordance with human nature. None of the distinctive operations that Butler attributes to self-love is especially characteristic of reason. Hence, it is not distinctively rational to take the point of view of self-love. For Butler, rational self-love has special insight into what is required for the benefit of the system that constitutes human nature. For Hume, there is no such system, and there is no distinctively rational self-love. Even if our nature requires certain kinds of actions, reason gives us no special access to them. In disagreeing with Butler about reason and natural action, Hume relies on his treatment of passion and reason.

---

[60] See Butler, §686.

[61] Butler sometimes affirms a hedonist account of the aim and object of self-love. Hume might easily suppose that he could agree with this characterization of self-love, and so take over Butler's argument, without seeing that Butler presupposes a conception of self-love for which Hume has no room.

[62] See §637.   [63] See §779.

731. Objectivism and Naturalism

This comparison of Hume's experimental approach to human nature with Butler's normative approach clarifies Hume's view of the main options in moral philosophy. He connects his approach with Hutcheson's, and cites Hutcheson's argument for the moral sense as an important discovery about the basis of morality.[64] Hutcheson has refuted Clarke's position, and thereby refuted objectivism.[65] The *Letter from a Gentleman* aligns Hutcheson (and others) with the ancients on one side, against Clarke and Wollaston on the other side.[66]

Hume's summary of Hutcheson distinguishes two positions. (1) The rationalist claims that (a) moral judgments are rational, and that (b) moral truths belong to the 'abstract nature of things' and are not confined to human nature. (2) The sentimentalist claims that (a) moral judgments belong to taste or sentiment rather than reason, and that (b) moral truths are confined to human nature. Hume treats the dispute as a dispute between Hutcheson and an opponent such as Clarke or Wollaston.

This summary of options in moral philosophy is worth comparing with Butler's summary.[67] Like Hume, Butler describes one approach as examining 'the abstract relations of things'; the other approach begins 'from a matter of fact, namely, what the particular nature of man is'. Butler agrees with Hutcheson and Hume in avoiding the first approach, though he does not repudiate it as they do; he pursues the second approach. But he does not agree that the second approach must make morality relative to the 'sentiment or mental taste of each particular being'. It makes morality relative to the nature of human beings, but facts about human nature are not primarily facts about the sentiments and tastes of human beings. Nor does Butler believe that moral judgments are expressions of sentiment and taste. He follows the rationalists in taking them to be rational judgments, though he does not endorse Clarke's view of what they are about.

Hume, in contrast to Hutcheson, does not treat Butler's view as an alternative to the extreme rationalism of Clarke. He rejects Hutcheson's attempted reconciliation of Butler with sentimentalism.[68] Here he is partly right and partly wrong. Hume is right to suggest that Butler's position does not fit sentimentalism. But Hutcheson is right to suggest that Butler's position is different from Clarke's. Hume ignores or overlooks this difference; probably he classifies Butler with Clarke as a theorist about the 'abstract nature of things'. This judgment is based on Butler's non-experimental and normative conception of nature. In Hume's view,

---

[64] The letter printed in Ross, 'Hutcheson on Hume', describes Hutcheson's initial favourable reaction to *T* i–ii. Hutcheson remarks that he has himself become more sympathetic to an Academic position. He does not reach a definite judgment on Hume's views.

[65] 'That faculty by which we discern truth and falsehood, and that by which we perceive vice and virtue, had long been confounded with each other, and all morality was supposed to be built on eternal and immutable relations which, to every intelligent mind, were equally invariable as any proposition concerning quantity or number. But a late philosopher has taught us, by the most convincing arguments, that morality is nothing in the abstract nature of things, but is entirely relative to the sentiment or mental taste of each particular being, in the same manner as the distinctions of sweet and bitter, hot and cold arise from the particular feeling of each sense or organ. Moral perceptions, therefore, ought not to be classed with the operations of the understanding, but with the tastes or sentiments.' (*IHU* ed. Hendel, 23n) See Kemp Smith, *PDH* 19.

[66] *LG* quoted in §751.   [67] Butler, *Sermons*, P 12–13, discussed in §678.

[68] On Hutcheson and Butler see §715.

the only philosophers who have the appropriate regard for human nature are those whose attitude is purely experimental and non-normative. To go further is to make untenable claims about 'abstract nature'.

Though Hume never, in his published works, argues against Butler by name, these disagreements with Butler are instructive; for Butler's version of naturalism is a plausible alternative to Hume's. We can now consider Hume's argument for an exclusively experimental and non-normative approach to human nature and morality. Butler believes that an examination of human nature supports a division between rational authority and appetitive strength. This division, in turn, supports the grounding of moral principles in rational authority. Since Hume rejects Butler's conception of human nature, he also rejects Butler's argument from nature to rational authority.

56

HUME: PASSION AND REASON

---

732. Aquinas, Hobbes, and Hume on the Passions

To attack views that connect nature, reason, and morality, Hume relies on his account of passion, practical reason, and their relation. He sets out his account of the passions in Book ii of the *Treatise*, before the chapter 'Of the Influencing Motives of the Will' (ii 3.3), which describes the roles of passion and practical reason. This account of the passions influences his discussion both of practical reason and of moral judgment. A comparison with Aquinas' account of the passions, on the one hand, and with Hobbes's account, on the other, highlights Hume's distinctive claims about the passions.

Aquinas emphasizes the relation of passions to desire for the good and to reason. Since he believes that human action on passions is normally voluntary and responsible, and that well-trained passions are essential to virtue and badly trained passions encourage vice, he seeks to explain how the passions are both distinct from and connected with the will and the good. He rejects the Stoic view that passions are false judgments about the good, but he accepts the Stoic claim that they involve desire on the basis of an appearance of some good. 'On the basis of' indicates not simply a causal relation, but also a justifying relation; the desire that belongs to the passion is guided by the appearance of goodness, and if we lose the appearance, we lose that passion. If the passion is connected to an appearance of goodness, it is open to criticism and evaluation. If the appearance is unjustified, the passion is unjustified, and we have reason to get rid of it. The passions are sources of voluntary action because they are subject to the consent of the will, which is moved not simply by an appearance of goodness, but by a belief about the universal good. They are the subjects of virtues because they can be guided by a will that is guided by prudence.

Hobbes and Hume reject Aquinas' description of the passions. Hobbes rejects the Scholastic division between will and passion. He identifies the passions with the various aspects of our motive power.[1] He entitles a chapter on the passions, 'Of the interior beginnings of voluntary motions; commonly called the passions . . . ' (*L*. 6, title). The will is not distinct from the passions; it is simply the 'last appetite, or aversion, immediately adhering to the action, or to the omission thereof'. The will is not essentially responsive

---

[1] ' . . . the power motive of the mind is that by which the mind giveth animal motion to the body wherein it existeth; the acts hereof are our affections and passions . . . ' (Hobbes, *EL* 6.9 = R 2).

to practical reason. Deliberation belongs to every passion; practical reason has no special role in, for instance, prescribing the pursuit of one's long-term good in opposition to one's more immediate impulses. Hobbes, however, does not always draw this conclusion. He treats prudence as the proper exercise of practical reason, prescribing concern for one's longer-term good. The prudent person is the one who deliberates best, by taking account of more consequences, and acts on this deliberation.[2]

Hume agrees with Hobbes in rejecting the division between passion and will. He sees that if we reject this division, we undermine Hobbes's belief in a special connexion between practical reason, will, and concern for one's overall good. Hobbes's belief is a Scholastic remnant, conflicting with the rest of Hobbes's position. Hume removes the conflict.

His analysis of the passions eliminates the aspects of a passion that allow rational evaluation and guidance. Aquinas believes that a passion is tractable because it includes an appearance of the goodness of its object, even though it does not rest on a belief about universal good. Hobbes retains this feature of Aquinas' account, since he takes each passion to involve its distinctive form of appetite or aversion, and therefore its distinctive view of something as good or bad (L. 6.2, 7). Hume, however, separates the passion from any appearance of goodness, taking the relation to be purely contingent. This aspect of his analysis explains some of his most surprising claims about the passions and their objects.[3]

733. The Object and the Cause of a Passion

Hume distinguishes the cause from the object of a given passion, and within the cause he further distinguishes the subject and the quality (T ii 1.2.6).[4] Since he takes causal relations to hold between 'objects', usually understood as events, we might take the subject (for instance, a house) and its quality (splendour) to be different constituents of the event that is the cause. Perhaps the object is a state of affairs or fact, so that I take pride in, say, the fact that I have a splendid house, or in my having a splendid house.

But when he speaks of the object of a passion, Hume does not refer to anything as complex as a fact or state of affairs. He seems to refer to the particular item in the world to which one's passion is directed. Hence he takes pride and humility to have the same object, oneself.[5] If we identified the cause with the object (as Hume understands 'object'), and distinguished passions by their objects, we would have to say that pride and humility are the same passion, because they have the same object. They are different, however, because they have different causes. Hume does not consider a description of the object of pride as 'something good about myself' or 'the fact that I am suitably connected to something good', or a suitably different description of humility.

---

[2] See L. 6.57, quoted in §473.

[3] Bennett, SSE 271, argues that Descartes, but not Spinoza, agrees with Hume in rejecting any cognitive element in a passion.

[4] Kemp Smith, PDH 180–5, discusses the object and the cause of a passion.

[5] 'Pride and humility, being once raised, immediately turn our attention to ourself, and regard that as their ultimate and final object; but there is something further requisite in order to raise them: something, which is peculiar to one of the passions, and produces not both in the very same degree.' (T ii 1.2.4)

He omits this possibility because he believes that the connexions between a passion, its cause, and its object are contingent features of the passion; we discover them by noticing correlations, not by grasping the necessary properties of a passion. When Hume asks how pride and humility take the self as their object (ii 1.3.4), he treats this as a reasonable question to be answered by empirical inquiry. If we took these passions to be essentially connected to specific objects, we would take such a question to rest on a misunderstanding. If the connexion were essential, a passion would not be pride if it involved no reflexion on oneself as suitably related to something good or admirable. If Hume admitted an essential connexion between pride and oneself, his question about how the self comes to be the object of pride would ask how a necessary connexion comes to be a contingent connexion. Since he is not asking this nonsensical question, he does not take the connexion between pride and oneself to be essential.

On this point he disagrees with Butler, whose analysis of resentment examines the essential character of resentment in order to discover some of our beliefs about justice and injustice. Butler assumes that these beliefs are essential to this specific passion, and that without them it would not be resentment. Similarly, Price argues that each affection 'has its particular end' that is essential to a given passion.[6]

If Butler and Price are right to believe in an internal connexion between passion and object, cause and object are less sharply separated than Hume supposes. Instead of saying that the house and its beauty are the cause of pride and I am its object, we may say that pride is directed towards good features of myself, so that in this case it is directed towards myself owning this beautiful house. 'Myself owning this beautiful house' would describe both the cause and the object of my pride; for the description of the object includes the description of the feature that makes it suitable for pride, and hence gives a reason for me to be proud of it. Though I might say I am proud of myself or proud of my house, a full description says that I am proud of myself as owner of this beautiful house. Similarly, I might say that I am afraid for myself or that I am afraid of a stray bullet, but a full description says that I am afraid of a stray bullet inflicting harm on me.

Since Hume does not recognize this connexion between passion and object, the question that we might find strange—about how pride and humility both have oneself for their object—is reasonable for him. His answer implies that the correlation between pride and its object is empirical.[7] It is a striking fact of experience, he supposes, that we cannot feel pride that is unrelated to ourselves; this fact reveals a constant tendency in human nature. If Hume had believed that it is logically impossible to feel pride unrelated to ourselves, he would not have taken this feature of pride to show something about the empirical tendencies of human beings.

If the relation of pride to oneself is natural and contingent, pride must have some further individuating property that allows the empirical discovery that we have pride only about

---

[6] Price, RPQM 69, explains his position: 'if . . . we desire everything merely as the means of our own good, and with an ultimate view to it, then in reality we desire nothing but our own good, and have only the one single affection of self-love'.

[7] 'Tis evident in the first place, that these passions are determined to have self for their object, not only by a natural but also by an original property. No one can doubt but this property is natural from the constancy and steadiness of its operation. 'Tis always self, which is the object of pride and humility; and whenever the passions look beyond, 'tis still with a view to ourselves, nor can any person or object otherwise have any influence upon us.' (T ii 1.3.2)

ourselves. If we had to distinguish pride from other passions by its object, we could not discover that something we already recognized as pride is always directed to oneself. Hume believes, then, that pride has some distinctive nature apart from its causes and objects. The distinctive nature is its introspectible quality. We discover cause and object empirically, because we find by experience that this specific introspectible feeling of pride is invariably associated with these causes and this object.

Hume's views about the individuation of passions, and their logical independence from causes and objects, are even clearer from some of his remarks about love and hatred. In his view, benevolence and anger are only contingently accompanied by love and hatred, 'by the original constitution of the mind' (ii 2.6 6). The relation that actually holds between love and benevolence 'abstractly considered, is not necessary', because the sensations of love and hatred could have existed without any desire, or connected with the opposite desires.[8] This division between the sensation and the desire implies that the sensation is the essential feature of the passion, contingently connected with the desire. This same view explains why passions are only contingently associated with their objects and causes.[9] According to this view, the sensation that we now have when we wish well to other people would still be love if it were conjoined with a desire to harm them or with complete indifference to their interests.

Hume may be right to claim that the sensation is part of the passion. The mere desire to benefit others is not enough for the passion of love, since we might have the desire for various reasons that would not cause the passion. But it does not follow that the desire is inessential to the passion. Hume's claim that the sensation is logically separable from the desire does not justify his claim that the mere sensation is the passion.

734. Passion and Evaluation

What does Hume's analysis of the passions imply for Aquinas' claims about the relation of the passions to will and reason? What Hume has said so far does not exclude some modification of passions by reason.[10] But the role he allows for reason is severely restricted.

Sometimes we decide that we are proud on the wrong occasions. Perhaps, for instance, we see that we ought not to be proud of the ingenuity we have shown in cheating people out of what justly belonged to them. According to Aquinas, we see that our pride lacks the object that is essential to it; pride is directed to our deceptive ingenuity on the assumption that it is good, and so the pride goes away once we abandon the assumption. The rational belief that deceptive ingenuity is nothing to be proud of does not automatically cancel our pride in deceptive ingenuity; for the appearance of goodness may be tenacious even when

---

[8] 'If nature had so pleased, love might have had the same effect as hatred, and hatred as love. I see no contradiction in supposing a desire of producing misery annexed to love, and of happiness to hatred. If the sensation of the passion and desire be opposite, nature could have altered the sensation without altering the tendency of the desire, and by that means made them compatible with each other.' (ii 2.6.6)

[9] Kenny, *AEW* 22–6, discusses Hume's view that emotions and their objects are only contingently connected. Russell, *FMS*, ch. 6, justly criticizes Hume on this point. Emotions and their objects are discussed by Lyons, *E*, ch. 6. See also Penelhum, *H*, ch. 5; Baier, *PS*, 158–60, 180–1; Reid, §849.

[10] For the moment, I set aside Hume's views about will and reason and concentrate on his views on the passions.

we abandon the belief. Still, the passion itself is open to rational criticism that tends to sustain or to undermine it, because of the internal connexion between the passion and the appearance.

Hume cannot allow this criticism of a passion, if the appearance of goodness is not an essential property of the passion itself, but simply part of the cause. Since beliefs can affect passions, the recognition that I have nothing to be proud of may cause me to abandon the passion.[11] But my recognition does not warrant criticism of my pride, since the belief or appearance of something to be proud of is not essential to the passion. The passion may be modified if we no longer attribute the property we used to attribute to its cause; but this is not criticism of the passion, but simply manipulation of it. Since the appearance of goodness is not part of the passion, an unreasonable or foolish appearance does not make a passion unreasonable or foolish.

735. Reason and Passion: Hume and Hutcheson

Hume's account of the passions, therefore, leaves open the possibility of causal influence, rather than rational criticism and evaluation, by the rational will.[12] But Hume does not exploit this possibility, since he does not separate the rational will from the passions; he argues that the will is a passion, with no essential connexion to practical reason. This is Hume's version of Hobbes's claim that the will is simply the last appetite in deliberation. Hume's version rests on a more precise account of a passion.

Hume takes himself to oppose a widespread view about the role of practical reason.[13] Though he does not mention Hutcheson, he defends Hutcheson's view that neither exciting nor justifying reasons can be derived from reason. But in contrast to Hutcheson, Hume suggests that his view 'may appear somewhat extraordinary' (ii 3.3.4).[14] He presents himself as an innovator challenging a consensus in favour of rationalism. Hutcheson, however, believes that this anti-rationalist view simply reasserts a Scholastic and Aristotelian view against modern rationalists.[15]

In the *Inquiry* Hume does not say he is an innovator.[16] He signals the importance that he attaches to the issue about reason and passion, by introducing it in the very first section of the work, and promising to present his own view of the issue in the course of the work as a whole. He recognizes that he is taking part in a controversy in which each side has

---

[11] This effect of beliefs on passions is emphasized by Baier, *PS* 158, who refers to Book i.

[12] This point is emphasized by Baier, *PS* 179–80.

[13] 'Nothing is more usual in philosophy, and even in common life, than to talk of the combat of passion and reason, to give the preference to reason, and to assert that men are only so far virtuous as they conform themselves to its dictates . . . On this method of thinking the greatest part of moral philosophy, ancient and modern, seems to be founded; nor is there an ampler field, as well for metaphysical arguments, as popular declamations, than this supposed pre-eminence of reason above passion.' (*T* ii 3.3.1)

[14] Hume's description of his view as perhaps appearing 'extraordinary' misleads Norton, *DH* 100, who takes this to imply that Hume does not derive it from Hutcheson. Hume's silence about his agreement with Hutcheson is parallel to iii 1.1.27, on 'is' and 'ought'. See §751.

[15] See Hutcheson, §657.

[16] Perhaps Hume is better informed than when he wrote *T* ii. Or perhaps (as in *LG*) he wants to show that his view is not outrageous.

already been defended.[17] Shaftesbury is the first modern writer to see the importance of distinguishing the contributions of reason and passion; he agrees with the 'ancient' view (as Hume conceives it) that makes taste and sentiment fundamental.

At the beginning of the *Inquiry*, Hume professes some sympathy for both sides in this dispute. But eventually he reasserts his anti-rationalism. In the first Appendix, he draws his conclusion from the argument of the *Inquiry*, and defends the position of the *Treatise*.[18] He relies on the argument that Hutcheson ascribes to Aristotle.

Hume needs to defend two claims: (1) The source of justifying and exciting reasons is not reason itself. (2) The source is passion. To reach the second claim from the first we must assume that the only two conceivable 'influencing motives of the will' are passion and reason, and that if reason fails, only passion is left. Hume assumes this; he devotes his efforts to a defence of his first claim, and says little to defend the dichotomy that underlies the second claim.[19] The assumptions that support the dichotomy are doubtful. Aquinas, for instance, believes that reason does not move us by itself, but does not infer that passion must be the only mover; for will, as Aquinas conceives it, is neither reason nor passion. If Hume conceives reason broadly, perhaps Aquinas' position fits into his dichotomy; but then we may need to reconsider the soundness of his argument to show that reason does not give us justifying or exciting reasons. What, then, does Hume mean by his first claim, and how does he defend it?

736. The Functions of Reason

To show that reason cannot provide justifying or exciting reasons, Hume claims to describe all the functions of reason, and then points out that these functions do not include exciting or justifying reasons.[20] He allows only two functions: (a) Reason points out that a desire rests on some false supposition, so that I desire x as F (F is x's desirability-characteristic), and reason points out to me that x is not F. (b) Reason points out to me that a desire for x as a means to y rests on a false supposition that x is in fact a means sufficient for y. The second function of reason is an instance of the first, informing me that the object of my desire lacks some feature that I thought it had, and that was the basis of my desiring it. Hume does not imply that whenever reason informs me that I have made a mistake about the properties of x, my desire for x will go away. He implies that if

[17] 'There has been a controversy started of late ... concerning the general foundation of morals; whether they be derived from reason, or from sentiment ... our modern enquirers, though they also talk much of the beauty of virtue, and deformity of vice, yet have commonly endeavoured to account for these distinctions by metaphysical reasonings, and by deductions from the most abstract principles of the understanding.' (*I*1.3) For the sentence omitted here, on the ancient moralists, see §725.

[18] 'It appears evident that the ultimate ends of human actions can never, in any case, be accounted for by reason, but recommend themselves entirely to the sentiments and affections of mankind, without any dependence on the intellectual faculties.... It is impossible there can be a progress in infinitum; and that one thing can always be a reason why another is desired. Something must be desirable on its own account, and because of its immediate accord or agreement with human sentiment and affection.' (*I*, App. 1.18–19)

[19] Stroud's succinct and lucid discussion, *H*156–66, makes clear the difference in Hume's treatment of the two claims.

[20] 'I shall endeavour to prove first, that reason alone can never be a motive to any action of the will; and secondly, that it can never oppose passion in the direction of the will.' (*T* ii 3.3.1)

I thought x was G, discover that it is not G, but still desire it, then I did not desire x as G.[21]

What sorts of reasons does Hume's argument cover? Hutcheson argues: (1) Reason provides no exciting reason; every action is caused by some desire that is independent of reason. (2) Reason provides no justifying reason: appeal to reason cannot show that one action deserves approval over another (except within the limits fixed by the functions of reason). Hume agrees with Hutcheson on exciting reasons, since he claims that 'reason alone can never be a motive to any action of the will'. He also seems to agree on justifying reasons. His claim that reason 'can never oppose passion in the direction of the will' includes justifying reasons, if 'direction' refers to prescriptions as well as to actual motivation. Moreover, Hume's account of the functions of reason undermines a justifying as well as an exciting role for reason alone.[22] In saying that what reason alone tells us cannot 'concern' us without some presupposed desire, he refers implicitly to justifying reasons. In saying that a desire must be presupposed before the objects of reason are 'able to affect us', he refers to exciting reasons.[23]

If Hume has identified the only two possible functions of reason, he has shown why Hutcheson is right: (1) Reason cannot by itself provide exciting reasons, since the two kinds of reasoning Hume recognizes cannot themselves motivate without some antecedent desire for an end about which reason discovers these facts. Simply discovering that x is F, or that x is a sufficient means to y does not move me to pursue x unless I already care about x's being F or being a means to y. (2) Nor can reason by itself provide justifying reasons; for the information that reason gives does not show that this or that action deserves to be approved. If I find that x is a sufficient means to y, I still have no justifying reason to approve x, unless I already want y. If reason supports my approval of x, I presuppose some prior approval of y, resting on some desire for y as an end or on some approval of y that in turn rests on a desire for some further end.

The narrow scope of reason implies that reason can prescribe neither the choice of an end nor the choice of the best means to an end. If I could book a flight from New York to London on one airline for $600 and on another airline for $700, and the two flights and airlines are otherwise equal, reason, as Hume understands it, is indifferent between them. Hume is right, given his view of the functions of reason, to deny that the preference for efficiency is rational. The choice of the best and most efficient means presupposes some preference for prudence and foresight, but this preference is not based on reason.

Hume rejects the Scholastic division between passion and will, because he does not treat will as essentially rational desire. According to Aquinas, will is rational because it aims at the

---

[21] In this respect, then, the character of a desire is not transparent to the subject. This lack of transparency is difficult to reconcile with Hume's usual view of impressions. Cf. i 4.2.5.

[22] He may have both roles of reason in mind in his familiar comparison of reason with passion: 'Thus it appears, that the principle, which opposes our passion, cannot be the same with reason, and is only called so in an improper sense. We speak not strictly and philosophically when we talk of the combat of passion and of reason. Reason is, and ought only to be the slave of the passions, and can never pretend to any other office than to serve and obey them.' (T ii 3.3.4) 'Pretending to an office' might include giving advice or prescriptions in opposition to passion.

[23] 'It can never in the least concern us to know, that such objects are causes, and such others effects, if both the causes and effects be indifferent to us. Where the objects themselves do not affect us, their connexion can never give them any influence; and 'tis plain, that as reason is nothing but the discovery of this connexion, it cannot be by its means that the objects are able to affect us.' (ii 3.3.3)

universal and final good; responsiveness to the believed effects of an action on my overall good makes will a rational desire. Hume does not deny that we might have a desire directed towards our longer-term rather than our shorter-term interest; we must have such a desire if we ever prefer the scratching of our finger to the destruction of the world. But he maintains that this is not a distinctively rational desire.

Hume believes that prudent action results from reasoning about what promotes my good as a whole, together with my overriding desire for my good as a whole. To this extent it is based on reason. But imprudent action may be based on reason to exactly the same extent. An intention resulting from the desire for my overall good and from deliberation about means to satisfy it is rational, if we mean only that it requires some reasoning (as Hume understands it). But such an intention is no more rational than an intention resulting from reasoning about how to satisfy a foolish and transitory desire. If we confine will to long-term desires, it is not distinctively rational. If we extend it to desires based on any reasoning at all, it has no special connexion with any overall good.

It is not contrary to reason, therefore, to prefer the destruction of the world to the scratching of my finger (T ii 3.3.6). If I see that x leads to the destruction of the world, and y to the scratching of my finger, I may choose x over y on the basis of this reasoning. The fact that the reasoning in question is not about my overall good does not make it any the less a case of reasoning; hence it does not make the action any less rational in any strict sense. Hume assumes that the relevant sense of 'rational' is 'resting on reasoning', and that the relevant sense of 'contrary to reason' is 'contrary to the conclusion of all reasoning'. This is why both the actions just mentioned are equally rational, and neither is contrary to reason.

Reason, therefore, cannot provide justifying reasons for the pursuit of one end over another.[24] Hume recognizes 'the maxims of common prudence and discretion' that advise us on how to achieve our various ends, by identifying instrumental means to them. But he argues that reason can provide nothing more.[25] The Sceptic claims that reason is incapable of discovering that anything is valuable in itself, and hence of justifying any ultimate ends.[26] He defends his claims about ultimate ends, first from 'diversity of sentiment', and then from the arguments in the *Treatise* about the source of moral distinctions. Hume's discussions of reason and passion and of moral distinctions have the common aim of undermining the conception of the philosopher as a 'cunning man' who can tell us which ends are worth pursuing, independently of whether we already pursue them or not. In denying that the philosopher is a 'cunning man', Hume denies that reason can provide justifying reasons independent of antecedent passions.

[24] This aspect of Hume's position is explored by Korsgaard, 'Instrumental' 220–34.

[25] 'What is it then you desire more? Do you come to a philosopher as to a cunning man, to learn something by magic or witchcraft, beyond what can be known by common prudence and discretion?—Yes; we come to a philosopher to be instructed, how we shall choose our ends, more than the means for attaining these ends; We want to know what desire we shall gratify, what passion we shall comply with, what appetite we shall indulge. . . . I am sorry, then, I have pretended to be a philosopher; For I find your questions very perplexing . . .' ('Sceptic' §§6–7, = EMPL163) On Hume's essays on the Epicurean, the Stoic, the Platonist, and the Sceptic, see Stewart, 'Stoic legacy'.

[26] 'If we can depend upon any principle, which we learn from philosophy, this, I think may be considered as certain and undoubted, that there is nothing, in itself, valuable or despicable, desirable or hateful, beautiful or deformed; but that these attributes arise from the particular constitution and fabric of human sentiment and affection.' ('Sceptic' §8 = EMPL164)

737. Objections to Hume on Justifying Reasons

Defenders of the Scholastic conception of the will should answer Hume's claim that reason cannot show one that one end deserves to be pursued over another. In particular they should answer his claim that reason cannot show that pursuit of one's longer-term good is more rational than pursuit of any other end.

To see how cogent Hume's argument is, we may compare it with Butler's claims about reasonable self-love. In his claim about the destruction of the world and the scratching of my finger, Hume rejects Butler's claim that it would be absurd to regard these two courses of action as equally rational.[27] Butler believes that, contrary to Hume, the relevant sense of 'rational' is 'resting on good reasons'. A choice that results from some reasoning may nonetheless be irrational, because it rests on bad reasons, or it may be less rational than another choice, because it rests on less good reasons.[28] Hence prudent action is rational and imprudent action is not.

Self-love is a superior principle, in Butler's view, because it evaluates the satisfaction of desires not by the comparative strength of desires, but by the weight of the reasons that can be given for satisfying one or the other. These reasons consider not only the comparative strength of desires, but also the effect of one or the other action on my overall good.[29] Hence a rational desire is formed by proper consideration of the weight of reasons. It is contrary to reason, therefore, to prefer my lesser good to my greater; such a preference could not be based on proper assessment of the weight of the reasons on each side.

This description of Butler's position rests on some conception of the 'weight' of reasons, which represents Butler's distinction between power and authority. Reid captures the same distinction by speaking of 'animal strength' and 'rational strength'.[30] To recognize this distinction is to reject the analysis of justifying reasons that Hume accepts from Hutcheson. In Hutcheson's view, we have a justifying reason for a given action only if we have an actual motive favouring that action; the recognition of the reason is the recognition of the presence of a motive, and the recognition of a stronger reason is the recognition of a stronger desire. According to Reid's development of Butler's position, this analysis of justifying reasons confuses rational strength (better reasons) with animal strength (stronger desire).

If rational strength differs from animal strength in this way, the recognition of rational strength does not require a stronger antecedent desire for the action favoured by stronger reasons. Hence the recognition of the comparative weight of reasons is a function of reason. Since it is not reducible to the functions of reason that Hume describes, Hume has not described all the functions of reason, and has not shown that reason cannot find justifying reasons independent of passion.[31]

---

[27] See Butler, *S* ii 17, quoted in §685.

[28] This account of 'less rational' might refer to subjectively good reasons (those the agent thinks good) or to objectively good reasons (those that are good, whether or not the agent thinks so). Whichever way we interpret 'less rational', Hume is open to objection.

[29] See also Reid, *EAP* iii 3.2 = H 580b–581a = R 862.   [30] See Reid, §832.

[31] An alternative defence of Butler might argue that recognition of the weight of reasons belongs neither to reason nor to passion. This defence accepts Hume's narrow conception of reason, but it denies that his division between reason and passion exhausts the possible sources of justifying reasons. The argument that follows can be adapted to support an objection to Hume based on this view.

If Hume is right, Butler's and Reid's conception of what is contrary to reason rests on some error, and the difference between comparative strength of desires and comparative weight of reasons is illusory. He has a good reason for disagreeing with Butler, if he has shown that reason can only trace causes and effects. But has he shown this?

He derives his conclusion about the functions of reason from his view that the understanding is concerned only with demonstrative reasoning or matters of empirical fact.[32] The substitution of 'understanding' for 'reason', and the description of the two functions of the understanding, refer to Book i of the *Treatise*. Hume relies on the assured results of the earlier book in settling the dispute about practical reason. He therefore assumes that reflexion on practical reason will not require us either (1) to re-examine our views about the understanding or (2) to consider whether practical reason has functions beyond the functions of the understanding. In disregarding the first possibility, Hume assumes that his theoretical philosophy is prior to his practical philosophy, and not to be reconsidered in the light of practical philosophy. In disregarding the second possibility, he assumes that theoretical reason is all there is to practical reason. These two assumptions distinguish Hume's method from Kant's.

Hume's assumptions are controversial. From Butler's and Reid's point of view, reflexion on practical reason justifies us in doubting at least one of Hume's assumptions. We need some plausible ground for rejecting Butler's conception of reason before we agree that Hume has described all the functions of reason.

This objection casts doubt on Hume's case for saying that reason cannot by itself provide justifying reasons for action. If reason discovers actions supported by better reasons, and if we have better reasons for pursuing our overall good than for avoiding the scratching of our finger, we act against reason in avoiding the scratching of our finger at the cost of our overall good. If Hume were to answer that justifying reasons all rest on a further desire that is independent of reasoning about our overall good, his argument would be circular.

In defending Butler's position against Hume's we have not argued that Butler is right to claim that self-love is moved by better reasons than those that would move us to prefer a particular passion over self-love. A supporter of Hume might be able to show that Butler is mistaken. But the argument that Hume offers to show that reason cannot be the source of justifying reasons does not defeat Butler's position, since it rests on a contestable claim about the functions of reason.

738. Prudence and Calm Passion

Hume would refute Butler, however, if he could show that what we say and believe about prudence can be understood without any reference to good reasons, and hence without appeal to any function of reason that refers to authority. He does not argue explicitly against Butler's position, perhaps because he does not see that Butler's claims about authority and

---

[32] 'The understanding exerts itself after two different ways, as it judges from demonstration or probability; as it regards the abstract relations of our ideas, or those relations of objects, of which experience only gives us information. I believe it scarce will be asserted, that the first species of reasoning alone is ever the cause of any action. . . . which leads us to the second operation of the understanding.' (T ii 3.3.2)

strength involve the rejection of Hutcheson's analysis of justifying reasons.[33] But he argues implicitly against Butler, through a diagnosis of our tendency to believe that reason supports prudence against imprudence. He argues that our claims about prudence and reason can be explained, though not endorsed, within his account of the role of reason and passion.

In Hume's view, we speak loosely when we describe imprudent action as irrational or unreasonable. We speak as though prudent action appealed to reason alone, because we do not see that it appeals to us only if we have the appropriate calm passion. We make this mistake because we tend to confuse the operation of reason alone with the operation of a calm passion. In the case of prudence, we confuse reason with 'the general appetite to good, and aversion to evil'. This appetite is a non-rational desire; it involves reason no more than any other passion does, but because it is not strongly felt, we do not realize that it is a passion.[34]

It is therefore no more reasonable, strictly speaking, to take the long-term point of view that is characteristic of prudence (T iii 2.7.5) than to be imprudent. But our calm passion gives us a tendency to take this point of view that is improperly called 'reasonable'. Since we often take this point of view, we try to counteract our known tendency to act on short-term views.[35] If in January I intend to buy a house in November, and I need $100,000 for a deposit, I do not (according to Hume) think about having the money for a deposit in the circumstances that will obtain in November, since I do not know now what all these circumstances will be. I simply think of having the money available versus being unable to buy the house: and since I prefer being able to buy the house, I deposit the money in an account from which I cannot withdraw it until November. My preference will waver in September, when the sight of a new car costing $20,000 arouses a violent passion that will be stronger than my calm passion for having the money to buy the house in November. But since I did not have this violent passion in January, I was able to make the prudent choice because of my calm passion.

Prudent action, therefore, can be understood without any appeal to a purely rational preference to act on a superior principle; we are simply moved by (a) a calm passion leading us to prefer our longer-term good, and (b) reasoning about what will satisfy that calm passion. In the case of imprudence we have (a) a violent passion, say, to take revenge on someone who has harmed us, and (b) reasoning about how to do it. Both passion and reason are present in both cases, but because the passion in the first case is less obvious, we suppose that in the first case we simply deliberate about what it is reasonable to do, without reference to any actual desire. We are wrong, because we really deliberate about what to do to satisfy our present calm passion.

If I act in the way Hume suggests, am I being prudent? If my future-directed preference is really based on ignorance of my future circumstances, it does not seem prudent to commit myself to the frustration of preferences that may arise in those circumstances. I ought not,

---

[33] This conjecture is supported by Hume's brief remark on Hutcheson and Butler on authority. See §779.

[34] On the use of calmness to replace an appeal to rational desire, see Hutcheson, §639; Stroud, H 163–6; Rawls, LHMP 36–50. Sturgeon, 'Passion', is a careful examination of the various roles that Hume allows to reason, in the various ways Hume understands it.

[35] 'When we consider any objects at a distance, all their minute distinctions vanish, and we always give the preference to whatever is in itself preferable, without considering its situation and circumstances. This gives rise to what in an improper sense we call reason, which is a principle that is often contradictory to those propensities that display themselves upon the approach of the object.' (T iii 2.7.5)

for instance, to decide in January to make $100,000 unavailable until November, if I have not considered whether in July I will need the money to pay for some expensive but necessary medical treatment. Contrary to Hume, a genuinely prudent decision to tie my hands in the future ought to rest on as much relevant information about the likely future circumstances as I can reasonably expect to acquire. And if the circumstances turn out to be different in important ways from what I expected, it might be foolishly rigid if, in the face of new information about the circumstances, I stuck to my earlier decision. In this case prudence may not require me to tie my hands or to stick to my earlier uninformed decision.

If Hume is right about the role of calm passions, prudent choices for the future depend on ignorance of future circumstances. If I made all these circumstances clear to myself, I might excite violent passions that would overcome the calm passion that underlies my prudent reasoning. His attempt to explain how we can see overriding reason to choose the prudent course of action removes the aspect of prudent action that makes it genuinely prudent. To explain and to undermine our belief that we consider the weight of reasons rather than the strength of desires, Hume concentrates on these cases where I do not know in advance what the prudent choice will cost me in the future. He fails to explain these cases.

He fails even more clearly to explain other cases of prudent choice. Sometimes it is clear to me in advance what the cost of my prudent choice will be; I may be well aware in advance how strongly I will be tempted to waste my money. According to Hume, such prior knowledge should excite a violent passion; hence it should prevent me from believing that the prudent course of action is better, since (in his view) my belief that it is better is simply the belief that it satisfies my currently predominant passion. But this claim of Hume's gives the wrong account of prudence. The more violent a passion I anticipate, and the more confidently I anticipate it, the better reason I have to counteract it in advance, if I am convinced that I will be better off if I do not follow it in the future.[36]

To see what is questionable in Hume's account of prudence, we ought to compare these two judgments: (1) It is rational to pursue my long-term good rather than my short-term satisfaction. (2) Given that I want my long-term good rather than my short-term satisfaction, I will achieve my end if I pursue my long-term good rather than my short-term satisfaction. Hume takes the second judgment to analyse the first. When we speak of what is rational, we presuppose, in his view, that we have only the calm passion favouring my long-term good; if we had a violent passion for a short-term satisfaction, we would also find it rational to pursue that satisfaction.

The second judgment, however, seems to say less than the first, and so seems not to analyse it. When we say that it is rational for me to pursue my long-term good, we imply that this ought to be my overriding desire, and that I am being irrational if it is not my overriding desire; we claim that one end is more rational than another, not simply because it achieves the means to some further end. Butler believes it is rational to pursue my long-term good because I am a creature with a constitution, and not just a collection of impulses. Since my future as well as my present desires belong to me, they deserve to be considered when I decide what to do. If I do not consider them, that is a failure of reason because I fail to take account of everything that deserves consideration in making a decision.

---

[36] For a similar appeal to distance and abstraction see §761.

If Hume's claim about calm passions does not capture what we say and presuppose when we make claims about prudence and rationality, he does not capture our view of practical reason. His account of the functions of reason is too restricted to explain what we say about the rational course of action and about what we have better reason to do. In his view, we say what we say about prudent action because we overlook the presence of a calm passion. But he is mistaken; for even if we recognize the presence of a calm passion favouring our long-term interest, we do not suppose that a course of action is rational simply because it is founded on reasoning about what satisfies that calm passion. If some people were to lack the relevant calm passion, that would not change the rational course of action for them.

From Hume's point of view, this objection may appear futile, because it assumes a function for reason that is not included in his exhaustive account of the functions of reason. But if he simply asserts that his account is exhaustive, and does not identify some further error in the claims about practical reason that he rejects, his argument should not move opponents who attribute some further function to reason. Since he does not adequately defend his account of the functions of reason, he is unwise to rely on it to support his account of justifying reasons. He would have a good case if he had shown that the justifying reasons we offer are good reasons only if we presuppose the relevant calm passions. But he has not shown this. Though some justifying reasons presuppose antecedent desires in the agent for whom they are good reasons, not all justifying reasons are of this kind.

If this defence of Butler is sound, Hume's view of passion and reason does not justify our ordinary view of prudence. If, therefore, he seeks to present a vindicating reduction of claims about practical reason to claims about Humean reason and calm passion, he fails.

Perhaps, however, he does not intend to offer a vindicating reduction of ordinary claims about prudence; or, even if he intends to offer it, his argument may support a more radical conclusion. He speaks as though he is attacking the theories of prudence offered by rationalist philosophers, rather than ordinary claims about prudence. But perhaps he believes that we—as agents, not just as philosophers examining agency—rely on unjustified claims about reason. Hume's experimental method might lead to a sceptical conclusion by showing that our claims about practical reason ascribe capacities to us that experience shows us we lack.

Experience might show us that we lack the relevant capacity, if we found that we have no rational basis, as the rationalist understands it, for regarding prudence as especially rational. Butler's argument moves from some claim about our nature as agents to a conclusion about what it is reasonable for us to do, and therefore about what we ought to do; and so he argues from 'is' to 'ought'. Hume believes such arguments are illegitimate. Hence, his basic dispute with Butler is about 'is' and 'ought'.

If this is the real basis of the dispute, two questions arise about Hume's argument on 'is' and 'ought': (1) Hume presents this argument in the course of his discussion of whether moral distinctions are derived from reason, but the argument ought not to apply only to moral distinctions. If Butler is wrong, a prudential 'ought' cannot be derived from an 'is' and therefore cannot be derived from reason. Does Hume's argument apply to prudential as well as to moral judgments? (2) If he is to rely on his argument about 'is' and 'ought' in order to refute Butler, that argument should not rest on the conclusion about reason and passion that rests on his claims about the functions of reason. For we have seen that he has not justified his claims about the functions of reason. If he relies on these claims, his argument against Butler will be question-begging. The argument about reason and passion, taken by itself, does not refute Butler. Has Hume a cogent argument about 'is' and 'ought' that is independent of his conclusion on reason and passion?

739. Can Desires be Unreasonable?

Hume believes that his opponents misunderstand both the functions of reason and the character of a passion. They not only believe that reason has more functions than it has, but also attribute to passions a structure that they lack. If the rationalists are right, reason can oppose a passion and show it to be unreasonable. But according to Hume, no desire can be either inherently rational or inherently opposed to reason. For desires are passions, and passions cannot be inherently either rational or opposed to reason.[37] If a passion were an idea purporting to represent an impression, we could reasonably ask whether it represents its original truly or not; but such a question is inappropriate for a non-representative state.

We might reply that a desire can be reasonable or unreasonable because it has an intentional content; it is a desire for x qua F, on the assumption that being F makes x desirable. A desire for x is unreasonable, then, if x's being F is not a good reason for wanting x. Since desires have content open to rational evaluation, desires are open to such evaluation.

This reply ignores Hume's conception of a passion. He takes a passion to be only contingently connected with any specific object and cause; beliefs are connected with a passion only causally, not logically. If a desire conforms to this model of a passion, the desire for x is a particular sort of sensation provoked by the thought of x, tending to cause us to try to get x. Since it is logically possible for us to have the very same desire irrespective of what we believe about x, no specific belief about x is essential to the desire, and so the desire itself cannot inherit the falsity or irrationality of any belief about x.[38]

Hume has theoretical reasons, therefore, for denying that desires are open to evaluation because of their intentional content. His opponent takes the relation to belief and reason to be part of the content of a desire, but in Hume's view the connexion is simply causal. He agrees that the desire for x tends to be caused by the belief that x exists and has some desired property, in accordance with his distinction between the subject and the quality of the cause of a passion (T ii 1.2.6). He admits, then, that passions may be contrary to reason 'in so far as they are accompanied with some judgment or opinion' (ii 3.3.6). But he asserts that desires have only these purely external relations to reason, because he takes desires to be sensations.

[37] 'A passion is an original existence . . . and contains not any representative quality, which renders it a copy of any other existence or modification. When I am angry, I am actually possessed with the passion, and in that emotion have no more a reference to any other object than when I am thirsty, or sick, or more than five foot high. 'Tis impossible, therefore, that this passion can be opposed by, or be contradictory to truth and reason; since this contradiction consists in the disagreement of ideas, considered as copies, with those objects, which they represent.' (ii 3.3.5)

[38] See Stroud, H158–62. Baier, PS 160–4, argues that this passage in ii 3.3.5 is 'at the very least unrepresentative' (160) of Hume's standard views about the connexion of passions to beliefs. But her defence of this claim does not take account of the fact that Hume regards the relevant connexions as purely causal and non-essential. Moreover, Hume recalls his conception of the passions as incapable of being contrary to reason, and reaffirms it at a vital point in his argument against rationalism in morals, at iii 1.1.9.

But this appeal to Hume's theory of the passions does not vindicate his claim about evaluation. Reasonable doubts about his theory of the passions encourage doubts about his conception of desires. It is even more difficult to believe that the desire for x is always logically separable from any beliefs about x than to believe that love is always logically separable from benevolence. Hume's opponent, then, may still reasonably maintain that since we desire x as F, our desire is contrary to the weight of reasons if the weight of reasons does not favour F.

If Hume could justifiably reject claims about the weight of reasons, this objection would fail. He could justifiably reject them if he could show that reason has only the functions that he attributes to it. But he has not shown that. In this case also, he has not answered Butler's claims about the functions of reason. His objections to rationalist claims about justifying reasons are not conclusive.

740. Objections to Hume on Exciting Reasons

A refutation of Hume's case about justifying reasons may not damage his case about exciting reasons. For even if reason gives us sufficient justifying grounds for approval, it may still be unable to move us by appeal to these grounds, unless we have some independent desire to act on them.[39] On the rationalist side we might argue that belief that an action is good for me is sufficient by itself to move me to do something about it; no independent desire is needed for me to be moved by the belief that something is or is not good for me.

Against the rationalist Hume might remark that in some cases we find that the belief about my good is not sufficient for me to act on it; I can act incontinently in preferring a known lesser good over a greater. But the rationalist might equally reply that passion by itself does not always provide a sufficient condition; we sometimes act continently by doing what we think better for us even though we have a stronger desire to do what we think is worse.[40] In Reid's view, a conclusion of practical reason has greater rational strength, even if the desire to follow a passion has greater animal strength; sometimes we are moved by rational strength and sometimes by animal strength.[41] Hume might reply that if we act continently, our desire to do the worse thing cannot be stronger; if we do what is better, we must have a stronger desire to do what is better. But why should we accept this reply, unless we already agree with Hume that reason alone cannot provide exciting reasons?

We might agree that there must be some difference beyond the fact that sometimes I fail to do what I believe to be better and sometimes I do it.[42] But why should the difference be a difference in the strength of some passion that is independent of reason? Why not say that the difference in motivation is explained by some difference apart from desire—for instance a difference in people's capacity to make clear to themselves the implications of the rationally compelling case? We have no introspectible evidence of this; but neither have we

---

[39] In speaking of grounds for approval, I try to distinguish two things that Hutcheson runs together: (a) giving us reasons for approving; (b) motivating us to approve. The examples that Hutcheson mentions in *IMS* 128–9 = R 363 seem to illustrate (a). But in arguing that reason is insufficient for justifying reasons, Hutcheson seems to refer to (b). Cf. §639.

[40] Cf. Aristotle, *De Anima* 433a1–8 (Aristotle's statement of the puzzles about reason and desire).

[41] See Reid, §841.   [42] This agreement relies on a determinist assumption that Reid rejects. See §832.

introspectible evidence of a passion, independent of reason, that favours continent action. Hume introduces calm passions here because they are needed to show that exciting reasons always involve a passion, not because he has any other good reason for introducing them.[43]

Hume makes clear a point that Hutcheson leaves implicit, that he intends to go beyond Aristotle's claim that thought does not move us without desire.[44] In rejecting pure rationalism about motivation Aristotle agrees with Hume that reason by itself cannot move us to action without desire; but he does not say that the desire that needs to be added to reason is desire that is independent of reason. The desire that Aristotle adds to reason is the desire for happiness, which is an essentially rational desire, open to modification through reflexion on the good. This sort of desire presupposes functions for practical reason that Hume denies.

And so Hume's denial that reason provides exciting reasons is more extreme than the apparently similar claims of Aristotle and Aquinas. He does not mean only that reason needs desire before we are moved to action; he also claims that the only source of motivation is desire without reason. In his view, a practical reason cannot modify a desire for an end, because the functions of reason do not apply to desire for ends. His claim about exciting reasons rests on his account of the functions of reason; but we have seen that this account does not refute Butler's position.

741. Passion, Will, and Freedom

The two sections before 'Of the influencing motives of the will' introduce the treatment of the will with a discussion of liberty and necessity. Hume does not explain why he treats this topic just here, except by saying that it 'occurs so naturally in treating of the will' (*T* ii 3.1.2). He mentions that people have attributed liberty, indifference, and spontaneity to the will, and that he proposes to show that the will operates by necessity. It is appropriate to discuss his argument here; for we will see that it rests on his claims about passion and practical reason.[45]

The discussions in the *Treatise* and in the *First Inquiry* differ about the belief in liberty. The *Treatise* appears to accept hard determinism, since it defends a doctrine of necessity and determinism that Hume takes to conflict with a belief in liberty. The *Inquiry* takes a compatibilist position, claiming that liberty, on any reasonable understanding of it, is not ruled out by necessity, on any reasonable understanding of it.[46]

The difference in substance between the two discussions is smaller than these different remarks about liberty might suggest. For the *Treatise* does not say that liberty, as the *Inquiry* understands it, is incompatible with necessity. Nor does the *Inquiry* claim that liberty, as the *Treatise* understands it, is compatible with necessity.

---

[43] Contrast the favourable assessment of Hume's argument by Harrison, *HME* 6 (often sharply critical of Hume) with the much more critical view of Mackie, *HMT*, ch. 3 (usually more favourable to Hume). The version of a 'Humean' theory of motivation defended by Smith, *MP*, ch. 4, lacks Hume's commitment to the pervasive role of desires that are independent of reason.

[44] See Hutcheson, §637.

[45] Equally, the treatment of reason and passion depends on the deterministic assumption that something explains why I sometimes act on my judgment about what is better and sometimes do not.

[46] Hume's reconciling project is discussed, with special reference to his conception of necessity, by Harris, *LN*, ch. 3.

But this degree of agreement does not make the difference between the two works trivial. The *Inquiry* seems to acknowledge, whereas the *Treatise* does not, that defenders of the doctrine of liberty often have a reasonable view independent of the more extravagant doctrines that Hume rejects. The *Treatise* recognizes this point briefly in suggesting that the liberty of spontaneity does not raise the difficulties raised by the liberty of indifference; indifference, but not spontaneity, commits us to incompatibilism.[47] Hume implicitly acknowledges that one might defend a doctrine of liberty as spontaneity without indifference, but he develops this point only in the *Inquiry*.[48]

Hume's two treatments overlook the view maintained by Aquinas, and to some extent by Cudworth and Locke, that freewill consists in determination by the will, as opposed to the passions.[49] Determination by will is freedom (according to Aquinas) because the will is not determined to one course of action apart from rational reflexion, but is moved by the rational reflexion that chooses among different possible actions. Hume follows Hobbes and Hutcheson in ignoring this alleged difference between will and passion. In listing the different sources of the false belief in freedom, he does not mention Locke's candidate—the capacity to suspend the operation of passions on the basis of rational consideration.

Hume's silence on this role of the will in freedom reflects his views on reason and passion. For he follows Hobbes and Hutcheson in rejecting the division between will and passion. Given his conception of practical reason, he cannot treat will as essentially rational desire. We may desire some overall long-term good, but we have no ground for claiming that this is an especially rational desire, or that it has any special role in freedom. Hume's silence about the standard division between will and passion results from his view of reason and passion; the will is nothing but 'the internal impression we feel and are conscious of' in initiating motion (*T* ii 3.1.2).

Hume is right, therefore, to place his chapters on liberty and necessity next to those on the influencing motives of the will. But they are in the wrong order. His view of the available options for giving an account of freedom presupposes his claims about reason and passion.

742. Responsibility

The rejection of a division between will and passion affects Hume's explanation and defence of compatibilism (in the *Inquiry*) and his conception of an acceptable notion of liberty (in the *Treatise*). Even in the *Treatise*, where he is an incompatibilist about determinism and freedom, he is a compatibilist about determinism and responsibility. In his view, to be responsible is to be an object of moral sentiments, and in particular of praise, blame, gratitude, anger, love, hatred. Determinism does not undermine these sentiments; indeed, we cannot be objects of

---

[47] 'Few are capable of distinguishing betwixt the liberty of spontaneity, as it is called in the schools, and the liberty of indifference; betwixt that which is opposed to violence, and that which means a negation of necessity and causes. The first is even the most common sense of the word; and as 'tis only that species of liberty, which it concerns us to preserve, our thoughts have been principally turned towards it, and have almost universally confounded it with the other.' (ii 3.2.1)

[48] Stroud, *H* 150–4, criticizes Hume's failure to explain why some people take the liberty of indifference, resting on a belief about alternative possibilities, to be necessary for freedom. He notices that the remarks on theological determinism (*IHU* 8.36) suggest that Hume is vulnerable to an incompatibilist argument.

[49] On Aquinas see §265.

these sentiments unless our characters and dispositions causally determine our actions (*T* ii 3.2.6). Our sentiments are directed at relatively persistent features of an agent's character, on the assumption that these have some reliable causal connexion with actions.

Hume is open to criticism for his claim that actions 'out of character' are not objects of praise and blame. The criticism is especially justified given that he claims to describe our actual reactions, not to tell us what reactions we ought to have. The mere fact of an action's being out of character does not relieve the agent from all praise or blame.

Still, part of Hume's position is reasonable. Some actions that are 'out of character', in the sense of being untypical and unusual for this person, are nonetheless explicable as (for instance) the result of weaknesses in his character that do not usually display themselves, or of a good side in him that he is capable of displaying occasionally. Such an explanation makes it intelligible that this sort of person acts in this way, and it makes praise and blame appropriate. An untypical action that could not be understood in relation to his character would not necessarily be exempt from all praise or blame, but we might reasonably decide that it is less subject to praise or blame than it would be if it were more centrally connected to the agent's character. Hume is right, then, in connecting praise and blame to character and relatively stable traits.

Something similar might be said about his suggestion that change of character removes responsibility for past actions. Normally this is not true. But if we were really convinced that someone had no more of his character in common with his past self than he had with any other random person, we would be reluctant to hold him responsible in the ordinary way for his past actions. We might, indeed, doubt whether, in such a case, we would be really dealing with the same person; such a doubt supports Hume.

If we go this far with Hume, however, we have a good reason to modify his simple demand for a stable condition of the agent. Some of the cases that seem to support his claims about the irrelevance of temporary aberrations are cases in which the agent is overcome by an irresistible desire that does not express his own values and outlook. But if this desire persisted, and the agent could not get rid of it despite his best efforts, the same considerations that would exempt him from responsibility for a short-term aberration would also remove him from responsibility for this long-term flaw; it would be a handicap for which he could not reasonably be blamed. In that case, we are justified in attending to the relation between the action and the agent's evaluative outlook expressed in his actions, including his actions on short-term passions and impulses.

This approach rejects Hume's less plausible claims about actions on temporary impulses, but adopts some of his suggestions about the relation of actions to character. But the approach also re-introduces the division between passion and will that Hume rejects. For the agent's character and values matter for judgments about responsibility because they express the outcome of his rational reflexion about the ends to pursue. If Hume were right about the functions of reason, such rational reflexion would be impossible, and so we would have no reason to focus on the agent's values. According to Hume's view of practical reason, rational reflexion is confined to questions about the reality of objects of passions and about means to ends that appeal to passions. If the desires resulting from such rational reflexion are not distinctively rational, they do not seem distinctively connected with responsibility. According to Aquinas, we are justified in treating the agent's will as the basis of freedom and responsibility because the ends we pursue are open to rational deliberation that reaches suitable objects of rational desire. Hume rejects this reason for considering the will.

Apparently, then, Hume's attempt to connect responsibility and character would be open to question, if he were right about the scope of practical reason and about the relation between will and passion. It is more plausible if it rests on the division between will and passion that he rejects. This conclusion gives us another reason for reconsidering his views on reason and passion; they cast doubt on his treatment of responsibility.

These difficulties in Hume are relevant to his moral theory. He tries to find the real basis of moral sentiments, not to show that they have no basis in facts about human actions and passions. He takes the same view about moral distinctions. This aim of vindicating moral sentiments is different from his sceptical attitude to our belief in external objects and in personal identity. In the metaphysical cases (he argues) common-sense beliefs are unjustified, but too tenacious to be undermined by sceptical arguments. Has he good reasons for claiming to vindicate our moral sentiments rather than subjecting them to sceptical doubt?

His arguments on reason and passion seem to support a sceptical position on responsibility. His appeals to temporary and permanent features of agents do not support our views on responsibility, because our views rest on a conception of practical reason and the will that Hume rejects. If we agree with Hume's view of practical reason and responsibility, our sentiments of praise and blame may not disappear; they may be stubborn, even if their rational basis is undermined. But we might doubt whether they will or should matter as much to us, if we decide that they rest on false or unjustified presuppositions about will and reason.

Here, then, we might be tempted to draw more sceptical conclusions than Hume draws.[50] His account of practical reason and prudence does not support ordinary claims about prudence, but conflicts with them. Similarly, his views about practical reason cast doubt on our conception of free and responsible agency. Contrary to Hume's intentions, his sceptical attitude to ordinary beliefs about objectivity and personal identity seems to provide a pattern for the attitude that we will take to moral beliefs if we grasp the significance of his arguments.

So far, then, discussion of Hume gives us a further reason to agree with Balguy's judgment on Hutcheson. According to Balguy, Hutcheson would be more sceptical about morality than he is, if he recognized the implications of his arguments. In the case of practical reason and responsibility, this judgment on Hutcheson seems to fit Hume as well. It is worth seeing how many aspects of Hume's position support Balguy's judgment.

---

[50] On the radical character of Hume's conclusion, cf. the discussion of Hutcheson in §654.

57

HUME: ERRORS
OF OBJECTIVISM

743. The Two Arguments against Rationalism

In the section 'Moral distinctions not derived from reason', Hume strengthens his defence of Hutcheson. He now defends anti-rationalism not only about practical reason and motivation, but also about morality. His discussion of reason and passion implicitly attacks Butler's views on superior principles and self-love; he now attacks Butler's views on conscience. Butler regards conscience as the expression of reason, as a source of moral requirements, and as a superior principle carrying authority. Hume rejects these claims.

Hume offers two distinct arguments to show that moral distinctions are not derived from reason. The first is his 'practical argument':[1] (1) Reason alone cannot move us to action. (2) But moral distinctions move us to action. (3) Hence moral distinctions cannot be derived from reason. The first step is derived from Hume's argument about the roles of reason and passion (in ii 3.3). Since Hume's defence of his first step is open to doubt, the doubt spreads to the practical argument.

Still, the practical argument is worth considering on the assumption that the first step is acceptable. The first step deals only with exciting reasons, and we might agree with Hume's anti-rationalism about exciting reasons even if we disagree with him about justifying reasons. The practical argument is important if it shows that acceptance of a Humean view of exciting reasons commits us to the rejection of rationalism about moral judgments.

Hume's second argument against rationalism is his 'metaphysical argument':[2] (1) Reason discovers only relations of ideas or matters of fact. (2) Moral truths correspond neither to relations of ideas nor to matters of fact. (3) Hence moral truths are not discovered by reason. Again we may concede the first step to Hume for the sake of argument. In the second step he seeks to show that the moral goodness or badness of an action cannot consist in any fact about the action itself apart from the feelings of the person judging the action good or bad.

The two arguments appear to be independent arguments for the same conclusion. At the end of the second argument Hume adds a further observation about the difficulty of

---

[1] This is stated briefly at iii 1.1.5–7, and elaborated in 8–16.
[2] This is presented in iii 1.1.17–25, and the main point is stated in 26.

deriving 'ought' from 'is' (iii 1.1.27). It is not clear whether he intends this observation to provide a third argument for the same conclusion, or a summary of one or the other or both of the previous arguments, or an argument for a different conclusion. We can try to answer these questions once we have discussed the two main arguments.

744. Moral Judgments and Motivation: What Does Common Experience Show?

Hume takes his practical argument to undermine every purely cognitive view of morality. He mentions three claims: (1) Virtue is 'nothing but a conformity to reason'. (2) There are eternal fitnesses that 'are the same to every rational being that considers them'. (3) Right and wrong impose an obligation on God as well as on human beings.[3] Hume speaks as though he is considering only views that treat moral judgments as a priori knowledge of 'relations of ideas' (as Hume calls them). Clarke and Price hold such views, but it is not clear that Butler agrees with them. Hume's argument is not confined, however, to conceptions of moral judgments as a priori; it seems to extend to all purely cognitive views (iii 1.1.26). According to such views, we can know that an action is right or wrong by knowing some fact about the world that is not constituted by the thoughts or feelings of the subject who knows.

Against a purely cognitive view of moral properties, Hume appeals to the practical aspect of morality.[4] We believe that 'morals have an influence on the actions and affections' (iii 1.1.6). To see what this belief commits us to, we need to see what Hume means by 'morals', 'morality', and 'moral distinctions'. He might have in mind (1) the properties of rightness or wrongness themselves, or (2) the moral condition—virtue or vice—of a person who acts rightly or wrongly ('a person of good morals'). A purely cognitive view of 'morals' in the first sense does not imply a purely cognitive view of 'morals' in the second sense. Even if moral properties are objects of rational cognition, virtue or vice need not be purely cognitive. The view that virtue is conformity to reason is not a purely cognitive view of virtue; for if a virtuous person's will must conform to reason, such conformity to reason is not a purely cognitive condition. If Hume simply appeals to the practical effects of 'morals', understood as virtue and vice, he does not refute a purely cognitive view of moral properties.[5]

---

[3] 'All these systems concur in the opinion that morality, like truth, is discerned merely by ideas, and by their juxtaposition and comparison. In order, therefore, to judge of these systems, we need only consider, whether it be possible, from reason alone, to distinguish moral good and evil, or whether there must concur some other principles to enable us to make that distinction.' (T iii 1.1.4)

[4] 'Philosophy is commonly divided into speculative and practical; and as morality is always comprehended under the latter division, 'tis supposed to influence our passions and actions, and to go beyond the calm and indolent judgments of the understanding.' (iii 1.1.5)

[5] Hume's use of 'moral distinction' fluctuates between (a) a subjective use, for our way of distinguishing virtue and vice, and (b) a non-subjective use, for the difference between virtue and vice or between moral good and evil. Some passages are ambiguous between the two uses; and this is not surprising, given Hume's view that the difference between moral good and evil is a difference in our sentiments, a distinction that we draw. Here are some examples: 'The merit and demerit of actions frequently contradict, and sometimes control our natural propensities. But reason has no such influence. Moral distinctions, therefore, are not the offspring of reason. Reason is wholly inactive, and can never be the source of so active a principle as conscience, or a sense of morals.' (iii 1.1.10) '. . . if moral distinctions be derived from the truth or falsehood of those judgments, they must take place wherever we form the judgments.' (iii 1.1.13) 'Extinguish all the warm feelings and prepossessions in favour of virtue, and all disgust or aversion to vice: Render men totally

He clarifies his view by giving some examples of the practical influence of morals. He claims that our duties and our moral opinions about justice and obligation influence our actions.[6] These examples are rather disparate. It does not seem obvious that the fact that something is my duty moves me to do it. If I am not aware that it is my duty, or I believe it is not my duty, it does not seem to influence my action. My duty seems to exist independently of my being motivated to act on it. Perhaps, then, Hume means that my belief that something is my duty moves me to do it; his other examples involve moral beliefs rather than moral facts.

Hume's argument against cognitivism, therefore, relies on one of two sorts of connexions between 'morals' and motivation:[7] (1) If he means that duty governs me, he asserts a connexion between the existence of moral properties and motivation. He needs this connexion if his claim about motivation is to defeat an objectivist conception of moral properties. (2) If he means that my awareness of duty governs me, he asserts a connexion between my recognizing the truth of a moral judgment and my being motivated to act on it. According to this view, it is essential to a moral judgment—not to the existence of the property mentioned in the judgment—that it moves the agent to act on it.

Hume is right to say that in common experience moral judgment and action are connected. We generally expect people to act on their moral judgments, and if people say they ought to do something that they do not do, we may infer that they do not really think they ought to do it. To say this is to say that moral judgments are regularly connected to action. In this respect, they do not differ from other judgments about questions that concern us. If I say that I believe the forecast of rain for today is completely reliable, you normally expect me to go out with a raincoat and umbrella; if I deliberately do not take them, you may reasonably infer (in some circumstances) that I do not take the forecast to be completely reliable. Meteorological judgments govern my action.

But this sort of connexion is not enough for Hume's purposes; for it allows a cognitivist account of moral judgments. If we can explain why we are normally concerned about moral questions, we can explain why moral judgments govern our action, even if they are as cognitive as judgments about the weather. To refute a purely cognitive view, Hume needs to argue that moral judgments are different from judgments about the weather because they motivate us by themselves. Is this a matter of common experience?

The task of answering this question is complicated by Hume's discussion of reason and passion. A cognitivist might agree with Hume's view that moral judgments by themselves can motivate us. This cognitivist believes: (1) Moral judgments by themselves motivate us.

---

indifferent towards these distinctions; and morality is no longer a practical study, nor has any tendency to regulate our lives and actions.' (I 1.8) 'Let these generous sentiments be supposed ever so weak; let them be insufficient to move even a hand or finger of our body; they must still direct the determinations of our mind, and where every thing else is equal, produce a cool preference of what is useful and serviceable to mankind, above what is pernicious and dangerous. A moral distinction, therefore, immediately arises; a general sentiment of blame and approbation . . .' (I 9.4)

[6] 'And this is confirmed by common experience, which informs us, that men are often governed by their duties, and are deterred from some actions by the opinion of injustice, and impelled to others by that of obligation. Since morals, therefore, have an influence on the actions and affections, it follows, that they cannot be derived from reason; and that because reason alone, as we have already proved, can never have any such influence. Morals excite passions, and produce or prevent actions. Reason of itself is utterly impotent in this particular. The rules of morality, therefore, are not conclusions of our reason.' (iii 1.1.5–6)

[7] This feature of Hume's argument is emphasized and explored by Brown, 'Internalist?', who argues that Hume's account of the moral virtues does not satisfy the specific internalist condition that he lays down here.

(2) Moral judgments are purely cognitive. (3) Therefore purely cognitive states sometimes motivate us. But Hume rejects this cognitivist position, because he believes: (4) Cognitive states can contribute to action only when they are suitably connected to passions that are independent of them. Hence Hume infers: (5) Moral judgments motivate us all by themselves because they imply passions and are not purely cognitive.

Hume's position, then, depends on our being persuaded to accept (4) while still accepting (1), so that we reject (2). But might we not take (4) to be a reason for denying (1) while accepting (2)? Hume agrees that we have the experience of moral judgments moving us to action all by themselves, without any further desire. But he disagrees with rationalists who interpret this experience as the experience of purely cognitive states moving us to action without any non-cognitive state. Hume rejects the rationalist interpretation because he thinks we must always be moved by a passion. When we seem to be moved by moral judgments without any passion, he believes we are really moved by a calm passion distinct from any reasoning.

But if we agree with Hume here, why should we not abandon our original view that we experience moral judgments by themselves moving us to action? Even if action requires passion, how can experience tell us that the relevant passion is part of the moral judgment? Introspection does not seem to be decisive; for if the appearance of a purely cognitive state moving us to action is misleading, might the appearance of a moral judgment by itself moving us to action not be equally misleading? Hume's claims about calm passions cast doubt on introspection; for calm passions tend to escape introspection, but we need to assume them to explain action that (to a rationalist) appears to be explained by reason alone. Hume's view on reason and passions seems to undermine his argument against a cognitivist account of moral judgments. If we agree with his account of reason and passion, we have no reason to trust introspection as much as we need to trust it if we are to agree that moral judgments by themselves move us to action.

Common experience, therefore, does not seem to show that moral judgments alone motivate us. But if it does not show this, it allows a purely cognitive view of moral judgments. Hume uses his conclusion about reason and passion as a premiss of his practical argument. But his arguments about reason and passion suggest that experience does not support the practical argument.

745. Questions about Internalism

Hume would have a more cogent argument to show that a moral judgment 'alone' motivates us if he could show that the appropriate calm passion is not simply a feature of a normal well-trained agent who makes moral judgments, but logically inseparable from every sincere moral judgment. He needs to assert an internal connexion between moral judgments and motivation, so that a moral judgment essentially motivates by itself, and hence it is logically impossible for a sincere moral judgment not to motivate us.[8]

This internalist thesis agrees with Hutcheson's claim that justifying reasons presuppose a moral sense, which implies some motivation in favour of the action favoured by the moral

---

[8] Falk, 'Ought' 31–3, suggests that 'ought' is ambiguous between internalist and externalist senses.

sense.[9] But a rationalist might reasonably doubt internalism.[10] Clarke asserts that some people 'will things to be what they are not, and cannot be', because they are corrupted by some particular interest or affection. Assent to a theoretical axiom is involuntary, but action on a moral axiom depends on the agent's will (Clarke, DNR = H ii 613 = R 232).[11] These claims about connexions between desires and beliefs do not imply either version of internalism. Nor does Price seem to agree with Hume. He accepts an internal connexion between moral judgments and recognition of reasons.[12] But this internalist thesis does not imply an internalist claim about moral judgments and motives.[13] Unless Price agrees with Hutcheson's view that recognition of a reason for doing an action implies a motive for doing it, he need not agree that moral judgments necessarily motivate.[14]

If we distinguish justifying from exciting reasons, we may doubt Hume's internalism about moral judgment and motivation. Some argument is needed to show that we intuitively accept the relevant logical connexion. If we take the connexion to be logical rather than empirical, we should treat 'I knew I ought to do it, but I didn't want to do it' as self-contradictory. But we do not treat it as self-contradictory; we do not assume that the mere knowledge of our duty moves us to act on it. On the contrary, we might answer Hume that only the knowledge of it together with a desire to do our duty moves us to act. Some people seem to be indifferent or hostile to morality, but capable of seeing the truth of moral judgments.

We might defend internalism by appeal to an assumption about sincerity. People's failure to act on a particular moral principle sometimes persuades us that they do not sincerely accept it. If someone is usually scrupulous about not stealing, but has no scruples about taking away the plastic knives and forks that come with a meal on a flight, he probably thinks there is nothing wrong with doing that. But this assumption about sincerity is not always reliable. If we discover that some people are willing to steal when it seems unusually tempting, we may not infer that they are insincere in claiming that it is wrong to steal; they may be doing something they believe to be wrong.

This appeal to intuition is not decisive. It implies the truth of the externalist assumption that it is possible for someone to recognize that a course of action is right, but still have no tendency to do anything about it. This is the alleged possibility that we reveal by imagining people doing what they believe to be wrong. Hume may reply that this alleged possibility is not really possible. When we suppose we imagine such cases, we really imagine people who do not make the relevant moral judgment; they do not sincerely believe it would be right to do what they do not want to do, but they are simply saying the words.[15]

Intuitions about imaginability and conceivability, therefore, may mislead us. If we did not know enough about what a triangle is, we might suppose we could imagine a triangle whose

---

[9] See Hutcheson, §639.   [10] Contrast Brown, 'Internalist?' 75–6, on Clarke.

[11] Balguy rejects internalism for similar reasons. See §655.

[12] '. . . to perceive an action to be right is to see a reason for doing it in the action itself. . .' (Price, RPQM 117n).

[13] See Price, §819.

[14] On internalism see Harrison, HME 15. Contrast Mackie, HMT 54. Mackie claims that internalism expresses 'how moral characterization has been understood throughout the whole history of moral philosophy' (55). He appeals (158n4) to the passages from Clarke and Price considered here.

[15] This is what Hare calls an 'inverted commas' use, at LM 171. The conflict between this claim and Hare's acceptance of Moore's Open Question Argument is parallel to the conflict between Hume's practical and metaphysical arguments. See §749.

interior angles add up to 190 degrees; but that would not be a good reason for believing such a triangle is possible, nor would we really be conceiving it. Similarly, a correct account of the relation of moral judgments to motivation may be expected to change our minds about whether it is possible or imaginable for a sincere moral judgment to fail to motivate.

Is Hume's internalism so plausible that it entitles him to dismiss our apparent ability to conceive moral judgment without motivation? Some believe that externalism gives the wrong account of how moral considerations can motivate. If motivation is something beyond the recognition of moral truths, then (it is suggested) we must suppose that morality motivates only when it conduces to the satisfaction of some antecedent desires, by being instrumental to non-moral aims. But to suppose this is to misunderstand the role of moral considerations.[16]

This defence of internalism, however, seems to assume a Humean view about the limitations of practical reason—that we can come to care about some truth that we previously recognize only if we see that it is instrumentally relevant to the satisfaction of our other desires. If we are not convinced by Hume's arguments about practical reason, we need not accept the argument against externalism. If we have a non-Humean conception of practical reason, we can defend externalism without saying that motivation to act on moral judgments presupposes the belief that morality is instrumental to antecedent aims and desires.

Internalism, therefore, does not seem immediately convincing enough in its own right to refute a purely cognitive conception of moral judgments. Moreover, it seems to lose plausibility for someone who reflects on Hume's claims about reason and passion. Just as these claims suggest a diagnosis of alleged experiences of moral judgments motivating us by themselves, they suggest a diagnosis of alleged intuitions favouring internalism. In both cases, we overlook the role of calm passions. Against internalism we may argue that the apparent impossibility of moral judgments without motivation simply reflects the regular presence of the relevant calm passions together with our moral judgments. Hume's earlier argument helps an opponent of his argument about moral judgments and motivation.

Though Hume represents his practical argument as a decisive refutation of a purely cognitive view of moral properties, he relies on controversial premises, and especially on contentious claims about logical possibility. He does not pursue all these questions, because he relies on some simple observations that 'conscience' or 'a sense of morals' is in some way an 'active principle' (iii 1.1.10), and that 'morals . . . have an influence on the actions and affections'. He supposes that these observations vindicate his specific view of how moral judgments are practical. But since he does not examine these observations closely, he leaves room for doubt about his position.

746. Moral Judgments and Moral Error

Having presented his practical argument, Hume seems to recognize implicitly that his opponents may not accept his premiss about the practical force of moral judgments; for he

---

[16] This reason for being an internalist is especially clear in Hutcheson, who connects externalism with egoism. See §§634–5 Cf. Smith's defence of internalism, MP, ch. 3.

considers possible defences of a cognitive position that do not take moral judgments to be essentially practical and motivating. Cognitivists suggest that an action may be 'obliquely' caused by a judgment that concurs with a passion, and that if this judgment is unreasonable, the action may be called unreasonable too. The action is obliquely caused by a judgment if the judgment contributes to the passion that directly causes the action. Though Hume regards it as 'an abusive way of speaking' to call the action reasonable or unreasonable because it is obliquely caused by a reasonable or unreasonable judgment, he allows this way of speaking, in order to show that it cannot support a cognitive account of moral judgments (iii 1.1.11).

According to Hume, judgments affect passions by informing them about the existence or the properties of the relevant object; if we make a false judgment about the existence of a glass of milk, or if we want a healthy drink and falsely believe that this glass of milk is healthy, our action of trying to get a glass of milk is (in the 'abusive' sense) unreasonable. But the cognitivist gains nothing by appealing to this sort of unreasonableness, since it is irrelevant to the moral properties of the action or the agent.[17] For if the cognitivist were right, errors of moral judgment would have to be these purely factual errors; but purely factual errors are not blameworthy, whereas errors of moral judgment are blameworthy; hence the cognitivist is wrong.

Cognitivists might try two answers to Hume: (1) They might deny his claim that no purely factual errors are blameworthy, even if they agree that he has given a full list of factual errors. His appeal to common sense shows that many factual errors are regarded as innocent; but it does not show that all factual errors, on whatever subject and in whatever circumstances, are blameless. If, for instance, it is easy and important for us to find out some fact, and we do not find it out, we may be blameworthy for not finding it out. (2) They might reject Hume's claim about what reason can find out, and in particular they might deny that reason can only find out about existence and about instrumental means to ends. Aristotle and Aquinas take moral error to be a form of deliberative error about what sorts of actions and states of character promote one's good. For the reasons we have considered, this is not purely instrumental deliberation; but error in such deliberation is error about some fact. Perhaps the Aristotelian view faces difficulties in explaining how this sort of error can be blameworthy; but it need not agree with Hume that an error about a fact is free from blame.

Since these answers are available to a cognitivist, Hume's argument about responsibility does not refute cognitivism.

747. The Character of Moral Facts

After this argument about culpable and non-culpable error, Hume concludes his practical argument (iii 1.1.16). He turns to a metaphysical argument against the belief in 'eternal

---

[17] '... 'tis easy to observe, that these errors are so far from being the source of all immorality, that they are commonly very innocent, and draw no manner of guilt upon the person who is so unfortunate as to fall into them. They extend not beyond a mistake of fact, which moralists have not generally supposed criminal, as being perfectly involuntary' (iii 1.1.12). On a similar argument in Scotus about factual and moral error see §366.

fitnesses and unfitnesses of things' (iii 1.1.17). He apparently waives his objection about the practical force of morality, and concentrates more directly on the question whether there are any moral properties of the sort that Clarke's and Butler's position requires.[18]

Clarke and Butler defend different versions of a rationalist belief in fitness. For Clarke, the rightness or wrongness follows directly from a description of the action itself, apart from its connexions with human nature; we see from the nature of a promise or a benefaction that fulfilment or gratitude is the right response, and that a broken promise or ingratitude to a benefactor is a contradiction in itself. This conception of the character of rightness and wrongness leads naturally to an attempt such as Wollaston's to make the contradiction clear by reducing wrongness to falsity. Butler's version of rationalism does not rely simply on Clarke's contradictions; that is why Butler rejects Wollaston's view, which avoids Butler's appeal to nature (Butler, P 13 = R 375).[19] Hume's criticisms affect these different versions of rationalism in different ways.

One of his objections attacks the anti-voluntarist view that moral right and wrong are not constituted by anyone's will, and that they equally oblige all rational agents, including God. He believes that the rationalist cannot defend this universal obligation; even if all rational agents knew the relevant principles, it might not motivate all of them, because knowing virtue does not imply conforming the will to it.[20]

This objection is surprising. If Hume allows the possibility of knowing virtue without motivation, he seems to contradict the internalist claims that underlie the practical argument. Perhaps, then, he means 'conforming the will' in a more demanding sense that does not simply imply some motivation, but requires overriding motivation. The objection, so understood, would be consistent with internalism. But it does not seem to damage Hume's opponents. Rationalists have no reason to agree with Hume that universal obligation implies universal motivation, since (as we have seen) they need not accept his internalism about exciting reasons.

If the question about obligation is confined to justifying reasons, it may be an awkward question for Clarke. Why should we be concerned with the abstract relations of consistency and contradiction that Clarke identifies with moral right and wrong? This objection, however, does not apply to Butler, who tries to show how acting on reason is acting in accord with nature.

Hume's second objection concerns the sort of relation that a rationalist must identify with moral rightness and wrongness.[21] He argues that the moral badness of ingratitude cannot consist in a relation between the agents, but must consist in a spectator's reaction to them. We should reject an objectivist answer, because the relation between the ungrateful

---

[18] On Hume's attack on Clarke see Raphael, 'Rationalism' 24–8.   [19] See §678.

[20] ' 'Tis one thing to know virtue, and another to conform the will to it. In order, therefore, to prove, that the measures of right and wrong are eternal laws, obligatory on every rational mind, 'tis not sufficient to show the relations upon which they are founded: We must also point out the connexion betwixt the relation and the will; and must prove that this connexion is so necessary, that in every well-disposed mind, it must take place and have its influence; though the difference betwixt these minds be in other respects immense and infinite.' (iii 1.1.22) Hume summarizes this objection: '. . . we cannot prove a priori, that these relations, if they really existed and were perceived, would be universally forcible and obligatory' (23).

[21] 'This is acknowledged by all mankind, philosophers as well as the people; the question only arises among philosophers, whether the guilt or moral deformity of this action be discovered by demonstrative reasoning, or be felt by an internal sense, and by means of some sentiment, which the reflecting on such an action naturally occasions.' (iii 1.1.24)

person and the victim of ingratitude can be found in other situations that involve nothing morally wrong. The choking of a tree by one of its saplings displays the same objective relations as the murder of a parent by a child; since the latter action is wrong and the former is not, its wrongness cannot consist in an objective fact, but must consist in our reaction to it.

One might reply that since trees are not voluntary agents, their actions are not blameworthy. Hume rejects this reply, arguing that even if the agent is different, the relation is the same, and therefore, according to the rationalist, the wrongness should still be present (iii 1.1.25). This seems an unfair dismissal; it seems arbitrary of Hume to insist that only the relation of killing between parent and child can constitute the relevant relation. One might say that if Hume were right about what constitutes the same relation, he should not stop with animate agents; apparently, 'the same' relation must also hold between inanimate things. If one star comes into being by separating from its 'parent' star, and then collides with the star it came from and destroys it, is the relation between the two stars not the same as the relation between the two plants and between the two human beings? If Hume replies that the relation is relevantly different when animate agents are involved, why should the rationalist not insist that the relation is relevantly different when voluntary agents are involved?

To show the rationalists that they cannot appeal to voluntariness or rationality to constitute wrongness, Hume presents an argument from relations between animals.[22] He argues that if incest is wrong among human beings, it must also be wrong among animals, since it is the same relation, and the fact that human beings are rational cannot be relevant to the wrongness of the action itself. He assumes that the only role for reason in different moral agents is its capacity to discover moral relations that already exist whether or not the agents involved are rational. Hence the fact that the incestuous relation holds between rational agents cannot affect whether it involves moral badness, but can only affect the capacity of the agents to recognize it.

Hume's assumption that reason cannot itself constitute morally relevant relations is dubious. If I deny a mouse the opportunity to learn to read, I do not harm the mouse, and I do not wrong it, if the mouse cannot learn to read; but I harm a human being to whom I deny this opportunity. Similarly, one might deny that a mouse has exactly the same right to life that a human being has, because of some differences between mice and human beings. Hume's assumption that an action that constitutes a wrong, if done by one human being to another, must be equally wrong, if done by one non-human to another, is therefore false in general, and not clearly true in the specific case of incest that he mentions.

But even if Hume's objection rests on a dubious assumption, it may still expose a flaw in Clarke's rationalism. To meet Hume's objection, we need to maintain that the relation of ingratitude that holds between voluntary agents is crucially different from the 'same' relation

---

[22] 'I would fain ask any one, why incest in the human species is criminal, and why the very same action, and the same relations in animals have not the smallest moral turpitude and deformity? . . . Animals are susceptible of the same relations, with respect to each other, as the human species, and therefore would also be susceptible of the same morality, if the essence of morality consisted in these relations. Their want of a sufficient degree of reason may hinder them from perceiving the duties and obligations of morality, but can never hinder these duties from existing; since they must antecedently exist, in order to their being perceived.' (iii 1.1.25)

that holds between non-voluntary agents. But why should this be, if the wrongness consists in the contradictoriness, rather than in the agents involved in the contradiction? Why should we pick out one instance of contradiction and neglect others? Clarke and Wollaston do not answer this question.

Butler answers the question, however. He does not identify moral properties simply with relational properties of actions; he also appeals to their connexion with human nature as a whole. This connexion makes it reasonable to distinguish relations between voluntary agents from the 'same' relations between other agents. Voluntariness is relevant because voluntary agents are capable of gratitude and of seeing the reasons for it; if they fail to see these reasons, they are culpable. It is appropriate and non-arbitrary to confine rightness and wrongness to the actions of agents who can reasonably be expected to appreciate certain considerations and to guide their actions by them.

This defence of the rationalist might not convince Hume, because he might regard it as an admission of the truth of his sentimentalist position. For he assumes that if our account of rightness and wrongness appeals to features of responsible agents that make them worthy of praise and blame, we must admit that rightness and wrongness are not properties of the agents and their actions in their own right. Hume assumes that if we admit this, we agree that rightness and wrongness consist partly in blameworthy features of the agents, so that rightness and wrongness are constituted by being praised and blamed by spectators. If moral deformity does not consist in purely 'external' features of agents and victims (features that do not include their being rational and responsible agents), it consists in being 'felt by an internal sense, and by means of some sentiment, which the reflecting on such an action naturally occasions' (iii 1.1.24).

Why does Hume assume that these are the only two options? Perhaps he assumes, as Hutcheson does, that if we say people are blameworthy, we mean that they are blamed, and so we take the wrongness of their action to consist in being blamed; we thereby introduce an internal sense and a sentiment. But Hume is not entitled to assume this. For, as Balguy points out against Hutcheson, to say that people are worthy of blame is not to say that they are blamed, still less that I am blaming them.[23] If they are blameworthy, there is a reason that would justify blame, whether or not anyone wants to blame them. Hutcheson might accept Hume's assumption, but a rationalist has no reason to accept it. We might accept it if we had already accepted Hume's argument about reason and passion; but in that case, the present argument simply relies on that earlier questionable argument.

748. 'The Object in Itself'

Hume presents a briefer and clearer objection to the rationalist position. He argues that moral judgments do not result from any possible operation of reason, concerning either relations of ideas or matters of fact (iii 1.1.26). If we consider a wilful murder by itself, without regard to our reactions to it, we cannot identify any property of the murder itself

---

[23] See §656.

with its moral badness.[24] Hence moral goodness or badness, like beauty, cannot be a quality of external objects.[25]

We might answer that the badness of a murder consists in its being a deliberate and unprovoked taking of the life of an innocent human being, which violates a right of a human being and violates a duty towards other people. Why is this not a description of precisely those features of the action itself that make it morally wrong? Admittedly, some of the properties mentioned are 'moral' properties that are perhaps too closely linked to moral badness to provide the right sort of basis for the moral judgment. But some reason needs to be given to show that such moral properties are not properties of the action itself.

Hume maintains that a complete description of the murder need not mention the properties that are its moral badness. But what is a complete description? From the point of view of the psychologist observing the agent's behaviour, perhaps a complete description can be given without mentioning the fact that deliberate killing of an innocent person is vicious. Similarly, from the point of view of some observers, a 'complete' description of my bodily movements could be given without saying that I am driving a car or steering a boat; the same bodily movements might constitute one or the other action in the right conditions. Still, it is a fact about the external events themselves that I am driving a car or steering a boat.

These examples suggest that a given description of the objective facts may be complete from some points of view and incomplete from others.[26] If a complete description includes everything that needs to be included, the same description may be complete for one purpose, and incomplete for another. Why should we not say that a description of a murder 'in itself' may be complete for the purposes of an insurance company without mentioning the moral badness, but incomplete for moral purposes unless it mentions the moral badness?

Perhaps Hume has in mind a further argument to show that a complete description does not include moral badness. He may argue: (1) If the moral badness of murder is a property of the murder itself, it must be identical to some objective property F-ness (where 'F' is some predicate other than 'moral goodness'). (2) But whatever we choose as F-ness, it is conceivable that two observers agree that murder is F, but disagree about whether it is morally bad. (3) If such disagreement is conceivable, Fness is not identical to its moral badness. (4) Hence no objective property of murder is identical to its moral badness.

This argument begs a question against Price, who does not accept the first premiss. Price agrees with this premiss only if 'complex property' or 'definable property' is substituted in the antecedent for 'property'. With this substitution, Price uses the argument to show that moral properties are simple and indefinable. Hume gives no reason for accepting his

---

[24] 'Take any action allowed to be vicious: wilful murder, for instance. Examine it in all lights, and see if you can find that matter of fact, or real existence, which you call vice. In which-ever way you take it, you find only certain passions, motives, volitions and thoughts. There is no other matter of fact in the case. The vice entirely escapes you, as long as you consider the object. You never can find it, till you turn your reflexion into your own breast, and find a sentiment of disapprobation, which arises in you, towards this action. Here is a matter of fact; but 'tis the object of feeling, not of reason. It lies in yourself, not in the object.' (T iii 1.1.26)

[25] The *Inquiry* offers a similar argument: 'Euclid has fully explained all the qualities of the circle; but has not in any proposition said a word of its beauty.' (App. 1.14). The same example is used in 'Sceptic' §16. Cf. Reid, *EAP* v 7 = H 677 = R 937; Ross, *RG* 120.

[26] See Anscombe, 'Facts'.

first premiss, and so he gives no reason for preferring his account of moral properties over Price's.[27] For similar reasons, Hume's argument might be adapted to support Moore's view that goodness is a simple non-natural property. According to Moore, Hume's first premiss is a mistake that Moore connects with the Naturalistic Fallacy.[28]

If we waive this objection to Hume's first step, and grant that if moral properties are objective, they are also complex and definable, we might still question Hume's third step. Perhaps A and B disagree because B supposes something self-contradictory. In that case, what A believes may still be true, and indeed necessarily true, even if B disagrees with it. Perhaps, then, Hume means to avoid this objection, by claiming that if 'F-ness is badness' can be denied without evident contradiction, F-ness is not identical to badness.

This reply is hardly convincing. Even if it does not appear self-contradictory to suppose that deliberately killing an innocent person is not bad, the deliberate killing may still be the moral badness in the action. We may grant that if two properties are really identical, their identity is necessary, but we need not agree that the necessity is logical necessity.[29]

749. Conceivability and Possibility

But let us concede that if F-ness is badness, 'F-ness is not bad' is self-contradictory. Hume still faces difficulties that raise a wider question about his strategy. He seems to assume that if something appears to be conceivable (murder's not being wrong, for instance), it is conceivable, and is therefore possible.[30] On this point he agrees with Moore's Open Question Argument. Moore maintains that if it does not immediately appear self-contradictory to say that x is F but x is not good, goodness is not F-ness. Both Hume and Moore make it too easy to reject proposed definitions.[31]

Hume's use of this argument is especially surprising in the light of his practical argument. For internalism implies that it is inconceivable, and therefore logically impossible, to judge that doing x is morally right without being moved to do x. If we understood that moral judgments include motivation, we would also understand that what we took to be conceivable is in fact impossible, and therefore inconceivable. If this is a reasonable defence of Hume's practical argument against a claim about conceivability, it suggests an objectivist answer to Hume's metaphysical argument. If we think it is conceivable for something to meet all the conditions for deliberate murder without being bad, we simply show our ignorance of badness.

Hume, therefore, assumes in his metaphysical argument a test for possibility that undermines his practical argument. In the practical argument he assumes that we must

---

[27] Cf. Price, §814. [28] See Moore, PE 72. [29] This point is exploited by Smith, MP 25–9.

[30] Stroud, H 177–8, argues that Hume faces a difficulty if he claims we can conceive murder without its being wrong: 'But can we really conceive of an act's leading to all that hardship and suffering without its being vicious? Hume must allow that there is a clear sense in which we cannot. According to his theory of human nature, we are so constituted that the contemplation of an act of that kind inevitably leads us to regard it as vicious, so any attempt on our part to conceive of an act with these characteristics without also regarding it as vicious is bound to fail.' Hume might have an answer to this objection. The fact that I cannot think of murder in detail without thinking it is wrong does not mean that I cannot imagine someone thinking of murder without thinking it is wrong; that sort of imaginability seems to meet Hume's normal tests for conceivability when he argues that conceivability implies possibility.

[31] See Moore, PE 65.

test and (if necessary) correct intuitions about conceivability in the light of prior judgments about possibility. In the metaphysical argument, however, he assumes that we must form judgments about possibility in the light of prior intuitions about conceivability. Since his assumptions about conceivability and possibility in each case are implicit, he does not see that they conflict. But since they conflict, his practical argument and his metaphysical argument cannot both be sound.

Hume would avoid this dilemma if his practical argument did not rely on the logical impossibility of separating moral judgments from motivation. If he could show that it is simply a well-confirmed empirical generalization that moral judgments motivate by themselves, his practical argument would not rest on a claim about conceivability and possibility that conflicts with the claim underlying his metaphysical argument. We saw, however, that empirical arguments face objections arising from Hume's doctrine of calm passions. He seems to have no easy alternative to an argument from logical impossibility; and therefore he seems to face the dilemma we have described.

750. 'The Object Itself' and Motivation

Hume might try a different objection against the claim that the badness of the murder is a property of the murder itself. He might point out that we could recognize all the properties of the murder itself and still be quite unmoved by them. This argument assumes that the badness of an action must be something that motivates the person making the judgment of badness to condemn the action or to avoid doing it.[32]

This assumption may be present in the parallel argument in 'The Sceptic'. After mentioning Euclid and the circle, the Sceptic considers a mathematician who reads Virgil's *Aeneid* simply to trace Aeneas' journey on a map. Such a reader might understand every Latin word, and might acquire a distinct idea of the whole narrative, without feeling the sentiment that makes us aware of the beauty of the poem.[33] Similarly, a complete grasp of the properties of a murder may not result in the sentiment characteristic of morality.

Hume's argument about the poem seems to assume that we cannot be aware of beauty without feeling the right sentiment.[34] Similarly, he assumes, we cannot recognize the moral properties of an action without being motivated to act. Since we can recognize all the properties of the object itself without being motivated, moral properties are not properties of the object itself.

This interpretation gives Hume the best argument. It offers to explain and to justify the assumption underlying the metaphysical argument. That argument assumes that moral

[32] Stroud, *H* 178–9, interprets the argument about 'the object itself' so that it relies on the practical argument.

[33] 'He knew, therefore, every thing in the poem: But he was ignorant of its beauty; because the beauty, properly speaking, lies not in the poem, but in the sentiment or taste of the reader. And where a man has no such delicacy of temper, as to make him feel this sentiment, he must be ignorant of the beauty, though possessed of the science and understanding of an angel.' ('Sceptic' §17)

[34] This argument might be understood in other ways: (1) The claim that beauty is not an objective property of the poem is a premiss from which we infer that the mathematician knows everything in the poem even without knowing its beauty. (2) The premiss says that he knows everything in the poem, and the conclusion says that beauty is not in the poem. (1) makes the argument useless for proving that beauty is not in the poem. (2) requires us to agree, without being given any reason, that the mathematician knows all the properties in the poem. Neither interpretation provides a good argument.

properties are not among the properties of the object itself, and this assumption is justified because moral properties are essentially connected with motivation, but facts about the object itself could not be essentially connected with motivation. If this is what Hume means, he believes that the practical character of moral judgments gives the basic reason for the failure of objectivism. So understood, the argument closes a gap. We noticed that the metaphysical argument simply assumed that moral goodness could not be a simple objective property, and so left room for Price's view (later revived by Moore). The practical argument closes this gap; a simple objective property would not be essentially connected with motivation, and hence could not be the moral property. Price and Moore can exploit the metaphysical argument to show that goodness is not a complex property describable by some predicate other than 'good', and can still maintain an objectivist conclusion. But they cannot so easily maintain objectivism against the metaphysical argument supported by the practical argument.

Hare's evaluation of Moore helps us to see the role of the practical argument in supporting the metaphysical argument.[35] Price and Moore identify goodness with a simple non-natural property because they take Hume's metaphysical argument (with the first premiss appropriately modified) to show that goodness is an objective property that cannot be identified with any other property. Hare argues that Hume's metaphysical argument (and hence Price's and Moore's argument) against identifying moral properties with ordinary non-moral properties is cogent only because it relies on the practical argument. Once we see this, we see that we cannot reasonably maintain an objectivist account of goodness since (Hare claims) an objective property cannot have the appropriate connexion to motivation. Hare suggests that Moore should not be an objectivist; for Moore's Open Question Argument succeeds because of the practical character ('prescriptivity') of moral judgments, and the practical character rules out objectivism. That is why Hare believes that Moore's rejection of the Naturalistic Fallacy relies on the same basic insight that Hume relies on in his argument against objectivism. Since Moore does not recognize that this is his basic insight, he sticks to an objectivist view. But if Hume intends to rest the metaphysical argument on the practical argument, his account of his argument is similar to Hare's account of Moore.

Since Hume's apparent attempt to rest the metaphysical on the practical argument (in the argument about the poem) is so influential in later meta-ethical argument, we may notice one difficulty that has emerged from our discussion of Hume's claims about conceivability. The internalist claim that moral judgments necessarily involve motivation assumes that non-motivational moral judgments are impossible, and therefore inconceivable, though they appear conceivable. The anti-objectivist claim—that we can know the objective properties of an action without any motivation—assumes that this complete knowledge is conceivable, and therefore possible, because it appears conceivable. Hence the internalist claim relies on a judgment about possibility that is taken to override judgments about apparent conceivability, whereas the anti-objectivist claim relies on a judgment about apparent conceivability to determine possibility. The two mutually destructive claims about conceivability that we noticed in Hume's two arguments now exert their mutually destructive forces within one argument.

---

[35] See Hare, *LM* 79–93.

This objection to Hume's argument does not rest on a peculiarity of his views about conceivability and possibility. The same objection faces later non-cognitivists who accept both Moore's Open Question Argument and internalism about moral judgments and motivation. Moore's argument relies on apparent conceivability to settle possibility, whereas internalism relies on impossibility to dismiss apparent conceivability. If we ought to rely on the Open Question Argument, we ought to reject internalism; if we ought to accept internalism, we ought to reject the Open Question Argument. This objection is particularly serious for Hare, who relies on internalism to explain the success of Moore's argument.

By anticipating some of the later uses of Hume's arguments, we have seen that he raises questions he does not explore. Since he states them quite briefly and leaves some of the crucial steps implicit, he does not see the conflict in his underlying assumptions. It is easy to suppose that his arguments must be basically right, since they appeal to some plausible suggestions about morality. We may readily agree that morality has some special connexion with motivation and action that distinguishes it from ordinary factual knowledge. We may readily agree that it seems much easier to establish non-moral facts about a situation than to settle moral questions. And we may well find it plausible to combine these plausible suggestions in the further claim that moral judgments are not about objective facts. This line of argument is appealing not only to Hutcheson and Hume, but also to later non-cognitivists who take the practical role of morality to explain why moral judgments cannot be factual judgments about objective properties of things. Since this line of argument is appealing, we may easily suppose that Hume is either right or nearly right in his general views about moral judgments. But it is difficult to make his arguments seem convincing; a little expansion reveals the difficulties that they raise.

751. Anti-realism: Hume and Hutcheson

After Hume has denied that moral judgments are about any matter of fact 'in the object', he says what they are really about.[36] Though we may suppose we attribute some property to the external situation, we are really talking about our feeling of approval or disapproval. The objectivist makes the mistake we would make if we thought that irritating people have a special property of irritatingness that they have independently of whether they irritate other people. But in fact, when we say that an action is right or wrong, we really refer both to the non-moral properties of the action, distinct from its rightness or wrongness, and to our sentiment towards the action.[37]

Hume believes that this account of moral judgment allows us to identify an error he has found 'in every system of morality, which I have hitherto met with' (iii 1.1.27).[38] He

[36] 'When you pronounce any action or character to be vicious, you mean nothing, but that from the constitution of your nature you have a feeling or sentiment of blame from the contemplation of it.' (T iii 1.1.26)

[37] 'Morality . . . is more properly felt than judged of, though this feeling or sentiment is commonly so soft and gentle, that we are apt to confound it with an idea . . .' (T iii 1.2.1)

[38] MacIntyre, 'Ought' 258–60, appeals to Hume's reference to 'vulgar systems of morality' to argue that Hume is not attacking other philosophical theories, but popular moral views (which MacIntyre illustrates from Allestree [?], WDM; cf. §726). But Hume's reference to every system he has ever met with casts doubt on MacIntyre's argument. 'Vulgar' probably just means 'commonly known', so that it includes philosophical theories. In any case, the end of the paragraph

exaggerates; for he is familiar with Hutcheson, and agrees with him about the nature of moral properties, even citing his comparison of moral properties to secondary qualities.[39] Since reflexion on Hutcheson probably influenced Hume's philosophical development, we might expect him to have mentioned Hutcheson here.[40] His silence is less surprising, however, in the light of a similar silence about Hutcheson in the discussion of reason and passion. There too Hume speaks as though he rejected a long-standing consensus on the other side; he does not mention that he agrees with Hutcheson.

In *A Letter from a Gentleman*, however, Hume acknowledges Hutcheson. To the charge that his system saps 'the foundations of morality' (*LG* 18) Hume answers that the charge applies no more to him than to Hutcheson and to the ancient philosophers, since they also recognize the role of sentiments.[41] The reference to Hutcheson is apposite in a letter that answers the charge that Hume's views on morality and religion made him unfit for a university chair in moral philosophy in Scotland. It is especially apposite in the light of Hutcheson's opinion that Hume was unfit for such a chair.[42]

Still, Hume's acknowledgment of Hutcheson is not simply a defence of himself in this particular controversy. He also acknowledges Hutcheson at the beginning of the *First Inquiry*.[43] In attributing sentimentalism to the ancients, he agrees with his suggestion in the *Second Inquiry* that the ancient moralists are sentimentalists in the details of their theory, despite their official rationalism.[44] He may also be alluding to Hutcheson's claim that anti-rationalism about practical reason is the ancient and scholastic view, and that the modern rationalists are innovators.

This passage in the letter confirms what we would gather in any case from the *Treatise*, that Hume means to defend Hutcheson's position. We need not suppose that his failure to mention Hutcheson and his reference to 'all systems' indicate an attempt to conceal

('this small attention would subvert all the vulgar systems of morality, and let us see, that the distinction of vice and virtue is not founded merely on the relations of objects, nor is perceived by reason') shows that Hume intends his argument to undermine the philosophical theories he has been discussing in this chapter.

[39] See Raphael, 'Rationalism'. The comparison with secondary qualities, and its significance for Hume's view of moral properties, are explored in detail by Sturgeon, 'Scepticism'.

[40] Kemp Smith, *PDH*, esp. chs. 1–2, 6, 9, explores the influence of Hutcheson on the development of Hume's views.

[41] 'He [sc. Hume] hath indeed denied the eternal difference of right and wrong, in the sense in which Clarke and Wollaston maintained them, viz. that the propositions of morality were of the same nature with the truths of mathematics and the abstract sciences, the objects merely of reason, not the feelings of our internal tastes and sentiments. In this opinion he concurs with all the ancient moralists, as well as with Mr Hutchinson, Professor of Moral Philosophy in the University of Glasgow, who, with others, has revived the ancient philosophy in this particular.' (*LG* 30)

[42] On the election to the chair of philosophy in Edinburgh see the letter of 1744, Greig, *Letters* i #24. Hume expresses surprise at Hutcheson's position: 'The accusation of heresy, deism, scepticism, atheism, etc etc etc, was started against me; but never took, being bore down by the contrary authority of all the good company in town. But what surprised me extremely was to find that this accusation was supported by the pretended authority of Mr Hutcheson and even Mr Leechman, who, 'tis said, agreed that I was a very unfit person for such an office. This appears to be absolutely incredible, especially with regard to the latter gentleman. For as to Mr Hutcheson, all my friends think that he has been rendering me bad offices to the utmost of his power . . . What can be the meaning of this conduct in that celebrated and benevolent moralist, I cannot imagine.' One might have expected Hume to be less surprised, given his previous correspondence with Hutcheson. Hume's replies show that Hutcheson had expressed reservations about Hume's lack of warmth towards morality, and had offered Hume advice about toning down some passages in the *Treatise*. See §758. Mossner, *LDH*, ch. 12, describes the election in Edinburgh. Stewart, *KI*, offers a more recent account. He remarks that 'there was a theological agenda to Hutcheson's ethics that is deliberately lacking in Hume, and . . . there was a degree of "self-concern" in Hume's account of moral motivation that would have been anathema to Hutcheson' (12).

[43] See *IHU*, ed. Hendel, 23.   [44] See §725.

his agreement with Hutcheson. On the contrary, Hume may simply have refrained from mentioning Hutcheson (as he often refrains from mentioning modern authors) because he expects his readers to be familiar with Hutcheson. It may be worth keeping his agreement with Hutcheson in mind when we consider any difficulties that may arise in interpreting the position that Hume reaches.

752. Is and Ought: Different Interpretations

Some difficulties of interpretation arise in the observation about 'is' and 'ought' that Hume appends to his anti-objectivist conclusion.[45] Other moralists make claims about facts about the world and go on to claim that something ought or not to be done. Instead of speaking of what is, they suddenly go on to speak of what ought to be. How are we entitled to make this transition from what is the case to what ought to be done, from the non-moral properties of things to their moral properties? Hume thinks this question about how we get from 'is' to 'ought' is a devastating question to raise about 'the vulgar systems of morality', and shows us that moral distinctions are not perceived by reason. Readers differ, however, about whether he raises this question in order to show that the transition from 'is' to 'ought' cannot be made, or to show how he can make it though other people cannot.[46]

Hume speaks of the view that 'ought' could be a 'deduction' from other relations that are different from it. This might suggest to us that he is concerned with deductive validity, and asking how 'ought' statements can follow deductively from 'is' statements. But he does not seem to intend such a narrow question.[47] For the paragraph that discusses 'is' and 'ought' immediately follows the paragraph in which Hume claims to show not only that morality does not consist in demonstrable relations 'that are the objects of science', but also that it does not consist in 'any matter of fact, which can be discovered by the understanding' (iii 1.1.26). He implies that moral properties cannot be discovered by reasoning about matters of fact (which, in his view, is not reasoning, strictly speaking).

He therefore attacks not only the cognitivist views of moral properties that take moral knowledge to be demonstrative, but also those that take it to be non-demonstrative knowledge about matters of fact. Since the paragraph on 'is' and 'ought' (27) is so closely connected with this one (26), it applies to the claim that non-deductive inferences about matters of fact grasped by reason can justify moral conclusions.

Hume might be taken to intend any one of these arguments: (1) The transition from 'is' to 'ought' not only 'seems altogether inconceivable' but is indeed altogether inconceivable;

---

[45] 'I cannot forbear adding to these reasonings an observation, which may, perhaps, be found of some importance, In every system of morality, which I have hitherto met with, I have always remarked, that the author proceeds for some time in the ordinary way of reasoning, and establishes the being of a God, or makes observations concerning human affairs; when of a sudden I am surprised to find, that instead of the usual copulation of propositions, *is* and *is not*, I meet with no proposition that is not connected with an *ought* or an *ought not*. This change is imperceptible; but is, however, of the last consequence.' (iii 1.1.27)

[46] The crucial passage is obscure: 'For as this *ought*, or *ought not*, expresses some new relation or affirmation, 'tis necessary that it should be observed and explained; and at the same time that a reason should be given, for what seems altogether inconceivable, how this new relation can be a deduction from others, which are entirely different from it.' (iii 1.1.27) This immediately follows the passage quoted above.

[47] MacIntyre, 'Ought' 253–4, suggests that Hume uses 'deduction' to refer to any kind of inference.

for if we could make this transition, we would show that moral distinctions are matters of fact grasped by reason. (2) What seems inconceivable is not inconceivable. We can make the transition if and only if we supply the right kind of 'is', referring to the feeling of the spectator. The fact that we need to supply this kind of 'is' shows that the cognitivist position is mistaken.[48] (3) What seems inconceivable is inconceivable. But what seems inconceivable is not every transition from 'is' to 'ought', but the transition from 'is' judgments about God or human affairs to 'ought' judgments. In this instance, the 'ought' expresses some new relation or affirmation that is illegitimate, because the relations from which one claims to derive it are entirely different from it. But 'is' statements about the feelings of the spectator refer to relations that are not entirely different from those referred to in 'ought' statements, and in these cases the transition to 'ought' is legitimate.

It is difficult to decide between these accounts of Hume's challenge, because he leaves some other aspects of his position quite uncertain. It is especially difficult to decide what he includes in 'is' and 'is not'. He should not include all sentences containing 'is' without 'ought'; for if he included them all, he would count 'x is good' and 'x is right' as 'is' judgments. But he does not suggest that the transition from 'It is right for me to do x' to 'I ought to do x' is questionable. Hence, he does not count judgments including 'is good' and 'is right' as 'is judgments'.

But how many other judgments are to be ruled out? What about judgments involving (so-called) 'thick' moral concepts, such as 'This is brave', or 'This is considerate' or 'This is deliberate and unprovoked murder'? One might argue that these are 'is' judgments, and that from them some 'ought' judgments can be legitimately derived (if they are understood as 'ought, some things considered' or 'ought, unless something more important counts against it'). These judgments raise a question parallel to the question that arose from Hume's claim that we can know all the properties of an action in itself without knowing whether it is right or wrong. If he disallows the predicates we have mentioned, by objecting that they allow the derivation of an 'ought' judgment and so cannot be 'is' judgments, he argues in a circle. But if he does not disallow them on this ground, we seem to have found 'is' judgments that give us a legitimate transition to 'ought'.

But let us waive this objection, and assume (contrary to fact) that we can satisfactorily identify the non-evaluative predicates that are allowed to appear in 'is' judgments. Hume may intend a further restriction of 'is'. The only examples of 'is' judgments that he gives are about the existence of a God or 'human affairs'. These are judgments about external objects. They are also judgments about matters of fact, but they are not the only such judgments. When we find a 'sentiment of disapprobation', this is a matter of fact, but 'an object of feeling, not of reason'. Hence some matters of fact are not objects of reason. He has also previously allowed this in saying that morality does not consist 'in any matter of fact, which can be discovered by the understanding' (26). The 'which' clause leaves open the possibility of other matters of fact, and this possibility is actualized in the reference to matters of fact that are objects of feeling.

Here Hume denies that the moral property is a property of, say, the wilful murder itself. But he does not make it clear whether matters of fact that are objects of feeling can be

---

[48] The first position is Atkinson's in 'Ought', and the second MacIntyre's in 'Ought'.

described in 'is' statements. He commits himself more definitely in his summary of the argument about 'is' and 'ought', when he asserts that the distinction of vice and virtue is not founded merely on the relations of 'objects'.[49] If this assertion states the point of the argument about 'is' and 'ought', we would expect 'is' judgments to be judgments about 'objects'. Now he could hardly deny that it is founded on relations of objects, if 'objects of feeling' count as objects; for he has not denied that moral properties are founded on relations of actions to sentiments. Hence he uses 'objects' in the more restrictive sense that he used in saying that the vice escapes us as long as we consider the object (26). He means 'external objects', in contrast to the 'objects of feeling' that we find when we turn our reflexion into our own breast.

Hume, therefore, seems to identify objective states of affairs with 'objects of reason', 'any matter of fact which can be discovered by the understanding', and 'matters of fact whose existence we can infer by reason'. These are a proper subset of matters of fact. He does not explicitly say whether the proper subset or the whole set is described by 'is' judgments. But if the argument about 'is' and 'ought' shows something about inferences from objective states of affairs to moral conclusions, the 'is' judgments should be about objective states of affairs.

This is still not quite right, however. We might take objective states of affairs to be contrasted with subjective conditions whose existence depends on the mental state of the subject of the condition. But Hume takes some of these subjective conditions to be among conditions that are 'in the object'. For judgments about matters of fact 'in the object' include judgments about 'certain passions, motives, volitions and thoughts' (26). Hence these should also be 'is' judgments.

Perhaps, then, Hume takes 'is' judgments to include judgments about subjective states of subjects other than the subject making the judgment. When I make judgments about other people's mental states, the truth of my judgment does not depend on my thoughts and feelings (though it depends on theirs); hence these are judgments about 'the object' and are 'is' judgments. They are included among the 'is' judgments from which people claim to derive 'ought' judgments. Hume's contrast is intelligible, if 'is' judgments involve the facts of the situation (including the mental states of the agents involved) apart from the reaction of an observer who makes these judgments. While this narrow use of 'is' and this broad use of 'in the objects' may confuse us, it is not surprising. Hume takes the scope of 'is' judgments to be defined by the claims of the 'vulgar systems' that he sets out to refute.

753. Is and Ought: Hume's View

If this is Hume's conception of 'is' judgments, what is his answer to his question about deriving 'ought' from 'is'? We might suppose that he thinks the vulgar systems fail to derive 'ought' from 'is' because they do not set out from the right 'is' judgments; they would derive 'ought' successfully, on this view, if the 'is' judgments included 'is' judgments

---

[49] 'But as authors do not commonly use this precaution, I shall presume to recommend it to the readers; and am persuaded, that this small attention would subvert all the vulgar systems of morality, and let us see, that the distinction of vice and virtue is not founded merely on the relations of objects, nor is perceived by reason.' (iii 1.1.27)

about the reactions of the subject.[50] This view of Hume's conclusion, however, conflicts with his restriction of 'is' judgments to facts about 'the object' in the sense we have explained.

Probably, then, Hume claims that 'ought' cannot be derived from 'is'. Admittedly, he says only that the derivation 'seems altogether inconceivable', not that it is inconceivable. But he says it seems altogether inconceivable 'how this new relation can be a deduction from others, which are entirely different from it'. He claims that the relation involved in 'is' judgments is entirely different from the relation involved in 'ought' judgments, not merely that it seems entirely different. If he allowed 'is' judgments to include judgments about our reactions, the relations they involve would not be entirely different from those involved in 'ought' judgments. Hence he does not treat judgments about our reactions as 'is' judgments. He confines 'is' judgments to those about objective states of affairs, those that involve 'relations of objects'. His account of moral judgments does not embody a legitimate transition from 'is' to 'ought', since it does not involve a derivation of the 'ought' relation from others that are entirely different from it. The 'ought' judgment is not derived from 'is' judgments alone, but from 'is' judgments plus judgments about our reactions.

But what is the 'ought' judgment? In declaring that moral properties are objects of feeling rather than reason, Hume compares them with the Lockean view (as Hutcheson understands it)[51] that secondary qualities 'are not qualities in objects but perceptions in the mind' (iii 1.1.26). If this parallel is exact, moral properties are also perceptions in the mind. In that case, they are not feelings and reactions, but judgments about them, just as the judgment that something is red is not itself the sensation of red. Since Hume takes a belief to be simply 'a lively idea, related to or associated with a present impression' (i 3.7.5), a moral judgment should be the lively idea associated with the sentiment of approval or disapproval.

If this view is right, Hume takes his discussion of 'is' and 'ought' to show that moral judgments are beliefs with a particular subject-matter, and that they are expressed by statements; they report and describe the spectator's reaction to actions and people.

754. Do Hume's Arguments Support Non-cognitivism?

Some readers, however, have drawn a different moral from the argument, because they take the division between 'is' and 'ought' to mark the division between the descriptive and the evaluative, or between indicatives and imperatives, or between judgments and sentiments. According to this view, Hume argues for a non-cognitivist account of moral judgments, and identifies them with the moral sentiments, not with judgments about them. This section of the *Treatise* has often been cited in the 20th century as an expression of an important insight. According to 'Hume's Law', no moral judgment follows from non-moral judgments, because no imperatives follow from indicatives.[52] Hume, therefore, discovers the logical

---

[50] This interpretation is suggested by Williams, reported by Hunter, 'Reply' 288–90, and rejected by Flew, 'Not proven' 293.

[51] See Hutcheson, §642.   [52] See Hare, *LM* 29–30.

gap between facts and values. These readers of Hume have taken the basic logical point to be closely connected to Moore's discovery of the naturalistic fallacy, as they understand it, and (in contrast to Moore) have taken it to support non-cognitivism. Since moral concepts and properties are not identical to any natural concepts and properties, we cannot validly derive moral from non-moral judgments.

A non-cognitivist interpretation gains only superficial support from Hume's use of 'is' and 'ought'. We have seen that his use of 'is' in the relevant contexts narrows the range of 'is' judgments to only a subset of statements containing 'is'. When I describe my own feelings, I make a statement, but I do not make one of Hume's 'is' judgments. The fact that he contrasts 'ought' with 'is' does not show that he means to distinguish the imperative from the indicative.

A better argument for a non-cognitivist interpretation rests on Hume's practical argument. This argument succeeds only if moral judgments by themselves are practical. But Hume's argument about reason and passion implies that the only mental items that are practical by themselves are passions. Hence moral judgments must be passions. If judgments about passions are distinguishable from passions, they do not motivate us in their own right. Even if they are simply lively ideas accompanying present impressions, and therefore inseparable from the passions they accompany, they depend on the passions for motivation. The practical argument, therefore, favours a non-cognitivist interpretation.

If this is true, the practical and the metaphysical argument seem to favour different conclusions. The passage on 'is' and 'ought' sums up the metaphysical argument. It concludes that moral judgments are beliefs about one's sentiments, not about objective facts. The practical argument suggests that moral judgments are really not beliefs at all, but sentiments. The difference between these accounts of moral judgments may not be clear to Hume. He argues that 'the vice entirely escapes you, as long as you consider the object' (iii 1.1.26); this is true whichever way he treats moral judgments. But it is not clear whether we make the moral judgment in describing and reporting our sentiment or in feeling it.

It is reasonable, then, for non-cognitivists to claim that Hume has anticipated them, and their claims should not be dismissed as anachronistic.[53] They ought not to claim that Hume is a non-cognitivist, since some of his arguments seem to support a subjectivist descriptive view of moral judgments. But they are right to claim that he offers arguments that support a non-cognitivist conclusion. The argument about 'is' and 'ought' supports non-cognitivism no better than it supports subjectivism, but the practical argument supports non-cognitivism.

The difference between subjectivism and non-cognitivism is probably not obvious to Hume, partly because it is not always clear whether he is discussing moral properties or moral virtues or moral judgments. He sets out from the general claim that 'morals' influence action, and his doctrine seeks to embody this claim by showing that 'morals' essentially include sentiments, so that we miss moral goodness and badness until we attend to our sentiments. But this might be true either because (1) 'morals' are moral judgments, which are essentially sentiments, or because (2) 'morals' are moral properties, which are sentiments, whereas moral judgments are first-person beliefs about these sentiments.

---

[53] Contrast Stroud, H 265n.

Hume's metaphysical argument and his discussion of 'is' and 'ought' favour a subjectivist view, whereas the practical argument favours a non-cognitivist view.

We need not, however, confine ourselves to Hume's arguments against objectivism and rationalism about moral properties and moral judgments. We may be able to understand his views more exactly by examining some details of his positive view of the nature of moral judgments and of their subject matter.

HUME: THE MORAL SENSE

755. Anti-realism and Sentimentalism

After rejecting cognitivist and objectivist views, Hume maintains that moral distinctions are not derived from reason, but from a moral sense. We must turn our reflexion into our own breast (iii 1.1.26), to our sentiments of approval and disapproval. This reference to our approval and disapproval introduces a moral sense.

This conclusion rests in different ways on Hume's practical and his metaphysical argument. Only the practical argument shows that the moral sense itself makes the moral judgment, because there is nothing to the moral judgment beyond the feeling of approval that belongs to the moral sense. This is Hume's position, if he sees the connexion between internalism and non-cognitivism. He relies on his view that 'morals' influence passions and actions. In saying this he might intend either of two claims: (1) The existence of moral goodness involves someone's having a motive to act on it. (2) The judgment that an action is morally good involves being motivated to do it.

The first view makes goodness something like sound, on the assumption that there are no unheard sounds. It would not be possible, on this view, for an action to be morally good if no one felt approval for it, since this feeling of approval is necessary (according to Hume) for motivation. The second view does not make this claim about moral properties directly, but appeals to the connexion between moral judgments and motivation.

The metaphysical argument also introduces the moral sense. It argues that moral properties do not consist in matters of fact 'in the object', independent of the reactions of the spectator; hence objectivism is false. Moral properties consist at least in part in the feelings of a spectator, and these feelings, in Hume's view, belong to a moral sense. It does not follow, however, from this argument that moral judgments are the reactions of a moral sense. Our grasp of moral properties might be purely cognitive, not involving any feeling of approval; it might be a report of the reactions of observers, either ourselves or other people. If I am both the judge and the observer, my moral judgment reports my feeling of approval, but the judgment may be distinct from the feeling of approval.

We have also noticed a version of the metaphysical argument that relies on the practical argument: (1) If a moral judgment were wholly about a (purported) a matter of fact in the object, it would be logically possible for us to recognize that matter of fact without being motivated by it. (2) If this were logically possible, moral judgments would not involve motivation. (3) Hence moral judgments cannot be wholly about any property of the object itself. If this is Hume's argument, he assumes that the motivating character of moral judgments is a logically necessary truth derived from the content of the judgments themselves. He cannot agree that it is a contingent truth about the making of the judgments in normal circumstances. This is the version of the metaphysical argument that Hume offers in 'The Sceptic'.[1]

None of these arguments supports the introduction of a moral sense unless Hume is right to suppose that moral judgments are logically connected with a reaction of approval; anything weaker than a claim of logical necessity leaves room for objective and cognitive views of moral judgments. For many judgments with different contents, made in the right conditions, can be used to express a speaker's motives, but the motivation need not be logically connected with the contents of the judgments. 'This aspirin will make my headache go away', said in the right conditions, often indicates a desire to take the aspirin, but it is neither a judgment about my desire nor an expression of desire; it is a statement about the objective causal properties of the aspirin. Similarly, then, a sincere utterance of a moral judgment by normal agents is usually evidence that they are inclined to the appropriate action, but the judgment need not be about their feeling of approval and need not express their inclinations.[2] Many objectivist views can explain why assumptions about approval and motivation are usually plausible, given the specific objective facts that moral judgments are about. Hume's conclusion follows only if we are entitled to assume that the connexion between judgment and approval is logically necessary.

Whichever of these accounts of Hume's arguments is correct, his conclusion rejects objectivism; he denies that moral goodness and badness, rightness and wrongness, consist in any properties that things have independently of the reactions of an observer. A moral property exists only if the observer has the appropriately favourable or unfavourable sentiment in response to it.[3] This is what Hume means in claiming that we cannot find the virtue or vice until we find the relevant sentiment within our own breasts.

Though he rejects objectivism, he does not deny that moral judgments are about objective features of things. If I judge that this benevolent action is right, or that this murder is wrong, I rely on a judgment that this action is benevolent or that action is an unprovoked killing of an innocent victim. But though I make the judgment about the moral property on the basis of these judgments about objective properties of the action and the people involved, my judgment about the moral property does not regard it as an objective property.[4] The moral property exists only if the observer has the relevant sort of response.

---

[1] See §748.

[2] See further Harrison, HME 15; Warnock, CMP 36–9 (a short and clear discussion of different ways of explaining the action-guiding force of moral judgments, equally applicable to questions about their motivating force).

[3] This needs to be qualified in the light of what Hume says about the postulated observer; see §§761–2.

[4] Norton, DH 120, overlooks this vital distinction. Hence he attributes 'moral realism' to Hume because of 'the view that there are moral distinctions grounded in real existences that are independent of the observer's mind . . .'. He is right in attributing this view to Hume if 'grounded in' means simply that our moral sentiments are excited by these real existences (killing of an innocent victim, e.g.). But to recognize that moral distinctions are grounded in real existences only in this sense is not to be a moral realist. Norton does not face the further question, whether moral properties themselves are (as opposed to being in some sense 'grounded in') real existences; but that is the question one needs to answer to decide whether Hume is a moral realist.

Hume does not mean that goodness or badness consists simply in the feeling of the observer. If he did mean this, his view would have absurd results; one might argue that if this is where the badness of murder is found, I acquire the badness of murder, and so become bad, simply by having a feeling of disapproval.[5] Hume means that the badness of the murder consists in the deliberate killing of an innocent victim and the resulting disapproval by the observer; he does not mean that the badness would exist if the feeling of disapproval existed but no murder had been committed.

756. The Meaning of Moral Judgments

If Hume reaches an anti-objectivist conclusion, what is his conclusion about? Is it about the meaning of moral judgments, and hence about the metaphysical claims that they imply? Or is it about the nature of moral facts themselves? His claim that in making a moral judgment about an action we 'mean' only that we have a sentiment about it does not answer all our questions.[6] For we might take the claim in at least three ways: (1) Moral judgments are statements about the speaker's feelings. (2) Moral judgments are not statements about feelings, but expressions of feelings. (3) When we make moral judgments, we are only talking about (referring to) feelings.

The first view faces a simple objection. If you judge an action to be right, and I judge the same action to be wrong, but I mean that I disapprove of the action and you mean that you approve of it, my judgment that the action is wrong does not contradict your judgment that it is right. But in fact we think the two judgments are contradictory. This is a good reason for supposing that Hume has not given the right account of the meaning of a moral judgment. Our view about when moral judgments contradict each other seems to presuppose that we take them to be judgments about 'the objects themselves', and not about our reactions.

Still, Hume has strong theoretical reasons for accepting this account of the meaning of a moral judgment. For, in his view, the meaning of the constituent terms must consist in some idea that is derived from some impression. What impression can underlie the idea expressed by 'ought' or 'right'? In his view, it cannot be any impression of the external world that is gained by the senses. All that can be left is an internal impression belonging to a passion. Hence, apparently, the meaning of the judgment that an action is wrong is some feature of our own passions.

The difficulty Hume faces here recalls his account of causation.[7] He recognizes that we seem to have an idea of a causal relation 'in the objects' that is more than temporal precedence and constant conjunction. Since this seems to be part of what we mean in speaking of a cause, some idea must correspond to our use of 'cause', and this idea must be derived from some impression. But the only impression Hume can find is our impression of the transition we immediately make from the idea of the first event to that of the second;

---

[5] See Stroud, *H*181.

[6] 'When you pronounce any action or character to be vicious, you mean nothing, but that from the constitution of your nature you have a feeling or sentiment of blame from the contemplation of it.' (iii 1.1.26)

[7] The comparison between moral judgments and judgments about causation is explored by Beck, ' "Was" '. See also Stroud, *H*176–9.

this is an impression that we mistakenly 'spread on external objects' (i 3.14.23). We have no idea of any necessary connexion in objects, since we have no impression of it.

If meanings correspond to ideas, it is difficult to see how we can mean that causation involves necessary connexion in objects. But we must be able to mean this if we are to say (falsely, in Hume's view) that causation is necessary connexion in objects. This difficulty that Hume faces points to a general difficulty in his attempt to connect meaning with ideas and impressions.

A similar difficulty seems to arise for moral properties. For he has argued that though some people think moral properties exist in objects, they are wrong, because we have no impression of them there. We have an impression of them only in ourselves, when we turn to our sentiments. Hence objectivists about moral properties seem to be similar to believers in objective necessary connexions; they mistakenly spread a feature of our minds on external objects.

But if Hume believes that objectivists spread a feature of our minds on external objects, how can he be right to say that our idea of moral properties is an idea of our own reactions? If objectivists have the false belief Hume says they have, must they not have some idea of moral properties in objects? Their false belief seems to presuppose such an idea, since the false belief seems to mean something, if Hume can contradict it.

Perhaps Hume need not accept this objection. In his view, the spreading of moral distinctions on objects is logically similar to the spreading of pleasures and pains on the objects that cause them. We do not normally spread pleasure and pain on objects; if I take a knife with wet green paint on it and stick it into my finger, I suppose that the green paint has passed from the knife to my finger but I do not suppose that a sharp pain has passed from the knife to my finger. This is because most of us clearly understand a pain as a sensation that cannot belong to a non-sentient object. But since we do not understand our moral ideas so clearly, we find ourselves saying things that are strictly self-contradictory, when we say that actions themselves are right or wrong.

This view that objectivists implicitly contradict themselves might allow Hume to explain why they disagree with his account of moral properties. It leads us into other questions about his conception of meanings and ideas, especially about the extent to which ideas are transparent to their subject.

The second view of what we 'mean' in speaking of moral rightness makes moral judgments into expressions of sentiments, rather than statements about them. This is the non-cognitivist interpretation of Hume's position. We have already considered some of the reasons for and against ascribing this view to Hume. Further discussion of non-cognitivism is better postponed until we come to more explicit statements and defences of it than we can find in Hume. In particular, we will want to consider whether later non-cognitivists are right to suppose that non-cognitivism does better than subjectivism in accounting for features of moral judgment that seem to favour objectivism. They claim, for instance, that non-cognitivism gives a better account of the apparent contradiction resulting from your saying that this action is wrong and my saying it is not wrong. Non-cognitivism implies that we express opposed attitudes towards the action, and that this why our judgments seem to be contradictory. We may well doubt whether this explanation gives non-cognitivism a significant advantage over subjectivism.

These two interpretations of Hume's claim about what we 'mean' both assume that he seeks to give an account of the meaning of moral terms. But the third interpretation is also worth considering, since it rejects that assumption. By 'mean' he may simply mean 'refer to' or 'talk about'. In that case he does not consider the semantics of moral terms, but makes the ontological claim that all we are talking about is our reaction to the action that we say is morally good or bad. We do not identify any further objective property beyond its non-moral properties, because it has no objective moral properties. According to this view, objectivists may have grasped the meaning of moral judgments, but they are wrong about the objective existence of moral properties of things.

This ontological interpretation captures part of Hume's position. Should it be preferred to the interpretation that also ascribes to him a claim about the meaning of moral judgments?

757. An 'Error Theory' of Moral Judgments?

We would have a good reason to prefer the third interpretation if we thought that Hume argues for a sceptical or nihilist conclusion about moral properties. According to this view, the meaning of our moral judgments implies that the objects themselves have moral properties, but, in Hume's view, the implication is false.[8] Objectivists are right about the meaning of moral judgments; hence they are right to say that moral properties, if they exist, are objective properties; but they are wrong to believe that there are any such properties.

One might regard Hume's eventual view of causation as an error theory. If he believes that objective necessary connexion is part of our concept of cause, but there are no necessary connexions, he should conclude that there are no causal connexions, and that we are mistaken in believing there are any. This conclusion does not commit him to giving up judgments about causal connexions; for he does not suppose that we give up, or ought to give up, all judgments that are undermined by sceptical or nihilist philosophical arguments.

It is doubtful, however, whether Hume regards his account of causation as an error theory; probably he does not agree that the concept of cause includes an objective necessary connexion. But his views about personal identity seem to attribute an error to common sense. He does not try to explain how our judgments about the identity of a person through time are true within his theory, but he tries to show how we can be misled into false beliefs (T i 4.6.5–7). He does not advise us to give up making the claims and assumptions about identity that rest on false beliefs. He takes our ordinary beliefs to rest on a tenacious error.

Does he hold such a view about moral judgments? He believes some people are wedded to a false assumption about the objectivity of moral properties. And he sees that false assumptions can affect concepts and meanings. He believes that, because of the malign influence of divines who recognize only voluntary states as moral virtues, 'reasoning, and even language, have been warped from their natural course' (IPM, App. 4.21).[9] If all the systems of morality Hume has ever met assume the legitimacy of a transition from external

---

[8] Mackie, E 42–6, defends an error theory, and in HMT 71–5 attributes to Hume some tendency towards such a theory (while recognizing the imprecision of Hume's actual views).

[9] See §§726, 776.

facts to moral properties, one might expect that language would have been warped by the prevalence of such systems. If it has been warped in this way, our moral concepts are concepts of objective moral properties of external objects, but, since external objects have no objective moral properties, there are no moral properties or facts. In that case, Hume ought to reach a nihilist conclusion.

He does not reach this conclusion, however. Though he acknowledges that the vulgar systems of morality are objectivist, he does not suggest that they are right about our moral concepts. In this respect our moral beliefs are different from our beliefs about personal identity, so that we do not refute them by refuting the belief in objective moral properties. Hume does not argue that if we believe colours are not features of objects, we should take a nihilist view of colours; he assumes that we have discovered the real character of colours. He assumes, then, that it is not essential to a tomato's being red that the redness belongs to the tomato itself. Similarly, he assumes that it is not essential to moral properties to be properties of the external objects themselves. If the first interpretation of what we 'mean' is correct, he holds that it is essential to moral properties to be subjective. If the first interpretation is wrong, he may hold that neither subjectivity nor objectivity is essential to moral properties.

In Hume's view, moral properties are essentially connected to motivation. His conviction is expressed in his internalism. It supports his denial of objectivism. If he had believed that moral properties are essentially both objective and motivational, his argument to show that these two features are incompatible would have shown that there are no moral properties. But since he does not take objectivity to be essential to moral properties, he avoids scepticism and nihilism.

Hume has a strong reason, therefore, not to hold an error theory. In rejecting rationalism and objectivism, he takes himself to reject the errors of philosophers, not the errors of ordinary moral agents and judges. He takes the presumed existence of moral goodness and badness to be part of ordinary life. His task is to find what moral goodness and badness consist in, not whether there are any such things.[10]

A sympathetic reader will consider Hume's degree of success in this task. We may fairly compare Hume's account of moral properties and moral judgments with ordinary conceptions of morality, to see how well it fits them. But we should leave open the possibility of adapting his views to support an error theory, so that his sentimentalism might offer a replacement of morality rather than an account of it.

758. A Correction of Hutcheson

Though Hume is not a nihilist or sceptic, he does not suppose that his rejection of objectivism leaves our other beliefs about morality unchanged. In fact, he believes that the implications of sentimentalism are broader than Hutcheson recognizes. He believes (as the *Letter from a*

---

[10] Mackie (just cited) holds an error theory, and to that extent disagrees with Hume (though not with Hume as Mackie interprets him). But he agrees with Hume in claiming that his philosophical theory does not undermine first-order morality. It is more difficult for Mackie than for Hume to defend this claim.

Gentleman shows) that his argument about the nature of moral distinctions is a defence of Hutcheson's sentimentalist position; for he takes that to be the only subjectivist option worth considering once objectivist views have been refuted. But Hutcheson does not appreciate all the implications of his sentimentalism, and does not notice how some of them undermine the conciliatory position that Hutcheson takes towards objectivism.

In a letter to Hutcheson, Hume asks for advice about the passage where Hume claims that moral properties lack objective reality, just as secondary qualities do. He wonders whether this passage is 'laid a little too strong', and asks Hutcheson whether it is prudent to publish it in that form.[11] He does not say why he thinks it would be imprudent to state his anti-objectivist doctrine forthrightly; it seems to go no further than Hutcheson has already gone in his comparison of moral properties to secondary qualities.[12]

Hume might reasonably believe, however, that Hutcheson is inexplicit about the sub-jectivist implications of his position. In his early work Hutcheson defends Shaftesbury's 'realist' position. He does not explicitly abandon that position in *Illustrations*, even though he affirms the subjective character of moral properties. He insists that his position does not question the 'reality' of our moral ideas, any more than it questions the reality of our idea of pleasure. By this he means that the idea of pleasure is a real and distinct idea, even though pleasure is subjective.[13] This sort of 'reality', however, is not the whole of Shaftesbury's moral realism; for Shaftesbury also treats moral properties as objective.[14] Hutcheson does not retain the objectivist element in Shaftesbury's realism, though he does not explicitly reject it either.

Perhaps, then, Hume believes that his denial of objectivism is more explicit than Hutcheson's. He insists that it has little or no influence on practice, because our ideas of pleasure and pain are real, and matter to us. This is a weaker claim than Hutcheson's affirmation of the reality of our moral ideas. Hume may suggest, therefore, that his own statement of his position disavows Shaftesbury's realism more clearly than Hutcheson disavows it. Hutcheson's reassuring remark that he is not denying the reality of moral ideas suggests that someone might suspect that subjectivism undermines morality. Hume's reassuring remark that subjectivism about moral properties has little or no influence on practice seems to be directed at the same sort of suspicion. The suspicion is expressed openly by the opponents of Hume who are cited in *A Letter from a Gentleman*.[15]

---

[11] 'I must consult you in a point of prudence . . . [Hume quotes part of *T* iii 1.26] Is not this laid a little too strong? I desire your opinion of it, though I cannot entirely promise to conform myself to it.' (Letter to Hutcheson, 16 Mar. 1740 = Greig #16 = R634) The passage from which Hume quotes is this: 'Vice and virtue, therefore, may be compared to sounds, colours, heat and cold, which, according to modern philosophy, are not qualities in objects, but perceptions in the mind: And this discovery in morals, like that other in physics, is to be regarded as a considerable advancement of the speculative sciences; though, like that too, it has little or no influence on practice. Nothing can be more real, or concern us more, than our own sentiments of pleasure and uneasiness; and if these be favourable to virtue, and unfavourable to vice, no more can be requisite to the regulation of our conduct and behaviour.' (*T* iii 1.1.26) On this passage see also §723.

[12] See Hutcheson, §642.   [13] See Hutcheson, *IMS* 163, quoted in §642.

[14] This summary conceals some obscurities in Shaftesbury's position. See §612.

[15] '[The author of the *Treatise* is charged] with sapping the foundations of morality, by denying the natural and essential difference betwixt right and wrong, good and evil, justice and injustice; making the difference only artificial, and to arise from human conventions and compacts . . .' (*LG*) 'I come now to the last charge, which, according to the prevalent opinion of philosophers in this age, will certainly be regarded as the severest, *viz.* the author's destroying all the foundations of morality.' (*LG*) Hume continues with the passage on Hutcheson quoted in §751.

759. Hume, Hutcheson, and Voluntarism

Hume's request to Hutcheson concerns the subjectivism and sentimentalism that Hutcheson also affirms. The same doctrine is relevant to Hume's further remark that Hutcheson has given no sufficient reason for accepting naturalism rather than voluntarism about God and morality.[16] Hutcheson rejects Balguy's allegation that sentimentalism implies voluntarism, and so he defends an important element in Shaftesbury's realism. In rejecting voluntarism he agrees with Butler. Hume, however, agrees with Balguy's objection that Hutcheson cannot escape voluntarism about God and morality.[17] Sentimentalism implies that moral properties exist only in relation to spectators with sentiments like ours. Hence they cannot, according to Hume, be assumed to exist in relation to God.[18] Whether or not it is right for God to do anything depends on how God reacts to it. If God's moral sense is different from ours, what is right for him is different from what is right for us. If he has no moral sense, nothing is right or wrong for him.[19]

Hume suggests that Hutcheson should discuss this issue more fully in print only if he thinks he can avoid the agnostic conclusion about God's moral outlook. If, like Hume, he believes the agnostic conclusion is correct, his 'character' (i.e., reputation) and 'situation' (as a professor of moral philosophy expected to support Christian morality) make it unwise for him to publish his views.

One might wonder whether this advice to Hutcheson is a little exaggerated. Certainly, naturalists (about God and morality) such as Balguy believe that we threaten the position of Christian moral theology if we make morality mutable in relation to sentiments. But voluntarists reply that the naturalist position threatens the freedom and sovereignty of God to legislate right and wrong. This voluntarist reply might claim support in some accounts of divine sovereignty, especially in those accounts sympathetic to a Calvinist

---

[16] 'I wish from my heart, I could avoid concluding, that since morality, according to your opinion as well as mine, is determined merely by sentiment, it regards only human nature and human life. This has often been urged against you, and the consequences are very momentous. If you make any alterations on your performances, I can assure you, there are many who desire you would more fully consider this point; if you think that the truth lies on the popular side. Otherwise common prudence, your character, and situation forbid you touch upon it. If morality were determined by reason, that is the same to all rational beings; but nothing but experience can assure us, that the sentiments are the same. What experience have we with regard to superior beings? How can we ascribe to them any sentiments at all? They have implanted these sentiments in us for the conduct of life like our bodily sensations, which they possess not themselves.' (Grieg #16 = R634) Kemp Smith, *PDH* 202, quotes this passage to show that Hume 'develops his views with a consistency that had not, he declares, been observed by his predecessors'.

[17] See §660.   [18] Blackburn, 'Errors' = *EQR* 153, tries to defend sentimentalism while rejecting voluntarism.

[19] Hume draws out further implications of sentimentalism for theological ethics at Grieg #21, on Leechman. According to Hume, we cannot defend, on a sentimentalist basis, any obligation to love God: 'It must be acknowledged that nature has given us a strong passion of admiration for whatever is excellent, and of love and gratitude for whatever is benevolent and beneficial, and that the deity possesses these attributes in the highest perfection and yet I assert he is not the natural object of any passion or affection. He is no object either of the senses or imagination, and very little of the understanding, without which it is impossible to excite any affection.' Hume's next remarks explain how he understands love to God: 'A remote ancestor, who has left us estates and honours, acquired with virtue, is a great benefactor, and yet 'tis impossible to bear him any affection, because unknown to us; though in general we know him to be a man or a human creature, which brings him vastly nearer our comprehension than an invisible infinite spirit. A man, therefore, may have his heart perfectly well disposed towards every proper and natural object of affection, friends, benefactors, country, children etc, and yet from this circumstance of the invisibility and incomprehensibility of the Deity may feel no affection towards him.'

outlook. Despite Hume's remark that naturalism is the 'popular side', one might expect that voluntarism would be taken seriously in Scotland no less than in England. Hutcheson's views brought him into conflict with ecclesiastical authority not because he was suspected of voluntarism, but because of a view that seems closer to naturalism, that we can know about good and evil before we know God.[20] The difficulties that arise for Hutcheson's sentimentalism do not seem any more serious than those that arise for voluntarism. Why could Hutcheson not exercise 'common prudence' by defending his sentimentalist position by the well-tried arguments that commend voluntarism to some Christian theologians?

Hume, therefore, seems to take a view that many Christian theologians, including many in contemporary Scotland, might be expected to reject, when he suggests that acceptance of sentimentalism undermines Christian moral theology. He is right to point out that a sentimentalist cannot say that God is bound by moral principles simply because God is a rational being. In discussing rationalist views, Hume takes them to hold 'that the measures of right and wrong are eternal laws, obligatory on every rational mind' (iii 1.1.22).[21] But he agrees with Hutcheson's view that (1) if A is obliged to do x, there is some reason for A to do x, and (2) if there is some reason for A to do x, A has some sentiment that favours doing x. Hence God cannot be obliged to do anything without a favourable sentiment. We cannot, therefore, take God to be obliged by moral principles unless we can attribute a moral sense to God.

Hutcheson might be expected to agree with all this, since he believes that God has benevolent sentiments and a moral sense. He believes that since we see that wise provision has been made for the needs of human beings in this world, and since such provision must proceed from a benevolent agent, we must attribute to God a moral sense that approves of this benevolence. Hume has reasons—developed in his critique of natural religion in the *Dialogues*—for objecting to the premisses of Hutcheson's argument, but his objections do not seem to aim specifically at the claim that God has a moral sense. They would apply equally to the claim that God is a rational being who is obliged by immutable moral principles.

Hume has a reasonable point about Hutcheson's position, but it is not exactly the one he emphasizes in his remarks about voluntarism. His reasonable point is that Hutcheson ought not to try to separate himself from theological voluntarists, and therefore ought to accept the arguments of rationalists who argue that his position agrees with the voluntarists in making morality mutable and dependent on God's preferences. That is an unwelcome result for Hutcheson, but Hume argues that it follows from his rejection of objectivism and acceptance of sentimentalism.

760. Objectivist Criticisms of Hume's Sentimentalism

Hume does not believe that these concessions to Balguy on voluntarism also undermine sentimentalism. Balguy and Hutcheson believe that if sentimentalism is committed to

---

[20] See Hutcheson, §645. [21] Quoted more fully in §747.

voluntarism, we have reason to doubt sentimentalism. Hume answers that voluntarism is simply a consequence that we have to live with.

Hume may be too hasty. For Balguy's argument about voluntarism is simply an application of a broader argument that seems to cast doubt on sentimentalism. This broader argument claims that sentimentalism makes moral facts mutable in ways that we know they are not mutable. We do not believe an action would cease to be right if the only facts that changed were facts about an observer's reactions.[22] If, for instance, the torture of innocent children for pleasure became so common that it no longer shocked observers, though it still hurt the victims just as much, it would not cease to be wrong simply because most people had become more callous.[23] But sentimentalists are committed to claiming that the moral facts change in such a case.

Hume agrees with Balguy's claim that sentimentalism implies this degree of mutability in moral facts and properties. But he does not agree that this casts doubt on sentimentalism. For he does not agree that moral facts and properties are immutable in the way that Balguy suggests. If they appear to us to be immutable, we are mistaken because we have not yet grasped the nature of moral properties. Once we see that moral facts depend on our reactions, we must simply accept their mutability.

This is a good reason for dismissing Balguy's objections only if the grounds for believing sentimentalism are stronger than the grounds for believing in immutability. Does Hume prove this point? His practical argument rests on internalism about motivation; but it is not clear that we are more convinced of internalism than of immutability. His metaphysical argument assumes that we can recognize all the objective facts without recognizing any moral fact; but Balguy might reply that we can equally recognize a change in observers' reactions without recognizing a change in the moral facts.

It would not be enough for Hume's purposes to show that internalism is no less plausible than Balguy's claims about immutability. If his claims and Balguy's claims are equally plausible, we should conclude that both internalism and objectivism are true. If these two conclusions are incompatible, we should conclude that moral facts and properties have incompatible features, and hence we should be nihilists or sceptics. Hume can avoid this conclusion if he can show that his internalist claims are more plausible than Balguy's claims about immutability. But it is difficult to be convinced of this without an explicit confrontation between the two lines of argument.

On this point one might argue that Hume's position is less plausible than Hutcheson's. Whereas Hutcheson tries to show that his version of sentimentalism can accommodate the reasonable intuitions that seem to support objectivism, Hume believes that Hutcheson's conciliatory efforts fail and that one should frankly embrace the sort of mutability that objectivists reject. To show that he is right to do this, he should show that the objectivist intuitions are not as reasonable as they seem.

Here, then, we have found a gap in Hume's argument. To see whether he does anything that might help to fill it, we may consider some of his positive account of the moral sense.

---

[22] This condition needs to be modified to deal with cases where it might be wrong to offend people, and so something might cease to be wrong if people cease to take offence at it. In this case the observer's reaction is not the only fact that changes.

[23] See §659.

Though he does not pretend to satisfy an objectivist about moral properties, he qualifies his claims about the moral sense so that they allow him to accept, or at least to explain, some objectivist intuitions without drawing objectivist conclusions.

761. Hume's Account of the Moral Sentiment

In Hume's view, moral judgments are, or require, expressions of sentiment, and do not simply describe external facts. Since he has argued that his opponents do not give sufficient conditions for moral judgments, he needs to show that the addition of a sentiment allows him to give sufficient conditions.

Not just any kind of sentiment will do. If we react to actions we believe to be wrong with a sentiment that rests on a belief that the actions are objectively wrong, the analysis of our moral sentiments suggests that we believe in objective wrongness. If this belief in objective wrongness is needed to distinguish moral sentiments from other favourable and unfavourable sentiments towards actions, Hume's account of moral properties conflicts with the account that our moral sentiments favour. This result would not vindicate our moral sentiments, but it would show that they do not support Hume's account of moral judgments.[24]

Hume recognizes that an objection he has urged against the rationalists may be urged against his account of moral judgments and properties. He argued that all the relations taken to constitute eternal fitnesses could hold between non-rational creatures as well, so that these relations are insufficient for moral facts and properties. His opponent now suggests that all sorts of things, including actions of non-rational agents, might provoke the favourable sentiment that, according to Hume, is sufficient for moral right and wrong, and so this sentiment cannot give us sufficient conditions for moral rightness and wrongness (iii 1.2.4).

We might try to defend Hume by replying that the sentiment appropriate to moral wrongness includes the belief that a rational agent has harmed the interests of others. If this belief—or a suitably refined statement of it—is essential to moral sentiment, the sentiments provoked by rocks falling on houses or young trees choking their parents are not moral sentiments. But this reply is not open to Hume. He denies that any belief about the objects of a sentiment is essential to the sentiment, since he holds that connexions between sentiments and beliefs are contingent.[25] The moral sentiment, then, must be distinguished from other passions by its character as a sensation, not by any connected beliefs. It is logically possible for the moral sentiment to be caused by actions of non-rational agents or movements of inanimate objects.

Still, Hume does not believe his position is open to the objection that damages his opponents' position. For he claims that the actions of rational agents produce a distinct sentiment; even though we feel favourable to the results of natural processes, to the behaviour of animals, and to actions of rational agents, the feeling is different in the different cases, just as both music and wine produce pleasures, but pleasures of recognizably different

---

[24] Broad, 'Moral sense', discusses questions relevant to this criticism of Hume.   [25] See §733.

kinds. Given Hume's account of the identity and individuation of passions, the pleasures from wine and from music must be different sensations, with different introspectible characters, one of which is always correlated only with wine and the other with music. Similarly, then, the contemplation of the actions of rational agents produces a phenomenally distinct feeling.

This suggestion faces a difficulty. For contemplation of the actions of rational agents results in many different passions. There seems to be no one passion that results from contemplation, and it is not plausible to identify all the resulting passions with moral sentiment. On contemplating an action I might feel thwarted or jealous or disappointed, and so might be moved to act one way or the other on contemplation of an action or a person. Hume agrees that none of these reactions is a moral judgment. He does not tell us to expand our conception of moral judgment to embrace all these reactions. An account of the moral sentiment should identify a sentiment that we feel in the cases where we naturally judge that something is right or wrong. 'Naturally' has to be added here to take account of Hume's objection to the divines. He does not follow their separation of genuine virtues from traits that we simply look on with favour. But he believes that, if we set aside the divines' conception of morality, we can still identify a class of judgments against which we can test our account of a moral sentiment.

He suggests, therefore, that we make moral judgments whenever we have a disinterested sentiment towards someone's action.[26] A disinterested point of view cannot be part of the sentiment or essential to the sentiment, given Hume's conditions for the identity of sentiments. Hume's claim should be understood as an empirical prediction; if we contemplate human actions while turning our attention away from their effects on ourselves in particular, we have a phenomenally distinctive feeling. This effort of attention may be difficult, and so it may be difficult to recognize the distinctive feeling resulting from disinterested contemplation. But once we get used to the effort of attention, we recognize the distinctive feeling.[27]

But this suggestion still seems to leave us with too many feelings, some of which do not seem to be the moral sentiment. The Emperor Heliogabalus is supposed to have killed Christians because he liked the combination of colours produced by red blood and green grass. If we had seen the results of one of these episodes and had admired the pleasing combination of colours, our reaction would have been quite disinterested, but it would not necessarily involve any moral appraisal at all. Hence, the point of view that causes the moral sentiment cannot be merely disinterested.

---

[26] '. . . an inanimate object, and the character or sentiments of any person may, both of them, give satisfaction; but as the satisfaction is different, this keeps our sentiments concerning them from being confounded, and makes us ascribe virtue to the one, and not to the other. Nor is every sentiment of pleasure or pain, which arises from characters and actions, of that peculiar kind, which makes us praise or condemn. The good qualities of an enemy are hurtful to us; but may still command our esteem and respect. 'Tis only when a character is considered in general, without reference to our particular interest, that it causes such a feeling or sentiment, as denominates it morally good or evil. 'Tis true, those sentiments, from interest and morals, are apt to be confounded, and naturally run into one another. It seldom happens, that we do not think an enemy vicious, and can distinguish betwixt his opposition to our interest and real villainy or baseness. But this hinders not, but that the sentiments are, in themselves, distinct; and a man of temper and judgment may preserve himself from these illusions' (T iii 1.2.4).

[27] Virtue is distinguished by the pleasure 'that any action, sentiment, or character gives us by the mere view and contemplation' (iii 1.2.10).

762. A Common Point of View

Hume answers this objection through a more careful description of the type of disinterested contemplation that he has in mind. He suggests that if we attend to the effects of actions on people's interests, we are moved by 'our sympathy with the interests of society' (iii 3.1.12). When I see you being pleased, I imagine myself being pleased, and I actually feel some of the sort of pleasure that you feel.

But Hume recognizes that this sort of sympathetic pleasure seems too variable to be identified with moral sentiment.[28] Though sympathy is directed to other people's interest, it seems to vary in ways that are inappropriate for moral judgments, since they remain stable while sympathy varies. If A protects B against C's aggression, we regard A's action as right. Our sympathy matches the moral judgment if it is directed towards B and the benefit that B gains from A. But if we think, in the same disinterested way, about C, we sympathize with C's frustration, and so we change our sympathy. But we do not conclude that A's action is both right and wrong, or neither right nor wrong. We attend to B rather than C, and this attention aligns our sympathetic pleasure with the correct moral judgment.

Why do we fix our sympathy on the potential victim rather than on the potential aggressor? We might be inclined to answer that it is because we believe that what A is doing is right and what C is trying to do is wrong, so that we believe B deserves our sympathy and C does not. This answer is not open to Hume, since it makes our sentiments depend on moral beliefs in the way that he tries to avoid. And so he offers a different answer. He suggests that a purely egocentric point of view makes it difficult for us to make up our minds or to have any steady view of the action we consider, because we find that other people contradict our egocentric sentiment. We are most likely to form a sentiment that avoids contradiction if we adapt ourselves to the general attitude to a given situation. In the case we have mentioned, most people attend to the benefit B receives rather than to the harm that C receives, so that we will be least liable to be contradicted if we share the general attitude and sympathize with B rather than C.[29]

This adaptation of our sentiments is similar, in Hume's view, to the correction of our perceptual appearances. Since we recognize that to most people a penny looks round, we judge that it is round, and we tell other people it is round, even if it looks elliptical to us. If we told them it is elliptical, we would be open to continual contradiction, which we avoid by conforming to the general view. We adapt our sympathy in the same way.[30]

---

[28] '... as this sympathy is very variable, it may be thought, that our sentiments of morals must admit of all the same variations. ... But notwithstanding this variation of our sympathy, we give the same approbation to the same moral qualities. ... The sympathy varies without a variation in our esteem. Our esteem, therefore, proceeds not from sympathy' (iii 3.1.4).

[29] 'When we form our judgments of persons merely from the tendency of their characters to our own benefit, or to that of our friends, we find so many contradictions to our sentiments in society and conversation, and such an uncertainty from the incessant changes of our situation, that we seek some other standard of merit and demerit, which may not admit of so great variation. Being thus loosened from our first station, we cannot afterwards fix ourselves so commodiously by any means as by a sympathy with those who have any commerce with the person we consider.' (iii 3.1.18)

[30] 'Such corrections are common with regard to all the senses; and indeed 'twere impossible we could ever make use of language, or communicate our sentiments to one another, did we not correct the momentary appearances of things, and overlook our present situation.' (iii 3.1.16)

This intriguing suggestion raises some questions. Some arise from the comparison with perceptual judgments about the external world. One might be inclined to answer Hume that we say the penny is round because we believe it is really round, no matter how it looks to people from a particular point of view. If I say that it looks elliptical to me, and you say it looks round to you, you do not contradict me; I could avoid being contradicted if I stuck to statements about how it appears, however egocentric they might be. I say it is round not because I want to avoid being contradicted by others, but because I want to say what I believe about its real shape. Hume's claims about contradiction do not seem to explain why I say the penny is round.

Something similar is true in the case of sympathy. Hume suggests that we want some constant point of view, to save us the trouble of continually changing our view of the action in the face of different people's egocentric views; these views present so many 'contradictions' to our own view that they loosen us 'from our first station' and leave us in a vacillating condition. But this suggestion is open to doubt; different people's egocentric views do not contradict mine, if they simply report that the same action affects other people differently. Why should I not decide to stick to my initial egocentric point of view? If I tell you I am grateful to A because A did me a good turn, you can understand my sentiment, and we can successfully communicate with each other, even though you do not yourself feel grateful to A. If I approve of A because I recognize that A is useful to me and I sympathetically disapprove of A because A is dangerous to you, my reactions to A do not contradict each other, and neither makes the other less stable. Similarly, if (in the case described above) some people approve of A's protecting B against aggression from C because they sympathize with B, while others disapprove of A's frustrating C because they sympathize with C, their reactions are consistent, and we can share both reactions without any conflict or vacillation.

These objections, however, may presuppose a non-Humean view of sentiments. If beliefs are internal to some sentiments, we can sometimes show that two sentiments are consistent because they rest on consistent beliefs. Hence 'I take pleasure in x because x gives pleasure to B' and 'I find x painful because x causes pain to C' are consistent, and we have no reason to expect that either will tend to displace the other. But Hume believes that the relation between a belief and a sentiment is always empirical and causal. The two sentiments we are to consider must be described independently of the beliefs we have mentioned, and hence we cannot rely on the beliefs to show that the sentiments are not contradictory. We must simply say that in these cases we find x both pleasant and painful.

But if we offer Hume this reply, we face a further question. If we do not make beliefs internal to sentiments, what makes sentiments contradictory? Hume's subjectivism about moral judgments makes it difficult to understand our assumption that if you say an action is right and I say it is wrong, we contradict each other. Since, in his view, you report your favourable sentiment and I report my unfavourable sentiment, neither of us contradicts the other. The same difficulty arises for his claim that sentiments contradict each other in a way that induces vacillation and so causes us to seek a steadier point of view.

Perhaps Hume could defend his main point by abandoning claims about contradiction. Perhaps he could claim instead that sympathy with B (the potential victim who is protected) and with C (the potential aggressor who is frustrated) are opposed, in that they tend to cancel or to weaken each other rather than to strengthen each other. Similarly, if something that I enjoy doing causes me to feel pride, the pride increases my pleasure, but if it causes me to feel shame, that reduces my pleasure. Perhaps the opposition that we find in these cases supports Hume's argument about sympathy.

This does not seem obvious, however. If we assume opposition rather than genuine contradiction, sympathy with B is opposed to sympathy with C no more than sympathy with B or C is opposed to pleasure caused by music; for this pleasure may also reduce my sympathy by distracting me. To avoid this sort of opposition, I need to attend to the music, or to B, or to C, to the exclusion of other things. I do not seem to need to take some different point of view that causes me to sympathize with B or to sympathize with C or to enjoy the music, to the exclusion of the other passions.

But even if we agree with Hume's claim that we need to resolve 'contradictions' in our sympathies by taking some more generally shared point of view, it is not clear that the sympathy we take from this point of view will be stable, or that it will match our moral judgments. To avoid contradictions, we might sensibly adopt the view of most people around us. But if these people are fickle, so that they incline to sympathize sometimes with B and sometimes with C, we will be no less inclined to shift in our sympathy, though they will not contradict us. If they shift in their sympathy, or if they are more inclined to sympathize with C (the potential aggressor) than with B (the potential victim), their sympathy does not match our moral judgments, and is still not moral sentiment.

763. The Point of View of Humanity

This criticism leads us to consider a different conception of the 'common point of view' that Hume offers, especially in the *Inquiry*. He describes the moral point of view as one that we can all share, irrespective of our private interests; this is the point of view of humanity.[31] Our moral judgments proceed from a sentiment that we all share, apart from our particular perspectives on actions, when we contemplate actions that affect human interests. In virtue of that sentiment, our moral evaluation expresses a common point of view.[32] When we take this point of view, we favour actions that promote the public good.[33] It is a frequent and widespread, and hence natural (in a sense of 'natural' that Hume accepts) fact about human beings that they are susceptible to feelings that are favourable to the public good. These are the feelings that match moral judgments. The relevant 'universal principle of the human frame' is benevolence, giving us 'a cool preference of what is useful and serviceable to mankind' (*I* 9.4).

---

[31] Selby-Bigge, Introd. to *I*, pp. xxiii–xxviii, argues plausibly that the relative prominence of benevolence and humanity in *I* marks a doctrinal difference from *T*.

[32] '...he expresses sentiments, in which he expects all his audience are to concur with him. He must ... move some universal principle of the human frame, and touch a string to which all mankind have an accord and symphony' (*I* 9.6).

[33] 'If he mean, therefore, to express that this man possesses qualities, whose tendency is pernicious to society, he has chosen this common point of view, and has touched the principle of humanity, in which every man, to some degree, concurs. While the human heart is compounded of the same elements as at present, it will never be wholly indifferent to public good, nor entirely unaffected with the tendency of characters and manners.' (*I* 9.6)

Hume's most plausible account of the moral sentiment is therefore this: (1) When we think impartially about the interests of those affected by an action, we form a distinctive sentiment about it. (2) This sentiment is benevolence, favouring the public good. (3) This sentiment is the moral sentiment; the actions it favours are those we intuitively judge to be right. These are all empirical claims. The first asserts that attention to certain features of an action tends to cause a sentiment. The second asserts that this sentiment tends to cause certain kinds of actions. The third asserts that the sentiment causing these actions is the one we feel when we make moral judgments.

In the first claim Hume describes a common point of view that expresses community and solidarity with other human people. This point of view involves the impartial consideration of the effects of actions on people's interests. We should be able to take this point of view without thinking about fairness, since Hume is trying to find the origin of moral sentiments without presupposing them. The common point of view on a theft, for instance, will recognize the pain suffered by the victim and the thief and by anyone else affected, but will leave out the fact that I or my friend or my enemy is the thief or the victim, or the beneficiary of the theft.

What sentiment do we form from this impartial point of view? It is difficult to see how we can be expected to agree on any one reaction. Perhaps I am more inclined to sympathize with the frustration, or greed, or whatever other motive might lead to theft, and you are more inclined to sympathize with the victim's feelings of loss. Apart from these difference in inclinations, we might have different views about how bad it is for people to lose what they have, compared with failing to get what they want. The fact that each of us takes an impartial point of view does not ensure agreement in our reactions, since we may have different inclinations and non-moral beliefs that affect our reactions.

But perhaps Hume wants us to abstract from these individual differences and to focus exclusively on the pain and pleasure of the thief and the victim. In that case, our reaction depends on whether the pain of the victim is greater than the pleasure of the thief, or the reverse. Perhaps this is why he identifies the common point of view with benevolence, understood as concern for the public good. This seems to be an empirical claim, about the result of taking the common point of view, rather than a description of what constitutes taking the common point of view. But if Hume intends the common point of view to abstract from everything except pleasure and pain, it is close to benevolence, as a hedonist utilitarian understands it.[34]

By introducing benevolence into his account of the moral sense Hume agrees with Hutcheson, but he simplifies Hutcheson's view. Hutcheson confines the moral sense to the moral judge who reacts favourably to the benevolence of an agent; he makes a second-order attitude of approval or endorsement of a sentiment essential to the moral sense. Simple benevolence without this further approval does not involve the moral sense, according to Hutcheson. The further approval is Hutcheson's analogue to the operation of conscience, as Butler conceives it.[35] According to Hume, however, in the passage we have just discussed, the moral sense does not require this second-order element. A benevolent reaction by itself

---

[34] Contrast Baier, *PS* 205, who argues that one ought to 'appreciate the hedonism, rather than the utilitarianism, of his thinking about ethics'.

[35] See Hutcheson, §§642, 715.

constitutes an expression of the moral sense. Our moral judgment is either this benevolent reaction itself (if Hume is a non-cognitivist) or a report of it (if he is a subjectivist).

764. Can We Isolate Moral Sentiment?

Has Hume found the moral sentiment? We may well doubt whether he has identified just one introspectibly distinct feeling for all and only the actions we regard as morally good. In some cases our reaction of moral approval might be enthusiastic, if the morally good coincides with our interest, or the agent is a friend of ours; in other cases it might be grudging, if the agent is an enemy or if the action harms us; in others it might be entirely neutral, if our interests and affections are quite uninvolved.

Hume admits that the moral sentiment may co-exist with others, but he maintains that with practice we can distinguish it. But even if we agree with him on this point, we may doubt his assumption that it has a distinct introspectible quality that is present on all occasions. It does not seem obvious that an introspectible quality is the common feature of the moral sentiment on all the occasions when it occurs with different tones. All the different reactions—eager, grudging, neutral—express the sentiment of disinterested approval, but not because they all contain the same phenomenally distinctive sensation. They share a certain kind of evaluative belief (or a disjunction of appropriate beliefs); but Hume's theory does not allow a doxastic element to individuate sentiments.[36]

Would Hume do better, then, to abandon his non-doxastic conception of sentiments? If he abandoned it, he would also have to give up some other views that matter to him. If he agreed that beliefs are essential to some sentiments, he would undermine his criticism of the divines, who want to restrict moral goodness and badness to voluntary actions and states. Hume argues against the divines by claiming that we have the same sentiments both towards voluntary and towards non-voluntary states. In this argument he seems to assume that the belief that a state is voluntary cannot be essential to the identity of a sentiment. But this assumption conflicts with the claim that the moral sentiment requires some belief.

Moreover, if Hume were to concede that some evaluative beliefs are essential to moral sentiments, he would leave room for a rationalist reply to his sentimentalism. If the moral sentiment essentially involves evaluative beliefs, why should we not identify moral judgments with these beliefs, and moral properties with the properties that are mentioned in these beliefs? In that case, Hume's attempted alternative to objectivism would apparently presuppose an objectivist account of the beliefs that partly constitute moral sentiment.

He avoids this objection if he affirms that moral sentiment consists simply in a feeling with a distinctive phenomenal character; beliefs cause this feeling, but they are not essential to it. These beliefs, then, are not moral judgments, and the properties they mention are not moral properties, because their relation to moral sentiment is only causal. According to this view, if we judge that an action promotes the public good, but we are not at all moved to favour the action, we have not made a moral judgment, since moral judgment requires motivation.

---

[36] See Smith's criticism of the moral sense, §789.

765. Moral Judgment Without Sentiment?

But though we might expect Hume to say this, he does not say it. For, in his view, I may learn to judge that something is good from the moral point of view, without the appropriate sentiment. In my moral judgment I say what someone would say who was directly affected by the action, I may not have the same feeling. Even if I have some feeling, I may not have equally strong feelings towards two actions that I judge to be equally wrong. My moral judgment, therefore, is neither the feeling nor a report on it.[37]

Our appeals to a general point of view do not automatically change our passions, 'nor do our passions often correspond entirely to the present theory' (T iii 3.1.18). A may agree that B's opposition to A's plans is morally blameless, but may still be angry at B for this opposition.[38] Though reason may favour impartiality, our passions do not always go along with it. Hume explains his mention of reason by arguing the so-called reason opposing our passions is really another passion, 'a general calm determination of the passions, founded on some distant view or reflexion' (iii 3.1.18).

In referring to a distant view, Hume relies on the assumption about calm passion that he uses to explain prudence.[39] When we take a 'distant' view, looking at a situation without reference to our own interest, our calm passions are excited. When we take a 'closer' view, and recognize how our interest is involved, more violent passions are aroused, and so our stronger feelings do not agree with our original calm passion. Hume might reasonably conclude, therefore, that moral judgments express or report the calm passion that is excited by sympathetic consideration of the interests of the people affected.

But this is not his conclusion. He does not say that if we judge that A and B are equally blameworthy, we express an equally strong calm passion towards A and B. Instead he takes our judgment to predict what would be felt in certain circumstances.[40] He therefore seems to abandon his sentimentalism. For he no longer seeks to correlate the stable moral judgment with a stable actual sentiment; the stable judgment is a prediction, not a report, about sentiments.

Some moral judgments, therefore, neither express nor report anyone's occurrent sentiment. They are still about sentiments, since they are predictions about sentiments rather than judgments about objective properties of actions and people. But, as we saw in discussing 'is' and 'ought', Hume counts judgments about other people's subjective states as judgments about what is 'in the object', and therefore as 'is' judgments. His present account of moral judgment seems to imply that moral properties are in the object, and that we can derive 'ought' from 'is'.

If moral judgments are predictions about sentiments, Hume's analysis does not support his claim that when you pronounce the action vicious 'you mean nothing but that . . . you

---

[37] 'Experience soon teaches us the method of correcting our sentiments, or at least, of correcting our language, where the sentiments are more stubborn and inalterable.' (T iii 3.1.16)

[38] 'Here we are contented with saying, that reason requires such an impartial conduct, but that 'tis seldom we can bring ourselves to it, and that our passions do not readily follow the determination of our judgment.' (iii 3.1.18)

[39] See §738.

[40] 'We blame equally a bad action, which we read of in history, with one performed in our neighbourhood the other day: The meaning of which is, that we know from reflexion, that the former action would excite as strong sentiments of disapprobation as the latter, were it placed in the same position.' (iii 3.1.18)

have a feeling or sentiment of blame . . .' (iii 1.1.26). Nor does it fit his internalist claim that moral judgments necessarily motivate the subject who makes them. His predictive analysis implies that his internalist and subjectivist account of moral judgment and moral properties is mistaken.[41]

Hume's account of the causes of moral sentiment even suggests that one might defend a more strongly objectivist account of moral judgments than the one he allows. In his view, the sentiment is aroused by the belief that a particular action is (for example) beneficial to those affected by it. Why should we not take this belief to be sufficient for a moral judgment? Hume's account of the content of the moral judgment seems to show how easily we can separate the making of the judgment itself from the attitude that it arouses in the judge. It is easy, on this view, to see why moral judgments are regularly connected with action; they characteristically express the point of view of humanity and appeal to our benevolent sentiments.

Once we see this, we may doubt whether moral judgments motivate all by themselves, and therefore cannot be derived from reason. For not everyone has benevolent sentiments to an equal degree, and on some occasions some people may have no benevolent sentiments. But they may still believe that this action promotes the public good, and therefore appeals to a benevolent person. Hume seems to have found objective properties that could be identified with moral goodness and badness. And so he seems to have undermined his efforts to show that moral distinctions are not founded in reason.

Hume rejects an objectivist account on the ground that it omits the internal connexion between moral judgment and motivation. But his counterfactual analysis referring to sentiments also omits that internal connexion. Once he has abandoned internalism, it is not clear why we should treat moral judgments as judgments about counterfactual sympathy rather than judgments directly about the properties of actions and people that tend to arouse the counterfactual sympathy.

If, therefore, we examine these details of Hume's account of moral judgment, we reach a different conclusion from the one we reach if we confine ourselves to the practical and metaphysical arguments and to the discussion of 'is' and 'ought'. These initial arguments support his internalism, subjectivism, and sentimentalism. But his account of the moral sentiment, and his substitution of counterfactual for actual sentiment, undermine his case against objectivism. He does not notice this, because he still maintains that moral judgments are about sentiments; he may suppose that this feature of moral judgments satisfies his internalist constraint.

If one believes that Hume's internalism and subjectivism are the most important and valuable aspects of his theory, one might restore consistency to his position by using a device favoured by later non-cognitivists. In cases where Hume admits that we make moral judgments without the appropriate sentiment, we might say that the moral terms in these judgments do not have their normal sense, but we use them in a 'non-standard' or 'inverted commas' sense. This resort to differences of sense would avoid the inconsistency that Hume introduces into his position. Hume might welcome this way to restore consistency, if he

---

[41] Brown, 'Internalist' 78–87, discusses aspects of Hume that are inconsistent with the internalism assumed in his argument against objectivism.

had noticed his inconsistency. But this move is costly; for it does not seem obvious that motivational and non-motivational uses of moral terms involve different senses. Further discussion of this issue is better postponed until we come to non-cognitivists who try to help Hume in this way.

766. The Possibility of Humean Objectivism

But in any case, a non-cognitivist's appeal to different senses, whether plausible or implausible, may not be the best way to restore consistency to Hume's position. One might be more inclined to emphasize the objectivist elements. Though internalism and subjectivism are prominent in his critical arguments and in his presentation of his own view, something worth considering survives the rejection of these claims. His suggestion that a moral judgment is one 'in which he expects all his audience are to concur with him' (I 9.6) correctly implies that moral considerations express a more common point of view than that of one person's interest.

What sorts of considerations are recognized from this common point of view? Hume's account of how we equally blame two actions that excite different sentiments implies that our judgment is a counterfactual judgment about how certain sorts of observers would react. If he offers this as a general account of moral judgments, the subject-matter of moral judgments is the sentiment of the observer taking the common point of view. Alternatively, we might concentrate on Hume's remarks about the actions that such an observer favours—those that promote the public good. These remarks might suggest that the subject matter of moral judgments is the public good.

In either case, Hume's view would be objectivist, insofar as it would make moral judgments true independently of the reactions of a particular moral judge.[42] In the second case, his view would be more strongly objectivist, since it would make them true independently of the reactions of any judge or observer. According to the first view, moral goodness and badness would change if observers taking the common point of view no longer favoured the public good. Whether this is possible or not depends on how the common point of view is to be defined. Is it no longer the common point of view if it ceases to be concerned with the public good? Alternatively, if everyone were to become indifferent to the public good, and were to agree in a general indifference to this aspect of actions, would the same common point of view now approve of something different?

It may be pointless to ask whether one or another of these possible views is Hume's view. His suggestions are not precise or detailed enough to make it clear what he means. And if he made them more precise, he would be more likely to notice the conflict between his non-sentimentalist remarks about the possibility of moral judgments without sentiments and the sentimentalist claims that he relies on in his initial arguments against rationalism and objectivism. The different elements in Hume's claims about moral judgments are instructive because they suggest why different views about the nature of moral judgments are attractive, and why nonetheless one needs to choose between them.

---

[42] Sharp, 'Hume' 53–6, emphasizes the objectivist tendencies in Hume's appeal to the impartial observer. At 158–9 he suggests that a Humean view might absorb some of Reid's claims about objectivity (see §670).

Our discussion of the position that Hume opposes to the 'vulgar systems of morality' has given us reason to believe that his conception of moral judgment is inconsistent.[43] Three different revisions of Hume leave us with some plausible and influential views: (1) If we take internalism to be most important, we will accept non-cognitivism, as later emotivists and prescriptivists do, sometimes for reasons that they take to be Hume's reasons.[44] (2) If we take Hume to be a subjectivist, we will take moral judgments to describe the sentiments of the spectator or of some class of actual, potential, or ideal spectators. This is the basis of Smith's account of moral judgments as statements about the impartial observer. (3) If we take Hume to oppose theories that separate moral goodness from empirical human feelings, we may take the objectivist utilitarian strand in his discussion to be the one that deserves defence and expansion; that is why Sidgwick treats Hume as a source for his utilitarianism.[45]

The utilitarian is right to emphasize Hume's assumption that the common point of view is a utilitarian point of view aiming at the public good. But one might be doubtful about Hume's reasons for believing that the common point of view underlying morality is utilitarian. Might one argue that the point of view of humanity is non-utilitarian? This issue is especially relevant when we consider Hume's views about the utilitarian and non-utilitarian elements in different aspects of morality.

[43] Garrett, CCHP, ch. 9, argues that Hume's account of the development of moral sentiment and moral judgments makes his account consistent. I doubt whether he resolves all the questions that can be raised about the role of sentiment.

[44] See Hare cited in §750. Contrast Stevenson, EL 273–6; though he is a non-cognitivist, he takes Hume to be a subjectivist. Laird, SMT 17–18, comes closer to ascribing non-cognitivism to Hume.

[45] Stephen, HET i 87, also treats Hume as a utilitarian: 'all must admire that the essential doctrines of utilitarianism are stated by Hume with a clearness and consistency not to be found in any other writer of the century. From Hume to J. S. Mill the doctrine received no substantial alteration.'

59

HUME: THE VIRTUES

767. Natural and Artificial Virtues

If we accept Hume's account of the moral sense, what account of morality do we commit ourselves to? Hume answers this question by listing the virtues and showing that they are objects of the sentiment that he ascribes to the moral sense. Before we consider his general account of the virtues and of their relation to the moral sense, it is useful to consider some of the specific virtues.

He divides the virtues into natural and artificial, on the basis of his general claim that we value virtuous actions only insofar as they express a virtuous character (T iii 2.1.2; iii 3.1.4). If we commend a particular action, it must be because we approve the state of character that it proceeds from, and this state of character must immediately appeal to our sympathetic feelings (those that belong to the principle of humanity) (iii 2.1.6). What state of character, then, appeals immediately to our sympathetic feelings?

Hume believes we cannot answer this question by saying that the virtuous state of character is the one that values virtuous actions precisely because they are virtuous or morally good; for he has already claimed that we value virtuous action only as expressions of a virtuous character. Hence the virtuous person who (supposedly) values virtuous actions simply because they are virtuous must in fact value them because they are signs of virtuous character. But we still do not know why she values virtuous character. If we say that she values it because of the virtuous actions it produces, we proceed in a circle.

Hume offers a way out of this circle of explanation, by introducing a non-moral motive. The virtuous agent must have some motive for doing the virtuous action, apart from the sense of its morality (its moral rightness or goodness); and the tendency to do this kind of action must appeal to morally enlightened judges apart from their sense of its morality.[1] If the agent and the judges could not be moved by these non-moral sentiments, we could not understand either the agent's motive or the judges' grounds for approval.[2]

---

[1] '...no action can be virtuous or morally good, unless there be in human nature, some motive to produce it, distinct from its morality' (T iii 2.1.7). See Reid, §850.

[2] See Mackie, HMT 76–82. At 78–9 (remarking that Hume conflates two questions), he seems to agree with Reid's criticism.

Different virtues, however, arouse our non-moral sentiments in different ways. The differences mark a division between natural virtues including benevolence, and artificial virtues, including justice.

My act of benevolence belongs to a natural virtue because of three features: (1) My action tends to benefit others. (2) I act out of a desire to benefit others. (3) My motive arouses approval in an impartial and sympathetic observer. Both my desire to help and the observer's reaction of approval are natural reactions to this action; for we have a natural sentiment of benevolence that explains both my desire and the observer's reaction.

In this case we face no difficulty in saying what it is about benevolent action that appeals to us as agents and observers. An act of justice, however, has neither of the first two features. It has the third feature; but this must be explained differently. A simple appeal to benevolence cannot explain our attachment to justice.[3]

768. The Difficulties about Justice

Hume tries to resolve two difficulties arising from Hutcheson's account of justice: (1) The first objection concerns Hutcheson's sentimentalism. Hutcheson rejects Hobbes's self-interested and instrumental explanation of justice, and claims instead that justice appeals to our sentiment of benevolence, which the moral sense approves of. But it is difficult to believe his claim that benevolence, understood as a sentiment involving an immediate reaction to actions and people, could support a utilitarian conception of justice that often acts against the interest of particular people who might be expected to arouse our benevolent sentiment. (2) But even if we could connect benevolence with utility, we would not have vindicated a utilitarian conception of justice. For we recognize just actions that do not promote utility.

These two difficulties in Hutcheson's position provoke two rationalist replies: (1) Balguy and Butler propose an alternative basis for benevolence. They introduce a rational principle of benevolence, and they rely on this principle, not on the sentiment of benevolence, to support moral principles that aim at the public good. (2) But even this rational principle of benevolence does not cover the whole of morality, and in particular does not cover justice. Principles of justice rest on a basis that is distinct from concern for the public good, and therefore cannot be explained by a utilitarian principle.

Hume sees the same difficulties in Hutcheson's position, but he offers an anti-rationalist solution.[4] In his view, benevolence cannot be the source of the just person's motive or of

---

[3] 'The only difference betwixt the natural virtues and justice lies in this, that the good, which results from the former arises from every single act, and is the object of some natural passion; whereas a single act of justice, considered in itself, may often be contrary to the public good, and 'tis only the concurrence of mankind, in a general scheme or system of action, which is advantageous. When I relieve persons in distress, my natural humanity is my motive; and so far as my succour extends, so far have I promoted the happiness of my fellow-creatures.' (T iii 3.1.12)

[4] See Hutcheson, §647; Balguy, §664. Hume criticizes Hutcheson's appeal to benevolence as the basis of justice, in a letter (Greig, LDH i #19, p. 47): 'You sometimes, in my opinion, ascribe the original of property and justice to public benevolence, and sometimes to private benevolence towards the possessors of the goods, neither of which seems to me satisfactory. You know my opinion on this head. It mortifies me much to see a person, who possesses more candour and penetration than any almost I know, condemn reasonings, of which I imagine I see so strongly the evidence. I was going to blot out this after having wrote it; but hope you will consider it only as a piece of folly, as indeed it is.' This is another point on which Hutcheson might be expected to find a lack of 'warmth' in Hume.

the observer's reaction; for this particular just action does not contribute to the good of others in the ways that provoke the sentiment of benevolence. Benevolence and humanity, in Hume's view, would often lead us both to do and to approve unjust action.[5] To see how concern for the public good could support justice, we have to look at the larger system of which particular just actions are a part, and we have to see that the system promotes the public good.

This point about benevolence does not clearly bear on the rational principle of benevolence, as Balguy and Butler understand it; for they regard it as a principle that considers the public good impartially and comprehensively, looking at the further as well as the nearer consequences of actions and policies. Hume's point applies only to the sentiment of benevolence as he and Hutcheson conceives it. He tries to overcome the objection to Hutcheson without resort to a rational principle.

In the *Treatise* his argument about justice assumes that we are not concerned for the public interest as such (iii 2.1.11), but only for the interests of individual people, because of the effects of sympathy. Even if every particular just action promoted the public interest, this would not explain our favourable attitude towards it, since we have no favourable sentiment towards the public interest. In the *Inquiry* Hume drops his objection about concern for the public interest; the point of view of humanity that produces the moral sentiment involves concern for the good of society, not just the good of this or that individual.[6]

But the acknowledgment of this concern for the public interest does not undermine Hume's main reason for counting justice as an artificial virtue. He argues that particular just actions do not seem to make any intelligible appeal to our concern for the public interest; for this concern would apparently often lead us to prefer the confiscation of a rich miser's property to benefit the poor, whereas justice requires us to respect the miser's right to his property. Here Hume recognizes the second rationalist objection to Hutcheson, but he does not agree with the rationalists in turning to a non-utilitarian conception of justice. He seeks to resolve the objection by showing how our concern for the public interest becomes attached to just actions that initially appear to conflict with the public interest.

According to the argument against Hutcheson, we cannot explain how our concern for the public interest, all by itself, could move us to take an interest in just actions. Hume argues that we need a two-stage account to resolve this difficulty for a utilitarian view. The first stage identifies our original motive for establishing justice. Here Hume gives a Hobbesian answer, referring to self-interest. The second stage explains our moral admiration for the rules of justice, once they have been established; at

---

[5] 'But if we examine all the questions, that come before any tribunal of justice, we shall find, that, considering each case apart, it would as often be an instance of humanity to decide contrary to the laws of justice as conformable to them. Judges take from a poor man to give to a rich; they bestow on the dissolute the labour of the industrious; and put into the hands of the vicious the means of harming both themselves and others.' (iii 3.1.12)

[6] See, e.g., *I* 5.45: 'It appears also, that, in our general approbation of characters and manners, the useful tendency of the social virtues moves us not by any regards to self-interest, but has an influence much more universal and extensive. It appears, that a tendency to public good, and to the promoting of peace, harmony, and order in society, does always, by affecting the benevolent principles of our frame, engage us on the side of the social virtues.' Such statements are more frequent and more emphatic than anything in *T*.

this stage Hume gives a non-Hobbesian answer, referring to concern for the public interest.[7]

769. The Origin of Justice

Hume rejects an initially plausible account of the origin of justice that might be ascribed to Hobbes. The observance of principles of justice results from our acting on the law of nature that enjoins the pursuit of peace and non-aggression. Hence we might trace the origin of justice to a promise—a Hobbesian 'covenant'—to refrain from aggression. Hume, however, believes that no appeal to a promise explains the observance of justice. A promise establishes a practice of mutual non-aggression only if we already recognize an obligation to keep the promise; but both the obligation to keep a promise and the recognition of this obligation[8] depend on an antecedent practice or 'convention' of non-aggression. Since the obligation to keep a promise presupposes the convention of non-aggression, it cannot explain the convention.[9]

We might take Hume to mean that we cannot found the moral obligations connected with justice in a promise, because the promise will be irrelevant unless we already recognize an obligation of justice to keep promises. This would be a reasonable point, but it would not be relevant to Hobbes's appeal to a covenant. Hobbes takes the relevant obligation to be prudential; he might argue that prudential obligation is the basis of the obligation to keep a promise, which then introduces moral obligation.[10] Such an argument does not require antecedent recognition of a moral obligation to keep a promise.

But Hume's point bears more directly on Hobbes's appeal to self-interest as the basis of a covenant. I will recognize a prudential obligation to keep a promise to you only if I take it to be in my interest. But I will believe it is in my interest to keep a promise to you only if I already have some reason to believe that you will also keep your promise to me. But how can I form such a belief if I have no previous experience of your keeping promises?

Hume answers that we need an antecedent practice or convention of non-aggression that gives me reason to rely on you. Two people may form such a convention to do their parts in rowing a boat, if the boat needs two people to row it, each of them wants to go to the same place, and neither sees a better way to get there. This convention may precede any promise, because we can establish a convention without having made any promise. We

---

[7] 'We now proceed to examine two questions, viz. concerning the manner, in which the rules of justice are established by the artifice of men; and concerning the reasons, which determine us to attribute to the observance or neglect of these rules a moral beauty and deformity. These questions will appear afterwards to be distinct.' (T iii 2.2.1) 'Thus self-interest is the original motive to the establishment of justice; but a sympathy with public interest is the source of the moral approbation, which attends that virtue.' (T iii 2.2.24) On Hume and Hobbes on justice see Sidgwick, OHE 205n.

[8] Hume does not explicitly distinguish the obligation from the recognition of it.

[9] 'This convention is not of the nature of a promise: For even promises themselves, as we shall see afterwards, arise from human conventions. It is only a general sense of common interest; which sense all the members of the society express to one another, and which induces them to regulate their conduct by certain rules. I observe that it will be for my interest to leave another in the possession of his goods, provided he will act in the same manner with regard to me. He is sensible of a like interest in the regulation of his conduct. When this common sense of interest is mutually expressed, and is known to both, it produces a suitable resolution and behaviour.' (iii 2.2.10; cf. ii 2.9.9; iii 2.5.1)

[10] See Hobbes, §493.

simply need to be aware of the mutual advantage that depends on co-ordinated action.[11] By seeing this advantage and acting on it, we establish a convention of mutually beneficial, co-ordinated action that requires no initial promise.[12] Rules about non-aggression, the use of language, and the use of money arise from convention in the same way. In all these cases the prudent action for each party individually depends on what the other party does, so that the conduct of the two (or more) parties is inter-dependent. Each of them gets the expected benefit only if both play their part. In these circumstances a mutually beneficial convention develops.

Self-interest, therefore, provides a reason and motive for observing these conventions, even though they may appear to frustrate self-interest. Our desire for possession, for instance, encourages us to grab other people's possessions, but we notice that we would frustrate our desire for possession if we were to indulge it by always grabbing what we can grab from other people, and thereby encouraging them to do the same to us. Hence the desire for possessions also gives us the motive to regulate it.[13] We do not need to introduce any specifically moral concern into the motives of people who establish a system of justice. Hence we have found a motive to produce just actions, 'distinct from their morality', as Hume requires.[14]

770. Hume v. Hobbes on Justice

This part of Hume's account, tracing justice back to self-interest, develops and modifies Hobbes's view of justice.[15] Hume is clearer than Hobbes about the distinct contributions of human nature and external circumstances to the conditions favourable for justice. He notices that complete selfishness is not necessary. He only assumes confined generosity; and he remarks that this would not result in aggression and conflict if we did not have to compete for scarce resources (iii 2.2.5–7). To form the state, we need no formal agreement to lay down our arms; and we need not explain how we can recognize an obligation to keep such an agreement. An appeal to convention explains how the appropriate practices can get started without any prior agreement.

Does Hume resolve the main difficulties in Hobbes? His examples of convention without explicit agreement are persuasive, but how much do they explain? Even if some practices satisfy Hume's conditions for conventions, and grow up without explicit agreements or moral sanctions, this pattern does not seem to fit most actual systems of justice. For these systems involve many individuals in complex interactions; the penalties of cheating may not

---

[11] 'whatever is advantageous to two or more persons, if all perform their part; but . . . loses all advantage if only one perform . . .' (*I* App 2.8; cf. *T* iii 2.2.10; iii 2.6.6).

[12] 'The actions of each of us have a reference to those of the other, and are performed upon the supposition, that something is to be performed on the other part. Two men, who pull the oars of a boat, do it by an agreement or convention, though they have never given promises to each other.' (*T* iii 2.2.10)

[13] 'It is by establishing the rule for the stability of possession, that this passion restrains itself.' (iii 2.2.14) 'After men have found by experience, that their selfishness and confined generosity, acting at their liberty, totally incapacitate them for society; and at the same time have observed, that society is necessary to the satisfaction of those very passions, they are naturally induced to lay themselves under the restraint of such rules, as may render their commerce more safe and commodious.' (iii 2.2.24)

[14] See §767.   [15] See Hobbes, §495. See Gauthier, 'Contractarian'.

be immediate and obvious, as they are in the case of the two rowers who can move the boat only by their joint efforts, and cheating may often offer me apparent benefits.

The apparent benefits of cheating raise difficulties for Hume and for Hobbes at some of the same points. Before an effective system is established, it is difficult to see how any agreement to 'lay down our arms' could be stable, since any given individual benefits if others lay down their arms and he does not. This is true no less of Humean conventions. Moreover, once a system of justice is working, Hobbes's dispute with the fool raises a more serious question about cheats and free-riders. Even if the existence and general observance of rules of justice benefits me, not every action falling under the rules benefits me. Why, then, should I refrain from cheating when I get the appropriate opportunity?

The answer to this question, in Hume's view, explains the origin of government. Following one line of thought in Hobbes, he traces the necessity for government to our tendency to act on our short-sighted passions.[16] The remedy for the effect of these passions is foresight and the calm passions it provokes. I can see that the long-term benefit to me of a stable system of non-aggression will be greater than the short-term benefit I will gain by cheating. When the opportunity for cheating is imminent, it will excite a violent passion that will be stronger than the calm passion favouring my long-term interest. But before the opportunity is imminent, my calm passion is stronger, and I can act on it by denying myself the opportunity to act on the violent passion that I know will be aroused. This is why Ulysses had himself tied to the mast, or I might pour the whiskey down the sink if I know I will want too much of it. The establishment of governments is a pre-emptive action against violent passions.

Hume seems to believe that pre-emption answers the challenge presented by the free-rider, by distinguishing the short-term from the long-term attitude to the rules and institutions of justice (iii 2.2.24). If free-riders steadily took the long-term view, they would see that they benefit from accepting and observing the rules of a system of justice, and they would take pre-emptive action against themselves.

To see whether this is a good answer to the free-rider, we need to separate two claims: (1) I am better off in the long term if I live under a system of justice that imposes these specific rules on me than I would be if I did not live under such a system. (2) I am never better off in the long term if I break one of these specific rules. Hume has a good defence of the first claim, and so a good argument for pre-emptive action. But a defence of the second claim is needed to answer the free-rider, if an answer must appeal only to Hobbesian motives.

We might come closer to answering the free-rider if we could find an indirect egoist defence of a system that excludes egoistic calculation.[17] We are all better off in certain respects if we habitually follow rules of justice without asking about our interest. A system in which people do not ask this question is more stable, and—in that respect—everyone benefits from it more than they would from a system in which they are always asking about their interest. In the latter system, people may calculate, falsely or truly, that violation of the rules is beneficial to them individually; if their calculations lead them to break the rules, the system will be less stable than the one that excludes egoistic calculation.

---

[16] For discussion of his account of prudence see §738.
[17] See Gauthier, *MA*, ch. 6, on constrained maximization.

This indirect egoist argument against calculation of self-interest is different from the one that Hume offers. Hume suggests that if I calculate my long-term interest correctly, I will see that it is in my interest to observe rules of justice. Indirect egoists, however, concede that sometimes a true calculation of my long-term interest favours a violation of the rules of justice, but then they argue that we are better off if we avoid this sort of calculation and observe rules of justice. This argument takes Hume's argument a step further.

But the indirect egoist argument does not offer Hume a good answer; it seems to share the basic limitation of his argument. If we grant that rigid observance of rules of justice makes us all better off than we would all be if each of us looked out for her own advantage, it does not follow that I always do better for myself if I form the habit of rigidly following rules of justice even when I would benefit more by cheating. In some conditions I might do better for myself if I were less rigid than other people in adhering to rules of justice. As the indirect egoist claims, I am better off if people in general are not prone to act on self-interested calculations; but if I am a free-rider, I ask why I should always observe the rules of the system that benefits everyone. An appeal to the benefits of the system for everyone does not answer this question.[18]

We may reasonably doubt, therefore, whether Hume's account of the origin of justice completely succeeds. His illuminating discussion of convention and of foresight suggests how a basically Hobbesian account might be made more plausible. But the improvements to Hobbes do not remove the basic difficulties that arise for attempts to find conclusive non-moral reasons for upholding a system of justice.

771. Justice and the Moral Sentiment

But even if these doubts are justified, they may not matter much to Hume's overall argument about justice. For, in contrast to Hobbes, he believes that our approval of justice rests not only on self-interest, but also on a moral sentiment. We approve of justice because of sympathy developed by artifice. Once we have set up a system that benefits everyone, sympathy causes us to respond to the benefits and harms to others and to the public, not merely to ourselves, that result from the observance and violation of rules of justice (iii 2.2.24). This sympathy is a natural reaction to the effects of the rules, though it is strengthened by deliberate artifice and training. Hume has explained why the actions required by a system of justice do not appeal in their own right to our moral sense, since they do not individually promote the good of particular people or the public good. But once a system of justice is working, we see that we benefit by its presence and would be harmed by its absence, and we see that the same is true of everyone. And so our sympathetic feeling is engaged by the system of justice, and attached derivatively to particular just actions and rules (T iii 2.2.24; iii 2.6.11).

In the *Inquiry* Hume recognizes a sentiment that is concerned directly with the public good. This is the sentiment engaged by a working system of justice. He appeals to this

---

[18] As Mackie points out, *HMT* 93, it is even less clear that the particular rules of justice envisaged by Hume would be most in the interest of purely self-interested agents.

sentiment to explain 'why utility pleases'.[19] In opposition to Hobbes, and in agreement with Hutcheson, he maintains that this concern for the public interest is distinct from our concern for our own interest. Both concerns engage us when we approve of justice. According to Hume, we regard justice as a moral virtue because it engages our other-regarding sentiment, which he calls sometimes 'benevolence' and sometimes 'humanity'.

In the light of his argument, what should we say about Hume's initial objection to the claim (accepted by Hutcheson) that benevolence is the basis of our approval of just actions? Earlier, he observed that our benevolence might be engaged by the prospect of distributing the rich miser's possessions rather than by observing the rules of private property. But now he suggests that reflexion on the benefits of the system of justice engages our benevolence on the side of observance of the rules of justice. Should we suppose, then, that our benevolence is engaged on both sides, since we see some benefit to others from redistribution and from the rules of property?

Hume does not suggest this answer; he seems to assume that benevolence will be engaged on the side of upholding the rules of property. When we think about all the benefits resulting from the system of justice, we see that we need to uphold its rules, and so our benevolence supports the maintenance of rights of property. If benevolence responds to these considerations, it must be a utilitarian attitude. But in that case it is puzzling that Hume initially claimed that benevolence would support redistribution rather than the rules of property.

Perhaps Hume's different claims about benevolence are more easily understood by appeal to indirect utilitarianism. He is less clear than Hutcheson about the distinctive character of indirect utilitarianism,[20] but closer attention to it might help his argument in some places. He suggests quite plausibly that if we look at a just action outside any system of justice, it will often seem contrary to the public interest. But a working system of justice changes things in two ways: (1) Within a system of justice (say, a system of rules of property), the particular action that otherwise would not be in the public interest is in the public interest. (2) Within a system of justice, it promotes the public interest to obey its rules whether or not obedience to them is in the public interest in particular cases.

Some cases seem to satisfy the second condition, but not the first. Stealing this loaf of bread here and now might be undetected, set no precedent, etc. Or telling this lie now might have no bad effects and many good ones. Such actions do not tend to undermine the general observance of the rule that prohibits lying and stealing. In these cases it might be better, given the particular situation, to violate the rule of justice. But it might be even better to have a system that prohibits violations in particular cases even when violations would be in the public interest. It is better if witnesses have the habit of telling the truth when they are questioned in court, or if lawyers try to make the best case for their clients, or if doctors focus on the health of their patients rather than on their social usefulness. If we are utilitarians, and we see the difference between these two cases, we will defend a system of justice by an indirect utilitarian argument.

---

[19] 'Thus, in whatever light we take this subject, the merit, ascribed to the social virtues, appears still uniform, and arises chiefly from that regard, which the natural sentiment of benevolence engages us to pay to the interests of mankind and society.' (I 5.43)

[20] In particular, he is less clear than Hutcheson's *SMP*. See §647.

The difference between the two forms of utilitarian argument is parallel to the difference between the two forms of egoist argument that might connect self-interest with a system of justice. We saw that Hume seems to confine himself to the first sort of egoist argument, and does not seem to consider indirect egoism. Similarly, he usually connects justice and utility by a direct argument, arguing that a system of justice makes a particular action promote the public interest. But he sometimes recognizes that the good consequences do not belong to particular actions but to the system of justice that requires these particular actions even when they have bad consequences.[21] Hence he sometimes accepts an indirect utilitarian account of justice, without sharply distinguishing it from a direct utilitarian account. According to the indirect account, our moral sentiment responds secondarily to a particular just action (whether or not it promotes the public interest in the long run) because it responds primarily to the beneficial tendency of the system that enjoins just actions.

772. Natural Virtues

Now that we have considered Hume's account of the moral sentiment underlying our concern for justice, we may return to his initial contrast between the artificial and the natural virtues. Has he shown that we can have no moral concern with a just action considered in itself?

In making this broad negative claim, Hume does not consider the possibility that we might care about equal treatment for relevantly similar actions, or equal responses to equal needs, apart from the benefit or harm to the agents involved. He therefore seems to set aside the deontological considerations that Butler opposes to all attempts to reduce morality to concern for the public interest. Hume seems to think he has disqualified all such considerations through his argument to show that the motive for being just cannot be regard for the justness of the action. He argues that such regard for the justness of the action would require an antecedent regard for the virtue of justice, and this is the very thing we are trying to explain (iii 2.1.9).

Hume's argument, however, does not distinguish the goodness of actions from the goodness of agents.[22] We might say that an action tending to treat people according to what they have done, or to match reward or punishment to the degree of intentional benefit or harm, is good in itself. Hence we might approve the attitude that cares about treating equal cases equally, matching reward and punishment to actions, and so on, because we value these actions. Such a motive constitutes justice, and it is not clear why it should not be a natural object of esteem.

Let us, however, waive these objections to Hume, and concede that we must derive the moral goodness of justice from its relation to some consequences that we approve of. In that case, his point about justice is that our approval has to depend on our views about the system of justice that prescribes this particular just action. If this is right, does it mark a difference between justice and the virtues that Hume regards as natural?

---

[21] '. . . every particular act of justice is not beneficial to society, but the whole scheme or system' (T iii 3.1.13; cf. 12).
[22] Hume's argument is criticized by Rawls, *LHMP* 53–4.

Actions proceeding from the natural virtues sometimes seem to result from consideration of their consequences or of the system of which they form a part. If your child has inherited money, and you do not allow him to spend it immediately as he pleases, but insist on its being saved or invested for his future use, your action is an act of benevolence. But Hume's sympathetic observer might notice that your action causes immediate distress and no obvious immediate benefit to the child. To see that the action is evidence of your benevolent motive, the observer must look at the general facts about people and societies that make this the best thing to do in the child's interest. Some of these facts are of the sort that Hume regards as conventions—arrangements about the use of money to buy commodities, about the accumulation of money from investment, and so on. But even though all this has to be taken into account, your action was benevolent, and evidence of a benevolent character.

If, then, Hume seeks to distinguish artificial from natural virtues on the ground that various social facts and consequences have to be considered if we are to understand the system that makes artificial virtues beneficial, he faces a difficulty. He does not show that justice is any more artificial than benevolence; for the same sorts of facts may be relevant to benevolence.

Hume does not discuss this question about his division, because he illustrates the natural virtue of benevolence with a rather narrow range of examples. He mentions benevolent actions in which, for instance, 'a parent flies to the relief of his child' (I, App 3.2), and no particular foresight or understanding is needed. Such examples are misleading, however, because benevolence is not confined to cases where the benefit is obvious. Concern for longer-term benefits does not distinguish the virtue of benevolence from the virtue of justice; it may simply distinguish one sort of benevolent action from another.

Hume's contrast between benevolence and justice may result from his treatment of benevolence as a sentiment that reacts to the immediate appearance of good and harm to others. If he thinks of benevolence as a natural virtue that rests on this sentiment, he might reasonably infer that it ignores consequences. This conception of benevolence makes it plausible to say that just actions often do not appeal to benevolence and unjust actions often appeal to it. But one might doubt whether the spontaneous expression of an unreflective sentiment of benevolence is really a virtue. Butler sees this point, and therefore distinguishes the passion of benevolence from the rational principle. While the consideration of consequences may be alien to the passion of benevolence, it is often necessary for a virtue of benevolence, which rests on the rational principle.[23]

Though Hume does not accept the basis of Butler's distinction, which rests on the division between passions and superior principles, he seems to recognize a type of benevolence that differs from the unreflective sentiment. For he sometimes describes the principle of humanity as benevolence; the benevolence he has in mind here must be sensitive to consideration of consequences. It is more plausible to count this reflective attitude as a virtue than to count the unreflective sentiment. Even if reflective benevolence is not utilitarian, it considers the long-term interest of the person or people who engage our benevolent concern. When

[23] Laird, *HPHN* 220–1, raises some related questions about conflicts in Hume's claims about benevolence.

we are clear about the relevant conception of benevolence, Hume's way of distinguishing natural from artificial virtues seems less convincing.

773. Is Justice an Artificial Virtue?

One might argue on Hume's behalf that these features of benevolence show only that social institutions and practices sometimes affect the demands of benevolence. Nonetheless (one might argue) our natural virtue of benevolence approves some actions apart from any social context, whereas we approve just actions only in the right social context. We approve actions that relieve suffering just because they relieve suffering, not because they belong to a beneficial system, whereas we do not approve rules of property in themselves; we always need to refer to a social context that shows us how they belong to a beneficial system that evokes our approval.

This claim about justice, however, seems open to question. We might concede that specific rules assuring the security of property rest on social institutions and practices, and that justice would not require respect for these specific rules outside a social context. But this does not seem to be true of all just actions. If B does a good turn for A and A returns evil for good, or if C harms A, and A harms the innocent B as well as the guilty C, or if A benefits B and harms C, though they have benefited or harmed A equally, we seem to recognize that A has acted unfairly and unjustly, and we readily disapprove of A's action, outside any social context. Hence we seem to disapprove immediately of some unjust actions in their own right. Different practices and conventions might make different types of actions unfair, but they do not affect the non-conventional injustice of treating equals unequally.

Hume's remarks on promising illustrate this point. We may grant that making a promise requires a convention. If I am to 'give my word' that I will meet you tomorrow, I must be able to say something to make it clear that I am not simply predicting that I will be in the same place as you are at a specific time, but I am treating the fact that I am telling you where I will be as a reason for my being there. The conventions that belong to promising make it clear when you are entitled to rely on my doing what I said I would do because I told you I would do it. If you could reasonably be expected to know that I was simply predicting what I would do, rather than undertaking to do it, you would not be entitled to complain if I did something different, and I would (in this respect) have done nothing wrong by not doing what I said I would do.

This does not prove, however, that the obligations of justice involved in promising are created by convention. The convention-based action of promising would not create an obligation if it were not already wrong to frustrate an expectation about my future action on which another person is morally entitled to rely. Without conventional ways of creating such expectations, it is more difficult to decide when someone is entitled to rely on some specific future action of mine; but the convention does not create the obligation that results from the entitlement.

We have a reason for recognizing non-conventional obligations of justice if we disagree with Hume about which conventions create obligations of justice. We might be inclined to say that only agreements or conventions formed in just or fair circumstances, for legitimate purposes, and based on legitimate expectations, create obligations of justice. If we are right about this, some non-conventional constraints of justice identify the appropriate circumstances, purposes, and expectations; otherwise we will face an infinite regress of conventions relying on conventions.

Hume believes he can avoid these non-conventional constraints of justice by claiming that all mutually advantageous conventions are just. If he is right, the only non-conventional constraints involve advantage, not justice, and all the obligations of justice result from convention. But his claim is open to doubt, if we can form mutually advantageous conventions that are nonetheless unjust, and therefore do not create obligations of justice. One of Hobbes's covenants suggests this sort of objection against Hume. If you are so powerful that you can credibly threaten me with death if I do not do what you want, and I cannot threaten you in the same way, it may be in my interest to promise to be your slave in return for your protection. Hobbes believes that justice requires me to keep such a promise; but we might reasonably disagree with him, because of the unfair and unjust circumstances that induced me to make the promise. Similarly, then, in similar circumstances, it might be mutually advantageous for you and me to establish a convention so that I serve you in whatever way you please on the understanding (without any explicit promise) that you will not kill me. Hume seems to be committed to the Hobbesian view that this convention creates an obligation of justice; the difference between explicit agreement and convention does not seem to matter for this point.

We might object, therefore, to Hume's position in the way we objected to Hobbes's position. The arrangement does not seem to be just, because the threats resulting from your superior power have made the circumstances of my compliance unjust. Hence I am not morally required to abide by it. This convention does not create an obligation of justice.[24] To determine which conventions are just, we need non-conventional principles of justice. And so not all obligations of justice depend on convention and social context.

Hume sees that he cannot explain obligations of justice by appeal to a promise, because any appeal to a promise would presuppose an unexplained obligation to keep a promise. He thinks he avoids this sort of objection by appealing to conventions rather than promises. But he does not avoid it; for conventions that create moral obligations depend, no less than promises do, on obligations that are prior to conventions. He has not proved, therefore, that the obligations of justice depend wholly on conventions. Since justice involves the fulfilment of legitimate demands and expectations, conventions determine the content of many duties of justice; for conventions create demands and expectations, and morally appropriate conventions create legitimate demands and expectations. But they would not do this unless some duties of justice were prior to conventions.

We may not be convinced, then, by Hume's reasons for believing that justice is an artificial virtue. These reasons depend on an over-simplified conception of a natural virtue, and on some controversial claims about the basis of obligations of justice. Hume relies on a Hobbesian view about the basis of justice, and does not answer all the arguments of Hobbes's successors for recognizing obligations of justice prior to any agreement or convention.

---

[24] Cf. Hobbes, §§494–5, 505.

774. Justice, Self-Interest, and Moral Sentiment

These questions about Hume's view of justice concern his account of the origin of just practices, and his attempt to explain them without reference to any prior concern for justice. Further questions arise about the moral sentiments that support an established system of justice. At this stage the natural operations of sympathy, together with the artifices of social pressure and moral education, produce a moral sentiment in favour of justice. Once we understand the ramifications and consequences of just institutions, they evoke the sentiment that Hume calls both 'benevolence' and 'humanity', because this sentiment is the one that results from recognition of utility.

We might expect, therefore, that Hume would treat self-interest as simply the origin of justice, not as the permanent basis of justice. If moral sentiment supports a system of justice that originally benefits everyone, but the system evolves so that it no longer benefits everyone but it now maximizes utility, by making some people worse off for the greater benefit of others, will our moral sentiment not still support it? In that case, might a system of justice survive with the support of moral sentiment alone, but without the support of self-interest?

Hume does not consider this possibility. But he seems to rule it out implicitly. For he does not suggest that justice requires me to learn to sacrifice my own interest to the public interest. He grants only that it requires me to sacrifice my short-term interest to the longer-term interest that I recognize when I think about how I benefit from the system of justice. Hence he seems to assume that I am always better off if I observe the rules of justice.

Why should this be a constraint on a system of justice? Hume might give different answers: (1) Hobbes is right to believe that the self-interested motives are basic and overriding, so that it is futile to rest the whole support of institutions on some other motive. (2) Though moral sentiments are no less basic, and may become no less strong, than self-interested motives, they are not sufficient in everyone, or on all occasions, to support a system of justice. (3) It would be irrational to accept just institutions for any non-egoistic reason. (4) Self-interest imposes a moral constraint on the provisions of justice: it is unfair or illegitimate to demand my acceptance of an institution that does not benefit me, but simply uses my contribution to benefit others.[25]

Hume favours the first claim in the *Treatise*. In the *Inquiry*, however, he appeals to the sentiment of benevolence that favours the public interest. He seems to have abandoned the doubts of the *Treatise* about the existence of such a motive. He is not entitled to the third claim, given his views about reason and passion. If it is not contrary to reason to prefer the destruction of the world to the scratching of my finger, it can hardly be irrational to prefer justice over self-interest. Hume's remarks in both works are consistent with the second claim, but he does not argue for it. Nor does he discuss the fourth claim.

Part of the reason for this obscurity in his view is his imprecise conception of the public interest and of utility. We have already noticed that it is not clear how we take the 'common point of view' that Hume regards as the mark of moral sentiment.[26] Similarly, when he

---

[25] See §§505–6 on a deontological interpretation of Hobbes's egoistic constraints and claims about equality.
[26] See §§761–2.

speaks of concern for the public interest, he might have two things in mind: (1) What is in the public interest is whatever advances the interest of everyone in common, resulting in benefit to each person; we may call this the 'common interest'. (2) What is in the public interest advances the interest of the public taken as a whole, but not necessarily the interest of each person; we may call this the 'total interest'. The two accounts of the public interest differ in their attitude to some action or policy that harms one person simply in order to benefit others to a degree that exceeds the harm to the victim. Such an action or policy advances the total interest, but not the common interest.[27]

Concern for the total interest, as opposed to the common interest, is characteristic of utilitarianism. Hutcheson is an explicit utilitarian because he attributes this maximizing aim to morality.[28] Hume's position is less clear. In the *Treatise* one might argue that he supports utilitarianism, because he explains our concern for the public interest by appeal to sympathy. I notice that the violation of rules of justice is sometimes prejudicial to myself; and so I imagine what other people feel when they are victims of these violations (*T* iii 2.2.24). If I add up all the sufferings of the public, my feeling in favour of the public interest is stronger than my feeling in favour of the interest of any particular people. According to this additive picture, concern for the public interest amounts to concern for the total interest.

The *Inquiry* appeals to a 'common point of view' or 'universal principle of the human frame' (*I* 9.6). It is not clear how far we need to abstract from our individual concerns and interests in order to reach the common point of view that belongs to morality. If we abstract from everything except pursuit of pleasure and avoidance of pain, no matter whose pleasure or pain it is, we reach the utilitarian outlook that favours the total interest. But we need some further argument to show that this point of view is common to all who contemplate an action without reference to their individual self-interest. If Hume simply defines the common point of view as the utilitarian outlook, he abandons his aim of understanding the moral outlook as the result of a sentiment that we form without antecedent moral convictions.

A different way to describe the common point of view might start from the assumption that we are looking for a point of view that self-interested people could share. Though I abstract from my specific concern for my own interest, I do not abstract from the fact that each person is concerned for their own interest. If, then, we look for a common point of view, we might favour a policy that offers something to everyone; for such a policy promotes everyone's interest, and so may be preferable to a policy that would promote my exclusive interest but would arouse most people's opposition.

If, then, the public interest is simply maximum utility, appeal to the public interest does not obviously 'touch a string to which all mankind have an accord and symphony'. But if the public interest is the common, not the total, interest, the accord and symphony are easier to understand, since the common interest offers something to everyone.

If the public interest is the common interest, the role of self-interest in his account of justice is easier to understand. Though different people might not benefit equally from the common interest, everyone has some reason to favour it, because it offers some benefit to

---

[27] This does not mean that the common interest requires everyone to benefit to an equal degree from every just policy, but that individual interests impose some limits on the extent to which it is legitimate to harm some to benefit others. Rawls's account of justice (see, e.g., *TJ* §§11–12, 29) tries to say what these limits might be.

[28] See Hutcheson, §644.

everyone, and does not sacrifice any person's interests simply to benefit other people. This policy would offer fair treatment of the interests of different people. Concern with total utility does not respect different people's interests in the same way.

A non-utilitarian principle of humanity does not refute Butler's claim that justice sometimes overrides utility. On the contrary, justice and moral sentiment, so understood, confirm Butler's conception of conscience as a part of human nature. Human nature includes some concern for common humanity—the fair and equal treatment of human beings as such. This feature of conscience helps Butler to explain why conscience has authority, so that we have some reason to obey it, apart from the strength of our desire to obey it. Butler's conception of authority presupposes—falsely, in Hume's view—the possibility of reasons distinct from strength of desire. Nonetheless, Hume helps us to see more clearly the attitude whose claim to authority needs to be justified.

This suggested non-utilitarian analysis of the principle of humanity does not express Hume's predominant view. Still, it is useful to consider the non-utilitarian elements that are suggested by the role he allows to self-interest and by his account of the principle of humanity. These elements make his account more complex than Hutcheson's more purely utilitarian account, and suggest ways in which a non-utilitarian might learn from his discussion of justice.

The non-utilitarian elements in Hume help us to understand the questions about justice and utility that arise for some of his successors. He tries to connect sentimentalism and utilitarianism by combining elements of Hobbes and Hutcheson. Some of his successors are not convinced by this combination.[29]

Price and Reid, following Butler, reject sentimentalism, and so reject the sentimentalist argument for utilitarianism. They believe that their meta-ethical rationalism and their non-utilitarian account of justice confirm each other, and that both views rest on ordinary moral convictions.

Sidgwick accepts some of the rationalists' premisses, but rejects their anti-utilitarian conclusion. He agrees with Butler, Price, and Reid against Hutcheson and Hume, in recognizing non-utilitarian elements in some common-sense morality, including our views about justice; Hume himself tacitly suggests these elements. But Sidgwick believes these non-utilitarian elements are rationally indefensible, and that only the utilitarian view, concerned with the total interest, is rationally tenable.

When Sidgwick confronts this account of morality with Butler's question about the authority of conscience, he finds he cannot explain why conscience, understood as endorsing utilitarianism, should be authoritative. To see whether Sidgwick has drawn the right conclusions from the problems we have raised for Hume, we need to see how far non-utilitarian elements in morality could be rationally defensible.

775. Personal Merit

Hume's discussions of benevolence and justice are two important parts of his examination of the different virtues. This examination leads him to the conclusion that a person's virtues are

---

[29] Cf. Smith on Hume, §799.

qualities that are useful or agreeable either to the person himself or to others. The utilitarian analysis, therefore, applies only to the virtues that are useful to others.[30]

Hume takes his conclusion to be easy and obvious.[31] We can reach it directly from the general principle that what is valuable is either useful (utile) or agreeable (dulce) and the further evident fact that a person's traits of character may be either useful or agreeable to oneself or to others. In Hume's view, his position represents the natural outcome of our reasoning, whereas other views express systems and hypotheses that pervert the natural course of our reasoning, as the outlook of the 'divines' does.[32]

We can see that Hume's conclusion is not obviously correct, once we notice that his twofold division of the valuable omits, as Hobbes does, the third element of the traditional division—the right (honestum). Perhaps he omits it because he supposes that he can analyse the right into the useful and the agreeable.[33] But if he assumes that, he takes a controversial position that needs some defence.

Perhaps Hume believes that his account of the virtues vindicates his assumption that the valuable includes only the useful and the agreeable. He sets out to describe the different elements of 'personal merit'.[34] In his view, we can give a complete description of these elements without attributing to them any sort of value beyond the two sorts he recognizes. If he is right about this, even those who doubt his initial claim about the twofold division must admit that this division captures our conception of the moral virtues.

To see whether Hume succeeds in this argument, we need to know what he means by asking whether a given trait is part of someone's personal merit. First, he suggests that such a trait makes a person an object of 'esteem and affection' or of 'hatred and contempt'; then he assumes that such a trait implies either 'praise or blame' and may enter into 'panegyric or satire' (I 1.10). He recognizes that affection and hatred are inadequate. We can feel these sentiments towards people who benefit or harm ourselves, but we recognize that these are not moral sentiments. To express moral sentiments we have to take the common point of view (I 9.6) that we expect others to share with us. Hence the elements of personal merit should be those that provoke affection, esteem, and praise from spectators in general, when each abstracts from his own individual advantage.

---

[30] Baier, PS, ch. 9, discusses virtues that, in Hume's view, focus on what is immediately agreeable, not on maximization over time.

[31] 'It may justly appear surprising, that any man, in so late an age, should find it requisite to prove, by elaborate reasoning, that personal consists altogether in the possession of mental qualities, useful or agreeable to the person himself, or to others. It might be expected, that this principle would have occurred even to the first rude, unpractised enquirers concerning morals, and been received from its own evidence, without any argument or disputation. Whatever is valuable in any kind, so naturally classes itself under the division of useful or agreeable, the utile or the dulce, that it is not easy to imagine, why we should ever seek farther, or consider the question as a matter of nice research or enquiry. And as every thing useful or agreeable must possess these qualities with regard either to the person himself or to others, the complete delineation or description of merit seems to be performed as naturally as a shadow is cast by the sun, or an image is reflected upon water.' (I 9.1)

[32] 'And it seems a reasonable presumption, that systems and hypotheses have perverted our natural understanding; when a theory, so simple and obvious, could so long have escaped the most elaborate examination.' (I 9.1)

[33] Cf. Hobbes, §477.

[34] 'We shall analyse that complication of mental qualities, which form what, in common life, we call personal merit. We shall consider every attribute of the mind, which renders a man an object either of esteem and affection, or of hatred and contempt; every habit or sentiment or faculty, which, if ascribed to any person, implies either praise or blame, and may enter into any panegyric or satire of his character and manners.' (I 1.10)

This would be an unhelpful account of personal merit if we could not identify the relevant attitude in spectators without ascribing correct moral beliefs to them. If the moral virtues are those that are correctly esteemed from the moral point of view, in the light of correct moral beliefs, we cannot find the moral virtues until we find the correct moral beliefs; and so we cannot use the point of view of the spectator to find the correct moral beliefs. Hume takes his account of personal merit to be more informative than this, because he believes he can describe the morally relevant outlook in spectators without ascribing correct moral beliefs to them.

Hume's sentimentalism and his theory of the passions force this belief on him. For if a moral judgment either is or reports a sentiment, and a sentiment conforms to Hume's account of a passion, a moral judgment on a person must be (or report) a passion that is identified by its intrinsic phenomenal quality. No beliefs are essential to a passion; hence no beliefs are essential to the moral sentiment. The traits that constitute personal merit are united by being the objects of a sentiment that is identified by a single phenomenal quality.

776. Hume and the 'Divines' on the Criteria for Virtue

We can illustrate some of the difficulties in these claims about the virtues by returning to Hume's rejection of the view of the 'divines' who take voluntariness to be necessary for genuinely moral virtues. He believes that this view about virtues displays ignorance of human nature, and that we can remove such ignorance by a proper exercise of the experimental method. When he says that his survey of the virtues reflects our natural understanding, and that 'systems and hypotheses' have perverted the natural course of our reasoning, he has the outlook of the divines and their 'monkish virtues' in mind (I 9.1, 3).

Hume's experimental method studies our sentiments towards different traits of character we admire, both voluntary and non-voluntary. In his view, we see that our sentiments towards voluntary and non-voluntary traits are the same, and hence we see that the divines are wrong. Hume relies on two claims: (1) If we have the same sentiment towards two traits, either both are virtues or neither is a virtue. (2) We have the same sentiment towards voluntary and non-voluntary traits. The first claim expresses Hume's sentimentalism; for the moment we may concede it and ask about his second claim.

This second claim rejects Butler's view that moral approval and disapproval depend on beliefs about whether an action or trait is voluntary.[35] Butler treats moral approval as a special kind of approval that rests on beliefs about the goodness and badness of people and actions.[36] Our 'moral approving and disapproving faculty' essentially involves beliefs about desert, and so does not simply involve favourable or unfavourable reactions. Our moral sentiments rest on moral judgments that presuppose our ability to evaluate reactions

---

[35] 'We never, in the moral way, applaud or blame either ourselves or others, for what we enjoy or what we suffer, or for having impressions made upon us which we consider as altogether out of our power; but only for what we do, or would have done, had it been in our power; or for what we leave undone, which we might have done, or would have left undone, though we could have done it.' (Butler, D 2)

[36] '. . . we naturally and unavoidably approve some actions, under the peculiar view of their being virtuous and of good desert; and disapprove others, as vicious and of ill desert.' (Butler, D 1)

and sentiments and to guide them by moral criteria. From Butler's point of view, then, it is reasonable to distinguish a particular kind of approval that he calls moral approval, resting on the application of rational standards, which include the demand for voluntary action.

Hume believes we lack the ability assumed by Butler, so that Butler is wrong to treat moral judgments as essentially involving the application of rational standards of evaluation to our sentiments. Hume's objections to the divines reflect one of his basic objections to his predecessors, that they regard morality as an expression of rational standards that guide sentiments and they regard moral philosophy as a normative discipline that can discover and justify these rational standards. This discipline is irreducibly normative insofar as it claims to discover principles about what we ought to do and have reason to do, and supposes that these principles do not simply describe psychological or social facts that can be fully described without reference to what we ought to do and have reason to do.

According to Hume, then, our sentiments do not follow Butler's rules. We can see this when we observe that we have the same sentiment towards voluntary and non-voluntary virtues. Hume assumes that we can observe this because we can observe phenomenally similar reactions towards these different traits of character. He individuates sentiments in the way in which he individuates passions, referring to their introspectible features. Experimental study of human nature shows that our feeling of admiration for an involuntary excellence is phenomenally similar to our feeling of admiration for a voluntary excellence. Hume infers that the two sentiments are the same, and that the divines have overlooked this introspectibly evident fact.

If Butler were confronted with Hume's objection that we have the same sentiment towards voluntary and non-voluntary virtues and vices, he might reasonably argue that moral applause and blame cast doubt on Hume's claim about the identity of sentiments. If our sentiment towards A rests on the belief that A acted voluntarily, but our sentiment towards B does not rest on that belief, the two sentiments are not the same (according to Butler), even if they are phenomenally similar in other ways. If I find that B's action was an accident resulting from circumstances that B could not reasonably have been expected to foresee, I am not indignant at B, even if I find myself feeling unfavourable towards B.

Apparently, then, Hume is wrong to claim that we have the same sentiments towards non-voluntary actions and states that we have towards voluntary actions and states. All he can claim is that their non-doxastic elements may be phenomenally indistinguishable. The objection that appeals to sentiments seems to rely on a questionable conception of the identity of a sentiment.[37]

But even if we agreed with Hume's view that we have the same sentiment towards voluntary and non-voluntary excellences, why should we also agree that the divines are mistaken to insist that only voluntary traits are virtues? He argues that they have warped reasoning and language from their natural course, by drawing distinctions that are not marked by the phenomenal character of our sentiments.[38] He suggests, therefore, that

---

[37] See Reid, §849, on moral approval and voluntariness.
[38] '. . . and as this latter science [sc. theology] admits of no terms of composition, but bends every branch of knowledge to its own purpose, without much regard to the phenomena of nature, or to the unbiassed sentiments of the mind, hence

(1) the distinctions marked by our sentiments determine the natural course of language and reasoning, and (2) we ought not to warp language and reasoning from this natural course.

These claims are difficult to evaluate. Which of Hume's senses of 'natural' has he in mind? If it is unusual to mark the distinction that the divines mark, that hardly counts against them; as Hume points out, heroic virtue is 'unnatural' in being unusual. If the divines' distinction involves artifice, that does not count against it either. Perhaps Hume means that our natural reaction is the one that inevitably or usually follows our awareness of a given action or trait. Perhaps we should rely on this reaction because it is pointless to try to get rid of it. The divines, in his view, have engaged in this pointless effort, since they have tried to draw a distinction that our sentiments have refused to acknowledge. It is more sensible to leave our natural reactions as they are. It would be foolish to try to persuade ourselves to give up our belief in external objects, simply because we do not think it is justified; the divines have been trying to persuade us to do something similar, and we are wasting our time if we listen to them.

Hume's form of argument may sometimes be reasonable, but in this case the divines have a reply. They can explain why we might have phenomenally similar reactions to genuine virtues and to some involuntary traits and accomplishments. They can even explain why it is useful and valuable if our sentiments are undiscriminating in this way. Perhaps it is sometimes difficult to decide how far a given trait is voluntary, but we want to encourage it as far as we can, or perhaps our favourable sentiment towards voluntary traits is strengthened if we also favour some involuntary traits. This account might also help to explain some other apparently undiscriminating reactions that might appear to support Hume. We have some feelings of regret at an accident we were causally, but not morally, responsible for; these are among the feelings that we also have when we think we are morally responsible for some harm to another person.[39] Our undiscriminating sentiments might be an appropriate support for discriminations that do not rest on these sentiments.

Hume's analysis of the voluntary raises a further question about his objections to the divines. In his discussion of liberty and necessity, he seems to assume (though he does not explicitly say so) that for an action to be voluntary is simply for it to be subject to praise and blame. In arguing that we are responsible only for actions that proceed from something durable and constant in us, he points out that these are the actions we are praised or blamed for (*T* ii 3.2.6). He does not consider the possibility that the same sentiments might be directed to non-voluntary actions as well. He seems to infer, then, that to be voluntary is to be the object of these sentiments. But against the divines he objects that we have these sentiments indifferently towards voluntary and involuntary actions. This objection is inconsistent with the view that voluntary actions are those towards which we have these sentiments. If Hume's analysis of the voluntary is correct, he agrees with the divines in treating moral virtues and vices as voluntary, since he says they are objects of the sentiments of praise and blame.

Some of Hume's arguments, therefore, rely on some of his own most questionable doctrines, while others seem to create more difficulties for him than they create for his

---

reasoning, and even language, have been warped from their natural course, and distinctions have been endeavoured to be established, where the difference of the objects was, in a manner, imperceptible' (*I*, App. 4.21).

[39] This point is relevant to Williams's discussion of 'agent regret' in 'Luck'.

opponents. The divines believe that we should rely on the division between voluntary and involuntary to form our sentiments, such as moral praise and blame, as Butler describes them. If we do not accept Hume's purely phenomenal individuation of sentiments, we can recognize distinct moral sentiments without distinct phenomenal features.

777. Objections to Hume's Account

This dispute with the divines suggests a general objection to Hume's method for finding a general account of the moral virtues. Some of his early critics attack his account of the ancients in order to attack his claims about the virtues. Beattie argues not only that the ancients require moral virtues to be voluntary,[40] but also that they are right to require this. He therefore attacks Hume's view that the different virtues surveyed in the *Inquiry* are all equally moral (*ENIT* 320), and Hume's rejection of any distinction between moral and intellectual virtues.

According to Beattie, Hume begs the question in claiming that whatever excites the same kind of disinterested sentiment is equally a virtue (324). Closer consideration shows that a sentiment—identified by Hume's criteria—is not sufficient for a virtue. James Balfour develops this criticism by trying to identify the elements of moral virtue that Hume ignores.[41] According to Balfour, a moral virtue must include a 'habitual purpose or intention to do good to others' (*DNOM* 125); a quality that Hume counts as a virtue is a real virtue only if the useful or agreeable trait is controlled by this intention. Balfour relies on the Socratic and Stoic view (later exploited by Kant) that virtue consists in the good use of other goods; he criticizes Hume for reducing virtues to assets or resources and leaving out the requirement of appropriate use.[42] He argues that Hume is wrong to claim the support of the ancients, and especially of Cicero (131–2). In fact Cicero follows the Stoic scheme of the cardinal virtues, which, according to Balfour, requires different useful and agreeable traits to be used well before they can belong to virtue.

These criticisms suggest that the catalogue of virtues in the *Inquiry* seems natural and plausible to Hume only because he relies on some of his more controversial claims. In supposing that the common feature of the virtues could only be found in our reaction to them, and that the relevant sort of reaction must be some sentiment, identified by its phenomenal character, he presupposes the argument of *Treatise* ii–iii on passion, reason, and the source of moral distinctions. From the start he rules out the possibility of an error theory of the virtues; for he assumes that we cannot identify the virtues on the basis of some criterion or distinction that he has undermined. If common sense assumed that a moral virtue requires practical reason to control passion, Hume's arguments would show that there are no moral virtues, as common sense conceives them. But he does not consider this possibility.

---

[40] See §726.   [41] Balfour, *DNOM*, ch 4.

[42] 'All those qualities, accounted virtues by our author in respect of their utility, are indeed useful; but in what sense? In this only, that they are capable of being put to a good use; but they may be also put to a bad one. Now what is it that determines betwixt these different and contrary effects, and gives the preference to the first? 'Tis virtue, or the virtuous disposition above noticed.' (Balfour, *DNOM* 125–6)

778. Kames and Sentimentalism

Kames's *Essays* express some reasonable dissatisfaction with Hume's combination of sentimentalism and utilitarianism, though Kames does not offer a satisfactory alternative. He agrees with Hume in recognizing a moral sense, but rejects Hume's and Hutcheson's attempt to reduce it to a favourable sentiment directed towards utility. In his view it involves a distinctive and unanalysable kind of approval recognizing the moral goodness of a means or an end (35). He does not claim that morality is to be defined as what the moral sense approves of. He seeks to show that 'the laws which are fitted to the nature of man and to his external circumstances are the same that we approve by the moral sense' (36).

In Kames's view, other philosophers cannot give an adequate account of the sense of duty and obligation without appealing to the distinct sort of approval that comes from the moral sense. He applies this criticism not only to sentimentalists such as Hutcheson, Hume, and Smith (38–40), but also to Butler (42).[43] Some of Kames's criticism of Butler rests, as we saw, on misinterpretation, since he treats Butler as a sentimentalist who simply reduces morality to what conscience approves of.

But this is not the whole of his objection to Butler. He also suggests that Butler's attempt to explain our awareness of moral obligation by appeal to the reflexive character of conscience fails to grasp the compulsory aspect of the sense of duty. Similarly, Kames argues that Clarke's appeal to fitness does not capture the recognition of moral obligation, unless we covertly rely on the moral sense.[44] This argument also commits Kames to the rejection of Price's account of moral judgment. His objection is rather similar to the complaint by Pufendorf and other voluntarists that naturalists cannot give an account of the compulsory character of moral principles. But Kames wisely avoids Pufendorf's appeal to divine commands; he rejects theological voluntarism on the ground that recognition of the goodness of God presupposes an antecedent sense of morality (102).

Though Kames recognizes this irreducible moral sense, not explicable by any further reference to approval or to recognition of rational requirements, he does not suggest that we can grasp the content of morality by simple intuition of moral rightness. On the contrary, he goes quite far in accepting Hume's utilitarianism as an account of the right. He concedes to Hume 'that the end of justice is public utility, and that its merit consists in contributing to that end' (130). He even claims that the utilitarian account of the end of justice is 'a proposition that no mortal controverts, namely, that public good is the sole end of justice' (134). He agrees with Hutcheson in treating benevolence as the foundation of a utilitarian outlook (146). Like Berkeley, Kames uses a providential argument in support of indirect utilitarianism. It is not for us to make judgments about overall utility, but we should leave that to God (whom we assume to be purely benevolent) (137).

Kames's main disagreement with Hume concerns the nature of our judgments and sentiments about justice. He denies that in recognizing something as just we recognize it as promoting utility. Hume's account would fail unless we presupposed some respect

---

[43] On Smith see §798. On Butler see §720.

[44] 'The doctor's error is a common one, that he endeavours to substitute reason in place of sentiment . . . His only mistake is that, overlooking the law written in his own heart, he vainly imagines that his metaphysical argument is just because the consequence he draws from it happens to be true.' (106)

for property and for fidelity to promises antecedent to any recognition of their benefits to oneself or to others (65). Kames argues effectively against Hume's argument that justice has a place only in the circumstances he describes, and would have no place in the better and worse circumstances that Hume envisages (132).

Kames's total position is not satisfactory. He owes us some explanation of why the moral sense, with the character he ascribes to it, approves of utility rather than some other feature of actions. Within his view, this seems arbitrary and inexplicable. This arbitrary aspect of his position tends to undermine his criticism of Hume's very broad conception of the range of the virtues (140). Kames justly remarks that this broad conception is supported by Hume's broad and ill-defined use of 'approval'. But though Kames believes that moral approval relies on some more definite criteria than Hume allows, he lacks the means to defend this belief, given his failure to describe the outlook of the moral sense. Unless we can say something more than he says, we cannot explain why the moral sense legitimately approves of honesty, disapproves of callousness, and has no particular moral attitude to physical strength or beauty.

Kames objects that if Hume were right, the difference between moral approval and other kinds would be arbitrary, since Hume just makes it a matter of greater or lesser strength. Hume might be willing to embrace this consequence, but Kames is right to suggest that it is an undesirable consequence. To avoid it, he needs to say more about the moral sense. Related difficulties arise from his acknowledgment that the moral sense needs the support of other motives, so that we cannot be required to maximize utility unless we have appropriate motives favouring it.[45] If we do not know why the moral sense approves of what it approves of, it is not obvious what motives we might reasonably encourage in its support.

One part of Kames's criticism of Hume goes too far, in rejecting any analysis of the moral sense. One part does not go far enough, since he uncritically accepts Hume's utilitarian account of the content of morality. Each part of Kames's position tends to undermine the other. A more effective reply to Hume needs a fuller account of the nature of moral judgment that is more plausibly connected with an account of the content of morality. In Kant's view, this is a task that his predecessors have left undone.

779. The Supremacy of Morality

In his account of the virtues, as in the rest of his moral philosophy, Hume claims to analyse our moral convictions, not to undermine them. He attacks rationalist philosophical theories, and argues that our moral convictions do not depend on such unreliable support. Rationalist opponents of sentimentalism claim that sound morality, not just sound moral philosophy, rests on convictions that sentimentalism rejects. Hume follows Hutcheson in rejecting this charge against sentimentalism. His defence of sentimentalism is more limited than Hutcheson's, since he endorses some of the rationalists' claims about the consequences of sentimentalism. But he argues that the truth of these claims has no bearing on morality. The *Inquiry* develops this argument with special emphasis, to show that other moralists

---

[45] 'Those moralists . . . who require us to lay aside all partial affection and to act upon a principle of equal benevolence to all men, require us to act upon a principle, which has no place in our nature.' (Kames, *EPMNR* 57)

obscure and confuse the natural understanding of morality, which allows us to see it in an attractive light.

Hume's discussion of justice, however, raises a question about how far he supports morality. Moral sentiment supports the demands of justice even if some of them appear to conflict with self-interest; but what have we reason to do in case of apparent conflict between moral sentiment and self-interest? This is the old question about the authority of morality and its claim to supremacy in relation to other practical principles. Hume is dissatisfied with the answers given by his predecessors, and he believes that his answer fits both his sentimentalism and the legitimate demands of morality.

The question about morality and self-interest is the question that Hobbes attributes to the fool. The fool does not see why he should observe moral principles if he will gain significantly by violating them. Hobbes's reply appears to argue unsuccessfully that the fool has good reason, in his own long-term interest, to refrain from self-interested calculation in the situations in which he would see a significant gain in violating principles of justice.[46]

Shaftesbury tries to answer the fool by emphasizing the higher degree of happiness that one gains from the happiness of others. Butler maintains that this sort of defence misunderstands the rational status of conscience. Since conscience expresses rational agency to a still higher degree than self-love does, it has authority over particular passions, as self-love does, and, moreover, has authority over self-love too.[47]

Butler's solution does not satisfy Hume, because it claims for conscience some degree of rational authority, as distinct from psychological strength. Hume's account of reason and morality is meant to undermine such claims to authority. Hutcheson tries to cast the moral sense in the role that Butler assigns to conscience, but Hume observes that Hutcheson overlooks the conflict between sentimentalism and authority.[48] According to Butler, conscience ought to prevail because we recognize it as prescribing what accords with our nature, and we agree that we have overriding reason to do what accords with our nature. Hume believes he has refuted Butler's claims about reason and nature. Hutcheson ought to have rejected them too, once he accepted sentimentalism. We cannot say that we recognize the rational authority of the moral sense, and so have rational grounds for believing that it ought to prevail. The sentimentalist agrees that our moral sense approves of itself on reflexion; but this second-order sentiment cannot be used, as Hutcheson tries to use it, as a basis for a claim to rational authority.

It would be inappropriate for Hume, no less than for Hutcheson, to try to answer Butler's question by arguing that it is always in one's own interest to be virtuous. This

---

[46] See §503.   [47] See §714.

[48] 'You seem here to embrace Dr Butler's opinion in his sermons on human nature; that our moral sense has an authority distinct from its force and durableness, and that because we always think it *ought* to prevail. But this is nothing but an instinct or principle, which approves of itself upon reflexion; and that is common to all of them. I am not sure that I have mistaken your sense, since you do not prosecute this thought.' (To Hutcheson, Jan. 1743 = Greig #19) When Hume says 'I am not sure that I have mistaken' where we might expect '. . . I have not mistaken', he probably uses 'I am not sure that' as equivalent to 'I doubt that' in Scottish idiom (where it means 'I suspect that'). Kemp Smith, *PDH* 201n, quotes this passage to show that '. . . there is, on Hume's theory of morals, no such thing as *moral* obligation, in the strict sense of the term. There is, that is to say, no intrinsically self-justifying good that with *authority* can claim approval. The ultimate verdict rests with the de facto constitution of the individual.' Hume is commenting here on Hutcheson, *MPIC*, Bk. i, ch. 1 §16. See §715 for evidence in his *SMP* of sympathy with Butler. Sharp, 'Hume' 164–6, discusses Hume's comment on Butler.

is Hobbes's answer (when the question is asked within a commonwealth); it rests on the special connexion that he recognizes between practical reason and the pursuit of one's own overall interest. In Hume's view, this supposed connexion is a relic of the normative view of practical reason that Hobbes ought to have discarded.

Nonetheless, since agents are in fact often concerned about their long-term interest, it is worth asking how far morality promotes it; that is why Butler defends the harmony of conscience and self-love while still maintaining the supremacy of conscience.[49] Though Hume is not concerned, as Butler is, about claims to authority, he has reason to believe that the degree of harmony or conflict between conscience and self-love is likely to affect the strength of people's motives for acting morally. He therefore has a good reason for examining the relation between the two principles.

In the *Treatise* he does not discuss this question. He gives an account of moral sentiment, and of the natural and artificial virtues. It is easy to see how the natural virtues appeal to the moral sentiment by arousing our sympathy. More argument is needed to show how justice comes to appeal to the moral sentiment. In neither case does Hume consider how far someone concerned for their own interest is likely to promote it by acquiring and exercising the virtues.

780. Self-Approval

Though Hume does not seek to attribute rational authority to the moral sense, he argues that second-order approval will have one of the effects of belief in rational authority, since it will strengthen our attachment to morality. When we study the moral sense and its origins, we present it and its origins to itself, as possible objects of approval or disapproval. Hume argues that since we can derive the moral sense from sympathy, and since the moral sense approves of sympathy, it will approve of itself more strongly once it recognizes that this is its origin.[50] If we discovered that the moral sense originates in deception (as Mandeville supposes)[51] or in resentment of superiority (as Nietzsche supposes),[52] our inquiry into its origins might be expected, in Hume's view, to change our attitude to the moral sense. But once we discover that it arises from sympathy, we confirm our approval of the moral sense, since we approve of sympathy from the point of view of the moral sense.[53]

Hume's defence of the moral sense as self-sustaining in the face of beliefs about its origin is reasonable. His letter to Hutcheson on Butler suggests that this self-approval on reflexion is the part of Butler's claims about authority that a sentimentalist can accept. But he argues that this does not justify Hutcheson in attributing authority to the moral sense in particular;

---

[49] See §708.

[50] 'But this sense must certainly acquire new force, when reflecting on itself, it approves of those principles, from whence it is derived, and finds nothing but what is great and good in its rise and origin. Those who resolve the sense of morals into original instincts of the human mind, may defend the cause of virtue with sufficient authority; but want the advantage, which those possess, who account for that sense by an extensive sympathy with mankind. According to the latter system, not only virtue must be approved of, but also the sense of virtue: And not only that sense, but also the principles, from whence it is derived.' (iii 3.6, 619)

[51] Mandeville, *FB* i 51.　　　[52] Nietzsche, *GM* i 10.

[53] Cf. Korsgaard, *SN* 55–66, on Hume and reflexive endorsement.

for, he suggests, this reflexive self-approval is common to all 'instincts' or 'principles'. If this is a fair objection to Hutcheson, it seems to apply equally to Hume's claim about the moral sense and sympathy. If all instincts and principles approve of themselves on reflexion, how do Hume's remarks about the origin of the moral sense tend to support it? Would it not have approved of itself—according to Hume's objection—whatever it had discovered about its origins?

Hume's defence of the moral sense is more convincing than his objection to Hutcheson. It is difficult to see why all instincts or principles must approve of themselves on reflexion. Not every instinct or principle seems to reflect on itself or approve of itself. If I hate my hatred, that is a passion or instinct directed against itself. But it does not seem to be a result of reflexion by hatred itself. I may conclude, from the point of view of self-love or morality, that my tendency to hate is bad and hateful.[54] Alternatively, I may decide that my hatred is appropriate, and therefore come to approve of my hatred; but it is conscience or self-love, not hatred, that approves.

To cope with this objection, we might restrict Hume's claim about self-approval to those instincts or principles that are capable of reflecting on themselves. In that case, he might claim that all these principles approve of themselves on reflexion, so that the self-approval of conscience does not show anything special about it. But this claim is also difficult to accept. For he seems to envisage the possibility that the moral sense might not approve of itself on reflexion. If that were not possible, he would need no argument to show that the moral sense approves of itself. For counter-examples to the claim about automatic approval, we might turn to some feelings of guilt or shame or hatred. If we recognize that these have origins we deplore, we might well disapprove of them.

In that case, self-approval by the moral sense is worth mentioning, since it justifies the expectation that the moral sense will be strengthened by this reflexion more than it would be if it had not approved of itself. This is also Hutcheson's substitute for Butler's claim about the authority of conscience.

It is not clear whether Hume thinks approval of the origin is necessary as well as sufficient for self-approval by an instinct. It does not always seem to be necessary. We might acknowledge that our moral outlook has arisen by a process that we do not entirely approve of. We might, for instance, accept a Freudian account, and disapprove of the process that it describes. Such disapproval need not lead us to disapprove of our current moral outlook; for we might believe that, irrespective of its origins, it is now sustained by beliefs, attitudes, and dispositions that we approve of, even if these are not the only things that sustain it.

Hume also recognizes, however, that though the moral sense approves of itself, we need not approve of the moral sense from every point of view, and we need not always believe we have overriding reason to follow it, given our other motives. But he does not suggest this is a serious difficulty. Those who have a moral sense and disobey it cannot 'bear their own survey'; their disapproval of immorality will keep them in line with the moral sense.[55]

---

[54] Smith notices this point about self-approval by a faculty. See §798.

[55] 'And who can think any advantages of fortune a sufficient compensation for the least breach of the social virtues, when he considers, that not only his character with regard to others, but also his peace and inward satisfaction entirely depend upon his strict observance of them; and that a mind will never be able to bear its own survey, that has been wanting in its part to mankind and society?' (T iii 3.3.6.6) For a comparison of Aristotle and Hume on vice see §111.

This claim is open to question. Occasional, or even fairly frequent, departures from the social virtues do not seem to make us unable to bear our own survey. Why should the moral sense insist on being followed on every occasion? Even if it does, why should we not be able to bear our own survey when we consider the advantages we gain by departing from the social virtues? Moreover, if we are often confronted by the apparent self-sacrifice imposed by morality, we might even become less able to bear our own survey if we find ourselves constantly moved to follow morality. The fact that the moral sense approves of itself does not imply that if we follow the moral sense we will always approve of what we do or of the motives that we act on.

These questions arise from Hume's claims about the strength of the moral sentiment. He acknowledges (*T* iii 3.1.18) that it may not always be strong enough to match our moral judgments. Later on, in his discussion of the connexion between our sentiments and our sense of merit, he suggests that discord between the strength of our sentiments and our judgments does not matter; we can share the general sense of merit and demerit without taking it as seriously as others do.[56] We might reasonably expect that someone could get on quite well with the moral sentiments accepted in society, and share them to some extent, without taking them so seriously that he cannot bear the thought of deviating from the social virtues.

The *Treatise*, then, suggests that self-approval by the moral sense strengthens our tendency to act on it and to disapprove of our failures to act on it. But it does not suggest that the moral sense demands any special place for itself among our other sentiments. Social pressure may cause us to form stronger moral sentiments, but the moral sentiments themselves offer us no reason to prefer them to be stronger than they are.

781. The Philosopher as Anatomist: Hume and Hutcheson[57]

This feature of the *Treatise* helps to explain Hutcheson's reaction to it. In a letter to Hutcheson Hume refers to Hutcheson's judgment that the *Treatise* lacked warmth in the cause of virtue.[58] Hutcheson found that Hume described virtue but did not advocate it. Hume answers that the *Treatise* is strictly an 'abstract inquiry', the work of an anatomist

---

[56] 'The intercourse of sentiments, therefore, in society and conversation, makes us form some general inalterable standard, by which we may approve or disapprove of characters and manners. And though the heart does not always take part with those general notions, or regulate its love and hatred by them, yet are they sufficient for discourse, and serve all our purposes in company, in the pulpit, on the theatre, and in the schools.' (iii 3.3.2)

[57] Sher, *CU* 168, discusses this analogy, and contrasts it with Hutcheson's outlook. *IMP*, ch. 1, surveys human nature from a practical and teleological point of view, describing it as the work of a benevolent God, and using this description as a protreptic to morality. Compared with this work of Hutcheson's, Hume's *T* might reasonably be said to lack warmth.

[58] 'What affected me most in your remarks is your observing, that there wants a certain warmth in the cause of virtue, which, you think, all good men would relish, and could not displease amidst abstract inquiries. I must own, that this has not happened by chance, but is the effect of a reasoning either good or bad. There are different ways of examining the mind as well as the body. One may consider it either as an anatomist or as a painter. . . . Any warm sentiment of morals, I am afraid, would have the air of declamation amidst abstract reasonings, and would be esteemed contrary to good taste. And though I am much more ambitious of being esteemed a friend to virtue, than a writer of taste; yet I must always carry the latter in my eye; otherwise I must despair of ever being serviceable to virtue. I hope these reasons will satisfy you; though at the same time, I intend to make a new trial, if it be possible to make the moralist and the metaphysician agree a little better.' (to Hutcheson, 17 Sept. 1739, Greig #13 = R630)

rather than a painter, because it tries to understand the origin and structure of the virtues rather than to present them in their attractive colours. If he had combined this anatomical study with advocacy of the virtues, he would have introduced extraneous 'declamation' that would be regarded as a breach of good taste.[59]

This answer to Hutcheson is surprising, since Hutcheson was hardly unfamiliar with 'abstract inquiries' or with normal conceptions of good taste, and might not seem to need instruction on these points. Scruples about good taste had not deterred him from including some 'warmth in the cause of virtue' in his abstract inquiries. Hume implies that Hutcheson committed a breach of good taste by combining a description of virtue with advocacy of it. This comment is typical of Hume's remarks on Hutcheson. He is respectful, even admiring, but he suggests that Hutcheson fails to see the implications of his own position.

In reply to Hume, one might argue that no irrelevant declamations are needed. Butler seeks to show that virtue consists in living in accordance with nature, and that we have conclusive reasons, considering human life and human nature, for accepting the principles of morality. Since these are consequences of the true theory of morality, pointing out these consequences is not irrelevant declamation. Hutcheson also believes that the true theory of morality gives us conclusive justifying reasons—as he understands them—for accepting morality.

Within Hume's theory, however, a defence of morality might seem to involve extraneous declamation. Since the theory gives no reason, as Butler or Hutcheson conceives it, for choosing morality in preference to other principles, a defence of morality is not part of the theory. Hume believes that Hutcheson ought to have said this too; his reply to Hutcheson's objection suggests this point obliquely. The suggestion about good taste conceals the point that, from the sentimentalist point of view, advocacy of virtue would have to be a task for rhetoric and declamation, not for philosophical argument. Butler does not add extraneous rhetoric in advocating morality, because he relies on the sort of argument that a sentimentalist believes is unavailable.

The contrast between the anatomist and the painter is drawn from the conclusion of Book iii of the *Treatise*. Hume comments briefly on the attractiveness of virtue, but stops himself, on the ground that it is irrelevant to his anatomical studies. But he does not take his work to be irrelevant or unhelpful to the advocate of virtue. An anatomical drawing is not a rival to a painting and does not make a painting any less appropriate. The fact that we have seen an anatomical drawing does not make a painting of the same figure, covered with flesh and clothing, any less beautiful; indeed, as Hume suggests, the painting may be executed better in the light of anatomical knowledge. Similarly, the advice of the moral theorist can help the advocate of morality to advocate it more persuasively.[60]

---

[59] Stewart, 'Two species', discusses the significance of Hume's contrast between the anatomist and the painter, with special reference to Hume's relation to Hutcheson and to the context of the *First Inquiry* (and especially Hume's unsuccessful candidacy for the chair in Edinburgh).

[60] 'But I forbear insisting on this subject. Such reflexions require a work a-part, very different from the genius of the present. The anatomist ought never to emulate the painter; nor in his accurate dissections and portraitures of the smaller parts of the human body, pretend to give his figures any graceful and engaging attitude or expression. . . . An anatomist, however, is admirably fitted to give advice to a painter; and 'tis even impracticable to excel in the latter art, without the assistance of the former. . . . And thus the most abstract speculations concerning human nature, however cold and unentertaining, become subservient to practical morality; and may render this latter science more correct in its precepts,

In Hume's view, we will be able to praise and recommend various traits of character more effectively if we know what feature of a trait of character produces our approval. The different virtues will appeal to us more if we see how they respond to our sentiment of humanity, because they are useful or agreeable to the agent or to others, and above all to the public interest.

But this is not the only possible effect of an anatomy. Knowledge of the underlying anatomy may not affect our judgments about beauty. But it may affect some of our judgments about goodness. If we are looking at a spacious, comfortable, and externally well-designed car, and it has performed well on a test drive, we may suppose we have found a good car; but we will change our mind if we learn that the engine is badly designed, the chassis is cracked, and some parts inaccessible to the onlooker have started to rust. In this case 'anatomical' knowledge may change our mind about whether this is a good car.

Similarly, the less obvious features of morality might show that it does not deserve the praise that we think it deserves, or that it does not meet the expectations we form for it. If we have looked at the inner workings of a car, we may be less warm in our praise of it.[61] The moral philosopher might ask whether an anatomical examination of morality warrants a similar decrease in warmth.

Hume's reply to Hutcheson's criticism of his lack of warmth implies that his anatomical inquiries are not the sort that encourage less warmth, but the sort that allow more effective praise of virtue. But we might wonder whether this is so, from the conclusion of the *Treatise*. Though our moral sentiment approves of itself, it is not clear why we should approve of it so strongly that we give it an overriding place. Sentimentalists cannot argue that we have overriding reason to prefer morality unless they can show that morality evokes some dominant passion, or at least evokes some calm passion that prompts us to take pre-emptive action against our more violent passions. But Hume has not shown that the moral sentiment has these effects.

782. The Sensible Knave

In the letter to Hutcheson, Hume acknowledges that the *Treatise* does not display warmth in the cause of virtue. Though he argues that this is not a defect in the *Treatise* given its aims, he promises that he will try again to make the moralist and the metaphysician agree a little better.[62] The *Second Inquiry* he fulfils this promise. At the end of the last section, he discusses

and more persuasive in its exhortations.' (iii 3.6.6) Hume returns to this comparison in the introduction to *IHU*: '. . . one considerable advantage, which results from the accurate and abstract philosophy, is, its subserviency to the easy and humane; which, without the former, can never attain a sufficient degree of its exactness in its sentiments, precepts, or reasonings. . . . The anatomist presents to the eye the most hideous and disagreeable objects; but his science is useful to the painter in delineating even a Venus or a Helen' (*IHU* 1.5)

[61] See further Smith, §801.

[62] Hume altered the text of *T* iii in response to Hutcheson's comments on a draft (Letter in Greig #15, 12 Nov. 1739). We do not know how he altered it, except that he tells Hutcheson: 'I intend to follow your advice in altering most of those passages you have remarked as defective in point of prudence; though I must own, I think you a little too delicate.' (Greig #13, 17 Sept. 1739). The 'prudence' Hume has in mind is caution towards readers who might take offence at his religious or moral views. Moore, 'Hume' 38–9, speculates without evidence on what Hume might have altered.

our 'interested obligation' to virtue, by asking whether we are well advised to practise the virtues if we are concerned about our happiness.[63]

He considers this question by introducing a 'sensible knave' who raises an objection raised by Hobbes's fool and by Glaucon and Adeimantus in the *Republic*. The knave accepts Hume's arguments to show that society, from which the knave benefits along with everyone else, depends on observance of the rules of justice. He even agrees that it is usually sensible to do what an honest person would do, but he believes that such general rules have exceptions and that an astute person violates the rules on some occasions when violation is his interest. He will not endanger the system of justice from which he benefits, but he will take advantage of the fact that not every violation endangers the whole system.[64]

Hume sees that it is difficult to answer the knave on his own terms. Someone who examines particular just actions to find out whether each one, considered by itself, is in his interest, cannot be satisfied. Hume contrasts such a person with the 'ingenuous natures' who would not consider the advantages of injustice worth the price. He suggests that these people are really happier than the sensible knave.[65] Cultivation of the moral sentiment produces antipathy to knavish calculations. This antipathy is confirmed whenever we see knaves being less sensible than they claim to be, and so taking foolish risks that betray their bad character to other people.

We might grant to Hume that honest people, given the preferences and revulsions he ascribes to them, will see no reason to adopt the outlook of the knave. To that extent, the outlook of honest people is stable and self-supporting, in contrast to the attitude that Glaucon and Adeimantus attribute to 'the many'.[66] But Hume gives no reason to suppose that a sensible knave will be less satisfied with a review of his own conduct.

A similar question arises about Hume's next argument against the knave. He believes that if we consider what the honest person enjoys compared to what even the successful knave enjoys, we will see that the honest person is better off. He enjoys the less expensive pleasures of life, and is satisfied with his own conduct, instead of wearying himself with the feverish pursuit of the expensive pleasures that engage the knave.[67]

This is a plausible reply to anyone who suggests that an honest person will practise honesty only reluctantly, and will envy the knave. Callicles, Glaucon, and Nietzsche suggest, for various reasons, that a morally virtuous person will suffer from envy, regret, or self-hatred. Hume replies that people who have cultivated the preferences of the virtuous person have no reason, given these preferences, to regret being the sort of people they are rather than knaves. But Hume seems to make the same doubtful assumption about the knave that

---

[63] '... whether every man, who has any regard to his own happiness and welfare, will not best find his account in the practice of every moral duty' (*I* 9.2).

[64] '... and though it is allowed that, without a regard to property, no society could subsist; yet according to the imperfect way in which human affairs are conducted, a sensible knave, in particular incidents, may think that an act of iniquity or infidelity will make a considerable addition to his fortune, without causing any considerable breach in the social union and confederacy' (*I* 9.2).

[65] 'Inward peace of mind, consciousness of integrity, a satisfactory review of our own conduct; these are circumstances, very requisite to happiness, and will be cherished and cultivated by every honest man, who feels the importance of them.' (*I* 9.2)

[66] Glaucon and Adeimantus on the many; see §50.

[67] '... but above all the peaceful reflexion on one's own conduct; what comparison, I say, between these and the feverish, empty amusements of luxury and expense?' (*I* 9.2).

others make about the honest person; for he suggests that the knave suffers feverish anxiety and self-hatred. This suggestion seems to presuppose that the knave has the attitude that the honest person would have to knavishness, or that knavishness inevitably leads to the excesses that Hume has in mind. These presuppositions do not seem justified.[68]

The conclusion of 'The Sceptic' is much more cautious about recommending morality. The Sceptic argues, following the outlook of the *Inquiry*, that in the ordinary circumstances of human life the virtues contribute most to one's contentment and ability to enjoy life without too much disturbance.[69] But he qualifies this defence of virtue by arguing that different people's temperaments, passions, and circumstances determine what is valuable for them, so that we cannot make universal and unqualified judgments about what states of character are worth acquiring. If someone is insensible to morality because he lacks the temper and passions that incline people to virtue, the Sceptic has no arguments that might reform him. It is no use to draw the insensible person's attention to the pleasures of being virtuous; for these pleasures are available only to people with a suitable temperament, which he lacks.[70] Hume does not simply mean that we cannot move an insensible person; he also believes we cannot show how he is worse off, whatever he may think about it, than a virtuous person.

The Sceptic reinforces his claims about the absolute dominance of natural temper by rejecting philosophical views—normally Stoic—about how to alter one's views of one's situation and life. If these views are too opposed to one's natural passions and tendencies, either they have no effect or their bad effects are at least equal to their good effects. If, for instance, we follow Stoic advice to cultivate indifference to misfortunes, we equally undermine ordinary attachments to individuals and communities.

Moreover, for some temperaments it may actually be worse to have some virtue than to have none. The abandoned villain is better off than the imperfect person with a sense of shame, because the imperfect person suffers from regret, shame, and guilt that the abandoned villain avoids.[71] While the completely virtuous person has no reason to want to change, it is not clear how many other people have reason to want to be virtuous. The abandoned villain may be no less content with himself than the virtuous person is. People who are neither abandoned villains nor completely virtuous may have a reason to change to one of the extremes; but they have a reason to change to the virtuous extreme only if it is easier than changing to the vicious extreme.

Examination of this essay, together with the *Inquiry*, suggests that, even though Hume displays some of the warmth that Hutcheson had missed in the *Treatise*, Hutcheson might

---

[68] These questions about the vicious person's attitude to himself are discussed by Plato, in *Republic* viii–ix, and by Aristotle, in *EN* ix 4. See §§59–60, 110–11.

[69] '...the happiest disposition of mind is the virtuous; or, in other words, that which leads to action and employment, renders us sensible to the social passions, steels the heart against the assaults of fortune, reduces the affections to a just moderation, makes our own thoughts an entertainment to us, and inclines us rather to the pleasures of society and conversation, than to those of the senses' ('Sceptic' §21).

[70] '...he might still reply, that these were perhaps, pleasures to such as were susceptible of them; but that, for his part, he finds himself of quite a different disposition. I must repeat it; my philosophy affords no remedy in such a case, nor could I do anything but lament this person's unhappy condition' ('Sceptic' §29).

[71] '...if a man be liable to a vice or imperfection, it may often happen, that a good quality, which he possesses along with it, will render him more miserable, than if he were completely vicious... A sense of shame, in an imperfect character, is certainly a virtue; but produces great uneasiness and remorse, from which the abandoned villain is entirely free' ('Sceptic' §54).

still be dissatisfied with the defence of morality that is offered in the *Inquiry*. Hume's defence shows that a sentimentalist can say something better than Hobbes could say in reply to the fool, and it dispels the suspicion that the virtuous person has something to regret, or that one can be attached to morality only as a means to one's own interest in this life or a future life. But this defence is also limited; while it recommends virtue to those who already have a taste for it, it does not explain how anyone else is missing anything by lacking a taste for it.

Hutcheson, therefore, might still reasonably object that Hume's defence fails to support one of our entrenched beliefs about morality. We do not think that morality is worth having only for those with a certain sort of temperament; we think the virtues are for human beings generally. Hume's argument tends to undermine this belief. But he suggests quite plausibly that Hutcheson could not consistently be dissatisfied with Hume's position without being dissatisfied with his own position as well.

783. How to Evaluate Moral Theories: Effects on Moral Practice

If Hutcheson is right to be dissatisfied with Hume's defence of morality, he points to a significant question about the sentimentalist position that they both accept. Hume makes two claims about the practical implications of his moral theory: (1) In judging its truth or falsity, we ought not to be concerned about whether it will have good or bad effects on moral practice.[72] (2) It does not tend to undermine morality; on the contrary, it presents morality in a favourable light.[73] These two claims are consistent, but each is open to doubt.

Hume's first claim is right, if it simply means that we ought not to rule out absolutely the prospect of discovering truths about morality that tend to raise questions about the appropriateness of our commitment to it. But he seems to have in mind the stronger claim that the practical implications of a theory have no proper role in our efforts to decide whether it is true. This claim is surprising, given Hume's attack on the 'monkish virtues' allegedly favoured by his opponents (*I* 9.3). But his account of his method makes his claim intelligible. His theory of morality is part of a science of human nature; the impartial and 'experimental' examination of our capacity for moral judgment and knowledge does not seem to depend on our views about moral practice.[74]

But though this view is intelligible, Hume's actual argument does not vindicate it. For his claims about moral distinctions rely on some intuitive judgments about morality. He assumes, for instance, that we cannot make sincere moral judgments without some motivation to act on them, and that we can assent to any factual judgments about external objects without accepting any moral judgment. Hume takes these intuitive judgments to

---

[72] 'There is no method of reasoning more common, and yet none more blameable, than in philosophical debates to endeavour to refute any hypothesis by a pretext of its dangerous consequences to religion and morality. (a) When any opinion leads us into absurdities, 'tis certainly false; but 'tis not certain an opinion is false, because 'tis of dangerous consequence. (b) Such topics, therefore, ought entirely to be forborne, as serving nothing to the discovery of truth, but only to make the person of an antagonist odious.' (*T* iii 3.2.3, letters added). In (a) Hume claims only that immoral implications do not make it certain that a theory is false. But in (b) he draws the sweeping conclusion that such implications should never be considered. Cf. *IHU* 8.26.

[73] See *T* iii 3.6.3–6; *I* 9.2. See also Ayer, 'Analysis'.

[74] Sturgeon, 'Difference', discusses some questions relevant to Hume's claim.

be introspectively evident judgments about conceivability and possibility. But one might argue that they are to be accepted or rejected in the light of the rest of our conception of morality.

In that case, we have reason to doubt Hume's denial of the relevance of practical implications. For part of our conception of morality is our view about its practical role in relation to other considerations that we take to matter. If, then, an account of morality makes its practical role more difficult to understand, might we not suspect that the theory is false, and might we not re-examine its premisses? Hume would apparently hesitate to present his theory with such vigour if he were convinced that reflexion on it would cause the moral sense to disapprove of itself. This appeal to practical implications is not the narrow pragmatic test that Hume rejects; it seems a reasonable question to raise about a moral theory.

If Hutcheson and Hume are right in their mutual criticisms, the appeal to practical implications presents them with a difficulty.[75] Hutcheson sees that Hume defends morality rather tepidly. Hume implicitly replies that this degree of tepidness is inseparable from a sentimentalist theory. For though such a theory may make virtue seem attractive to those who already have suitable sentiments, and though it may confirm them in preferring virtue over vice, it gives no reason to believe that it is better to be a virtuous person than a sensible knave.

This is not our normal attitude to morality. We do not normally take it to be preferable only from the virtuous person's point of view. We believe that we have reason, whether or not we initially share the virtuous person's preferences, to acquire them. We believe we would be worse off if we were to acquire the preferences of the sensible knave, and not simply because we do not welcome them from our present point of view.[76] If we accepted sentimentalism, we could not believe we had this sort of external reason for preferring morality. Since the belief that we have this sort of external reason is a basic feature of our moral outlook, we have a reason to doubt sentimentalism.

Hume recognizes, and sees that Hutcheson does not recognize, that a sentimentalist must reject this feature of our moral outlook. He believes that his account of reason and passion exposes the basic confusion in any belief in external reasons. But if sentimentalism excludes external reasons, we have a reason to reconsider Hume's account of reason and passion. We may reasonably ask whether it is so persuasive that we ought to stick to it even if we think it undermines our conception of morality.

It is not clear, therefore, that Hume's sentimentalist account of morality is 'a considerable advancement of the speculative sciences' that 'has little or no influence on practice' (T iii 1.1.26). He argues that his denial of objectivism saps the foundations of morality no more than Hutcheson's theory saps them. In answer to Hutcheson's doubts about his failure to recommend virtue strongly, he argues that Hutcheson is no better off. But if he is right in this estimate of Hutcheson's position and his own, his conclusions about morality seem more sceptical than he believes they are. They seem to cast doubt not only on philosophical views of morality, but also on some of the beliefs underlying morality.

---

[75] On Hutcheson and Hume see Sidgwick, ME 104.
[76] On preference-independent and external reasons see §259.

But even if Hume conceded this point, he would not concede that his arguments undermine morality itself. In his view, the sentiments supporting morality are too tenacious to be undermined by philosophical argument. We do not stop believing in the external world if we are convinced by a sceptical argument. Similarly, he might argue, the discovery that our moral beliefs are unjustified will not make our moral sentiments go away.[77]

Would he be right to claim that moral scepticism does not undermine moral beliefs and sentiments? He might be right to claim that the sentiments will remain in some form, even in the face of convincing sceptical challenges to their justification. But our attitude to them will not necessarily be the same; if we agree that they are unjustified, we may not take them so seriously. Perhaps the sentiments that would be left if we were to accept sentimentalism would serve some of our purposes 'in company, in the pulpit, on the theatre, and in the schools' (iii 3.3.2), but it might not serve all our present purposes.

We ordinarily believe, for instance, that it is important for everyone to accept morality, not simply because it is convenient for other people, but also because it is the outlook that everyone has good reason to accept. Hence we do not believe we are simply trying to make people fit in with other people's expectations; we also believe they have a good reason to accept these expectations. If we agreed with Hume, we would no longer believe these things. This seems to be a practical implication of his conception of morality, and an implication that we might reasonably take into account if we wonder whether to accept his conception.

784. Hume's Contribution to the Defence of Morality

Though it is fair to emphasize the sceptical side of Hume's moral theory more than Hume emphasizes it, it would be one-sided to concentrate exclusively on it. In his view, he supports morality by freeing it from indefensible doctrines that rationalists maintain in a misguided effort to find rational foundations for morality. Even if he is wrong to claim that morality as a whole is left undamaged by the rejection of rationalism, he might still be right to maintain that sentimentalism explains important elements of morality. The traits and tendencies that develop from our sentiments, by the process that Hume describes, are important elements in the moral virtues, even if they are not the virtues themselves.

A rationalist has good reason to believe that the foundations of morality include the non-rational foundations that Hume identifies. For any plausible theory of morality needs to explain both (1) why morality is as tenacious as it is, and (2) why it does not seem to everyone to rest on a foundation of rational conviction. Hume's account helps a rationalist to answer these questions. Since certain elements of morality can be explained by Hume's explanatory scheme, it is intelligible that a rationalist theory does not appear to be mandatory for a correct understanding of morality. A person's moral outlook does not consist of just one set of beliefs, states, or dispositions that are either present or absent as a whole; in different people, or in the same person at different times, some elements may be stronger

---

[77] '. . . there is sufficient uniformity in the senses and feelings of mankind, to make all these qualities the objects of art and reasoning, and to have the greatest influence on life and manners' ('Sceptic' §17n).

than others. Hume identifies elements that do not require a rational foundation. He is right to say that they can arise and persist in the absence of rational conviction in the moral agents themselves, and that they can be understood without appeal to a philosophical theory that proves that they are rationally justified.

To say this is not to reject rationalism. For even if we agree that Hume identifies important elements of morality that do not require a rational foundation, we may nonetheless insist that these are only parts, and not the whole, of morality, and that they need to be modified by reflexion on a rational foundation. To grasp the truth in Hume's position is also to recognize its incompleteness.

785. Hume's Reaction to Hutcheson and Hobbes

A useful way to grasp some of the central points in Hume's position is to recapitulate the points of comparison with Hutcheson.[78] We noticed two leading tendencies in Hutcheson: (1) He seeks to defend a position close to what Shaftesbury calls 'moral realism', opposed to the egoist and voluntarist conception defended by Hobbes. (2) He rejects the rationalist defence of this moral realism that appeals to intuitions of fitness, and he replaces it with a moral sense theory.[79] Hutcheson's rationalist critics, Burnet and Balguy, argue that the two sides of Hutcheson's position conflict, because the moral sense theory is subject to the basic objections that refute Hobbes's position.

Hutcheson, therefore, agrees with his rationalist opponents in believing that the objections of Cudworth and Shaftesbury undermine Hobbes's position, and that they identify conditions of adequacy for any moral theory. He disagrees with them insofar as he believes that he can meet their objections to Hobbes without accepting rationalism.

Just as we can see two sides of Hutcheson's position, we can also see two sides of Hume's reaction to Hutcheson: (1) He accepts Hutcheson's anti-rationalism about practical reason and about moral properties and judgments, and accepts a moral sense theory. (2) But he believes that he grasps the implications of such a theory more fully than Hutcheson grasps them, and that they undermine Hutcheson's reply to his rationalist critics.

These two sides of Hume's reaction help to explain why he can reasonably present himself as a follower of Hutcheson despite his sharp disagreements with him. Some contemporaries regarded Hutcheson as a defender of morality and religion and Hume as a dangerous sceptic. They might understandably be surprised and offended by Hume's expressions of agreement with Hutcheson; some modern critics agree with them. But such a reaction does not take proper account of the degree of agreement between Hutcheson's rationalist critics and Hume. Hume follows Balguy and Burnet in their assessment of the implications of

---

[78] Moore, 'Hume', argues against the common tendency to regard Hume as a follower of Hutcheson. See also Stewart, *KI* 12 (quoted in §751). In his view, 'Hume's moral philosophy was not at all Hutchesonian in origin or inspiration; it derived rather from a tradition of moral philosophy, the substantive Epicurean tradition adopted by Bayle and other modern sceptics, which was opposed by Hutcheson...' (53). The denial that Hutcheson inspired Hume is exaggerated; the fact that Hume disagrees with Hutcheson on some important points does not preclude deep Hutchesonian influence. Hume believes that Hutcheson ought to agree with Hume if he were more consistent.

[79] See §632.

Hutcheson's position.[80] Hutcheson rejects their criticisms, but, if Hume is right, the critics expose a conflict in Hutcheson's position.[81]

Hume, therefore, agrees with the attacks of Hutcheson's rationalist critics. But he rejects a point on which Hutcheson agrees with these critics; for he does not believe that Cudworth's and Shaftesbury's criticisms of Hobbes are decisive, and so he does not believe that an acceptable moral theory must avoid the mutability of moral properties that Cudworth finds in Hobbes and Balguy finds in Hutcheson. Hume concludes that Hutcheson is wrong to resist the arguments of his rationalist opponents about the consequences of his sentimentalism, but also wrong to suppose that these arguments need to be resisted; for the consequences are not as damaging as both Hutcheson and Balguy take them to be.[82]

We can see how Hume reaches this assessment of Hutcheson if we recall some earlier points. First, Hume agrees with some of Hutcheson's central claims:

(1) He agrees with Hutcheson's conception of practical reason. Reason provides neither exciting nor justifying reasons, but simply finds means to the satisfaction of desires proceeding from passions. Hence we must reject the traditional division between will and passion, and we must reject any account of freedom and responsibility that relies on this division.

(2) He agrees both with Hutcheson's introduction of a moral sense and with the subjectivist conclusion about moral properties that Hutcheson draws from his claims about the moral sense. In Hume as in Hutcheson, internalism about moral properties and motivation supports subjectivism. Since Hutcheson believes that justifying reasons require a desire resulting from the exercise of the moral sense, and he assumes that a true moral judgment implies the existence of a justifying reason for the person judging, he infers that in correctly judging that I ought to do x, I imply that I have some desire arising from my favourable attitude to x. Hume agrees with this general connexion between moral judgment, moral properties, and motivation, and so he agrees with Hutcheson's conclusion that moral properties are secondary qualities. This conclusion rests on Hutcheson's understanding of Locke's view, which takes secondary qualities to be states of the perceiver, not objective properties of external objects.

(3) He agrees with Hutcheson in rejecting Hobbes's account of justice. Hobbes does not suggest any role for any motive other than self-interest in his account of the social contract, or in his account of the motives and concerns that move us to maintain the commonwealth once it has been founded. Hume agrees with Hutcheson in believing that some sentiment in favour of the public interest must be invoked in a satisfactory account of our attitudes to justice.

The fact that Hume agrees with Hutcheson on these points is not difficult to discover. Hume acknowledges the basic agreement on subjectivism and the moral sense.

The points of disagreement with Hutcheson all follow from these points of agreement:

(4) Hutcheson tries to defend some elements of Butler's position within the moral sense theory. Hume notices that Hutcheson attributes to the moral sense some of the

---

[80] Anon., 'Review' (*Bibl. Raisonnée*) 9, regrets the fact that Hume does not discuss the views of Burnet and Hutcheson on the moral sense.

[81] Stewart, *KI* 20, also points out that Hume criticizes some aspects of Hutcheson's views that conflict with anti-rationalist versions of Calvinism. See §§645, 759.

[82] Thomas Brown argues in defence of Hutcheson and Hume. See §881.

authority that Butler attributes to conscience as supreme principle. Butler's claims about authority, however, rest on the distinction between power and authority, which Hutcheson undermines by taking reasons to refer to actual desires, rather than to what one ought to desire. Hume sees, therefore, that the approval of our moral sense cannot claim the rational authority that Butler claims for conscience, so that Hutcheson ought not to appeal to Butler's claims about authority and supremacy.

(5) Hutcheson follows Butler in claiming that morality accords with human nature, but Hume argues that Hutcheson is not entitled to Butler's naturalism. Butler's conception of nature includes claims about actions that are appropriate for human beings as whole systems. The relevant conception of appropriateness relies on the assumption that some actions are rationally appropriate, whether or not they are the objects of our predominant desire. Hume argues that Hutcheson is not entitled to rest any claim of rational authority on an appeal to nature, and that therefore he must give up Butler's specific appeal to nature. The only basis for an appeal to nature as a source of rational authority is an overtly theological basis, which confronts Hutcheson with further questions.

(6) Hume makes it clear that he seeks to correct Hutcheson from Hutcheson's own premises, in his discussion of the moral attributes of God. Moral properties exist only insofar as human beings actually have certain reactions; they do not exist as sources of requirements that human beings ought to respond to whether or not they actually do. Hence we cannot say that human beings ought to conform to moral principles or standards irrespective of how they actually react to them. We introduce an 'arbitrary and positive' character into moral properties (as Balguy says in discussing Hutcheson). A voluntarist claims that nothing is right or wrong apart from acts of will and command, and so makes moral goodness and rightness mutable in relation to will and command. A sentimentalist makes moral goodness and rightness mutable in relation to sentiments of most judges or of the usual judges. This is what Hume means when he says he wishes he could avoid this conclusion about morality, which has often been urged as an objection to Hutcheson.[83] If moral principles have not been shown to have authority for all rational beings, we cannot take God to be bound by them, and so we cannot take them to be antecedent to God's moral sense, if God has one. Even if we could overcome the difficulties that Hume raises for the attribution of a moral sense to God, we would still have to make moral properties mutable in relation to God's moral sense.

(7) Hutcheson relies on the moral sense and on its approval of benevolence to explain why morality includes principles of justice. He gives a utilitarian explanation of principles of justice, and takes utility to be the concern of benevolence. Hume agrees in trying to connect the moral sense with justice, but he rejects Hutcheson's claim that justice rests on benevolence. We cannot explain the tenacity of our rules of justice without appealing to a shared recognition of self-interest. The moral sense enters only when we have fixed some relatively stable rules based on this shared recognition of self-interest.

(8) In reply to Hutcheson's criticism that the *Treatise* lacks warmth in the cause of virtue, Hume claims that his role as an anatomist requires some restraint in warmth. But even when he says something warmer, as he does in the *Inquiry*, Hume does not display the warmth

---

[83] Letter in Greig, *LDH* #16 = R 634, quoted in §758.

that Hutcheson displays. This is not surprising, since Hume does not suggest that we have any reason to care about the moral virtues if we are not already among those who have ends to which virtuous actions would be means. If our sentiments and passions already dispose us to approve of virtuous actions, we have reason to cultivate the virtues. If we have selfish purposes to which virtuous actions are means, we have reason to cultivate the virtues to that degree. But Hume does not propose any reason that ought to influence people who lack the appropriate antecedent purposes and sentiments. This position ought not to surprise Hutcheson, since it follows from his views about justifying reasons, the moral sense, and the nature of moral properties.

The general tendency of all these disagreements with Hutcheson is the same: Hume argues that because Hutcheson agrees with him as much as he does, he ought also to agree with his criticisms of Hutcheson. In his view, Hutcheson has no escape from the implications of the sentimentalist point of view that Hume points out to him.

Hume's differences from Hutcheson do not bring Hume all the way back to Hobbes. He departs from Hobbes in recognizing an irreducible unselfish sentiment, and in taking this to be essential for explaining our support of morality within an established social order.[84] On this point Hume rejects an aspect of Hobbes that might be called 'scepticism', and so he affirms the reality of moral distinctions. Hence he insists on the reality of unselfish sentiments, in agreement with Hutcheson. This is one issue that both Hume's predecessors, from Shaftesbury onwards, and his contemporaries recognize as a clear mark of division between Hobbes and his opponents, and on this issue Hume is clearly against Hobbes.[85] He supports, as Hutcheson does, one aspect of the position that Shaftesbury calls 'realism'.

But this disagreement with Hobbes helps to support some of Hobbes's basic claims about morality. We might welcome Hume's account of the moral sentiment as offering Hobbes a credible account of our motivation for supporting morality within the commonwealth. Hume supports Hobbes's basic claim that morality deserves our concern only insofar as we have the desires and passions that make moral requirements instrumentally appropriate for us. He abandons Hobbes's residual tendency to speak as though prudence were uniquely rational, and so he develops Hobbes's predominant tendency to attribute a purely instrumental role to practical reason. Hume's anti-rationalism and anti-realism show how some of Hobbes's basic views are more defensible when they are separated from Hobbes's egoism.[86] Johnson may or may not have had good reasons for calling Hume a Hobbist, but his judgment captures part of the truth.[87]

---

[84] The irreducibility of this sentiment is much clearer in *I* than in *T*. See §763. In the first work, Hume seems more inclined to reduce unselfish sentiment to the operations of sympathy and association. The arguments of Kemp Smith, *PDH* 139–43, against Green to show that Hume is not an egoistic hedonist about the passions are much easier to support from *I* than from *T*.

[85] This is the aspect of Hume's position that Norton, *DH*, ch. 3, has in mind when he represents Hume as a 'common-sense' moralist, and even as a moral 'realist'. See §643.

[86] Anon., 'Review' (*Bibl. Raisonnée*) says of *T* iii: 'It is, as we see it, Hobbes's system presented in a new form. Had this philosopher [sc. Hume] presented it in this manner, I doubt that he would have been welcomed into the world' (10). The reviewer is speaking primarily of Hume's treatment of justice, and does not make it clear whether the same judgment applies to Hume's theory as a whole.

[87] For Johnson's view see §727.

60

SMITH

---

786. The Practical Unimportance of the Epistemology and Metaphysics of Morality

Smith recognizes two main topics of inquiry in moral philosophy: (1) An inquiry into the character of virtue. (2) An inquiry into the faculty that 'recommends' virtue to us.[1] The first topic is the primary concern of ancient moralists; the second is the concern of the moderns. In Smith's view, only the first is of practical importance; the second is a purely theoretical question that makes no difference to practice. This attitude to the second question agrees with Hume's attitude to the epistemology and metaphysics of morals. Hume takes the conception of moral properties as secondary qualities to be 'a considerable advancement of the speculative sciences; though . . . it has little or no influence on practice' (T iii 1.1.26). To show that the second question has no practical importance, Smith argues it makes no difference to our judgment about what is right and wrong in particular cases.[2]

It is difficult to agree with Smith about the practical unimportance of his second question. If we are convinced by a sentimentalist theory of the nature of moral judgment, we may find that some common moral judgments do not fit that theory. Must we not either reject these common judgments or reject the theory? If, for instance, we agree with Hume's view that, contrary to the 'divines', moral virtues include some involuntary traits, must we not allow as virtues some traits that the 'divines' disallow? Acceptance of this sentimentalist theory would surely affect some of our particular moral judgments.

But even if Smith were right to say that meta-ethical questions do not affect moral judgments about particular cases of right and wrong action, he would not have shown that meta-ethical questions are practically unimportant. Our judgments about whether it is right

---

[1] 'First, wherein does virtue consist? Or what is the tone of temper, and tenour of conduct, which constitutes the excellent and praise-worthy character, the character which is the natural object of esteem, honour, and approbation? And, secondly, by what power or faculty in the mind is it, that this character, whatever it be, is recommended to us?' (vii 1.2, 265) I cite TMS by book, chapter, section, and page from the edition of Raphael and Macfie (cited as RM).

[2] '. . . I must observe, that the determination of this second question, though of the greatest importance in speculation, is of none in practice. The question concerning the nature of virtue necessarily has some influence upon our notions of right and wrong in many particular cases. That concerning the principle of approbation can possibly have no such effect. To examine from what contrivance or mechanism within, those different notions or sentiments arise, is a mere matter of philosophical curiosity' (vii 3.introd.2, 315).

to tell this lie here and now, or to inflict this undeserved harm on this innocent person in the public interest, are not the only practically important moral judgments. Our conduct does not depend simply on our judgments about which actions are morally right or wrong; it also depends on how much we think morality matters. Hume envisages the possibility of our coming to believe that moral judgments result from a sentiment that we disapprove of on reflexion; Nietzsche's genealogy exploits this possibility. If we were convinced by such a genealogy, might we not take morality less seriously?

The assertion that meta-ethical conclusions are practically unimportant is part of Smith's defence of sentimentalism. Some opponents of sentimentalism claim that it undermines morality. Hume answers that the debate between sentimentalism and rationalism concerns a question of purely theoretical interest, so that a decision in favour of sentimentalism could not tend to undermine morality. Smith adds nothing to Hume on this point.

He believes that moral judgment must be traced back to sentiments, because he agrees with Hutcheson and Hume in believing that moral distinctions are not derived from reason. Like Hutcheson, he accepts some of the rationalist critique of Hobbes, but he believes that Hutcheson has shown that the true points in this critique do not require the acceptance of rationalism. He agrees with Cudworth's argument against Hobbes's positivism, but he believes that Cudworth was wrong to assume that the moral principles prior to law are rational principles. Cudworth's error was excusable, since in his time no option besides reason had been considered.[3] But Hutcheson made the further advances in the science of human nature that settle the issue about reason.[4] In Smith's view, Hutcheson's discussion of the role of reason shows how we can accept what is sound in Cudworth's criticism of Hobbes without embracing rationalism.[5]

If Smith is right to agree with Hutcheson against the rationalists, Balguy is wrong to suppose that Cudworth's argument against Hobbes's legal positivism also undermines Hutcheson's sentimentalism. In that case, rationalist arguments against voluntarism and positivism do not apply to sentimentalism. Hutcheson argues, against Balguy, that he allows the corrigibility of the moral sense. He relies on the parallel with the external senses, and hence allows the correction of one person's sense by reference to the normal perceiver, where 'normal' is understood not normatively but statistically. According to Hutcheson, this degree of corrigibility allows us to reject Hobbesian positivism without embracing rationalism.

Balguy replies that Hutcheson's account of corrigibility does not answer the case against Hobbes. For if moral judgments allow only the sort of correction that Hutcheson describes, we can adjust them to the normal judge's reactions, but we cannot criticize the normal moral judge. But morality (in Balguy's view) is not mutable in relation to the reactions of

---

[3] '. . . the abstract science of human nature was but in its infancy, . . . before the distinct offices and powers of the different faculties of the human mind had been carefully examined and distinguished from one another. . . . no other faculty had been thought of from which any such ideas could possibly be supposed to arise' (vii 3.2.5, 319).

[4] 'Dr Hutcheson had the merit of being the first who distinguished with any degree of precision in what respect all moral distinctions may be said to arise from reason, and in what respect they are founded upon immediate sense and feeling. In his illustrations upon the moral sense he has explained this so fully, and, in my opinion, so unanswerably, that, if any controversy is still kept up about this subject, I can impute it to nothing, but either to inattention to what that gentleman has written, or to a superstitious attachment to certain forms of expression . . .' (vii 3.2.9, 320–1).

[5] Price, RPQM 281–2, writing in 1787, before the last edition of TMS, notices Smith's dogmatic anti-rationalism, and looks forward to Reid's EAP for argument on the rationalist side.

the normal judge. According to Balguy and Price, we regard the moral sense as correct only if it corresponds to some principles of right and wrong that are independent of it; that is Cudworth's reply to Hobbes's appeal to law as the basis of right.

Hume, in contrast to Hutcheson, rejects the rationalist objections to Hobbes, and so does not believe that sentimentalists need to answer Balguy and Price. Once we examine our moral judgments and the sort of properties they must be about, we can see that there is nothing more to being right and wrong than being approved or disapproved by our moral sense. If we suppose that the moral sense is open to moral appraisal, we are misled. And so, while Hobbes was wrong to appeal to law, he was basically right, and Cudworth was basically wrong. Hume supposes that moral judgments are the result of our accommodation to the reactions of other people and their point of view. Morality has no basis for criticizing our attitudes or for arguing about whether other people's reactions are reasonable and appropriate.

Smith does not comment on this disagreement between Hutcheson and Hume about the 'positive and arbitrary' character of the moral sense (as Balguy puts it). But their disagreement raises another question about practical significance. If we agree with Hume that we have no rational or moral basis for critical evaluation of our moral sense, we may not take morality as seriously as we would take it if we thought we had the sort of critical basis that the rationalists suppose we have. Hume concedes this point to the rationalists. Hutcheson and Smith do not; but Smith does not say what is wrong with Hume's argument against Hutcheson.

Hume's lack of concern about this aspect of his theory may be connected with a feature of his treatment that caught Hutcheson's attention. Hutcheson notices that in Hume's *Treatise* 'there wants a certain warmth in the cause of virtue'. Though Hume suggests that he will try to remedy this in his later writings, and though the *Inquiry* is warmer than the *Treatise*, Hutcheson would probably have reacted to the *Inquiry* in the same way.[6] Smith, however, is warm in the cause of virtue; he does not suggest that reflexion on the nature of moral virtue or of moral judgment will or should lead us to take morality less seriously or to be less warm in its defence. He returns to Hutcheson's position, but he gives no reason for preferring it to Hume's position.

Smith, therefore, is rather complacent in his assurance that disputes between rationalism and sentimentalism are 'a mere matter of philosophical curiosity'.[7] Balguy argues against this claim that sentimentalists can legitimately take morally seriously. Though Hume claims that his sentimentalism 'has little or no influence on practice',[8] he concedes Balguy's points about the positive and arbitrary character of the moral sense. These points suggest that the theoretical dispute may also be significant in practice. By dismissing such questions, Smith overlooks a worthwhile direction of inquiry into the implications of sentimentalism.

787. Arguments for Sentimentalism

Smith's unreasonably dismissive attitude to these questions may result from his conviction that the dispute between rationalism and sentimentalism has been settled. However seriously

---

[6] See §781.   [7] vii 3.introd.2, 315.   [8] *T* iii 1.1.26, quoted in §758.

we take morality, we cannot (he assumes) accept Balguy's arguments as good reasons for favouring rationalism; for we already have decisive reasons for accepting sentimentalism. But Smith's reasons for confidence in sentimentalism are open to doubt. His main ground for rejecting rationalism about moral distinctions seems to be his acceptance of a version of internalism about virtue and motivation. In his view, virtue necessarily pleases us, but this effect would not be necessary if our judgment that something is a virtue were a purely rational judgment. If the judgment were purely rational, it would be a contingent fact that virtue pleases some people and displeases others. But since it would be self-contradictory to judge that something is virtuous and not to find it pleasing, moral judgment must include feeling.[9]

It is difficult to accept Smith's claim about the necessary connexion between virtue and pleasure. One might accept some necessary connexion between virtue and desirability, if this means that virtue necessarily deserves to be desired.[10] But this internal connexion does not support Smith. He needs a further internal connexion between virtue and actual pleasure and desire. But what is this connexion? He cannot mean that justice, for instance, is a virtue only if everyone desires it and finds it pleasant. Perhaps, then, he means that A regards justice as a virtue only if A desires it and finds it pleasant.

In reply to Smith, we might suggest that we could recognize justice as a virtue and still be indifferent to it. If Smith seeks to rule this answer out by appeal to a conceptual claim, he is on weak ground. But if he simply means that every virtue must be an object of desire and pleasure to a well-disposed person, anti-rationalism does not follow. For we may answer that a well-disposed person desires justice and takes pleasure in it because justice promotes interests or safeguards rights that every well-disposed person wants to promote or safeguard. We can easily accept this answer while still maintaining a rationalist position about the nature of justice and our knowledge of justice.

Smith would be on stronger ground if he appealed to a different anti-rationalist argument, more clearly presented by Hume than by Hutcheson. According to this argument, reason itself cannot discover appropriate ends, but can only discover instrumental means to ends, and hence cannot be a source of ultimate justifying reasons. If virtues are sources of ultimate justifying reasons, reason cannot discover the virtues. The virtuous person, according to Hutcheson, regards the good of other people as worth pursuing for its own sake; but we cannot discover by reason that the good of others is worth pursuing for its own sake; and so the virtuous concern must result from something other than a discovery of reason. Reid exposes a weakness in this argument for sentimentalism: even if virtue involves a specific belief about ultimate ends, and even if this belief cannot be further justified, it does not follow that it is a sentiment.[11]

---

[9] '...nothing can be agreeable or disagreeable for its own sake, which is not rendered such by immediate sense and feeling. If virtue, therefore, in every particular instance, necessarily pleases for its own sake, and if vice as certainly displeases the mind, it cannot be reason, but immediate sense and feeling, which, in this manner, reconciles us to the one, and alienates us from the other. Pleasure and pain are the great objects of desire and aversion: but these are distinguished not by reason, but by immediate sense and feeling. If virtue, therefore, be desirable for its own sake, and if vice be, in the same manner, the object of aversion, it cannot be reason which originally distinguishes these different qualities, but immediate sense and feeling' (vii 3.2.7–8, 320).

[10] Smith recognizes that the desire for praise is different from the desire to be praiseworthy (iii 2.2, 114), and we might fairly insist on a parallel distinction between the desired and the desirable, taking the desirable to be what is worthy of desire.

[11] See Reid, §848.

Smith, therefore, does not offer convincing direct arguments for Hutcheson's and Hume's anti-rationalism. He is not much concerned with the epistemology and metaphysics of morals, and in these areas he has little to add to Hume.

788. A Descriptive and Causal Theory

On these basic questions about the truth of sentimentalism, we may be disappointed by Smith's arguments. Though his investigation of moral sentiments presupposes sentimentalism, he does not defend his presupposition effectively. But he contributes indirectly to the defence of sentimentalism. He begins from the positive aim of Hume's second *Inquiry*, to 'discover the true origin of morals' (*I* 1.10). Hume offers an 'explication' of benevolence and justice, expecting that this 'will probably give us an opening by which the others may be accounted for'. In the course of examining the different virtues, Hume argues that they are all qualities agreeable or useful to the agent or to others, and that this is the causal origin of our tendency to praise them as virtues. Smith follows Hume in recognizing this causal and explanatory inquiry as a task of the moral philosopher.

Hutcheson and Hume do not complete this task. Hutcheson confines the moral sense to the approval of benevolence. He fails to account for those aspects of our moral judgments that, as Butler sees, go beyond benevolence or even against it; his efforts to incorporate Butler's views about conscience into his own view of the moral sense reveal the conflict between Butler and himself. Hume improves on Hutcheson by partly detaching the moral sense from benevolence. But he attaches it to the approval of utility (now distinguished from benevolence); hence he fails to explain the moral judgments that seem not to be limited to recognition of utility to the possessor of the virtue or to others.[12]

Smith advances this discussion through a fuller constructive account of the moral sentiments than Hume offers. He supports the sentimentalist position by describing sentiments that we might plausibly regard as the basis of our moral judgments. If he offers a descriptively adequate account that traces our various moral judgments to their sources in sentiments, he shows that sentimentalism fits the actual range and variety of moral judgments.

This account of moral sentiments may be valuable even if sentimentalism is false. For even if we do not believe that moral judgments consist basically or entirely in sentiments, we have good reason to believe that they are characteristically connected with sentiments, and that the formation of appropriate sentiments partly forms moral character. Smith may have found an important part of the truth about morality, even if he has not found the basic constituent of moral virtue.

789. Moral Sentiments v. Moral Sense

Though Smith agrees with Hutcheson and Hume in rejecting rationalism, he rejects their arguments for tracing moral judgments to a moral sense. In his view, Hutcheson introduced

---

[12] The same is true when we add the virtues that Hume explains by agreeableness rather than utility.

a moral sense because he had correctly eliminated reason and self-love as the source of moral judgments, but could not find their source in any other recognized mental capacity; hence he needed some new capacity. He called it the moral sense because he took it to be somewhat analogous to the external senses, and also somewhat analogous to the 'reflex senses' whose operations result from the operations of other senses (vii 3.3.5–6, 321–2).

Smith criticizes Hutcheson on three grounds: (1) We make moral judgments about our moral sentiments themselves. (2) Moral judgments are too various to be expressions of a single sentiment or emotion. (3) Even if we exclude reason and self-interest, other recognized mental capacities can explain moral judgments, and so we do not need a new one.

The first line of criticism is reasonable. It exploits Balguy's objection that the moral sense is corrigible because we apply moral criticism to someone's moral sentiments, on the assumption that they are capable of improvement, and that they reflect moral credit or discredit on a person (vii 3.3.8–10, 322–4). Hutcheson tries to explain some criticisms of a particular agent's moral sense, by reference to the moral sense of the 'normal' observer. But if 'normal' just means 'statistically most frequent', he does not answer Balguy's objection. Smith implicitly agrees with Balguy; for if Hutcheson's appeal to the normal observer refuted Balguy, it would refute Smith too. Can Smith explain the moral criticism of someone's moral sense by reference to something more than Hutcheson's standard of normality?

The second objection to an appeal to the moral sense is more relevant to Hume than to Hutcheson. Though Hume follows Hutcheson in appealing to a moral sense, he does not rely as strongly on an analogy with the other senses. Often he speaks of a certain kind of feeling. Smith is right to suppose that—given Hume's view of feelings—this account of moral judgment requires the relevant feeling to be introspectively similar in all moral judgments.[13] If we were to claim that the identity of the moral sentiment consists in the judgment on which it is based, we would no longer make the moral sense primary; hence Hume assumes that introspective similarity is the common feature of all expressions of the moral sense.[14] Against this assumption Smith points out that the sentiments connected with approval of different kinds of actions and characters vary with the objects of our approval. They have no specific feeling in common.[15]

These two objections prepare for the third objection, which rests on a positive account of moral judgment. Smith rejects any appeal to a distinct moral sense. He regards this notion

[13] '. . . whatever variations any particular emotion may undergo, it still preserves the general features which distinguish it to be an emotion of such a kind, and these general features are always more striking and remarkable than any variation which it may undergo in particular cases. Thus anger is an emotion of a particular kind: and accordingly its general features are always more distinguishable than all the variations it undergoes in particular cases' (vii 3.3.13, 324). Cf. Hume, §761.

[14] 'We do not infer a character to be virtuous, because it pleases: But in feeling that it pleases after such a particular manner, we in effect feel that it is virtuous. The case is the same as in our judgments concerning all kinds of beauty, and tastes, and sensations. Our approbation is implied in the immediate pleasure they convey to us.' (Hume, T iii 1.2.3) Part of the next paragraph is quoted in §781.

[15] 'If approbation and disapprobation, . . . were, like gratitude and resentment, emotions of a particular kind, distinct from every other, we should expect that in all the variations which either of them might undergo, it would still retain the general features which mark it to be an emotion of such a particular kind, clear, plain, and easily distinguishable. But in fact it happens quite otherwise. If we attend to what we really feel when upon different occasions we either approve or disapprove, we shall find that our emotion in one case is often totally different from that in another, and that no common features can possibly be discovered between them.' (Smith, TMS vii 3.3.13, 324–5)

as an unnecessary innovation.[16] His account of moral judgment is intended to show that the relevant features of moral judgment can be explained without reference to a special sense. In his view, the relevant facts about moral judgment are to be explained by the operation of sympathy. The feeling connected with moral approval varies according to our sympathetic reaction to the trait of character that we approve of.[17] Moreover, we approve of proper approval by another, and disapprove of improper approval. In this case our moral attitude is to be understood as coincidence or opposition between our sentiments and those of the other person. Why, he asks, should the same not be true in every case (vii 3.3.14, 325)?

In these arguments Smith does not draw the extreme conclusion that no sort of sentiment is essential to moral judgment. He believes that the common feature of moral judgments is not the similarity of sentiment, considered in its own right, but the fact that we find the same relation of our own sentiment to the sentiment of another. The common feature is the operation of sympathy.

In opposition to the moral sense theory, Smith claims that the different operations of sympathy give an account of moral judgments.[18] The successive stages in our reactions help us to answer both of the main questions of ethical theory, about which traits are virtues, and about how we judge that they are. A trait is a virtue insofar as it arouses sympathy from different points of view; and we judge that a trait is a virtue insofar as we react to it sympathetically. The close connexion between Smith's answers to these two questions raises even more doubts about his claim that the first is practically important and the second is not.

790. Sympathy and Fellow-Feeling

Though Smith criticizes Hutcheson and Hume for introducing a moral sense, he agrees with their aim of finding a reductive account of moral judgment. His description of the moral sentiments is intended to capture the content and nature of moral judgments. Hence his account is open to objection if the sentiments he describes are either insufficient or unnecessary for some clear cases of apparent moral judgment.

---

[16] 'Against every account of the principle of approbation, which makes it depend upon a peculiar sentiment, distinct from every other, I would object; that it is strange that this sentiment, which Providence undoubtedly intended to be the governing principle of human nature, should hitherto have been so little taken notice of, as not to have got a name in any language. The word moral sense is of very late formation, and cannot yet be considered as making part of the English tongue.' (vii 3.3.15, 326) Contrast Reid, §842.

[17] 'Thus the approbation with which we view a tender, delicate, and humane sentiment, is quite different from that with which we are struck by one that appears great, daring, and magnanimous. Our approbation of both may, upon different occasions, be perfect and entire; but we are softened by the one, and we are elevated by the other, and there is no sort of resemblance between the emotions which they excite in us. But according to that system which I have been endeavouring to establish, this must necessarily be the case. As the emotions of the person whom we approve of, are, in those two cases, quite opposite to one another, and as our approbation arises from sympathy with those opposite emotions, what we feel upon the one occasion, can have no sort of resemblance to what we feel upon the other.' (vii 3.3.13, 325)

[18] 'First, we sympathize with the motives of the agent; secondly, we enter into the gratitude of those who receive the benefit of his actions; thirdly, we observe that his conduct has been agreeable to the general rules by which those two sympathies generally act; and, last of all, when we consider such actions as making a part of a system of behaviour which tends to promote the happiness either of the individual or of the society, they appear to derive a beauty from this utility, not unlike that which we ascribe to any well-contrived machine.' (vii 3.3.16, 326)

The first definition of sympathy takes it to be 'our fellow-feeling with any passion whatever' (i 1.1.5, 10). The simplest way to understand fellow-feeling is to treat it as a sort of reproduction or copy of the original passion.[19] We assume that passions are contagious; A's awareness of B's feeling a given passion causes A to feel the same passion.

This simple account neglects many cases of fellow-feeling, as Smith sees. If A is aware that B is angry at C, A does not necessarily come to share B's anger. A is also aware of how C suffers from B's anger, and comes to sympathize with C. If A is to sympathize with B or with C, A must have some idea of what has provoked B; for A's evaluation of the occasion for B's anger will affect A's tendency to sympathize with B or with C. In these cases 'sympathy does not arise so much from the view of the passion as from that of the situation which excites it' (i 1.1.10, 12).

Hence we may sympathize with others even if we do not believe they feel any passion about the event that is the basis of our sympathy. If, for instance, A is polite, but B is boorish, and A sees B behaving rudely, A judges that if A were in B's actual situation, A would be embarrassed; this judgment causes A to be embarrassed for B. A's sympathy is directed towards A-imagined-in-B's-situation. A has no fellow-feeling with B's passion, since the boorish B feels no passion.[20]

It is difficult to understand the counterfactual that explains A's imagination of A's embarrassment in B's situation. Ought not A to recognize that if A were in B's situation and were as rude as B, A would not be embarrassed by A's rude behaviour? Moreover, if A would be embarrassed by A's behaving rudely in B's situation, A would not behave as rudely as B is actually behaving. It seems irrational for A to have fellow-feeling for B on the assumption that B shares some passion with A that B evidently does not share.

Smith's explanation suggests that A's being embarrassed by B's rudeness is parallel to a case in which fellow-feeling is more clearly misplaced. If C likes Beethoven and hates jazz, but D has the reverse preferences, it would be irrational for C to feel disappointed for D when D misses a Beethoven concert and to feel frustrated on D's behalf when D sits through a jazz concert. It seems irrelevant that this is how C would feel if C were in D's situation; C's 'fellow-feeling' would be irrational if it rested on this basis. On the contrary, C ought to feel pleased for D sitting through a jazz concert, because C recognizes that D's tastes in music, and therefore D's passions, are different from C's. But in that case one might expect that if the polite A is rational, A will recognize that the boorish B is not embarrassed by B's rudeness, and therefore A will not be embarrassed for B.

Smith sometimes recognizes the appropriate counterfactual basis for fellow-feeling. He sees that sympathy requires not that I consider myself with my feelings in your situation, but I consider myself being you and having the feelings that you have or would have.[21]

---

[19] 'The passions, upon some occasions, may seem to be transfused from one man to another, instantaneously, and antecedent to any knowledge of what excited them in the person principally concerned.' (i 1.1.6, 11)

[20] 'We sometimes feel for another a passion of which he himself seems to be altogether incapable; because, when we put ourselves in his case, that passion arises in our breast from the imagination, though it does not in his from the reality. We blush for the impudence and rudeness of another, though he himself appears to have no sense of the impropriety of his own behaviour; because we cannot help feeling with what confusion we ourselves should be covered, had we behaved in so absurd a manner.' (i 1.1.10, 12)

[21] '... though sympathy is very properly said to arise from an imaginary change of situations with the person principally concerned, yet this imaginary change is not supposed to happen to me in my own person and character, but in that of the person with whom I sympathize. When I condole with you for the loss of your only son, in order to enter into your grief I do not consider what I, a person of such a character and profession, should suffer, if I had a son, and if that son was unfortunately to die: but I consider what I should suffer if I was really you, and I not only change circumstances with

Hence he seems to imply that A's embarrassment at B's rudeness is a case of irrational sympathy.

But even the more plausible account of the counterfactual basis of sympathy does not seem to cover all cases of appropriate sympathy. Smith recognizes some cases in which sympathy seems appropriate, but seems not to be based on my imagining what you feel: (1) We feel anguish at the sight of people who have lost their reason, even if they seem quite cheerful about it. The counterfactual suppositions on which this anguish is based are inconsistent; I suppose myself suffering terribly if I were aware of myself in that situation, though at the same time I suppose that if I were in that situation I would not be aware of it, and hence would not suffer.[22] (2) A mother feels agony for her child suffering from a disease, even though the child cannot have the fears for the future that explain the mother's anxiety. (3) We feel sorry for the dead because we imagine ourselves both being dead (and so having no consciousness) and being aware of being dead (and so being conscious).[23]

In the third case Smith believes that fellow-feeling is irrational. If so, it seems to be irrational in the first and second cases as well. Ought we not, therefore, to try to discount such fellow-feeling in our deliberation and action? If the conclusions that we might reach on the supposition that a figure is both round and square are not to be taken seriously, it seems equally irrational to act on the supposition that we both have and lack a certain sort of belief or passion. And yet it often seems appropriate to feel compassion for people who have lost their reason, and for young children with fatal diseases. If Smith's analysis is right, these morally appropriate reactions rest on inconsistent suppositions that we should not act on.

To see why such reactions are appropriate, we should distinguish two kinds of 'fellow-feeling'. (1) One kind is a passion in us that corresponds to a passion in the other person. This is the reaction advised by St Paul in 'Rejoice with those who rejoice and weep with those who weep'.[24] (2) Another kind is a passion in us that is directed to the other person's situation. Smith recognizes these two passions, but he tries to explain the second by reference to the first, by introducing counterfactual passions that are reproduced in actual passions.

A better account of the second kind of passion might attribute to A the judgment that B's situation is bad, and therefore deserves compassion; the compassion results directly from

you, but I change persons and characters. . . . A man may sympathize with a woman in child-bed; though it is impossible that he should conceive himself as suffering her pains in his own proper person and character' (vii 3.1.4, 317).

[22] 'The anguish which humanity feels, therefore, at the sight of such an object cannot be the reflexion of any sentiment of the sufferer. The compassion of the spectator must arise altogether from the consideration of what he himself would feel if he was reduced to the same unhappy situation, and, what perhaps is impossible, was at the same time able to regard it with his present reason and judgment.' (i 1.1.11, 12)

[23] 'We sympathize even with the dead, and overlooking what is of real importance in their situation, that awful futurity which awaits them, we are chiefly affected by those circumstances which strike our senses, but can have no influence upon their happiness. . . . The idea of that dreary and endless melancholy, which the fancy naturally ascribes to their condition, arises altogether from our joining to the change which has been produced upon them, our own consciousness of that change, from our putting ourselves in their situation . . . It is from this very illusion of the imagination, that the foresight of our own dissolution is so terrible to us, and that the idea of those circumstances, which undoubtedly can give us no pain when we are dead, makes us miserable while we are alive.' (i 1.1.13, 12–13) Smith does not intend to reduce the influence of this 'illusion', since he immediately considers its social utility: 'And from thence arises one of the most important principles in human nature, the dread of death, the great poison to the happiness, but the great restraint upon the injustice of mankind, which, while it afflicts and mortifies the individual, guards and protects the society.' Cf. ii 1.2.5, 71; Griswold, *ASVE* 89.

[24] *Rm.* 12:15. Butler uses this as the text for his fifth Sermon, which Smith recalls inaccurately in i 3.1.1, 43; see RM ad loc.

A's judgment about the facts of B's actual situation, not from A's judgments about what A would feel if A were in B's situation. Our reaction to people who lose their reason, to young children suffering from fatal diseases, and to the dead, is reasonable if it rests on a reasonable judgment about the badness of these situations. We need not also imagine what we would feel in their situations. Hence we need not rely on the inconsistent suppositions that Smith describes.

The difference between passions based on evaluative judgments and passions based on counterfactual passions can be seen more clearly in cases where the two kinds of passions conflict. Suppose that A sees B taking cruel pleasure in causing pain to C, and that A knows both that A also tends to enjoy the pleasures that a cruel person would enjoy and that A is insensitive to pain. Smith's analysis requires A to reflect: 'If I were in B's situation, I would enjoy causing pain to C, and if I were in C's situation, I would not care much about the pain I suffered from B'. According to Smith, then, A will have fellow-feeling for B rather than C. But if A is a moderately good person, this analysis does not fit; for A recognizes that these features of A are not a good reason for denying that B is doing unjustified harm to C. Hence A's sympathy for C rests on A's judgments about the badness of B's cruelty and the severity of C's suffering, not on the feelings that A would have in B's and C's situation. If A is a moderately good person, these evaluative judgments cause A to sympathize with C, not with B.

This explanation of one kind of sympathy conflicts with one of Smith's main aims. For the explanation takes sympathy to rest on prior evaluative judgments, contrary to Smith's aim of explaining evaluative judgments through the operation of sympathy. His reductive account of evaluative judgments does not capture the range of morally appropriate reactions. If his account implies that some morally appropriate actions rest on contradictory assumptions or illusions, the account is open to doubt. Perhaps the doubt is not decisive; we may decide that the illusory character of the suppositions underlying a reaction does not affect the moral appropriateness of the reaction itself. But before we decide this, we may reasonably ask whether Smith's account is so plausible that we have to accept its less appealing implications.

791. A Reductive Account of Approval

These doubts about Smith's account of sympathy, and about his rejection of unreduced evaluative judgments underlying fellow-feeling, suggest further doubts about his account of approval, and his attempt to reduce it to sympathy.

In the cases we have considered, A's feeling does not correspond to B's, but rests on a judgment about A's counterfactual feeling. But in cases where A's feeling and B's agree, Smith claims that A approves of B's feelings.[25] In such cases B's feelings appear to A to be 'just and proper and suitable to their objects', and hence A makes favourable evaluative

---

[25] 'When the original passions of the person principally concerned are in perfect concord with the sympathetic emotions of the spectator, they necessarily appear to this last just and proper, and suitable to their objects . . . To approve of the passions of another, therefore, as suitable to their objects, is the same thing as to observe that we entirely sympathize with them . . . The man who resents the injuries that have been done to me, and observes that I resent them precisely as he does, necessarily approves of my resentment.' (i 1.3.1, 16)

judgments about B's passions.[26] This is a reductive account of evaluative judgments by reference to sympathy. When A approves of B's feeling, A simply records the fact that A feels the same as B feels. The analysis refers to no evaluative judgment, but only to a judgment about one's present feelings.

Smith recognizes, however, that this analysis is too narrow.[27] I may recognize that a joke is funny, though I am not in the mood to laugh, and that a stranger's mourning is appropriate even though I do not know enough about him, or have not attended enough to him, to be able to share his grief (i 1.3.4, 17–18). In such cases A approves of B's feelings even though A does not feel what B feels, and hence A's and B's feelings do not agree. Smith explains A's approval as a judgment by A about A's counterfactual reactions. The earlier examples we discussed involved the presence of a passion in myself despite its absence in the other (sympathizing with dead people); but approval sometimes involves the presence of a passion in the other and its absence in myself. In this case I judge that I would share your feelings if I considered your situation more closely.[28] Smith suggests that our approval is 'founded upon' our belief about counterfactual sympathy, as though the approval were something more than this belief. But what more could it be? Smith identified approval with awareness of sympathy (i 1.3.1, 16); since he has replaced 'sympathy' with 'conditional sympathy', we would expect the consciousness of conditional sympathy to be the approval itself.

The appeal to conditional sympathy raises questions parallel to those we raised for the claim that judgments about counterfactual passions underlie fellow-feeling. For I might know that, because of some peculiarity of mine, I would not feel sympathy if I were better informed about your situation. I might know that I am a rather cold person, or that I am rather prone to sentimental excesses, and that full information about your situation might result in indifference or in excessive displays of grief or joy. But since I know I have these defects, I might believe your reactions are about right, so that I approve of them. In this case, as in his discussion of fellow-feeling, Smith overlooks the role of evaluative judgments, as distinct from predictions about actual or counterfactual feelings. Hence he does not notice how judgments about my counterfactual feelings in your situation differ from evaluative judgments about your feelings in your situation.

To support his identification of approval with recognition of shared feelings, he relies on a parallel with belief. He argues that we cannot approve of another person's opinions without sharing them, and that therefore the same applies to sentiments.[29] This parallel with belief

---

[26] Perhaps 'appear' might be taken to refer to a mere appearance of appropriateness that A does not necessarily endorse. But Smith does not seem to recognize any gap between an appearance of appropriateness and the belief that the passion is appropriate.

[27] 'There are, indeed, some cases in which we seem to approve without any sympathy or correspondence of sentiments, and in which, consequently, the sentiment of approbation would seem to be different from the perception of this coincidence. A little attention, however, will convince us that even in these cases our approbation is ultimately founded upon a sympathy or correspondence of this kind.' (i 1.3.3, 17)

[28] '. . . we know that if we took time to consider his situation, fully and in all its parts, we should, without doubt, most sincerely sympathize with him. It is upon the consciousness of this conditional sympathy, that our approbation of his sorrow is founded, even in those cases in which that sympathy does not actually take place' (i 1.3.4, 18).

[29] 'If the same arguments which convince you convince me likewise, I necessarily approve of your conviction; and if they do not, I necessarily disapprove of it: neither can I possibly conceive that I should do the one without the other. To approve or disapprove, therefore, of the opinions of others is acknowledged, by every body, to mean no more than to observe their agreement or disagreement with our own. But this is equally the case with regard to our approbation or disapprobation of the sentiments or passions of others.' (i 1.3.2, 17)

invites two objections: (1) In some cases we can distinguish approval of another's belief from sharing the belief. If you and I have access to different evidence bearing on the truth or falsity of p, I might approve of your belief, as being reasonably based on your evidence, even if I hold a different belief, based on different evidence. (2) But even if Smith is right about some types of belief, beliefs are different from sentiments. If I take your belief that p to rest on conclusive reasons, I must also recognize that these are conclusive reasons for me to believe that p. But the connexion between recognition of reasons and the resulting attitude does not hold in the same way for sentiment; even if I recognize conclusive reasons for abandoning my anger, it does not follow that I abandon my anger. If, then, I take your moderate reaction to an offence to rest on conclusive reasons, I approve your moderate reaction, but I may not have the same reaction.

These objections to Smith's account of sympathy and of approval affect the reductive aspect of his account. He tries to avoid any appeal to evaluative beliefs about the other person, by explaining sympathy and approval as the sharing of sentiments, without reference to evaluative beliefs. His attempted explanation fails; it does not capture the ways in which approval may depart from shared sentiment. Since approval differs from shared sentiment, a correct account of approval has to refer to evaluative beliefs about the object of approval.

792. Approval and Propriety

Smith's discussion of particular cases of shared sentiments and approval exposes a tension in his position. On the one hand, he relies on the analysis of approval as shared sentiment. On the other hand, he also insists that in some cases approval comes apart from shared sentiment, so that we can have one without the other. His second line of argument creates a difficulty for the first, but it does not cause Smith to revise his analysis of approval.

His discussion of the 'propriety' of different sentiments illustrates the first line of argument. He assumes that if I am to induce other people to recognize my sentiments as appropriate for me in my situation, I have to adjust my sentiments to the type and intensity of sentiments that they are ready to feel for me in my situation. Not only must the spectator exercise imagination to find out what she would feel in the agent's situation; the agent must also adjust her feelings to those she expects a spectator to feel. Though we cannot achieve complete harmony of sentiments in this way, we can achieve enough 'for the harmony of society', so that we do not diverge too much in our response to various situations.[30]

Different ways of achieving harmony mark a difference between 'amiable' and 'respectable' virtues. The amiable virtues are those that we approve of by fellow-feeling with the unmodified responses of the other person. Gentleness and kindness involve passions that a spectator readily shares, and therefore endorses. Other virtues however, require some

---

[30] 'He must flatten, if I may be allowed to say so, the sharpness of its [sc. his passion's] natural tone, in order to reduce it to harmony and concord with the emotions of those who are about it. What they feel will indeed always be, in some respects different from what he feels, and compassion can never be exactly the same with original sorrow; because the secret consciousness that the change of situations, from which the sympathetic sentiment arises, is but imaginary, not only lowers it in degree, but, in some measure, varies it in kind, and gives it a quite different modification.' (i 1.4.7, 22)

adjustment of our original passion to the likely reactions of the spectator. The dispositions to modify passions in these ways are the respectable virtues, the ones that involve self-command.[31] When someone exercises this command beyond the ordinary level, we recognize a virtue of self-command (i 1.5.6, 25).

Smith speaks without distinction of two processes of adjustment: (1) We adjust our sentiments to those that an impartial spectator would approve of.[32] (2) We adjust them to those that an impartial spectator would feel. His account of approval explains why he does not distinguish the two processes. But his examples suggest that the two processes are different, and hence they raise further doubts about his account of approval. If A is resentful at B for B's killing A's children, it does not seem obvious that A ought to be no more resentful than S (an impartial spectator) would be. It is true that A ought to demand no worse punishment for B than S would approve, and also true that A ought not to feel more resentment than S would approve.[33] But this does not mean that A ought to feel no more resentment than S would feel.

Smith admits that S will normally feel a weaker passion, as a result of imagining what S would feel in A's situation, and so he infers that we ought not to demand exact matching of sentiments. But his account of approval implies that if A could adjust A's sentiments so that they agreed more closely with S's, A would thereby be more deserving of S's approval. This is not necessarily so; S might think it appropriate for A to feel more resentment than S would feel, and in that case S would approve of A only if A did not adjust A's sentiments to S's.

Smith points out this appropriate difference between A's and S's sentiments, in order to expose the error in the Stoic position. The Stoics (he supposes) advise us to match our emotions in bereavement to the emotions of the impartial spectator contemplating someone else's bereavement.[34] Smith rejects their advice, arguing that we ought not to feel only the sentiments that the impartial spectator would feel.[35] But this reasonable objection to the (supposed) Stoic position applies equally to Smith's account of adjustment.

The virtue of self-command, therefore, is not the disposition that Smith describes. We ought not always to adjust our sentiments to those an impartial spectator would have in our situation, or those that other people actually have towards our sentiments. Self-command requires us to adjust our sentiments to those an impartial spectator would approve. But

---

[31] '... we admire that noble and generous resentment which governs its pursuit of the greatest injuries, not by the rage which they are apt to excite in the breast of the sufferer, but by the indignation which they naturally call forth in that of the impartial spectator; which allows no word, no gesture, to escape it beyond what this more equitable sentiment would dictate; which never, even in thought, attempts any greater vengeance, nor desires to inflict any greater punishment, than what every indifferent person would rejoice to see executed' (i 1.5.4, 24).

[32] The point of Smith's emphasis on the impartiality of the spectator is explained by Raphael, *IS* 34–6.

[33] This claim about the impartial spectator rests on the assumption, so far unexamined, that this spectator's point of view is the right one for deciding whether actions and passions should be approved.

[34] ' "When our neighbour" says Epictetus, "loses his wife, or his son, there is nobody who is not sensible that this is a human calamity, a natural event altogether according to the ordinary course of things; but, when the same thing happens to ourselves, then we cry out, as if we had suffered the most dreadful misfortune. We ought, however, to remember how we were affected when this accident happened to another, and such as we were in his case, such ought we to be in our own." ' (iii 3.11, 141)

[35] 'The sense of propriety, so far from requiring us to eradicate altogether that extraordinary sensibility, which we naturally feel for the misfortunes of our nearest connexions, is always much more offended by the defect, than it ever is by the excess of that sensibility. The stoical apathy is, in such cases, never agreeable, and all the metaphysical sophisms by which it is supported can seldom serve any other purpose than to blow up the hard insensibility of a coxcomb to ten times its native impertinence.' (iii 3.14, 143)

since Smith analyses approval as shared sentiment, he does not mark the difference between a sentiment that impartial spectators approve of and a sentiment that they share.

793. Sharing of Passions v. Approval of Passions

Smith's treatment of sympathy and approval influences his description of the different passions and the ways in which they can be proper or improper. He describes them in accordance with the general principle that makes sympathy primary; hence he assumes that we judge these passions appropriate insofar as we approve of them, and that we approve of them insofar as we sympathize with them.[36] He relies on two related assumptions: (1) If we cannot easily share a given feeling, we disapprove of it. (2) If we find it easy to share a feeling, we approve of it.

His discussion of romantic love relies on the first assumption. He suggests that the lover's passions are 'but little sympathized with' (i 2.2.1, 31). This is true (we may grant), if we take 'sympathize' in Smith's sense, which requires actually sharing the lover's particular feelings. But inability to share the lover's feelings need not inhibit us in 'fellow-feeling' or in approval. Someone who listens sympathetically to a lover need not share his passion. If we recognize that lovers tend to find love all-absorbing and to be distracted from other things, and we show special consideration to the lover in these circumstances, that is a way of showing sympathy for the lover. To treat the lover's sentiments as ridiculous simply because we do not share them would be unreasonably harsh. This example also suggests that we may treat other people sympathetically because of their passions without approving of the passions. We may think they are misguided in particular attachments, but nonetheless show them special consideration. Neither reaction depends on our sharing or not sharing a particular passion, as Smith assumes.

A similar assumption underlies Smith's claim that we approve of self-command and self-restraint in the display of grief because we cannot share the feelings of those who react more strongly.[37] His explanation omits an aspect of self-command that Aristotle notices; the virtuous person bears misfortune calmly 'not because of insensibility to pain (*analgêsia*), but because he is noble and magnanimous' (*EN* 1100b32–3). As uninvolved spectators we contemplate the misfortune of other people calmly, because we are insensible to the pain of the victims. But if we thought the victims were equally insensible, we would not think they displayed any special virtue, but we might simply think they were callous. On Smith's view, however, the more callous we become towards our own misfortunes or to those of people close to us, the more other people will, and ought to, approve of us.

Perhaps Smith might appeal to the Stoics to show that we are wrong in objecting to this conclusion.[38] He expects us to admire them; but are they not callous, since they are

---

[36] 'And if we consider all the different passions of human nature, we shall find that they are regarded as decent, or indecent, just in proportion as mankind are more or less disposed to sympathize with them.' (i 2.introd.2)

[37] 'His firmness, at the same time, perfectly coincides with our insensibility. He makes no demand upon us for that more exquisite degree of sensibility which we find, and which we are mortified to find, that we do not possess. There is the most perfect correspondence between his sentiments and ours, and on that account the most perfect propriety in his behaviour.' (i 3.1.13, 48)

[38] See iii 3.11, 141, quoted in §792.

indifferent to their misfortunes? The Stoics, however, are free of passion because they do not think misfortunes are to be taken as seriously as most people take them, since they are not genuine harms to us. If they did think misfortunes are genuine harms, but did not care about them, they would be callous, and would thereby cease to be praiseworthy.[39]

Smith agrees with Aristotle's remark that callousness is not the same as self-command. Self-command presupposes an intensity of feeling that the impartial spectator lacks; nonetheless the impartial spectator approves of this self-command.[40] How are we to understand this approval, however, within Smith's analysis? We might say that the reaction of someone with self-command accords with the 'sentiment'—the evaluative judgment—of impartial spectators, but not with their 'sentiment'—their feeling. But Smith cannot consistently recognize these two senses of 'sentiment'; his analysis of moral judgments into sentiments rather than judgments requires strict adherence to the second sense, referring to emotions as distinct from judgments. Reid sees that Smith uses 'sentiment' in this second sense.[41]

Reflexion on the Stoics may suggest a different reason for approval of self-command. Someone who reacts to misfortune without self-command may easily over-estimate its importance, or may react to it in ways that damage other important aims. If parents grieving for the loss of a child neglected their other children, they would be unduly dominated by their grief. If we think domination by grief is inappropriate, we do not imply that parents ought to imitate the uninvolved spectator who is relatively indifferent to their loss; we recognize that other things besides their grief have a claim on them.

If we think of self-command in this way, we change Smith's emphasis on the reactions of the spectator to an emphasis on the situation of the agent. It is difficult to see how the reactions of someone who has not suffered the loss that a grieving parent has suffered could be a reasonable measure of the grief appropriate for a grieving parent. The judgment of appropriateness should be a judgment about that agent in that situation. By trying to reduce the judgment of appropriateness to similarity of sentiment, Smith transforms a reasonable judgment—that your reaction is inappropriate because your situation demands a different reaction—into an unreasonable judgment—that your reaction is inappropriate because it is not how I would react to your situation. Perhaps this criticism of Smith is unfair; for he observes that a spectator may sometimes approve of other people's reactions without sharing their feelings. But his account of approval does not allow him to take proper account of this observation, since he analyses approval as actual or counterfactual sharing of sentiments.

In contrast to cases where we approve of someone's sentiment without sharing it, Smith also considers cases where we share someone's sentiment but do not approve of it. We tend to sympathize with the prosperity of the rich and powerful, because we imagine ourselves

---

[39]   On the Stoics see §§191–2.

[40]   'Concerning the subject of self-command, I shall only observe further, that our admiration for the man who, under the heaviest and most unexpected misfortunes, continues to behave with fortitude and firmness, always supposes that his sensibility to those misfortunes is very great, and such as it requires a very great effort to conquer or command. The man who was altogether insensible to bodily pain, could deserve no applause from enduring the torture with the most perfect patience and equanimity. The man who had been created without the natural fear of death, could claim no merit from preserving his coolness and presence of mind in the midst of the most dreadful dangers.' (iii 3.44, 156)

[41]   Reid, EAP v 7 = H 674b–675a. See §842.

sharing the feelings of satisfaction that we (falsely) attribute to people in their situation.[42] Smith notices that this tendency is socially useful, because it supports 'the distinction of ranks, and the order of society' (i 3.2.3, 52), apart from any expectation of benefit from our superiors. But he does not approve of it without qualification; on the contrary, he mentions it as a source of the 'corruption' of our moral sentiments (i 3.3.1, 61). We go wrong because we allow our sympathy for the powerful and prosperous to create respect and admiration for them, even though such respect and admiration should be reserved for wisdom and virtue. Similarly, we treat failure and poverty with the contempt that we should reserve for vice and folly.

In contrast to Hume, Smith does not argue that because we find these qualities agreeable to us, we have a moral sentiment in favour of them. On the contrary, he denies that our sympathy with wealth and power constitutes moral approval of them. A little attention shows us the difference between our sentiments towards wealth and those towards virtue; we corrupt our moral sentiments if we do not attend to the difference.[43] But Smith's view about the nature of approval seems to make the confusion he complains of both difficult to avoid and difficult to criticize. In his view, approval of the rich and powerful simply amounts to sympathy with them, as a result of our imagining what we would feel in their situation and the sympathetic feeling that we have towards that imagined feeling. According to his view of approval, then, we approve of the rich. If our tendency to imagine ourselves enjoying being a film star is unavoidable, our tendency to approve the life of a film star must also be unavoidable; and so the 'corruption' of our moral sentiments is unavoidable as well.

Smith's example illustrates the irrationality of some sentiments that are founded on my imagining my sentiments in the agent's situation. If I am poor, I may correctly believe that if I were rich I would be in a position to satisfy all the desires that I have now, and so I may correctly infer that if I were rich and had all and only my present desires, I would make myself happy. I would be wrong, however, to infer that if I were rich I would be happy; for if I were rich, my desires would also have changed from my present desires, and being rich might not be enough to satisfy the desires I would have then.[44] My error in assuming that a rich person is happy illustrates the error in forming my attitude to someone else's situation by imagining my counterfactual attitudes in the other person's situation.

But even if I am subject to irrational attitudes formed through this imaginative activity, I need not approve of the person for whom I form this favourable feeling. To approve of the person is to make an evaluative judgment about their situation. Smith sees that our imagination may mislead us into approving of things that we ought not to approve of. But

---

[42] 'When we consider the condition of the great in those delusive colours in which the imagination is apt to paint it, it seems to be almost the abstract idea of a perfect and happy state. It is the very state which, in all our waking dreams and idle reveries, we had sketched out to ourselves as the final object of all our desires. We feel, therefore, a particular sympathy with the satisfaction of those who are in it. We favour all their inclinations, and forward all their wishes.' (i 3.2.2, 52)

[43] 'The respect which we feel for wisdom and virtue is, no doubt, different from that which we conceive for wealth and greatness; and it requires no very nice discernment to distinguish the difference. But, notwithstanding this difference, those sentiments bear a very considerable resemblance to one another. In some particular features they are, no doubt, different, but, in the general air of the countenance, they seem to be so very nearly the same that inattentive observers are very apt to mistake the one for the other.' (i 3.3.3, 62)

[44] As Hare explains it in MT, ch. 5, my failure to take account of how my desires would change if I were rich confuses my now-for-then preferences with my then-for-then preferences.

his view of approval makes it more difficult to explain why this process is misleading or avoidable; for he supposes that the mistaken sentiments formed on the basis of imagination constitute approval. His attempt to avoid any reference to evaluative judgment, as distinct from shared sentiments, is the common element in several of his questionable claims about sentiments and approval.

794. Desert

Smith's account of desert rests on his account of approval. In his view, we attribute desert to those towards whom we approve gratitude or resentment.[45] Since approval is sympathy, understood as similarity of sentiment, the sense of desert must also be explained by reference to sympathy. Approval of punishment, therefore, must be a sympathetic feeling towards those who feel resentment towards the offender. If we share the gratitude of the recipients when we imagine ourselves in their situation, we approve of their reaction, and thereby take the agent to deserve reward.

This account seems to be open to counter-examples. If a gangster pleases his wife by giving her an expensive car that he has bought with the money gained by fraud, we might be moved by the gratitude of the wife so that we tend to sympathize with it (in Smith's sense). But might we not still disapprove of the gangster and of his action, and take it to deserve punishment rather than reward?

Smith deals with some counter-examples of this sort by insisting that a judgment about desert requires not only approval of the consequences of the action, but also of the motives of the agent. It is not enough, therefore, to sympathize with the wife's gratitude; we must also approve of the gangster's motive in giving his wife the car. In this case, Smith might argue, we disapprove of the gangster's criminal motive, because we sympathize with the resentment of his victims.

This resort to the agent's motive, however, does not answer the basic objection to Smith's analysis. The gangster's motive is dishonest (since he does not mind buying presents for his wife with the profits of his criminal activities), but nonetheless benevolent towards a particular person. If the bad effects of his criminal actions on other people are relatively indirect (he engages in fraud, but not in murder), we might find it hard not to share the favourable sentiment of his wife (or other beneficiaries of his largesse), and hard to share the imagined resentment of his victims (who might not even know they are being cheated and so might not be resentful). In that case our reaction to his motive, according to Smith's account of approval, is approval, and so we must regard him as deserving of reward.

This account ignores the possibility of recognizing that we sympathize more with the beneficiaries than the victims and so find ourselves sympathizing with the agent's motive, but we still disapprove of it, because we judge the motive to be inappropriate, and therefore judge the agent to deserve punishment. This possibility is not open in Smith's account, given

---

[45] 'Gratitude and resentment, therefore, are the sentiments which most immediately and directly prompt us to reward and punish. To us, therefore, he must appear to deserve reward, who appears to be the proper and approved object of gratitude; and he to deserve punishment, who appears to be that of resentment.' (ii 1.1.7, 69)

the connexions he sees between judgments of desert, approval, and sympathy. His remarks about the propriety of the agent's motive do not allow judgments of desert to depart from sympathetic reactions. But since our judgments seem to depart from sympathetic reactions, his account does not capture judgments of desert.

The weakness of Smith's account appears in judgments of desert in cases where the agent has killed an innocent victim. Smith has to rely on his previous account of sympathy with the plight of the dead (ii 1.2.5, 70–1). If A has made B suffer, we have some genuine suffering in B to sympathize with, but if A has killed B, B is no longer (we may assume) suffering. Hence we have to imagine the suffering we would feel if we were both dead and subject to the pains we would suffer if we were alive and were (say) being dismembered. Since we attribute this suffering to the dead B, we also attribute to B the resentment that we imagine B feeling, even though we believe B feels nothing of the sort. This explanation of approval through sympathy commits Smith to the view that our belief that A deserves punishment is based on a true belief about B's suffering if B is alive, but on a false belief if B is dead. Why should we not suppose, then, that A is more deserving of punishment if A does not kill B than if A kills B? For since it is easier to sympathize with B if we know B is alive and suffering than if we believe B is dead and incapable of suffering, we apparently ought to sympathize with B more if we believe B is alive than if we believe B is dead. This would be a strange conclusion about desert. Smith implies that our attitude towards the dead is based on a basically inconsistent and irrational exercise of imagination. If we believe our attitudes are consistent and rational, we cannot accept Smith's analysis of approval.

So far we have ignored Smith's restriction of the people whose sympathetic reactions count for determining desert. Sometimes he attributes the relevant sympathetic reactions to 'every reasonable man', and to 'everybody who knows of it' (ii 1.2.3, 70), as though these were the same people. Unless everyone, or every reasonable person, sympathizes with the gratitude of the gangster's wife, we cannot say that the gangster deserves reward.

But how can we tell whether everyone sympathizes with a particular reaction? The sympathetic reactions of other people who know about an offence may vary in accordance with the different beliefs and emotions of these people. Why ought we to follow the reactions of everyone, as Smith suggests, or even of most people? Why not follow the reactions of the people we most often have to deal with, even if other people react differently?

Perhaps Smith is not really thinking of everyone's reaction, but only of the reaction of an impartial spectator. Instead of considering most people, or a specific group of people, perhaps we should consider the reactions of a spectator whose personal concerns and interests are not directly involved with those of the agent or the victim. But this appeal to the impartial spectator does not help us to determine our own reaction. Some spectators who are impartial in this sense may be callous, while others may be especially susceptible to certain kinds of appeals to their emotions. These different impartial spectators will react differently; hence they do not provide a guide for our reactions.

Could Smith answer by substituting the reactions of the 'reasonable man' for those of the impartial spectator? Without some explanation of 'reasonable', we are none the wiser about what his reactions would be. If the explanation includes the reasonable man's tendency to follow correct evaluative judgments, it relies on an account of evaluative judgments that Smith has so far not provided.

795. Justice and the Impartial Spectator

The impartial spectator has a special role in explaining the special attitudes that are connected with justice. If a requirement is part of justice, our performance of it can legitimately be demanded, we can be compelled to perform it, and we are appropriately punished for violating it. Justice requires us to avoid harm to our neighbour, though it does not require us to refrain from vigorous competition, or to be beneficent.[46] The morally significant asymmetry between failure to benefit others and actual harming of them is not clear from the point of view of self-love, but it is clear from the point of view of the impartial spectator. Since an individual wants to adjust his attitude to himself to the attitude of the impartial spectator, he curbs his tendency to look at himself from the point of view of self-love. I recognize that other people will never take me as seriously, in comparison to other people, as I take myself, and my knowledge of their less inflated view of me helps me to take a less inflated view of myself. This change of my perspective on myself helps me to see myself as others see me, and thereby to make the appropriate room for other people in my attitude to myself.[47]

How can reference to the impartial spectator produce this change in perspective? If S is an impartial spectator of A's conduct, S's sympathy or lack of sympathy with A results from S's imaginative placing of S in A's situation. Smith suggests that when S considers A competing against B, and so making B's condition worse relative to A's, S sympathizes with A, but when S considers A injuring B by violating the demands of justice, S sympathizes with B rather than A. S recognizes that if S were in A's position, S would care about A more than about B, and that if S were in B's position, S would care about B more than about A. Hence S is subject to sympathy with A in A's pleasure at getting the better of B, and subject to sympathy with B in B's pain at losing to A. Apparently the relative intensity of A's pleasure and B's pain should determine the sympathy that predominates in S's attitude to A and B. It is not clear why the difference between A's successfully competing against B and A's unjustly harming B determines whether S's predominant sympathy is with A or with B.

Smith's position would be stronger if we also knew that (1) S believes A's injustice to B is a more serious harm than A's succeeding at B's expense, and that (2) S's sympathy is guided by this belief. But if we know only that S is an impartial spectator, we cannot take either of these things for granted about S. Different impartial spectators may have different views about the relative badness of injustice and competitive loss, and may be influenced by their evaluative judgments to different degrees.

---

[46] 'There can be no proper motive for hurting our neighbour, there can be no incitement to do evil to another, which mankind will go along with, except just indignation for evil which that other has done to us. To disturb his happiness merely because it stands in the way of our own, to take from him what is of real use to him merely because it may be of equal or of more use to us, or to indulge in this manner, at the expense of other people, the natural preference which every man has for his happiness above that of other people, is what no impartial spectator can go along with.' (ii 2.2.1, 82)

[47] 'But though the ruin of our neighbour may affect us much less than a very small misfortune of our own, we must not ruin him to prevent that small misfortune, nor even to prevent our own ruin. We must, here, as in all other cases, view ourselves not so much according to that light in which we may naturally appear to ourselves, as according to that in which we naturally appear to others. . . . When he views himself in the light in which he is conscious that others will view him, he sees that to them he is but one of the multitude in no respect better than any other in it. If he would act so as that the impartial spectator may enter into the principles of his conduct, which is what of all things he has the greatest desire to do, he must, upon this, as upon all other occasions, humble the arrogance of his self-love, and bring it down to something which other men can go along with.' (ii 2.2.1, 82–3)

Why is it important to view ourselves from an impartial point of view, and what does this point of view consist in? Should we adopt it because it adjusts our views to those of others, or because it adjusts our views to reasonable views? These two reasons for adopting it are not equivalent; for whether or not a particular group of other people holds reasonable views depends on how reasonable these people are. It is not clear that their mere impartiality—not taking the interest that we take in our good—makes them reasonable.

If, then, we seek to adjust our sentiments to reasonable views, not simply to the views of others, we need more than impartiality. Admittedly, impartiality is relevant to the just and reasonable point of view, since this point of view is not distorted by self-interest. In speaking of distortion we assume that it is possible to form a true view, and that we can appeal to this true view to correct distortions. Smith is right, therefore, to believe that the impartial spectator, whom he also calls the 'impartial judge' (ii 2.2.4, 85), is important. But impartiality is not enough for reasonableness. Some spectators who are not moved by their own self-interest may nonetheless be misanthropic and malevolent towards the interests of the people they consider; others may be merely indifferent. If the reasonable judge should be impartially concerned for the interests of those affected, disinterested malevolence or indifference does not make us reasonable judges. When Smith assumes that impartial spectators approve of justice and of respect for others, the views he attributes to them do not follow from his account of sympathy and approval.

In Smith's view, however, these objections overlook the fact that our judgments about merit and demerit display precisely the sort of irregularity that we ought to expect if his analysis is correct. We suppose that our approval of other people rests on a general principle about their good or bad intentions; it seems unfair to blame one person more than another if their intentions are the same.[48] But in fact our judgments about praise and blame violate this principle; for some of our reactions do not simply reflect our views about the agents' will and intentions, but are also affected by the outcomes of their intentions. We think more highly (say) of the Duke of Wellington than of some other general who was just as able, but who happened to live in a time of peace between Britain and its neighbours, and we think more highly of Dietrich Bonhoeffer than we think of some other Christian who was just as brave, but who did not live under a tyranny. Similarly, we punish attempted murder less severely than successful attempts, even though the intention to murder may have been just the same.

Smith suggests that his analysis explains why we violate a maxim that we profess to accept. In his view, our tendency to deviate from the maxim that ties praise to intention supports a sentimentalist account of approval, and refutes an account relying on unreduced evaluative judgment. If evaluative judgment determined our approval, we would not deviate from the judgment about praise and intention as often as we actually do. But if shared sentiments determine approval, the 'irregularity' (as Smith calls it, ii 3.introd.6, 93) of our judgments is intelligible. For when we think of Wellington's successes, our sympathy is engaged, and influences our readiness to praise him; conversely, when we think of the

---

[48] 'To the intention or affection of the heart . . . to the propriety or impropriety, to the beneficence or hurtfulness of the design, all praise or blame, all approbation or disapprobation, of any kind, which can justly be bestowed upon any action, must ultimately belong.' (ii 3.introd.3, 93)

victim of the successful murderer, our sympathy is aroused by suffering, and influences us in blaming the murderer. If the intentions were unfulfilled, there would be nothing to excite our sympathy. Hence (Smith infers) the variations in our judgments about praise and blame reflect the operations of sympathy, rather than adherence to an abstract rational principle.

We need not draw this conclusion. Instead we might doubt Smith's claim that we accept the simple maxim that he mentions. Reflexion on the cases he mentions suggests that 'approbation or disapprobation of any kind, which can justly be bestowed on any action' does not depend entirely on the agent's intention. We might, for instance, distinguish approval of the agent from approval of the agent's actions. We might also suggest some discrimination between different types of approval of the agent for different things; judgments about the character of agents might not always accord with judgments about what should be done to agents on the basis of their actions. We might also want to separate questions about whether praise and blame are justified from questions about when it is appropriate to express praise and blame, or appropriate to express them through the state's mechanisms of reward and punishment. Once we consider action by the state to enforce judgments of merit or demerit, we introduce many epistemic and practical questions that may reasonably affect the application of our evaluative judgments.[49]

These cases need not result from 'irregularity of sentiments'. They may be reasonable exceptions to, or qualifications of, the rule of measuring approval and disapproval by intention. We can see that they are not random or ad hoc exceptions if we consider why they are reasonable provisions. The relevant kinds of approval reflect evaluative judgment rather than irregular sentiments.

If we rely on evaluative judgments, they may guide us to a change of mind about whether a given exception to the rule about intentions is reasonable. As Reid remarks, we learn to distinguish the reactions that are appropriate for responsible agents from those that are not.[50] Children may be angry at tools or animals because they are frustrated or disappointed, and in some circumstances it is difficult for any of us to separate frustration, disappointment, grief, envy, spite, and related emotions from the appropriate reactions to responsible agents. This may explain our failure to distinguish the different degrees of responsibility underlying manslaughter and murder (ii 3.2.8, 103).

In such cases, we may agree with Smith's view that our judgments are influenced by sentiments that are strictly irrelevant to judgments of responsibility. But if we can form judgments that diverge from our sentiments, these judgments are not simply the products of our sentiments. If we have formed these judgments, but our sentiments have not changed to match them, we may find that we do not approve of our sentiments because they do not match our judgments. Approval, therefore, does not consist simply in sharing sentiments.

---

[49] Smith recognizes some of these: '. . . if the baseness of the thought which had given birth to no action, seemed in the eyes of the world as much to call aloud for vengeance as the baseness of the action, every court of judicature would become a real inquisition. There would be no safety for the most innocent and circumspect conduct. Bad wishes, bad views, bad designs, might still be suspected; and while these excited the same indignation with bad conduct, while bad intentions were as much resented as bad actions, they would equally expose the person to punishment and resentment.' (ii 3.3.2, 105)

[50] See Reid, §849.

796. Being Praised and Being Praiseworthy

Smith does not want his claims about the impartial spectator to suggest to us that all we really care about, or ought to care about, is approval and praise by others.[51] He recognizes that we care about deserving the praise of others and ourselves, not simply about being praised, and he approves of this concern with praiseworthiness.[52] How does desire for praiseworthiness, in contrast to mere praise, fit Smith's views about sympathy and approval?

In his view, our approval is directed towards the character and conduct of others (iii 2.3, 114). When we begin to sympathize with the character and conduct that they sympathize with, we care about having this character and conduct. To identify the appropriate character, we must look at ourselves from the point of view of others.[53] The actual praise of other people confirms that we have been right in our belief about what is praiseworthy, and so it is welcome to us for that reason; but it is praiseworthiness that primarily concerns us. When I sympathize with the sentiments of others, I sympathize with their sentiments as including some belief about the object of their sentiments. If you are gratified by the company of a friend, your pleasure is pleasure in the company of a genuine friend, not in someone who is pretending to be your friend. And so, if I sympathize with your reactions, and I want to be the sort of person you sympathize with, I will approve of being a genuine friend rather than a pretender. Hence if I want the character and conduct that other people sympathize with and praise, I want to be that sort of person, not simply to be praised. In this case my sympathy includes the intentional object (a real friend, a genuinely generous person) of their sympathy.

But Smith does not make it is clear why sympathy with others must extend to the intentional object of their sympathy. People also approve of people who in fact appear to be friends but are not real friends (though they do not approve of them under this description), and so we must apparently sympathize with this reaction to undetected pretenders. If, then, we sympathize with those whom other people sympathize with, why should we not want to be undetected pretenders? It is not obvious from Smith's account why sympathy must lead an impartial spectator to approve of the genuine character rather than the undetected pretender.

Smith concedes this point. He does not maintain that we have some reason to prefer praiseworthiness over praise. He takes it to be a brute fact that we prefer it. The desire to be praiseworthy is more beneficial to society than the simple desire to be praised would be, but individuals themselves are not moved by the good of society; their preference rests on no further reason.[54]

[51] In a letter Smith explains one of his aims in iii 2: 'You will observe that it is intended both to confirm my doctrine that our judgments concerning our own conduct have always a reference to the sentiments of some other being, and to show that, notwithstanding this, real magnanimity and conscious virtue can support itself under the disapprobation of all mankind.' (Letter to Gilbert Elliot = *Corresp.* #40)

[52] 'The love of praise-worthiness is by no means derived altogether from the love of praise. These two principles, though they resemble one another, though they are connected, and often blended with one another, are yet, in many respects, distinct and independent of one another.' (iii 2.2, 114)

[53] 'We must at least believe ourselves to be admirable for what they are admirable. But, in order to attain this satisfaction, we must become the impartial spectators of our own character and conduct. We must endeavour to view them with the eyes of other people, or as other people are likely to view them.' (iii 2.3, 114)

[54] 'Nature . . . has endowed him, not only with a desire of being approved of, but with a desire of being what ought to be approved of; or of being what he himself approves of in other men. The first desire could only have made him wish to appear to be fit for society. The second was necessary in order to render him anxious to be really fit.' (iii 2.7, 117)

If people generally prefer praiseworthiness over praise, what is it that they prefer? We might assume that a praiseworthy action or trait is one that deserves to be praised whether or not it is praised; this is the conception of the honestum that Price derives from Cicero.[55] If we assume this, we assume that other people may be mistaken in the kinds of traits that they select for praise. If we want to be praised for being praiseworthy, we want to be praised for the traits that people ought to praise. Sometimes Smith seems to accept this evaluative conception of praiseworthiness; he describes it by reference to 'what, we imagine, ought to be the judgment of others' and to a 'fair and impartial spectator'.[56] We might suppose that Smith attributes to us a moral judgment about what the spectator ought to judge or about what a fair person would judge. If that were what he meant, reference to the impartial spectator would not give a reductive analysis of moral judgment, since a moral judgment would be part of the analysis.

Smith, however, sometimes presents a reductive analysis. He suggests that we find satisfaction in knowing that we are praiseworthy because we possess the qualities that other people praise, whether or not they actually praise us for having them.[57] If, therefore, people normally select (say) aggressiveness for praise, and they praise me because they mistakenly believe I am aggressive, then, according to Smith, aggressiveness is praiseworthy, but I am praised without being praiseworthy. He does not ask whether people ought to praise or to condemn aggressiveness. Nor does he give us any grounds for deciding this question one way or the other. Hence he distinguishes (1) being praised from (2) being praiseworthy by distinguishing (1) what people actually praise on a particular occasion, given their beliefs about this occasion, from (2) what they intend to praise. His analysis of praiseworthiness is non-normative insofar as it mentions only what people praise and would praise, not what they ought to praise.

797. A Non-normative Account of the Impartial Spectator

Is Smith's account of the impartial spectator equally non-normative? He distinguishes three points of view: (1) The actual views of other people. (2) The outlook of an individual and

---

[55] See Price, RPQM 62, discussed in §819.

[56] 'Whatever judgment we can form concerning them [sc. our own sentiments and motives], accordingly, must always bear some secret reference, either to what are, or to what, upon a certain condition, would be, or to what, we imagine, ought to be the judgment of others. We endeavour to examine our own conduct as we imagine any other fair and impartial spectator would examine it. If, upon placing ourselves in his situation, we thoroughly enter into all the passions and motives which influenced it, we approve of it, by sympathy with the approbation of this supposed equitable judge.' (iii 1.2, 108–9)

[57] '. . . it often gives real comfort to reflect, that though no praise should actually be bestowed upon us, our conduct, however, has been such as to deserve it, and has been in every respect suitable to those measures and rules by which praise and approbation are naturally and commonly bestowed. We are pleased, not only with praise, but with having done what is praise-worthy. . . . The man who is conscious to himself that he has exactly observed those measures of conduct which experience informs him are generally agreeable, reflects with satisfaction on the propriety of his own behaviour. When he views it in the light in which the impartial spectator would view it, he thoroughly enters into all the motives which influenced it. He looks back upon every part of it with pleasure and approbation, and though mankind should never be acquainted with what he has done, he regards himself, not so much according to the light in which they actually regard him, as according to that in which they would regard him if they were better informed' (iii 2.5, 115–16).

fallible spectator, 'the supposed impartial and well-informed spectator . . . the man within the breast, the great judge and arbiter of their conduct' (iii 2.32, 130). (3) The outlook of a properly impartial spectator who is free of these errors. We need to distinguish the second from the third point of view, because the 'man within the breast' is not always a properly impartial spectator. He does not always keep his attention firmly on the praiseworthy, but is sometimes influenced by the actual praise and blame of other people, and so he sometimes identifies the praiseworthy with what is actually praised.[58] In contrast to this judge who is easily confused by what people actually praise, the properly impartial spectator concentrates on the praiseworthy.

The properly impartial spectator approves of the traits that people praise in general and intend to praise in particular cases. Even if generosity is one of the traits that we praise, we may nonetheless praise Croesus for generosity even though he is not really generous; we are taken in by the scale of his charitable contributions and we overlook the fact that he contributes only to causes that advance his own schemes. The truly impartial spectator would not be dazzled by Croesus' multi-millions in gifts, but would see that Croesus really lacks the trait that we praise. Similarly, he would notice that the widow giving her mite is really generous; he would not be misled by the small size of her gift. In this respect, he approves of praiseworthy traits, but not necessarily of traits that on particular occasions are praised by misguided people.

Nonetheless, Smith's account of the properly impartial spectator is basically non-normative. This spectator does not ask himself whether the traits that people generally praise really ought to be praised. He corrects ignorant and weak people who are easily misled about whether someone is really generous. But he does not ask himself if people are generally ignorant or weak in their selection of qualities for praise. He identifies the qualities that people intend to praise, but does not ask whether these qualities ought to be praised. If the moral point of view asks whether these qualities ought to be praised, Smith's impartial spectator does not take the moral point of view.

The limitations in the normative judgments of the impartial spectator raise difficulties for Smith's account of conscience. He identifies approval by one's own conscience with 'the testimony of the supposed impartial spectator' (iii 3.1), and he compares the impartial point of view of conscience, correcting our initial view of our actions, with the perceptual point of view that corrects our initial distorting perspective.[59] This comparison,

---

[58] 'The supposed impartial spectator of our conduct seems to give his opinion in our favour with fear and hesitation; when that of all the real spectators, when that of all those with whose eyes and from whose station he endeavours to consider it, is unanimously and violently against us. In such cases, this demigod within the breast appears, like the demigods of the poets, though partly of immortal, yet partly too of mortal extraction. When his judgments are steadily and firmly directed by the sense of praise-worthiness and blame-worthiness, he seems to act suitably to his divine extraction: But when he suffers himself to be astonished and confounded by the judgments of ignorant and weak man, he discovers his connexion with mortality, and appears to act suitably, rather to the human, than to the divine, part of his origin.' (iii 2.32, 131)

[59] 'As to the eye of the body, objects appear great or small, not so much according to their real dimensions, as according to the nearness or distance of their situation; so do they likewise to what may be called the natural eye of the mind: and we remedy the defects of both these organs pretty much in the same manner. . . . I can form a just comparison between those great objects and the little objects around me, in no other way, than by transporting myself, at least in fancy, to a different station, from whence I can survey both at nearly equal distances, and thereby form some judgment of their real proportions. . . . In the same manner, to the selfish and original passions of human nature, the loss or gain of a very small interest of our own, appears to be of vastly more importance, excites a much

however, raises a question that Smith does not clearly answer. We view or imagine things from different points of view because we suppose that our current angle of vision is likely to mislead us about the real size and shape of something; hence Smith speaks of 'their real proportions'. But is the same true in the moral case? Smith suggests that we are looking for 'a proper comparison' of other people's interest with our own, and that the impartial point of view leads us to this proper comparison. Does he mean that the impartial point of view, as he defines it, constitutes moral rightness? This is not true of the visual case; we imagine or view things from different points of view because we think they have a real size that we will grasp more readily by taking these different points of view. Similarly, we think we can explain why the different points of view are better at detecting the real size. If Smith means that the impartial point of view is good at detecting what is really right, he needs some argument. It is not obvious that a true prediction of the sentiments of an impartial spectator is a correct judgment of what is really right.[60]

According to Butler, conscience is a superior principle that claims authority; it claims to judge by 'rational' rather than 'animal' strength (as Reid puts it). Smith cannot allow this division between rational and animal strength; his conception of approval dissolves rational strength into animal strength. To approve of someone else's sentiments is to share those sentiments, not to judge that the other person is right. Hence, approval by the impartial spectator must be a sentiment evoked by consideration of the reactions of different people. If approval is a rational judgment about the rightness or wrongness of an action, we might have good reason to stick to it despite other people's disagreement, if we are right to distrust their judgment. But if we take Smith's view, we cannot understand conscience in this way, and therefore we cannot explain why it might be right to disagree with other people's views. Smith's attempt to capture Butler's claims about conscience within his own conception of approval is no more successful than Hutcheson's attempt to capture them within his conception of the moral sense.[61]

---

more passionate joy or sorrow, a much more ardent desire or aversion, than the greatest concern of another with whom we have no particular connexion. Before we can make any proper comparison of those opposite interests, we must change our position. We must view them, neither from our own place nor yet from his, neither with our own eyes nor yet with his, but from the place and with the eyes of a third person, who has no particular connexion with either, and who judges with impartiality between us.' (iii 3.2–3, 135) Cf. Hume, *T* iii 3.1.16 (discussed in §762), and RM ad loc.

[60] Smith's use of the impartial spectator to perform the functions of conscience is discussed by Raphael, *IS* 36–42.

[61] See §715. See also Stewart, *PAMP* ii 7.2 = Hamilton, 330–1 = Reeder, *OMS* 123: '. . . Mr Smith's theory . . . confounds the *means* or *expedients* by which nature enables us to correct our moral judgments, with the principles in our constitution to which our moral judgments owe their origin. . . . The intention of such expedients . . . is merely to obtain a just and fair view of circumstances; and after this view has been obtained, the question still remains, what constitutes the obligation upon me to act in a particular manner? In answer to this question it is said that, from recollecting my own judgments in similar cases in which I was concerned, I infer in what light my conduct will appear to society; that there is an exquisite satisfaction annexed to mutual sympathy; and that, in order to obtain this satisfaction, I accommodate my conduct, not to my own feelings, but to those of my fellow-creatures. Now I acknowledge that this may account for a man's assuming the appearance of virtue . . . ; but in the important concerns of life, I apprehend there is something more,—for when I have once satisfied myself with respect to the conduct which an impartial judge would approve of, I feel that this conduct is *right* for me, and that I am under a moral obligation to put it in practice.' Stewart is wrong to attribute a hedonist motive to Smith's agent. But he is right to argue that we can recognize the question about rightness as a distinct question from the question about the reactions of the impartial spectator.

798. The Sense of Duty

The section of *TMS* that we have been discussing (Section iii) is entitled 'Of the sense of duty'.[62] Here Smith tries to accommodate the features of moral judgment that may appear to conflict with sentimentalism.[63] He introduces the impartial spectator in order to separate moral judgments from the expressions of feelings that we share with particular other people. The 'man within the breast' is a 'great judge and arbiter' who does not simply follow the reactions of other people. In being guided by this 'great judge', we try to follow the impartial spectator, since this is the point of view we try to achieve, even though a particular person's conscience is liable to be unduly swayed by the views of particular other people.

The impartiality of the great judge helps us to reach the moral point of view, which corrects the errors of our egocentric perspective. Smith improves on Hume's account (in the *Second Inquiry*) of the sentiment of humanity, by distinguishing it from the feeling of benevolence. He notices that benevolence is too weak and too partial to explain our moral judgments. If I think of the suffering of 100 million unknown people, it will affect me less, even if I am benevolent, than the amputation of my little finger. But our moral sentiments are not limited by our benevolence.[64] When we follow the impartial spectator, we act justly and fairly, without inappropriate bias towards the interest of any of the people affected by our action. This is the point of view that Hutcheson mistakenly traced to the sentiment of benevolence. It incorporates the attitudes that persuaded Butler that conscience could not be identified with benevolence.

Reference to the impartial spectator and his reactions explains the origin of moral rules and principles. The spectator does not make moral judgments relying primarily on moral principles or rules, but his sympathy is the both the basis for our moral judgments and the criterion of their correctness. A moral rule is a prediction that this kind of action excites the relevant reactions in an impartial observer.[65]

---

[62] This section was extensively revised in the 6th edn. of *TMS*. See RM, Introd. 43.

[63] In iii 5.5 Smith distinguishes his view from Hume's claims about reflexive approval: 'Our moral faculties are by no means, as some have pretended, upon a level in this respect with the other faculties and appetites of our nature, endowed with no more right to restrain these last, than these last are to restrain them. No other faculty or principle of action judges of any other. Love does not judge of resentment, nor resentment of love. Those two passions may be opposite to one another, but cannot, with any propriety, be said to approve or disapprove of one another. But it is the peculiar office of those faculties now under our consideration to judge, to bestow censure or applause upon all the other principles of our nature.' Cf. Hume, §780.

[64] 'When our passive feelings are almost always so sordid and so selfish, how comes it that our active principles should often be so generous and so noble? . . . It is not the soft power of humanity, it is not that feeble spark of benevolence which Nature has lighted up in the human heart, that is thus capable of counteracting the strongest impulses of self-love. . . . It is reason, principle, conscience, the inhabitant of the breast, the man within, the great judge and arbiter of our conduct. It is he who, whenever we are about to act so as to affect the happiness of others, calls to us, with a voice capable of astonishing the most presumptuous of our passions, that we are but one of the multitude, in no respect better than any other in it; and that when we prefer ourselves so shamefully and so blindly to others, we become the proper objects of resentment, abhorrence, and execration. It is from him only that we learn the real littleness of ourselves, and of whatever relates to ourselves, and the natural misrepresentations of self-love can be corrected only by the eye of this impartial spectator. . . . It is not the love of our neighbour, it is not the love of mankind, which upon many occasions prompts us to the practice of those divine virtues. It is a stronger love, a more powerful affection, which generally takes place upon such occasions; the love of what is honourable and noble, of the grandeur, and dignity, and superiority of our own characters.' (iii 3.4, 137)

[65] 'It is thus that the general rules of morality are formed. They are ultimately founded upon experience of what, in particular instances, our moral faculties, our natural sense of merit and propriety, approve, or disapprove of. We do not

The process that Smith describes is important in the formation of sentiments, including moral sentiments. He is right to emphasize the significance of our capacity to sympathize with the reactions of others, and especially of others who have no particular favourable emotion towards us. This process allows us to escape from being dominated by the 'moral stupidity' in which (as George Eliot puts it) we take 'the world as an udder to feed our supreme selves'.[66] The capacity to imagine the reactions of others and to react in accordance with their reactions affects our ability to take the moral point of view and to react in accordance with it. But Smith also claims that to take the moral point of view is simply to judge and to react in accordance with the reactions of the impartial spectator. Does he justify this stronger claim?

An answer to this question depends on the description of the impartial spectator. In describing him as impartial, Smith abstracts from the attachment to a particular person or particular people that is characteristic of all of us in some of our reactions. This abstraction, however, does not give us an adequate description of the spectator; he might lack particular attachments, but still might be cruel or callous or thoughtless or ignorant. We have to add, therefore, that he is well-informed and sympathetic to an ordinary degree. Smith suggests that if we leave him with our sympathetic reactions and remove our interested and partial reactions, we have found the moral point of view.

To see whether Smith is right, we need to return to his initial description of sympathetic reactions. No doubt we have some non-moral sympathetic reactions, but these do not seem enough to generate moral judgments. Smith stretches them so that they approach moral judgments, but only because he assumes irrational sympathies—with the sufferings of dead people, for instance—to match the moral judgments that he tries to accommodate. He cannot, within the reductive aims of his argument, explain our sympathy with the dead by appeal to our judgment that it is bad for us to be dead; hence he has to appeal to irrational sympathy based on inconsistent assumptions (that someone is dead and so feels nothing, but yet feels something).

Sympathy as Smith conceives it is different from sympathy as we normally conceive it because it leaves out any moral element. If I sympathize with the sufferings of an innocent victim of a cruel practical joke, my sympathy rests partly on the thought that the victim did not deserve to suffer in this way, and that the practical jokers had no right to do what they did; I do not think simply about what the victim suffers, but also about how the suffering came about. Our ordinary sympathetic reactions seem to be based on judgments about welfare, harm, desert, and fairness; hence they seem to rest on moral rules and principles. Smith cannot allow this sort of sympathy to the impartial spectator; for if the reactions of the spectator rest on moral judgments, they cannot be, as he claims, the foundation of moral rules. But if Smith sticks consistently to non-moral sympathy, he does not explain the scope of our moral judgments.[67]

---

originally approve or condemn particular actions; because, upon examination, they appear to be agreeable or inconsistent with a certain general rule. The general rule, on the contrary, is formed, by finding from experience, that all actions of a certain kind, or circumstanced in a certain manner, are approved or disapproved of. . . . His detestation of this crime, it is evident, would arise instantaneously and antecedent to his having formed to himself any such general rule. The general rule, on the contrary, which he might afterwards form, would be founded upon the detestation which he felt necessarily arise in his own breast, at the thought of this, and every other particular action of the same kind.' (iii 4.8, 159)

[66] George Eliot, *Middlemarch*, ch. 21 end (Norton 146).
[67] Some similar questions arise about Firth's adaptation of Smith's position in 'Observer'.

The moral limitations of the impartial spectator cast doubt on Smith's implicit answer to Balguy's attack on Hutcheson's sentimentalism. According to Balguy, sentimentalism is open to the objections about mutability that Cudworth urges against Hobbes. In Reid's view, Smith is also open to these objections.[68] If a true moral judgment is a true prediction of the reactions of an impartial spectator, a change in these reactions would make different moral judgments true, and hence would change what is morally right. But we do not believe that if impartial spectators became more callous, or more rational (so that they ceased to sympathize with dead people), moral rightness and wrongness would change too. Smith, therefore, does not answer all Balguy's objections to Hutcheson's attempt to explain praiseworthiness by reference to actual praise. He does not avoid the main charge of eliminating judgments about desert in favour of predictive judgments.[69]

A closely related objection of Balguy's, developed by Price, alleges that Hutcheson fails to capture the character of obligation by reducing it to motivation; the existence of an obligation implies the existence of a reason, but facts about motivation do not by themselves provide the relevant sort of reason. Smith tries to answer this sort of criticism; by devoting a whole section to the sense of duty, he tries to show that his reduction of the sense of duty vindicates our belief in duties and obligations. Nonetheless, the main rationalist criticism still applies. Kames argues that this criticism of Hutcheson and Hume also applies to Smith's use of sympathy.[70] Reid agrees with the criticism.[71] According to Kames and Reid, we take ourselves to be morally obliged insofar as we believe we have a specific sort of reason; our moral judgment (in Butler's terms) has authority.[72]

Smith's distinction between the praised and the praiseworthy is meant to accommodate Butler's claims about authority. But his resources for accommodating them are too limited to answer reasonable criticisms. For we can recognize not only a mere logical possibility, but also a genuine moral question about whether the reactions of the impartial spectator are justified, and whether they ought to be obeyed. Since these reactions are subject to moral criticism, they cannot wholly constitute moral judgment. Smith criticizes Hutcheson's

---

[68] '. . . it is obvious that according to [Smith's] system there is no fixed standard of virtue at all; it depends not upon our own actions but upon the tone of our passions, which in different men is different from constitution. Nor does it solely depend upon our own passions, but also upon the sympathetic passions of others, which may be different in different persons, or in the same person at different times. Nor is there any standard according to which either the emotions of the actor or the sympathy of the spectator is to be measured; all that is required is that they be in harmony or concord. It is evident that the ultimate measure and standard of right and wrong in human conduct, according to this system of sympathy, is not any fixed judgment grounded upon truth or upon the dictates of a well-informed conscience, but the variable opinions and passions of men. So that we may apply to this system what Cicero says of the Epicurean . . .'. Reid continues by quoting Cic. *Fin.* ii 22. (Reid, 'Sketch' 81). Cf. Ross, *LAS* 192. Reid's criticism of Smith is discussed by Duncan and Baird, 'Reid on Smith', answered by Norton and Stewart-Robertson, 'Reid on Smith'.

[69] On Hutcheson and Balguy see §656.

[70] 'Neither is the author of the treatise upon human nature more successful [sc. than Hutcheson], when he endeavours to resolve the moral sense into pure sympathy. According to this author, there is no more in morality, but approving or disapproving an action, after we discover, by reflexion, that it tends to the good or hurt of society. This would be by far too faint a passion to control our irregular appetites and passions.' (Kames, *EPMNR* ii 3 = Moran32 = SB 927) Kames's reference to the faintness of the moral sense, as Hume and Smith conceive it, does not identify the main issue. A sentimentalist might answer that it is arbitrary of Kames to assume that the moral sense cannot be strong enough to motivate us on enough occasions to ensure good behaviour.

[71] 'I have always thought Dr S-'s system of sympathy wrong. It is indeed only a refinement of the selfish system; and I think your arguments against it are solid. But you have smitten with a friendly hand, which does not break the head; and your compliment to the author I highly approve of.' (Reid, Letter to Kames, 30 Oct. 1778 = H 92)

[72] Kames goes on (Moran 33 = SB 931) to criticize Butler on authority. His criticism is unwarranted. See §720.

appeal to a sense on these grounds, but his resort to a sentiment does not avoid the criticism.

On the main issues about moral reasons and obligation Smith does not advance beyond Hutcheson and Hume. His account of the moral sentiments is more accurate, subtle, and complex than anything they offer. But if we are convinced by the main rationalist objections to Hutcheson and Hume, Smith ought not to change our mind. Balguy, Price, and Reid argue convincingly that a sentimentalist analysis does not capture moral judgment.

799. Utilitarianism

Smith examines the moral sentiments in detail partly in order to show that sentimentalism does not lead to utilitarianism. Hutcheson supposes that the moral sense approves of benevolence, which takes a utilitarian point of view. Hume is more cautious; but sometimes (especially in the *Inquiry*) he brings the sentiment of humanity close to benevolence. Against these views Smith argues that utility is only one object of approval for the impartial spectator. The spectator does not take the view that Sidgwick calls 'the point of view of the universe', which is guided wholly by the demands of practical reason (as Sidgwick understands them).[73]

The self-regarding virtues help Smith to illustrate his point. We value superior reason and understanding for their own sakes, apart from any practical advantage. Similarly, the impartial spectator admires self-command, because he is less prone than we are to be moved by short-term desires.[74] Smith relies on his dubious assimilation of approval to fellow-feeling, arguing from the fact that the spectator does not feel the solicitations of our present appetites to the conclusion that he does not approve of our acting on them. The argument is open to question; for though the spectator does not feel our affection to our immediate family either, he approves of it. Still, Smith's observation suggests a reasonable point closely connected to his previous point about our admiration for superior reason apart from its consequences. The reasonable spectator approves of practical reason for its own sake, and therefore admires the operation of practical reason in someone else's life, apart from any judgment about whether it is useful to the agent all things considered.

Admiration of other-regarding virtues seems to offer equally little support to the utilitarian. Someone who displays self-sacrificing bravery or public spirit may not be concerned about the consequences of the action; indeed, if he asked himself which consequences he preferred, he might well prefer the self-preservation that would result from a less brave or less generous action. Our immediate admiration of him is equally independent of the consequences that

[73] Sidgwick comments on Smith at *ME* 424, 463.

[74] 'The spectator does not feel the solicitations of our present appetites. To him the pleasure which we are to enjoy a week hence, or a year hence, is just as interesting as that which we are to enjoy this moment. When for the sake of the present, therefore, we sacrifice the future, our conduct appears to him absurd and extravagant in the highest degree, and he cannot enter into the principles which influence it. On the contrary, when we abstain from present pleasure, in order to secure greater pleasure to come, when we act as if the remote object interested us as much as that which immediately presses upon the senses, as our affections exactly correspond with his own, he cannot fail to approve of our behaviour: and as he knows from experience, how few are capable of this self-command, he looks upon our conduct with a considerable degree of wonder and admiration.' (iv 2.8, 189–90)

we anticipate; we admire the self-sacrifice for its own sake.[75] If we did not respond at all to the views that other people take of our actions, we could still reflect on utility, but we would be incapable of moral evaluation, since we would lack the appropriate attitudes to our own behaviour and character.[76] The moral point of view necessarily refers to the views of others, even if the others are represented by the judge within the agent.

We may not agree with Smith's claim that moral evaluation is necessarily other-directed in this way. But we might nonetheless agree that if utilitarian considerations matter morally, they matter because they meet some distinct standard of moral appropriateness, not because they themselves constitute the relevant standard. He makes a reasonable case for the view that our moral sentiments do not respond immediately to utility, and that, even on reflexion, they do not respond only to utility. In rejecting a utilitarian analysis of moral sentiment, Smith disagrees with Hutcheson and with Hume.

Nonetheless, Smith agrees on one point with utilitarianism. Though our sentiments themselves do not consider utility, the general tendency of our acting on our sentiments is to promote utility, because of a 'happy adjustment' by Nature.[77] We might understand Smith's reference to Nature theologically, so that he agrees with Berkeley and with the position entertained by Butler, treating God as a utilitarian who has given us non-utilitarian principles to maximize utility. He is inclined to agree, without definitely agreeing, with Hutcheson against Butler that God's character is purely benevolent (vi 2.3, 235–7; vii 2.3.18, 305).[78] Alternatively, he might be referring to some quasi-evolutionary process, according to which some social processes select the reactions that tend to maximize utility. Here, as in his better-known reference to the 'invisible hand', Smith alludes to some co-ordinating mechanism without describing it very precisely.[79]

---

[75] 'To every bystander, the success or preservation of this other person may justly be more interesting than their own; but it cannot be so to themselves. When to the interest of this other person, therefore, they sacrifice their own, they accommodate themselves to the sentiments of the spectator, and by an effort of magnanimity act according to those views of things which, they feel, must naturally occur to any third person.' (iv 2.10, 191) 'In these and in all other cases of this kind, our admiration is not so much founded upon the utility, as upon the unexpected, and on that account the great, the noble, and exalted propriety of such actions. This utility, when we come to view it, bestows upon them, undoubtedly, a new beauty, and upon that account still further recommends them to our approbation. This beauty, however, is chiefly perceived by men of reflexion and speculation, and is by no means the quality which first recommends such actions to the natural sentiments of the bulk of mankind.' (iv 2.11, 192)

[76] 'He would not be cast down with inward shame at the thought of this deformity; nor would he be elevated with secret triumph of mind from the consciousness of the contrary beauty. He would not exult from the notion of deserving reward in the one case, nor tremble from the suspicion of meriting punishment in the other. All such sentiments suppose the idea of some other being, who is the natural judge of the person that feels them; and it is only by sympathy with the decisions of this arbiter of his conduct, that he can conceive, either the triumph of self-applause, or the shame of self-condemnation.' (iv 2.12, 193)

[77] 'And Nature, indeed, seems to have so happily adjusted our sentiments of approbation and disapprobation, to the conveniency both of the individual and of the society, that after the strictest examination it will be found, I believe, that this is universally the case. But still I affirm, that it is not the view of this utility or hurtfulness which is either the first or principal source of our approbation and disapprobation. These sentiments are no doubt enhanced and enlivened by the perception of the beauty or deformity which results from this utility or hurtfulness. But still, I say, they are originally and essentially different from this perception.' (iv 2.3, 188)

[78] But Smith seems to attribute to God concern for justice for its own sake. See ii 2.3.12, 91. On the passage from earlier editions deleted in the final edition see RM, App. ii. Cf. Hutcheson, §645.

[79] 'The rich only select from the heap what is most precious and agreeable. They consume little more than the poor, and in spite of their natural selfishness and rapacity, though they mean only their own conveniency, though the sole end which they propose from the labours of all the thousands whom they employ, be the gratification of their own vain and insatiable desires, they divide with the poor the produce of all their improvements. They are led by an invisible hand to

Why does he believe that the working of the moral sentiments coincides with the utilitarian principle? The traits that appeal to the impartial observer are beneficial to society in general, insofar as they encourage actions that are likely to benefit many members of society or to forward some common good. But it does not follow that these traits tend to maximize the total good summed over all the individuals affected. The utilitarian claim implies that the virtues approved by the impartial observer do not support values and principles that interfere with maximum utility. The claim is plausible only if indirect utilitarianism can justify friendship, justice, and other traits that tend to diverge from direct utilitarianism. Since Smith does not offer an indirect utilitarian justification, his concession to utilitarianism is premature.

Sidgwick cites Smith's concession in support of his own view that the morality of common sense is unconsciously utilitarian (*ME* 424), and that a clear understanding of common sense supports a preference for utilitarianism. Smith, however, does not agree that we ought to prefer utilitarianism, or that we ought to reform our non-utilitarian rules and principles, if necessary, so that the ideal observer becomes more sensitive to utilitarian considerations. He does not suggest that if we were to discover a conflict between utilitarianism and the virtues he describes, we ought to resolve the conflict by reforming our conception of the virtues to match the utilitarian standard. The reformer's judgment, like all moral judgments, is simply a prediction about the reactions of impartial spectators; hence it cannot take a perspective outside these reactions, and so cannot be used to reform them. If the impartial spectator does not prefer utility over other principles, we ought not to prefer it. Here Smith sticks consistently to the reductive anti-rationalism that is his guiding aim and assumption.

800. Stoicism

Though Smith's argument begins from his question about the source of moral judgment—the question that he takes to be practically irrelevant—it leads him to an answer to the question that he takes to be practically relevant, about the nature of virtue. His conclusions about the nature of virtue may be summarized by a comparison with Stoicism. This is the moral theory that he discusses most fully, and for good reasons. Both the points of agreement with Stoicism and the points of disagreement make clear the main features of his own position.

Smith emphasizes Stoic indifference to external circumstances. In his view, the Stoics hold an adaptive conception of happiness; they take virtue to be sufficient for happiness because it guarantees the appropriate tranquillity in the face of external conditions.[80] He takes the

---

make nearly the same distribution of the necessaries of life, which would have been made, had the earth been divided into equal portions among all its inhabitants, and thus without intending it, without knowing it, advance the interest of the society, and afford means to the multiplication of the species.' (iv 1.10, 184) See RM ad loc; Smith, WN iv 2.9. Cf. Griswold, *ASVE* 319.

[80] 'The never-failing certainty with which all men, sooner or later, accommodate themselves to whatever becomes their permanent situation, may, perhaps, induce us to think that the Stoics were, at least, thus far very nearly in the right; that, between one permanent situation and another, there was, with regard to real happiness, no essential difference: or that, if there were any difference, it was no more than just sufficient to render some of them the objects of simple choice or preference; but not of any earnest or anxious desire: and others, of simple rejection, as being fit to be set

Stoic claims about happiness to imply that we need not take preferred and non-preferred indifferents seriously, since we can adapt ourselves to living without them. That is why the Stoics regard human life as a mere 'two-penny stake'. We play the game not because we care about winning but because we care about playing it well (vii 2.1.24, 279).[81]

This mistaken interpretation of the Stoics incorporates some aspects of the Epicurean conception of happiness as tranquillity (*ataraxia*). It has some excuse, since the Stoics emphasize the undisturbed and 'smooth-flowing' character of the sage's life. But it assumes falsely that the Stoics believe a natural advantage deserves to be taken seriously only if it constitutes or promotes one's happiness. Smith does not attend to the Stoic conception of the life in accordance with nature, which requires the achievement of preferred indifferents. He cites the requirements of nature as though the Stoics ignored them.[82] His misinterpretation reflects his conception of happiness, which he reads into the Stoics.

Having attributed this form of indifference to the Stoics, Smith explains their endorsement of it by reference to the cosmic aspect of their theory. If we attend to the order of the universe as a whole, and recognize that the ups and downs of our life make no significant difference to it, we will see that it is pointless to be anxious about our own insignificant fortunes. We can be confident in cosmic providence to order the universe properly, and can concentrate on the propriety of our own behaviour, which consists in adapting ourselves to the universal order (vii 2.1.21, 277).

Though Smith believes that the cosmic aspect of Stoicism explains Stoic indifference, his account introduces a conflict into the Stoic position. For indifference, in his view, rests on the conception of happiness as tranquillity; and it is not clear how tranquillity is consistent with the Stoics' admitted concern to keep their own character in harmony with cosmic providence. This concern must surely cost them some anxiety, at least before they become sages. For it is not always easy to find the virtuous course of action, or to stick to it in the face of other apparently attractive options. If tranquillity were really our overriding concern, it is not clear why we should attach such importance to our co-operation with providence by becoming virtuous. If we pursue virtue only for the sake of tranquillity, it does not seem the most effective means to that result.

Smith does not see this conflict in the Stoic position as he presents it. Had he seen it, he might have answered that it is a genuine conflict in the Stoic position, not only in his presentation of it. But in order to be convinced on this point, we would have to be convinced by his claims about the role of tranquillity in the Stoic conception of happiness. These claims express Smith's views about happiness, not the Stoics' views.

Smith approves of some aspects of the Stoic position, as he interprets it. He agrees about happiness and tranquillity, and he believes the Stoics are right to look at their actions and characters from an impartial point of view. In this respect they grasp an essential feature of the morality. He disagrees, however, with their attempt to make the cosmic point of

---

aside or avoided; but not of any earnest or anxious aversion. Happiness consists in tranquillity and enjoyment. Without tranquillity there can be no enjoyment; and where there is perfect tranquillity there is scarce any thing which is not capable of amusing.' (iii 3.30, 149)

[81] Quoted and discussed in §182. The influence of Stoicism on Smith is discussed by Vivenza, *ASC*, ch. 2. She does not discuss the difference between the Stoics and Smith on happiness.

[82] See vii. 2.1.46, quoted below. Smith might be influenced by the appeal to nature against Stoicism in Cic. *Fin.* iv.

view their only point of view. As he argues in opposing a utilitarian account of the moral sentiments, the impartial point of view is not the same as the global and universal point of view; for we can sympathize directly with one victim's sufferings, or admire one brave person's heroic action, without any of the comparisons and weighings that a global and maximizing point of view would require. The Stoic outlook is sometimes useful for helping us to look at ourselves from the impartial point of view.[83]

In appealing to nature and its prescriptions Smith rejects the suggestion that we ought to take the Stoic point of view on ourselves, even if we do not find it easy to do this. He does not believe that moral philosophy ought to criticize the outlook of impartial spectators. They do not adopt a Stoic cosmic attitude to their ordinary concerns, and so we have no ground for attributing a Stoic attitude to the moral point of view.

Nonetheless, the Stoics recognize an important function of morality. Smith believes that Stoic impartiality may help us to cultivate the outlook of the impartial spectator, by helping us to detach ourselves from our self-centred point of view. He rejects the Stoic claim that the impartial outlook should eliminate the self-centred demands of nature, but he agrees that it ought to modify these demands.[84] He does not say how far we ought to go in modifying our emotions in the light of the impartial point of view. He rejects this sort of question, because it introduces a normative element that his theory tries to eliminate.

801. The Importance of Irrational Sentiments

Here as elsewhere Smith rejects a normative conception of moral philosophy that tries to criticize or reform our moral sentiments on rational grounds external to them. Our sentiments are not rational, and in some respects they are even irrational; but he does not advise us to try to change or to eliminate them. His analysis of the moral point of view implies that moral principles are incapable of offering the fundamental rational criticisms that his rationalist opponents claim to offer.

This anti-rationalist tendency, however, is mitigated by another tendency that we have noticed in Smith. He sometimes suggests that our sentiments are not merely non-rational and immune from rational moral criticism, but are also systematically co-ordinated. He claims that 'Nature' organizes them wisely for its own ends, which may not be apparent

---

[83] 'Nature has not prescribed to us this sublime contemplation as the great business and occupation of our lives. She only points it out to us as the consolation of our misfortunes. The Stoical philosophy prescribes it as the great business and occupation of our lives. . . . By the perfect apathy which it prescribes to us, by endeavouring, not merely to moderate, but to eradicate all our private, partial, and selfish affections, by suffering us to feel for whatever can befall ourselves, our friends, our country, not even the sympathetic and reduced passions of the impartial spectator, it endeavours to render us altogether indifferent and unconcerned in the success or miscarriage of every thing which Nature has prescribed to us as the proper business and occupation of our lives.' (vii 2.1.46, 292–3)

[84] 'The reasonings of philosophy, it may be said, though they may confound and perplex the understanding, can never break down the necessary connexion which Nature has established between causes and their effects. The causes which naturally excite our desires and aversions, our hopes and fears, our joys and sorrows, would no doubt, notwithstanding all the reasonings of Stoicism, produce upon each individual, according to the degree of his actual sensibility, their proper and necessary effects. The judgments of the man within the breast, however, might be a good deal affected by those reasonings, and that great inmate might be taught by them to attempt to overawe all our private, partial, and selfish affections into a more or less perfect tranquillity. To direct the judgments of this inmate is the great purpose of all systems of morality.' (vii 2.1.47, 293)

to us as agents. It is not clear, however, how this observation from the 'speculative' or theoretical point of view should affect the outlook of agents. If we become aware of (say) the utilitarian tendencies of some moral sentiments, we have no moral obligation, from Smith's point of view, to modify our other sentiments to fulfil utilitarian goals; but we also have no reason not to modify them. If, on the other hand, we could not see the hand of 'Nature' in our moral sentiments, should this make any difference to our view of them? Smith's moral theory obliges him to answer No. But the fact that he forestalls the question by assuring us that Nature organizes our sentiments for utilitarian ends suggests that he allows a moral question that his theory ought to disallow.

Some questions about the relation between a purely psychological attitude and a critical attitude to moral sentiments converge in Smith's treatment of the accumulation of wealth and other non-moral goods. He agrees with the Stoics that these are not necessary for happiness, because he imputes to the Stoics his own conception of happiness as contentment and tranquillity. He believes that we sympathize with the rich and powerful because we imagine how happy we would be if we were in their position, and we do not take account of the different desires that we would have if we were in their position (i 3.2.2, 52). Our sympathy is irrational, insofar as it is based on a false supposition, but it is nonetheless socially important.[85] Our deferential tendencies are useful for the order of society, but they go beyond the limits that can be justified by appeal to their utility. But Smith does not advise us to try to replace these deferential tendencies with a degree of subordination that might be more justifiable and might avoid the bad effects of the deferential tendencies. In appealing to 'Nature' he suggests that it would be hazardous to interfere with our sentiments; but in this case it is at least not obvious that 'Nature' maintains the 'wise order' that he attributes to it elsewhere.

The social importance of irrational attitudes explains our sympathy not only for the rich and powerful, but also for the accumulation of wealth. Since it is only a means to happiness, we have good reason to value it only insofar as we attach non-instrumental value to the end that it promotes. Since Smith identifies happiness with tranquillity, he believes that a rational valuation of wealth would lead us to a rather cautious estimate of it, since increased wealth by no means guarantees greater happiness. Strenuous and successful efforts to increase wealth often lead only to disappointment.[86] Nonetheless, we irrationally admire the plentiful means of happiness without making it clear to ourselves how few of these means we actually need.[87] In this case nature's contrivance is wise, since our irrational

---

[85] 'Upon this disposition of mankind, to go along with all the passions of the rich and the powerful, is founded the distinction of ranks, and the order of society. . . . Neither is our deference to their inclinations founded chiefly, or altogether, upon a regard to the utility of such submission, and to the order of society, which is best supported by it. Even when the order of society seems to require that we should oppose them, we can hardly bring ourselves to do it. That kings are the servants of the people, to be obeyed, resisted, deposed, or punished, as the public conveniency may require, is the doctrine of reason and philosophy; but it is not the doctrine of Nature.' (i 3.2.3, 52–3)

[86] 'Through the whole of his life he pursues the idea of a certain artificial and elegant repose which he may never arrive at, for which he sacrifices a real tranquillity that is at all times in his power, and which, if in the extremity of old age he should at last attain to it, he will find to be in no respect preferable to that humble security and contentment which he had abandoned for it.' (iv 1.8, 181)

[87] 'If we consider the real satisfaction which all these things are capable of affording, by itself and separated from the beauty of that arrangement which is fitted to promote it, it will always appear in the highest degree contemptible and trifling. But we rarely view it in this abstract and philosophical light. We naturally confound it in our imagination

attachment to these means to happiness actually increases the happiness of others.[88] Our irrational sentiments encourage the accumulation of the means of happiness, in the false belief that it increases the happiness of the accumulators. It is socially useful, however, to encourage these irrational sentiments, since the accumulation increases the happiness of others. 'Providence' and the 'invisible hand' are utilitarians.[89]

This link between Smith's moral and economic theory displays some indecision about the role of critical reason. In claiming that 'it is well that nature imposes upon us in this manner', he offers a justification that might appeal to someone who demands a rational defence of our moral sentiments, and takes the rational outlook to be utilitarian. But he does not demand this rational defence. He does not suggest that our moral sentiments would be open to criticism if they could not be represented as the wise contrivances of a utilitarian nature. It is fortunate that our sentiments have good results, but nothing would be wrong with them, in his view, if they did not have these results.

Since Smith does not consider rational criticism of our moral sentiments, he does not consider any revision in our sentiments about wealth and happiness. We might argue that, since we would rather be rich than poor, even if the rich are usually no more contented than the poor, wealth promotes our welfare even if it does not increase our contentment, and so happiness consists in something more than contentment. Though rich people may be no more content than poor people, they usually have opportunities for pursuits that are not open to those who have to struggle for necessities; and so we might suppose that attention to these pursuits will throw some light on our conception of happiness. This argument presupposes that our sentiments have some claim to be rational, and that therefore we ought to find an account of them that makes them reasonably coherent.

Since Smith rejects the presupposition, he concludes that our tendency to admire different ways of life is inconsistent with our conception of happiness. The degree of non-rationality and irrationality that he sees in our moral sentiments results from his initial assumptions about the irrelevance of reason to morality. He does not contemplate any reconsideration of his claims about happiness in the light of our views about which lives we admire.

Smith's comments on the psychological basis of accumulation illustrate the ways in which he nearly transforms moral philosophy into a purely descriptive social science, and the ways in which he falls short of that result. If moral philosophy describes, and does not attempt to justify, our moral sentiments, we have no room to argue that the sentiments favouring accumulation are unjustified. Smith is simply telling us how accumulation happens and why we favour it; he denies that we have any philosophical room to stand back and ask whether

with the order, the regular and harmonious movement of the system, the machine or economy by means of which it is produced. The pleasures of wealth and greatness, when considered in this complex view, strike the imagination as something grand and beautiful and noble, of which the attainment is well worth all the toil and anxiety which we are so apt to bestow upon it. And it is well that nature imposes upon us in this manner. It is this deception which rouses and keeps in continual motion the industry of mankind.' (iv 1.9–10, 183)

[88] 'When Providence divided the earth among a few lordly masters, it neither forgot nor abandoned those who seemed to have been left out in the partition. These last too enjoy their share of all that it produces. In what constitutes the real happiness of human life, they are in no respect inferior to those who would seem so much above them. In ease of body and peace of mind, all the different ranks of life are nearly upon a level, and the beggar, who suns himself by the side of the highway, possesses that security which kings are fighting for.' (iv 1.10, 185) Sidgwick, ME 155 n1, draws attention to this passage, remarking that it is 'striking' to find it in the author of WN.

[89] The passage just quoted follows the reference to the 'invisible hand', quoted in §799.

we ought to favour it. If moral philosophy confines itself to describing our moral sentiments, and recognizes no further normative task of arguing that our sentiments are justified or unjustified, it becomes a purely descriptive social science. Hume suggests such a conception of moral philosophy; Smith executes it in some detail.

Still, he does not avoid all questions about justification; nature enters to reassure us about the overall results of our moral sentiments. Smith does not always assume that the natural process or result is the morally desirable one; he recognizes that the natural habit of deference goes further than we might prefer it to go. But at crucial points in his argument he combines his purely descriptive account of the operations of our moral sentiments with an appeal to the utilitarianism of nature. Even within a theory that leaves no room for an external critical perspective on our moral sentiments, Smith seems to acknowledge that we look for such a perspective.

61

PRICE

802. Price's Aims

Price's book is suitably entitled a *Review*. He not only examines the main contributions to moral theory since Hobbes, but also surveys the relevant disputes in epistemology. He examines Locke, Shaftesbury, Hutcheson, Hume, and comments (briefly, in a later edition) on Smith, Reid, and Paley.[1] He is the first moralist who clearly uses Cudworth's *Eternal and Immutable Morality*. He follows Butler, Clarke, and Balguy on many points, but his historical and philosophical horizon extends beyond them; he uses his first-hand knowledge of Plato and the Stoics to defend the rationalist side of the argument.[2]

Whewell admires Price as a healthy corrective to the decline, as Whewell regards it, in 18th-century English moral philosophy, He praises Price for returning to the defence of 'immutable' and 'independent' morality against Hume and Paley.[3] He comments that Price's views 'seem to me to be capable of being developed into a very valuable correction of the errors of his contemporaries'.[4]

Whewell's attitude to Price is over-simplified. Both of them tend to represent the rationalism of Clarke and Balguy as the only reasonable alternative to Hume. Neither of them clearly recognizes that Butler offers a significant option distinct both from Clarke's rationalism and from sentimentalism. Price takes himself to maintain the position of Butler against the errors of Shaftesbury and Hutcheson. He does not discuss the significant differences between himself and Butler.[5] Still, Price's statement of a rationalist position is

---

[1] On Paley see §880. See Whewell, *LHMPE* 183; Rivers, *RGS* 171.

[2] Price's connexion with Butler goes back to their education in Dissenting academies. See Thomas, *Price* 12; Thomas, *HM* 9. One of Price's teachers, Vavasour Griffiths, had been a student of Samuel Jones at Tewksbury Academy. Jones's students also included Thomas Secker (Butler's friend, later Archbishop) and Butler. Jones had been a student of Perizonius in Leyden.

[3] 'Hutcheson the Irishman, and Hume the Scotchman, thus seemed to trample on the very ruins of the old fortress of immutable morality, which English moralists had abandoned. But a champion, and a very able one, soon issued from Wales, and did no little to restore the fortunes of the fight. I speak of Dr Price . . . in this work there are, perhaps, the germs of a greater change in the prevalent philosophy of the subject than has yet take place.' (*LHMPE* 182)

[4] According to Schneewind, 'Whewell 1852 does not discuss Price, perhaps because Price was Welsh. Yet in his own moral theory Whewell is closer to Price than to any other predecessor . . .' (*IA* 385n11). Whewell's comment on Price shows that he is well aware of his debt to him.

[5] After expressing agreement with part of Shaftesbury's account of virtue (see §817), Price adds a general comment: 'His account of virtue in his Inquiry is indeed on several accounts extremely deficient, particularly on account of his

fuller and better defended than Clarke's and Balguy's. Price and Reid help us to understand what can be done for rationalism without traditional naturalism.[6]

803. Psychology and Epistemology

Rationalists and sentimentalists tend to be opposed in moral psychology, meta-ethics, and normative ethics. Sentimentalists believe that sentiment or passion is prior to reason in motivation and in justification, that moral judgment is determined by feeling rather than reason, and that moral rightness consists in the tendency to maximize utility, since this appeals to the benevolent (or sympathetic) agent (or judge). Rationalists tend to take the opposite view on all three questions. Cumberland and Balguy are the rationalists who show most sympathy to utilitarianism, but even they do not endorse it.

Hume draws more extreme conclusions from Hutcheson's anti-rationalism than Hutcheson draws. He rejects Hutcheson's sympathy for Butler's views about nature, and he insists more clearly that the basis of moral philosophy is purely psychological; moral philosophy describes the sentiments of a certain type of observer, and cannot justifiably claim to present reasons that are independent of these sentiments. In reaction to Hutcheson and Hume, Price defends rationalism. Like Hume, he presents his moral philosophy as part of a systematic philosophical outlook; he argues that rationalist ethics gains support from its relation to his general epistemological position.[7]

In contrast to Hobbes, Butler, Hutcheson, and Hume,[8] Price begins not with an account of human nature, but with questions in moral epistemology. His epistemological argument is fundamental; 'if I have failed here, I have failed in my chief design' (3). His most original contribution to moral theory is perhaps his special emphasis on epistemology rather than on psychology. His epistemological emphasis does not abandon moral psychology, but imposes a condition of adequacy on any account of human nature. If our account of human nature leaves us without the capacity to acquire the sort of knowledge that our epistemology tells us we acquire, or if it leaves us with no account of how this knowledge could guide our action, the account has to be revised.

In Hutcheson psychology determines epistemology; for he believes that the sort of moral knowledge that rationalists attribute to us could not influence our actions in the way that moral knowledge plainly does, and so he infers that his moral psychology shows the error in rationalist epistemology.[9] Price seems to reverse Hutcheson's direction of argument. He claims that since the kind of knowledge that clearly guides our action does not fit

limiting virtue so much . . . to the cultivation of natural affection and benevolence, and overlooking entirely, as Dr Butler observes, the authority belonging to virtue and the principle of reflexion' (*RPQM* 190n). He goes on to regret the bad effects of Shaftesbury's prejudices against Christianity. On Butler and Shaftesbury see §§677, 714. I cite *RPQM* from Raphael's edition. Page references without any title refer to this work.

[6] Broad, 'Moral sense' 131, emphasizes the importance of Price's defence of rationalism.

[7] 'I should be sorry that any one should fix this as his judgment, without going through the whole treatise, and comparing the different parts of it, which will be found to have a considerable dependence on one another' (3).

[8] This point applies to Hutcheson's most systematic presentation of his position, in *IMGE*.

[9] This is also Hume's main argument against rationalism in moral philosophy, though he certainly has broader epistemological objections against rationalism.

into Hutcheson's moral psychology, that moral psychology must be wrong. He does not, therefore, discuss the questions in moral psychology very extensively in their own right. In some cases he allows his answers to emerge from his epistemology. But he also relies on Butler's account of human nature, assuming that Butler has done the work for him. It is worth asking whether Price's rationalism is consistent with his reliance on Butler's naturalism.

804. Hedonism and Value

Price approaches questions about self-love and other affections through a general view of affections (69). Affections are distinguished by their objects, and their objects essentially include distinctive ends; curiosity, for instance, is the love of what is new and uncommon, and ambition is the love of fame. Hume includes affections of this sort under the passions, which he takes to be distinguished by their distinctive sensations, connected only empirically with their objects. Price, by contrast, takes a distinctive object and a distinctive end to be internally connected to a given affection. Hence, he claims, psychological egoism—understood as the doctrine that we desire everything simply as a means to our own good—implies that we really have only one affection, self-love.

In affirming this internal connexion between affection, object, and end, Price maintains that pride is necessarily pride in some apparent good, and humiliation necessarily responds to an apparent evil. Hume, on the contrary, takes these connexions of emotions to objects to be contingent. Hence he believes that passions cannot be reasonable or unreasonable, because they do not admit of truth or falsehood. Price takes the more plausible view that passions may be reasonable or unreasonable, and some actually are reasonable.

He uses his account of affections and their objects to support Butler's attack on psychological hedonism (74–6). He argues that any pleasure in obtaining x presupposes a prior affection for x. Since we have an affection for x only if we desire x for its own sake, the pleasure in obtaining x presupposes a desire for x for its own sake; hence we cannot consistently claim that we take pleasure in obtaining the object of our desires and that the only thing we desire for its own sake is pleasure.

Price fails, as Butler fails, to show that every pleasure presupposes an independent desire for its object.[10] But the exaggeration does not defeat Price's main point. If any pleasures are value-dependent, they raise a difficulty for psychological hedonism.

The internal connexions between pleasure and desire, and between desire, object, and end, suggest to Price that a pleasure is internally connected to its object.[11] If our pleasure in friendship is essentially directed towards friendship, pleasure cannot be all we want. If we could gain pleasure equivalent to or greater than the pleasure of friendship, but without friendship, we would still want friendship in addition to this added pleasure.

---

[10] See Butler, §688.

[11] ' . . . nothing can be more proper than to consider; whether, supposing we could enjoy the same pleasure *without* the object of our desire, we should be indifferent to it. Could we enjoy pleasures equivalent to those attending knowledge, or the approbation of others, without them, or with infamy and ignorance, would we no longer wish for the one or be averse to the other?' (75).

Price supposes—at least for the sake of argument—that we could gain some pleasure 'equivalent' to the pleasure we take in friendship. On this supposition, a large enough supply of pleasure of the sort we get from a warm bath might outweigh the pleasure we get from friendship. He might have strengthened his argument if he had questioned this supposition.[12] If we cannot always find an amount of one pleasure that we are willing to substitute for another pleasure, we have reason to believe that we desire the objects of the pleasures for their own sakes, and that therefore pleasure is not the only thing we desire for its own sake.

If hedonism is meant to give us an account of the one object that we aim at for its own sake, the pleasures pursued in different actions cannot be different in kind in some way that would prevent the substitution of a sufficient quantity of one for another.[13] Moreover, 'substitution' must be understood as the replacement of one thing by something else of strictly equivalent value, not simply as its replacement by something that is the best we can find in the circumstances (as when we speak of an 'inferior substitute'). Apparently, however, we cannot enjoy 'the same pleasure without the object of our desire', as Price puts it; the pleasures of different actions and states cannot be strictly equivalent substitutes, so that some quantity of the pleasure of warm baths would be strictly equivalent to the pleasure of friendship. The appeal to pleasure does not reveal just one object of desire that we pursue for our own sake, but as many different kinds of objects as there are types of pleasure.

805. Pleasure, Happiness, and Self-Interest

Price follows Butler not only in his rejection of psychological hedonism, but also in a concession to prudential hedonism, identifying the object of rational self-love with happiness, and identifying this happiness with pleasure. He seems to take the equivalence of happiness and pleasure for granted. When he argues against the view that virtue secures happiness, he contents himself with listing the painful incidents that sometimes result from virtue. Indeed, when he considers (without saying so) the arguments offered by Greek moralists to show that virtue promotes happiness, he does not seem to realize what they have in mind.[14]

In replying to Plato's argument in the *Republic* to show that the just person is always better off than the unjust, Price assumes that Plato means that the just person will gain more pleasure than the unjust person.[15] Plato, however, believes that the just person gets more

---

[12] This would be an Aristotelian question. See §95. Aristotle's view of pleasure would have strengthened Butler's and Price's objections to hedonism.

[13] This point arises for Mill, in *Utilitarianism*, ch. 2.

[14] 'Though in equal circumstances, it [sc. virtue] has always greatly the advantage over vice, and is alone sufficient to overbalance many and great inconveniences; yet it would be very extravagant to pretend, that it is at present completely, and without exception, its own happiness; that it is alone sufficient to overbalance *all possible* evils of body, mind, and estate; or that, for example, a man who, by *base* but *private* methods, has secured a good estate, and afterwards enjoys it for many years with discretion and credit, has less pleasure than another, who, by his benevolence or integrity, has brought himself to a dungeon or stake, or who lives in perplexity, labour, self-denial, torture of body, and melancholy of mind.' (257) Lecky argues at length in favour of Price's view at *HEM* i 58–66.

[15] Price's objection is partly reasonable, since Shaftesbury (sometimes) and Butler defend the hedonistic thesis, and Price's reply is appropriate for their arguments. Moreover, Plato thinks the just person gets more pleasure than the unjust (this claim is defended in *Rep*. ix; cf. Price 230n).

pleasure because he is happier; and he thinks the pleasure is greater because its objects are better. Plato does not claim that by Price's tests we can discover that the just person gets more pleasure. Price relies on the conception of pleasure and happiness that is assumed by his hedonist opponents, and wrongly applies it to non-hedonist eudaemonist arguments. He agrees with John Brown's objection to Shaftesbury, and hence underestimates the non-hedonist elements in Shaftesbury's position.[16] We have seen that Shaftesbury sometimes defends himself by a non-hedonistic conception of a person's good as defined by rational nature. Price does not see that this is a reasonable way to interpret the claim about virtue and happiness that we find in the Greek moralists.

His attitude to Plato is surprising, in the light of his attitude to hedonism. Even if he were right to understand Plato's or Shaftesbury's claims about happiness as claims about pleasure, he might reasonably have remarked that if they take virtue to be a source of pleasure, they do not necessarily claim that virtue is simply a means to the greatest pleasure. If the greatest pleasure is pleasure taken in the greatest non-instrumental good, we do not refute Plato's claim that virtue promotes the greatest pleasure if we show that the virtuous person does not gain the greatest pleasure, as the non-virtuous person would estimate it. Price's criticism of eudaemonism seems not to take account of the complications resulting from his view of pleasure and its objects.

Price admits that Plato might mean that virtue is of greater 'intrinsic excellence' than vice; but he argues that this true claim about virtue does not show that virtue is more beneficial for the virtuous person.[17] On this point he disagrees with Plato, Aristotle, and the Stoics, who all claim that virtue is profitable precisely because they think it is to be chosen for its own sake. They take the good for an agent to include both the useful (utile, commodum) and the morally good (honestum). This connexion between the honestum and the good is especially clear in Suarez's discussion. Price does not recognize this feature of some eudaemonist views. He seems to make Scotus' mistake of supposing that in aiming at our good, we must aim at advantage, understood as a good that belongs exclusively to the agent.[18]

From the eudaemonist point of view, then, Price's objection is ambiguous and unsuccessful. From his point of view, it is clear and decisive, because his hedonist conception of happiness blinds him to the possibility of non-hedonistic eudaemonism, and therefore blinds him to the character of eudaemonist defences of morality.

---

[16] On Brown see §867.

[17] 'It may, 'tis true, be justly said, that virtue, though in the most distressed circumstances, is preferable to vice in the most prosperous, and that expiring in flames ought to be chosen, rather than the greatest wages of iniquity. But the meaning of this is not, that virtue in such circumstances is more *profitable* than vice (or attended with more pleasure) but that it is of *intrinsic* excellence, and obligation; that it is to be chosen for itself, independently of its utility; and remains desirable and amiable above all other objects, when stripped of every emolument, and in the greatest degree afflicted and oppressed.' (257–8) For non-hedonist eudaemonists, including Plato, Aristotle, the Stoics, Aquinas, and Shaftesbury (sometimes), the facts about virtue mentioned in Price's first sentence prove that virtue promotes happiness more than anything else does; and these same moralists appeal to the point he mentions at the end of the passage ('but that it is of intrinsic . . . '). Price, however, seems to intend his remarks to count against the eudaemonist defence of virtue; and his reason is given by the contrast ('But the meaning of this is not . . . ') between choosing virtue for itself and choosing it because it is 'profitable'. If we interpret 'profitable' as referring to instrumental value, the eudaemonists agree with Price about virtue, but do not take this point to count against the eudaemonist defence. If we interpret 'profitable' as meaning simply 'promoting happiness', and assume a non-hedonist conception of happiness, eudaemonist moralists do not maintain the position Price ascribes to them.

[18] On Scotus see §§363–4. Suarez objects to the confusion of conveniens with commodum; see §438.

On this issue a defender of Price might claim that he sees the implications of Butler's position more clearly than Butler sees them. According to Sidgwick, Butler sees the distinction between prudence and morality that is obscured by Greek moralists.[19] But he agrees with eudaemonists in arguing for the harmony of conscience and self-love. Since Butler accepts a hedonist conception of happiness, he apparently ought to accept the fairly simple observations that Price uses to show that there is no reason to expect a general coincidence between virtue and pleasure; hence, apparently, Butler ought to admit that the same observations undermine any claim about the coincidence between virtue and happiness.

Perhaps, however, we ought not to draw this conclusion from Price and Butler. Instead of concluding that Butler should agree with Price in rejecting the harmony of conscience and self-love, perhaps we ought to conclude that both Butler and Price should reject a hedonist conception of happiness. If they pursued the implications of their views about pleasure and goodness, they would have good reason to agree with Butler, against Price, on the harmony of conscience and self-love.

806. Passions v. Affections

We can perhaps confirm these doubts about Price's hedonist conception of happiness if we notice that this conception of happiness raises questions about the claim, accepted by both Butler and Price, that self-love is a rational principle. We have noticed how Butler raises some of these difficulties for himself. Price's position makes them even clearer, as Reid perhaps sees.[20]

Price defends the rational character of self-love by arguing that our desire for happiness cannot be the product of instinct.[21] To suggest that a desire is instinctive, as Price understands the term, is to suggest that we could have been the same sorts of beings as we are but have lacked this particular desire. If, for instance, we tend to prefer the taste of sweet things over sour things, but could have been the sorts of beings that we are without this preference, our preference is instinctive.

On this basis, Price distinguishes affections from passions. Affections are 'desires founded in the reasonable nature itself, and essential to it; such as self-love, benevolence, and the love of truth' (74). They belong to reasonable natures because they are reasonable desires to have, not because they happen to be found in reasonable creatures.[22] A creature would not be reasonable if it did not see the reasons that support such desires and were not moved by these reasons. Affections in this general sense may be strengthened by 'instinctive

---

[19] See Sidgwick, OHE 197–8, quoted in §708.   [20] Cf. Butler, §869, and Reid, §836, on self-love and hedonism.

[21] 'Is then all desire to be considered as *wholly instinctive*? Is it, in particular, owing to nothing but an original bias given our natures, which they might have either wanted or have received in a contrary direction; that we are at all concerned for our own good or for the good of others?' (70)

[22] 'It seems beyond contradiction certain, that every being must *desire* happiness for himself; and can those natures of things, from which the *desire* of happiness and *aversion* to misery necessarily arise, leave, at the same time, a rational nature totally indifferent as to any *approbation* of actions procuring the one, or preventing the other? Is there nothing that any *understanding* can perceive to be amiss in a creature's bringing upon himself, or others, calamities and ruin?' (45)

determinations'; we not only recognize, and act on, the reasonableness of concern for our own interest, but we also have a non-essential feeling that favours it, and this feeling (we might say) gives us a Humean exciting reason that supports the non-Humean exciting reason that belongs to us as reasonable creatures.

Once he has distinguished affections from passions, Price denies that the desire for happiness is simply a passion.[23] Since it is not instinctive, it is a rational principle, and it is contrary to reason to refrain from pursuing happiness, either for oneself or for others (71).

Sometimes Price states too weak a condition for being non-instinctive. We might say that if some desire is necessary to our survival, it cannot be merely instinctive, since we could not have existed if we had been given the contrary desire. This test, however, would generate too many rational principles. Price normally intends the more complex counterfactual claim that we would not have been the same kind of agents if we had lacked the desire in question. If we ask what we would have been like without this desire. and if this question is not really about ourselves, but about some other sort of agent, we have found a desire that is necessary for being a rational agent.

807. Reasonable Self-Love

The abstractions that are required or permitted here are sometimes difficult to decide; some of the difficulties recur in Kant's claims about necessary features of rational agency and its relation to human beings. Still, this is the question that Price seems to intend. The question draws attention to an important aspect of eudaemonism. We might wrongly take a eudaemonist to rely on an empirical, though universal, feature of human beings, that they desire happiness. This is how Kant interprets the desire for happiness.[24] Price rejects this interpretation, because he believes the desire is necessary for a rational agent.

Price's conception of happiness, however, does not fit his claim that the desire for happiness is necessary for a rational agent. The pursuit of happiness does not seem rationally necessary, if happiness and pleasure (as a hedonist understands it) are identified. Unless pleasure is defined so as to imply a necessary connexion between pleasure and the fulfilment of desire, it does not seem obvious that every rational agent must pursue pleasure. Even if we take pleasure to be a by-product of fulfilled desire, it does not seem obvious that rational agents must actually pursue pleasure; why could they not care simply about the fulfilment of their desire and be indifferent about the pleasure resulting from it? Price makes it difficult to see why the desire for happiness expresses a rational principle that is necessary for a rational agent.

His claim about the desire for happiness, however, fits a non-hedonist conception. Aquinas believes that self-love is a rational principle and that desire of one's own happiness is necessary for a rational being. This is not because he thinks we all necessarily pursue pleasure or that

---

[23] 'The full and adequate account of it, is, *the nature of happiness*. It is impossible, but that creatures capable of pleasant and painful sensations, should *love and choose* the one, and *dislike and avoid* the other. No being, who knows what happiness and misery are, can be supposed indifferent to them, without a plain contradiction. Pain is not a *possible* object of *desire*; nor happiness, of *aversion*.' (70)

[24] See Kant, *KpV* 25–6.

something about pleasure makes it appropriate for pursuit by a human being.[25] He believes that happiness is the proper combination of intrinsic goods, and hence is necessarily suitable for a rational agent. Once we understand rational desire and happiness, we must, in Aquinas' view, agree that rational agents necessarily pursue their happiness. Butler and Price accept Aquinas' conclusion, but rely on a different conception of happiness. Aquinas' conception of happiness gives a better account of rational self-love and its relation to particular passions and desires. Butler and Price neglect non-hedonist eudaemonism, and their neglect weakens their argument.

If we accept hedonism, it is plausible, contrary to Butler and Price, to regard the desire for happiness simply as a non-rational instinct. This is how Hobbes regards it. Hume sees, though Hobbes and Hutcheson do not, that once we regard the desire for happiness in this way, we have no ground for supposing that it is a distinctively rational desire.[26] Though Price rejects Hume's conclusion, he does not see how many of Hume's premises need to be questioned.[27]

While a non-hedonist conception of happiness supports Butler's and Price's claims about the rational character of self-love, it casts doubt on their attacks on egoism. If we conceive self-love as a concern for the whole self and its aims, it becomes more difficult to assert the superiority of conscience over self-love. From an Aristotelian point of view, self-love accepts the point of view of conscience; the self that accepts conscience is defined by its pursuit of happiness. Self-love seems to be supreme, since it takes the comprehensive view from which the claims of conscience can be recognized and accepted. Once we reject hedonism, and attribute a comprehensive outlook to self-love, we make it a much more plausible candidate for being a supreme principle.

Perhaps Butler or Price could show that this is the wrong way to compare the points of view of self-love and of conscience. Perhaps it can still be argued that conscience is more comprehensive than self-love in a way that justifies its claim to supremacy. Their case for distinguishing conscience from self-love and asserting the superiority of conscience does not rest entirely on their hedonistic conception of happiness. Even without a hedonist account of self-love, we might take the impartial character of conscience to distinguish conscience from self-love. But they need a better argument than they offer.

808. Reason and Will

Price rejects the sentimentalist conception of moral judgment and the anti-rationalist conception of will and action on which it rests. He seems to be a rationalist about motivation in general, not just about morality. He believes that some objects have a 'natural aptitude' to please or displease us.[28] Relying on his distinction between affections and passions, he argues that we have certain desires and reactions not because we are first reasonable beings and then acquire the appropriate affections, but simply because we recognize reasons.

---

[25] Aquinas believes these things about pleasure, but they do not explain his claims about happiness.
[26] On Hobbes and Hutcheson see §§479, 634.   [27] Reid does better; see §§836–7.
[28] '. . . a reasonable being, void of all superadded determinations or sense, who knows what order and happiness are, would, I think, unavoidably receive pleasure from the survey of an universe where perfect order prevailed; and the contrary prospect of universal confusion would offend him' (58–9).

Price applies this general claim to the particular case of happiness. To show that our pursuit of happiness is not simply the product of instinct (in his sense), he argues that a being 'purely reasonable . . . would not want [i.e., lack] all principles of action, and all inclinations' (70–1). In fact 'the nature of happiness also would engage him to choose and desire it for *himself*' (71). It is as evident that happiness is better than misery as it is that a whole is greater than one of its parts.[29] No prior desire for happiness explains why a rational agent pursues happiness; the mere knowledge of what happiness is moves us by itself to pursue it.[30]

Price's comparison of 'happiness is better than misery' to 'the whole is greater than one of its parts' does not really clarify his position. The statement about whole and parts is analytic; we will assent to it as soon as we know the meaning of 'whole' and 'part'. The statement about happiness, however, does not seem to be analytic (especially if we accept Price's conception of happiness); and even if it were, Price would not have explained why the belief that something is better for us should be supposed to move us to action by itself.

One might reply that the belief that something is good for us will move us if we are rational agents; this is part of what it is to be a rational agent. This reply might not secure Price's main point, however. If we are rational agents, our desires are responsive to considerations of relative importance and coherence; this order in an agent's desires constitutes, in Aquinas' view, a desire for happiness. It is not clear, then, that Price avoids the ascription of desire to a rational agent who is moved by considerations of what is best. Though the desire for one's own good is not an instinct, it does not follow that the belief that something is good for us moves us by itself. Still, part of Price's position may be defensible; for he would be justified in claiming that, even if we acknowledge the necessity of desire for action, desire does not explain why we act on the belief that something is worth pursuing. Our having a desire to pursue what is worth pursuing simply follows from the fact that we act on this sort of belief.[31]

809. Freewill

Price affirms that responsibility requires self-determination.[32] Agreeing with Cudworth, he claims that we ourselves, and not some causes outside us, are the genuine causes of our actions. This self-determination conflicts with a doctrine of necessity that makes something external to us the only real cause of our actions, in such a way that we are not their causes. But Price does not say very clearly what claims commit us to this sort of doctrine of necessity.

---

[29] 'It cannot therefore be reasonably doubted, but that such a being, upon a comparison of happiness and misery, would as unavoidably as he perceives their difference, *prefer* the one to the other; and *choose* the one rather than the other for his fellow-beings.' (71) Here Price refers to the choice of happiness for other people, but what he says is also meant to apply to one's choice of happiness for oneself.

[30] Cf. Reid's discussion of Price, §839.

[31] This is how Nagel, *PA* 29–32, understands a consequential desire that follows from our believing that (for instance) something is in our interest and acting on our belief.

[32] 'Determination requires an efficient cause. If this cause is the being himself, I plead for no more . . . In short; who must not *feel* the absurdity of saying, *my* volitions are produced by a *foreign* cause, that is, are not *mine*; I determine *voluntarily*, and yet *necessarily*?' (181–2)

In his view, motives are not 'physical efficients and agents' (211; cf. 183n);[33] they cannot effect our determination, and our judgments are not physically connected with our action (183n).

We might take these remarks in either of two ways: (1) Motives cannot be parts of sufficient causal conditions for our actions, because our actions have no sufficient causal conditions. (2) Even if our motives cause our actions, we are still the causes of our actions. The first interpretation commits Price to indeterminism. The second simply commits him to some account of the cause of our actions that makes ourselves the cause. If such an account can be offered within determinist assumptions, it should satisfy the demands implied in the second claim.

Price seems to recognize that responsibility may not require indeterminism.[34] If a doctrine of necessity can be explained so as to retain his claims about agency, it allows moral responsibility. But he does not say what sort of doctrine of necessity would satisfy him. Hume, for instance, presents a doctrine of necessity that he takes to be compatible with the freedom that is relevant to moral responsibility. But Price does not say whether Hume's version of the doctrine of necessity safeguards responsibility. He might reasonably claim that Hume's view deprives the self and the rational will of an appropriate role in free action.

It is unfortunate that Price comes no closer than Cudworth comes to identifying the crucial errors in the Hobbesian doctrine of necessity. Cudworth's emphasis on the importance of rational motives raises doubts about Hobbes's and Hume's version of compatibilism, since they allow any sort of motive to be equally sufficient for the relevant sort of freedom. Price ought to agree with Cudworth on this point, given the rest of his rationalist view; but he does not make his position clear.

810. The Objectivity of Moral Properties

Since Price rejects sentimentalism about desire and action, he has no reason to favour sentimentalism about moral properties. In his view, it is not only unnecessary for capturing the connexion between morality and action, but also morally inadequate. He argues for a combination of rationalism and realism. He assumes, as Cudworth does, that rationalism and realism are inseparable.

---

[33] At 183n Price refers to his correspondence with Priestley, published in FD. Here he insists especially on the connexion between self-determination and activity: 'This definition implies that in our volitions or determinations we are not acted upon, Acting and being acted upon are incompatible with one another . . . Man therefore would not be an agent, were all his volitions derived from any force or the effects of any mechanical causes.' (FD 136). Following Clarke, he distinguishes 'the operation of physical causes' from 'the influence of moral causes'; a moral cause of my doing x does not take it out of my power to do x and not x. Hence (137) 'a benevolent man will *certainly* relieve misery when it falls in his way; but he has the *power* of not relieving it.' He concludes: 'That the causality implied in the views and dispositions of beings is entirely consistent with moral obligation and responsibility: But that all effects brought about by mechanical laws are inconsistent with them.' (143)

[34] 'If, upon examination, any of the advocates of the doctrine of necessity should find, that what they mean by necessity is not inconsistent with the ideas of *agency* and *self-determination*, there will be little room for further dispute; and that liberty, which I insist upon as essential to morality, will be acknowledged; nor will it be at all necessary to take into consideration, or to pay much regard to any difficulties relating to the nature of that influence we commonly ascribe to motives.' (183)

We might question this assumption. For might we not accept rationalism and still believe that our moral knowledge is knowledge of the tendencies of our own reason, rather than knowledge of objective moral properties?[35] Alternatively, might we not reject rationalism and believe that sense, either the ordinary senses or an additional sense, gives us moral knowledge of external reality?[36] Price concentrates on realist rationalism and an anti-realist doctrine of a moral sense because he rejects a moral sense and embraces rationalism.

He allows that if Hutcheson's doctrine of the moral sense asserted only that moral judgments are immediate, it would be innocuous. But it is not innocuous when Hutcheson adds that moral properties have the status of secondary qualities. Price agrees with Hutcheson in believing that secondary qualities are not genuine differences in objects themselves, but simply reflect features of ourselves and our reactions (14).[37] He does not endorse Reid's more robustly realist account of the senses and their objects, and so he does not regard belief in a moral sense as a reliable support for objectivism about moral properties (280–3).[38]

According to Price, moral properties would be objects of a moral sense only if they did not belong to actions and people themselves, but belonged only to our reactions.[39] Hutcheson derives this conclusion illegitimately from the immediacy of moral judgments.[40] In Price's view, we must support the intellectual character of moral judgments and their correspondence to external reality, by rejecting the moral sense.

He rejects a moral sense theory by rejecting empiricism in general. He argues, for reasons similar to Cudworth's, that many of the ideas that Locke takes to be derived from the senses are in fact derived from the understanding. He claims, for instance, that some ideas about causation are derived from understanding, since the senses give us experience only of succession. While Price agrees with Hume about what we learn from experience, he does not agree with Hume's conclusion about the idea of necessary connexion (25–8). The understanding is the source of its own simple ideas, which are preconditions, not products, of reasoning (40). A moral sense theory is wrong because moral properties are not the sorts of properties that we grasp through a sense.

To prove his point, Price appeals to our intuitive belief that moral properties belong to actions in themselves, not simply to our reactions to them; when we call an action wrong,

---

[35] On rationalism without realism see §718.

[36] This is the view that Whewell and Norton ascribe to Hutcheson. See §§633, 643.

[37] 'For the term *sense*, which he applies to it, from the rejection of all the arguments that have been used to prove it to be an intellectual power, and from the whole of his language on this subject; it is evident, he considered it as the effect of a positive constitution of our minds, or as an implanted and arbitrary principle by which a relish is given us for certain moral objects and forms and aversion to others, similar to the relishes and aversions created by any of our other senses.' (14)

[38] These notes on Reid were written before the appearance of Reid's *EAP*; see 282 (Note D). See §842.

[39] 'Virtue (as those who embrace this scheme say) is an affair of taste. Moral right and wrong, signify nothing in the objects themselves to which they are applied, any more an agreeable and harsh; sweet and bitter; pleasant and painful; but only certain effects in us.' (15)

[40] 'All that can appear from the objections and reasonings of [Hutcheson] . . . is only . . . that the words *right* and *wrong, fit* and *unfit*, express simple and undefinable ideas. But that the power perceiving them is properly a sense and not reason; that these ideas denote nothing true of actions, nothing in the nature of actions; this he has left entirely without proof. He appears, indeed, to have taken for granted that if virtue and vice are immediately perceived, they must be perceptions of an implanted sense. But no conclusion could have been more hasty.' (42)

we attribute a property to the action itself, not to its effect on us as spectators.[41] He admits that this intuitive belief is open to dispute, since it may be dismissed as the product of false 'objectification', the tendency of our mind to 'spread itself' (as Hume says) on objects (46 #1). In reply he points out the absurdities (as he considers them) that result from the subjectivist position. He uses a version of Cudworth's argument about mutability, claiming that his opponents' view makes moral properties mutable in relation to certain other properties that in fact make no difference to moral properties.[42]

Defenders of a moral sense theory reject this criticism. In reply to Burnet and Balguy, Hutcheson argues that the senses are corrigible, but sensory qualities do not exist independently of our perceptions of them. This defence of the subjectivist position does not answer Price. For if the views of the normal perceiver constitute correctness, moral properties are still mutable, not in relation to any particular perceiver, but in relation to changes in normal perceivers. People in general may become, say, more or less prone to approve compassion, benevolence, or honesty. But these qualities themselves do not become better or worse with these changes in perceivers. Hence, according to Price, sentimentalism mistakes the character of moral properties.

Price argues that if moral properties were mutable in the way that follows from sentimentalism, all actions would be indifferent in their own right.[43] In that case we would have no reason not to alter our reactions so that we did not care about doing what we at present take to be right. Rejection of objective right and wrong removes our reason for resisting any anti-moral tendencies.[44]

Subjectivists resist Price's effort to represent them as enemies of morality. Hutcheson recognizes that our moral reactions have a compulsory character that is inconsistent with the view that we are simply aiming at pleasure and the absence of pain; it is not indifferent whether we have them or not, but we are in some way required to have them.[45] We do not treat them as we might treat feelings of pain that we would rather get rid of. Hutcheson can therefore answer Price by pointing out that our moral outlook ascribes to moral judgments the compulsory character that Price recognizes. We need not believe in objective moral properties, therefore, if we treat our moral judgments as compulsory.

Price, however, need not accept this defence of Hutcheson. The moral sense theorist can show that it is psychologically possible to regard our moral judgments as compulsory. But

---

[41] 'Or is it no determination of judgment at all, but a species of mental taste? Are not such actions really right? Or is every apprehension of rectitude in them false and delusive, just as the like apprehension is concerning the effects of external and internal sensation, when taken to belong to the causes producing them?' (45)

[42] 'How strange would it be to maintain, that there is no possibility of mistaking with respect to right and wrong; that the apprehensions of all beings, on this subject, are alike just, since all sensation must be alike true sensation? Is there a greater absurdity, than to suppose, that the moral rectitude of an action is nothing absolute and unvarying; but capable, like all the modifications of pleasure and pain, of being intended and remitted, of increasing and lessening, or rising and sinking with the force and liveliness of our feelings?' (47)

[43] '. . . if no actions are, in themselves, either right or wrong, or any thing of a moral and obligatory nature, which can be an object to the understanding; it follows that, in themselves, they are all indifferent. This is what is essentially true of them, and this is what all understandings, that perceive right, must perceive them to be' (48).

[44] 'If this is judging truly; how obvious is it to infer, that it signifies not what we do; and that the determination to think otherwise, is an imposition upon rational creatures? Why then should they not labour to suppress in themselves this determination, and to extirpate from their natures all the delusive ideas of morality, worth, and virtue? What though the ruin of the world should follow? There would be nothing really wrong in this.' (48)

[45] See Hutcheson, *IMGE* 2.8 = L 111 = SB 104, quoted at §633n15.

this proof (if we concede it) of psychological possibility does not capture the reason we think we have for regarding our judgments as compulsory. Price points out that sometimes we regard our judgment as compulsory because it is constrained by the nature of the objects of our judgment. A purely psychological explanation of why we regard the relevant judgments as non-optional would miss the point; for we regard the non-optional character of the judgment that fire burns wood as the result of a fact about fire. Price argues that in the same way we regard the non-optional character of our moral judgments as the result of facts about right and wrong actions.[46] We do not simply find that we cannot bring ourselves to regard the harming of innocent people as right; we also believe that if nothing changed about the world, we would be mistaken in changing our reaction. Changing our moral judgments at will would be misguided because it would lead us away from being guided by the facts about the actions. The moral sense theorist's explanation gets things the wrong way round.[47]

Even if Price over-simplifies his opponents' position, his criticism is reasonable. Hutcheson does not believe that the moral sense is arbitrary, or that it detects no genuine feature of actions. He believes that it responds to benevolence, and therefore is guided by objective properties of actions. But he does not satisfy Price's demand for an explanation of why the moral sense picks out benevolence. He cannot say that benevolence really deserves approval, because he cannot say that any quality of the action itself really deserves approval, whether or not it is approved. To deserve approval is to be the subject of a justifying reason, which depends (according to Hutcheson) on the reactions of our moral sense.[48]

Price's criticism does not refute sentimentalism, but it shows that sentimentalism does not vindicate our moral judgments. Sentimentalists do not show that our moral judgments rest on the grounds that we take them to rest on. They should admit that they reject our moral judgments and they try to replace them with other judgments that will serve some of the purposes of our moral judgments.

Though Price (like other rationalists) does not attend as he should to the possibility of this defence of sentimentalism, the defence does not completely answer him. He shows that if we are to become sentimentalists, we must modify our initial view of moral judgments more than the sentimentalist initially acknowledges. If we acknowledge this, we need arguments that justify us in discounting the initial credibility of our moral judgments. We must become justifiably more confident in the soundness of sentimentalist arguments against objective moral properties than we are in the conviction that we are right to approve of benevolence because benevolence is really good.

If sentimentalists are held to this standard of proof, their arguments are less plausible. If they were simply explaining why our moral judgments are true or justified, their account would not have to be strong enough to override our initial conviction of the truth of our moral judgments; for it would not compete with that conviction. But if sentimentalism rejects our moral judgments, it competes with our initial conviction, and so assumes a heavier burden of proof.

---

[46] 'Whatever any thing is, that it is, not by will, or decree, or power, but by nature and necessity. Whatever a triangle or circle is, that it is unchangeably and eternally. It depends upon no will or power, whether the three angles of a triangle and two right ones shall be equal . . . ' (50)

[47] For attempts to avoid this objection see Blackburn, *EQR* 153.   [48] See Hutcheson on justifying reasons, §639.

Price believes that an anti-realist about morality faces a further difficulty, because the arguments for anti-realism about moral properties support anti-realism in other areas as well. Protagoras and other ancient philosophers were right to extend anti-realism from ethics to other areas.[49] Though Price rests his claim about extension on his view that moral principles are self-evident, it need not depend on this epistemological view. Anti-realists deny that facts about right and wrong themselves explain why moral judgments and sentiments of approval are sometimes correct and sometimes mistaken. If we reject realist assumptions about the explanatory role of moral properties, why should we not also (Price asks) reject analogous assumptions in other areas?

This question does not refute anti-realism about moral properties, but it shows that anti-realists may have to pay a higher price than they recognize. Most anti-realists try to maintain moral anti-realism without maintaining anti-realism as a general metaphysical position. We are entitled to do this if the arguments for moral anti-realism are peculiar to moral properties, so that we cannot argue by parity for general anti-realism. As Price remarks, Protagoras believes that arguments against moral realism allow this extension to general anti-realism. If moral anti-realists cannot refute Protagoras on this point, moral anti-realism is more difficult to accept; our reasons for accepting it must be better than our reasons for rejecting general anti-realism.

Price has a reasonable point against moral anti-realism. Many later moral anti-realists have rejected general anti-realism, and so they have supposed that their arguments are peculiar to morality. If, as Price believes, the arguments are not peculiar to morality, part of the strategy of later moral anti-realism is open to doubt.

811. Voluntarism and Moral Properties

In arguing that morality is 'eternal and immutable' (50), because it is not mutable in relation to our judgments, Price agrees with Cudworth. He improves Cudworth's argument by showing how his opponent is committed to accepting the consequences of treating actions as being in themselves morally indifferent. He also agrees with Cudworth in taking the objectivity of moral properties to rule out a voluntarist account of morality and will that would make morality consist in divine commands.

Mediaeval voluntarists deny that the will necessarily chooses the greater apparent good, on the ground that such necessity implies lack of freedom. Hobbes and the sentimentalists reject this libertarian aspect of voluntarism, since they think the will is determined to follow the strongest motive, and that it is not up to the will to decide which the strongest motive will be. But they also reject the rationalist view that there is some good for the will to discover and that the greater apparent good, rather than the stronger desire, explains the choice of the will. On this point Hobbes and the sentimentalists agree with voluntarism

---

[49] 'And indeed it seems not a very unnatural transition, from denying absolute *moral* truth, to denying *all truth*; from making right and wrong, just and unjust, dependent on perception, to asserting the same of whatever we commonly rank among the objects of the understanding. Why may not he who rejects the reality of rightness in beneficence, and of wrong in producing needless misery, be led, by the same steps, to deny the certainty of other self-evident principles?' (53)

against rationalism. According to Hobbes, the laws of nature are divine laws, dependent on God's will. God does not command what he sees to be antecedently right.[50]

Cudworth argues against Hobbes's attempt to identify what is morally right with what is commanded by a sovereign. We can reasonably ask whether what a commander commands is right or not; we find that in some circumstances it is (if the commander has the relevant authority) and otherwise it is not. The fact that we can raise this question shows that rightness is something independent of the existence of a command by someone with superior power. Price endorses this argument (52, 105–7),[51] and uses it against other accounts of what is morally right and obligatory.

The broader meta-ethical implications of Hobbes's voluntarism about morality are clearer in Hutcheson; for his view about the relation between the moral sense and the quality that it approves of is parallel to Hobbes's view of God's will and the quality that God approves of. He argues that the goodness of a person or action consists in being approved of by the moral sense, and he denies that the moral sense could be wrong by failing to approve of something that is morally good independently of our reactions to it. This implication of the sentimentalist view is even clearer in Hume, who takes variations in our sentiments to establish differences in the qualities that constitute personal merit, and takes the uniformity of our sentiments to establish the uniformity of moral qualities.[52]

Price follows Cudworth in rejecting voluntarism about God and morality. Believing that moral rightness is eternal and immutable, he cannot identify it with the content of a positive law made by God or regard it as wholly dependent on God's will. The voluntarist view is tempting because an act of will can sometimes make an act right that would otherwise be indifferent. If I promise to pay you $5, paying you $5 now becomes right, and not paying it becomes wrong; if a legislature requires driving on the left, driving on the right becomes wrong. These examples, however, do not support voluntarism; for acts of will change the moral status of particular actions only because they presuppose the rightness of keeping promises and obeying laws. If these actions were not right, acts of will could not affect the rightness and wrongness of particular actions in the way they do.[53] Similarly, we ought not to try to explain the whole basis of morality by claiming that the morally wrong is whatever incurs rewards and punishments; for punishment presupposes wrongdoing that deserves punishment whether or not it is actually punished (108). The cases that appear to support voluntarism actually refute it.

In reply to the charge that this position makes morality independent of God in a way that undermines God's omnipotence, Price replies that though morality does not depend on the will of God, it is not independent of God's nature (87), since it is essential to God to be morally good. If morality is independent of God's will, it does not follow that God is

---

[50] Hobbes also believes that we recognize that the laws of nature are counsels of self-preservation, and therefore choose them as requirements of right reason. This does not make him a rationalist; for they are requirements of right reason only insofar as they fulfil our inclination to self-preservation. See Hobbes, §478.

[51] Price's argument is discussed by Passmore, RC 103. See §§546–7.   [52] See §776.

[53] '...it is by no means to be inferred from hence, that obligation is the creature of will, or that the nature of what is indifferent is changed: nothing then becoming obligatory which was not so from eternity; that is, *obeying the divine will, and just authority*. And had there been nothing right in this, had there been no reason from the natures of things for obeying God's will; it is certain, it could have induced no obligation, nor at all influenced an intellectual nature as such.' (52)

not omnipotent.[54] God is omnipotent as creator, and this omnipotence does not make facts about right and wrong subject to God's legislation.[55] If moral facts were in God's power, there would be no moral obligation and no moral reasons.

To support this objection, Price explores the consequences of making moral obligation depend entirely on the will of a superior. He asks the theological voluntarists what they say about an atheist or Epicurean; would he 'feel no moral obligation, and therefore be not at all accountable?' (107). His answer to this question, on behalf of the voluntarist, is that the atheist would feel no obligation. Hobbes, Cumberland, Pufendorf, and John Clarke believe that if we abstract from divine commands, we still have some reason to follow moral principles, to the extent that observance of them is useful for securing non-moral goods. But if they are right, we have no distinctively moral reason in such circumstances for observance of moral principles.

This answer exposes the voluntarist to another of Price's objections. If we allow no morality or moral obligation without commands and prohibitions, we make it difficult to see how command and prohibitions alone could introduce moral obligation. Commands and sanctions may affect prudential obligation, but the voluntarists believe that prudential obligation is not moral obligation; for they believe that without commands there is only prudential and no moral obligation. Commands create moral obligations only if they are commands of a commander who is morally entitled to command in this area; hence, in Price's view, they presuppose morality. Pufendorf's appeals to love or gratitude towards God fail to establish the moral legitimacy of obeying God's commands.[56]

Price's conclusions may at first seem too sweeping. Many defenders of the view that morality depends on the divine will do not agree that it depends on any human will; that is why Cudworth deals with divine command theories only after he has dealt with views that identify morality with positive human law. Price, however, argues that if we make morality depend on the divine will, we really make it depend on will in general.[57] Either we say that any will equally creates moral obligation, or we appeal to some morally relevant features of the will of God. The only morally relevant feature of the divine will is the fact that God is especially good at recognizing what is obligatory, or that God has some right to command us. In either case, we recognize something that is right and is not created by God's command.

Price considers a Hobbesian reply.[58] In Hobbes's view, the divine will differs from other wills by being especially powerful and by imposing an especially severe sanction; that is why we have an obligation to obey the sovereign and God, but no obligation to obey just anyone who feels like giving us orders. Price answers that this is not a morally

---

[54] 'Omnipotence does not consist in a power to alter the nature of things, and to destroy necessary truths (for this is contradictory, and would infer the destruction of all wisdom, and knowledge) but in an absolute command over all *particular, external* existences, to create or destroy them, or produce any possible changes among them.' (50)

[55] On creation v. legislation cf. Suarez, §424; Pufendorf, §566.   [56] See Pufendorf, §577.

[57] 'What an absurdity it is, then, to make obligation subsequent to the Divine will, and the creature of it. For why, upon this supposition, does not all will oblige equally? If there be anything which gives the preference to one will above another; that, by the terms, is moral rectitude. What could any laws or will of any being signify, what influence could they have on the determinations of a moral agent, was there no good reason for complying with them, no obligation to regard them, no antecedent right of command? To affirm that we are obliged in any case, but not in virtue of reason and right, is to say, that in that case we are not obliged at all.' (111–12)

[58] In the last sentence of the passage just quoted ('To affirm . . . ').

relevant reason, and that Hobbes is really saying we have no obligation. He assumes, quite reasonably, that we can distinguish a source of moral obligation from a threat of sanctions if we fail to do what we are told. Threats may be effective, but they do not explain why we recognize the authority as legitimate. This argument shows why an appeal to divine commands cannot provide a plausible basis of moral obligation. A proponent of such views might offer them as a way of understanding the closest thing to moral obligation that we can find.

812. Open Questions

Price has exploited Cudworth's arguments for the 'eternal and immutable' character of morality to argue against both theological voluntarism and sentimentalism. He relies on these arguments to impose general conditions on the adequate definition of a moral property.

The first condition emerges from his attack on Locke's view that rectitude signifies the conformity of actions to rules or laws (of God, or the magistrate, or custom).[59] Locke's account implies that it would be absurd to ask whether a law is right; for a law could be right only if it conformed to a second law, about which the same question would arise, leading to an infinite regress.[60] According to Locke, the question 'Are the laws right?' should not be a reasonable question, since rightness simply consists in conformity to law. In this case the question 'Are the laws wrong?' should be equally unreasonable. Price answers that both questions are reasonable. He relies on this answer to formulate a general necessary condition for an adequate definition: (C1) If definition D makes right and wrong consist in conformity and non-conformity to F, but it is reasonable to ask 'Is F itself right or wrong?', because the answer is not clearly 'neither', then D is unacceptable.

A second condition for an adequate definition emerges from Price's attack on some unacceptable definitions.[61] Whereas the first condition concerned a question raised about the standard of rightness (law etc.), the second concerns a question raised about acting in accordance with the standard. In this case we ask whether it is right (e.g.) to obey a law. If rightness consisted in obeying a law, it would be absurd to ask whether it is right to obey a law; for that question would simply ask whether obeying a law is obeying a law. But Price observes that the question is not at all absurd, and that therefore the definition is unacceptable.

He therefore offers a second condition of adequacy: (C2) If definition D defines right action as doing F, but it is reasonable to ask 'Is doing F right or wrong?', because the answer is not clearly 'right', then D is unacceptable. In the previous case, where Price appealed to

[59] 'From whence it follows, that it is an absurdity to apply *rectitude* to rules and laws themselves; to suppose the divine will to be directed by it; or to consider it as *itself* a rule and law.' (43)

[60] See Cudworth, §548.

[61] 'Right and wrong when applied to actions which are commanded or forbidden by the will of God, or that produce good or harm, do not signify merely, that such actions are commanded or forbidden, or that they are useful or hurtful, but a *sentiment* concerning them and our consequent approbation or disapprobation of the performance of them. Were not this true, it would be palpably absurd in any case to ask, whether it is *right* to obey a command, or *wrong* to disobey it; and the propositions, *obeying a command is right*, or *producing happiness is right*, would be most trifling, as expressing no more than that obeying a command, is obeying a command, or producing happiness, is producing happiness.' (16–17)

(C1), the answer to the question 'Is F right or wrong?' should be 'neither', if the definition is adequate. In the present case, relying on (C2), the answer should be 'obviously right'.

If the two conditions (C1) and (C2) mark two ways in which a definition of a moral property is unacceptable, a definition is acceptable only if questions of the first sort are clearly ill-formed, resting on a misunderstanding, and the answer to questions of the second sort is, as Price says, 'most trifling', a near-tautology. If we have found the standard of rightness, the question 'Is F right?' should be ill-formed, and 'Conformity to F is right' should be as trivially analytic as 'A brother is a male sibling'. Price objects to proposed definitions by pointing out that some questions are reasonable that ought not to be reasonable if the definitions were correct. We may therefore say that he identifies 'open questions'.[62]

Price deploys both sorts of open question in his argument against Hobbes. He deploys them equally, following Burnet and Balguy, in his rejection of Hutcheson's appeal to the moral sense. In this case the two questions to be considered are (1) 'Is the moral sense right or wrong?', and (2) 'Is what the moral sense approves of right?' The first question would not be an open question, if the moral sense theory were right; for the only way to answer it within the moral sense theory would be to appeal to a second moral sense approving of the first one, and then we would face an infinite regress. The first question, then, ought to be ill-formed. The affirmative answer to the second question ought to be trivially analytic.

In Price's view, however, both questions are open. It is sensible, and not absurd, to say that the moral sense is right or wrong, because we can think of further considerations that would determine whether it is right. Similarly, it is not trivial to say that following the moral sense is right. If it is right to follow the moral sense, that is because following the moral sense meets some further condition for rightness, and we accept the moral sense only to the extent that we think it meets this further condition.

Price's use of open questions persuades him that rightness is simple and indefinable. We might expect him to say that every attempted definition of rightness results in an open question. But this is not his view. For he admits that some statements of the form 'It is right to do F' do not result in an open question, but he argues that nonetheless rightness cannot be defined as F-ness, because such statements give us merely synonymous expressions. Simplicity does not imply that every attempted account raises an open question; it only implies that every attempted account going beyond mere synonymies raises an open question.[63]

On this ground he argues that the accounts of rightness offered by Clarke and Balguy do not show that rightness is complex and definable. 'Acting suitably to the nature of things' and so on are useless for defining virtue, since 'they evidently presuppose it' (125). Instead of saying that rightness, fitness, obligatoriness can be defined through each other, Price

---

[62] Price does not use 'open question', but it is a useful description of his form of argument. It suggests correctly that his argument, on one interpretation, anticipates Moore's argument. On Moore and Price see Raphael, *MS* 1n, 111–15.

[63] 'He that doubts this, need only try to give definitions of them, which shall amount to more than synonymous expressions. Most of the confusion in which the question concerning the foundation of morals has been involved has proceeded from inattention to this remark. There are, undoubtedly, some actions that are ultimately approved, and for justifying which no reason can be assigned; as there are some ends, which are ultimately desired, and for choosing which no reason can be given. Were this not true, there would be an infinite progression of reasons and ends, and therefore nothing could be at all approved or desired.' (41)

believes they are all indefinable and 'convey . . . ideas necessarily including one another' (105).[64]

Here Price imposes a third condition of adequacy on a definition: (C3) If a proposed definition D says that rightness is F-ness, we must be able to understand F-ness independently of understanding rightness. A proper definition must be informative because we understand the definiens independently of the definiendum. According to this condition, rightness may still be indefinable even if many synonymous expressions connect it with other moral properties.[65]

813. Naturalism, Rationalism, and Moral Properties

Price's account of moral properties is intended to defend the anti-voluntarist position that, as we saw, has both naturalist and rationalist elements. In Aquinas and Suarez, naturalism and rationalism support each other; we grasp moral properties by reason, by discovering what is suitable for rational nature. These are the immutable moral properties, not mutable in relation to any legislative will, but mutable in relation to rational human nature. This naturalist element may still be present in the position that Cudworth develops against Hobbes.[66] Clarke appeals to fitness; he emphasizes the rationalist side of the argument against voluntarism, at the expense of the naturalist side.

In contrast to Clarke, Hutcheson emphasizes the naturalist argument against voluntarism, and takes it to support sentimentalism rather than rationalism. Balguy, however, argues that sentimentalism repeats the meta-ethical errors of voluntarism. Butler returns to the traditional combination of rationalism with naturalism, in opposition to Wollaston's defence of Clarke.

In this debate about different elements of Scholastic naturalism, Price supports rationalism without naturalism. He follows the lead of William Adams, who rejects Clarke's appeal to fitnesses. Adams and Price are perhaps influenced by the objections of theological voluntarists who complain that rationalist explanations of fitness are either unhelpfully vague, or misleading (because they imply it is morally wrong to address a French-speaker in English[67]), or collapse into utilitarianism. If the supposed explanation of rightness by fitness is either a bad explanation or a non-explanation, it is better to admit that it is a non-explanation, and that the rationalists were wrong to suppose that the nature of rightness could be explained by appeal to fitness.

Adams and Price conclude that we should simply speak of a perception of rightness, without attempting to ground it in knowledge of any other property. No other property can explain rightness in a way that satisfies the voluntarists. In Price's view, knowledge of rightness is not to be grounded in knowledge of anything else, because rightness is not identical to any other property; no non-synonymous account of the essence of moral rightness can be given.

[64] On 'mere synonymy' as a sign of an unsatisfactory definition see §656. On irreducibility as distinct from simplicity see §845.

[65] On criteria for definition see Thomas, *HM* 47–8. He does not mention C3.   [66] See Cudworth, §547.

[67] See Brown, §867.

From Price's point of view, traditional naturalist accounts of rightness and goodness are no less misguided than sentimentalist accounts. If the right cannot be what is approved by the moral sense, it cannot be what accords with rational nature or what is eternally fit. Price's position is more extreme than anything that Clarke says. It is difficult to say how far it goes beyond what Clarke means, since Clarke does not offer much explanation of fitness. But Price implies that Wollaston and Balguy were wrong to try to explain fitness, and he rejects the position of Butler and of traditional naturalism.

This aspect of Price's position is not completely clear, because of his third condition. For he might claim that Clarke's and Butler's accounts of moral properties do not really raise open questions, because they only offer synonymies, which cannot be understood without understanding the term that is being defined. Clarke and Butler might offer the sort of clarification of moral properties that he thinks possible and desirable. But if this is what he means, his claim about simplicity is true only in a restricted sense, so that moral properties are not definable in simpler terms. They might be complex and definable in many other ways.

In Price's view, appeals to fitness cannot provide a definition of virtue. We need some further account of why it is right to act according to fitness, and then we 'find ourselves obliged to terminate our views in a simple perception, and something ultimately approved for which no justifying reason can be assigned' (127). This does not show that rightness is indefinable. Even if explanations cannot be infinitely long, an appeal to fitness may explain something about rightness. We may understand action better, for instance, by treating it as the outcome of belief and desire, even if our account of belief and desire eventually mentions their relation to action. Instead of saying that the account of action is non-explanatory, we should infer that action, belief, and desire are to be understood through one another. Something similar might be true about fitness, rightness, appropriateness, obligation, and related features of morality. Price's objection is sound only if appeals to fitness are entirely non-explanatory.

To see whether Price is right, we need to distinguish two objections that he might intend: (1) Alleged definitions of moral rightness (etc.) by reference to fitness do not eliminate terms such as 'ought' and 'right'. (2) These alleged definitions do not eliminate moral terms. These two objections are not the same. For even if we cannot explain normative properties by appeal to exclusively non-normative properties (those that can be understood without 'ought', 'right', 'good', and concepts explained through them), we might be able to explain moral normative properties by appeal to non-moral normative properties. Perhaps Clarke and Butler explain the moral through the non-moral, not the normative through the non-normative.

Similarly, Price does not show that appeals to fitness provide no criterion of virtue (127). He assumes that the relevant sort of criterion is one that we could appeal to, in a particular case, to resolve a doubt about whether an action is right. He points out that if we cannot see whether an action is right, it will not help us to ask whether it has the relevant sort of fitness, and so he infers that fitness is not a criterion. But that is not the only sort of criterion one might seek. An appeal to fitness might say what makes a right action right, and in this way provide a criterion, even if we cannot use it in a particular case to settle difficulties in moral judgments.

After raising these objections to appeals to fitness, Price explains the sense in which he thinks they are acceptable. Clarke's is right if he means that moral properties are real, objective properties that can be rationally discovered and recognized.[68] Price seems to reject Clarke's and Butler's further claim, that we understand moral properties better by appealing to fitness or to naturalness. But his reasons for rejecting this further claim rest on a narrow conception of explanation. Our defence of Clarke and Butler against his objections does not show that they provide an explanation; but it identifies more precisely what they need to show in order to meet Price's criticism.

814. Price's Criteria for Definitions

Price's three conditions are supposed to show that the moral properties he discusses are indefinable and simple. He intends to distinguish moral properties from other properties on this point; he does not suppose he has shown that no properties are definable. If, then, his conditions imply that no property is definable, they are open to question.[69]

We may reasonably doubt his conditions, once we apply both the second and the third to a proposed definition. C2 tells us that if rightness is correctly defined as F-ness, then 'F is right' is trivially analytic and does not raise an open question. But C3 tells us that the correct definition of rightness as F-ness would have to be informative, not a mere synonymy in which our understanding of F-ness presupposes some understanding of rightness. We might suspect that any definition meeting the demand for informativeness and independent understanding of the definiens will thereby fail to meet the demand for trivial analyticity that leaves no open question. If this suspicion is correct, Price's conditions for definition are mistaken, since they imply that nothing can be defined.

He might reply that some definitions are informative, because we understand the definiens independently of the definiendum, but they still yield the right trivially analytic consequences that avoid open questions. Perhaps some definitions are of this sort. If we ask the meaning of 'vixen' and are told that a vixen is a female fox, we may understand the definiens independently of the definiendum. If we realize that we are being told the meaning of 'vixen', we may also realize that it is trivially analytic that a vixen is a female fox. Perhaps this sort of definition of a moral property would satisfy Price, since it would conform to both C2 and C3.

This sort of example, however, does not show that all acceptable definitions satisfy C2 and C3. The example of 'vixen' and 'female fox' is untypical for two reasons: (i) We assume that the definition is offered to someone who does not grasp the meaning of the word. Here, it is assumed, we have no previous beliefs involving 'vixen' that might make us competent users of the word without grasping the definition. (ii) There is nothing to being a vixen beyond being a female fox.[70] We have no other beliefs about vixens in the light of which we might find 'This vixen is a female fox' trivial or non-trivial. Neither feature of the example

---

[68] He believes they express the fact that 'morality is founded in truth and reason; or that it is equally necessary and immutable, and perceived by the same power, with the natural proportions and essential differences of things.' (128)

[69] On Price's arguments about definition see Hudson, *RR*, ch. 1   [70] This ignores metaphorical uses.

applies to proposed definitions of moral properties. In these cases we are not asking to have the word explained to someone who is wholly ignorant of its meaning, and we have many background beliefs against which the consequences of a proposed definition may or may not seem trivial.

In the case of proposed definitions of any properties that differ from our example of 'vixen', anything that meets C3 seems to violate C2. If a definition is informative, it must tell us something more than is obvious to a competent user of the term defined. Price thinks it is obvious that if we can use 'right', 'fit', and so on, we see that they are connected; that is why he denies that a definition that simply exhibits their connexions is satisfactory or informative. But then any informative definition of them seems to raise an open question. Since we do not already know, for instance, that rightness is what maximizes utility (if we did know that, the definition would be uninformative, a mere synonymy), the proposed definition must surprise us, and it will hardly seem 'most trifling' that it is right to maximize utility. In general, until we have thought harder about the meaning of 'F', we may be surprised to be told that 'F' means 'G', and so the question 'Is F G?' still seems open. But this hardly shows that F cannot be defined as G.

For this reason, Price's three conditions exclude so many proposed definitions that they cast doubt on his argument to show that moral properties are indefinable. Apparently we cannot satisfy the demand for both informativeness and triviality at the same time.

815. Meanings and Properties

Before considering how to revise Price's conditions for definition, we may raise a broader difficulty about his whole argument. He sometimes says he is asking about our 'ideas' of right and wrong. We might infer that he is asking about meanings or concepts; and sometimes he is clearly concerned with them (104).[71] Usually, however, he seems to be talking about the properties of rightness and wrongness; for properties belong to actions (for instance) apart from our view of the actions. If properties are, or exactly correspond to, meanings of words, the conditions for 'nominal' definitions of words and concepts will also be conditions for 'real' definitions of properties. But if properties are different from meanings, different questions may arise about the different appeals to open questions.

Price's appeal to open questions recalls Cudworth's argument against Hobbes, and Balguy's arguments against voluntarism and sentimentalism. Cudworth's argument against Hobbes is a development of the argument in Plato's *Euthyphro* about piety and what the gods love.[72] But the relation between Price's arguments and these earlier arguments is not

---

[71] 'Signify' (16) by itself need not imply a concern with meaning. Cf. Hudson, *RR* 21, who cites Price's use (39) of 'idea' as evidence of interest in meaning.

[72] See Passmore, *RC* 42: 'Cudworth's argument . . . depends upon a certain interpretation of his predecessors. . . . [P]utting the matter in the form which Moore has made familiar, they have asserted, both that "God always wills what is good" is a non-tautological proposition and that to be good simply means to be willed by God.' Rashdall, *TGE* i 136, claims that the indefinability of 'good' 'was taught with sufficient distinctness by Plato . . . , Aristotle, and a host of modern writers who have studied in their school—by no one more emphatically than by Cudworth'. He gives no reference. Prior, *LBE* 18, takes Cudworth's criticism of Hobbes differently: 'This is not quite Professor Moore's point that if obligatoriness is a character which may be significantly predicated of some person's commands, then it cannot

clear. We have seen that open semantic questions and open moral questions lead to different arguments. They also raise different questions about Price.

If Price seeks to raise open semantic questions, we may doubt whether he succeeds.[73] A utilitarian might argue that it is absurd to ask whether it is right to maximize utility, but we do not see this if we are surprised to discover that 'right' means 'what maximizes utility'. Presumably, Price believes that even when we know the meaning of 'F' and have got over our surprise at it, there will still be some genuine open questions, and he may argue that 'Is what maximizes utility right?' is clearly one of these questions. The utilitarian, however, may answer that we believe the question is open only because we have not considered the meaning of 'right' carefully enough. Since there are non-trivial and non-obvious equivalences of meaning, the fact that there is room for dispute does not show that the dispute is not about the meaning of the word.

Suppose, however, that utilitarians concede that Price is right about meaning, and that 'maximizing utility' is not the meaning of 'right'. They might still be right to claim that the property of rightness is the property of maximizing utility, so that maximizing utility is the feature of the world that we refer to when we speak of rightness. Our moral theory tells us that the properties referred to by 'right' and by 'maximizing utility' are in fact the same. We discover (in Locke's terms) the real essence of rightness, and we express our discovery in a real definition.

Price's argument has less force against a proposed real definition than against a proposed nominal definition. Any interesting discoveries of the identity of two properties must rely on facts beyond those that are obvious to those who know the meanings of the words well enough to communicate; otherwise they would not be interesting discoveries, In that case, people who have not learned the relevant facts can raise an apparently open semantic question (e.g., 'Is the Morning Star really Venus?' or 'Is temperature really mean kinetic energy?'). To refute a proposed real definition, he needs to find open moral questions. These are the questions that concern Cudworth.[74]

The difference between Cudworth and Price may be clearer if we attend to different ways of understanding properties. Ross, following Moore, distinguishes the property of rightness itself from the right-making property.[75] This distinction is quite alien to Plato, who takes

just *mean* being commanded by that person . . . The point is rather that it is impossible to deduce an ethical conclusion from entirely non-ethical premisses. We cannot infer "We ought to do X" from, for example, "God commands us to do X", unless this is supplemented by the ethical premiss, "We ought to do what God commands"; and it is quite useless to offer instead of this some additional non-ethical premiss such as "God commands us to obey his commands".' In referring to deduction, Prior takes Cudworth to mean that Hobbes's argument is logically, rather than morally, defective. Darwall, *BMIO* 118n, seems to agree. He remarks that 'Cudworth's argument has an obvious affinity with G. E. Moore's argument that every attempt to define "good" commits the naturalistic fallacy'. He refers without dissent to Passmore's and Prior's interpretations. Prior, 'Eighteenth century' 171–2, offers further evidence to show that some of the earlier moralists have something like Price's and Moore's argument in mind. He mentions Cudworth, *EIM* i 2.1. Cudworth says he is arguing for the reality of moral good on evil 'if they be not mere names without any signification, or names for nothing else but willed and commanded, but have a reality in respect of the persons obliged to do and avoid them'. Prior takes this to imply that Hobbes's position would make sense if 'good' and 'just' simply meant 'commanded'. (See also *LBE* 17.) Cudworth does not seem to be making this concession to Hobbes, however. He assumes, as common ground between him and Hobbes, that 'good' and so on have some meaning distinct from 'commanded'. Price and Moore on open questions are compared by Hudson, *RR* 5–8.

[73] On semantic and moral open questions see §661.   [74] See §551.
[75] See Ross, *RG* 10 (the property of rightness v. the right-making characteristic).

the right answer to his question 'What is the F itself that Fs have in common?' to be exactly what makes F things F, or that 'by which' F things are F. While Ross assumes that properties match concepts, Plato does not. If Cudworth's conception of a property is closer to Plato's than to Ross's conception, it is reasonable for him to argue against an account of a moral property by offering moral objections rather than purely conceptual objections. Hence he considers a different type of open question from the one that Price considers. Price's question is relevant to arguments about concepts, but not necessarily to arguments about properties.

If Cudworth's open questions are relevant to definitions of moral properties, we ought to reject Price's condition (C2) requiring a definition to be trivially analytic. A proposed definition 'Rightness is F-ness' ought not to be rejected simply because it does not seem trivially analytic that it is right to do F. The fact that this is not trivially analytic does not show that it creates an open moral question. An open moral question arises when we have good reason to believe that doing F is not right simply by being F.

Is the open moral question any more useful than the open semantic question? It may appear to provide a less readily applicable test than the test Price offers, and its application may appear to be more controversial. This is not clear, however. Price's test for a definition appeals to judgments about self-contradiction and tautology; but these judgments may be controversial, and if we insist on finding uncontroversial tautologies and self-contradictions, we will find it difficult to accept many definitions. By contrast, the open moral question seems to yield plausible results in some cases. If we have some basis for judging that F actions are right or wrong, besides the fact that they are F, F-ness cannot be moral rightness.

The appeal to an open moral question rests on the claim that the property of rightness is the one that explains the various characteristics of right actions; an open moral question about the rightness of F actions shows that F-ness cannot be the relevant explanatory property, since some further property of F actions beyond their F-ness explains why they are right. The appeal to counterfactuals is appropriate, since counterfactual dependence is closely connected with explanation.

We might question appeals to open moral questions. Do they confuse epistemological (or perhaps psychological) questions with metaphysical questions? The fact that we come to know or believe that x is F by recognizing that x is H rather than that x is G does not show that F-ness is H-ness rather than G-ness; for it might still be true that G-ness constitutes F-ness and explains x's being F.[76] Even if we appeal to something other than utility to convince ourselves than an action is right, it does not follow that the property of maximizing utility is not identical to the property of rightness. Berkeley may have this point in mind in his defence of utilitarianism; some have also attributed it to Butler.[77]

This objection shows us that the moral open question should not be used rashly, and that we cannot always decide, without appeal to further moral beliefs, whether it has been used correctly. Still, that does not show it is useless. For though we have to exercise our moral judgment to consider the relevant counterfactuals, it does not follow that we are learning only about our moral judgments. If we have good reason for claiming that if an action were F but not G it would still be right, but it is false that if an action were G but not F it would still be right, then we have a good reason for believing that an action is right because it is F

---

[76] Cf. R. Adams, 'Wrongness', on divine commands and rightness.   [77] See §§699–700.

and not because it is G, and for believing that G actions are right because they are also F, but it is false that F actions are right because they are G.

When Price appeals to open semantic questions, he introduces open questions that do not arise from Cudworth's arguments. Not all of his open questions are relevant to arguments about moral properties, understood as explanatory. Sometimes, however, they are relevant; he appeals to moral open questions, or at least his argument can be recast so as to raise them. In his arguments against divine command theories and moral sense theories, he exploits and generalizes the arguments used by Cudworth and Balguy, and presents a plausible general strategy. He introduces more open questions than we can introduce if we focus on open moral questions. He ought, therefore, to drop C2; he ought not to require an acceptable definition to yield trivially analytic truths of the sort he considers.

He ought also to drop C3; its demand for independent understanding of the definiens seems too strict. He is right to say that if we understand F simply through G and G simply through F, neither helps us to understand the other. But not all circles of understanding need be so small. We may come to understand 'right' better when we grasp its connexions to 'ought', 'obligation', 'duty', 'fitness', and so on.

C3 is even less plausible for real definitions. To apply C3 to moral properties is to insist that a moral property is definable if and only if it is reducible to some non-moral property that has precisely the explanatory role that we attribute to the moral property. This is a very strong reductive claim. We ought not to accept such a condition for specifying the nature of any genuine moral property; and so we have no reason to accept C3 as an appropriate condition on definitions of moral properties. Price does not show, therefore, that moral ideas or moral properties are simple and indefinable. His arguments for this claim rest on his questionable conditions for definition.

To abandon this claim, however, is not to abandon Price's objections to Hobbes and Hutcheson. These objections show not that moral properties are indefinable, but that they are irreducible to the non-moral properties proposed by Hobbes and Hutcheson. The arguments for irreducibility rest on a proper use of an argument about an open moral question. Cudworth helps us to see the part of Price's argument that is worth taking seriously after we reject Price's exaggerated claims.

816. Objections to Sentimentalism

Our reservations about Price's actual argument, and these suggestions about possible revisions of his argument, are relevant to the objection that he raises, following Balguy and Burnet, to Hutcheson's attempt to identify rightness with what is approved of by the moral sense. He argues that Hutcheson's belief in the supremacy of the moral sense over all 'kind affections' is inconsistent with his normal conception of moral approval as a favourable sensory reaction.

Price considers the question 'what ought to be the end of our deliberate pursuit, private or public happiness?', or 'which ought to give way (that is which it is right should give way) in case of opposition, the calm selfish, or the calm benevolent affections?' (217n). In asking this question we acknowledge some point of view superior to both selfish and benevolent affections; this is what Butler has in mind in speaking of the supremacy of conscience. Price notices that Hutcheson endorses Butler's claims about conscience, and that he applies them to the moral sense, in his *System of Moral Philosophy* (215n). In Price's view, these concessions to Butler conflict with Hutcheson's conception of the moral sense.[78]

Since we can ask whether we ought to follow, and whether it is right to follow, private or public happiness, Hutcheson's account of the nature of moral rightness is mistaken.[79] When we ask whether something is right, we do not take ourselves to be asking what we feel favourable towards. The latter question is answered by a report on our feelings and reactions at the time; but the question we are asking seeks a reason for forming our reactions one way or another.

This application of Price's open question argument presents a fair objection to Hutcheson's theory. It uses Hutcheson's objection to a theological voluntarist account of moral rightness.[80] The objection is not decisive. It shows that the meaning of the question 'What is right?' is not 'How do we react to this or that course of action?', so that a reference to the moral sense does not tell us the meaning of the question. But Hutcheson might still maintain that in fact we are simply consulting our moral sense, though our question suggests that we are doing something else.

Hume implicitly supports this answer to Price's objection.[81] When he says that in making moral judgments about actions we 'mean' nothing more than that we have a favourable sentiment, Hume need not suppose that we believe we are talking about a sentiment. He may suppose that we believe we are talking about the action itself, but we are in error. Hutcheson has good reason to attribute this sort of error to us; for we suppose we are asking about properties of actions and people, not about our own reactions.

Price's objection, therefore, forces sentimentalists to present their theory of moral properties and moral judgments as an 'error theory'. They must argue that Price's question results from an error about the nature and capacity of moral judgment and about the character of moral properties. If they frankly present their theory in this light, his arguments do not refute it. Still, his objections have some force. For if Hutcheson must revise our normal views about the character of our moral judgments in this way, we may ask whether the revision is reasonable.

The revision must be extensive. If we think we can sometimes have good reason to believe that our moral sense ought to be stronger than it is, or that we ought to listen to it more often than we do, our judgments do not seem to fit Hutcheson's view; for it is not clear that they are simply reactions of the moral sense. Hutcheson might say that these judgments rest on an illusion, because no reasons support our judgment about what is right or obligatory, apart from the reactions of our moral sense. But if he says this, he must agree that some of our moral judgments are simply mistaken. He cannot offer any interpretation that makes them true. Price's question forces Hutcheson to admit that he is

---

[78] See §642.

[79] 'This question, I say, plainly implies, that the idea of *right* in actions is something different from and independent of the idea of their flowing from kind affections, or having a tendency to universal happiness; for certainly, the meaning of it cannot be, which will proceed from kind affection, or which has a tendency to promote universal happiness, following our desire of private or of universal happiness.' (217n)

[80] See §660.   [81] See §756.

offering to replace moral judgment with something else, rather than giving an account of our actual moral judgments. Price's open question argument is legitimate, if it is applied without Price's exaggerations.

817. The Evaluation of Character

Price's examination of our attitude to moral character develops a further argument against a sentimentalist account of moral judgment. If Hutcheson's moral sense theory is right, our approval of the character of others consists in a favourable reaction by our moral sense to their benevolence.[82] Price argues that this account of approval leaves out an essential element in moral evaluation of a person. He agrees with Shaftesbury and Butler in claiming that we expect reflexion and rational choice in the genuinely virtuous person.[83] Merely instinctive benevolence, separated from any rational conviction of the value of benevolent action, is not the proper object of moral esteem.[84] Price does not discuss over-determined actions, where both our rational reflexion on what is right and our instinctive benevolence seem to be sufficient to move us to action, so that rational reflexion would have caused us to act even if the instinctive benevolence had not. It is not clear that the presence of instinctive benevolence subtracts moral worth from the action.[85]

Still, Price's main point is plausible. If the moral sense theory were right, disinterested favourable feeling towards another person's benevolent feeling would be moral approval of the other person's character. But Price points out that we draw a distinction between these two ways of looking at another person; character requires more than simple benevolent feeling.[86] Hutcheson's moral sense theory does not give the right account of our conception of moral worth or moral approval.[87] If Hutcheson recognized this, he would have to answer that we are mistaken to suppose we can draw Price's distinction.

Hutcheson does not believe he attributes to us the errors that he in fact attributes to us, if Price is right. Price's criticism, therefore, exposes an important consequence of Hutcheson's theory. Though Price is too quick to assume that this consequence refutes Hutcheson's theory, or the modified version of it that would be needed to respond to his criticisms, he offers a serious objection. For if a theory requires a radical revision of our initial view of the character of our moral judgments, we have to ask whether the arguments underlying the theory are cogent enough to outweigh our reasons for taking the view we take of moral

---

[82] Price also seems to have Hume in mind, at 189 para. 2.

[83] 'If a person can justly be styled *virtuous* and *praise worthy*, when he never reflects upon virtue, and the reason of his acting is not taken from any consideration of it, intelligence certainly is not necessary to moral agency, and brutes are fully as capable of virtue and moral merit as are we.' (189) He notices that Shaftesbury agrees with him on this point, and quotes from Shaftesbury.

[84] 'But *instinctive benevolence* is no principle of virtue, nor are any actions flowing merely from it virtuous. As far as this influences, so far something else than reason and goodness influences, and so much I think is to be subtracted from the moral worth of any action or character.' (191) Balguy gives a similar argument, to show that Hutcheson has to allow virtue to non-rational animals. See §657.

[85] On this issue about subtraction and addition in motivation see §669.

[86] 'Whenever the influence of mere natural temper or inclination appears, and a particular conduct is known to proceed from hence, we may, it is true, love the person, as we commonly do the inferior creatures when they discover mildness and tractableness of disposition; but no regard to him as a *virtuous* agent will arise within us.' (191)

[87] The point that Price insists is one of the 'verbal disputes' that Hume discusses in *IPM*, App. 4. See §726.

judgments. Once this question is raised about Hutcheson's theory, the theory looks less plausible.

818. Obligation

Price's rejection of voluntarism and his analysis of moral concepts prepare us for his analysis of obligation. He takes this to be the most important concept to explain ('the term most necessary to be here considered', 105), because it underlies fitness and rightness (104–5).[88] Just as Price uses his arguments about open questions to attack both voluntarists and sentimentalists, he defends an objective conception of obligation against the errors that he takes to be common to these other positions. His attack on the sentimentalist position endorses Maxwell's attack on Cumberland's voluntarist reduction of obligation to the necessity imposed by a threat of punishment (114–16n).

According to the sentimentalist, 'obligation' refers to a psychological state; I have an obligation to do x when I have a motive sufficient for me to do x or at least causing me to tend to do x. Balguy the rationalist follows the sentimentalists in accepting a subjective account of obligation as 'a state of the mind into which it is brought by perceiving a reason for action' (114).[89] Price rejects this and all other psychological definitions on the ground that they do not distinguish the objective basis of the feeling of obligation from the feeling itself, and they do not recognize that the obligation is the objective basis, not the feeling.[90]

A true moral judgment, in Price's view, recognizes an obligation that is already there whether or not we recognize it; that is the difference between a genuine obligation and something that we feel like doing or even feel compelled to do.[91] If genuine recognition of

---

[88] '. . . if no actions are, in themselves, either right or wrong, or any thing of a moral and obligatory nature, which can be an object to the understanding; it follows, that, in themselves, they are all indifferent . . .' (48). '. . . there being nothing intrinsically proper or improper, just or unjust; there is nothing obligatory . . . Moral right and wrong, and moral obligation or duty, must remain, or vanish together. They necessarily accompany one another, and make but as it were one idea' (49). 'Obligation to action, and rightness of action, are plainly coincident and identical; so far so, that we cannot form a notion of the one, without taking in the other. This may appear to anyone upon considering, whether he can point out any difference between what is right, meet or fit to be done and what ought to be done. It is not indeed plainer, that figure implies something figured, solidity resistance, or an effect a cause, than it is that rightness implies oughtness (if I may be allowed this word) or obligatoriness.' (105)

[89] See Balguy, §656. On subjective aspects of obligation see also Cockburn, §876. Adams's account of obligation appears similar to Balguy's: '. . . right implies duty in its idea. To perceive that an action is right is to see a reason for doing it in the action itself, abstracted from all other considerations whatsoever. Now this perception, this acknowledged rectitude in the action, is the very essence of obligation; that which commands the approbation and choice, and binds the conscience of every rational being' (Adams, NOV 17). The reference to 'perception' might suggest that obligation is a mental state, but 'rectitude in the action' might suggest a more objective conception of obligation, similar to Price's. At 58 Adams calls obligation a reason for action that 'makes the action a duty'.

[90] 'The meaning of it [Balguy's definition] is plainly that obligation denotes that attraction or excitement which the mind feels upon perceiving right and wrong. But this is the effect of obligation perceived, rather than obligation itself. Besides, it is proper to say that the duty or obligation to act is itself a reason for acting; and then this definition will stand thus: *obligation is a state of the mind into which it is brought by perceiving obligation to act.*' (114)

[91] 'It is not exactly the same to say, it is our *duty* to do a thing; and to say, we *approve* of doing it. The one is the quality of the action, the other the *discernment of that quality*. Yet such is the connexion between these, that it is not very necessary to distinguish them; and, in common language, the term *obligation* often stands for the sense and judgment of the mind concerning what is fit or unfit to be done. It would nevertheless, I imagine, prevent some confusion, and keep our ideas more distinct and clear, to remember, that a man's consciousness that an action ought to be done, or the

obligation essentially recognizes something other than our belief and feeling as a ground for our action, a purely psychological account of obligation is wrong. The state of mind that belongs to obligation should include a characteristic feeling that results from recognition of an obligation that is not a state of mind. Both obligation and the feeling of obligation are unintelligible unless we recognize that the obligation is the basis of the feeling.

The objective conception of obligation conflicts both with sentimentalism and with the legislative conception accepted by voluntarists. According to voluntarists, 'obligation' explains 'right', 'wrong', 'duty', and so on. All of these other moral concepts include a reference to obligation—as Price agrees—and obligation refers to legal imposition. Price rejects this direction of explanation; rightness consists wholly in facts about objective properties of things that are independent of the will of any legislator. Though obligatoriness and rightness imply some law binding us to do what is obligatory and right, this law does not require any legislator. The law results simply from the fact that some things are right, and that therefore we ought to do them.[92]

A moral ought, therefore, contains an obligation and a law without any act of legislation. The relevant type of law is an authoritative binding principle; we discover such a principle by discovering that we have no rational alternative to acting as the principle prescribes. Rightness itself provides us with the relevant sort of principle. This analysis refers to the sort of rightness that Suarez calls 'intrinsic rightness'.[93]

Both sentimentalists and voluntarists have to say that our belief in intrinsic rightness rests on an error. According to sentimentalists, the error is the belief that something external to us is obligatory. Our ordinary way of speaking of colours suggests that the redness of a body is an objective quality of it, independent of our perception; but Hutcheson and Hume believe that Locke has proved that there is no objective redness, and that we are really talking about a state of our consciousness. Something similar, in the sentimentalist view, is true of obligation.[94]

The voluntarist takes the error to be not the belief in obligation that is external to us, but the belief that it is intrinsic to an external state of affairs independently of an act of legislation. Hence voluntarists and sentimentalists agree in rejecting states of affairs that are obligatory independently of anyone's view of them. Price answers both conceptions of obligation by arguing that they make the recognition of obligation unintelligible; for unless we recognize intrinsic obligation, we have no grounds for recognizing obligation, in contrast to inclination, and we cannot explain why legislation has moral force.

Price does not accept—or even consider—the option defended by Suarez, confining obligation to legislation and allowing intrinsic rightness and wrongness without obligation. This option tries to explain why the voluntarist position seems plausible, by allowing that

---

judgment concerning obligation and inducing or inferring it, cannot, properly speaking, be *obligation itself*; and that, however variously and loosely the word may be used, its primary and original signification coincides with *rectitude*.' (117)

[92] 'From the account given of obligation, it follows that rectitude is a law as well as a rule to us . . . Reason is the guide, the natural and authoritative guide of a rational being. . . . But where he has this discernment, where moral good appears to him, and he cannot avoid pronouncing concerning an action that it is fit to be done, and evil to omit it; here he is tied in the most strict and absolute manner . . . That is properly a law to us, which we always and unavoidably feel and own ourselves obliged to obey . . . Rectitude, then, or virtue, is a law. And it is the first and supreme law, to which all other laws owe their force, on which they depend, and in virtue of which alone they oblige. It is an universal law.' (108–9)

[93] See §437.   [94] Mackie, *E* 39–46, offers an error theory in response to an argument similar to Price's.

legislation introduces a distinct type of moral requirement. But its recognition of intrinsic rightness agrees with Price on the basic issue.

819. Obligation and Motivation

Sentimentalism about obligation rests partly on internalism. An obligation seems to be a reason for action, and reasons are connected to motivation. Since sentimentalists accept the Hobbesian aim of reducing normative properties to psychological properties, they argue that, since obligations are reasons, they are internally connected to motives. Some voluntarists accept a similar internal connexion between obligation and motivation, taking a command by a superior with appropriate sanctions to provide us with a motive for acting on an obligation; this is part of (for instance) Hobbes's and John Clarke's voluntarism.

If this is why sentimentalists and some voluntarists are internalists about obligation and motivation, we might expect Price to be an externalist.[95] Indeed he comes close to externalism; he distinguishes the obligation, which is external to the agent, from the sense of obligation, which is a state of the agent. Though he asserts a close connexion between an obligation and a motive, he does not claim that obligation implies our actually being moved to action.[96] Such a claim would not fit his clear distinction between the existence of an obligation and our recognition of it. Nor would it fit Price's contrasts between his view of obligation and Hutcheson's. According to Hutcheson, 'a person is obliged to an action, when every spectator, or he himself upon reflection, must approve his action and disapprove omitting it' (116). Price replies that the obligation is what we recognize as the basis of our approval of an action; it is not the approval itself.[97]

---

[95] Hudson, *RR* 66, criticizes Price's theory for its failure to explain the internal connexion between the acceptance of a moral judgment and assent to an imperative. Hudson proceeds on the assumption (which he takes from Hare, *LM*) that there is an internal connexion that needs to be explained.

[96] 'What, in these instances, produces confusion, is not distinguishing between perception and the effect of it: between *obligation* and a *motive*. All motives are not obligations; though the contrary is true, that wherever there is obligation, there is also a motive to action.' (114) The last sentence, taken by itself, suggests that whenever it is right that A do x, A has a motive to do x. This strong internalist claim would suggest that we can never fail to recognize, and hence to act on, any obligation we actually have. Price thinks basic moral truths are self-evident, but he does not think all moral truths are as transparent to everyone as they would have to be if the strong internalist thesis were correct. Moreover, the strong thesis does not fit the immediately preceding sentence ('What, in these . . . ') When Price says 'there is a motive', he may use motive in the sense in which the police use it in trying to identify people who 'have a motive' to commit a crime. These are people whose interests and circumstances give them reasons to want the victim to be dead; the police do not mean that all such people actually want the victim dead.

[97] 'This account, however, is not perfectly accurate; for though obligation to act, and reflex approbation and disapprobation do, *in one sense*, always accompany and imply one another; yet they seem as different as an *act* and an *object* of the mind, or as perception and the truth perceived.' (116–17) The quotation continues in the previous note. In a footnote explaining 'in one sense' Price appeals to his distinction between absolute and relative virtue, and applies this to his claim about obligation: 'There are then two views of obligation, which, if not attended to, will be apt to produce confusion. In one sense, a man's being obliged to act in a particular manner depends on his knowing it; and in another sense, it does not. Was not the former true, we might be contracting guilt, when acting with the fullest approbation of our consciences: And was not the latter true, it would not be sense ever to speak of showing another what his obligations are, or how it is incumbent upon him to act.' (116n) The obligations of absolute virtue do not depend on an agent's knowledge, but those of relative virtue depend on it. In the relative sense, we are obliged to do what we believe to be obligatory, but in the absolute sense, it is possible to discover that what we believed to be obligatory is something we are not obliged to do at all. Price's claims do not seem entirely relevant to his main point. For even in the relative case

Price's considered view distinguishes three things: (1) I am under an obligation to do x. (2) I recognize that I am under this obligation. (3) I am motivated to do x by recognizing that I am under the obligation. Though he does not always mention all three, he seems to intend to distinguish the existence of the obligation (in (1)) from my recognition of it (in (2)). When he says that obligation and approbation, in one sense, always accompany each other, he appears to mean that recognition of an obligation is always accompanied by motivation; and so he seems to use 'approbation', as Hutcheson does, in a sense that implies motivation.[98] He asserts an internal connexion between knowledge of an obligation to do x and being moved to do x, not between the existence of the obligation to do x and being moved to do x.

He does not take this internal connexion to imply an internal connexion between knowledge of obligation and feeling of obligation. He recognizes that feeling is relevant to moral judgment and motivation, but denies that it is essential to them. In a passage that recalls Butler, he allows a significant role to feeling, but he commits himself to a rationalist position.[99] He thinks moral judgment is primarily a 'perception of the understanding', and that the appropriate 'feeling of the heart' is a consequence of the perception.[100] Price's claim about an internal connexion between recognized obligation and motivation presupposes an internal connexion between obligation and reasons. Someone who maintained that reasonableness gives no reason might well be thought to be inconsistent. But without some further premises about the connexion between the recognition of reasons and the presence of motives the move from reasons to motives is open to dispute.[101]

820. Obligation and Reason

In clarifying the internal connexion between recognized obligation and motivation, Price claims that being moved by moral considerations is part of being a 'reasonable being'.[102]

---

the obligation does not consist simply in the consciousness of obligation; the point is that we have an obligation (distinct from our consciousness) to follow our consciousness of obligation.

[98] This view is suggested by a later remark: 'But further, it seems extremely evident, that excitement belongs to the very ideas of moral right and wrong, and is essentially inseparable from the apprehension of them. The account in a former chapter of *obligation* is enough to show this.—When we are conscious that an action is *fit* to be done, or that it *ought* to be done, it is not conceivable that we can remain *uninfluenced*, or want a *motive* to action.' (186) Price cites Cic. *Fin.* ii 45.

[99] 'The truth seems to be that, "in contemplating the actions of moral agents, we have both a perception of the understanding, and a feeling of the heart; and that the latter, or the effects in us accompanying our moral perceptions, depend on two causes. Partly, on the positive constitution of our natures: But principally on the essential congruity or incongruity between moral ideas and our intellectual faculties"' (62) In a footnote Price quotes from Seneca ('Placet suapte natura . . . virtus', *Ben.* iv 17) and Cicero ('Etiamsi a nullo laudetur, natura est laudabilis', *Off.* i 14) to illustrate his claim about essential congruity. In explaining and (as he may suppose) paraphrasing his claim Price throws more light on what he means: 'It would be to little purpose to argue much with a person, who would deny this; or who would maintain, that the *becomingness* or *reasonableness* of an action is no reason *for* doing it . . . An affection or inclination to rectitude cannot be separated from our view of it. The knowledge of what is right, without any approbation of it, or concern to practise it, is not conceivable or possible.'

[100] The similarity and the difference between Butler and Price are remarked by Mackie, *HMT* 43.

[101] On Hume and internalism see §745.

[102] 'Why a *reasonable* being acts *reasonably*; why he has a disposition to follow reason, and is not without aversion to wrong; why he chooses to do what he knows he *should* do, and cannot be wholly indifferent, whether he abstains from that which he knows is evil and criminal, and *not to be done*, are questions which need not, and which deserve not to be answered.' (187)

We should not, in his view, ask, 'Given the fact that we are reasonable beings, what else needs to be true of us if we are to be moved by moral considerations?'. Given the nature of moral considerations and the nature of reasonable beings, it follows that we will be moved by moral considerations. Just as reasonable beings are necessarily moved by considerations of their happiness, they are necessarily moved by recognized obligations; if they lacked these motives, they would not be reasonable beings.[103]

This claim does not assert an internal connexion between recognized obligation and motivation. It says that the features that make us reasonable beings also include the sorts of motives that cause us to act on our recognition of moral obligation. If moral considerations were addressed to some different sort of being, they would not necessarily motivate.

These remarks, therefore, suggest a connexion between morality, being a reasonable agent, and motivation. If Price intends this sort of connexion, he does not imply either that recognition of obligation motivates independently of desire, or that it includes a desire. He claims only that our being reasonable agents includes having motives that make us susceptible to moral obligations.

If this is Price's view, he does not even imply that every reasonable agent always acts on the recognition of obligation. In his view, no further motive besides those implied in reasonable agency is needed to explain why we act on moral obligations. Some failure of reasonable agency underlies failure to act on moral obligations. But since Price does not believe that every reasonable agent always acts reasonably, he allows that we may fail to act on recognized moral obligations. But he rejects Hume's claim that a person's reasonableness is independent of their acting on moral obligations. His position reflects a dispute with Hume about what can be attributed to practical reason.

Price does not pursue this question further. Since he does not say what feature of rational agency implies a disposition to act on moral considerations, he does not dispel the suspicion that his claim is either trivial or mysterious. His claim is trivial if it says no more than that 'rational' means 'disposed to be moved by moral considerations'. This account of the meaning of the term is eccentric, and it does not tell us how rational agents are moved by morality. If he claims that 'rational' means 'moved simply by the belief that something is morally required', he tells us something about how a rational agent is moved, but he does not convince us that there are any rational agents in this special sense. His claim is obscure, however, if it means that rational agents, as we ordinarily understand them, are moved simply by the thought of moral obligation all by itself. This claim suggests that recognition of moral considerations has some capacity to move us, but throws no light on what the capacity is.

Price would remove the appearance of triviality or obscurity if he could present a plausible account of rational agency that did not assume that a rational agent is moved by morality, and if he could then present a plausible account of morality that showed how it would move a rational agent of the sort previously described. The argument might proceed in these stages: (1) A rational agent (as we can see without relying wholly on our views about moral motivation) must be moved by a characteristic reason. (2) Morality (as we can see by appeal to moral judgments, not simply by appeal to our conception of rationality) appeals to this same characteristic reason. (3) Hence a rational agent must be moved by morality.

---

[103] On the desire for happiness see §§805, 807.

What, then, is the characteristic reason? Butler tries to answer this question by connecting conscience and morality with nature. Even though moral agents thinking about their obligations do not think about nature, the fact that fulfilment of their obligations is suitable to their nature explains why they have reason to follow morality. Since Price rejects naturalism, he cannot give this explanation of why it is rational to be moved by morality. His moral epistemology discourages any such explanation. For his excessive use of the open question argument leaves no room for a clear account of the reason that is characteristic of morality; and so it is not clear what necessary aspect of rational agency corresponds to a necessary aspect of moral obligation. Price's moral epistemology seems to interfere with his argument about moral motivation.

He does not leave us completely at a loss, however. For though his normative theory is influenced by his epistemological intuitionism, it identifies some characteristics of the moral attitude. In particular, he emphasizes the implicit impartiality and reciprocity of moral principles. Could some account of rational agency show that a rational agent must be moved by principles embodying the appropriate sort of impartiality and reciprocity? Recognition of the gaps in Price's theory might lead us towards a theory such as Kant's.

821. Virtue and Vice

We have seen that Price sometimes seems to suggest that my belief that x is morally obligatory moves me by itself to do x. This is his strongest thesis about obligation and motivation. But we have also noticed that some of his remarks avoid this strong thesis. A more moderate thesis claims that rational agency itself includes the tendency to act on moral considerations, and that failure to act on moral considerations is a failure in rational agency. The strong thesis implies that vicious people are unaware of their moral obligations. According to the moderate thesis, they may be aware of their obligations, but they fail to act on them because of some defect in rational agency.

Price needs to explain how his view explains degrees of virtue and vice, and especially the possibility of progress or regress from one to the other, or from one intermediate state to a better or worse one. He does not claim that the moral motive is always the strongest, or that knowledge of obligations always moves us to act on them.[104] Following Butler's distinction between authority and power, he argues that the supremacy that he attributes to knowledge of moral obligations does not always result in action. He takes incontinence to illustrate strength separated from authority.[105] Once we admit the distinction between authority and strength, we can readily, in Price's view, recognize the possibility of incontinence.

---

[104] 'It being therefore apparent that the determination of our minds concerning the nature of actions as morally good or bad, suggests a motive to do or avoid them; it being also plain that this determination or judgment, though often not the prevailing, yet is always the first, the proper, and most natural and intimate spring and guide of the actions of reasonable beings . . .' (188)

[105] 'In other words; we have a *particular tendency or appetite* to *present good*, from whence it happens, that good is far from always affecting and influencing us, in proportion to the apprehended degree of its absolute worth. The view of *present good*, therefore, getting the better of the calm and dispassionate views of our *greatest interest upon the whole*, is only one instance of what happens continually in the world, namely, "blind desire, unintelligent inclination or brute impulse, getting the better of motives and considerations, known by the mind to be of incomparably greater weight".' (194n)

Vice has to be explained differently; for it does not seem so obvious that in this case we know that the virtuous action we reject rests on stronger considerations. Nonetheless, Price speaks of comparative strength in this case too.[106] The vicious person is not simply the victim of overwhelmingly strong desires. On the contrary, he is all the more vicious because he does not act under the influence of overwhelming influences; he seems to choose deliberately not to follow the moral obligation that he recognizes. But what sort of choice can this be, given Price's account of the moral motive? If the vicious person compares his obligations with his immoral preferences, on what basis does he compare them? Price does not say.

Our attitude to virtue is not fixed and unalterable. Price remarks that practice in facing difficulties may strengthen the virtuous motive.[107] But how does this happen? Is it just a natural fact that the more we try, in some sort of non-rational trial of strength, to act on the virtuous motive, the more likely we are to succeed? That is not our normal conception of training and practice. We are inclined to think that if we focus more sharply on the characteristics of the virtuous action and think about them more, we will find that the virtuous action seems more reasonable and attractive. It is not an easy matter to say what we discover about virtuous action when we focus on it in this way; Price gives us no help.

It is clear to Price that deliberately vicious action is more blameworthy than impulsive bad action under the influence of overwhelming desires. Since he thinks that praise and blame rest on the assumption that we are responsible for, and hence the self-determined causes of, the relevant actions, he has to show what is self-determined and responsible about the choice of virtuous and vicious actions. But his account of rational choice and its relation to moral motivation does not answer the question about responsibility.

Some of the difficulties that Price faces would be removed or reduced within a eudaemonist theory of morality and rational choice; in fact the desire to answer some of the questions that Price cannot answer suggests a reason for accepting eudaemonism. Price does not give a fair hearing to eudaemonism, because he connects it with a hedonist doctrine about the nature of happiness. Perhaps he could show that even a eudaemonist theory that is immune to his objections still fails to give the right account of the status of morality.[108] But what he says does not discredit eudaemonism.

822. Objections to Utilitarianism[109]

Price accepts Butler's objections to utilitarianism as a theory of morality as a whole, and develops them further by going beyond Butler's intuitive counter-examples. He takes

[106] 'When an action is reflected upon as evil, but the motives to commit it are very strong and urgent, the guilt attending the commission of it is diminished, and all that can be inferred is, not the *absolute*, but the *comparative* weakness of the virtuous principle, or its inferiority in strength to some other principles.—The more deliberately any wrong action is done, the more wicked it appears to us; because, in this case, reason and conscience have time to gather their whole force, and exert their utmost strength; but nevertheless are conquered.' (202)

[107] 'And though, at first, the virtuous principle may be scarcely able to turn the balance in its own favour, or but just prevail; yet every repeated instance, in which the inward spring of virtue thus exerts its utmost force, and overcomes opposition, gives new power to it . . .' (205)

[108] Reid tries to refute eudaemonism on the basis of a more accurate understanding; see §854.

[109] Price's anti-utilitarian arguments are discussed by Hudson, *RR*, ch. 4.

Butler's cases to be 'clear and decisive' (131–2), and adds both examples and arguments of his own.

One might suppose that Price's meta-ethical position makes it too easy for him to refute any normative theory. When he relies on logical open questions to refute other views of rightness, he concludes that rightness must be simple and indefinable. If he has already proved this conclusion, has he not proved that rightness is not what maximizes utility? Apparently, he only needs to point out that it is not evidently self-contradictory to assert that it is right to keep one's promises (for instance) even though it does not maximize utility. Moore uses a similar argument against a utilitarian account of good.[110]

If Price appealed to an open semantic question to argue against utilitarianism, he would be mistaken. For the most important utilitarian thesis is not vulnerable to such arguments. If these arguments show anything, they show what is wrong with some accounts of the concepts 'good', 'right', and so on. If utilitarians concede that they are not offering an account of the concept of rightness, they may still claim to be identifying the 'right-making characteristic'.[111]

We might still wonder, however, whether any account of this characteristic could be acceptable within Price's account of the 'idea' of rightness. For if he has shown that our concept of rightness is a concept of something simple and indefinable, how could we show that any definable characteristic is right-making? Our only constraint on the identification of the right-making characteristic is that it must make something have the simple and indefinable property of rightness. But if the resulting property is simple and indefinable, why should we believe that one characteristic rather than another causes, makes, or constitutes it? From this point of view, neither utilitarianism nor any other normative theory seems to satisfy Price's constraints.

This argument overlooks the restrictions on Price's claim that rightness is simple and indefinable. He denies that rightness can be analysed into simpler, independently understood elements that would allow a reductive definition. Though he rejects such an analysis, he allows that we can describe rightness informatively, and that we can connect it with other properties. All these descriptions and connexions give us 'synonymous descriptions' rather than genuine definitions, but they embody necessary truths about rightness. Such descriptions, therefore, may tell us enough about rightness to allow a decision about whether utilitarianism or some other normative theory is correct. Price's claim about simplicity does not disqualify all attempts at normative theory.

His diagnosis of the utilitarian error draws on Butler's treatment of psychological hedonism.[112] Price refuses to confine the issue to questions about whether the actions prescribed by the different virtues actually promote utility. Even if they did not always promote it, the utilitarian could argue that they generally promote it, so that we form 'a habit of considering them [sc. vices] as of general pernicious tendency, by which we are insensibly

---

[110] See Moore, PE 72.   [111] See §815.

[112] 'It has been urged against those who derive all our desires and actions from self-love, that they find out views and reasonings for men, which never entered the minds of many of them; and which, in all probability, none attended to in the common course of their thoughts and pursuits.—The same may be urged against those, who derive all our sentiments of moral good and evil from our approbation of benevolence and disapprobation of the want of it; and both, in my opinion, have undertaken tasks almost equally impracticable.' (136)

influenced, whenever, in any particular circumstances or instances, we contemplate them' (135). The question is whether this is the right explanation of the moral judgments we actually make. Even if utilitarians made the same moral judgments as non-utilitarians, that would not vindicate the utilitarian position.

Price does not refute the utilitarian case if he simply observes that we do not consciously think in utilitarian terms. Utilitarians need not attribute explicit utilitarian reasoning to us; but they must argue that we care about utilitarian considerations enough to adapt our moral judgments to them. We answer this utilitarian claim if we show that we would still see moral reasons for acting as we do if we were convinced that no utilitarian defence of our action could be given. These moral reasons may not always be overriding, if utilitarian considerations also contribute to overall rightness. But they refute a utilitarian account of rightness.

Price applies this counterfactual test against utilitarianism. We are often quite unsure about the effects of a particular action or rule on overall utility, but our uncertainty may not make us uncertain about whether it is right or wrong. One of his examples concerns the role of desert in distribution of benefits. In his view, 'vice is of essential demerit; and virtue is of itself rewardable' (81). We have some bias in favour of distributing benefits to the worthy and not to the unworthy, and we take this to be right. Price does not deny that beneficial effects are relevant to distribution; but he argues that they are not the only things that matter. We would still favour distribution according to merit even if we did not consider the utilitarian effects.[113]

Price's argument does not rely on his questionable views about the force of open semantic questions.[114] He does not argue simply that there would be no contradiction in supposing an action right but non-optimific. He argues for the stronger claim that a judgment about an action's being optimific does not settle the question about its rightness; other features of it besides its tendency to promote utility are relevant to its being right or wrong.

In this case, then, Price relies on an open moral question against utilitarianism. Though he appeals to our judgments about what is certain and uncertain, he does not confuse epistemic with explanatory reasons. If rightness is the tendency to promote utility, an enlightened person's certainty or uncertainty about the tendency of an action to promote utility should produce corresponding certainty or uncertainty about whether the action is right.

Should this argument move utilitarians? Admittedly, they need not be moved by the fact that our tendency to believe an action right may persist despite doubts about its tendency to promote utility. Still, they must agree that if we are rational, and take account of our doubts about utility, our conviction about rightness ought to be weakened also. If, then, our convictions about rightness do not change in the way that they would change if we were utilitarians, our moral judgments do not support utilitarianism.

The utilitarian might reply that indirect utilitarianism explains why it is generally beneficial for us to take the non-utilitarian attitude that Price describes. But this reply does not defeat

[113] 'But why right? Not merely on account of the effects; (which in these instances, we are far from taking time always to consider) but immediately and ultimately right; and, for the same reason that beneficence is right, and that objects and relations, in general, are what they are.' (80) On the relevance of this argument to Hutcheson's position see §648.

[114] Similarly, Moore, PE 76, does not take the failure of 'analytic utilitarianism' (as we may call it) to imply the failure of normative utilitarianism.

Price's basic objection. For, according to the indirect utilitarian, if we are enlightened about the basis of moral rules (or motives, or traits of character), our attachment to them depends on some conviction about their effects on utility. If Price is right, this utilitarian claim is mistaken.

A utilitarian who agreed with Price so far might argue that any attachment that is independent of utilitarian defences of a moral rule is irrational. Price denies this, but his denial is less convincing given his intuitionist account of moral judgment. For it might seem difficult to distinguish the intuitive and correct conviction of the rightness of non-utilitarian rules from an irrational attachment to them; on Price's view, we can give no further account of what we find rationally compelling about different types of right action.

He might argue, however, that if this is a difficulty for him, it is a difficulty for the utilitarian as well, since we have a good reason to accept the utilitarian principle only if we have an intuition of its rightness. If the utilitarian has to allow one principle grasped by intuition, why not accept the apparent fact that several principles, rather than just one principle, are intuitively compelling? Similarly, if we appeal not to rational intuition, but to what is immediately approved of by a moral sense, we have no reason to claim that our moral sense reacts only to benevolence and utility, and not to several irreducibly different features of right actions and of virtuous people (137).[115]

We might be able to resolve this dispute between monism and pluralism about ultimate principles if we could find a rational basis for accepting utilitarian or non-utilitarian principles, and could show that they do not rest simply on intuition without further support. But we could exploit this possibility only if we revised Price's moral epistemology.

Price suggests how we might show that opposition to utilitarianism is more than irrational stubbornness. Acceptance of utilitarianism would imply drastic revision in our views about rights.[116] We do not suppose that people's rights are conditional on a proof that such rights promote utility; but the aggregative aspects of utilitarianism conflict with the attitudes that underlie our views about rights. Utilitarianism is open to objection because of its aggregative weighing of the benefits and harms to one person against those to other people.[117]

Price suggests that the utilitarian attitude results from treating questions about distribution of happiness among different people as though they were parallel to questions about distribution within a single person.[118] He could have strengthened his objection by remarking

---

[115] Thomas, *HM* 82–6, discusses Price's objections to utilitarianism in relation to the debate between Bayes, Balguy, and Grove over divine benevolence. See §662.

[116] 'Were nothing meant, when we speak of the *rights* of beings, but that it is for the general utility, that they should have the exclusive enjoyment of such and such things; then, where this is not concerned, a man has no more right to his liberty or his life, than to objects the most foreign to him; and having no property, can be no object of just or unjust treatment.' (159)

[117] 'But besides, if public good be the sole measure and foundation of *property*, and of the *rights* of beings, it would be absurd to say *innocent* beings have a right to exemption from misery, or that they may not be made in any degree miserable, if but the smallest degree of *prepollent* good can arise from it. Nay, any number of innocent beings might be placed in a state of absolute and eternal misery, provided amends is made for their misery by producing at the same time a greater number of beings in a greater degree happy.' (159–60)

[118] 'What makes the difference between communicating happiness to a *single being* in such a manner, as that it shall be only the excess of his enjoyments above his sufferings; and communicating happiness to a *system of beings* in such a manner that a *great* number of them shall be totally miserable, but a *greater* number happy?' (160) Price's views on rights play an important role in his political theory. For instance, Laboucheix, *RPMPPT* 62, connects Price's insistence on the rights of minorities with his political outlook, and especially with his support for the rights of the American colonies.

that the utilitarian does not even have to suppose that more people benefit from harm to fewer people. If it does not matter how pleasure is distributed, more people might justifiably be harmed in order to make fewer people happier, as long as the resulting happiness of the minority would be great enough.

This objection draws attention to a conflict between utilitarianism and intuitive moral judgments. In connecting it with the issue about rights, Price suggests what might be needed to make his objections more than simply intuitive.[119] If he could show that the attitude to inter-personal distribution that resists utilitarian aggregation is a basic feature of our moral judgments, he would have shown that utilitarianism requires the replacement of morality by something else, rather than a mere revision of morality. But he does not develop his criticism far enough to present this general objection.

823. Normative Ethics and Intuition

In Price's view, we need intuition about ultimate moral principles, just as we need it about all ultimate principles.[120] He believes that an appeal to intuition is not a peculiar feature of his normative outlook, but a necessary feature of any normative outlook that seeks to trace its claims about the rightness and wrongness of specific actions to ultimate principles.[121] If it is not a reasonable option to reject intuitionism, it is not a reasonable option to question it simply because it leads to pluralism. We must simply recognize several moral principles and virtues that all rest on equally self-evident foundations, and we must resist any attempt to reduce them to one set of principles. As Price recognizes, this position requires us to admit the possibility of moral conflicts and dilemmas, where the requirements of two virtues cannot both be satisfied in the same situation.

He opposes this outlook to Paley's majoritatian utilitarianism. Price's political views as well as his Arianism may explain Johnson's antipathy to him. Boswell reports: 'I was present at Oxford when Dr Price, even before he had rendered himself so generally obnoxious by his zeal for the French Revolution, came into a company where Johnson was, who instantly left the room' (*LJ*, Sept. 1783 = Hill-Powell iv 238n (but cf. 434).

[119] Rights are central in Price's conception of good government: 'Our first concern as lovers of our country must be to enlighten it. Why are the nations of the world so patient under despotism? . . . Give them just ideas of civil government and let them know that it is an expedient for gaining protection against injury and protecting their rights, and it will be impossible for them to submit to governments which, like most of those now in the world, are usurpations on the rights of men and little better than contrivances for enabling the few to oppress the many.' ('Country' 181)

[120] 'It is on this power of intuition, essential, in some degree or other, to all rational minds, that the whole possibility of all reasoning is founded. To it the last appeal is ever made. Many of its perceptions are capable, by attention, of being rendered more clear; and many of the truths discovered by it, may be illustrated by an advantageous representation of them, or by being viewed in particular lights; but seldom will admit of proper proof.—Some truths there must be, which can appear only by their own lights, and which are incapable of proof; otherwise nothing could be proved, or known; in the same manner as, if there were no letters, there could be no words, or if there were no simple and undefinable ideas, there could be no complex ideas.' (98)

[121] Ross, *FE* 82, defends intuitionism and pluralism: 'The objection that many people feel to Intuitionism can hardly be an objection to the admission of intuition; for without that no theory can get going. The objection rather is that Intuitionism admits too many intuitions, and further that it admits intuitions that in practice contradict one another.' Ross's answer to the first objection is similar to Price's: 'After all, there is no more justification for expecting a single ground of rightness than for expecting a single ground of goodness . . . It is, to my mind, a mistake in principle to think that there is any presumption in favour of the truth of a monistic against a pluralistic theory in morals, or, for that matter, in metaphysics either.' (83)

He argues that the recognition of conflicts does not raise any difficulty for his intuition-ism.[122] The existence of some difficult cases does not imply that the principles themselves are not clear and self-evident. Price emphasizes that a moral judgment about an action in a particular case cannot rest on mere inspection, but has to depend on a careful examination of all the aspects of the action that are relevant to its rightness or wrongness.

Nonetheless, conflicts seem to raise a difficulty for Price's intuitionism. For even if we ought not to expect a moral theory to provide a solution for all difficulties, we might expect some answers to questions of priority; but Price seems to force many such questions on us, and to provide no answers. On one way of looking at it, the demands of justice and benevolence often conflict, since goodwill towards someone might often result in some desire to benefit him unjustly. If justice and benevolence are independent and self-evident principles, we ought to have no basis for deciding between their conflicting claims in such cases.

This conclusion may exaggerate the degree of disorder and conflict that we find in our moral beliefs. We need not claim that we can always decide between benevolence and justice, or that there are no genuine dilemmas. Still, we raise a serious difficulty for Price if we agree that it is often clear that we ought not to confer a trivial benefit at the cost of some great injustice. This is a fairly obvious feature of our moral convictions, but how does Price's theory explain it? The self-evident principles that, in his view, tell us that some moral weight is to be attached to justice and to benevolence do not seem to tell us about their comparative weight; if they gave us complete answers to comparative questions, they would be unimaginably complex. Alternatively, Price might seek to add self-evident principles about priority to the self-evident principles prescribing the individual virtues. But this answer seems to multiply the number of self-evident principles beyond credibility.

A more serious objection arises, however. For if we think about why a small favour does not justify a serious injustice, we are not completely at a loss about why this is so. We have some idea of the principles underlying both justice and benevolence, and we can give reasons to justify the conclusion that we reach in this case. We do not argue as we would argue if we believed that each duty rests on nothing more than an intuitive grasp of its rightness.

Price agrees that we often prefer the public good over other considerations.[123] He does not say that in every case where the public interest conflicts with some other moral principle, it ought to override, or even that when it carries considerable weight it must override, but only that in this situation it may override other principles. But in fact we seem to have some basis for identifying situations where the public interest or some other moral consideration ought to override. We can identify them partly because we have some conception of the principles that underlie both our concern for the public interest and our concern for other duties. Would we have access to this large, though sometimes imprecise and untidy, body of moral reasoning if Price's theory were right?

---

[122] 'The principles themselves, it should be remembered, are self-evident; and to conclude the contrary, or to assert that there are no moral distinctions, because of the obscurity attending several cases wherein a competition arises between the several principles of morality, is very unreasonable.' (168)

[123] 'What will be most beneficial, or productive of the greatest public good, I acknowledge to be the most general and leading consideration in all our enquiries concerning *right*; and so important is it, when the public interest depending is very considerable, that it may set aside every obligation which would otherwise arise from the common rules of justice, from promises, private interest, friendship, gratitude, and all particular attachments and connexions.' (153)

Price might reply that this reasoning is not about the relation between ultimate principles of right, but about whether specific actions have the right-making properties. Though ultimate principles of right must be grasped by intuition, the properties that make actions right may well be complex, and reasoning may be needed to decide whether specific actions have these properties. Intuition tells us that fair and impartial actions are right, but we may need more than intuition to know which actions are fair and impartial.

This distinction between rightness itself and right-making properties does not entirely answer the objection we have raised. If we can argue and reason about when and why the public interest ought or ought not to override considerations of justice or friendship, we seem to have some view about the relations between the relevant principles too. It seems arbitrary to insist that our moral reasoning tells us nothing about the character of rightness itself.

A further difficulty for Price's intuitionism seems to arise from his insistence on a version of the inseparability of the virtues. He argues that the different 'heads' of virtue 'all run up to one general idea, and should be considered as only different modifications and views of one original, all-governing law' (165). Since all the virtues are commanded by the same 'eternal reason', virtue is 'necessarily *one* thing. No part of it can be separated from another' (165). Acceptance of any virtue requires acceptance of them all.[124]

Price's claim is puzzling. In the objective, or (as he calls it) absolute, sense of 'obligation', each virtue imposes the same obligation, and so an objective ground for any one is equally an objective ground for all the others that we know by the same rational intuition. But it is not clear why Price should deny (or whether he means to deny) that we can have a clear intuition of the obligation imposed by one virtue without any intuition of the obligations imposed by the others. His intuitionism does not seem to rule out a complete and perfect intuition of just one virtue.

He would have a much stronger case if he were to argue that the reasons that require us to regard justice as a virtue also require us (say) to regard generosity and temperance as virtues. In that case it would be clear that someone who did not recognize generosity and temperance as virtues would be failing to grasp something essential to justice as well, and might well be said to lack knowledge of it. But this argument suggests that there is some further property that makes all these virtues right and obligatory—something further that should be identified with their rightness. Once we try to say what this feature is, we will have great difficulty in showing that it does not raise the sort of open question that Price takes to refute other attempted accounts of rightness.

Once again Price's intuitionism seems to interfere with a reasonable argument that he offers. Price is rightly concerned to avoid the premature reduction of all moral rightness to utility. But it would be equally premature to suppose that his frequent appeals to intuition are the only reasonable alternative to utilitarianism.

---

[124] 'He, therefore, who *lives* in the neglect of any one of them, is as really a rebel against reason, and an apostate from righteousness and order, as if he neglected them all. . . . True and genuine virtue must be uniform and universal.' (165)

62

REID: ACTION AND WILL

---

824. Reid's Main Contributions

Price argues against sentimentalism by defending an epistemological position that allows us to know about objective moral properties, not simply about how we react to things that lack moral properties. Reid agrees with him in claiming that we have this sort of moral knowledge. His distinctive contribution is his discussion of questions that are less discussed by Price, on will and action. The most important parts of *Active Powers* concern the topics of Book ii of Hume's *Treatise*, on passion, reason, and will.

Reid's discussion reflects a conviction that he shares with Butler about the importance of moral psychology for the grasp of moral principles. He offers a full account of practical reason, will, and freewill that supports his objections to sentimentalist views in moral psychology. Butler takes moral psychology to be the centre of his argument against Hobbes; and Reid tries to state more systematically the conception of will and practical reason that Butler accepts and that Hutcheson and Hume wrongly reject.

Stewart's memoir mentions that Reid regarded Butler as an antidote to excessive reliance on principles derived from Locke.[1] This favourable estimate of Butler is confirmed not only by the explicit references in *Active Powers*, but also by the general character and tendency of Reid's argument. It is useful to approach Reid's essays by asking what he offers to support Butler's position, and whether he succeeds in his aim of supporting it.

Reid has the advantage of comparing Butler's position with Hume's attack on Butler's naturalism. He often develops his positive views through a detailed criticism of Hume. Since the points on which Reid criticizes Hume are some of the main points on which Hume attacks Butler's naturalism, an examination of Reid's criticisms of Hume will help us to decide how far Hume's criticisms expose fatal flaws in Butler.

---

[1] 'In his views of both [sc. natural religion and Christianity] he seems to have coincided nearly with Bishop Butler, an author whom he held in the highest estimation. A very careful abstract of the treatise entitled "Analogy" drawn up by Dr Reid, many years ago for his own use, still exists among his manuscripts; and the short "Dissertation on Virtue" which Butler has annexed to that work, together with the "Discourses on Human Nature" published in his volume of Sermons, he used always to recommend as the most satisfactory account that has yet appeared of the fundamental principles of morals; nor could he conceal his regret that the profound philosophy which these discourses contain should of late have been so generally supplanted in England by the speculations of some other moralists who, while they profess to idolize the memory of Locke, "approve little or nothing in his writings, but his errors".' (*Works*, ed. Hamilton i 32b) I refer to Reid's works by pages and columns of Hamilton's edition (H).

825. Will as the Source of Active Power

Reid begins with our awareness of active power in ourselves.[2] We cannot give a 'logical definition' of power that would reduce it to simpler elements, as Locke and Hume try to do (H 514b), but we all recognize active power, because all our 'volitions and efforts' presuppose our attribution of active power to ourselves.[3] Why does he believe this?

A minimal notion of active power might be derived from the general presumption that some internal state of ours makes a difference to what happens to us; I notice this about myself in the first-personal transactions that Reid mentions, and I assume it about others in third-personal transactions. If this were all that Reid meant, however, we would recognize active power in ourselves whenever we noticed that seeing a mouse causes us to jump or thinking about eating oysters causes us to feel ill. But if this were active power, Reid would not ask 'whether beings that have no will nor understanding may have active power' (H 522a, title of ch. 5). His answer to this question is No. In agreement with Locke, he claims that active power requires will.[4]

To see why Reid claims that only will can give us a power to give certain motions to our bodies, we need to stress the active force of 'give'. If we 'gave' motion to our bodies by simply having internal states that are sources of the motion, our seeing a mouse and jumping would 'give' motion to our bodies. But Reid replies that we ourselves do not give this sort of motion. Our intuitive sense of ourselves giving motion rests on an intuitive sense of who we ourselves are. This intuitive sense identifies ourselves with our will.

Reid shares Aquinas' interest in distinguishing activity from passivity, and he agrees with Aquinas in connecting activity with will. Aquinas also tries to clarify the ways in which the passions are modes of passivity, and the ways in which non-rational animals are passive rather than active.[5] He explains these contrasts between activity and passivity by appeal to the rational character of the will, claiming that human beings control their actions through will and reason. The same assumptions underlie Reid's claims about active power. Understanding active power is important for understanding our sense of control over our actions and accountability for them.[6] Reid connects an action's being in our power with its being dependent on our wills. We have effective wills if and only if we have active power.

---

[2] Reid's views on active power and will are discussed carefully and well by Yaffe, MA.

[3] 'All our volitions and efforts to act, all our deliberations, our purposes and promises, imply a belief of active power in ourselves; our counsels, exhortations and commands, imply a belief of active power in those to whom they are addressed.' (H 517b)

[4] '. . . the only clear notion or idea we have of active power is taken from the power which we find in ourselves to give certain motions to our bodies, or a certain direction to our thoughts; and this power in ourselves can be brought into action only by willing or volition. From this, I think it follows, that, if we had not will, and that degree of understanding which will necessarily implies, we could exert no active power, and consequently would have none . . . It follows also, that the active power, of which only we can have any distinct conception, can be only in beings that have understanding and will. Power to produce any effect implies power not to produce it. We can conceive no way in which power may be determined to one of these rather than the other, in a being that has no will' (H 523a).

[5] On passivity in Aquinas see §§243–4.

[6] 'It is of the highest importance to us, as moral and accountable creatures, to know what actions are in our own power, because it is for these only that we can be accountable . . .; by these only can we merit praise and blame; . . .' (H 523b) 'Every man is led by nature to attribute to himself the free determination of his own will, and to believe those events to be in his power which depend upon his will. On the other hand, it is self-evident that nothing is in our power that is not subject to our will.' (H 524a)

To clarify active power, we need to clarify the relevant notion of the will.[7] An act of will must have an object, 'some conception, more or less distinct, of what he wills. By this, things done voluntarily are distinguished from things done merely from instinct, or merely from habit' (H 531b). In order to will, we must will an action that we believe to be in our power (H 532b). If this claim is taken strictly, it suggests that the agent must have a conception of itself and of its will and of things being up to it.

826. Will and Judgment

What sorts of agents meet these conditions for having wills, and therefore for having active powers? Reid's discussion is complicated by his assumption that will does not require reason and judgment. In his chapter, 'On the influence of incitements and motives on the will' (H 533a), he implies that the will is not essentially rational. First, he sets aside what we do by instinct and by habit, 'without any exercise either of judgment or will' (H 533b). The imputation of an action to an agent requires will.[8] But the intervention of will does not require any judgment or reason; for in some actions 'the will is exerted, but without judgment' (H 533b). An example is our choice of how much to eat; Reid suggests that we are better off if we follow our tastes than if we try to work out the exact amounts and times for ourselves, and he implies that if we follow our tastes we act on will without judgment.

In the explanation of action Reid distinguishes mechanical, animal, and rational principles.[9] While mechanical principles require neither attention nor deliberation nor will, it is not so clear how animal principles differ from rational. Reid believes animal principles lack judgment and reason; since deliberation seems to require judgment and reason, animal principles seem to lack deliberation.[10] Hence Reid seems to imply that they require will without deliberation.

To illustrate will without reason and judgment, Reid mentions conflicts of motives that are not resolved by reason. A soldier may be afraid of certain death on retreating more than of probable death on advancing, and so he advances. A dog may be hungry, but more afraid of being beaten for eating, and so he does not eat, because 'the strongest force prevails'. From these examples Reid concludes that will does not require judgment.[11] These actions also

---

[7] 'Every man is conscious of a power to determine, in things which he conceives to depend upon his determination. To this power we give the name of *Will*.' (H 530a) '[Will] may more briefly be defined.—The determination of the mind to do or not to do something which we conceive to be in our power.' (H 531a) Since this account relies on our understanding of 'in our power', which takes us back to a notion of power, it is not a logical definition of will.

[8] 'In the strict philosophical sense, nothing can be called the action of a man, but what he previously conceived and willed or determined to do. In morals we commonly employ the word in this sense, and never impute anything to a man as his doing, in which his will was not interposed. But when moral imputation is not concerned, we call many things actions of the man, which he neither previously conceived nor willed. Hence the actions of men have been distinguished into three classes—the voluntary, the involuntary, and the mixed. By the last are meant such actions as are under the command of the will, but are commonly performed without any interposition of will.' (H 543a)

[9] 'There are some principles of action which require no attention, no deliberation, no will. These, for distinction's sake, we shall call mechanical. Another class we may call animal, as they seem common to man with other animals. A third class we may call rational, being proper to man as a rational creature.' (H 545a)

[10] 'They [sc. animal principles] are such as operate upon the will and intention, but do not suppose any exercise of judgment or reason; and are most of them to be found in some brute animals, as well as in man.' (H 551b)

[11] 'Thus we see, that, in many, even of our voluntary actions, we may act from the impulse of appetite, affection, or passion, without any exercise of judgment, and much in the same manner as brute animals seem to act.' (H 534a)

illustrate the operation of will without deliberation.[12] 'Voluntary' actions without judgment seem to be those in which the will is exerted without judgment. According to Reid, then, all voluntary actions involve an exercise of the will, but do not all involve an exercise of judgment.

Non-rational animals, children, and madmen are agents who act voluntarily, but are not accountable for their actions, because either they lack rational judgment or it is not effective in their actions (H 614b).[13] Reid does not say that non-rational animals have wills. But he seems to imply that they have wills, if he allows that children both have wills and act on them.

827. What is a Non-rational Will?

This claim that non-rational agents have wills is difficult to grasp. They have more than mechanical principles of action, in which Reid includes instincts and habits. Their cognitive and affective responses are too flexible to be simply instincts or habits. But why does he not simply ascribe appetites and desires to them? Why must they also have wills?

An appeal to Reid's account of will does not seem to answer this question. If he simply regarded the will as the last appetite in deliberation, as Hobbes does, and if he held Hobbes's view of deliberation, his position would be intelligible. For non-rational agents can have a series of impulses tending in different directions; such a sequence is Hobbesian deliberation. The strongest impulse in this series is the one that we act on; and so that, according to Hobbes, is the will.

We might argue that Hobbes's picture is incomplete, because we need something other than appetites and desires to resolve a conflict between them; this resolution might be the task of the will. Reid rejects any such argument. For he supposes that the comparative strength of impulses is all we need to explain the choice of one option over another; we do not need to assume the 'interposition' of the will.

The ascription of wills to non-rational agents seems to conflict with Reid's account of the conviction that belongs to agents with wills. He argues not only that 'we are efficient causes in our deliberate and voluntary actions' (H 603b), but also that in acting on our will we have this conviction.[14] In his view, the conviction that the effect is in our power is characteristic

---

[12] 'Our determination, or will to act, is not always the result of deliberation, it may be the effect of some passion or appetite, without any judgment interposed. . . . In such cases we act as brute animals do, or as children before the use of reason. We feel an impulse in our nature, and we yield to it.' (H 539a)

[13] 'But it ought to be observed, that he [man] is a voluntary agent long before he has the use of reason.' (H 558a) 'Animal principles of action require intention and will in their operation, but not judgment.' (H 579b) 'If, therefore, there be any principles of action in the human constitution, which, in their nature, necessarily imply such judgment [sc. of things abstract and general], they are the principles which we may call rational, to distinguish them from animal principles, which imply desire and will, but not judgment.' (H 580a) 'What kind, or what degree of liberty belongs to brute animals, or to our own species, before any use of reason, I do not know. We acknowledge that they have not the power of self-government. Such of their actions as may be called *voluntary*, seem to be invariably determined by the passion or appetite, or affection or habit, which is strongest at the time.' (H 600a)

[14] 'An exertion made deliberately and voluntarily, in order to produce an effect, implies a conviction that the effect is in our power . . . The language of all mankind, and their ordinary conduct in life, demonstrate, that they have a conviction of some active power in themselves to produce certain motions in their own and in other bodies, and to regulate and direct their own thoughts. This conviction we have so early in life, that we have no remembrance when, or in what way we acquired it.' (H 603b)

of acting on our will in general; but he does not suggest that the conviction is present in every action that meets his broader conditions for voluntary action. If a child's actions on passions and appetites are voluntary, the conviction that they are in one's power must go back to very early childhood; but Reid does not actually assert anything as strong as this. He might reply that the conviction that he refers to arises only from action that is not only voluntary, but also deliberate. But that reply seems to conflict with his initial definition of acting on our will; for he took it to involve the conviction that the action is in our power.

Perhaps Reid thinks non-rational agents have the relevant kind of conviction if they seem to make choices that rest on the assumption that one course of action is feasible and another is not. If we could train a chimpanzee to get a banana off a high branch by using a stick, then we took the stick away, and the chimpanzee gave up trying to reach the banana, we might say that previously the chimpanzee thought it was in its power to reach the banana, but no longer thinks so. If this sort of belief is sufficient for the exercise of will, we must allow will to non-rational animals.

But if this is sufficient for the conviction that an action is in one's power, the conviction does not seem to help Reid's argument to show that we have a conviction of an active power in ourselves. The belief that we can ascribe to a chimpanzee amounts only to the belief that one course of action rather than another will succeed. If Reid attributes to children and non-rational animals some stronger conviction that their actions are in their power, the conviction is apparently false; for Reid believes that only free agents perform actions that are strictly in their power.

Reid could point to a conviction that is more suitable for his argument. Some agents form the conviction in some cases that they face alternative courses of action and that it is up to them to choose between them. This conviction includes the conviction that they are not simply passive spectators of a conflict between internal forces. Sometimes I might feel entirely or partly passive; I might wonder how long it will be before the pain of having my tooth drilled makes me shout, or how long I will be able to listen to a lecture without falling asleep. In other cases I believe that I am not just watching the interaction of forces that are out of my control. This belief seems more like a conviction of agency; for I distinguish these cases from cases of sheer or partial passivity.

Such a conviction fits Reid's account of will as 'a power to determine, in things which he conceives to depend upon his determination' (H 530a). Agents with wills recognize that they must make up their minds and 'determine' because the impulses they are aware of do not settle the question of what they should do. Such a view of the will makes it reasonable for Reid to say that impulses and desires 'operate upon the will' (H 551b), and that passion both 'gives a strange bias to the judgment' (H 571a) and 'gives a violent impulse to the will' (H 571b). When passion misleads us, it 'first blinds the understanding, and then perverts the will' (H 573a). The will seems to be distinct from appetites and desires; it is not simply the last and strongest desire in a sequence of desires. When the will is involved, I recognize that I need to decide which of these impulses, if any, I am to follow, and that it is up to me to decide which I follow. This conviction of agency seems quite different from the belief that we might ascribe to the chimpanzee trying or not trying to get the banana.[15]

---

[15] It is the conviction that is reflected in Aquinas' doctrine of consent. See §252.

828. The Rational Aspect of Will

Some of Reid's other remarks on the will confirm these tendencies to treat a will as requiring judgment and understanding. His contrast between desire and will suggests that the will is rational.[16] Since we can will what we cannot desire, will is not simply a desire, either first-order or second-order. But it is difficult to see how a non-rational agent could act on a will that is different from a desire. Reid, therefore, seems to assume that a will is some sort of rational state.

The connexion between will and imputation also tends to suggest that acting on passion is insufficient for acting on one's will, and hence that non-rational agency does not imply will. When we act on passion, our actions 'are partly imputed to the passion; and if it is supposed to be irresistible, we do not impute them to the man at all' (H 534a). This feature of the passions helps to explain why non-rational animals are not responsible for their actions.[17] Reid implicitly appeals to Butler's notion of a superior principle, without yet having explained it. He suggests that we need superior principles if we are to be accountable for our actions. Imputability and responsibility require judgment in an agent guided by a superior principle.[18] Since accountability follows from having a will and active power, Reid implies that non-rational agents, not being accountable, lack will and active power. Similarly, human beings dominated by passions seem not to be exercising their active power.

Reid seems to accept this claim that will involves judgment and a superior principle; for he connects will with accountability.[19] He believes we act on the conviction that we are accountable for those actions in which we take ourselves to exercise our active powers by acting on our wills. Hence we should apparently take judgment, which is necessary for accountability, to be necessary for will.

One might reasonably suggest, therefore, that the will is moved by superior principles, and that we act on will rather than passion insofar as we are moved by consideration of the weight of reasons instead of simply registering the strength of desires. People who act wrongly under the influence of a strong passion are blameworthy if they ought to have restrained their passion; still, their action is not imputed entirely to them, but partly to the passion. Reid contrasts this case with a case of 'perfectly' voluntary action,[20] suggesting that actions may

---

[16] 'With regard to our own actions, we may desire what we do not will, and will what we do not desire; nay, what we have a great aversion to. ... Desire, therefore, even when its object is some action of our own, is only an incitement to will, but it is not volition. The determination of the mind may be not to do what we desire to do.' (H 532a)

[17] 'We conceive brute animals to have no superior principle to control their appetites and passions. On this account, their actions are not subject to law. Men are in a like state in infancy, in madness, and in the delirium of a fever. They have appetites and passions, but they want that which makes them moral agents, accountable for their conduct, and objects of moral approbation or of blame.' (H 534a)

[18] 'Sometimes, however, there is a calm in the mind from the gales of passion or appetite, and the man is left to work his way, in the voyage of life, without those impulses which they give. Then he calmly weighs goods and evils which are at too great a distance to excite any passion. He judges what is best upon the whole, without feeling any bias drawing him to one side. He judges for himself as he would do for another in his situation; and the determination is wholly imputable to the man, and not in any degree to the passion.' (H 534a)

[19] 'Every man is led by nature to attribute to himself the free determinations of his own will, and to believe those events to be in his power which depend upon his will.' (H 524a) 'Every man knows infallibly that what is done by his conscious will and intention, is to be imputed to him as the agent or cause; and that what is done without his will and intention cannot be imputed to him with truth.' (H 524a)

[20] 'But if a man deliberately conceives a design of mischief against his neighbour, contrives the means, and executes it, the action admits of no alleviation, it is perfectly voluntary, and he bears the whole guilt of the evil intended and done.' (H 536a)

be voluntary to different degrees. An action is voluntary to the extent that it proceeds from the will, and it proceeds from the will to the extent that it proceeds from a superior principle, involving consideration of reasons rather than mere registering of strength of desires.

According to this argument, Reid ought to confine will to agents who are capable of acting on superior principles. This account of will seems to give a clearer conception of what it means to have the relevant sort of conviction that an action is in our power. We suppose that the action is up to us because we think about the merits of different courses of action, and our decision on this point determines what we do. This connexion between deliberation and active initiative is familiar in Aquinas.

This restrictive conception of the will gives Reid a strong argument against Hume's conception. He criticizes those philosophers who take the will to include 'not only our determination to act or not to act, but every motive and incitement to action' (H 531a). He thinks this broad conception of will is mistaken.[21] But he seems to invite the same objection to his view, by allowing voluntary action (explicitly) and will (less explicitly) to agents that act on these other conative states.

Reid might answer that this objection misconceives the distinction that he intends between passion and will. He compares it to the difference between advice and the 'determination' that we reach as a result of the advice.[22] One might try to understand the division between motives and determination as the division between the impulses that incline us one way or the other, and the 'decisive' or effective impulse. This is Hobbes's conception of the will as the last appetite. But this minimal understanding of 'determination' does not fit everything that Reid says about the will and about its connexion with the awareness of power. For we could have a 'determining' impulse without any awareness of the action's being up to us, or of our having the power to determine which of our impulses we act on.

To maintain his distinction between passion and will, Reid should argue that the relevant sort of 'determination to act or not to act' results from rational deliberation. He agrees with both mediaeval voluntarists and mediaeval rationalists who distinguish will from passion, and so he rejects the sentimentalist tendency, derived from Hobbes, to assimilate the two. But he faces the difficulties that a voluntarist faces in recognizing the rational character of the will.

Reid might object to our connecting will with rational deliberation; for our will is relevant to actions that are not themselves the immediate product of rational deliberation. But this does not refute the claim that the will involves practical reason and deliberation. For some actions may be voluntary because they are open to the influence of rational deliberation, even though no rational deliberation is engaged in them, and because we consent to them and thereby recognize that they are open to deliberation.[23] Reid believes that this feature

---

[21] 'It is this, probably, that has led some philosophers to represent desire, aversion, hope, fear, joy, sorrow, all our appetites, passions, and affections, as different modifications of the will; which, I think, tends to confound things which are very different in their nature.' (H 531a)

[22] 'The advice given to a man, and his determination consequent to that advice, are things so different in their nature, that it would be improper to call them modifications of one and the same thing. In like manner, the motives to action, and the determination to act or not to act, are things that have no common nature, and, therefore, ought not to be confounded under one name, or represented as different modifications of the same thing. For this reason, in speaking of the will in this Essay, I do not comprehend under that term any of the incitements or motives which may have an influence upon our determinations, but solely the determination itself, and the power to determine.' (H 531a)

[23] On consent see §827.

of such actions makes them imputable to the agent; and he could give the same account of what makes them voluntary. He need not say that they actually express the agent's will.

829. Reason v. Passion

Some of the difficulties in Reid's position emerge in his comparison of the division between will and passion with the division between reason and passion. He agrees with both common sense and ancient philosophers in separating two parts 'which have influence upon our voluntary determinations'.[24] He takes the rational part to include superior principles, which are the basis of the authority of the rational part. Reid traces Butler's division to the Platonic division between the non-rational and the rational part, which he identifies with a division between *hormê* and *nous* (or the *hêgemonikon*).[25]

Reid does not treat the will as a superior principle. The rational and non-rational parts are sources of different kinds of influence on the will and our 'voluntary determinations' (H 536a). Neither the rational nor the non-rational part is characteristic of, or essential to, the will. On this point his division differs from Aquinas' description of the will as essentially rational desire (appetitus rationalis).[26] But his position does not seem consistent unless he holds Aquinas' view. For he repeats his usual claim about the connexion between judgment and accountability (H 536a). If he takes will to imply accountability, he should take rational judgment to be essential to will.

It is difficult, however to express the essential connexion between reason and will. Reid wants to say that we can act on our will without being guided by the rational part. In such cases we might say that we deliberately refuse to follow the superior principle that we recognize. One might ask how something that is essentially rational could refuse to follow reason.

Reid suggests an answer to this question (though he does not apply it directly to his description of the will). In some cases we seem to choose simply by inclination, as when we choose between cheese and lobster. But he argues that our choice does not result simply from inclination; we correctly believe it is all right to follow inclination because we judge that the two tastes are equally good and that it is reasonable to follow inclination instead of trying to reason about which to prefer (H 534b). Rational judgment tells us how to decide the first-order question about which action to prefer.

An application of this pattern might help to explain how the will, while being essentially rational, can reject reason. We may reach a rational, even if mistaken, conclusion that in this case it is all right to follow passion without reflecting further on the merits of the course of action that our passion inclines us to do. This way of understanding will explains how Reid

---

[24] 'There is an irrational part, common to us with brute animals, consisting of appetites, affections and passions; and there is a cool and rational part. The first, in many cases, gives a strong impulse, but without judgment, and without authority. The second is always accompanied with authority.' (H 536a) '. . . there is a leading principles in the soul, which, like the supreme power in a commonwealth, has authority and right to govern. This leading principle they [sc. the ancients] called reason. It is this which distinguishes men that are adult from brutes, idiots, and infants. The inferior principles, which are under the authority of the leading principle, are our passions and appetites, which we have in common with the brutes.' (H 588b)

[25] He cites Cic. *Off.* i 101.

[26] See Aquinas §241. Aquinas gets confused when he speaks of the will as rational by participation; see §257.

can distinguish it from the influence of practical reason, but also insist on its connexion with accountability, which requires judgment.

830. Animal v. Rational Principles

Reid's further remarks about the will make his position no less perplexing. He distinguishes mechanical, animal, and rational principles of action. Mechanical principles require no will or intention; animal principles require will and intention, but not judgment; and rational principles require judgment (H 558a, 579b, 580a, 599b). While everyone acknowledges mechanical and animal principles, some philosophers deny any rational principles. Reid sets out to show that we must recognize them. Since animal principles do not require the reason and judgment that are characteristic of human agents, they belong to other animals too (H 551b).

It is particularly difficult to see what he means by claiming that the operation of animal principles requires will and intention. These principles are present in non-rational animals as well as rational; does Reid mean that in non-rational animals will and intention are involved in the operation of animal principles? It is difficult to see why they should be. For in rational agents will and passion are distinct; passions provide motives and can influence the will, but Reid does not believe that they are effective only when will endorses them. If they can move rational agents independently of will, why can they not move non-rational agents in the same way?

When Reid claims that the operation of animal principles involves will, he might not be referring to non-rational agents. He might mean that we normally act voluntarily when we act on animal principles, since normally we are accountable for how we act on animal principles. If we are accountable, will is involved, since will is the source of accountability. But if he has this role in mind for will, he cannot reasonably separate will from judgment; for, as we have seen, he takes accountability to vary with the role of judgment in an action.

Reid's discussion of animal principles corresponds to Aquinas' discussion of the passions, but in one respect it is inferior to Aquinas. Reid ought to explain how animal principles are the source of some of the voluntary actions for which we are accountable. Aquinas explains this by appeal to the consent of the will, understood as essentially rational desire. Reid follows him in taking accountability to require some role for the will, but he does not explicitly describe the will as essentially rational.

831. Superior Principles

We can perhaps clarify some of Reid's views about will and reason if we turn to his explicit discussion of action on rational principles. He follows Butler in ascribing superiority and authority to these principles.[27] Acting on rational principles involves some sort of judgment. But evidently not every sort of judgment will do. If we act on purely instrumental reasoning about ways to satisfy a particular appetite, we do not necessarily act on a rational principle.

---

[27] 'Thus we see, that, in many, even of our voluntary actions, we may act from the impulse of appetite, affection, or passion, without any exercise of judgment, and much in the same manner as brute animals seem to act.' (H 534a)

We recognize an authoritative principle insofar as we recognize that some consideration apart from the strength of my desire favours one course of action over another. Sometimes one appetite may be restrained by a stronger contrary appetite, as in the earlier example of a hungry dog who leaves his food alone from fear of punishment; the dog does not act on a superior principle.[28] Reid suggests that without superior principles non-rational agents yield passively to the stronger impulse; he returns to the connexion between will and active power. Though he does not say that acting on our will is acting on a superior principle, he attributes the common character of active, rather than passive, reaction to both of them.

Moreover, an authoritative principle tends to provoke self-approval (if we follow it) and shame or remorse (if we violate it).[29] Our reactions to such a principle rest on the considerations that underlie it. Since we think we have some reason to follow it apart from our desire for the end that it enjoins, we have some basis for reproaching ourselves. We do not simply notice that our predominant desire in the past is no longer predominant.

So far Reid follows Butler. He exploits this conception of a superior principle in order to defend a conception of rational self-love that is not explicitly present in Butler. He sees that when Butler speaks of superior principles and claims that they are in accordance with the agent's nature, he is not simply explaining what he means by 'superior principle' or 'nature'. On the contrary, Butler claims that acting on principles that consider value as well as psychological strength fits our nature as temporally extended agents.

Reid points out that superior principles reflect our conception of our good on the whole, which results from our conception of ourselves as temporally extended agents whose good is to be considered. Since we are temporally extended agents, we have interests that cannot be achieved by simply following the stronger current impulse; and so we discover that in our own interest we have to follow principles that rely on authority rather than mere strength.[30] In Reid's view, this account of superior principles and of self-love is not his innovation or Butler's. It captures arguments that lead Greek moralists to recognize an ultimate end that underlies all rational desire.[31]

This comparison with Butler and with the eudaemonism of Aristotle and Aquinas is appropriate, but it does not fit Reid's view of the will. Aquinas presents his theory of the will as a simplifying and unifying account of (1) the difference between will and passion;

---

[28] 'Do we attribute any virtue to the dog on this account? I think not. Nor should we ascribe any virtue to a man in like case. The animal is carried by the strongest moving force. This requires no exertion, no self-government, but passively to yield to the strongest impulse.' (H 554a) 'One principle crosses another. Without self-government, that is which is strongest at the time will prevail. And that which is weakest at one time may, from passion, from a change of disposition or of fortune, become strongest at another time.' (H 578b)

[29] 'We may resist the impulses of appetite and passion, not only without regret, but with self-applause and triumph; but the calls of reason and duty can never be resisted, without remorse and self-condemnation.' (H 536a)

[30] 'We learn to observe the connexions of things, and the consequences of our actions; and, taking an extended view of our existence, past, present, and future, we correct our first notions of good and ill, and form the conception of what is good or ill upon the whole; which must be estimated, not from the present feeling, or from the present animal desire or aversion, but from a due consideration of its consequences, certain or probable during the whole of our existence. That which, taken with all its discoverable connexions and consequences, brings more good than ill, I call good upon the whole. That brute animals have any conception of this good, I see no reason to believe. And it is evident, that man cannot have the conception of it, till reason be so far advanced, that he can seriously reflect upon the past, and take a prospect of the future part of his existence. It appears therefore, that the very conception of what is good or ill for us upon the whole, is the offspring of reason, and can be only in beings endowed with reason.' (H 580a)

[31] 'I pretend not in this to say any thing that is new, but what reason suggested to those who first turned their attention to the philosophy of morals. . . .' (206 = H 581a) He quotes Cic. *Off.* i 11, quoted in §176n3.

(2) conditions for responsibility; (3) the necessity of the pursuit of happiness. All of these questions are answered by Aquinas' account of the will, because the will is an essentially rational desire that is focussed on the pursuit of the ultimate end that is happiness, and because we are responsible for actions in which our desire for happiness has some causal role.[32] This is not how Reid explains his position. While he takes will to be necessary for responsibility, he does not take it to involve the desire (confined to agents with rational principles) for one's good as a whole. Hence he does not believe that responsibility involves a causal role for this desire. He differs from Aquinas on this point partly because he does not always take the will to be essentially rational.

This disagreement with Aquinas carries a cost for Reid. He agrees with Aquinas in taking the will to be essentially connected with responsibility. But he also takes judgment to be necessary for responsibility. Aquinas agrees on both points, and explains the connexion between them, by taking will to require rational judgment (appropriately understood). Reid does not explain the connexion in this way. By failing to explain it, he leaves obscure the roles of will and judgment in responsibility.

832. Will and Freedom

Some of the obscurities in Reid's conception of the will are easier to explain if we turn to his views about the freedom of the will, which he takes to be incompatible with determinism. His argument for indeterminism rests on our convictions about agency, which he takes to conflict with the truth of causal determinism.

He assumes we have a conviction of liberty as an agent's 'power over the determination of his own will' (599a). But he adds a second condition on freedom, rejecting necessitation.[33] This condition seems to tell us that the relevant power comes only from ourselves. But why should we need this information? If the source of the power is not wholly within ourselves, why should we abandon our claim to have the power?

Reid answers that the two conditions, referring to the possession of the power and to its source, are not really separate; the requirement of power implies the absence of necessitation. He argues that if we have the power to do x here and now, we must have all the means necessary for doing x.[34] If we would not have done x without the occurrence of some event that happened before we were born, we lack the power to do x.[35] Once we

---

[32] See Aquinas §267.

[33] 'But if, in every voluntary action, the determination of his will be the necessary consequence of something involuntary in the state of his mind, or of something in his external circumstances, he is not free; he has not what I call the liberty of a moral agent, but is subject to necessity.' (H 599b)

[34] 'All that is necessary to the production of any effect, is power in an efficient cause to produce the effect, and the exertion of that power: for it is a contradiction to say, that the cause has the power to produce the effect, and exerts that power, and yet the effect is not produced. The effect cannot be in his power unless all the means necessary to its production be in his power.' (H 603b) 'Were it not that the terms *cause* and *agent* have lost their proper meaning, in the crowd of meanings that have been given them, we should immediately perceive a contradiction in the terms *necessary cause* and *necessary agent*. ... To say that man is a free agent, is no more than to say, that in some instances he is truly an agent and a cause, and is not merely acted upon as a passive instrument. On the contrary, to say that he acts from necessity, is to say that he does not act at all, that he is no agent...' (H 607b)

[35] On Reid's conception of power and its connexion to his indeterminism see Lehrer, *TR* 260–1.

recognize what follows from our being genuine agents and active causes with the power to produce effects, we can see that indeterminism is true.

These arguments about liberty introduce a new element in Reid's views on will and responsibility. So far we have found reasons to ascribe three views to him: (1) According to his broad view, acting on will is necessary and sufficient for accountability. In one place he says that 'the free determinations of his own will' are attributed to the agent,[36] but immediately afterwards he speaks of actions that are 'subject to the will' and 'what is done by his conscious will and intention'[37] as attributable to the agent. (2) According to a more restrictive view, actions are attributable to the agent to the extent that they proceed from will and judgment. These actions are 'perfectly voluntary' and the whole guilt is attributed to the agent (73).[38] (3) According to the most restrictive view, actions are attributable to the agent only if they proceed from will and judgment and are done freely. This is the account of responsibility that Reid defends in his arguments about liberty.

When he defends the most restrictive view, Reid suggests that some actions proceeding from will and judgment may not be attributable to the agent, because they are not free.[39] In order to show that will does not imply accountability, Reid cites actions dependent on will for which the agent is not accountable. From these cases he argues that freedom is an additional condition for accountability, not automatically satisfied by actions dependent on will.

One might reasonably doubt, however, whether in these cases we take a person's action to proceed from his will without accountability. Reid mentions the actions of brute animals, children, madmen, and people acting on irresistible motives (H 614b, 619a). But if we really believe that these motives and emotions are irresistible, we need not agree that when we act on them we act on our will. In such cases we seem to act as non-rational animals do; we are moved simply by the strongest desire (H 534a),[40] where 'strongest' is taken to imply 'animal strength', as Reid explains it (H 611a).[41]

Reid claims that even when we act solely on the strongest animal motive, and when this motive is so strong that we are not accountable for acting on it, our will is engaged. But he does not give a good reason for introducing the will. The will seems to have no distinct explanatory role in the process that Reid conceives as simply an interplay of forces. The mere

---

[36] Quoted in §825.　　[37] Quoted in §828.　　[38] Ibid.

[39] 'If there can be a better and a worse in actions on the system of necessity, let us suppose a man necessarily determined in all cases to will and to do what is best to be done, he would surely be innocent and inculpable. But, as far as I am able to judge, he would not be entitled to the esteem and moral approbation of those who knew him and believed this necessity.' (600b) 'This moral liberty a man may have, though it do not extend to all his actions, or even to all his voluntary actions . . . In the first part of his life, he has not the power of self-government any more than the brutes. The power over the determinations of his own will, which belongs to him in ripe years, is limited . . .' (H 600b) 'I acknowledge that a crime must be voluntary; for, if it be not voluntary, it is no deed of the man, nor can be justly imputed to him; but it is no less necessary that the criminal have moral liberty. In men that are adult and of a sound mind, this liberty is presumed. But in every case where it cannot be presumed, no criminality is imputed, even to voluntary actions.' (H 614b) '. . . we do not conceive every thing without exception to be in a man's power which depends upon his will. There are many exceptions to this general rule.' (H 619a). 'There are cases, however, in which a man's voluntary actions are thought to be very little, if at all, in his power, on account of the violence of the motive that impels him.' (H 619b)

[40] Quoted in §826.

[41] 'They [sc. brute animals] do not appear to have any self-command; an appetite or a passion in them is overcome only by a stronger contrary one. On this account, they are not accountable for their actions, nor can they be the subjects of law.' (H 611b) '[Rational motives] do not give a blind impulse to the will as animal motives do . . . Brutes, I think, cannot be influenced by such motives. They have not the conception of *ought* and *ought not*.' (H 611b)

fact that the process reaches some 'determination' does not show that we need anything more than a Hobbesian 'last appetite'; it does not show that we have the determinative power that Reid ascribes to a will. Hence it is not clear that action on irresistible passions and emotions engages the will; hence these actions do not show that will is insufficient for accountability.

If, then, the will is involved in fewer actions than Reid supposes, his examples do not involve will, and hence they do not show that accountability requires freedom in addition to will and judgment. If we are convinced that will and judgment have the appropriate causal role in someone's actions, we have a good reason for taking the agent to be accountable for the actions.

In speaking of an 'appropriate' causal role for will and judgment, we may appear to be evading the issue that Reid raises, about the character of the appropriate causal role. Still, we seem to be entitled to recognize a causal role for our will and judgment that falls short of freedom, as Reid conceives it. When Reid takes freedom to be a further condition, he suggests that our actions might 'depend on' will and judgment, even if we are not free in performing those actions. But his remarks about will, judgment, and accountability suggest that dependence on will and judgment implies accountability.

833. Why is Freedom Necessary for Accountability?

Reid might answer us by pointing out that we take will to be relevant to accountability because we take it to involve the exercise of active power. But we cannot exercise active power, in his view, if we are necessitated. In claiming that we ourselves are the agents of our actions, we deny that our actions result from a deterministic process that results from events outside us and our will. If our actions resulted from such a deterministic process, the agents responsible for our actions (if any) would be external to us, and we ourselves would not exercise active power (280).

Reid takes seriously the claim that we ourselves are the causes of our actions. He takes it to require a doctrine of agent causation, so that, strictly speaking, the cause of our actions is ourselves, not some event, process, or state in us.[42] Though he recognizes that we use 'cause' in looser senses that do not require the complete causal self-sufficiency of a cause or agent, he believes that the strict sense fits our convictions about our agency, and hence about our accountability.

These claims raise a difficulty for Reid. He admits that we habitually use 'cause' and 'agent' loosely, so that we do not always take them to imply his strict conditions. How, then, does he know that our experience of agency, formed by our deliberate and voluntary action, is a conviction that we are causes in his strict sense, and not only in the looser sense consistent with necessitation?[43]

---

[42] 'If the person was the cause of that determination of his own will, he was free in that action, and it is justly imputed to him, whether it be good or bad.' (H 602ab) 'To suppose any other cause necessary to the production of an effect, than a being who had the power and the will to produce it, is a contradiction; for it is to suppose that being to have power to produce the effect, and not to have power to produce it.' (H 626b)

[43] This question is connected to Reid's acceptance of a principle of efficient-causal exclusivity, discussed by Yaffe, MA 45–7.

It is difficult even to understand Reid's strong conception of power. Some restriction on its apparent scope seems to be needed. We normally suppose that we have the power to move a pen or kick a football. We lack a necessary means, however, for exercising this power unless the pen and the football exist. Their existence may not be in our power; it is not in our power to create all the instruments we use, still less to create them immediately before we use them. In any case, our own existence is presumably a necessary condition of our exercising any power, but it is not itself in our power.

Reid might reply that we do not really have the power to kick a football, but only have the power to move our foot in a particular way or (since the existence of our foot and its connexion to our brain are not in our power) to make a certain kind of choice that can be described without reference to a foot or a football. But his position is actually more complicated. He concedes that there may be intermediary processes of which we are ignorant, coming between our decision to raise our arm and the rising of our arm.[44] His treatment of 'indirect causation' seems relevant to questions about determinism. For here he admits that my responsibility for shooting my neighbour does not depend on my act of will's being sufficient, all by itself, for his being shot. The shooting must somehow appropriately depend on my will. It may be difficult to describe this dependence precisely, but Reid has good reason to claim that we can recognize an appropriate causal connexion that carries accountability.[45]

Why, then, might we not take the same view about the causal sequence that precedes the contribution of my will? If I deliberately will to shoot my neighbour and set in motion the train of events that I believe will result in the shooting, am I not accountable for shooting him, even if I am not the only cause of my deliberate will? Reid suggests, quite reasonably, that we need not be concerned, for purposes of responsibility, about whether other unknown processes intervene between my will and the shooting. Why, then, should we not be similarly indifferent to whether my will is ultimately the outcome of unknown deterministic processes? Even if the ultimate determinant of my neighbour's being shot is some sequence of events in the early history of the universe, that does not affect the fact that my will contributes causally to the shooting.

Reid might reply that our will is taken to fix responsibility only in cases where it is the exercise of the appropriate sort of power. If I want to score a goal, and I am a skilled footballer, but no one will play football, I cannot in these circumstances score a goal. I cannot exercise my ability (as we might call it[46]) to score a goal in the present circumstances unless the present circumstances make it possible for me to do something that leads to my scoring a goal; and so I might say that I lack the power to score a goal.

---

[44] 'This may leave some doubt whether we be, in the strictest sense, the efficient cause of the voluntary motions of our own body. But it can produce no doubt with regard to the moral estimation of our actions. The man who knows that such an event depends upon his will, and who deliberately wills to produce it, is, in the strictest moral sense, the cause of the event; and it is justly imputed to him, whatever physical causes may have concurred in its production . . . Philosophers may therefore dispute innocently, whether we be the proper efficient causes of the voluntary motions of our own body; or whether we be only, as Malebranche thinks, the occasional causes. The determination of this question, if it can be determined, can have no effect on human conduct.' (H 528b)

[45] We cannot say that the relevant sort of dependence makes my will a necessary condition for my neighbour's being shot, because of cases of over-determination and pre-emption.

[46] Cf. Scotus' treatment of capacity, §269.

But this requirement (that if I am able to do x here and now, circumstances must make it possible to do something that leads to doing x) falls far short of Reid's demand for an absolutely self-sufficient power that depends on no antecedent conditions external to the agent. Why, then, should we ever ascribe to ourselves the sort of absolutely self-sufficient power that he mentions? If we do not think we have absolutely self-sufficient power, his argument from our conviction of power to the truth of indeterminism must collapse.

834. Objections to Reid's Indeterminist Account of Agency

The same objection faces Reid's appeal to our convictions about causation. He argues: (1) We think we are the causes of our actions. (2) A genuine cause must be an undetermined cause. (3) Hence the truth of our conviction in (1) rests on the truth of indeterminism. The weakness in Reid's argument lies in his effort to combine his first two claims. Let us grant the second claim for the sake of argument, and allow that the only genuine cause is an undetermined cause. But is this the sense of 'cause' that properly applies to the common-sense conviction stated in the first claim? In believing that we are causes, do we believe that we are undetermined causes?[47]

Reid admits that we tend to use 'cause' loosely so that it applies to determined (let us call them) 'quasi-causes'. Why, then, should we not suppose that when we believe we are causes, we use 'causes' to refer to quasi-causes? If Reid could show that we hold the views about power and ability that require us to be undetermined causes, he would be entitled to claim that we take ourselves—implicitly at least—to be undetermined causes. But his arguments to show that we attribute absolutely self-sufficient power to ourselves are open to objection.

Reid argues that we have a firm belief in freedom that cannot be uprooted by any doctrine of necessity, even in those who find the doctrine convincing (H 616b, 618a). His observation is a legitimate objection against any 'hard' determinist (someone who combines incompatibilism with determinism). But it is an argument for his indeterminist position only if our conviction conflicts with the truth of determinism. To show that it conflicts with determinism, Reid must rely on the arguments about causation and power that we have previously disputed. He cannot claim the support of common sense and universal conviction for his indeterminist analysis of freedom and power.

He tries to show that some of the beliefs connected with our convictions about freedom are reasonable only if determinism is false. He argues that praise and blame are wrongly directed at human agents if determinism is true, since accountability presupposes power.[48] If determinism were true, reward and punishment would have a purely prospective justification. Since a law was broken, the inducement to keep it must have been too weak; and that is the legislator's mistake. It is misguided to attribute the fault to the lawbreaker.[49]

---

[47] Rowe, TRFM, ch. 4, discusses Reid's views more fully and more sympathetically than I have discussed them.

[48] 'That no man can be under a moral obligation to do what it is impossible for him to do, or to forbear what it is impossible for him to forbear, is an axiom as self-evident as any in mathematics.' (H 621a) Reid's argument on obligation and freedom is examined by Lehrer, TR 273–5.

[49] 'We might as well impute a fault to the balance, when it does not raise a weight of two pounds by a force of one pound. Upon the supposition of necessity, there can be neither reward nor punishment, in the proper sense, as these

Reid is right to suppose that obligation and responsibility presuppose that the agent is in some sense the cause of the good or bad action and that in some sense it is possible for the agent to do or not to do the action. But what are the relevant senses of 'cause' and 'possible'? Reid is entitled to rely on our convictions about accountability and obligation only if he can show that they rely on his strongest conditions for causation and possibility. But he has not shown this. Admittedly, we do not blame agents for actions that their beliefs and values seem not to affect, or for actions on beliefs and values that seem to have been formed in the wrong way. But when we praise or blame people, we do not explicitly assume that their choices are not caused by any previous events.[50] We do not try to assure ourselves about the absence of external causation, and we do not change our minds about the agent's responsibility simply because we learn a causal account of the origin of the agent's values.

Indeed, one of Reid's favourite arguments from common sense seems to work against him here. When he discusses intermediate causes (in ascribing responsibility for shooting one's neighbour), he assumes that our knowledge, will, and intention are decisive, and that the causal mechanisms by which they achieve their effects do not matter for purposes of accountability. We might reasonably argue that this is also the point of view of common sense on determinism; we are interested in the role of our will and intention and not in all the processes by which our will and intention came about. Instead of claiming that our intuitive convictions about agency exclude the truth of determinism, Reid would be better advised to claim that they are indifferent to determinism.

835. The Free Will and the Rational Will

Reid's indeterminist conception of freewill seeks to answer the objection (urged by, for instance, Hobbes and Hume) that indeterminism gives an unintelligible account of decision and choice. From the determinist point of view, the introduction of indeterminism implies that on some occasions nothing in particular causes me to choose one way rather than another, and so my choice is unexplained and capricious, contrary to what we expect of a rational agent, let alone of a virtuous agent. Reid answers these objections by arguing that indeterminism does not introduce caprice.

Reid admits that 'rational beings, in proportion as they are wise and good, act according to the best motives' (H 609a); but he thinks this admission raises no difficulties for an indeterminist position. He is right, 'according to' means simply that a good person does what good motives prescribe. But this meaning does not capture our conception of a good person; someone who did what good motives prescribe, but for the wrong reason, would not be a good person. Good agents not only conform to good motives, but also act as they do because of what the good motives prescribe. And how is this 'because of' to be explained except by saying that good agents are causally determined by the prescriptions of good motives? We might support this demand for causal determination by good motives from

---

words imply good and ill desert. Reward and punishment are only tools employed to produce a mechanical effect.' (H 613a)

[50] Reid does not think choices are uncaused, but he believes they are caused by the agent, not in virtue of any previous event.

Kant's description of the person who acts from duty in contrast to the one who acts merely in accord with duty.[51] If, as Reid argues, no motives causally determine us, we apparently cannot be good agents.

Reid rejects this inference. He argues that we can draw a distinction between capricious and non-capricious action even if we reject determinism for human actions.[52] He suggests that someone who resists animal motives 'when duty requires' is a good person. But apparently the mere conjunction suggested by 'when' does not make someone a good person. We also require a good person to resist animal motives because duty requires. If my recognition that duty requires this action does not explain my doing this action, I am not a good person; but my recognition that duty requires it does not seem to explain my action unless it is a causal determinant of the action. Reid has not explained how the causal claims involved in our judgment of a person's character can be justified without belief in causal determination.

He might argue that the determinist interpretation of common-sense causal assumptions cannot be correct; for surely we can apply common-sense judgments without holding a metaphysical thesis about the truth of determinism? This argument is worth considering, but Reid is not in a good position to press it. Perhaps common-sense moral judgments are flexible in relation to controversial metaphysical theses that do not seem to be explicitly accepted by common sense. But this general principle casts doubt on Reid's attempt to derive indeterminism from common-sense judgments about responsibility no less than it casts doubt on any determinist attempt to argue from common-sense judgments about character.

Reid believes that agents choose the courses of action that make them virtuous or vicious. Why do they do this? An intellectualist account of the will argues that the vicious person has made a mistake about the good, and has chosen some apparent or partial good that appeared to him to be the right way to secure his ultimate good. Reid rejects the determinist assumptions of this view; for he thinks the will must be free to choose for or against the greater apparent good. He agrees that we are accountable for this choice, and therefore we make it freely. To explain how we make the choice, he asks what people will do if they have the freedom that he attributes to them. He assumes that wise people may be expected to choose the greater long-term good over the immediately pleasant.[53] But what justifies this expectation? If the will is likely to pick the pleasant or the overall good, these two objects are likely to seem attractive; but whether they are attractive or not seems to depend on what sorts of considerations actually determine the will. If nothing determines the will, we have no reason to expect that these will be the most likely objects of choice.

Moreover, why is it wise or foolish to choose one or the other option in the situations Reid mentions? A choice shows foolishness in the agent not because it reaches the wrong

---

[51] See Kant, G 397. For the argument that reasons for an action are best understood as causes of the action see Davidson, 'Actions' 693–700.

[52] 'To resist the strongest animal motives when duty requires, is so far from being capricious, that it is, in the highest degree, wise and virtuous. And we hope this is often done by good men.' (H 612b)

[53] 'It may surely be expected, that of the various actions within the sphere of their power, they will choose what pleases them most for the present, or what appears to be most for their real, though distant good. When there is a competition between these motives, the foolish will prefer present gratification; the wise, the greater and more distant good.' (H 612b)

conclusion, but because it rests on some error about what is most important or most choiceworthy. But if Reid is right, ought we to assume that an agent's choice of immediate pleasure in preference to overall good betrays foolishness? If the will were determined by our judgment of what is best, failure to choose what is best would show lack of understanding. But if the will can recognize what is best, and still choose something else, the choice of something else does not seem to be evidence of foolishness. Reid does not seem entitled to his assumptions about wisdom and folly.

He faces these difficulties because he believes we are accountable for our choice of good and bad courses of action only if we freely choose them. If this choice is to be free, it cannot, in his view, be determined by any specific sort of consideration; in particular it cannot be determined by consideration of the greatest apparent good, as the rationalist supposes. But in that case, the choice by the will must rest on no considerations at all. If nothing causes the will to choose the greater good over immediate pleasure, how can the choice be relevant to accountability?

In supposing that an undetermined choice underlies claims about accountability, Reid seems to undermine the conception of choice that allows it to play a role in judgments about accountability. Normally we think an agent's choice matters because we think it is made in the light of considerations, and we suppose that these considerations are the appropriate or inappropriate ones to determine an agent's actions. But a choice that is not based on, or determined by, anything at all does not seem important for judgments about accountability.

Reid has not described a credible alternative to an intellectualist conception of the will. Though he claims that intellectualism cannot explain freedom and accountability, the alternative conception he offers is unsatisfactory. It should prompt us to ask whether the objections to the intellectualist view are as decisive as he thinks they are. Reid's indeterminism is not justified by our beliefs about freedom and responsibility.

If we recognize these objections to Reid's position, we ought not to go to the other extreme and to argue, as Hume does, that the truth of determinism is necessary for judgments about accountability. A reliable and non-accidental connexion between recognizing the appropriate considerations and acting on them may fall short of a deterministic connexion; even if it did not always hold, it might hold reliably enough to support our normal judgments about agents, wills, and characters. Reid does not show how his position fits common-sense judgments about actions and character. He recognizes the importance of reconciling his position with these judgments; indeed, his main objection to his opponents is that they fail in the task of reconciliation. He does not show that his indeterminist position is any better on this point.

These objections to Reid rest on his remarks about will and accountability in the earlier essays (i–iii) before he turns to questions about freedom (in Essay iv). In arguing that common sense commits us to indeterminism, he departs from the description of common sense that he relies on the earlier essay. We have illustrated this point from his different claims about will, judgment, and accountability. His claims about will and judgment in the earlier essays are not completely consistent; but they are clear enough to cast doubt on the incompatibilist claims that he attributes to common sense in Essay iv.

Reid's indeterminism is probably not the only reason for his attempt to separate the will from reason and judgment, but, as in Scotus, his indeterminism and his voluntarism tend to support each other. In offering a voluntarist account of the will, he fails to explain how acting on our will necessarily differs from acting on our strongest passion. If he had followed Aquinas, and taken will to involve judgment, he would have been able to make clear the sense in which rational agents do not simply act on their strongest passion, even in cases where they choose to act against reason or to ignore reason. This role of judgment in will would also explain why human action is free and why we are accountable for it. These features of Aquinas' view are absent from Reid; instead he defends a voluntarist and indeterminist account of will and responsibility. But his claim that common sense supports voluntarism and indeterminism is not convincing. The convictions that he seeks to enlist in support of his position give stronger support to Aquinas.

836. Self-Love and Happiness

Though Reid does not follow Aquinas in taking the desire for happiness to be the distinguishing feature of a free agent, his conception of it makes it quite suitable for that role. His views about happiness are closer to those of the Greek and mediaeval moralists than to those of his immediate predecessors; he is an exception to the general tendency to accept a hedonist conception of self-love and happiness.[54] He gives a much fairer account of the Greek conception of happiness than we find in his predecessors. He therefore corrects some of Butler's and Price's claims about happiness and one's own good, so that Reid's conception of reasonable self-love is more suitable than Butler's own conception for the role that Butler has in mind for self-love.[55]

In Reid's view, reasonable self-love aims at 'our good on the whole'. Sometimes he identifies this good on the whole with happiness. He discusses the position of the ancient moralists as a position about our good on the whole:[56] In discussing their view, he asks 'How can he be happy, who places his happiness in things which it is not in his power to attain . . . ?' (H 583a). He means that these things do not contribute to our good on the whole.

Reid's other remarks about happiness are easily understood if he identifies happiness with one's good on the whole.[57] He refers to the same thing when he considers the connexion between one's own happiness and the happiness of others. We discover that we are 'social creatures, whose happiness or misery is very much connected with that of our fellow men' (H 584a). It would be difficult to understand these remarks if 'happiness' referred to something narrower than our overall good. Similarly, he speaks of happiness in a remark

---

[54] Sidgwick comments: 'It is to be observed that whereas Price and Stewart (after Butler) identify the object of self-love with happiness or pleasure, Reid conceives this "good" more vaguely as including perfection and happiness; though he sometimes uses "good" and happiness as convertible terms, and seems practically to have the latter in view in all that he says of self-love.' (OHE 228n)

[55] See Butler, §689.

[56] 'It has been the opinion of the wisest men, in all ages, that this principle, of a regard to our good upon the whole, in a man duly enlightened, leads to the practice of every virtue. This was acknowledged, even by Epicurus; and the best moralists among the ancients derived all the virtues from this principle [of a regard to our good upon the whole]. For, among them, the whole of morals was reduced to this question, What is the greatest good? Or, what course of conduct is best for us upon the whole?' (H 582b)

[57] 'We see, indeed, that the same station or condition of life, which makes one man happy, makes another miserable, and to a third is perfectly indifferent. . . . The evils of life, which every man must feel, have a very different effect upon different men. What sinks one into despair and absolute misery, rouses the virtue and magnanimity of another . . . He rises superior to adversity, and is made wiser and better by it, and consequently happier.' (H 583a)

about the superior principle concerned with one's own good. In his view, both our pursuit of our own overall good and our regard for morality reflect rational principles; his statements of this view speak indifferently of regard for our happiness and of regard for our good on the whole.[58]

Sidgwick is right, then, to claim that Reid does not speak of self-love and one's own good in purely hedonist terms. He is wrong, however, to suggest that Reid's view of the object of self-love is vague or inconsistent. Reid seems to conceive it consistently as one's own good, which includes more than pleasure. Sidgwick perhaps supposes that Reid is inconsistent in speaking of the object of self-love sometimes as one's happiness and sometimes as including more than pleasure.[59] Sidgwick finds these remarks inconsistent because he assumes, without any warrant, that Reid uses 'happiness' in a hedonist sense. Reid's view is (for all Sidgwick shows) quite clear and consistent.

Sidgwick's criticism of Stewart's restatement of Reid's position faces similar objections. He mentions Stewart as one of the modern moralists who identify one's own good with happiness, and therefore—Sidgwick assumes—with pleasure. Since Sidgwick attributes a hedonist conception of happiness to Stewart, he argues that Stewart misrepresents the eudaemonism of the ancient philosophers by identifying eudaimonia, as the ancients understand it, with happiness.[60] Sidgwick's criticism would be fair if Stewart accepted a hedonist conception of happiness.[61] But in fact Stewart follows Reid closely; he assumes that 'happiness' means 'good on the whole'.[62]

Stewart's presentation of eudaemonism agrees with his remarks about happiness. He praises Aristotle for rejecting the view that self-love is the source of vice.[63] He then rejects

[58] 'What I would now observe . . . is that the leading, principle, which is called *reason*, comprehends both a regard to what is right and honourable, and a regard to our happiness on the whole.' (H 588b) In speaking of 'our happiness on the whole', Reid refers to what he has described as 'our good on the whole'.

[59] Sidgwick's comment may refer to Reid's claim that 'whatever makes a man more happy, or more perfect, is good, and is an object of desire, as soon as we are capable of forming the conception of it' (204). But we need not infer that Reid takes happiness to exclude perfection; we might equally read the 'or' as meaning 'i.e.'.

[60] 'Thus when Stewart . . . says that "by many of the best of the ancient moralists . . . the whole of ethics was reduced to this question . . . What is most conducive on the whole to our happiness?", the remark, if not exactly false, is certain to mislead his readers. For Stewart always uses "happiness", as most English writers do, as equivalent to "sum of pleasures"; and he uses "self-love", as most exact writers after Butler have done, to denote the impulse which prompts us to seek the greatest amount of such pleasure obtainable.' (ME [1] 76n, abbreviated in ME [7]) Later Sidgwick comes back to the same criticism: '. . . when "Reasonable Self-love" has been clearly distinguished from Conscience, as it is by Butler and his followers, we find it is naturally understood to mean desire for one's own Happiness: so that in fact the interpretation of "one's own good", which was almost peculiar in ancient thought to the Cyrenaic and Epicurean heresies, is adopted by some of the most orthodox of modern moralists. Indeed it often does not seem to have occurred to these latter that this notion can have any other interpretation.' (ME 405) A footnote mentions Stewart as one of the 'orthodox modern moralists' whom Sidgwick has in mind.

[61] Sidgwick claims that Stewart is clearer than Reid on issues about self-love: '. . . he is more definite and consistent than Reid in conceiving as "happiness" that "good on the whole" of the individual which he takes to be the object of the "rational and governing principle of action", which he consents after Butler to call self-love—though he offers some just criticism on the term' (OHE 232). Sidgwick has no basis for his claim that Stewart differs significantly from Reid on this point. When Stewart identifies the object of self-love with happiness, he is not disagreeing with, or even clarifying, Reid's view unless he identifies happiness with pleasure.

[62] 'There is another, however, and a very important respect, in which the rational nature differs from the animal, that it is able to form the notion of happiness, or of what is good for it upon the whole, and to deliberate about the most effectual means of attaining it.' Stewart continues by quoting the passage from Cicero's *De Officiis* that Reid quotes for the same purpose. (Stewart, *PAMP* ii 1, p. 212)

[63] Stewart, *PAMP* ii 1.

the opposite view, that virtue is to be reduced to self-love, so that ethics is simply an inquiry into what promotes the agent's happiness.[64] Stewart neither asserts nor suggests that ancient moralists reduce virtue to a means to one's own pleasure. In his statement of their outlook Stewart follows Reid, who uses 'our good upon the whole', where Stewart uses 'happiness'. Both Stewart and Reid identify one's good on the whole with happiness.

Stewart says nothing misleading, therefore, in reporting the Greek moral philosophers as holding that 'the whole of ethics was reduced to the question, what is the supreme good? or, in other words, What is most conducive, on the whole to our happiness?' It is misleading of Sidgwick, however, to suggest that Stewart's remark is misleading. Sidgwick is so convinced that 'happiness' is to be understood in a hedonist sense that he does not see that Reid and Stewart hold a non-hedonist conception of happiness. That is why he claims to find vagueness, obscurity, and misleading suggestions where they are not to be found.

837. Superior Principles and Ends

Reid relies on his conception of superior principles in order to answer people who claim that ultimate ends are simply a matter of taste, and that reason has no role in the evaluation of ends. He considers an argument that begins from an admitted difference in taste—over the taste of lobsters and cheese.[65] Reid answers that it is wrong to say there is no room to apply rational judgment to the question about cheese and lobsters. On the contrary, rational judgment tells us that both tastes are equally good, and that there is nothing wrong if the cheese lover and the lobster lover follow their different tastes. In the case of the life of virtue and the life of pleasure, rational judgment is just as competent as it is the case of cheese and lobster. In this case it says that the two lives are not equally good; we can justly reproach the person who leads the life of pleasure.

Reid points out that when people deny that reason can judge between ends, their favourite example of incompatible tastes really works against them. For in that case they have to appeal to the rational judgment that there is really nothing better about one taste than about the other.[66] The fact that reason delivers this judgment shows that it is competent in such cases; and so such cases give us no ground for concluding that reason is incompetent in cases where it judges that two alternatives are not equally good.

The presence of rational judgments in the choice of ends implies an important modification of Butler's account of action. We might infer from Butler that sometimes we choose between

[64] 'As some authors have supposed that vice consists in an excessive regard for our own happiness, so others have gone to the opposite extreme, by representing virtue as merely a *matter of prudence*, and a sense of duty but another name for a *rational self-love*. This view of the subject was far from being unnatural; for we find that these two principles lead in general to the same course of action; and we have every reason to believe, that if our knowledge of the universe was more extensive, they would be found to do so in all instances whatever. Accordingly, by many of the best of the ancient moralists, our *sense of duty* was considered as resolvable into self-love, and the whole of *ethics* was reduced to the question, *what is the supreme good?* or, in other words, What is most conducive, on the whole to our happiness?' (Stewart, ii 2, 219)

[65] In this case, '. . . it is vain, say they, to apply judgment to determine which is right. In like manner, if one man prefers pleasure to virtue, another virtue to pleasure, this is a matter of taste, judgment has nothing to do with it' (H 534b).

[66] 'Nay, I apprehend that the two persons who differ in their taste will, notwithstanding that difference, agree perfectly in their judgment, that both tastes are upon a footing of equality, and that neither has a just claim to preference.' (H 534b)

alternatives simply on the basis of the comparative strength of our desires; Reid's choice between cheese and lobster seems to be an example in which we simply have to register the comparative strength of our desires. If this were a complete account, our choices in such cases would be no different from the choices of agents without superior principles.

Reid points out that this conclusion is false. In cases where the choice is a matter of taste, a rational agent who has superior principles recognizes that this is so. To recognize that there is nothing to choose between cheese and lobster on rational grounds, and that therefore it is all right to choose either, is an operation of rational judgment. If we are guided by this rational judgment and choose on the basis of our taste for cheese or lobster, we are acting on superior principles no less than when we choose directly on the basis of a superior principle.

Aquinas captures this point in his claim that the desire for happiness is a feature of genuinely human action as a whole. He does not confine it to actions in which there is something to be said for one alternative over the other. In choices where neither option is better than the other, the desire for happiness is still active, by permitting us to choose either. Aquinas and Reid draw attention to the permissive role of superior principles as well as their more direct intervention in our choices.[67]

838. Against Hume on Reason and Passion

Reid's account of a superior principle clarifies his dispute with Hume on the roles of reason and passion in motivation and justification. In his view, the dispute is not simply about words, about whether something that both Reid and Hume recognize is to be called 'reason' or not. In Reid's view, Hume loses an important distinction if he denies that sometimes we act on passions and sometimes on reason. The effect of Hume's view, according to Reid, is to deny the obvious truth that we act on superior principles.[68]

In Reid's view, Hume claims that reason has only the instrumental role of finding means to the ends that we pursue on the basis of passion without reason; Hume therefore ignores an essential function of practical reason.[69] Reid agrees that if Hume has correctly described the functions of reason, Hume wins his case; and so Reid seeks to show that there are distinctively rational principles that provide justifying and exciting reasons not included in Hume's description of reason. The principles Reid has in mind are those that cause us to pursue what appears good for us on the whole and to follow what appears to us to be our duty.

Reid describes our conception of our good as the product of reasoning that considers what is good or bad for us over the whole of our existence. As such, it is clearly the product of reasoning, not available to non-rational animals. Reid takes this to be a traditional view.[70] He claims that when we act on our conception of our good on the whole, we act according to reason, and reason prevails over passion.[71] Hume does not see this point, because he

---

[67] Cf Aquinas, §248.   [68] Reid's argument against Hume is discussed by Raphael, *MS* 160–5.

[69] '. . . some philosophers, particularly Mr Hume, think that it is no part of the office of reason to determine the ends we ought to pursue, or the preference due to one end above another . . . If this be so, reason cannot, with any propriety, be called a principle of action' (H 580a = R 859).

[70] See the passage Reid quotes from Cicero (quoted in §176n3).

[71] '. . . as soon as we have the conception of what is good or ill for us upon the whole, we are led, by our constitution, to seek the good and avoid the ill . . .' (H 581a). 'It appears that it is not without just cause, that this principle of action has

relies on a 'gross and palpable abuse of words'. Hume's claim that there is nothing especially rational about prudence relies on an unjustifiably narrow use of 'reason' and 'rational'. [72]

Hume may seem to have an easy reply. Prudent action (aiming at my good on the whole, as I conceive it) rests on reasoning about my good as a whole. But imprudent action may equally rest on reasoning. It is not contrary to reason to prefer the destruction of the world to the scratching of my finger (*T* ii 3.3.6). If I see that x leads to the destruction of the world, and y leads to the scratching of my finger, I choose x over y on the basis of this reasoning. The fact that the reasoning in question is not about my overall good does not make it any the less a case of reasoning, and hence it does not make the action any less rational in any strict sense.

If Hume is right about this, it is useless to say that we commonly tend to call action based on prudent reasoning rational action, or commonly tend to say that it is based on reason rather than passion, and tend not to say this about action based (in the same sense) on imprudent or positively anti-prudent reasoning. It is true that I have to be a rational agent in order to engage in prudent reasoning; but equally I have to be a rational agent in order to form some crazy desire for some satisfaction I will gain in ten years that will make me miserable for the rest of my life.

Reid might concede this point, but argue that the two cases still differ. In imprudent action, I am guided both by reasoning and by a foolish and irrational desire; in prudent action, I am guided (he might claim) by prudent reasoning, and not by desire. Hume disagrees, claiming that prudent action depends, no less than imprudent action does, on a prior non-rational desire for the end to which reason shows us the means. In the case of prudent action, this non-rational desire is a 'calm passion', and so we do not normally notice it. When we notice it, we can see that prudent and imprudent action have the same types of rational and non-rational antecedents, and that neither is the product of reason alone.

Our overlooking the role of calm passions is the source of all those 'confused harangues' (as Hutcheson calls them) about the superiority of reason. Once we see the source of the error, it seems pointless to appeal, as Reid does, to the common use of 'reason'; for this common use is simply the product of the confused harangues that overlook the role of calm passions. If we concede all this, Hume has won on the point of substance, even if the ordinary use of 'reason' has not yet caught up with his conclusions.

839. Prudence and Reason

Reid, however, should not be satisfied with Hume's reply. Hume's account of the origin of prudent desires and actions appeals to the effect of abstraction and distance in causing me to think of a future event without its attendant circumstances. [73] Abstraction causes me to form

in all ages been called reason . . . [It] not only operates in a calm and cool manner, like reason, but implies real judgment in all its operations. The . . . passions are blind desires of some particular object, without any judgment or consideration, whether it be good for us upon the whole, or ill.' (H 581b = R 863)

[72] '. . . he must include under the passions, that very principle which has always, in all languages, been called *reason*, and never was, in any language, called a *passion*. And from the meaning of the word *reason* he must exclude the most important part of it, by which we are able to discern and to pursue what appears to be good upon the whole' (H 581b).

[73] See Hume, §738.

a desire for a future good, and this desire causes me to follow the prudent course of action. The transitions from one desire to another must be purely causal and psychological, not at all based on justifying reasons. If Hume is wrong about this, his appeal to a calm passion and to instrumental reasoning is not sufficient to explain the role of practical reason in prudence.

One might sometimes suppose that Reid regards the prudent outlook as the result of a purely psychological process.[74] Hume might suppose he could easily accept this, as a purely natural, psychological fact about the empirically observed tendency to pursue our overall good once we have formed the conception of it.

But Reid does not refer to a purely empirical tendency. He suggests, in agreement with Price, that it is essential to rational agents to desire their overall good, and that no special sense or feeling is needed to cause us to act on beliefs about our own good.[75] In Reid's and Price's view, it is irrational to fail to pursue one's own happiness, whether or not we assume a calm passion of the sort Hume recognizes.

Reid and Price over-state their objection to Hume's view of prudence in suggesting that it is strictly self-contradictory for agents to know that something promotes their good and to recognize no reason for pursuing it. But they have good reason to maintain that it is not a mere psychological fact that agents form a desire to do what promotes their overall good. They suggest that it would be irrational to the point of unintelligibility if agents did not recognize their own good as a justifying reason for an action, and if this justifying reason did not sometimes provide an exciting reason.[76]

Reid's conviction of the rationality of prudence rests on the connexion between prudence and awareness of one's past and future.[77] He connects awareness of my existence as a temporally extended agent with awareness of the reasonableness of pursuing my overall good. He assumes that I care about my present desires partly because they are mine, not simply because they are present. For even if the desires are present, the satisfaction of them comes in the future; and if my future self is no concern of mine, why should I bother with my present desires? If, then, I recognize that my self extends through time, and I can take a more detached view of what will satisfy this extended self, my reason for attending to my present desires also seems to give me a reason for attending to my future desires. To deny that there is any such reason, I must either deny the reality of my future self or deny that I have any reason to be concerned about my present desires.

Why not try this second reply, and agree that I have no reason for my self-concern?[78] This seems to be Hume's reply. For he does not deny that we can form a conception of our

---

[74] 'I observe, in the *next* place, that as soon as we have the conception of what is good or ill for us upon the whole, we are led, by our constitution, to seek the good and avoid the ill . . .' (H 581a)

[75] 'I am very apt to think, with Dr Price, that, in intelligent beings, the desire of what is good and aversion to what is ill, is necessarily connected with the intelligent nature; and that it is a contradiction to suppose such a being to have the notion of good without the desire of it, or the notion of ill without aversion to it.' (H 581a) 'To prefer a greater good, though distant, to a less that is present; to choose a present evil, in order to avoid a greater evil, or to obtain a greater good, is, in the judgment of all men, wise and reasonable conduct . . .' (H 581b) Cf. Price, *RPQM* 45, quoted in §806.

[76] I add 'sometimes' to make it clear that Price and Reid are not committed to the claim that one's own good always provides an exciting reason, or an overriding exciting reason. The use of 'justifying reason' here does not follow Hutcheson's use; see §639.

[77] See H 580b, quoted in §831.

[78] Hume does not consider the first reply, since, for the purposes of his moral philosophy, he does not deny a person's persistence through time. See §770.

overall good and can form a desire for it; he simply denies that it is irrational not to care about one's overall good. If Hume is right about this, we ought to be able to conceive agents who are entirely indifferent to their overall good, but display no other defect that would justify us in calling them irrational. Can Reid show that indifference to one's own good is a symptom of some more basic irrationality?

840. Theoretical and Practical Rationality

Reid does not pursue this broader issue that is raised by his objections to Hume, but it is worth seeing how it might be pursued. Rational believers who discover contradictions in their beliefs try to remove the contradictions by giving up some of the beliefs that lead to the contradiction. In some cases we cannot immediately identify the beliefs to be given up. We may know that the conjunction of q and r implies not-p, and that p seems overwhelmingly plausible, but further investigation may be needed to decide whether to reject q or r. If it mattered to us whether we believe q or r, and it seemed fairly easy to investigate which is true, but we were unwilling to undertake this investigation, and did not change any of our attitudes to q and r as a result of seeing the conflict with p, we would not be rational believers.[79]

But why should we bother to examine our beliefs? The result will be available only to our future selves; if we do not care about their beliefs, why should we bother to try to get rid of the contradictions in our present beliefs? A fairly simple and basic condition for rationality in belief seems to presuppose concern for the states of our future self. This is not surprising, since the decision to modify our beliefs rests on desires for our future beliefs, and so must rest on some sort of prudential consideration.

Contrary to Hume, then, there is something irrational about our seeing no reason to care about our future states; if we saw no reason to do this, we would not respond to the sorts of considerations that a rational believer responds to. When Reid argues that concern for one's overall good is rational, and that indifference to it is contrary to reason, he is not simply quarrelling about the use of a word. He might argue that indifference to my future states reflects a degree of irrationality that would disqualify me from being a rational believer. The feature of practical reason that Reid appeals to is relevant to theoretical reason too; Hume overlooks it when he claims to give an exhaustive account of the functions of reason.[80]

This argument might not move Hume; for it rests on a conception of belief that he may not share. He describes a belief as a lively idea associated with a present impression.[81] This conception of belief leaves us no reason to get rid of contradictory beliefs. According to Hume, we may see overwhelming reasons for believing not-p, but still believe p, and do nothing to try to resolve the conflict. He thinks this happens when we consider the arguments against the existence of external objects, but they do not shake our belief in external objects.

---

[79] It might be very difficult and time-consuming to decide between q and r; hence it would not necessarily be rational to give up one of them as a result of investigation into their truth. But if we did not give up one of them, it would be rational to rely on them less confidently in cases where it matters which one is true.

[80] Cf Hume, §737.   [81] Reid criticizes this doctrine of Hume's at H 671a; cf. 433b.

Perhaps, then, Hume's account of belief does not imply that the conditions for rational belief include a constraint that exposes the irrationality of ignoring one's future states. But it is doubtful how far Hume could afford to press this objection. For his account of passions and morals is not supposed to rely on his radically sceptical epistemological and metaphysical claims; if it did, he could not even admit that my future states are the states of the person who has these present states. When he is thinking of ordinary beliefs in ordinary contexts (as opposed to the special context of metaphysical and sceptical argument), he cannot dispense with the normal assumption that rational believers try to remove conflicts in their beliefs. Indeed, one part of his account of how we take the moral point of view assumes that we try to avoid contradictions.[82]

If Hume accepts this much, it is fair to argue that agents who are indifferent to the states of their whole selves lack an elementary feature of rational believers. In that case Reid is right, though he does not explain why he is right, to argue that recognition of the reality of our future states is all that is needed to justify concern for them, and that failure to see a reason to be concerned for our good as a whole would be a mark of deep irrationality.

If Reid is right on this point, Hume is wrong, because he has not mentioned all the functions of reason. The recognition that it is rational to pursue my own good is not the result of reasoning about causes and effects in general, or about means to ends in particular. Though imprudent actions may rest on the same sort of causal reasoning that underlies prudent actions, it does not follow that they are as rational as prudent actions.

Reid, therefore, is not merely saying that we call prudent action rational; he is claiming that such action really is rational, insofar as it involves a correct exercise of practical reason that is absent from imprudent action. Hume does not answer this objection to his argument. He cannot fairly assume that his opponents accept his account of the functions of reason, and so have to show that prudent action is more rational, on these terms, than imprudent action is. Reid rejects this assumption, since he rejects Hume's account of the functions of reason.

841. Prudence, Justification, and Motivation

We might defend part of Hume's position by confining Reid's objection to justifying reasons. Perhaps it would indeed be irrational not to recognize my own good as a good reason for action; but, Hume might still answer, this recognition will not provide an exciting reason unless it is subordinate to some independent overriding desire for my own good.

Reid denies that we are determined to action by the strongest motive (H 610a = R 882).[83] First he asks how we are to understand the comparative strength of motives. If a motive's being stronger consists merely in its actual prevalence—in the fact that we act on it—the claim that we act on the strongest motive is trivially analytic. But two other conceptions of strength of motive make it non-trivial to claim that we act on the strongest motive: (1) The 'animal test' measures strength by the conscious effort required to resist a desire. (2) The

---

[82] See Hume, §762.

[83] This argument against Hume is independent of Reid's indeterminism, and for the moment I have not mentioned the indeterminist aspects of his position.

'rational test' measures strength by considering 'that which it is most our duty and our real happiness to follow' (H 612ab).[84]

Either test of strength shows, in Reid's view, that the strongest motive does not always prevail. For we sometimes act against the motive that is stronger by either test. If Reid's two tests are exhaustive, he wins. Hume needs to show that there is some third type of strength or motivational force that is different from each of Reid's two types, and explains action and motivation.

Hume might argue that unless there is some third type of strength besides Reid's two types, we cannot explain why we sometimes follow the rationally strongest motive and sometimes do not. The difference must lie in some motivational force associated with the rational motive in some cases and not in others; and in these cases we must have some further desire or passion supporting our rational judgment. As we have seen, however, it is not clear why the crucial difference must rest in a passion, as opposed to defective understanding or attention.[85]

Reid's distinction between two types of strength rests on Butler's distinction between authority and power; 'rational strength' simply indicates greater authority. If Hume were correct in supposing that there is nothing distinctively rational about prudence, the distinction between power and authority would disappear. For prudence consists in being moved by the weight of reasons and not simply by the strength of one's desires. If someone just happened to prefer his longer-term over his shorter-term satisfaction because of some irrational tendency to favour the more distant over the more immediate future, he might often choose what a prudent person would choose, but he would not thereby be a prudent person.[86] For the prudent person responds to the case that can be made for one or another course of action, regarding this case as something different from the current strength of non-rational desires in favour of the different courses of action.

In believing that two kinds of motivation differ in this way, we are not making any of the mistakes about reason that Hume identifies. We recognize a type of response that seems clearly rational; it is a different sort of response from the sort that Hume can recognize. According to Hume, we understand prudence simply by recognizing the relevant calm passion. A calm passion, however, is not responsive to the weight of reasons; as Hume conceives a calm passion, it can only respond to the strength of desires. Since Hume allows us no capacity to respond to the weight of reasons, he does not recognize practical rationality. But prudence seems to involve rationality, since it seems no less rational to fit our desire to the weight of reasons than it does to fit our belief to the weight of evidence.

Hume answer this objection by rejecting the theoretical parallel to practical reason; for he might deny that there is any such thing as fitting our belief to the weight of evidence, in contrast to simply following our stronger inclination. His analysis of belief in Book i of the *Treatise* suggests that the division between following the weight of evidence and following the stronger inclination is misconceived. But if Hume has to appeal to this radically sceptical side of his epistemology, Reid wins his main point. Hume does not want his moral

---

[84] Yaffe, *MA* 118–31, discusses Reid's views on different types of strength.

[85] See Hume, §740. For further discussion, tending to support Reid, see Balguy, §655.

[86] He would agree with a prudent person often, but not always; for prudence does not always involve a preference for the longer-term over the shorter-term end.

philosophy to depend on his radical scepticism, and his case becomes less persuasive if it depends on the epistemological doctrines that are most difficult to accept.

He might try a more moderate reply to Reid by arguing that in the practical case, though not in the theoretical case, we are wrong to distinguish the weight of reasons from the strength of desire; though we seem to see a difference, there is none. If Hume says this, he accepts part of the Hobbesian strategy of reducing normative to psychological properties; though we believe the purely psychological differs from the normative, all we are actually talking about are purely psychological properties involving strength of desire. But if Hume goes this far, his position is more nihilistic than he recognizes; he has to say that our deliberative practice rests on false beliefs and that it could not be expected to survive the discovery of the falsity of these beliefs.

Reid's discussion of Hume, therefore, is not conclusive, because it is, from one point of view, superficial. Because he attacks Hume for disagreeing with common sense and ordinary usage, we might criticize him for failing to grasp the ways in which Hume intends to replace common assumptions and prejudices with a true account based on a sound psychology. This criticism of Reid, however, would be unfair. By making clear the extent of Hume's commitments to scepticism or to nihilism, he shows how extreme a position Hume has to take. Since this is a more extreme position than Hume acknowledges, Reid raises a fair question about whether we ought to accept all the claims that commit us to the implications of Hume's position.

63

REID: KNOWLEDGE
AND MORALITY

842. Reid's Defence of the Moral Sense

Reid agrees with Price in affirming the intuitive character of moral knowledge, the rejection of psychological hedonism, the irreducibility of conscience to self-love, and the rejection of utilitarianism. But he adds some important arguments to the rationalist position.

In arguing that moral beliefs rest on intuitive first principles that are evident to common sense, Reid relies on his general view that we have no rational alternative to trusting common sense. He does not rely as heavily as Price does on a parallel between moral principles and geometrical principles (though he accepts the parallel). Instead, he takes moral knowledge to be analogous to ordinary perceptual knowledge, believing that the same sort of defence is appropriate in each case.

To this extent it would be misleading to call him a rationalist. Cudworth, Clarke, and Price argue that moral knowledge should be contrasted with ordinary perceptual knowledge of the physical world, and so should be treated as some sort of a priori knowledge of necessary truths, rather than the sort of knowledge we might acquire from a special sense; Reid sees no need to insist on this sharp contrast, and so he recognizes a moral sense.[1]

In taking moral judgments to be expressions of a moral sense, Hutcheson and Hume intend these claims: (1) Moral 'judgments' are immediate reactions, not reached by reasoning and inference from prior judgments and principles. (2) They are sensory and emotional reactions, rather than strictly judgments based on recognition of evidence. (3) They are about the effect of external objects (actions, people, etc.) on us, not about the objects themselves.

These points embody Price's understanding of Hutcheson's position. He sees that Hutcheson reaches these conclusions by supposing these are all features of the senses. According to Hutcheson, we are right to speak of a moral sense because our moral judgments share all these features with sensory reactions. Since Price broadly agrees with Hutcheson's view of a sense, he rejects Hutcheson's belief in a moral sense; he rejects the

---

[1] Reid's belief in a moral sense is examined by Raphael, *MS* 172–92.

anti-intellectualist epistemology embodied in the second alleged feature of moral judgments, and the anti-realist metaphysics embodied in the third.[2]

Reid, following Price, agrees with Hutcheson's first claim about moral judgments, that they are in some way immediate.[3] He also follows Price in rejecting the inference from immediacy to anti-realism. But he separates himself from both Hutcheson and Price in rejecting their common assumption that to speak of a moral sense is to commit oneself to anti-intellectualism and anti-realism.

One might suppose that Reid is simply arguing for a more generous construal of 'sense' than either Hutcheson or Price allows. He argues, against Smith, that the belief in a moral sense has respectable historical antecedents, and is not a mere invention of the 18th century.[4] Reid's usage agrees with Butler's. For when Butler mentions 'moral sense' as one of the possible descriptions of conscience (D 1), he does not endorse any particular theory of moral judgment, let alone Hutcheson's conception of a moral sense.

Reid, however, is not simply claiming the right to use 'moral sense' as broadly as Butler does. He also believes that Price and Hutcheson are wrong to suppose that a more precise analogy with the senses commits us to anti-intellectualism and anti-realism.[5] In his view, both empiricists and rationalists lack 'just notions of the offices of the external senses', because they attribute too few intellectual functions to ordinary perception. Their conception of the external senses determines their conception of a moral sense; that is why the empiricists attribute moral judgments to a moral sense, and that is why rationalists reject any moral sense.[6]

If we recognize an analogy between the moral sense and the external senses, we need not take the analogy to deny the objectivity of moral properties. Hutcheson's use of the analogy with the senses expresses, according to Reid, a basic error about the senses in general.[7] In calling the senses 'powers by which we judge', Reid means that they allow us to detect actual features of external objects, and that our judgments that external objects have these features are immediate and reliable judgments. Among judgments of the senses he includes the judgment that one sound is loud, another soft, and that synchronous sounds are discordant or concordant (H 590a). These are not purely sensory states, but include beliefs and judgments that inform us reliably about the objective features of external objects. If Price had accepted Reid's conception of a sense, he would have had to qualify his opposition to the moral sense.

Reid sees the same error in his opponents' references to moral 'sentiments'. He takes sentiments to include the operations of reason and judgment.[8] This is a legitimate objection

---

[2] See Price, *RPQM* 14, quoted in §810.   [3] See Price, *RPQM* 42, quoted in §810.

[4] 'Some philosophers, with whom I agree, ascribe this to an original power or faculty in man, which they call the moral sense, the moral faculty, conscience. . . . by an original power of the mind, when we come to years of understanding and reflexion, we not only have the notions of right and wrong in conduct, but perceive certain things to be right, and others to be wrong. This name of the *moral sense*, though more frequently given to conscience since Lord Shaftesbury and Dr Hutcheson wrote, is not new. The *sensus recti et honesti* is a phrase not unfrequent among the ancients, neither is the *sense of duty* among us.' (H 589b) Cf. Turnbull's description of the moral sense, quoted in §715.

[5] 'It has got this name of *sense*, no doubt, from some analogy which it is conceived to bear to the external senses. And if we have just notions of the office of the external senses, the analogy is very evident, and I see no reason to take offence, as some have done, at the name of the *moral sense*.' (H 589b)

[6] Smith also rejects a moral sense, on grounds different from Price's. See §789.

[7] 'They are represented as powers by which we have sensations and ideas, not as powers by which we judge.' (H 590a)

[8] 'Authors who place moral approbation in feeling only, very often use the word *sentiment* to express feeling without judgment. This I take likewise [sc. like the similar use of 'sense'] to be an abuse of a word. Our moral determinations

to Hume and Smith. In tracing moral distinctions to a moral sense or to moral sentiments, they offer a reductive anti-rationalist account, showing that these distinctions (i.e., our drawing these distinctions) between right and wrong depend on sense or emotion rather than on reason and judgment. But if they rely on a false account of a sense and a sentiment, they do not succeed in eliminating reason and judgment from moral distinctions.[9]

843. The Errors of Sentimentalism

If we agree with Reid on the role of judgment in the operation of the moral sense, we reject Hume's conclusion that 'morality . . . is more properly felt than judged of' (T iii 1.2.1), and that the matter of fact we discover 'is the object of feeling, not of reason' (T iii 1.1.26). In taking the moral sense to be parallel to the external senses, Reid denies that we can discover some more immediate object of the senses that is an internal impression, as opposed to the external object that we make a perceptual judgment about. But we do not need to go so far in rejecting the 'way of ideas'. Even if we allow a more immediate object, we might argue that a moral judgment is analogous not to a judgment about an immediate object, but to one of the perceptual judgments that Reid mentions.

From this point of view, belief in a moral sense is reasonable for Reid, who holds the opposite view to Hutcheson's about the objectivity of moral qualities and about the relation of the moral sense to the feeling of approval. In attending to perceptual judgments, Reid also rejects Hutcheson's view of the place of reason and feeling in moral judgments. Hutcheson identifies the moral sense with the feeling of approval, and supposes that the moral goodness we approve is a state that depends on the observer's perception (in accordance with Locke's account of secondary qualities, as Hutcheson interprets it). Reid, however, believes that the moral sense informs us about objective properties; its judgments are the appropriate basis for our feeling of approval, not the feeling itself (H 590ab). He develops the position that Burnet and Balguy maintain against Hutcheson.[10]

Part of Hutcheson's reason for treating moral judgment as the product of a moral sense, and hence as a mode of reaction, is his internalism about moral properties, moral reasons, obligation, and motivation.[11] He believes, plausibly, that something's being right creates a reason and an obligation for agents; but he also assumes that all reasons refer to an actual motive in an agent; and so he concludes that moral properties essentially include an actual motive in the agent. If Reid rejects Hutcheson's anti-realist conception of a sense, he should also reject either internalism or Hutcheson's defence of it.

may, with propriety, be called *moral sentiments*. For the word *sentiment* in the English language never, as I conceive signifies mere feeling, but *judgment accompanied with feeling*. It was wont to signify opinion or judgment of any kind, but of late is appropriated to signify an opinion or judgment that strikes and produces some agreeable or uneasy emotion. So we speak of sentiments of respect, of esteem, of gratitude; but I never heard the pain of the gout, or any other mere feeling, called a sentiment.' (H 674b) Hamilton ad loc. protests that Reid's claim about 'sentiment' is 'too unqualified an assertion'. But Reid's claim agrees with Price, *RPQM* 16 (see Raphael ad loc.). On Butler see §719. Evidence on the use of the term is collected by Brissenden, ' "Sentiment" '. At 106 he supports Reid's observation on Hume's use. On the broad use of 'sentiment', with both cognitive and affective uses see Jones, *HS* 203n12.

[9] Cf. Smith, §791, on the 'sentiments' of the impartial observer.   [10] See §659.   [11] See Hutcheson, §639.

His position on this question is not clear. He seems to accept some sort of internalism.[12] But it is not clear whether he means that it would be self-contradictory to ascribe to someone a moral judgment without the corresponding affection or emotion. Nor does he say whether the relevant connexion between judgment and affection is present in every sincere moral judgment.

He seems to mean, however, that the connexion between moral judgment and affection is not simply a product of early training or of one's social environment. He seems to have a less contingent connexion in mind when he speaks of the 'constitution of our nature'. He suggests that we have not only the capacity to form moral judgments, but also the capacity to make our emotional reactions conform to our judgments of worth; that is why our attitudes of admiration, esteem, and indignation, directed both to others and to ourselves, follow our moral judgments.

Reid's claims rely on one necessary truth about emotions. If we had an emotion that was not guided by moral judgments of worth, that emotion would not be esteem or indignation; for these specific emotions depend on the relevant judgments of worth. It is not the same sort of necessary truth, however, that we have such emotions as esteem and indignation. It does not seem self-contradictory to suppose an agent capable of moral judgment but lacking the capacity to form the corresponding emotions.

In reply to Hume, therefore, Reid does not seem to maintain the connexion between moral judgments and sentiments that constitutes Hume's internalism.[13] He maintains that it is essential to human agency that we have the capacity to form emotions that follow our moral judgments; if we lacked this capacity, our moral judgments would not have the role in human agency that they actually have. Since this is Reid's position, he has no reason to accept Hume's argument from internalism to anti-rationalism and anti-realism. He agrees that the role of the moral sense in human agency requires a connexion with sentiments, but he does not infer that the moral sense is a tendency to have these sentiments. He maintains that it is the capacity to form the relevant sorts of moral judgments.

844. The Errors of Empiricism and Rationalism

Reid therefore believes that previous rationalists were wrong to deny that moral judgments belong to a moral sense. They were wrong because they had the wrong idea of a moral sense, and they had this wrong idea because they assumed too much Lockean empiricism. Moral and perceptual knowledge are sharply distinct only if the empiricists are right about the character of perceptual knowledge. If empiricism leads to scepticism, we ought to reject the first moves that lead us along this sceptical path. Hence we ought to reject the empiricist account of perceptual knowledge. In Reid's view, moral knowledge is not

---

[12] 'Our moral judgments are not, like those we form in speculative matters, dry and unaffecting, but from their nature are necessarily accompanied with affections and feelings. . . . we approve of good actions, and disapprove of bad; and this approbation and disapprobation, when we analyse it, appears to include not only a moral judgment of the action, but some affection, favourable or unfavourable, toward the agent, and some feeling in ourselves.' (H 592a) '. . . esteem and benevolent regard not only accompany real worth, by the constitution of our nature, but are perceived to be properly due to it; and . . . on the contrary, unworthy conduct really merits dislike and indignation.' (H 592b)

[13] See Hume, §§744–5.

especially controversial. We have good reason to claim knowledge of objective moral facts and properties if we accept a non-sceptical account of perceptual knowledge.

Hutcheson and Hume rely on an empiricist account of perceptual knowledge, in order to defend a parallel account of moral knowledge. The rationalists, assuming that this account of perceptual knowledge is more or less right, insist that moral knowledge cannot be understood in the same way. Reid disagrees more fundamentally with the empiricists, and so need not deny that moral knowledge is similar in important ways to perceptual knowledge.

This criticism is especially effective against Hume, because Hume believes that his rationalist opponents have to make moral judgment mysterious. He argues that we cannot treat it as demonstrative knowledge, and we cannot understand how it could be ordinary perceptual knowledge of matters of fact in the object. Reid accepts Hume's first point, but rejects his second. According to Reid, moral judgment is no more mysterious than ordinary perception. Since we must treat the external senses as involving judgments about features of the objects themselves, we have no reason to reject the moral sense simply because it also involves judgments about features of the external objects.

Reid believes that Hume's *Treatise* embodies the errors that are implicit in the whole empiricist position derived from Locke.[14] In an exchange of letters with Reid, Hume sees that Reid takes him to have articulated the implications of an empiricist position.[15] Reid agrees; and so he claims that a refutation of Hume is also a refutation of apparently more moderate positions that really lead to Hume's conclusions.[16] To refute Hume's scepticism, then, we need to question the apparently plausible principles that constitute the apparently more moderate empiricist position of Locke. If we refute the empiricist principles, we have a firmer basis, according to Reid, for a true account of moral knowledge.

845. Moral Knowledge

Like Price, Reid is a cognitivist and a realist. He also agrees with Price in restricting the definability of moral properties. He does not argue as elaborately as Price does by appeal to an open question argument; but he claims that some basic moral concepts (e.g. 'duty', 'will') cannot be given a 'logical' definition (H 587a). In objecting to proposed definitions of 'duty' he

---

[14] 'That system [i.e. Hume's] abounds with conclusions the most absurd that ever were advanced by any philosopher, defended with great acuteness and ingenuity from principles commonly received by philosophers.' (H 518a) Reid's claim about Hume and empiricism is supported at length by Green, in *IHTHN*, Part I §5 (pp. 5–6), Part II §20 (pp. 321–2). Hence Passmore, *HI*, 84–5, quite reasonably speaks of the 'Reid–Green' interpretation of Hume. Cf. Kemp Smith, *PDH* 80.

[15] '...if you have been able to clear up these abstruse and important subjects, instead of being mortified, I shall be so vain as to pretend to a share of the praise; and shall think that my errors, by having at least some coherence, had led you to make a more strict review of my principles, which were the common ones, and so to perceive their futility.' (Hume, Letter to Reid, 25 Feb. 1763 = Greig 201)

[16] '...I shall always avow myself your disciple in metaphysics. I have learned more from your writings in this kind than from all others put together. Your system appears to me not only coherent in all its parts, but likeways justly deduced from principles commonly received among philosophers: principles which I never thought of calling in question until the conclusions you draw from them in the Treatise of human Nature made me suspect them. ... I agree with you therefore that if this system shall ever be demolished, you have a just claim to a great share of the praise, both because you have made it a distinct and determinate mark to be aimed at, and have furnished proper artillery for the purpose.' (Reid to Hume, 18 Mar. 1763 = Greig 376n4 = H 91)

says we can define it 'only by synonymous words or phrases, or by its properties and necessary concomitants' (H 587a). He makes a similar claim about the definability of active power.[17]

It is easy to see why Reid rejects attempted definitions that simply provide concomitants, such as 'duty is what is in itself laudable, though no man should praise it'.[18] These attempts do not explain what makes duty laudable. He also objects to attempted definitions that provide only synonymous expressions (e.g., 'duty is what we ought to do', or 'duty is what is fair and honest'). Logical definitions must be reductive. We give a reductive account if we define F as G, and we can understand what Gs are without understanding what Fs are. Since he imposes this condition only on logical definitions, Reid's rejection of definitions for moral properties leaves room for definitions that do not meet his strict conditions.[19]

The difference between Reid's conception of synonymy and a more familiar conception becomes clearer once we notice that some definitions stating synonymies—as we would normally suppose—seem to meet his conditions for a reductive definition. We could know what a fox is and what a female is without knowing what a vixen is, and there seems to be nothing more to being a vixen than being a female fox. The same sort of test would perhaps allow more ambitious claims about identity of properties to count as definitions; 'temperature is mean kinetic energy' seems to count. At least, since Reid does not appeal to Price's open question argument, he seems to raise no objection in principle to such an account of a property.

In Reid's view the fact that we cannot give a 'logical' definition of something is no reason for denying the existence of the definiendum.[20] He begins his discussion of active power by arguing that we cannot give a logical definition, but he objects to Hume's inference that we therefore have no idea of power. Hume objects that 'the terms *efficacy, agency, power, force, energy*, are all nearly synonymous; and therefore it is an absurdity to employ any of them in defining the rest' (H 520b).[21] Reid answers that there is nothing absurd about this.[22] We should not be surprised by the failure of logical definition if the definiendum is simple.

This claim about simplicity is not entirely justified. In admitting that our 'definitions' are synonymies and not logical definitions, we do not imply that the definiendum is simple; we may mean that the different elements we introduce in our definition cannot be understood without reference to one another. If the definiendum has an organic structure, the whole cannot be understood without reference to the parts, nor the parts without reference to the whole. Reid, therefore, does not show that the failure of logical, reductive definitions indicates the simplicity of the definiendum. Simplicity need not be the only explanation of irreducibility.

Reid's concentration on simplicity affects his conclusions about the definability of moral properties. Since he takes simplicity to be the only ground of logical indefinability, he argues

---

[17] See §825.   [18] Quoted from Cicero. Cf. §819.   [19] On the use of 'synonymy' see §§656, 812.

[20] I use 'definiendum' to avoid deciding whether Reid is speaking primarily of words, concepts, or properties, or of all three indifferently.

[21] Reid quotes (and abbreviates) from Hume, *T* i 3.14.4.

[22] 'Surely this author was not ignorant, that there are many things of which we have a clear and distinct conception, which are so simple in their nature, that they cannot be defined any other way than by synonymous words. It is true that this is not a logical definition, but that there is, as he affirms, an absurdity in saying it, when no better can be had, I cannot perceive.' (H 520b)

from the indefinability of moral concepts and properties to their simplicity; they have no simpler elements that might provide the basis for a logical definition. It would be more plausible to appeal to irreducibility. If different moral concepts can be defined by reference to one another, but cannot be defined reductively through non-moral concepts, they may be complex but irreducible. Perhaps 'ought', 'right', 'obligation', and 'reason' are to be defined by reference to one another, and none of them can be defined without reference to at least one of the others. This explanation of the irreducibility of moral concepts is better than the explanation that appeals to simplicity.

If we detach irreducibility from simplicity, we can also detach Price's and Reid's arguments against logical definitions of moral concepts from their specific epistemological views about simplicity and immediacy. We have good reason to do this if we are doubtful about these epistemological views. The arguments about irreducibility do not depend on intuitionism about moral knowledge.

In saying that the only definitions we can give of duty are mere synonymies, Reid seems to mean that we can give no reductive definition of the kind that we can give (for different reasons) for 'vixen' and for 'temperature'. His view that no such reductive account is possible is defensible, but Reid is not clear about the sort of defence that it might need. The fact that a particular account (for instance a utilitarian account) initially seems unintuitive does not show that it is unsuccessful; many reductive accounts seem unintuitive until we understand the theory that underlies them. We cannot, then, refute reductive definitions just by looking at them without reference to the relevant theory. Reid examines and rejects reductive arguments that would allow us to explain the crucial moral concepts by reference to self-interest, or to the reactions of a particular kind of agent, or to maximization of utility. These arguments need to be considered if we are to evaluate his claims about the sense in which moral properties are indefinable.

Reid claims not only that moral properties are indefinable, but also that basic moral truths are self-evident, not grounded on any further truths. He believes this for foundationalist reasons. In his view all knowledge must have foundations 'on which the whole fabric of the science leans' (H 637a), and which have no further foundation. When a question arises about them, we must appeal not to some further justifying argument, but to common sense (H 637a; cf. 590b–591a).[23] The defence of the analogy between moral knowledge and ordinary perceptual knowledge also makes it reasonable, in Reid's view, to treat both perceptual judgments and moral judgments as foundations.

Even if moral beliefs must have some foundation, the foundation need not be moral beliefs. If the sort of reduction that Reid rejects for moral concepts and properties were possible, a foundationalist might argue that the self-evident foundation for moral beliefs consists in non-moral beliefs. Reid's version of foundationalism rests partly on his argument against reduction.

How are we supposed to find that a principle is self-evident? Reid suggests that if p is self-evident, we ought to find on reflexion that we are more certain about the truth of p than we are about the truth of anything that implies not-p or about anything that might be cited

---

[23] '... the first principles of morals are the dictates of this [moral] faculty; and ... we have the same reason to rely on these dictates, as upon the determinations of our senses, or of our other natural faculties' (H 592a).

as a defence of p.[24] He believes we ought not to seek any proof of a first principle, since our search may raise unnecessary doubts that would not otherwise have arisen.

Reid's objection to attempts to defend first principles is not convincing. I might find that my belief in p is more confident than my belief in any principle that is used in an argument for p, and so I might still regard it as apparently self-evident. But it is always fair to ask whether I am justified in retaining my confidence in p; though I find that I cannot give up my belief in p, how do I remove any question about whether my confidence does not simply reflect my irrational stubbornness? I might find this question troublesome if p appears to conflict with q and r, which seem quite plausible to me, though less plausible than p.

Our doubts about our attitude to p would be removed or reduced if we could show that in fact q and r support p. We have better grounds for our confidence that p is more certain than our other beliefs if we find that our other beliefs rely on the truth of p. This form of argument defends p by appeal to beliefs that appear less certain than p. Such a defence should not shake our belief in p.

This argument raises doubts about foundationalism in general. For once we ask whether our impressions of greater certainty are reliable in a particular case, we may reasonably consider the relation of a fundamental belief to other beliefs. Once we do that, we imply that an appeal to coherence confers some degree of justification.[25] Reid is right to claim that his foundationalism excludes the sort of defence of basic principles that we have described. But his objection that such a defence raises new doubts is unfounded; instead of rejecting the possibility of such a defence, he should have re-examined his foundationalism.

846. Against Hume on Moral Judgment

Reid defends his cognitivist and realist account of moral judgments in his Chapter 7, 'That moral approbation implies a real judgment', where he discusses Hume's anti-realist and anti-rationalist position.[26] He starts from his disagreement with Hume about the character of a moral judgment. According to Reid, it is a real judgment about the qualities of external objects, and it provides the basis for the feeling of approval to which Hume wants to reduce it. According to Reid, Hume's attempted reduction of judgment to feeling is the product of Hume's general epistemological position.[27] Reid argues that the common belief that reason is the source of moral judgments is correct, and that Hume is wrong to reject it.

The two Humean theses, that (1) reason is not the source of motivation, and that (2) moral 'judgments' are really feelings in the observer, are distinct. We can accept Hume's first thesis without the second, if we reject internalism about moral judgment and motivation; for Hume relies on internalism in his arguments to show that moral distinctions are not

---

[24] '...when we attempt to prove by direct argument, what is really self-evident, the reasoning will always be inconclusive; for it will either take for granted the thing to be proved, or something not more evident; and so, instead of giving strength to the conclusion, will rather tempt those to doubt of it, who never did so before' (H 637a).

[25] Relevant issues are discussed by Brink, MRFE 116–25.

[26] Reid's criticism of Hume is discussed by Cuneo, 'Moral' 251–6.

[27] 'Before the modern system of ideas and impressions was introduced, nothing would have appeared more absurd than to say, that when I condemn a man for what he has done, I pass no judgment at all about the man, but only express some uneasy feeling in myself.' (H 670b)

derived from reason. As we have seen, Reid seems—though his position is not clear—to reject internalism.[28] But he does not draw attention to this issue. Hume's second thesis is particularly important for Reid's purposes; for, if we accept it, we lose one reason for believing that rational judgments can move us to action. Reid, therefore, argues directly against Hume's second thesis, independently of the first.

He argues against Hume and Hutcheson that we do not speak of moral judgments as though we identified them with feelings of approbation. He remarks that moral judgments appear to claim truth and falsehood and to be open to contradiction, in a way that separates them from feelings (H 673ab). This sort of argument is useful, though inconclusive. For it forces sentimentalists to admit that they do not give an account of our ordinary conception of moral judgment; they really argue that this conception is mistaken and should be replaced. Once we see that sentimentalists reject the ordinary conception, we can focus on the main question, about where they think the ordinary conception is mistaken.

Hume implicitly supports Reid by his failure to maintain his sentimentalist view consistently. Though he relies on internalism in arguing that moral judgments are feelings or involve feelings, he later agrees that we can make moral judgments without having the feelings that would dispose us to act on them.[29] This change of mind shows that it is difficult to abandon the view that moral judgments are genuine judgments about something other than our own feelings.

847. Against Hume on 'Is' and 'Ought'

Reid relies on some of his epistemology, and especially on some of his claims about the moral sense, in order to shift the burden of proof that Hume tries to place on his opponents. He takes Hume's questions about how we can reach 'ought' from 'is' to express an illegitimate demand for an explanation of 'ought' and 'ought not'. In Reid's view (H 675b–676a), these cannot be explained by a reductive, 'logical' definition, but they can be explained by a 'synonymous' definition of 'ought'. Unless Hume can show that the absence of a reductive definition shows that 'ought' is unintelligible, his objection has no force.

Hume asks why we should infer an 'ought' judgment from 'is' judgments—why, for instance, we should infer from the fact that A killed B without provocation the conclusion that A acted wrongly. Reid does not say how exactly he understands Hume's question. But we might reasonably take Hume to observe that it does not seem analytic that unprovoked homicide is wrong, and then to ask what makes it wrong. Reid seems to understand Hume to ask this question. He answers that the question is illegitimate. Basic moral judgments (e.g., 'harming an innocent person is wrong') are not to be derived from anything more basic, since they are themselves first principles. Since we must eventually come to first principles, we have no reason to reject an appeal to judgments that rest on no further judgments. Hume has not shown why moral judgments should not play this role. If we are foundationalists, our foundation need not be non-moral.

---

[28] See §843.   [29] See Hume, §765.

These arguments show that Hume's doubts rest on controversial assumptions about what needs explanation and what an adequate explanation would have to be like. His assumptions are not neutral between different conceptions of moral judgment. Reid argues that they assume the falsity of the conception of moral judgment that Hume claims to refute.

848. Rightness 'in the Object'

Reid argues against Hume's criticism of the view that moral rightness or wrongness is a quality of the object. If we consider ingratitude, we will never, according to Hume, find its demerit or blame if we just examine the external circumstances themselves.[30] Reid disagrees on this point. But he agrees with Hume that the wrongness of an action produces a sentiment, provided that a sentiment is taken to include a judgment as well as a feeling.

Reid ought not to agree that the property making the action wrong is its tendency to produce a certain judgment in the observer. Such an account of the wrong-making property conflicts with Reid's account of the observer's judgment; for, in his view, the observer's judgment includes the belief that the action itself has some moral property independent of this judgment. And so, even if the wrongness of an action tends to produce a certain effect in an observer, Reid should insist that the wrongness itself consists in the property of the object, not in the tendency to provoke the observer's judgment. He implicitly insists on this point when he speaks of the judgment being true (H 676b). If ingratitude provokes a true judgment of (say) condemnation in the observer, it must have whatever property warrants condemnation; this property, not the tendency to provoke condemnation, is the wrongness of the ingratitude.

Hume believes that this conception of moral judgment is untenable, because no intelligible account can be given of the property that (on the view he rejects) we attribute to the object. According to Hume, we can know all the relevant matters of fact about the object before we raise a moral question about it:[31] Reid argues that if Hume were right on this point, there would be no further room for a judge's understanding to operate after the evidence has been given. As Reid insists, the judge has a further fact to discover—'whether the plaintiff has a just plea or not' (H 677a).

Reid could have strengthened this point by observing that in other cases also, we have to use our judgment to draw a conclusion from available evidence about the nature of a situation. We ask, for instance, whether Tom's doing what he did in Dick's presence constituted making a promise to Dick, and whether what Dick did in Harry's presence

---

[30] Hume concludes: '. . . this crime arises from a complication of circumstances, which being presented to the spectator, excites the sentiment of blame, by the peculiar structure and fabric of his mind' (quoted by Reid, H 676a). Reid agrees with this account of what makes ingratitude wrong, and disagrees with Hume's reasons for supposing that it supports a sentimentalist analysis of moral judgment. He tries to expose Hume's mistake: 'He could be led to think so, only by taking for granted one of these two things. Either, 1st, that the *sentiment of blame* means a feeling only, without judgment; or, 2dly, that whatever is excited by the particular fabric and structure of the mind must be feeling only, and not judgment.' (H 676b) Reid accepts neither of Hume's assumptions.

[31] 'After these things are known, the understanding has no further room to operate. Nothing remains but to feel, on our part, some sentiment of blame or approbation.' (H 676b–677a)

constituted an insult or a threat to Harry. In such cases, we are not consulting our own reactions; we are asking whether one sort of fact constitutes another sort.[32]

Hume assumes that in the moral case our conclusion or verdict cannot introduce a further fact about the object besides the ones he has mentioned. But he does not justify this assumption. He would have justified it if he had shown that any further fact must be specifiable through reductive definition in non-moral terms; but Reid casts reasonable doubt on whether Hume has shown this.

To show that Hume has no sound basis for his claim that the wrongness of an action cannot be a further fact about it besides the non-moral facts, Reid considers Hume's argument for restricting the range of facts about the object. Hume suggests a parallel between moral goodness and beauty. He argues that 'Euclid has fully explained all the qualities of the circle; but has not in any proposition said a word of its beauty' (IPM, App. 1.14); he infers that the moral goodness or badness, like beauty, cannot be a quality of external objects. Reid answers that Euclid concerns himself only with the geometrical properties of the circle, and does not attempt to describe all its properties (H 677ab). Hume's reasons for denying that wrongness is a property of an object show at most that it is not a non-moral property of an object; but Reid correctly challenges Hume's assumption that moral properties, if there are any, are reducible to non-moral properties.

Finally, Reid considers Hume's argument from ultimate ends. Hume argues that since ends cannot be infinitely regressive, some ends rest on no further reasoning, and therefore rest on feeling rather than reason. Reid points out (H 678ab) that this argument moves illegitimately, as Hutcheson does, from foundationalism about ends to sentimentalism about our grasp of ends.[33] If any argument can be made for sentimentalism from the fact that not all ends can be justified by reference to higher ends, it must be a more complicated argument than the one offered by Hutcheson and Hume.

Reid's criticisms of Hume depend partly, but not wholly, on his foundationalism and on his specific views about the nature of the moral sense and the indefinability of moral properties. He sometimes claims that Hume asks for inappropriate explanations through failure to see that some moral judgments are fundamental. But not all of Reid's case against Hume depends on questionable epistemological assumptions. He argues effectively that Hume neglects some reasonable arguments that might be offered for the factual and objective character of moral judgments. On some points, indeed, it may be easier to answer Hume if we abandon Reid's foundationalism for a more holist position. His main objections challenge Hume's assumption that a satisfactory account of moral properties would have to be reductive. Once we see that Reid's rejection of logical definitions leaves us with more room than he recognizes to explain the character of moral properties, we should also find it easier to answer Hume.

849. Approval of Virtue

Following Price, Reid claims that the content of our moral judgments conflicts with sentimentalism. If the moral sense and moral approbation were a special sort of favourable

---

[32] The point of Reid's objection, therefore, is explained by Anscombe in 'Facts'. See Hume §748.
[33] See Hutcheson, §638; Hume, §736.

feeling, we could not account for the judgments we pass on agents. Many aspects of people might cause a favourable feeling towards them, but only some favourable feelings on certain specific grounds belong to moral judgments about their goodness or badness.

Reid mentions the connexion between moral judgment and voluntariness. Not only must a morally good action be voluntary (H 589a), but it must also result from the right kind of voluntary process.[34] If we accept these constraints on moral approval, we cannot also, according to Reid, accept Hume's account of moral approval.

Reid argues that Hume's account of what we approve is warped by his conception of approval. If moral approval consists simply in some feeling, not in a judgment, what kind of feeling is it? Hume takes it to be distinctive of moral approval that it results 'upon contemplating certain characters or qualities of mind coolly and impartially' (H 651a). Then he asks what qualities in fact provoke this feeling, and he argues that it arises from all the qualities of mind that are useful or agreeable to their possessor or to others (H 651a). The qualities provoking the feeling of approval need not be confined to voluntary states of character and actions. Indeed, the attempt to connect morally good action and character with the voluntary is an error of Christian morality.[35]

If this account of moral virtues were correct, there would be no reason, in Reid's view, to confine them to qualities of mind in particular.[36] But we do not agree with Hume.[37] We recognize many useful and agreeable qualities in other people, and in other animals, without supposing that they have the merit that belongs to moral virtue. Virtue is in fact also useful or agreeable, but this is not the only feature of virtue that we approve of.[38] Hume's description of approval does not account for everything that we actually approve of in virtue.

Reid's objection emphasizes the connexion between his account of moral judgment and his account of the object of moral approval. If moral judgment were simply a feeling of approval, we could hardly limit it to voluntary actions; we have no reason to predict that only voluntary actions and qualities will provoke a favourable feeling.

If we were to reply, in partial defence of Hume, that moral approval is the feeling provoked by useful or agreeable qualities in the circumstances where we believe they are voluntary, we would be abandoning the main point (in Reid's view) of Hume's account of moral judgment. For this belief about the voluntariness of actions and qualities would have to be a constituent of moral approval, and it would limit the conditions in which moral approval is justified. In that case our moral judgment would be a belief about an objective fact providing a basis for the feeling of approval.

Reid's objection, then, identifies a basic difference between his position and Hume's. If Hume conceded Reid's point about the role of voluntariness, he would introduce belief into

---

[34] '. . . no action can be called morally good, in which a regard to what is right has not some influence. Thus a man who has no regard to justice, may pay his just debt, from no other motive, but that he may not be thrown into prison. In this action there is no virtue at all' (H 598a). In 'some influence' Reid shows that he holds a 'co-operative' rather than a 'subtractive' view. See Hutcheson, §633; Balguy, §669.

[35] See Hume, §726.

[36] 'Nor does there appear any good reason why the useful and agreeable qualities of body and of fortune, as well as those of the mind, should not have a place among moral virtues in this system. They have the essence of virtue; that is, agreeableness and utility, why then should they not have the name?' (H 651b–652a)

[37] See Beattie on Hume, §777.

[38] 'But virtue has a merit peculiar to itself, a merit which does not arise from its being useful or agreeable, but from its being virtue. The merit is discerned by the same faculty by which we discern it to be virtue, and by no other.' (H 652b)

his account of the moral feeling, and so would destroy the whole point of his account. His account of the moral sentiment follows his general view of passions; since the connexion between passion and belief is contingent, the passion cannot be individuated by the presence of a specific belief.[39]

Hume relies on this account of passions and sentiments in opposing the 'divines'. He complains that in the doctrine restricting virtues to voluntary states and actions, 'reasoning, and even language, have been warped from their natural course'.[40] He implies that if our sentiments are guided by some belief about objective facts, so that they would not survive the loss of this belief, we warp our reasoning and language from their natural course. According to Hume, if we have a certain feeling towards (say) tall and handsome people, and we have a phenomenologically similar feeling towards just people, we approve of both sorts of people in the same way. If we were to argue that moral approval of just people rests on the belief that their states are voluntary, and that our approval would not be moral approval otherwise, Hume would answer that we were warping our natural feelings of approval. He rejects any belief-based distinction between phenomenologically similar sentiments. If, then, Hume attempted to meet Reid's objection by restricting moral approval to a sentiment based on belief, he would undermine a central element in his own conception of moral sentiments, and indeed a central element in his conception of the emotions.

Reid claims that the demand for voluntariness is basic; we do not take voluntariness to be a reliable indicator of something that we value for some other reason. We are not concerned with voluntary actions and qualities simply because we think they are the most likely to be stable, and therefore the best basis for predicting that the agent will keep the useful or agreeable traits in question. Hume's attempt to reduce moral approval to approval of the agreeable or useful omits an essential element in moral approval and moral sentiment.

850. Actions and Agents

Once he has explained his view about the object of our moral approval, Reid considers a central puzzle in Hume's account of justice. In Hume's view, 'no action can be virtuous or morally good, unless there be in human nature some motive to produce it, distinct from its morality' (H 648a, 667b). Hume argues that the justice does not consist in the action itself, since we regard actions as just only insofar as they are the sign of a just character. But the agent's reason for acting justly cannot simply be regard for a just character; for we do not know what a just character is unless we understand what a just action is. Hume seems to believe, then, that unless there is some further motive for doing one action rather than another besides the desire to act justly, we have not explained acting justly.[41]

Reid rejects Hume's contention that we cannot take any moral attitude to actions apart from the motives of the agents. If an action relieves the sufferings of a person in distress, then we rightly approve of it. As Reid says, we think it 'ought to be done by those who have the power and opportunity, and the capacity of perceiving their obligation to do it' (H 649a). We can think this about the action even if we think the agent acted from bad motives.

---

[39] See Hume, §733.   [40] Quoted in §726.   [41] On Reid's argument see Lehrer, *TR* 241–4.

Indeed, if we did not approve of actions apart from our views about the motive, we would deprive ourselves of an important part of the explanation of our approval of motives. For part of our basis for approval of motives is our approval of the actions that they tend to cause. If our approval of the actions in turn depended on our approval of the motives, we would be caught in a vicious circle. Reid seeks to remove the appearance of circularity by distinguishing formal from material goodness (H 649b–650a). Hume has given no reason for rejecting that distinction.

Hume would be right to say that we praise agents for their actions, and regard the actions as an aspect of personal merit, only because of our belief about the motives of the agents, and that in this respect approval of actions is secondary to approval of agents. But it does not follow that we take all the moral goodness of the action to be merely a sign of goodness in the agent. As Reid suggests, we predicate goodness of the action and of the character in different, though related senses. Hume seems to have confused the issue because he speaks indiscriminately of 'the goodness of an action' and 'the virtue of an action'. Reid suggests, therefore, that we remove any appearance of paradox once we distinguish the goodness appropriately ascribed to an action from that ascribed to an agent.

Perhaps, however, Hume has noticed a different difficulty that he does not distinguish from the one that he describes. Our explanation would go in a vicious circle if we could say only that the just person is the one who does just actions and that just actions are the sort of actions that a just person would do. One or the other of the just action and the just person must be independently specified if we are to understand either just actions or just agents. For similar reasons just people must be able to describe their just actions as more than simply 'what a just person would do'; for we want to explain why just people choose these actions rather than some others, and we must cite something about the actions themselves. Just people are not indifferent to the properties of just actions; nor do they choose just actions simply as means to the exercise of just character.[42]

But we need not infer that, as Hume supposes, just action rests on some motive apart from the sense of its morality. If we suppose that just action requires equal distribution between equally deserving recipients, we need some conception of what equal distribution is and who a deserving recipient is; and a just person needs some conception of these things in order to act as a just person does. But it does not follow that just people must have some further motive for valuing equal distribution apart from the fact that it is just.

We might suggest, therefore, that to be a just person is to be concerned about equal distribution because it is just, and not because of some further benefit that we care about. We may then ask why we should attach moral importance to equal distribution. On this sort of question Reid tends to appeal to intuition when we might reasonably seek some further explanation. But the further explanation need not introduce a non-moral motive for caring about equal distribution.

Reid's main point is sound. A reasonable distinction between the goodness of actions and of agents undermines the general point that Hume wants to derive from considerations about 'the morality of an action'. Perhaps Hume thinks of feelings of approval without differentiation, and does not consider the different sorts of judgments that apply to agents

---

[42] Hume makes this point in his letter to Hutcheson, referring to Cic. *Fin.* iv. See §726.

and to actions. To distinguish these judgments is to admit, contrary to Hume, that judgments are essential to moral approval. Hume's sentimentalist account of moral approval affects his view on some normative questions.

But even if Reid's account of moral judgment and moral approval is more accurate than Hume's, might the sentiments described by Hume be preferable to those described by Reid? Perhaps Hume has shown that Reid's sentiments are baseless. Even though Hume believes he is describing moral approval, and not replacing it with something else, his position may appear more plausible if it is understood as a form of nihilism rather than reductionism about morality. We have often noticed that a nihilist presentation of Hume's position would be contrary to Hume's intentions, but might be taken to fit his arguments.

If we take Hume to argue implicitly for the abandonment of moral judgments and sentiments in favour of Humean sentiments that do some of the work of moral judgments, we must take the main weight of his argument to rest on (1) his account of the passions and their objects; (2) his arguments about passion and practical reason; (3) his arguments to show that moral judgments are really sentiments rather than judgments and are really about us rather than about the objects. But his arguments for these parts of his theory of morality are open to question; they do not clearly justify the abandonment of moral judgment and approval.

In this as in other cases, we might initially suppose that Reid's answer to Hume is superficial because it rests on common-sense claims that Hume might appear to have undermined. But the more radical Humean arguments that would undermine the common-sense claims are not convincing enough to justify radical Humean conclusions. Reid's criticisms mark weak points in Hume's position.

851. Justice v. Utility

According to Reid, Hume accepts the Epicurean reduction of all considerations of moral goodness to considerations of pleasure and utility; as Reid puts it, he reduces the *honestum* to the *utile* and the *dulce* (H 651ab). Reid recognizes that Hume rejects the Epicurean reduction of benevolence to self-love.[43] Nonetheless he thinks Hume is open to the objection raised against the Epicurean system, that it 'was justly thought . . . to subvert morality, and to substitute another principle in its room' (H 651b). Since Reid takes Hume's account of justice to embody these mistakes about morality, he examines it at length.

Reid attacks Hume's account of the origins of justice in self-interest and his utilitarian account of rules of justice. He argues that (1) our belief that some things are just and that just action is obligatory does not depend on the existence of rules or conventions that are in everyone's selfish interest, and that (2) our belief about what is just and about why just actions are obligatory does not depend on any belief about utility.

When Hume claims that justice is an artificial virtue, he has both these points in mind. For it is difficult to give a convincing utilitarian account of justice (replying to Reid's second point) unless we can tie principles of justice to some appropriate set of rules and

---

[43] This anti-reductive attitude to benevolence is more prominent in *IPM* than in *T*. See §763.

conventions (replying to Reid's first point). Hume points out that while the utilitarian benefits of benevolence are easily seen (as long as we are not very careful to distinguish immediate from long-term utility), we cannot easily give a parallel account of justice.[44] In order to respond to Butler's objections, he has to appeal to the effects of a system of rules.

None of this implies that the system of rules must benefit each of us individually; but Hume's account of moral judgment makes this conclusion difficult to avoid. For, given this account of the nature of moral judgment, some feeling of approval towards the public interest would be necessary to get a system of justice started, if we do not appeal to self-interest. But what feeling of approval could this be? Hume correctly argues that the feelings of approval that might move us to approve of particular other-regarding actions cannot be counted on to move us to approve of a distant goal such as long-term public interest.[45] Hence the basis of our approval of justice must ultimately be self-interest.

Reid argues against Hume's contention that justice depends essentially on systems of rules. Hume considers only the branches of justice that concern property and contracts. Since the institution of property (or at any rate of some kinds of property) appears to rest on rules or conventions, it is easy to see why the branch of justice concerned with property is also concerned with rules. We might be inclined to believe something similar about contracts (though Reid thinks this would be a mistake). But Reid argues that there are four other areas of justice, to do with injuries to one's person, family, liberty, or reputation, and that Hume has ignored them.[46] We will deny that these other cases of injustice are wrong independently of any rules or conventions, if we agree with Hobbes's view about the dependence of right and wrong on the existence of positive law. Hume does not clearly endorse Hobbes's view; but unless he endorses it, his restriction of justice seems arbitrary.

This is not a purely verbal dispute, about what should be called 'justice'. For if the non-conventional branches of justice neglected by Hume rest on principles that also explain why certain rules about property are just, Hume neglects a non-conventional basis for rules about property.

Reid points to moral sentiments that, in his view, presuppose a sense of justice that would also explain the justice in rules about property. He appeals to the sense of being owed something, and takes this sense to be present in elementary moral sentiments of gratitude and resentment.[47] Reid returns to his critique of Hume's attempt to describe moral sentiments without moral beliefs. If moral approval is to be analysed into sentiments, it must be analysed into distinctively 'moral sentiments, not into any old favourable feeling. But Reid argues that we cannot identify characteristically moral sentiments without attributing

---

[44] Hume criticizes Hutcheson's attempt to make benevolence the basic moral sentiment. See §768.

[45] Hume does not seem to think this criticism applies to the sentiment of humanity introduced in *IPM*. But he does not rely on this sentiment as a sufficient basis for justice. See §771. These difficulties help to explain why one might want to rest utilitarianism on a rationalist account of moral judgment, as Sidgwick does.

[46] 'He seems, I know not why, to have taken up a confined notion of justice, and to have restricted it to regard to property and fidelity in contracts. As to the other branches he is silent. He no where says, that it is not naturally criminal to rob an innocent man of his life, of his children, of his liberty, or of his reputation; and I am apt to think he never meant it.' (H 657a)

[47] 'As soon, therefore, as men come to have any proper notion of a favour and of an injury; as soon as they have any rational exercise of gratitude and of resentment; so soon they must have the conception of justice and of injustice; and if gratitude and resentment be natural to man, which Mr Hume allows, the notion of justice must be no less natural.' (H 655b)

specific moral beliefs to the agents who have the sentiments.[48] These sentiments presuppose the belief that other people sometimes do things for us that they owe us as a matter of justice, sometimes go beyond what they strictly owe, and sometimes fail to give us what they owe us. Gratitude is appropriate only when people do us favours beyond what they owe us, and resentment is appropriate only when they fail in something that they owe us. We have some sense of what is owed and due to us independently of all rules and conventions, and this sense does not depend on any conviction about our own interest.

Reid's other appeals to non-utilitarian convictions about justice rest on similar grounds. We are concerned about fairness, reciprocity, and connected features of justice, outside the contexts where Hume finds justice. In the cases where Hume thinks justice does not apply (H 659ab), he overlooks some apparently relevant convictions about justice. If, for instance, conditions of great scarcity require the suspension of ordinary rules of justice and property, the most convincing case for this suspension will show that the suspension is just and fair in the circumstances (H 659b–660a). Similarly, Reid urges, against Hobbes and Hume, that war does not make principles of justice irrelevant.[49]

This argument is limited, since it overlooks, as Reid often does, a more radical reply. Hume's account of justice may not accord with our convictions about justice, but it may still explain them. Perhaps our tenacious attachment to justice irrespective of utility shows why these convictions about justice maximize utility; if we held them less tenaciously, for consciously utilitarian reasons, they would be less stable, and would tend to promote utility less well.

Reid might fairly reply that even this utilitarian effect of our principles does not explain our attachment to justice. Some utilitarians might reply that any attachment to justice that cannot be explained on utilitarian grounds is irrational. Hume cannot give exactly this answer, since he does not claim that the sentiment in favour of utility is especially rational, or that a moral sentiment is open to objection because of its irrationality. In his view, a sentiment that is indifferent to utility will disappear, or at least weaken, in the face of our awareness that it does not promote utility.

852. Utilitarianism and Intuitionism

This dispute between Reid and utilitarians raises more general questions about what to expect from moral theories. We may be dissatisfied by Reid's appeal to intuition and to first principles, especially if his alleged intuitions seem open to question. This dissatisfaction, however, does not undermine his criticism of the utilitarian position. A utilitarian explanation of our moral convictions raises a question about the utilitarian principle itself. Since it cannot be defended on sentimentalist grounds, the utilitarian may appeal instead, as Sidgwick does, to a rational intuition. Perhaps, then, the utilitarian needs Reid's appeal to intuition.

According to Reid, the intuitive status that utilitarians claim for the principle of utility really belongs to a number of moral principles.[50] If our moral convictions cannot all be explained by the utilitarian principle, but can be explained by other principles that are at least

---

[48] Cf. Butler on resentment, §705.   [49] Cf. Clarke on Hobbes, §626.   [50] Here he agrees with Price. See §822.

as intuitively clear as the utilitarian principle, a non-utilitarian conviction is not necessarily irrational.

We might welcome some argument that takes us beyond these competing appeals to intuition. If we could find some reason for believing that a utilitarian or a non-utilitarian reconstruction of ordinary beliefs has some claim to be a better reconstruction, we would have some more systematic reason for preferring it. Reid's basic epistemological outlook opposes the search for a more general account of basic moral principles. But since the examination of issues in moral theory seems to justify a search for some such general account, perhaps the epistemological outlook that causes Reid to stop the argument where he does should be re-examined. The fact that we would like to go further does not imply that an attempt to go further is bound to succeed. If it fails, Reid's position may be best; perhaps we have failed to do something that cannot be done. But if we see the questions that he leaves unanswered, we have some reason to take some of Kant's questions seriously.

853. Duty and Interest: In Defence of Self-Love

Reid's view of morality is similar enough to Butler's and Price's view to raise similar questions about the relation between interest and duty, and between self-love and conscience. On these issues the three moralists offer different answers.

Butler argues that self-love and conscience are independent principles, and that conscience is superior to self-love, even though they almost always coincide. We have seen that Butler's position may be attacked from two different directions: (1) One might argue against him from a eudaemonist point of view; his argument for the distinctness of self-love and conscience relies on the restricted conception of self-love that results from identifying happiness with pleasure. (2) One might argue that he concedes too much to eudaemonism in arguing that self-love and conscience agree; for the account of self-love that separates conscience from self-love also seems to undermine arguments for the agreement of the two principles.

Price rejects the first objection to Butler, but endorses the second, since he argues against Butler's belief in the general agreement of the two principles. His argument depends on identifying happiness with pleasure, and perhaps even on identifying it with selfish pleasure; he does not take account of the sort of argument that, for instance, Plato offers in the *Republic*.

Reid differs from Price; for he gives a much better account of the conception of happiness that supports the efforts of Greek moralists to reconcile morality and self-interest. He exploits this conception of happiness to argue for the systematic agreement of self-love with morality, in defence of Butler against Price. But he does not accept eudaemonism. He argues, as Butler does, that, despite the coincidence of the two principles, morality is distinct from and superior to self-love.[51] If Reid is right, a plausible conception of happiness does not weaken the case for the independence of conscience from self-love.

Reid's generally favourable attitude to Greek eudaemonism rests on his account of the characteristic Greek conception of happiness. He sees that the Stoics' conception of happiness as our good on the whole, and their arguments about the role of practical reason in reducing

---

[51] See Butler, §§704–5.

irrational dependence on external goods, underlie their defence of the virtues of character. He attributes the same view, free of Stoic exaggerations, to Socrates and Plato (H 583a). This eudaemonist argument 'leads directly to the virtues of prudence, temperance, and courage' (H 584a).

His attitude to the other-regarding virtues is more complex. He recognizes that a eudaemonist argument offers some defence of them.[52] In fact, he seems to combine two arguments: (1) Since our good consists in satisfying our affections, and since our affections include other-directed affections, satisfaction of other-directed affections is part of our good. (2) Since we are 'social creatures' and our 'happiness or misery' is connected with the circumstances of others, our good consists in fulfilling our nature, and sharing the good of others is part of our nature; hence sharing the good of others is also part of our good.

These two arguments rest on different conceptions of a person's good. The first relies on a conative conception, finding one's good in the satisfaction of desire. The second relies on a naturalist conception, finding one's good in the fulfilment of one's nature. Reid's account of happiness supports the second argument. It is easy to run the two arguments together, if one recognizes that one's natural affections are parts of one's nature. But they are still distinct arguments, since one can satisfy one's natural affections without fulfilling one's nature. If, for instance, our natural affection for our own good or the good of others is not strong enough to direct us to the appropriate pursuit of its object, we might satisfy it without doing enough for our own good or the good of others, and so without fulfilling our nature. This is one of Butler's reasons for distinguishing the rational principles of self-love, benevolence, and conscience from our natural affections.

If the naturalist argument is primary, Reid should appeal to our nature as social creatures. According to this argument, the fulfilment of our nature requires the fulfilment of our capacity to live in societies that involve concern for the good of others for their own sakes. If this is what Reid has in mind, he appeals to the sort of argument that Aristotle and Aquinas offer in defence of friendship.[53]

It is not clear, however, whether he means to endorse such arguments for the social virtues. If he endorses them, he recognizes eudaemonist arguments for the motives and intentions characteristic of the virtuous agent; for he recognizes that the right intention is necessary if we are to judge that the agent is good, and not simply that the action was good (H 649a).[54] But he seems to hesitate on this aspect of eudaemonism. After saying that eudaemonism argues for 'the practice of every virtue', he also agrees that it leads to the virtues themselves (H 638a). But he seems to qualify this agreement, since he adds that the eudaemonist's motive is not the motive of the virtuous person.[55] This contrast

---

[52] 'And when we consider ourselves as social creatures, whose happiness or misery is very much connected with that of our fellow men; when we consider, that there are many benevolent affections planted in our constitution, whose exertions make a capital part of our good and enjoyment; from these considerations, this principle leads us also, though more indirectly, to the practice of justice, humanity, and all the social virtues. It is true, that a regard to our own good cannot, of itself, produce any benevolent affection. But, if such affections be a part of our constitution, and if the exercise of them make a capital part of our happiness, a regard to our own good ought to lead us to cultivate and exercise them, as every benevolent affection makes the good of others to be our own.' (H 584a)

[53] See §§122, 336.   [54] See also Reid's remarks on the influence of the moral faculty, at H 598a.

[55] 'And though to act from this motive solely, may be called *prudence* rather than *virtue*, yet this prudence deserves some regard upon its own account, and much more as it is the friend and ally of virtue, and the enemy of all vice; and as it gives a favourable testimony of virtue to those who are deaf to every other recommendation. If a man can be induced

between loving virtue for its own sake and loving it for the sake of happiness suggests that Reid does not firmly accept the traditional eudaemonist argument that makes virtue a non-instrumental good that is part of happiness.

854. Duty and Interest: Objections to Self-Love

Though Reid agrees that a reasonable conception of happiness leads us indirectly to the practice of the social virtues, he nonetheless insists that the principle of self-love is defective 'if it be supposed, as it is by some philosophers, to be the only regulating principle of human conduct' (H 584b).[56] What conception of self-love underlies these claims about its defects?

We might suppose Reid simply argues against the view that all our affections are reducible to forms of self-love. Butler ascribes this position to Hobbes, and rejects it. But Reid also seems to deny that self-love is (to use Butler's terms) the supreme practical principle. He argues that 'disinterested regard to duty' is an independent principle not subordinate to self-love (H 584b). Eudaemonism, therefore, is wrong to make self-love superior to every other principle, and thereby to distort the role of conscience.

Reid offers three arguments against the supremacy of self-love: (1) The eudaemonist reasoning that justifies the moral virtues is too complicated for everyone to follow, and will not necessarily move everyone as sharply as a sense of duty moves us.[57] (2) Eudaemonism provides the wrong motive for cultivating the virtues.[58] Our demand for the appropriate motive in the virtuous person conflicts with the supremacy of self-love. (3) The eudaemonist attitude is self-defeating; for if we do not take happiness as our only ultimate end, we will in fact achieve more happiness than if we are eudaemonists.[59]

The first argument maintains that if we all treated moral obligation as dependent on our conception of happiness, many of us would not be appropriately moved by moral obligation. Reid does not dispute the soundness of the eudaemonist argument to show that our overall good requires the moral virtues; he simply argues that it is hazardous to make everyone's commitment to morality depend on acceptance of an argument that most people may not grasp. It is morally desirable, therefore, to find non-eudaemonist grounds that give us sufficient reason to be moral.

---

to do his duty even from a regard to his own happiness, he will soon find reason to love virtue for her own sake, and to act from motives less mercenary.' (H 638a)

[56] Reid's argument is discussed by Rowe, *TRFM* 125–8.

[57] 'There is reason to believe, that a present sense of duty has, in many cases a stronger influence than the apprehension of distant good would have of itself.' (H 584b)

[58] Yet, after all, this wise man, whose thoughts and cares are centred ultimately in himself, who indulges even his social affections only with a view to his own good, is not the man whom we cordially love and esteem. . . . Even when he does good to others, he means only to serve himself; and therefore has no just claim to their gratitude or affection. Our cordial love and esteem is due only to the man whose soul is not contracted within itself, but embraces a more extensive object: who loves virtue, not for her dowry only, but for her own sake: whose benevolence is not selfish, but generous and disinterested: who, forgetful of himself, has the common good at heart, not as the means only, but as the end . . .' (H 585a)

[59] Reid considers a hypothetical case: 'We may here compare, in point of present happiness, two imaginary characters; the first, of the man who has no other ultimate end of his deliberate actions but his own good; and who has no regard to virtue or duty, but as the means to that end. The second character is that of the man who is not indifferent with regard to his own good, but has another ultimate end perfectly consistent with it, to wit, a disinterested love of virtue, for its own sake, or a regard to duty as an end' (H 585b).

This practical argument does not show that there are grounds independent of happiness for moral obligation; it simply shows that we ought to look for them, and that if we find them, we ought to welcome them. But we may concede to Reid that his arguments about the moral sense show that we have such grounds. Still, agreement on this point does not settle the issue about subordination; for it does not settle how far we have reason to stick to moral obligations when they conflict with other aspects of our good. If we agree that we have some rational grounds independent of our overall good, we may still ask how these grounds are to be compared with our grounds for pursuing other goods. To answer this question, we may still, for all Reid has shown, need to appeal to happiness.

The second argument is more directly relevant to the question about subordination. Even if eudaemonists recognize virtue as a primary element of one's good, they must (in Reid's view) take a 'mercenary' attitude to virtue. What is this mercenary attitude that prevents our valuing virtue at its proper worth? We might understand it in two ways: (1) It is the attitude that values virtue purely instrumentally. (2) It is the attitude that values virtue because of its contribution to happiness. Reid's different remarks suggest that he has each of these views in mind in different places, and that he probably does not distinguish them.

If Reid refers to the first attitude, he is right to say that it is incompatible with the ordinary understanding of a virtuous person. But a eudaemonist need not accept it. For many eudaemonists argue that virtuous action is worth choosing for its own sake, and is therefore a part of happiness; we can value virtue for its own sake and still be eudaemonists. If Reid has the second attitude in mind, he is right to say that eudaemonists are committed to it. But it does not require a purely instrumental approach to the virtues. Reid might believe that our normal attitude to virtue requires a strongly disinterested concern that conflicts with eudaemonism. But he does not justify this belief.

The third argument seeks to present a paradox of eudaemonism parallel to the paradox of hedonism. But it suffers from the obscurity that we have found in the second argument. Reid might mean: (a) We will achieve more happiness if we value virtue for its own sake than if we value it purely instrumentally. (b) We will achieve more happiness if we have a strongly disinterested concern for virtue than we will achieve if our concern is related to our happiness. The first claim is plausible, but does not conflict with eudaemonism. The second claim conflicts with eudaemonism, but is it plausible?

Eudaemonism does not require us to claim that happiness is the only thing worth choosing for its own sake. In fact, some eudaemonists argue that happiness is the ultimate end because it is composed of ends that are worth choosing for their own sakes. Hence we introduce no conflict in our beliefs if we believe both that something other than happiness is worth choosing for its own sake and that happiness is the only ultimate end. Reid would raise a genuine difficulty for eudaemonists if the belief that maximizes happiness is the belief that some particular non-ultimate end would still be preferable to anything else if something else promoted my happiness better. But he has not shown that someone maximizes happiness by holding this belief.

Reid's third objection, then, rests on the sort of misunderstanding that also underlies his second objection. He seems to be wrong about the implications of the eudaemonist claim that happiness is the ultimate end. He seems to suppose that this claim implies a purely instrumental status for other goods; but the eudaemonist has no reason to agree with him.

855. Eudaemonism and the Moral Motive

Reid's criticisms of eudaemonism assume, therefore, that a eudaemonist treats virtues as purely instrumental to happiness in some objectionable sense. He doubts whether a eudaemonist argument, treating self-love as the supreme principle, can justify the virtues, because he doubts whether it can justify our valuing the virtues for their own sakes, as a virtuous person values them. He takes this criticism to apply even to 'the best moralists among the ancients', including the Stoics.[60] But this objection to Stoicism is puzzling, given his other remarks.

Since Reid rejects the supremacy of self-love, he recognizes a distinct superior principle of duty.[61] In his view, the irreducibility of duty is recognized by ordinary people and philosophers of all times and nearly all schools. Reid cites the Greek concept of the *kalon*, rendered in Latin by 'honestum'. He believes, as Price does, that this concept expresses the right and the honourable, and marks the requirements of duty as opposed to interest.[62] The morally virtuous person, according to Reid, recognizes that conscience and the sense of duty constitute an independent and sufficient rational principle. Reid takes the Stoics to acknowledge that the moral motive has this status; they clarify the devotion to duty and the moral motive that Reid takes to be characteristic of the morally good person.[63]

This judgment on the Stoics seems to conflict with Reid's view that they are eudaemonists. He does not say how this apparent conflict is to be resolved. Indeed, in the contexts where he emphasizes the devotion of the Stoics to the honestum, he does not mention that they are eudaemonists. His objections to eudaemonism cast doubt on at least some of his views about the Stoics; for either his claims about the Stoics, or the Stoics' own claims, seem to be inconsistent, and Reid does not try to remove the appearance of inconsistency. If the Stoics are eudaemonists, do they not take the mercenary attitude to virtue that is inconsistent with their devotion to the honestum? But if their position is consistent, Reid's description of their position casts doubt on his criticism of eudaemonism.

---

[60] 'These oracles of reason led the Stoics so far as to maintain . . . that virtue is the only good . . . This noble and elevated conception of human wisdom and duty was taught by Socrates, free of the extravagancies which the Stoics afterward joined with it.' (H 583a)

[61] '. . . the notion of duty cannot be resolved into that of interest, or what is most for our happiness. Every man may be satisfied of this who attends to his own conceptions, and the language of all mankind shows it' (H 587a)

[62] 'What we call *right* and *honourable* in human conduct, was, by the ancients, called *honestum, to kalon*; of which Tully says, "Quod vere dicimus, etiamsi a nullo laudetur, natura esse laudabile". [Cic. *Off.* i 14.] All the ancient sects, except the Epicureans, distinguished the *honestum* from the *utile*, as we distinguish what is a man's duty from what is his interest. The word *officium, kathêkon*, extended both to the *honestum* and the *utile*: so that every reasonable action, proceeding either from a sense of duty or a sense of interest, was called *officium*.' (H 588a) Stewart follows Reid: 'This distinction [sc. between duty and interest] was expressed, among the Roman moralists, by the words *honestum* and *utile*. Of the former Cicero says, . . . [quotation as above]. *To kalon* among the Greeks corresponds, when applied to the conduct, to the *honestum* of the Romans.' (PAMP ii 2, 220) Here Stewart cites Reid in his support, and continues with Reid's comments on different aspects of the *kathêkon*. The passage from Cicero is also quoted (for a different, though related, purpose) by Price, *RPQM* 62. See also Suarez, §438.

[63] 'The authority of conscience over the other active principles of the mind, I do not consider as a point that requires proof by argument, but as self-evident. For it implies no more than this, that in all cases a man ought to do his duty. He only who does in all cases what he ought to do, is the perfect man. Of this perfection in the human nature, the Stoics formed the idea, and held it forth in their writings as the goal to which the race of life ought to be directed. Their *wise man* was one in whom a regard for the *honestum* swallowed up every other principle of action.' (H 597b–598a)

This doubt affects Reid's argument as a whole. He introduces the Stoic conception of the honestum in support of Butler's belief in the distinctness and independence of conscience from self-love. But the Stoics do not seem to support Butler, since they do not separate the honestum from happiness. They recognize that the belief that an action is morally right is different from the belief that it contributes to my happiness. They also agree that belief in moral rightness provides a motive that is distinct from the desire for my happiness. But they do not infer that moral rightness gives me a justifying reason that is independent of any contribution to happiness.

Reid perhaps overlooks this distinction between the character of the moral motive and the justifying reason it provides. He goes too far in claiming that the Stoic sage was someone 'in whom a regard to the honestum swallowed up every other principle of action' (H 589a). The claim that the moral motive 'swallows up' other principles of action is obscure on the crucial point. The Stoics believe that no other principle of action conflicts with the moral motive in the sage. But they do not believe that nothing else matters to sages besides the moral motive; sages also insist that action on the moral motive is the only element in their happiness, and the crucial element in the way of life that they aim at.[64]

Reid might answer that this division between the moral motive and the eudaemonic justifying reason does not make the Stoic position consistent. For he might believe that acceptance of a eudaemonic justifying reason implies a mercenary attitude to virtue, and thereby excludes the right attitude to moral obligation. This answer depends on our accepting Reid's claim—implicit in some of his arguments—that the moral motive is not only distinct from the desire for happiness, but also requires indifference to happiness. But Reid has no good defence of this claim. Hence his case against the supremacy of self-love is not cogent.

856. The Supremacy of Conscience

Reid rejects eudaemonism, and believes that conscience constitutes a rational principle distinct from self-love. He therefore faces Butler's question about which principle is superior, and why. He rejects the opinion that he attributes to some mediaeval mystics, that we should pay no attention to our happiness in this life or the afterlife. This is also the view of the Quietists whom Butler opposes as 'enthusiasts'.[65] Reid takes his objections to the 'mercenary' aspects of eudaemonism to apply to the position accepted by Aquinas. The opposing view he rejects does not say simply that conscience is superior to self-love, but that we should renounce self-love altogether.

Reid agrees with Butler's view that conscience is supreme.[66] He also agrees with Butler's belief in the harmony of self-love and conscience. In his view, the opposition between conscience and self-love is 'merely imaginary', because following our conscience is in fact always for our good.

---

[64] This is the 'life in accordance with nature', which includes the preferred indifferents as well as happiness.

[65] 'This seems to have been the extravagance of some mystics, which perhaps they were led into, in opposition to a contrary extreme of the schoolmen of the middle ages, who made the desire of good to ourselves to be the sole motive to action and virtue to be approvable only on account of its present or future reward.' (H 598b) On enthusiasm cf. Butler, §717.

[66] '. . . the disinterested love of virtue is undoubtedly the noblest principle in human nature, and ought never to stoop to any other' (H 598b).

The reconciliation of conscience with self-love rests partly on the eudaemonist arguments that Reid has endorsed, even though he has rejected them as a reason for subordinating conscience to self-love. In the present context he especially emphasizes the theological reasons for believing in the harmony of the two principles. Those who believe in God and believe that God rewards virtue with eternal happiness need not consider their own happiness, as long as they follow their conscience in the questions that concern conscience.

Reid does not believe, however, that our only assurance of the harmony of duty and interest is theological. He describes someone who rejects the harmony of the two principles.[67] In agreeing with Shaftesbury's judgment on this case, Reid apparently disagrees with Butler, who rejects Shaftesbury's claim that the case is without remedy.[68]

The disagreement with Butler is, at first sight, surprising. For Butler criticizes Shaftesbury for neglecting the difference between strength and authority. He answers that, once we recognize the rational supremacy of conscience, we have sufficient reason to follow conscience, even if our inclinations or sentiments conflict and our benevolent sentiments are no stronger than our selfish ones. Reid should accept this criticism of Shaftesbury, since he agrees with Butler in insisting on the difference between strength and authority—as he puts it, between animal strength and rational strength.

Still, as Reid sees, Butler's answer to Shaftesbury does not eliminate every possibility of a conflict between conscience and self-love. Reid is considering a different point from the one that Butler considers in answering Shaftesbury. He considers self-love not simply as an inclination or particular passion, but as 'a leading principle' of one's nature. Reid recognizes that Butler's naturalism is difficult to defend without the harmony of self-love and conscience.[69] Denial of their harmony casts doubt on the claim that human nature constitutes a system, and that, as both Reid and Butler insist, action on each of these principles is natural.

If Reid is to show that action on conscience is natural, he needs to rely on the eudaemonist arguments he has given for accepting the content of morality, even though he denies that they capture the moral motive. These are the arguments that a sceptic about the harmony of virtue and happiness has failed to grasp. Reid believes that the sceptic makes a mistake about virtue and happiness that is distinct from the mistake of being an atheist. Reid's position, then, depends on the cogency of these eudaemonist arguments.

In considering the consequences of denying the harmony of duty and interest, Reid faces Sidgwick's dualism of practical reason. Sidgwick believes in a dualism because he thinks that both self-love and conscience claim to be supreme; each claims that it is ultimately reasonable to follow it rather than any other principle. That is why we face a 'fundamental contradiction' (Sidgwick, ME 508) in practical reason, not simply an awkward practical conflict on possible particular occasions. If Sidgwick is right about what each principle says, no assurance of their practical harmony removes the fundamental difficulty raised by their contradictory claims about supremacy.

---

[67] 'Indeed, if we suppose a man to be an atheist in his belief, and at the same time, by wrong judgment, to believe that virtue is contrary to his happiness upon the whole, this case, as Lord Shaftesbury justly observes, is without remedy. It will be impossible for the man to act, so as not to contradict a leading principle of his nature. He must either sacrifice his happiness to virtue, or virtue to happiness; and is reduced to this miserable dilemma, whether it is best to be a fool or a knave.' (H 598b)

[68] See Butler, §714.   [69] See Butler, §710.

Reid, like Butler, rejects Sidgwick's dualism; he does not believe that the two principles threaten the contradiction that Sidgwick describes. He asserts that conscience claims supremacy, but he does not assert that self-love claims it. He seems to follow Butler in treating self-love as a superior principle, but conscience as supreme.

If this is his view, should he infer that those who reject the harmony of the two principles face a miserable dilemma? He assumes that they must choose between (as it will appear to them) being a fool and being a knave. But he seems to exaggerate their difficulties. If we accept both principles as superior, we will presumably follow each of them on many occasions—we will neither be purely mercenary nor purely self-denying. We will violate either principle only on those occasions where the demand of the other seems to be especially urgent. We need not think of ourselves as knaves (on the occasions where we decide that the cost to self-love is too great for us to follow conscience) or fools (on the occasions when we sacrifice self-love for the sake of conscience). While Reid is justified in asserting the importance of belief in the harmony of duty and interest, he seems to exaggerate the bad effects of not recognizing their harmony.

857. The Authority of Conscience

If Reid affirms, with Butler, the supremacy of conscience, how does he justify himself? He claims that we can see how conscience is a rational principle, and therefore a superior principle; but why is it supreme? Reid's appeal to self-evidence is too hasty.[70] One ground for judging that we ought to do x is the fact that x is our duty.[71] But, contrary to Reid, this is not the ground that decides whether conscience is superior to self-love. Even if conscience claims that there are moral grounds for preferring morality, it does not follow that moral grounds are to be preferred over purely prudential grounds. The moral ought-judgment needs to be supported by claims about overall reasonableness that go beyond the moral judgment. Reid's argument to show that the superiority of conscience is self-evident is, therefore, dubious. If he appeals to a further self-evident principle that it is reasonable overall to follow conscience against self-love, he relies on intuition to settle a question that seems open to argument, and therefore does not seem to have a self-evident answer.

Can Reid show something more about the character of the moral point of view that would prove that conscience is supreme? One might ask why acceptance of the supremacy of conscience is natural. Something about the content of conscience should show us that in following it we express the systematic character of the different impulses and principles that constitute the nature of rational agents.

Reid suggests a possible partial answer to this naturalist demand. The first principles of morals include a principle enjoining reciprocity—that we should act towards others as we would judge it right for them in the same circumstances to act towards us (H 639a).[72] He justifies this principle by arguing that we recognize its force whenever we are the victims

---

[70] See H 597b–598a quoted in §855.
[71] Alternatively, we might say that the sense of 'ought' in which it is evident that we ought to do our duty is the moral sense of 'ought'.
[72] Clarke also emphasizes this feature of moral judgment. See §631.

of an offence.[73] Reid suggests that we cannot rationally avoid the impartial application of moral principles. We are ready to apply them to others, and we have no rational basis, if we are honest with ourselves, for refusing to apply them to ourselves as well.

In demanding what we think is owed to us, we do not simply assert that we want something; for we do not resent the refusal to give us what we want unless we believe we deserve or are entitled to it. In believing this about ourselves, we apply a principle that rests on authority, since we appeal to reasons, and not simply to the strength of our desires. Hence the application of these authoritative principles to ourselves commits us to accepting the authority of conscience.

This point about authority might allow a defence of the rational supremacy of conscience. Reid argues that if we accept moral principles in their application to other people, but deny their application to ourselves, we rely on some assumption about what is special about ourselves. But when we think about it honestly, we reject this assumption. This argument presupposes that we rest our claims against others on authoritative principles. Hence we might avoid the conclusion by denying we rely on authoritative principles in our treatment of others; we might claim to be simply asserting our desires against them. Reid assumes that we cannot escape his conclusion in this way, if we admit that we are rational agents who guide our actions by authoritative principles.

Much more needs to be said in defence of this argument. One needs to show, for instance, that morality expresses an impartial and authoritative conception of what people deserve and are entitled to, so that it binds anyone who makes claims against others on the basis of entitlement. Butler briefly defends his view that this conception of morality underlies the exceptions to utilitarianism. Reid's argument will be convincing only if he shows that Butler's view gives an account of the basic principle of morality. Like Price, he sketches an argument that Kant explores more fully.

858. Rationalism v. Naturalism

Reid's defence of a rationalist position against Hume gives us an opportunity to sum up some of the issues in the debate between rationalists and sentimentalists. This debate begins with Hobbes's attack on a traditional view of the relation of morality to human nature. This traditional view is contained in Suarez's defence of Aquinas' general position. Though Suarez does not agree with Aquinas on all the main questions of moral and political theory, he defends some of the main claims that distinguish Aquinas from his voluntarist critics and from Hobbes and his successors.

In Suarez's view, principles of morality (1) describe what is appropriate for rational nature, which is not constituted by anyone's beliefs or desires. He takes this conception to be equivalent to the conception of them as (2) principles of practical reason aiming at the human good. The first claim is more prominent in Suarez, and the second is more prominent

---

[73] 'It is not want of judgment, but want of candour and impartiality, that hinders men from discerning what they owe to others. They are quicksighted enough in discerning what is due to themselves. When they are injured, or ill treated, they see it, and feel resentment. It is the want of candour that makes men use one measure for the duty they owe to others, and another measure for the duty that others owe to them in like circumstances.' (H 639a)

in Aquinas; but, given the view of rational nature common to Aquinas and Suarez, the two claims agree. Sentimentalists reject the first claim. In their view, morality depends on will or sentiment, or both, not simply on facts about rational nature and what is appropriate for it.

Some rationalists also reject the first claim. They agree that moral principles describe facts not constituted by human choice, will, desire, or sentiment. But Clarke, Price, and Reid reject the connexion between morality and rational nature. In their view, moral principles are true about moral facts that have no essential reference to rational nature; their rightness does not depend on the relation of morality to anything outside it.

In claiming that moral principles describe eternal relations of fitness grasped by reason, Clarke agrees with Suarez. Indeed, Suarez may be Clarke's indirect source, since Clarke is probably inspired by views similar to those of Cudworth, and Cudworth follows Suarez. The essential point that Clarke omits from Suarez is the appeal to rational nature. This element is restored by Butler in his account of morality, which comes much closer to Suarez's account. But Price and Reid follow Clarke in deleting the appeal to nature.

859. Intuitionism v. Naturalism

This difference between the naturalism of Suarez and the rationalism of Clarke, Price, and Reid is epistemologically and metaphysically significant. If true moral principles describe what is fitting for rational nature, we have some basis for argument about moral questions; apparently, we can test a purported moral principle by seeing whether it really fits rational nature. Admittedly, this appearance may be misleading; for we may be unable to reach a sufficiently detailed understanding of rational nature. But at least we seem to have something to argue about.

Once the appeal to rational nature is dropped, we have nothing further to argue about if we ask whether a purported moral principle is true or not. We have to see the answer to such questions by inspection, since we have nothing we can infer it from. It is understandable, then, that the rationalists are also intuitionists about our knowledge of moral principles.

If we separate moral facts from facts about fitness for rational nature, we also deprive ourselves of an apparently reasonable answer to questions about their metaphysical status. If Suarez is right, moral facts may be facts about human beings, or, more broadly, about rational beings. This is not completely obvious; for we might argue that facts about rational beings can be completely stated without any reference to what is fitting for their nature. Suarez does not take this view; he believes that the nature of rational beings determines what is fitting for them, so that an account of all the facts about human nature will determine the facts about fittingness. Whatever metaphysical status we attribute to facts about human and rational nature must also be attributed to moral facts.

Since the rationalists reject this connexion with facts about rational nature, they cannot say anything further about the sorts of facts that moral facts are; hence, they must regard them as sui generis. This metaphysical claim is expressed in their claim that moral properties are indefinable.

Reid provides a fuller and more articulate defence of this position than Clarke and Price provide. He argues, taking up suggestions of Price, that moral truths are not the only ones of which we must give an intuitionist account. Since empiricism, in his view, cannot account for our knowledge of the external world, and since we have to rely on intuition here too, we cannot reasonably object to an intuitionist treatment of moral knowledge. Reid does not explicitly reject Butler's naturalism, insofar as it supports claims about the superior status of self-love and the supremacy of conscience. But he does not use naturalism against intuitionism.

860. Reasons for Rejecting Naturalism

The rationalists do not make it clear why they reject the naturalist account of moral facts and our knowledge of them. Two reasons are worth considering: (1) We have noticed the broader philosophical and scientific grounds for rejecting an appeal to nature, if nature is taken to include immanent teleology, without reference to the legislative will of God. (2) Balguy's and Price's arguments against Hutcheson suggest that they believe any concession to naturalism is an admission of inappropriate mutability in moral properties, and therefore a concession to the Hobbesian errors exposed by Cudworth.

Suarez follows Aquinas in explaining fitness to rational nature by reference to the ultimate end of a rational agent. Aquinas' eudaemonism connects his account of morality with his account of will and freedom. On this point he differs from the rationalism of Clarke and his defenders. According to Aquinas, pursuit of a final good is not an empirically known feature of rational beings; it is an essential property of rational agents, and it is essential to the freedom that is peculiar to rational agents.

Price and Reid abandon this central role of the final good. They deny that it is essential to freedom; they offer an indeterminist account of freedom that has no essential role for a rational desire for the good. Though Reid stays closer than Butler or Price do to Aquinas' conception of happiness and prudence, he does not rely on the final good for his explanation of the difference between will and passion, or for his explanation of freedom. In contrast to Aquinas, he does not believe that in attributing freedom to rational agents, we attribute the desires and aims that are the basis for the moral virtues.

In rejecting Aquinas' eudaemonism and his account of the will, rationalists seem to be influenced by the similarities between these doctrines and some doctrines of their sentimentalist and voluntarist opponents. If we take happiness to be pleasure, it is clear why acceptance of eudaemonism seems to commit us to Hobbesian claims about the basis of morality. This is why Hutcheson, Balguy, and Price all reject eudaemonism.

This reason for rejecting eudaemonism does not fit Reid, who has a more accurate conception of the ultimate good, as Aristotle and Aquinas conceive it. It still seems to him an inadequate basis for morality. But his reasons for rejecting it are quite weak, in the light of his description of the good and happiness.

Similarly, Reid's objections to Aquinas' explanation of freewill seem to reflect his antipathy to Hobbes's and Hume's versions of compatibilism. In their view, freedom is simply causation by desires rather than external force. Reid objects that this simple compatibilist view fails to recognize some crucial distinctions between will and passion. But he does not refute the more complex compatibilist view that can be derived from Aquinas.

861. Difficulties for Non-naturalist Rationalism

In accepting some elements of the outlook of Aquinas and Suarez and rejecting other elements, the rationalists expose themselves to objections that the naturalist does not face. Perhaps the most serious objection arises from the extent to which the rationalists are committed to intuitionism.

This objection does not rest on the mere fact that they sometimes rely on intuition. Price and Reid reject a single principle of rightness, such as the principle of utility, and recognize the possibility of conflicts among principles that cannot simply be settled by appeal to a supreme principle. This pluralism does not discredit their position.

They are open to more damaging objections for their appeal to intuition as a substitute for an account of the nature of moral facts, and for reasons that might be given for taking morality seriously. They claim that morality involves indefinable properties, sui generis facts, and principles that must be grasped by intuition without any further room for argument, defence, or explanation. These claims tend to undermine part of the rationalists' initial motive for maintaining their position. They believe, reasonably, that a sentimentalist conception of moral principles does not take them seriously enough, since it makes them subordinate to sentiments, and does not recognize their regulative role in relation to sentiments. But if they cannot say what feature of morality gives it a regulative role, they cast doubt on their claim to be vindicating this regulative role of morality.

These considerations suggest that rational intuition of independent sui generis facts is not a satisfactory conclusion for a rationalist to reach. If we find the rationalist position unsatisfactory, we may react in different ways: (1) We may decide that sentimentalism is right after all. (2) We may decide that the appeal to independent facts is mistaken. (3) We may decide that the separation of moral truths from truths about rational agents is mistaken.

The first reaction is open to question; for the rationalists' objections to sentimentalism may still seem cogent, even when the weakness in their position is recognized. The second reaction is justified only if independent facts would have to be the sorts of facts that the rationalists describe. The view that objectivism implies intuitionism has sometimes persuaded opponents of intuitionism to oppose objectivism as well.[74]

But we will not immediately share this second reaction if we consider rationalism against the background of naturalism. The mediaeval naturalist point of view favours the third reaction to the rationalism of Price and Reid. Aquinas' ethical theory is not intuitionist, and it does not treat moral facts as sui generis. The aspects of naturalism that the rationalists reject are the ones that make it unnecessary to introduce the strongly intuitionist aspects of rationalism. When we see this, we ought to ask whether the rationalists are right to reject these aspects of naturalism.

862. Rationalism, Naturalism, and Kant

This summary of the disputes between naturalists, sentimentalists, and rationalists may help to introduce the examination of Kant. For, in ethics as in epistemology and metaphysics,

---

[74] This line of argument is especially clear in Strawson, 'Intuitionism'.

Kant is dissatisfied both with empiricism and with the rationalism that leads to undefended intuitions. Part of his strategy can be described as an expression of the third reaction; for he takes the connexion between a theory of rational agency and a theory of morality to be much tighter than it appears to be in rationalist conceptions. To this extent he develops a central aspect of Butler's position (despite his ignorance of Butler) that is obscured by Price and Reid (despite their knowledge of Butler).

Still, Kant does not revive mediaeval naturalism; he rejects it even more clearly than the rationalists do. His rejection is implicit; he does not seriously consider the Aristotelian position defended by Aquinas and his 16th-century supporters, and his explicit references to Greek ethics are rather brief and inexact. We will have to examine his reasons for rejecting the naturalist position, and see how far they leave him from the position common to Aquinas and Butler.

This question is connected with a question about the nature of Kant's rejection of rational intuition; does this lead him to a version of the second reaction as well as the third? Some of his views encourage interpreters to believe that his rejection of rationalism includes the rejection of objectivism. We need to see whether this is Kant's position, and whether he has a good reason for regarding it as the most reasonable reaction to the intuitionist aspects of rationalism.

64

VOLUNTARISM, EGOISM, AND UTILITARIANISM

863. Voluntarists as Critics

We noticed earlier that theological voluntarism is a persistent feature of English moral philosophy in the 17th and 18th centuries.[1] We might have expected to find it in Scottish philosophy too, given its affinity to some trends in Calvinism, but we do not find it. Probably this is not because it was unpopular in Scotland, but because the major Scottish philosophers belonged to the theological moderates who reacted to Calvinism.[2] Complaints against Hutcheson suggest that some of his opponents may have been voluntarists.[3]

No English moralist sets out a voluntarist position as fully as Pufendorf does. But the English voluntarists are worth examining as critics of rationalism and sentimentalism. John Clarke sets out the main points of criticism. In his view, both Samuel Clarke the rationalist and Hutcheson the sentimentalist leave obscurities and unanswered questions that a voluntarist account removes. He identifies two main flaws in their position: (1) They cannot give a perspicuous account of moral duty and obligation without reference to divine commands. (2) They cannot give a perspicuous account of reasons and motives without an egoistic appeal to God's promises of rewards and punishments.

These voluntarist criticisms are worth discussing partly because they may help us to identify genuine difficulties and obscurities in rationalism and sentimentalism. We might

---

[1] See §§525–6. Pattison, 'Thought', offers a fairly sympathetic treatment of moral philosophy in conjunction with English theology in the 18th century. At 61–2 he connects developments in moral philosophy with different interpretations of Paul's remark on natural law in *Rm.* 2:14: 'Since the time of Augustine, the orthodox interpretation had applied this verse, either to the Gentile converts, or to the favoured few among the heathen who had extraordinary divine assistance. The Protestant expositors, to whom the words "do by nature the things contained in the law" could never bear their literal force, sedulously preserved the Augustinian explanation . . . The rationalists, however, find the expression "by nature", in its literal sense, exactly conformable to their views . . .' Pattison's contrast misrepresents the position of many Protestant expositors; for evidence of the error in his first sentence see §§226, 412.

[2] Sher, *CU* 57, mentions Witherspoon's satire on moderate ministers in *EC*. The moderates should make sure to know only Leibniz, Shaftesbury, Collins, Hutcheson, and Hume's Essays, and to avoid scriptural and theological learning (*EC* 26). The moderates' 'Athenian Creed' includes the article: 'I believe in the divinity of L. S-y, the saintship of Marcus Antoninus, the perspicuity and sublimity of A-e, and the perpetual duration of Mr H-n's works, notwithstanding their present tendency to oblivion. Amen.' (27)

[3] See the charges brought before the Presbytery of Glasgow, quoted in §645. Voluntarists might have been especially likely to object to Hutcheson, though neither of the two grounds of objection is confined to voluntarists.

sympathize with critics who claim that the rationalists appeal too quickly to 'fitnesses' and related notions that appear to promise some understanding of moral concepts, but really presuppose understanding of them. Similarly, we might doubt whether an appeal to a moral sense explains the distinctive features of moral judgments and moral properties. Rationalists and sentimentalists criticize each other on these grounds; voluntarists are more convinced by the criticisms than by the defences.

We have a further reason for taking voluntarist criticisms seriously. When critics object to obscurity in their opponents' position, they rely on some explicit or implicit views about which concepts or judgments are clear and which are obscure, and on what standards of clarity are appropriate for the subject-matter. The voluntarists' demand for clarity leads them to a reductive analysis of moral concepts and properties to concepts and properties (command, motive, interest) that can be explained and understood without reference to moral properties.[4] Neither rationalists nor sentimentalists meet the standards of clarity that voluntarists demand.

Voluntarists, therefore, raise a useful question about whether we ought to demand this sort of clarity from an account of morality. In this way they anticipate utilitarian criticism of other moral theories. Bentham and Mill believe that utilitarianism is superior to its main rivals in its clarity. Sidgwick is more cautious in his claims, but he basically agrees with Bentham and Mill; he often objects to other theories because their accounts of moral properties are obscure or unhelpfully circular. In the 20th century naturalists and non-cognitivists raise similar objections to non-naturalism. Non-naturalists agree with their critics that their analyses fail to provide certain kinds of clarification, but they disagree about whether that matters.

The English voluntarists maintain three major claims: (1) An imperative account of morality as consisting in obligations imposed by commands. (2) A utilitarian account of the content of morality. (3) An egoist account of moral motivation. These claims are logically separable, but voluntarists pass easily from one to the other. They are especially prone to combine the first claim, about the metaphysics of morality, with the third claim, about moral motivation. They are influenced by the different aspects of obligation, which they take to include both metaphysical and motivational elements.

In trying to treat these different elements separately, we are imposing distinctions that are not easy to mark in the relevant texts. But the distinctions may nonetheless be useful, to point out the different parts of a voluntarist position that one might accept or reject. Though the voluntarists themselves think of them as a package, it is worth noticing that we might accept one thesis without the others. This selective attitude to the voluntarists is characteristic of later utilitarians.

864. Enthusiasm[5]

Voluntarism expresses one widespread reaction to Shaftesbury and the French Quietists who raise questions, from different points of view, about the role of self-interest in the

---

[4] I speak of concepts and of properties because it is not clear which of them the voluntarists are trying to explain.
[5] See §§611, 717.

Christian outlook. Shaftesbury—according to one interpretation—takes it for granted that Christian morality appeals to self-interest, because it offers the prospect of happiness in an afterlife as the reward for virtue in this life. Since this is the orthodox outlook, he infers that the orthodox outlook is open to moral objections. He argues that, from the Stoic point of view, Christian morality fails to value the honestum for its own sake.

The French Quietists also express doubts about appeals to self-love. They rely on a strict interpretation of Augustine's contrast between self-love and the love of God, and they argue that Christianity requires an entirely self-forgetful love of God in which believers even forget that they achieve their own happiness in the love of God. In contrast to Shaftesbury, they do not agree that the genuinely Christian outlook makes self-love primary; they attack any outlook that gives any place to self-love as a perversion of Christianity.

Despite these differences between Shaftesbury and the Quietists, they share an attitude that English writers attack as 'enthusiasm', a fanatical rejection of normal human motives in favour of an unhealthy degree of self-renunciation. In France Bossuet argues against Quietism by re-affirming the legitimacy of eudaemonism within a Christian outlook.[6] In England a series of critics attack both Quietism and Shaftesbury's version of Stoicism as aspects of the same enthusiastic rejection of self-love.

We might reject the enthusiastic outlook by affirming the legitimacy of both self-love and disinterested motives. This is Butler's position. His Sermons assume the moral appropriateness of self-love and defend the harmony of self-love and conscience. He warns against an extreme reaction to enthusiasm that would deny the reality or moral appropriateness of disinterested motives.

Despite Butler's warning, the English voluntarists accept the extreme reaction, and so reject appeals to disinterested motives. Perhaps they are impressed not only by the dangers of enthusiasm, but also by Mandevile's sceptical doubts about disinterested motives. Mandeville suggests that since true virtue depends on pure and disinterested motives, and since we can usually find some self-interest in the antecedents of allegedly virtuous actions, we may reasonably doubt the reality of true virtue. One might suppose that the safest reply to Mandeville is to concede his point, given his understanding of true virtue, but to deny its relevance. If we can defend morality without assuming disinterested motives, we need not worry about his doubts.

This reply concedes rather a lot to Mandeville. His doubts rest on alleged observations about mixed motives. He generalizes from cases in which someone who gives a charitable gift is also attracted by the thought that he will gain a good reputation for his charity, so that it will be good for business. But such cases show only that sometimes people act from mixed motives. These mixtures do not threaten the reality of disinterested motives; they show only that disinterested motives often co-operate with self-interested motives. Such

---

⁶ Bossuet's eudaemonism is rather severely examined by Ward, NG, ch. 3. In 'Instruction' (Pref. §9) Bossuet defends eudaemonism as authentically Christian: 'c'est donc une illusion d'ôter à l'amour de Dieu le motif de nous render heureux' (Calvet 613). He insists that happiness has to be understood to include more than one's own advantage (utilité, intérêt). He acknowledges that Anselm and Scotus have understood happiness as advantage, but argues that they have not lost sight of its broader scope (which includes 'l'honnêteté et la justice') (614). Once we keep the right conception of happiness in mind, we ought to love God as the source of our own happiness, and we should not try to cultivate a purely disinterested love of God (the attitude in which 'on aimerat Dieu, quand par impossible il faudrait l'aimer sans récompense', 617).

co-operation is no threat to the reality of moral virtue, unless we assume that virtue requires wholly unmixed motives. Some moralists, however, including Balguy, assume this about virtue, and so leave themselves open to Mandeville's doubts.[7] Balguy's position makes it easier to understand why voluntarists prefer not to rely on disinterested motives.

865. Obligation and Imperatives

John Clarke's *Foundation of Morality in Theory and Practice* sketches the different elements of the voluntarist position, and shows how they are connected. He defends himself against both Samuel Clarke and Hutcheson, arguing that they both overlook the necessary connexion between moral rightness, duty, divine commands, and self-interest.

According to John Clarke, Samuel Clarke is mistaken in trying to identify moral properties with facts about the nature of things apart from law. John Clarke agrees with Cumberland and Pufendorf in holding that law is the necessary basis of duty.[8] But Samuel Clarke need not disagree. As Gregory of Rimini and Suarez put it, we may find an 'indicative law' in the nature of things, giving us compelling reason to act one way rather than another. This is law in the larger sense recognized by Hooker.[9] Samuel Clarke's appeal to fitness acknowledges this sort of indicative law. To refute Samuel Clarke, therefore, John Clarke needs to show that morality requires an imperative law (as Gregory puts it) and not just an indicative law.

To fix the connexion between morality and imperative law, John Clarke relies, as many English writers do, on his conception of obligation.[10] He argues that since obligation implies motivation, and since 'ought' and 'obliged' are equivalent, morality requires an imperative law supported by sanctions; for this sort of law is needed to create the sort of motive that belongs to obligation. The motivational conception of obligation makes it reasonable to accept both voluntarism and egoism.

Thomas Johnson uses some of Pufendorf's arguments to defend voluntarism.[11] He quotes and endorses Pufendorf's view that obligation, and therefore morality, needs to be imposed by a superior.[12] He takes over Pufendorf's argument against Grotius, claiming that if natural

---

[7] See §669.

[8] 'Duty is founded in law, and supposes it; for that, and that only, is so called, which is supposed to be required by some law.' (J. Clarke, *FMTP* 9)

[9] See §414 on Hooker; §425 on Suarez.

[10] 'The same may be said of obligation, which, in the sense it always has, I think, in treatises of morality, signifies the necessity a person lies under, to comply with some law, or suffer the penalty denounced against the violation of it. So that obligation implies law too, in the philosophical use of the word, and therefore has no place where there is no law. There is indeed another vulgar acceptation of the word, wherein no reference is had to law, but only to some inconvenience or prejudice, considered as the natural or likely consequence of acting or forbearing to act so or so. . . . It is visible, in the first sense of the word, men cannot be said to lie under any obligation with respect to moral rules, if they are not supposed to be laws, that is, the positive will and command of God. And in the second and vulgar acceptation of the word, under the supposition that the observation of moral rules should be attended with nothing but pain and misery, men would be so far from being obliged to the observation, that they would be obliged on the contrary to the breach and violation of them. What has been said, may be applied to the term Ought; for Ought and Obliged signify the same.' (J. Clarke, *FMTP* 9)

[11] Johnson's essay *EMO* seeks to settle the dispute between Waterland and the supporters of Clarke over the status of moral and positive duties; see §869. He defends Waterland's side of the dispute by arguing for a voluntarist account of morality. Like Waterland, he believes he is on the side of orthodox Christianity, because rationalism leads to Deism (70).

[12] Johnson, *EMO* 8, quotes Pufendorf, *DOH* 2.2.

and social creatures exist only because of the divine will, voluntarism is correct (*EMO* 12). Here he follows Pufendorf and Barbeyrac in misunderstanding the issue about naturalism and voluntarism.[13] But he also argues more pertinently for Pufendorf's view, by maintaining (against Chubb) that a law without a sanction is a law with no obligation, and hence is not a law (48).[14] Samuel Clarke speaks of the laws of nature, but does not take them to be commands imposed by a divine legislator; Johnson argues that Clarke's position is inconsistent.

Johnson also follows Pufendorf in trying to avoid some of the apparently unwelcome moral implications of voluntarism. Though he appeals to God's will as the source of moral principles, he also relies on God's goodness and wisdom (*EMO* 16). These moral properties of God explain why God's only purpose is the diffusion of happiness (19). This assumption about goodness and happiness allows Johnson to combine voluntarism with utilitarianism. He does not consider the implications of ascribing goodness and wisdom to God, and so he does not discuss the difficulties that arise for this version of voluntarism.

866. Objections to Sentimentalism and Rationalism

Rutherforth defends a voluntarist position similar to John Clarke's, in opposition to Shaftesbury's account of morality, as he conceives it. He argues that, contrary to Shaftesbury, a disinterested attitude to other people's good would not be a strictly moral outlook, but would be morally undesirable. If we could cultivate the disinterested benevolence advocated by Shaftesbury, we would be enthusiasts, and would not act on a sense of duty. Though some people may be as disinterested as Shaftesbury claims, their disinterested motives cannot be a basis for morality, because they cannot be a basis for obligation. They cannot be a basis for obligation (according to Rutherforth's motivational conception of obligation), because they do not always ensure sufficient motivation.[15]

Rutherforth has a reasonable objection to the view that disinterested benevolence alone is the necessary and sufficient basis of morality. One might fairly argue that agents who are merely benevolent and are not benevolent on principle are missing some important element of morality. The appropriate explanation of 'on principle' is not easy to find, but it suggests a weakness in a purely sentimentalist analysis of the moral outlook.[16] If Shaftesbury identified morality with benevolence, he would be open to Rutherforth's objection. The objection fits Hutcheson's claims about benevolence, but on this point Hutcheson seems to go beyond Shaftesbury. Butler agrees with the objection to mere benevolence; that is why he distinguishes the passion from the principle of benevolence, and further limits benevolence by the other moral principles that guide conscience.

---

[13] Cockburn points out this misunderstanding. See §876.

[14] He supports his claim that a law requires sanctions (60) by citing Pufendorf, *DOH* 2.7; Cumberland, *LN*, Proleg. §6.

[15] 'I would have him [sc. the grave moralist] recollect . . . how few instances there are of persons that have really been enthusiasts of this sort, amongst the many who would be thought such: they have certainly been too few to show that this affection is part of the human constitution.' (Rutherforth, *NOV* 110). 'But suppose we had an instinctive approbation of virtue, suppose the reluctance that we feel when we act other than virtuously to be owing to this principle; I see not how this can be made the cause of moral obligation: unless they who think so will grant that the obligation to virtue is quite precarious, and that our true principle of action is a very unsteady one.' (*NOV* 113–14)

[16] Cf. Hawkins on Fielding and Shaftesbury, §652.

Rutherforth, however, assumes that if we reject benevolent instinct as the basis of morality, voluntarism is the only reasonable alternative. Samuel Clarke, Balguy, and Price agree with him that mere benevolence is insufficient for the recognition of a moral requirement, because it leaves out the compulsory element of morality. But they deny, contrary to Rutherforth, that the compulsory element results from a command. In their view it is a rational requirement. Rutherforth rejects appeals to fitness, and equally rejects any supplementary appeals, such as we find in Balguy, to the nature of the agent and the action (*NOV* 138). Rutherforth does not discuss Butler's attempt to understand 'nature' normatively, treating human nature as a goal-directed system. His criticisms assume the conception of nature that Butler objects to in Wollaston. He implies that some of Wollaston's criticisms of naturalism also apply to Wollaston's and Clarke's conception of fitness.[17]

Voluntarists argue, therefore, that rationalist explanations of the rational requirements in morality are obscure, unintelligible, or unhelpful. Edmund Law defends voluntarism by arguing against Clarke's account of rightness as fitness. Law agrees with Bayes[18] in claiming that the idea of fitness that is relevant to morality is fitness for some end. He also believes, as Bayes does, that the only relevant end is happiness. But he seems to differ from Bayes about how happiness is relevant. Bayes introduces happiness to show that we need to explain fitness by reference to utility, the general happiness. Law, however, suggests that actions are right by being fit to promote the agent's interest.[19]

It is not clear why Law believes that the appropriate clarification of fitness leads us directly to egoism, and only indirectly to utilitarianism.[20] He seems to assume, as John Clarke does, that morality obliges and that obligation includes motivation. But he does not go so far as to deny the possibility of choosing virtue for itself. He supposes that we can choose virtue for itself if we mistake the means for the end.[21] The appropriate end is conformity with the will of God. Law seems to believe that this is not only the feature of morally right actions that makes them right, but also the end that the virtuous person ought to have in mind. The virtuous outlook looks on right actions as having no value in their own right and as having value only as means to fulfilling the divine will.

Law does not explain why the virtuous person's only non-instrumental aim should be conformity with the divine will. We might defend his position by arguing that morality essentially obliges and that obligation requires divine commands. If these claims about morality and obligation are right, someone who cares about the morally right as such cares about it as commanded.

[17] Cf. 13 on Wollaston, 146 on Clarke on the fitness of worshipping God.

[18] At King, *EOE*, ch. 1 §3 (pp. 83–8) Law cites Bayes, *DB*, discussed in §662. Cf. Law's note on ch. 1 §3 (p. 51).

[19] In reply to a discussion of abstract fitness Law argues: 'For to say a thing is essentially good or evil, to call it by hard names, and to affirm that it hath a natural turpitude; or, to put a compliment upon it, and call it a moral rectitude, and such like scholastic terms—without offering a particular reason of interest, why we should do the one or avoid the other, is as much as to say, a thing is good for nothing; or it is bad, but we know not why; or it is good or bad, for a woman's reason, because it is . . .' (Law in King, *EOE*, ch. 1 §3, p. 86).

[20] Law may not be disagreeing radically with Bayes. When Bayes defends the utilitarian explanation, he is explaining divine benevolence rather than the fundamental character of morality.

[21] 'If . . . we follow virtue for its own sake, its native beauty or intrinsic goodness, we lose the true idea of it, we mistake the means for the end; and though we may indeed qualify ourselves for an extraordinary reward from God for such a state of mind, yet we do really nothing to entitle ourselves to it . . .' (Law 273), because we do not do it explicitly in obedience to the will of God.

Law's psychological explanation of the choice of virtue for its own sake appeals, as Gay and Hartley do, to association of ideas. He does not suggest that his explanation vindicates the attitude he describes. He believes he exposes a mistake that we should be able to correct once we notice that we have no reason to ascribe non-instrumental value to virtue.

Similarly, Johnson defends voluntarism against an appeal to a moral sense. He does not treat rationalism separately, because he claims that Samuel Clarke and Butler, no less than Hutcheson, are committed to belief in a moral sense (29). He believes this on the strength of Clarke's remark that we feel shame and compunction if we violate a moral obligation and that we are indignant at other people's failure to respect our rights. In Johnson's view, Clarke believes that moral rightness is constituted by these reactions. He ascribes the same subjectivist view to Butler, and so assimilates the rationalist view of Clarke and Butler to Hutcheson's sentimentalism.[22] He therefore supposes he can refute the rationalist view by refuting Hutcheson. He claims to refute Hutcheson by arguing that our valuing moral virtue for its own sake is a result of confusion of the means with the end (37).

Johnson agrees with Law in supposing that when we identify the psychological origin of the belief that virtue has non-instrumental value, we also show that this belief is mistaken and that we ought to avoid it. That is why the ancient moralists who chose virtue for its own sake suffered from an 'enthusiastic' error.[23] Their mistake anticipates the mistake of Shaftesbury, Clarke, and Hutcheson.

867. Fitness and Utilitarianism

A distinct, but closely related, criticism of rationalism claims that Samuel Clarke's appeal to fitness can be given a definite content only through a utilitarian interpretation. According to John Clarke, the natural foundation for obligation consists in fitness to promote human happiness. He follows Culverwell and Pufendorf in allowing some natural fitness, but denying that this is sufficient for moral rightness.[24] He does not ask whether it is contingent or necessary that God commands us to do these naturally fitting actions. This is a difficult question for Pufendorf, who wants to avoid having to say that God commands arbitrarily, but wants to preserve divine freedom in relation to morality.[25]

John Clarke seems to concede that something makes these actions naturally 'fit for practice' apart from divine commands. If we recognize this fitness, we see a good reason for acting on moral principles, though we do not yet recognize them as divine commands. But John Clarke believes that we recognize their moral character if and only if we treat them as divine commands, because only divine commands carry the obligation that is necessary for morality.

---

[22] For other treatments of Butler as a sentimentalist see §720 on Kames and Selby-Bigge.

[23] The Stoics 'mistook the means for the end . . . and ran into the enthusiastic notion (for such I must call it) of virtue being a lovely form, amiable in itself, and desirable without further end' (Johnson, EMO 62).

[24] 'There is, to be sure, a fitness or unfitness in different things or actions to promote the happiness or misery of mankind. . . . And therefore I grant that upon account of that fitness or unfitness, those moral rules, called the laws of nature, suppose there was no God, or that they were not the positive will or injunctions of God, would be good rules of convenience; and very fit for practice, generally speaking; but that they would be, in strict propriety of language, law, obligatory, or matters of duty, I deny.' (J. Clarke, FMTP 20)

[25] See Pufendorf, §§576–7.

John Clarke believes that utilitarianism provides the best interpretation of Samuel Clarke's claims about fitness. Given the goodness of God, divine commands specify moral rules that promote the general happiness of human beings.[26] John Clarke assumes, agreeing with Berkeley and Hutcheson, that if God is morally good, and expresses this moral goodness in the moral rules that embody divine commands, moral rules are utilitarian. We assume, therefore, that utility gives us a standard for moral rightness. But while this standard allows us to identify morally right actions, it is not the ultimate standard; for utilitarian rules are correct only because they state divine commands.

Brown and Rutherforth support John Clarke's attack on appeals to fitness apart from utility.[27] They argue that a reference to human happiness answers the questions that rationalist accounts cannot answer. This utilitarian criticism of rationalist views about fitness does not imply either voluntarism or egoism. But both Brown and Rutherforth criticize fitness from a voluntarist and egoist point of view. If there is some sort of intrinsic rightness that we can both recognize and act on, we have a strong case against voluntarism. Brown and Rutherforth believe that once the rationalist account of intrinsic rightness is rejected, we have no plausible alternative to theological voluntarism.

Brown examines Shaftesbury's belief in the intrinsic goodness and admirability of virtue; he correctly takes this to be a predecessor of the appeal to fitness in Clarke, Balguy, and Wollaston, and he finds them all deficient in the same ways. Similarly, Rutherforth raises reasonable questions for Clarke and Balguy; he seeks a clearer explanation of fitness, and especially a clearer account of the specific kind of fitness that is to be identified with moral rightness.

According to Brown, Shaftesbury's aesthetic conception of moral rightness is too vague. The rationalists' conception is either equally vague, or, if it is made more precise, clearly unsatisfactory. When Shaftesbury represents virtue as fine and admirable in itself, he does not say what it is about virtue that is the proper object of this admiration. When the rationalists answer this question by appeal to fitness, they imply that, for instance, it would be wrong to speak to someone in a language he does not understand; this would be treating him (in Wollaston's phrase) as what he is not (SB 740). But this is clearly insufficient for immorality. If rationalists refuse even the degree of clarification that Wollaston offers, their account of the right 'is really no more than ringing changes upon words' (78).

In Brown's view, any attempt to supplement or clarify Shaftesbury or the rationalists introduces a reference to human happiness.[28] Here he moves too quickly. He is right to say that in many cases virtues refer to someone's interest. But it does not follow that they

---

[26] 'All morality, all the laws of nature, are founded entirely upon the consideration of pleasure and pain, happiness and misery . . . such kind of conduct being enjoined thereby as are [sic] proper to promote the peace, welfare, and happiness of mankind . . . for that reason, and upon account of that tendency only. To assert the contrary is to unhinge morality, contradict nature, and leave mankind in a state of darkness wherein it will be for ever impossible for them to know what they have to do. . . . In this tendency therefore precisely consists the moral good and evil of human actions; that is, their agreeableness or disagreeableness to the will of God. For the law of nature is founded upon the supposition of the divine goodness. From thence we justly conclude that such actions as are necessary or conducive to the peace and happiness of the world, are agreeable to his will, and the contrary displeasing.' (J. Clarke, FMTP 16)

[27] J. Brown, ECLS.

[28] 'In all these instances, the reference to human happiness is so particular and strong, that from these alone an unprejudiced mind may be convinced, that the production of human happiness is the great universal fountain, whence our actions derive their moral beauty.' (Brown, ECLS 130 = SB 741)

always refer to the maximization of total human happiness, as the utilitarian understands it. Brown does not consider the objections that Butler raises to utilitarianism.

In connecting utilitarianism with morality, the voluntarists do not decide between two ways of understanding the connexion; (1) We might argue that since we have reliable convictions about what is morally right, and since utilitarianism is true, our moral convictions should guide us in deciding what promotes utility. (2) Alternatively, we might argue that our convictions about what promotes utility should guide and modify our convictions about moral rightness.

Each of these directions of argument might be appropriate in different circumstances. But unless the second is sometimes appropriate, we will not learn much about morality by connecting it with utility. Mill accuses the theological voluntarists of holding the first view, and therefore of holding a conservative view of utility.[29] His criticism of Paley on this point is justified. But the view of earlier utilitarians is not so clear. If they take the first view, relying on other moral judgments to decide questions about utility, their attitude is 'conservative' insofar as it tends to hold moral convictions fixed in estimates of utility. But it is not necessarily thereby 'conservative' in a social and political sense. If we believe an institution is (say) unjust, this first form of utilitarianism does not allow us to change our mind by reflexion on utility; hence it rejects a utilitarian device for reconciling ourselves to existing institutions. The utilitarian attitude is socially conservative only if it both estimates rightness by utility and estimates utility by the standard of prevailing practices and institutions.

868. Utilitarianism and Egoism

Voluntarists who accept a utilitarian account of morality re-introduce benevolence into their theory, even though they reject Hutcheson's attempt to identify the moral outlook with the benevolent outlook. According to John Clarke, benevolence is God's motive for commanding the observance of these divine commands rather than others. But if God were not benevolent, God's commands would still constitute morality; for as long as divine commands with sanctions are imposed, we are under moral obligation. Even though the utilitarian character of morality reveals God's benevolence, moral obligation consists in having a sufficient motive, and so it rests on one's own interest.[30] The reasonableness and fitness of actions must ultimately refer to one's own good, and therefore to the fact that God will reward us for these actions.[31] Though sometimes morality requires us to prefer

---

[29] See Mill, 'Whewell' = CW × 170.

[30] 'And though the observation of moral rules be never so good, never so beneficial to the world about a man, if he himself receives no advantage, directly or indirectly, in this life or another, from such an observation, it cannot be said to be good for him. Nor can the consideration of other people's being the better for it, be any motive at all to dispose him thereto, so long as he finds his happiness utterly unconcerned in the case, and still the less so, if misery be the unavoidable consequence of such an observation. He that says the contrary will find it incumbent on him to prove that rational beings are obliged (if the word Obligation in this case can have any meaning) to have a greater regard to the happiness of others than themselves, and that absolutely and finally, which it seems impossible and a contradiction to suppose they should. If by good be meant morally good, that term will coincide with duty and obligation, which have already been considered.' (J. Clarke, FMTP 11)

[31] 'Whence it is manifest, the terms reasonable and fit have a final reference to the happiness of the agent, with respect to whose actions they are applied, and by consequence nothing can be said to be reasonable or fit for him that is not

the general interest over our own, God makes sure that we do not lose by this.[32] Unless God guaranteed the coincidence between morality and self-interest, we would have no good reason for the sacrifices that morality requires of us.[33]

These claims about morality and self-interest seem to express doubts about the rationality, and even the possibility, of disinterested moral motivation. One might be readier than John Clarke is to allow moral motivation independent of self-interest, and to allow that it is reasonable to act on it, while still insisting that it would be unreasonable to act on it consistently if it tended to destroy our own happiness. This position would be a demand for the reconciliation of moral motives with self-interested motives. Such a demand would be close to Samuel Clarke's and Butler's position. John Clarke, however, seems to take a more extreme position, in making any reason for morally right action depend on self-interested reasons.

John Brown's case for egoism also rests on a conception of obligation as involving motivation. He assumes a hedonist account of motives, and on this basis shows that we can act on no motives or reasons apart from our own happiness, understood as pleasure.[34] Shaftesbury sometimes agrees with this account of motives, according to Brown; for he recommends virtue as being in itself a source of happiness, and therefore admits that nothing can be rationally recommended except as a means to one's pleasure.

In support of this claim Brown quotes Shaftesbury's remarks on self-love.[35] He assumes that Shaftesbury intends a hedonist conception of happiness. Contrary to Brown, however, most of Shaftesbury's views are more intelligible on the assumption that he is a eudaemonist, but not a hedonist. Once this obscurity—not unusual among English moralists—about happiness is removed, it is no longer so obvious that Shaftesbury accepts Brown's psychological hedonism about the relation of virtue to happiness.

Brown concedes that some people find their greatest pleasure in being virtuous, but he does not think this fact is of much use in a defence of virtue. If there are such people,

proper to promote his welfare.' (J. Clarke, *FMTP* 12) It is a mistake to look for a principle higher than self-love, 'since there neither is nor can be any other principle of human conduct than self-love, or a regard to interest in this life or a future' (15).

[32] 'God . . . has enforced on us the preference of the general good before our particular interest at present, by future rewards and punishments, and by that means rendered our compliance with his own disposition and good pleasure, practicable and fitting, which otherwise would have been impossible, or at least highly unreasonable to be expected.' (*FMTP* 18)

[33] 'The only seeming reason that can be alleged is that such an adherence to virtue, though attended with nothing but pain and misery to a man's self, may yet be good for others, may at least have some tendency to the good of the world about him. Very true, but what then? This can be, as the supposition is put, no reason, no motive to a man to act at all. That charity begins at home, is the voice of nature confirmed by revelation. God, who knows human nature best, expects no such conduct from us, as to prefer the happiness of others to our own absolutely and finally, but has made a steady adherence to virtue under all extremities, or the preference of the public to his own private good, in this life, a man's truest interest, by a promise of endless and unspeakable happiness hereafter for it.' (J. Clarke, *FMTP* 22) 'That a man should love his neighbour as himself, is the voice of nature, confirmed by revelation; but that he should love his neighbour better than himself is, I think, the voice of neither, as appearing utterly and absolutely impossible.' (36) For Biblical support he cites *1 Cor.* 15:32; *Heb.* 12:2 (24).

[34] 'And as it hath already been made evident that the essence of virtue consists in a conformity of our affections and actions with the greatest public happiness; so it will now appear that the only reason or motive by which individuals can possibly be induced or obliged to the practice of virtue must be the feeling immediate or the prospect of future private happiness.' (Brown, *ECLS* 107 = SB 748)

[35] See Shaftesbury, §610.

their attachment to virtue is a result of inborn taste and temperament.[36] Those who lack this unusual temperament may approve of Shaftesbury's view when they read it, but may find they are incapable of living up to it.[37] For most people, then, an appeal to external sanctions is the only way to secure compliance with the requirements of virtue. The only sufficiently comprehensive sanctions are those that appeal to rewards and punishments in an afterlife.

869. Waterland on Moral and Positive Duties

These objections to Samuel Clarke's rationalism are philosophical, insofar as they rely on claims about the interpretation of fitness and about the nature of obligation. A distinct series of objections rests on theological grounds, arguing that Clarke's attitude to morality conflicts with orthodox Christianity. Waterland expresses these objections most forcefully.[38] His attack on Samuel Clarke provoked a number of replies, including those by Chilton and Chubb, who defend rationalism against voluntarism.

Waterland rejects Clarke's view that positive duties imposed by God, including those imposed in the Christian sacraments are always subordinate to, and therefore inferior to, moral duties.[39] Against Clarke, he cites Abraham's obedience to God's command; this is a fulfilment of a positive duty, not at all inferior to a moral duty. If we grant that it is a moral duty, then we must grant that some positive duties, which are also moral duties, are to be preferred over other moral duties.[40] According to Waterland, Clarke's preference for natural morality over the positive commands declared in Scripture is a device used by deists in order to attack Scripture, tradition, and orthodox Christianity.[41]

In opposition to rationalism Waterland claims that all moral principles, including those that belong to natural law, are expressions of divine commands. He does not consider the

---

[36] 'Thus, as according to these moralists, the relish or taste for virtue is similar to a taste for arts; so what is said of the poet, the painter, the musician, may in this regard with equal truth be said of the man of virtue—nascitur, non fit.' (Brown, ECLS 193 = SB 769)

[37] 'Thus a lively imagination and unperceived self-love, fetter the heart in certain ideal bonds of their own creating: till at length some turbulent and furious passion arising in its strength, breaks these fantastic shackles which fancy had imposed, and leaps to its prey like a tiger chained by cobwebs.' (Brown, ECLS 187 = SB 765)

[38] On Clarke's views see §672.

[39] Waterland claims that, in Clarke's view, positive duties 'have the nature only of means to an end, and . . . therefore they are never to be compared with the moral virtues'. Waterland protests: 'I cannot understand why positive institutions, such as the two Sacraments especially, should be so slightly spoken of. Moral virtues are rather to be considered as a means to an end, because they are previous qualifications for the Sacraments, and have no proper efficacy towards procuring salvation, till they are improved and rendered acceptable by these Christian performances. By moral virtues only we shall never ordinarily come at Christ, nor at heaven, nor to the presence of God: but by the help of the Sacraments superadded, to crown and finish the other, we may arrive to Christian perfection . . .' (Waterland, 'Remarks' = Works iv 45)

[40] 'In short, if the love of God be moral virtue, such obedience, being an act of love, is an act of moral virtue, and then there is no ground for the distinction: but if there must be a distinction made, then let one be called moral virtue, and the other Christian perfection, and let any man judge which should have the preference. Indeed they should not be opposed, since both are necessary, and are perfective of each other.' (Waterland, 'Remarks' = Works iv 46)

[41] 'If Scripture is once depreciated, and sunk in esteem, what will become of our morality? Natural religion, as it is called, will soon be what every man pleases, and will show itself in little else but natural depravity; for supposing the rules of morality to be ever so justly drawn out, and worked up into a regular system, yet as there will be no certain sanctions (Scripture once removed) to bind it on the conscience, no clear account of heaven or hell, or future judgment to enforce it, we may easily imagine how precarious a bottom morality will stand upon.' ('Remarks' = Works iv 48)

view of Suarez that there can be moral duties without obligation and law. He approves of Cumberland's voluntarist account of the basis of morality,[42] and endorses John Clarke's attack on Samuel Clarke's attempt to ground obligation in the nature of things without divine legislation. Without reference to God, he believes, we have rules of convenience, but no morality.

In Waterland's view, naturalism not only fails to give an account of the obligation inherent in morality, but also compromises the supremacy of God. He agrees with Pufendorf's allegation that naturalism sets up a principle extrinsic to God; hence he follows Pufendorf in believing that anyone who understands the implications of recognizing God as creator must accept a voluntarist account of morality. Similarly, he approves of Parker's criticism of Grotius 'for supposing the rules of morality obligatory without the supposition of a Deity'.[43]

Once we recognize that moral principles are the product of divine commands, we can see that they need not take precedence over positive divine commands; Abraham and Mary show that it is sometimes obligatory to obey positive commands rather than moral principles (447). On this basis Waterland rejects the position of Tillotson, who reduces the laws of the first table of the Decalogue to the laws of the second table.[44] According to Waterland, Tillotson has reversed the proper relation of the two tables. Obedience to God comes first, and this should be the basis for the imitation of God through observance of the moral law.[45] The deists go to the opposite extreme from the antinomians who reject the moral element in Christianity; they defend morality as a way of attacking revealed religion.

Waterland's critics urge some of the standard naturalist objections to voluntarism. Chubb argues that obedience to divine law presupposes a moral law that is independent of divine commands. We recognize that this moral law applies to God also, and this is why God's commands are reasonable and not arbitrary.[46] Waterland rejects this argument, and in

---

[42] 'Every law, properly so called, is moral, is regula moralis or regula morum, a moral rule, regulating the practice of moral agents. But moral law in a more restrained sense signifies the same with natural law, a law derived from God, consonant to the nature and reason of things, and therefore of as fixed and unmoveable obligation as the nature and reason of things is.' (Waterland, 'Sacraments' = *Works* iv 57) 'All obligation arises from some law, and it is the Divine law that constitutes moral good and evil. Things many be naturally good or bad, that is, may have a natural tendency to promote happiness or misery, may be materially good or evil, that is, useful or hurtful, previous to any law: but they cannot be formally and morally good and evil without respect to some law, natural or revealed; for "where no law is, there is no transgression."' ('Sacraments' = *Works* iv 61)

[43] Waterland, 'Supplement' = *Works* iv 108–12. On Parker see Locke §560.

[44] He quotes from Tillotson: 'What is religion good for, but to reform the manners and dispositions of men, to restrain human nature from violence and cruelty, from falsehood and treachery, from sedition and rebellion?' (Tillotson, Sermon xix in *Works* i 445). Waterland comments: 'The thought is free and bold, and probably in some measure shocking to many a serious reader; who may suspect there is something amiss in it, though it is not presently perceived where the fault lies' ('Sacraments' = *Works* iv 76). Waterland's use of the quotation is not completely fair. Tillotson's point is not that revealed religion is nothing more than morality, but that revealed religion without true morality is worse than atheism: 'Thus to misrepresent God and religion is to divest them of all their majesty and glory. For if that of Seneca be true, that "sine bonitate nulla maiestas", "without goodness there can be no such thing as majesty", then to separate goodness and mercy from God, compassion and charity from religion, is to make the two best things in the world, God and religion, good for nothing' (444). This was a suitable point for a sermon to the House of Commons on 5 November.

[45] 'Sacraments' 462. Cf. Grove, §877.

[46] 'I would likewise observe, as a further consequence of the distinction between moral and positive laws, that if it is the moral law that is the ground of our obedience to positive precepts, as I have before shown; then the obligation of the moral law does not arise from the positive will of God, but from the reasons and fitnesses of things; which we are sensible of, are capable by comparing the aspects, relations, and influences things have on one another, of finding

particular denies that God is obliged to follow moral principles.[47] But he also denies that God's choice of moral principles is an arbitrary exercise of will. He answer's Chilton's objection on this point by insisting that God is necessarily good and trustworthy.[48] He does not say how he can explicate this claim without departing from voluntarism; hence he seems to be open to Leibniz's objections against Pufendorf.[49]

Since Waterland takes morality to imply obligation and divine commands, he believes that those who recognize no divine commands cannot recognize morality either. Hence he takes a strict line on pagan virtue. In reply to Chubb's questions, he asserts that pagan virtue is only 'nominal' virtue.[50] His view about morality and obligation seems to lead him back to Baius' position.[51]

Waterland's discussion of moral principles and divine commands takes an extreme line in answer to the Deist view that reduces the demands of Christianity, and revealed religion in general, to the demands of morality. It is an extreme line insofar as it resorts to voluntarism in its defence of distinctively Christian moral duties against Deism. A few years after the publication of Waterland's essays (in 1730), Butler's *Analogy* (published in 1736) agrees with Waterland in rejecting Deist reductionism, but argues that naturalism does not lead to Deism. In Part II, chapter 1, 'Of the importance of Christianity', Butler argues that Christianity is both a 'republication of natural religion' including natural morality (§4), and a 'revelation of a particular dispensation of Providence' that enjoins new duties (§14). The facts of revelation themselves involve new moral relations apart from commands.[52] Christianity also includes 'positive' duties, those that result from commands. Though these positive duties may be contrasted with moral duties, they nonetheless have moral force, and hence result in moral obligations.[53]

Having argued for distinctive duties that belong to Christianity, Butler nonetheless defends his naturalist account of morality. He argues that if a positive duty were to conflict with a moral duty (i.e., a duty arising from natural morality without any command), the moral duty would take precedence. We have a positive duty when we do not see the reason

---

out; cannot but approve of when our minds are not corrupted, and think that certain things become us, others are unsuitable to our nature and character; and have not only a speculative, but a practical sense of, and a natural motive to them; are uneasy with ourselves and self-condemned, when we violate these fitnesses, from whence arises the strongest obligation.' (Chubb, *CEOMPD* 17)

[47] Waterland, 'Supplement' = *Works* iv 110.   [48] Waterland, 'Supplement' = *Works* iv 114.

[49] Leibniz on Pufendorf, §590.   [50] 'Supplement' = *Works* iv 132.   [51] Baius, §417.

[52] 'Christianity, even what is peculiarly so called, as distinguished from natural religion, has yet somewhat very important, even of a moral nature. For the office of our Lord being made known, and the relation he stands in to us, the obligation of religious regards to him is plainly moral, as much as charity to mankind is; since this obligation arises, before external command, immediately out of that his office and relation itself.' (Butler, *Anal.* ii 1.16)

[53] 'Moral precepts are precepts, the reasons of which we see: positive precepts are precepts, the reasons of which we do not see. Moral duties arise out of the nature of the case itself, prior to external command. Positive duties do not arise out of the nature of the case, but from external command; nor would they be duties at all, were it not for such command, received from him whose creatures and subjects we are.' (*Anal.* ii 1.21) '... positive institutions in general, as distinguished from this or that particular one, have the nature of moral commands; since the reasons of them appear. Thus, for instance, the external worship of God is a moral duty, though no particular mode of it be so. Care then is to be taken, when a comparison is made between positive and moral duties, that they be compared no further than as they are different; no further than as the former are positive, or arise out of mere external command, the reasons of which we are not acquainted with; and as the latter are moral, or arise out of the apparent reason of the case, without such external command.' (ii 1.23)

for the action we are commanded to do; we have a moral duty when we see the reason for the action. In case of conflict, we ought to do what we see a reason to do rather than what we see no reason to do.[54]

In this defence of naturalism Butler implies that Waterland's reaction to Deism is excessive. In Butler's view, the right understanding of the moral force of divine commands rests on a naturalist conception of morality as consisting in principles distinct from divine commands. If we do not recognize such principles, therefore, we cannot explain the source of our obligation to observe the positive duties enjoined by divine commands. Butler's argument about the priority of moral duties to positive precepts seems to conflict with Waterland's appeal to Abraham and Mary, and Butler does not make it clear how his principle of priority copes with these cases where positive precepts seem to be prior. His answer has to rely on his view that such cases—allegedly involving dispensations from moral law—are not really cases of violating moral duty, because the special circumstances of Abraham's action make it no longer a violation of moral duty.[55] Though Butler does not develop the details of an argument against Waterland, his statement of his position suggests how the argument might go.

870. Voluntarism as the Consensus

Some of the arguments we have considered support voluntarism polemically, by arguing that other positions are unsatisfactory. Gay tries a different sort of argument. Instead of attacking other positions for denying voluntarism, he argues that they tacitly accept it, and that therefore voluntarism captures the real sense, as opposed to the superficial meaning, of different moralists.[56] Gay is impressed by the extensional equivalence of different moral systems, and so believes that voluntarism succeeds if it comes out with the same moral conclusions as rationalism.

To see why non-theological accounts of morality seem plausible, we need to see the difference between the criterion and the essence of morality. Gay understands 'criterion' epistemologically, so that the criterion of morality is our means of distinguishing what is morally right from what is wrong.[57] But to find the criterion, we need to know what it is the criterion of, and hence we need to grasp the 'idea' of virtue. According to Gay, this idea

---

[54] '. . . suppose two standing precepts enjoined by the same authority; that, in certain conjunctures, it is impossible to obey both; that the former is moral, i.e. a precept of which we see the reasons, and that they hold in the particular case before us; but that the latter is positive, i.e. a precept of which we do not see the reasons: it is indisputable that our obligations are to obey the former; because there is an apparent reason for this preference, and none against it. Further, positive institutions, I suppose all those which Christianity enjoins, are means to a moral end: and the end must be acknowledged more excellent than the means. Nor is observance of these institutions any religious obedience at all, or of any value, otherwise than as it proceeds from a moral principle' (ii 1.24).

[55] Butler on dispensations: §717.

[56] 'And if a man interpret the writers of morality with this due candour, I believe their seeming inconsistencies and disagreements about the criterion of virtue, would in a great measure vanish; and he would find that acting agreeably to nature, or reason, (when rightly understood) would perfectly coincide with the fitness of things; the fitness of things (as far as these words have any meaning) with truth; truth with the common good; and the common good with the will of God.' (Gay, FPV xxviii = SB 850)

[57] 'The criterion of any thing is a rule or measure by a conformity with which any thing is known to be of this or that sort, or of this or that degree.' (Gay, FPVM §1, xxxii = SB 856)

consists primarily in obligatory action for the sake of general happiness.[58] From this idea we can try to discover the criterion of virtue.

Gay agrees with other voluntarists in taking obligation to be the central element of morality. But he does not discuss obligation as an act of the obliger, and hence (according to the voluntarists) as a command. He considers it as a state of the obliged, and so takes it to include motivation. The relevant motivation must be a desire to do what promotes my own happiness. Hence the principles of morality are those that it is necessary for me to follow for the sake of my happiness.[59] Since God is the ultimate source of happiness and misery, moral obligation consists in conformity to the will of God; this, therefore is the primary criterion of virtue.[60] Since God is benevolent, we can assume that God intends the general happiness, and so the general happiness is a secondary criterion of virtue (R 465 = SB 864). Promotion of utility is not strictly essential to morality, but it is reliably connected to morality, given what we believe about the divine will.

Hence theological voluntarism allows us to agree with moralists who regard utility as the basis of morality. They have found a secondary criterion, and this criterion allows them to form reliable views about which actions are morally obligatory. But their views are not counterfactually reliable. On this issue voluntarists agree with Hutcheson and Hume. In the sentimentalist view, morality is what our moral sense approves of, and it is a contingent fact that the moral sense approves of utility. If our moral sense were to change, morally right action would no longer promote utility. Voluntarists take the same view, substituting the divine will for the moral sense.

Gay's argument assumes that we are wrong if we regard utility as the essence of morality, because that account of the essence does not capture the essentially obligatory character of morality. Obligation requires sufficient motivation, and hence—given an egoist account of motivation—requires divine commands supported by sanctions that appeal to one's self-interest.

This account will seem implausible and dogmatic to those who believe in disinterested moral motivation. John Clarke's anonymous critic attacks voluntarism on this ground.[61] The critic argues that self-love needs control, and that benevolence is distinct from, and irreducible to, self-love (22, 27). The critic prefers Hutcheson's position to John Clarke's, though he believes that Hutcheson goes too far (following Shaftesbury) in rejecting a defence

---

[58] 'Virtue is the conformity to a rule of life, directing the actions of all rational creatures with respect to each other's happiness; to which conformity every one in all cases is obliged: and every one that does so conform, is or ought to be approved of, esteemed and loved for so doing. What is here expressed, I believe most men put into their idea of virtue.' (Gay, FPVM §1, p. xxxv = R 462 = SB 860)

[59] 'Obligation is the necessity of doing or omitting any action in order to be happy: i.e. when there is such a relation between an agent and an action that the agent cannot be happy without doing or omitting that action, then the agent is said to be obliged to do or omit that action. So that obligation is evidently founded upon the prospect of happiness, and arises from that necessary influence which any action has upon present or future happiness or misery. And no greater obligation can be supposed to be laid upon any free agent without an express contradiction.' (Gay, FPVM §2, p. xxxvi = R 463 = SB 862)

[60] '. . . a full and complete obligation which will extend to all cases, can only be that arising from the authority of God; because God only can in all cases make a man happy or miserable: and therefore, since we are always obliged to that conformity called virtue, it is evident that the immediate rule or criterion of it, is the will of God' (Gay, FPVM §2, pp. xxxvi–xxxvii = R 464 = SB 863).

[61] See Anon., A Letter to Mr John Clarke . . . 19.

of morality by relation to self-love.[62] John Clarke's position is worse than Hutcheson's because it makes charity and love of one's neighbour impossible by denying the reality of benevolence (34).

871. Association and the Moral Sense

Gay tries to answer such criticisms of voluntarist egoism by conceding something to them. He admits that unselfish motives, as they now are in us, are distinct from selfish motives, but he denies that this gives them any authority distinct from that of selfish motives. He argues that they can be explained by appeal to a doctrine of association (R 477–8 = SB 881–7).

Hartley develops this view further within a general account of association and its physiological basis. He argues that the various associations that build up the moral sense from different occasions of pleasure and pain also account for its authority.[63] Hartley tries, as Hutcheson does, to capture Butler's belief in the authority of conscience, but it is difficult to see how authority emerges from Hartley's genetic account. The variety of associations that lead to the reactions of the moral sense does not show why these reactions have the authority of the whole nature of the person making the judgment.

On the basis of his appeal to association, Hartley rejects any moral sense as an 'instinct' that might have access to 'eternal reasons and relations of things' independently of anything that might be grasped by the senses and association (499). This description of the view he opposes seems to combine an element of sentimentalism (in speaking of an 'instinct') with an element of rationalism (in speaking of eternal reasons and relations), suggesting that Hartley thinks he has disposed of both views at once. But the case he has presented seems more effective against a sentimentalist conception of a moral sense. Butler understands authority by contrasting the weight of reasons with the strength of desires; but Hartley's appeal to association does not capture this feature of moral judgment.

Gay also argues from claims about association to doubts about a moral sense. He admits that Hutcheson is right about the moral phenomena, but he rejects any moral sense that is irreducible to the sense of one's own private advantage. He believes that the moral phenomena are explained if we assume that pleasure and pain are attached to actions not directly related to our own good, because they were originally connected with rewards and punishments, and the pleasure and pain are later attached to the actions without the further rewards and punishments.[64]

One might argue that this associationist explanation really concedes the essential point to Hutcheson, since it concedes that we have disinterested affections, however we got them.

---

[62] 'It seems to me, that he [sc. Hutcheson] has carried the point of a moral sense too far, and has said too much in behalf of a disinterested virtue, without propounding a needful distinction. And in consequence of carrying these things too far, he appears to pay but a low regard to the Christian motives, taken from rewards and punishments.' (*Letter* . . . 33)

[63] 'This moral sense therefore carries its own authority with it, inasmuch as it is the sum total of all the rest, and the ultimate result from them; and employs the force and authority of the whole nature of man against any particular part of it, that rebels against the determinations and commands of the conscience or moral judgment.' (Hartley, *OM* 497)

[64] 'And this will appear by showing that our approbation of morality, and all affections whatsoever, are finally resolved into reason pointing out private happiness, and are conversant only about things apprehended to be means tending to this end; and that whenever this end is not perceived, they are to be accounted for from the association of ideas, and may properly enough be called habits.' (Gay, *FPVM* xxxi = SB 855)

This is not Gay's view. He believes he has shown that disinterested affections cannot claim any rational authority apart from the selfish affections from which they arise.

Voluntarists, therefore, take different views about the possibility and the moral relevance of disinterested motivation. Some of them doubt whether it is possible; some of these appeal to association to explain why it appears to be possible. Others, however, appeal to association to explain how disinterested motivation is possible, not to deny its possibility. But even those voluntarists who admit the possibility of disinterested motivation deny that it is essential to morality. Since it does not carry the obligation that is essential to morality, we have to look elsewhere; we find the relevant obligation only if we identify morality with divine commands supported by sanctions.

One might wonder whether the voluntarists have conceded too much if they allow the possibility of disinterested motivation. If the obligatory element of morality consists in motivation, might we not argue that for those who have strong enough disinterested motives, moral obligation is found in these motives? In that case moral obligation would be different things for different people with stronger and weaker motives of different sorts.

A voluntarist such as Rutherforth[65] might reply that his objection to disinterested motivation does not refer only to its weakness. Even if we had strong disinterested motives, they would not give us a grasp of morality; for we have to recognize morality as rationally compelling, not simply a matter of disinterested sentiment. This is a reasonable objection to Hutcheson and to Shaftesbury (as Rutherforth understands him). But then one might doubt whether one recognizes the relevant sort of rationally compelling principles if one simply appeals to divine commands. Must we not also regard these as right and reasonable in themselves? A plausible defence of voluntarist objections to sentimentalism seems to lead us back to rationalism.

872. Waterland v. Butler on Self-Love and Benevolence

Gay and Hartley try to accommodate the phenomena of moral motivation within an associationist explanation, so that they can allow a moral motive that at least appears distinct from ordinary self-love. Waterland defends egoism more aggressively; he defends the position of John Clarke against Butler by arguing that nothing is wrong with self-interest as a motive for morality.

He understands self-love as loving oneself in everything and loving oneself most. Self-love itself is neither morally good nor morally bad. The fault in immorality and selfishness is not self-love, but misguided self-love.[66] It would be neither reasonable nor possible to adhere

---

[65] See §866.

[66] 'Self-love, considered in the general, abstracting from particular circumstances, is neither a vice nor a virtue. It is nothing but the inclination or propension of every man to his own happiness. A passionate desire to be always pleased and well satisfied; neither to feel nor fear any pain or trouble, either of body or mind. It is an instinct of our nature common to all men, and not admitting of any excess or abatement.' (Waterland, 'On self-love' = *Works* v 447) Practical reason relies on self-love: 'Reason and thought hold out the light, and show us the way to happiness, while the instinct of self-love drives us on in the pursuit of it. The latter without the former would be no better than blind instinct; and the former without the latter would be but useless speculation, and dull lifeless theory.' (448) Lecky mentions Waterland among those who believe that 'virtue is simply prudence extending its calculation beyond the grave' (*HEM* i 15).

to virtue and religion if we were going to lose by it on the whole, and there could be no obligation to it.[67] Similarly, Clarke's appeal to fitness does not justify us in rejecting the supremacy of self-interest.[68]

Some of Waterland's remarks are compatible with disinterested action that neither promotes nor harms our interest. In these remarks he does not rule out an Aristotelian and Thomist view about self-love and morality. Sometimes, however, he seems to hold a stronger egoist thesis. He seems to suggest that only divine rewards and punishments make an action morally right, because otherwise nothing would be left but calculation of worldly interest.[69]

Waterland agrees with John Clarke in taking God to be benevolent, but denying that we act from any motive similar to divine benevolence.[70] We follow the rules imposed by a benevolent God because God creates a connexion between observance of the rules and our self-interest, through rewards and punishments in the afterlife. The only reason for observing the requirements of morality is the fact that God has commanded them and has supported these commands with sanctions.

Whewell answers that Waterland has chosen a 'very harsh and repulsive mode of stating that side of the question' (*LHMPE* 129). He questions Waterland's view that there is no genuine morality in just action based on a calculation of narrow self-interest in this life, but there is genuine morality if we calculate narrow self-interest in an afterlife.[71] In reply to such criticisms, Waterland argues that the self-interested attitude he defends is the only rational moral outlook; the view that we should act on anything other than self-love is misguided and irrational.[72] In supposing that virtue consists in a purely instrumental

---

[67] 'For this would be obliging us to hate ourselves, which is impossible: it would be obliging us to something under pain of being happy upon refusal, and in the hope of being rewarded with misery, which is all over contradictory and absurd; and therefore no obligation.' ('On self-love' = *Works* v 449) Cf. Clarke and Balguy on duty and interest, §673.

[68] 'It is fitting and reasonable and just that a man should love and serve himself, equally at least with others; and it is unfitting, unreasonable, and unjust (were it practicable) for a man to love his neighbour better than himself. There is no wisdom or virtue in being wise for others only, and not for one's self also, first or last; neither can any man be obliged to it.' ('Supplement' = *Works* iv 111)

[69] 'Abstract from the consideration of the divine law, and then consider what justice and gratitude would amount to. To be just or grateful so far as it is consistent or coincident with our temporal interest or convenience, and no farther, has no more moral good in it than paying a debt for our present ease in order to be trusted again; and the being further just and grateful without further prospects, or to be finally losers by it, has as much of moral virtue in it as folly or indiscretion has; so that the Deity once set aside, it is demonstration there could be no morality at all.' (Waterland, 'Supplement' = *Works* iv 114) Whewell, *LHMPE* 134, quotes this passage and comments: 'I do not think a genuine moralist, or even a person of genuine moral feeling, could really assent . . .'

[70] 'But the wisdom and goodness of Almighty God is highly conspicuous in this affair; that whereas the general happiness of the whole rational or intellectual system is what himself proposes as the noblest end, and holds forth to all his creatures; yet since no one can pursue any good but with reference to himself, and as his own particular good, God has been pleased to connect and interweave these two, one with the other, that a man cannot really pursue his own particular welfare without consulting the welfare of the whole. His own private happiness is included in that of the public: and there is, in reality, no such thing as any separate advantage or felicity, opposite to the felicity of the whole, or independent of it.' ('On self-love' = *Works* v 449)

[71] Stephen, *HET* ii 108, criticizes this aspect of Waterland: 'Socrates was not virtuous because he did not do right with a view to posthumous repayment. Rather, it seems, he should be called a fool or a madman.'

[72] 'It may perhaps be objected that this way of resolving virtue makes it look like a mean and mercenary thing, because it is supposed to stand only upon a view to one's own happiness, when it ought rather to be entirely disinterested and above all selfish views. To which I answer, that this way of resolving virtue is just and rational: for what more rational than to pursue our greatest happiness? Or what more irrational than to neglect it, or to praise anything above it? Let some declaim as they please upon disinterested benevolence, we maintain that it is sufficiently disinterested if it contemns all

attitude to virtuous action, Waterland agrees with John Clarke's extreme opposition to any 'enthusiastic' supposition of unselfish motivation.

Perhaps, however, Waterland does not always confine himself to this unrelieved appeal to rewards and punishments. Sometimes he seems to be thinking of the connexion in this life between my happiness and the happiness of others.[73] He might intend an Aristotelian argument, not just an appeal to rewards and punishments.[74] The role of self-interest suggests to Waterland that disinterestedness is not characteristic of virtue. It would perhaps be easier for him to make a convincing case on this point if he did not rely so heavily on a hedonist conception of happiness. He takes this conception of happiness for granted, however, as Balguy often does,[75] in an argument that otherwise draws quite heavily on traditional distinctions between types of self-love.

Waterland sometimes recognizes moral principles of the sort that rationalists also accept. In his sermon 'The duty of loving our neighbour as ourselves explained', he emphasizes that the commandment is not to love our neighbours as much as ourselves; it allows gradations for self, people close to us, people further away, and so on. The sense in which 'as yourself' applies is: 'as you would love yourself in the same circumstances'. We should help a stranger in distress if, when we think about it, that is what we would reasonably want a stranger to do for us in distress.

This argument appeals to fairness, reciprocity, and impartiality as a basis for benevolence. Waterland does not say that these principles have any rational status apart from being imposed by God; but he seems to appeal implicitly to their reasonableness. Some of his remarks might be interpreted so as to agree with an Aristotelian conception of self-love, but that interpretation conflicts with the narrow egoistic doctrines that he sometimes embraces. It is difficult to see how his opposition to Butler could be defended without appeal to the extreme egoism that is open to Butler's objections.

873. Happiness

Brown and Rutherforth agree with Waterland's objections to disinterested moral concern. Though they give a utilitarian account of moral rules, they do not follow Balguy and Hutcheson in recognizing disinterested benevolence that pursues universal happiness for its

---

narrow, low, or sordid views, and looks only at securing an eternal interest in God. What other foundation of virtue can any man lay, which is not plainly fanciful and chimerical? They may say they follow virtue for virtue's sake: as if virtue were the end, when it is evidently but the means; and happiness is the end it leads to, happiness either of ourselves or others.' ('Supplement' = Works iv 115)

[73] 'What happiness can any thinking man propose separate from God, the centre of all happiness? And if man be made a sociable creature, it is vain for him to propose any separate independent happiness from the rest of the kind. Man was designed to live in consort, and to be happy, if so at all, in the mutual friendship and enjoyment of each other. It is the law of their creation, the condition of their being: and therefore any pretended happiness, separate from the common good of mankind, is a mere dream and a delusion, a contradiction to the reason and nature of things.' ('On self-love' = Works v 461–2)

[74] On self-love see Aristotle, §124; Aquinas, §336; Scotus, §365.

[75] See Balguy, FMG ii 11 = TMT 132: '. . . I do not understand how nature can recommend any particular objects to our choice and pursuit, any otherwise than by annexing pleasure to the perception of them. If they have no absolute objective worth, they must have some relative goodness: and what can this be but either pleasure or a tendency thereto?'

own sake. In their view, the only possible basis for obligation is the prospect of one's own happiness.[76] Since Brown accepts psychological hedonism, he infers that 'no affection can, in the strict sense, be more or less selfish or disinterested than another'.[77] Hence there can be no disinterested concern for virtue.

For similar reasons, he finds it difficult to see what Shaftesbury means in recognizing concern for something for its own sake. In Brown's view, love of virtue for its own sake means only that 'we find immediate happiness from the love and practice of virtue without regard to external or future consequences' (SB 749). Brown has some excuse for taking this view. For Shaftesbury does not always make it clear whether he regards pleasure taken in virtue as the result of a conviction of the value of virtue in its own right; to make this clear, we need to attend to Butler's account of the relation between satisfaction of a desire and pleasure taken in it.[78]

Since Brown does not use Butler's distinction, he takes the question about whether virtue leads to happiness to be a predictive question about whether people will in fact find most pleasure as a result of being virtuous. It is intelligible, though incorrect, for a reader of Shaftesbury to interpret the question in this way; Price interprets it in the same way.[79] Traditional eudaemonism understands the question differently. According to the traditional view, which Shaftesbury sometimes accepts, happiness is the human good, which is to be identified with the fulfilment of human nature. To decide whether virtue promotes happiness, we ought not to survey what different people enjoy, but we ought to rely on a true account of the human good and of human nature. This conception of happiness brings us back to some of the questions about fitness that were raised earlier; for if we explain fitness by reference to human happiness, we do not necessarily explain it as a means to pleasure.

874. Voluntarism and Eudaemonism

Brown does not connect this aspect of Shaftesbury with the eudaemonist aspect of Greek ethics. Rutherforth, however, notices the relevance of the Greek moralists; he tries to show that they agree with him that the only possible reason for virtuous action is regard for our own selfish interest. He sees that the Stoics might appear to disagree, since they attribute inherent goodness to virtue. Stoic views are especially relevant because Shaftesbury and Clarke often rely on them to support their own views about disinterested pursuit of virtue, and Butler relies on them to support his view that virtue consists in following nature.

Rutherforth argues at some length, and with appropriate citations of the sources,[80] that the Stoics agree with other ancient moralists in taking happiness to be primary.[81] He seems to assume that the ancients who assert the primacy of happiness agree with him about the primacy of selfish self-interest. When he finds them asserting that virtue is to be chosen

---

[76] Brown identifies an obligation with a motive: 'a natural motive or obligation to virtue' (ECLS 181); 'internal motive or obligation to virtue' (184).

[77] Brown, ECLS 163 = SB 751.   [78] On Shaftesbury see §610.   [79] See Price, §805.

[80] At NOV 169–88 Rutherforth cites, among other passages, Cic. Fin. v 6; Plutarch, SR 1070b; Seneca, Ep. 118, on agreement with nature; Cic. TD iv 15; Fin. ii 14 (which he takes to conflict with eudaemonism).

[81] '…all…seem…amidst all their disputes to agree upon it as a thing self-evident and indisputable, that the sovereign good is the principal point in view, or the last end of each action' (NOV 169).

for its own sake without regard to consequences, he remarks that these claims appear to conflict with the primacy of happiness. To remove the appearance of conflict, he suggests that the Stoics take virtue to be an immediate means to happiness, even if it does not produce external goods. He assumes that if they are eudaemonists, they must take virtue to be an instrumental means to a feeling of satisfaction.[82] According to Rutherforth's solution, the Stoics claim that virtue is 'the only true enjoyment of man' (193), understood as the only means to maximum pleasure.

These references to the ancient moralists support Rutherforth's criticism of Samuel Clarke's and Balguy's attempt to divorce moral understanding and moral motivation from any reference to one's own ultimate end. Balguy goes so far as to claim that morality is concerned with what is 'good in itself' as opposed to what is 'good for me'.[83] Clarke and Balguy appeal to Stoic sources for this division, but Rutherforth reasonably doubts whether they are entitled to do this, if they reject the eudaemonist framework within which the Stoics place their claims about the morally good and the fine (honestum).

Rutherforth, however, is not justified in taking ancient eudaemonism to confirm his general position. For if a correct conception of one's own happiness has to include regard for virtue as a good to be chosen for its own sake, a correct eudaemonist doctrine affirms the possibility and rationality of unselfish concern for virtue. This objection to Rutherforth is urged, though not clearly explained, in Catharine Cockburn's criticism.[84] She points out that when Aristotle and the Stoics speak of happiness, they have in mind the fulfilment of human nature, and they insist on the social aspects of human nature. She argues, therefore, that Aristotle maintains the supremacy of virtue in one's own good. The eudaemonism maintained by Aristotle and the Stoics does not support Rutherforth, but opposes him.

Given the tendency of Shaftesbury, Butler, and Balguy to assimilate happiness to pleasure, we can see why Rutherforth supposes that Greek eudaemonism supports his selfish theory. He misunderstands Greek eudaemonism partly because his rationalist opponents also misunderstand it. They miss the opportunity to appeal to the ancients in support of their position, and so they encourage Rutherforth to cite the ancient moralists on the wrong side. While Butler supports traditional naturalism, he does not connect it, as he should, with eudaemonism. The controversy between Rutherforth and Cockburn makes clear an issue that ought to have been clear to their predecessors. Reid and Stewart still obscure some aspects of the issue.[85]

875. Warburton's Compromise

Gay's attempt to accommodate other positions in a voluntarist framework concedes only that non-voluntarists have found a secondary criterion of morality, and insists that the

---

[82] '... Cicero speaks for Chrysippus when he affirms that it is impossible there should be any virtue, unless it is disinterested. But how is this consistent with saying that virtue is not worth our notice if it can be miserable? Or how shall we make his opinions intelligible who at one time maintains that virtue and interest are the very same thing, and at another represents them as quite different, by describing the nature of virtue to be such as will necessarily approve itself to us, even though it should fail of producing our interest?' (NOV 189). 'Disinterested' translates 'gratuita', Cic. Ac. ii 46.
[83] See §658.   [84] See Cockburn, Remarks = Works i 82–3.   [85] See Reid, §854.

voluntarists have found the essence and primary criterion. Warburton makes a more serious effort to combine the elements of truth that he sees in different positions. The objection that voluntarism reduces morality to arbitrary divine commands encourages him to construct a modified voluntarist view that absorbs some elements of rationalism and sentimentalism. In *The Divine Legation of Moses*[86] he recognizes three sources of morality: the moral sense, moral reason recognizing eternal fitnesses, and the will of God (*DLM*, Bk i §§4, 36). He defends this 'threefold cord' against those who try to rest morality entirely on one of the three sources, to the exclusion of the other two (39).[87] In Warburton's bizarre view of the history of ethics, each strand of his threefold cord is found in the ancient moralists. Plato is the patron of the moral sense, Aristotle of essential and natural differences between right and wrong, and Zeno of the arbitrary will of God (*DLM* 42).

We have a moral sense, according to Warburton, insofar as we have a taste for moral goodness and we are repelled by badness. But we cannot say why this taste should be trusted if we cannot say what we detect by it, and why its detection is reliable. Warburton's claim may be defended by appeal to Balguy's criticism of sentimentalism. Agreeing with Shaftesbury and Doddridge, Warburton separates a question about the existence of a moral sense from the sentimentalist conclusion that Hutcheson draws from it.

The questions that we cannot answer by appeal to the moral sense are answered by moral reason, recognizing the difference between goodness and badness. Warburton agrees with the rationalists in recognizing these differences; he does not suggest, as critics of rationalism usually do, that the eternal fitnesses are empty, or do not capture anything of interest to morality.

Nonetheless, Warburton believes that both the moral sense theory and Clarke's rationalism fail to capture moral obligation. He rejects Bayle's view that an atheist can both recognize and fulfil the demands of morality. He agrees with Bayle in allowing that an atheist can have some grasp of morality. What the atheist lacks, according to Warburton, is a grasp of moral obligation, which requires recognition of post-mortem rewards and punishments. This is the aspect of morality that an atheist cannot grasp.[88]

Warburton has different reasons for this claim, though he does not separate them. (1) He suggests that Clarke confuses natural differences with moral (49), because he fails to distinguish the passive character of the understanding from the active character of the will (46). An account of how we recognize the natural difference between good and evil does not explain how our will is guided by it, since the will is a capacity distinct from the passive capacity to recognize the truth. (2) Obligation involves a law (46). Since Hobbes (according to Warburton) did away with a divine legislator, he had no alternative but to make law depend on human legislation (97). But since moral law does not depend on human legislation, we cannot eliminate a divine legislator. (3) Merely natural good—either one's own happiness or the perfection of the universe—cannot yield moral obligation (47–8).

---

[86] Whewell, *LHMPE* 123–30, discusses Warburton's views and the influence that resulted from their apparently welcome simplification of questions about obligation.

[87] Threefold cord: *Eccl.* 4:12. For Culverwell's use of the same metaphor in a similar context see *LN* 53–4, quoted in §559. Since he recognizes elements of truth in non-voluntarist views, Warburton is willing to write a commendatory preface to Cockburn's defence of Clarke against Rutherforth, even though Cockburn goes much further than Warburton is prepared to go in defence of Clarke.

[88] Cf. Bayle, *HCD* 401 (Clarification I), quoted in §228.

Perhaps Warburton means that it is up to us to be concerned about either of these ends, whereas moral obligation has a compulsory aspect. (4) Moral obligation must be imposed by an obliger who is different from the person obliged. For anyone who can impose an obligation can also release from it; and so, if we could impose an obligation on ourselves, we could also release ourselves (45).[89]

Warburton might have conceded that facts about the nature of things are sufficient for the existence of moral right and wrong, and then argued that divine commands are necessary to make us pay enough attention to these natural facts. On this view, commands would be necessary for moral motivation, but not for the existence of morality. But Warburton does not confine himself to this claim about motivation. He also accepts the metaphysical claim that without obligations and commands we have nothing distinctively moral, as opposed to prudential. This is Culverwell's and Pufendorf's position; Warburton agrees with their view that commands are necessary not only for moral obligation (as Suarez agrees, given his conception of obligation), but also for morality itself. He also seems to connect genuine obligation with sufficient motivation, and so he requires not only a command, but also sufficient sanctions to produce a strong enough motive to be moral.

This introduction of divine commands tries to capture an element of morality that some critics believe we cannot grasp if we identify morality with what Suarez calls 'intrinsic morality' apart from prescriptive laws and commands. We have noticed a similar view in Anscombe's assessment of modern moral philosophy and in modern Roman Catholic moralists who take 'formal', as opposed to merely 'fundamental', morality to require a divine legislator.[90]

Warburton does not consider all the difficulties that arise for his attempt to combine the different strands in his 'threefold cord'. He does not really incorporate Hutcheson's moral sense theory. For Hutcheson's theory seeks to tell us what moral properties are, not simply how we come to know them. If our approval by the moral sense really constitutes the rightness and wrongness of things, Clarke's realism is mistaken. The aspect of sentimentalism that Warburton incorporates is simply the belief in a moral sense.

Warburton's attitude to Clarke's position depends on his answer to questions that arise for Pufendorf and Barbeyrac. It is quite consistent to maintain that actions are right and fit in themselves, but are not morally right or wrong unless God commands them. But it is more difficult to give a satisfactory account of why God commands them. If God simply commands them, not because they are right and fit, God's commands seem arbitrary. But if God commands them because they are right and fit in themselves, rightness and fitness in themselves seem to impose moral requirements on God; hence they do not seem to fall short of morality.

A similar question arises about our obedience to God's commands. If we recognize these as imposing moral obligation, must we not already recognize a moral obligation, independent of commands, to obey God's commands? If obedience to divine commands is intrinsically right, why suppose it is the only case of intrinsic rightness that is independent of divine commands? Alternatively, if obedience to divine commands is not intrinsically right, but if

---

[89] Barbeyrac uses this argument in answering Leibniz on behalf of Pufendorf. See §596.   [90] See §602.

we obey the commands out of fear, non-moral admiration, or love of God, do we recognize a moral obligation to obey the commands at all?

Warburton does not discuss the difficulties that arise for his voluntarism, given his concessions to sentimentalism and rationalism. While he is right to say that we might combine some elements of the three views that make his threefold cord, he does not show that we can reasonably combine the elements he combines. He does not make it unnecessary to choose between the views that he tries to combine.

876. Cockburn's Defence of Clarke

Defences of voluntarism and egoism provoke some acute replies by Catharine Cockburn' in her remarks on Law, Gay, and Johnson, and in the instructive (though repetitive) series of letters between Cockburn and Thomas Sharp.[91] Cockburn identifies one of the motives of the voluntarists, especially Waterland, when she protests against the charge that rationalism supports Deism.[92] Deists exploit rationalism, arguing that if morality consists in intrinsic facts independent of the divine will, God cannot make any difference to morality. Cockburn argues that this Deist inference rests on a misunderstanding of the implications of Clarke's views on fitness. She protests that her opponents go to unreasonable extremes in their opposition to rationalism and especially to its non-egoistic aspects.

She finds the source of this opposition in the hostility aroused by Shaftesbury's comments on rewards and punishments.[93] Some egoist voluntarists argue that it would be irrational to care about the interests of others if we could not look forward to the prospect of post-mortem rewards (421). Cockburn answers that people who argue for the selfish position 'argue against the common sentiments of humanity', and 'contradict the most natural sentiments of their own minds'.

In her defence of Clarke she tries to clarify some of the concepts that have raised objections. She denies that Clarke conceives fitnesses to be independent of any effects on the happiness of the people involved. The good effects of an action are often a reason for believing that it is fit to be done, and so the connexion between the rightness of an action and its good effects on others is no objection to Clarke's doctrine. Still, she denies that Clarke is a utilitarian. Duties to parents and benefactors do not depend on their good effects on either side; nor do duties to God lapse if happiness is assured.[94]

---

[91] See Cockburn, *Works* ii 353–460. Price commends these letters at *RPQM* 177 (ch. 8, on absolute v. relative virtue), 233 (ch. 10, on 'foundation of virtue'). These references in the 1st edn. are absent from the 3rd edn. (printed in Raphael's edn.).

[92] Cockburn, *Virtue = Works* i 430.

[93] 'And now, because a celebrated author has represented any regard to future rewards as dangerous to virtue, tending to render it selfish or mercenary; those writers must needs have it that without a certainty of future rewards, or without selfish regards, there could be no obligation to virtue, no duty at all.' ('Seed' 143–4) 'This author [Seed], among the rest, tells us, that what would be highly rational, and consequently virtue, upon the supposition of a future state, would be madness, and consequently not virtue, if that were left out of the account. When I first met with this notion, I thought it so singular and extravagant, that it needed only to be taken notice of as such; but I now find it is the common topic of those writers.' (144)

[94] '... it sufficiently appears in many places of the Doctor's works, that natural good is to him the criterion of moral good, as it respects ourselves, or our fellow creatures; though reward and punishment is not. ... But let it here be

She also defends Clarke against those who take him to mean that the fitness of an action is a wholly non-relational property, to be determined by the action itself without reference to its circumstances. She argues that fitness involves a relation between the action and the circumstances, and so may be changed by an alteration in the circumstances.[95] The mere fact that the same action (in one way of understanding it) may be right in some circumstances and wrong in others does not count against Clarke's claim that rightness consists in fitness.

These remarks about fitness and its relation to effects and circumstances help to clarify some of Clarke's remarks on fitness; but they also raise further questions. In Cockburn's view, the welfare of those affected by an action is an important aspect, but not the whole, of fitness; hence she rejects the reduction of fitness to utility (as suggested by Gay). But she does not say why or in what circumstances good consequences do or do not determine the fitness of an action. She seems to need a more detailed conception of the nature of the agents and of the people affected by an action. This defence of a rationalist position seems to lead us back to the naturalism of Suarez and Butler.

Cockburn clarifies her defence of Clarke in her letters to Sharp. Sharp sympathizes with Warburton's aim of reconciling rationalism with voluntarism, and argues that Clarke and Warburton only appear to disagree, because they use 'obligation' and 'foundation of virtue' in different senses. 'Obligation' in the broadest sense is equivalent to 'ought' ('unalienable right'). But Sharp also marks a narrower sense in which 'obligation' implies 'enforcement' on 'reluctancy'. In this sense, obligation requires some motive strong enough to 'enforce' the action we are obliged to do despite our reluctance, and hence it requires a strong enough sanction. In Sharp's view, this is the sense of 'obligation' that is relevant to morality. While he agrees with Clarke in recognizing objective fitnesses, he believes that these are only the basis of moral obligation; they are insufficient for moral obligation, and hence for morality. He reaches a position similar to Culverwell's and Warburton's.[96]

Cockburn agrees with Sharp in recognizing a subjective aspect of obligation. If I am obliged not to commit murder, facts about the nature of murder, including its objective unfittingness, are not enough. I must also perceive it in such a way that I would condemn

observed, that though the fitness of moral actions consists in their general tendency to produce natural good to the objects of them, yet there are particular cases, where the fitness remains, though no natural good should be consequent upon it. Respect to parents, gratitude to benefactors, are always fit in themselves, that is, have a rectitude in them, that makes them fit to be chosen, whether any benefit can accrue from them to either side or not' (Cockburn, *Virtue* = *Works* i 405–6).

[95] 'The mistake of the author of the Essay [sc. Johnson] lies, in supposing, that independent fitnesses (as he affects to call them, though improperly) have no relation to any end, and are not alterable by any change of circumstances. Whereas the fitness of moral actions has always a respect to some end, and is entirely dependent on the nature and relation of things, considered in their various circumstances. The same action may be fit and right in some circumstances of things, which would be unfit in others; for an action is then only morally fit, when it is suitable to the agent, and the object, according to their various relations and circumstances.' (*Virtue* 431–2)

[96] 'Take it in a grammatical sense, and it implies something, that enforces upon reluctancy; and in this sense of it (when used in morality) it should seem most properly founded in the sanctions of rewards and punishments; or in the will of him, who has the power to reward and punish. Take it in a legal sense, and it implies an obliger; and there must be two persons at least, that is, two intelligent agents, or two free wills to create obligation in either of them. And in this view obligation in morals will certainly be founded in the will of God. Take it in a third sense, viz. as an unalienable right, that truth has to be preferred over falsehood, good before bad, by all rational creatures, that can distinguish them; and then its foundation will be in the essential differences of things, and their eternal ratios, fitnesses, etc.' (Sharp in Cockburn, *Works*, ii 368–9)

myself if I committed murder.[97] This is not very satisfactory; it seems to identify obligation with the perception of obligation. Moreover, in saying that the relevant perception 'forces' me to condemn myself if I do what I am obliged not to do, Cockburn seems to pass over the very point that needs to be explained. We need to know how the content of the relevant perception 'forces' us to condemn ourselves for violation. Sharp and Warburton believe that the relevant sort of 'force' comes from a sanction. Cockburn disagrees; but she does not explain that the sort of 'force' she has in mind is the force of (as we say) compelling reasons rather than powerful motives.

In taking obligation to include this subjective and motivational element Cockburn agrees with Clarke and Balguy. They leave it obscure whether they believe an action can be wrong if we have no obligation to avoid it. If they believe that wrongness implies obligation, they imply that wrongness cannot exist unless we perceive the relevant inducement not to act. But if they believe that wrongness does not imply obligation, do they believe that wrongness implies that we ought not to do it? If so, what is the relation between oughts and obligations? The questions raised by this rationalist account of obligation threaten to obscure the objectivist elements of the rationalist account of moral properties. They would clarify their position if they followed Suarez in distinguishing oughts from obligations. Price tries a different clarification, by identifying oughts with obligations and defending a purely objective account of obligation.[98]

Despite the obscurity that results from her claims about obligation, Cockburn's main aim is to show that objective rightness and wrongness are primary in morality, and that therefore morality does not need an external legislator imposing commands and sanctions. To show that this is not simply a verbal dispute about what is to be called 'moral', she argues that voluntarists need her account of oughts and obligations if they are to explain why one ought to obey the divine will.[99] If voluntarists agree that we have a moral obligation to obey God's command because God is just, good, and wise, they concede that these features of a commander give moral reasons for obedience. These moral reasons do not include the fact that God commands us to obey; for the question at issue is why we ought to obey commands.

Cockburn uses the main point of Cudworth's argument against Hobbes. It does not refute voluntarists. They can avoid it by denying that we have moral reasons to obey God. But if they choose this way out, they have to deny that a moral question arises in an area where it plainly appears to arise. It is not surprising that both Pufendorf and Sharp are unwilling to embrace the Hobbesian answer to Cudworth's and Cockburn's objection.

Cockburn supplements her defence of Clarke's conception of obligation with a clarification of his claims about intrinsic rightness and wrongness. Sharp follows Pufendorf in alleging that

---

[97] The explication that Cockburn offers Sharp is similar to the one she offers in *Remarks* (on Rutherforth), *Works* i 380: 'such a perception of an inducement to act, or to forbear acting, as forces an agent to stand self-condemned, if he does not conform to it'.

[98] See Price, *RPQM* 114, 117, quoted in §818.

[99] 'But I would ask, if the will of God is supposed to be the only foundation of moral obligation, upon what grounds are we obliged to obey his will? I can conceive no other, but either his absolute power to punish and reward; or the fitness of obedience from a creature to his creator. The first of these would bring us down, I fear, to those low principles [sc. of self-interest] the Doctor [sc. Sharp] disapproves; and if that is rejected, the other returns us to that reason, nature, and essential differences of things, into which, I apprehend, all obligation must at last be resolved.' (Cockburn, *Works* ii 359)

if we believe in intrinsic morality (as Suarez describes it), we contradict the Christian doctrine of creation. In his view, Clarke takes moral rightness and wrongness to be 'antecedent' to the divine will. But since the necessary relations of fitness involve agents who would not exist if God had not willed to create them, they cannot be antecedent to the divine will, and so voluntarism is correct. Cockburn answers that Clarke's view does not make intrinsic morality independent of God; she implicitly relies on Suarez's distinction between the creative and the legislative aspects of God.[100] Sharp accepts this explication, and says he had previously misunderstood Clarke on antecedency (386). His misunderstanding repeats Pufendorf's and Barbeyrac's misunderstanding of Grotius.[101]

877. Objections to Voluntarism: Doddridge and Grove

This argument about how moral rightness is not 'antecedent' to the divine will is only one part of the voluntarists' case to show that that their position gives the appropriate place to God in morality. But their case is open to question. Some of the reasons for Christian moralists to oppose voluntarism may be gathered not only from some of the most prominent British moralists—Clarke, Butler, Price, and so on—but also from less well-known writers. The treatises of Doddridge and Grove, used in Dissenting academies, illustrate some of the criticisms of voluntarism.[102]

Doddridge accepts the rationalist view of Clarke and Balguy that moral rectitude consists in acting according to the moral fitness of things.[103] But in contrast to Wollaston, he sees no conflict between this rationalist appeal to fitness and the outlook of the ancient moralists who make virtue consist in living according to nature (120). Here he agrees with Butler.[104]

Since he agrees with Clarke and Butler, he rejects voluntarism, claiming that 'the foundation of virtue and vice cannot depend upon the mere will of any being whatever' (106). He does not believe that naturalism is open to the theological objections that Pufendorf urges against Grotius, and that might especially appeal to a Calvinist critic. He argues, as Cockburn does, that naturalism does not require us to recognize some standard that is prior to God, or to deny God's omnipotence, properly understood.[105] He warns against a rash interpretation of the counterfactuals that naturalists might use to express their position. They ought not to maintain, for instance, that if God were to change his mind, other things

---

[100] 'But if God created a system of beings, conformably to certain relations and fitnesses eternally perceived by the divine understanding; and if he gave them no other law but what resulted from their nature, discoverable by their natural faculties: Then the query is, whether that law of nature does not itself oblige them to conform to it, before any discovery either by reason or revelation of the will of God concerning it?' (*Virtue* 382) Cockburn explains her point more fully in an appendix (450–5).

[101] See §§566, 582.

[102] Doddridge's book is professedly based on his lectures. Since it does not present itself as an original work in moral philosophy, but as a compendium of received and plausible views (with references to current literature on each topic), it offers some evidence of the diffusion of arguments for and against voluntarism. Grove was also the head of a Dissenting academy. He not only published a systematic treatise on moral philosophy, more elaborate and argumentative than Doddridge's textbook, but also contributed to the *Spectator* on moral questions. Bond in *Spectator* i, p. lxxix, ascribes nos. 588, 601, 626, 635 to Grove.

[103] See Doddridge, *Course* 106.　　　[104] On Butler see §679.

[105] '. . . it is no more injurious to the divine being to assert that he cannot alter his own sense of some moral fitnesses, than that he cannot change his nature or destroy his being' (Doddridge, *Course* 107).

would continue the same; for if God were to change his mind, he would no longer be God. Doddridge's concerns justify Suarez's care in explaining the appropriate counterfactuals.[106]

This naturalist account of morality supports a similarly naturalist account of natural law. Doddridge argues that the rules of intrinsic morality (as Suarez puts it) are laws of nature apart from the will of God.[107] He agrees with voluntarists who believe, with Pufendorf, that natural law expresses the 'divine will and purpose', but he takes this point to be consistent with naturalism.

Doddridge agrees with the anonymous critic of John Clarke who defends Samuel Clarke.[108] The critic argues that Samuel Clarke speaks legitimately of being 'obliged by the reason of things and the right of the case' (Letter 13). Indeed, Christian moralists cannot do without this aspect of Samuel Clarke's naturalism; for John Clarke does not satisfactorily explain what it means to say that God is just and righteous. A satisfactory explanation relies on some antecedent conception of morality derived from the nature of things themselves.[109]

Doddridge applies his criticism of voluntarism to Hutcheson's sentimentalism. He agrees with Hutcheson on the existence of a moral sense, but rejects Hutcheson's metaphysical claims about the connexion between the existence of moral rightness and approval by the moral sense; hence he argues that the moral sense is not the foundation of virtue. On this issue Doddridge agrees with Balguy's criticism of Hutcheson's tendency towards voluntarism. He argues that Hutcheson's metaphysical thesis about moral rightness goes beyond the views of Shaftesbury that Hutcheson claims to defend. Shaftesbury does not take virtue to be essentially what the moral sense approves of; he takes it to be essentially agreement with the 'eternal measure and immutable relation of things' (121).

Grove takes the same position, attacking voluntarism from both the philosophical and the theological point of view. He begins his *System* with a defence of the usefulness of moral philosophy for a Christian reader. He takes this defence to be necessary because of doubts about the discipline raised by contemporary opponents from different theological perspectives. On the Dissenting side, some treat moral philosophy as 'impiety presented in the form of an art'.[110] On the Anglican side, Butler's opponent Waterland attributes the growth of Deism to the study of moral philosophy.[111] In his view, the various forms of non-voluntarist moral philosophy agree in dispensing with any appeal to the will of God in fixing the nature of morality and the moral motive.

---

[106] See Suarez, §§424, 428.
[107] 'Those rules of action which a man may discover by the use of his reason to be agreeable to the nature of things, and on which his happiness will appear to him to depend, may be called the law of nature; and when these are considered as intimations of the divine will and purpose, they may be called the natural laws of God.' (Doddridge, *Course* 192)
[108] Anon., *A Letter to John Clarke* . . .
[109] 'Sir, when you are to settle this point, that God is a just and righteous being, must not you have ideas of just and right? And from whence can you have them, but from things as existing in their differences, respects, and relations, with the proper application of them? Now seeing we receive ideas of just and right, from the reason and relation of created things, we may also be very sure, that those ideas belong to the divine being, and that his nature is righteous.' (Anon., *A Letter to John Clarke* . . . 15)
[110] 'impietas in artis formam redacta'. Grove, *SMP* 111, quotes this from Mather, *MM* 39–40: 'As for ethics . . . of that whereon they employ the plough so long in many academies, I will venture to say, it is a vile thing . . . It is all over a sham; it presents you with a mock-happiness; it prescribes to you mock-virtues for the coming at it; and it pretends to give you a religion without a Christ, and a life of piety without a living principle; a good life with no other than dead works filling of it.'
[111] Waterland, 'Sacraments'.

Against these opponents Grove believes that we need moral philosophy to guard against the moral errors that infect some theological outlooks.[112] He has in mind Calvinists who rely on voluntarism to defend absolute predestination and reprobation. Such a defence is different from the one that Calvin offers. According to Calvin, predestination is an exercise of God's hidden wisdom, which we do not understand, but which we would nonetheless see to be right if we were wise enough.[113] Though Calvin believes that what God wills must be right, he does not draw the voluntarist conclusion that nothing apart from the mere fact of willing makes God's willing right.

The voluntarist, however, claims that there is no further fact about the rightness of God's decisions apart from God's willing them, so that God is immune to the possibility of moral evaluation. Grove attacks this view on the ground that voluntarism pays too high a price for exempting God from moral criticism; it deprives us of any room to admire or love God's moral attributes in their own right, apart from the fact that they express God's inscrutable and arbitrary will.

878. Grove on Egoism

Just as Grove rejects voluntarism, he rejects the egoism that the voluntarists use to connect divine commands with motivation and obligation. But he concedes some points to the egoist that blur some of his objections, and separate him from eudaemonism.

He identifies happiness with pleasure, which he calls 'formal happiness'. The sorts of things that Aristotle regards as parts of happiness Grove describes as 'objective happiness'; parts of objective happiness are not parts of happiness itself but simply objects from which we gain our pleasures (SMP 63). On this basis he rejects the traditional threefold division of good into the pleasant, the useful, and the morally good (honestum); the first two are enough to cover all goods, and the third is simply one element in the useful (74). Consistently with this view, Grove rejects any non-hedonist conception of the good; for instance, he rejects Cumberland's conception of the good as perfection, because it violates hedonist principles (72).

Though he accepts hedonism, Grove does not accept egoism. In some of his essays in the *Spectator* he defends the reality of disinterested benevolence, on lines similar to Hutcheson's and less precise than Butler's.[114] To disarm critics who appeal to examples of selfishness, Grove argues that benevolence, though part of human nature, is less prominent than we might expect it to be.[115] The influences of society, custom, and education encourage us to develop narrower concerns that inhibit our natural benevolence.[116] Grove argues that the natural 'diffusiveness' of human heart and its benevolent characteristics are inhibited by contingent and removable obstacles, arising from 'an unhappy complexion of body', 'love of

---

[112] Grove attacks the extreme version of Calvinist doctrines that assumes the 'unworthy idea of the Deity, which in effect leaves out his moral attributes, or most miserably disfigures and misrepresents them' (SMP 13).

[113] See Calvin, *Inst.* i 17.2, quoted in §412.   [114] *Spectator* v 10–14 (no. 588).   [115] *Spectator* v 54–8 (no. 601)

[116] ' 'Tis a property of the heart of man to be diffusive; its kind wishes spread over the face of the creation; and if there be those, as we may observe too many of them, who are all wrapped up in their own dear selves, without any visible concern for their species, let us suppose that their good-nature is frozen, and by the prevailing force of some contrary quality restrained in its operations.' (*Spectator*, no. 601, 54)

the world', and 'uneasiness of mind' resulting from needs or demands or emergencies that seem to make it more urgent to take care of oneself.[117] We tend to place our happiness in zero-sum goods, in contrast to those that grow by being shared.[118] If, however, we could attend to the pleasures that we gain from shareable, non-competitive goods, we would more readily recognize the possibility of disinterested motives.

In this popular essay Grove does not try to reconcile his claims with his hedonism. According to hedonism, benefit to others cannot be itself a part of our good; it must be an instrumental good that causes pleasure in us without any further effect on our selfish interest. He is right to claim that this possibility of 'disinterested' action is open to us even within the hedonist scheme. But this conception of disinterested action leaves out an essential element of genuinely disinterested action, as we normally conceive it, and as Grove conceives it in his *Spectator* essay. For we usually suppose that disinterested concern for the good of others takes their good as our end in its own right, apart from its causal results.

In another essay Grove re-affirms the reality of a sentiment of benevolence that is irreducible to self-love and to practical reason. Human beings are both reasonable and sociable; two principles of action, self-love and benevolence, correspond to this double capacity. Society could not flourish with self-love alone.[119] This argument is quite similar to Hutcheson's claims about reason, self-love, and benevolence.[120] It agrees with him in accepting a purely instrumental view of practical reason, in contrast to Cumberland's view that practical reason prescribes concern for the common good as reasonable in itself, apart from further instrumental benefits. Sentimentalism rests on rejection of Cumberland's non-instrumental view of practical reason.

Whatever he thinks about disinterested action, Grove believes that a virtuous person needs to attend steadily to the ultimate good (*SMP* 79). The Stoics who claim to find their happiness in virtue alone are mistaken; they are misled by their pride and their exaggerated belief in their self-sufficiency (86, 112).[121] In fact no creature can leave us completely satisfied, and so none can be the chief good (92). Grove therefore approves of Plato's view (on a possible interpretation) that the chief good consists in the contemplation of God (94).

He concludes, therefore, that virtue must be directed towards God as its ultimate end.[122] This conclusion does not commit him to theological voluntarism, because the virtuous person seeks God's favour in the belief that God is supremely good, not simply as a source of

---

[117] He concludes: 'Place the mind in its right posture, it will immediately discover its innate propension to beneficence' (58).

[118] 'If that which men esteem their happiness were, like the light, the same sufficient and unconfined good, whether ten thousand enjoy the benefit of it, or but one, we should see men's good will and kind endeavours would be as universal.' (*Spectator*, no. 601, 56) '. . . virtue . . . grows by communication, and so little resembles earthly riches that the more hands it is lodged in the greater is every man's particular stock' (57). For his example of the light Grove quotes Ennius in Cic. *Off.* i 51, quoted at §195.

[119] 'Reason, tis certain, would oblige every man to pursue the general happiness as the means to procure and establish his own; and yet, besides this consideration, there were not a natural instinct, prompting men to desire the welfare and satisfaction of others, self-love, in defiance of the admonitions of reason, would quickly run all things into a state of war and confusion.' (*Spectator*, no. 588, p. 12)

[120] Hutcheson; §635.

[121] Grove's criticism suffers from lack of attention to the Stoics' views on indifferents.

[122] 'For what men call virtue is either a shoot from religion, being directed by the will of the supreme cause as its rule and measure, and animated by his favour as its ultimate reward, or grows upon other principles, and is nourished by other views. If this latter be understood, it is the shadow of virtue, not the vital substance; it is vanity, or interest, or at best a natural generosity of temper.' (*SMP* 113)

rewards. But it is not clear how Grove reconciles this account of virtue with his recognition of disinterested concern for the good of others. If disinterested concern is necessary for virtue, should the good of others not be at least a part of the ultimate end that the virtuous person pursues? Grove makes this point difficult to express within his position, because of his hedonism about the good.

Grove's argument illustrates the wide appeal of some aspects of the voluntarist position, even to someone who rejects the position as a whole. If we accept hedonism about the good, but we find it difficult to see how pursuit of our own pleasure could lead us directly to the acceptance of morality, we may easily be inclined to rely on some artificial connexion between morality and our own pleasure. Hobbes finds this connexion in the institutions of a particular society; if we think these are not enough, we will find it plausible to appeal to divine rewards and punishments. Grove rejects this conclusion, but his initial concessions to hedonism make his argument less convincing.

879. Tucker and Paley

We have traced some stages in the debates about voluntarism between opponents and defenders of Shaftesbury and Clarke. We may now turn to the later statements of a voluntarist position by Tucker and Paley. These are important links between voluntarism and the utilitarianism of Bentham. Paley's *Principles* is an especially brief, clear, and influential re-statement of the combination of voluntarism, utilitarianism, and egoism that John Clarke, Brown, and Gay all defend. Paley acknowledges a debt to Tucker's unbearably prolix and rambling work; fortunately, he reduces the main lines of argument in Tucker and his predecessors to a reasonable length.[123]

Tucker's argument for utilitarianism rests on a connexion between rightness and good consequences (*LNP* 123–5). He connects rectitude with rules, and denies that rules could be correct in themselves apart from the results of observing them.[124] He argues plausibly that if a rule is right, it rests on some right-making reason, but then he assumes more controversially that an appropriate reason has to refer to the effects of observing the rule.

Having argued that nothing is right in itself, and reduced the right to what produces good consequences, Tucker denies that virtue could be a good in itself (127). His argument rests on the assumption that the mental state of satisfaction is the only non-instrumental good; from this assumption it is easy to infer that virtue must be only a means to satisfaction. He argues that 'the advantage of virtue over vice lies not in the act, but in the consequences' (128). Similarly, he finds the foundation of justice in utility, relying on an argument similar to Hume's (145–6).

---

[123] I cite Tucker, *LNP*, from Hazlitt's very welcome abridgment, which includes an amusing preface by Hazlitt, warmly commending Tucker. Hazlitt, however, dissents from Tucker's egoism (p. xxi). He suggests (p. xvi) that Tucker is pulled between Locke and Kant on self-love and benevolence. Stephen, *HET* ii 110, also speaks warmly of Tucker.

[124] 'The idea of rules being right in themselves, I conceive arose from our observing that they often grow out of one another, so that we are contented to trace them back a certain way, but do not think it necessary to inquire into the foundation of the more remote and general ones, which we therefore look upon as right in themselves, because we feel their good effects without being at the trouble to inquire into their origin. But no rule is right without a reason that renders it so . . .' (Tucker, *LNP* 125)

He recognizes, however, that appearances do not support the view that benevolence is reducible to selfish motivation, and he criticizes the easy arguments for egoism that argue from the fact that we want to satisfy our desires to the conclusion that all we want is satisfaction for ourselves.[125] He therefore seems to reject (without discussing it in detail) the psychological egoist reduction of benevolence. But he accepts rational egoism; though he allows distinct psychological reality to benevolence, he does not allow it rational authority. He believes it is reasonable for selfish motives to predominate in case of conflict. Plato's example of Gyges' Ring (not so called) appears to Tucker to present a serious problem.[126] A solution to the problem needs to show that the instrumental advantages of morality in the long run outweigh the instrumental disadvantages noticed by Plato.

Tucker tries to explain the fact that some people believe that morality is valuable enough to deserve to be followed despite its disadvantages. He suggests, in agreement with Gay and Hartley, that we pursue morality for its own sake because we have formed a persistent habit that we retain even when we gain nothing by it.[127] But though this is psychologically possible, Tucker maintains that it is irrational.[128] The ultimate defence of morality, and hence the ultimate basis of obligation, has to rest on long-term rewards. Tucker affirms the voluntarist combination of egoism and utilitarianism.

Paley uses Tucker to formulate a clear re-statement of the position of Gay and his successors. He does not try to complicate voluntarism, as Warburton does, in order to meet the objections of sentimentalists and rationalists. He prefers to attack the assumptions that might lead us to doubt the adequacy of the voluntarist account of morality. We will be impressed by anti-voluntarist arguments if we trust our intuitive judgments about the difference between moral requirements and commands backed by threats. But Paley believes that no intelligible alternative to the voluntarist analysis can be offered, and so we should simply reject the relevant intuitive judgments. The supposed obscurity of rationalist claims about disinterested concern and motivation by perception of intrinsic rightness encourages Paley to conclude that the questions raised by rationalists are spurious.

---

[125] 'Wearing woollen clothes or eating mutton does not make a man sheepish, nor does his looking into a book every now and then render him bookish; so neither is every thing selfish, that relates to oneself.' (Tucker, *LNP* 149)

[126] 'It may be said that if satisfaction, a man's own satisfaction is the groundwork of all our motives; that if virtue and benevolence are recommended by reason only as containing the most copious sources of gratification, then are they no more than means, and deserve our regard no longer than while they conduce to that end. So that if a man should have an opportunity of gaining some great advantage secretly, and without danger to himself, though with infinite detriment to all the world besides, and in breach of every moral obligation, he would do wisely to embrace it.' (*LNP* 155)

[127] 'I knew a tradesman, who, having gotten a competency of fortune, thought to retire and enjoy himself in quiet; but finding he could not be easy without business, was forced to return to the shop, and assist his former partners gratis. Why then should it be thought strange that a man, long inured to the practice of moral duties, should persevere in them out of liking, when they can yield him no further advantage?' (156)

[128] 'Upon the whole, we are forced to acknowledge, that hitherto we have found no reason to imagine that a wise man would ever die for his country, or suffer martyrdom in the cause of virtue. The only way in which we can extend the obligations of virtue to every circumstance that can happen, is by supposing that the end of life is not the end of being; that death is but a removal to some other stage, where our good works shall follow us, and yield a plentiful harvest of happiness which had not time to ripen here.' (159)

He therefore supposes that he has cleared up an unnecessary air of mystery surrounding morality and obligation.[129] His argument implies that there is nothing distinctive about obligation in contrast to being induced. In his view 'a man is said to be obliged when he is urged by a violent motive resulting from the command of another' (ii 2 = R 848). In the case of morality, the commander is God, and the violent motive results from the prospect of reward and punishment.

By taking this view of obligation Paley reverts to the position of Hobbes, and rejects the distinction between obligation and inducement on which Cudworth rests his opposition to Hobbes. In assuming that obligations all rest on the same desire for reward and fear of punishment, he denies that a legitimate or authorized commander or legislator differs from one who is powerful enough to hold out effective threats and offers.

Paley also follows Hobbes in accepting a utilitarian explanation of moral rules. Hobbes connects the laws of nature with the preservation of the state rather than with any more general maximization of the good. Paley follows those who attribute a utilitarian outlook to God, and so he agrees with Gay in making utility a subordinate criterion of morality. He answers the question that Gay does not answer, about our capacity to discern the actions that maximize utility. According to Paley, we promote utility by following the accepted rules and institutions of society.

He does not make a serious effort to show, by appeal to some independent grasp of utility, that these specific rules actually maximize it. Nor does he appeal to a less optimistic view of our capacities that makes accepted moral rules our best guide to the benevolent will of God; this is the view that Berkeley endorses and that Butler suggests, without endorsing it. Paley cuts short all these questions by treating the moral rules he is familiar with as being in general a reliable guide to utility.

After making all these simplifying assumptions, Paley is able to present his moral philosophy in a lucid and concise form. The use of his book as a textbook in Cambridge reflects its success in summarizing the voluntarist side of the 18th-century debate. The book remained popular for many years. It was first published in 1785, and by 1811 it had reached its 19th edition. It remained popular enough in the 1850s to allow the publication of annotated editions. Whately commented from an anti-utilitarian position, and Bain defended the core (as he saw it) of Paley's utilitarianism. Paley's book helped to provoke Whewell's defence of a non-utilitarian rationalist position. Whewell remarks that Paley had been (since 1786)[130] and still was (in 1852)[131] prescribed for study in Cambridge, and that he summed up the theological voluntarist outlook that had been prominent in Cambridge for many years.[132]

---

[129] 'When I first turned my thoughts to moral speculations, an air of mystery seemed to hang over the whole subject; which arose, I believe, from hence,—that I supposed, with many authors whom I had read, that to be obliged to do a thing, was very different from being induced only to do it; and that the obligation to practise virtue, to do what is right, just, etc., was quite another thing, and of another kind, than the obligation which a soldier is under to obey his officer, a servant his master; or any of the civil and ordinary obligations of human life.' (Paley, *PMP* ii 3 = R 851)

[130] Whewell, *LHMPE* 165: '. . . the principles upon which Paley's book is based, the doctrine that actions are good in as far as they tend to pleasure, and obligatory in as far as they are commanded by a powerful master, had already long been taught in this university [sc. Cambridge], and had undoubtedly taken a strong hold of the minds of men. They had accustomed themselves to look upon it as the only rational and tenable doctrine; and one which was as superior in these respects to the vague and empty doctrines, of loftier sound, which had preceded the time of Locke, as the philosophy of Newton was to that of Aristotle.'

[131] Whewell, *LHMPE*, p. xxv.   [132] On later opponents and defenders of Paley see Le Mahieu, *MWP* 155–62.

880. Whately's Criticisms of Paley

It is useful to survey a few of Whately's comments on Paley. They are not especially original; they recapitulate some of the earlier criticisms of voluntarism that we find, for instance, in Price, who also disapproves of Paley's book.[133] They also agree largely with Whewell's comments on Paley. These criticisms give some idea of the objections that a utilitarian might be fairly expected to answer, and some reasons for thinking that theological voluntarism does not provide the best defence of utilitarianism. Whately believes it is important to discuss Paley critically because of the influence of his book.[134] He especially attacks Paley's theological voluntarism, but he also disapproves of the account of moral obligation and of Paley's utilitarianism, for reasons that go beyond voluntarism.

In Whately's view, theological voluntarism defeats its own ends, for reasons related to those that Socrates urges against Euthyphro.[135] One might defend Paley against this objection. The voluntarist is committed to explaining 'God's will is right and good' as 'God's will is God's will' only if voluntarism offers an account of moral concepts. If it allows a non-voluntarist account of moral concepts, but offers a voluntarist account of moral properties, voluntarists may agree that 'God's will is right' is not a tautology, but still claim that the property referred to by 'right' is being willed by God. But it is not clear that Paley can use this defence; he seems to offer voluntarist analyses of moral concepts.

But even if we allowed Paley this defence against Whately's conceptual argument, it would not answer Whately's main point. If we recommend Christian morality for its moral excellence, our recommendation is more plausible if we appeal to some standard of moral excellence distinct from Christian morality itself. The mere fact that it expresses the will of God is not sufficient for its meeting the appropriate standard for morality. Whately argues that we need a distinct standard of morality, and that the Christian doctrine of God as creator encourages us to look for it.[136] The mere fact that voluntarists attribute more than naturalists attribute to the will of God does not show that voluntarism fits orthodox Christianity better.

Indeed Paley himself, in Whately's view, implicitly concedes some independent criterion of morality.[137] Whately believes that the role Paley allows to moral knowledge without

---

[133] Price on Paley; *RPQM* 342. Many of Whately's comments are repeated from *ILM*. Prior, *LBE* 100, discusses the meta-ethical implications of some of Whately's arguments.

[134] 'Having long been an established text-book at a great and flourishing university, it has laid the foundation of the moral principles of many hundreds—probably thousands—of youths while under a course of training designed to qualify them for being afterwards the moral instructors of millions. Such a work therefore cannot fail to exercise a very considerable influence on the minds of successive generations.' (Whately, *PMP*, Pref.)

[135] '. . . its inevitable consequence is to derogate from God's honour and to deprive the Christian revelation of part of its just evidence . . . To call the will of God righteous and good, if our original ideas of righteousness and goodness imply merely a conformity to the divine will, is an empty truism. It is in fact no more than saying that the will of God is the will of God; and if we dwell on the excellence of the Christian morality at the same time that we make Christianity the whole and original standard of moral excellence, we are evidently arguing in a vicious circle, and merely attributing to the Gospel the praise of being conformable to the rules derived from itself' (Whately, *PMP* 64).

[136] 'If the author of the universe and the author of Christianity, the giver of reason and of revelation, be, as we contend, the same being, it is to be expected that the declarations of his will which we meet with in revelation should correspond with the dictates of the highest and most perfect reason; and the testimony of the heathen moralists proves that such is the fact.' (*PMP* 66)

[137] Paley, i. 4: '. . . the Scriptures commonly presuppose in the persons to whom they speak a knowledge of the principles of natural justice; and are employed not so much to teach *new* rules of morality, as to enforce the practice of it by *new* sanctions, and by a *greater certainty* . . .' (quoted by Whately, *PMP* 16).

revelation conflicts with Paley's support of voluntarism.[138] Paley might reply that Whately attributes a more extreme position to him than he holds. A voluntarist metaphysics does not require us to deny that people may be partly aware through natural reason of principles that are moral principles because God commands them. People are aware of the principles, but not of what makes them moral principles.

But this reply on Paley's behalf does not completely dispose of Whately's criticism. If we concede natural knowledge of the actions that are morally right, it is difficult not to concede some natural knowledge of the standard of morality as well. Once we concede this, we seem to allow recognition of the relevant standard without reference to divine commands.

We might try to find support for voluntarism in the fact that we sometimes have to take God's word for some action's being right. Whately answers that this sort of trust in God does not support voluntarism.[139] For we can also trust moral advice from other people on similar grounds, without supposing we have no access to any independent standard of morality. The independent standard warrants us in taking their advice when we do not know what to do.

Not only are the arguments for voluntarism weak; its consequences are also unacceptable. Whately particularly objects to Paley's account of obligation as a violent motive.[140] Paley's attempt to explain moral concepts and judgments really changes the subject. Whately implies that Paley is open to the objections that expose the inadequacy of a Hobbesian account of obligation.[141]

If Paley were right about our moral concepts, we would not mark distinctions that in fact we do mark, and we would not agree with the ancient moralists in marking them.[142] Paley's

---

[138] 'For supposing man a being destitute of all moral faculty, and deriving all notions of right and wrong that he can ever possess, entirely from a consideration of the will of God, and the expectation of reward and punishment in the next world from him, one does not see how those to whom our Scriptures were addressed . . . could have had any notion at all of "natural justice".' (Whately, PMP 16) 'He admits that we attribute goodness to the Most High on account of the conformity of his acts to the principles which we are accustomed to call "good"; and that these principles are called "good" solely from their conformity to the divine will. It is very strange that when he was thus proceeding in a circle, this did not open his eyes to the erroneousness of the principle which had led him into it.' (24) Whately comments on Paley, i 9.

[139] '. . . this is from our general conviction that God is wise and good; not from our attaching no meaning to the words wise and good except the divine will. Then and then only can the command of a superior make anything a duty, when we set out with the conviction that it is a duty to obey him' (PMP 25; cf. 62).

[140] 'But the most amazing circumstance in that remarkable chapter . . . is the total unconsciousness which the author seems to exhibit of there being anything peculiar or specific in our feeling of moral approbation. He seems to think that, as soon as he has shown that the approval which we bestow upon things because they are useful, may become by habit immediately attached to them, after the perception of their utility has dropped out of the mind, he has done all that could be reasonably expected by his antagonists; or, in other words, he seems to imagine that no one can possibly suppose the emotion which approves the virtue of a man, to differ specifically from that which commends the proportions of a doorway, or the elegance of a tweezer-case.' (PMP 30)

[141] 'A planter's slave, for instance, is urged by a violent motive—a very violent motive—to work in the fields at his master's command, and sometimes to assist in flogging his fellow-labourers. But though he is obliged to do this, few, except slave-owners, would call this a moral obligation . . . If it should be said that the master has no just right over him, and is not therefore a rightful "superior", this would be to recognize a moral faculty. But if every one is a superior who has power to enforce submission, the slave-owner is such . . .' (58)

[142] 'And all the ancient heathen writers use words which evidently signify what we call "virtue", "duty", "moral goodness"; which words could not possibly have found their way into the languages of men destitute (as most of them were) of any belief in a future state of retribution, if Paley's theory were correct. It is disproved not by any supposed truth and soundness in the views of the ancient writers, but by the very words they employ.' (PMP 62) 'Yet it is an indisputable fact that the ancient heathen did, without the knowledge of a future state, entertain a notion of duty. . . . The fact that they did entertain some is a disproof of the theory in question.' (63)

principles make us unable to distinguish between what is bad because prohibited and what is prohibited because bad (72).[143] To illustrate the fact that moral obligations are independent of acts of will, Whately cites the oath taken by the king to observe the laws; this does not create obligation, but recognizes a pre-existent obligation (121). Paley might reply that these distinctions that we think we draw are spurious, and cannot be explained with sufficient clarity. But this abandonment of moral distinctions needs more argument than he offers for it. He claims to be explaining morality, but he fails.

Paley does not explain in detail how his hedonistic utilitarianism justifies the specific moral rules he defends. Whately suggests that such an explanation would be difficult to give. He does not simply object that hedonistic calculation is likely to give the wrong answers; he also rejects it as morally inappropriate. 'Disgust' at utilitarian answers is understandable if utilitarians believe that calculation of pleasures is the right basis for recognition of moral obligation.[144]

Whately's objections do not settle the issues about voluntarism, They are even less decisive about utilitarianism, which is not his main concern. But they expose some serious difficulties not only in Paley's position, but also in any position that tries to explain moral requirements by appeal to something like Paley's 'violent motive'. Paley's combination of egoistic hedonism with utilitarianism may seem initially appealing, and it certainly seems so to Bentham as well as the theological voluntarists; but Whately exposes some of its flaws.

881. Thomas Brown's Criticism of Paley

Some of the main points of Whately's rationalist criticisms of Paley agree with the objections of Thomas Brown, who attacks Paley on sentimentalist grounds. He affirms the 'original' character of moral reactions, against any reductive account, either egoist or associationist (such as Gay and Hartley offer).[145] But he differs from Hutcheson in rejecting the analogy with a sense (181). Hutcheson's account suggests that moral judgment consists partly in receiving ideas from external reality, whereas Brown believes we only need to recognize the specific feeling of approval, which is only one component of Hutcheson's analysis.

Brown rejects Clarkean rationalism, claiming (as Hutcheson and Hume claim) that it cannot account for the practical aspects of morality. In particular, he claims that reasoning cannot give us a reason or motive to pursue one end rather than another; he accepts

---

[143] 'You can easily prove, therefore, that when people speak of a knowledge of the divine will being the origin of all our moral notions, they cannot mean exactly what the words would seem to signify; if, at least, they admit at the same time that it is a matter of duty, and not merely of prudence, to obey God's will, and that he has a just claim to our obedience.' (*PMP* 90)

[144] 'And if the pleasures of sense "differ only in intensity and duration" from the pleasures of filial and parental affection, we ought to know how many days of luxurious living are equivalent to the pleasure of saving a father's life, that we may decide rightly when these things happen to come in competition. If utilitarian moral obligation consists in being regulated by such calculations, we cannot be surprised at the disgust with which so many persons speak of the scheme which refers us to the "calculations of utility".' (*PMP* 42)

[145] 'All which a defender of original tendencies to the emotions that are distinctive of virtue and vice can be supposed to assert is that, when we are capable of understanding the consequences of actions, we then have those feelings of moral approbation or disapprobation which . . . I suppose to constitute our moral notions of virtue, merit, obligation.' (Brown, *LE* 120)

Hutcheson's view about the purely instrumental character of reason (64–74). He does not discuss Hume's arguments to show that moral distinctions are not derived from reason (which are quite similar to his own arguments). The aspect of Hume's theory that he selects for discussion is utilitarianism. He disagrees with Hume, arguing that neither the agent nor the spectator is primarily concerned with utility; Hume (he believes) has been misled by the general coincidence between moral sentiment and utility into believing that moral sentiment is essentially utilitarian (Lecture 5).

His examination of Smith (Lectures 8–9) is sympathetic and acute, raising a major difficulty for Smith's derivation of moral sentiments from sympathy. Brown notices that if Smith's derivation is to achieve its aims, the sympathy from which moral sentiment is derived cannot itself contain or presuppose any moral judgment. But he argues that, contrary to Smith, we cannot explain the crucial instances of sympathy unless we suppose that they rest on moral judgment, so that we cannot take this moral judgment to be the product of sympathy. In some cases we do not form sympathetic feelings towards the feelings of others except on the basis of a moral judgment about these feelings; if, then, these moral judgments determine the scope and limits of our sympathy, they do not depend on non-moral sympathy (150).[146]

Though Brown rejects the 'selfish system' for familiar reasons, he keeps his sharpest criticism for the theological voluntarism of Paley, which he regards as an especially degrading form of selfish system because it tells us that God is 'not to be loved, but to be courted with a mockery of affection' (131). He also rejects the other side of Paley's position, his theological voluntarism about moral obligation; he argues on familiar naturalist grounds for the independence of moral sentiment and moral obligation from belief in God (137–42).

Since he defends a sentimentalist position, Brown faces the objections raised by Price and Reid, and repeated by Stewart.[147] Price, following Balguy, rejects sentimentalism on the ground that it makes morality unstable. Brown admits that morality is liable to vary with our sentiments, but does not regard this as an objection to his position. The rationalists point out that moral judgments and properties are liable to counterfactual changes if moral emotions change, but Brown does not think this sort of mutability matters, because the relevant counterfactuals are too remote to concern us.[148]

This seems an over-simple reply to Price's criticism, for two reasons: (1) It is not clear that the counterfactuals are as remote as Brown suggests. It is reasonable to suppose, as Hutcheson admits, that people's actual sentiments vary. Sentimentalists tend to resort to the normal perceiver, but it is not clear that a purely statistical, non-normative, notion of normality gives a satisfactory account of moral properties. (2) Brown rejects voluntarism on the basis of naturalist arguments about the independence of moral sentiments from

---

[146] Brown summarizes his main objection: '[Smith's theory] . . . would still be liable to the insuperable objection, that the moral sentiments which he ascribes to our secondary feelings of mere sympathy are assumed as previously existing in those original emotions with which the secondary feelings are said to be in unison.' (*LE* 157).

[147] At 188–92 Brown cites Stewart, *OMP*. In §190 Stewart mentions the alleged consequence of Hutcheson's position, that it makes morality arise from an arbitrary relation between our constitution and external objects. Stewart thinks this consequence can be avoided if Reid's conception of a moral sense is substituted for Hutcheson's conception.

[148] 'It is a very powerless scepticism, indeed, which begins by supposing a total change of our nature. We might perhaps have been formed to admire only the cruel, and to hate only the benevolent . . . But if the moral distinctions be as regular as the whole system of laws which carry on in unbroken harmony the motions of the universe, this regularity is sufficient for us while we exist on earth . . .' (*LE* 192)

God's will. This independence is shown by appeal to counterfactuals about mutability. Balguy and Price argue that these objections to voluntarism can be adapted to undermine sentimentalism. Since Brown accepts naturalist arguments against voluntarism, either he needs to show that the same arguments do not defeat his sentimentalism or he needs to give up some of his arguments against theological voluntarism.

Brown's account of morality is a significant development of the sentimentalism of Hutcheson and continued by Smith. He includes some acute criticisms of his sentimentalist predecessors, though he does not show that his position is exempt from the general objections to sentimentalism.

882. Wainewright's Defence of Paley

To illustrate the persistence of Paley's views, it is worth noticing a later defence against his early 19th-century critics, the *Vindication* by Wainewright. In reply to various critics, Wainewright defends the use of Paley's work as a textbook in Cambridge (2), and tries to separate him from such utilitarians as Hume and Godwin (6). He separates him from these utilitarians because Paley's survey of consequences extends to the afterlife, and because Paley refers to utility only when some question arises about the rightness of an action. Wainewright argues that (as Gay puts it, though not using Gay's terms) the will of God is the primary criterion of morality and utility is only a secondary criterion. He also qualifies Paley's utilitarianism by arguing, against Stewart, that he is not an unqualified act-utilitarian, but insists on the importance of observing general rules (9). Similarly, Stewart is unjustified in claiming that Paley assimilates duty to interest; in distinguishing our interest in this life from our interest in the afterlife, he draws the appropriate distinction (28).

On these points Wainewright's attitude is defensive; he admits that the charges against Paley would be damaging if they were true, and so he argues that they are false. On some other points his vindication is more aggressive; he admits the truth of some allegations, but believes that Paley is right to hold the views that the critics reject. His answer to the Euthyphro question seems to favour Euthyphro, since he says that Paley defines right as 'consistency with the will of God' (27). But he also seems to say that Paley takes right to be essentially what maximizes happiness. It is a result of God's creative will that in our circumstances these actions achieve happiness, and hence (Wainewright infers) voluntarists are right to say that what is right depends on the will of God.[149] This formulation seems to reflect the failure to distinguish the creative from the legislative will of God that we have found in Pufendorf and others. Nor do Paley and Wainewright make it clear whether it is necessary or contingent that God chooses the principles that maximize utility.

---

[149] 'It will scarcely be disputed that no moral laws are framed, and that no actions and dispositions have been enjoined by the Deity, which do not tend to promote the happiness of his intelligent creatures. What is termed the essential difference between right and wrong entirely depends on this tendency to produce happiness or misery: on no other account is the one commanded, and the other prohibited. That some actions and dispositions are productive of human enjoyment, and others of uneasiness and pain, must result from the relations arising from the circumstances in which man finds himself pleased; but as these circumstances could not have any existence if no such being as man had been created, so far the consequent relations may be said to originate with the Creator.' (Wainewright, *VPTM* 78)

Wainewright defends Paley's egoism by appeal to a motivational account of obligation, claiming that any obligation refers to what is necessary for one's own happiness.[150] A further defence relies on an egoist account of justification. Wainewright answers those who criticize Paley for the selfish aspects of his system. He calls Thomas Brown's objections 'extravagant' (115). He answers that the desire for happiness is a perfectly acceptable motive from the moral point of view, and that Kant was wrong to deny this (119). If Paley's position is selfish, Christianity (he claims) is also selfish, since it appeals to rewards in the afterlife (123).

Wainewright's argument suffers from failure to distinguish the appeal to self-interest as one acceptable motive from the exclusive appeal to self-interest. The latter appeal seems to be characteristic of Paley, but not (or not obviously) of Christianity. The critics of Paley whom he attacks object to Paley's reduction of all moral motives to self-interest. This criticism is not answered by the observation that self-interest is one legitimate motive. Wainewright's only concession to critics of the selfish position is the observation that Paley allows virtue to become habitual, without constant reflexion on divine rewards; for this purpose Paley uses Tucker's example of the merchant who still wanted to stay in business after he had retired (117–18). This observation, however, does not meet the main point that Paley's critics urge against him.

The obscurity in this part of Wainewright's argument is easier to understand in the light of his attack on all defences of morality that rely on disinterested motives.[151] He accuses his opponents of favouring Stoicism (142).[152] Though one might suppose that he is only attacking those who reject interest altogether in favour of virtue, he seems to include in his attack those who allow any role to disinterested motives. Hence he accuses Clarke of inconsistency because he appeals both to fitness and to the prospect of rewards in the afterlife.

Though Wainewright does not make much progress towards an answer to the attacks on Paley, or even towards a clear account of the questions in dispute, he makes one suggestive remark about the relation of Bentham's utilitarianism to Paley's. He suggests that Bentham is inconsistent in his views about why we ought to promote utility, and that his most plausible answer to the question relies on Paley's egoism.[153] If Bentham thinks the promotion of

---

[150] '. . . nothing can be said to oblige us which is not in some way or other necessary to our happiness. The supposition of physical force is of course entirely excluded;—and in what other way can the will be influenced, except through the instrumentality of motives?' (VPTM 87).

[151] 'Constituted as the human faculties and affections are at present, to endeavour to persuade the great mass of mankind, or indeed any but visionary speculatists, who never mingle in the business and tumults of the world, that they ought to practise virtue either exclusively for its own sake, or from no other motive than the feeling of approbation which it inspires in the heart, is, I cannot help believing, to the last degree, idle and preposterous.' (VPTM 136) In his support Wainewright quotes Berkeley, Alc., Dialogue 3: 'Seized and rapt with this sublime idea, our philosophers do infinitely despise and pity whoever shall propose or accept any other motive to virtue'. This is part of Berkeley's attack on Shaftesbury; see §614.

[152] He quotes with approval La Bruyère, Caractères, ch. 11 (De l'homme) §3, on Stoicism. La Bruyère attacks the allegedly unrealistic character of the Stoic doctrine of apatheia. (On the Stoics' actual view see §191.) In his view, the Stoics' unrealistic advice is also useless: 'Ils ont laissé à l'homme tous les défauts qu'ils lui ont trouvés, et n'ont presque relevé aucun de ses faibles'. Wainewright believes that the pursuit of disinterested motivation is equally unrealistic.

[153] 'When he [sc. Bentham] describes "the greatest amount of happiness" to be the rule of our conduct, which he does in his first chapter, he so far agrees with Paley; and where he considers it as the sole obligation (chap ii, sect 19), his opinion is very closely allied to that of Hume. His commentators, however, maintain, that the great object he has in view (though it is certainly mentioned in a very summary way, chap. xvii, sect 6 & 7) is to show that every man, by consulting the greatest happiness of the community, adopts the surest method of securing his own. If the truth of Revelation be

utility is our sole obligation, he must believe we have a reason and motive to promote it for its own sake (given that obligation implies motivation). But if Bentham maintains that we need to reconcile promotion of the general happiness with promotion of one's own happiness, he assumes—according to Wainewright—that the sole obligation is to promote one's own happiness, and that promotion of the general happiness is subordinate to this.

It is not completely clear whether Bentham accepts the egoism that Wainewright ascribes to him here. But at least Wainewright raises a reasonable question about why Bentham thinks we are obliged to promote the general happiness. If he gives the egoist reason, his rejection of Paley's theological voluntarism leaves him with an unanswered question about how egoist reasons either generate or justify concern for the general happiness. This question for the utilitarian occupies both Mill and Sidgwick.

admitted, there can be no question that this position may be fully established; but without this admission the attempt would as clearly fail.' (*VPTM* 110)

65

ROUSSEAU

883. Hobbes's Errors

Rousseau's works do not include any treatise on moral philosophy, but they include different sorts of material that is relevant to moral philosophy. Several of his main works are primarily relevant to social philosophy, since they deal with interactions between individuals and different sorts of social contexts.

One of Rousseau's preoccupations arises from his objections to Hobbes. According to Hobbes, the most illuminating way to understand society, and especially the state, is to contrast it with the condition of human beings without society, in the state of nature. When we consider non-social human beings, we can see that each individual needs society, and in particular needs a commonwealth with coercive power, in order to satisfy the desires that we form without any commonwealth. The commonwealth offers peace, which we can see, from the point of view of the state of nature, to be better than the war of all against all that is characteristic of the state of nature.

Rousseau believes that Hobbes's question is illuminating, but not for the reasons that Hobbes supposes. Hobbes's argument succeeds only if the evils removed by the commonwealth are present in the non-social state of nature. But Rousseau believes that they are not present in Hobbes's state of nature. If we follow Hobbes's instructions to begin from a non-social starting point, we will not find the sorts of desires and conflicts that create the war of all against all. Hobbes has attributed to a non-social condition desires and aims that really belong to people in society. This is one common error in appeals to the state of nature.[1] Those who make the error suggest the state as the remedy for a disease that the state has created in the first place.

This may not be a very effective criticism of Hobbes. If Hobbes's argument is to work, he must be right about the predicament of human beings without a commonwealth—that is to say, without a state exercising coercive power in order to secure peace. For the

[1] 'The philosophers who have examined the foundations of society have all felt the necessity of going back as far as the state of nature, but none of them has reached it. ... all of them, continually speaking of need, greed, oppression, desires, and pride transferred to the state of nature ideas they had taken from society; they spoke of savage man and depicted civil man.' (*DOI*, Introd. §5 = P iii 132 = C 38) At §33 = P 252 = C 52 Rousseau criticizes Hobbes for saying that the human condition in the state of nature is miserable. I cite the *DOI* by paragraphs, and by pages in the Pléiade edition (P) and Cress's translation (C).

purposes of this argument, it would not matter if some of the desires that create the predicament of the state of nature require some form of society. Hobbes is refuted only if these desires presuppose a commonwealth. But Rousseau does not show that, for instance, greed and pride require a Hobbesian commonwealth. He shows at most that they require some form of social relations. We must (let us grant) have enough interactions with other people so that we care about impressing them or showing our superiority to them. But we could apparently interact enough to form these desires without being members of a commonwealth.

To defend Rousseau's objection to Hobbes, we might argue that the forms of society that allow the formation of greed and pride (for instance) must be fairly stable and long-lasting. In that case, one of two things follows. Either (1) Hobbes will say that such societies require a commonwealth, so that Rousseau is right to object that Hobbes relies on desires that require a commonwealth; or (2) such societies do not require a commonwealth, and so Hobbes is wrong to maintain that stable societies require a commonwealth.

The dilemma offered to Hobbes does not necessarily damage his position. He might allow the possibility of societies that are stable enough to allow the formation of greed and pride, but are still not stable enough to guarantee peace. Families, clans, alliances might persist in favourable circumstances without the degree of security that results from the assurance of peace. It is not obvious, therefore, that Hobbes's argument relies on attributing these various passions to completely non-social individuals, without ties to family, friends, or other associates.

One might wonder in any case whether Hobbes's argument essentially depends on the inevitability of 'competitive' desires such as those that Rousseau mentions.[2] This question leads into a series of difficult questions about Hobbes. But at least one line of argument may allow Hobbes to dispense with any essential appeal to such desires. Even if we have moderate desires for food, drink, shelter, and other objects that do not essentially involve a sense of superiority over others, we may be drawn into conflict if they appear to us to be in short supply, or if we see some danger to their continued supply, or if we think other people will form such beliefs. However pre-social we may be, we seem to be liable to these sources of conflict, and hence we have reason to desire the increased security that would come from peace. Even if the fears we might form are irrational, they still undermine security.

This argument might make Hobbes's case for a commonwealth less universal. It would be confined to circumstances of less than complete abundance, and would not apply to circumstances in which no one could see any threat to the supply of resources for satisfaction of their non-competitive desires. But if circumstances of less than complete abundance are frequent enough, Hobbes's argument applies to many instances of the state of nature. Rousseau does not adequately answer this argument by simply observing that people in the state of nature have moderate desires.

This dispute between Hobbes and Rousseau introduces some of Rousseau's reflexions on the state of nature. In one respect, as we have seen, his account of the state of nature

---

[2] On Hobbes see §491.

is more austere than Hobbes's, since he takes it to be prior even to the elementary forms of society that Hobbes perhaps includes, or might consistently include, in the state of nature. The point of this austere account is not to ask Hobbes's questions about a more exactly described state of nature, but to argue that Hobbes's questions are misconceived. If we consider a wholly non-social state of nature, we find human beings at such a primitive material and mental level that they have none of the needs that are satisfied by the state. Society creates these needs, and does not take them for granted.

884. The Errors of Traditional Naturalism

Rousseau's view of Hobbes's argument separates him from naturalist appeals to human nature as the foundation of a state. Though he agrees with the naturalist tradition, as he finds it in Grotius as well as Burlamaqui, in thinking one ought to begin with human nature, he believes that this tradition proceeds from mistaken views.[3]

According to Grotius, natural right consists in what is appropriate to rational and social nature.[4] Following Aristotle and the Stoics, Grotius assumes that human beings are fundamentally rational and social.[5] The aims and needs that result from these human characteristics belong to the natural basis that explains and justifies the existence of a state. We ought not to try to justify the state by reference to its instrumental functions in providing security; the attempt to find such a justification is the error of Epicurus, followed by Carneades and by Hobbes.

Though Rousseau disagrees with Hobbes's conception of the state of nature, he disagrees even more with the traditional naturalist conception. Hobbes excludes all the alleged aspects of human nature that would impose moral constraints on the character of a commonwealth beyond the demands of peace and security. He takes these Aristotelian constraints to be a source of dispute and faction within a state. Rousseau agrees with him on this point. He believes that the 'rational and social' aspects of human beings do not belong to human nature in its own right, but are the product of society. Like Hobbes, the traditional naturalists take features of human beings that depend on society and treat them as though they were independent of society.

Because he thinks Hobbes and the naturalists include too much in human nature in isolation from society, Rousseau's conception of isolated human nature is quite minimal,

---

[3] 'For it is no light undertaking to disentangle what is original from what is artificial in man's present nature, and to know accurately a state which no longer exists, which perhaps never did exist, which probably never will exist, and about which it is nevertheless necessary to have exact notions in order accurately to judge of our present state. . . . It is this ignorance of the nature of man that causes such uncertainty and obscurity on the genuine definition of natural right; for the idea of right, says M. Burlamaqui, and still more that of natural right, are manifestly ideas relative to the nature of man. . . . It is not without surprise and scandal that one notes how little agreement prevails about this important matter among the various authors who have dealt with it.' (*DOI*, Pref. §§4–6 = P 123–4 = C 35)

[4] For the inclusion of 'and social' see Grotius, §464.

[5] Grimsley in *SC* 55: 'Rousseau's stress on freedom is linked up with his rejection of the Aristotelian idea that since man is a "political animal", politics consist mainly of developing some pre-existent capacity and of constructing the State in accordance with a fixed pattern or model'.

and in particular excludes sociability.[6] He believes the traditional naturalist argument ascribes to nature the sociability that it ought to ascribe to society.[7]

How effectively does Rousseau argue against a traditional naturalist view? We may concede that it would be a mistake to conceive the standard manifestations of rationality and sociability as though they were totally independent of society. But it is not clear how much this point matters. The naturalist may concede that different forms of social life may develop rational and social characteristics to different degrees. The point of naturalism is to claim that those forms of social life that repress these characteristics, or do not allow them a controlling place in human action, are to be rejected, because they are inappropriate for the nature of human beings. It does not matter, for this purpose, that society affects the development or expression of different traits in human beings. The naturalist argument says that not all developments are equally acceptable from the moral point of view, and that the unacceptable ones are unacceptable because they are inappropriate for the nature of the people whose traits are being developed.

To avoid this appeal to naturalist principles, we might argue that the relevant moral criteria are applicable only from a point of view that is the product of a certain kind of social life. If social life has formed us so as to be predominantly rational and social, then (according to this view) we ought to take this point of view in evaluating society. If it has formed us so as to be predominantly creatures of our passions, or indifferent to the interests of others, this formation gives us a different point of view for evaluation of society. None of these points of view can claim to be more appropriate than the others for human beings.

If this objection to naturalism is sound, different forms of society and education are not subject to external moral criticism for the ways they treat the human beings whose characters they affect. They may still be subject to criticism for failing to achieve their own ends. If, for instance, a given society weakens itself because it makes its citizens lazy, selfish, or quarrelsome, it is open to criticism from its own point of view. But it is not subject to any external criticism for its formation of its citizens.

This conclusion is unwelcome to Rousseau. For his major work on education, *Emile*, is devoted to external criticism of current forms of education, on the ground that they rest on errors about human nature, and therefore mistreat people. In his view, the correct education achieves the goal of nature. Our education comes from 'nature, from human beings, or from things' (*Emile* i, P 247 = Bloom 38), and the human contribution ought to fit the character resulting from nature.[8] He seems to agree, therefore, with the naturalist view that some

---

[6] 'Hence disregarding all the scientific books that only teach us to see men as they have made themselves, and meditating on the first and simplest operations of the human soul, I believe I perceive in it two operations prior to reason, of which one interests us intensely in our well-being and our self-preservation, and the other inspires in us a natural repugnance to seeing any sentient being, and especially any being like ourselves, perish or suffer. It is from the co-operation and from the combination our mind is capable of making between these two principles, without it being necessary to introduce into it that of sociability, that all the rules of natural right seem to me to flow . . .' (*DOI*, Pref. §9 = P 125–6 = C 35)

[7] Derathé, *RSPST* 142–51, has a good discussion of Rousseau's objections to traditional naturalism. At 148 he takes Rousseau to agree that human beings are potentially social (in the 'Confession' in *Emile*; see, e.g., Bk iv = P 596, 600 = Bloom 287, 290); but he does not remark that Rousseau here accepts the basic naturalist claim.

[8] 'Nature, we are told, is merely habit. What does that mean? Are there not habits formed only by force, habits which never stifle nature? Such, for example, are the habits of plants whose vertical direction one obstructs. The plant, once let go free, keeps the direction that one has forced it to take, but still the sap has not changed its course at all, and any new

features of human beings constitute their nature, and that these ought to be some sort of guide for the proper treatment of human beings in society.

His conception of nature seems to raise some difficulties for him. If he simply considers it as a collection of natural tendencies, how can he says that education ought to harmonize with them all? Some of them may conflict, and then we will have to choose. We might choose to make education harmonize with the tendencies that are most rigid, and most difficult to counteract. But that might not be a wise choice. Perhaps some primitive fears are difficult to remove, but we would be wrong to assume that we should be guided by them as far as possible, or that we ought not to cultivate habits that require us to repress them.

To avoid these unwelcome results, Rousseau seems to need something like Butler's conception of human nature as a system including passions that are organized by practical reason. Though this system is not present in a child, the child's capacity for developing the system is a ground for one sort of upbringing rather than another. Similarly, even though human beings manifest this system to different degrees, their capacity for manifesting it is a ground for treating them one way rather than another. Butler, for instance, maintains that we are appropriate objects of resentment, gratitude, and the attitudes connected with responsibility.

Rousseau does not seem to want to deny these claims about human nature as a system. Indeed, it is difficult to understand the progress of education, as described in *Emile*, if he does not take something like this for granted. But if he takes it for granted, he has no good reason for excluding it from the state of nature, as traditional naturalism conceives it.

Perhaps Rousseau rejects traditional naturalism because he supposes that it appeals to pre-social desires and pre-social expressions of human nature. If we remove the influences of society, individual human beings (we may grant) do not manifest the characteristic expressions of a rational and social nature. Hence Rousseau may be right to say that the expression of rational and social nature depends on society, and cannot be presumed in human beings conceived in isolation from society. In this respect, naturalism would make the mistake that Rousseau ascribes to Hobbes.[9]

It would be a mistake, therefore, to try to justify states on the ground that they satisfy desires that can only appear as a result of society and education; for people in the state of nature will lack these desires, and so, to this extent, will not want to enter a state in order to satisfy them. If the state of nature includes only the manifest desires that people are actively trying to satisfy, Rousseau is right (we may concede) to claim that it does not include rationality and sociality.

But traditional naturalists do not deny this. In claiming that human beings have a rational and social nature, they do not mean that every human being isolated from any social

---

growth the plant may make will be vertical again. It is the same with a man's inclinations; while the conditions remain the same, habits, even the least natural of them, hold good; but as soon as the situation changes, the habit ceases, and the natural returns. ... Everything should therefore be brought into harmony (rapporter) with these primitive dispositions.' (*Emile*, Bk. i = P 247–8 = Foxley 6–7 = Bloom 39)

[9] 'The mistake of Hobbes is not, therefore, to have established the state of war between human beings who are independent and have become social, but to have supposed that this state is natural to the species, and to have cited it as the cause of vices of which it is the effect.' (SC [1st version] i.217 = P 288) See Grimsley, *SC* 239. As Derathé, *RSPST* 108, puts it, Rousseau thinks Hobbes is right about the state of nature, except in making it natural. Hobbes's account fits man in society: 'Aussi reproche-t-il seulement à Hobbes de l'avoir présenté comme un tableau de l'état de nature, alors qu'elle s'applique parfaitement aux hommes vivant en société'.

influence manifests the explicit desires of a rational and social being. They mean that a human being in such circumstances is nonetheless a rational and social being. The point of appealing to natural rationality and sociality is not primarily to identify desires that seek satisfaction, but to identify the capacities that ought to be developed as part of the system of human nature. Against this naturalist position Rousseau's argument about the absence or weakness of certain desires in the state of nature is irrelevant and ineffective.

Rousseau might, however, answer this defence of traditional naturalism by arguing that human beings have no rational and social nature. To argue for this claim, he would have to show that reason and sociality are not part of a system of human nature, but are a deforming influence on it. If we are too close to other people, it may be bad for our health, if we pick up diseases from them; in this respect it is clear how society has a deforming influence on human nature.[10] If it could be shown that the development of one's rational capacities has an equally deforming influence, we would refute the naturalist claims about reason and nature.

One interpretation of Rousseau's remarks about primitive human beings might indeed support this conclusion about the deforming influence of developed rationality. We might understand his discussion of the origin of inequality to contrast a 'golden age' of non-rational life and activity with the corruptions resulting from the development of society and rationality. If this is what Rousseau means, reason and sociability are not parts of the system of human nature, but deformations of it. In that case, naturalists who appeal to natural rationality and sociality have grasped the reverse of the truth. According to this interpretation, Rousseau is a naturalist who takes human nature as the appropriate basis for the moral order of society, but he rejects the rational and social aspects normally attributed to human nature.

According to a more moderate interpretation, Rousseau believes that the rational aspects of human beings are products of society, but does not claim that they are really deformations of human nature. Such a view rejects any attempt to criticize the ways in which society moulds human beings. If we think the development of rational and social capacities is a good or a bad thing, we are taking a point of view within the outlook of a given society; we are not standing outside it to criticize it. Rousseau's myth of a golden age might be taken as a means of seeing the basic error in traditional naturalism. If we reject the story of original goodness and later corruption by society as a myth, we should recognize the equal unreality of the naturalist story of a fixed human nature that is either fulfilled or frustrated by society.

Naturalist views are a bit too stubborn, however, to be refuted by this sort of argument. For Rousseau can hardly avoid the sort of evaluation that (according to this argument) he wants to deny to the naturalist. Even if we do not take completely seriously his myth of a golden age in which people had simple wants and lived without conflict, one part of his attack on the effects of social life is meant seriously. He believes that society harms us in encouraging the competitive desires that arise with inflamed 'amour propre'. In wanting to excel other people, we try to accumulate wealth and power over them; since society accepts this outlook, it tends to form people who accept it, and so the competitive tendencies of individuals are inflamed still more by society. Rousseau does not treat inflamed amour

---

[10] Rousseau comments on health and illness at *DOI* i §9 = P 138 = C 42.

propre as a product of society beyond moral judgment; he believes political theory ought to counteract the effects of this attitude. In his view, some aspects of the development of society have harmed both the winners and the losers in the competition resulting from inflamed amour propre.

Rousseau's discussion of inflamed amour propre brings him closer to traditional naturalism. For, in speaking of an inflamed form of amour propre, he allows the possibility of a healthy form that is not subject to the same criticisms. Emile has this healthy form of amour propre, since he wants to be admired by others, but only to a limited extent. He wants to be the strongest and most skilful, because these are advantages whether or not other people value them. He does not care about goods that are goods only because other people value them.[11]

We cannot reject amour proper as a whole, because we cannot regard concern for the good opinion of another as avoidable or undesirable. Rousseau suggests that it arises from love and the desire to be loved.[12] Our desire for love helps to explain why we turn our attention on others, and compare ourselves with them.[13] But the mere fact that we want to excel others in certain respects does not make it inevitable that our amour propre will be insatiable.

Rousseau believes, therefore, that moderate amour propre is healthy, because of its relation to other human motives. An attempt to eliminate all amour propre would have to eliminate all concern for the good opinion of others, and all desire for another person's preferential esteem for oneself over others. But we could not eliminate those desires without eliminating love and friendship involving discriminatory relations between individuals. Rousseau clearly believes that these relations are necessary and appropriate for the good of human beings. He does not regard them as mere necessities, since he does not suggest that we reduce them to the necessary minimum in order to eliminate the dangers arising from temptations to amour propre. He relies on some assumptions about the good of human beings. Hence he relies on some conception of human nature as forming a system. It is difficult to see how he could avoid including reason and sociality in this system.

885. The Growth of Rational and Social Characteristics

Our discussion of Rousseau's objections to traditional naturalism has introduced some aspects of his contrast between the primitive human condition and the later development of society. It will be useful to consider some of the details of this contrast.

[11] 'Although his desire to please does not leave him absolutely indifferent to the opinion of others, he will concern himself with this opinion only in so far as it relates immediately to his person, without concerning himself about arbitrary appreciations that have no law but fashion or prejudice.' (*Emile* iv = P 670 = Bloom 339 = Foxley 304)

[12] 'To be loved, one has to make oneself loveable. To be preferred, one has to make oneself more loveable than another, more loveable than every other, at least in the eyes of the beloved object. This is the source of the first glances at one's fellows: this is the source of the first comparisons with them; this is the source of emulation, rivalries, and jealousy. ... With love and friendship are born dissensions, enmity, and hate. From the bosom of so many diverse passions, I see opinion raising an unshakeable throne, and stupid mortals, subjected to its empire, basing their own existence on the judgments of others. Expand these ideas, and you will see where our amour propre gets the form we believe natural to it, and how self-love, ceasing to be an absolute sentiment, becomes pride in great souls, vanity in small ones, and feeds itself constantly in all at the expense of one's neighbour.' (*Emile* iv = P 494 = Foxley 175–6 = Bloom 215)

[13] 'And the first sentiment aroused in him by this comparison is the desire to be in the first position. This is the point where love of self turns into amour propre, and where begin to arise all the passions which depend on this one.' (*Emile* iv = P 523 = Foxley 197 = Bloom 235)

In the primitive human condition people differ from other animals by being free and by having the capacity to perfect themselves (*DOI* i §16–17 = G 141). Freedom involves the capacity to acquiesce in impressions or to resist them. Perfectibility involves the capacity to improve one's own condition, and to transmit this improvement to other people. These capacities explain why human beings do not necessarily retain their initial outlook throughout their lives or throughout generations. But these features of human beings do not make rationality or sociality original features of human nature.[14] Hence Hobbes is wrong to claim that people in the state of nature have the vices that in fact come from society.[15] Rousseau assumes that the only source of vice is social, because it results from the competitive outlook that is absent from human beings in the state of nature.

To explain the actions of human beings in their natural condition we must attribute to them love of self (amour de soi), to explain their self-preserving activity. But Rousseau believes we must also attribute pity to them. To explain why he ascribes pity to non-social and non-rational human nature, Rousseau refers to the behaviour of animals—horses who are reluctant to trample living bodies, and so on.[16]

Why does Rousseau believe that in the state of nature human beings have self-love without amour propre? He clarifies his position in distinguishing the two sentiments.[17] Amour propre is absent from the state of nature because 'every individual human being views himself as the only spectator to observe him' (*DOI*, n 15 = P 219 = C 106), and does not regard others as judges of his merit. But why does Rousseau assume this?

Perhaps he is thinking of the parallel with other animals, and assuming that they display no tendency to compare themselves with others. This assumption is difficult to maintain in the face of hierarchies among groups of animals. But perhaps Rousseau means that other animals do not regard others as providing a standard or norm for themselves. But if that is true, it may be because other animals do not regard themselves as acting on a standard or norm at all. Does Rousseau mean, then, that our applying standards to our actions is an effect of society, and absent from the state of nature?

If that is what he means, it is difficult to see how other people could be responsible for the growth of amour propre. If amour propre grows because I want the approval of other people

---

[14] '... it is at least clear, from how little care nature has taken to bring men together through mutual needs and to facilitate their use of speech, how little it prepared their sociability, and how little of its own it has contributed to all that men have done to establish its bonds' (*DOI* i §33 = P 151 = C 51).

[15] 'Above all, let us not conclude with Hobbes that because he has no idea of goodness man is naturally wicked, that he is vicious because he does not know virtue ... Hobbes did not see that the same cause that keeps savages from using their reason, as our jurists claim they do, at the same time keeps them from abusing their faculties, as he himself claims that they do; so that one might say that savages are not wicked precisely because they do not know what it is to be good; for it is neither the growth of enlightenment nor the curb of the law, but the calm of the passions and the ignorance of vice that keep them from evil-doing ...' (*DOI* i §35 = P 153 = C 53)

[16] 'There is, besides, another principle which Hobbes did not notice and which, having been given to man in order under certain circumstances to soften the ferociousness of his amour propre or of the desire for self-preservation prior to the birth of amour propre, tempers the ardour for well-being with an innate repugnance to see his kind suffer.' (*DOI* i §35 = P 154 = C 53)

[17] 'Self-love is a natural sentiment which inclines every animal to attend to its self-preservation and which, guided in man by reason and modified by pity, produces humanity and virtue. Amour propre is only a relative sentiment, factitious and born in society, which inclines every individual to set greater store by himself than by anyone else, inspires men with all the evils they do one another, and is the genuine source of honour. This being clearly understood, I say that in our primitive state, in the genuine state of nature, amour propre does not exist.' (*DOI* i, n 15 = P 219 = C 106) Contrast this description of amour propre with Dent, *R* 25.

for my actions, I must already conceive my actions as either deserving or not deserving approval; hence I must already have thought of myself as a judge who could make the relevant judgments about my own actions. In that case, amour propre seems to be present in me without reference to other people; or at least, it presupposes something more than the mere desire for self-preservation that Rousseau attributes to the state of nature.

We might understand amour propre differently, without any reference to judgment by standards. When we recognize that we need other people's help, and that others are a danger to us, we might both want their favourable opinion of us and want to excel them, so that they both honour us and fear us. But these attitudes to others might simply recognize them as possible instruments and possible obstacles to the pursuit of our own aims. If amour propre is the result of these attitudes, it does not necessarily involve self-assessment or attention to assessments by others; it simply involves these things as means of making other people less dangerous to us. This purely instrumental conception of amour propre, however, falls short of what Rousseau seems to intend. He claims that 'it is reason that engenders amour propre' (*DOI* i §35 = P 156 = C 54); amour propre seems to respond to some demand of reason that was present from the beginning.

To confirm this suggestion that the rational basis of amour propre is present from the beginning, we might appeal to Rousseau's claim that in the most primitive condition human beings are free and perfectible (*DOI* i §§16–17 = P 142–3 = C 45). To explain how freedom and perfectibility affect human action, we might appeal to our responsiveness to reasons. We recognize our freedom when we notice that we are inclined to do x, but see better reasons to do y, and therefore choose to do y. Because we can recognize the better course of action, and can act on our recognition, we can take steps towards something better, and to that extent we are perfectible. But this account of freedom and perfectibility implies that we judge our actions by reasons and norms; we see that we ought to act one way, even if we are inclined to act another way. Hence we consider ourselves as 'others' judging our future and past actions. We do not have to wait for other people to impose standards on us by their judgments.

Rousseau's description suggests, therefore, that the state of nature contains more than he acknowledges. It seems to include those aspects of self-assessment that make us responsive to the judgments of qualified judges—whether ourselves or other people. This initial responsiveness to qualified judges seems more important than the mere presence of other people.

A defender of Rousseau might reply that this objection does not affect his general view. We ought to expect that the state of nature will include something that explains why we care about other people's judgment of us; otherwise the growth of amour propre would be difficult to understand. In pointing out the implications of Rousseau's remarks on freedom and perfectibility, we simply explain why human beings in the state of nature are capable of development in the direction that he describes.

It is not so easy to defend Rousseau on this point, however. For his whole account of the state of nature emphasizes the guidance of self-love and pity, without the critical and reflective judgments that are characteristic of practical reason and morality. He supposes that in the state of nature human beings are not rational and social. But if we have correctly interpreted his claims about freedom and about perfectibility, critical rational judgment is present from the beginning. Once we recognize a standard for judgment external to our immediate inclinations, we can recognize it in other people as well as ourselves. Rousseau's picture of an initial state in which we are guided by unreflective self-love and pity does not seem to fit even the presuppositions of his own account.

The growth of society and culture begins with social contacts, initially casual, but gradually becoming more permanent. People gradually come to pay more attention to other people and to their opinion.[18] But this degree of attention to others does not yet introduce the specific forms of modern society. It still falls short of the inflamed amour propre of modern life.[19] The distinctive aspects of modern society depend on the expansion of desires that makes co-operation and inter-dependence necessary for the satisfaction of our various desires. Since some people can determine the terms of co-operation, co-operation introduces inequality; inequality introduces arrogance, on the one hand, and envy and humiliation, on the other.

Exaggerated amour propre is partly the effect and partly the cause of this development.[20] The desire to be admired by other people encourages us to appear to have the qualities that they admire; hence amour propre encourages deception. Once this cycle begins, it reinforces itself. Amour propre encourages inequality, and inequality inflames amour propre, both in the arrogant winners and in the angry losers.

This cycle of inequality, arrogance, and anger produces the condition that Hobbes identifies with the state of nature. Rousseau suggests that Hobbes is right to regard the state as a way out of the war of all against all. He disagrees with Hobbes in arguing that the war of all against all is not the state of nature, but the product of a development that includes a level of amour propre that was absent from the state of nature.

This disagreement with Hobbes leads Rousseau to question one of Hobbes's assumptions about the difference between the state of nature and the commonwealth. Hobbes seems to assume—though this is not always clear—that conflict in the state of nature results from one's insecure possession of one's share of a limited stock of goods, and that once the state ensures secure possession, the source of conflict will disappear. Rousseau suggests that conflict results not from insecurity alone, but also, and more basically, from the competitive aspects of amour propre. We can find some support for this view in Hobbes also.[21] In that case the foundation of a commonwealth does not ensure the end of the conflict that arose in the state of nature. It removes the tendency towards conflict that arises from insecure possession; but it does not remove the tendency that arises from amour propre, or from the passion that Hobbes calls 'glory'.

[18] 'Everyone began to look at everyone else and to wish to be looked at himself, and public esteem acquired a price; . . . from these first preferences arose vanity and contempt on the one hand, shame and envy on the other . . .' (*DOI* ii§16 = P 169–70 = C 64)

[19] 'Thus, although men now had less endurance, and natural pity had already undergone some alteration, this period in the development of human faculties, occupying a just mean between the indolence of the primitive state and the petulant activity of our amour propre, must have been the happiest and the most lasting epoch.' (*DOI* ii§18 = P 171 = C 65)

[20] 'Here, then, are all our faculties developed, memory and imagination brought into play, amour propre interested, reason become active, and the mind almost at the limit of the perfection of which it is capable. . . . consuming ambition, the ardent desire to raise one's relative fortune less out of genuine need than in order to place oneself above others, instils in all men a black inclination to harm one another, a secret jealousy that is all the more dangerous as it often assumes the mask of benevolence in order to strike its blow in greater safety; in a word, competition and rivalry on the one hand, conflict of interests on the other, and always the hidden desire to profit at another's expense; all these evils are the first effect of property, and the inseparable train of nascent inequality.' (*DOI* ii§27 = P 174–5 = C 67)

[21] See *L*. 17.8 quoted in §491. Derathé, *RSPST* 139–40, compares Rousseau with Hobbes on the role of pride.

Rousseau sees this implication of his emphasis on amour propre, and so he notices that the state further increases inequality, and hence increases the possible occasions for conflict.[22] Rousseau's conception of the state is on this point closer to Plato's than to Hobbes's. He does not represent the state as a complete solution to the disadvantages of the state of nature. It is only a partial solution; for it also increases inequality, arrogance, and competition, and so tends to promote further conflict and instability (*DOI* ii §§47–56 = P 186–91 = C 76–9).

Though Rousseau describes this development as a story of corruption and increasing misery, his account of it is not purely negative. He suggests that if we value the intellectual and moral excellences of developed reason, we cannot consistently reject the amour propre that has produced them. It would be simple-minded to interpret him as proposing, or even wishing for, the abolition of those features of modern society that have increased inequality, amour propre, and conflict. Indeed, one might take him to argue that it is pointless to compare the characteristics of human beings in modern society with some standard of 'human nature' applicable to all societies and all circumstances. If we examine the state of nature, we see how futile and misguided are the arguments both of traditional naturalists and of Hobbes, who all try to assess the legitimacy of states by reference to an irrelevant conception of human nature.[23]

But if Rousseau intends this anti-naturalist conclusion, his argument, conveyed in the quasi-historical narrative, does not support it. If he were right, we ought to be at a loss to say whether the particular social and cultural developments he describes are appropriate or inappropriate for human beings, given their nature. But we do not seem entirely at a loss for an answer to this question. If Rousseau's story is roughly accurate, we may concede that we ought not to draw hasty conclusions from a comparison between the different historical conditions of human beings. We might even concede that some increase in inequality, competition, and amour propre is necessary for the development of mental characteristics that we take to be important in a rational and reflective agent. We might agree with Rousseau's version of Plato's claim that we must look at the 'swollen city', not at the 'city of pigs', to find genuine virtues, as opposed to people who naturally do the right thing without virtue.[24] But the fact that the natural capacities of human beings are most easily seen in a form of social life in which they have been more fully developed ought not to surprise us. Nor should it convince us that these capacities are not really part of human nature.

Rousseau's quasi-historical story raises a question that leads us back to a naturalist outlook. If we grant that inflamed amour propre, competition, inequality, avarice, deception, and so

---

[22] 'Such was, or must have been, the origin of society and of laws, which gave the weak new fetters and the rich new forces, irresistibly destroyed natural freedom, forever fixed the law of property and inequality, transformed a skilful usurpation into an irrevocable right, and for the profit of a few ambitious men henceforth subjugated the whole of mankind to labour, servitude, and misery.' (*DOI* ii §33 = P 178 = C 70)

[23] 'In thus discovering and retracing the forgotten and lost paths that must have led man from the natural state to the civil state . . . any attentive reader cannot but be struck by the immense distance that separates these two states . . . He will sense that, since the mankind of one age is not the mankind of another age, the reason why Diogenes did not find a man is that he was looking among his contemporaries for the man of a time that was no more. . . . In a word he will explain how the human soul and passion, by imperceptible adulterations, so to speak change in nature; why in the long run the objects of our needs and pleasures change; why as original man gradually vanishes, society no longer offers to the eyes of the wise man anything but an assemblage of artificial men and factitious passions which are the product of all these new relationships, and have no true foundation in nature.' (*DOI* ii §57 = P 191–2 = C 80)

[24] Plato, *Rep.* 372e.

on, have been historically necessary for the expression of rational and social capacities, we may still ask whether they are necessary to sustain and to develop these capacities further. If they are, we may decide that we have to put up with them. If they are not, we may ask whether we can reasonably try to get rid of them or to reduce them. We may grant that if the tendencies to conflict and inequality continue, they will also tend to produce desires that cannot be satisfied without their continuation; but this does not show that we ought or ought not to allow these tendencies to continue.

Rousseau shows, therefore, how we might ask reasonable questions about whether certain kinds of economic, social, and political developments are or are not on the whole harmful to the people whose lives and desires are formed by them. The fact that we can ask these questions shows that we have some conception of what people are like that is distinct from their having the desires that are formed by a given social or political condition. This conception is a conception of human nature.

For these reasons, reflexion on Rousseau's narrative in the *Discourse* may lead us in different directions. On the one hand, Rousseau appears to argue for an anti-naturalist conclusion, rejecting the possibility of external moral criticism of a given form of society. But, on the other hand, he also argues that modern society is in some ways better and in other ways worse than its predecessors. This argument tends to support naturalism, since the judgments about better and worse rest on some conception of human nature, apart from the effects of a particular society. Rousseau's observations, therefore, are more congenial to traditional naturalism than he intends them to be.

886. The Relation of the *Social Contract* to the *Discourse*

The last part of the *Discourse* contains a short account of the origin of states and governments (*DOI* ii §§31–4 = P 177–9 = C 69–70), which Rousseau defends against other people's views. He argues that an agreement to set up the state is a remedy for the ills of the Hobbesian war of all against all. Rousseau believes that the state is both a remedy for these ills and a source of further ills. It appeals to people who 'had too much greed and ambition to be able to do for long without their masters' (*DOI* ii §32 = P 177 = C 69). But in safeguarding possessions and assuring security states also reduce freedom.[25] From the point of view of people suffering from inflamed amour propre and its effects, the state is not wholly satisfactory, but it is the best option in the circumstances.

The *Social Contract*, published seven years later, seems to begin with the situation that the *Discourse* tries to explain.[26] When he dismisses the question of how human beings lost their primitive freedom, he seems to dismiss a question similar to the one he discusses in the

---

[25] 'All ran toward their chains in the belief that they were securing their freedom; for while they had enough reason to sense the advantages of a political establishment, they had not enough experience to foresee its dangers; those most capable of anticipating the abuses were precisely those who counted on profiting from them, and even the wise saw that they had to make up their mind to sacrifice one part of their freedom to preserve the other, as a wounded man has his arm cut off to save the rest of his body.' (*DOI* ii §32 = P 177–8 = C 69)

[26] 'Man was [or "is"?] born free, and everywhere he is in chains. The one who thinks he is master of others does not avoid being more of a slave than they are. How did this change happen? I do not know. What can make it legitimate? I believe I can resolve this question.' (*SC* i 1.1 = P 352 = C 141) I cite *SC* by book, chapter, and paragraph.

Discourse. There he offers an account not of how the change from primitive freedom to the state did happen, but of how it might have happened. The *Social Contract* does not explicitly raise this question, but Rousseau seems to set it aside together with the question about how the change did happen. In *Emile* his summary of political theory seems to introduce the social contract in order to explain how states could have come about.[27] But this is not the question that seems to concern him in the *Social Contract*. Here he asks about the legitimacy of the condition of subjection that we find in states. If we agree that human beings are born free, we may ask how it could be legitimate to introduce subjection.

Does a Hobbesian account of the state, or the sort of account that Rousseau offers in the *Discourse*, answer the question about legitimacy? These accounts do not commit the error that Rousseau criticizes in the *Social Contract*; for they do not treat the state simply as the result of conquest or superior force. They try to give reasons for accepting it that are not simply reasons for acquiescing in a conquest or for acceding to a threat of force. Rousseau argues that in the circumstances created by inflamed amour propre, the sacrifice of some freedom is reasonable if we are to preserve other freedoms, just as we have an arm cut off to save ourselves from death. This does not seem to be purely prudential legitimacy. One might argue that from the moral point of view it is reasonable, in the circumstances that Rousseau describes, to sacrifice some liberties for the sake of others.

This is how Rousseau seems to conceive the condition for which the social contract is to be a solution.[28] One might take a 'legitimate' solution to be one that improves the situation of conflict and instability in the state of nature, because it is better overall than the state of nature, even if it is worse in some respects. We might call this 'relative legitimacy' or 'legitimacy in the circumstances'. According to this conception, it is relatively legitimate to do x rather than y if, given the circumstances, x and y are the only options and x is better than y.

But this relative legitimacy does not ensure a more demanding sort of legitimacy, which we may call 'legitimacy simpliciter'. If we ought not to have got into the circumstances where we face a choice between x and y, it is possible that neither x nor y is legitimate simpliciter, even though x rather than y may be legitimate in the circumstances. If our acting wrongly leads us into a situation where our only options are all wrong, it does not become legitimate simpliciter to do the least wrong, but only legitimate in the circumstances. If the circumstances are alterable, then perhaps we ought not to do any of the actions that are legitimate in the circumstances, but ought to alter the circumstances.

These simple thoughts about legitimacy affect our interpretation of Rousseau's question about the legitimacy of the state. Does he simply try to show that it is legitimate in the circumstances, given the bad aspects of the state of nature? Or does he believe it is legitimate simpliciter, because it is better in a wider range of circumstances? We might gather from the *Discourse* that we would be better off without the state if we did not suffer from the bad effects of the more primitive forms of social life that are both effect and cause of amour propre. Is this still the view of the *Social Contract*?

---

[27] See *Emile* v = P 839–40 = Bloom 460 = Foxley 424.

[28] 'I suppose that human beings reached a point where the obstacles to continuing in the state of nature were stronger than the forces that each individual was able to employ in order to maintain himself in this state. This primitive state, therefore, can endure no longer, and the human race would have perished if it had not changed its manner of existence.' (*SC* i 6.1 = P 360 = C 147)

The questions that arise here are similar to those raised by 'remedial' views of virtue and morality. Hume describes the circumstances of moderate scarcity and limited benevolence in which justice is a genuine virtue.[29] Similar limitations in external conditions and in human beings might be obstacles for which other virtues are remedies. The claim that the virtues are remedial is plausible, if it means only that they have this remedial function. It is more controversial if it means that their remedial function exhausts their character as virtues, and that they would not be virtues if the ills that they remedy no longer existed. Similarly, we might ask Rousseau whether we would have to take the state to be illegitimate if we made less pessimistic assumptions about the evils we would face without it.

These questions about what Rousseau means by 'legitimacy' are connected to questions about the point of his argument about legitimacy. Does he intend to decide whether existing states are morally acceptable by deciding whether they meet his conditions for legitimacy? If we find that a particular state is not legitimate, by his conditions, must we take ourselves to be morally obliged, or morally free, to disregard its laws and institutions? Or might legitimacy come in degrees, so that a state might approach legitimacy closely enough to have a moral claim on us?

These questions become important if Rousseau's conditions for legitimacy prove to be demanding, so that all or most actual states fail them. Should we conclude that Rousseau requires us to be anarchists? Or that his conditions are pointlessly strict and irrelevant to social and political reality? Or that his argument about legitimacy serves some other moral or political purpose apart from the condemnation of existing states?

887. Why is a Social Contract Needed?

Rousseau clarifies his demand for a legitimation of the state by his critical review of other people's attempts to answer the question. He seeks to show that (as the title of chapter 5 says) 'we must always go back to a first convention'. We ought to be able to see why the first convention, or social contract, satisfactorily answers a question that other people cannot answer with their alleged sources of legitimacy.

The alleged 'right' of the strongest cannot answer the question about legitimacy because it does not answer a moral question.[30] We do not answer the question about legitimacy simply by showing that it is prudent to accept a state. We answer it only by showing that we have a moral duty. But mere superior force does not by itself create a moral duty. A moral duty arises only when the superior force is exercised legitimately.[31] This is the argument that Cudworth uses against Hobbes to show that the sovereign's superior power or command does not create a right to rule, but leaves open the further question about moral legitimacy.

Any attempt to extend a right of conquest to legitimate the dominion resulting from conquest is equally hopeless. Rousseau argues against this 'right' by pointing out that it

---

[29] See Hume, T iii 2.2.16; I 3.1–6. Reid comments at H 659ab. See §851. On a remedial conception of virtue see §326.

[30] 'Strength is a physical power; I do not see at all what morality can result from its effect. To yield to force is an act of necessity, not of will; it is at most an act of prudence. In what sense could it be a duty?' (SC i 3.1 = P 354 = C 143)

[31] 'Let us agree, then, that strength does not create right, and that one is only obliged to obey legitimate powers.' (i 3.3 = P 355 = C 144)

would include a right to enslave, and that no such right can be admitted. The position he opposes claims that the relation between master and slave is morally legitimate because it imposes on the slave a moral duty to obey. Rousseau does not directly discuss the view that slavery is legitimate because moral questions are not involved in it. He rejects the moral case for slavery because it assumes simultaneously that the slave is a moral subject (having moral duties) and is not (having no rights).

Why should we not answer him by claiming that a slave has moral duties but no moral rights? Rousseau argues that such a claim conflicts with the essential freedom of a moral subject.[32] One might suspect that Rousseau equivocates on different kinds of freedom here. Elimination of free will would indeed (we may agree) eliminate moral agency at all; we could not have moral relations between two agents one of whom lacked free will, and in particular an agent without free will could not be subject to moral obligation. But the freedom of action denied to a slave seems to be compatible with the free will belonging to a moral agent.

Rousseau might argue that he is not equivocating, because the freedom that is denied to a slave is not simply freedom of action, but also the freedom presupposed by moral obligation. If I am subject to moral obligation, I act on reasons that seem good to me from some degree of rational reflexion, not simply on impulses. But in treating someone as a slave, I do not treat him as an agent who acts on reasons. I hold myself to be entitled to treat him as though he were not moved by rational reflexion at all; for I do not recognize an obligation on me to offer him moral reasons at all, and hence I do not impose any moral obligation on him. Rousseau supports this claim by arguing that the alleged convention establishing slavery is one that moral agents could never find any reason for accepting.[33] If I claim the right to treat you as I like irrespective of any reasons you may recognize, I do not treat you as a subject of moral obligation; hence I cannot coherently claim that you are obliged to accept this treatment.

If this is the right way to understand slavery, Rousseau's argument is plausible. But it does not cope with a defence of something very like slavery. If A tells B that A is so much wiser than B, and B is so weak in relation to A, that B would be better off by agreeing to obey A absolutely, to allow A free use of B's property, control over B's movement, and so on, Rousseau's argument would not work. Nor would it work if A argued that B's ancestors had willed B to A as A's property, and that one always ought to follow the provisions of wills. In such circumstances B would in fact be no freer than Rousseau's slaves. But Rousseau is right to say that this relation between A and B is at least a moral relation. A moral reason is being offered to B, and, if it is a good moral reason, it justifies A's demand for B's obedience; A is not claiming the absolute right to treat B without any reference to reasons that might appear to B to constitute an obligation.

---

[32] 'To renounce one's liberty is to renounce one's quality of being a human being, one's rights of humanity, even one's duties. There is no indemnity possible for renunciation of everything. Such a renunciation is incompatible with the nature of a human being; and to remove all liberty from one's will is to remove all morality from one's actions.' (i 4.6 = P 356 = C 144–5)

[33] 'The convention, in short which stipulates on one side an absolute authority, and on the other side an obedience without limits is vain and contradictory. Is it not clear that one who has the right to demand everything from another is not engaged to anything in relation to him, and that this exclusive condition, without equivalent, without exchange, implies the nullity of the act?' (i 4.6 = P 356 = C 145)

Once again, Rousseau rejects an unsuccessful account of legitimacy because it fails to explain why a moral duty is present. He does not show that we could not have prudential reasons to accept slavery. He shows that we could not have moral reasons to have ourselves treated as though we had no moral reasons. If that is what slavery involves, the idea of slavery being morally justified is incoherent.

Instead of trying to find the basis of a state in an analogy with conquest, we may appeal to a deliberate act of constituting someone as ruler. In this spirit Rousseau considers Grotius' suggestion that a people can 'give itself' to a king (i 5.2).[34] If this act of 'giving' is a collective decision, we still need to understand how such a decision is possible. If we say that it is possible because we can bind ourselves by a majority vote, we need to explain why a majority vote is binding (i 5.3). It is binding only if we are obliged to accept the result of a vote even when we have voted in the minority. But in what circumstances are we obliged to accept the result of a vote? I am not obliged to act in accordance with the views of a public opinion poll. Nor am I obliged to accept the result of a vote if I am in prison with five guards who all vote for me to stay in prison, and I am the only one who votes for my release.

Rousseau is right to argue that an appeal to a majority vote simply raises further questions about legitimacy. But such questions are not necessarily answered by appeal to a unanimous vote to accept the results of a majority vote. We can also ask why this unanimous vote should be binding. Why should I not be allowed to change my mind and reconsider my vote for the policy of majority voting? I am not morally free to change my mind in this way if my initial vote for acceptance of majority votes was really an irrevocable promise. But why am I obliged to make an irrevocable promise rather than simply to cast a vote for a system that I might want to change in future?

This simple extension of Rousseau's own argument shows that a mere appeal to a unanimous vote does not settle questions about moral legitimacy. We need to say something more about the circumstances or the content of the vote in order to see why we are obliged to follow its provisions even if we change our mind. Even if we convert the vote into a promise, we still do not explain why this particular promise should be regarded as binding. We need to say more about the circumstances in which we make it, or about the nature of what we promise to do.

And so when Rousseau argues (in i 5) that we must always go back to an original 'convention' or agreement, he underestimates the significance of his previous arguments. For he has shown that resort to a unanimous agreement does not answer all his questions. A unanimous agreement does not by itself oblige; we need to say something about what we have agreed to do. But if we agree that an agreement is not sufficient, should we agree that it is necessary? If we consider the content of what we (allegedly) agree to do, may we not find that we are obliged to do these things whether or not we have agreed to do them?

It is not obvious, therefore, from Rousseau's argument why we must resort to a convention. It is clear why the accounts he has discussed require us to go back further in order to find the moral basis of a state. But it is not equally clear that what we must go back to is an original agreement. To see whether Rousseau is right, we need to look more closely at the sort of agreement that he thinks will answer the questions that have so far remained unanswered.

---

[34] Grotius, *JBP* i 3.8.

888. The Nature of the Contract

In i 6, Rousseau discusses the character of a social contract that will explain the legitimacy of a state. He assumes that we need some concentration of our powers in order to remove the bad features of the state of nature. But how can we legitimately concentrate our powers?[35] We begin from the assumption that an individual owes it to himself to protect and preserve himself, and that he cannot violate this obligation in agreeing to a concentration of powers.

Rousseau argues that we can satisfy this condition only through an association in which an individual 'uniting himself to everyone, nonetheless obeys only himself and remains as free as he was before' (i 6.4). The social contract is meant to satisfy this condition. But why is it a reasonable condition? We might ask some questions about it: (1) Why is self-protection the only aim that deserves to be considered? (2) Why should we insist that each person remain as free as he was before?

The first question might be taken to indicate Rousseau's neglect of natural sociality. If we took the state to fulfil the social aspects of human nature, we would not need to restrict its functions to the protection of all of the constituent individuals. We might recognize that an individual could reasonably consider other aims that are not necessarily instrumental to self-preservation.

This question leads us into the second question. Rousseau seems to defend his claim by arguing that each person's freedom is one of the primary means of his self-preservation, so that it could not be reasonable for him to give it up. But if we ought to consider other things besides self-preservation, might it not be reasonable to consider giving up some freedom in return for some other significant good, especially a good that fulfils our rational and social nature?

Perhaps Rousseau might reply to this objection in the way he replies to defences of slavery, by arguing that in removing freedom we also remove moral agency. But this does not seem to be the sort of freedom that he has in mind in speaking of the freedom that is instrumental to self-preservation. This freedom seems to be the external liberty from other people's instructions, leaving me free to act as I see fit to protect myself. I could surely give up some of this external independence without making myself into something other than a moral agent.

Though Rousseau's argument for the claim that a morally legitimate state must require no sacrifice of freedom is not cogent, perhaps he is alluding to a more general question about freedom. If we follow Hobbes, we may think of the state as a compromise, containing both advantages and disadvantage in comparison with the state of nature, but the best that can be achieved in the circumstances. This is how Glaucon and Adeimantus think of justice, as a compromise between the best but unattainable situation, in which we can commit injustice with impunity, and the worst situation, in which we suffer injustice that we cannot deter or repel.[36] From this Hobbesian point of view, it is unreasonable to insist that when we enter the state we must be as free as we were before. Hobbes's view is just the contrary; we lay

---

[35] 'Such a concentration of powers cannot arise except from the concurrence of a number of people. But, the power and freedom of each person being the primary means of his preservation, how will he pledge them without harming himself and without neglecting the care that he owes to himself?' (i 6.3 = P 360 = C 147–8)

[36] See Plato, *Rep.* 359a.

down our natural liberty in return for something better. Though Rousseau's reference to self-preservation suggests that he accepts Hobbes's starting point, perhaps he does not really accept it. Perhaps he does not really agree that the formation of a state requires us to give up some liberty worth having, and to accept a lesser liberty in return for some other good. But if this is his view, he has not yet argued for it.

His further clarifications of the claim that freedom is undiminished in the state are also unconvincing. He suggests that the interest of the individual and of the whole cannot conflict, because the whole is nothing more than the individuals composing it (i 7.5). This quasi-ontological argument is not very powerful; it seems quite easy to imagine that some measure would promote the preservation of most people by sacrificing some individuals. Rousseau rules out this possibility only if he relies on his doctrine of the general will, which he develops only later.

It is equally difficult to understand how Rousseau justifies two claims that deny the Hobbesian view of the state as a compromise or bargain. (1) Each individual must surrender all his rights (i 6.6). (2) In surrendering these rights, each individual gives himself to all, and thereby gives himself to no one (i 6.8). The second claim counteracts the impression that we may gain from the first claim, that participation in a social contract involves a significant reduction of freedom.

The argument for the first claim is derived from the need for unity in the state.[37] Rousseau assumes that if individuals reserve rights against the state, there could be no common authority to pronounce on them. But his assumption is difficult to understand. If I retain, for instance, a right to property or to privacy, I might also want to set up laws and agencies to define this right, and to protect the appropriate degree of privacy. But even if Rousseau were right on this point, he would not be entitled to infer that if some things are left to private judgment, everything must be.

It is equally implausible to claim that if everyone equally renounces each right, no one really restricts his freedom or rights, or makes any sacrifice. If each of us has $20, and each contributes $10 to a common fund, no one worsens his position relative to anyone else. But still each of us becomes $10 poorer, and if each of us has to pay $20 for rent, none of us can afford the rent any longer. This may be a misleading analogy for what Rousseau has in mind in speaking of equally giving oneself to all; but he does not explain why it is misleading.

His claim that when we enter a state we are as free as we were before affects his argument for coercion by the state. He allows that an individual may have an individual will different from the general will that he has as a citizen.[38] The general will has the common interest as its object. Each person has the general will insofar as he is a citizen, but this is not his only will. He is not indifferent to the common interest, but he supposes that a little free-riding,

---

[37] 'For should there be any rights left to individuals, since there would be no common superior empowered to pronounce between them and the public, each person, being his own judge on some point, would soon claim to be judge on all points.' (i 6.7 = P 361 = C 148)

[38] 'His particular interest can speak to him quite differently from the common interest; his absolute and naturally independent existence can make him regard what he owes to the common cause as a free (gratuite) contribution, the loss of which will be less harmful to others than its payment is burdensome for him; and looking on the moral person constituting the state as a being of reason because it is not a man, he would enjoy the rights of the citizen without wanting to fulfil the duties of the subject—an injustice whose progress would cause the ruin of the political body.' (i 7.7 = P 363 = C 150)

offering large benefits to him and only a small harm to the common interest, is sometimes rational for him. In that case the state coerces him, but it does not merely coerce him.[39] The coercion involves forcing him to be free, because it forces him to stick to the terms of the initial agreement.

This claim introduces a new complication in Rousseau's views about freedom. We have seen that he believes the state does not reduce our freedom, since it leaves us as free as we were before. But now he also suggests, in his defence of coercion, that we are freer when we follow the general will than we are in following our individual will. If this were not so, coercing us to follow the general will would not force us to be free; we would be free in any case, if we simply followed our individual will. Forcing us to conform to the general will might not make us less free; but it is not obvious so far why it should increase our freedom.

889. What is the Civil State?

So far Rousseau's efforts to explain why the state is morally legitimate have not been very successful. He has introduced a series of unsupported claims: that one does not become less free, but actually freer, in a state; that as a citizen one has a general will aiming at the common interest; that one gives up all one's rights, but still remains free. But in chapter 8, 'on the civil condition (état)', the point of his argument becomes clearer. Until now he has followed Hobbes in supposing that we view the state as a means of self-preservation. The general will and the common interest, as far as we can gather from what we have been told, are concerned with this particular aim. But in chapter 8, Rousseau shows that this is not his point of view in evaluating the state.

He now attends to the ways in which the state changes and re-directs the individual to justice from instinct and from appetite to reason and morality.[40] Though we lose some advantages that we had in the state of nature, we gain benefits of far greater value. By this Rousseau does not mean what he meant in earlier chapters, that the state is more effective for our self-preservation than we would be without its help. He means that the changes in our outlook resulting from the state are clearly preferable to our previous outlook.

How are we to take this claim? Rousseau defends it from the point of view of someone who has passed from the state of nature to the civil state.[41] We take the point of view of someone looking back to his previous state, and feeling grateful that he is no longer in that old state. But what would be the result of a comparison in the other direction? Do people in the state of nature prefer the civil state to the one they are currently in? It is difficult to see

---

[39] '... whoever refuses to obey the general will will be coerced to it by the whole body. And this signifies just that one will force him to be free; for such is the condition which, giving each citizen to his country, guarantees him against all personal dependence' (i 7.8 = P 364 = C 150).

[40] 'It substitutes justice for instinct in his conduct, and gives to his actions the morality that they previously lacked. It is only then that, the voice of duty succeeding physical impulse and right succeeding appetite, a man, who until now had regarded nothing but himself, sees himself forced to act on other principles and to consult his reason before listening to his inclinations.' (i 8.1 = P 364 = C 150–1).

[41] '... if the abuses of this new condition did not often degrade him to a point below the one he has left, he would have to bless without ceasing the happy moment that took him from that old condition for ever, and that made him, from a stupid and limited animal, into an intelligent being and a man' (i 8.1 = P 364 = C 151).

how they could, if they are really 'stupid and limited' animals. If preference is being used as an index of superiority, we have no better reason to say that the civil state is superior to the natural state than to draw the contrary conclusion. We must rely on some other basis for the judgment that one of the two conditions is better than the other.

To see what Rousseau means, we have to recognize an ambiguity in his account of the change that results from the civil condition. He might mean either of two things: (1) Once we have entered the civil condition, we begin a process of education and development that eventually makes us rational persons rather than unintelligent animals. (2) Insofar as we are in a civil condition we are rational persons rather than unintelligent animals. According to the first claim, the civil condition is the environment in which we develop the relevant characteristics. According to the second claim, the civil condition is simply the condition that follows from our being rational agents.

These two claims have contradictory implications. According to the first, we cannot already be intelligent rational agents when we enter a civil state; rational agency must be its product rather than its starting point. According to the second claim, our being in a civil condition already includes rational agency. But though we must choose between the two claims on this question, they are compatible on some other points. For we might agree that rational agency implies the civil condition while still arguing that if we exercise our civil condition by behaving like rational agents, we strengthen our tendency to behave in this way, so that stable and fully developed rational agency may be a product of the civil condition.

To decide what Rousseau means, or what would fit his argument best, we have to face the wider question about how to interpret the historical form of his descriptions of human nature. In the *Discourse* he described the formation of various human traits preceding the state and making it necessary. Some such description seems to underlie the *Social Contract* also. If we take this historical account seriously, we may conclude that there is no definite human nature for which the state is especially appropriate; different forms of social life create the relevant types of human nature, and there is no fixed human nature present both in the social forms preceding the state and in the civil condition.

But we need not take Rousseau to describe a historical development. We may instead take the 'pre-civil' natural condition to be an abstraction from human nature, to show us what human beings would be like without their civil condition. Our civil condition, so understood, is not added to human nature; it is simply the aspect of human nature that makes us capable of relations to others as fellow-citizens.

This second way of understanding Rousseau's historical story makes it easier to see the point of comparing the natural condition with the civil condition. When we compare the two, we see that by being in a civil state, we act as rational and free agents, whereas we do not actualize these aspects of ourselves in the types of action that do not involve the relations that belong to a civil state. This account of the civil state explains why we can reasonably compare it with the non-civil state and judge it better.

Such a defence of the civil state, however, raises a difficulty for Rousseau's argument against traditional naturalism. He suggests that naturalism makes the same mistake as Hobbes makes, in attributing to human nature properties that are really the outcome of historical and social development. But now we have seen that his comparison of the civil state with the natural state is convincing if and only if we take the civil state to realize the capacities that are already present in human beings, rather than creating a different human nature. In that case, Rousseau has no basic objection to the traditional naturalist claim that political association is appropriate for rational and social nature.

890. What Difference does the Civil State Make?

The civil state, according to Rousseau, differs from the state of nature because it introduces the rule of reason rather than passion. He expresses this contrast in different ways; sometimes he opposes physical impulse (impulsion physique) to duty (devoir), at other times appetite to right (droit), or self-regard to other principles, or inclinations (penchants) to reason, or animal to human being, or the impulse of appetite to obedience to one's own law. These do not seem to be different contrasts. Rousseau's freedom in passing from one to another suggests that he takes them all to express the same basic difference.

What is this basic difference? Rousseau cannot mean, consistently with his other views, that a human being in the state of nature is altogether lacking in practical reason, or simply at the mercy of appetites. If he meant this, he would be rejecting the elaborate and subtle account of the natural condition of human beings, their amour propre, and the development of the Hobbesian state of nature. This account assumes that people have a conception of themselves as mattering to other people, that they want to matter more to them, and that they take steps to increase their significance to others. Nor would it be plausible to claim that a person in this condition is concerned only with himself. Even apart from the other-directed concerns that may arise from amour propre, Rousseau recognizes pity as a primitive impulse that extends an individual's concerns outside herself.

Even if we were to suppose that in the *Social Contract* Rousseau has forgotten or rejected all these claims in the *Discourse*, we have to face another apparent contradiction within the *Social Contract* itself. For the account of the state of nature would be incomprehensible if it did not describe the reactions of rational agents to their circumstances. In the *Social Contract* as in the *Discourse*, people in the state of nature are aware of the dangers they face, and of the prospect of security to be found in the state, and they are capable of taking action to reach the more secure conditions of the state. One has to recognize these aspects of rational agency outside the civil state.

In fact the issues are not so simple. We noticed in discussing Hobbes that the official Hobbesian account of practical reason may not be adequate for the official Hobbesian account of our escape from the state of nature. Hobbes suggests that deliberation and practical reason may be understood as reasoning about how to satisfy our prevalent desire; it is because we have a prevalent desire for security that reason suggests the articles of peace (L. 13.14). If this is an adequate account of the state of nature, we can reach the state without actually being guided by reason; we are guided simply by our prevalent desire, and reason has a purely instrumental function. If Rousseau agrees with Hobbes on this point, he can defend his claim that outside the civil state we behave as animals rather than rational agents.

But if this is Rousseau's position, it is difficult to see how he can claim that the civil state makes such a difference. Hobbes believes that even when we are in a commonwealth his account of practical reason remains true of us. Admittedly, once we are in a commonwealth, private appetite ceases to be the measure of good and evil (*L.* 15.40); but this is simply a demand of Hobbesian instrumental reason, since peace and security require private appetite to cede this function. The basic reason for formulating and for obeying moral principles is our (presumed) overriding desire for peace. Perhaps Rousseau believes we ought not to be convinced by Hobbes's description of the civil state; but if we are not, how can we be convinced by his account of our escape from the state of nature? It is difficult to see how Rousseau could recognize only Hobbesian instrumental practical reason in the state of nature, but genuine control by reason in the civil state.

Here we have a further reason for rejecting a developmental account of Rousseau's claims about the natural and the civil state; he seems to damage his own position if he claims that the civil state is a later stage resulting from our emergence from the natural state. It is more plausible to treat the natural state as an abstraction—what we are left with if we remove the relations that belong to the civil state. Rousseau claims, according to this view, that without the civil state all we have left is Hobbesian agency.

This does not mean that we have to be members of an actual political body in order to be rational agents. Rousseau may be referring to the relations that make us capable of being citizens, and arguing that these relations are necessary for rational agency. If he is right about this, states are appropriate for human beings because they fulfil their rational capacities, not simply because they fulfil the Hobbesian functions of providing peace and security.

891. How does the Civil State Realize Freedom?

What, then, is the distinctive feature of the civil state that justifies Rousseau in claiming that it results in rule by reason rather than impulse? This is not obvious from what he has already told us about the state. We know that it involves the surrender of rights without a decrease in freedom, and the adoption of a general will aiming at the common interest; these features justify the state in forcing us to be free if we do not feel inclined to agree with the general will. Why should we believe that if we live under such a system we are ruled by our own reason?

Rousseau answers this question at the end of chapter 8, in claiming that the civil condition includes moral freedom.[42] We should not regard the civil condition as simply a limitation on freedom. It rests on the principles that a free person chooses, because it rests on principles founded in practical reason rather than in non-rational impulse.

The claim that a significant type of freedom consists in being governed by reason rather than by impulse is plausible and familiar. If we take freedom to require guidance by the will and not simply by inclination, and we take the will to be essentially rational, freedom consists in guidance by practical reason. Rousseau is therefore justified in claiming that if we require someone to act on principles prescribed by practical reason, we are in a certain respect forcing him to be free. We are not forcing him to be free if we simply force him to

---

[42] '...moral freedom, which alone makes a person truly master of himself. For the impulse of appetite alone is slavery, and obedience to the law that one has prescribed to oneself is freedom.' (i 8.3 = P 365 = C 151)

act as he would act if he were guided by practical reason; if we were doing that, we would simply be requiring him to do what a free person, guided by practical reason, would do. Rousseau is wrong if he means to claim that compelling action is forcing to be free. He would be right, however, if he meant that if the state makes it obligatory to be guided by practical reason, it forces us to be free; it obliges us to be guided by principles that may sometimes conflict with our inclination.

But why are we acting on practical reason only if we take the point of view of Rousseau's citizen? We can find a partial and inadequate answer if we return to the Hobbesian element in Rousseau's argument. If we are guided by practical reason, we see that we have good reason to enter a state to avoid the bad aspects of the state of nature; this is not simply a conclusion of instrumental reason following a prevalent impulse. Hence acceptance of the state is characteristic of the outlook of practical reason.

But this does not suffice to make us the sort of citizen that Rousseau has in mind in speaking of the civil state. If we simply treat the state as a means to secure peace, it is not obvious why we should take the point of view of the general will concerned with the common good. I may find it useful to see what the common good requires, if that is the best way to secure peace. But it is not obvious that I will care about the common good for its own sake. If other people are so indifferent or blind to their own interest that they are willing to support the state even if they do not gain from it, that does not matter to me if I care only about the preservation of peace.

Rousseau assumes that the general will concerned with the common interest for its own sake uniquely expresses the point of view of practical reason. Reason, he assumes, treats us all equally as rational agents. This assumption becomes explicit only at the end of Book i.[43] This moral equality is the equality of rational agents. From the rational point of view, rational agency is an appropriate basis for equal treatment.

Why does Rousseau claim this? He might mean that sometimes my inclinations lead me to distort my view so that I act irrationally; and he may infer that any time I prefer myself to someone else, that is because of my own inclinations leading me to act irrationally. This would not be a reasonable inference; for we still need to be convinced that only an irrational inclination could lead me in general to suppose that my own interests matter more than other people's.

He implies that, from the point of view of practical reason, I count for myself as a rational agent; it is my being a rational agent that makes it reasonable for me to treat myself as I do. Hence the rational point of view on myself makes it reasonable for me to treat other rational agents in the same way, and hence to recognize the equality (in this respect) of rational agents.

This interpretation of Rousseau's position makes it easy to see why Kant found some aspects of his views attractive.[44] It does not seem unreasonable to describe Rousseau as implicitly Kantian. But the assumptions he relies on are not exclusively Kantian. We have

---

[43] 'I will end this chapter and this book with a remark that ought to serve as the basis for the whole social system. It is that in place of (au lieu de) destroying natural equality, the basic compact substitutes on the contrary a moral and legitimate equality for whatever physical inequality nature may have placed among human beings, and that, while being unequal in strength or in intellect, they all become equal through agreement (par convention) and by right.' (i 9.8 = P 367 = C 153)

[44] See Beck, *CKCPR* 200. Beck, *EGP* 489, quotes Kant's remark on Rousseau from Kant, *GS* xx 44. The relation of Kant to Rousseau is discussed by Schmucker, *UEK*, ch. 4.

seen that the connexion between the rational outlook, impartiality, and morality is present in Butler's conception of conscience. The political interpretation of this conception of morality is as old as Aristotle, who describes law as 'understanding without desire'.[45]

Rousseau's description of the civil state, therefore, is not primarily a description of members of a political society, but of members of a moral community. I am in a civil state in relation to other people insofar as I am guided by impartial moral reason in my treatment of myself and others as moral equals. If we all take this point of view, we will consent unanimously to the basic principles that guide our conduct; hence we can agree with Rousseau that we are bound by a unanimous agreement. But unanimity itself is not important. We might equally say that if we all take the appropriate point of view, any one person's deliberation will be authoritative for the actions of all the others, since each person takes the same impartial point of view. It is not the fact that we have made a contract, or that we have all agreed to something, that confers moral legitimacy; it is the fact that the principles that guide us are justifiable from the moral point of view. The civil condition is really the moral condition.

Hence Rousseau's claims about the differences between the state of nature and the civil state do not really vindicate political society, and do not show that it has the effects he describes. If the 'civil' state is really the moral state, he claims that human freedom, involving guidance by practical reason, is realized in the impartially rational view of morality. I am in a civil state in relation to anyone whom I consider from this moral point of view. Rousseau gives us no reason to suppose that this relation requires the distinctive institutions of a state. On the contrary, membership of a state will promote the civil condition, as Rousseau describes it, only in states that are guided by the impartial moral principles that define the civil condition.

This does not mean that the description of the civil condition is useless for answering Rousseau's original question about the legitimacy of states. His argument implies that a state is legitimate when it accords with the moral principles that represent the civil condition defined by the moral point of view. If it is acceptable to all, or to any one, of the people who take the point of view defined by the civil state, a state is morally legitimate.

Since this condition for legitimacy relies on the content of the moral point of view, Rousseau has not told us much about how to establish legitimacy, since he has not told us much about the moral point of view. But he has told us something. If the institutions of a given state can be justified only on the assumption that the interests of some of its citizens matter more than the interests of others, those institutions are morally illegitimate.

Though this test is still vague, it allows us to avoid a misleading suggestion of Rousseau's argument. Sometimes he appears to be specifying the sort of constitution and government that would make a state legitimate. We might imagine, for instance, that a city-state that established its constitution by unanimous agreement and designed the institutions of government according to Rousseau's prescriptions would thereby be legitimate. This appearance is misleading because the formal devices that Rousseau describes do not guarantee moral legitimacy, as he conceives it. Direct democracy, even requiring unanimous votes on some issues, does not make a state legitimate, since some or all of the voters may fail to take

---

[45] Aristotle, *Pol.* 1287a32 (*nous aneu orexeôs*).

the impartial point of view of morality and some may be too easily persuaded to vote for institutions that cannot be justified from this impartial point of view. The moral conditions for legitimacy are not automatically satisfied by any particular form of constitution; for they require us to choose from the rational and impartial moral point of view that is not guaranteed by any particular constitutional arrangement.

A reasonable interpretation of Rousseau's views on legitimacy should also warn us against treating legitimacy as an all-or-nothing question. In one way, his moral conditions for legitimacy are quite demanding, since they do not allow the automatic endorsement of any particular form of government or constitution. In another way, they are more flexible than (for instance) an endorsement of direct democracy would be. For we might be able to argue that some aspects of a given state are acceptable from a moral point of view, and some are not. If, for instance, a state fails in distributive justice, but achieves a reasonable degree of corrective justice, it may be illegitimate in one respect and legitimate in another. In such a case it may be reasonable neither to endorse it completely nor to regard oneself as free of any moral obligations in relation to it.

We should not necessarily suppose, then, that emphasis on the moral aspect of Rousseau's conditions of legitimacy is bound to make his position more abstract and less practically relevant. This is true in some respects, insofar as the relation between legitimacy and forms of constitution is less clear than he suggests it is. But an emphasis on the moral aspect of his views may also lead to a more realistic and plausible conclusion about the legitimacy of different aspects of different states.

892. How do we Discover the General Will?

We can illustrate this general point about Rousseau by looking more closely at some of his claims about the general will. For they make clear the uneasy relation between 'formal' or 'procedural' and 'substantive' elements in his theory. The 'procedural' elements are those that try to establish moral legitimacy by reference to the ways in which a decision is reached, without reference to any morally substantive assessment of the decision. Though this is a crude division between the procedural and the substantive elements of a decision, it is clear enough to identify some of the different tendencies in Rousseau's position.

Rousseau has introduced the general will in Book i, taking it to aim at the 'common interest' (i 7.6). Each citizen is supposed to have a general will as well as a particular will that may deviate from the common interest. This is an implausible claim if it is taken to mean that each actual member of a state must care about the common interest as well as his particular interest. But a more plausible claim emerges from the explanation of the civil condition. Rousseau means that each person who takes the rational point of view that gives us moral freedom is concerned for a common interest, insofar as each considers each person's interest equally.

This understanding of the general will allows us to see Rousseau's point at the beginning of Book ii, where he traces a consequence of his argument in Book i.[46] He seems to claim

---

[46] 'The first and most important consequence of the principles so far established is that the general will can alone direct the powers of the state in accordance with the end for which it was instituted, which is the common good. For

that a general will aiming at a common interest is needed for the survival of any society. But such a claim seems exaggerated. Perhaps the survival of a given society requires some fairly large proportion of its citizens not to be strongly convinced that they would be better off in some different form of society that they could achieve, or at least not to be convinced that they are being seriously harmed by the present society; but that condition falls a long way short of Rousseau's claim that a society must pursue a common good, or that (if he means this) that people must believe that it pursues a common good. If his claim is taken as a claim in political psychology or sociology, we have good reason to reject it.

But his claim is more plausible if we interpret it in the light of the argument in Book i (as his first words suggest we should), and take it to be about the character of a morally legitimate community. If it is governed by the impartial rational principles that count each person equally, it will aim at some common interest. The interest must be common, since the moral point of view does not pursue the interest of a given person in particular, but aims equally at the interest of any person. The claim that a state should be governed by a general will aiming at the common interest is a claim about the principles that should govern interactions between moral agents. If we accept this claim, we need not agree that every viable state must meet this condition for moral legitimacy, and we need not agree that we should (for instance) uphold or obey only the laws of states that count as wholly legitimate by this standard.

The discussion of 'whether the general will can err' (ii 3) reveals some of the different aims and tendencies in Rousseau's argument. He begins by affirming that it follows from his previous discussion that the general will is always right, and that it always aims at 'public utility' (ii 3.1). This is true because the general will is simply the will that is defined by the impartial and rational outlook of morality. Rousseau sees that this account of the general will excludes one simple procedural account of it. We might have been tempted to infer, from some remarks in Book i, that unanimous consent guarantees a decision of the general will. But now he rejects that simple way of identifying the general will; for he argues that the will of all is different from the general will and cannot be assumed to agree with it (ii 3.2).

Though the general will is inerrant, it does not guarantee the correct conclusion about what the laws should be.[47] References to 'the people' and 'the public' suggest that some group of people in some specific role or aspect can be identified with the general will. In this spirit Rousseau suggests that we can reach the general will from the will of all by removing the 'pluses' and 'minuses' that cancel out (ii 3.2). He mentions an apparently empirical device for removing the individual pluses and minuses of particular wills. Adequate information and inability to communicate would result in the general will.[48] Factions and smaller groups

if the opposition of particular interests has made the establishment of societies necessary, it is the agreement between these same interests that has made it possible. It is what different interests have in common that forms the social tie; and if there were not some point in which all the interests agree, no society could exist. Now it is solely on this common interest that a society can be governed.' (ii 1.1 = P 368 = C 153)

[47] 'The people of itself always wishes the good, but of itself it does not always see it. The general will is always right, but the judgment that guides it is not always enlightened. . . . Individuals see the good that they reject; the public wishes the good that it does not see. . . . Individuals must be obliged to conform their wills to their reason; the public must be taught to recognize (connaître) what it wishes.' (ii 6.10 = P 380 = C 162)

[48] 'If, when the people, sufficiently informed, deliberated, the citizens had no communication among themselves, from the great number of small differences the general will would always result, and the deliberation would always be good.' (ii 3.3 = P 371 = C 156)

within the state prevent the expression of the general will; to reach the general will, these groups should be eliminated, and each citizen should form his opinion only for himself (n'opine que d'après lui, ii 3.4).

These methods for discovering the general will are subtler than a mere appeal to unanimous consent, but they still face objections. Perhaps Rousseau thinks that if we can discount the influence of factions who influence individual decisions systematically over time, we will find that the merely individual differences over questions of public policy are relatively small and the area of consensus is much wider; perhaps this is what he means by removing the pluses and minuses. But it is difficult to see how this process reaches the general will. Complete information plus isolation from others seems to guarantee only that individual prejudices will dominate our decisions; and if we try to extract the pluses and minuses from individual prejudices, we seem to be left only with shared prejudices. We have no reason to suppose that this process will result in a will that aims at the common interest.

The devices for reaching the general will are more plausible if we take them to be aspects of the impartial point of view of morality. We can think of each person deliberating by himself without communication if we assume that he is taking the impartial moral standpoint. For since this standpoint regards the interests of rational agents equally, I do not need other people to urge me to consider their interests; I consider them already if I take the moral point of view. Factions are dangerous to this sort of deliberation because they induce me to give disproportionate weight to some interests that are closely related to my own. This weight is disproportionate in relation to the demands of morality for equal consideration.

Rousseau's devices are therefore defensible if they are taken to be parts of a description of the general will as the outlook of morality. But they are also less significant than we might at first have supposed. For they identify some secondary features of the general will without mention of its most important aspects. His most important claim about the general will is the claim that it expresses a uniquely rational point of view that is also the point of view of morality, giving equal weight to different people's interests. This claim is implied by the assertion that in belonging to a community guided by the general will we achieve the distinctive freedom that consists in being guided by reason rather than inclination.

We may understand Rousseau's account of the state as a description of a moral community—a community governed by the moral outlook that we may reasonably call Kantian. But his attempts to connect this description with claims about constitutions and forms of government are quite implausible. A fuller understanding of the moral point of view, as he conceives it, is needed to give further precision to his description of the general will.

Rousseau partly, but only partly, grasps this point. His attempts to describe effective methods for finding the general will suggest that he has not entirely given up a purely procedural conception, as though it could be adequately described by a set of restrictions on voting. But the difficulty of seeing what these restrictions imply suggests that he does not think a purely procedural description is good enough. The further moral conditions for a general will remain in the background.

893. The Common Good and the General Will

Since the general will wills a common good, the complexities in Rousseau's conception of the general will reappear in some of his claims about the common good. He is not content to claim that the common good should be defined as whatever the general will wills. In saying that the object of the general will is the common good, he offers some further specification of the general will; hence he can reasonably be asked for some argument to show that the general will, as he conceives it, aims at the common good, as he conceives it.

Rousseau treats the common good as good for each person. We achieve it through actions that result from mutual obligation.[49] The reference to mutuality suggests that not every principle willed by the general will must itself promote the common good; mutual obligation ensures that the services I do for others are balanced by those that others do for me. This reciprocity and balance seems to be necessary to make sure that everyone gains by following the general will.[50]

One might conceive the common good as an equal division of goods between all the individuals involved. If there are not enough goods to go round, this equal division will fall short of what I need for my own good, so that I have to be willing to sacrifice my own good. But Rousseau seems to deny that I will face this choice. Perhaps he simply means that achieving my own good at other people's expense is not a real option for me in the circumstances, so that I do the best I can for myself in willing the common good.

If we explain mutuality in this way, we admit that Hobbes's 'fool' raises a relevant question, in suggesting that, without returning to the state of nature, I can sometimes do better for myself if I do not aim at the common good, but try to benefit myself at other people's expense. Does Rousseau's advocacy of the common good depend on the dubious claim that Hobbes's fool always miscalculates his own advantage?

His explanation of the appeal to self-interest is complex. He argues that self-interest is necessary if the general will is to have its appropriately impartial character.[51] This point rests on his previous claim that each person must include himself and his own interest in the common interest. He seems to argue that because each person aims at his own good, but cannot secure it without securing everyone's good, he can will the general good. If, on the other hand, we were judging something 'alien to us', because alien to our good, we would have no principle of equity.

This is difficult to understand, because we might think that even if our good is included in the common good, the fact that the two goods are not identical implies that the common good is something 'alien' to us. But Rousseau's point about self-interest may not be open to this objection. If I think about my own happiness and about its importance to me, and I

---

[49] 'The engagements that bind us to the social body are obligatory only because they are mutual, and their nature is such that in fulfilling them one cannot work for others without working also for oneself.' (ii 4.5 = P 373 = C 157)

[50] 'For why is the general will always right, and why do all will constantly the happiness of each of them, except because everyone appropriates to himself this word "each" and thinks of himself in voting for all?' (ii 4.5 = P 373 = C 157)

[51] 'This proves that the equality of right and the notion of justice that it [sc. the general will] produces derives from the preference that each person gives himself, and consequently from human nature; that the general will, in order to be truly such, must be the general will in its object no less than in its essence; that it must set out (partir de) from all in order to apply to all; and that it loses its natural rightness when it tends to some individual and determined object, because in that case, judging about what is alien (étrange) to us, we have no genuine principle of equity to guide us.' (ii 4.5 = P 373 = C 157)

also recall that every rational agent has equal reason to aim at happiness for every rational agent, I will be equally concerned with the happiness of each rational agent. That is why the principles that I accept from this impartial point of view aim at the common good.

If Rousseau takes these features of the moral point of view for granted, he is right to claim that in aiming at the common good I do not necessarily renounce my own happiness; for the common good embraces my own happiness as well as everyone else's. But the fact that I do not necessarily renounce my own happiness does not show that I necessarily achieve it. For even if I aim at everyone's happiness, that may not be achievable; some people's good may require harm to others, and an equal degree of happiness for everyone may prevent anyone from fully achieving happiness. This possibility is especially relevant if everyone's or some people's happiness includes competitive and comparative elements. If, for instance, at least two people's good requires them to excel everyone else in the same respect, what is good for everyone cannot achieve everyone's good, since everyone's good includes the demand that A excel everyone else (including B) and that B excel everyone else (including A).

We might, indeed, expect Rousseau to be particularly attentive to this possibility, since he emphasizes the role of amour propre in generating the conflicts that make it advisable to form a state. If we suppose that we have changed from a primitive condition, so that our good requires the satisfaction of our inflamed amour propre, I must after all sacrifice some element of my good if I am to pursue the common good. Hence the achievement of the common good would not achieve my own good.

Rousseau seems to deny this possibility, since he denies that the social contract implies any renunciation by individuals. We make a profitable exchange, of uncertainty for security, of natural independence for freedom, of power to harm others for protection from harm, of one's own unreliable power to defend oneself for the right that is defended by the state (ii 4.10). The exchanges considered here do not include the objects of amour propre, if these objects are included, it is more difficult to see how the exchange involved in acceptance of the general will is wholly profitable, from the point of view of individuals who have not yet accepted the point of view of the general will.

This difficulty takes us back to our earlier comparison of the *Discourse* with the *Social Contract* on the formation of the state. The *Discourse* suggests a Hobbesian account; we need the state for greater security. But here Rousseau admits that we need it partly because of the effects of our amour propre, which is not entirely checked, and is even given new opportunities to develop within the state. If this is such a prominent motive as Rousseau takes it to be in the *Discourse*, must we not suffer a significant loss in taking the point of view of the general will? For the impartial concern of the general will seems likely to frustrate the outlook of amour propre.

Rousseau has an answer to this objection if he does not take the satisfaction of inflamed amour propre to be part of one's good when one is in the civil condition. We would expect him to say this, given his description of the civil condition. For in the civil condition we replace mere independence with the genuine freedom that consists in being guided by reason rather than impulse. If we take guidance by reason to be a predominant part of one's good, and we take the civil condition to secure this guidance by reason, we can see why acceptance of the outlook of the general will does not imply a sacrifice of any part of one's real good.

But why should we agree that an agent guided by reason will not be influenced by inflamed amour propre? The competitive aspects of amour propre may be traced to a desire to assert oneself in relation to others. This desire to assert oneself may in turn to be traced to a demand for recognition of one's status by others—a demand to be recognized as counting for something.[52] The moral point of view respects this demand for recognition; for it begins from rational self-concern, and accords the same sort of concern impartially to everyone. If we view one another from the point of view of morality, we recognize that each person counts in her own right. We do not need to acquire some competitive advantage in relation to other people in order to count for something in their eyes, or in our own eyes; for our counting for something does not rest on our comparative status, but simply on our status as moral agents.

If Rousseau is right about the outlook of morality, he has a good reason for saying that acceptance of the social contract does not involve renunciation. For, even though the social contract impedes the pursuit of the aims that result from inflated amour propre, it does not involve a genuine loss. For we no longer regard the aims of inflated amour propre as promoting our real good. We now find that the moral point of view includes the appropriate respect for each person. We need not pursue the aims of inflated amour propre in order to secure this respect from other people.

This aspect of Rousseau's position corresponds to Kant's distinction between the predisposition to humanity and the predisposition to personality.[53] The outlook of mere humanity treats practical reason as purely instrumental, and hence does not find in it the source of non-instrumental value in oneself or in others. Rousseau does not explain why the distinctive features of the civil state cancel the effects of inflated amour propre. But he needs to explain this, in order to show why acceptance of the social contract involves no renunciation of genuine goods. An explanation is available to him in the distinctive attitude of the civil state towards practical reason. The civil state is appropriate for people who value the exercise of practical reason for its own sake, and hence value themselves for their own sakes as rational agents. That is why they can claim to pursue a common good in which each person's individual good is achieved. This claim would be false if inflated amour propre rested on a true conception of one's good. But we can undermine the conception of one's good that encourages inflated amour propre, once we discover the value that belongs to us in our own right as rational agents.

The different claims about the state in the *Discourse* and the *Social Contract* represent, therefore, different conceptions of the appropriate relations to others, and of the appropriate conception of oneself and one's value that underlies our relation to others. The *Discourse* develops one strand in a Hobbesian conception of the state. Unlike Hobbes, Rousseau takes inflamed amour propre to be an essential element in human nature, because it results inevitably from one's demand for recognition of one's importance. Hence the state is partly a product of inflamed amour propre, partly a means to avoid its most destructive aspects, but partly also a means to the further expression and satisfaction of amour propre. Rousseau's overall view is on this point less optimistic than Hobbes's view, since he believes that the state removes some sources of conflict and insecurity, but at the same time creates other sources, by offering new opportunities to our competitive motives.

---

[52] Dent, *R*, ch. 2, discusses some of the different aspects of amour propre.   [53] See Kant, *Rel*. 26.

Though Rousseau does not say so, the state as envisaged in the *Social Contract* rejects inflated amour propre. When we are in the civil condition, we do not regard our own practical reason as purely instrumental, and we do not regard other people as mere rivals. We attribute non-instrumental value to each person as a rational agent. Rousseau's description of these attitudes is combined with, and partly distorted by, his attempt to translate them into specific political institutions and forms of government. The most important claims underlying his political theory are basically moral claims. Though he relies on these claims, he does not defend them; for a defence we have to turn to Kant.[54]

This conclusion shows that Rousseau does not really abandon the naturalist view that takes the state to be justified by its appropriateness to human nature, understood as rational and social. His historical or quasi-historical narrative shows that this is not all there is to human nature, and that both traditional naturalist and Hobbesian accounts overlook the significance of motives that are neither desires for bare self-preservation nor distinctively rational desires. But his account of the civil condition shows that he thinks the outlook of amour propre is not the basis for the correct understanding of human beings and their value. He believes that the civil state is the state that reveals the true nature of human beings as rational agents.

[54] Some connexions between Rousseau and Kant are explored by Cassirer, 'Kant and Rousseau'.

BIBLIOGRAPHY

Abercrombie, N. J., *The Origins of Jansenism*. OUP, 1936.

Adams, R. M., 'A modified divine command theory of ethical wrongness', in *The Virtue of Faith and Other Essays in Philosophical Theology*. OUP, 1987, ch. 7.

——*Finite and Infinite Goods*. OUP, 1999.

Adams, W., *The Nature and Obligation of Virtue*, 3rd edn. Shrewsbury, 1776 (1st edn., 1754).

Albee, E., *A History of English Utilitarianism*. London: Swan, Sonnenschein, 1902.

——Review of Selby-Bigge, *BM*. *PR* 7 (1898), 82–6.

Alberigo, J., et al., eds., *Conciliorum Oecumenicorum Decreta*, 3rd edn. Bologna: Istituto per le Scienze Religiose, 1973.

Alphonsus Liguori, *Theologia Moralis*, 2 vols. Turin: Marietti, 1847 (repr. of 9th edn., 1785).

Andrew of Neufchâteau, *Questions on an Ethics of Divine Commands*, ed. J. M. Idziak. Notre Dame, Ind.: University of Notre Dame Press, 1997.

Anon., *A Letter to Mr John Clarke . . . wherein it is showed that he hath treated the learned Dr Clarke very unfairly, that he hath carried the principle of self-love much too far. And that his heavy charge against the author of Beauty and Virtue, may, with more reason, be retorted upon himself*. London: Roberts, 1727.

——Review of Hume, *Treatise*, Book III, in J. Fieser, ed., *Early Responses to Hume*, i (Bristol: Thoemmes, 2004), 1–14. From *Bibliothèque Raisonnée* 26.2 (1741), 411–27.

Anscombe, G. E. M., *Collected Philosophical Papers*, iii: *Ethics, Religion, and Politics*. Minneapolis: University of Minnesota Press, 1981.

——'Modern Moral Philosophy', in *Papers* iii, ch. 4. From *Phil.* 33 (1958), 1–19.

——'On brute facts', in *Papers* iii, ch. 3. From *Analysis* 18 (1958), 69–72.

Aquinas, Thomas, *De Malo* in *Quaestiones Disputatae*, 2 vols., ed. R. Spiazzi et al. Turin: Marietti, 1949.

——*In Decem Libros Ethicorum Aristotelis ad Nicomachum Expositio*, 3rd edn., ed. R. M. Spiazzi. Turin: Marietti, 1964.

——*In Epistulam Pauli ad Romanos*, in *Expositio et Lectura super Epistulas Pauli Apostoli*, 8th edn., 2 vols., ed. R. Cai. Turin: Marietti, 1953.

——*Quaestiones Quodlibetales*, in *Opera Omnia*, 25 vols. Parma: Fiaccadori, 1852–68, vol. ix.

——*Summa Theologiae*, 3 vols., ed. P. Caramello. Turin: Marietti, 1952.

Aristotle, *De Anima*. OCT.

——*Ethica Nicomachea*. OCT.

——*Politics*. OCT.

Atkinson, R. F., 'Hume on is and ought: a reply to Mr MacIntyre', in Chappell, ed., *Hume*, 265–77. From *PR* 70 (1961), 231–8.

Augustine, *De Civitate Dei*, 2 vols., J. E. C. Welldon, ed. London: SPCK, 1924.

——*De Libero Arbitrio*, in *Opera Omnia*, Benedictine edn., 11 vols. Paris: Gaume, 1836–90, vol. i.

Ayer, A. J., *Language, Truth, and Logic*, 2nd edn. London: Gollancz, 1946 (1st edn., 1936).

——'On the analysis of moral judgments', in *Philosophical Essays*. London: Macmillan, 1954, ch. 10. From *Horizon* 20 (1949).

Backus, I., ed., *The Reception of the Church Fathers in the West*, 2 vols. Leyden: Brill, 1997.

——'The Fathers in Calvinist orthodoxy: Patristic scholarship', in Backus, ed., *RCFW*, ch. 21.

Baier, A. C., *A Progress of Sentiments: Reflexions on Hume's Treatise*. HUP, 1991.

Baier, K., 'Moral obligation', *American Philosophical Quarterly* 3 (1966), 210–26.

—— *The Moral Point of View: A Rational Basis of Ethics*. Ithaca, NY: Cornell UP, 1958.

—— *The Rational and the Moral Order*. Chicago: Open Court, 1995.

Balfour, J., *A Delineation of the Nature and Obligation of Morality*, 2nd edn. Edinburgh: Hamilton and Balfour, 1763.

Balguy, J., *A Collection of Tracts Moral and Theological*. London: Pemberton, 1734.

—— *Divine Rectitude: Or a Brief Inquiry concerning the Moral Perfections of the Deity*. London: Pemberton, 1730. Repr. in *TMT*.

—— *The Foundations of Moral Goodness*, Part 1 (1st edn., 1728) and Part 2 (1st edn., 1729). Repr. in *TMT*.

Barbeyrac, J. 'Historical and critical account of the science of morality, and the progress it has made in the world, from the earliest times down to the publication of this work', preface to Pufendorf, *JNG*, tr. B. Kennett, 5th edn. London: Bonwicke et al., 1749.

Barker, E., *Political Thought of Plato and Aristotle*. London: Methuen, 1906.

Barrow, I., *Works*, ed. J. Tillotson, 5th edn., 3 vols. London: Millar, 1741.

Barry, B. M., 'Warrender and his critics', in *HR*, ed. Cranston and Peters, 37–65. From *Phil.* 43 (1968), 117–37.

Bayes, T., *Divine Benevolence: Or an Attempt to Prove that the Principal End of the Divine Providence and Government is the Happiness of his Creatures*. London: J. Noon, 1731.

Bayle, P., *Historical and Critical Dictionary: Selections*, tr. R. H. Popkin. Indianapolis: Bobbs-Merrill, 1965.

Beattie, J., *An Essay on the Nature and Immutability of Truth, in Opposition to Sophistry and Scepticism*, 9th edn. London: Mawman, 1820 (1st edn., 1770).

Beck, L. W., *Commentary on Kant's* Critique of Practical Reason. Chicago: University of Chicago Press, 1960.

—— *Early German Philosophy*. HUP, 1969.

—— ' " Was-must be" and "is-ought" in Hume', *Philosophical Studies* 26 (1974), 219–28.

Beiser, F. C., *The Sovereignty of Reason*. PUP, 1996.

Bennett, J. F., *A Study of Spinoza's Ethics*. Indianapolis: Hackett, 1984.

—— *Locke, Berkeley, Hume: Central Themes*. OUP, 1971.

Bentham, J., *Deontology*, ed. A. Goldworth. OUP, 1983.

Berkeley, G., *Alciphron*, in *Works* iii.

—— 'Passive Obedience', in *Works* vi 1–50.

—— *Works*, 9 vols., A. A. Luce and T. E. Jessup, eds. London: Nelson, 1948–64.

Berman, D., ed., *Alciphron in Focus*. RKP, 1993.

Biel, G., *Collectorium circa quattuor libros Sententiarum*, 4 vols., W. Werbeck and U. Hoffman, eds. Tübingen: Mohr, 1979.

Blackburn, S. W., *Essays in Quasi-Realism*. OUP, 1993.

Blair, H., 'Hutcheson's moral philosophy', *Edinburgh Review* 1 (1755), 9–23.

Bogue, D., and Bennett, J., *History of Dissenters*. London: 1809.

Bolton, M. B., 'Universals, essences, and abstract entities', in Garber and Ayers, eds., *CHSCP*, ch. 8.

Bonar, J., *The Moral Sense*. London: Allen and Unwin, 1930.

Boonin-Vail, D., *Thomas Hobbes and the Science of Moral Virtue*. CUP, 1994.

Bossuet, J-B., 'Instruction sur les états d'oraison', selections in *Bossuet: oeuvres choisies*, J. Calvet, ed. Paris: Hatier, 1917.

Boswell, J., *Boswell's Life of Johnson: Together with Boswell's Journal of a Tour to the Hebrides*, ed. G. B. Hill and rev. L. F. Powell, 6 vols. OUP, 1950.

Bowle, J. W., *Hobbes and his Critics: A Study in Eighteenth-Century Constitutionalism*. London: Cape, 1951.

Boyle, R., *A Free Enquiry into the Vulgarly Received Notion of Nature*, E. B. Davis and M. Hunter, eds. CUP, 1996 (Orig. pub. 1686).

_____ *The Christian Virtuoso, showing that by being Addicted to Experimental Philosophy a Man is rather Assisted than Indisposed to be a Good Christian*. London: James, 1690.

Bramhall, J., *A Defence of True Liberty*. Selections in Hobbes, *LN*, ed. Chappell. From *Works* iv.

_____ *Castigations of Mr Hobbes*, in *Works* iv.

_____ *Discourse of Liberty and Necessity*. Selections in Hobbes, *LN*, ed. Chappell. From *Works* iv.

_____ *The Catching of Leviathan or The Great Whale*, in *Works* iv.

_____ *Works*, 5 vols. Oxford: Parker, 1842–5.

Brandt, R. B., 'The concepts of obligation and duty', *M* 73 (1964), 374–93.

Brender, N., and Krasnoff, L. eds., *New Essays on the History of Autonomy: A Collection Honoring J. B. Schneewind*. CUP, 2004.

Brink, D. O., *Moral Realism and the Foundations of Ethics*. CUP, 1989.

Brissenden, R. F., ' "Sentiment": some uses of the word in the writings of David Hume', in *Studies in the Eighteenth Century*, i. R. F. Brissenden, ed., Canberra: ANU Press, 1968, 89–107.

Broad, C. D., 'Berkeley's theory of morals', *Revue Internationale de Philosophie* 7 (1953), 72–86.

_____ 'Egoism as a theory of human motives', in D. R. Cheney, ed., *Broad's Critical Essays in Moral Philosophy*. London: Allen and Unwin, 1971, ch. 11.

_____ *Five Types of Ethical Theory*. London: RKP, 1930.

_____ 'Some reflexions on moral-sense theories in ethics', *PAS* 45 (1944–5), 131–66.

Brown, C., 'Is Hume an internalist?', *JHP* 26 (1988), 69–87.

Brown, J., *Essays on the Characteristics of Lord Shaftesbury*. London: Davis, 1751.

Brown, K. C., ed., *Hobbes Studies*. Oxford: Blackwell, 1965.

Brown, T., *Lectures on Ethics*. Edinburgh: Tait, 1846.

Buckle, S., *Natural Law and the Theory of Property*. OUP, 1991.

_____ 'Voluntarism, morality, and practical reason', in Haakonssen and Thiel, eds., *RWN* 98–123.

Burlamaqui, J. J., *Principles of Natural Law*, tr. T. Nugent. London: Nourse, 1748.

Butler, J., *The Analogy and Fifteen Sermons*, ed. J. Angus. London: Religious Tract Society, 1855.

Butler, J., *The Works of Bishop Butler*, ed. J. H. Bernard, 2 vols. London: Macmillan, 1900.

_____ *The Works of Joseph Butler*, ed. W. E. Gladstone, 2 vols. OUP, 1896.

Cajetan (Tomasso de Vio), Commentary on Aquinas, *Summae Theologiae*, printed in Aquinas, *Opera Omnia*, editio Leonina. Rome: Typographia Polyglotta, 1882–(incomplete).

Calvin, J., *Ioannis Calvini Opera Selecta*, 5 vols, P. Barth and W. Niessel, eds. Munich: Kaiser, 1952–9.

_____ *Institutes of the Christian Religion*, 2 vols., tr. F. L. Battles, ed. J. T. McNeill. London: SCM, 1960.

_____ *Institutes of the Christian Religion*, tr. H. Beveridge. Edinburgh: Calvin Translation Society, 1845.

Carmichael, Gershom, *Pufendorfi De Officio Hominis . . . auxit et illustravit*. Edinburgh: Mossman, 1724. ET in *Natural Rights on the Threshold of the Scottish Enlightenment: The Writings of Gershom Carmichael*, J. Moore and M. Silverthorne, eds. Indianapolis: Liberty Fund, 2002.

Cassirer, E., 'Kant and Rousseau', in *Rousseau, Kant, Goethe*. PUP, 1945.

_____ *The Platonic Renaissance in England*. London: Nelson, 1953.

Cathrein, V., *Philosophia Moralis in usum Scholarum*. Freiburg: Herder, 1915.

Chappell, V. C., ed., *Hume: A Collection of Critical Essays*. London: Macmillan, 1968.

Chroust, A.-H., 'Hugo Grotius and the Scholastic Natural Law Tradition'. *New Scholasticism* 17 (1943), 101–33.

Chubb, Thomas, *The Comparative Excellence and Obligation of Moral and Positive Duties . . .* London: Roberts, 1730.

Cicero, *Academica*. BT.

_____ *De Finibus Bonorum et Malorum*. OCT.

_____ *De Legibus*. BT.

Cicero, *De Officiis*. OCT.

———— *De Oratore*. OCT.

———— *De Republica*. OCT.

———— *Tusculan Disputations*. BT.

Clarke, J., *Foundation of Morality in Theory and Practice*. York: Gent, 1726.

Clarke, S., *A Demonstration of the Being and Attributes of God* [= *DBAG*], in *Works*, ed. Hoadly, ii.

———— *A Discourse concerning the Obligations of Natural Religion, and the Truth and Certainty of the Christian Revelation* [= *DNR*] in *Works*, ed. Hoadly, ii.

———— *The Works of Samuel Clarke*, 4 vols., ed. B. Hoadly. London: Knapton, 1738 (repr. Bristol: Thoemmes, 2002). Cited as H.

Cockburn, C., 'Remarks on Mr Seed's Sermon on moral virtue', in *Works* ii.

———— *Remarks upon . . . Dr Rutherforth's essay . . .* (1747), in *Works* i 7–107.

———— *Remarks upon some writers in the controversy concerning the foundation of moral virtue . . .*, in *Works* i, 381–455.

———— (Trotter), *Works*, 2 vols. London: Knapton, 1751 (repr. Bristol: Thoemmes, 1992).

Coleridge, S. T., *Marginalia*, ii, ed. G. Whalley. RKP, 1984.

Colley, L., *Britons: Forging the Nation, 1707–1837*. New Haven: Yale UP, 1992.

Colman, J., *John Locke's Moral Philosophy*. Edinburgh: Edinburgh UP, 1983.

Council of Trent; see Denziger and Schönmetzer, *ES*.

Cranston, M., and Peters; R. S., eds., *Hobbes and Rousseau*. Garden City, NY: Doubleday, 1972.

Cronin, T. J., *Objective Being in Descartes and Suarez* (Analecta Gregoriana 154). Rome: Gregorian UP, 1966.

Cudworth, R, *A Treatise concerning Eternal and Immutable Morality, with a Treatise of Freewill*, S. Hutton, ed. CUP, 1996.

———— *A Treatise of Freewill*. Included in *Eternal and Immutable Morality*, ed. Hutton.

———— *A Treatise of Freewill*, J. Allen, ed. London: Parker, 1838 (repr. (together with Scott, *ICTEIM*) Bristol: Thoemmes, 1992).

———— *The True Intellectual System of the Universe*, J. Harrison, ed. Notes by J. Mosheim. 3 vols. London: Tegg, 1845 (repr. Bristol: Thoemmes, 1995).

Culverwell, N. *An Elegant and Learned Discourse of the Light of Nature*, R. A. Greene and H. MacCallum, eds. Toronto: University of Toronto Press, 1971 (repr. Indianapolis: Liberty Fund, 2001). (Orig. pub. London, 1652.) Cited as *LN*.

Cumberland, R., *De Legibus Naturae*. London: Nathanael Hooke, 1672. ET in *A Treatise of the Laws of Nature*, tr. J. Maxwell. London: J. Knapton, 1727 (repr. ed. J. Parkin, Indianapolis: Liberty Fund, 2005).

Cuneo, T., 'Reid's moral philosophy', in *The Cambridge Companion to Thomas Reid*, T. Cuneo and R. van Woudenberg, eds. CUP, 2004, ch. 10.

Cunliffe, C., ed., *Joseph Butler's Moral and Religious Thought*. OUP, 1992.

Curley, E. M., *Behind the Geometrical Method*. PUP, 1988.

Darwall, S. L., 'Autonomy in modern natural law', in Brender and Krasnoff, *NEHA*, ch. 5.

———— *The British Moralists and the Internal 'Ought'*. CUP, 1995.

Davidson, D., 'Actions, reasons, and causes', *JP* 60 (1963), 685–700.

Dent, N. J. H., *Rousseau: An Introduction to his Psychological, Social, and Political Theory*. Oxford: Blackwell, 1988.

Denziger, H., and Schönmetzer, A., eds., *Enchiridion Symbolorum*, 36th edn. Freiburg: Herder, 1976. Cited as 'Denz.' or 'D'.

Derathé, R., *Rousseau et la science politique de son temps*, 2nd edn. Paris: Vrin, 1970 (1st edn., 1950).

Descartes, R., *Oeuvres de Descartes*, C. Adam and P. Tannery, eds. 11 vols. Paris: Cerf, 1894–1913.

De Scorraille, R., *François Suarez*, 2 vols. Paris: Lethielleux, 1913.

Bibliography

Dictionnaire de Théologie Catholique, A. Vacant et al., eds. 15 vols. Paris : Letouzey et Ané, 1903–46.

Diogenes Laertius, *Vitae Philosophorum*. OCT.

Doddridge, P., *A Course of Lectures on the Principal Subjects in Pneumatology, Ethics, and Divinity*, 2nd edn., ed. S. Clarke. London: Buckland, 1776 (1st edn., 1763).

———*Correspondence and Diary*, ed. J. D. Humphreys. London: Colbourn and Bentley, 1829–31.

Dudden, F. H., *Henry Fielding, his Life, Works, and Times*, 2 vols. OUP, 1952.

Duffy, E., 'Wesley and the Counter-Reformation', in J. Garnett and C. Matthew, eds., *Revival and Religion since 1700*. London: Hambledon, 1993, ch. 1.

Duncan, E. H., and Baird, R. M., 'Thomas Reid on Adam Smith's theory of morals', *JHI* 38 (1977), 509–22.

Dworkin, R. M., 'Hard cases', in *Taking Rights Seriously*. HUP, 1977, ch. 4.

Edwards, J., *The Eternal and Intrinsic Reasons of Good and Evil*. CUP, 1699.

Eliot, G., *Middlemarch*, ed. B. G. Hornback. New York: Norton, 1977. (1st pub. 1872.)

English Articles, in Schaff, *CC* iii.

Falk, W. D., ' "Ought" and motivation', in *Ought, Reasons, and Morality*. Ithaca, NY: Cornell UP, 1986, ch. 1. From *PAS* 48 (1947–8), 492–510.

Farrell, W., *The Natural Law according to St Thomas and Suarez*. Ditchling: St Dominic's Press, 1930.

Fiddes, R., *A General Treatise of Morality, formed upon the Principles of Natural Reason only*. London: Billingsley, 1724.

Finnis, J. M., *Natural Law and Natural Rights*. OUP, 1980.

Firth, R., 'Ethical absolutism and the ideal observer', *PPR* 12 (1952), 317–45.

Flew, A. G. N., ' "Not proven"—at most', in Chappell, ed., *Hume*, 291–4.

———'On the interpretation of Hume', in Chappell, ed., *Hume*, 278–86. From *Phil.* 38 (1963), 178–81.

Fowler, T., *Shaftesbury and Hutcheson*. London: Sampson Low, 1882.

Frankena, W. K., 'Concepts of rational action in the history of ethics', *Social Theory and Practice* 9 (1983), 165–97.

———'Hutcheson's moral sense theory', *JHI* 16 (1955), 359–75.

———'Obligation and motivation in recent moral philosophy', in *Perspectives on Morality*, ed. K. E. Goodpaster. Notre Dame, Ind.: University of Notre Dame Press, 1976. Also in Melden (ed.), *EMP* 40–81.

———'Sidgwick and the history of ethical dualism', in B. Schultz, ed., *Essays on Henry Sidgwick*. CUP, 1992, ch. 6.

Frankfurt, H. G., 'Freedom of the will and the concept of a person', in *The Importance of What We Care About*. CUP, 1988, ch. 2. From *JP* 68 (1971), 5–20.

Frassen, C., *Scotus Academicus, seu Universa Doctoris Subtilis Theologica Dogmata*, 12 vols. Rome: Bernabo, 1721.

Frey, R. G., 'Butler on self-love and benevolence', in Cunliffe, ed., *JBMRT*, ch. 12.

Garber, D. E., and Ayers, M. R., eds., *The Cambridge History of Seventeenth-Century Philosophy*, 2 vols. CUP, 1998.

Garnett, J., 'Bishop Butler and the Zeitgeist: Butler and the development of Christian moral philosophy in Victorian Britain', in Cunliffe, ed., *JBMRT*, ch. 4.

Garrett, D., ed., *Cambridge Companion to Spinoza*. CUP, 1996.

———*Cognition and Commitment in Hume's Philosophy*. OUP, 1997.

———'Spinoza's ethical theory', in *CCS*, ed. Garrett, ch. 6.

Gascoigne, J., *Cambridge in the Age of the Enlightenment: Science, Religion and Politics from the Restoration to the French Revolution*. CUP, 1989.

Gaudium et Spes, in Alberigo et al., *Decreta*.

Gauthier, D. P., 'David Hume: contractarian', in *MD*, ch. 3. From *PR* 88 (1979), 3–38.

———*Moral Dealing: Contract, Ethics, and Reason*. Ithaca, NY: Cornell UP, 1990.

———*Morals by Agreement*. OUP, 1986.

Gauthier, D. P., Review of Skinner, *RRPH*, *JP* 94 (1997), 94–7.

———— 'Taming Leviathan', *PPA* 16 (1987), 280–95.

———— *The Logic of Leviathan: The Moral and Political Theory of Thomas Hobbes*. OUP, 1969.

———— 'Thomas Hobbes: moral theorist', in *MD*, ch. 1. From *JP* 76 (1979), 547–59.

———— 'Three against justice: the foole, the sensible knave, and the Lydian shepherd', in *MD*, ch. 6. From *Midwest Studies in Philosophy* 7 (1982), 11–29.

Gay, J., *A Dissertation concerning the Fundamental Principle and Immediate Criterion of Virtue, as also the Obligation to and Approbation of It, with some Account of the Origin of the Passions and Affections*, in King, *OE* (tr. Law).

Gemmeke, E., *Die Metaphysik des sittlich Guten bei Franz Suarez*. Freiburg: Herder, 1965.

George, R. P., ed., *Natural Law, Liberalism, and Morality*. OUP, 1996.

Gert, B., 'Hobbes and psychological egoism', *JHI* 28 (1967), 503–20.

———— 'Hobbes, mechanism, and egoism', *PQ* 15 (1965), 341–9.

———— 'Hobbes's psychology', in Sorell, ed., *CCH*, ch. 7.

Gladstone, W. E., *Studies Subsidiary to the Work of Bishop Butler*. OUP, 1896.

Grave, S. A., 'The foundations of Butler's ethics', *AJP* 30 (1952), 73–89.

Green, T. H., *Complete Works*, 5 vols. (incl. 2 additional vols.), ed. P. Nicholson. Bristol: Thoemmes, 1997. 3 vols. (repr. from *Works*, ed. R. L. Nettleship, 3 vols. London: Longmans, Green, and Co., 1885–8).

———— *Introductions to Hume's Treatise of Human Nature*, in *Works* i 1–371.

———— *Prolegomena to Ethics*. OUP, 1883 (repr. in *Works* iv).

Gregory of Rimini, *Gregorii Ariminensis OESA Lectura super primum et secundum Sententiarum*, 7 vols., A. D. Trapp and V. Marcolino, eds. Berlin: De Gruyter, 1981–7.

Grisez, G. G., 'The first principle of practical reason', in A. J. P. Kenny, ed., *Aquinas: A Collection of Critical Essays*. London: Macmillan, 1970, 340–82.

———— *The Way of the Lord Jesus* i. Chicago: Franciscan Herald Press, 1983.

Griswold, C. L., *Adam Smith and the Virtues of Enlightenment*. CUP, 1999.

Grotius, H., *De iure belli et pacis*, ed. and tr. W. Whewell. 3 vols. CUP, 1853. (Orig. pub. 1625.)

———— *De iure praedae*, tr. G. L. Williams and W. H. Zeydel. OUP, 1950. (Orig pub. 1604.)

Grove, H., *System of Moral Philosophy*, 2nd edn., T. Amory, ed. London: Waugh, 1749.

———— *Wisdom the First Spring of Action in the Deity*, 2nd edn. London: Fenner, 1742.

Gueroult, M., *Spinoza*, 2 vols. Paris: Aubier-Montaigne, 1968.

Haakonssen, K., 'Hugo Grotius and the history of political thought', *Political Theory* 13 (1985), 239–65.

———— *Natural Law and Moral Philosophy*. CUP, 1996.

———— 'Protestant natural law theory', in Brender and Krasnoff, eds., *NEHA*, ch. 4.

———— and Thiel, U., eds., *Reason, Will, and Nature* (*History of Philosophy Yearbook* 1). Canberra, 1993.

Hamilton, B., *Political Theory in Sixteenth-Century Spain*. OUP, 1963.

Hampshire, S. N., *Spinoza*, rev. edn. Harmondsworth: Penguin, 1987 (1st pub. 1951).

———— *Two Theories of Morality*. OUP, 1977.

Hampton, J., 'Hobbes and ethical naturalism', *Philosophical Perspectives* 6 (1992), 333–53.

———— *Hobbes and the Social Contract Tradition*. CUP, 1986.

Hare, R. M., *Moral Thinking*. OUP, 1981.

———— *The Language of Morals*. OUP, 1952.

Harris, J. A., *Of Liberty and Necessity: The Free-Will Debate in Eighteenth-Century British Philosophy*. OUP, 2005.

Harrison, B., *Henry Fielding's Tom Jones: The Novelist as Moral Philosopher*. London: Chatto and Windus, 1975.

Harrison, J., *Hume's Moral Epistemology*. OUP, 1976.

———— *Hume's Theory of Justice*. OUP, 1981.

Hart, H. L. A., 'Legal and moral obligation', in Melden, ed., *EMP* 82–107.

———— *The Concept of Law*. OUP, 1961.

_____ and Honoré, A. M., *Causation in the Law*. OUP, 1959.

Hartley, D., *Observations on Man, Part 1*, 2nd edn. London: Johnson, 1791 (1st edn. 1749).

Hawkins, J., 'The Life of Johnson', in *The Works of Samuel Johnson*, ed. Hawkins. 11 vols. London: Buckland et al, 1787, vol. i.

Hobbes, T., *De Cive* (Latin and English), H. Warrender, ed. 2 vols. OUP, 1983. (Orig. pub. Latin 1642; English 1651.)

_____ *De Cive*, S. P. Lamprecht, ed. New York: Appleton-Century-Crofts, 1949.

_____ *De Cive*, ed. R. Tuck, tr. M. Silverthorne. CUP, 1998.

_____ *De Homine* = *OL* ii. Excerpt in Hobbes, *MC*, ed. Gert.

_____ *English Works*, W. Molesworth, ed. 11 vols. London: Bohn, 1839–45.

_____ *Hobbes and Bramhall on Liberty and Necessity*. V. C. Chappell, ed. CUP, 1999.

_____ *Leviathan*, E. M. Curley, ed. Indianapolis: Hackett, 1994. (Orig. pub. London, 1651.)

_____ *Leviathan*, tr. F. Tricaud. Paris: Sirey, 1971.

_____ *Man and Citizen*, B. Gert, ed. Garden City, NY: Doubleday, 1972.

_____ *Opera Latina*, 5 vols., W. Molesworth, ed. London: Bohn, 1839–45.

_____ *The Elements of Law: Human Nature and De Corpore Politico*. J. C. A. Gaskin, ed. OUP, 1994. Cited as *EL*.

Hochstrasser, T. J., 'Conscience and reason; the natural law theory of Barbeyrac', *HJ* 36 (1993), 289–308.

_____ *Natural Law Theories in the Early Enlightenment*. CUP, 2000.

Hooker, R., *Of the Laws of Ecclesiastical Polity*, in *The Works of Richard Hooker*, 7th edn., 3 vols., J. Keble, ed. OUP, 1888.

_____ *Of the Laws of Ecclesiastical Polity*, in *The Works of Richard Hooker*, W. S. Hill, ed., 6 vols. Binghamton: Center for Mediaeval and Renaissance Texts and Studies, 1993.

Hudson, W. D., *Reason and Right*. London: Macmillan, 1970.

Hume, D., *A Letter from a Gentleman to his Friend in Edinburgh*, E. C. Mossner and J. V. Price, eds. Edinburgh: Edinburgh UP, 1967.

_____ *A Treatise of Human Nature*, D. F. Norton and M. J. Norton, eds. OUP, 2000. (Orig. pub. 1739–40.)

_____ *Dialogues concerning Natural Religion*, N. Kemp Smith, ed. Edinburgh: Nelson, 1947. (Orig. pub. 1779.)

_____ *Essays, Moral, Political, and Literary*. OUP, 1963. (Orig. pub. 1741–2.)

_____ *Inquiry concerning Human Understanding*, T. L. Beauchamp, ed. OUP, 1999. (Orig. pub. 1748.)

_____ *Inquiry concerning Human Understanding*, C. W. Hendel, ed. Indianapolis: Bobbs-Merrill, 1955.

_____ *Inquiry concerning the Human Understanding* and *Inquiry concerning the Principles of Morals*, 2nd edn., L. A. Selby-Bigge, ed. OUP, 1902.

_____ *Inquiry concerning the Principles of Morals*, T. L. Beauchamp, ed. OUP, 1998. (Orig. pub. 1751.)

_____ *The Letters of David Hume*, Greig, J. Y. T., ed. 2 vols. OUP, 1932.

_____ *New Letters of David Hume*, Klibansky, R., and Mossner, E. C., eds. OUP, 1954.

Hunter, G., 'Reply to Professor Flew', in Chappell, ed., *Hume*, 287–90. From *Phil.* 38 (1963), 182–4.

Hutcheson, F., *A Short Introduction to Moral Philosophy*, 2nd edn. Glasgow: Foulis, 1753 (1st edn., 1747). ET of *MPIC*.

_____ *A System of Moral Philosophy*, 2 vols. Glasgow: Foulis, 1755.

_____ *An Essay on the Nature and Conduct of the Passions and Affections: With Illustrations on the Moral Sense*, A. Garrett, ed. Indianapolis: Liberty Fund, 2002. (Reprint of 1st edn. (1728) with later variants.)

_____ *An Inquiry concerning Beauty*, in *Inquiry into the Original of our Ideas of Beauty and Virtue*, ed. W. Leidhold. Indianapolis: Liberty Fund, 2004. (Repr. of 2nd edn. (1726) with later variants.)

_____ *An Inquiry into Moral Good and Evil*, in *Inquiry into the Original of our Ideas of Beauty and Virtue*, 5th edn. London: Ware, 1753. (1st edn., 1725.)

_____ *An Inquiry into Moral Good and Evil*, in *Inquiry into the Original of our Ideas of Beauty and Virtue*, ed. W. Leidhold. Indianapolis: Liberty Fund, 2004. (Repr. of 2nd edn. (1726) with later variants.)

Hutcheson, F., *Illustrations on the Moral Sense*. ed. B. Peach. HUP, 1971. From *An Essay on the Nature and Conduct of the Passions and Affections: With Illustrations on the Moral Sense*, 3rd edn. London: A. Ward et al., 1742. (1st edn., 1728.)

—— *Moralis Philosophiae Institutio Compendiaria*, 2nd edn. Dublin: McKenzie, 1787. (1st edn., 1742.)

—— *On Human Nature* (= *Reflexions on our common systems of morality* and the *Inaugural Lecture on the social nature of man*), T. Mautner, ed. CUP, 1993.

—— *Thoughts on Laughter, and Observations on the Fable of the Bees in Six Letters*. Repr. Bristol: Thoemmes, 1989. (Orig. Glasgow: Foulis, 1758.)

Jackson, R., 'Bishop Butler's refutation of psychological hedonism', *Phil.* 18. (1943), 114–39.

James VI and I, *Political Writings*, ed. J. P. Sommerville. CUP, 1994.

James, S., *Passion and Action*. OUP, 1997.

Johnson, T., *An Essay on Moral Obligation: With a View towards Settling the Controversy concerning Moral and Positive Duties*. London: Knapton, 1731.

Johnston, M., 'Dispositional theories of value', *SPAS* 63 (1989), 139–74.

Jones, P., *Hume's Sentiments*. Edinburgh: Edinburgh UP, 1982.

Jordan, G. J., *The Reunion of the Churches: A Study of G. W. Leibniz and his Great Attempt*. London: Constable, 1927.

Kames, Lord (Henry Home), *Essays on the Principles of Morality and Natural Religion*, 3rd edn., ed. M. C. Moran. Indianapolis: Liberty Fund, 2005. (Orig. pub. Edinburgh: John Bell, 1779.) (1st edn., 1751; 2nd edn., 1758.)

Kant, I., *Gesammelte Schriften*, xx. Berlin: De Gruyter, 1942.

—— *Religion and Rational Theology*, tr. and ed. A. W. Wood and G. di Giovanni. CUP, 1996.

—— *Groundwork of the Metaphysics of Morals* (cited as *G*), *Critique of Practical Reason* (cited as *KpV*), and *Metaphysics of Morals* (cited as *MdS*) in *Kant: Practical Philosophy*, tr. M. J. Gregor. CUP, 1996.

Kavka, G. S., *Hobbesian Moral and Political Theory*. PUP, 1986.

Kemp Smith, N., *The Philosophy of David Hume*. London: Macmillan, 1941.

Kenny, A. J. P., *Action, Emotion, and Will*. RKP, 1963.

Kilcullen, J., 'Natural law and will in Ockham', in K. Haakonssen and U. Thiel, eds., *Reason, Will, and Nature* (*History of Philosophy Yearbook* 1). Canberra, 1993, 1–25.

King, W., *An Essay On the Origin of Evil*, tr. and ed. E. Law., with essay by J. Gay. 3rd edn. Cambridge: Thurlbourn, 1739 (1st edn. 1731).

Kirk, K. E., *Conscience and its Problems*. London: Longmans, 1927.

—— *The Vision of God*, 2nd edn. London: Longmans, 1932.

Kirk, L., *Richard Cumberland and Natural Law*. Cambridge: James Clarke and Co., 1987.

Kivy, P., *The Seventh Sense: Francis Hutcheson and Eighteenth-Century British Aesthetics*, 2nd edn. OUP, 2003.

Knox, R. A., *Enthusiasm*. OUP, 1950.

Korkman, P., *Barbeyrac and Natural Law*. Helsinki, 2001.

Korsgaard, C. M., 'The normativity of instrumental reason', in G. Cullity and B. Gaut, eds., *Ethics and Practical Reason*. OUP, 1997, ch. 8.

—— *The Sources of Normativity*. CUP, 1996.

Laboucheix, H., *Richard Price as Moral Philosopher and Political Theorist*. Oxford: Voltaire Foundation, 1982.

La Bruyère, J., *Les Caractères*, ed. R. Garapon. Paris: Garnier, 1962. (Orig. pub. 1688.)

Lactantius, *Divinae Institutiones*, ed. S. Brandt. Vienna: Tempsky, 1890. (= *CSEL* xix 1).

Laird, J., *A Study in Moral Theory*. London: Allen and Unwin, 1926.

—— 'Hobbes on Aristotle's *Politics*', *PAS* 43 (1942–3), 1–20.

—— *Hume's Philosophy of Human Nature*. London: Methuen, 1932.

Larmore, C. E., *The Morals of Modernity*. CUP, 1996.

Law, Edmund: *see* King.

Lecky, W. E. H., *History of European Morals from Augustus to Charlemagne*, 2 vols. London: Longmans, 1920 (Orig. pub. 1869).

Lehrer, K., *Thomas Reid*. RKP, 1989.

Leibniz, G. W., *Die philosophischen Schriften*, C. I. Gerhardt, ed. 7 vols. 2nd edn. Berlin: Weidmann, 1875–90.

_____ *New Essays on Human Understanding*, P. Remnant and J. Bennet, eds. and trs. CUP, 1996.

_____ *Oeuvres*, L. A. Foucher de Careil, ed. 2nd edn. 7 vols. Paris: Didot, 1867–75.

_____ 'On nature itself', in *PLP* 498–508.

_____ *Opera Omnia*. L. Dutens, ed. 6 vols. Geneva: De Tournes, 1768.

_____ 'Opinion on the Principles of Pufendorf', in Dutens, ed., *OO* iv 275–84. Tr. in Riley, *PW* 64–75.

_____ *Philosophical Letters and Papers*, 2nd edn., L. E. Loemker, ed. and tr. Dordrecht: Reidel, 1969.

_____ *Political Writings*, P. Riley, tr and ed. 2nd edn. CUP, 1988.

_____ *Textes Inedits*, G. Grua, ed. Paris: Presses Universitaires de France, 1948.

_____ *Theodicy*, tr. E. M. Huggard. RKP, 1951.

Le Mahieu, D. L., *The Mind of William Paley*. Lincoln: U of Nebraska Press, 1976.

Lewis, D., 'Dispositional theories of value', *SPAS* 63 (1989), 113–37.

Lincoln, A., *Some Political and Social Ideas of English Dissent, 1763–1800*. CUP, 1938.

Locke, J., *An Essay concerning Human Understanding*, P. H. Nidditch, ed. OUP, 1975. (Orig. pub. 1700 (4th edn.).)

_____ *An Essay concerning Human Understanding*, A. C. Fraser, ed. OUP, 1894.

_____ *Essays on the Law of Nature*, W. von Leyden, ed. OUP, 1954 (3rd imp. 1988).

_____ *The Correspondence of John Locke*, E. S. de Beer, ed. 8 vols. OUP, 1976–89.

Loeb, L. E., *From Descartes to Hume*. Ithaca, NY: Cornell UP, 1981.

Lyons, W., *Emotion*. CUP, 1980.

McAdoo H. R., *The Spirit of Anglicanism: A Survey of Anglican Theological Method in the Seventeenth Century*. London: Black, 1965.

_____ *The Structure of Caroline Moral Theology*. London: Longmans, 1949.

McGuire, J. E., 'Boyle's conception of nature', *JHI* 33 (1972), 523–42.

MacIntyre, A. C., 'Hume on is and ought', in Chappell, ed., *Hume*, 240–64. From *PR* 68 (1959), 451–68.

Mackie, J. L., *Ethics: Inventing Right and Wrong*. Harmondsworth: Penguin, 1977.

_____ *Hume's Moral Theory*. RKP, 1980.

Mackintosh, J., *Dissertation on the Progress of Ethical Philosophy: Chiefly during the Seventeenth and Eighteenth Centuries*, 4th edn., with perface by W. Whewell. Edinburgh: Black, 1872 (1st pub., 1836).

McNaughton, D. A., 'Butler on benevolence', in Cunliffe, ed., *JBMRT*, ch. 13.

McNeilly, F. S., 'Egoism in Hobbes', *PQ* 16 (1966), 193–206.

McPherson, T. H., 'The development of Bishop Butler's ethics', *Phil.* 23 (1948), 317–31, and 24 (1949), 1–22.

Mahoney, J., *The Making of Moral Theology*. OUP, 1987.

Mandeville, B., *The Fable of the Bees*, ed. F. B. Kaye. OUP, 1924.

Marcus Aurelius, *Meditations*, 2 vols., ed. A. S. L. Farquharson. OUP, 1944.

Martineau, J., *Essays, Reviews, and Addresses* iii. London: Longmans, 1891.

_____ *Types of Ethical Theory*, 2nd edn. OUP, 1886. (1st edn., 1885.)

Martinich, A. P., *The Two Gods of Leviathan*. CUP, 1992.

Mather, C., *Manuductio ad Ministerium*. Republished by J. Ryland. London: Dilly, 1781.

Maxwell, J., 'A Treatise concerning the obligation, Promulgation, and observance of the Law of Nature'. Appendix to his translation of Cumberland.

_____ 'Concerning the City, or Kingdom, of God in the Rational World, and the Defects in Heathen Deism' and 'Concerning the Imperfectness of the Heathen Morality'. Two introductory essays bound with his translation of Cumberland.

Melden, A. I., ed., *Essays in Moral Philosophy*. Seattle: University of Washington Press, 1958.

Mercer, C., 'Leibniz, Aristotle, and ethical knowledge', in R. Pozzo, ed., *The Impact of Aristotelianism on Modern Philosophy* (Washington: Catholic University of America Press, 2004), ch. 5.

Meijering, E. P., 'The Fathers in Calvinist orthodoxy: systematic theology', in Backus, ed., *RCFW*, ch. 22.

Mill, J. S., *An Examination of Sir William Hamilton's Philosophy*, in *CW* ix.

—— 'Bentham', in *CW* x.

—— *Collected Works*, 33 vols., J. M. Robson (gen. ed.). Toronto: U of Toronto Press, 1963–91.

—— *Utilitarianism*, in *CW* x.

—— 'Whewell on moral philosophy', in *CW* x.

Millar, A., 'Butler on God and human nature', in Cunliffe, ed., *JBMRT*, ch. 14.

—— 'Following nature', *PQ* 38 (1988), 165–85.

Millican, P., ed., *Reading Hume on Human Understanding*. OUP, 2002.

Mintz, S. I., *The Hunting of Leviathan*. CUP, 1962.

Molhuysen, P. C., 'The first edition of Grotius' *De Iure Belli ac Pacis*', *Bibliotheca Visseriana*, 5 (1925), 101–49.

Moore, G. E., *Principia Ethica*, 2nd edn., ed. T. W. Baldwin. CUP, 1993 (1st edn., 1903).

Moore, J., 'Hume and Hutcheson', in Stewart and Wright, eds., *HHC*, ch. 2.

—— and Silverthorne, M., 'Natural sociability and natural rights in the moral philosophy of Gerschom Carmichael', in Hope, ed., *PSE*, ch. 1.

Moore, M. S., 'Good without God', in George, ed., *NLLM*, ch. 12.

Moran, R. A., *Authority and Estrangement*. PUP, 2001.

More, H., *Enchiridion Ethicum*. ET. New York: Facsimile text society, 1930. (Orig. pub. 1690.)

Mossner, E. C., *The Life of David Hume*, 2nd edn. OUP, 1980.

Nagel, T., 'Hobbes's concept of obligation', *PR* 68 (1959), 68–83.

—— *The Possibility of Altruism*. OUP, 1970.

Nietzsche, F., *On the Genealogy of Morality*, ed. K. Ansell-Pearson. CUP, 1994.

Norton, D. F., *David Hume: Common-sense Moralist, Sceptical Metaphysician*. PUP, 1982.

—— and Stewart-Robertson, J. C., 'Thomas Reid on Adam Smith's theory of morals', *JHI* 41 (1980), 381–98; 45 (1984), 309–21.

Oakeshott, M. B., 'Introduction', in *Hobbes: Leviathan*, ed. M. Oakeshott. Oxford: Blackwell, 1946 (repr. in Oakeshott, *RP*).

—— *Rationalism in Politics and Other Essays*. London: Methuen, 1962.

Oberman, H. A., *The Harvest of Mediaeval Theology: Gabriel Biel and the Late Mediaeval Nominalism*. HUP, 1963.

Ockham, W., *Opera Theologica*, 10 vols. St Bonaventure: Franciscan Institute, 1967–86.

Osler, M. J., ed., *Atoms, Pneuma, and Tranquillity*. CUP, 1991.

Oxford Dictionary of National Biography, 61 vols., ed. H. G. C. Matthews and B. Harrison. OUP, 2004.

Paley, W., *Principles of Moral and Political Philosophy*, ed. D. L. Le Mahieu. Indianapolis: Liberty Fund, 2002. (1st edn., orig. pub. 1785.)

Palmer, R. R., *Catholics and Unbelievers in Eighteenth Century France*. PUP, 1939.

Palladini, F., *Discussioni seicentesche su Samuel Pufendorf*. Bologna: Il Mulino, 1978.

—— *Samuel Pufendorf, Discepolo di Hobbes*. Bologna: Il Mulino, 1990.

Parfit, D. A., *Reasons and Persons*. OUP, 1984.

Parker, S., *A Demonstration of the Divine Authority of the Law of Nature and of the Christian Religion*. London: Royston, 1681. (Cited as *DA*.)

Parkin, J., *Science, Religion, and Politics in Restoration England*. Woodbridge: Boydell Press, 1999.

Passmore, J. A., *Hume's Intentions*, 2nd edn. London: Duckworth, 1968.

—— *Ralph Cudworth: An Interpretation*. CUP, 1951.

—— 'The moral philosophy of Hobbes', *AJP* 19 (1941), 31–43.

Patrick, S. [?], *A Brief Account of the New Sect of the Latitude-Men*. Augustan Reprint Society no. 100. Los Angeles, 1963. (Orig. pub. 1662.)

Patrides, C. A., ed., *The Cambridge Platonists*. HUP, 1970.

Pattison, M., 'Religious thought in England', in *Essays*, ed. H. Nettleship, 2 vols. OUP, 1889, vol. ii, ch. 13.

Penelhum, T., *Butler*. RKP, 1985.

―――― *Hume*. London: Macmillan, 1975.

―――― *Themes in Hume*. OUP, 2000.

Plamenatz, J. P., 'Mr Warrender's Hobbes', in Brown, ed., *HS*, ch. 4 (1). From *PS* 51 (957), 295–308.

Plato, OCT.

Plutarch, *Moralia*, Loeb. Works cited: *Adversus Colotem* (vol. xiv); *De Stoicorum Repugnantiis* (vol. xiii).

Price, R., 'A discourse on the love of our country', in *Political Writings*, ed. D. O. Thomas. CUP, 1991, 176–96.

―――― *A Review of the Principal Questions in Morals*, 3rd edn., ed. D. D. Raphael. OUP, 1974 (orig. 3rd edn., 1787; 1st edn., 1758).

―――― and Priestley, J., *A Free Discussion of the Doctrines of Materialism and Philosophical Necessity, in a Correspondence between Dr Price and Dr Priestley*. London: J. Johnson and T. Cadell, 1778.

Prior, A. N., 'Eighteenth-century writers on twentieth-century subjects', *AJP* 24 (1946), 168–82.

―――― *Logic and the Basis of Ethics*. OUP, 1949.

Pufendorf, S., *De iure naturae et gentium*, tr. C. H. Oldfather and W. A. Oldfather. OUP, 1934.

―――― *De iure naturae et gentium*. Amsterdam: Hoogenhuysen, 1688. (1st edn., Lund, 1672.)

―――― *De iure naturae et gentium*. ET: *Of the Law of Nature and Nations*, tr. B. Kennett. London: Walthoe, 4th edn., 1729.

―――― *De officio hominis et civis juxta legem naturalem*. Lund, 1682 (repr. OUP, 1927). ET: *On the Duty of Man and Citizen according to Natural Law*, J. Tully, ed., M. Silverthorne, tr. CUP, 1991.

―――― *Elementa jurisprudentiae universalis*, tr. W. A. Oldfather. OUP, 1931. (Orig. pub., Cambridge, 1672.)

―――― *Eris Scandica*, in *GW* v.

―――― *Gesammelte Werke*, W. Schmidt-Biggemann, ed. 5 vols. Berlin: Akademie-Verlag, 1996–.

―――― *Les Devoirs de l'Homme et du Citoyen*, 4th edn., tr. J. Barbeyrac. Amsterdam: Pierre de Coup, 1718.

Radcliffe, E. S., 'Hutcheson's perceptual and moral subjectivism', *HPQ* 3 (1986), 407–21.

Rae, J., *Life of Adam Smith*, repr., with introd., by J. Viner. New York: Kelly, 1965 (1st pub. 1895).

Raphael, D. D., 'Bishop Butler's view of conscience', *Phil.* 24 (1949), 219–38.

―――― ed., *British Moralists, 1650–1800*, 2 vols. OUP, 1969.

―――― 'Hume's critique of ethical rationalism', in W. B. Todd, ed., *Hume and the Enlightenment* (Edinburgh: Edinburgh UP, 1974), 14–29.

―――― 'Obligations and rights in Hobbes', *Phil.* 37 (1962), 345–52.

―――― *The Impartial Spectator*. OUP, 2007.

―――― *The Moral Sense*. OUP, 1947.

Rashdall, H., *Theory of Good and Evil*, 2 vols., 2nd edn. OUP, 1924 (1st edn., 1907).

Rawls, J., *A Theory of Justice*, 2nd edn. HUP, 1999 (1st edn., 1971).

―――― *Lectures on the History of Moral Philosophy*. HUP, 2000.

Raz, J., ed., *Practical Reasoning*. OUP, 1978.

Reeder, J. ed., *On Moral Sentiments: Contemporary Responses to Adam Smith*. Bristol: Thoemmes, 1997.

Reginaldus, Valerius, *Praxis fori pœnitentialis ad directionem confessarii in usu sacri sui muneris*, 2nd edn., 2 vols. Mainz, 1617.

Reid, T., 'A Sketch of Dr Smith's Theory of Morals', in Reeder, ed., *MS* 69–88.

―――― *Essays on the Active Powers of the Human Mind*, in *Works* ii.

―――― *Works*, 2 vols., ed. W. Hamilton, 6th edn. Edinburgh: Maclachlan and Stewart, 1863.

Rickaby, J., *Moral Philosophy*, 4th edn. London: Longmans, 1918.

Rivers, I., *Reason, Grace, and Sentiment*, 2 vols. CUP, 1991 (vol. i), 2000 (vol. ii).

Ross, I. S., 'Hutcheson on Hume's Treatise: an unnoticed letter', *JHP* 4 (1966), 69–72.

——— *The Life of Adam Smith*. OUP, 1995.

Ross, W. D., *Foundations of Ethics*. OUP, 1939.

——— *The Right and the Good*. OUP, 1930.

Rousseau, J.-J., *Basic Political Writings*, tr. D. A. Cress. Indianapolis: Hackett, 1987.

——— *Discourse on the Origin of Inequality*, in *BPW*, tr. Cress.

——— *Emile*, tr. A. Bloom. New York: Basic Books, 1979. (Orig. pub. 1762.)

——— *Emile*, tr. B. Foxley. London: Dent, 1911.

——— *Oeuvres Complètes* iii–iv, B. Gagnebin and M. Raymond, eds. Paris: Gallimard, 1964, 1969 (Bibliothèque de la Pléiade).

——— *Social Contract*, ed. R. Grimsley. OUP, 1972. (Orig pub. 1762.)

Rowe, W. L., *Thomas Reid on Freedom and Morality*. Ithaca, NY: Cornell UP, 1991.

Russell, C., 'Divine right in the early seventeenth century', in *Public Duty and Private Conscience in Seventeenth-Century England*, J. Morrill, P. Slack, and D. Woolf, eds. OUP, 1993, ch. 7.

Russell, P., 'A Hobbist Tory: Johnson on Hume', *HS* 16 (1990), 75–9.

——— ' "Atheism" and the title page of Hume's *Treatise*', *HS* 14 (1988), 408–23.

——— *Freedom and Moral Sentiment: Hume's Way of Naturalizing Responsibility*. OUP, 1995.

——— 'Scepticism and natural religion in Hume's *Treatise*', *JHI* 49 (1988), 247–65.

Rutherforth, T., *An Essay on the Nature and Obligation of Virtue*. Cambridge: Thurlbourn, 1744.

Rylaarsdam, J. C., 'Exodus', in *The Interpreter's Bible*, G. A. Buttrick, et al., eds., 12 vols. Nashville: Abingdon-Cokesbury, 1952, vol. i.

Saastamoinen, K., *The Morality of the Fallen Man: Samuel Pufendorf on Natural Law*. Helsinki: SHS, 1995.

St Leger, J., *The 'Etiamsi Daremus' of Hugo Grotius*. Rome, 1962.

Salisbury, John of, *Metalogicon*, ed. C. C. J. Webb. OUP, 1929.

Sanderson, Robert, *De Obligatione Conscientiae*. W. Whewell, tr. and ed. CUP, 1851 (orig. 1647).

——— *Sermons*, R. Montgomery, ed. 2 vols. London: Ball, Arnold, 1841.

Saxenhouse, A. W., 'Hobbes and the beginnings of modern political thought', in *Hobbes: Three Discourses*, N. B. Reynolds and A. W. Saxenhouse, eds. Chicago: U. Chicago Press, 1995, Part 3.

Scanlon, T. M., *What We Owe to Each Other*. HUP, 1998.

Schaff, P., *The Creeds of Christendom*, 6th edn., 3 vols. New York: Harper & Row, 1931.

Schmucker, J., *Die Ursprünge der Ethik Kants*. Meisenheim: Hain, 1961.

Schneewind, J. B., 'Barbeyrac and Leibniz on Pufendorf', in F. Palladini and G. Hartung, ed., *Samuel Pufendorf und die europäische Frühaufklärung*, ed. F. Palladini and G. Hartung. Berlin: Akademie Verlag, 1996, 181–9.

——— 'Kant and natural law ethics', *Ethics* 104 (1993), 53–74.

——— 'Locke's moral philosophy', in *The Cambridge Companion to Locke*, ed. V. C. Chappell. CUP, 1994, ch. 8.

——— ed., *Moral Philosophy from Montaigne to Kant*, 2nd edn. CUP, 2003.

——— 'Pufendorf's place in the history of ethics', *Synthese* 72 (1987), 123–55.

——— *The Invention of Autonomy*. CUP, 1997.

——— 'The misfortunes of virtue', *Ethics* 101 (1990), 42–63.

——— 'The use of autonomy in ethical theory', in T. C. Heller, M. Sosna, and D. E. Wellbery, eds., *Reconstructing Individualism*. Palo Alto: Stanford UP, 1986, 64–75.

Schopenhauer, A., *On the Basis of Morality*, tr. E. F. J. Payne. Indianapolis: Bobbs-Merrill, 1965.

Scott, J. B., 'Introduction', in *Suarez: Selections from Three Works* ii (OUP, 1944), pp. 3a–38a.

Scott, W. R., *An introduction to Cudworth's Treatise concerning Eternal and immutable Morality*. London: Longmans, 1891. Reprinted in Cudworth, *FW*.

894

_____ *Francis Hutcheson*. CUP, 1900.

Scotus, Duns, *Opera Omnia*, 12 vols., ed. L. Wadding. Lyons: Durand, 1639 (repr. Hildesheim: Olms, 1968). Cited as OO.

Selby-Bigge, L. A., ed., *British Moralists*, 2 vols. OUP, 1897.

Selden, J., *De iure naturali & gentium, iuxta disciplinam Ebraeorum*. London: Bishop, 1640.

_____ *Table Talk of John Selden*, ed. F. Pollock. London: Quaritch, 1927.

Seneca, *De Beneficiis*, in *Dialogi*. OCT.

_____ Epistulae Morales. OCT.

Sextus Empiricus, *Adversus Mathematicos*. BT. Cited as '*M*'.

_____ *Pyrrhoneae Hypotyposes*. BT. Cited as '*P*'.

Shaftesbury, Earl of *Characteristics of Men, Manners, Opinions, Times*, L. E. Klein, ed. CUP, 1999. (Orig. pub. 1714.)

_____ *Characteristics*. 2nd edn., 3 vols. London, 1714.

_____ *Inquiry concering Virtue or Merit*, ed. D. E. Walford. Manchester: Manchester UP, 1977.

_____ *The Moralists: A Philosophical Rhapsody*, in *Characteristics*, ed. L. E. Klein. (Orig. Pub. London: Wyat, 1709.)

_____ *Letters to a Student in the University*. London, 1790.

_____ Preface to Whichcote, *Select Sermons*. London: 1698.

_____ *The Life, Unpublished Letters, and Philosophical Regimen of Anthony, Earl of Shaftesbury*, ed. B. Rand. London: Swan Sonnenschein and Co., 1900. Cited as PR.

Sharp, F. C., 'Hume's ethical theory and its critics', M 30 (1921), 40–56, 151–71.

_____ 'The ethical system of Richard Cumberland and its place in the history of British ethics', M 21 (1912), 371–98.

Sharp, T., Letters to Catharine Cockburn, in Cockburn, *Works* ii.

Sharrock, R., *Hupothesis Ethike*. Oxford: Typis Lichfieldianis, 1660.

Shaver, R., 'Grotius on scepticism and self-interest', AGP 78 (1996), 27–47.

Sher, R. B., *Church and University in the Scottish Enlightenment*. PUP, 1985.

Shoemaker, S., 'Realization and mental causation', in *Identity, Cause, and Mind*, 2nd edn. OUP, 2003.

Shorey, P., *Platonism, Ancient and Modern*. Berkeley: UC Press, 1938.

Sidgwick, H., *Outlines of the History of Ethics*, 3rd edn. London: Macmillan, 1892.

_____ *The Methods of Ethics*, 7th edn. London: Macmillan, 1907. 1st edn., 1874. (Earlier edns. cited as [1], [2]. etc.)

Silvester, T., *Moral and Christian Benevolence*. London, 1734.

Simons, W., 'Introduction' to Pufendorf, *JNG*, tr. Oldfather.

Skinner, A. S., and Wilson, T., eds., *Essays on Adam Smith*. OUP, 1975.

Skinner, Q. R. D., *Reason and Rhetoric in the Philosophy of Hobbes*. CUP, 1996.

_____ *The Foundations of Modern Political Theory*, 2 vols. CUP, 1978.

Sleigh, R., Chappell, V., and Della Rocca, M., 'Determinism and human freedom', in Garber and Ayers, eds., *CHSCP*, ch. 33.

Smith, A., *An Inquiry into the Nature and Causes of the Wealth of Nations*, E. Cannan, ed. London: Methuen, 1925. (1st edn. orig. pub. 1776.)

_____ *Correspondence of Adam Smith*, E. C. Mossner and I. S. Ross, eds. OUP, 1977.

_____ *The Theory of Moral Sentiments*, 6th edn., ed. D. D. Raphael and A. L. Macfie. OUP, 1976 (1st pub. 1790; 1st edn., 1759). (This edn. cited as RM.)

Smith, M., 'Dispositional theories of value', SPAS 63 (1989), 89–111.

_____ *The Moral Problem*. Oxford: Blackwell, 1994.

Sommerville, J. P., 'From Suarez to Filmer', HJ 25 (1982), 525–40.

_____ 'John Selden, the law of nature, and the origins of government', HJ 27 (1984), 437–47.

Sorell, T., ed., *Cambridge Companion to Hobbes*. CUP, 1996.

S.P. *See* Patrick, S.

Spectator, ed. D. F. Bond. 5 vols. OUP, 1965.

Spinoza, B., *Collected works of Spinoza* i, tr. E. M. Curley. PUP, 1985.

———— *Complete Works*, tr. S. Shirley. Indianapolis: Hackett, 2002.

———— *Ethics*, in Spinoza, *CWS* (tr. Curley) and *CW* (tr. Shirley).

———— *Tractatus Theologico-Politicus*, in Spinoza, *CW* (tr. Shirley).

Stamm, J. J., and Andrew, M. E., *The Ten Commandments in Recent Research*. London: SCM Press, 1967.

Stephen, L., *History of English Thought in the Eighteenth Century*, 2 vols. London: Smith, Elder, 1876.

Stevenson, C. L., *Ethics and Language*. New Haven: Yale UP, 1944.

Stewart, D., *Dissertation on the Progress of Metaphysical, Ethical, and Political Philosophy*, in *Works* i.

———— *Outlines of Moral Philosophy*, ed. J. McCosh. London: Allan, 1864.

———— *Philosophy of the Active and Moral Powers*, in *Works* vi.

———— *Works*, ed. W. Hamilton, 11 vols. Edinburgh: Constable, 1855–60.

Stewart, M. A., 'An early critic of *Alciphron*', *Berkeley Newsletter* 6 (1982–3), 5–9.

———— *The Kirk and the Infidel*. Inaugural Lecture: Lancaster: Lancaster University, 1995.

———— 'The Stoic legacy in the early Scottish enlightenment', in Osler, ed., *APT*, ch. 14.

———— 'Two species of philosophy', in Millican (ed.), *RHHU*, ch. 2.

———— and Wright, J. P., eds., *Hume and Hume's Connexions*. University Park, Pa.: Penn State UP, 1995.

Strawson, P. F., 'Ethical intuitionism', *Phil.* 24 (1949), 23–33.

———— 'On referring', *M* 59 (1950), 320–44.

Stroud, B., *Hume*. RKP, 1977.

Sturgeon, N. L., 'Hume on Reason and Passion', in D. Ainslie, ed., *Hume's Treatise: A Critical Guide*, CUP, forthcoming.

———— 'Moral scepticism and moral naturalism in Hume's Treatise', *HS* 27 (2001), 3–83.

———— 'Nature and conscience in Butler's ethics', *PR* 85 (1976), 316–56.

———— 'What difference does it make whether moral realism is true?' *SJP* 24 Suppl. (1986), 115–41.

Suarez, F., *De Bello*, in *OO* xii.

———— *De Bonitate*, in *OO* iv.

———— *Defensio Fidei Catholicae*, in *OO* xxiv.

———— *On the Essence of Finite Being* (*DM* xxxi), tr. N J. Wells. Milwaukee: Marquette UP, 1983.

———— *Opera Omnia*, C. Berton, ed., 28 vols. Paris: Vivès, 1866.

———— *Selections from Three Works*, 2 vols. (vol. i, text; vol. ii, tr. G. L. Williams et al.). OUP, 1944.

———— *The Metaphysics of Good and Evil according to Suarez*, J. J. E. Gracia and D. Davis trs. Munich: Philosophia Verlag, 1989.

———— *Tractatus de Legibus ac Deo Legislatore*, 8 vols., ed. and tr. L. Perena et al. Madrid: Consejo Superior de Investigaciones Cientificas, 1971–81.

Taylor, A. E., 'Some features of Butler's ethics', in Taylor, *Philosophical Studies*. London: Macmillan, 1934, ch. 8 From *M* 35 (1926), 273–300.

———— 'The ethical doctrine of Hobbes', in Brown, ed., *HS*, ch. 2 (2). From *Phil.* 13 (1938), 406–24.

Taylor, C., 'What is human agency?', in *Human Agency and Language* i. CUP, 1985, ch. 1. From T. Mischel, ed., *The Self*. Oxford: Blackwell, 1977, 103–35.

Taylor, J., *Ductor Dubitantium*, in *The Whole Works*, R. Heber, ed., 15 vols. London, Ogle, Duncan, 1822, vol. xi.

Thomas, D. O., *The Honest Mind: The Thought and Work of Richard Price*. OUP, 1977.

Thomas, R., *Richard Price, Philosopher and Apostle of Liberty*. OUP, 1924.

Tierney, B., *The Idea of Natural Rights*. Atlanta: Scholars Press, 1997.

Tillotson, J. *Works*, 12 vols. London: Ware et al., 1742–4.

Tindal, M. *Christianity as Old as the Creation. or, the Gospel, a Republication of the Religion of* Nature. London, 1731.

Toland, J., *Christianity Not Mysterious: Or a Treatise Showing that there is Nothing in the Gospel Contrary to Reason, nor Above it, and that No Christian Doctrine can be Properly Called a Mystery*, 2nd edn. London: Buckley, 1696. (Repr. Bristol: Thoemmes, 1995.)

Treloar, J. L., 'Moral virtue and the demise of prudence in the thought of Francis Suarez', *ACPQ* 65 (1991), 387–405.

Tuck, R., 'Hobbes's moral philosophy', in Sorell, ed., *CCH*, ch. 8.

_____ *Natural Rights Theories: Their Origin and Development*. CUP, 1979.

_____ *Philosophy and Government, 1572–1651*. CUP, 1993.

_____ 'The "modern" theory of natural law', in A. Pagden, ed., *The Languages of Political Theory in Early-Modern Europe*. CUP, 1987, ch. 5.

Tucker, A., ('Edward Search'), *The Light of Nature Pursued*, 5 vols. London: Payne, 1768. Abridged by W. Hazlitt, London: Johnson, 1807.

Tulloch, J., *Rational Theology and Christian Philosophy*, 2 vols. 2nd edn. Edinburgh: Blackwood, 1874.

Turnbull, G., *The Principles of Moral Philosophy*. London: Millar, 1740.

Tyrrell, J., *A Brief Disquisition of the Law of Nature*. London: Baldwin, 1692.

Urban, L. W., 'A revolution in Anglican moral theology', *Anglican Theological Review* 53 (1971), 5–20.

Vasquez, G., *Commentaria ac Disputationes in Primam Secundae Sancti Thomae*, 2 vols. Ingolstadt, 1606.

Villey, M., *La formation de la pensée juridique moderne*. Paris: Montchrestien, 1968.

Vivenza, G., *Adam Smith and the Classics*. OUP, 2002.

Wainewright, L., *A Vindication of Dr Paley's Theory of Morals*. London: Hatchard, 1830.

Wallace, R. J., 'How to argue about practical reason', *M* 99 (1990), 355–85.

Walton, 'Life of Sanderson', in Sanderson, *Sermons* i.

Warburton, W., *The Divine Legation of Moses Demonstrated*, 2nd edn., 4 vols. London: Fletcher Gyles, 1738.

Ward, W. G., *On Nature and Grace*. London: Burns and Lambert, 1860.

Warnock, G. J., *Contemporary Moral Philosophy*. London: Macmillan, 1967.

Warrender, H., 'The place of God in Hobbes's philosophy: a reply to Mr Plamenatz', in Brown, ed., *HS*, ch. 4 (2). From *PS* 8 (1960), 48–57.

Waterland, D., 'A supplement to . . . the nature, obligation, and efficacy . . .', in *Works* iv 105–48. (Orig. pub. 1730.)

_____ 'On self-love'. Sermon 3 in Sermons collected 1741–2, in *Works* v 446–62.

_____ 'Remarks upon Dr Clarke's exposition of the Church Catechism', in *Works* iv 1–50.

_____ 'The duty of loving our neighbour as ourselves explained', in *Works* v 436–45.

_____ 'The nature, obligation, and efficacy of the Christian sacraments considered', in *Works* iv 53–104. (Orig. pub. 1730.)

_____ *Works*, W. van Mildert, ed., 6 vols. OUP, 1856.

Watkins, J. W. N., *Hobbes's System of Ideas: A Study in the Political Significance of Philosophical Theories*. London: Hutchinson, 1965.

Watson, G. L., 'Free agency', in *Free Will*, ed. Watson. OUP, 1982, ch. 7. From *JP* 72 (1975), 202–20.

Wesley, J., *Sermons*, in *The Works of John Wesley* i, A. C. Outler, ed. OUP, 1984.

Whately, R., *Introductory Lessons on Morals*. London: Parker, 1855.

_____ *Paley's Moral Philosophy, with Annotations*. London: Parker, 1859.

Whewell, W., ed., *Butler's Three Sermons on Human Nature*. Cambridge: Deighton, 1848.

_____ *Lectures on the History of Moral Philosophy in England*. London: Parker, 1852.

_____ *Lectures on Systematic Morality*. London: Parker, 1846.

Whewell, W., Preface to J. Mackintosh, *DPEP*.

Whichcote, B., *Moral and Religious Aphorisms*, ed. J. Jeffery and S. Salter. London: Payne, 1753.

—— *Select Sermons*. London, 1698.

White, A. R., 'Conscience and self-love in Butler's Sermons', *Phil.* 27 (1952), 329–44.

Whiteley, C. H., 'On duties', *PAS* 52 (1952–3), 95–104.

Wiles, M. F., *Archetypal Heresy:Arianism through the Centuries*. OUP, 1996.

Williams, B. A. O., 'Moral luck', in *Moral Luck*. CUP, 1981, ch. 2.

—— 'Voluntary acts and responsible agents', in *Making Sense of Humanity*. CUP, 1995, ch. 2.

Wilson, J. M., and Fowler, T., *Principles of Morals*. OUP, 1886.

Winkler, K. P., 'Hutcheson's alleged realism', *JHP* 23 (1985), 179–94.

Wishart, W., *A Vindication of the Reverend D—B—from the scandalous imputation of being the author of a late book, intitled Alciphron or the Minute Philosopher*. Edinburgh: Wilford, 1734.

Witherspoon, J., *Ecclesiastical Characteristics, or the Arcana of Church Polity, being an Humble Attempt to Open Up the Mystery of Moderation . . .*, 2nd edn. Glasgow, 1754.

Wolfson, H. A., *The Philosophy of Spinoza: Unfolding the Latent Process of his Reasoning*, 2 vols. in 1. HUP, 1948 (1st pub. 1934).

Wright, C., 'Moral values, projection, and secondary qualities', *SPAS* 72 (1988), 1–26.

Yaffe, G., *Manifest Activity: Thomas Reid's Theory of Action*. OUP, 2004.

Zagorin, P., *Ways of Lying*. HUP, 1990.

INDEX